LINDA LESLIE

Psychology

COVER

A Sunday Afternoon on the Island of La Grande Jatte *is the best-known work of the French artist Georges Seurat, who painted it over a three-year period a few years before his death, at 31, in 1891. This picture seems an appropriate choice to introduce a psychology textbook because Seurat deliberately applied scientific principles of visual perception to his color relations and shapes. Seurat trusted theoretical principles, among them those offered in the scientific treatise on color contrast by the chemist Chevreul, and applied them systematically. This attitude resembled that of a scientist, although it was uniquely combined with an artist's sensitivity to direct visual observation.*

Seurat attempted to reconcile art and science in a method of painting called divisionism. He replaced the traditional irregular brush strokes with meticulously placed dots of color. Instead of mixing paints on his palette he allowed the mixture to be accomplished optically, that is, in the eye of the onlooker placed at a proper distance. From Chevreul he learned that under such conditions complementary colors, e.g. green and red or blue and orange, add up to luminous greys.

A scientist can present his statements without describing the individual experiences from which they were derived, but such direct display of principle may endanger an artist's spontaneity and his work may end up appearing coldly theoretical. In fact, Seurat has been criticized for the geometrical precision of his shapes and for the somewhat mechanical application of colored dots.

Seurat's visual arrangements of human figures, however, can be thought of as reflecting the social isolation of urban man, brought about by the industrial revolution. Seurat portrays his fellow citizens as isolated individuals, unaware of one another and spread across the wooded park at the water's edge without the interplay of mutual response. At the same time, the seemingly random display of these forty or so figures is highly controlled by the painter's sense of spatial arrangement. In this way, Seurat has created a visual symbol of accidental relation—a profound, intuitive judgment by which the artist rivals the scientific analyst as a critical observer of the world.

Rudolf Arnheim

Psychology

GARDNER LINDZEY

UNIVERSITY OF TEXAS, AUSTIN

CALVIN S. HALL

UNIVERSITY OF CALIFORNIA, SANTA CRUZ

RICHARD F. THOMPSON

HARVARD UNIVERSITY

WORTH PUBLISHERS, INC.

Credits for Chapter Opening Photographs:

Cover and frontispiece, Courtesy of the Art Institute of Chicago; Chapter 1, Photographed by Toni Frissell, Courtesy Frissell Collection, Library of Congress; 2, Wynn Bullock; 3, Tringali, dpi; 4, Arthur LaZar; 5, Photo by Dorothea Lange, The Oakland Museum Collection; 6, Janine Niepce, Rapho Guillumette; 7, Anna Kaufman Moon; 8, Philippe Halsmann; 9, The British Museum; 10, J. A. Pavlovsky, Sygma; 11, Leonard Freed, Magnum; 12, Sabine Weiss, Rapho Guillumette; 13, Laurence Le Guay; 14, Wynn Bullock; 15, Dennis Stock, Magnum; 16, Edward Steichen; 17, Bettmann Archive; 18, Charles Gatewood, Magnum; 19, Richard Noble; 20, Vilem Kriz; 21, Jan Lenica, poster for *Wozzeck*; from *Quality*, ed. Louis Kronenburger, Atheneum, 1969.

Fourth Printing, July 1976

WORTH PUBLISHERS, INC.

444 Park Avenue South

New York, New York 10016

Preface

This book is for students taking their first course in psychology. We hope it will not be their last. Human behavior is a fascinating and amazingly complex subject. We would be delighted if our readers caught from this text an enthusiasm for psychology that carried their studies beyond the beginning level.

Most fields of scientific study begin with a set of scattered facts and hypotheses and evolve toward a unified, logical pattern of basic concepts. Psychology, in a sense, can be seen as a science in its youth, vigorous but full of contradictions and conflicts. We have attempted, in the organization of our book, to bring order to this wealth of information by moving from past to present, from the individual to the group, from normal to abnormal.

Our wish to offer a balanced account of theories and experiments guided our decisions at every stage; the result is an eclectic text. We have no interest in emphasizing favorite, personal notions and have presented competing theories and differing views of controversial issues. Although our book covers a wide spectrum of psychology, we have tried to treat each topic in enough depth to give the reader a sense of its significance.

We should like to show psychologists in action—to allow students to see that psychologists strive constantly for better answers; that in the process they sometimes make mistakes (and sometimes learn from them!); that they often discover more than one useful answer to a question; and that no answer is absolutely final. Thus, we try not to tell students what to think; instead, we tell them what has been observed and how it was observed; and we present the sometimes-conflicting interpretations of these observations. On occasion, we show how successive experiments have altered and even overturned theories that once seemed well grounded in observation or common sense, or both. Our conviction is that the proper study of man is man himself, so we pay special attention to *human* behavior. Nonetheless, references to animal experiments are essential, as well as stimulating, so we include these wherever they can help us make a principle or process clear. This is particularly necessary in the chapter on learning, which could scarcely be written without reference to animal work, such as that done by Pavlov, Thorndike, Köhler, Hull, Tolman, and Skinner.

As with all areas of the academic world, psychology is cluttered with jargon. Although a lot of these words have their uses for psychologists, they can be tedious and even confusing to students. We have stayed clear of technical terms wherever possible. Those that do appear are defined immediately. In addition, we have put a list of key terms at the end of each chapter and a glossary at the end of the book. These aids should help students secure the vocabulary they need in order to follow our narrative and enjoy the course.

A detailed knowledge of the anatomy and physiology of the nervous system or of statistics is not essential for understanding the material presented in this book. These two topics are nevertheless included; the highlights of descriptive and inferential statistics in a 16-page appendix at the back of the book, and the anatomy and physiology of the nervous system in an 18-page appendix to Chapter 3 on the brain and behavior. Throughout the book we refer to specific neurophysiological structures and events, but whenever we do we provide sufficient explanation and illustration to make reference to the appendix unnecessary.

Organization. It is difficult to describe in a few sentences how all of this book's parts fit together, but a brief sketch of its skeleton may be useful. Chapter 1 is meant to provide a glimpse at the entire range of topics in psychology and leave our readers with a feeling for various research problems, strategies, and points of view. We follow with a chapter on human evolution and the genetic mechanisms of heredity. It places in perspective the physical and psychological character of *Homo sapiens* and lays down some basic principles of genetics as they relate to human behavior, with schizophrenia used as a specific example. From this discussion of heredity and behavior we move to the brain and behavior (Chapter 3—with an appendix on the human nervous system and endocrine system), perception (4), states of awareness (5), learning (6), memory and language (7), thinking (8), and dreams and symbols (9).

Chapters 2 through 9 focus on basic processes of human behavior and their applications in the day-to-day lives of ordinary people. With Chapter 10, we move on to more dynamic aspects—the motivations and emotions that shape and direct our behavior. Thus, chapters on motivation (10) and emotion (11) lead to those on aggression (12) and sexual behavior (13).

All of the first 13 chapters are concerned with psychological phenomena common to humans in general. The next four chapters—development (14), intelligence and its measurement (15), and personality theories (16) and assessment (17) point up individual differences that distinguish one person from another.

The next two chapters—attitudes (18) and groups (19)—carry us into the complex world of social psychology, where the basic processes that we derived from our study of individuals are now at hand to assist in the analysis of social situations.

So far we have been concerned primarily with so-called normal behavior. The final two chapters cover behavior disorders (20) and their treatment (21).

Special Topics. We have included a few chapters that most other introductory psychology books do not contain—chapters on states of awareness, dreams and symbols, aggression, and human sexual behavior. These topics have a strong bearing on the individual and on society and are, at present, especially active areas of investigation. In order to sustain this sense of contemporary research activity, we also invited a number of distinguished psychologists to write original essays on subjects related to their research—subjects that are also related to the needs and interests of college students. We are grateful to the following scholars who kindly contributed special pieces for us:

Rudolf Arnheim	Visual Perception in the Arts
Gordon Bower	Memorizing with Imaginary Maps
Daniel X. Freedman	Alcoholism
Harry Harlow & Stephen Suomi	Generalizations from Monkey to Man
Dorothea Jameson & Leo Hurvich	Color Vision
Eleanor Maccoby & Carol Jacklin	Psychological Differences Between the Sexes—and their Implications
Neal Miller	Control of Bodily Functions through Biofeedback
Martin Orne	Hypnosis
Zick Rubin	What Is This Thing Called Love?
Gary Schwartz	Meditation
Phillip Shaver	Psychology and Jury Selection
	On the Tip of My Tongue: Two Approaches to Memory Failure
Janet Spence	Highlights of Descriptive and Inferential Statistics (Appendix)
Elliot Valenstein	Psychosurgery
Eric Wanner	Understanding Understanding

Aids for Students. Probably a good way to deaden a beginning student's first blush of excitement in a new course is to hand him or her a textbook as fat as this one. We wish that we had been able to keep it leaner, but we ran into the same difficulty that confronts most writers of introductory books. There is a lot of ground to cover, and the student has a lot to learn. We have tried to make the student's task easier by providing a number of learning aids. Although we stayed clear of graphics that serve no purpose beyond adornment, there are abundant illustrations that amplify and supplement the narrative. At the end of each chapter is a summary that presents the basic facts of the chapter in numbered, short paragraphs. This is followed by a list of suggested readings.

Besides these learning aids in the text itself, there is a student study guide. The study guide includes for each chapter an outline, a list of objectives, a semi-programmed review, a post-test, and application questions. The review questions are to be used immediately after the student has read the chapter, so that he or she can check understanding of the material. The post-test provides a quick review of major concepts, and the application questions help the student to see the relationship between theoretical concepts and everyday experiences.

We realize that it is an act of presumption to assume knowledge broad enough and deep enough to do justice to an entire discipline, particularly one as multifaceted as psychology. Certainly no one of the three authors would have been comfortable about taking on this task alone. There is comfort in numbers, however, and we felt that the sum total of our separate experiences in research and teaching—spanning psychology's main areas—gave us a reasonable base upon which to erect a comprehensive textbook for beginning students.

Acknowledgments. Of course no three people can write a well-balanced text without ample help. Our most important collaborators are those hundreds of men and women who by their scientific activities have made psychology what it is today. We dedicate this book to them and hope we have represented their work sensibly and well.

We had to call upon many other people for assistance. Most significant of those who assisted us are the individuals who prepared draft materials for various chapters. These include Hazel Markus (Chapter 18), Irwin Sarason (Chapter 20 and 21), Sandra Scarr-Salapatek (Chapter 14), Timothy Teyler (Chapter 6, 7 and 15), and Robert Zajonc (Chapter 18 and 19). Several other people helped us in various ways. They are Arno Baule, Ralph Berger, Linda Burdette, David Marlowe, Vernon J. Nordby, and Richard A. Roemer. Our publisher gave us advice and guidance from many psychologists active in teaching and research. To these critics, often wisely blunt in their complaints, we owe a great deal. Any errors that remain are our responsibility. To the following reviewers we give our most sincere thanks: Vernon L. Allen (University of Wisconsin), Leonard Blau (Chabot College), James Butcher (University of Minnesota), Deborah Fein (Trenton State College), Gillian Hamilton (Hunter College), Andrew Hansson (Grand Rapids Junior College), Sidney Hochman (Nassau Community College), Lester M. Hyman (Michigan State University), Carol Jacklin (Stanford University), Ruth Koch (Manhattan Community College), Ronald W. Mayer (San Francisco State College), Sharon Nash (Stanford University), Carnot Nelson (University of South Florida), Craig Polite (SUNY, Stony Brook), Jay T. Rusmore (San Jose State College), Arthur Seagull (Michigan State University), Ronald E. Smith (University of Washington), Stephen Suomi (University of Wisconsin), Shelley Taylor (Harvard University), David G. Tierman (California State College, Hayward), Eric Wanner (Harvard University), and Sheldon Weintraub (SUNY, Stony Brook).

We are fortunate in having a publisher whose skill in producing introductory textbooks of high quality and pleasing design is widely recognized. The editorial staff worked hard to make our sentences clear and easy to read. We appreciate their genuine interest in the needs of teachers and students and their desire to produce a useful book. Indeed, whatever literary and esthetic merits this book may have are due in large part to the good taste and good sense of its publisher.

G. L.
C. H.
R. F. T.

January 1975

Contents

Chapter 1 Introduction

. . . . a man like me cannot live without a hobby-horse, a consuming passion—in Schiller's words a tyrant. I have found my tyrant, and in his service I know no limits. My tyrant is psychology.

—Sigmund Freud
(1895, in a letter to Wilhelm Fliess)

When, then, we talk of "psychology as a natural science," we must not assume that that means a sort of psychology that stands at last on solid ground. It means just the reverse; it means a psychology particularly fragile, and into which the waters of metaphysical criticism leak at every joint, . . . A string of raw facts; a little gossip and wrangle about opinions; a little classification and generalization on the mere descriptive level; a strong prejudice that we have states of mind, and that our brain conditions them: but not a single law in the sense in which physics shows us laws, not a single proposition from which any consequence can causally be deduced. . . . This is no science, it is only the hope of a science.

—William James
(Psychology: Briefer Course)

Introduction

Perhaps no course in the college curriculum has promised undergraduates more and delivered less than the first course in psychology. Many students expect that the study of psychology will enable them to understand and eliminate the bewildering inconsistencies, the persistent insecurities, the conflicts and unacceptable impulses that seem to be an inescapable part of their lives. They may anticipate that their relations with others will become smoother, more effective and rewarding. Quite reasonably, they may believe that with a firmer grasp of the principles of behavior, they will be able to understand the puzzling responses they often observe in those about them—including parents, brothers, sisters, friends, and even teachers.

However, the information actually presented under the heading of psychology may seem to some students more related to rats than to humans, more concerned with computers or statistics than with personal difficulties, more occupied with the mythical average person than with any particular individual, and more inclined toward abstract theories than toward practical solutions to the immediate problems of human behavior.

No book, or course, can satisfy every student's expectations. Nonetheless, we have tried to avoid some of the most persistent areas of disappointment. Wherever possible, we concentrate on human problems and studies rather than on research involving lower animals. We do not ignore the latter, however, for they have an important and legitimate role in psychology. Our use of statistics is sparse and simple. We consider problems of the individual and the social group much more often than findings that apply to the average but fictitious person.

We believe that most students will understand more about their own behavior after reading this book and that they will be able to understand better the consistencies and inconsistencies that they observe in others. We invite the reader to continually examine what is said on the following pages in the light of his or her own experience. We do not mean to imply that the ultimate test of the adequacy of a psychological generalization is its fit with one's own experience or with common sense. However, we would be surprised, and somewhat alarmed, if the reader's observations did not correspond at all with those of psychologists. More important, the process of examining our own observations of behavior in the context of the findings of psychologists does serve to enhance our understanding of ourselves and others.

What Is Psychology?

In a sense, each of us is a psychologist. We all observe human behavior, attempt to predict it, understand it, and, on occasion, control it. We not only observe and puzzle over our own behavior; we also attend to what those about us are doing and why. While this clearly overlaps the activities of the professional psychologist, we would not call it psychological inquiry, because the distinctive features of science are missing from these everyday observations.

For the psychologist, psychology is the _scientific study of behavior_. Psychologists and laymen define the term behavior in much the same way. Psychologists have argued over whether internal, subjective, mental events, such as images, memories, thoughts, and feelings, are within the domain of psychology. But most now agree that the term behavior is to be used broadly and includes all responses—motor acts and overt physiological responses as well as mental events. Thus, behavior includes both external and easily observable events and events that can only be inferred indirectly from verbal reports or from physiological indicators, for example, an increase in the rate of breathing or perspiring.

Scientific study has certain distinguishing features. The major ones are objectivity, repeatability, communication with others, and a systematic approach. _Objectivity_ involves providing definitions that are precise and fully understandable to any appropriately trained person, as well as making observations in such a manner that they accurately reflect what exists in the real (objectively observed) world. Adequate definitions allow one to measure something (whether it is height, dominance, intelligence, a motor skill, or motivation) so that it can be _quantified_—that is, numbers can be assigned to the observations in some meaningful and useful way. A major aim of these attempts to introduce objectivity is the elimination of the observer's personal biases, preconceptions, and convictions, which could easily distort or blur the event or object being observed. Investigators take great pains to minimize or eliminate subjectivity and the experimenter's bias from their psychological studies. For example, we may wish to test a drug's effects on behavior by comparing subjects who have taken the drug with a control group that has not had the drug. We make certain that the subjects do not know whether they have been given the drug. But we also keep this information from the experimenter, so that he does not know whether he is observing subjects who have taken the drug or those who have had a placebo (inactive substance). Such an experimental design, referred to as "double blind," is commonly used in psychology.

Not only must the data be collected in an objective fashion; the findings must be _repeatable_. Let us say the investigator reports that "A response followed by a reward will be more likely to occur again than a response not followed by a reward." With adequate definition of these terms, other psychologists should be able to observe this relationship regularly on many different occasions and in different settings. In this way, psychologists seek to establish and confirm empirical generalizations about significant aspects of behavior. A scientific finding must be capable of being shared with others not only in the sense of being communicated to them but also in the sense of being repeated by others in different laboratories. In short, *science must be public.*

A final commitment of a scientific discipline is to deal in an *orderly* and *comprehensive* manner with the events being studied. An investigator cannot treat isolated, interesting topics while leaving significant and related questions unanswered. A major contribution of psychological theory is to organize existing knowledge and to point out those areas of relative ignorance that are in need of investigation. While an amateur observer or hobbyist might pursue some special aspect of human behavior—such as the perception of triangles, changes in sensation when under the influence of hypnosis, or the psychological aspects of chess playing—psychology as a field is committed to dealing with the full range of significant human behavior.

Is the point of psychological theory, then, to make rational and systematic the psychologist's quest for an understanding of behavior? Indeed it is! In fact, one of the major contributions of theory is to provide both a network within which existing findings can be incorporated and seen in some relationship to one another and also a map of those questions that are relevant but have not yet been studied. For example, we may know that schizophrenia is characterized by certain intellectual deficiencies and that there is a strong hereditary contribution to the disorder. But what is the relationship between the intellectual deficiencies and the hereditary factors? In general, the psychologist's task is to explore behavior *systematically*—not by whim, personal interest, or even fashion, but so that eventually the total behaving organism will be described and understood in all its aspects.

Who Psychologists Are

When the American Psychological Association was founded in 1892, it consisted of 31 members, 17 of whom attended the first annual meeting at the University of Pennsylvania. Today, the membership is approximately 40,000 and attendance at annual meetings sometimes exceeds 15,000. How rapid this expansion has been can be shown by plotting the annual growth rate of psychologists against the annual increase in the U.S. population: If the two rates were to remain constant, it is possible to demonstrate the ridiculous—that before too many decades every citizen of the United States would be a psychologist! However, this prospect is not at all likely. Indeed, the rate of increase in the number of psychologists is already beginning to decline, as are the growth rates of virtually all academic disciplines.

A recent study of psychologists who have a Ph.D. degree (National Academy of Sciences, 1974), which included almost 25,000 respondents, permits us to make a number of generalizations about who doctoral psychologists are and where they work. About 20 percent are women—a far greater percentage than in most sciences. Only 2 percent are minority group members, a figure that is somewhat but not strikingly above comparable figures for other sciences. Currently, the American Psychological Association and many universities are making strenuous efforts to increase this figure.

As a group, doctoral psychologists are young. More than 25 percent are under 34 and almost 75 percent are under 50. More than 60 percent of these psychologists work in educational institutions, although only about 48 percent list teaching or research as their primary activity. More than 26 percent list consulting and professional activities as their primary work. The remaining 40 percent are in private practice, work for state or federal agencies, for profit-making businesses and industries, or for clinics and hospitals. The median salary for the entire group is $20,000; for those who received Ph.D.s in 1972, the median salary is approximately $16,000. Clearly, most psychologists have some association with schools, colleges, or universities, although many of them are serving as counselors, administrators, psychological testers, and investigators rather than as teachers.

To balance this picture, we must point out that many (perhaps most) people working as psychologists do not possess the doctoral degree. Particularly in such important areas of applied psychology as school psychology, counseling, and industrial and clinical psychology, most psychologists do not have training beyond the master's degree. It is estimated that there are approximately 10,000 high school teachers offering courses that deal in part or whole with psychology. While few of these teachers have more technical training than an undergraduate major in psychology, they serve a vital function by introducing psychology to a wide range of students.

Table 1-1, which lists the divisions of the American Psychological Association, gives some indication of psychologists' diversity of interests and professional activity. These groups vary in size from about 400 to 5,000 members; each holds meetings at which technical papers are presented, and each publishes its own newsletters or journals. Many psychologists belong to more than one of these divisions.

What Psychologists Do

Psychologists can be categorized in many ways. One can divide them according to their level of training (doctoral or master's degree, and so on), where they work (university, college, high school, hospital, private practice, government agency, and so on), level of income, or in terms of demographic factors, such as sex or ethnic status. Perhaps the most significant distinction is based on what psychologists do, the activities in which they are engaged.

The most general classification in terms of activity divides psychologists into those who teach psychology, those who investigate psychological problems, and those who apply techniques or skills derived from

Table 1-1 Divisions of the American Psychological Association

Title of Division	Number of Members
Division of General Psychology	1531
Division on the Teaching of Psychology	2522
Division of Experimental Psychology	1158
Division on Evaluation and Measurement	887
Division of Physiological and Comparative Psychology	635
Division on Developmental Psychology	985
Division of Personality and Social Psychology	4705
The Society for the Psychological Study of Social Issues	2104
Division on Psychology and the Arts	367
Division of Clinical Psychology	3870
Division of Consulting Psychology	563
Division of Industrial and Organizational Psychology	1209
Division of Educational Psychology	3668
Division of School Psychology	2453
Division of Counseling Psychology	2248
Division of Psychologists in Public Service	611
Division of Military Psychology	432
Division of Adult Development and Aging	381
Society of Engineering Psychologists	418
Division of Rehabilitation Psychology	859
Division of Consumer Psychology	335
Division of Philosophical Psychology	490
Division for the Experimental Analysis of Behavior	1431
Division of the History of Psychology	463
Division of Community Psychology	1025
Division of Psychopharmacology	1461
Division of Psychotherapy	2435
Division of Psychological Hypnosis	433
Division of State Psychological Affairs	1268
Division of Humanistic Psychology	647
Division on Mental Retardation	401

psychological study. Obviously, this distinction between teaching, research, and application is blurred because many teachers also do research and many are also consulting, or applied, psychologists. Even with this relatively high degree of overlap, we still can place most psychologists in one, or perhaps a few, of the categories described below. First, let us deal with those fields that are primarily involved in teaching and research. Then we shall turn to the areas more concerned with the applications of psychology.

Developmental Psychology. Traditionally, *developmental psychologists* have been concerned with the study of child development, but in recent years adolescence, adulthood, and the aged have drawn increasing interest. Every area of human functioning has a place in this specialty, whether it is intelligence, motor skills, the senses, morality, behavior

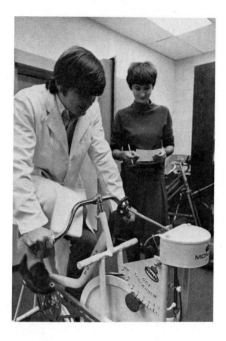

1-1
A human experimental psychologist focuses on testing in the laboratory. (Top) The mirror-drawing test is concerned with motor-skill learning. With only the reflected view of her movements to guide her, the subject attempts to draw a line through the maze without touching its border lines. (Bottom) The subject exercises before going into a sleep chamber; the effect of such physical activity on dreaming is then investigated. (Van Bucher, Courtesy of University of Florida)

pathology, or language. Each phenomenon is viewed in a developmental frame of reference. Thus, this study comprises general psychology but with special attention to changes over time and, often, to particular age groups.

Most of the work in this area is still done with children; many centers and institutes are devoted to the study of infant and child behavior. Some investigators have focused their efforts on longitudinal studies in which the same subjects are studied over periods of time—sometimes over many years. A major concern of developmental psychologists has been the process of socialization—how the immature, asocial and relatively helpless infant is transformed into a functioning member of society. An important part of socialization is the process whereby language is acquired, and this is now an area of vigorous research activity. Though developmental psychology has been with us since the very beginning of psychological study, its current popularity clearly is increasing.

Human Experimental Psychology. The broad domain of *human experimental psychology* includes all topics that are especially amenable to experimentation. In particular, sensory psychology, and the study of perception, learning, and thinking, have been the key topics over the years. Although in principle it is possible to conduct experiments on any aspect of human behavior, the simpler the process and the more readily it can be isolated for study, the more likely it is that many well-designed experiments will be conducted. Thus experiments on vision, hearing, thinking, and learning had been conducted decades before the experimental method was introduced into social and personality psychology. Experimental psychology exists on the borderline between the physical sciences and the behavioral sciences. Its methods and problems and even the background of its investigators share much with such areas as physics. Together with animal experimental psychology, it is the most rigorous and self-consciously scientific of all the areas of psychology. Human experimental psychology was also the primary concern of those who founded psychology as a scientific discipline.

Animal Experimental Psychology. This psychological specialty has much in common with human experimental psychology, except for the fact that the research is conducted with lower animals—typically rats, mice, dogs, pigeons, cats, apes, and monkeys, although at one time or another almost every kind of animal has been subjected to behavioral study. The bulk of research in animal experimental psychology has focused upon the learning process; much of modern learning theory was based initially on findings secured with lower animals.

Casual observers often are puzzled that psychologists should show so much interest in nonhuman subjects when their field is centered on the study of human behavior. Several compelling factors account for this apparent paradox. First, there are a variety of important questions having to do with human behavior that cannot be pursued with humans but can be explored with rats, pigeons, or such. The reasons for this include the relatively short life-span of many organisms, the relatively small expenses of working with animals as opposed to humans, and the ethical restraints that sometimes apply less to lower animals than to humans. Second, the physiological similarities and differences between species often provide the basis for important new insights into the factors that determine the behavior of the species in question. For example, if a hypothesis says that a particular part of the brain is essential to a given type of perception and if it can be demonstrated that this type of perception can be made by lower animals lacking this part of the brain, the original hypothesis may need to be revised or perhaps abandoned. Third, many psychologists share the biologists' keen interest in the evolution of species; and a proper understanding of the process of evolution depends on the study of many species.

Physiological Psychology. Just as experimental psychology is the portion of psychology closest to the physical sciences, *physiological psychology* is the area closest to the biological sciences. Indeed, whether one labels a problem in physiological psychology as part of the biological or psychological world becomes quite arbitrary. Even the new interdiscipline between these fields is referred to either as psychobiology or biopsychology.

Individuals working in this area are concerned with the physiological determinants and consequences of behavior. Interest in the relation between brain function and behavior has increased in recent years. The relationship between hormone action and behavior continues to be a topic of great significance and growing concern. The role of genetic variation in normal and pathological functioning has led to the emergence of a new subdiscipline — behavior genetics. Psychopharmacology, the study of drugs and behavior, is another recent subfield that has generated great interest. Psychopharmacology ranges from studies dealing with the gross behavioral effects of drugs to molecular research into the neural and metabolic processes involved in producing a drug's effects.

Quantitative Psychology. The primary aim of *quantitative psychology* is to develop mathematical, statistical, and quantitative methods of studying and understanding human behavior. Many individuals in this area are concerned with *applied statistics* — the design of experiments and the analysis of data to arrive at reasonable and dependable conclusions. Others want to develop tests or scales that yield numerical scores representing significant aspects of human behavior. All psychological test development is closely associated with quantitative methods.

Psychologists have recently attempted to go beyond statistical analysis and to develop mathematical models to represent (and predict) significant areas of behavior. This subfield, known as *mathematical psychology*, is related most closely to sensory psychology, learning, and decision-making.

Personality Psychology. *Personality psychologists* are concerned with the individual and with differences between individuals. They are particularly interested in the motivational aspects of behavior. Their interests range from the normal and even creative personality to the deviant or pathological personality. Much of the effort in this field has sought to develop means of classifying individuals in some useful and predictive manner, or at least devising dimensions that can be used to compare or

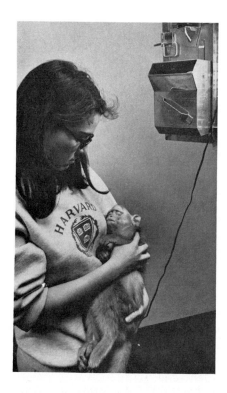

1-2
The results of experimental studies of animals often may be generalized to human behavior. (Top) A rhesus monkey is recovering from an operation in which the two halves of its brain were split. We discuss split-brain studies in Chapter 3. (Bottom) Chimps in a "playroom" are observed to determine how they interact after isolation. (Van Bucher, Photo Researchers; Jim Amos, Photo Researchers)

contrast different people. Not surprisingly, the development of personality measures to predict normal and pathological behavior has long been an active area of study.

While much of psychology may be accused justifiably of displaying a greater interest in the generalized individual than the unique individual, personality psychologists are particularly interested in the qualities that distinguish one individual from another. Indeed, some psychologists have considered the field of personality to be devoted solely to the study of the individual's unique qualities. While this point of view is not common among psychologists, most personality psychologists share an interest in case histories and a concern for the individual and his distinctive features.

Social Psychology. *Social psychologists* study man as a social animal who interacts frequently, if not continually, with other humans and lives in groups ranging from the family to the society. We have already discussed areas of psychology that are oriented toward the biophysical sciences; social psychology is an area closely associated with the other social sciences, particularly sociology. Indeed, many individuals who are trained and employed as sociologists call themselves social psychologists.

The social psychologist is concerned with the effect of the group (whether family, peer, professional, subcultural, or societal) upon the individual, and vice versa. But he is also interested in a wide variety of other personal interactions. For example, the factors that determine interpersonal preferences, the development and maintenance of prejudice and discrimination, the formation of attitudes, the effect of groups upon problem-solving, the appearance of mass phenomena such as mobs or crowd behavior, and socially deviant behavior are all significant problems for social psychologists.

Educational Psychology. In a field closely related to human experimental psychology, particularly in the study of learning, *educational psychologists* deal with all the psychological aspects of the educational process. In addition to the principles of learning, educational psychologists study such topics as the ways in which educational performance is influenced by individual differences in motivation, personality factors, and social interaction. Their research examines such variables as teacher-student interaction, the effects upon learning and morale of class size, type of instruction, and grouping by ability. On a larger scale, they may investigate the social organization of schools and the selection and training of teachers and school psychologists. Because of their interest in individual differences, educational psychologists are often expert in measurement and applied statistics.

Applied Psychology

Thus far we have discussed areas in which the psychologist is primarily an investigator or teacher of psychology. At least as important in terms of numbers and human significance are the *applied psychologists*. The distinguishing activity of these psychologists is that they apply their

1-3
Social psychologists study interactions between groups—the family, classmates, whole communities— and the individual. These people are singing "We Shall Overcome" at the funeral of Martin Luther King, Jr. (Steve Larson)

skills to the psychological problems faced by individuals and groups. It is essential to train individuals to occupy these roles and many of the specialized areas of applied psychology described below are also topics of instruction in colleges and universities. Courses are offered at both graduate and undergraduate levels in clinical psychology, industrial psychology, and related topics. Research may also be a significant part of the applied psychologist's practice.

Clinical Psychology. Probably the area of application that is most familiar to the general public is *clinical psychology.* Clinical psychologists may do many different things, but they always are concerned with helping other individuals toward psychological well-being. Traditionally one thinks of the clinician as having three functions: research, diagnosis, and treatment. In reality, the individual clinical psychologist may perform only one or two of these functions. When it comes to treatment, as we shall discover, there are almost as many techniques as there are therapists. The difference between clinical psychologists and other psychological healers, such as psychiatrists, is that they do not ordinarily use physical methods of treatment, for example, those involving drugs or surgery.

Psychologists use many diagnostic techniques, including interviews and psychological tests. Psychological tests range from the highly structured and standardized to the completely unstructured and nonstandardized. The clinical psychologist's research is wide-ranging, but usually focuses on psychologically disturbed subjects or on a topic that may shed light on a psychopathological process. Clinical psychologists may work in a university, clinic, or hospital, or in private practice. Most psychologists in private practice are clinical psychologists.

Community Mental Health. For many years considered specialists within clinical psychology, psychologists in *community mental health* have in recent years asserted the relative independence of their field, arguing that its differences in approach from clinical psychology as traditionally practiced are greater than its similarities. Workers in community mental health are less concerned with psychotherapy and psychodiagnosis than with the environmental setting within which behavioral disturbances appear or might appear. They are interested more in environmental intervention—for example, in altering how a school is organized and administered or how an entire community deals with its adolescents and children—than in changing the behavior of any single individual. Their training is more likely to include some sociology and anthropology than is the training of the clinical psychologist. If the clinical psychologist can be seen as a close relative of the psychiatrist, then the community mental health worker is comparably closer to the social worker.

Counseling Psychology. *Counseling psychologists* work primarily with people who have only minor problems, such as those associated with educational or vocational choices. A large proportion of these psychologists work in colleges, helping students to adjust to the demands of campus life or to plan their academic futures or careers. An important

1-4
The clinical psychologist attempts to diagnose an individual's inner conflicts and concerns. Various kinds of tests may be used, including the Rorschach test shown here. In Chapter 17, this technique of personality measurement is discussed. (Van Bucher, Photo Researchers)

part of a counseling psychologist's role is assessing the individual's relative strengths and weaknesses. Often he will use psychological tests to help make this appraisal. Unlike the clinical psychologist, he probably will not work with the extremes of behavior deviation. Also, unless he is counseling people who have physical disabilities, he is less likely to be working in a medical or hospital setting. In general, the counseling psychologist helps relatively normal individuals to use their strengths to the fullest.

School Psychology. *School psychologists* have much in common with both community mental health workers and counseling psychologists. However, their role is limited to primary and secondary school settings, and they are more likely to refer individuals to other specialists for specific treatment than to give this treatment themselves. Within the school, their activities include vocational and educational testing and advising, organizing training programs that help teachers relate better to students and other teachers, and conducting research designed to answer questions of practical significance to the school and its administrators. The school psychologist may conduct studies to determine the effectiveness of new teaching programs, study the morale of students or teachers, or investigate the incidence of illegal drug use and the usefulness of educational programs in changing the patterns of drug use.

Industrial Psychology. *Industrial psychologists*—also called business psychologists—may work directly for a particular industry or company or they may work as consultants to many organizations. In any case, they deal with a range of problems that have to do with the human element in the business setting. They are often concerned with classifying people and jobs, helping to select more reliably and with greater efficiency the most suitable applicant for a particular job, and also helping to ensure that employees are used in a manner that enhances their potential contribution to themselves and the company. Psychological tests and interviews are essential tools. Industrial psychologists also develop training programs that may increase technical skills, improve the individual's ability to deal with others, raise morale, or decrease tension in groups of workers. They may study a company as a human organization and recommend changes that are intended to increase the productivity and morale of the employees.

An important area of industrial psychology involves the study of the specific relations between men and machines—often referred to as *engineering psychology*. Engineering psychologists attempt to make the man-machine relationship as efficient and rewarding as possible. Consequently, they are often involved in the design of equipment or machines to ensure that workers can use them easily and reliably. Recent attempts to devise spacecraft so that the astronauts can operate them and live in them with the greatest efficiency and comfort are a clear illustration. Another is the continuing attempt to design automobiles that enhance the motorist's safety and comfort.

A related practitioner is the *consumer psychologist.* Consumer psychologists explore those psychological factors that determine product and brand preferences. They seek to learn why consumers prefer one product to another or why they buy—or shun—a particular product.

Most psychologists who work in marketing or advertising fall into this category. Generally, they rely heavily upon surveys or questionnaires to find out from potential consumers what their response to particular products is or might be. There is also an important role to be played by consumer psychologists in informing the public how to make wise purchasing decisions.

Methods of Psychology

It is easy to say that the methods of psychology are the methods of science; it is also true. Nevertheless, there are some distinctive features to the ways in which psychologists characteristically go about answering questions, and it is useful to identify these.

The Experimental Method

One can have a science without experiments—this is more or less the case with astronomy and geology—but it is not easy. Moreover, among scientists, the inability to experiment entails a certain loss in status. This follows from the fact that the *experimental method* provides an elegant and powerful means of answering questions and is more definitive and rigorous than other methods. Among the advantages of the experiment are the investigator's ability to control just when and where the observations are to be made. Thus, he is in the best possible position to make objective and accurate observations. Second, the experimental method permits the investigator to repeat his studies, or to have others repeat them, thus lessening the role of personal bias or chance factors. Third, the experimenter approaches his problem in a systematic manner in which all of the steps are explicitly set forth.

Two essential ingredients in an experiment are manipulation and control. An investigator must be able to manipulate (vary systematically) a condition or variable whose effect he wishes to understand. This variable, which ordinarily is called the *independent variable*, is the antecedent variable. The experimenter wishes to discover its effects upon some consequent variable—usually referred to as the *dependent variable*. A learning psychologist, for example, may vary the presence or the frequency of reinforcement (reward) after a subject has successfully completed a learning task, such as running a maze or memorizing a verbal passage. Then he will examine the effect upon subsequent performance of reward versus no reward, or reward on every trial as opposed to reward on alternate trials, or on randomized trials. Another experimenter may vary the level of light and examine the accuracy with which people perform a motor skill under different lighting conditions. Another may vary the degree of psychological stress and measure the subsequent variation in the strength of a person's motivation to be with others (affiliation motivation). In all of these cases, the experimenter is able to determine that manipulations of the independent variable (the reward, illumination, or stress), will have a particular, measurable effect upon the dependent variable (rate of learning, or accuracy, or need to affiliate with others). He can repeat his experiment as many times as necessary to satisfy himself and others of the stability of the finding.

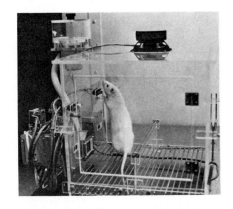

1-5
The experimental method involves the manipulation of independent variables to see their effect on dependent variables. The rat in the shuttle box (see Chapter 10) presses the lever to escape a shock. (Beckwith Studios)

In an experiment, the investigator is studying the effect of one variable's controlled change upon another variable. To make dependable generalizations about the relationship between these two variables, however, the experimenter also must control any other variables that might influence the dependent variable. Thus, an investigator using food as his reward obviously must control his subjects' hunger—food does not reinforce a well-fed subject. The experimenter must introduce a control, such as the interval since the subject has last eaten. Or, if he is working with lower animals, he may use them in experiments when their weight is a certain proportion below their normal weight. While controlling every variable is virtually impossible, this is the experimenter's ideal goal—so he attempts to hold constant every variable that he knows or suspects will affect the dependent variable.

One usually thinks of an experiment in terms of varying a single independent variable and assessing its consequences on a single dependent variable. However, with modern methods of statistical analysis, the experimenter can vary a number of variables and assess their effect on one or more dependent variables. Indeed, in many areas of psychology, the effects of more than one variable *must* be examined at the same time because this is how they occur in the real world. Their joint influence on behavior may be considerably more important than their effects when examined individually.

Initially, the experimental method was considered the exclusive property of psychologists working in the traditional areas of experimental psychology—the study of perception, learning, and such. But for many years experimentation has been accepted as a useful tool in such areas as social and personality psychology—even though such studies are often more difficult to contrive and may involve a lower degree of control of relevant variables than the traditional areas of experimentation.

Systematic Observation

Although all people observe human behavior, their observations show varying degrees of accuracy. *Systematic observation* makes more sensitive and consistent the capacity to observe others and to infer what they are doing. It includes a wide variety of approaches, from informal observation, to simple rating scales (the observer simply estimates how often a subject does something), to highly complicated mechanical devices with which the observer can record the type, duration, and intensity of particular kinds of behavior.

Anthropology is a discipline built largely upon systematic observation. Social anthropologists observe the members of a tribe or society over a long period of time. In addition, they record their observations in great detail while they are still fresh in the mind. Such scientists may direct their attention toward particular types of behavior because of their special interests. Thus, an anthropologist may be especially interested in religion, economics, sexual behavior, or tribal organization; each topic will direct his observations in a somewhat different direction.

Like anthropologists, psychologists must identify the variable or variables they wish to observe and then define these as precisely as possible. They also try to record observations as soon as they make them. Using

A

B

1-6
Psychologists systematically observe human behavior in natural settings to determine the type and frequency of behavior exhibited. They might, for example, be interested in noting the tendency to behave aggressively toward a doll (A) or in the interactions of children at play (B). (A. J. W. Cella, Photo Researchers; B. Bruce Roberts, Rapho Guillumette)

several observers to watch the same event is a common way to check the reliability of one's observations and lessen the likelihood that observer bias will prejudice the observations.

Survey Methods

Survey methods involve questionnaires and/or interviews to measure attitudes or opinions of sizable segments of a population. Surveys, or polls, are best known as political barometers—ways to predict election results or public reaction to policy decisions of broad importance, such as income tax reform and national health care programs.

The survey method demands careful attention to two important considerations: Are the respondents truly representative of the population being surveyed (adequacy of sampling)? Are the questions truly unbiased? Questions must not suggest a particular response, but they must cover fully the area of opinion in question. While we shall discuss these methods in greater detail in Chapter 18, let us note here that survey methods have achieved great descriptive and predictive success in recent decades. Polls and surveys are not infallible, but when used by a properly trained social scientist to answer a reasonable question, they can be very accurate.

Case Studies

The experiment is the ideal means of answering a question when a good deal is known about the factors that influence the behavior being studied. But when the investigator is working in a relatively uncharted area and has neither good hypotheses nor a firm sense of the key variables, then a *case study*, a detailed study of an individual, may provide an understanding that could never be obtained from the examination of experimental findings. Examination of individual case studies may enable the investigator to arrive at hypotheses that can be experimentally tested.

As this suggests, the case study has a greater role in the formation of hypotheses than in the testing of them. For example, psychoanalysis rests upon the individual therapeutic case—Freud's patients provided the basic data upon which psychoanalytic theory was structured—and psychoanalysis has been one of the most productive and influential sets of psychological ideas yet uncovered. Still, one can accept generalizations from a case study only tentatively; their validity must be confirmed by some more objective means.

Correlation Approaches

The study of individual differences has a long and hallowed tradition in psychology. From the very beginning, psychologists have recognized the obvious—that individuals differ—and have attempted to qualify and study these differences. In fact, research psychologists can be divided roughly into experimentalists (who usually find individual differences a nuisance because they are looking for general laws) and students of individual differences, who are less likely to resort to experiments and more likely to use methods of correlation. *Correlation techniques* are means of estimating the extent to which two variables or events tend to covary or go together.

Psychologists have devoted much of their energy to measurement. They have assessed almost every conceivable aspect of behavior, and certain areas of behavior have been the focus of concerted measurement efforts for many years. The measuring devices are tremendously varied—one of the most common and best known is the psychological test—but all of them provide a score to be assigned to a dimension of behavior. The *psychometric* tradition has produced hundreds of tests of intelligence, personality, interests, values, motivation, and other psychological variables. In addition, psychologists often employ measures of various physical, physiological, biochemical, and social variables that are highly relevant to behavior.

With all of these measures available to them, it is inevitable that psychologists are interested in learning how the measures relate to one another. As mentioned above, correlation techniques provide a means of assessing the degree of association between two or more measures. For example, let us say we wish to assess the degree of association between height and leadership effectiveness. If we have ways to measure both variables, a *correlation coefficient* will tell us whether they tend to be positively or negatively related or not related at all (actually they tend to have a low positive correlation). Or, if we wish to relate IQ to socioeconomic status we again can resort to a correlation coefficient; this time we would find a moderate positive correlation.

Knowing that two variables are highly correlated is an interesting and potentially significant bit of information. However, it does not ordinarily tell us much about causation. For example, if we are interested in social dominance and find that our measure of dominance is highly correlated with a measure of dietary adequacy, this does not tell us whether diet influences dominance, or dominance determines food intake, or a third variable (such as heredity) determines both dominance and food intake. This difficulty with inferring causation from correlation is one of the reasons that many psychologists favor the use of experiments, where causal inferences can be made with more confidence.

A Brief Historical Perspective

Once man's brain became large enough and sufficiently differentiated to permit thought and reflection, one of the first targets of this new capacity was undoubtedly man himself. Certainly when our ancestors became literate they devoted a sizable proportion of their writing to observation and speculation about human nature. Traditionalists sometimes claim that the writings of Plato and Aristotle contain most of the wisdom that has been re-acquired so painfully in the intervening centuries through controlled observation and experimentation.

Despite these early stirrings of formal interest in human behavior, psychology as a scientific discipline usually is considered to have originated in middle Europe in the late 19th century as a complex hybrid of philosophy and the newly emerging discipline of experimental biology. Scientists such as Wundt, Helmholtz, Ebbinghaus, and Brentano played a large part in these developments. During this period, every American scholar who aspired to become a psychologist went to Europe (usually Germany) to secure his doctoral degree. It was not until the second or third decade of the 20th century that any sizable number of American psychologists received their advanced training in this country.

Psychology in this period was dominated by a limited number of "schools." Each school was characterized by a particular theoretical approach, an interest in certain limited aspects of behavior, its own preferred methods of studying behavior, and a set of ardent believers. Among the most significant of these schools were structuralism, Gestalt psychology, behaviorism, and psychoanalysis. We shall discover that although psychologists today are not divided into competing schools of thought, some of these viewpoints have maintained lively traditions within contemporary psychology.

Structuralism

An approach initiated by Wilhelm Wundt in Leipzig, Germany, in what is generally regarded as the first laboratory of experimental psychology, became known as *structuralism*. Edward Titchener, an Englishman who was a dominant figure in American psychology during the first three decades of this century, brought the theory of structuralism to America. This first school of psychology was modeled on the physical sciences and their success in identifying the fundamental elements of the physical world. The structuralists developed a technique called *introspection*, which employed subjects trained to report in precise detail their subjective experiences under various laboratory conditions. In this way, the structuralists sought to identify the fundamental elements of

1-7
Wilhelm Wundt, who founded the world's first psychology laboratory in Leipzig, Germany in 1879. (The Bettmann Archive)

1-8
Edward Titchener brought structuralist theories to America. (The Granger Collection)

mental experiences and thus the structure of the mind. Introspection was supposed to reveal the content of the normal, conscious human mind. It was assumed that the mind was so generalizable that even a small number of subjects, intensively studied, could reveal its basic mental elements and structure. For Titchener, psychology was the scientific study of consciousness and introspection was the preferred method of scientific observation.

Wundt and Titchener's detailed concepts and findings are no longer significant. Some have been absorbed into special areas of psychology, especially the study of the senses, while others have quietly disappeared. Structuralism's major contemporary significance is that it provided a point of view against which other theories could be pitted. Thus, Gestalt psychology, behaviorism, and psychoanalysis were as much attempts to correct structuralism's perceived deficiencies as they were efforts to develop new theoretical positions. Gestalt psychology opposed dividing the mind into elements; behaviorism rejected the whole notion that consciousness could be studied objectively; and psychoanalysis pointed out that there is much more to the mind than consciousness.

Gestalt Psychology

While structuralism sought to resolve the mysteries of behavior by analyzing mental events into their fundamental parts, the *Gestaltists* saw the most significant aspect of experience as being its wholeness and interrelatedness. For them, any attempt to analyze behavior into parts was doomed to fail because it lost the most important and distinctive characteristic of experience—its wholeness, organization, and pattern. No stimulus has constant significance or meaning; everything depends upon the pattern of surrounding events. Lukewarm water feels hot when your hand has been immersed in ice water but it feels cold when your hand has been in hot water. A six-footer appears short when he plays basketball with a professional team, but he looks like a giant if he stands among pygmies.

Gestalt psychology, like structuralism, focused upon subjective experience and the exploration of consciousness. However, it did not rely so heavily upon trained subjects and was much more interested in reports

1-9
Kurt Koffka and Wolfgang Köhler, two of the founders of Gestalt psychology, which emphasized the wholeness of experience. (The Granger Collection)

made by untrained observers of experiences occurring outside the laboratory. This unstructured reporting of experience, referred to as the *phenomenological approach,* led to Gestalt psychology's interest in the processes of thinking, reasoning, and problem-solving. The other area in which Gestalt psychology has made an impact is perception—particularly visual perception.

In some respects, Gestalt psychology has always seemed to be less closely linked to the physical sciences than structuralism and behaviorism. Consequently, Gestalt psychologists appear less attracted to the rigors of controlled experimentation. Their studies have been more informal and bear more resemblance to those of the speculative philosopher than those of the physicist. Today, relatively few psychologists identify themselves as Gestaltists, but all branches of psychology recognize the importance of context and pattern.

Behaviorism

Structuralists used the method of introspection in attempting to identify the basic elements of consciousness; Gestaltists argued that the pursuit of elements was fruitless and could only destroy the most characteristic and fundamental aspect of experience—its wholeness. In striking contrast to both positions, *behaviorists* were perfectly willing to analyze behavior into fundamental elements but they completely dismissed both consciousness and the method of introspection. Instead, they devoted themselves to the objective observation of overt behavior.

Many individuals contributed to the founding of behaviorism, including particularly the brilliant Russian physiologist Pavlov, whose classical conditioning work with dogs is one of the cornerstones of modern learning theory. However, it was John B. Watson who made behaviorism a rallying point for American psychologists in the early part of this century. Watson was a handsome, talented, dogmatic, and driven man who left his mark upon psychology in half a lifetime, before a sensational divorce drove him from the academic world into advertising, where he also became a significant figure.

Watson emphasized the importance of environmental events, rejected all aspects of the individual that could not be observed externally and objectively, and believed that all behavior could be understood as a result of conditioning (learning). Thus, he advocated a psychology that rejected the nonobservable and subjective, and relied solely upon the objective and observable. Psychology became the study of overt behavior and the learning process instead of internal events and introspection.

Watson, unlike Titchener, believed in applications of psychology. His extension of behaviorism to child development had an impact on our society's child-rearing patterns that can be compared only with that of Sigmund Freud and Dr. Spock. Watson recommended that mothers never hug and kiss their children or let them sit on their laps. "If you must," he said, "kiss them once on the forehead when they say goodnight. Shake hands with them in the morning" (Watson, 1928). The advice has earned him infamous immortality.

Although Watson's version of behaviorism is no longer significant, many points of view derived from it also emphasize learning and the ob-

1-10
J. B. Watson, one of the founders of behaviorism, believed that psychology was the study of observable events. (Culver Pictures)

1-11
Most of B. F. Skinner's theories about human behavior are based on laboratory experiments with animals—especially pigeons and rats. (Ken Heyman)

jective approach to studying behavior. These forms of behaviorism continue to be dominant influences in modern psychology. Indeed, B. F. Skinner, who in many ways is the closest parallel to Watson on the current scene, is unquestionably one of the most influential psychologists in the world today—both in his direct effect upon the field of psychology and in his impact on the world at large. He, too, has had something to say about the rearing of children, as well as the building of social groups and even societies—as we shall see in Chapters 6 and 14.

Psychoanalysis

The schools of psychology we have just discussed all had their beginnings in the experimental laboratory. Quite the contrary is true of psychoanalysis, which had its origins in the treatment of mental patients. Sigmund Freud was, and remains, the major figure in this tradition. Although he and many of his followers were trained in medicine rather than psychology, the impact of Freud's ideas and techniques upon psychology has been far-reaching. In fact, psychoanalysis is the early school that has most successfully carried over into the modern world of psychology.

Psychoanalysis is a method of studying human behavior; a theory of behavior; and a method of treatment. As a method of study, it combines the use of free association—the subject speaks the first thought that comes to mind without inhibition or censorship—a permissive setting, and typically a couch on which the patient reclines looking away from the therapist. Under these circumstances, and with a minimum of intervention by the psychoanalyst, the patient usually reveals a host of material that is not only private—in that he has not told others about it—but also unconscious in that he himself was not consciously aware of it. It is difficult to overstate the extent to which the revelations elicited by this method depart from those usually available even in our most intimate relationships. Freud devised a window to aspects of the person that previously had been known only to mystics, priests, and psychotics.

1-12
Sigmund Freud, the father of psychoanalysis. (Culver Pictures)

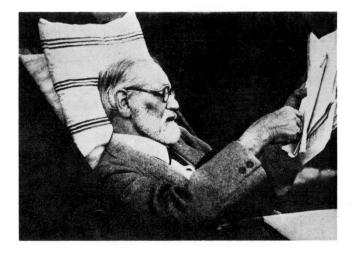

We shall have much more to say about psychoanalysis as a theory of behavior in Chapters 16 and 21. But, in brief, Freud's theory emphasized the overriding importance of early (particularly infantile) experience, of sexual drives, and of the unconscious, in determining adult behavior. In combination, these assumptions about behavior lead quite naturally to the belief that the individual's early relations with other members of his family, particularly with his parents, are vital in his development.

As a method of therapy, psychoanalysis involves use of the couch, free association, and occasional interpretation by the psychoanalyst as an aid to bringing the unconscious into consciousness and resolving the infantile conflicts whose residues in the unconscious interfere with current adjustment. In general, the analyst plays a relatively passive role, making interpretations infrequently.

No sooner had Freud and his revolutionary ideas gained acceptance than the cohesive group that had formed about him in Vienna began to divide and divide again. On both personal and intellectual grounds, many variants of psychoanalysis appeared; some of the best-known schools were those led by Jung, Adler, and Rank. Psychoanalysis in its various forms came to dominate American psychiatry and had a pervasive influence upon psychology—particularly upon personality theory and the practice of clinical psychology. While some see a waning of this influence, it continues to be a contemporary position of great importance.

The Contemporary Scene

As we have observed, psychologists no longer classify themselves into competitive schools of thought that can be distinguished readily by their different concepts, assumptions, methods, and the behavior they study. Most modern psychologists are eclectic (drawing from several theories) to some degree. A fair number of psychologists will identify themselves proudly (even aggressively) as behaviorists or as believers in classical psychoanalysis, but this is far from typical. Most psychologists borrow assumptions and concepts from various theories according to the needs of the particular situation at hand.

The recent development of *humanistic psychology* in many ways resembles the appearance of the classical schools of psychology. Often referred to as the "third force" in modern psychology—in contrast to the major existing forces of behaviorism and psychoanalysis—humanistic psychology undoubtedly has been the most rapidly developing theoretical position in modern psychology. Its growth owes much to the writings of Abraham Maslow, Gordon Allport, and Carl Rogers. More attuned to literature and the humanities and less attentive to the scientific disciplines, humanistic psychologists generally emphasize man's positive features and growth capacity. They consider their position a healthy antidote for what they regard as the negativistic and mechanistic view of man espoused by Freud and the behaviorists.

In recent years, another trend has emerged—a move away from general theories about all or most of human behavior toward micro-theories that focus on special areas of behavior, such as hearing or vision, rote learning, psychological stress, or decision-making. These theories do not, of course, solve the problem of dealing with the whole person. But currently, we appear to be in a phase in which psychologists are pulling together the available knowledge about limited or specialized areas of behavior before they turn once again to the task of developing broad or generalized theories of human behavior.

We have seen something of the numbers, the diversity and the origins of psychologists. We also have seen that they share many characteristics with all scientists—particularly in their use of experimental methods—but that they possess certain distinctive features—especially their focus upon human behavior. In addition, psychology's use of particular techniques, such as the case study, surveys, and correlational methods, distinguishes it from most other fields of science. The psychologist's diverse activities take him from settings that resemble the biologist's or physicist's laboratory to research settings designed to study social behavior. Among today's psychologists are individuals engaged in field studies in schools, homes, and other nonlaboratory situations as well as applied psychologists working in clinics, hospitals, private offices, industrial settings, and government agencies. Theoretical changes in the contemporary American psychological scene appear to have involved a move away from general theories as well as some developments that seem related to changes going on in the society about us.

Summary

1. Psychology is the scientific study of behavior.

2. Scientific objectivity requires precise definitions understandable to any appropriately trained person as well as observations that accurately reflect what exists in the real world.

3. Experiments must be repeatable. Other people must be able to perform the same procedures with the same type of subjects and produce the same results.

4. A theory provides a conceptual framework that organizes and relates existing findings while drawing attention to questions that are relevant but as yet unexamined.

5. Developmental psychology is primarily concerned with child development, although adolescence, adulthood, and old age are receiving increasing attention.

6. Human experimental psychology includes all topics amenable to experimentation, but particularly perception, learning, and thinking.

7. Animal experimental psychology differs from human experimental psychology in that the subjects are lower animals. Much of modern learning theory is based on the results of animal studies.

8. Physiological psychologists deal with the ways in which the biological life processes determine and are affected by behavior.

9. Quantitative psychologists attempt to develop mathematical, statistical, and quantitative approaches to the study of human behavior.

10. The personality psychologist studies individual differences among people, particularly their motivations; he has a special interest in the unique aspects of the individual.

11. Social psychologists study people in groups and how individuals affect and are affected by the groups to which they belong.

12. The educational psychologist deals with the psychological aspects of the educational process, including learning, motivation, personality factors, and social interaction.

13. The clinical psychologist usually deals with psychologically disturbed subjects and uses such diagnostic techniques as the interview and various psychological tests.

14. Community mental health workers attempt to modify the environment in ways that will reduce behavioral disturbances.

15. The counseling psychologist works with people who have difficulties with educational or career choices.

16. The school psychologist usually works in primary and secondary schools with students, teachers, and administrators.

17. One of the industrial psychologist's typical activities is matching people to jobs, in order to provide greater work satisfaction for the employee and greater efficiency for the company. Engineering psychology attempts to make the man-machine relationship more rewarding and efficient.

18. The consumer psychologist analyzes the public's buying habits, generally through surveys and questionnaires.

19. In the experimental method, the investigator controls the variables under study. He manipulates the independent variable to discover its effect on a dependent variable.

20. The purpose of systematic observation is to make more sensitive and consistent the capacity to observe others and to infer what they are doing. Techniques include informal observation, rating scales, and devices with which the observer can record the type, duration, and intensity of particular kinds of behavior.

21. Questionnaires and interviews are survey methods for measuring the attitudes or opinions of a population. When used by a properly trained social scientist to answer a reasonable question, polls can be very accurate.

22. The case study is useful when the investigator is working in a relatively uncharted area and has neither good hypotheses nor a firm sense of the key variables. In such situations, the detailed study of an individual may provide hypotheses that can then be tested.

23. Correlation techniques allow the psychologist to estimate the extent to which two variables or events tend to co-vary or go together.

24. Psychology as a scientific discipline originated in middle Europe in the late 19th century as a complex hybrid of philosophy and the newly emerging discipline of experimental biology. Psychology remained a European, and particularly a German, discipline until the 1920s when the first substantial numbers of Americans began taking their doctoral degrees in this country.

25. The four major schools of psychological thought that emerged early in this century were structuralism, Gestalt psychology, behaviorism, and psychoanalysis.

26. Through the use of introspection by trained subjects, the structuralists—Titchener, for example—sought to identify the fundamental elements of mental experiences and thus the mind's structure.

27. Gestalt thinkers saw the wholeness and interrelatedness of experience as its most important aspect. Like the structuralists, Gestaltists focused on subjective experience and the exploration of consciousness. However, they relied upon reports of experiences occurring outside the laboratory. This unstructured reporting of experience is referred to as the phenomenological approach. Major figures were Kohler and Koffka.

28. The behaviorist is concerned with the objective observation of overt behavior. One of his dominant beliefs is that behavior can be understood in terms of the conditioning that led to it. Major figures in the behaviorist school are Pavlov, Watson, and Skinner.

29. Psychoanalysis is a method of studying human behavior, a theory of behavior, and a method of treatment. Freud is the father of psychoanalysis; variant forms of the process were devised by Jung, Adler, Rank, and others.

30. The third force in modern psychology—besides behaviorism and psychoanalysis—is humanistic psychology. This school, which owes much to the writings of Maslow, Allport, and Rogers, generally emphasizes positive aspects of human nature, such as man's capacity for personal growth.

Important Terms

objectivity

developmental psychology

human experimental psychology

animal experimental psychology

physiological psychology

quantitative psychology

mathematical psychology

personality psychology

social psychology

educational psychology

applied psychology

clinical psychology

community mental health

counseling psychology

school psychology

industrial psychology

engineering psychology

consumer psychology

experimental method	structuralism
independent variable	introspection
dependent variable	Gestalt psychology
systematic observation	phenomenological approach
survey methods	behaviorism
case studies	psychoanalysis
correlation techniques	humanistic psychology
psychometrics	

Suggested Readings

AMERICAN PSYCHOLOGICAL ASSOCIATION. *A career in psychology.* Washington, D.C.: American Psychological Association, 1970.

A pamphlet designed to acquaint the reader with the field of psychology, its various specialties, and its national organization, the American Psychological Association.

AMERICAN PSYCHOLOGICAL ASSOCIATION. Special issue: Psychology's manpower: The education and utilization of psychologists. *American Psychologist,* 1972, **27**(5).

The official journal of the American Psychological Association, in an oversized issue, examines many aspects of the careers of psychologists including job markets, salaries, the status of women, specialized types of employment, and future prospects.

BORING, E. G. *A history of experimental psychology* (2nd ed.) New York: Appleton-Century-Crofts, 1950.

Easily the best introduction to the history of psychology, even though somewhat dated. When combined with the carefully selected readings in the volume by Herrnstein and Boring, it provides a balanced view of the origins of modern psychology.

BORING, E. G., & LINDZEY, G. (EDS.) *A history of psychology in autobiography.* vol. 5. New York: Appleton-Century-Crofts, 1968.
LINDZEY, G. (ED.) *A history of psychology in autobiography.* Vol. 6. Englewood Cliffs, N. J.: Prentice-Hall, 1974.

These two volumes present twenty-eight autobiographies of outstanding contemporary psychologists. These life stories provide a vivid illustration of the diversity of backgrounds from which psychologists come, the differences in how they define psychology, and what they actually do.

CLARK, K. E., & MILLER, G. (EDS.) *Psychology* (*Behavioral and social sciences survey*). Englewood Cliffs, N. J.: Prentice-Hall, 1970.

A survey of the current status and prospects of the major areas of contemporary psychology. Each chapter is written by a distinguished psychologist.

HALL, C., & LINDZEY, G. *Theories of personality* (2nd ed.). New York: Wiley, 1971.

Surveys the major contemporary personality theories, which are the modern successors to the older schools of psychology. Each theory is presented in brief historical perspective and in a generally positive light, though with some critical evaluation.

HERRNSTEIN, R. J., & BORING, E. G. (EDS.) *A source book in the history of psychology.* Cambridge, Mass.: Harvard University Press, 1965.

See Boring.

NORDBY, V. J., & HALL, C. S. *A guide to psychologists and their concepts.* San Francisco: W. H. Freeman, 1974.

Brief biographies of 42 prominent contemporary psychologists and a clear presentation of their most important ideas. Written for the beginning psychology student.

WEBB, W. B. (ED.) *The profession of psychology.* New York: Holt, Rinehart and Winston, 1962.

Discusses a number of factual questions concerning psychology as a profession, its organization, and particularly the various specialties in which psychologists work.

Chapter 2   Evolution and Heredity

The chimpanzees were unceasingly alert and curious. They seized every opportunity to bring variety into their lives, taking different paths down the hill on different occasions and continually changing their gait and their mode of locomotion. They were fascinated by everything new and unusual. They carefully examined all the objects I laid in their path and even collected some of them. Once I saw a chimpanzee gaze at a particularly beautiful sunset for a full 15 minutes, watching the changing colors until it became so dark that he had to retire to the forest without stopping to pick a papaw for his evening meal.

Another respect in which the animals resembled human beings was in their doubting and uncertain natures. They appeared to ponder such problems as whether to turn to the left or the right, or whether or not a papaw tasted good. Often, just like laboratory chimpanzees puzzling over a difficult problem in an intelligence test, the chimpanzees I observed scratched themselves elaborately while making these decisions.

—Adriaan Kortlandt
(*"Chimpanzees in the Wild"*)

Evolution and Heredity

The subject matter of this book is man and his behavior. It is altogether fitting, therefore, to begin with some basic questions about man. How did man as a distinct species originate? How did modern man become the way he is? What is man's place in nature?

We are all familiar with two accounts of the origin of man. One is to be found in the first book—appropriately called Genesis—of the Old Testament. In Genesis we read that God created the world, including man. The creation of man and woman, their idyllic life in the Garden of Eden, and their banishment from this paradise for eating the forbidden fruit are regarded by most people today as lovely myths, rich in symbolic and moral significance.

The other account, known as evolution, was formulated by the English scientist Charles Darwin and published in 1859, in his celebrated book: *The Origin of Species.* The modern scientific version of Darwin's theory of evolution is quite rightly called the greatest unifying theory in biology. It provides a framework for the relatedness of all living creatures and explains the ways in which species change to become adapted to their environments. In this chapter, after a brief description of the evolution of man over the last few million years, we will introduce the modern theory of evolution, including the genetic factors upon which much of it is based. The chapter concludes with some specific examples, in particular a study of the heritability of schizophrenia, that point out a few of the countless ways in which man's genetic makeup affects his behavior.

The Emergence of Man

Our closest living relatives are the great apes—the chimpanzee, gorilla, gibbon, and orangutan. However, the lines leading to man and the great apes began to diverge about 14 million years ago, long before the emergence of man or chimp. The ancestors of both lines were relatively small primates with smaller canine teeth than those of modern apes. These creatures lived in Africa, probably on open grasslands dotted with clusters of trees. Such a territory favored ground-living over tree-dwelling.

AUSTRALOPITHECUS

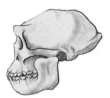

HOMO ERECTUS

NEANDERTHAL

CRO-MAGNON

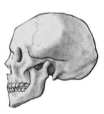

HOMO SAPIENS

2-1
The skulls of ape-man and man through evolutionary history. *Homo sapiens* is the only surviving species of the hominids, the family of man's ancestors that began with *Homo erectus*. Note the changes in shape from a relatively small brain case to a much larger one.

Australopithecus (Southern Ape)

The first creature that could be called an ape-man rather than an ape was *Australopithecus*, who appeared in Africa about 4 million years ago. He had an upright posture and walked on two legs. His skull was balanced above the backbone in human fashion. He was the size of today's pygmies, but his brain was only half the size of the modern human brain.

The evidence indicates that *Australopithecus* was a tool maker. This is a most important point. Man did not develop a large brain by chance and then stand up and start making tools. Upright posture came first; by freeing his hands, it enabled early ape-man to use rocks and branches as tools and weapons. The upright posture raised his head above the grasses and helped him to see distant game and enemies. The increasing complexity of man's tools and the growth of his brain went hand in hand. The early ape-man's first tools were simply chipped stones that could serve as weapons or cutting and scraping implements.

Australopithecus was a hunter, and an impressively successful one, judging by the animal bones found with his remains. Indeed, from this early beginning to the emergence of modern *Homo sapiens*, man has been the most awesomely successful hunter ever to appear on the face of the earth. For example, when the ancestors of the American Indians crossed the Bering Strait to enter the western hemisphere 30,000 years ago, their numbers were not large—but as they spread across the continent, many species of game animals quite suddenly became extinct. It seems likely that they were wiped out by man's skilled and relentless hunting.

Homo erectus

The next step in human evolution, the hominid called *Homo erectus* (at one time referred to as *Pithecanthropus*), appeared about 800,000 years ago. He was intermediate in form between *Australopithecus* and modern man, with a brain significantly smaller than that of modern man and a less-developed thumb. The thumb is an important characteristic, because our manual skill depends on having a thumb that can form a strong pincerlike movement with the fingers. Thus, improved tools depended on the evolution of a more efficient thumb as well as a larger brain. *Homo erectus* not only made stone tools but also used fire; he was a very successful creature surviving virtually unchanged for more than half a million years. Modern man evidently developed from *Homo erectus*; primitive forms of modern man began to appear about 200,000 years ago, just as *Homo erectus* was disappearing.

Neanderthal Man

In 1856, the remains of an extinct race of man were found in the Neanderthal valley near Düsseldorf, West Germany. It is estimated Neanderthal man appeared about 100,000 years ago. He was a most interesting creature. A bit shorter than modern man, he was broad, squat, and brutish-looking with a low, sloping forehead, huge brow ridges, and a receding chin. Neanderthal's brain was as large as our own, but rather different in shape, with smaller frontal areas. Neanderthal developed a vigorous culture that spread throughout Europe, North Africa, and the Near East. His culture included flaked stone tools and a characteristic hand axe. Ritual burial sites indicate that Neanderthal may have had some form of religion; it seems likely that he possessed a kind of language as well.

Homo sapiens

Modern man—*Homo sapiens* ("man of wisdom")—first appeared about 50,000 years ago. Our species may have originated in western Asia, but it soon spread throughout the world. The culture of *Homo sapiens* seems almost from the beginning to have included the stone blade and, as evidenced by burial practices, religion. Although we have no direct evidence, it is likely that modern *Homo sapiens* has always possessed language.

When *Homo sapiens* appeared on the scene, Neanderthal suddenly and totally disappeared. Our species may have exterminated Neanderthal or absorbed him. (Knowing *Homo sapiens*, both methods were probably tried.) As one anthropologist has described it: "A . . . breed in possession of one well-defined cultural tradition (the hand axe) was directly confronted and dispersed by men of modern type with a totally different material culture" (Hawkes, 1963).

The cultural development of modern man has been incredibly rapid and without precedent. In the short span of about 20,000 years, the stone blade became the spear; the bow and arrow were developed; sculpture and painting appeared—for example, the exquisite cave paintings done in France and Spain about 15,000 years ago; animals were domesticated, grains cultivated, and the modern races spread throughout the world.

Recent Discoveries. Recent fossil finds in Africa by the Leakey family and others may require modification of this account of the evolution of man. The newly discovered fossils may indicate that the emergence of a recognizably human being occurred earlier than was formerly thought. The Leakeys have also suggested that man's family tree may have several branches. Doubtless, discoveries of the future will provide new knowledge of the evolution of man, but the important point to keep in mind is that *Homo sapiens* did evolve from prehuman species.

Evolution

The study of evolution and genetics leads to an increased understanding of the biological heritage and potentials of man. As Charles Darwin made clear, evolution occurs as a result of *natural selection* acting on *genetic diversity*. The individual members of any species of animal living in a state of nature show great diversity in their genetic makeup. This diversity makes it likely that some individuals will have character-

2-2

Darwin's careful observations of finches on the Galapagos Islands were the basis for many of his ideas about the evolution of species. Thirteen different species of finches live on the islands. All of them are believed to have arisen from one common ancestral group, perhaps transported to the Galapagos by a particularly severe storm from the mainland of South America 600 miles away. The most remarkable of the finch species is the woodpecker finch, which employs a trait rare in birds, tool use, to extract its diet of grubs from trees. The woodpecker finch first selects a twig, inserts it into the bark (or in the space between wooden blocks, as shown here), and prods out a grub. The bird carries the twig about to hunt for more grubs. (Dr. Robert I. Bowman, San Francisco State University)

istics which enable them to adapt unusually well to their environment. Such individuals are the most likely to survive and produce offspring; in other words, they are the most likely to be naturally selected. Man has been able to utilize this principle by selectively breeding strains of plants and animals that have certain desirable characteristics. The psychologist Tryon (1940), by breeding smart male rats with smart females for several generations, was able to develop a strain of rats that could learn a maze exceptionally rapidly. Other psychological characteristics, such as emotionality, have also been selectively bred in animals. Some people known as *eugenicists* have urged that selective breeding be applied to human beings. Their views have not prevailed except for a brief period in Nazi Germany, when they were used to justify Hitler's infamous programs for exterminating the "unfit."

Natural selection, in the form of a diversified environment that is sometimes benign and sometimes exceedingly hostile, acts on the wide genetic variety of individuals in the species. As a rule, many more individuals are produced than survive the rigors of the environment to produce young of their own. The characteristics and abilities that make us *Homo sapiens* have been shaped by natural selection. We are what we are because we have survival value—not just as individuals but as a species that has reproduced from a few million, spread very thinly over the earth 10,000 years ago, to 4 billion today and to an estimated 7 billion by the year 2000. In fact, the growth rate of the human species soon may prove to be catastrophic due to overpopulation.

Evolution works *after* the fact of genetic composition, not before it. Man is not the ultimate product of some evolutionary master plan. We are the largely accidental result of particular environmental pressures acting on the available genetic material. Indeed, we carry many compromises and even physical defects as a part of our genetic inheritance. Our S-shaped spinal column is a most imperfect adaptation of the horizontal, arch-shaped backbone of the four-legged animal to an upright, two-legged position. The high incidence of lower back pain, slipped discs, and hernias among humans can all be blamed on evolution.

The Emergence of Modern Races

The evolution and migration of the modern races is still an uncertain story. Cro-Magnon, the branch of *Homo sapiens* that invaded Europe about 35 or 40 thousand years ago, already possessed the skull features of the white race. A skull of about the same age from China resembles the early Mongoloid. No Negro skulls of this age have yet been found, yet it is believed that all racial differences are more than 35,000 years old.

The distribution of the races of man in 8000 BC and 1000 AD is shown in Figure 2–3. Asia was initially occupied largely by the early Mongoloids—people closely resembling modern American Indians. They crossed the Bering Strait about 30,000 years ago and occupied the New World. Modern Negroes seem to have appeared first in northern Africa; southern Africa was populated by a quite different and ancient race, the Bushmen. They are lightly built, with light yellowish-brown skin and a "five-cornered" skull. They possess one other unusual and distinct feature; if well nourished, the women accumulate a large amount of stored fat in their buttocks. In the 9,000 year span shown in Figure 2–3, the modern Negro expanded through much of Africa, the whites occupied northern Africa and the remainder of northern Europe, much of which had been covered by glaciers in 8000 BC, and the late Mongoloids (modern Asians) occupied all of Asia and the northermost part of the New World.

2-3
The distribution of the races of man in 8000 BC and 1000 AD. According to available evidence, it is believed that by 8000 BC (map at top) early Mongoloids had already spread from the Old World to the New World, while late Mongoloids inhabited a large part of northern Asia. Distribution in 1000 AD (map at bottom) has late Mongoloids dominating Asia, northern Canada and southern Greenland, and early Mongoloids dominating the America's. The Pygmies and Bushmen of Africa began a decline that has continued up to the present. (From W. H. Howells. *The Distribution of Man.* Copyright © 1960 by Scientific American, Inc. All rights reserved.)

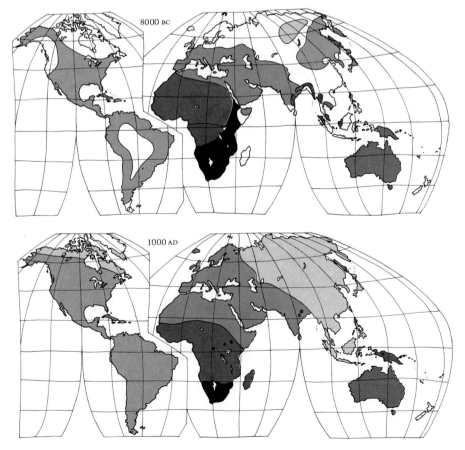

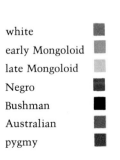

white
early Mongoloid
late Mongoloid
Negro
Bushman
Australian
pygmy

GENERALIZATION OF BEHAVIOR FROM MONKEY TO MAN

Harry F. Harlow and Stephen J. Suomi   *University of Wisconsin*

Scientists and laymen always have been uncertain about the extent to which behavioral data on subhuman species can be generalized to man. The issue is whether conclusions derived from experiments upon monkeys, rats, pigeons, and the other creatures that experimental psychologists work with in their laboratories contain insights into man's behavior. Some purists properly point out that to engage in this sort of scientific inquiry for its own sake is hardly wrong. Studying the behavior of hummingbirds and hoot owls because one finds hummingbirds and hoot owls interesting as species is an innocent and rewarding pastime. However, those people not caught up by the fascinations of science simply for the sake of science, and this includes the tormented taxpayer whose dollars support most research, seldom take much interest in hoot owls but do quite sensibly care about research that yields insights into their own behavior and that of other human beings. Under the pressure to produce experimental results that can be applied to the solution of man's problems in the real world, none of us should be surprised to hear most animal researchers plead that their findings really do improve our understanding of what people do and why they do it. On the other hand, some psychologists who carry out research using people rather than animals as their subjects are inclined to belittle animal researchers' efforts to apply to man the things they have learned about the behavior of non-human subjects. As you might expect, those of us who work at the Primate Center find that animal and human nature are profoundly similar in many important ways.

The two of us have been studying rhesus monkeys for most of our sci-entific lives, and we are acutely concerned about the degree to which our research findings can be applied to man. Happily, rhesus monkeys are phylogenetically far closer to man than most of the animal species one finds in psychology laboratories. This simple fact of evolution helps to support our practice of generalizing from monkey to man. In any case, we take seriously the need to show how our monkey findings apply to human behavior and we believe we have demonstrated the validity of such generalization. Most animal re-searchers just study animals, then try to find some portion of human behavior that seems to relate to their findings. We at Wisconsin take the opposite approach.

To achieve the greatest generality between our laboratory work on monkeys and human data, we exam-ine well-documented and formulated behavioral data that are derived from studies of human beings and deter-mine the degree to which our simian subjects, under rigorous laboratory conditions, duplicate or simulate this human behavior. The results have been illuminating.

For example, our first excursions into generality related to learning. Since human mental tests have shown that learning in man pro-gresses and improves in an orderly manner throughout most of life, we tested for a comparable progression in monkeys. After devising and ad-ministering a series of mental tests to monkeys, we were able to show that monkey maturation of learning resembled man's, save for the fact that the mental age of the monkeys increased four times as fast as man's at the outset but then slowed down. Specifically, the 1-year-old monkey was found to be twice as bright as the 1-year-old human, but the 6-year-old human was twice as bright as the 6-year-old monkey.

Subsequently, we conducted re-search on affectional and social behavior in monkeys, modeling these researches on information obtained from observations and experiments others had carried out with humans. We demonstrated that the interpreta-tions of some of the human data had been limited or even wrong. With laboratory controls we were able to correct the erroneous human as-sumptions, particularly with respect to the relationships between the newborn offspring and its mother. For example, authorities on human behavior had believed that love for the mother was learned by the child's associating the mother's face or breasts with hunger satisfaction. We were able to show that newborn monkeys, and newborn humans too, love their mothers for the sheer plea-sure of contact with her body, a phe-nomenon we call "contact comfort" (Figure A).

Having clarified some aspects of learning and loving we are now studying insanity, using the same techniques that had served us well in our previous research. We studied established human psychotic syn-dromes and engendered similar syn-dromes in our monkeys. First we fo-cused our efforts on experiments designed to simulate human child-hood depression and discovered that infant monkeys displayed the same human developmental stages de-scribed by Spitz and Bowlby. This research has given us a better sense of the origins of childhood depression and has generated useful notions about how it can be avoided or treated. Adult depression in both human and subhuman forms is more complex, but it is not beyond our capabilities and skills to produce and

A

An infant monkey receiving "contact comfort" from surrogate mother. (Courtesy Harry Harlow, Wisconsin Primate Laboratory)

B

A previously isolated monkey (above) learning contact and play from younger normal "therapist" monkey (below). (Courtesy Harry Harlow, Wisconsin Primate Laboratory)

study these affects. Depression destroys more adult people than any other disease. We have some hope that our studies of subhuman species will help eradicate this damaging affliction. Other human disorders currently being investigated with monkeys include sociopathology and schizophrenia.

The proper therapeutic techniques could rehabilitate many human psychotics. Since we have an abiding faith in the soundness of generalizing from monkey to human behavior, we think we stand a chance of discovering such techniques as we attempt to rehabilitate our psychotic monkeys. The first attempts have worked well. We reared monkeys in total social isolation. Then we placed these monkeys, which exhibited psychotic behavior, with 3-month-old normal monkeys, which we call "therapists." The previously isolated monkeys had no fear of the infant therapists, and this left the therapists free to rehabilitate the isolates through progressive development of contact and play (Figure B). We find it heartening to see that many human therapists are using similar techniques in the effort to treat human psychotics.

Although the human is an atypical animal, we are convinced that much of his behavior is similar to that of other animal species. While generalization is not identity, the surprising point is the enormous degree of behavioral similarity between man and other animals when, anatomically, human and other animal bodies and brains are so different. Clearly, many basic psychological needs and the behavioral skills used to accommodate these needs run well beyond the boundaries of specific species. We have learned a lot about ourselves by studying animals, and we can learn a lot more.

There is much speculation and little fact concerning the origins of racial characteristics. Some racial characteristics seem adaptive, that is, they make it easier to live in a particular environment, but others are less clearly so. Among the "white" races (those possessing similar bone structure and other features), skin color is closely related to the amount of ultraviolet radiation in sunlight, varying from light blond along the Baltic to dark brown in India. However, the often prominent noses of whites seem to offer no adaptive benefits. The facial features of the late Mongoloids, who apparently originated in northern Asia, are well adapted to extremely cold climates. The eyes and cheeks are padded with fat and the nose and forehead are flat, providing excellent protection of the eyes, nose, and sinuses against the bitter cold. If these facial characteristics indeed resulted from natural selection through such pressures as pneumonia and sinus infection, the late Mongoloid race must have been the most recent to develop. It evidently appeared after the American Indians (the early Mongoloids) crossed into the western hemisphere.

Actually, the closest correlations between climate and body features are not racial at all. Both humans and other animals tend to be bulkier in cold areas. Further, the arms, legs, ears, and noses are generally smaller in cold climates. Thus, man tended to be lanky and long-limbed in hot deserts and dumpy and short-limbed in the Arctic, independent of race. These differences are adaptive in each case; compact bodies conserve heat, while lanky bodies radiate it more efficiently.

The topic of race and racial differences is surrounded by emotion today. What little evidence we have suggests that the modern races of man began to develop as minor variations in the ancestral stock about 50,000 years ago. More important than the minor physical differences is the fact that all the modern races faced the primitive world with the same ability to survive and the same high culture of technology, art, religion, and language. We are but one breed of man, probably exceeding earlier forms of man, such as our cousin Neanderthal, both in wisdom and in destructiveness.

Human Evolution Today

The development of civilization as we know it began with the earliest agriculture, about 10,000 years ago. There has been no appreciable evolution or change in the human race in this short period. Viewed in the context of evolution, the human race is scarcely at the dawn of its existence as a species. The average time taken for one species of mammal to evolve from another is about 8 million years. Yet we have existed for only about 50,000 years. If you think this is a long time, consider that if you traced your family tree back more than about 2,000 generations, your ancestors would begin to look distinctly nonhuman.

From the first appearance of *Australopithecus,* some 4 million years ago, until the development of agriculture, our species evolved as a hunter. This fact does not necessarily mean that we became more and more aggressive. The ability to cooperate in the hunt must surely have been important. Communication in the form of language would

A

B

2-4

Man as a hunter. (A) A modern depiction of *Cro-Magnon* men cooperating to kill a large-tusked mammoth. (B) A rock painting (from Alpera, Spain) of an archer, drawn about 10,000 years ago when bows and arrows first were invented. (Courtesy of the American Museum of Natural History)

be of great benefit. A group of men acting together can chase a herd of buffalo off a cliff and feast for months—apparently a common practice in prehistoric Europe, judging by the fossil remains, and a peculiarly human kind of behavior.

We are still evolving, of course. However, the pressures of natural selection now are different from those that have shaped us, because we have found ways to alter many of the old pressures. Wisdom teeth provide a common example; many people have impacted wisdom teeth that must be removed, while other people do not have wisdom teeth at all. Popular articles on evolution claim that we are gradually losing our wisdom teeth—but this is a misconception. Wisdom teeth will disappear from the human race only if people with wisdom teeth stop having children. Before this century, the improper growth of wisdom teeth led to infection and death in many adolescents, and this did reduce the frequency of wisdom-teeth genes. But thanks to modern medicine and dentistry, wisdom teeth no longer reduce our fitness to have offspring. Man's inventiveness has ended the relationship between wisdom teeth and number of offspring today, and so, the trait will remain. Science has intervened to change many other situations—virtually wiping out several deadly diseases through vaccination and innoculation programs, for example. Despite these interventions, the old law still holds. The only traits and characteristics that will change and evolve are those that influence the reproductive success of the individuals who possess them.

Genetic Factors in Evolution

Several factors are responsible for the genetic variation that exists in any natural population of animals. Some of these are *sexual recombination, mutation, fitness, isolation,* and *genetic drift.* Each will be described briefly in this section.

Sexual Recombination

A _chromosome_ is a complex structure composed of many genes threaded together like a string of beads. A _gene_ is the basic unit of heredity. Each gene is composed of a biochemical substance called DNA, which provides the basic hereditary information and controls. Normal chromosomes always exist in matched pairs and are present in virtually all cells in the body. Humans have 23 pairs of chromosomes in each cell—46 different chromosomes in all. Each gene controls some specific aspect of body structure or function. Genes in the same position in a pair of chromosomes work together to control the same characteristic—eye color, for example. However, the two genes often differ; one may be a brown-eyed gene inherited from one parent and the other a blue-eyed gene inherited from the other. In such cases, one generally dominates the other; brown-eyed genes dominate blue-eyed genes, for instance. When sex cells (the female egg or male sperm) are formed, they contain only half the normal number of chromosomes. Each sex cell

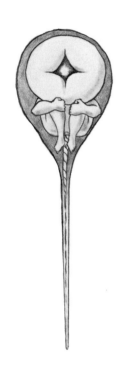

2-5
What the animalculists, or spermists, of the 17th and 18th centuries believed they saw when they looked through a microscope at sperm cells. This is a homunculus ("little man"), a future human being in miniature, enclosed within a sperm cell. It was mistakenly thought that, except for "prenatal influences," the mother's only contribution to the forming of the child was to carry it in her womb.

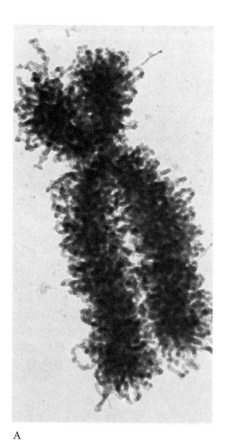

A

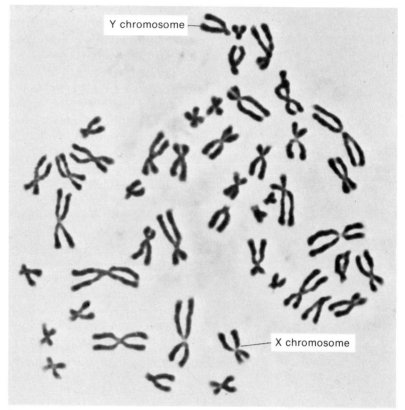

Y chromosome

X chromosome

B

2-6
Every normal human cell has 46 chromosomes. These long strands carry the genes that determine our genetic heredity. (A) A double chromosome, magnified 30,000 times its normal size. (B) The 46 chromosomes of a human cell. The X and Y chromosomes indicate these are from a male. (A. Lester V. Bergman; B. Omikron)

contains only one chromosome from each pair. The single chromosome from each pair is selected entirely by chance for each sex cell. Thus, if a brown-eyed person has one blue-eyed and one brown-eyed gene, half of his or her sex cells will have blue-eyed genes and the other half will have brown-eyed genes.

When the egg is fertilized, the chromosomes from the egg and sperm combine so that there are again 46 chromosomes existing in 23 matched pairs. This is known as *sexual recombination*. Each complement of 23 chromosomes is a chance assortment of half of each parent's chromosomes, and which sperm out of the millions that are contained in an ejaculation will fertilize the egg is also largely a matter of chance. Consequently, except for identical twins, every human is a unique genetic entity with a genetic makeup quite different from that of any other human. Since there are about 4 billion people alive today, this represents an incredible genetic diversity.

Mutation

Sexual recombination produces genetic diversity but it does not change the nature of the genes. A change in the chemical composition of a gene is called a *mutation*. Genetic mutations occur both "spontaneously" and as a result of exposure to x-rays and chemical actions. The so-called "spontaneous" mutations actually may be caused

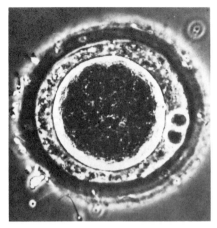

A

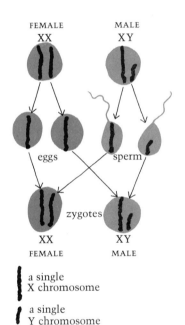

a single
X chromosome

a single
Y chromosome

B

2-7

(A) At the moment of fertilization, one sperm cell out of millions manages to fuse with the egg. (B) In the union of sperm and egg, the sex of the resulting new cell, or zygote, is determined by the sperm, as illustrated by this diagram. The zygote will develop into a female if the sperm contributes an X chromosome, a male if the sperm contributes a Y chromosome. (A. Dr. L. B. Shettles)

by agents as yet unknown. Mutation is not very common. In humans, the spontaneous mutation rates seem to vary from about 1 in 10,000 to 1 in 250,000 for those few genes that have been studied. Many genes probably have far lower rates. As an example, it has been calculated that 1 sex cell in every 50,000 individuals carries a new mutant gene that causes a cancer of the eye in children. However, these low "spontaneous" mutation rates were measured before the days of nuclear radiation, smog, and synthetics, all of which may make mutation much more common in the future. Most mutations that have been observed have harmful effects. The vast majority probably result in early miscarriages—the effects of the mutation are so severe that the human cannot develop normally during the prenatal stage. However, during the evolution of a species some mutations must have had beneficial effects. Otherwise, it is difficult to see how man could have become man.

Fitness

The extent to which a mutation will be transmitted to the gene pool of the species depends on its _fitness_—which refers to the individual's success at reproducing itself. Fitness for survival, in terms of evolution, does not refer to the individual. Suppose a combination of heredity and environment produces a large and powerful _Homo sapiens_ who can kill a lion with his bare hands. He is individually well fitted for survival in the primitive state. However, if he has no children, his "Darwinian fitness" is zero—he does not contribute to the gene pool of humanity. An actual example of fitness is provided by achondroplastic dwarfism, which is caused by a gene mutation. People with this mutant gene develop normal heads and trunks but very short arms and legs. Though they apparently have perfectly normal health, they reproduce much less than the normal population. For every 100 children produced by normal individuals, the same number of achondroplastic dwarfs produce only 20 children. Consequently, the dwarf gene mutation contributes little to the total gene pool of the human species. Such individuals, although healthy, have low Darwinian fitness.

Isolation

Another factor producing genetic diversity is physical _isolation_, an important reason for the separate development of the many different forms of ape-man in the course of human evolution. A small tribe might live in a mountain valley in complete isolation from other hominids for many thousands of years. Inbreeding within this tribe would develop many genetic traits that could even result in a new breed—though such close inbreeding almost always leads to deterioration in higher animals. Laboratory experiments show that for every ten inbred strains of mice that are started, nine die out. The deleterious effects of close inbreeding are particularly evident in humans. The death rate among children of first cousins is three times higher than it is for the population at large. Children that are the result of nuclear incest (parent and child or brother and sister) have an even higher incidence of abnormalities. In one study of 18 such children, 11 had serious defects: 5 died at a young age, 2 were mentally retarded, 3 were of borderline intelligence, and 1 had a cleft palate. It has been suggested (Lindzey, 1967) that the universal taboo against nuclear incest is an evolutionary necessity. Cultures that did not have the taboo must have perished.

Genetic Drift

Another kind of genetic change occurs in small isolated populations quite independently of natural selection. _Genetic drift_—relatively large increases or decreases in the frequencies of certain genes from generation to generation—appears when the group is too small for truly random selection to take place. For example, everyone in a randomly selected group of 10 people may have blue eyes, but such a coincidence would be virtually impossible in a group of 100 people.

Consider a trait that occurs in 2 percent of the individuals in a population. In a population of a million, 20,000 individuals possessing this trait would be present in the gene pool. But in a population of 50, only one person might have the trait. If this individual should die before leaving offspring, this trait would be lost from the gene pool. Similarly, if 10 of the 49 without the trait died, the frequency would jump from 1 in 50 to 1 in 40. These sudden and large changes in the frequency of certain genes in a small population are examples of genetic drift.

Genetic drift has been studied in several modern human groups. The "Dunkers" are a small, isolated religious sect who came from Germany to Franklin County, Pennsylvania a century ago. The frequency of blood group A is now 60 percent among the Dunkers, in contrast to 45 percent in Western Germany and 40 percent in the United States. They also have a significantly higher percentage of individuals with unattached ear lobes than exists in either parent or host country. It is difficult to imagine that these characteristics have any adaptive value, particularly over the few generations that the Dunkers have lived in isolation. However, an increased frequency of one blood group might be associated with other blood factors that relate to disease resistance and immunity. Genetic drift has caused these random fluctuations in gene frequency, but the long-term effect could someday influence survival and Darwinian fitness.

The two major causes of racial differences in man were genetic drift and natural selection, both acting on the normal range of variation in characteristics. Mutations probably played a very minor role.

Genetics and Behavior

We have seen how man has evolved, and how he has even learned by selective breeding to intervene in the evolutionary process in limited ways. Now we will look more closely at the interactions between our genetic inheritance and our behavior.

Genes do not generate behavior, organisms do. Genes are simply chemical molecules in the nucleus of the cell. However, genes are responsible for the production of proteins, the chemical substances which in turn form the structures of the organism, including the brain. Proteins also

2-8
The Old Order Amish are an isolated religious sect founded by only three couples some 200 years ago. Genetic drift and inbreeding have resulted in there being among this group an unusually high frequency of genes that cause extra fingers and dwarfism. This Amish child is a six-fingered dwarf. (Victor A. McKusick)

form chemicals called enzymes, which regulate the chemical processes of the organism. From conception until death, the development and behavior of each human is the result of a complex interaction between genetic and environmental influences. Geneticists use two words to distinguish between the genetic constitution of cells and the outward expression of the genes: _genotype_ — the genetic makeup, and _phenotype_ — the expression of this makeup. Phenotype can refer to anything from a simple physical characteristic like blue eyes to complex behavioral traits like intelligence.

Sickle-cell anemia, a serious human disease, illustrates the distinction between phenotype and genotype. The disease is named from the sickle shape of the red blood cells, which contrasts with the normal disc shape. Individuals suffering from the disease die in early adulthood or remain severely ill throughout life. The illness apparently results from the tendency of the oddly shaped red blood cells to clump or clot. A surprising aspect of the disease is that it occurs mostly in blacks who live in the central coastal zones of Africa, or whose ancestors came from this region. The disease is due to the action of a single gene pair. An individual who inherits the gene from both parents will have the disease. The genotype matches the phenotype. In contrast, individuals who have one normal and one sickle-cell gene are perfectly healthy under normal circumstances. However, such individuals may become ill at high altitudes, indicating that the sickle-cell gene has some partial effect on the red blood cells. At high altitudes, reduced atmospheric pressure requires the red blood cells to carry larger amounts of oxygen than are required at lower altitudes. If some of the cells are reduced in size by the sickle-cell gene they will be unable to carry the necessary amount of oxygen and the person will feel ill.

In the United States about one-quarter of 1 percent of blacks have the disease (have both sickle-cell genes), while about 9 percent are carriers (individuals with one sickle-cell gene and one normal gene). In some African tribes, 40 percent are carriers and 4 percent have the disease, an amazingly high incidence for a virtually lethal gene. But individuals who are carriers are much more resistant to malaria than either normals or individuals with the disease. In short, the sickle-cell gene is an evolutionary adaptation to malaria and occurs only in those regions of Africa where malaria is prevalent (see Figure 2–9). It actually _increases_ the

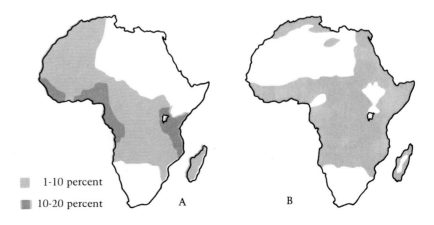

2-9
As these maps show, there is a clear overlap between areas with a high incidence of sickle-cell anemia (A) and areas with a high incidence of malaria (B). In a malaria-infested region, someone with one sickle-cell gene and one normal gene (a carrier) has a better chance of survival than someone with only the normal genes. (Alland, 1973)

 1-10 percent
 10-20 percent

A   B

Darwinian fitness of African blacks, many of whom would otherwise die of malaria before they were old enough to reproduce. The incidence of the sickle-cell gene among blacks in the United States, were there is no malaria, is steadily declining—a striking example of human evolution occurring today.

Heritability

Let us consider the nature-nurture question: Are human abilities and characteristics genetically determined or learned? Phrased in this way, the question cannot really be answered. All human behavior is phenotypic. Environment certainly influences complex behavior and may even affect simple reflex actions. A common way of expressing genetic influence is to state that genes set the limits of abilities and environment does the rest. But even this is too simple. Abilities, from running to writing, develop as a continuous interaction between the person and his environment.

For this reason, behavior geneticists—biologists and psychologists who study the genetic roots of behavior—have developed a somewhat different approach. They use a measure called _heritability_. Instead of asking to what extent a given trait is due to nature (genes) or to nurture (environment), behavior genetics asks to what extent the observed _differences_ among people are due to differences in genes and to what extent they are due to differences in environment. This is not a mere quibble over words, as we shall see.

Thanks to that most fortunate experiment of nature, identical twins, we can measure the differences in performance on any test of ability or personality scored by two individuals with the identical genetic makeup. Because the two genotypes are identical, any phenotypic differences _must_ be due to differences in environment. Identical twins occur when a single fertilized egg (_zygote_) divides once and each of the two cells, with identical chromosomes, develops as a separate individual. They are termed _monozygous_ or MZ twins. Nonidentical twins develop from two separate zygotes (_dizygotic_ or DZ twins) and have different genetic compositions. Dizygotic twins have the same genetic similarity as nontwin brothers and sisters (siblings). MZ twins can be compared with DZ twins raised in a similar environment. Such comparisons are not perfect—subtle environmental differences can develop even for

2-10

Example of an hereditary trait. The "Habsburg lip" appeared in all generations of the Hapsburg family for over 350 years. Shown here from left to right are Rudolph I (1218–1291), King of Germany; Maximilian I (1460–1519), Holy Roman Emperor; Charles V (1500–1558), Holy Roman Emperor; and Ferdinand I (1503–1564), Holy Roman Emperor. (The Bettmann Archive)

MZ twins within a single family—but they are far better than previous approaches to the problem.

Environmental similarities and differences often are varied by chance circumstances. Some identical twins have been separated shortly after birth and raised in different families, for example. Researchers also can look for differences in the occurrence of a trait among children of parents possessing the trait. This is done by comparing such children, raised by their natural parents, with similar children who were adopted and raised by parents not having the trait. All these approaches involve measuring the differences in traits of people who have varying degrees of genetic or environmental similarity.

The Heritability of Schizophrenia—An Example of Behavior Genetics. The behavior genetics approach has revealed a great deal about the heritability of schizophrenia, a severe mental disorder. Schizophrenia is discussed in greater depth in Chapter 20; we use it here as an example of genetic influences on complex attributes of human nature.

Schizophrenia is the most serious and prevalent form of mental disorder throughout the world. The most common symptoms are disorganized thought processes, personality disintegration, and bizarre behavior. One percent of the world's population is schizophrenic—about 40 million people. Schizophrenia occurs at about the same rate in all societies and cultures. This fact is in itself an argument for genetic cause—cultural differences seem to have little effect on the rate at which populations develop schizophrenia.

A number of studies have compared the incidence of schizophrenia in MZ and DZ twins when one member of each twin pair has been diagnosed as schizophrenic. The results consistently indicate a strong genetic influence. Approximately 50 to 60 percent of identical twin individuals will be schizophrenic if their twin has been so diagnosed. For DZ twins, the rate is only about 10 percent (Slater, 1968; Gottesman & Shields, 1972). What of the 40 to 50 percent of identical twin members who do not have the disease even though their twins do? If schizophrenia were entirely due to genetic factors, particularly a single gene, *all* identical twin pairs should be the same—either both twins should be afflicted or neither one.

Heston (1970) re-examined the twin data, paying particular attention to the personality characteristics of the nonschizophrenic MZ twins of schizophrenics. He found that most of these twins had some form of personality impairment, described by various investigators as schizoid (schizophreniclike) or borderline schizophrenic. In short, although they did not fit the formal diagnosis of schizophrenia, they exhibited similar abnormalities. When both schizophrenic and schizoid descriptions were included, 88 percent of these identical twins showed serious personality impairment. Heston argued that the problem was one of diagnosis—it may be incorrect to distinguish between schizophrenic and schizoid; they may simply be different degrees of expression of the same underlying genetic defect. In brief, he proposed that one dominant gene produces "schizophrenic or schizoid" individuals.

It has long been known that relatives of schizophrenics are much more likely to be schizophrenic than members of the general population. The

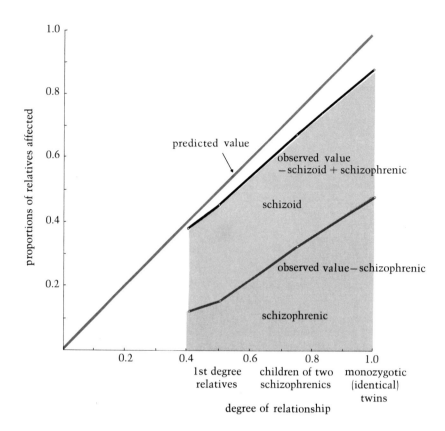

2-11

Graph of the occurrence of schizophrenia and schizoid behavior as a function of a person's degree of relationship to others who are schizophrenics. The closer the relationship, the more chance there is of the person developing schizophrenia or a related maladjustment. (From Leonard L. Heston, "The genetics of schizophrenia and schizoid disease." *Science*, January 16, 1970, vol. 167, p. 253. Copyright © 1970 by the American Association for the Advancement of Science)

closer your relationship to a schizophrenic, the more likely you are to be schizophrenic. Figure 2–11 shows the incidence of schizophrenia and schizoid characteristics as a function of degree of relationship to schizophrenics. If we assume that schizophrenia is due to a single gene paired with a normal gene, then the incidence should be 100 percent for identical twins, about 50 percent for first-degree relatives (brothers and sisters of one schizophrenic parent), and 75 percent for children whose parents are both schizophrenic. The correspondence between these predicted values and the actual combined incidence of schizophrenia plus schizoid personality is striking. However, the absence of schizophrenia in 12 percent of the MZ twins of schizophrenics indicates that some environmental factors also are at work.

A different study by Heston (1966) provides another kind of evidence for the heritability of schizophrenia. He tracked down individuals born between 1915 and 1945 to chronic schizophrenic mothers confined in an Oregon state psychiatric hospital. All of them had been taken from their mothers within three days of birth, placed in foster homes or foundling homes, and later adopted. No information was obtained about the fathers. A control group of children from normal parents, placed for adoption at a similar age, was matched with the experimental group for age, type of eventual adoption, and length of time in child-care institutions. Heston was able to find, interview, and test 47 of the grown children of schizophrenic mothers. Fifty control subjects were studied. The results are shown in Table 2-1. Five of the experimental group were schizophrenic in contrast to none of the control group. Eight experi-

Table 2-1   Results of a Study of Individuals Born to Schizophrenic Mothers and Reared in Adoptive or Foster Homes and of Controls Born to Normal Parents and Similarly Reared. (Heston, 1966)

Item	Control	Experimental
Number of subjects	50	47
Number of males	33	30
Age, mean (years)	36.3	35.8
Number adopted	19	22
Number with schizophrenia	0	5
Number with mental deficiency (I.Q. <70)	0	4
Number with antisocial personalities	2	9
Number with neurotic personality disorder	7	13
Number spending more than 1 year in penal or psychiatric institutions	2	11
Total years incarcerated	15	112
Number of felons	2	7
Number serving in armed forces	17	21
Number discharged from armed forces on psychiatric or behavioral grounds	1	8
Social group, first home, mean	4.2	4.5
Social group, present, mean	4.7	5.4
I.Q., mean	103.7	94.0
Years in school, mean	12.4	11.6
Number of children, total	84	71
Number of divorces, total	7	6
Number never married, >30 years of age	4	9

mentals were discharged from the army for psychiatric reasons, as opposed to one control. Indeed, more than half of the children of schizophrenic mothers scored significantly worse on all measures of personality adjustment and psychological health. Twenty-six of them had significant and serious impairments, compared with only nine in the control group.

Heston found two subgroups among the 26 impaired subjects. These groups exhibited personality impairments other than schizophrenia or mental deficiency. As Heston described them:

The first group is composed of subjects who fit the older diagnostic category, "schizoid psychopaths." This term was used by Kallman (1938) to describe a significant sub-group of relatives of schizophrenic persons. Eight males from the present study fall into this group, all of whom received a diagnosis of sociopathic personality. These persons are distinguished by anti-social behavior of an impulsive, illogical nature. Multiple arrests for assault, battery, poorly planned impulsive thefts dot their police records. . . . These subjects tended to live alone—only one was married—in deteriorated hotels and rooming houses in large cities, and locating them would have been impossible without the cooperation of the police. They worked at irregular casual jobs such as dishwasher, race-track tout, parking attendant. When interviewed they did not acknowledge or exhibit evidence of anxiety. Usually secretive about their own life and circumstances, they expressed very definite though general opinions regarding social and political ills. In spite of their suggestive life histories, no evidence of schizophrenia was elicited in interviews. No similar personalities were found among the control subjects.

A second sub-group was characterized by emotional "lability" . . . six females and two males from the experimental group as opposed to two control subjects were in this category. These persons complained of anxiety or panic attacks, hyper-irritability, and depression. The most frequent complaint was panic when in groups of people as in church or at parties, which was so profoundly uncomfortable that the subject was forced to remove himself abruptly. Most subjects described their problems as occurring episodically; a situation that they might tolerate with ease on one occasion was intolerable on another. The women reported life-long difficulty with menses, especially hyper-irritability or crying spells, and depressions coincident with pregnancy. These subjects described themselves as moody, stating that they usually could not relate their mood swings to temporal events. Four such subjects referred to their strong religious beliefs much more frequently than other respondents. Psychophysiological gastrointestinal symptoms were prominent in five subjects. The most frequent diagnosis advanced by the raters was emotionally unstable personality.

Of the 9 persons in the control group who were seriously disabled, 2 were professional criminals, careful and methodical in their work, 2 were very similar to the emotionally labile group described above, one was a compulsive phobia-ridden neurotic, and 4 were inadequate or passive-aggressive personalities.

The 21 experimental subjects who exhibited no significant psychosocial impairment were not only successful adults but in comparison to the control group were more spontaneous when interviewed and had more colorful life histories. They held the more creative jobs: musician, teacher, home-designer; and followed the more imaginative hobbies: oil painting, music, antique aircraft. Within the experimental group there was much more variability of personality and behavior in all social dimensions.

If schizophrenia is entirely a genetic disease, why does it continue to occur at the high rate of 1 percent of the population? The Darwinian fitness of diagnosed schizophrenics is less than that of normals—they have fewer children. However, recent data suggest that the brothers and sisters of schizophrenics may have larger families than is true for the general population (see McClearn & DeVries, 1973). In his study, Heston noted that nonschizophrenic children of schizophrenic mothers tended to be more creative and interesting people than the controls. Perhaps the "schizophrenic gene," like the sickle-cell gene, will turn out to increase Darwinian fitness in certain circumstances. We know too little about it to rule out such speculations at this point.

Summary

1. The earliest ape-man, *Australopithecus,* appeared in Africa about 4 million years ago.

2. *Australopithecus* was succeeded by *Homo erectus* about 800,000 years ago, followed by Neanderthal, 100,000 years ago, and modern man, *Homo sapiens,* 50,000 years ago. Each species produced an increasingly sophisticated form of culture.

3. Evolution results as natural selection acts on genetic diversity. Thus, man's biological heritage and potential are the outcome of particular environmental pressures acting on the available genetic material.

4. The modern races of man probably began to emerge as minor variations of *Homo sapiens* about 50,000 years ago. Racial characteristics were influenced both by natural selection and genetic drift.

5. Some genetic factors that influence evolution are sexual recombination (the chance assortment of half of each parent's chromosomes during fertilization), mutation (the appearance of new traits in a species as a result of a physical change in a gene's chemical composition), fitness (the individual's reproductive potential), isolation (a cause of inbreeding with a population), and genetic drift (the random fluctuations in genetic frequency that occur in a small gene pool).

6. The nature-nurture controversy seeks to determine the extent to which human abilities and characteristics are genetically determined or learned. A person's genotype is his genetic makeup, and his phenotype is the expression of this makeup in his particular environment.

7. To measure heritability, researchers examine the extent to which observed differences among people are due to environment or genes. Experiments using identical twins are particularly useful in this research. For example, the heritability of schizophrenia has been studied extensively in twins and their families.

Important Terms

Australopithecus	chromosomes
Homo erectus	genes
Neanderthal	mutation
Homo sapiens	fitness
Cro-Magnon	isolation
evolution	genetic drift
natural selection	genotype
genetic diversity	phenotype
sexual recombination	nature-nurture issue

behavior genetics

dizygotic twins

heritability

schizophrenia

monozygotic twins

Suggested Readings

EIBL-EIBESFELDT, I. *Ethology: The biology of behavior.* New York: Holt, Rinehart & Winston, 1970.

A comparative examination of the functions of behavior patterns in animals and man. The author investigates the behavior of the total organism and its relationship with the organic and inorganic environment.

HIRSCH, J. (ed.) *Behavior-genetic analysis.* New York: McGraw-Hill, 1967.

A collection of chapters written by biological and behavioral scientists concerned with various aspects of genetics and the study of behavior.

HOWELLS, W. *Mankind in the making.* Garden City, N.Y.: Doubleday, 1967.

An anthropological survey tracing evolution from the mammals through prehistoric man. The study also includes discussion of the physical characteristics of the earth at various periods, views on race, genes and function, and adaptation.

MUNN, N. L. *Evolution and the growth of human behavior.* Boston: Houghton Mifflin, 1955.

A textbook of genetic psychology with an eclectic point of view. It is a revision of the author's *Psychological Development: An Introduction to Genetic Psychology* (Boston: Houghton Mifflin, 1938), which is a comprehensive summary of phylogenetic and ontogenetic development of behavior.

SAVAGE, J. M. *Evolution.* New York: Holt, Rinehart and Winston, 1969.

Using evolution as a central unifying concept of biology, the author focuses on the changes in biological organization that the interaction of genetic variation and environmental selection produces.

STERN, C. *Principles of human genetics.* San Francisco: Freeman, 1973.

Written with authoritative scholarship, this broadly based book is academic in tone and a classic in its field.

Chapter 3   The Brain and Behavior

With every day, and from both sides of my intelligence, the moral and the intellectual, I thus drew steadily nearer to that truth, by whose partial discovery I have been doomed to such a dreadful shipwreck, that man is not truly one, but truly two. . . . If each, I told myself, could but be housed in separate identities, life would be relieved of all that was unbearable; the unjust might go his way, delivered from the aspirations and remorse of his more upright twin; and the just could walk steadfastly and securely on his upward path, doing the good things in which he found his pleasure, and no longer exposed to disgrace and penitence by the hands of his extraneous evil. It was the curse of mankind that these incongruous faggots were thus bound together — that in the agonized womb of consciousness, these polar twins should be continuously struggling. How, then, were they dissociated?

—Robert Louis Stevenson
(*The Strange Case of Dr. Jekyll and Mr. Hyde*)

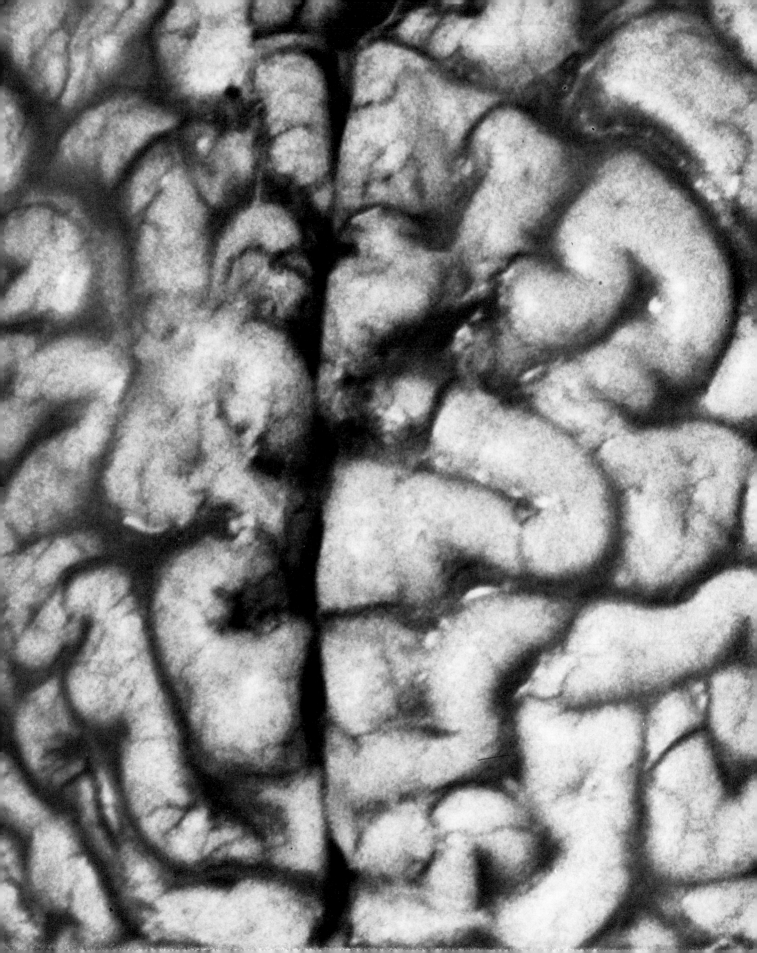

The Brain and Behavior

As we learned in the last chapter, the human brain* is the supreme achievement of man's evolution. Let us ponder this three pounds of soft, spongy tissue encased within a rigid skull and resting like a crown atop the body. The human brain is the most complex physical structure in the known universe. It consists of 10 to 12 *billion* nerve cells (called *neurons*) and 120 *billion* glial ("glue") cells, which apparently nourish and support the neurons. In a single human brain, the number of possible interconnections among the neurons is greater than the number of atomic particles in the entire universe.

The Cerebral Cortex

As psychologists we are primarily interested in the part of the brain called the *cerebral cortex*, for within the cortex lies the secret of man's consciousness, his superb sensitivities to the external world, his remarkable memory, his motor skills, his aptitudes for reasoning and imagining, and above all his unique language abilities. As one writer (Gray, 1958) has described it:

This roof brain (cerebral cortex) is the supremely distinctive organ of the human species. What goes on within its network of cells makes the fundamental difference between man and brute. The functioning of the cerebral cortex not only distinguishes man from the animals, but more than any other faculty it distinguishes man from man. It marks the fateful difference between the meek follower and the dynamic leader, between the scholar and the artist, between the genius and the moron.

The *cerebral cortex* is the brain's outer covering of cells. It is a layer about 2 millimeters (1/25th of an inch) thick that overlies the rest of the brain; it is composed of nerve cells and other kinds of cells. When

3-1

The human brain. The surface you see is the cerebral cortex, a complex layering of neurons that covers the brain. It is the most recent region of the brain to have evolved. (Trangali/Palmeri, dpi)

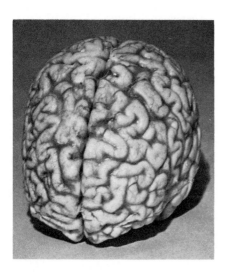

* At the end of this chapter (page 69) you will find an Appendix on brain anatomy and physiology. It describes in pictures and text the features of the human brain that are of interest to psychologists.

you see a picture of the human brain, the surface you see covering the two brain hemispheres is the cerebral cortex.

Medical studies of patients who had suffered various types of brain damage yielded the first clues that certain regions of the cerebral cortex are specialized for very complex abilities and aspects of consciousness. In right-handed people, damage to a part of the cerebral cortex's left hemisphere essentially abolishes the person's ability to understand or speak language intelligently. Damage to the corresponding part of the right hemisphere has no effect on language skills. However, right-handed people with right-hemisphere damage have great difficulty performing spatial tasks. They lose their way, forget well-traveled routes, and have difficulty understanding complex diagrams and pictures.

The cerebral cortex is the most recent evolutionary development of the vertebrate nervous system. Fish and amphibians have no cerebral cortex, and reptiles and birds have only a rudimentary indication of cortex. Much of the cerebral cortex in these lower forms is "old cortex," which has close interrelationships with the more primitive olfactory (smell) system. Certain areas of the mammalian brain also have such cortex. In our discussion of the cerebral cortex, we shall be concerned only with the _neocortex_, the "new" cortex that has become elaborated more recently in the evolutionary process. More primitive mammals, such as the rat, have a relatively small, smooth cortex. Moving from more primitive to more complex mammals, following the general course of evolution, the amount of cortex relative to the total amount of brain tissue increases in fairly regular proportions. Primate brains display this same relationship. Relatively primitive monkeys, such as the marmoset and squirrel monkey, have smoother cortical surfaces compared with higher forms. More advanced primates, such as the rhesus monkey, chimpanzee, and man have enormous and disproportionate increases in the amount of cerebral cortex. Of the approximately 12 billion nerve cells in the human brain, 9 billion are in the cerebral cortex.

All the sensory systems, such as the visual and auditory systems, project information to the cortex, each to a specific region. The motor systems, which ultimately control the muscles and glands, originate in the region known as the motor cortex. Interestingly, the basic organization of the cortical sensory and motor areas does not appear to differ markedly from rat to man. However, as one ascends the mammalian scale of evolution, the relative amount of _association cortex_ (cortex that is neither sensory nor motor and often has been assumed to be involved in higher or more complex behavioral functions) increases strikingly. Figure 3-2 shows rough scale drawings of the cerebral cortex of rat, cat, monkey, and man. Note the remarkable increase in the brain's absolute size as well as the increase in the relative amount of association cortex. Man, incidentally, does not have the largest brain. Porpoises, whales, and elephants all have larger brain masses, although the density of their brain cells may be lower than man's.

Fissures and Lobes of the Cortex

In higher forms, which have a fairly high density of nerve cells in the cortex, many fissures have developed. A _fissure_ is simply an infolding of

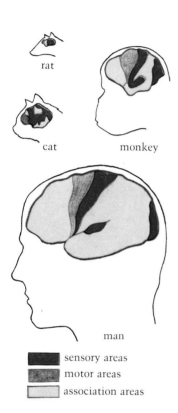

rat

cat   monkey

man

■ sensory areas
▨ motor areas
▢ association areas

3-2
Diagram comparing the brains of a rat, cat, monkey, and man. In addition to the increase in absolute size, there is also a relative increase in association cortex. This "elite" cortex is not directly involved in sensory processing or movement control but rather in more complex aspects of behavior, including short-term and long-term memory processes, thinking and, in man at least, speech and language

Diagrams comparing the fissure patterns of three primates: squirrel monkey, rhesus monkey, and man. The fissures are the infoldings and convolutions that increase the area of cortex. As we ascend the evolutionary scale, the number and complexity of fissures increases dramatically.

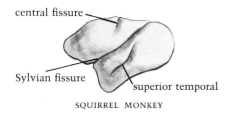

SQUIRREL MONKEY

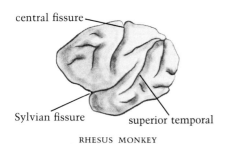

RHESUS MONKEY

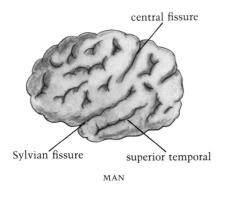

MAN

3-4
Diagram of the major subdivisions of the brain's cerebral cortex.

cortex, such as would occur if a ruler were pressed into the skin of an orange. Cortex is present on both banks of a fissure and has the same thickness except at the bottom, where it usually is thinner. Fissures have permitted an enormous increase in the amount of cortex in higher primates, without undue enlargement of the rigid skull casing. A comparison of the fissure patterns of the squirrel monkey, rhesus monkey, and man illustrates this point (see Figure 3-3). More than three-quarters of the total amount of cerebral cortex in the human brain has been estimated to lie within fissures. Two fissures serve as major cerebral landmarks; the *central fissure* (*fissure of Rolando*), which separates the cerebrum into anterior and posterior halves; and the *temporal* or *Sylvian fissure.*

Some rather complex terminology has developed to designate various brain regions in relation to fissures. However, we need remember only a few major subdivisions. The anterior portion of the cortex, which lies in front of the central fissure, customarily is divided into precentral and frontal regions. The *frontal lobe* extends from the front of the brain back to the precentral cortex. The *temporal lobe* lies below and behind the temporal fissure. The remaining postcentral cortex usually is divided into the *occipital lobe,* which is the posterior portion, and *parietal lobe,* which extends from the occipital lobe to the central fissure. Remembering these subdivisions may be easier if you keep in mind this somewhat oversimplified set of relationships between cortical structure and function: occipital lobe = vision; parietal lobe = skin and muscle senses; part of the temporal lobe and temporal fissure = hearing; precentral cortex = motor or movement control. All remaining parietal, preoccipital, temporal, and frontal areas—which seem to be neither sensory nor motor—have been called "silent" or association areas.

The Split Brain

The body is said to be bilaterally symmetrical because its right side mirrors its left side—we have right and left eyes, ears, arms, and legs. The cerebral cortex is also divided into a right side and a left side. These two sides are called *hemispheres.* The two hemispheres are connected

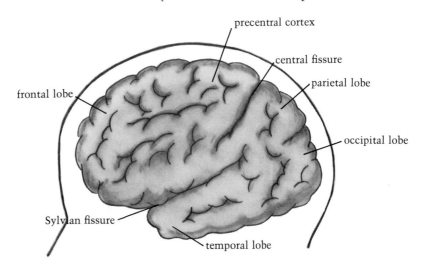

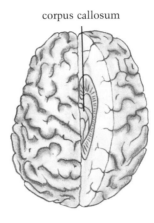
corpus callosum

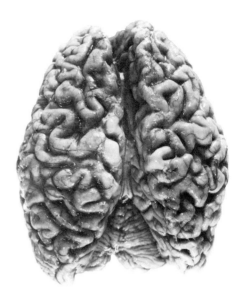

Left   Right

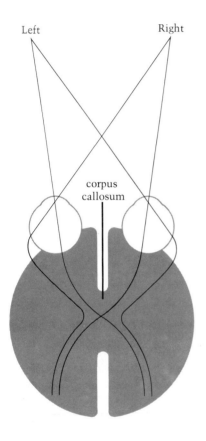

corpus callosum

by a band of millions of nerve fibers called the *corpus callosum.*

What happens when this band of neurons is cut so that all communication between the two hemispheres is abolished? The first observations of split brains were made on patients suffering from a form of epilepsy that begins with abnormal brain activity in one of the hemispheres and spreads to the other hemisphere. Neurosurgeons found that some of these patients could be helped if the corpus callosum was cut. The most surprising result of this drastic brain surgery was that it seemed to have no ill effects on the patients. They showed no loss of intelligence and none of the typical signs of brain damage.

Roger Sperry and his associates (Sperry 1966; Gazzaniga & Sperry, 1969) have conducted a number of fascinating studies of split-brain patients. In order to understand Sperry's work, it is necessary to know the relationship of the two hemispheres to vision and to bodily movement.

In the visual system, each side of each eye projects visual information through nerve pathways to a different side of the cerebral cortex. The left side of both the left and right eyes projects to the left cerebral cortex, and the right side of each eye projects to the right cerebral cortex (see Figure 3-6). The right half of the visual field projects to the left half of each eye. If you look at a particular point on the wall opposite you, everything you see to the right of that point projects to the left hemisphere of the cerebral cortex and everything you see to the left of your point of gaze projects to the right hemisphere. Normally, of course, the corpus callosum interconnects these two hemispheres of cortex. Consequently, you see a unified visual world rather than two half-worlds. The split-brain patients have quite different experiences, as Sperry and his associates discovered.

Roger Sperry's studies of the patients involved procedures for testing the functions of the two hemispheres independently. He was able to measure the output from each hemisphere by noting the responses of each of the patient's hands, which were placed behind a screen blocking the patient's view of his hands (see Figure 3-7). The patient looks at a fixation point while visual information—words, drawings, pictures—is flashed briefly to his left or right cerebral cortex. He responds verbally or with movements of either hand behind the screen. Sperry's patients were all right-handed. For all right-handed and most left-handed people the speech area is in the left hemisphere. The left hemisphere of the cerebral cortex also controls the body's right side, including the right hand, while the right hemisphere controls movements of the body's left side.

Sperry's findings are strikingly clear. When a word was flashed to the patient's right visual field and hence to his left hemisphere, the patient could immediately say it and write it with his right hand because his speech and his right hand were controlled by the left hemisphere of his brain. In marked contrast, if the word was flashed to the right hemisphere, the patient could neither say nor write it. Despite this, it soon became apparent that the right hemisphere could easily recognize objects. The trick was to find a way for the right hemisphere to tell the experimenter. A picture of a fork might be flashed to the right hemisphere. If the left hand (controlled by the right hemisphere) were allowed to feel many different objects behind the screen, including a fork, it would immediately select the fork and hold it up. While the right hemisphere is nonverbal, it is not incompetent. Having correctly identified the fork, the patient still cannot say what it is. However, if the right hand is allowed to take it from the left, the patient immediately says "fork."

Actually, the right hemisphere did show some limited verbal comprehension. If simple words rather than pictures of objects were flashed to it, the patient often could identify the object by pointing to it with his left hand. Similarly, if an object like a pencil were placed in his left hand behind the screen, and the experimenter then flashed a series of words, including pencil, to his right hemisphere, the patient could correctly signal with his left hand when the word pencil was flashed. However, he still could not say the word.

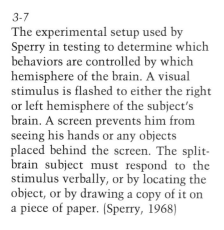

3-7
The experimental setup used by Sperry in testing to determine which behaviors are controlled by which hemisphere of the brain. A visual stimulus is flashed to either the right or left hemisphere of the subject's brain. A screen prevents him from seeing his hands or any objects placed behind the screen. The split-brain subject must respond to the stimulus verbally, or by locating the object, or by drawing a copy of it on a piece of paper. (Sperry, 1968)

Sperry (1968) made this observation:

In one particularly interesting test the word "heart" was flashed across the center of the visual field, with the "he" portion to the left of the center and "art" to the right. Asked to tell what the word was, the patients would say they had seen "art"—the portion projected to the left brain hemisphere (which is responsible for speech). Curiously when, after "heart" had been flashed in the same way, the patients were asked to point with the left hand to one of two cards—"art" or "he"—to identify the word they had seen, they invariably pointed to "he." The experiment showed clearly that both hemispheres had simultaneously observed portions of the word available to them and that in this particular case the right hemisphere, when it had had the opportunity to express itself, had prevailed over the left.

The patients became very adept at "cross-communicating" between hemispheres by using peripheral cues:

We had a case of such cross-cuing during a series of tests of whether the right hemisphere could respond verbally to simple red or green stimuli. At first, after either a red or a green light was flashed to the right hemisphere, the patient would guess the color at a chance level, as might be expected if the speech mechanism is solely represented in the left hemisphere. After a few trials, however, the score improved whenever the examiner allowed a second guess.

We soon caught on to the strategy the patient used. If a red light was flashed and the patient by chance guessed red, he would stick with that answer. If the flashed light was red and the patient by chance guessed green, he would frown, shake his head and then say, "Oh no, I meant red." What was happening was that the right hemisphere saw the red light and heard the left hemisphere make the guess "green." Knowing that the answer was wrong, the right hemisphere precipitated a frown and a shake of the head, which in turn cued in the left hemisphere to the fact that the answer was wrong and that it had better correct itself! We have learned that this cross-cuing mechanism can become extremely refined. The realization that the neurological patient has various strategies at his command emphasizes how difficult it is to obtain a clear neurological description of a human being with brain damage.

In contrast to the left hemisphere's involvement in speech, the right hemisphere is distinctly superior to the left in tasks involving perception and manipulation of spatial patterns. Experiments in which simple designs were presented to one hemisphere at a time and copied by the opposite hand bring out this difference. Drawings made by the left hand were clearly superior to those made with the right hand even though the patients were "right-handed."

Finally, the right hemisphere handled "emotional" perception and responsiveness quite well, although nonverbally.

In one of our experiments . . . we would present a series of ordinary objects and then suddenly flash a picture of a nude woman. This

3-8

The split-brain patient in this experiment was instructed to copy each of the drawings on the left, first with the left hand and then with the right. All of his drawings were somewhat awkward-looking because he was not allowed to see what he was doing. However, his left-hand drawings resembled the real thing more than his right-hand drawings even though he was right-handed. The patient's performance on the drawing task indicates that the right hemisphere controls visual-spatial activities. (Sperry, 1968)

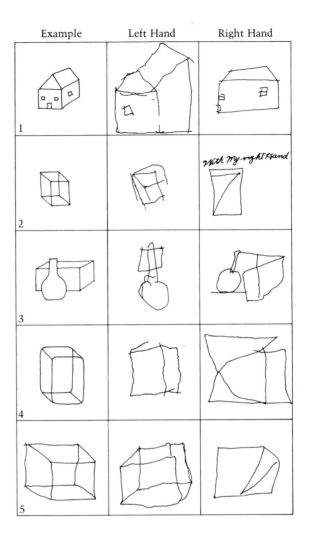

evoked an amused reaction regardless of whether the picture was presented to the left hemisphere or to the right. When the picture was flashed to the left hemisphere of a female patient, she laughed and verbally identified the picture as a nude. When it was later presented to the right hemisphere, she said in reply to a question that she saw nothing, but almost immediately a sly smile spread over her face and she began to chuckle. Asked what she was laughing at, she said: "I don't know . . . nothing . . . oh—that funny machine." Although the right hemisphere could not describe what it had seen, the sight nevertheless elicited an emotional response like the one evoked from the left hemisphere.

Gazzaniga (1967) summarizes some of the implications of these studies in the following passage:

All the evidence indicates that separation of the hemispheres creates two independent spheres of consciousness within a single cranium, that is to say, within a single organism. This conclusion is disturbing to *some people who view consciousness as an indivisible property of the human brain. It seems premature to others, who insist that the capacities revealed thus far for the right hemisphere are at the level of an automaton. There is, to be sure, hemispheric inequality in the present cases, but it may well be a characteristic of the individuals we have studied. It is entirely possible that if a human brain were divided in a very young person, both hemispheres could as a result separately and independently develop mental functions of a high order at the level attained only in the left hemisphere of normal individuals.*

In a stimulating recent book (*The Psychology of Consciousness*, 1972), Robert Ornstein develops a somewhat controversial but most interesting view of consciousness. He starts from the work we have reviewed on the functions of the two hemispheres of the cerebral cortex. By drawing on several different cultural histories, Ornstein makes the point that most human cultures consider "right" to be rational and analytic, and "left" intuitive, dark, and mysterious. The French word for law is *droit*—right. Similarly, our word sinister comes from the Latin word *sinistra*—"left." The Mojave Indians have a similar interpretation; they believe the left hand is passive and maternal while the right hand is the active father.

In sum, Ornstein proposes two different modes of consciousness, noting that different cultures and religions have emphasized one or the other mode. Western rational culture and science are "left hemisphere" and the meditative, mystical religions and cultures of the East and certain American Indian tribes are "right hemisphere."

Ornstein suggests we should attempt to integrate the two approaches to wisdom—the rational and intuitive. Indeed, there is an old cultural tradition in the Western world of the two sides of man, often at war with one another, epitomized by Freud's conception of the id versus the ego (see Chapter 16). This concept has been compellingly described in Robert Louis Stevenson's *The Strange Case of Dr. Jekyll and Mr. Hyde.*

3-9
A split face (*a*) used in tests of patients whose brains have been surgically divided is made up from two of the faces shown in the selection (*b*). The patient, wearing a headgear that restrains eye movements, sees the picture projected briefly on a screen. The left side of the brain recognizes the pictures as being the one of the child; the right side sees the woman.

A

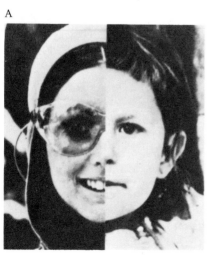

B

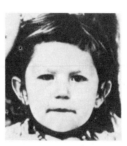

That 19th-century novel's central idea is set forth in the quotation that opens this chapter. It is dramatically illustrated by some of Roger Sperry's descriptions of Jekyll-and-Hyde behavior in split-brain patients. For example, a split-brain man might grab a woman roughly with his left hand, only to have his right hand seize his left and pull it away. Another split-brain subject's right hand was fumbling with a block-arrangement test when his left hand, more skilled at such tasks, impatiently pushed aside its clumsy rival and completed the task.

Stevenson and Ornstein provide us with fascinating speculations. However, from a scientific "right-sided" (left hemisphere) view, we must be content with the data demonstrating differences in performance between the left and right hemispheres of the cerebral cortex. This information does seem to suggest that the nature and functions of consciousness may differ substantially between the two hemispheres.

The Electrical Signs of Brain Activity

How can we study the activities of the brain? Direct observation of such a complex organ is, of course, impossible. Parts of the brain can be removed or destroyed during experiments on lower animals, but this procedure cannot be used with human beings. Brain-damaged persons can be studied to see how the damage has affected their behavior, and this method has revealed important information. And as the split-brain experiments show, brain surgery sometimes provides us with important information about cortical activities. But we also can study the brain activities of perfectly normal people by means of the electroencephalogram or EEG, as it is abbreviated. This method makes use of the fact that nerve impulses traveling along the nerve fibers are electrical in character. This electrical activity within the brain emits signals that can be measured, even though these signals are very weak—in the microvolt (millionth of a volt) range. Electrodes glued to the scalp record the electrical signals generated by the underlying brain. The signals flow to an amplifier and then are displayed on a polygraph—usually an ink record made on moving paper.

Historically, the EEG was the first kind of electrical brain activity to be recorded. In 1895, Caton, an English scientist who was working with anesthetized animals, put electrodes on their brains and reported variations in voltage. Because he had only an extremely primitive electrical recording device, he could not specify more about the brain's activity. Considerably later, meaningful recording of the EEG was first done with humans. Hans Berger, an obscure German psychiatrist in Jena, placed large metal discs on the head of a human volunteer and connected them to a primitive recording device, a galvanometer. In his first paper, published in 1929, Berger noted that in the relaxed adult subject regular sequences of waves occurred at the rate of about 10 per second. These waves were most visible when the subject was relaxing with his eyes closed. Berger named these the alpha waves. He also discovered smaller amplitude waves that were faster in frequency, ranging from about 18 to 50 per second, which he called the beta waves. At first, scientists ignored Berger's discovery. However, in the 1930s they began to repeat

3-10

The electroencephalogram (EEG) is a graphic record of the electrical activity emitted by the brain as measured by the electroencephalograph. The active electrode is attached to the surface of the scalp; the other electrode to a neutral point such as the ear. The brain's weak signals must be amplified before being recorded on an ink writing galvanometer or displayed on an oscilloscope and recorded by a camera.

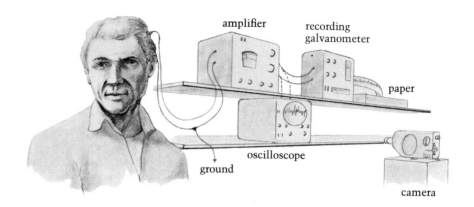

his observations, using animal subjects. With the development of vacuum tube amplifiers, this field of study expanded rapidly.

To date, electroencephalography has been used chiefly for clinical studies of human brain dysfunction. As a tool in the diagnosis and location of certain forms of epilepsy and brain damage, electroencephalography has been very successful. However, it also is a widely used research device for the study of the human brain's normal functions.

Alpha Waves

As we noted, *alpha waves* are the waves Berger found issuing at a rate of 10 per second from widespread regions of the brain when the subject was awake but physically relaxed in an environment free of sudden stimuli. Alpha waves can be recorded in the adult and the young adult ranging down to about 12 years of age. An alpha wave's size or amplitude can range from a few microvolts to a few hundred microvolts. The more relaxed a subject is, the larger and more prominent are his alpha waves. Interestingly, some people do not show clear alpha. However, most subjects do. If you suddenly startle or arouse a subject showing alpha waves, they stop; this is called *alpha blocking.* Shining a light in a subject's eyes will stop alpha immediately. In short, alpha seems to relate inversely to arousal. Unaroused, a subject is likely to continue producing alpha. When a subject is aroused, alpha will stop.

Other Types of Brain Waves

Beta Waves.   Berger first defined *beta waves* as fast, rhythmic, low-voltage waves occurring at the rate of 20 to 50 per second. Jasper subsequently divided this class of waves into *beta waves*, ranging from 18 to 30 per second, and *gamma waves*, ranging from 30 to 50 per second. We know less about beta and gamma waves, probably because we have not studied them as much as alpha waves. Beta and gamma waves occur at higher states of arousal or alertness than alpha waves.

Delta Waves.   A fourth type of wave, the *delta wave*, is a very slow, large amplitude wave occurring at the rate of about 2 or 3 per second. Normally, delta waves occur only in *slow wave* sleep, where the EEG shows the very large, slow synchronized waves. However, delta waves also are common in more unusual circumstances, such as unconsciousness, whether it is induced by anesthesia, head injury, or convulsions, and in certain types of brain injury. If present in a waking subject, delta waves may indicate severe brain malfunction or brain damage.

Theta Waves. Another wave, which is just slightly slower than the alpha wave, is called the *theta wave.* With a frequency of about 5 to 7 waves per second, it is found particularly over the head's temporal (sides) and frontal (front) regions. Theta waves are particularly prominent in children and adolescents. Data from animal studies suggest that theta waves may occur as alpha is blocked in the cerebral cortex. Thus, when an animal is aroused, his cortical alpha stops while his theta grows more intense. Under many such circumstances these two rhythms seem to show a reciprocal relationship. When alpha stops, theta gets larger, and vice versa.

Kappa Waves. One EEG wave that has been surrounded by controversy is the so-called *kappa wave.* This alphalike rhythm at the temples, described by Kennedy and his associates in 1948, was thought to be associated with intellectual processes. The kappa wave has a frequency of about 8 to 12 per second, similar to the alpha rhythm. It tends to occur (on the polygraph) in spindle-shaped bursts and reportedly can be increased by reading and mental arithmetic, difficult discrimination, memory tasks, and problem-solving. Eye movements cause voltage changes that show up on an EEG record in a kappa wave pattern, and some authorities believe that eye movements are the cause of kappa waves. The issue remains unclear. However, a recent study by Chapman (1972) suggests that some subjects may show a reliable kappa rhythm correlated with mental activity rather than eye movements.

3-11
The frequencies and amplitudes of the different brain waves. (Woodbury, 1965)

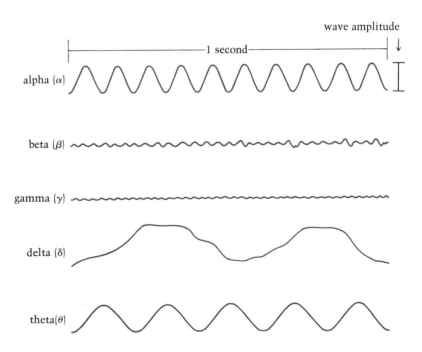

EEG Arousal

With the possible exception of some very irregular beta waves, an alert, attentive subject typically does not show a regular pattern of waves in the EEG. This finding has led to the descriptive phrase, "low-voltage activity," or "arousal," for the alert or aroused EEG pattern. As a typical arousal EEG shows, the electrical activity is small in amplitude and fast and irregular in frequency. However, because the same arousal EEG also is characteristic of the deep-sleep state, we must take care to distinguish between behavioral arousal and EEG arousal. EEG arousal refers only to the brain's electrical activity pattern, not to the person's interior state.

One interesting aspect of the EEG is its progressive development in children. Figure 3-12 shows the EEG record of an individual from infancy through young adulthood. Incidentally, these records were taken by the pioneering electroencephalographer Dr. Donald Lindsley on his son, David Lindsley. David himself is now a well-known neurophysiologist. As the record shows, no alpha is found in infancy. In the newborn, no regular brain rhythm at all is apparent. Regular brain rhythm over the occipital region first occurs at 3 or 4 months of age with a frequency of 3 to 4 waves per second. By about 12 months, the wave's frequency increases to about 5 or 6 per second. Gradually, its frequency continues to increase until at about 10 years of age the alpha's frequency reaches the adult level of about 10 per second.

Today, the alpha wave is quite widely discussed on a popular and commercial level. Companies are selling devices which are said to allow the buyer to "control" his own alpha. These poor man's electroencephalograms turn on a tone or some other signal when the subject is generating alpha waves. The subject then tries to keep the tone on as much as possible, that is, to train his alpha to occur more frequently. Apparently, many subjects can do this. Elaborate claims are made for these devices and for the value of the alpha state, which is merely another way of describing normal, relaxed waking. If you can generate more alpha, it simply means that you can relax. There is nothing wrong with such relaxing; people who are normally tense may benefit from it. However, alpha is not a mystical force; it is only an index of relaxed wakefulness. Interestingly, in the state called "transcendental meditation," alpha intensifies and may become slower in frequency. Whether transcendental meditation is merely a very relaxed, wakeful state or another state is yet to be determined (see Chapter 5).

Effects of Experience on the Growth of the Brain

If the cerebral cortex is the center for intelligent behavior, as everyone assumes it is, does the cortex grow larger with use in the same way that muscles become larger with exercise? The answer, at least for laboratory rats, is yes.

Studies by Bennett, Diamond, Krech, and Rosenzweig (1964) have demonstrated that the kind of environment a rat is raised in can powerfully affect the growth and development of its brain. In their classic experiment, they raised rats in "enriched" or "impoverished" environments, somewhat analogous to the environments of rich children and slum

3-12

Alpha rhythm of a subject (Lindsley's son) from age 1 month to 21 years. Note that after this rhythm is established during the fourth month its frequency increases and its voltage (amplitude) decreases until the subject is 10 years old; thereafter the average frequency is the same as an adult's. (Lindsley, 1960)

Scale:
frequency: 1 second ⊢———⊣
amplitude: 50 microvolts ⏉

children. The rich rats and slum rats were litter mates from the same genetic strain. Their genetic background was the same; only their environments differed. Slum rats lived in the standard small rat cage. Figure 3-13 shows the rich rat's more stimulating environment, which was full of objects to play with and explore.

Environment's effects on the rats' brains were quite striking. Rich rats had bigger and heavier brains; their cerebral cortex was actually thicker. More subtle chemical differences also were found. And the rich rats' brains had many more glial cells. Finally, a recent study by Globus, Rosenzweig, Bennett, and Diamond (1973) demonstrated that the nerve cells in the rich rats' cerebral cortexes had more dendritic spines and synapses than the nerve cells of slum rats. (Synapses and dendritic spines are the interconnections between nerve cells; they are described in the appendix to this chapter.)

Obviously, these fundamental studies of environment's effects on brain development are important. They suggest that a rich environment enhances the growth and complexity of brain development while a slum environment retards it. A natural conclusion from this point might be that, similarly, mental abilities and capacities are enhanced by a rich environment and retarded by a slum environment. Studies of children from slum and enriched environments tend to support this conclusion, though in human studies, it is difficult to distinguish between the influences of heredity and environment.

The Brain and Language

In concluding this chapter, let us consider the localization in the brain of the most complex of human activities—language. The brain mechanisms that underlie speech and language are good illustrations of the way the nervous system receives, processes, and generates information. When words are spoken, the resulting sound waves activate receptors in your ear which initiate activity in the auditory nerve. This information is relayed through a network of nerve cells that lead to the auditory area of the cerebral cortex. From here, having been transformed again in complex ways we do not yet understand, it is transmitted to association areas of the cerebral cortex. At this point you "understand" the spoken words.

When we read a word, a similar analysis and transmittal from the eye to the visual area of the cerebral cortex takes place. Again, it is then mysteriously transformed and projected to association areas. At this point we "understand" the word we have read.

To speak a word we must first "think of" the word, then project it to the anterior motor speech areas. This activates the motor cortex and the descending motor systems—which control tongue, lips, and throat—to generate actual speech.

Essentially all our information about the brain mechanisms of language is drawn from studies of patients who have suffered damage to the speech areas. This causes a language defect known as *aphasia*. It may be a sensory disorder in which the ability to read or to understand speech is impaired, or it may be a motor disorder in which the ability to write or speak language is impaired. Figure 3-14 shows the approximate locations of the major regions of the cerebral cortex involved in language. In the normal adult, language is localized entirely in one hemisphere of the brain—the left for 97 percent of all people (all right-handed and most left-handed individuals). Penfield (1954) has produced a "scale" which places in order of severity the general damage that might impair the various areas. Damage to the superior area (in the general region of the supplementary motor cortex) causes speech difficulties or aphasia for only a few weeks. Damage to *Broca's area* (an area in the left frontal lobe of the cerebral cortex) causes much more prolonged aphasia but recovery generally occurs. Many authorities believe that damage to Broca's area affects motor control of words and word sequences more than the conceptual aspects of language. The most devastating and permanent aphasias result from damage in a rather large region of the left posterior association cortex termed *Wernicke's area*. An adult suffering severe injury to this entire region is likely to remain permanently aphasic.

3-14
The speech areas of the brain.

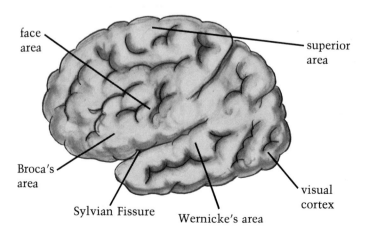

In young children, the effect of brain damage on language is dramatically different. If the entire dominant (left) hemisphere is destroyed, the child will be completely aphasic but generally will recover over a period of months and ultimately develop perfectly normal language.

When searching for abnormalities in the brain, Penfield (1954) observed the effects of electrical stimulation of the cerebral cortex on language in epileptic patients. When the brain's language areas are electrically stimulated, the normal language function is blocked. With the use of this effect, Penfield was able to draw up stimulation maps of the speech areas that agree well with the clinical literature on brain damage. Individuals with early brain damage to language regions of the dominant hemisphere develop the language function in the corresponding regions of the brain's other hemisphere.

Characteristically, damage to Broca's area results in very slow, poorly articulated speech. Such patients typically produce little speech. Apparently, the trouble is not only motor control of the tongue, since small words and endings are omitted. In contrast the patient with damage to Wernicke's area can produce rapid, well-articulated sound and even proper phrases and sequences of words easily, but not language. Such a patient's "speech" has the correct rhythm and general sound of normal speech but conveys no information. These patients can understand neither spoken nor written language, although they have basically normal hearing and vision.

On the basis of these observations and others Geschwind (1972) emphasizes how important for language the *interconnections* among sensory, association, and speech areas in the brain are.

For example, a lesion limited to the region interconnecting Wernicke's area and Broca's area produces what is called *conduction aphasia.* This patient has perfect comprehension of spoken and written language, but his speech is severely abnormal and resembles that of patients with damage to Wernicke's area—fluent words but no sense.

Many years ago the French neurologist Dejerine described a patient who had lost the ability to read and write but could understand spoken language and could speak. His disorder is called *alexia* (inability to read) with *agraphia* (inability to write). An autopsy of Déjerine's patient revealed a lesion in his auditory-visual association area. He had seen words and letters correctly but they were meaningless visual patterns to him since the visual pattern first must be connected to the auditory form before the word can be understood. The auditory pattern of hearing a word must be transformed into the visual pattern before it can be spelled and rewritten. However, heard words could be processed through the auditory cortex and Wernicke's area for understanding and thence to Broca's area for speech.

Another of Déjerine's patients awakened one morning to discover he could not read. He was found to be blind in the right half of his visual field due to occlusion (blocking) of a cerebral artery, the result of a stroke. The visual cortex of his left hemisphere was completely destroyed, explaining his half-blindness but not his inability to read. The patient could speak and comprehend spoken language. Vision in the left side of his visual field was normal. He also could write. Postmortem examination revealed that the stroke had destroyed not only the left visual cortex but also the posterior region of the corpus callosum, which carries visual information between the hemispheres. Consequently, although visual information got to the patient's right visual cortex and association area, it could not cross to the critical region for integration of visual and auditory functions—nor to the left Wernicke's area.

Geschwind completed anatomical studies of 100 normal human brains, comparing a portion of Wernicke's area for the two hemispheres. On the average, the left region was one-third larger than the right. Juhn Wada (1969) published similar results in which he found that the left Wernicke's area was larger in human infants who had died soon after birth. Apparently, a larger left Wernicke's area is genetically determined. Perhaps the most significant result from the studies of aphasia is the critical importance of the intercortical connections in the human brain. It seems quite possible that many complex human attributes and properties, in addition to language, may depend on particular pathways interconnecting specific regions of the cortex and subcortical structures.

Summary

1. Containing 10 to 12 billion nerve cells, as well as other cells, the human brain is the most complex structure in the known universe.

2. The cerebral cortex, which is the outer covering of the brain, seems to mediate the more complex aspects of behavior, as well as control the sensory and motor aspects of behavior. The relative amount of this brain material distinguishes lower from higher animals.

3. Fissures, or infoldings of the cortex, increase the cortex's surface area without requiring greater space and thus a larger skull. Fissures also divide the brain into various regions or lobes: frontal, parietal, occipital, and temporal.

4. Studies by Roger Sperry and associates, in which the two hemispheres of the brain had been disconnected by severing the nerve fibers (corpus callosum) joining them, reveal that the functions of the two sides of the brain are in many ways different and independent—the left side usually controls language, and the right side controls visual and spatial abilities.

5. Alpha waves are electrical activity from the brain which occur at the rate of about 10 waves per second when the subject is awake, physically relaxed, and in an environment free of sudden stimuli.

6. Beta waves, ranging from 18 to 30 per second, and gamma waves, ranging from 30 to 50 per second, occur at higher states of arousal or alertness than alpha.

7. Delta waves are very slow, large-amplitude waves, occurring about 2 or 3 per second in slow-wave sleep or in unconsciousness.

8. Theta waves have a frequency of about 5 to 7 per second and are particularly prominent in adolescents and children.

9. Kappa waves occur at 8 to 12 per second, but are recorded in spindle-shaped bursts, and are tentatively associated with such mental activity as problem-solving.

10. Studies of the effects of the environment on brain development, using rats raised in "enriched" or "impoverished" environments, show that the rats in enriched environments had bigger and heavier brains, thicker cerebral cortexes, and more glial cells and synapses.

11. Our information about the brain mechanisms of language is largely drawn from studies of patients who have suffered damage to the speech, sensory, and association areas of the brain, and their interconnections. There are many sorts of aphasia (language disability), depending not only on whether a sensory or a motor disorder is involved, but also on whether the brain damage is suffered as a child or as an adult.

Important Terms

cerebral cortex

corpus callosum

central fissure (fissure of Rolando)

temporal or Sylvian fissure

frontal lobe

temporal lobe

occipital lobe

parietal lobe

electroencephalogram (EEG)

alpha waves

alpha blocking

beta waves

gamma waves

delta waves

theta waves

kappa waves

aphasia

conduction aphasia

alexia

Broca's area

Wernicke's area

Suggested Readings

GAZZANIGA, M. S. *The bisected brain.* New York: Appleton-Century-Crofts, 1970.
   A fascinating account of the experiments by Sperry, Gazzaniga and their associates on split-brained human patients.

ORNSTEIN, R. E. *The psychology of consciousness.* San Francisco: Freeman, 1972.
   An intriguing and speculative approach to human consciousness.

ECCLES, JOHN C. *The understanding of the brain.* New York: McGraw-Hill, 1973.

A very clear and readable introduction to the brain by the world's foremost neurophysiologist.

SINGH, D. & MORGAN, C. T. (EDS.) *Current status of physiological psychology: Readings.* Monterey, Cal.: Brooks-Cole, 1972.

A current and comprehensive collection of papers in the field.

TEITELBAUM, P. *Physiological psychology.* Englewood Cliffs, N.J.: Prentice-Hall, 1967.

A concise, readable introduction to some topics in physiological psychology by one of the field's most eminent researchers.

TEYLER, T. J. *A primer of psychobiology.* San Francisco: Freeman, 1975.

A concise and lucid presentation of the relations between brain and behavior. This delightful little book assumes no background on the part of the reader.

THOMPSON, R. F. *Introduction to physiological psychology* (2nd ed.) New York: Harper, 1975.

Clear and comprehensive text on the biological bases of behavior. Designed for a first undergraduate course in physiological psychology.

THOMPSON, R. F. (ed.) *Physiological Psychology: Readings from Scientific American.* San Francisco, Freeman, 1971.

A fascinating collection of articles from *Scientific American* by experts in all aspects of psychobiology.

ZEIGLER, H. P. *Learning and memory.* New York: Harper, 1969.

A compendium of important research papers in these fields.

Appendix to Chapter 3

A Survey of the Human Nervous System

This appendix surveys the anatomy and function of the human nervous system—the brain, the spinal cord, and the many nerve cells that conduct information throughout the body. This description of the nervous system lays the physiological foundation for many of the psychological processes discussed throughout the book.

Neuroanatomy

The _brain_ is the vast network of cells and cell fibers in the upper portion of the skull. As this cellular mass leaves the skull, it becomes the _spinal cord_. The _central nervous system_ (CNS) includes both the brain and the spinal cord; it is made up of nerve cell bodies and a variety of other types of cells, such as blood vessels and supporting tissues. A complete _nerve cell_ with its cell body and fibers is called a _neuron_. The word _nerve_ refers to a collection of nerve fibers (not including the cell bodies). Collections of nerve cell bodies are called _nuclei_ when they are inside the CNS and _ganglia_ when they are outside.

_A-1_
Electron photomicrograph of a nerve cell. The dark oval area within each cell body is the cell nucleus. (The Carolina Biological Supply Co.)

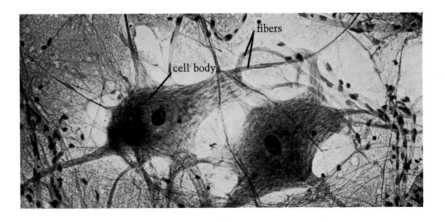

The CNS, like the human body itself, is bilaterally symmetrical; that is, most of its structures have left and right sides which are mirror images of each other. A number of CNS systems are *crossed;* for example, areas in the left hemisphere of the brain are functionally related to body structures on the right, and vice versa.

Organization of the Central Nervous System

We can best understand the CNS organization in terms of groups of nerve cell bodies interconnected by fiber tracts. Nuclei are clusters of cell bodies belonging to neurons that are involved in a similar activity; tracts are bundles of nerve fibers involved in the performance of a particular function. In the spinal cord, nuclei lie in the central core surrounded by fiber tracts. Connecting tracts that travel the farthest tend to lie toward the outside while short tracts lie closer to the central core. The central core area, made up of clusters of cell bodies and short fibers, is called *grey matter;* the surrounding area, composed of tracts of long fibers, is called *white matter.* The brain also is made up of grey matter and white matter. White and grey are the actual colors of these areas in live tissue. The protective myelin sheath surrounding each nerve fiber gives white matter its characteristic color. The fibers that constitute white matter connect the cell bodies that are located in different regions of grey matter. Throughout the spinal cord and brain stem, cell bodies and fibers receiving sensory input from the sense receptors in the body tend to lie at the back (dorsal) side; those concerned with motor-output messages from the brain to the muscles tend to lie toward the front (ventral) side. (Motor fibers are those nerve cell fibers that direct the action of skeletal muscles.)

Peripheral nerves. Nerves lying outside the spinal cord are called *peripheral nerves.* Peripheral nerves carry messages between the CNS and the various parts of the body. Throughout most of their length they are *mixed.* They contain both incoming (*afferent*) sensory fibers carrying information to the spinal cord from receptors in the skin, muscles, and joints; and outgoing (*efferent*) motor fibers conveying instructions from

A-2

Two views of the spinal cord: (A) a cross section and (B) a lateral view.

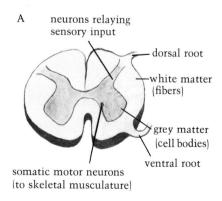

A neurons relaying sensory input

— dorsal root

—white matter (fibers)

—grey matter (cell bodies)

ventral root

somatic motor neurons (to skeletal musculature)

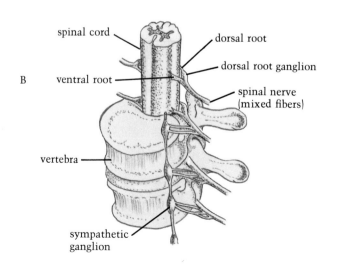

B ventral root

spinal cord

dorsal root

dorsal root ganglion

spinal nerve (mixed fibers)

vertebra

sympathetic ganglion

the spinal cord and brain stem motor neurons to the muscles and glands. Afferent and efferent neuron fibers enter and leave the spinal cord in groups, known as roots. Afferent fibers enter the spinal cord through dorsal roots and efferent fibers leave the spinal cord through ventral roots. Efferent fibers then join with afferent fibers to form mixed nerves, which travel to various body structures. As they approach their target regions, the motor and sensory fibers again separate and go to their appropriate locations.

Efferent fibers have their cell bodies in the ventral part of the cord's central grey matter. Sensory or afferent nerves differ somewhat from efferent nerves; their cell bodies are located in a series of separate cell bodies, called dorsal root ganglia, outside the spinal cord. Peripheral receptors—which are the senses detecting pain, temperature, pressure, joint movement, smell, color, and taste—activate the sensory fibers, which then convey information to the spinal cord through the dorsal roots.

Autonomic Nerve Fibers. The nerves we have just described are called *somatic* nerves, because they innervate (supply with nerves) the striated skeletal musculature—that is, somatic or body muscles. These are voluntary muscles that we can consciously control. *Autonomic nerve fibers,* on the other hand, govern structures such as smooth muscle (involuntary muscle of the internal organs excluding the heart), heart muscle, and those glands involved in autonomic responses, such as crying, sweating, heartbeat, or stomach ache, which commonly are related to "emotional" behavior. Autonomic means involuntary and spontaneous. The muscle action driving such internal body elements as intestines, heart, and glands long was regarded as entirely involuntary and not subject to conscious control. However, as we shall see in Chapters 6 and 11, experiments by Neal Miller have shown that some functions of the autonomic system (for example, heart rate and blood pressure) can be brought under conscious control.

The *autonomic nervous system* (ANS) has two divisions: the sympathetic and the parasympathetic. *Sympathetic* fibers have their cell bodies in the spinal cord. They run out through the ventral roots and a short length of mixed nerves to the sympathetic ganglia. The fibers form a connected chain which runs parallel to, but outside of, the spinal bony vertebrae. From the sympathetic ganglia, peripheral nerve fibers extend out to the heart, stomach, and various other organs.

The *parasympathetic* division of the autonomic nervous system differs somewhat in its organization. Its motor fibers branch off from cranial nerves coming directly from the brain (or from sacral nerves—nerves extending from the part of the spinal cord that is directly connected to the pelvis at the end of the spinal cord) and travel to ganglia located near the target organs they innervate. Thus, the parasympathetic and sympathetic divisions of the autonomic system come from different regions of the CNS and have their ganglia in different locations.

Often, the two divisions of the autonomic system work against each other. Activation of the sympathetic system causes such reactions as artery contraction, heart acceleration, inhibition of stomach contraction and secretion, and dilation of the pupils. In contrast, activation of the

A-3
The autonomic nervous system. As
this diagram shows, the sympathetic and parasympathetic divisions
act on the same organs but in different ways, as described in the table
below.

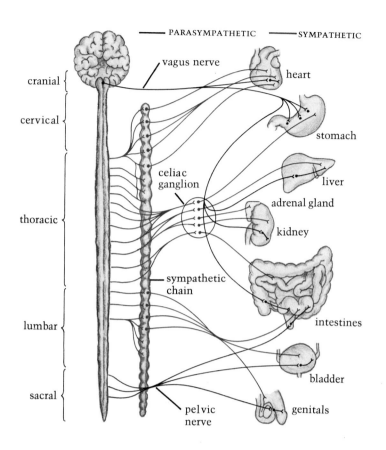

Table A-1   *Functions of Autonomic Nervous System*

Organ	Sympathetic Division—Function	Parasympathetic Division—Function
Heart	Acceleration	Inhibition
Blood vessels		
In skin	Constriction	None
In muscle	Dilation, constriction	None
In heart	Dilation	Constriction
In abdominal organs	Constriction	None
Pupil of eye	Dilation	Constriction
Tear glands	(Possibly a secretory function)	Secretion
Sweat glands	Secretion	None
Hair on skin	Erection of hair	None
Adrenal glands	Secretion	None
Liver	Release of sugar	None
Salivary glands	(Possibly a secretory function)	Secretion
Stomach	Inhibition of secretion and peristalsis (some excitation)	Secretion, peristalsis (some inhibition)
Intestines	Inhibition	Increased tone and movement
Rectum	Inhibition	Feces expelled
Bladder	Inhibition	Urine expelled
Genital organs (male)	Ejaculation	Erection

parasympathetic system causes dilation of arteries, inhibition of the heart, contractions and secretions in the stomach, and constriction of the pupils. These opposed effects have led to the commonly accepted generalization that the sympathetic system works to mobilize the body's resources for emergencies, while the parasympathetic system works to conserve and store body resources. Thus, in a sudden emergency or stress a person will have an increased heartbeat, inhibited stomach activity, and widened pupils, all due to the action of the sympathetic system. (One can think of the system as acting in sympathy with the emotions.) On the other hand, such conservative functions as digestion will be carried on by the parasympathetic system in the intervals between stresses. These two divisions of the autonomic system are under the control of the limbic system, which will be described shortly.

In summary, motor fibers have their cell bodies in the ventral regions of the cord's grey matter and run out to muscles or autonomic ganglia. The sensory fibers have their cell bodies in the dorsal root ganglia and enter the spinal cord to convey information from receptors. Sensory fibers convey this information either directly to the motor neurons (in reflexes) or to more central regions of the CNS (brain) for further information processing and control.

Spinal Reflexes. The spinal cord handles two general categories of activity: spinal reflexes and supraspinal activity. Supraspinal activity refers to the passage to and from the brain of all the sensory and motor stimuli we have been describing. *Spinal reflexes* are automatic muscular responses to bodily stimuli; they occur without the mediation of the brain, and occur even if the spinal cord is severed from the brain, as is the case with paraplegic accident victims.

Burning your hand on a hot stove can serve as an example. Receptors translate the skin temperature into stimuli that travel along afferent neurons to the spinal cord. At this point, the neurons branch. Some take the message to your brain, whereupon you become conscious of pain. But your hand will already have jerked away. This happens because some of the sensory neurons that carried the original message to the spinal cord pass the message to interneurons within the spinal cord, and these, in turn, pass it to motor neurons that cause the muscles in your arm to contract, pulling your hand away from the source of injury. The circuit from hand to spinal cord to muscles (that is, from receptors to afferent neurons to interneurons to motor neurons to muscles) is called a *spinal reflex pathway* or *spinal reflex arc.*

Overall Structure of the Brain

The basic organization of the vertebrate brain and spinal cord can be most easily observed in certain invertebrates. The fundamental plan, that of a segmented tube, is evident in the earthworm. Each body segment has nerves running to and from the corresponding segment of the tubular nervous system. Even in the worm, the "head" end of the nerve cord is enlarged. The specialization of the anterior end of the worm for feeding and exploring is reflected in this early precursor of the brain. The human brain maintains this basic tubular organization from the

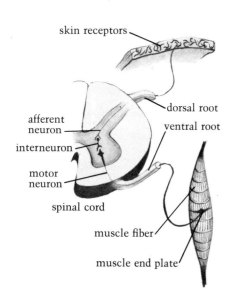

skin receptors

dorsal root

afferent neuron

ventral root

interneuron

motor neuron

spinal cord

muscle fiber

muscle end plate

A-4
A spinal reflex. Messages from sensory receptors are carried by afferent neurons to the spinal cord, where they are passed to interneurons, and ultimately to efferent neurons that carry messages from the spinal cord to the appropriate muscles or glands.

A-5
The increasing complexity of brains, from earthworm to man. (Thompson, 1967)

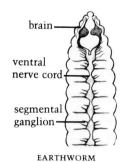

brain

ventral nerve cord

segmental ganglion

EARTHWORM

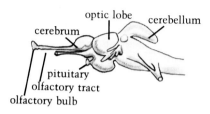

optic lobe

cerebellum

cerebrum

pituitary

olfactory tract

olfactory bulb

CODFISH

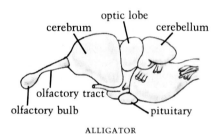

optic lobe

cerebrum

cerebellum

olfactory tract

olfactory bulb

pituitary

ALLIGATOR

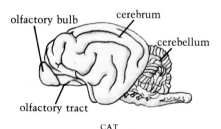

olfactory bulb

cerebrum

cerebellum

olfactory tract

CAT

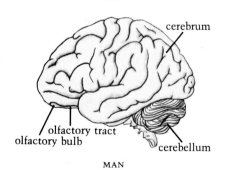

cerebrum

olfactory tract

olfactory bulb

cerebellum

MAN

spinal cord up to about the middle of the brain. However, the tube's front end, the *forebrain*, is enormously expanded and laid back over the core tube to form most of the matter we normally call the "brain." Chapter 3 focuses on this most recent evolutionary development of the vertebrate nervous system, made up primarily of the *cerebral cortex*. As we mentioned in the chapter, the cerebral cortex is the multiple layer of nerve cells, about 2 millimeters thick, overlying the *cerebrum*. It is this enlargement of the forebrain that distinguishes men from monkeys and monkeys from lower animals. The human hindbrain continues the spinal cord's tubular organization. In mammals, however, there is only a very narrow central canal filled with *cerebrospinal fluid*. Thus, the tube is mostly wall composed largely of nerve cell bodies, fibers, glial cells, and blood vessels.

Brain Stem. The term <u>brain stem</u> refers to everything between the spinal cord and the cerebrum. The major structures, going from cord to cortex, are *medulla, pons, midbrain,* and *thalamus.* The medulla, pons, and midbrain are a forward continuation of the tubular spinal cord and contain a large number of nuclei and fiber tracts.

The <u>cranial nerves</u> are nerves that enter and leave the brain from the brain stem rather than the spinal cord. There are 12 cranial nerves. Psychologists are most interested in the optic and the auditory cranial nerves, which convey information from receptors of the eye and ear.

The <u>medulla</u> is the first continuation of the spinal cord in the brain and contains all the fiber tracts interconnecting brain and spinal cord, together with a number of important nerve cell nuclei. Most of the cranial nerves enter and exit at the medulla and the bordering region of the pons. In addition, the medulla contains several nuclei concerned with such "vital" (life-sustaining) functions as respiration, heart action, and gastrointestinal activity. These nuclei are associated with the autonomic nervous system.

A-6
The human brain, showing the major structures that would be visible with the left hemisphere removed.

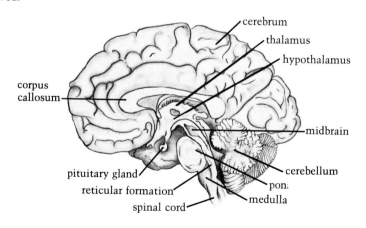

cerebrum

thalamus

hypothalamus

corpus callosum

midbrain

cerebellum

pituitary gland

pons

reticular formation

medulla

spinal cord

74 Chapter 3 Appendix: The Human Nervous System

The *pons* is an upward continuation of the brain stem; it contains ascending and descending fiber tracts and many additional nuclei. A large bundle of crossing fibers lies in the lower portion of the pons. This bundle interconnects the brain stem and cerebellum, and also contains the motor fibers going from cortex to spinal cord. The pons houses several cranial nerve nuclei that play a major role in feeding and in facial expression. In addition, the pons contains higher-order relays for the auditory system, nerve cells that act to inhibit and facilitate behavioral movements, and additional respiratory nuclei.

The *midbrain* is the uppermost extension of the brain stem that retains the spinal cord's basic tubular structure. It merges into the thalamus and hypothalamus. The midbrain's upper portion (the tectum) contains two pair of important relay nuclei for the visual and auditory systems. The midbrain's lower portion (the tegmentum) contains nuclei for cranial nerves that control eye movement, all of the ascending and descending tracts interconnecting the brain's upper and lower portions, and the upper portion of the reticular formation.

The medulla, pons, and midbrain developed early in the course of evolution and, from fish to man, are surprisingly uniform in structure and organization. Of course, some variations exist among species. Lower vertebrates, such as the shark or frog, which have little cerebral cortex have essentially no tracts from cortex to spinal cord. It is a general principle of neural organization that the size and complexity of a structure is related to the behavioral importance of that structure. Thus, in fish, which have no cerebral cortex, the midbrain is relatively large because it is the center of seeing and hearing. Among mammals, the bat, for example, has a large midbrain auditory relay nucleus, which correlates with the bat's extensive use of auditory information. As you probably know, the bat employs a system much like sonar. It emits very high frequency sound pulses to determine the location of objects in space by the echoes of the reflected pulses. This principle relating the size of a brain structure to its behavioral importance has produced a number of clues about the possible functions of particular brain structures.

The *reticular formation* of the brain stem has extremely important functions that have been appreciated only recently. Anatomically, the formation is a complex network ("reticulum") of cell bodies, fibers, and nuclei that extends from the spinal cord to the thalamus. A major function of the ascending reticular formation is its influence on the cerebrum. Moruzzi and Magoun (1949) demonstrated that stimulation of the ascending reticular formation produced an arousal response of the EEG—a pattern of low-voltage, high-frequency cortical activity characteristic of the waking animal. An animal whose midbrain reticular formation has been destroyed is usually sleeping or stuporous. The ascending reticular formation thus appears to be crucially involved in the control of sleeping and waking. It also seems to play a fundamental role in behavioral alerting or "attention" (Lindsley, 1958).

In summary, the brain stem contains all the fiber systems interconnecting the higher brain structures and the spinal cord; it also contains the cranial nerves and their nuclei (except for the olfactory and optic nerves); the nuclei regulating vital functions and emotional expression;

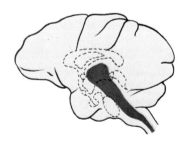

A-7
The reticular formation (in color) extends through the brain stem up toward the thalamus and hypothalamus.

and many of the higher-order nuclei concerned with various senses. When all brain tissue above the midbrain is removed in an animal such as a cat, it still can exhibit an amazing variety of behavior. Such animals will live for long periods, can walk, vocalize, eat, sleep, display some components of emotional expression, and may even be capable of very limited "learning" (Bard & Macht, 1958).

Cerebellum. The _cerebellum_ is a very old structure from an evolutionary point of view; it probably was the first to become specialized for sensory-motor coordination. The cerebellum overlies the pons and typically looks convoluted, having a large number of lobules (little lobes) separated by fissures. As in the cerebral cortex, the nerve cell bodies of the cerebellum form a surface layer about 2 millimeters thick. Although it probably is involved in a number of other functions as well, the cerebellum is primarily concerned with the regulation of motor coordination. Removal of the cerebellum produces a characteristic syndrome (a set of symptoms) of jerky, uncoordinated movement and halting speech (because speech involves an intricate pattern of muscle movement). In short, while muscle movements are not initiated by the cerebellum, the smoothness of such movements is made possible by it.

Thalamus. The _thalamus_ is a large grouping of nuclei located just above the midbrain. The thalamus is shaped somewhat like a football. The major nuclei of the thalamus are the _sensory relay nuclei._ These neuron groups receive impulses from specific ascending sensory pathways and relay them to specific sensory regions of the cerebral cortex. One major nucleus in this class receives visual fibers and relays their signals to the visual cortex; another receives auditory fibers and relays to the auditory cortex, and a third receives somatic fibers and relays to the somatic sensory areas of the cerebral cortex. If the cerebral cortex is removed, all of these nuclei in the thalamus degenerate and disappear completely because their terminals in the cortex have been destroyed. Other regions of the thalamus have interconnections with the reticular formation and with various structures of the limbic system, which we shall describe shortly. These regions of the thalamus appear to play a significant role in the regulation of spontaneous EEG activity in the cortex and are involved in the control of such processes as sleep, waking, and attention.

Hypothalamus. The term _hypothalamus_ refers to a grouping of small nuclei that lie generally in the cerebrum's ventral portion at the junction of the midbrain and thalamus. Diagrams cannot clearly show their rather complicated spatial layout. The various nuclei lie along the base of the brain (above the roof of the mouth), next to the pituitary gland. The pituitary gland is actually innervated by nerve cells from the hypothalamus. In recent years, these hypothalamic-pituitary interrelationships have been found to regulate endocrine gland function. In this way, the nuclei composing the hypothalamus are crucially involved in eating, sexual behavior, drinking, sleeping, temperature regulation, rage and violence, and behavior generally.

There are two kinds of glands in the body—duct or _exocrine glands_ and ductless or _endocrine glands._ The exocrine or duct glands (sweat glands,

A-8

Diagram of the relationship between the hypothalamus and the pituitary gland. Pituitary hormones are actually made in the hypothalamus. Nerve fibers (in color) connecting the hypothalamus and the posterior lobe of the pituitary transmit the hormones that are stored in and released from the posterior lobe. The anterior lobe is connected with the hypothalamus by a network of capillaries. Neurosecretory cells of the hypothalamus secrete hormones designed for the anterior pituitary directly into these capillaries.

A-9
The location of the endocrine glands.
The table below briefly describes
their principal functions.

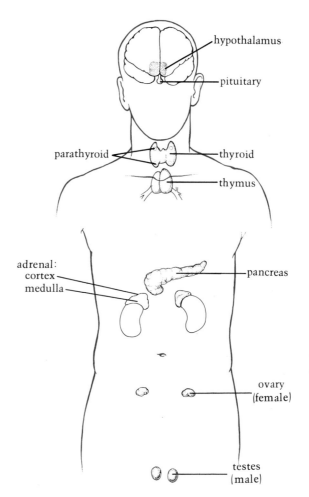

Table A-2   Some Typical Functions of Some of the Endocrine Glands

Gland	Activities Regulated
Pituitary—anterior	Growth (dwarfism, giantism); as "master gland" influences secretions of thyroid, pancreas, adrenal glands, and gonads.
—posterior	Water metabolism, etc.
Thyroid	Metabolic rate; body weight.
Thymus	Important in regulation of the lymphoid system, and in the development of immune reactions of the body.
Parathyroid	Calcium metabolism; maintenance of normal excitability of the nervous system.
Pancreas	By means of insulin, controls sugar metabolism; excess insulin leads to state of shock.
Adrenal—cortex	Secretes life-maintaining regulators; control of salt and carbohydrate metabolism.
—medulla	Active in emotion through the effects of epinephrine and norepinephrine.
Gonads	Secondary sex characteristics.

digestive glands, tear glands, salivary glands) make secretions onto the body's surface or into body cavities (stomach, mouth, and so on). The endocrine or ductless glands are internally secreting glands. Cells in the gland secrete their products, called _hormones_, which travel out through the cell membrane to the blood capillaries. Hormones enter the bloodstream directly from the glands for transport to various parts of the body. Hormones powerfully affect such diverse events as physical growth, blushing, fight or flight reactions, sexual responses, and many other physical expressions of mental states. Figure A-9 on the preceding page locates the endocrine glands within the body; Table A-2 gives some idea of each gland's function.

The Limbic System. The hypothalamus interconnects with many regions of the brain. Many anatomists regard a number of these structures—including the old cortex, the hippocampus, the septal (wall) area, and the hypothalamus itself—as an integrated network of structures known as the _limbic system_. Many of these structures seem to be involved in such aspects of behavior as emotion and motivation. They once were called the visceral system because some of the signals that control digestion and related visceral (internal) processes come from this part of the brain.

All parts of the limbic system are interconnected by nerve pathways that also are connected to many other parts of the nervous system. The precise role of each component remains unknown, but the limbic system as a whole clearly is involved in the expression of emotional states. Although the subjective experiences of fear, rage, aggression, euphoria, and other emotions may take place somewhere in the frontal lobe of the cerebral cortex, the behavioral expression of such emotions seems to originate in the limbic system. For example, by placing electrodes in specific areas of the cat's hypothalamus, experimenters can make the animal salivate, increase or decrease its blood pressure, cause its hair to rise, slow down or speed up its breathing, generate rapid or sluggish movement of the intestinal walls, and bring about many other physical symptoms of emotional states. Indeed, electrical tampering with the appropriate parts of this system can put a tranquil cat into the grip of fierce rage, abject terror, or frantic sexual behavior.

Experimental arrangements that allow an animal to stimulate electrically parts of its own limbic system indicate that some parts of the system generate unpleasant feelings when stimulated and other parts generate feelings of high pleasure. If a lever-activated electrode is placed in the limbic "pleasure center" of a rat's hypothalamus, the rat will hit that lever continually, 2,000 times an hour for 24 hours or more, until it is exhausted (see Chapter 10).

It is possible that stimulation of certain limbic areas sets off neurons that usually fire only upon the gratification of some basic need, such as sex or hunger. In any case, one can see in the dramatic physical results of limbic stimulation (abrupt changes in heart rate, blood pressure, muscle tension, and so on) a clear example of how activity in the brain can have strong effects on various parts of the body. Similarly, anxiety, though a subjective state, can cause such physical manifestations as

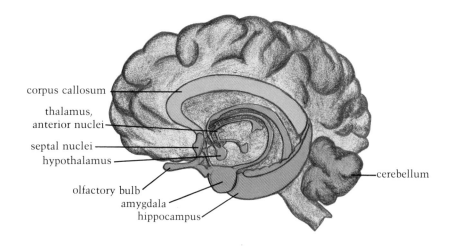

corpus callosum

thalamus, anterior nuclei

septal nuclei

hypothalamus

olfactory bulb

amygdala

hippocampus

cerebellum

skin rashes, hemorrhoids, ulcers, and sundry other *psychosomatic* (mind-body) ailments.

Homeostasis. Many houses have thermostats that automatically control room temperature. If the device is set at 70°F, it will turn on the furnace when room temperature drops below that point and will turn the furnace off again when the temperature reaches 70° once more. The body has similar feedback devices that control temperature and various other physical and chemical factors that must be kept at relatively constant levels. The process is called <u>homeostasis</u> (homeo = same; stasis = standing), the maintaining of a stable internal environment.

The controls that regulate our body temperature, for example, are very tight. Normally, a person's internal temperature, as measured by a rectal thermometer, does not vary more than a few tenths of a degree. This remarkable constancy of temperature is maintained by an automatic system—a thermostat—in the hypothalamus, which precisely measures the body temperature and triggers the appropriate control mechanisms. Receptor cells in this center monitor the temperature of the blood servicing the cells of the hypothalamus. Although the surface of the skin is covered with receptors for hot and for cold, these are not directly involved in the regulation of internal temperature, as has been demonstrated by some interesting experiments with human subjects. For example, in a room in which the air is warmer than body temperature, if the blood circulating through a person's hypothalamus is cooled, he will stop perspiring, even though his skin temperature continues to rise. The skin receptors signal changes in external temperature only, and these signals travel to the centers of consciousness in the brain, bypassing the unconscious center in the hypothalamus. The elevation of temperature known as fever is due not to a malfunction of the thermostat but to a resetting. Thus, at the onset of fever, an individual typically feels cold and often has chills; although his body temperature is rising, it is still lower than his thermostat setting.

This quick survey of the brain could lead to erroneous notions about the nature of brain organization and function. Many brain structures have distinct physical shapes and have been given particular names. Thus, one might easily come to conceive of the brain as a very complicated hi-fi system with many components—an amplifier here, a tuner there, and so on. Yet the brain is not like that at all. It is a continuous series of interconnections among nerve cells. Many of the nerve cell bodies have been grouped into clusters and shapes, but it is a mistake to think that a given "thing" in the brain is in fact a structure with a particular function.

Much of our information about the possible functions of brain structures still comes from the crudest experimental technique—the *lesion* method. An experimenter damages or destroys a specific part of the brain and notes the loss of ability or the behavioral defects. To jump from this kind of observation to the conclusion that particular structures have particular functions is wrong, especially for the brain's higher regions. It is like trying to determine the function of one part of a television circuit by smashing it with a hammer and noting how the television set then misbehaves.

Neurophysiology

The nervous system contains two distinct kinds of cells: nerve cells and glial cells, or glia. Blood vessels and other cells found in all tissues are also present, but we shall emphasize nerve cells—and with good reason. Our present state of understanding indicates that nerve cells are the primary functional elements, though glia may play important roles as well. In terms of numbers, the brain's 12 billion nerve cells are outnumbered 10 to 1 by its 120 billion glial cells, so we will glance first at the glia.

Researchers once thought that glial cells only held the nerve cells in place, as do connective-tissue cells in many body organs. However, glia are now thought to do much more. Many complex chemical interactions occur between nerve cells and their neighboring glial cells. It even appears that in some systems, such as the retina (the light-sensitive region at the back of the eye), the electrochemical activity of glial cells can directly modify the electrical activity, and hence the information transmissions, of nerve cells. Quite possibly, glial cells eventually will be found to play critical roles in the control of nerve cell activity in the brain, and hence in higher processes such as perception and learning.

The Nerve Cell

A typical *nerve cell* has several characteristics. The *cell body* contains the *nucleus* and has many short fibers, called *dendrites*, extending out from it; the dendrites receive stimuli from adjacent cells and conduct the resulting impulses to the cell body. The long fiber which transmits this activity to other nerve cells or to muscles and glands is the *axon*. Actually, if the axon is stimulated, it will conduct in both directions; however, impulses can cross the interconnections (synapses) between nerve cells in only one direction, from the axon of one cell to the cell body or

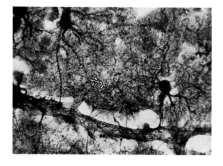

A-11
Electron photomicrograph of two glial cells surrounded by nerve cells. Both glial cells have extensions to the blood vessel running along the bottom of the picture. (Lester V. Bergman)

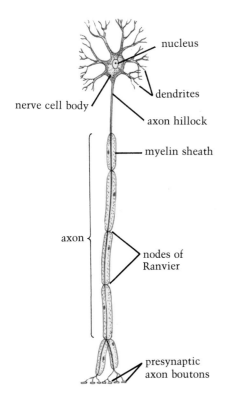

nucleus

dendrites

nerve cell body

axon hillock

myelin sheath

axon

nodes of Ranvier

presynaptic axon boutons

dendrites of another. Longer axons, such as the one shown here, have a surrounding _myelin sheath_ of fatty material interrupted at intervals by constrictions called _nodes of Ranvier_. Some axons are very long, extending, for example, from the brain to the base of the spinal cord or from the base of the spinal cord to the tip of the toe. The initial portion of the axon, called the _axon hillock_, is unmyelinated as it leaves the cell body. The presynaptic _axon terminals_ or _boutons_ at the end farthest from the cell body are typically fine and unmyelinated as they branch and terminate close to other nerve cells.

Afferent neurons carry messages into the CNS from our joints and muscles and senses. They receive these messages either from _receptors_ at their ends or from separate but closely connected receptors in the sense organs. These receptors detect physical or chemical events and translate them into electrochemical impulses that travel along the afferent neuron to the brain or the spinal cord. Each kind of receptor responds to a specific form of energy. Those in the eye respond to electromagnetic energy, those in the nose to the shapes of certain molecules, and so on for touch, taste, balance, etc.

Our experience of the outside world is limited by the capabilities of our receptors. For example, we cannot see radio waves or x-rays or any other part of the electromagnetic spectrum beyond the narrow band that constitutes visible light. In short, the capacities and limitations of our nervous system have a crucial influence on the way we perceive the world and the way we behave.

Efferent neurons carry information away from the central nervous system to the effector organs, the muscles and glands. (Those efferent neurons that connect to skeletal muscles are known as _motor neurons_.)

Interneurons, which make up 97 percent of all nerve cells in the human body, are located _within_ the CNS. Among other things, they carry the signals we experience as thoughts, memories, and such.

The Nerve Membrane.   Most chemical elements in the body exist as ions—charged atoms or molecules. Nerve cells, like every other cell in the body, are enclosed by a cell membrane. This membrane is _semipermeable_ to ions—some can pass through it but not others. Chloride ions can cross the membrane with relative ease, potassium ions less easily, and sodium ions normally cannot cross at all.

In order to picture this selective transport of ions, imagine that the nerve membrane has different-sized pores or gates, one for each type of ion. The chloride gate (negative ions) opens freely, the potassium gate (positive ions) has a moderately stiff spring, and the sodium gate (also positive) is locked.

The Resting Nerve Membrane Potential

When a nerve cell is not active, ions are unequally concentrated on the inside and the outside of the membrane. Most sodium ions (Na^+) are outside, most potassium ions (K^+) are inside, and most chloride ions (Cl^-) are outside. Because of these unequal distributions, a net electrical potential exists across the membrane. It is more negative inside than outside.

A-13
A schematic diagram of a nerve fiber. (A) The membrane is in its resting state. (B) An action potential has begun as sodium rushes in to the fiber due to a change in the membrane potential.

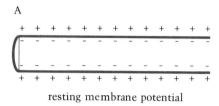

resting membrane potential

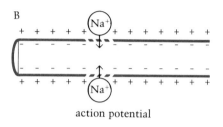

action potential

A-14
Measurement of the net electrical potential across the nerve cell membrane. (A) If the recording electrodes are both placed on the outer surface of the axon, no electrical potential is recorded. (B) Similarly, no electrical potential is recorded if both of the electrodes are inserted within the axon. (C) If one electrode is on the outside and one on the inside, however, an electrical potential of −70 millivolts is registered. This is the resting potential. (D) An action potential is produced experimentally by stimulating the membrane electrically; this action potential travels down the axon. (E) An action potential occurring at any time on a particular axon or at any place will be the same; that is, it will have the same duration and the same voltage.

A variety of experiments—particularly studies by Hodgkin and Huxley in England, for which they were awarded the Nobel Prize—have demonstrated that the different concentrations of potassium ions inside and outside the nerve cell membrane comprise the mechanism that generates the *resting membrane potential.* If the potassium concentration is changed, the membrane changes its permeability to ions.

The Action Potential or Nerve Spike

In its resting state, the nerve cell membrane is 30 times more permeable to potassium than to sodium. What would happen if the sodium ion gates at some part of a neuron's membrane should suddenly be unlocked and thrown open, allowing sodium to rush in? That part of the cell's interior, ordinarily negative in relation to the exterior, would abruptly become positive. That is what happens when a nerve cell "fires," when it transmits a stimulus. The locks on the sodium gates can be unlocked simply by a change in the membrane potential. If we apply a voltage to the nerve cell, the gates unlock and the sodium rushes in. But the membrane adjacent to this action potential is still at its resting state, negative on the inside, positive on the outside. Thus two adjacent points along the membrane carry a different charge, causing a horizontal flow of ions from one point to the other. This flow of ions changes the membrane potential at the second point, causing the opening of its sodium ion gates and thus the generation of its own action potential, which in turn causes an action potential right next to it. In this way, the action potential (inrush of sodium) travels rapidly down the axon. The sodium gates are unlocked only for a brief period—about 1/1000 of a second—during the action potential. At the peak of the action potential, the membrane's permeability to sodium ions is 600 times greater than it

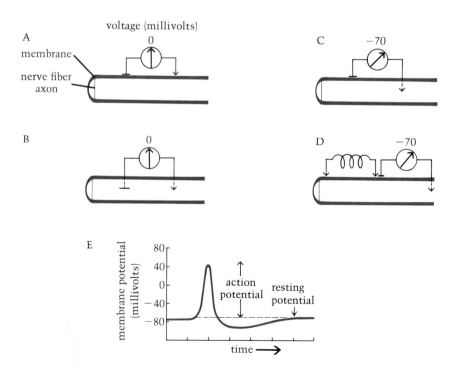

Diagram of the ion concentrations inside and outside a nerve membrane as an action potential travels down the axon.

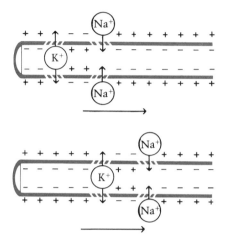

Schematic of the synapse. The chemical transmitter is stored in the vesicles. When the stimulus is transmitted down the axon to the presynaptic terminal, the transmitter is released and travels by diffusion across the synaptic space to the postsynaptic terminal.

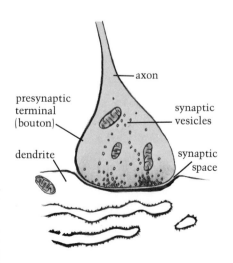

is during the resting state. After the peak, the membrane's permeability to sodium ions drops sharply. The sodium gate is slammed shut. As the permeability to sodium decreases, permeability to potassium increases. Now potassium ions, which are also positively charged, leave the cell, drawn toward the negatively charged exterior, until the cell membrane returns to its resting potential, once again negative on the inside and positive on the outside.

To summarize, the nerve spike action is due to a brief unlocking of the sodium gates which travels down the axon. Normally, this unlocking first occurs at the point where the axon leaves the cell body—the axon hillock.

An action potential occurs only when the initiating stimulus has reached a critical magnitude, or *threshold*. If you pull the trigger of a loaded gun all the way back, it will fire. If you squeeze the trigger only part of the way back, it will not fire. So it is with a nerve cell. The stimulus will be strong enough to set off an action potential or it will not. The action potential is an all or nothing electrical event which travels rapidly down a nerve cell axon to the axon terminals and in this way conducts information to other nerve cells. The action potential is an electrical potential of constant amplitude traveling at a fixed speed along a given fiber.

Synaptic potential is the activity that one nerve cell induces in another nerve cell. When an action potential in a nerve fiber reaches the axon terminals or *boutons*, it induces synaptic activity in the postsynaptic or target nerve cell. The number of nerve terminals activated on the target nerve cell determines the amplitude or amount of this synaptic activity.

In order to understand how the message proceeds from cell to cell, we will have to take a close look at the structure of the synapse itself.

The Synapse

The *synapse* is the key to the nervous system. It is the point of interaction between nerve cells. So far as we know, synapses are the only places where nerve cells can influence other nerve cells. The synapse is not an actual physical connection but rather a close approximation to one. The synaptic space between the terminal bouton of one nerve cell and the dendrite or the cell body of another is extremely small. A typical nerve cell in the brain has thousands of synaptic terminals from other nerve cells on its cell body and dendrites. It, in turn, may form synapses on many other nerve cells.

Figure A-16 is a schematic drawing of a nerve cell forming a synapse on another nerve cell. Technically, the term synapse includes everything shown in the figure: the *presynaptic terminal* and *membrane;* the space between the presynaptic terminal and the *postsynaptic terminal* of the postsynaptic cell; and the membranes and close structures of the postsynaptic region. The presynaptic terminal contains many small round spheres or *vesicles*. At present, these are thought to contain the transmitter substance, a chemical that is released to cross the synapse and causes the impulse to be taken up in the postsynaptic nerve cell.

As we mentioned, most nerve cells have several *thousand* synapses on

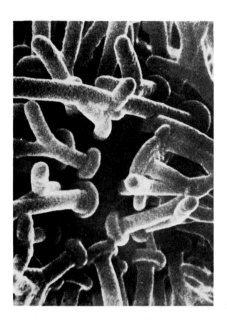

A-17
Electron photomicrograph of dendritic spines magnified 1500 times actual size. (UPI)

them. One type of synapse characteristically has small bumps or knobs on the postsynaptic membrane. These knob synapses occur on the dendrites of nerve cells and are called *dendritic spines* (see Figure A-17). The spines are the little thornlike structures covering the dendrites. Each tiny spine is a separate synapse. Ramon y Cajal, the great neuroanatomist, first described the synapse in 1888; however, the significance of dendritic spines was not appreciated until recently. Each spine on the nerve cell has a synaptic terminal.

Synaptic Transmission

The first step in synaptic transmission is to get the synaptic transmitter—the chemical that actually crosses the synapse—down the axon to the terminal bouton. This transmitter chemical seems to be synthesized (made) in the cell body. The transmitter—or a substance closely resembling the transmitter that can easily be converted to the transmitter chemically—must be transported down the inside of the axon to the terminal. This is called *axoplasmic transport.* When the transmitter arrives at the bouton, it is stored, probably in the vesicles.

Most synapses between nerve cells also have glial cells close by. At synapses, some glial cells are believed to help hold down the amount of transmitter substance. They act like vacuum cleaners to keep the synapse "clean."

We now can trace the events that occur in synaptic transmission. The transmitter moves down the axon and is stored in the vesicles of the bouton. Any transmitter that "leaks" out of the bouton is destroyed by the *breakdown enzyme* in the glial cells and postsynaptic cell. When a spike action potential travels down the axon to the bouton, the chemical transmitter is released into the synapse. We do not know how this happens but the critical event is a movement of calcium ions into the bouton. This movement is triggered by the membrane spike potential and, in turn, it triggers release of the transmitter. Incidentally, this role for calcium in normal brain functioning is one reason why it is an essential element in the human diet.

The transmitter travels across the synaptic space to the postsynaptic membrane by diffusion; there it activates receptors that cause the postsynaptic cell membrane to develop a potential change and eventually an action potential. The transmitter is then broken down or inactivated by the breakdown enzyme and the synapse is ready to function again. To give a specific example, one transmitter is called acetylcholine (ACh). It is made from acetyl and choline. The breakdown enzyme is called acetylcholinesterase (AChE). When ACh contacts AChE, it is immediately broken down into acetyl and choline and consequently inactivated as a transmitter.

Synaptic Excitation

The chemical transmitter from a single synapse on a single nerve cell opens the target nerve cell's ion gates only a crack. If several synapses act together on a given nerve cell, more gates open and the synaptic potential becomes larger. To start an action potential going in a nerve cell,

A-18
The formation, transmission, and breakdown of ACh, one of the transmitter chemicals.

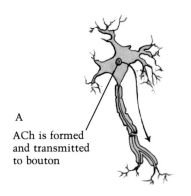

A
ACh is formed and transmitted to bouton

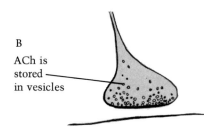

B
ACh is stored in vesicles

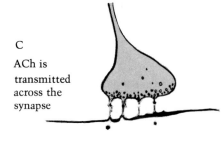

C
ACh is transmitted across the synapse

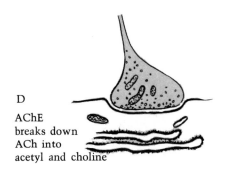

D
AChE breaks down ACh into acetyl and choline

a threshold point must be crossed. The synaptic potential must be large enough to enable the membrane resting potential at the beginning of the axon to shift to an action potential. Thus, synaptic activity is *graded;* the more synapses sending transmitter substances, the larger the synaptic potential.

Synaptic Inhibition

We have just described synaptic excitation—the process by which one nerve cell causes another to fire. Another synaptic process is *synaptic inhibition.* Nerve axon terminals release a synaptic transmitter that is a chemical inhibitory substance. It opens only some ion gates while keeping all sodium gates completely closed. As a result, the inner cell membrane becomes more negative than the resting level. The nerve cell is then inhibited; and other excitory synapses may be unable to make it generate an action potential.

The 12 billion nerve cells of the brain are in a constant state of flux, with ever-changing potentials in each cell. It is these changing potentials that generate the EEG and all other electrical signs of brain activity.

Drug Action

Chemicals and drugs can act on any one or more of the steps of synaptic transmission. This is why drugs affect the brain in so many different ways. In addition, the brain probably contains many different kinds of synaptic transmitter chemicals at various regions and synapses.

Acetylcholine (ACh). The best understood synaptic transmitter is ACh. It has been proved to be the transmitter at the neuromuscular junction—the synapses made by motor nerves on skeletal muscle fibers—and at certain peripheral autonomic synapses. ACh is also believed to be a transmitter in certain brain regions, for example, regions of the hypothalamus and the cerebral cortex. We know as much as we do about ACh because it is easy to remove a neuromuscular junction (together with a piece of the nerve and muscle) and study its function *in vitro,* that is, in a dish.

ACh is formed in the cell bodies of neurons and transported down the axons to synaptic terminals with skeletal muscle fibers. When an action potential arrives at the junction, ACh is released, crosses the synapse and activates the muscle fiber just as we described above for the transmitter action of a nerve cell. The breakdown enzyme AChE then breaks down ACh into acetyl and choline, which are reabsorbed into the nerve cell to be reformed into ACh.

Some common drugs affect the ACh synapse. The best known of these is *curare,* the poison some South American Indians use on their arrows. Curare blocks ACh from activating the postsynaptic receptor. The curare molecules are thought to occupy the sites on the receptors that ACh normally activates. Curare itself does not activate the postsynaptic receptors (that is, muscle fibers). Consequently, ACh is blocked from acting. The effect of curare is total paralysis. The muscles will no longer respond to nerve commands because the transmission of the commands is blocked at the synapse between nerve and muscle.

The deadly food poison, *botulinus toxin,* produces another kind of blocking action at ACh synapses. The toxin appears to block the release of ACh from the presynaptic bouton. Again, total paralysis results, because once again transmission at the synapse between nerve and muscle is blocked. However, this blocking mechanism is quite different. Curare blocks ACh from postsynaptic receptors and the toxin blocks ACh release from the presynaptic terminal. Yet the two poisons have exactly the same final effect—paralysis. This example illustrates how difficult it can be to determine the impact of various drugs on unknown synaptic transmitters. Diverse drugs can affect synapses quite differently and yet produce similar effects.

LSD and mescaline (from cactus peyote buttons) are two more examples of the blocking phenomenon. They are quite different chemicals and may act very differently, yet they affect awareness in similar ways, producing bizarre hallucinations and psychoticlike experience. In addition, they show cross-tolerance. With repeated use of LSD, for example, more of the chemical is required to produce the same effect; this is tolerance. The same LSD user would also need more than a normal dosage of mescaline, even though he had never used it before; this is *cross-tolerance.* Both LSD and mescaline may be acting in different ways on the same brain synapses to yield the same net effect.

A third way to influence the ACh synapse is to block the action of the enzyme AChE. A drug called *prostigmine* does just this, producing prolonged and uncontrollable muscle contractions. The ACh is not broken down because AChE is blocked; hence ACh continues to act on the postsynaptic receptor, causing repeated activation of the muscle.

Chapter 4   Perception

Illusion, you will find, is hard to describe or analyze, for though we may be intellectually aware of the fact that any given experience must *be an illusion, we cannot, strictly speaking, watch ourselves having an illusion. If the reader finds this assertion a little puzzling, there is always an instrument of illusion close at hand to verify it: the bathroom mirror. I specify the bathroom because the experiment I urge the reader to make succeeds best if the mirror is a little clouded by steam. It is a fascinating exercise in illusionist representation to trace one's own head on the surface of the mirror and to clear the area enclosed by the outline. For only when we have actually done this do we realize how small the image is which gives us the illusion of seeing ourselves "face to face." To be exact, it must be precisely half the size of our head. I do not want to trouble the reader with geometrical proof of this fact, though basically it is simple: since the mirror will always appear to be halfway between me and my reflection, the size on its surface will be one half of the apparent size. But however cogently this fact can be demonstrated with the help of similar triangles, the assertion is usually met with frank incredulity. And despite all geometry, I, too, would stubbornly contend that I really see my head (natural size) when I shave and that the size on the mirror surface is the phantom. I cannot have my cake and eat it. I cannot make use of an illusion and watch it.*

—E. H. Gombrich
(*Art and Illusion*)

Perception

The brain, as we saw in the last chapter, is a marvelous, mystifying organ. It enables us to experience the world, to remember past experiences, to learn new habits and skills, to think creatively and critically, and to communicate our thoughts to others by means of language. However, the brain cannot function in a vacuum; it requires a constant supply of information from the external world and from the rest of the body. As we all know, information is obtained from the sense organs which in their own right are just as marvelous as the brain, but a good deal less mystifying. They have the capability of responding selectively and analytically to forms of energy in the world—to light waves, sound waves, pressures, temperatures, and chemicals. These energies are produced by objects—sound waves, for example, are given off by vibrating objects—or they are reflected from objects as in the case of light waves.

Information is transmitted by the sensory nerves from the sense organs to the brain, where it is processed to form our perceptions of the world. Perception is the way in which the world appears to our brain. It is *the* basic psychological process; lacking perception there would be no memory, learning, or thinking—in fact, no mind.

The sequence of events that results in a *perception* can be summarized as follows: *An object gives off energy that stimulates a sense organ; the sense organ codes the energy into the language of nerve activity; this activity is conveyed to the brain, where it is processed, resulting in a perception of the object.*

Under most ordinary conditions, the perception of an object is a reasonably faithful likeness of the object.

As we shall see later in this chapter, another step needs to be considered—the person's response to a perception. How he reacts to a perception influences the perception. In fact, evidence suggests that such reactions are necessary for perception.

Astonishingly, we are not aware of any of these steps except the final one of perception. We are certainly not aware of the physical and chemical events that occur when our sense organs respond to energy from the outside world; nor are we aware of the transmission of messages along our nerves and the ways in which the brain translates these messages into perceptions. Awareness is limited to perception; indeed, awareness *is* perception.

And though our perceptions actually take place in the brain, we experience them as events taking place in the external world. That is, we unconsciously refer the brain's perceptions back to their energy sources—the objects in the external world. We do not see images in the brain; we see objects in the world. This projection is a very strange and wonderful phenomenon; no less strange or wonderful because we take it for granted.

Even when some part of the body is stimulated, we refer the perception back to the area that has been stimulated. A stomachache is felt in the stomach not in the brain. Perhaps you have heard of the "phantom limb" experienced by an amputee. He still feels sensations of pain and pressure in the limb that has been amputated. These sensations actually arise in the stump of the limb but they are referred back to a region of the leg or arm that no longer exists.

At any given moment there are an infinite number of objects in the world that are capable of stimulating the sense organs. Yet we pay attention only to a small fraction of these objects at any one time. Since what we perceive depends on what we attend to, we shall first discuss the process of attention.

Attention

Attention is a complex process. Consider the following example. You are absorbed in reading a book when someone asks you a question in a normal voice. Your awareness and response might be any of the following:

You are completely unaware that anything was said.

You are vaguely aware that something was said, but not what.

Several minutes later you become aware that a question was asked, but you can't recall what it was.

Several minutes later you become aware of the question and answer it.

You hear and understand the question, but don't bother to answer it at the time.

You hear and answer the question immediately.

There are two important aspects to this example of *selective attention*. First, the questioner spoke in a perfectly audible manner. If you had been "paying attention," you would have heard the question clearly. Second, you were paying attention to another sensory input, in this case a visual one. It was not a simple matter of one sound obscuring and masking another. If you have tried to attend to two stimuli in such situations, you know how difficult it is. Your attention tends to shift back and forth between the two sources of input. It is as though you have a *limited channel capacity* and cannot easily attend to more than one message at a time.

The problem is even more difficult for the psychologist who wants to determine whether you have heard and understood the question. You might have heard nothing; heard something but not understood it; or heard and understood it. You know your own experience—but the psy-

4-1
Attention plays a part in all human behavior—physical as well as mental. It is most obvious in competitive sports; the athlete focuses all his senses on the play at hand. Another familiar example of attention occurs in the teaching situation. (Charles Gatewood, Magnum)

chologist, the questioner, or anyone else interested in your behavior, cannot know what you experience unless you tell him. If you report your experience honestly, there will be a good correspondence between what you have experienced and what you say. However, a rat in a psychologist's experiment cannot tell him what it experienced.

Here is a major problem we must deal with if we want to study the process of attention. Suppose you have trained an animal to respond to a sound. If you now present the sound and the animal does not respond, is it because it was not paying attention? Perhaps. However, you might have trained him using food rewards and he might not be hungry at the moment. Or perhaps he was accidentally hurt the last time he responded to the sound and now fails to respond out of fear of being hurt again. Or he may not have heard the sound at all. Attention, like other psychological processes, can only be studied objectively by measuring the organism's responses. Lack of attention often leads to failure of response, but many other factors can also lead to response failure. For all of these reasons, progress in the experimental analysis of attention has come largely from studies of selective listening in humans.

The Cocktail Party

A British scientist, E. Colin Cherry, dubbed the feat of selective listening the "cocktail party" phenomenon (1953), because it is so easily observed there. Picture yourself standing in a crowded room with sounds of voices and music all about you. You are probably talking with one or two other people. However, you may be more interested in what someone else is saying, particularly if he or she is talking about you. You can quite easily pay more attention to this other conversation than to the louder but less interesting words of your immediate neighbor. And, no doubt, you will remember much more of this conversation than the one you are ignoring.

In a typical cocktail party, we have a number of cues that allow us to determine the direction and source of different voices. Obviously, we can tell what direction a voice comes from. We can correlate the voice with the lip movements and gestures of the appropriate person. Voices can also be distinguished in terms of pitch, loudness, character, whether they are male or female, and so on. Accents differ and so will the topics of conversation. We utilize all these cues and others too at a cocktail party and we utilize them very well indeed.

Experimental Evidence. Cherry did some experiments on the perception of simultaneous spoken messages. He recorded different messages on two separate tapes and then played one tape into the subject's right ear and the other into his left ear. In such a *dichotic listening* experiment, the subject can attend to either the right-ear or the left-ear message. He "knows" that one speaker is directly to his right and the other is directly to his left. Even when Cherry played similar, cliché-ridden speeches into each ear, subjects could tell there were two messages, but they could not listen to them simultaneously.

This general method is the best yet developed for analyzing attention. The physical stimuli going into the two ears are identical in terms of voice, volume, and tone; only the messages differ. The subject has equal opportunities to listen to both. If humans had an information-processing system that could handle more than one message simultaneously, we would have no trouble listening to both equally. However, this does not seem to be possible. Cherry had his subjects repeat the message they were attending to as they heard it. The subjects repeated perfectly, although their words lagged behind those from the record. Interestingly, the subjects spoke in a dull monotone with very little emotional response, regardless of the content of the message. Evidently, the subjects work hard at attending to the correct message and repeating it, and so they cannot attend to its meaning or its emotional content. In addition, they cannot repeat any of the message delivered to the unattended ear.

Selective Understanding. Can the subject understand anything at all about the message delivered to the unattended ear? Apparently not, as the following experiment shows. Cherry started the unattended-ear message in English. After the subject was comfortably repeating the message from the right ear, the left-ear message was changed to German spoken by an Englishman. When the subject was asked what language the ignored left-ear message was in, he reported that he really didn't know, but assumed it was English. It seemed that the unattended message, though delivered to the left ear, was simply not "heard" or processed by the subject.

Donald Broadbent (1958) developed a *filter model* to explain Cherry's study and his own similar findings. He proposed that the nervous system contains a selective filter that can be tuned to accept the attended message and reject others. His basic assumption was that the human information-processing system is a limited-capacity channel—it can only process so much information at a time. Broadbent suggested that a selective filter, located between the initial sensory process and the brain, simply blocks out the unattended message. In short, attention is the directional or differential action of this selective filter. This idea seemed to explain some aspects of selective listening, though it did not describe the nature of the selective filter or how it is controlled.

Broadbent's idea of a selective filter has since been challenged by an experiment performed by Anne Triesman (1964). Triesman also had the subject listen to two messages in his two ears, attending to one and not to the other. But when she included the subject's name in the unattended message, the subject immediately responded to it. Like Cherry and Broadbent, Triesman found that if she changed the unattended message from a man's voice to a woman's, or changed the language, the subjects did not notice. But important words—the subject's name, or material relevant to the message being attended to—*were* noticed immediately. If the subject were completely filtering out the message to the unattended ear, he could not possibly notice his name or any other aspect of the unattended message. Clearly, he *was* paying some sort of attention to the "unattended" message.

This paradox has obliged us to abandon Broadbent's simple selective filter notion of attention. The mechanism of selective attention must be more complicated than that. "Unattended" messages are not just filtered out. Rather, they are somehow given a preliminary evaluation and then either stored in memory or else discarded as useless.

We are still left with something of a paradox. We assumed that the purpose of selective attention was to permit us to concentrate on analyzing and responding to one input by filtering out all others. But Triesman's experiment indicates that we do complicated processing of both the attended and the unattended inputs, and we reject the unattended input only *after* we evaluate it and decide it is unimportant. This suggests that perhaps there is no such thing as a selective mechanism. Maybe selective listening only *appears* to be selective.

The Role of Memory

Before we abandon the whole idea of selective listening, we should consider the relationship of memory to attention. Clearly, if we want to know how much of each input our subject has heard, we must ask him either to "shadow" (immediately repeat) the message or else report afterward what he remembers of each message. But even shadowing requires him to use his memory for a brief instant. In other words, "filtering" may be a process of deciding which messages are placed into memory storage.

A number of scientists have suggested alternatives to the filter-system model of selective attention. Donald Norman (1969) has developed an intriguing model of selective attention involving memory. He assumes that *every* incoming signal is checked for meaning by being compared with the material already in the subject's memory store. This brief analysis would be the minimum amount necessary to determine whether the material is important or not. Memory is obviously a crucial element in this model of attention. And in fact it does seem necessary to invoke memory if we want to explain Triesman's findings. How do we determine whether a particular word embedded in a message is going to be significant for us? We could not recognize our name or other words unless they match or correspond to something we have in memory, or at least call out some kind of association with items stored in memory. A word with no associations for us would be a meaningless word.

The general model of human information processing that Norman and others have developed is schematically shown in Figure 4–2. The basic idea is that physical signals are picked up by sensory systems, such as the ear and the eye; then the stimuli are analyzed by the receptors and sensory pathways of the brain. For example, your ear picks up and passes on frequencies, intensities, and patterns of sound; your brain analyzes and interprets these stimuli as spoken sentences. This analyzed sensory input is then recorded in some form of storage system—something like a computer data bank, perhaps. (Norman pictures this as a large rectangle in the center of his diagram.) From this storage system, messages flow out to various other complicated (and hypothetical) systems involving our expectations, our use of language, and other factors, from which responses that focus our attention or select certain information for more permanent memory are returned to the storage system. This is an intricate process but it works with remarkable efficiency and speed.

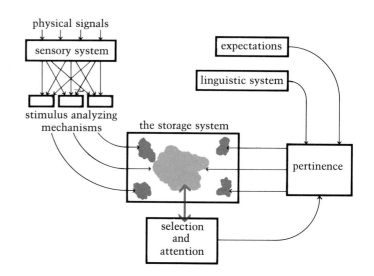

4-2

Norman's model of selective attention. Physical signals are received by the appropriate sense organ, analyzed into their elements, and then passed into the storage system. Each of the irregular shapes in the rectangle representing the storage system is an item being considered for further attention. If one's expectations, for example, give meaning to one of these items, it is selected for further attention and storage in long-term memory. (From Donald A. Norman, *Memory and attention.* © 1969. Reprinted by permission of John Wiley & Sons, Inc.)

As we have seen, memory evidently plays a part in this rapid process. In fact, there is a good deal of evidence that memory may be of two sorts: *short-term* and *long-term*. (These and other types of memory will be discussed in greater detail in Chapter 7.) Short-term memory lasts a few seconds at most—the time you can remember a new telephone number if you don't repeat it. Long-term memory is much more permanent—your memory of your own telephone number, for instance. If we accept this assumption, then a reasonable interpretation of Norman's model is that all incoming information passes through the short-term storage system. However, it is placed in long-term memory only after it has been analyzed and found to have significance and meaning. If it is irrelevant or not significant for the person, it will simply be dropped from short-term store. As you may have realized, this assumption about short-term memory also enables us to explain Triesman's findings. Of course, Norman's diagram is only a picture of a theory. The colored and shaded areas in it do not refer to specific parts of the brain but merely to hypothetical functional systems.

Though we have a wealth of evidence and theories, there is still a great deal more to be learned about the basic nature of stimulus selection in higher animals and man.

Hearing

Because our perceptions are so dependent upon how the sense organs receive, analyze, and code incoming energies, let us see how these organs work. We shall examine the organs of hearing and vision in some detail. Our senses of smell, taste, touch, balance, and so on also contribute to our perception, but to a much smaller degree than vision or hearing.

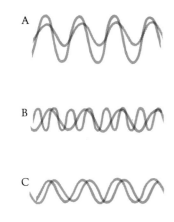

4-3

A schematic illustration of the differences between the amplitude, frequency, and phase of a sound. (A) Two sounds with the same phase and frequency but different amplitudes; (B) phase and amplitude are the same, but the frequencies are different; and (C) amplitude and frequency are the same, but the phases are different.

Psychological Dimensions of Sound

Waves in the air make sound possible. Any source of sound causes successive condensation and rarefaction in the air, generating pressure waves which radiate outward from the source. These pressure waves strike the eardrum, making it vibrate at the same frequency as the sound waves. Thus the *pitch* of the sound—how high or low it is—is determined by the frequency of the sound waves. The more frequently the waves strike, the higher the pitch. But pitch is not identical with frequency. Pitch is a *psychological* dimension, corresponding to our experience; *frequency* is a *physical* dimension, corresponding to the number of cycles per second of the sound wave. The two do not agree. For example, if you play middle C on a piano and then play C above middle C, one octave higher, the second note does not sound twice as high—but it is. Middle C has a frequency of 256 Hz (hertz, or cycles per second), while C above middle C has a frequency of 512 Hz. It is twice as high in physical frequency, but sounds only a bit higher.

Another important aspect of sound waves is their *amplitude*—how big are the condensations and rarefactions in the sound wave? Once again, we must make a distinction between a physical property of the sound pressure wave and our psychological experience of it. To keep this distinction clear, we refer to the physical property of amplitude as the *intensity* of a sound. *Loudness* refers to our psychological experience of a sound. Like frequency and pitch, intensity and loudness do not correspond exactly.

A third dimension of sound is its tonal quality. Middle C on a piano sounds very different from middle C on a violin, for example. The physical explanation for this is that most sounds are complex combinations of waves. When you play middle C on a musical instrument, you produce numerous secondary vibrations above the basic 256 Hz tone. Our psychological experience of this combination of tones is described as the *tone color* or *timbre* of a sound.

Physiology of the Ear

(see fig. 4-4)

The process of hearing begins when sound waves cause the *eardrum* to vibrate. These vibrations are transmitted by the bones of the middle ear (the *hammer*, *anvil*, and *stirrup*) to the *oval window*, a membrane covering a fluid-filled, coiled tubular structure—the *cochlea*. The vibrations set up standing wave patterns of pressure in the fluid of the cochlea. These wave patterns excite receptor cells, known as *hair cells*, which are connected to the *auditory nerve fibers*. Here at the cochlea, the frequency, intensity, and other complex properties of the sound are translated from vibrations or pressure waves into activity in the auditory nerve fibers.

Different frequencies cause maximum pressure at different regions of the cochlea. This differential pressure is most evident for higher frequencies. For example, a high soprano voice, which may include tones of several thousand cycles per second, would be coded largely in the cochlea. But for very low frequencies, a different kind of mechanism

4-4

The human ear. Sound waves cause vibrations of the eardrum, which are carried to the oval window; vibrations at the oval window set up patterns of pressure in the cochlear fluid, which stimulate the hair cells (*see below*), where sound waves are translated into neuronal activity.

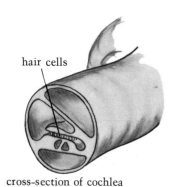

cross-section of cochlea

seems to operate. A sound of about 100 cycles per second, which is at the lower end of the human voice spectrum, would be coded largely by the auditory nerve fibers firing 100 times per second. All these complex activities take place in an organ the size of a pea, yet they permit us to hear sounds as rich and orchestrated as those that make up a symphony.

The Sensitivity of the Ear

Although some of us (young people primarily) can hear sounds between 20 and 20,000 Hz, our hearing is keenest between about 400 Hz and 3,000 Hz. Not surprisingly, this is roughly the range of human voices. Like most species, we are best equipped to hear our own vocalizings. Our *most* sensitive hearing is for frequencies a bit above the highest normal frequencies of speech. This puts both soprano arias and high-pitched screams at the upper end of our best hearing range. There is a general relationship between the size of an animal and its range of most sensitive hearing. A mouse has a much higher best-frequency range than we do, and an elephant has a much lower one.

Like most animals, humans have incredibly sensitive hearing. We can actually detect vibrations of our eardrum that are smaller than the diameter of the hydrogen atom. If our hearing were any more sensitive than it is, we would hear random molecules bouncing off our eardrums in a continual rumble which would mask other faint sounds. As it is, we can hear our own blood flowing if we cup a hand over an ear. In short, our hearing is as good as it can possibly be, at least at those frequencies we hear best.

It is probable that evolution has led to more and more sensitive hearing. The ability to detect and analyze faint sounds is an obvious aid to survival, particularly if you are hunting—or being hunted. Unfortunately, those of us who live in cities are in some ways the victims of our remarkably sensitive hearing mechanisms since we must suffer the loud, annoying, and even dangerous noises that have recently become a commonplace aspect of our environment.

Localization of Sounds

One important feature of the auditory system is that sounds going to one ear project to both sides of the brain. As we explained in Chapter 3, the human brain, like the brains of all higher animals, is *bilaterally symmetrical*. It exists as two interconnected half-brains side by side. The left half of the brain controls movement of the right torso, arm, and leg; the right half of the brain controls movement of the left torso, arm, and leg. Similarly, touch sensations from the right hand are analyzed in the left side of the brain, and vice versa.

However, each ear projects almost equally to both sides of the brain. This is a great help in determining the source of a sound. You know the experience of trying to figure out where a faint sound is coming from. You turn your head, and the sound gets progressively louder in one ear and softer in the other. When the sound is equally loud in both ears, you assume that you are looking in the direction from which it comes. This way of localizing a sound source would not be possible unless information from each ear went to both sides of the brain. In order to determine the exact location of the source of a sound, some common mechanism—nerve cells, for example—must receive input from both ears and compare the signals from each source.

We actually use two kinds of cues to determine the source of a sound. If it is fairly high-pitched, like a squeak, we tend to locate it by balancing the loudness of the sound at each ear. But if it is quite low in pitch, like a low vibration or rumble, we listen for a difference in the *phase.* Phase refers to the differential pressure exerted by the sound wave. Sound waves are like sea waves; each has a crest when the pressure is high and a trough when the pressure is low. A difference in phase between the two ears simply means that a sound is exerting high pressure on one ear while it is exerting low pressure on the other. When we can hear a difference in phase, we turn our head until the phase is the same in each ear—that is, maximum pressure at both ears occurs at the same time so that we are looking in the direction of the sound source.

Vision

Vision is one of the most remarkable events in nature. The human eye has about 130 million separate light-receptor cells. A complex system of nerve cells at the back of the eye links these cells to the one million separate fibers of the optic nerve that convey this visual information to the brain.

The Eye

(see fig. 4-5)

The eye is structurally and functionally similar to a camera. Each has a *lens*, which focuses an image of the external world on a light-sensitive sheet—the camera's film or the eye's *retina*. Each also has a device that governs the amount of light striking the sensitive sheet—a diaphragm in a camera and an *iris* in the eye. It contracts in bright light and opens up

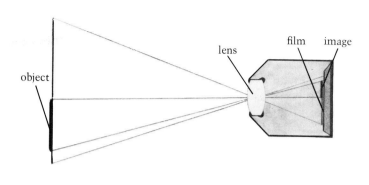

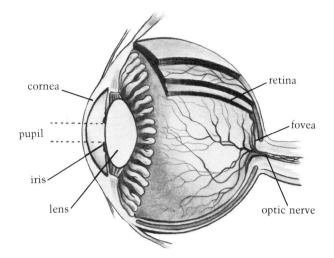

4-5
The human eye compared with a camera. The lens of the eye focuses an image on the retina at the back of the eye, much as the lens of a camera is focused to project light on the film in the back of the camera.

(see fig. 4-6)

when the light is dim. The eye focuses on nearby or distant objects by changing the shape of the lens; a camera lens must be moved out or in. The compound lens of a fine camera is actually superior to a human eye in one respect; it can compensate better for color distortion.

The retina—the photosensitive sheet of receptor cells at the back of the eye—functions much like the film in a camera. When light strikes the film, it induces chemical reactions in light-sensitive silver particles. Developing the film makes these reactions visible. When light falls on the eye's receptor cells, it induces a chemical reaction in the photosensitive chemicals or pigments there (called *rhodopsin* and *iodopsin*). The light bleaches the chemicals, and this process activates the nerve cells in contact with the receptor cells. The pigments are extremely sensitive; one photon, the smallest amount of light energy possible, falling on a receptor cell will activate a nerve cell. If as few as seven receptor cells are activated at once and conditions are perfect, we will see light. In practical terms, this means that we can see a single candle 30 miles away if the night is dark and the air is clear.

The retina of the human eye has two types of light-sensitive receptor cells. The most sensitive type is called a <u>rod</u>. Rods give us a visual impression that is like a black and white photograph; they show us everything, including colors, as shades of grey. Our night vision depends on these extremely sensitive receptors—which means that we cannot distinguish colors in a moonlit scene. Rods are scattered throughout the eye, but they are more common at the sides of the eye than at the back. That is why it is easier to see a faint star at night if you turn your head very slightly to one side. You probably will find yourself doing this automatically.

Our receptors for color vision are called <u>cones</u>. Because they are less sensitive than rods, cones function only in daylight or relatively bright light. Cones are concentrated in the *fovea*, an area at the very center of the retina where the lens focuses the image. There are relatively few cones at the sides of the retina.

A

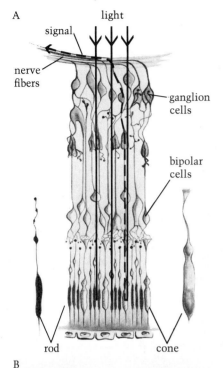

light

signal

nerve
fibers

ganglion
cells

bipolar
cells

rod   cone

B

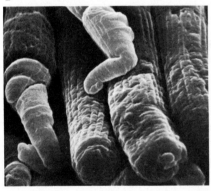

4-6

(A) The retina of the eye. Light
must pass through a layer of cells
to reach the photoreceptors (the
rods and cones) at the back of the
eye. Signals from the photoreceptor
cells are then transmitted through
the bipolar cells to the ganglion
cells, whose axons converge to become the optic nerve. The transmission paths involve elaborate interconnections. (B) Electron photomicrograph of rods and cones. The
cone in the center has partially
collapsed; the one at the left is
intact. The rods are in the foreground. (E. R. Lewis)

The Visible Spectrum and Color Vision

Like sound, light travels in waves. The total range of electromagnetic radiation extends from gamma rays, with wavelengths as short as the diameter of an atom, to radio waves over a mile long. The wavelengths we can see—the *visible spectrum*—make up only about one tenquadrillionth of the total spectrum. Visible spectrum wavelengths range from about 380 nanometers at the ultraviolet end to about 750 nanometers at the infrared end. (A nanometer is one billionth of a meter.) Green light, for example, has a wavelength of about 520 nanometers—a length shorter than the diameter of the eye's smallest nerve cells or receptor cells. The colors associated with the various wavelengths of the visible spectrum are shown in Plate 1 on page 102. The wavelengths merge into one another all along the color spectrum. But when we look at the spectrum, we can easily distinguish bands of violet, blue, blue-green, green, yellow, orange, and red. This translation of wavelength signals that we eventually perceive as colors occurs in the retina.

We will investigate that translation process shortly, but first we must look more closely at the nature of color itself. The colors we see are almost always mixtures of several wavelengths; only laser beams come close to true "pure" color. Colors can be mixed in two different ways, with differing results. If we project colored lights on a white card, we are adding wavelengths together. If we project the three primary light colors, red, green, and blue, we will get white—the sum of all the *additive* colors. Mixing paints, on the other hand, is a *subtractive* process. Paints, like most nontransparent colored objects, absorb all but a few wavelengths. Blue paint absorbs most wavelengths other than blue; yellow absorbs most wavelengths other than yellow. The green wavelengths, in between blue and yellow, are the only wavelengths not absorbed by a mixture of blue and yellow paint. If we mix the three primary paint colors of red, yellow, and blue together, we will get a muddy color close to black.

Why is it that we and all other organisms sensitive to light—including plants that use light energy for photosynthesis (the process by which plants manufacture carbohydrates)—can sense only this very narrow region of the vast electromagnetic spectrum? George Wald, who won the Nobel Prize for his studies of the eye (1949), has pointed out some reasons for this narrow sensitivity. If we were exposed to ultraviolet light below 300 nanometers, our eyes would immediately be destroyed. This light disrupts proteins and would prevent normal cell development. At the other end of the scale, infrared light above about 2,000 nanometers is so hot it would cook the cells in our eyes. Fortunately, the ozone layers in the upper atmosphere absorb ultraviolet light and the moisture in the atmosphere absorbs infrared light. Not surprisingly, our eyes evolved to be most sensitive to the wavelengths that most effectively penetrate the earth's atmosphere—specifically, 510 nanometers in the blue-green range.

Only three of the eleven phyla (major divisions of the animal kingdom) of animals have developed eyes: arthropods (insects and crabs), molluscs (octopi and squid), and vertebrates. These three phyla developed eyes independently in the course of their evolution, yet their eyes function in the same way and all three use essentially the same light-sensitive chemicals.

Theories of Color Vision.   A number of theories have been proposed to explain color vision. The *Young-Helmholtz theory* (developed in 1867 by Thomas Young, an English physicist, and Hermann von Helmholtz, a German physiologist and psychologist) assumes that there are three types of color receptors in the retina—one sensitive to blue, one to green, and one to red. Any color in the visible spectrum can be reproduced by some combination of these three primary colors. Presumably, the color receptors in the retina note the proportions of each primary color and pass these notations to the brain, which "mixes" them to re-create the original color.

The other major theory of color vision, first developed by Hering (1861) and later expanded by the Hurviches (1955), assumes that there are three *systems* of receptors in the retina—one for red-green, another for blue-yellow, and a third for black-white. Each system contains two opposing types of receptors. For example, some red-green receptors would respond positively to red and negatively to green, while others would respond negatively to red and positively to green. Coding a color would involve balancing each of the opposing pairs and then blending the three resulting color mixtures to reproduce the original color. This is called the Hering-Hurvich *opponent-process theory*. Current evidence indicates that color vision is an extremely complex process involving *both* the Young-Helmholtz and Hering-Hurvich processes. The retina evidently *receives* a color as Young and Helmholtz predicted. When the image of a colored object falls on the retina, it is coded by three different light-sensitive pigments in three different types of cones. These pigments are sensitive to blue, green, and yellowish-red—primary colors that can be mixed together to produce any color of the spectrum. However, the retina does not *transmit* a color to the brain in terms of three primary colors. Rather, it codes the color in an opponent process like that proposed by Hering and the Hurviches before transmitting it to the brain over the optic nerve fibers.

This process has been explored in great detail by DeValois and his colleagues (1965)—and by Rushton (1958) and MacNichol (1964) as well—who used a microscopically small electrode to detect the responses of individual nerve cells (neurons) in the thalamus and cerebral cortex of the rhesus monkey. (The rhesus monkey was selected because its color vision is identical to that of the normal human being.) DeValois found two categories of neurons in the lateral geniculate body (the part of the thalamus activated by the optic nerve fibers) that respond to light. One category responds to all the visible wavelengths of light, just as the rods do. DeValois termed these "non-opponent" cells. The other category of nerve cells responds to much narrower bands of wavelengths and behaves in what he called an "opponent" manner.

Some of these cells are excited by blue and inhibited by yellow light. Other nerve cells are excited by yellow and inhibited by blue. A third type is excited by green and inhibited by red, and the fourth type is excited by red and inhibited by green. These are the only four types of opponent cells found by DeValois. In short, the nerve cells in the retina and the lateral geniculate body code color perceptions in an opponent manner, just as Hering suggested, but the system is more complex than Hering thought. Though the details are complicated, all it means is that the optic nerve fibers fire more red signals and fewer green signals or more yellow and fewer blue signals, and so on.

In summary, it appears that both Young and Hering were partially correct. To oversimplify, the receptor cells are Young cells and the nerve cells are Hering cells. The cones have three types of photosensitive chemicals: red, green, and blue (Young's theory). However, interactions at the retina recode messages from the receptors so that the neurons in the higher visual centers of the brain will respond in an opponent manner (Hering and Hurvich theory). The two opponent categories are red-green and blue-yellow. In addition, there are opponent cells that are either excited or inhibited by all the visible wavelengths of light; these cells presumably deal with shades-of-grey messages from the rods. These findings by DeValois and others permit us to reconstruct the subjective experience of color from the patterns of discharge of nerve cells in the lateral geniculate body of the thalamus.

Psychological Dimensions of Color. Our experience of color actually has three dimensions. _Hue_ is the name we give to the psychological experience of an object's color—our translation of the wavelengths recorded by our cones. _Saturation_ refers to the purity and richness of the color. Fire-engine red is highly saturated; brick-red is not. Saturation is determined by the number of different wavelengths present in the color. The more wavelengths there are in a color, the _less_ saturated it is. A laser beam having only one wavelength will also have a completely saturated color. _Brightness_—the range of a hue from light to dark—is the third dimension of color. Brightness is determined by the amount of energy an object emits in the form of light. Dark objects absorb most of the light energy that strikes them; light objects reflect most of it.

The relationships between these three psychological dimensions of hue, brightness, and saturation are shown in Plate 2, a portion of the *color solid.* The hue is in the lower lefthand corner. Saturation is represented along the horizontal axes, going from a pure saturated color on the outside to grey at the center; brightness is represented by points along the vertical axis. The most highly saturated colors are those of medium brightness. As colors increase or decrease in brightness from this middle range, they approach the extremes of white or black, which are really colors without hue and therefore of zero saturation.

Afterimages. If you look intently at a colored object for a while and then look at a piece of grey paper, you will see a colored image of the first object. However, the color of the afterimage will be complementary to the color of the object. In other words, the afterimage color will be opposite the original color on the color wheel (Plate 3). These experiences are referred to as _negative afterimages._ Although there is no really simple explanation for negative afterimages, the Hering-Hurvich opponent theory can handle them rather nicely. When you look at yellow, the yellow-receptor neural process dominates its opponent blue process. When you look away, the yellow process ceases and this results in a rebound of the blue process.

THE COLORS WE SEE

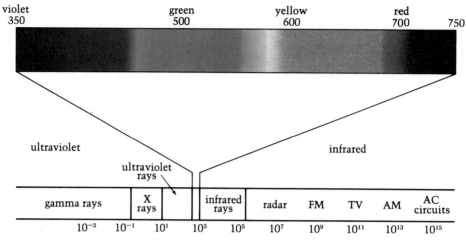

Plate 1

The entire range of electromagnetic radiation. The human eye sees only a miniscule portion of the existing wavelengths. A few animals and insects can see a bit more of the spectrum. The bee, for example, can see ultraviolet light.

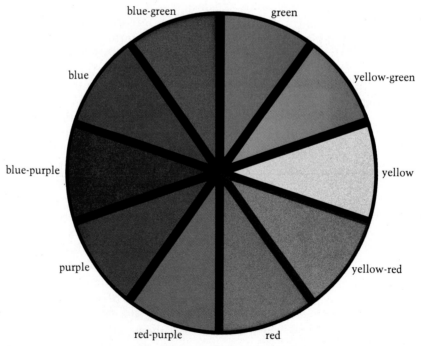

Plate 2

The colors are arranged around the circumference of the color wheel. Colors directly opposite each other are complementary; if they are added together, they produce white.

Plate 3

This portion of the color solid illustrates the three dimensions of color. The purple hue is found in the lower left hand corner. As black is added to the basic hue, its saturation decreases, from pure saturation in the left corner to the least saturation in the right corner. Brightness ranges along the vertical axis.

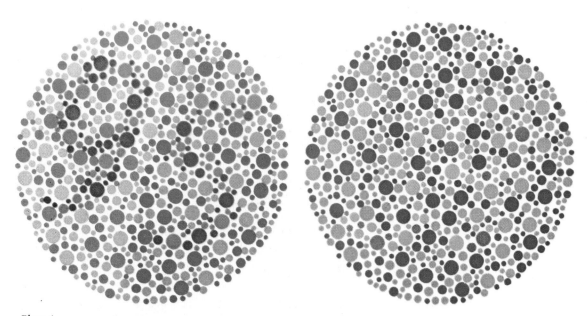

Plate 4

The Dvorine Pseudo-Isochromatic Plates typically are used to test for color blindness. The person must be able to distinguish the number in the center of the circle. If he is color blind, everything meshes together and the number is invisible; only the color separates the number from its background. (Reproduced from the Dvorine Pseudo-Isochromatic Plates, copyright © 1944, 1953, by Harcourt Brace Jovanovich, Inc. Reproduced by special permission of the publisher. Published by Harcourt Brace Jovanovich, Inc. Copyright 1958, SCIENTIFIC PUBLISHING CO., Baltimore, Md.)

COLOR VISION

Dorothea Jameson and Leo M. Hurvich *Columbia University and University of Pennsylvania*

The puzzles of color vision have, over the centuries, posed an intellectual challenge to persons of surprisingly diverse interests, many of whom are as well or better known for accomplishments unrelated to the problem of how we see color.

Isaac Newton, whose work on gravitational force was a cornerstone in the building of physics as a science, was also the first to show how white light that is passed through a prism can be broken up into colored rays. Johann Wolfgang von Goethe, who plumbed the depths and heights of human experience in his poetry and dramatic writings, was unsatisfied with Newton's emphasis on the physics of light and proposed his own analysis that emphasized the perceptions of colored objects. Thomas Young, who deciphered the hieroglyphics on the Rosetta Stone, proposed that as few as three different mechanisms in the eye could account for all the thousands of colors we see. Hermann von Helmholtz, giant of 19th-century physics and physiology, whose name is associated with the science of acoustics, the ophthalmoscope, and the principle of conservation of en-

ergy, can also be found linked with Young as the proponent of a theory of color vision that dominated the textbooks of the late 19th and early 20th centuries. James Clerk Maxwell, whose fundamental electromagnetic equations are known to every student of physics, also carried out light-mixture experiments to determine color equations that are known to every student of color vision. Ewald Hering, concerned with the neural control of breathing and the physiology of space localization and binocular vision, wanted to show how the phenomena of color vision could be used to study the behavior of the nervous system. This list could be continued to the present day. Many others have sought explanations for the nature of colors and how we see them; but this touch of history will suffice to show that color vision, which most of us accept in a matter-of-fact way every day of our lives, is really an intricate interaction between electromagnetic energy and exquisite physiological processes in the eye and brain, an interaction that has fascinated some of the greates artists and scientists of the last 200 years.

Puzzles often contain the key to their own solution. The prism that Newton used is a good point at which to start. Figures A-1, A-2, and A-3 show three ways of obtaining white light from a mixture of colored lights. Figure A-1 contains the essence of Newton's famous prism experiment: as a beam of white light passes through it, the prism of glass bends the rays of different wavelengths to different degrees and produces the color spectrum. Reversing the process, by sending the colored rays through the prism from the other side, recombines the rays to produce white light again. Although not surprising, it was a demonstration that Newton had to make to prove that the glass had not somehow given off the colors.

A mixture of the whole spectrum of different wavelengths is not needed to produce white. Figure A-2 is a fairly accurate visual representation of what happens when two narrow wavelength bands, one at about 475 nanometers (a nanometer is one billionth of a meter) that looks blue and another at about 575 nanometers that looks yellow, are mixed with each other in proper proportions.

A-1
Diagram of Newton's prism experiment. White light passing through the prism produces the color spectrum. Reversing the process, white light is reconstructed.

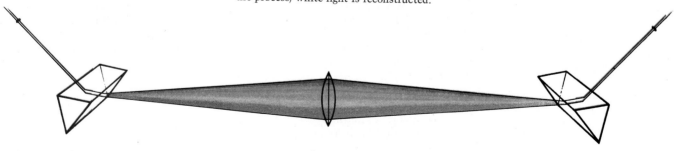

A-2

Graphic representation of the mixing of blue (475 nanometers) and yellow (575 nanometers).

A-3

Graphic representation of the mixing of blue-green (490 nanometers) and yellowish-red (650 nanometers).

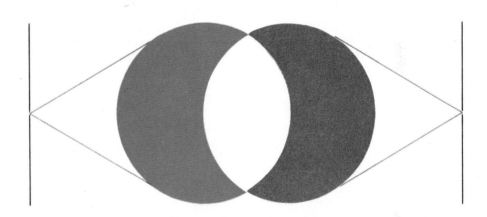

This mixture of two bands of light produces the same white quality as Newton's entire spectrum. Figure A-3 illustrates the same effect from a different pair of narrow wavelength bands, a blue-green one at about 490 nanometers and a yellowish-red one near 650 nanometers. The illustration expresses two basic facts about color vision. One is the principle of color mixture. The visual system is an integrative one; the same perceived color can result from a variety of different light mixtures. The principles of color mixture were the aim of Maxwell's experiments and of many other more precise ones that followed, and color-mixture data have played a dominant role in the development of theoretical models that stemmed from Young's idea and Helmholtz's later espousal of it.

The illustrations in Figure A need not have been limited to mixtures that produce white; a series of different light mixtures can mimic any hue. We chose white for the illustration because it makes a second basic point about color vision. Certain colors, when combined, cancel each other out. Notice that when we start with a light that looks blue, we add to it a light that looks yellow to get white; when we start with a greenish light, we get white by adding a light that looks reddish. If the greenish light also has a blue hue, then the reddish light needed to get white must have a yellow hue. Were we to start with a yellowish-green, then the red that combines with it to produce white will have to be a bluish-red. Clearly, something in the visual system prevents blue and yellow or red and green hues from being seen in the same place at the same time. Stimuli that give rise to these hues seem to cancel each other when combined, producing the hueless white. Facts of this sort led Ewald Hering to conclude that an inherent opponent or antagonistic process in the visual physiology characterizes the responses associated with these particular paired hues.

Other phenomena lead to a similar conclusion. Figure B is a facsim-

B

Bust of a young girl in the reversed colors of an afterimage. Stare at the girl for a minute or so and then turn to look at a white piece of paper. (After a painting by Goethe, Nationale Forschungs-und Gedenkstätten der klassischen deutschen Literatur in Weimar.)

ile of a painting of Goethe's. Fix your eyes on a spot on this figure. While keeping your head steady, continue to look at the spot without moving your eyes for a minute or so. Then shift your gaze quickly to a spot within the blank square area adjacent to the figure. The ephemeral lady you now see is, of course, an afterimage of her pre-exposed counterpart. Afterimages of this sort suggest that, while the figure's retinal light image activates the physiological process associated with yellowness, the paired physiological antagonist is somehow building up its opposite force. When direct stimulation of yellowness is removed as the gaze shifts to the blank area, the antagonistic process is released, showing itself in the blue afterimage in the place where yellow had just been seen. The situation is similar for redness and greenness, and also for whiteness and blackness: dark areas in the viewed figure are light areas in the afterimage and vice versa.

The physiological antagonists not only oppose and tend to counterbalance each other in time, they also do so in space—a lesson that every artist must master to be an effective colorist. The inset square frames on the different backgrounds of Figure C are physically identical. The important thing to notice is not simply that the frames look different; notice also the systematic way in which the darker background forces the inset toward a lighter color, the red background forces it toward a greener color, the yellow background toward a bluer color, and so on. This antagonistic pairing is the same kind that shows up in the color-mixture hue cancellation of Figure A and the afterimage of Figure B. It is said that, when hanging his paintings for a gallery opening, Joseph Turner, the 18th-century British artist, knew precisely how to make last-minute alterations in the colors on his canvasses in order to diminish the effectiveness of the colors in rival paint-

ers' works hung next to his own.

In our own work we have observed, measured, and analyzed a variety of visual phenomena, including color mixture and hue cancellation, adaptation and the after-effects of colored light stimulation, contrast effects, visual discriminative capacities, and the changes in all of these properties in individuals with defective or abnormal color vision. We did this work to develop a systematic theoretical account of how the color vision mechanism operates. Basic to our account is the three-variable nature of this mechanism and its organization into three pairs of antagonistic neural processes that are color-coded as red or green, blue or yellow, and black or white.

Neurophysiologists have measured the responses of individual nerve cells in the retina and visual centers of the brain. These measurements have confirmed that antagonistic processes do regulate the electrical activity occurring in individual cells

C

A grey square against backgrounds of different colors.

of the visual system when the retina is exposed to different wavelengths, energies, and patterns of light. The electrode recordings of cellular behavior were taken, by necessity, from the visual systems of fish, monkeys, and other animals. Considered alone they are difficult to extrapolate to human vision with any degree of certainty. It is therefore important to know that our theories about the way the human visual system operates have certain basic features in common with the physiological events that can be studied directly in animals.

The opponent neural organization, expressed so clearly in color vision, has implications that reach far beyond the visual system itself. Essentially the opponent organization is an equilibrium-seeking device that achieves and maintains an adaptive balance between competing excitations. The principle expresses itself in such learning situations as Pavlovian excitation and inhibition, in the phenomena of novelty versus habituation, in the reflex control of muscle antagonists, and it lies at the heart of antigen-antibody interactions. The role of opponent processes

in the concepts of balance, symmetry, and equilibria shows up in many aspects of intellectual history. The subtleties of the opposing forces of Yin and Yang, for example, permeate Oriental thought (see Chapter 9). We do not want to suggest that the processes basic to color vision can be taken directly to explain in detail a variety of other psychological phenomena. However, we do suggest that these opponent processes may serve as useful guiding principles.

VISUAL PERCEPTION IN THE ARTS

Rudolf Arnheim *Professor Emeritus, Harvard University*

Why do we see the shapes and colors in the world around us the way we do? How do they express what they do? The psychologist asks these questions; but perhaps they are of even more vital interest to the painter, the sculptor, the designer, or the architect. For his experiments in perception, the psychologist prefers simple patterns of a few shapes and colors; and it is not always evident how the principles derived from such a simple set of variables apply to the complexity of a colorful street scene or landscape around us. This is true also for much of the realistic painting and sculpture of the past or for highly ornamented furniture and architecture. Our eyes manage to cope with these riches, but how does the scientist fare who wishes to explain their visual effects?

Fortunately, in the arts of our century many works meet the psychologist halfway. For reasons of their own, many artists have come to prefer plain-colored surfaces bounded by simple contours. This trend towards simplification of form pervades much of our design in buildings, furniture, packaging, posters, and traffic signs. Driving on a highway one appreciates the incisive clarity of a twisted black arrow on a yellow ground; it warns the motorist of a curve without complicating the visual message by all the details of the actual situation. The eyes are given the essentials, and the mind profits from it.

The arrow shows up clearly because one distinguishes it as the figure on a ground. Such a tidy distinction between foreground and background has been favored also by some artists of the past—for example, when a portrait was outlined against a plain blue or golden background or when a temple or castle placed on a high hill was set off against an empty sky.

Some modern artists have enjoyed experimenting with ambiguity by giving the ground some of the properties of the figure, so that shapes protrude or recede whimsically, playing hide-and-seek with the viewer.

Another perceptual principle is that of similarity. Psychologists have noted that when visual objects or parts of objects share the same perceptual feature the mind of the observer will connect them almost automatically. The shared property may be a color, a particular shape, the direction of a movement, or the degree of brightness. For example, when a painting contains two areas of a similar red, the eye will see them as related, even when they are placed at some distance from each other. Artists have used this spontaneous grouping of similar items intuitively to guide the viewer's attention in accordance with the intended message and to tie the various parts of a composition together. In offices and machine shops, color keying facilitates orientation and distinction, and telephone installation workers would be at a loss without the various colors distinguishing their wires.

Painters and draftsmen often are concerned with the representation of three-dimensional space on a flat surface. If such pictures are obtained by optical projection, as are photographs or indeed as are the retinal images created by the lenses in the eyes, serious deformations occur because distant objects produce smaller images than nearby objects. Psychology tells us that these distortions are reduced substantially during the processing of retinal images in the nervous system. It is because of this "constancy of size" that at early levels of pictorial representation sizes and shapes often are shown exactly as they are physically: the right

angles of a table top are depicted as right angles, and a human figure shown at a distance is as large as one in the foreground. Since the Renaissance, however, painters have preferred to use the geometrical construction of central perspective, which resembles optical projection in many ways. This helped to make photography acceptable when it was invented. The expansions and contractions of perspective distortion also have been shown to yield powerful pictorial expression. Nevertheless, many artists today have preferred to return to the directness of early space representation.

Perceptual images are not static agglomerations of shapes and colors but are loaded with what may be called visual dynamics. For example, a sculptor knows that when he uses large convex volumes they expand visually and invade the surrounding empty space, whereas narrow and concave shapes possess a passivity that invites the background space to press against the figure and eat into it from the outside. Similarly in architecture, every style of building can be said to be characterized by a particular ratio between the horizontal dimension of masses resting securely on the ground and the vertical dimension of their rising boldly toward the sky. The degree to which a building seems to defy the force of gravity is read by the human mind symbolically as a metaphor depicting man's struggle for freedom from burdens that hold him in comfortable inertia.

A

A traffic sign is a highly abstract visual statement. It demonstrates the human mind's ability to grasp the essentials of a perceptual situation. In the present instance, the dangerous curves of the mountain road ahead are all that matters to the driver. He has learned to accept the simple arrow as a picture of a landscape and he will recognize the twists of the road in the complexity of the actual setting. In less obvious ways, works of art typically present abstracted interpretations of familiar objects. (Bjorn Bolstad, Photo Researchers)

B

Some of Robert Indiana's stenciled letters and digits in his *Autoportrait 1965* rest securely on their white or red backgrounds. They are perceived as "figure" covering "ground." However, by cleverly breaking up the unity of color and brightness in the two principal shapes of his painting, Indiana prevents the viewer from seeing the star consistently in front of the disk. Thus the pie-shaped red area at the bottom appears in front of the white ground when looked at by itself and only reluctantly accepts its role as a part of the big star's background when the picture is viewed as a whole. (Eric Pollitzer)

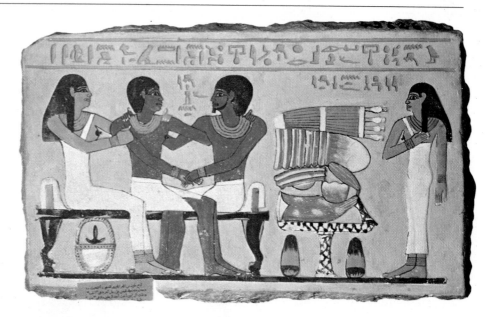

C

By distributing similar colors and similar shapes all over the surface of his sculpture, Jean Dubuffet gives unity to the unruly complexity of his standing figure. The viewer's eyes feel compelled to spin webs of formal relations. They tie all the reds together and also all the blues. An overall similarity of crookedness of shape or stripedness, regardless of direction, is sufficient to activate the integrating perceptual mechanism. (Jean Dubuffet, *Bidon L'Esbroufe*, December 11, 1967. The Solomon R. Guggenheim Museum Collection)

D

Instead of blaming the painters of Ancient Egypt or our modern children for ignoring perspective, many psychologists and art educators appreciate the "naive" procedure of rendering size and shape of objects undistorted. The most characteristic dimension of each object is presented in the picture plane: dinner plates preserve their roundness by being shown from above, whereas chairs, chandelier, rabbit, and flowers are given in elevation. The Egyptian painter offers a clear view of his profile figures by retaining the frontal symmetry of shoulders and eyes; and he displays the foodstuff on the table in an arrangement that avoids any disturbing superposition. [Painted Limestone Stele of Amenemhet (from Thebes) Cairo Museum. (Scala New York/Florence)]

E
Realistic perspective, as first developed in the 15th century, serves not only to create a strong depth effect; it also makes a long hallway converge as though its sides, top, and floor were approaching each other with increasing distance. The squeezing of the hollow volume by means of perspective gives the hospital corridor a dynamic tension, characteristic of many paintings by Vincent van Gogh. (*Hospital Corridor at Saint Remy.* (1889–90). Gouache and watercolor, 24⅛ × 18⅝″. Collection, The Museum of Modern Art, New York)

F

Empty space is quite active perceptually. From all sides it closes in on the emaciated shapes of Alberto Giacometti's *Walking Man* as though the compressive power of surrounding forces caused his thinness. The flourishing complexity of the shapes employed by Gaston Lachaise creates an equally dynamic interplay between space and figure. His figure of a *Walking Woman* seems to expand from

the center. The figure invades the surrounding space and pushes it back [Alberto Giacometti, *Walking Man* (bronze, 1947–8) Hirshhorn Museum & Sculpture Garden, Smithsonian Institution; Gaston Lachaise, *Walking Woman* (1919) Hirshhorn Museum & Sculpture Garden, Smithsonian Institution (Scala New York/Florence)

G

The architectural expression of the horizontal and the vertical is illustrated by two buildings of our century, a one-family home by Frank Lloyd Wright and a medical research building by Louis I. Kahn. Wright said that horizontal planes identify the house with the ground and constitute the earth line of repose. By contrast, Kahn's towers, containing the staircases and the air-intakes for the laboratories, rise with the defiant pride of a medieval fortress. The particular ratio between ground-hugging security and bold elevation determines the pattern of visual forces on which the character of a building's appearance depends. (Hedrich-Blessing, Jaimini Mehta)

Visual Acuity

When we look at an object, both of our eyes focus on it. Seeing with two eyes is called _binocular vision_. The object is projected onto the center of the back of each eye, the foveal area of the retina. The fovea is the region of maximum _visual acuity_; vision is sharpest when objects are focused on it. The fovea is made up entirely of cones. Though cones enable us to see color, as well as the smallest details, they cannot function if the light gets too dim. This is the basic distinction between daylight vision and night vision. It takes about 30 minutes for our eyes to _dark-adapt_—that is, for the rods to become fully sensitive to very dim light. Conversely, cones take only a few minutes to _light-adapt_.

Although the fovea is a very small part of the retina, the fovea's cones project to about half of the visual cortex. In other words, their representation in the brain is enormous relative to their actual numbers at the retina. When you look at a wall, you actually focus on one small point on the wall. That very small point on which you are focusing occupies half of the entire visual cortex; the rest of the wall occupies the remaining half. Of course, you do not see the wall as a point of sharp focus surrounded by vast blur—it appears to you as a continuous, sharply-focused image.

The Blind Spot. There is a spot near the fovea where the optic nerve fibers leave the eye to go to the brain. At this point, there are no receptors on the retina. This is the so-called _blind spot_. You can locate the blind spot in your own eye by using the diagram in Figure 4–7. When you find the blind spot, you will notice that the black circle disappears from your vision. What is there in its place? Is it a hole in the piece of paper? A blank spot? A dark spot? No. It looks like the rest of the piece of paper.

This is a most important point. There is a permanent hole in your visual world, but normally you are not aware of it. The visual nervous system somehow fills in this blind spot. This is also true of some people who have suffered damage to their visual cortex. In one region of their visual field, they are completely blind—they cannot see any objects at all. Nonetheless, they see this blind part of their visual field as continuous, just as we do with the blind spot. The visual brain fills in the missing region with whatever the surroundings may be. The blind spot is one example of the difficulties we encounter when we try to explain our awareness of perception in words. Without the trick picture, we would never know there is a hole in our visual field. When asked if there is one, we would say no, because we are never aware of it. Yet it is always there.

4-7
This visual test will show that you have a blind spot in each eye. Cover your left eye and, holding the book about 12 inches from your face, look steadily at the X as you slowly bring the book toward your face. At some point the image of the dot will disappear. Try the same thing with your right eye covered; as you fix your gaze at the dot, the X will vanish.

X ● / /

Form Perception

The eye does not have specialized receptors for perceiving form. The lens projects an image of the object onto the retina, where it is picked up by the cones or rods. This image is recorded *as a whole*. Then it is coded and transmitted through the visual nervous system from the eye up to the cerebral cortex.

Our knowledge of form perception owes much to the Gestalt school of psychology, particularly the theories of Köhler, Koffka, and Wertheimer. They argued that our perception of form is an innate property of the visual system. When you look at an object against a background, it stands out from the background. They termed this the *figure-ground relationship.* This process has been observed by several people who were born with cataracts in their eyes and therefore could see nothing but vague sensations of light (Hebb, 1949). The cataracts were surgically removed when these people were adults. When the bandages came off, they got their first clear look at the world.

They reported that at first the world was an overwhelming confusion of visual sensations. However, they immediately became aware of two things: figure-ground and color. A simple object, such as a cube, was perceived an object against the background of the walls of the room. However, they could not identify the object by looking at it. As soon as they were given the cube to touch and feel—the sense in which they were highly sensitive—they immediately identified it. But the next time they saw it they often were unable to identify it visually. It took these people some time to learn the names of objects they saw, even though they knew the names immediately if they were allowed to feel the objects.

A

4-8
What do you see as you look at these pictures? It depends on what you see as the figure and what you see as the ground. This is known as *reversible figure-ground.* In (A) you may see a white vase against a black background; in (B) a similar reversible figure-ground relationship has been enhanced by making the figures three dimensional in the foreground. (B. Escher Foundation, Haags Gemeentemuseum, The Hague)

B

They had similar problems with the names of colors. They were immediately impressed with the existence of colors and the differences between colors, but learning the names took time. Young children have the same difficulty. Even a very young child can put the red things together and the green things together. However, it is only much later, around age three, that they can easily name the different colors correctly. In short, it appears that the figure-ground relationship and the experience of color are innate responses to visual sensations, just as the Gestalt psychologists argued. What must be learned are the correct *names* for objects and colors.

Perceptual Grouping. Another important aspect of visual form perception is *grouping*. We tend to organize our visual field or world into meaningful groups of objects, patterns, or stimuli. Look at Figure 4-9A. You see pairs of parallel lines, each pair "grouped" together. If extensions are added to these lines, as in 4-9C, different pairs of lines become

4-9

Grouping: A Gestalt rule of perceptual organization whereby items are grouped in terms of proximity, similarity, symmetry, closure, and continuation.

A

PROXIMITY. Items closest to each other are perceived as whole. We see three sets of two lines each; we do not see six separate lines.

B

△ ○ △

△ ○ △

△ ○ △

SIMILARITY. Items that most closely resemble each other are perceived as units. The rows of circles and triangles are seen as two vertical rows of triangles and one of circles; we do not see three horizontal rows of circles and triangles.

C

[ ][ ][ ]

SYMMETRY. Items that form symmetrical units are grouped together. We see three sets of brackets; we do not see six unconnected lines.

D

CLOSURE. Items are perceived as complete units, even though they may be interrupted by gaps. We see a horse and rider rather than a series of broken squibs. Closure is the basis for camouflage.

E

CONTINUATION. Items with the fewest interruptions are perceived as units. We see a curved line and a straight line; we do not see a straight line with small semicircles above and below it.

grouped together. Grouping clearly illustrates the general Gestalt notion that the whole is different from the sum of its parts. How you see a whole scene depends on how you see the figure-ground relationship and on how the various parts of the scene are organized in relation to each other.

How the brain codes our perception of form has remained a mystery until quite recently. Hubel and Weisel (1962) placed small recording electrodes (wires) in the visual areas of the brain in animals (cats and monkeys) and studied the responses of single nerve cells to visual stimuli. They found that some cells code edges, others code lines, and some even code right angles. The right angle detector cell, for example, only responds to an angle stimulus made up of two joined lines. Furthermore, it responds best to a right angle. These findings suggest that even very complicated and abstract visual stimuli may be coded by individual visual nerve cells. Presumably, there are a number of such cells for each kind of visual stimulus, or at least for each level of complexity.

4-10
Diagram showing how a single nerve cell in a cat's visual cortex responded selectively to various movements of a bar-shaped object across the visual field. The movements of the bar are shown on the left. On the right are the cell's responses to this stimulus. Note that the cell is most active as the bar moves down and to the left in the center of the visual field (B and C) and when it moves back and forth at this same angle (H). The colored lines above the activity charts show the times during which the stimulus was presented. (Hubel & Weisel, 1962)

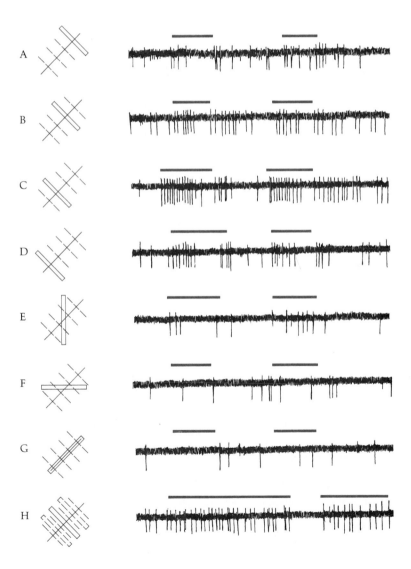

THE MEASUREMENT OF SENSATION

Our sensations and perceptions of stimuli form the basis of all human communication. In order to relate to our fellow humans, we must communicate our perceptions to them. But though sensations are basic to human behavior, the scientific study and analysis of sensations has been a most difficult and challenging process. In fact, modern psychology really began when such pioneering 19th-century scientists as Weber and Fechner first attempted to measure and study human sensations. We will look at two aspects of sensation here: the judgment of how strong or intense a stimulus is—the *magnitude* of sensations; and the measurement or detection of *absolute thresholds* for faint stimuli. Each of these seemingly simple problems has given rise to an entire field of psychology.

The Magnitude of Sensations

The field of *psychophysics* relates the magnitude of sensations—the human experience of how strong a stimulus is—to the physical stimuli that produce them. We all find it easy to judge how loud sounds are—the TV or hi-fi often is too loud or too soft. It does not seem difficult to judge one sound as being twice as loud as another. But surprisingly, such judgments do not have a simple, direct relationship to the physical intensity of the sound waves. A tone that is physically twice as intense as another sounds a little louder to us, but certainly not twice as loud. A sound that you would judge to be twice as loud as another is actually several times more intense. Our subjective scale of loudness greatly compresses the actual physical scale of sound intensity. This has an obvious advantage for us; we can compress a wide range of sound intensities into a reasonable range of experience. For this

reason, the decibel scale (dB) of sound measurement is a *subjective* scale. Absolute threshold, defined as a physical stimulus that is perceived half the time, is 0 dB. Hearing damage and sensations of pain begin to occur at about 110 to 120 dB. This range covers a many thousandfold increase in the physical intensity of sounds.

Current understanding of our judgment of stimulus intensity comes largely from the work of S. S. Stevens (1962). He demonstrated that the relationship between stimulus intensity and our subjective sensations of stimulus intensity can always be described by a special mathematical formula—the *power law*. The power law can best be illustrated graphically; Figure A shows the relationship between the subjective sensation of intensity and the physical intensity of stimuli for three kinds of stimulation—electric shock, apparent length, and brightness of light.

The three types of stimuli seem to have very different curves. Judgment of electric shock strength increases rapidly above a certain level of stimulus intensity. Judgment of apparent length of lines has a linear relationship, meaning that we are consistently accurate in this judgment. Brightness judgments rise rapidly at first and then taper off. Actually all of these are very adaptive relationships. Our judgment of the sizes of objects corresponds closely to their actual sizes; if it did not, we would certainly have trouble dealing with our environment. This fact is actually merely a graphical demonstration of the law of size constancy (see p. 122).

Judgment of the loudness of sounds is, like the brightness of light, a compression of the physical scale. A fairly large increase in the physical

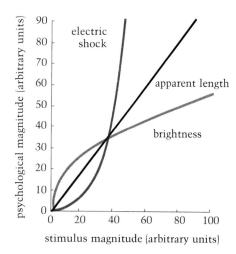

A

Graphic representation of Stevens' power law, showing the relationship between the magnitude of physical stimuli—electric shock, apparent length, and brightness, in this case—and our psychological perception of the stimuli. (Stevens, 1962)

intensity of an already intense sound causes only a small increase in our psychological perception of the loudness. We can encompass comfortably the vast range of sound intensities from a breaking twig to a crash of thunder.

Electric shock is a potentially damaging stimulus. At low intensities, below pain threshold, it is not very important for us to judge how strong it is. However, as shock crosses the pain threshold and begins to cause tissue damage, it becomes vitally important for us to detect small changes in shock intensity. The point at which the curve for electric shock in Figure A begins to rise rapidly is the pain threshold. At a stimulus magnitude of 30 units, a small increase in the physical intensity of the shock causes a large increase in our judgment of how strong the shock seems. Stevens' discovery, which led to his power law, was that these three very different curves can all be described by the same general mathematical expression. The formula, $\psi = kS^n$, describes a relationship between ψ, the subjective experience of a stimulus; k, a constant that depends on the unit of measurement; and S, the physical magnitude of a stimulus. Thus, all curves relating stimuli intensity to our experience for all different types of stimuli—from the sourness of tastes to the brightness of lights, and possibly even to esthetic judgments of how strongly we like art—are described by his power law formula.

Signal Detection Theory and the Absolute Threshold

For a long time, psychologists agreed with the common assumption that there are absolute thresholds for stimuli. If a sound is made progressively weaker, it will reach a precise point where it can no longer be heard. Indeed, such absolute thresholds were measured in the laboratory for years—but different scientists often arrived at very different values for the absolute threshold of a given stimulus, such as the 1000 Hz tone. A few years ago, telephone company engineers working on the problems of communication developed a different approach. They decided that there was no such thing as an absolute threshold. They found that some noise is present under any conditions, even in sound-proofed laboratory test rooms. Thus, when a signal is given to a subject, it occurs against a background of noise. When the signal is not present, there is still noise, which might fool the subject into thinking a stimulus was given.

This discovery led to the development of the *signal detection theory*, which states that detection of a signal depends on a person's previous experience, expectations, and motivation as well as the intensity of the actual stimulus. Consequently, in any judgment of absolute threshold there are four possible outcomes: (1) judgment of signal present when signal is present (called a hit on a signal trial); (2) judgment of signal present when signal is absent (false alarm on a catch trial); (3) judgment of signal absent when signal is present (false alarm on a signal trial);

and (4) judgment of signal absent when signal is absent (hit on a catch trial). Judgments 1 and 4 are correct; 2 and 3 show the two kinds of possible errors—commission and omission.

Psychologists and engineers studying the problem soon discovered that the most important variable determining the occurrence of errors and hits was the subject's decision criterion. If the subject is very cautious, he will make many errors of omission but few of commission. If he is bold and guesses frequently, he will make many errors of commission but few of omission. These two types of subjects will also appear to have different thresholds.

The most valuable contribution of signal detection theory is its emphasis on the critical importance of the subject himself—his "set" or tendency to respond. This is far more influential than the actual physical intensity of stimuli. Consequently, there is no such thing as one absolute threshold for each stimulus. Modern signal detection theory has led to significant increases in our understanding of how people make judgments about sensations.

Depth Perception

Binocular vision is one of the two basic mechanisms that enable us to judge how far away an object is. If you look at a nearby object, each of your eyes turns slightly inward, so that they both can focus on the same point. This is termed _convergence._ If you look at your finger and then move it toward the tip of your nose, your eyes will cross as they continue to focus on the finger. In effect, our eye muscles send to the brain signals that carry information about how much our eyes are turned inward, and our brain is able to interpret these signals in a way that relates inward eye movement to the distance between us and the object we are looking at. This eye movement assists in the process of _depth perception._ Our other means of perceiving distance or depth involves the lens of the eye. When our eye focuses on an object, muscles actually change the shape of the lens. This is called _accommodation._ It gives us muscular cues about where the lens is focused. Thanks to this mechanism, a person with one eye still has depth vision. In short, we get information from each eye individually and from both eyes together about how far away an object is.

In addition to these mechanisms, we rely on a variety of visual cues to aid us in depth perception. Figures 4–11 and 4–12 illustrate four of the most common _monocular cues_ to depth and relative distance.

Many visual illusions and distortions of perception depend on the fact that we use two-dimensional drawings to represent three-dimensional objects. Two-dimensional drawings require the viewer to supply the missing dimension of depth with the aid of various cues.

Three-dimensional visual illusions are not uncommon, as magic shows demonstrate. However, it is impossible to maintain a three-dimensional visual illusion if the viewer is allowed to move around. This makes good adaptive sense. If our vision allowed us to be continually fooled about where objects were in the world or what they were like, we would not survive long.

4-11
The monocular cue of linear perspective is typically illustrated by railroad tracks that appear to meet in the distance. Equally often we encounter the long, narrow road edged by trees and brush. (Henri Cartier-Bresson, Magnum)

Perceptual Constancies

Why does a familiar object always look the same no matter what angle it is viewed from? This is because of the perceptual constancies.

Shape Constancy

Every time you look at a car, the actual image projected on your retina is different. You probably have never seen the identical image twice, yet you always see it as the same automobile. To take a simpler example, a coin held in front of you at right angles to your line of vision looks like a circle, and you identify it as a coin. If you rotate the coin, it becomes an elipse, then a very narrow elipse, and finally a straight bar when you look directly at its edge. Its image on your retina changes from round, to elipse, to bar, and yet you see it always as a round coin. It has _shape constancy;_ no matter what shape our retinal image is, we always perceive it as the same shape. A great many visual cues, both monocular and binocular, support our impressions of constancy. These same cues can mislead us at times.

4-12
Monocular cues for the perception of depth. (A) Clearness: sharper images are seen as being closer; (B) Interposition: An object that appears to be in back of another object is seen as being further away; and (C) texture-gradient: the more details that are visible, the closer the object is.

4-13
Optical Illusions. (A) The Ponzo illusion. The upper horizontal line appears longer than the lower one, although both are the same length. (B) The center circles are the same size, but the one surrounded by larger circles appears smaller. (C) and (D) The Hering illusion. The vertical lines do not appear to be parallel. (E) The Müller-Lyer illusion. Both vertical lines are actually the same length. (F) Both figures are actually identical.

Size Constancy

Learning plays a role in the development of certain kinds of constancies. For example, Leibowitz and his students (1965) have demonstrated the role of learning and other variables in *size constancy*, the tendency to perceive objects as always the same size by adjusting retinal image according to distance. The basic experiment is simple. Subjects are shown a large round disc about 10 feet away. The same disc is then shown at progressively greater distances (of course, the subjects do not see it being moved). As the disc is moved further away, the size of its image on the retina grows smaller, of course. But adults continue to judge accurately the actual size of the disc—that is, they judge that it remains the same size, even though their retinas record a progressively smaller image. They are accurate because binocular cues like convergence and monocular cues like accommodation make most of us very good judges of depth and distance.

If the viewing conditions are artificially simplified by progressively removing depth cues, the judgment becomes progressively more difficult. Thus, if the subject is required to use only one eye (no convergence) and look through a tiny hole smaller than his own pupil (no accommodation) and the object is against a completely featureless black background (no learned distance cues), a normal adult will judge the object as remaining at the same distance and growing progressively smaller, though it is in fact the same size and moving further away.

In experiments comparing adults and children, Leibowitz and his students showed the effect of experience on size constancy quite clearly. First, they simply compared adults and children in the basic experiment—a constant-size disc moved progressively further away under normal viewing conditions. Adults judged that the disc remained constant in size, but children reported that it was growing smaller. The judgment of 8-year-olds was not based entirely on the retinal image size, but fell partway between the real size of the object (constancy) and the diminishing size of its retinal image.

Zeigler and Leibowitz (1957) turned the tables on their subjects in one experiment and used progressively larger discs at greater distances so the retinal image remained constant. Adults continued to judge correctly; that is, they judged the more distant, larger discs as larger. However, 8-year-old children judged the object as getting somewhat larger at greater distances, but not as large as it was. Evidently, they have developed only partial size constancy; they rely more on the size of the retinal image than do adults.

Color Constancy

A red apple looks red in all lights: in sunlight, in bright or dim artificial light, or even in reddish or bluish light. As is true for size and shape constancy, both the physical stimulus itself and learning are responsible for *color constancy*, the tendency to perceive objects as always the same color. If the apple is viewed in bluish light near a blue book, it looks more red than the book, even though the actual wavelengths of light it reflects may not be very red. The relative brightness, hue, and saturation

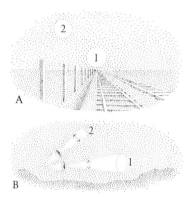

4-14
The moon illusion is a well-known example of how size constancy may be affected by the environment in which the object is perceived. (A) According to Kaufman and Rock (1962), distance cues from objects on the horizon cause the illusion. The moon looks larger because it is beyond these objects that we know are far away. When the moon is overhead, we judge its size accurately because there are no nearby objects to compare it with; thus we judge it by the size of its image alone. (B) The moon illusion can be demonstrated in daylight. Stare at a bright light for 30 seconds. Look away. You will continue to see the light. If you then look at the sky, the image appears larger on the horizon than it does high in the sky. (From Julian E. Hochberg, *Perception.* © 1964. Reprinted by permission of Prentice-Hall, Inc., Englewood Cliffs, New Jersey.)

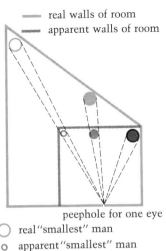

— real walls of room
— apparent walls of room

○ real "smallest" man
○ apparent "smallest" man
● real "medium" man
● apparent "medium" man
● "largest" man

peephole for one eye

4-15
The Ames room. When normal binocular cues of vision are removed, size constancy is eliminated. The Ames room removes all such cues, because it is viewed with one eye through a peephole. Actually the room has no right angles and the ceiling is higher on the left than on the right. Thus, the man on the left appears to be much smaller than the man on the right. Actually, all three men are the same height. (William Vandivert)

all contribute to a red object like an apple appearing red. The other set of factors is due to learning. We know that a given type of apple is red. Hence we judge it to be red even when it reflects no red light at all. If we used painted balls of various colors instead of red apples, our judgment of color would come much closer to the actual wavelengths of light reflected by the balls.

Vision and Hearing in Perspective

Vision and hearing are the most important *distance* senses we possess. (The human sense of smell, although very sensitive to odor quality, cannot locate the odorous object very well.) The senses of vision and hearing have played a vital role in the evolution of the human body and brain. Dinosaurs were visual animals—they were active by day and relied on vision to feed and hunt. Much of the information they needed about the distance and size of objects was analyzed in the eye rather than in the brain. Consequently, dinosaurs did not need large brains to respond effectively in a visual world.

Because dinosaurs ruled the day, the only safe period for the first mammals was night. The most useful distance sense at night is hearing. Consequently, those mammals that developed sensitive hearing mechanisms were able to survive. To survive, these early nocturnal mammals also needed to sharpen their ability to localize sounds in space. But such localizing ability required larger brains. The necessary comparison of input from two ears cannot be done at the level of the auditory receptors. It was at this period in the evolution of mammals that the ratio of brain weight to body weight jumped significantly.

Another example of the importance of the auditory system in evolution is the development of speech in humans. We had to develop large and specialized areas of the cerebral cortex to develop and use language. It is probable that language and the size and complexity of the human brain grew together.

The basic properties of vision and hearing are summarized in Table 4-1. As the table shows, obvious parallels can be found between hearing and vision, in terms of both the physical stimuli and our experience of them. Another surprising similarity exists between vision and hearing. If we calculate the total number of different lights we can discriminate on the basis of wavelength and amount of light, it comes to roughly 340,000. If we make the same calculation for all the different sounds we can discriminate on the basis of differences in frequency and intensity, it comes to roughly 340,000. Even though light and sound are very different, and our eyes and ears are obviously different, both systems are able to handle the same total number of different stimuli—they both have the same maximum information capacity. We do not yet know why this surprising observation is true. It probably reflects the underlying ability of the human brain to deal with sensory information.

Table 4-1   Summary of Vision and Hearing

Sense	Stimulus	Receptor Cell	Physical Property	Psychological Property
Vision	electromagnetic radiation	rods and cones in the retina	frequency or wavelength amplitude number of wavelengths	hue brightness saturation
Hearing	sound waves	hair cells in the cochlea	frequency amplitude waveform	pitch loudness timbre

Perception of Movement

The ability to detect movement is far more important to organisms than perception of stationary objects and scenes. Indeed, neither predator nor prey animals would survive long if they were not good at detecting movements. It is no accident that prey animals like the rabbit and deer have their eyes set far to the sides of their head; they can thus detect movements from behind as well as in front. If you have ever tried to sneak up on such an animal, you know that it can be done only if you move very slowly. Any sudden movement and they flee.

Simpler animals like the frog actually have movement perception coded in the eye itself. Nearly one-fourth of all the nerve cells conveying information from the frog's eye to its brain respond only to irregular movements of small dark objects. Lettvin, Maturana, McColloch, and Pitts, who discovered this remarkable fact in 1959, have termed these nerve cells from the eye "bug-detectors."

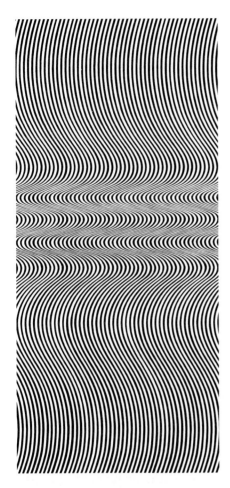

4-16

Apparent movement is the illusion of movement where none exists. Stare at this picture for a few seconds; the lines will appear to move. (Bridgett Riley. Collection, The Museum of Modern Art, New York. Philip Johnson Fund.)

In humans, coding of movement is done both at the eye and in the brain. Movement is of key importance in human visual perception. As one expert (Rushton, 1962) said:

Its (the eye's) purpose is not to fix a picture upon the retina, but rather to transmit in a code of nerve impulses the more dramatic features of the ever-changing retinal scene. Our rods and cones are 100 million reporters seeking "copy." That which continues unchanging is not "news" and nothing will induce them to report it.

Even more remarkably, it seems that movement of the visual image is necessary for perception in humans. The eye makes continuous small, rapid movements so that the image of the visual world is constantly jiggling. We do not perceive this as movement, of course. Riggs and his associates (1953) found a way to cancel out the effects of this jiggling. They put small mirrors on contact lenses and then presented visual stimuli to subjects by reflecting them off the eye mirrors onto a large screen. This technique was termed the *stabilized image,* because no matter where the subjects looked on the screen, the stimulus was projected to exactly the same place on the retina. Under these conditions, the stimuli—lines, geometric forms—rapidly vanished!

Humans and other higher animals have two types of perception of movement—perception of *real movement* and perception of *apparent movement.* In the case of real movement, there is a clear change in the energy flux or activation of different regions of the retina. If you are looking at a stationary object and a ball flies past, its image clearly will cross the retina. Conversely, if you follow the ball with your eyes, the background moves across the retina. In both cases, there is real movement of objects and thus real movement of images across the retina.

Real-movement perception could be explained simply in terms of changing patterns of light energy on the retina. However, central brain processes and perceptual events play a profound and important role in movement perception. This is best illustrated by perception of apparent movement. As we all know from seeing movies and TV, perception of apparent movement is a most believable experience. There is no real movement in a movie. A series of still pictures are flashed on the screen in rapid succession, and the movement is provided by our brain—that is, by our perception.

Illusions of apparent movement were first analyzed formally by Gestalt psychologists, who referred to the process as the *phi phenomenon.* The simplest example is two lights a short distance apart that flash alternately in rapid succession. This creates a powerful illusion that one light is actually moving from side to side. It is due entirely to the phi phenomenon that we can enjoy movies and TV.

Another intriguing form of apparent movement is the *autokinetic phenomenon.* If you stare at a small, dim pinpoint of light in a completely dark room for a few minutes, the light will appear to move about the room. The movements can be large and dramatic and the experience is quite eerie—you know the light is not really moving, and yet it is. This phenomenon has not yet been put to practical use, except perhaps by certain mystics who fixate on a small light during meditation. The auto-

kinetic phenomenon has been a source of real danger to pilots. During night flights in the early days of flying, navigational beacon lights seemed to move because of the autokinetic effect. This was dangerously disorienting to pilots until someone thought of a simple but effective solution. The steady beacon was replaced with a flashing light.

Eye movements have been shown to play a role in the autokinetic phenomenon. Matin and MacKinnon (1964) used the stabilized image technique and found a marked reduction in the extent of autokinetic movement. However, this is not the entire explanation. In classic experiments on the importance of suggestion in perception, Sherif (1936) had stooges suggest to subjects that the autokinetic light was moving in particular directions. Although the light was stationery, subjects experienced what was suggested to them. It is even possible for subjects to be instructed to see the light tracing out letters. These observations help to clarify the process of suggestibility as well. If subjects were asked to see a light move in a lighted room, where the autokinetic effect does not occur, they of course would not. Suggestion works best when the subjects cannot test the validity of the suggestion.

Sensory-Motor Integration and the Development of Perception

One fundamental question in psychology concerns the mechanisms through which we develop our complex, integrated perceptions of the external world. There are two extreme views of this question. One holds that perception is entirely the result of inborn factors—the genetic "programming" of the eye and the brain. The other view holds that perception is entirely learned.

In species below birds, most perception seems to be inborn. Birds show some completely predetermined perceptions and some perceptions that must be learned. A particularly clear example of *inborn perception* is the food pecking of newborn chicks studied by Fantz (1957). As soon as the chicks hatched, Fantz showed them a number of small objects of different shapes. The chicks pecked much more often at small spheres, the objects closely resembling the chicks' normal food, than they did at pyramids, flat discs, or other shapes of similar size. Evidently, newborn chicks with no previous visual experience have an innate perceptual preference for small, round shapes. They do not have to learn to select objects that are most likely to be edible.

Hess (1959) tried to alter young chicks' visual experience by fitting them with prism goggles. The prisms displaced the apparent location of objects a few degrees to one side. To get food grains, the chick would have to learn to peck a few degrees away from where the grains seemed to be. The chicks never learned. They went on pecking exactly where the object seemed to be. These innate perceptual-motor mechanisms seem very resistant to modification.

In higher organisms, such completely predetermined perceptual abilities do not seem to exist. Riesen (1950) demonstrated that if infant

4-17
A chick wearing prism goggles that shift its vision to the left. (Wallace Kirkland, *Life*) The top pattern of peck marks was made by a chick without goggles; the bottom one made by a chick wearing goggles that altered the location of the seedlike object. The chicks could not adapt to altered vision. (Eckhard H. Hess)

4-19
Two kittens, one relatively free and the other constrained in a gondola, were later tested for visual-motor coordination. Both kittens were raised in the dark except for their daily experiences in this experimental situation. The free kitten adapted easily to the visual world, but the gondola kitten reacted as though blind. (Held & Hein, 1963)

kittens can in fact be modified by experience. They raised kittens with goggles that had horizontal or vertical stripes. After some weeks, the goggles were removed and electrodes were implanted in the nerve cells of the kittens' visual cortexes. The kittens were then shown various objects, some striped vertically, some striped horizontally, and some without stripes at all. Using the electrical activity of the cortex as a measure of response, the researchers discovered that those kittens that had worn goggles with vertical stripes on the glass responded most to stimuli that were patterned with vertical stripes and those that had worn the horizontal goggles responded most to horizontally striped stimuli. Consequently, there does seem to be some important perceptual learning in the visual system during development.

Distorted Perception

It seems that our visual pathways and our visual cortex are not simply altered as we learn to perceive. We also learn to respond differently because of our total experience, including our transactions with the environment. Striking examples of this have come from experiments with goggles that invert or displace the visual world. Kohler (1962) performed an extensive series of such experiments. When his subjects first put on the goggles, the world looked rather displaced or else upside down and markedly distorted. The subjects were very clumsy and did poorly on even the simplest motor tasks. However, they showed amazing improvement. By the end of a month, subjects could bicycle, fence, and generally perform skilled visual-motor tasks almost as well as before. Interestingly, when the distorting goggles were permanently removed, the subjects again showed very poor visual-motor performance and had to relearn motor behaviors.

Does such a subject come to see an upside-down world as right side up? Is his learning limited simply to a reorganization of visual experience, or does he learn to respond appropriately to a now upside-down world? The latter seems to be the case. Held and Freedman (1963) did an experiment on human adults somewhat similar to Held's kitten study. The subjects wore prisms which displaced the visual world to one side. An active group of subjects walked about for several hours with the prisms on. A passive group, also wearing prisms, was pushed over the same route in wheelchairs. The subjects then were tested on simple visual-motor tasks involving locations of visual targets. The results were striking. The active group showed impressive and marked improvement on the task, but the passive group showed no improvement, even though they had experienced the same visual distortion and stimuli as the active group.

A consistent theme emerges from the studies of perceptual development and perceptual reorganization in higher animals and man: motor activity and movement are crucial. To develop normal perceptions of the world, we must respond *physically* to the world. Perception is sensory-motor integration, the development of appropriate responses to incoming sensory messages. Our experience of the world is due both to the pre-wired organization of our sensory receptors and brain, and to our actions. The process of perceptual learning is a lifelong process that involves learning to make the appropriate responses to this visual world.

Sensory Deprivation

For generations, shipwrecked sailors have told of floating for many days lost and alone on a raft in the ocean. Typically, these survivors have described bizarre sensations and hallucinations. The common factor in these experiences seems to be extreme boredom due to the absence of changing sensory stimulation. This has been termed *sensory deprivation.*

Heron (1957) undertook an extensive and systematic study of sensory deprivation. The subjects, volunteer male college students, were paid $20 a day to participate in the experiment. They were isolated in lighted cubicles, where they lay on comfortable beds for a minimum of 24 hours at a time. They wore translucent plastic visors which let in diffuse light but no pattern vision. Cotton gloves and cardboard cuffs extending beyond their fingertips restricted their touch perception. Their heads lay on rubber pillows. A continuous low hum masked any other sounds.

The experimenters carefully studied the subjects' verbal reports of their experiences, and also evaluated the effects of the sensory depriva-

4-20
In their studies at McGill University, Heron and his colleagues isolated subjects from all sensory stimulation. After a time, most subjects reported bizarre sensations, including hallucinations similar to those produced by mind-altering drugs. (From W. Heron. *The pathology of boredom.* Copyright © 1957 by Scientific American, Inc. All rights reserved.)

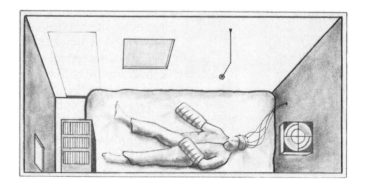

tion with three types of pre-tests and post-tests. One group of tests involved arithmetic, anagrams, and word associations. Another tested motor skills: copying designs, speed of copying a prose paragraph, substituting symbols for numbers, and simple concept tests like picking out the odd picture in a series of pictures. The third test was a form of brainwashing—a tape recording arguing strongly for the reality of ghosts and other supernatural phenomena. This was played both before and after sensory deprivation.

The experimenters found that the subjects' performances were significantly impaired on every test given. Performance after sensory deprivation was much poorer than that of a control group of students who took the tests twice without isolation. One significant result involved the brainwashing. When the tape arguing for the reality of ghosts was played to the subjects after sensory deprivation, they found it quite believable. Some of them reported that for several days after the experiment they were afraid of seeing ghosts.

The subjects' psychological experiences during sensory deprivation were remarkable. Their thoughts gradually changed. At first they tended to think about commonplace worries, such as grades and minor personal problems. After a while, they began to think more about past events—their families and close friends. To occupy their minds, some tried actively to think about things, such as remembering a movie in great detail. Some simply counted numbers, starting at one and going to many thousands. Eventually, some subjects reached a state where they found it too difficult to concentrate and think about anything and they just let their minds drift. One subject said, "My mind just became full of songs and colors and I could not control it." Several subjects experienced blank periods when they were not aware at all. All the subjects became markedly irritable as time went on. They lost their sense of perspective in terms of social behavior and began to behave in more and more childish ways.

Many of the subjects who were isolated for periods longer than 24 hours began to see images. One reportedly saw a vision of a rock shaded by a tree. Another kept seeing pictures of babies and could not get rid of them. Several subjects reported that they were having dreams while wide awake. These images were genuine hallucinations. One of the experimenters himself went through the experiment to verify this and reported that his hallucinations were clear, very colorful, and strange. They evidently resembled the hallucinations that occur under the influence of mind-altering drugs. The subjects' hallucinations usually began with simple forms—dots of light, lines, simple geometric patterns. Then they became more complex, resembling wallpaper designs, and finally integrated scenes, such as a procession of squirrels with sacks over their shoulders marching purposefully across the visual field; prehistoric animals roaming in a jungle; processions of eyeglasses walking down a street.

At first, the subjects were surprised and looked forward eagerly to what was going to happen next. The pictures alleviated their boredom. They described them as being much like movie cartoons. After a while, however, the pictures became so vivid and disturbing that they interfered with sleep. The subjects had no control over the content of their hallucinations. One saw nothing but dogs, another nothing but eyeglasses. Hallucinations were auditory as well as visual. Subjects heard talking and music. One man saw the sun rise over a church and heard a choir singing in full stereophonic sound.

The subjects reported many sensations that were vague and difficult to describe. Some spoke of feelings of otherness or bodily strangeness. One said, "My mind seemed to be a ball of cotton wool floating above my body." Another said, "Something seemed to be sucking my mind out through my eyes." After emerging from isolation, many of the subjects reported that things looked different. Near things looked large and far things looked small, in contrast to their normal perception of size constancy. Many objects looked curved. One of the most consistent aftereffects was that stationary objects seemed to be moving. When subjects emerged after several days of isolation, they reported that the whole room appeared to be in motion. These powerful hallucinations and distortions of perception occurred simply as a result of a relative absence of sensory input for a period of a few days and nights.

The experimenters also recorded the electrical activity of the subjects' brains, and found some changes during the period of sensory deprivation. The most noticeable was a gradual increase in the number of alpha and slower waves; the alpha waves also intensified and slowed a bit. This is strikingly similar to the brain-wave changes observed during transcendental meditation, as we will see in the next chapter.

A more extreme test of sensory isolation was developed by Lilly (1956). His subjects, wearing scuba equipment and dark goggles, drifted below the surface of a large tank of water at body temperature. Under these conditions, they had no sensations of light or bodily weight and no feeling of touch whatever. The only sensation was that of breathing. Lilly tried this himself many times and reported that after just a few minutes, he began to develop striking subjective feelings. He states that his experience resembled those reported by religious mystics; intense feelings of understanding and awareness.

These striking and profound effects of isolation or deprivation are not simply a curiosity—they are also a very real problem in the world today. Long-distance truck drivers and pilots on intercontinental flights quite commonly report the development of hallucinations as they sit at the wheel, numb with boredom. Their minds wander; they find it increasingly difficult to pay attention to the task at hand. To quote Heron:

A changing sensory environment seems essential for human beings. Without it, the brain ceases to function in an adequate way and abnormalities of behavior develop. In fact, as Christopher Birny reported in his remarkable account of his stay in solitary confinement, "variety is not the spice of life, it is the very stuff of it."

Summary

1. Perception refers to the way things look, sound, feel, taste, and smell. Perception, which depends on the physical nature of the objects, the way the subject's sensory receptors and brain systems work, and his

previous experiences, occurs when stimuli are coded into the language of nerve activity and processed by the brain.

2. Attention is our conscious focus on particular sensory information.

3. Selective listening experiments use the technique of simultaneously playing different spoken messages into each ear. These physical stimuli are identical in voice, volume, and tone; only the message content differs.

4. Norman's model of selective attention suggests that every incoming signal passes through the short-term memory storage system and is evaluated. If it is found to have significance and meaning, it is placed in long-term memory.

5. Physical and psychological dimensions of sound differ. Frequency corresponds to the number of cycles per second of the sound wave; pitch refers to our perception of how high or low it is. Intensity is the amplitude or size of the condensations and rarefactions in the sound wave; loudness refers to our perception of its strength.

6. The process of hearing begins when sound waves cause the eardrum to vibrate. The vibrations pass along the bones of the middle ear to the oval window membrane and then to the cochlea, where they are translated into neuronal activity.

7. Because sounds project to both sides of the brain almost equally, it is possible to determine the location of a sound by balancing the loudness of the sound at each ear (for high-pitched sounds) or by balancing the phase or maximum pressure of the sound at both ears (for low-pitched sounds).

8. Vision is accomplished through a system analogous to the camera. The eye has a lens to focus, a retina to serve as film, an iris resembling a diaphragm, and photosensitive chemicals or pigments.

9. The wavelengths of the visible spectrum are translated into colors in the retina. However, the eye perceives only a minute portion of the total electromagnetic spectrum—the range from 380 to 750 nanometers.

10. The rods and cones are the light-sensitive receptor cells on the retina at the back of the eye. Rods are found along the sides of the retina and are most sensitive in dim light. Cones are concentrated in the fovea of the retina and are responsible for color vision and vision in bright light.

11. The two major theories of color vision are the Young-Helmholtz theory, which assumes three types of color receptors (sensitive to red, green, and blue); and the Hering-Hurvich opponent-process theory which assumes that the neurons in the higher visual centers recode this initial response into opponent categories of red-green, blue-yellow, and black-white. Color vision evidently involves both of these processes. The retina does contain three types of color receptors. However, DeVaolois has shown that the visual nervous system functions in an opponent-process manner, as the Hering-Hurvich theory predicted.

12. Complementary colors are directly opposite each other on a color wheel; when combined, they produce grey. Psychological experience of an object's color relies on hue, saturation, and brightness.

13. Negative afterimages tend to be complementary. According to the opponent-process theory, the colored afterimage represents a rebound of the opponent color.

14. Maximum visual acuity occurs when an image is projected onto the center of the back of each eye, the fovea.

15. Because there are no receptors on the retina at the point where the optic nerve leaves the eye, a blind spot exists there. However, we perceive complete scenes because the brain somehow fills in the blind spot.

16. In form perception, the image is recorded as a whole and is then coded and transmitted through the visual nervous system from the eye to the cerebral cortex. Research suggests that a number of visual nerve cells exist for each kind of visual stimulus (such as curves and angles). Form perception is influenced by figure-ground relationships and our tendency to organize our visual field into meaningful patterns (grouping).

17. Two basic mechanisms allow us to experience depth perception: convergence or the inward turning of the eyes to focus on an object (a binocular cue), and accommodation or the muscular changes that focus the lens of the eye (a monocular cue).

18. Perceptual judgments of the constancy of an object's shape, size, or color rely on visual cues, learning, and physical stimulus conditions.

19. Two types of apparent movement are the phi phenomenon and the autokinetic phenomenon.

20. In lower animals, the ability to perceive shape, three-dimensionality, size, and distance seems to be inborn and very resistant to modification; in higher organisms, such completely predetermined perceptual ability does not seem to exist and learning plays an important role in perception.

21. Studies of perceptual development and perceptual reorganization in higher animals and man indicate that movement and motor learning, in addition to sensory learning, are crucial to the development of normal perceptions of the world.

22. Experiments in sensory deprivation show that when deprived of stimuli the subject's ability to perform simple intellectual and motor-skill tests decreases, he becomes susceptible to brainwashing, and he experiences hallucinations and strange feelings and sensations.

Important Terms

perception

attention

selective listening

limited channel capacity

pitch

frequency

intensity

hertz (Hz)

loudness

timbre

eardrum

hammer

anvil

stirrup

oval window

cochlea

hair cells

phase

lens

retina

iris

rhodopsin

iodopsin

rod

cone

fovea

visible spectrum

additive process

subtractive process

Young-Helmholtz theory

Hering-Hurvich opponent-process theory

saturation

hue

brightness

color solid

negative afterimage

binocular vision

visual acuity

dark adaptation

light adaptation

blind spot

figure-ground relationship

grouping

convergence

accommodation

monocular cues

shape constancy

size constancy

color constancy

apparent movement

phi phenomenon

autokinetic phenomenon

sensory deprivation

Suggested Readings

ALPERN, M., LAWRENCE, M., & WOLSK, D. *Sensory processes.* Belmont, California: Brooks/Cole, 1967.

> The authors describe a series of sensory experiments on animals using the latest tools in electrophysiology, biochemistry, and physics. They show how the results of these experiments can be applied to human sensation and perception.

BARTLEY, S. H. *Principles of perception.* New York: Harper & Row, 1969.

> The author attempts to develop a useful view of perception and to define it in a way that will best fit into a science of human behavior. He is also concerned with the relationship of perception to other

aspects of behavior, how it is dealt with in the laboratory, and its role in human social relations.

GELDARD, F. A. *The human senses*, 4th ed. New York: Wiley, 1972. A clear and comprehensive review of the human senses, structures and function of receptor systems and how translated into perseption.

GREGORY, R. L. *Eye and brain*. New York: McGraw-Hill, 1966. Introductory discussion of the psychology of seeing, including material on color, brightness, and illusions. Clearly written and well illustrated; an excellent overview of perceptual mechanisms.

HELD, R., & RICHARDS, W. (EDS.) *Perception: Mechanisms and models.* San Francisco: Freeman, 1972.

An up-to-date collection of articles, including authoritative research on the development of perceptual mechanisms, on the sensory systems, and on rules of perceptual organization.

HOCHBERG, J. *Perception*. Englewood Cliffs, N.J.: Prentice-Hall, 1965. A carefully illustrated monograph that begins with a discussion of the importance of the study of perception. The author then proceeds to develop specific topics, including how sensations are measured, the ways in which we perceive elementary events, and how objects are perceived as structures. A great deal of perceptual research is described.

MUELLER, C. G. *Sensory psychology*. Englewood Cliffs, N.J.: Prentice-Hall, 1965. The five senses, along with the kinesthetic sense, are described and explained from the standpoint of the stimuli for each sense and the manner of responses. In each case, the varied stimuli are studied in detail.

UTTAL, W. R. *The psychobiology of sensory coding.* New York: Harper & Row, 1973. Brilliant and fairly comprehensive analysis of the physical and neural basis of sensation and perception.

Chapter 5 States of Awareness

I had the greatest difficulty speaking coherently and my field of vision fluctuated and was distorted like the reflections in an amusement park mirror. I also had the impression that I was hardly moving, yet later my assistant told me that I was pedaling at a fast pace. So far as I can recollect, the height of the crisis was characterized by these symptoms: dizziness; visual distortion; the faces of those present appeared like grotesque colored masks; strong agitation alternating with paresis (partial motor paralysis); the head, body and extremities sometimes cold and numb; a metallic taste on the tongue; throat dry and shriveled; a feeling of suffocation; confusion alternating with a clear appreciation of the situation; at times standing outside myself as a neutral observer and hearing myself muttering jargon or screaming half madly.

Six hours after taking the drug (LSD), my condition had improved. The perceptual distortions were still present. Everything seemed to undulate and their proportions were distorted like the reflections on a choppy water surface. Everything was changing with unpleasant, predominantly poisonous green and blue color tones. With closed eyes multihued, metamorphosing fantastic images overwhelmed me. Especially noteworthy was the fact that sounds were transposed into visual sensations so that from each tone or noise a comparable colored picture was evoked changing in form and color kaleidoscopically.

—Albert Hofmann
(in *Drugs and Youth*)

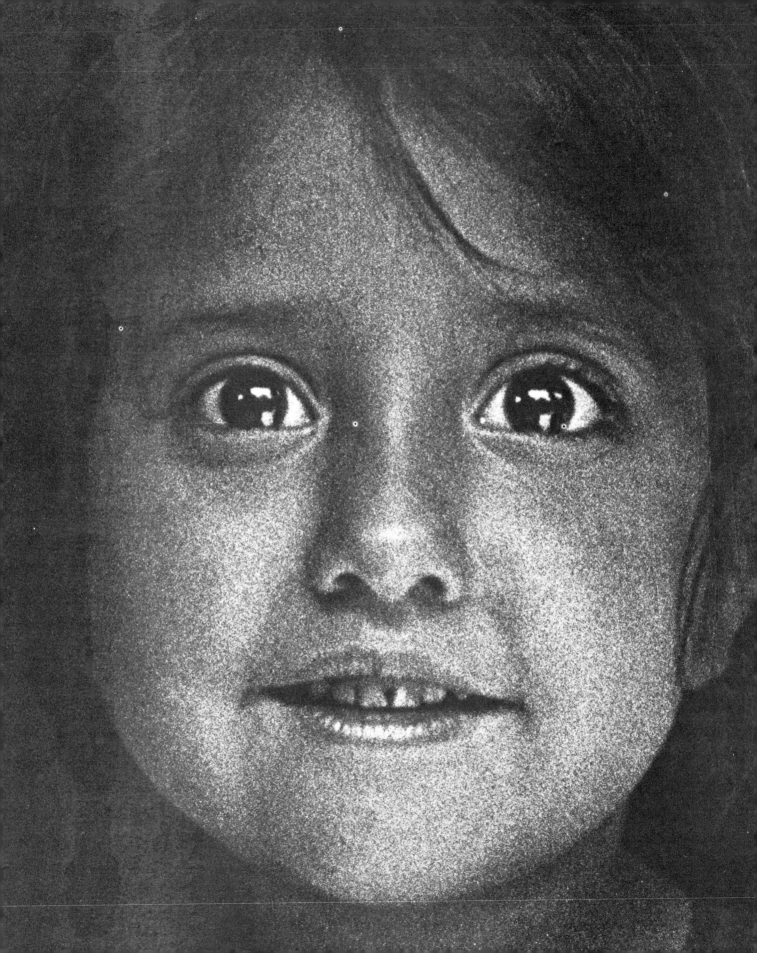

States of Awareness

Usually, we think of awareness as the sensory perception of the sights, sounds, and smells around us. But our awareness extends to many more perceptions. Any person who takes the time to look into himself will become aware, first, of a number of bodily sensations. He will notice the rhythm of his breathing and heartbeat, feel stomach movements, the saliva in his mouth, the texture and weight of his clothing, small aches, itches, perhaps even passing pains. Besides these physical sensations, the introspective person also becomes aware of vague emotions—drifts toward pleasure, irritation, or boredom. And, depending on his emotional makeup, an individual may be acutely or dimly aware of the passage of time, the future, his own mortality, the continuity of his awareness, and the essential separateness of his conscious self.

Though it is difficult for individuals to describe their self-awareness with any degree of precision, the sense of one's own being is nonetheless animated by a great warmth, immediacy, and richness. This complex, often poignant, perception of oneself is particularly evident in times of emotional fullness, as when making love or when feeling great sorrow. However, it is always present to some extent, even in the dullest, most ordinary moments of one's life. Psychology is just beginning to develop tools to observe and register these aspects of awareness. We still must rely in large part on verbal descriptions, supplemented by relatively simple recordings of heart rate, respiration, gland secretions, and the brain's overall electrical activity.

The familiar level of awareness is conscious thought. Even if a person sits quietly and becomes introspective, he is always thinking. Ideas, no matter how trivial, continually pass through his awareness. Most normal thinking, furthermore, appears to be accompanied by behavioral responses—whenever a person thinks, his tongue and throat muscles usually make small movements. If he is not actively thinking, he is probably daydreaming. The average person has about 200 daydreams every day (Singer, 1966).

Awareness, then, is the sum of everything that one can discover about one's experience at a given time. There is, of course, much more to a person than his immediate awareness. He also has innumerable memories—which are unconscious unless called forth by association or request—as well as many unconscious motivations and intentions. Together, these factors constitute a person's identity as a psychological being.

Sleep: A Natural State

We all know that our world is in continual flux. Furthermore, our own awareness of the world is not constant. We fluctuate from one state of awareness to another. Indeed, some states of awareness are not what most of us would refer to as being aware at all. While we are sleeping, for example, we are hardly aware of what is happening around us, but we are aware to some degree. Any loud noise or other abrupt stimulus will almost certainly awaken us. Even the meaning of a particular stimulus is important when we are asleep. While it may take a loud noise to awaken a normal, single adult, a new parent may be awakened by very small noises made by the baby. We are able somehow to evaluate the significance of stimuli even when asleep, and from time to time we are very much aware of dreaming. Dreaming as a special state of awareness is discussed in Chapter 9. Sleep does not block our awareness; it merely alters and lessens it. Other states of awareness can be induced by hypnosis, meditation, and drugs. Following our discussion of sleep, we shall examine each of these three states.

Biological Clocks

All higher animals exhibit 24-hour activity cycles; they are more active at certain times during the 24-hour period than at others. These biological rhythms are called *circadian rhythms* (circadian is Latin for "about a day"). Typically, predators are most active at night and sleep during the day. But some prey animals sleep at night and are active during the day. Primates, including man and other animals that rely on vision to guide their behavior, are more likely to be active in the daytime and asleep at night. Humans can adjust to sleeping during the day as well as during the night. However, anyone who has passed through several time zones while flying east or west knows how difficult it can be to change from one sleep schedule to another. This "jet lag" can be so debilitating that many corporations will not allow their executives to enter negotiations for at least 2 days after such a trip. At least a week is needed to adapt to major shifts in time zones. A complete shift in the 24-hour bodily temperature cycle, which is normally lower during the night than during the day, takes even longer. In a normal individual, the temperature cycle is closely associated with the sleep cycle. We sleep during the time of the 24-hour period when our temperature is at its lowest point, usually at night.

One of the greatest mysteries about sleep is that it occurs at all. It seems to be necessary—animals die and humans often experience bizarre hallucinations if kept awake for very long periods of time (Thompson, 1975)—but we do not understand why. The body consumes substantially the same energy in both the quiet waking and sleep states. No known poisons or toxins require sleep to be dissipated. There seems to be absolutely no reason why we should sleep, yet we must.

The Sleep States

All the higher mammals experience two sleep states. They are called *REM* (rapid eye movements) sleep and *NREM* (no rapid eye movements) sleep. (The REM state also is called D for dreaming, because dreaming was supposed to occur only during this state; the NREM state is called S for sleep.) While eye movements are the outward signs distinguishing REM sleep, there is, of course, more to it than simply eye movements. Associated changes in brain activity and muscle tension also occur (see Table 5-1). Sleep researchers have subdivided sleep into various other stages. Some of these represent transitions between the major states.

Before REM sleep was discovered accidentally by Aserinsky and Kleitman in 1953, scientists thought there were only two biological states—waking and sleeping. Dreaming was generally believed to occur only very briefly, when we were awakening. "State" implies a set of measurable events that occur together in a reliable pattern, making one state easily distinguishable from another. Some psychologists would argue that waking and sleeping and dreaming are simply a continuum of a single state, with a range reaching from "very responsive" to "very unresponsive." This is in part a quibble over words. In fact, we can distinguish the states of waking, REM sleep, and NREM sleep quite easily. Researchers have even been able to calculate the exact proportion of each night's sleep spent in each state. In particular, they have found that the proportion of REM sleep decreases from about 50 percent at birth to about 22 percent at age 4 or 5, and remains fairly constant thereafter.

REM Sleep and Brain Activity. When Aserinsky and Kleitman discovered REM sleep, they also discovered some interesting corresponding brain activity. As we discussed in Chapter 3, this activity is measured by the electroencephalogram (EEG), which monitors the brain's electrical signals at the scalp. The investigators found that a very character-

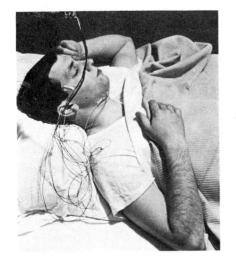

5-1
Subject wired to record the rates of brain waves, eye movements, breathing, and other physical functions during sleep. (National Institutes of Health)

Table 5-1 *Physiological Activities During Wakefulness and Sleep*

Behavioral State	Eye Movements	Neck Muscles	Finger Muscles	EEG
1. alert waking (eyes open)	present	active	active	arousal pattern (see Figure 5-2)
2. relaxed-drowsy waking (eyes closed)	absent	active	relaxed	alpha
3. NREM sleep	absent	active	relaxed	delta
4. REM sleep	present	relaxed	active	arousal pattern

5-2

Brain activity from the awake state through the stages of sleep originally identified by Dement and Kleitman. Stages 2 and 3 are transitions between 1 (REM) and 4 (NREM). (Dement, W. & Kleitman, N. The relation of eye movements during sleep to dream activity: An objective method for the study of dreaming. *Journal of Experimental Psychology*, 1957, **53**, 339–346. Copyright (1957) by the American Psychological Association. Reprinted by permission.)

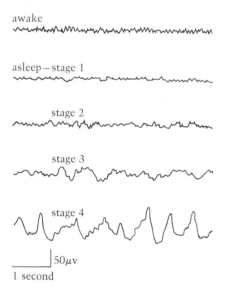

awake

asleep — stage 1

stage 2

stage 3

stage 4

|50μv

1 second

5-3

Graph of the amount of time spent in NREM and REM sleep as a function of age. As infants, we spend 50% of our sleeping hours in REM sleep. By the ages of 5 to 9 this proportion has dropped to about 18.5%. (Roffwarg, 1966)

istic EEG pattern of brain activity seemed to occur at the same time as the rapid eye movements.

During the alert waking state, EEG activity of the brain is rapid, irregular, and of small amplitude. This is called the arousal pattern — low-voltage, fast, brain EEG activity. The EEG pattern recorded from the scalp surface is generated by many millions of nerve cells in the brain. In the alert, waking state, the nerve cells seem to be functioning out of synchrony with each other — they are acting irregularly in time. Consequently, recordings of many millions of nerve cells show no clearly evident pattern, but a jumble of fast random activity.

In contrast, in the quiet resting state with eyes closed, a very clear and regular wave — the alpha wave — appears in the EEG. These fairly large amplitude waves occur at a rate of 8–12 per second and are very easy to detect in the EEG. Presumably, many millions of neurons are pulsing together in the brain to generate this regular wave pattern. The alpha pattern is characteristic of the normal resting-awake state.

In marked contrast, the brain activity in NREM sleep is characterized by the large, slow, irregular delta waves. Because of the marked difference between the NREM sleep state and waking, the NREM state has been called the slow-wave sleep state.

Aserinsky and Kleitman discovered to their surprise that when periods of rapid eye movements began, the EEG shifted abruptly from the slow-wave sleep pattern to the waking low-voltage, fast EEG. This continued as long as eye movements continued. At first they thought this occurred simply because the subject was beginning to wake up. However, they soon discovered that it was harder to wake the subject from this stage than from the slow-wave sleep state. This is why REM sleep has been termed *paradoxical sleep*. The EEG in REM sleep is that of an alert, awake person, yet the sleeper is difficult to awaken.

Other Characteristics of REM Sleep. REM sleep has a number of characteristics besides eye movements and brain activity. In NREM sleep, heart rate is slow and steady. However, in adult REM sleep it is highly irregular, ranging from 45 to 100 beats per minute. This rate is similar to that of normal waking when we are periodically engaged in vigorous

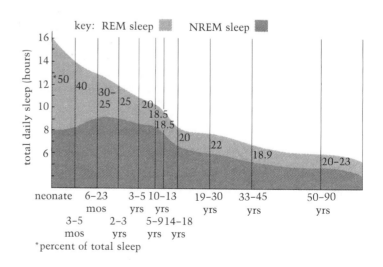

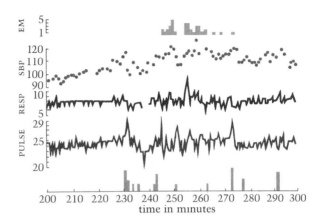

5-4

Twelve subjects were studied for a total of 30 nights of uninterrupted sleep by simultaneous recordings of their eye movements (EM), blood pressure (SBP), respiration, and pulse rate. The 100-minute sample shown here contains an interval — from 242 to 273 — that is considered to be REM sleep, even though eye movement is not continuous. The bar graph at the bottom indicates the occurrence of gross body movements. (Snyder, F., Hobson, J. A., Morrison, D. R., & Goldfrank, F. Changes in respiration, heart rate, and systolic blood pressure in human sleep. *Journal of Applied Physiology*, 1964, **19**, 417–422.)

activity. Similarly, the breathing rate is slow and regular in NREM sleep but highly variable and irregular in REM sleep. REM-sleep eye movements are conjugate; that is, the eyes move together, shifting rapidly every 1/20 of a second. The body musculature at the same time shows a general and marked reduction in tone. Neck muscles relax so much that the head flops over if it is not supported. In spite of the lowered muscle tension, characteristic jerks and twitches of the face, throat, hands, and feet occur during REM sleep.

Another characteristic of REM sleep, in the male, is the penile erection. Partial-to-complete erection occurs throughout each REM period, but not during NREM sleep. Yet REM sleep erection does not necessarily correlate in any way with sexual dream content. Erection occurs during REM sleep in infants as well as adults.

Sleep Deprivation. One of the most carefully studied cases of sleep deprivation was the case of Peter Tripp, a New York disc jockey who stayed awake for 200 hours. Luce and Segal (1966) describe his marathon graphically:

In 1959, New York City beheld one of the most disturbing ordeals a man can undergo. Day and night, while the public gathered in a spirit of carnival curiosity around a Times Square recruiting booth, a well-known disc jockey was staying awake for 200 hours to benefit the Polio Fund of the National Foundation. He looked weary, but no radio listener or casual onlooker could have imagined the truth of his experience. It resembled a medieval torture. . . . When Peter Tripp decided to forego sleep for over eight days, scientists tried to dissuade him from a courageous but risky undertaking. Tripp was determined. He set up broadcasting headquarters in a glass-walled Army recruiting booth in Times Square. Across the street in the Hotel Astor a suite was converted into a psychological laboratory. An impressive crew of psychologists, psychiatrists and medical specialists offered to participate under the direction of Louis Jolyon West, of Oklahoma, and Harold L. Williams, then of Walter Reed. A preliminary checkup and some baseline tests were made to establish Tripp's normal functions. Then a regular daily routine involved medical and psychological tests, including tests of mental ability. EEG recordings were to be made at Columbia University each day, and blood samples and urine collected and analyzed. For more than eight days Tripp was never away from the watchful care of doctors and nurses. He broadcast his regular program and a dozen spot comments on his progress from the booth, and every few hours he was escorted to the Hotel Astor laboratory where he could also clean up and change clothes. If there was any known safeguard to be obtained under the circumstances, Peter Tripp had it.

Almost from the first the overpowering force of sleepiness hit him. Constant company, walks, tests, broadcasts helped, but after about five days he needed a stimulant to keep going. Although his health was good and he stayed on a high-protein athletic diet, he soon remarked that he felt like "the last pill in the bottle." After little more than two days, as he changed shoes in the hotel, he pointed out to West a very interesting sight. There were cobwebs in his shoes—to his eyes, at least. West had warned him that he would have visual illusions. Specks on the table began to look like bugs. He thought he saw a rabbit in the booth. He was beginning to have trouble remembering things.

By 100 hours, only halfway, he had reached an inexorable turning point. Now he could perform only one or two of the daily battery of tests. Tests requiring attention or minimal mental agility had become unbearable to him and the psychologists testing him. As one later recalled, "Here was a competent New York disc jockey trying vainly to find his way through the alphabet." By 170 hours the tests were torture. A simple algebraic problem that Tripp had earlier solved with ease took such superhuman effort that he was frightened, and his agonized attempts to perform were painful to watch.

Loss of concentration and mental agility were not the worst, however. By 110 hours there were signs of delirium. As one of the doctors recalled, "We didn't know much about it at the time because he couldn't tell us." From his later statements, his curious utterances and behavior at the time, it became clear. Tripp's visual world had grown grotesque. A doctor walked into the recruiting booth in a tweed suit that Tripp saw as a suit of furry worms. A nurse appeared to drip saliva. A scientist's tie kept jumping. This was frightening, hard to explain, and sometimes Tripp grew angry wondering if this were a bona fide experiment or a masquerade. Around 120 hours, he opened a bureau drawer in the hotel and rushed out calling for help. It seemed to be spurting flames. Tripp thought the blaze had been set deliberately to test him. In order to explain to himself these hallucinations—which appeared quite real—he concocted rationalizations resembling the delusions of psychotic patients.

By about 150 hours he became disoriented, not realizing where he was, and wondering who he was. He developed a habit of glancing oddly at the large clock on the wall of the booth. As the doctors later found, the clock bore the features of an actor he knew, made up like Dracula for a television show. He began to wonder whether he was Peter Tripp or the actor whose face he saw on the clock. Still his teen-age admirers, radio audience, and onlookers would not have guessed his torment.

Sometimes he would back up against a wall and let nobody walk behind him. Yet from 5 to 8 P.M. all his forces were mysteriously summoned, and he efficiently organized his commercials and records and managed a vigorous patter for three hours. Although he had passed the breaking point, he never made careless indiscretions, profanities, or the kind of impulsive utterances he made when off the air. His broadcast time occurred at the peak of his diurnal temperature cycle. It was later, when his temperature was low, that he showed the worst symptoms. Although he managed to act awake continuously, his brain waves were like those of deep sleep.

On the final morning of the final day a famous neurologist arrived to examine him. The doctor carried an umbrella although it was a bright day, and had a somewhat archaic manner of dress. To Tripp he must have appeared funereal. He always insisted that patients undress and lie down on the examining table. Tripp complied, but as he gazed up at the doctor he came to the morbid conclusion that the man was actually an undertaker, there for the purpose of burying him alive. With this gruesome insight, Tripp leapt for the door with several doctors in pursuit. Nightmare hallucination had merged with reality, and the only explanation seemed to be that the doctors had formed a sadistic conspiracy in which he was the victim.

With some persuasion, Tripp managed to get through the day, give his final broadcast, and then, following an hour of tests, he sank into sleep for 13 hours. When he awakened, the terrors, ghoulish illusions, and mental agony had vanished. He no longer saw a visual world where objects changed size, specks turned into bugs, and clocks bore human faces. Now it was no effort to remember a joke and solve simple problems. In 13 hours that unspeakable purgatory had vanished, although a slight depression lingered for three months. The strain and publicity had probably contributed to the ordeal, but it had been a valuable one for research. (Reprinted by permission of Coward, McCann & Geoghegan, Inc. from Sleep *by Gay Gaer Luce and Julius Segal. Copyright © 1966 by Gay Gaer Luce and Julius Segal.)*

Peter Tripp's experiences and symptoms are similar to those reported by many people who have stayed awake for long periods. Although there are no modern documented cases of death from sleeplessness, medieval historians describe executions being done simply by forcing the victims to remain awake. Similarly, forced wakefulness is an essential element of the process known as brainwashing. After a certain point is reached, the victim genuinely cannot distinguish dreaming from reality and may be convinced he is dreaming when he signs a "confession."

In sum, the effects of sleep deprivation are devastating, both in terms of behavior and experience, and in terms of physiology.

REM and NREM Deprivation. One of the familiar effects of sleep deprivation is that when the deprived person is finally permitted to sleep without interruption, he sleeps for a longer time than he normally does. Suppose, however, that he is deprived only of REM sleep by awakening him every time his eyes begin to move. This procedure has two interesting consequences. First, the time between REM periods during the night decreases markedly. In some cases, a person has to be awakened every few minutes because his eyes begin to move shortly after he falls back to sleep. A second consequence is that when a person is allowed to sleep without interruption throughout the night after several nights of REM deprivation, the amount of time the eyes move during the night of uninterrupted sleep is greatly increased over the normal amount. This is known as the *rebound effect*. A similar rebound effect is observed when a person is deprived of NREM sleep. Apparently, we not only have a need to sleep; we also have a need to spend a fixed amount of the sleep period in REM sleep and NREM sleep. For if either the amount of REM or NREM sleep is reduced, we will make up for it on succeeding nights.

Hypnosis

Hypnosis has fascinated people for many years. This phenomenon — the production of a temporary trance-like state — seems to exert very powerful control over behavior. For a long time a subject in a hypnotic trance was thought to be in a different physiological state. Demonstrations by a stage hypnotist might lead you to agree. For example, a hypnotized person, told that he is as rigid as a slab of steel, can lie with his head on one chair and his feet on another. His muscular control seems quite different from that of the waking state. However, in recent years, careful physiological measurements of hypnotized persons have indicated that brain activity (the EEG) and all other physiological measurements, such as respiration and heart rate, seem to be typical of the normal waking state. Thus, hypnosis appears to be a variation of the normal waking state.

5-5
At the suggestion of the stage hypnotist, a subject can be induced to assume an absolutely rigid position. (The Bettmann Archive)

Hypnotic Suggestion

In recent years, research on the nature of hypnosis (Hilgard, 1965, 1970) has isolated two characteristics of the hypnotic state. The first is *suggestibility*. Unless the hypnotized subject is told to behave in a certain way, he does nothing; he remains passive. However, when he is told to perform a particular act, he bends all his attention to this one task. While people normally are somewhat suggestible, suggestibility apparently increases very notably in the hypnotic state. A hypnotist can suggest to a subject that he is a small child and he will behave like one. He can suggest that a small, friendly dog is standing before the subject, and he will pet and play with the nonexistent animal.

Hypnosis may be followed by a second characteristic effect called *posthypnotic amnesia*. Hypnotized subjects who are told that they will not remember the events that occur during the hypnotic state later have substantially poorer memories of those events than hypnotized subjects who are not told that they will forget the events.

Hypnotic suggestion can dramatically and profoundly affect both the subject's behavior and his experiences. One psychiatric case history illustrates the point. A man sought help because whenever he went out at night he was pursued by a giant black dog. Every time he turned a corner, he saw the dog creeping after him. Since the dog never actually attacked him, he was not sure the dog was real. However, he was becoming very sure that he was losing his mind. Upon questioning, it turned out that the patient had served as a subject for a stage hypnotist a few months before. The stage hypnotist had suggested to the patient that he was being pursued by a ferocious black dog. The patient ran all over the stage in an attempt to escape from the dog, greatly amusing the audience. At the end of the trance session, the hypnotist suggested that he would forget all about the experience. At the time he sought help, the patient had no recollection of the trance state or the suggestions of the hypnotist. He remembered only that he had gone to the performance. But the hypnotic "experience" of the large black dog apparently stayed with him.

Hypnosis and Pain

Another striking phenomenon of hypnosis is its apparent power to render a person incapable of feeling pain. Since pain is perhaps our most compelling subjective experience, this is a most remarkable power. Under hypnosis, a subject will sit calmly and permit the demonstrator to repeatedly penetrate his skin with needles. The subject will show no sign of discomfort whatever and may later report no awareness of the experience. Again, this kind of effect would seem to argue that hypnosis is a different physiological state. However, careful studies of the characteristic physiological responses accompanying painful stimuli indicate otherwise. In one such study, experimental subjects were placed in a hypnotic trance and given moderately painful stimuli (Barber, 1963, 1971). Physiological measurements such as heart rate, respiration, and sweating of the palms, the so-called *galvanic skin response* (GSR), were recorded. Control subjects who were given the same painful stimuli

5-6
Police departments throughout the country have recently discovered hypnosis as a valuable aid in solving criminal cases. Under hypnosis, a witness of a crime, whose descriptions of events often become distorted, generally will remember and report the events more accurately. (Ron Sherman)

displayed physiological responses substantially greater than the hypnotized subjects. However, a third group, unhypnotized and each paid a sum of money not to respond to the painful stimuli, showed responses exactly equivalent to those of the hypnotized subjects.

In this experiment, the hypnotized subject's behavior was changed, but the change was no more than could be produced by providing a normal, unhypnotized subject with a strong incentive to cooperate. The major difference is that when a hypnotized subject is told that he will feel no pain and that he will not remember the pain stimuli, he does not report the pain when questioned later. This reliance on the subject's reports is the central difficulty in measuring a person's subjective awareness directly. If he in fact reports no perception of pain, there are several possibilities. Did he in fact perceive the pain and then forget it, did he not perceive it, or did he perceive it and remember it but not report it? Today we have no way to answer this question directly. We know that he perceived the pain at some level because during the occurrence of the pain stimuli he exhibited physiological responses—increased heart rate and respiration and sweating of the palms. However, his awareness may have been altered at the time. Certainly his memory seems to have been altered later. Whatever the basic mechanism, the apparent absence of both the awareness and the memory of pain has very practical applications. In dentistry, hypnosis is widely used for minor surgical procedures that would otherwise be quite painful. Hypnosis also is used in obstetrics to make possible "painless" deliveries. Undoubtedly, other applications will be developed in the future.

Hypnotic Susceptibility

Many people think of hypnosis as an almost magical phenomenon in which a hypnotist with a strong personality "casts a spell" over the subject. All that is actually required to induce hypnosis is a cooperative subject. The most common technique of hypnosis is to repeat monotonous statements—for example, tell the subject he is becoming relaxed and sleepy over and over again. Hilgard has developed a *hypnotic susceptibility scale,* which indicates the degree to which hypnosis can be induced in a given subject (see Table 5-2). A hypnotist or investigator suggests to the hypnotized subject the various behaviors in sequence: first postural sway, then eye closure, and so on down the list to the amnesia test, at which point the subject is instructed not to recall what has happened during the trance. If the subject meets the criteria through item 9 (if he tries to brush an imaginary fly away), he is given a passing score on the scale.

Hilgard and his colleagues tested normal college students who had never before undergone hypnosis. As the distribution of scores, shows, most subjects scored above 4—they passed the first 4 items, but no more. Only a few subjects passed all 12 during the first session. With repetition, most subjects will progress further up the scale. Hilgard found in a study of over 500 university students that only about one-quarter of the students could reach item 12, posthypnotic amnesia. Fewer than 10 percent exhibit posthypnotic visual hallucinations with eyes open. Hilgard concludes that hypnosis apparently is influenced by early childhood experiences.

Interviews with hundreds of subjects, before and after induction of hypnosis, have pointed to the importance of early childhood experiences. Experiences of a particular kind appear to either generate or maintain the abilities that enter into hypnotizability. (Hilgard, 1970)

A capacity to become deeply involved in imaginative experiences derives from parents who are themselves deeply involved in such areas as reading, music, religion, or the esthetic appreciation of nature. Another experience leading to hypnotizability is rather severe punishment in childhood. The conjecture is that a history of punishment may produce hypnotizability in either (or both) of two ways: first, through instilling a habit of automatic and unquestioned obedience; second, through a tendency to escape the harassment by moving off into a realm of imagination, thus practicing the dissociations that are later to be used in hypnosis. (Morgan, Davert, & Hilgard, 1970)

5-7

Graph showing the behavior of subjects under hypnosis for the first time. As Table 5–2 indicates, there are twelve tasks that a readily hypnotizable subject should be able to perform. The largest group of subjects had a score of 4; very few subjects obtained a high score of 12. Thus, of 533 subjects, only 22 were totally susceptible to hypnosis. (© 1965 by Harcourt Brace Jovanovich, Inc. and reproduced with their permission. From Ernest R. Hilgard, *Hypnotic Susceptibility*.)

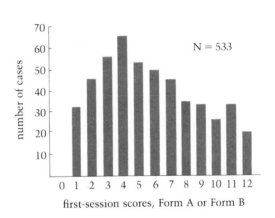

Table 5-2   Items of the Stanford Hypnotic Susceptibility Scale, Form A

Suggested Behavior	Criterion of Passing
1. Postural sway—"You are falling over"	Falls without forcing
2. Eye closure—"Your eyelids are getting heavy"	Closes eyes without forcing
3. Hand lowering (left)	Lowers at least six inches by end of 10 seconds
4. Immobilization (right arm)—"You cannot move your arm"	Arm rises less than one inch in 10 seconds
5. Finger lock—"You cannot separate your hands"	Incomplete separation of fingers at end of 10 seconds
6. Arm rigidity (left arm)	Less than two inches of arm bending in 10 seconds
7. Hands moving together	Hands at least as close as six inches after 10 seconds
8. Verbal inhibition (name)—"You cannot say your name"	Name unspoken in 10 seconds
9. Hallucination (fly)	Any movement, grimacing, acknowledgment of effect
10. Eye catalepsy—"You cannot stop yourself from blinking"	Eyes remain closed at end of 10 seconds
11. Posthypnotic (changes chairs)	Any partial movement response
12. Amnesia test	Three or fewer items recalled

Reprinted with permission of the publishers from the *Stanford Hypnotic Susceptibility Scale,* Forms A and B, by Andre M. Weitzenhoffer and Ernest R. Hilgard (Stanford: Stanford University Press, 1959; distributed by Consulting Psychologists Press) p. 27.

HYPNOSIS

Martin T. Orne *Institution of Pennsylvania Hospital and University of Pennsylvania*

Under hypnosis, some subjects seem able to experience the world as it is suggested to them—they see, hear and feel what is told to them, apparently oblivious to other stimuli; they can forget what has happened or remember what has not occurred.

Ever since this phenomenon was first described by the Marquis de Puysegur, one of Mesmer's students, controversy has persisted about the effects, the nature, and even the very existence of hypnosis.

Thanks largely to the way hypnosis has been depicted in fiction and presented by stage magicians, most people think of it as a means of controlling behavior. However, systematic studies have shown that all items of behavior carried out by deeply hypnotized individuals can also be elicited from nonhypnotized control groups. I often illustrate this point in the context of a lecture by asking students to carry out a number of mildly embarrassing, nonsensical requests such as giving me their wallet, taking off their left shoe, and so on. After these tasks have been carried out, I asked if they had been hypnotized, and they correctly answer, "Of course not." I can then point out to observers that if these same students had been hypnotized first and then carried out the very same behaviors, they would have said, "Oh, they did that *because* they were hypnotized." Of course, the students had merely been cooperative, assuming—correctly, I hope—that some legitimate reason for these peculiar requests would ultimately emerge.

If the subject's willingness to do what is demanded of him does not characterize hypnosis, what does? Again try a simple experiment. Consider the hippopotamus—no doubt you have seen one at the zoo. Think about the hippopotamus. Now try to forget it. Try very hard. You will note that the harder you try, the less likely you are to succeed. However, a deeply hypnotized individual can forget with ease, although most of us usually find it almost impossible to "will" forgetting. What characterizes hypnosis, then, is not the hypnotist's control over a subject's behavior but rather the subject's potential to alter his or her subjective experiences in accordance with the suggestions of the hypnotist. What makes hypnosis unusual is not the behaviors that subjects can be induced to carry out but rather the changes in subjective experience that seem to be reflected by these behaviors.

Let's look at one of the many striking and fascinating hypnotic phenomena—suggested age regression. A deeply hypnotized person, told that he is 6 years old, will begin to behave like a 6-year-old. Typically, he will print in an unmistakably childlike fashion rather than write. His tone of voice, his mien, and even his movements will resemble a child's. His performance is so convincing that many observers readily accept the regression as genuine. Because of age regression's implications for cognitive psychology in general and memory and development in particular, and because of its clinical importance in psychotherapy, investigators have sought to document this effect in a number of careful studies.

Among the most compelling findings were studies showing that the Babinski reflex (extension and fanning of the toes in response to stimulation of the sole of the foot), which is characteristic of early infancy, could be reinstated in subjects who were age-regressed to that period (Gildro-Frank & Bowers-Buch, 1948) and studies that showed performance on both intelligence tests and projective tests (such as the Rorschach) characteristic of actual children at the age to which hypnotized subjects

A

Original drawings done at age 6.

B

Drawings done while subject was "regressed" for the first time.

had been regressed (Spiegel, Shor, & Fischman, 1945). A particularly influential study (Reiff & Scheerer, 1959) used Piaget-type tasks (for example, matching the lengths of two lines; see Chapter 14) to assess the level of cognitive development in age-regressed subjects and employed, as a comparison group, others who were simply instructed to play-act. These experiments showed that hypnotized individuals could perform the Piaget-type tasks as actual children would perform them, while role-players could not. Perhaps the simplest and therefore most striking demonstration involved regressing subjects back to their birthdays at ages 10, 7, and 4, and asking them the day of the week. Hypnotized individuals performed at far better than the chance rate on this task, whereas others did not (True, 1949).

These studies seemed to prove that age regression involves almost miraculous changes, suggesting that all information once available to consciousness remains somehow stored and available if we can but learn to unlock the filing system. However, further research, which threw a dif-

ferent light on these findings, illustrates the immense problems confronting the scientist seeking an objective explanation of subjective events. For example, it is true that the Babinski reflex usually reflects either an organic injury in adults or an immature nervous system, but some adults suffering from hysteria display a reaction resembling the Babinski reflex. Furthermore, the subjects in the Gildro-Frank and Bowers-Buch study were medical students and nurses whose training gave them ample opportunity to learn how and at what age the Babinski reflex changes. Because of the erroneous assumption that the change in the Babinski reflex was necessarily beyond an individual's volitional control, the experimenters had not employed a control group.

The Reiff and Scheerer study was particularly instructive. On closer examination, it became apparent that those experimenters knew which subjects were play acting and the subjects instructed to play-act knew that the experimenters were aware of their status. In an extended replication, a minor but crucial variation of

the original Reiff and Scheerer experiment was introduced. In addition to play-acting subjects, another group of unhypnotizable subjects was asked to "fake" hypnosis for a hypnotist who did not know which subjects would be faking. These subjects realized they could succeed in their task of deceiving the hypnotist—and they did! On the particular tests employed, the performance of the faking subjects was indistinguishable from that of deeply hypnotized individuals. Not only is it likely that Reiff and Scheerer treated subjects they knew to be hypnotized differently from their play-acting controls, but play-acting subjects behaved differently from subjects who were faking for a hypnotist who they knew was unaware of their true status. This difference seems to account for most of the reported findings.

A particularly interesting aspect of the replication was the inclusion of groups of actual children. To everyone's surprise, their behavior was entirely different from that of either the hypnotized subjects or those who were faking (O'Connell, Shor, & Orne, 1970). For example, in a seem-

C

Two weeks later: "Regressed" for the second time.

D

Drawings in "regression" after seeing originals in awake state for the first time.

E

Drawings in "regression" done after awakening and repeated showing of the originals in awake state.

F

Drawing executed in awake state imagining how he might have drawn at the age of 6.

ingly ingenious procedure, Reiff and Scheerer had their subjects make mudpies while they were regressed to age 4. After their hands were caked with mud, the subjects were offered a lollipop, which the experimenter held by the stick. The hypnotized subjects were willing to grasp the candy part with muddy hands while role-players insisted on taking their lollipop by the proper end. In the replication, both the subjects who were faking—without the experimenter's knowledge—and the truly hypnotized subjects put their hands on the candy before placing it in their mouths. However, when actual 4-year-old children were tested, they all insisted on taking the lollipop by the stick—much to the surprise of the experimenters!

The study involving the identification of the day of the week on which the 10th, 7th, and 4th birthdays fell is perhaps the most difficult to understand. Several investigators tried unsuccessfully to replicate it; yet their failure did not explain the reported findings. The answer finally emerged in a personal communication with the author of the original study. He indicated that an editor had shortened his published paper and that it was important that

subjects be asked, "Is it Monday?" "Is it Tuesday?" "Is it Wednesday?" Further inquiry revealed that during the experiment, the hypnotist knew the correct answer since he had a perpetual calendar before him. One explanation might be that the experimenter had inadvertently communicated the correct answer to the hypnotized subjects. Further analysis of the published data showed that the subjects while regressed to age 4 reported the day of the week almost as accurately as when they were regressed to age 7. However, checks with real children show that, when asked what day it is, hardly any 4-year-olds can correctly name the day of the week while almost all 7-year-olds can. This strongly supports the likelihood that those original findings had been due to the experimenter's inadvertent bias.

This situation illustrates the issues confronting the investigator hoping to understand hypnosis. First, he is impressed with dramatic effects only to find with truly careful study that the apparent changes are largely illusory or within the behavioral repertoire of normal waking individuals. Not surprisingly, skeptics have from the very beginning raised questions about the reality of hypnosis.

When a nonscientist observes hypnotic age regression and asks if it is real, he is asking two different questions. First, is the subject actually like a child and does he accurately remember events that occurred when he was 6 years old? Second, does the subject really feel like a child? Is he really deluded into thinking he is a child, and not merely "putting me on" and consciously making believe? The answer to the first question is for the most part "no," the hypnotized person's mental processes remain those of an adult. While his memory may be somewhat improved, especially for traumatic, emotionally charged events, it is not otherwise different in kind. However, the answer to the second question is a resounding "yes." The deeply hypnotized subject is deluded; he does at the time believe he is a child; and his behavior cannot be explained as simply conscious play-acting.

It is paradoxical that some of the most compelling evidence for the genuineness of hypnotic age regression emerges from some of the obvious inconsistencies seen in subjects' behavior. For example, an individual regressed to age 6 printed in a typical childlike fashion but in perfect spelling: "I'm conducting an experi-

G
Drawing in "regression" after originals were shown during hypnosis.

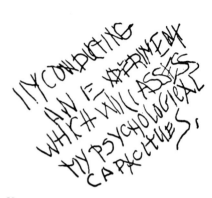

H
Dictation written in "regressed" state.

ment which will assess my psychological capacities." Even more dramatic, a German-American subject who spoke English well but who had not learned English by age 6 replied to my question, "Do you speak English?" in his native German, "Nein" (no). When asked, again in English, if he understood any English at all, he reiterated, "Nein." When asked whether his parents spoke English, his answer was "Ja. Damit ich's nicht verstehe." (Yes. So I won't understand). I rephrased the question 10 times in English and each time received an appropriate response in German, clearly indicating that he understood while his verbal assertions maintained that he could not understand. No subject who is play-acting is sufficiently careless or naive not to recognize the blatant inconsistency in such behavior. Indeed, we have observed that in this sense subjects simulating hypnosis do a more "believable" job than those actually hypnotized. Yet this very inconsistency is typical of the hypnotized individual; it is an honest behavioral reflection of altered experiences rather than the consequence of a subject's thinking about how to behave correctly.

While hypnotic age regression cannot miracuously reverse psychological or physiological changes brought about by aging any more than it can cause an individual to shrink in size, it does produce profound experiential changes that often can be useful in the course of psychotherapy. Traumatic events that are so painful they are pushed out of consciousness while still exerting important effects on the individual can be brought to consciousness so that the person can deal with them. Other important therapeutic applications of hypnosis range from controlling pain to mobilizing the patient's motivation to help him accomplish difficult goals.

Research has shown that individuals differ widely in their ability to enter hypnosis. As we noted, the hypnotist does not directly control the subject's behavior; rather, through mechanisms closely related to fantasy and imagery, he can alter the subject's experience. The extent of the subject's response depends more on his desires and skill than on the hypnotist's ability. With a willing subject, hypnosis requires no special technical skill. Certainly, an ability to hypnotize people does not qualify an individual as a therapist. Hypnosis is a technique to be em-

ployed by trained therapists. As such, it should be used only by individuals who have broad therapeutic training and are equally competent with other therapies.

Even more important than the present-day therapeutic use of hypnosis may be the lessons hypnosis can teach us about the nature of man. Preeminently, hypnosis illustrates the difficulty inherent in the objective study of subjective events. The investigator needs to avoid both an irrational belief in magic and an equally irrational skepticism that may lead him to deny events merely because he finds them difficult to understand.

Finally, hypnosis is a uniquely human phenomenon that can teach us much about human potentialities. When we can understand adequately why some individuals have the capacity to be hypnotized while others do not, why such simple procedures as hypnotic induction can produce such profound changes, and how imagination can be temporarily stimulated to override sensory experience, we may better understand the mechanisms responsible for much of psychopathology as well as for some of man's artistic achievements.

Hypnosis: What Is It?

There is no doubt that a subject under hypnosis behaves differently. Subjects have undergone surgical procedures ranging from tooth extraction to amputation of an arm with no more anesthetic than hypnosis and afterward reported no discomfort or pain, although they exhibit the normal physiological responses to pain. Is hypnosis a separate state of awareness? We really cannot answer this question yet.

Meditation and Religious Experience

All human cultures from the very dawn of history have valued the mystical or religious experience. Man always seems to be searching for some form of higher consciousness or awareness. Certain Indian tribes in the American Southwest chew cactus peyote or mushrooms—which contain mind-altering drugs—to produce a kind of religious ecstasy. The Yogis of India and the Zen Buddhists in the Orient are famous for their mystical experiences. But the mystical experience is not limited to remote regions or primitive cultures. Mysticism has been a very common element in Western Christian civilization. Dramatic examples abound in the history of the early Christian martyrs. William James wrote a most interesting book on the mystical experiences of Christians called *The Varieties of Religious Experience.* All such experiences share one trait: they cannot be described very well in words. When such descriptions are attempted, they almost always are peppered with terms that denote something indescribable, such as "ineffable." These descriptions also usually contain many adjectives indicating joy or extremely positive and powerful emotions. Unfortunately, very little scientific study of religious ecstasy has been done. One reason is that the feelings cannot be generated on command. However, one form of semireligious experience that has become widespread in recent years can be done at will. It is called *meditation.*

Transcendental Meditation

Thérèse Brosée, a French cardiologist, conducted one of the most interesting studies of meditation among Yogis. She took a portable electrocardiograph to India in 1935 and recorded the remarkable finding that one subject made his heart stop completely. This dramatic observation has not been repeated, nor has the Yogi been subsequently tested (or seen again!). In more recent and extensive tests with newer equipment, no Yogi has been found who could stop his heart completely. However, all the Yogis studied have been able to induce marked changes in many physiological responses. They can, for example, slow both their heart and respiration rates.

In earlier days, many years of training were thought necessary before a person could achieve the proper state of meditation. But in recent years, thanks to the teachings of Maharishi Mahesh Yogi and others, a form of meditation has become very popular. The procedure for *transcendental meditation* is simple. The subject sits quietly in a comfortable position

In some forms of meditation, subjects achieve a state of relaxation during which they generate alpha waves. By concentrating on a musical tone that sounds when alpha waves are produced, the people shown here are learning to control their alpha rhythm. This technique is known as alpha feedback training. (Aquarius Electronics)

with his eyes closed. He attends to a pleasant-sounding word or phrase and, without attempting to concentrate specifically or think logically, allows his mind to wander through the thought and to experience it freely, meanwhile attempting to relax as much as possible. Those who practice transcendental meditation maintain that their thoughts reach a more developed and more creative level in an easy and natural manner.

Unlike hypnosis, where physiological measurements indicate no change from the normal waking state, some changes from the normal waking condition clearly occur during transcendental meditation. These changes are all in the direction of a slowing down of normal physiological processes—the kinds of changes that accompany reduction of tension and anxiety. Subjective reports about meditation are difficult to quantify or analyze, but the subjects seem to find the experience relaxing and restful. One study (Dickman, 1963), devoted to the personal experiences of the subjects, reported that most subjects said the time spent in meditation seemed shorter than it was. They also reported some alterations in perception. When they were asked to observe a blue vase fixedly, the vase seemed both to fill the visual field and not to fill it—perception of the vase was conflicting and changing. At the same time, other external stimuli attracted less attention than they normally would. Apparently, extraneous stimuli were being blocked out. Finally, subjects reported that meditation was a strongly pleasurable experience, very rewarding and reinforcing.

Biofeedback. EEG alpha rhythm intensifies during transcendental mediation. And as we noted in Chapter 3, alpha feedback machines also are used to "turn on" alpha waves. But it is not clear that subjects using these feedback machines have in fact achieved a shortcut method of transcendental meditation. However, both transcendental meditation and alpha feedback training seem to increase alpha waves, and subjective reports suggest that in both cases the subject is pleasantly relaxed when the alpha rhythm is intensified. This is not particularly surprising, since alpha activity is normally associated with a relaxed and slightly drowsy state.

MEDITATION

Gary E. Schwartz *Harvard University*

In recent years, the practice of meditation has been introduced into Western societies as a legitimate and effective aid to human health. Proponents of meditation claim that its regular practice can profoundly affect human consciousness, personality, and general well-being. Maharishi Mahesh Yogi, the founder of Transcendental Meditation (TM), believes that TM can make its practitioners happier, more relaxed, less aggressive, better able to cope with stress, more alert, and more fulfilled. Despite personal accounts of teachers and practitioners of meditation, very little scientific research has been done to test the claims of TM. Given the theoretical as well as the clinical importance of such claims, our challenge is to try to evaluate and understand them.

What is meditation? All meditation practices share at least one component—sustained self-regulation of attention—but the manner of controlling attention varies greatly. Some practices are *passive*, taking place in a quiet, relaxed manner. In certain forms of Zen meditation, the practitioner simply breaths in and out for twenty to thirty minutes without making any conscious attempt to control his breathing. In TM, the practitioner quietly attends to the sounds of a *mantra* that he repeats silently to himself. (A mantra is one of many Sanskrit words selected by the teacher of meditation.) Other meditation techniques are very *active* and highly *concentrated*, sometimes requiring strenuous effort to hold the object in one's attention. In this class are certain Yoga techniques which require the person to maintain specific postures and to deliberately manipulate aspects of his breathing or other bodily functions. These techniques have physiological correlates very different from those of passive meditation.

Since much of our present knowledge is based on the passive-relaxation types of meditation, we shall discuss meditation in terms of these techniques.

Words seem inadequate to describe the changes in consciousness that occur in meditation. Many reports are couched in religious or spiritual terms alien to Western culture and science. Nonetheless, we can see some common threads running through all the reports. The Zen monk's ultimate state is *satori* or "enlightenment." *Satori* is described as a state of "nothingness," a complete quieting of mind and body—yet practitioners say that a person in this state feels a complete "oneness" with his experience. Distinctions between subjective and objective, person and thing, mind and body are replaced by total awareness. Erich Fromm writes about the experience of Zen:

He who awakens is open and responsive to the world, and he can be open and responsive because he has given up holding onto himself as a thing, and thus has become empty and ready to receive. To be enlightened means the full awakening of the total personality. (Fromm, Suzuki, & de Martino, 1960)

Similar experiences are claimed by those practicing TM. During meditation one "transcends" normal consciousness, going beyond the act of thinking to arrive at the source of the thought—a state of pure awareness; of nothingness. As a result, practitioners say, one experiences the world directly and profoundly, yet one is relaxed and peaceful. In his poem, *Four Quartets*, T. S. Eliot employs a metaphor more common to Western experience:

Music heard so deeply
That it is not heard at all, but you
are the music
While the music lasts

How does such an experience arise? Most practitioners of passive techniques meditate in quiet, serene settings. They direct their attention inward toward their breathing, or toward a pleasant-sounding word or phrase that they repeat for twenty or thirty minutes. By focusing their attention in this way, they block distracting thoughts or feelings. Whenever problems or images threaten to attract the meditator's attention, he again quietly focuses on his breathing or *mantra*. With time, he retains in his consciousness only the desired object of attention. However, as Ornstein (1971) points out, repetition may remove even this stimulus by the process of habituation—leaving the awareness of *nothing* or "pure consciousness." While most of us have had our minds "go blank," this usually occurs accidentally and is not desired. However, practitioners of TM deliberately cultivate this kind of experience as an attentional skill and value it highly.

Achieving a prolonged state of mental and physical "nothingness" is not easy; it requires a great deal of practice. Complicating the task is the fact that in the initial stages of relaxation, people commonly experience *increases* in imagery, and sometimes even hallucinations and delusions. Research on sensory isolation tells us that as we reduce levels of external stimulation, spontaneous internal stimulation normally increases. However, the sensory isolation experiments differ from meditation in a number of important respects. The person who takes up meditation (1) voluntarily *seeks* the situation and the resulting experiences, (2) *expects* the outcome to be positive and valuable, (3) has some *prior knowledge* as to what will happen, and (4) has particular *tasks* to perform in the situation. Our present understanding of the phenomenon is thus made more difficult, since we must take into account many ingredients, including set (expectation) and suggestion. Clearly, more research is needed to identify the combinations of factors that produce positive meditation experiences.

Studies of Zen meditation in Japan and TM in America have reported marked decreases in several physiological systems, including heart rate and blood pressure, lactic acid in the blood (high lactic acid has been associated with anxiety), respiration rate, and general body metabolism. While the EEG activity superficially resembles a drowsy state and the decrease in body metabolism (about 20 percent) actually is greater than that typically found during sleep, the meditators claim to be awake and alert. This finding led Wallace (1970) to classify passive meditation as a unique "fourth state of consciousness"—distinct from waking, sleeping, and dreaming. Benson has renamed this pattern of responses the "relaxation response." He reports that subjects who simply attend passively to their breathing while sitting quietly and saying the word "one" after each breath (an English substitute for a mantra,) can bring about large decreases in their body metabolism (Berry & Benson, 1974).

A number of studies have reported personality and health changes with TM. Benson and Wallace (1972) found that, with the regular practice of TM, meditators can reduce or eliminate their use of drugs (including cigarettes), and they claim to be generally healthier. Benson suggests that individuals with essential hypertension (high blood pressure) can reduce this affliction by using TM as a relaxation technique (Benson, Rosner, & Marzetta, 1973). Other studies suggest that TM increases "self-actualization," as measured by the Personal Orientation Inventory, showing increases in the subjects' capacity for intimate contact, self-regard, and spontaneity. Schwartz and Goleman (in Schwartz, 1973) observed that meditators are less anxious and appear less neurotic, as measured by Eysenck's Personality Inventory; they also are less extraverted and aggressive. To date, such drug, personality, and health findings are quite consistent with the clinical literature that interrelates these variables, thus supporting some of the claims made for TM. However, many of these studies are surveys and do not control for important variables such as expectancy and self-selection. In fact, Otis (1974) claims that some of the positive meditation results are inflated because only those people who are motivated and find the experience rewarding continue to meditate and are measured; the studies do not account for all those who have abandoned meditation as unsatisfactory.

Despite its apparent simplicity, passive meditation poses a fascinating paradox. Subjectively, the meditator claims to be more alert and responsive to outside stimuli (colors seen more vivid after meditation, for example) while being more relaxed, less bothered by outside stresses! This split between perceptual awareness and emotional responsiveness is evident at the physiological level. Studies of meditation suggest that EEG responses to auditory and visual stimuli habituate very little or not at all, while sweat-gland responses actually habituate faster. In his 1974 book, *Psychophysiology of Zen*, Hirai calls this state "relaxed awareness." In America, Goleman and Schwartz (in Schwartz, 1974) describe this state more explicitly as increased cortical arousability plus decreased subcortical or limbic reactivity—although they point out that even this is an oversimplification. Goleman and Schwartz also note that the strength of this response pattern will vary, depending on the conditions under which the person meditates. For example, when subjects meditated in anticipation of watching a stressful movie, the response pattern was markedly accentuated; meditators were more cortically vigilant in preparation for the stress, yet at the same time they were relaxed emotionally.

The claim that TM increases "creative intelligence" is probably the most controversial. By creative intelligence, the Maharishi does not mean an enhanced ability to produce creative products or raise IQ; instead, he describes it as a more global change in one's perceptions of the world and other people, as well as better choices of activity. Creativity and intelligence are both difficult to define and measure. Some evidence indicates that meditation as well as other relaxation procedures, such as deep muscle relaxation, can improve a person's performance on specific intellectual tasks, particularly if the test subject had been anxious previously.

Should we conclude that relaxation is the most adaptive state for all kinds of activities? Basic research on physiology and human performance indicates that too much or too little arousal can lead to inferior performance; each person doing a given task appears to have an optimal level of arousal. Schwartz (1973) has obtained data suggesting that teachers of meditation show enhanced creativity on tasks whose performance benefits from low arousal; yet performances by those subjects hold steady or decline on other creative tasks best performed under higher levels of arousal. We can expect that investigations of the effective use of meditation and relaxation training for education will be a significant area of psychological research for years to come.

5-9
Standard biofeedback techniques may be used to detect emotions. Electrodes are implanted on four facial muscles, and the signals are passed to an oscilloscope screen for interpretation. Subjects are first asked to try to express a certain emotion with their facial muscles and then to think sad or happy thoughts without expressing them facially. A comparison of the two tests enables the experimenter to determine the emotion being felt, whether or not it is expressed. Recent applications of this as yet unperfected technique, called facial electromyography, include the checking of progress of clinically depressed patients receiving drugs. Eventually, such biofeedback may be used to treat such patients, who are often unwilling to communicate with the doctor. (Newsweek, 1974)

In recent years, the general topic of *biofeedback* has evoked a great deal of interest. Learning to control one's own alpha rhythm is one example of biofeedback. The basic concept of biofeedback is simple. If a person can observe in himself some biological event of which he is not normally aware—such as the presence of alpha rhythm in his brain activity—then he can be trained to modify that event. The subject may be trained to produce more alpha rhythm and perhaps thereby induce the state of relaxed awareness associated with alpha activity. This apparent capability is in itself interesting. Its significance grows in the light of some possible applications of biofeedback training. A person with high blood pressure might be trained to alleviate his condition. You will recall that in the state of transcendental meditation, many processes *are* slowed down. Equipped with monitors that showed him the state of these physiological indices, an individual might be able to control them even more effectively. Such research—called *biocybernetics*—is in its infancy. We are just beginning to provide interactive systems between man and computer in which the computer can immediately analyze and feed back to the subject the state of his own physiology, particularly his brain activity. Someday, through computers interacting with human subjects, we may be able to increase effectively man's awareness far beyond anything now achieved. Science fiction? Several years ago few people would believe that a person could learn to control his own brain waves.

Drugs

A drug is any chemical substance that affects humans and other animals. We shall discuss drugs that have particularly strong influences on awareness, experience, and behavior. The study of such drugs is called *psychopharmacology*. It is a study of growing importance as drug use, whether for medical or nonmedical reasons, increases steadily, especially in the developed countries. We can classify drugs in many ways. We can group them according to chemical structure, the way they act on an organism's physiology, or the effects they have on experience or behavior. Most pharmacology texts classify psychopharmacological agents by their specific effects on experience and behavior. Thus, some drugs are called *sedatives* or *hypnotics* because they have a calming or tranquilizing effect. Others are called *stimulants* because they accelerate physiological activity; and still others are called *psychotomimetics* because they induce psychoticlike effects. A few major drug categories and typical actions are shown in Table 5-4 on p. 168. We will discuss several of these but we will emphasize the drugs that strongly affect behavior and awareness. (For more information on the drugs discussed in this section, see Goodman & Gilman, 1970, and Julien, 1975.)

Sedatives and Hypnotics

Barbiturates, a widely used family of sedatives and hypnotics, are general depressants; in larger doses they act as general *anesthetics,* sub-

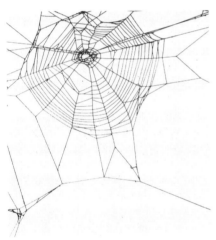

5-10
Phenobarbital was administered to an adult female spider. At the top is shown the normal delicate web spun by this spider; the web at the bottom shows the effects of phenobarbital on her web-spinning ability. (UPI)

stances that relieve pain. However, unlike most general anesthetics, barbiturates block consciousness first and then pain perception. For a patient to gain a significant anesthetic effect from a barbiturate, he must be given enough of the drug to render him unconscious. In smaller doses barbiturates are widely used as a relaxant for patients about to undergo surgery and as sleeping pills. *Sodium pentathol,* the so-called truth serum, is an interesting barbiturate. The right dose of this drug produces a kind of twilight state in which the drugged individual responds as though he were hypnotized. He will answer questions and describe events and feelings, yet have no memory of the experience afterward. Most barbiturates have this effect, to some extent.

There are several commonly available barbiturates: *nembutal*— "yellow jacket" on the street; *seconal*—called "redbird" on the street; and the "purple hearts," *phenobarbital* and *amobarbital.* Nembutal and seconal are short-lived depressants; phenobarbital, amobarbital, and other barbiturates have longer and stronger effects.

Barbiturates relax nerves and muscles. They slow muscle responses and depress the nervous system. Medically prescribed doses generally are enough to relax the user and to put him to sleep. Higher doses, such as those taken by addicts, cause enormous depression, slurred speech, staggering, and other loss of coordination. Memory and thinking are severely impaired, and confusion and even amnesia may result. Accidental death from unintentional overdose—which must be very large—is common among barbiturate addicts (see Table 5-3). The chronic user may be quarrelsome, irritable, and short tempered; he often acts as though he were drunk.

If barbiturates generally depress all functions, why are they such a common street drug? There are two reasons. First, as with all anesthetic agents, the initial reaction to a barbiturate is a period of excitation. The person who takes a heavy "goofball" dose often experiences a strong "high" on the way to oblivion. Second, a barbiturate's general depressant effects seem to reverse in the strongly addicted user after long and repeated use. Instead of slowing down and sleeping, the addict reports feeling calm, "away," or high. He claims he can cope better with his problems, and he feels more alive. At this stage the user is already strongly addicted to barbiturates. Barbiturates hold another danger. They have a strong effect when taken with alcohol. One barbiturate pill and one drink of whiskey have a much more potent depressing effect than two of either alone. This effect is termed *drug potentiation.* Often one drug will augment the effects of another.

Withdrawal from barbiturates may produce symptoms that are more severe than those of heroin. Sudden withdrawal often kills the addict. Withdrawal symptoms usually appear in this sequence: severe cramps, nausea, and convulsions, followed by delirium, dizziness, and extreme anxiety. Assuming gradual withdrawal, it still takes several months to withdraw an addict to the point where he no longer has a physiological craving for the drug.

Tolerance to barbiturates can be built up to high levels. But the development of tolerance varies with the dose employed, the frequency of that dose, and the length of time the drug effects endure (Hug, 1972). Nonetheless, many addicts take as many as 50 sleeping pills a day to ob-

Table 5-3   Comparison of Drug-Related Suicides to Total Number of Suicides[a]

		Percentage of Total Suicides	Percentage of Drug Suicides
Total No. of Suicides (1963)	20,819[b]		
No. related to barbiturates	1,997	10%	75%
No. related to nonbarbiturate sedatives (e.g. Miltown)	243	1%	11%
No. related to minor tranquilizers	64	.3%	3%
No. related to morphine and other opiates	7	.03%	.3%
Miscellaneous			10.7%

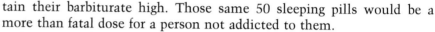

Source: Berger, F. M. Drugs and suicide in the United States. *Clin. Pharmacol. Ther.,* 1967, **8**, 219–223.
[a] Note that death due to drugs is often the result of accidental overdose. The number of such deaths has risen steadily. For example, in Santa Clara, California there were 10 in 1968–69, 26 in 1969–70, 30 in 1970–71, and 46 in 1971–72 (Finkle, 1972).
[b] This number is four times larger than the number in 1953 (Richman & Orlaw, 1965).

5-11
Alcoholism is the most serious drug problem in the United States and throughout the world. (Kay Lawson, Rapho Guillumette; Henri Cartier-Bresson)

tain their barbiturate high. Those same 50 sleeping pills would be a more than fatal dose for a person not addicted to them.

The terms tolerance and addiction are often confused. *Tolerance* simply means that when a drug is taken repeatedly, progressively larger doses are necessary to produce the same effect. The patient or street user develops a tolerance to the drug's actions. Tolerance is developed to many drugs—morphine and barbiturates, for example—but not to all drugs. *Addiction* has several meanings, all relating to increased need or use of drugs. At a behavioral level, addiction means that the person (or animal—mammals all seem to develop quite similar addictions to certain drugs like heroin, amphetamine, and cocaine) takes it repeatedly and has difficulty kicking the habit. Addiction also refers to the occurrence of withdrawal effects when use of a drug is stopped. Interestingly, not all drugs that show marked tolerance are addicting. LSD, for example, has pronounced tolerance effects but does not appear to be addicting.

Barbiturates tend to reduce the percentage of the night spent in REM sleep and dreaming. On nights after an addict's abrupt withdrawal, a REM sleep rebound effect occurs. He spends a much higher than normal percentage of the night in REM sleep, with a high incidence of nightmares.

Alcohol is another general sedative. It is, of course, the most widely used of all sedatives and, contrary to popular opinion, is the most dangerous drug in widespread use in society today—when it is judged by its deleterious effects on human behavior. Several million Americans are alcohol addicts. This number may increase dramatically as more and more teenagers turn from drugs to alcohol. National surveys show that 14 percent of all high school seniors get drunk at least once a week; on a smaller scale, 60 percent of all New York City teenagers use alcohol (Nemy, 1974).

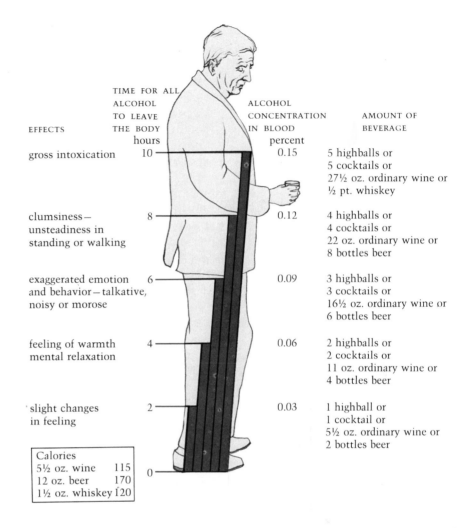

5-12
Diagram showing alcohol levels in the blood after drinks of whiskey taken on an empty stomach by a 150-lb. person. (Dr. Leon Greenberg, chart by W. Hortens, *Time*, 1974)

EFFECTS	TIME FOR ALL ALCOHOL TO LEAVE THE BODY hours	ALCOHOL CONCENTRATION IN BLOOD percent	AMOUNT OF BEVERAGE
gross intoxication	10	0.15	5 highballs or 5 cocktails or 27½ oz. ordinary wine or ½ pt. whiskey
clumsiness— unsteadiness in standing or walking	8	0.12	4 highballs or 4 cocktails or 22 oz. ordinary wine or 8 bottles beer
exaggerated emotion and behavior—talkative, noisy or morose	6	0.09	3 highballs or 3 cocktails or 16½ oz. ordinary wine or 6 bottles beer
feeling of warmth mental relaxation	4	0.06	2 highballs or 2 cocktails or 11 oz. ordinary wine or 4 bottles beer
slight changes in feeling	2	0.03	1 highball or 1 cocktail or 5½ oz. ordinary wine or 2 bottles beer
	0		

Calories
5½ oz. wine 115
12 oz. beer 170
1½ oz. whiskey 120

When alcohol addicts attempt to "go on the wagon," they find that alcohol withdrawal symptoms are severe, somewhat resembling those of barbiturates. Despite the serious risks attached to drinking, our culture condones the use of alcohol—partly because Western culture has used alcohol as a social relaxant for thousands of years. Because of this long usage and because most people can drink within reason, we tend to forget that this congenial sedative can produce shattering addiction in many individuals. Chapter 21 contains a more detailed discussion of alcoholism and its effects.

Narcotics

The *opium alkaloids* are among the oldest drugs. For centuries, they have been used to relieve pain. The pain caused by chronic ills ranging from toothache to terminal cancer may be relieved by *morphine*. When morphine was first introduced as a medical aid, physicians hailed it as a great advance because of its effective pain-relieving properties. They prescribed it widely. As physicians increased their use of morphine, addiction grew in their patients. When this was discovered, morphine use became much more selective and careful. It matters very little if a patient with terminal cancer is severely addicted to morphine. In fact, one might say so much the better, as long as his pain is relieved. However, prescribing repeated doses of morphine for relatively minor pain is quite a different matter.

Morphine is derived from the *opium* poppy. Opium itself has been known from antiquity; it was first used in China about 2000 BC. In the Orient, it was usually smoked, mixed with tobacco. Morphine, an early product of modern chemistry, was isolated from crude opium plant products in about 1804. During the 19th century in the United States, addiction to both opium and morphine became widespread. Most people did not realize that virtually all of the patent medicines, the "snake oil" sold by the traveling medicine man, were composed mainly of opium or morphine. Patent medicine users from teenagers to the elderly became opium addicts. Fortunately, addiction is less severe when the drugs are eaten or drunk rather than injected. Injection was introduced in about 1853 when the syringe was invented. From this time on, severe cases of morphine addiction developed in the Western world.

<u>Heroin</u> is made from morphine. Ironically, the name heroin derives from the Greek god Heros who was the "savior of mankind." When first discovered, heroin was used enthusiastically as a cure for morphine and opium addiction. A few months later, physicians realized their error. They found that heroin not only causes further addiction; its addictive properties are three times stronger than morphine's (The Drug Abuse Survey Project, 1972).

Of all drug dependencies, heroin addiction is probably the most difficult to break and to cure. First, many addicts die from overdoses, some of them intentional. Second, the addict always "mainlines" the drug (injects it directly into a vein), often developing either local infections from unsterile needles, or hepatitis—sometimes fatal—from introducing a dirty needle into his bloodstream. Third, a heroin addict does not eat regularly and many develop severe malnutrition, which can be fatal. Thus, while heroin's direct effect, when given in proper doses, is not by itself physically damaging, its side effects and the final addiction are frequently fatal.

How does heroin affect the user? In normal dosages, it does not produce illusions or hallucinations. Instead, it produces an intense feeling of pleasure, particularly when the heroin is mainlined (injected). Though the sensation seems difficult to describe, it is often reported to resemble a prolonged orgasm. Heroin does have a remarkable effect on perception of pain and response to it—this *analgesic* effect is the reason the drug in the form of morphine has been so widely used in medicine. The major effect is not so much to raise the pain threshold as to change the response to pain—heroin makes pain bearable. Similarly, the person under the influence of heroin does not seem to be bothered by tensions and anxieties.

In the United States, heroin addiction began in the slums and ghettos. Now it is widespread in both the slums and suburbs. Why does a normal healthy person become addicted to heroin? There is no simple answer—as the following quotes from "What Everyone Needs to Know about

5-13
Opium is derived from the poppy plant (Paparer somniferum). Poppies, such as the one shown here, are grown in India, Turkey, and parts of Mexico, Egypt, China, and Russia.

Drugs" (*U.S. News & World Report*, 1970) show. A 17-year-old former addict describes his reasons:

I just wasn't doing anything. Life was kind of meaningless, aimless. Everyday was just there. I wasn't actively involved in anything and I wasn't really enjoying anything. The way I see it, the people who are into drugs, nothing holds their interest and there's no real meaning for them so this is what they get to.

This youth was from a wealthy suburban subculture. However, the reasons he gives—nothing much to hold his interest, nothing to aim for, nothing to do—seem to be exactly the ghetto youth's reasons for turning to heroin. The drug provides a stimulant, a change, an excitement, in an otherwise dull and hopeless life. Another motivation, of course, is the strong kick that occurs with heroin injection.

The kids (that take drugs regularly) are mostly looking for adventure. They got most of what they want and they are looking for something else. It's just this thing they hear about, these groovy highs, and they want to experiment. It seems as if there is just something in heroin, something that gets into your veins the first time you do it and even if it's not a physical addiction, there's just a calling that's in you once you do it.
I thought I could handle it.

One ex-addict says, "Don't start. Heroin may be dynamite stuff but you can't beat it. Nobody beats it. Horse is king and you'll end up its slave."
Addicts will go to almost any extreme to inject heroin:

They'll shoot dope anywhere they can get it, an abandoned house, an old car; they'll use a dirty spike, anything to get the drug in the vein. If they don't have a spike, they'll bum one from someone else. It doesn't matter if its rusty. And they know what dirty spikes can do. A rusty needle—it'll pull your skin in as soon as an abscess, then you lose an arm or a hand because your skin rots away, but it just doesn't seem to matter.
Some people have deep veins. They may try coke needles (long needles used for shooting cocaine), but if that doesn't work they'll shoot some place else. The same thing happens to guys who use it for a long time. Their veins sink down and they can't hit them. I've seen guys take an hour or more trying to hit a vein. Some so frustrated they start crying. But once the arm veins are gone they'll shoot some place else. Where? In the neck, the legs, under the fingernails, anywhere.

Some people do overcome their heroin addiction. A young woman who kicked the habit "cold turkey"—without medication—describes how she felt:

It's like a terrible case of flu. Your joints move involuntarily. That's where the phrase "kick the habit" comes from. You jerk and twitch and you just can't control it. You throw up. You can't control your bowels either and this goes on for four or five days and afterwards, for fifteen days afterwards, you can't sleep and you're gagging all the time and you cough up blood, because if you're on drugs, you don't eat and that's all there is to cough up.

Addiction

Why are addicting drugs so habit-forming? We really do not know, but addiction is not hard to spot. As the user repeatedly takes any addictive drug, he gradually needs more and more of the drug to produce the same effect. A severe addict may take fifty times the initial dose, enough to kill a person who is not addicted. As we indicated, a patient severely addicted to any one of the addicting drugs—heroin, barbiturates, alcohol—has severe withdrawal symptoms which may be fatal. One general theory attempting to explain drug addiction is called the *hypersensitivity theory*. This theory rests on a basic fact: Whatever effect a drug has will appear in opposite form during withdrawal. For example, if stomach contractions are diminished by a drug, they will become abnormally strong and produce severe stomach cramps during withdrawal. Amphetamine, a drug we shall discuss later, produces a sense of euphoria and well-being, a strong "high." During amphetamine withdrawal, the patient becomes severely and even suicidally depressed.

How this reversal effect comes about can be illustrated by the effects of a drug at a nerve synapse (see the Appendix to Chapter 3). Suppose that a given type of excitatory nerve synapses on the heart and acts to sustain a normal heart rate—that is, the synapse releases a chemical transmitter substance regularly to keep the heart beating at its usual rate. Suppose now that we are given a drug like a barbiturate which tends to slow the heart. The drug acts at this synapse to partially block or decrease the effect of the nerve on the heart. The heart rate will slow down. However, the brain and body will strive to counter the effect of the drug; that is, they will attempt to raise the heart rate to the normal level. They can do this by increasing the amount of chemical transmitter substance released at the excitatory synapse. If the drug is taken often and repeatedly by an addicted person, the synapse will stabilize at a new and much increased level of activity to maintain a normal heartbeat. It now releases much more of the chemical transmitter substance all the time. If the drug is now stopped, the synapse will continue releasing more than the normal amount of chemical transmitter for a considerable period of time, perhaps even for several days. Consequently, the heart rate will be much higher than normal and an abnormally fast heartbeat will be one of the symptoms of withdrawal. The hypersensitivity theory accounts very nicely for the opposite effects that occur when undergoing withdrawal from the drug. Indeed, we can predict the withdrawal symptoms of addicting drugs quite accurately merely by observing the effects of the drug itself. All these effects will be reversed during withdrawal.

Another approach to the possible mechanisms underlying drug addiction relates to the notion that the brain has strong positive pleasure centers. The experience that mainliners report on the injection of heroin resembles, in many ways, reports from patients who have received electrical stimulation in these pleasure centers of the brain. It is almost as though the drug acts directly on the pleasure centers. Although many addicts describe heroin's "kick" as somewhat like an orgasm, it is more like a general but strong pleasure feeling than a sexual orgasm. An intense feeling of pleasure is the way addicts consistently describe it. Similarly, that is the only way patients who have received electrical stimulation in the pleasure centers can describe their experience. They want it, it's great, it's a kick, they want more. Severely addicting drugs may somehow act on the brain's basic or primary need and reward system. Because of this pleasure reward system in the brains of vertebrates, addiction becomes possible. When we fully understand the physiological basis of pleasure and reward, we also may understand the basis of drug addiction.

Stimulants

Many varieties of drugs are classified as *stimulants*. Even *strychnine*, although a deadly poison, can be used as a stimulant, if taken in extremely small amounts. In the 19th century, strychnine and opium were combined to make a common ingredient in patent medicines. The smallest pinch of strychnine will affect the nervous system because it blocks an inhibitory transmitter substance from being released by certain synapses in the brain. This inhibitory transmitter substance normally prevents the brain from becoming overactive. Thus strychnine allows the nervous system to run away with itself. We see the extreme form of this malfunction in strychnine poisoning; the brain goes into severe seizures, resembling extreme epilepsy, which produces convulsions and death.

At the opposite extreme within the stimulant class are the very mild drugs used widely in our society. We hardly think of them as drugs: caffeine, which is found in coffee, tea, and cocoa; and nicotine in tobacco. One cup of coffee contains about 1/5 gram of caffeine, a large enough dose to produce noticeable stimulation. However, caffeine's effect is relatively mild. It increases motor activation and wakefulness, preventing drowsiness and fatigue, but seems to have few or no side effects for most people.

Between the deadly strychnine and the harmless caffeine lie a number of potent stimulants the effects of which depend on how they are used. *Cocaine*, one of the first local anesthetics, is one of these stimulants. In the mountains of South America, this drug can be found in high concentrations in the leaves of the coca bush. For many centuries, the natives living in the Peruvian Andes have eaten coca leaves. They eat them not because of their local anesthetic properties, but because, like most local anesthetics, cocaine also acts as a stimulant to the central nervous system, producing a sense of well-being.

The natives of Peru consume several million pounds of cocaine-bearing leaves each year. In the United States, cocaine addiction was widespread around the turn of the century and then became relatively rare. With the emergence of the drug subculture in the 1960s, cocaine addiction again became common in this country. Cocaine in its pure state is a white, flaky substance—hence its street name, "snow." Addicts take it by sniffing it or by mainlining it. Sometimes they mix it with heroin and inject this combination, called "speedball." Repeated mainlining of cocaine usually results in addiction. The same is true of Novocain (procaine hydrochloride), a local anesthetic that is a synthetic substitute for cocaine.

Sigmund Freud did the first detailed studies of cocaine, both as a local anesthetic and as a stimulant to the central nervous system. In one case, Freud successfully used the drug to break a colleague's morphine addiction. He was too successful. He converted the man from a morphine addict into a cocaine addict.

Freud himself tried cocaine on a few occasions. He reported that he felt an increased sense of self-control and considerable euphoria. Moreover, he felt the euphoria was more normal than that produced by many other drugs. He described the cocaine effect as a lessening of depression that allowed a feeling of well-being to grow. Neither Freud nor others knew, at the time, about the severely addictive properties of mainlined cocaine. Nor did they know that relatively small cocaine overdoses can kill the user.

Amphetamines are potent stimulants. Amphetamines and various related drugs stimulate the brain and the peripheral autonomic system, particularly the portion that mobilizes the body in emergencies.

An amphetamine has several effects. It reduces appetite, fatigue, the need for sleep, and depression. It increases alertness, performance, and motor and verbal behavior. Amphetamines also raise one's spirits and induce euphoria. All of these seemingly beneficial effects occur to some extent when moderate doses are taken. That may be 5 milligrams; an addicted person, on the other hand, may take 100, 200, or 1,000 milligrams a day.

Amphetamine's most common medical use is as a stimulant for patients who tend to be overweight or sleepy, such as pregnant women. The drug's effect on appetite varies in humans. For some people it seems to decrease appetite, for others it doesn't have much effect at all. However, if a dog is given a dose one hour before feeding, it will refuse to eat. Given repeated doses of amphetamine, it will literally starve to death even when food is readily available.

The Japanese first synthesized amphetamine about 1919; it was used extensively by both the Axis and the Allied forces during World War II. Amphetamines also have been used extensively by truck drivers, who originated many of its street names—cartwheels, coast-to-coasts, West-Coast turnarounds, truck drivers, and copilots. Grinspoon and Hedblom (1972) describe the derivation of the term "copilot."

The last term (copilot) presumably was derived from the now legendary accident that occurred when one exceedingly lucky driver, who had stayed behind his wheel for more than two days on speed, decided to take a brief nap in his sleeping berth while moving at 60 miles per hour. When finally extricated from his totally demolished vehicle, he stated that he had been sure that his assistant was competent to handle the truck in broad daylight. The "copilot," however, was an amphetamine-induced illusion; the driver had been alone for the entire forty-eight-hour period.

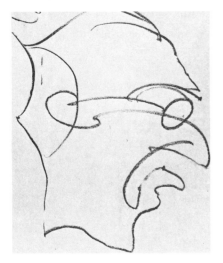

5-14
Drawings done before and after LSD was taken. (Drs. H. W. Leeman & R. W. Frei)

Amphetamine or "speed" addicts may begin with small daily doses of 10 to 20 milligrams and build up to the point where they are mainlining 1000 milligrams (a whole gram) at a time. Mainlining speed gives the addict a sudden flash or rush of intense pleasure that envelops his body seconds after the drug enters his bloodstream. Describing the sensation, one girl said that her whole brain seemed to be vibrating and that shocks surged up and down her spine. When speed is injected directly into the bloodstream, it produces an enormous and rapid increase in blood pressure, which can lead to sudden cerebral hemorrhages (strokes) and heart failure.

Many speed addicts inject dose after dose of amphetamine for the rush and to maintain a high. Sometimes they remain awake for a week and can, in the process, lose up to 20 pounds. When they stop injections, the inevitable "crash" follows. Physically exhausted, they may sleep for 48 hours and wake up feeling profoundly depressed and fatigued. They suffer from severe headaches and are inevitably irritable.

Considerable evidence suggests that repeated use of amphetamines leads to brain damage. In San Francisco's Haight-Ashbury district, speed addicts who had been on amphetamines for months displayed markedly depressed mental functions, even after withdrawal. They could not think clearly, and their memory was substantially impaired—effects that seem to be permanent. The typical speed addict is an emaciated person, afflicted by constant nervous tremors and twitches. His teeth grind continually and his muscles and joints ache severely. He has tooth abscesses, ulcers, and skin infections. If he continues to inject speed, he probably will live only a short time.

Among addictive drugs, amphetamines are unique for one effect. Their repeated use leads to a clinical condition indistinguishable from genuine psychosis (a severe mental disorder), namely paranoia. Paranoid individuals are convinced that others are trying to hurt them. Such persons can be extremely dangerous because they act irrationally, "retaliating" for harmless, everyday acts they misconstrue as hostile.

Psychotomimetic Drugs

The most widely known *psychotomimetic drugs* (commonly known as hallucinogens) are *LSD*, or acid; *mescaline*, derived from the peyote cactus; *psilocybin*, derived from mushrooms; and *marijuana*. All of these drugs induce psychoticlike symptoms.

LSD, Mescaline, and Psilocybin. These three drugs seem to have similar effects on perception and awareness. They all cause distortions, hallucinations, and bizarre experiences. Although the effects of these three psychotomimetic drugs may differ somewhat, the major difference is in the dosage required. LSD, the most powerful, produces its effects with doses as low as 100 millionths of a gram. Much higher doses of mescaline and psilocybin are needed to produce the same effects.

D-lysergic acid diethylamide—LSD's chemical name—is one of the most potent of all drugs. In the quote at the beginning of this chapter, Albert Hofmann, the chemist who first synthesized LSD, describes his first experiment with "acid." Since then, volumes have been published on

Table 5-3 A Few Types of Drugs, Medical Uses, Symptoms Produced, and Dependence Potentials (Question Marks Indicate Difference of Opinion)

Name	Slang Name	Chemical or Trade Name	Source	Medical Use
SEDATIVE				
Barbiturates	Barbs, Blue Devils, Candy, Yellow Jackets, Phennies, Peanuts, Blue Heavens	Phenobarbital, Nembutal, Seconal, Amytal	Synthetic	Sedation, Relieve high blood pressure, epilepsy, hyper-thyroidism
NARCOTICS				
Heroin	H., Horse, Scat, Junk, Smack, Scag, Stuff, Harry	Diacetyl-morphine	Semi-Synthetic (from Morphine)	Pain relief
Morphine	White stuff, M.	Morphine sulphate	Natural (from Opium)	Pain relief
Codeine	Schoolboy	Methylmorphine	Natural (from Opium), Semi-Synthetic (from Morphine)	Ease pain and coughing
Methadone	Dolly	Dolophine amidone	Synthetic	Pain relief
STIMULANTS				
Cocaine	Corrine, Gold Dust, Coke, Bernice, Flake, Star Dust, Snow	Methylester of benzoylecgonine	Natural (from coca, NOT cacao)	Local anesthesia
Amphetamines	Bennies, Dexies, Speed, Wake-Ups, Lid Poppers, Hearts, Pep Pills	Benzedrine, Dexedrine, Desoxyn, Meth-amphetamine, Methedrine	Synthetic	Relieve mild depression, control appetite and narcolepsy
PSYCHOTOMIMETICS				
LSD	Acid, Sugar, Big D, Cubes, Trips	d-lysergic acid diethylamine	Semi-Synthetic (from ergot alkaloids)	Experimental study of mental function, alcoholism
Mescaline	Mesc.	3,4,5-trimeth-oxyphenethyl-amine	Natural (from Peyote)	None
Psilocybin		3(2-dimethyl-amino) ethylin-dol-4-oldihydro-gen phosphate	Natural (from Psilocybe)	None
Marijuana	Pot, Grass, Hashish, Tea, Gage, Reefers	Cannabis sativa	Natural	None in U.S.

How Taken	Effects Sought	Long-Term Symptoms	Physical Dependence Potential	Mental Dependence Potential	Organic Damage Potential
Swallowed or Injected	Anxiety reduction, Euphoria	Addiction w/ severe withdrawal symptoms, Possible convulsions, toxic psychosis	Yes	Yes	Yes
Injected or Sniffed	Euphoria, Prevent withdrawal discomfort	Addiction, Constipation, Loss of Appetite	Yes	Yes	No
Swallowed or Injected	Euphoria, Prevent withdrawal discomfort	Addiction, Constipation, Loss of Appetite	Yes	Yes	No
Swallowed	Euphoria, Prevent withdrawal discomfort	Addiction, Constipation, Loss of Appetite	Yes	Yes	No
Swallowed or Injected	Prevent withdrawal discomfort	Addiction, Constipation, Loss of Appetite	Yes	Yes	No
Sniffed, Injected or Swallowed	Excitation, Talkativeness	Depression, Convulsions	No	Yes	Yes?
Swallowed or Injected	Alertness, Activeness	Loss of Appetite, Delusions, Hallucinations, Toxic psychosis	No?	Yes	Yes?
Swallowed	Insightful experiences, Exhilaration, Distortion of senses	May intensify existing psychosis, panic reactions	No	No?	No?
Swallowed	Insightful experiences, Exhilaration, Distortion of senses	?	No	No?	No?
Swallowed	Insightful experiences, Exhilaration, Distortion of senses	?	No	No?	No?
Smoked, Swallowed, or Sniffed	Relaxation, Increased euphoria, perceptions, sociability	See note on p. 171	No	Yes?	?

Adapted from *Resource Book for Drug Abuse Education*, October 1969. Washington, D.C.: U.S. Department of Health, Education, and Welfare, Public Health Service, National Clearinghouse for Mental Health Information.

LSD's powerful and sometimes catastrophic effects on subjective experience and on behavior. When using LSD, the subject quite typically experiences striking and pervasive hallucinations and odd feelings and emotions of all kinds.

Vision is the most profoundly affected sense. Commonly, illusions develop first. External objects and people appear to change color, shape, and perspective. Colors become more intense and vivid. On the other hand, if the user is depressed, colors appear grey and washed out. Objects change their shapes and sizes, shrinking and growing with marked variations in perspective. Space itself seems to glow.

Hallucinations also emerge. People report hearing voices and even conversations; they hallucinate odors, tastes, and other sensations. Some early enthusiasts for psychotomimetic drugs, including author Aldous Huxley, reported transcendental experiences in which they seemed to approach mystical and ethical truths. After recovering from the drug's effects, however, they could not describe or even accurately remember any of these experiences or insights. Even under LSD, the individual retains a certain awareness. Generally, the LSD user recognizes his hallucinations as such. This is quite different from the psychotic (undrugged) individual, who often mistakes his hallucinations for reality.

An interesting phenomenon in LSD trips, noted in the Hofmann quote, is _synesthesia_; one mode of stimulation seems to be experienced in another mode. Or, as Hofmann said, when he heard music playing, it seemed to come out in colors. Similarly, visual stimuli sometimes seem to be heard or even smelled.

For a while, LSD was thought to be a useful tool for the study of psychoses, since LSD's symptoms and effects are similar to the internal experiences reported by psychotics. However, there are distinct differences. For the LSD user, illusions and hallucinations, particularly the latter, are primarily visual. For the psychotic, they are most commonly auditory. Despite these differences in effect, many case histories document the fact that individuals with no psychotic background became severely and sometimes permanently psychotic after only a few acid trips. Similar research has shown that LSD's effects can range from temporary impairment of behavior to permanent destruction of the personality. Such a person, with his tendency to act irrationally, may be a great danger to himself and others.

Short of these serious, long-range effects, hallucinogens occasionally cause a "bad trip." The person under the drug's influence develops an overwhelming impression of blackness, deep gloom, and isolation. Everything becomes ugly. He sometimes sees his own body as extremely distorted, his limbs decaying, his flesh melting away, his face a mask.

5-15
Marijuana is extracted from the female Cannabis sativa. Marijuana plants have been found in the exotic Far East and in the pragmatic West—in back yards, on highway divider strips, and even behind a police station.

Marijuana

Marijuana is the most widely used psychotomimetic drug. It is a resin produced by the Indian hemp plant, _Cannabis sativa_. The resin actually oozes to the surface of the leaves on the female plant and can be separated for harvesting. In India, the resin from the lower leaves, called _bhang_, is extracted for popular consumption. Rather than being smoked, it is swallowed. In most states of India the use of *bhang* is legal. Many thousands of small stores have renewable licenses to sell it. Because it has an unpleasant bitter taste, it is commonly combined with ice cream. Throughout India it is very easy to buy a drink of *bhang* legally and its use is not considered to have created serious legal, public health, or moral problems. Furthermore, crushed marijuana leaves are a favorite ingredient in Indian cooking. In the 19th century, visiting English ladies were often served afternoon tea cakes prepared with marijuana.

In the United States, two terms for the *cannabis* plant have come into widespread use. *Marijuana* is the chopped and dried plant itself, which is smoked. <u>Hashish</u>, which is much more concentrated, refers to various preparations of the resin alone. Subjective experiences with marijuana vary from person to person and depend in part on the user's expectation. The drug takes effect fairly slowly. About 10 minutes after a person has inhaled the smoke, a sense of heaviness and warmth suffuses the muscles. He does not find the heaviness unpleasant; it simply feels like an increased awareness of his body's tone and presence. Next, he begins to see his surroundings differently. He sees shapes, colors and textures in a way that he had not seen them before. His perceptions are not necessarily more profound, but they are certainly different. His focus of interest narrows; time slows. His experience seems to have a greater concreteness. Shapes, sounds, and colors are examined very carefully. Some people report that listening to music becomes a total experience. Many subjects say the pleasure of sexual intercourse seems greatly enhanced and drawn out in time. The 19th century French poet Baudelaire, who was fond of hashish, describes the experience:

It sometimes happens that your personality disappears, and you develop objectivity . . . to such an abnormal degree that the contemplation of outward objects makes you forget your own existence, and you soon melt into them. Your eye rests upon an harmoniously shaped tree bowing beneath the wind. Within a few seconds, something that to a poet would merely be a very natural comparison becomes to you a reality. You begin by endowing the tree with your own passions, your desire or melancholy; its groanings and swayings become your own, and soon you are *the tree. In the same way, a bird soaring beneath a blue sky at first merely* represents *the immortal yearning to soar above human life; but already you are the bird itself.*

But marijuana does not always produce these effects. The dose normally used in one cigarette of marijuana produces milder effects. Indeed, many of the reported effects of marijuana are often *placebo* effects. That is, the smoker describes what he thinks he ought to be experiencing. However, in doses higher than those normally used in a marijuana cigarette, the drug is a severe psychotomimetic agent producing psychotic-like behavior, hallucinations, and delusions.

The obvious physiological effects of smoking marijuana do not seem to be drastic. A smoker may have dilated pupils, bloodshot eyes, a rapid pulse rate, increased blood pressure, more rapid breathing, diarrhea, and sometimes nausea. However, there may be hidden effects; we still do not know why it produces the effects it does, though we now have some clues. Some preliminary reports raise the possibility that certain undesirable side effects may result from repeated use of marijuana—for example, a partial loss of cellular immunity (Nahas, Suciu-Foca, Armand, & Morishima, 1974) and a decrease in male fertility (*The New York Times*, April 18, 1974). However, much more research is needed before we can be certain of these and other possible effects of the drug.

While the hallucinogenic drugs as a class can be highly harmful, users do not become addicted to them—at least not physiologically addicted. However, physical need for a drug is not the total definition of addiction. An individual can also become psychologically dependent. He may begin to need the *feelings* that come with hallucinogenic drugs. It is not uncommon for a person who starts taking marijuana to continue taking it. One effect of this chronic use may be that he begins to lose interest in other activities. The time he spends under the influence of the drug becomes more real and more important to him than more demanding activities such as going to work or school.

As we have seen, drugs come in many varieties, with many different effects. If they are used with care, that is, taken under supervision in the amounts appropriate to treat various conditions both physical and mental, many drugs can have significant beneficial effects. With the addictive drugs, of course, one always runs the risk of developing physiological dependency and perhaps emotional dependency. And with the psychotomimetic drugs, though the possibility of physical addiction is not present, the chance of psychological addiction is a real possibility

5-16
The relationship between the ages of current smokers, alcoholic beverage consumers, and people with marijuana experience. The numbers in parentheses indicate the number of people interviewed in each age group. (The National Commission on Marijuana and Drug Abuse, 1973)

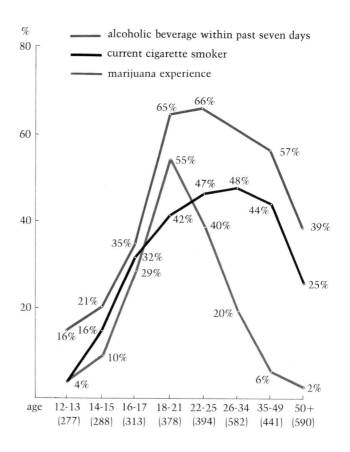

172   Chapter 5   States of Awareness

for many people. Future research may reveal both how and why physical and psychic addiction can develop and how they can be remedied.

Summary

1. Awareness is the sum of everything that one can discover about one's experience at a given time.

2. Although awareness is lessened and altered in sleep, we are nevertheless able to evaluate the significance of some stimuli even in sleep.

3. All higher animals exhibit 24-hour activity cycles called circadian rhythms. Interruptions in these cycles cause sleep-schedule and temperature-cycle maladjustments.

4. Two sleep states exist for all higher mammals: REM (rapid eye movements) sleep and NREM (no rapid eye movements) sleep.

5. Electroencephalogram (EEG) readings of brain activity during REM sleep paradoxically show the low-voltage, fast EEG pattern typical of the alert waking state. This contrasts with NREM sleep, in which large, slow, irregular waves, called delta waves, occur.

6. Hypnosis, the production of a temporary trancelike state, is characterized by increases in the subject's suggestibility. Another significant effect, which follows hypnosis, is called posthypnotic amnesia. Some people are more susceptible to hypnosis than others.

7. Under hypnosis, a subject's awareness and memory of pain are altered so that he appears not to have perceived it. However, heightened physiological responses indicate that he perceived the pain at some level, but that the hypnotic state supplied a strong incentive not to respond with normal overt reactions.

8. Transcendental meditation is a form of experience that can be generated on command. Unlike hypnosis, this state shows some differences from the normal waking condition, including reduced oxygen consumption and carbon dioxide elimination, a decline in sweat gland activity, and an increase in alpha rhythm. It also is said to produce a strongly rewarding pleasurable experience.

9. The basic concept of biofeedback is that if a person can observe some biological event in himself, such as the alpha rhythm in his brain, he then can be trained to modify that event. Applications of this concept are being studied in biocybernetics, in which computers interact with the subject to analyze and control his physical state.

10. Drugs are chemical substances that affect humans and other animals. The study of drugs that influence awareness, experience, and behavior is called psychopharmacology.

11. Barbiturates, widely used as sedatives and hypnotics, are general depressants of the nervous system. Abuse of these drugs leads to unconsciousness, depression, loss of coordination, slurred speech, impaired memory, and confusion. Withdrawal symptoms are severe.

12. Alcohol is the most commonly used addictive sedative. Alcoholism is the most serious drug problem throughout the world.

13. Tolerance means that when a drug is taken repeatedly, progressively larger doses are needed to produce the same effect. Addiction involves the increased need or use of drugs and the occurrence of withdrawal effects when the drug is no longer used.

14. Derived from the opium poppy, morphine is an addictive narcotic which under careful supervision, is used medically to relieve pain. Heroin, made from morphine, has even stronger addictive properties.

15. Two theories that attempt to explain drug addiction are the hypersensitivity theory and the effect of the drug on strong, positive pleasure centers in the brain.

16. Among the better known and less harmful stimulants are caffeine in coffee and nicotine in tobacco, which increase motor activation and wakefulness. More dangerous stimulants are: cocaine, which is addictive and produces euphoria, and amphetamines, which reduce appetite, tiredness, and depression, while inducing a sense of well-being. Addiction to amphetamines or "speed" decreases mental functions and may produce emaciation, nervous tremors, skin infections, and paranoia.

17. LSD, mescaline, and psilocybin are psychotomimetic drugs or hallucinogens. These three drugs affect perception and awareness similarly; they cause distortions, hallucinations, and bizarre experiences, usually visual.

18. Marijuana is the most widely used psychotomimetic drug. Produced from the Indian hemp plant, it can result in heightened awareness and appreciation of perceptions. Although it is nonaddictive, high doses can produce psychoticlike behavior, hallucinations, and delusions.

Important Terms

circadian rhythms	sedatives
REM or D sleep	hypnotics
NREM or S sleep	barbiturates
paradoxical sleep	anesthetics
hypnosis	drug potentiation
hypnotic suggestion	tolerance
posthypnotic amnesia	addiction
hypnotic regression	narcotics
meditation	opium
transcendental meditation	morphine
biofeedback	heroin
psychopharmacology	hypersensitivity theory

stimulants

cocaine

amphetamines

psychotomimetic drugs

LSD

mescaline

psilocybin

marijuana

hashish

Suggested Readings

BARBER, T. X. *LSD, marijuana, yoga, and hypnosis.* Chicago: Aldine, 1970.

A description of the psychological and physiological effects of yoga, hypnosis, and psychedelic drugs. Of particular interest is the author's controversial view of hypnosis; he argues that hypnosis is not really a separate state of awareness, but rather a variation of the state of wakefulness.

DEMENT, W. C. *Some must watch while some must sleep.* San Francisco: Freeman, 1974.

A readable account of the findings of recent sleep experiments by one of the outstanding investigators in this area.

ERIKSEN, C. W. (ED.) *Behavior and awareness.* Durham, N. C.: Duke University Press, 1962.

The central question dealt with in this symposium of research and interpretation is whether we can perceive and learn without being aware of the relationships between environmental stimuli and our own responses. The roles of awareness in areas such as learning are explored here as they emerged from the authors' research experiments.

JULIEN, R. *A primer of drug actions.* San Francisco: Freeman, 1975.

A clear, readable, and important account of what drugs are, how they act, and why. Emphasis is placed on drugs that profoundly influence human behavior and experience.

KLEITMAN, N. *Sleep and wakefulness.* Chicago: University of Chicago Press, 1963.

A comprehensive text including research on experimental, pathological, and theoretical aspects of sleep and wakefulness; by the leading authority in this area.

ORNSTEIN, R. E. *The psychology of consciousness.* San Francisco: Freeman, 1972.

An attempt to define "consciousness" by synthesizing the approaches of experimental and esoteric psychology.

ORNSTEIN, R. E. (ED.) *The nature of human consciousness.* San Francisco: Freeman, 1973.

A book of readings concerning the nature of "consciousness," from the viewpoints of both experimental and traditional psychologists, as well as believers in the more esoteric approaches to consciousness, such as mysticism, Zen, and meditation.

SHOR, R. E., & ORNE, M. T. (EDS.) *The nature of hypnosis.* New York: Holt, Rinehart and Winston, 1965.
Comprehensive collection of articles on hypnosis, including conflicting viewpoints. Orne, who is a practicing hypnotherapist, argues that hypnosis depends to a great extent on what the subject thinks the hypnotist expects of him.

TART, C. T. *Altered states of consciousness.* New York: Wiley, 1969.
A discussion of the increasingly widespread use of drugs, self-hypnosis, and other methods of producing altered states of consciousness. Results and long-term effects of these experiments are analyzed from a scientific perspective.

THE DRUG ABUSE SURVEY PROJECT. *Dealing with drug abuse.* New York: Praeger, 1972.
A clearly written, comprehensive analysis of all types of drugs, from sedatives to narcotics. Drugs are classified and described in terms of their psychological and physiological effects. Programs for dealing with addiction are also discussed and evaluated.

Chapter 6 Learning: Basic Processes and Issues

All . . . institutions use personal reinforcers to achieve their appropriate effects. A city government may induce its citizens to stop at intersections by fining those who do not stop. Teachers use failure or the birch rod, on the one hand, or grades, diplomas, and prizes, on the other, to induce students to study. Economic systems use money, which is exchangeable for personal reinforcers. But these institutions also claim a more general return. They justify themselves by pointing to certain entities long associated with value systems. Governments are said to promote justice, security, and peace, religious piety and salvation, economic wealth, educational knowledge and skills, and psychotherapeutic mental health. These are some of the values often cited when people raise questions about values. And they are the kinds of values which are now being strongly challenged.

Young people in particular are beginning to ask some embarrassing questions:

Why should I serve my fellow man?
Why should I seek to be admired by other people?
Why should I avoid censure or criticism?
Why should I die for my country?

. . . . We cannot answer these questions by pointing to absolutes. There is no absolute truth in value judgments. No one has that kind of truth or can answer questions by appealing to it. It is not a question of what people should do or ought to do, or what is right. The question is why certain cultures have made certain things reinforcing or have failed to do so. If these values are now being challenged, it is presumably because the culture has engineered them badly.

—B. F. Skinner
(*Beyond Freedom and Dignity*)

Learning: Basic Processes and Issues

This chapter was drafted by Timothy Teyler, Department of Psychology and Social Relations, Harvard University.

In 1971, the publication of a controversial book, *Beyond Freedom and Dignity*, startled the reading public. In that book, Harvard psychologist B. F. Skinner examines our society, finds it sick, and prescribes a cure. Skinner's thesis is that man and thus society is controlled by a haphazard assortment of rewards and punishments. Because the rewards and punishments are administered capriciously, rather than rationally and consistently, they often lead to the perpetuation of the behavior they are designed to eliminate. As evidence, Skinner cites the fact that in America, such undesirable behaviors as crime, violence, drug addiction, and alcoholism are continually increasing.

Skinner proposes a technology of behavior that would supersede all of the presently known means of controlling behavior. He points out that all of us are controlled by our physical surroundings as well as by other people. Such control may be blatant or subtle, but it is always present. *The fundamental mechanism of control is reinforcement.* We learn to do the things that either reward us or permit us to avoid pain. In short, reinforcement determines our behavior. Clearly, this view clashes with the concept of man as a free and autonomous being. Skinner replies that today's complex and frightening world compels us to revise such traditional concepts. He argues for a technology of behavior that would arrange the environment and the interpersonal rewards and punishments of our society into a logical system.

Assuming that such a technology is possible, who controls this new technology? Who determines the rewards and punishments? Who determines which behaviors shall be rewarded and which punished? Who sets the goals for the society? And, who controls the controller?

Two basic issues are at stake. The first is whether Skinner is correct when he says that human behavior can be controlled. Do we really know enough about learning and the effects of reward and punishment to control other human beings? The second issue is one of values. *Should* we deliberately control human behavior?

Skinner's views have grown from his laboratory experience with the behavior of organisms. The learning principles that he would apply to human behavior are those of *operant conditioning*. While reading this chapter, bear in mind that most learning phenomena are more than laboratory curiosities; they are realities that permeate our lives.

Varieties of Learning

Learning commonly refers to the modification of behavior by experience. Formal learning in the classroom and on the job are only the tip of the iceberg. It is difficult to imagine any period of our waking lives when we are not learning something. Often we are not aware that we are learning. While walking down a street we continually modify our behavior in response to the environment. We avoid telephone poles, fire hydrants, and mailboxes. We observe other people and react to them. We register the environment of the street and our emotional reactions to it. Later, we can draw on these incidental impressions (this is known as *incidental* or *latent* learning; we shall discuss it later in this chapter). Queried about some feature of the street, we may find ourselves able to give a surprisingly accurate reply. Yet while we were walking down the street we were hardly aware that we were "learning" anything at all.

Much of our experience consists of learning that a thing is not particularly important to us. We learn that the words on a billboard do not especially relate to us, so we ignore them. On the other hand, when driving, we learn that many traffic signs and route markers are important, so we attend to them. We learn that the sounds of people talking while we are studying in the library are not relevant, so we ignore them. Yet, if someone mentions our name, we immediately attend to this "meaningful" stimulus.

Association is a process basic to most kinds of learning. Before we can react appropriately to some facet of the environment we must associate it with something else or with some consequence. An association also may be formed between an object and its name, as in language. We know a good deal about the most (and least) efficient ways of arranging stimuli to achieve associations. The two major forms or aspects of learning to be discussed in this chapter, *classical* and *operant* conditioning, are both forms of associative learning. Stimuli and responses are associated together, as in learning that a red light means stop.

Perhaps the most important kind of learning we do is *verbal* learning. It is certainly the most important for college students. Verbal learning is generally classed as a form of associative learning. *Motor-skill* learning also involves the association of many stimuli with many responses to achieve complex and integrated patterns of movements. Typists, machinists, and brain surgeons, to name a few skilled workers, all display complex motor skills learned through long practice. Verbal and motor-skill learning will be treated in Chapter 7.

Still more complex forms of learning have been studied in the laboratory. *Learning set*, or learning-to-learn, is a case in point (we shall be discussing this type of learning toward the end of this chapter). Most readers will know from their own experience that if they practice a particular kind of learning, of foreign languages, for example, it seems to become easier. The term *cognitive* learning often is used to refer to such learning, so complex that it seems to involve reorganization of one's perceptions or ideas.

In short, learning suffuses our lives. If we were incapable of learning we would be unable to exist in our complex world.

Habituation and Sensitization

Not all forms of learning are permanent. Some stimuli produce only temporary behavior changes. For example, a person usually will turn toward a sufficiently strong stimulus, like an auto backfire. This *orienting response* is a temporary behavior. If the stimulus has no other consequences and occurs repeatedly, the response will diminish and may disappear. This phenomenon is *habituation* or *adaptation*. Human beings have a great capacity for habituating or not responding to a large number of things—nagging wives and untidy husbands, crying children, a roommate's snoring, a blaring radio, and an offensive odor. We can get used to almost anything, even very unpleasant experiences, if they are repeated often enough.

Sensitization is the opposite of habituation. We all have experienced sensitization. A person watching Alfred Hitchcock's film *Psycho* is a good example. If another person snaps his fingers during a particularly hair-raising scene, the viewer is likely to jump. Normally, his reaction to a snap of the fingers is small, if he has any at all. But the film has so sensitized him that virtually any stimulus will provoke a vigorous response. Laboratory studies of sensitization usually involve more standard stimuli than *Psycho*. For example, if a mildly painful stimulus is used, an animal at first responds by trying to escape the shock. With each repetition of the shock, the animal becomes more and more agitated and responds more and more strongly; he tries harder and harder to escape the shock. After a while, however, he realizes that he cannot avoid the continuing shocks. At that point, he habituates to the shock; he accepts it as inevitable and no longer tries to escape.

Many psychologists regard habituation and sensitization as examples of the simplest kind of learning. We can at least agree that they are elementary. No new responses are brought into play; existing responses merely increase or decrease.

Survival of an organism depends to a large degree on its reactions to potential danger. A rabbit would not last long if it ignored the stimuli that signal the presence of a fox. In the urban environment, humans would be maladaptive if they did not respond to the flow of automobile traffic or an open manhole. On the other hand, an organism also would be maladaptive if it reacted strongly to every stimulus in its environment. Because most stimuli are meaningless, habituation is a very adaptive response to a complex environment. The organism "conserves" its responses. Both sensitization and habituation increase an organism's chances of survival.

Most organisms are particularly responsive to certain kinds of stimuli. A housecat reacts more attentively to a rustling sound than does a dog.

6-1
Humans survive because they are sensitized to dangers in the environment. (Copyright, 1974, United Press Syndicate)

In addition, the cat's response to this stimulus is less likely to habituate than the dog's. The reason: rustling sounds, usually associated with the scurrying of small prey, are more meaningful to a cat.

Sometimes stimuli that differ only slightly provoke completely divergent behaviors. The response of young turkeys to a cardboard model of a bird flying overhead is a good example. (See Figure 6-2.) Moving the model to the left over the young birds elicited no sustained reaction. However, moving it to the right elicited a vigorous escape reaction that sensitized, that is, increased with repetition. The explanation seems clear. Moving to the left, the model bird appeared to have a long neck and a short tail like a flying goose. Geese do not prey upon turkeys. However, moving the model to the right produced the illusion of a bird with a short neck and a long tail. Hawks, which prey on young turkeys, fit this description. Interestingly, the young turkeys had never seen a live hawk. Yet they responded vigorously to the "hawk" model. It is tempting to conclude that this response is instinctive.

The Interaction of Habituation and Sensitization

Habituation involves another important related behavior. If any aspect of the habituated stimulus changes, the organism's response will revert toward its initial level. If we present an infant with a new stuffed toy, the infant will display an orienting response. It will examine and perhaps handle the toy; eventually, the response habituates. But if we tug a string attached to the toy, the infant immediately regains its interest. This return to the initial level of response after the change in the stimulus is called _dishabituation_. Dishabituation is the superimposing of sensitization on habituation.

The interaction of habituation and sensitization has been illustrated in an experiment dealing with the rat's startle response (Groves & Thompson, 1970), a good animal model of the human orienting response. Rats were placed on a device that measured the magnitude of their startle response (jumping) to a loud tone. The jumping became sensitized briefly and then habituated. Just before trial 15, half of the animals were subjected to a bright flashing light. The light dishabituated (sensitized) the rats' startle response, but only for one trial. This indicates that the increased or dishabituated response after the light flash was due to superimposition of sensitization on habituation. If the

6-2
Drawing of the cardboard model of a bird flying overhead and the baby wild turkeys' responses to it. When the model was moved to the left, the turkeys remained passive and calm. When it was moved to the right, the turkeys fled. Moving to the left, it appeared to be a goose; moving to the right, it appeared to be a hawk. (N. Tinbergen, _The study of instinct_. The Clarendon Press, Oxford, 1951)

light flash had actually disrupted the habituation, then the rats would have continued to show a large startle response that would have rehabituated slowly.

The physiological mechanisms underlying habituation and sensitization were recently traced to particular groups of neurons in the central nervous system. These neurons exhibit either habituation or sensitization (Groves & Thompson, 1970). Presumably, they send their information to other neurons, which control the organism's actual response. It is possible that physical analysis of simple forms of learning, such as habituation and sensitization, may lead to an understanding of the brain mechanisms employed in complex learning.

Habituation and Adaptation

Humans can habituate to meaningful stimuli as well as to irrelevant stimuli. An individual living under the landing approach to a large airport is periodically subjected to the sound of screaming jet engines, which interrupts conversation, disturbs radio or TV reception, and impairs concentration. He would at first be upset and angry. However, after accepting the inevitability of the noise, he probably would habituate to the disturbance. Later, he might even be surprised when visitors react to the noise as he did initially. He has adapted to the noise.

In many environments, habituation is vital to an individual's successful adaptation. *Urban Stress*, a recent book, argues that habituation is essential for survival in cities:

We regard adaptation (habituation) as the key to understanding modern life — at least those aspects of it involving man-environment interactions. The most remarkable feature of current urban existence is not how stressful the city has become, but how unaffected day-to-day functioning of the city dweller is despite the indignities heaped upon him. The effects of stress are not only neurophysiological. It isn't merely as if the ear were becoming less sensitive to sound, or pressure receptors were losing their ability to report the jostlings and bumpings of a busy street. What also happens is that complex events, for example, hurried meals, hectic traffic, brusque and even hostile interpersonal exchanges, also lose their apparent power to disrupt. It is this fascinating loss of reactivity to stimuli generally regarded as aversive that makes the general issue of adaptation not only pertinent to our studies but a sine qua non *for understanding urban stressors.* (Glass & Singer, 1972)

It should be pointed out, however, that failing to attend consciously to the stresses and strains of city living does not mean that they may not have harmful bodily effects. Psychological habituation could actually be maladaptive under such circumstances, because we are not warned of damage to our bodies. Consciously we may be able to get used to anything, but do our bodies habituate as well? Considerable evidence indicates that they do not.

As important as habituation and sensitization are, some psychologists object to calling them "learning," especially when they are shown to occur in the "unintelligent" spinal cord. Many physiological psychologists use the term _plasticity_ to refer to such elementary behavioral changes resulting from experience.

Classical Conditioning

"Father's voice had an ominous tone in it as he called me into the study. I dreaded facing him. My heart was pounding, my hands were cold and clammy, and I had a funny feeling in my stomach."

Many of us have had this feeling. The youngster's response to his father's voice is a _conditioned response._ We can assume that in the past the youngster had heard a similar tone in his father's voice. We also can infer that the earlier confrontation did not end in the child's favor. He has associated the tone of his father's voice with a painful outcome. So the tone alone now evokes the feeling that the unpleasant experience itself had evoked.

Thus, in _classical conditioning,_ stimuli associated with a meaningful event tend to become substitutes for the event itself, eliciting similar reactions. Just as the father's voice evokes a reaction, the mere sight of a loved one can elicit strong emotional responses. Similarly, to a hungry individual, the smell of food is a powerful conditioned stimulus.

A single word may trigger a classically conditioned response. For instance, many people are disgusted by rats. This is not an innate reaction. Biologically, rats are on a par with other rodents, such as squirrels and chipmunks. Yet, throughout their lives, people have been told that rats bite, carry disease, and are generally the scum of the animal world. In some cases, the sound of the word "rat" alone is enough to set off a negative reaction. In another culture the phrase "you dirty squirrel" might arouse equal feelings of revulsion.

Although it is commonly attributed to _Ivan Petrovich Pavlov,_ classical conditioning was actually developed by another Russian, the physiologist Sechenov. He was interested in the body's reflexes. He used the model of the familiar knee-jerk response to a tap just below the kneecap. Pavlov built his own experiments on the framework erected by Sechenov.

Ivan Pavlov himself was a renowned physiologist who won the 1904 Nobel Prize for his work on the physiology of digestion. In his research on digestion, Pavlov used a minor surgical procedure that enabled him to collect samples of salivary fluid from the dogs that were his experimental subjects. He wanted to analyze the chemical constituents of salivary fluid, so a dog was trained to stand in an apparatus similar to the one shown in Figure 6-4. To stimulate the saliva flow, meat powder was put in the dog's mouth. Pavlov noted that after a few such experiments, a dog would salivate at the sight of the experimenter. After several more experiments, the dog began to salivate to the sound of a tuning fork, a light being turned on, or a bell being rung. Pavlov called this a "psychic reflex" and vigorously pursued the new line of research opened up by this observation.

Pavlov's observation is a classic example of _serendipity,_ the chance discovery of something while seeking an entirely different goal. Pavlov's

6-3
The child reflexively pulls away from the shock of an electric current and learns to associate the electrical outlet with pain. He is conditioned to refrain from pushing metal objects into electrical outlets.

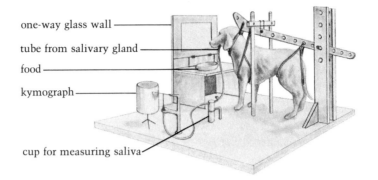

one-way glass wall

tube from salivary gland

food

kymograph

cup for measuring saliva

6-4
The apparatus used by Pavlov in his original classical conditioning experiments. The dog's saliva was drained into a cup. The amount of saliva was recorded on a moving drum known as a kymograph. The appearance of saliva was a measure of conditioning to a tuning fork, for example, and the amount of saliva was a measure of strength of conditioning.

contributions to behavior study have been reinforced through the decades by hundreds of investigations and legions of experimenters. The timing of Pavlov's discovery was significant because prior to Pavlov psychology had been subjective. Introspection was regarded as the means of studying behavior. Pavlov firmly established the study of behavior as a discipline that could be subjected to rigorous scientific analysis. In the United States, Edward Thorndike independently developed a similar approach to studying behavior in his work on operant conditioning, which we shall discuss later in this chapter.

Procedure and Terminology

Classical conditioning has developed its own specialized terminology. The natural stimulus, such as food, that elicits the initial response, such as salivation, is called the _unconditioned stimulus (US)_. Responses to such unconditioned stimuli are called _unconditioned responses (UR)_ because they are unlearned and innate to the organism. Effective conditioning requires that the unconditioned stimulus produce a clear and reliable unconditioned response. In classical conditioning, the unconditioned stimulus is also the reward or _reinforcer_ that makes it likely that the desired response will be repeated by the subject.

Stimuli with which the unconditioned stimulus is paired, such as the sight of the experimenter, are called _conditioned stimuli (CS)_. The responses to the conditioned stimuli that develop after a number of pairings are the _conditioned responses (CR)_. "Conditioned" can be translated to mean "learned" because only the dog's past experience makes it salivate at the sight of the experimenter. Relatively neutral stimuli generally are used as conditioned stimuli. The repeated pairing of a neutral conditioned stimulus with a meaningful unconditioned stimulus is the essence of classical conditioning. The conditioned response that develops to the conditioned stimulus is usually similar to the subject's unconditioned response to the unconditioned stimulus.

Timing. The timing of the two stimuli is very important. When the conditioned stimulus precedes the unconditioned stimulus by about one-half second, the conditioned response is established rapidly and efficiently. If the _interstimulus interval_ is longer or shorter, the conditioned response is learned less well. If the unconditioned stimulus precedes the conditioned stimulus (called _backward conditioning_) very little, if any, learning seems to occur.

unconditioned stimuli	responses	conditioned stimuli
meat powder	salivation	lights
electric shock	limb movement	tones
electric shock	heart rate changes	touches
air puff to eye	eyeblink	odors
emotional stimuli	galvanic skin response changes	words
food	gastrointestinal movement and secretions	pictures
insulin injection	insulin shock	
injection of toxic substances	immune reaction	
frightening objects	fear responses	
bright light	electroencephalographic changes	

6-5

Lists of typical unconditioned stimuli, conditioned stimuli and the responses they produce under classical conditioning.

6-6

The timing of classical conditioning. Delayed conditioning is the most effective sequence. The vertical arrows indicate the approximate time of the appearance of the conditioned response once conditioning has occurred.

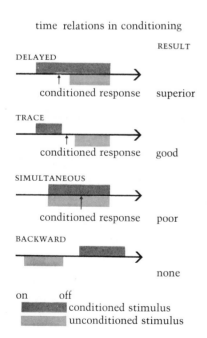

time relations in conditioning

Trace conditioning, in which the conditioned stimulus is no longer present when the unconditioned stimulus appears, results in reasonably good conditioning. However, delayed conditioning, in which the unconditioned stimulus is delivered while the conditioned stimulus is still present, is superior. The trace procedure is particularly interesting because it suggests that some brain mechanisms must "remember" the conditioned stimulus during the interstimulus interval. The term "trace" implies that some underlying physical brain event, a short-term memory trace, must result from the conditioned stimulus and remain in effect until the unconditioned stimulus is presented, in order for there to be a learned response. The simultaneous or delayed procedures, where the two stimuli overlap in time, do not require a stimulus "trace" to persist for any length of time.

Limits of Classical Conditioning

Organisms differ dramatically in form and function, both between species and among those members of the same species that are at different stages in their development. Conditioning can occur over astonishingly wide phylogenetic (different species) and ontogenetic (growth and development within a species) ranges. The single-celled protozoan, paramecium, is the simplest species to be successfully trained. A group of these microscopic animals (slightly over 1/10 of a millimeter long) were placed in a dish of water. A needle containing bacteria (food to the paramecia) was repeatedly dipped into the water. The needle was the conditioned stimulus, the bacteria the unconditioned stimulus, and the protozoans' movement toward the needle was the response. The test of learning occurred when a sterile needle was put into the water. The paramecia congregated around the unbaited needle (Gelber, 1952). (Unfortunately, this experiment has been questioned because it did not include adequate controls for other factors.)

We know that organisms young and old can be conditioned. However, the efficiency of learning is not equal across the age spectrum—the very young and very old are slightly inferior. Yet, some evidence suggests that conditioning can occur in the womb. In one experiment, a vibratory

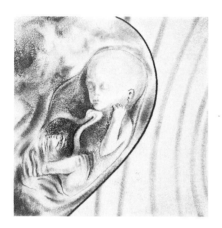

6-7
The fetus being conditioned to respond to vibrations. The vibrations (CS) are paired with a loud noise (US) until they alone elicit the CR of kicking.

stimulus to the mother's belly served as the conditioned stimulus and a loud noise directed at the mother's belly served as the unconditioned stimulus. After pairing, the fetus's conditioned response to the vibration was akin to its startle reaction from the loud noise (Spelt, 1948). This is another illustration of why classical conditioning is said to be a universal phenomenon occurring over a wide range of organisms and at all ages.

Applications of Classical Conditioning

One of the most fascinating examples of classical conditioning occurred in an experiment involving a learned insulin reaction. Insulin, a hormone normally present in the bloodstream, regulates cellular uptake of blood sugar and thus cellular metabolism (the processes involved in providing energy for vital bodily activities). An overdose of insulin results in an insulin coma. In the experiment, a light was paired with an insulin overdose. After a number of pairings, an ineffective saltwater injection replaced the insulin. The animals were clearly conditioned, judging from the comas produced by the harmless saltwater solution (Sawrey, Conger, & Turrell, 1956). A similar result was obtained in an experiment in which laboratory animals were injected with morphine paired with a neutral stimulus. The CS alone eventually elicited the nausea caused by the injection of morphine. In sum, even bodily defense reactions can be brought under stimulus control by conditioning.

Conditioned nausea has been used to great advantage in the treatment of alcoholics. This treatment, known as *aversive conditioning*, will be discussed in detail in Chapter 21.

Emotional responses to a good many stimuli are established through conditioning. A scene, a face, or a word may be the conditioned stimulus for a long-standing emotional response. Often these responses were established without our awareness or when we were very young. As a result, we often are at a loss to explain our emotional reactions to such things as spiders, loved ones, rainy days, beards, and flags.

In an ingenious experiment, human volunteers were subjected to conditioning while under hypnosis (so that they reported they could not remember the procedures). In one instance, a click was paired with the presentation of a geometric design on a screen. In the posthypnotic test, the subject was asked to look at a blank card and tell what he saw. Naturally he reported seeing only a blank card. When he was asked to imagine hearing a click, the geometric design appeared on the card. All the subjects reported being completely puzzled by these strange "hallucinations." All of us have passed through times in our lives when we have felt "down," fearful, or uneasy, yet we were unable to explain why. It may be that some long-forgotten conditioning is responsible for such inexplicable "moods."

Pavlov was the first researcher to notice that a neurosis (a seemingly inexplicable fear or anxiety) can be created in the laboratory. The procedure was rather complicated. The first step was to train a dog to salivate to a drawing of a circle. Then an ellipse was drawn nearby. The circle was paired with food and the ellipse was not. The dog quickly learned to discriminate between the circle and the ellipse. However, unknown to the subject, the experimenters were gradually altering the two stimuli. They made the circle more and more elliptical and the ellipse more and more circular. The animal continued to respond correctly to the "more circular" stimuli. Eventually, the stimuli were made so similar that the dog could not discriminate between them. At this point, it began to display neurotic behavior. The normally placid dog thrashed about, barked, and appeared fearful (Pavlov, 1927).

While it may be difficult to define neurosis in dogs, a number of the animal's behavior patterns were identical to those of neurotic humans. For example, not only did the animal behave abnormally; it also did nothing to help solve its problem. In addition, its behavior was remarkably resistant to elimination. Some *experimental neuroses* in animals have lasted for years, just as neuroses commonly do in humans. As you will see in Chapter 20, these characteristics of neurosis in animals are very similar to some aspects of human neurosis.

Operant or Instrumental Conditioning

A hungry dog seeks out food and eats it. Going down stairs, we place our feet squarely on the steps to avoid a fall. A deer flees at the sight of a hunter. A prospective medical student works for good grades to insure his admission to medical school. All these actions are examples of *operant* or *instrumental conditioning*. Operant conditioning means learning what response to make in a situation, what operation to perform, in order to obtain a reward or avoid an undesirable or harmful event.

The procedure in operant conditioning is quite simple. Teaching a dog to roll over is a good example. Usually, the trainer coaxes the dog to perform a part of the behavior, however approximate it might be. He might gently push the dog to the floor while saying "roll over." When the dog performs this part of the behavior, the trainer will praise, pet, and feed it. In the same way, the trainer will coax the dog into displaying progressively more and more of the behavior—rewarding it every time with food and affection.

A dog can be taught many other tricks to obtain rewards of food and praise. To make the final stages of training work best, the trainer must withhold the reward until the animal has completed the entire behavior it has learned. If the trainer were, for example, to continue to reward the initial lying-down behavior, the animal, seeking to get the most food and affection, would simply repeat that behavior over and over. Similarly, a child will tend to continue his infant "talk" if his parents continue to reward that behavior by responding to it.

At about the same time that Pavlov began studying classical conditioning in dogs, the first operant conditioning experiments were conducted by *E. L. Thorndike.* Unlike Pavlov, Thorndike was a psychologist by training. His studies, which he called "trial-and-error learning," were the precursors of what was to be known as instrumental or operant conditioning.

In classical conditioning, the organism's response has no bearing on the receipt of reinforcers; the response occurs automatically to the unconditioned stimulus. In operant, or instrumental, conditioning the organism's behavior operates on, or is "instrumental" in, determining whether the subject receives a reward or avoids a punishment. In operant conditioning, responses are not *elicited* from the organism as they are in classical conditioning. Rather, responses are spontaneously *emitted* by the organism and are then reinforced by the reward or the avoidance of punishment.

Thorndike, like Pavlov, used as his subject a common pet — the house cat. He confined cats, unfed, in "puzzle boxes" which he had designed. In each case, the locked doors would open if the cats tripped certain levers or latches; they then could get to the food waiting in full view outside.

Thorndike (1898) observed that when they were first introduced to the boxes, the cats' behavior was quite random. They cried, bit, scratched, and tried to squeeze through the bars. However, these acts gradually disappeared as the animals learned that only certain acts would free them from the confining box. Such learning is often called *trial-and-error* learning. Contrast this behavior with that produced by classical conditioning. The "end" response of operant conditioning is not already present and ready for association with a stimulus. Instead, the animal must "figure out" (or discover by accident) the response it must make to obtain the reinforcement. In classical conditioning the dog's salivation did not produce the meat powder. The meat powder appeared whether or not the animal salivated. However, in Thorndike's operant conditioning experiment, the organism, in quest of its reward, had to push the correct combination of latches in order to make the door open. While the procedures and the behaviors are different in these two learning methods, classical and operant conditioning still have much in common. They both involve learning new associations between stimuli and responses.

Operant conditioning's tremendous impact on psychology and society is primarily the result of the experimentation and writing of B. F. Skinner. Most of our knowledge about schedules of reinforcement comes from the work he carried out in the *experimental chamber,* or so-called *Skinner box.* Through his books — *Walden Two, Beyond Freedom and Dignity,* and *About Behaviorism* — Skinner has brought the social implications of operant learning to the layman's attention.

Procedures and Terminology

One of operant conditioning's distinguishing marks is the degree to which it has avoided subjective explanations of inferred inner states. Instead, it emphasizes an accurate, objective description of the situation and behavior. Events are described in "operational terms." Rather than say that an organism was very hungry, the description says "food and water deprived for 24 hours." Another common practice is to concentrate on the response itself rather than on the means by which a subject can make that response. For example, a child who must push a blue button to gain a candy reinforcer can respond in a variety of ways. He can push the button with his finger, his elbow, or his toe. How the response is performed is secondary to the response's actual appearance.

A learning measure common in operant conditioning is the *rate of response.* A pigeon, for example, will peck at objects at a fairly high and steady rate. Its rate of responding can be increased or decreased by operant techniques. In such experiments, a device called a *cumulative recorder* keeps track of the subject's responses. The recorder moves a strip of paper at a constant speed past a time-marking pen and a response-marking pen. Whenever the apparatus in the experimental chamber registers a response, the pen moves over one step. The slope of the response line on the paper reflects the subject's rate of responding.

Of the great variety of behaviors displayed by higher organisms, some are much more likely to occur than others. These behaviors can be arranged in a hierarchy of occurrence. In an operant training procedure, a particular behavior or response is selected for reinforcement. It may be a pigeon's pecking at a lighted disc or a person's smiling. The reinforcement, by increasing the probability that the response will be repeated, makes the response stronger and more predominant.

The initial level of responding is termed the *operant level.* A behavior well up in the hierarchy of occurrence (*high operant level*) will come under the reinforcement's control quite rapidly. A rare behavior (*low operant level*) requires more time to become firmly established. A response outside an organism's behavioral repertoire will not come under reinforcement control unless special steps are taken.

6-8

B. F. Skinner demonstrates, with the assistance of a rat, how the experimental chamber is used. In the course of investigating its new surroundings, the rat discovers that pressing the lever will release a food reward. (Nina Leen, Time-Life Picture Agency)

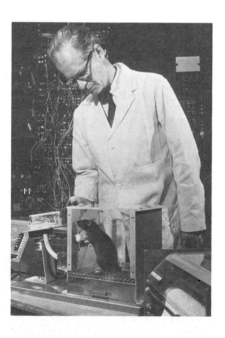

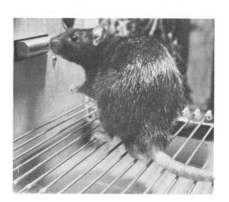

6-9
The cumulative recorder provides the researcher with a clear record of the animal's response rate over a period of time. With each response the response-marking pen moves a step away from the time-marking pen.

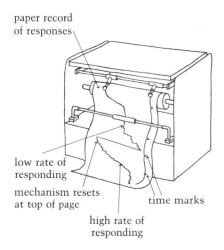

paper record of responses

low rate of responding

mechanism resets at top of page

high rate of responding

time marks

Shaping

A parent who wanted to use strict operant conditioning to teach his child to turn a somersault would have to wait until the somersault occurred naturally before reinforcing it. He might wait a long time. To establish such a response—not in the child's repertoire of normal behaviors—the parent would have to resort to a training aid known as *shaping*. Because reinforcers can establish behaviors, we can use them to mold or shape the desired response or series of responses.

Suppose then that we want to teach a 3-year-old child to turn a somersault without letting him know he is being taught. We can shape the behavior by reinforcing those bits of the child's behavior that are part of, or similar to, the somersault behavior. First, we tell the child what we want him to do. Although he understands our words, he must practice some to accomplish the somersault. When the child gets down on the floor on his hands and knees, we would immediately reinforce that behavior with some candy. After a few reinforced trials, the child would drop to his hands and knees to obtain more candy. We would now withhold further reinforcement until the child placed his head near the floor. After both some random and rewarded movements, the child would discover which movements earned him a reward. We could build the entire behavior in this way. Thus, the final behavior would be "created" by reinforcing *successive approximations*—by shaping the child's behavior, piece by piece, into the desired response. In using shaping, each step must be small enough for the subject to master it. For this reason, shaping is a difficult process that requires a skilled trainer.

A

B

C

D

6-10
Shaping is a basic technique of operant conditioning. Through proper reinforcement, the rats learn that working together they can obtain a food reward. In (A) one rat holds the ladder while another prepares to descend; the third rat is in an open box suspended outside of the chamber. In (B) the two rats pull chains to draw the box closer so that the third rat can join them. In (C) the rats sequentially step on three different buttons, which causes the door to raise. In (D) they enjoy the fruits of their teamwork. (Frank Lotz Miller, Black Star)

Teaching a child to turn a somersault is an example of shaping. The child is reward by his mother's encouraging and appreciative words and gestures at successive stages until he learns to perform the entire behavior pattern.

The tricks that circus animals perform are amazing. But they were all built slowly by the skillful application of shaping techniques.

Schedules of Reinforcement

A poker player does not win every time he plays. Similarly, organisms interacting with the environment usually are reinforced for relatively few of their responses. Yet card playing and many other human activities do not seem to decline for lack of a consistent reward. Thus, *partial reinforcement,* which means rewarding only a percentage of the total responses, is an effective means of controlling behavior.

Of the many different schedules of reinforcement, four are both the most commonly used and the most representative. Basically, these four schedules can be divided into two types. In type A, the reinforcement occurs after either *a fixed or variable amount of time* has elapsed between responses. In type B, the reinforcement occurs after either *a fixed or variable number of responses.* The names of the four reinforcement schedules are the fixed interval, the variable interval, the fixed ratio, and the variable ratio.

Fixed-Interval Schedule. Organisms operating under a *fixed-interval schedule* are reinforced for the first correct response that occurs after a fixed period of time has elapsed since the previous reinforced response. On a 2-minute fixed-interval schedule, the subject would be reinforced for the next correct response he made after 2 minutes had passed since his previous reinforced response.

Performance under a fixed-interval schedule of reinforcement follows a characteristic pattern. The responses fall off sharply immediately after a reinforcement. As the interval proceeds, the response rate gradually picks up until the organism is responding at a high rate near the interval's end. The behavior of the organism (man or beast) suggests that it is keeping track of elapsed time and responding appropriately. Since there is no reinforcement immediately after a reinforced response, adaptive behavior suggests to the subject that he should not "waste" responses during the early portion of the interval. The gradual increase in rate toward the end probably occurs because the organism cannot keep an exact account of elapsed time.

The typical cumulative response record under fixed-interval reinforcement shows "scallops" as the organism alternately pauses and accelerates time and time again. Fixed-interval responding produces the fewest responses per unit of time (note the relatively slight slope of the fixed-interval line) and the least consistent rate of response (as indicated by the scalloping). Considering the rather poor showing on fixed-interval responding, it comes as a mild surprise to realize that normal college practice is to give examinations on a fixed-interval schedule. Examinations are scheduled at mid-term and at the end of the term. Presumably, the reinforcement is to avoid a low grade, earn a high grade, or both. The response is studying. "Cramming" immediately prior to an exam corresponds to the animal subject's bursts of responding seen prior to a reinforcement on a fixed-interval schedule. After the exam, most students put their books on a shelf for a while until the next "reinforcement" draws near.

Variable-Interval Schedule. In the <u>variable-interval schedule</u> the reinforcement is available after a period of time that varies from one reinforcement to the next. The result is that the organism can no longer accurately judge when the next reinforcement will be available and

6-12

Graph comparing a subject's response rate under each reinforcement schedule. The fixed-interval schedule is obviously the least effective (the subject pauses for a time after each reinforcement). Under a variable-ratio schedule the response rate is very high; the subject does not know when reinforcement will be given and so responds consistently and rapidly. (From *A primer of operant conditioning.* G. S. Reynolds, Copyright 1968 by Scott, Foresman and Company. Reprinted by permission of the publisher.)

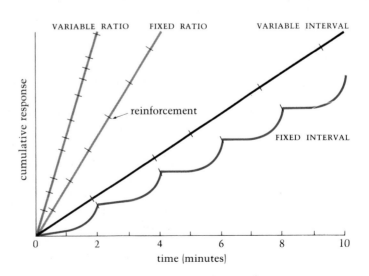

responds at a fairly constant low rate. Consequently, a variable-interval schedule eliminates the uneven rate of responding or scalloping that occurs under fixed-interval schedules.

If a college instructor had attempted to solve the problem of fixed-interval examinations by substituting variable-interval examinations he would, no doubt, be less popular but his students might be more consistently attentive to his course. Since the essence of variable-interval reinforcement is that the subjects do not know when the next reinforcement will occur, the instructor would employ unannounced "pop quizzes." Variable-interval responding is somewhat higher than fixed-interval and considerably more regular. In Figure 6-12 the interval's length would vary randomly between 0 and 4 minutes, producing a reinforcement on the average of one every 2 minutes.

Fixed-Ratio Schedule. A high rate of responding is typical of the *fixed-ratio schedule*. Reinforcement is available after a set number of non-reinforced responses. Industrial companies, for example, might base their employees' pay upon the number of units produced. If an employee can turn out 50 items a day at the pay rate of one dollar per item, he can earn $50 a day. If he increases his production, he can earn even more. Conversely, if he slows down he will earn correspondingly less. The worker's wage is a result of the speed at which he works. Obviously, if the reward is a sufficient motivator, the rate of responding can be quite high.

One difficulty in the use of the fixed-ratio schedule is that with high ratios—40 or 50 responses per reinforcement—the subject often pauses briefly after the reinforcer. To eliminate such pauses, the ratio of responses to reinforcers should be relatively low.

Variable-Ratio Schedule. As in fixed-ratio schedules, reinforcement under a *variable-ratio schedule* is available after a number of nonreinforced responses, but the number of them varies from reinforcement to reinforcement. The gambler's behavior is the most striking example of variable-ratio schedules of reinforcement. People have played slot machines nonstop for days, with random payoffs occurring throughout the period. The consequence of this schedule is that the individual never knows when be will hit the jackpot. It may occur on the next pull on the "one-armed bandit" or it may occur on the 100th pull.

Responding faster and faster, as subjects will in the variable-ratio schedule, means that the reinforcement will come more rapidly, as in fixed-ratio schedules. But the brief post-reinforcement pauses typical of fixed-ratio schedules do not occur, because the subject is eager to respond; his next response may pay off. If a consistently high rate of responding is the goal, the variable-ratio is the schedule to use.

The variable-ratio test schedule might be used to insure continuous studying, for example. Each student would be tested after he had completed study of a variable *amount* of material. In the traditional classroom, such a system would cause chaos. But used with today's teaching machines—some of which employ computers—and programmed textbooks, the student can pace himself, going as rapidly or as slowly as he chooses. After he has reviewed the unit of study matter, the book or the machine "examines" him. If he "passes," he goes on to

6-13
The slot machine is the classic example of a variable-ratio schedule of reinforcement. The player never knows when the machine will pay off. Payoffs—in small amounts—are given periodically to keep the player interested enough to continue to feed his quarters into the slot. (Elliott Erwitt, Magnum).

the next section; if he "fails," the better books and machines of this type will advise him to back up and repeat a particular bit of material. As another alternative, the machine, especially if it is linked to a computer, may put the student on a "remedial education" course to correct the deficiency the exam detected. Obviously, this teaching method works better with some subjects than with others. English literature may not fare as well as Spanish grammar or algebra. Nevertheless, such teaching devices promise efficient use of time for both student and teacher in many disciplines.

Reinforcement schedules have played a part in the space exploration program. The program's scientists drew on the knowledge that animals operating under a high-ratio schedule, either fixed or variable, are sensitive to disturbances about them; and their sensitivity is reflected in the changes in their rate of responding. In the early years of space exploration, many trained rats, pigeons, and monkeys were sent on brief orbital and lunar space shots. Scientists studied the effects that high acceleration, zero gravity, cosmic rays, and other forces had on the animals' rates of response. Russia's space project used animals in a similar way. However, following the Pavlovian tradition, they sent aloft dogs that had been classically, rather than operantly, conditioned. Significant changes in the environment were reflected in changes in the animals' conditioned responses.

Positive and Negative Reinforcement

We are accustomed to thinking of a reinforcement as something given—a candy, a food pellet, a coin. And these are indeed reinforcers—*positive reinforcers,* because they are stimuli whose presentation strengthens the responses that led to their presentation. But there also are *negative reinforcers.* They usually involve the removal of pain or discomfort and are defined as stimuli whose withdrawal increases the likelihood of the responses that led to their withdrawal. A rat that learns to press a lever which shuts off an electric shock is being conditioned with a negative reinforcer—the shutting-off of the electrical current.

The vast majority of positive reinforcers have few bad side effects. Obvious exceptions, of course, are such extremely powerful positive reinforcers as addictive drugs and, perhaps less obviously, electrical stimulation of the brain. In such cases, experimental animals will neglect all other behavior to obtain the reinforcer. Human drug and alcohol addicts, as well as some "obsessive" people—for example, a person fixated on personal success to the exclusion of all else—will display similar fixated behavior.

Escape Learning

The rat that learns to do something to turn off a shock is exhibiting what is called *escape learning* in its simplest form. No conditioned stimulus is present, only the punishing shock and some means of ending it—a lever to press or a place to escape to. Escape learning occurs widely and rapidly in the natural state for most organisms, including humans. Witness the difficulty of keeping prisoners in jails.

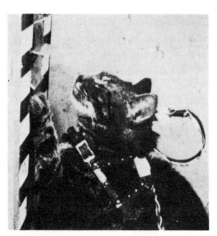

6-14
The cat learns to escape a shock by rotating a paddle wheel. Eventually, the cat is able to *avoid* the shock by rotating the wheel at the sound of a warning signal. (Courtesy Neal E. Miller)

In a particularly clear example of escape conditioning, Mowrer (1940) delivered a shock lasting for many minutes to rats in an experimental chamber. The shock was gradually increased from zero to a painful level and was maintained there. The first time rats were placed in this situation, they began to show agitated behavior after about a minute. As the shock grew stronger they began jumping, running, squealing, biting the shock floor grid—in short, trying every way they could to escape. On the first trial, it took 3 to 6 minutes for them to hit the lever accidentally. By the *tenth* trial they pressed the lever as soon as the shock was perceptible, long before it hurt.

Avoidance Learning

If we provide a warning or stimulus cue that punishment is on its way, animals and people will learn very quickly to avoid the punishment. If a tone is given just prior to shock and a rat can avoid the shock entirely by pressing a lever, he will quickly learn to do so when the tone comes on. Indeed, *avoidance learning*—learning to avoid an unpleasant stimulus or situation—is one of the most widespread forms of behavior control used in society. We avoid fines, jail, humiliation, and even boredom by engaging in appropriate and approved behaviors.

Sometimes, learned avoidance behavior can be inappropriate. When small children are being toilet-trained, they may be punished for "going" in their pants. As a result, they may try to avoid "going" at all, with certain and disastrous consequences. Punishment by itself often merely suppresses behavior. A related laboratory example of this was provided by Fonberg (1956). Dogs were conditioned to lift a leg to avoid shock. Later they were being trained in a different situation to tell the difference between two tones. When it became difficult to tell, they began lifting their legs—they were clearly telling the experimenter that the situation was unpleasant and they would like to avoid it.

Very high rates of behavioral response can be generated by avoidance training. An ingenious experiment by Sidman (1953) illustrates the point. Rats were given a shock every 20 seconds. If they pushed a lever between shocks, the next shock was postponed for a few seconds but eventually was given. Under these conditions rats pressed the lever at very fast rates and thus postponed the shock indefinitely.

Interesting studies by Garcia and others (Garcia & Ervin, 1968; Garcia & Koelling, 1966) have demonstrated clear limits to the effectiveness of certain combinations of stimuli and punishment in avoidance learning. The basic phenomenon is "bait-shyness," known for centuries to hunters and ranchers. It is almost impossible to poison a predatory wild animal that has once been poisoned and survived. They become wary of the taste of the poison and even of the bait itself. Garcia trained groups of rats in an avoidance task using either a visual or a taste conditioned stimulus. Two kinds of punishment were used for different groups—electric shock and sickness induced by exposing the animals to x-radiation. Results were strikingly clear. Animals trained with visual cues to avoid shock learned very well. Similarly, animals trained with taste to avoid radiation-sickness learned very well. However, animals could not learn to avoid shock by a taste warning stimulus and could not learn to avoid radiation sickness with a visual warning stimulus. In both the natural behavioral world and the brain sensory systems, taste and sickness go together and visual cues and shock (external body pain) go together. It is a common human experience that some odors and tastes nauseate us but tones and lights most certainly do not.

Conditioned Fear. Anxiety that has been learned to neutral stimuli because of their pairing with negative reinforcement is called conditioned fear. The classic experiment was done by Neal Miller (1948). Rats were placed in a white compartment and given a strong inescapable shock. Later, they were put back in the white compartment without shock but now with a wheel that, when turned, allowed them to escape. They quickly learned to escape, even though shock had never been paired with escape. They learned to fear the white compartment and this conditioned fear then served as a learned or acquired motivation which led to subsequent avoidance learning. The basic mechanism in conditioned fear is probably classical conditioning, but it serves to motivate much subsequent avoidance learning. Such acquired fears are probably much more important than direct fear of pain in adult human behavior. An extreme pathological form of conditioned fear is called a *phobia*, a totally unreasonable fear of some neutral object like running water or dolls.

Punishment

Punishment is a conditioning tool which, like negative reinforcement, employs an unpleasant or painful stimulus to produce a response. However, punishment is substantially different from negative reinforcement. In negative reinforcement, the existing painful stimulus is withdrawn to produce a response; in punishment, it is imposed to produce a response. There is another important difference. Negative reinforcement is used to build up a response; punishment is used to undermine and discourage a response.

Punishment is firmly ingrained in our method of interpersonal and societal control. We spank children, fine or imprison lawbreakers, flunk students, and hit dogs. Does it work? What are the consequences? Obviously, punishment works to suppress the behavior that elicits the punishment—at least to a degree. Most social customs, such as imprisonment, have evolved because they are to some extent effective. However, an individual often seeks ways to avoid the punishment rather than cease his own undesirable behavior.

As we shall discuss in a later section, a learned response—and many punished behaviors are learned—can be eliminated by nonreinforcement or extinction. Unfortunately, we often are not in control of the reinforcer. The parents of a young boy who has taken up with a neighborhood gang of juvenile thugs might strongly disapprove. However, they cannot eliminate the reinforcement their son receives when he associates with the gang.

If mild punishments are regularly used to discourage an undesirable behavior, it may be temporarily suppressed. If, at the same time, the subject is shown alternate, acceptable behaviors associated with positive reinforcement, he may exchange his undesirable behaviors for acceptable ones. If an infant is scolded for hitting his dog while he is shown how to "pet" the dog, the child can retain the reinforcement he gets from interacting with his dog. Only his mode of expression changes.

On the other hand, if mild punishments are given intermittently and no attempt is made to build in acceptable behaviors, the subject's behavior will change little. Indeed, the individual will probably try to avoid punishment, and often will resort to trickery and devious behaviors to attain the forbidden goal without punishment.

Strong punishments affect behavior quite differently. Inflicting a severe punishment every time an undesirable behavior is performed can suppress the behavior completely. However, this procedure may produce side effects. First, the severe punishment could prompt avoidance responses that not only may apply to the specific undesirable behavior, but also may generalize to the entire situation. A youngster who is severely punished for misbehaving during religious services may avoid church altogether because of the aura of pain he associates with it. Second, severe punishment may produce a strong, unresolvable conflict within the individual. He is torn by two opposing forces. On the one side is the positive reinforcer, which he associates with pleasure and the performance of the undesirable behavior, and on the other side is the harsh punishment, which he associates with fear and inhibition of the same behavior. The resulting conflict may produce a neurotic individual. This syndrome is fairly common in persons severely punished for "forbidden" sexual activity—itself a strong positive reinforcer.

In sum, punishment may effectively control behavior when it is paired with opportunities to learn new responses to replace old ones.

Autonomic Conditioning

For decades, psychologists and physiologists had assumed that the autonomic nervous system, which controls heart rate and blood pressure, could not be brought under operant control. A few years ago, their assumption was disproved. Miller (1969) showed that the heart rate and blood pressure of rats could be operantly conditioned. He began by measuring the heart rate of his subjects and by rewarding some with brain stimulation for speeding up their heart rate and others for slowing it down (as we shall see in Chapter 10, stimulation of areas of the hypothalamus seems to produce pleasurable feelings). Miller found that the animals could increase or decrease heart rate by at least one-third. Several animals, trained to slow their heart rate, lowered it so much that they died.

In other experiments, Miller has demonstrated that operant conditioning can control salivation, intestinal contractions, and kidney and stomach functions. A rat can even be trained to increase the blood flow in one ear. Miller and his associates performed a comprehensive series of control experiments which showed that such effects did not result from general arousal, muscular activity, or other factors.

Miller's discovery offers a possible way to treat the causes of psychosomatic illnesses, which are real physical disorders that appear to have psychological rather than physiological roots (see Chapter 20). For ex-

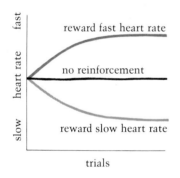

6-15
Graph of an experiment in which rats were rewarded (with brain stimulation) for increasing or decreasing their heartbeats. Brain stimulation is such a strong reinforcer that the animals performed exactly as desired. (Adopted from N. E. Miller & A. Banuazizi. Instrumental learning by curarized rats of a specific visceral response, intestinal or cardiac. *Journal of Comparative and Physiological Psychology*, 1968, **65**, 1–7. Copyright © 1968 by the American Psychological Association. Reprinted by permission.)

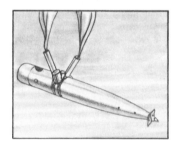

ample, many young children are pampered when ill. They may learn that they can gain attention or get their way by being "sick." Illness becomes an effective, though unhealthy, means to deal with parents—and others, if the response generalizes. This is only one way in which psychosomatic ills might develop.

Current operant techniques may alleviate existing psychosomatic illnesses to some extent. High blood pressure, or hypertension, is one example of a psychosomatic illness. Inordinately high pressure severely strains the heart and blood vessels. Miller and his colleagues proposed that hypertensive persons be trained to use operant methods to lower their own blood pressure. If humans can be trained to regulate their own blood pressure and other autonomic functions effectively, the symptoms of many illnesses could be relieved. Actually, direct human control of autonomic functions should not surprise us. For centuries, Indian mystics have been slowing their hearts at will.

Significance of Operant Conditioning

It would be difficult to overstate the significance of operant conditioning in human life. In our daily routines, we try to maximize pleasure and avoid pain, even if we must endure temporary "pain" to gain eventual pleasure. Man has used operant conditioning for many many years, but only in this century has it been studied scientifically. Still, there is much that psychology does not know about human or animal behavior. Information from future operant conditioning studies certainly will provide us with greater opportunities to increase our understanding and control of human behavior. In Chapter 21, we shall discuss two operant methods—token economies and behavior therapy—which already have provided a good deal of information about controlling and restructuring human behavior.

To convince yourself of the subtle power of operant conditioning, try this experiment. Sit down with another person at a table from which you can unobtrusively watch a clock. Talking over coffee is ideal. Have a piece of paper in front of you. Doodle on it. For the first 10 minutes note on the paper the number of opinions your companion states. Tally up all of the "I think . . ." and "It seems to me . . ." statements. For the next 10 minutes positively reinforce those opinions by emphatically agreeing with them. (This may be difficult!) Again keep a tally. For the final 10-minute period you can do one of two things: Deny reinforcement of the opinions by keeping silent or changing the topic; or, negatively reinforce the opinions by emphatically disagreeing with each and every one. Again keep a tally. You may be surprised at the experiment's outcome. Your companion also will be surprised when you tell him what you were doing. If you are skillful, he will have been totally unaware that you were controlling his behavior.

6-16
Operant conditioning is used by the Navy to teach pilot whales to make deep ocean recoveries of experimental torpedoes. The whale was shaped to attach "grabber claws" to the torpedo. (When attached the claw releases a balloon which floats the torpedo to the surface.) Shaping is accomplished by rewarding the whale with food for each successive approximation to the desired behavior pattern. Frogmen shaped the whale's behavior by working with it in shallower water. (Naval Photographic Center)

Basic Processes in Learning

Classical and operant conditioning, the fundamental forms of learning, share a number of basic processes and conditions. Both types of learning are associative, as we have said. Reinforcement, the receipt of reward or punishment, is critical in both types of learning, as is the time relationship or contiguity between reward and behavioral response. Other phenomena of learning include forgetting or extinction, and generalization and discrimination.

Contiguity

The fundamental element shared by classical and operant conditioning is _contiguity_—the closeness in time of the two stimuli to be associated. Up to a point, the more coincident the stimuli, the more efficient the learning. The operant conditioning of a rat is a good illustration. The animal is placed in an experimental chamber, or Skinner box. Eventually, the rat will press the lever in the box. If the animal immediately receives a food pellet each time it presses the lever, it will link lever-pressing with the receipt of food—and quickly learn the association. However, if the food arrives a minute after the rat presses the lever, the rat will take a very long time to learn the association. Between the pressing of the lever and the arrival of food a minute later, the rat would perform many other behaviors. If the rat happened to be scratching its nose when the food arrived, that behavior would become associated with food. A hungry rat could be expected to spend more and more time scratching its nose.

In a laboratory experiment to show the effects of contiguity, three groups of rats were rewarded with food for choosing the correct goal box in a maze shaped like a T. One group received food immediately upon entering the goal box. The other groups received food after delays of 5 seconds and 30 seconds. The graph shows the rats' performance in terms of how often they chose the correct goal box. Since the rats initially chose the wrong side as often as the right side, they started at 50 percent. The animals ran 10 trials per day. Those receiving food immediately (0-second delay) and the 5-second-delay group learned at a faster rate than the 30-second-delay group, which did not learn beyond the 65 percent correct level. In this experiment, the contiguity between correct behavior and reward had a marked effect.

Contiguity also affects human behavior. A mother who defers punishing (or praising) a child until Daddy comes home is violating the rule of contiguity. The child will not alter his behavior much as a result of such long-delayed punishments or rewards. Instead, the child will frequently develop a fear of his father for dispensing seemingly unwarranted punishments.

Superstition. Operant conditioning provides a very clear explanation for human superstitions. _Superstition_, the belief that the repetition of a behavior will elicit or prevent an event, results when an individual mistakenly thinks that a certain incidental action or situation is the cause that elicits or prevents that event. Skinner discovered that if

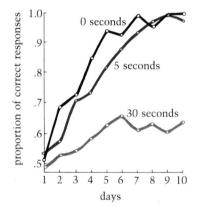

6-17
Graph of the relationship between timing of reinforcement and learning. Rats receiving food 0 or 5 seconds after performing the correct response learned the correct response substantially better than rats that received reinforcement after a 30 second delay. (Unpublished data from Atkinson)

rewards are simply given to an animal (or human) at random times with no relation to the behaviors generated by the animal, very peculiar kinds of behavior develop. One pigeon, for example, might be circling around the experimental chamber when food arrives. Subsequently, it will spend more time circling and will be more likely to be circling the next time food arrives. Soon the pigeon will be circling madly and continuously around the cage. Circling was the behavior that was reinforced initially merely because, by chance, it occurred at the same time that the reward was given.

Human superstitions provide endless examples of the power of contiguity. Walking under a ladder must, on occasion, lead to punishment—the painter drops his pail, for example. An athlete who wins an important game sometimes wears the same cap or jacket or other article of clothing in other games because it brought him good luck the first time. Every reader can think of things that she or he does regularly because they were reinforced once or twice by chance. One of the authors of this book developed the habit of going to grade Z movies before each big exam in college because the first time he did so he got an A. The grade was due, obviously, to having studied and not to having watched a terrible movie. However, he found the movie-going behavior very difficult to eliminate.

Superstitious behavior resulting from chance combinations of some behavior and an unrelated reward have a surprising degree of meaning for individuals. Indeed, many religious beliefs can be traced to chance contiguity between some action and reward. Good crops *sometimes* grew after the Aztecs tossed the sacrificial victim off the pyramid. Partial reinforcement is enough—the behavior does not need to be "rewarded" every time, only occasionally. We tend to remember the rewarded times more than the failures.

Reinforcement

Simple contiguity is not enough to insure learning. In the previous example, the rat in the experimental chamber would not have learned the association between lever-pressing and food if it had not been hungry. By the same token, punishing a child by depriving it of dessert is ineffective if the child detests the strawberries and cream anyway. Both the rat's pellet and the child's dessert are examples of the vital importance of selecting the right reinforcement. Reinforcers may satisfy basic biological needs for warmth, sex, food, drink, and air—all common reinforcers in animal experiments.

Another basic biological goal and a powerful reinforcer is the removal of pain or discomfort. To take an action that prevents discomfort also is reinforcing. Thus, donning a warm coat on a cold day is reinforcing. We have learned that it is more pleasant (more reinforcing) to put on a coat to prevent being cold than to become cold and afterward put on a coat to remedy the situation.

Reinforcers are not always related to basic biological needs. In the United States, most people do not often experience severe hunger, thirst, or cold. On the other hand, we are under the control of a large number of reinforcers that arise out of our interpersonal relations. A

6-18
Superstitions develop when we are accidentally rewarded for a particular behavior. Superstitions also are passed from generation to generation. While most of us have never encountered bad luck after walking under a ladder, stepping on a crack, breaking a mirror, and so on, we feel curiously reluctant to test these age-old beliefs.

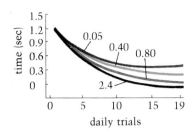

6-19
Graph of the relationship between amount of reinforcement and learning. The group of rats that received the greatest amount of food at the goal box took less time to start on subsequent runs down the alley than those receiving proportionately less food. The numbers above the curves indicate the amount of food reward each group received. (After D. Zeaman. Response latency as a function of the amount of reinforcement. *Journal of Experimental Psychology*, 1949, **39,** 466–483. Copyright © 1949 by the American Psychological Association. Reprinted by permission.)

smile can be a reinforcer, as can school grades, peer approval, money, and the avoidance of humiliation.

Reinforcers are so important to most kinds of learning that Thorndike made them the pivotal element in his *law of effect*. This law states that an organism tends to repeat and learn a behavior that has a satisfying or reinforcing outcome. The opposite often is true. However, the effects of punishment are so uncertain and undependable that organisms frequently will repeat a behavior that has an unpleasant or nonreinforcing outcome.

A particular reinforcer does not have the same effect on all individuals. An experience which reinforces one person may not reinforce another. Some people would relish, and thus find reinforcing, a meal of squid or snails but many others would not. One challenge of the teaching profession is discovering which reinforcers to use. Unfortunately, some students respond only to threatened negative reinforcers (low grades); others, of course, are also interested in learning the subject matter. Actually, an individual may be unaware of many of the reasons why he works and strives for various goals. Much motivation appears to be unconscious—a topic we will explore further in Chapter 10.

The amount of reinforcement given an organism affects its learning. However, learning *speed* rather than *amount* of learning is most affected by the quantity of reward. In other words, the amount of the reinforcement would have a greater impact on how fast the organism learned rather than on how much it learned. The graph in Figure 6-19 shows the results of an experiment in which several groups of rats each received a different amount of food as reward for running down a straight pathway to a goal box. Each group's running speed was graphed and compared to its amount of reinforcement. The animals that received more reinforcement ran faster.

Conditioned Reinforcement. As we have noted, money is a powerful reinforcer. Money, like many other *conditioned reinforcers*, attains its power from its association with other reinforcers. Obviously, money is not good to eat or drink, will not keep you warm or entertain you. Yet it will buy all of those things—and that is the source of its reinforcing value. It is associated with basic *unconditioned reinforcers*.

In modern societies, such conditioned reinforcers as money, praise, success, and approval are more commonly used than are unconditioned reinforcers. One side effect of using conditioned reinforcers is that the accumulation of them tends to become an end in itself. Plain need is replaced by other motives. People accumulate much more money than they can spend; students strive for straight A's, forgetting that their purpose is to gain an education; and some people strive for success neglecting other goals that might well bring them more lasting happiness. One common trait shared by the Beatniks of the 1960s and the Hippies of the early 1970s was their rejection of some of the conditioned reinforcers that are widely accepted in our society.

Extinction and Spontaneous Recovery

If the reinforcement for a learned behavior is removed, the behavior slowly disappears or *extinguishes*. How fast extinction occurs depends

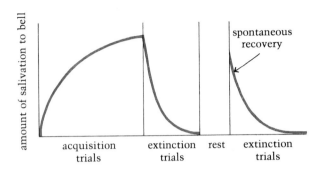

amount of salivation to bell

spontaneous recovery

acquisition trials · extinction trials · rest · extinction trials

6-20

In conditioning, if the unconditioned stimulus or the reinforcement is withdrawn, learned responses to the stimulus will extinguish. If conditioning trials are resumed after a period of rest, the animal exhibits spontaneous recovery. This schematic illustrates the course of acquisition, extinction, spontaneous recovery and subsequent extinction.

on how often the behavior was performed, the amount of reinforcement, and many other factors. If we wait long enough, a learned response will disappear completely. Has it been forgotten? Usually, the answer is no.

Figure 6-20 depicts extinction in an experiment in which a dog was trained to salivate to the sound of a bell. In the conditioning phase, called *acquisition,* the bell was repeatedly paired with meat powder placed in the mouth. Eventually, the bell elicited salivation *before* the reinforcing meat powder was delivered. At this point, the meat powder was discontinued, leaving only the bell. The salivary response eventually disappeared. However, if the dog rested and then was tested again, the learned salivary response reappeared! Such *spontaneous recovery* indicates that an extinguished response is not totally eradicated. Apparently, the subject suppresses rather than forgets the learned response.

Generalization

Many years ago, the American psychologist J. B. Watson performed an experiment on a small child named Albert. Watson placed Albert in a room with a tame white rat. Every time Albert reached for the rat, Watson made a loud noise which startled the infant and made him cry. After several such trials, Albert whimpered at the mere sight of the rodent. This is a classic example of conditioned fear.

In addition, Albert demonstrated a remarkable behavior. Whenever anything resembling a white rat was placed near him, he cried. Furry objects and other animals were the most effective in eliciting tears from Albert (Watson & Rayner, 1920). Albert was exhibiting a learning behavior called *generalization,* in which objects similar to a particular stimulus will elicit similar responses. The more marked the similarity, the more vigorous the response. Reportedly, Albert survived this episode and later became a psychologist, perhaps an example of overgeneralization.

Generalization declines as the test stimulus begins to differ from the training stimulus (for example, as the furry object becomes less and less similar to the white rat). The point is well illustrated by an experiment in which the subject's galvanic skin response (GSR) was conditioned to a particular tone (Hovland, 1937). The GSR, one measure in a lie-detector test, represents the change in skin resistance measured on the palms of the hands; the resistance results from increased sweat gland

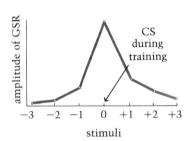

amplitude of GSR

CS during training

−3 −2 −1 0 +1 +2 +3

stimuli

6-21

Graph of an experiment in which a subject's GSR was conditioned to the sound of a tone (represented by 0). His GSR generalized to similar tones. As the tones became less like the original tone, the subject was better able to discriminate among the tones. +1, +2, and +3 are tones of higher pitch and −1, −2, and −3 are tones of lower pitch than the original tone. (After Hovland, 1937)

Basic Processes in Learning **203**

activity, usually accompanying an emotional response. The tone in this experiment was paired with an electric shock. At first, only the shock produced a GSR. But after several pairings, the tone assumed significance and also produced a GSR. When testing with tones higher or lower in pitch than the training tone, the more the test stimulus resembled the training stimulus the greater the generalization and the greater the GSR response.

Humans generalize a good deal. If we visit a strange town and are impressed with the few people we meet, we tend to have a good feeling about the whole town. Similarly, if our first encounter with a person from some other racial or social group is unpleasant, we tend to overgeneralize from the individual to his entire group.

Discrimination

Discrimination is the opposite of generalization. A discriminating buyer is able to distinguish between closely related items and choose the one that best suits his needs. The same is true of discrimination in learning: a response is established toward one stimulus in the presence of others. Discrimination is best established by reinforcing only one of several stimuli. The other stimuli may be unreinforced or even negatively reinforced. In the latter case, the organism is rewarded for responding to one stimulus but punished for responding to others.

Thus, generalization prompts similar responses to similar stimuli, while discrimination prompts different responses to similar stimuli. To return to the experiment just described, the subject only somewhat generalized his GSR response to a tone different from the training tone. Generalization is the extent to which he gave the same response to both stimuli. Discrimination is the extent to which he did not give the same response. Whether you call the initial response generalization or whether you call it discrimination depends on how you measure it. A familiar example of both generalization and discrimination occurs in the infant's development of language (Brown, 1965). When he is first learning to speak, all adults are "da-da," including the mailman and little old aunts. Similarly, all animals are "woof-woof," from cats to chickens. When the child calls a chicken a "woof-woof," the parent might say, "No, that's a chicken," or "No, that's a bird." Thus, the child is differentially reinforced and learns to discriminate the dogs from chickens. Did dogs and chickens "look" the same to the child initially? It seems unlikely. What he learns is to make differential responses.

In the operant conditioning laboratory, a stimulus whose responses are positively reinforced is a _positive discriminative stimulus_ or S^D. A stimulus whose responses are not reinforced or negatively reinforced is called a _negative discriminative stimulus_ or S$^\Delta$ (pronounced S delta). As we have noted, subjects can often discriminate among objects that are only slightly different. Man's ability to discriminate among stimuli underlies those tasks in intelligence tests that require one to select identical complex images presented in different positions.

Discrimination learning has still another use. Researchers have used it to investigate sensory functioning in many organisms. For example, by requiring dogs to discriminate between a stimulus of one color (S^D) and

A

B

6-22
In this discrimination test, the rat is learning the concept of "two-ness." In (A) it is reinforced for jumping through the door on which two children's faces appear. To discover whether it has learned the concept, the rat is tested later with diagonal lines. It obviously has learned the concept of two-ness, since it jumps through the door with two diagonal lines on it. This is a typical discrimination test. (Experiment by Professor Loh Seng Tsai; photo by Frank Lotz Miller, Black Star)

a stimulus of another color (S^Δ), experimenters can determine whether dogs can see colors. They know that the dog can learn analogous non-color discriminations. When the experiment is controlled for differences in brightness and other variables, they find that a dog cannot learn to discriminate colors, and conclude correctly that the dog does not have color vision.

Cognitive Learning

Complex intellectual activities like thinking, problem-solving, and insightful learning merge into one another. The term *cognitive learning* has no precise definition. It refers generally to those aspects of learning associated with more complex aspects of behavior. However, even relatively simple forms of learning, such as latent learning, which we shall discuss shortly, are often called cognitive. The psychologist Tolman gave cognitive learning a sound experimental base. He argued that all higher organisms, from man down at least to rat, form cognitive maps of the world in their minds (or brains, if you prefer). Behavior is guided not only by past and present rewards and punishments but also by our expectations, based on a general view or understanding of the world that we have built up through a lifetime of experience. The cognitive aspects of behavior are treated at length in Chapter 8. We shall discuss here only those aspects most clearly related to learning.

Learning as an Active Process

The following passage on learning and education by Jerome Bruner, a leading cognitive psychologist, conveys a sense of the modern cognitive approaches to learning. The key idea in Bruner's view of learning is that learning is an active process. Thus, rather than being merely passive receptacles of associations, each of us imposes active effort, our own frame of reference, and our personal intellectual style on what we learn and how we learn it. Or, as Bruner says:

Learning a subject seems to involve three almost simultaneous processes. First there is acquisition of new information—often information that runs counter to or is a replacement for what the person has previously known implicitly or explicitly. At the very least it is a refinement of previous knowledge. Thus one teaches a student Newton's laws of motion, which violate the testimony of the senses. Or in teaching a student about wave mechanics, one violates the student's belief in mechanical impact as the sole source of real-energy transfer. Or one bucks the language and its built-in way of thinking in terms of wasting energy by introducing the student to the conservation theorem in physics, which asserts that no energy is lost. More often the situation is less drastic, as when one teaches the details of the circulatory system to a student who already knows vaguely or intuitively that blood circulates.

A second aspect of learning may be called transformation—the process of manipulating knowledge to make it fit new tasks. We learn to unmask or analyze information, to order it in a way that permits ex-

trapolation or interpolation or conversion into another form. *Transformation comprises the ways we deal with information in order to go beyond it.*

A third aspect of learning is evaluation, checking whether the way we have manipulated information is adequate to the task. Is the generalization fitting, have we extrapolated appropriately, are we operating properly? Often a teacher is crucial in helping with evaluation, but much of it takes place by judgments of plausibility without our actually being able to check rigorously whether we are correct in our efforts. (Bruner, 1960)

Latent or Incidental Learning

It is likely that much of the learning we do in our ordinary daily lives is incidental. When you are caught up in an absorbing movie or television program you do not make an active effort to *remember*. You do not review a movie as you would do with lecture notes or a text while preparing for an exam. Yet you remember much of the movie—you can see long scenes in your mind's eye. We all have had the experience of seeing what we believe to be a new program or movie on television, only to discover quickly that we have seen it before. To our irritation, we can predict every scene and action and we lose interest. Despite such accurate recall, we were not trying to remember it the first time we saw it. Our learning of the movie may be termed *incidental* or *latent*. We use the term latent because generally no subsequent test of learning is conducted. We would not know you had seen the movie before (and you might not either) until you saw it again and remembered it.

The classic study of latent learning was done by Tolman and Honzik (1930). In brief, they trained one group of rats in a maze with a food reward at the end of each trial and two groups without reward. The groups "trained" without reward showed only small improvements in performance. On day 11 one of the previously unrewarded groups was suddenly given food at the end of each run through the maze. The performance of these rats improved dramatically, rising to the level of the regularly rewarded group. Clearly, the "unrewarded" animals had learned something about the maze when allowed to explore it without reward. Tolman would say they had developed a <u>cognitive map</u> of the

6-23

An illustration of latent learning. The food-rewarded rats negotiate the maze with fewer errors than the rats not rewarded with food during the first ten days. When the nonrewarded rats are rewarded on and after day 11, the number of errors they make drops dramatically. Errors do not decrease much for a third group which is given no reward throughout the 17 days. These results show that the nonrewarded rats have been learning the maze during the first ten days, but their learning is latent and does not manifest itself until they are rewarded. (Tolman & Honzik, University of California Press, 1930)

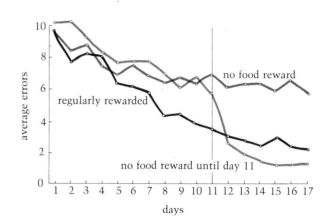

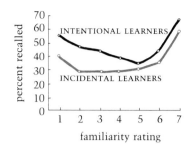

6-24
Graph showing how incidental learning may improve as a function of familiarity. While subjects who intentionally learn material have a consistently better rate of recall, the performance of the incidental learners is almost as good when the material to be learned is familiar to them. (L. Postman, P. A. Adams, & L. W. Phillips. Studies in incidental learning. II: The effects of association values and of the method of testing. *Journal of Experimental Psychology*, 1955, **49**, 1–10. Copyright © 1955 by the American Psychological Association. Reprinted by permission.)

maze which they had no reason to *show* until there was a payoff. Their learning remained latent.

A similar laboratory phenomenon is *sensory preconditioning.* In the pioneering study of Brogden (1939) dogs first were simply given paired lights and tones. They were then trained to avoid shock by responding to a warning light. In testing the strength of their avoidance conditioning, the experimenter replaced the light with a tone. The dogs responded to the tone much more quickly and correctly than did control dogs that had not earlier experienced the tone and light paired together (Thompson, 1972). The first set of dogs remembered that the two stimuli had occurred together earlier, even though they were not rewarded at the time.

There is now considerable interest in human latent learning. Research in the laboratory is somewhat difficult—it obviously would not work well to ask intelligent college student subjects *not* to learn some aspects of a task. One approach has been to instruct the subjects to learn one kind of task and then later test them on some seemingly irrelevant aspect of the task. Postman and associates (for example, Postman, 1964) compared learning of verbal materials (both "incidentally" and "intentionally") as a function of the material's meaning to the subject. For example, two lists of words—one meaningful and the other meaningless—might be presented to the subjects. One group would be told that they were being tested on how well they could recall the lists. The other group was simply asked to read the list several times. Interestingly, if the material to be learned holds a great deal of meaning for the subject, little difference can be found between the amount learned incidentally and intentionally. But material with little meaning is learned much better intentionally than incidentally. This experiment explains why we remember good movies so well without even trying. A good movie is almost by definition very meaningful. In fact, extremely bad movies also are often "meaningful"—even if we do not like the meaning. This observation also provides some justification for the use of audiovisual aids in education. If a learning experience can be made sufficiently absorbing and meaningful, as in movies, students will remember well even if they do not try to learn the material.

Learning Set or Learning-to-Learn

There is an old argument in psychology and education about the value of formal memorization. You may remember stories by your grandparents about how they had to memorize countless pages of poems in school. The notion was that the "faculty" of memory was thereby improved. William James tested this notion many years ago in a heroic self-experiment. He set himself to learn 40 lines a day of Milton's *Paradise Lost.* When he had memorized the entire poem he found that his memory for other information had not improved at all.

Although James's conclusion about rote learning of poetry was largely correct, learning-to-learn is in fact a very real phenomenon. Adults have probably already learned to learn meaningful verbal materials as well as they possibly can—after all, we practice almost from birth. Harry Harlow has provided perhaps the clearest laboratory demonstrations of

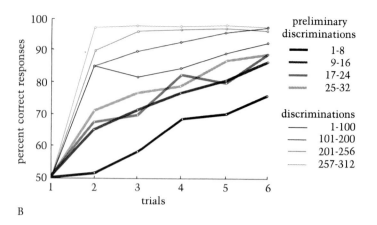

6-25

(A) Photograph of a monkey performing one of Harlow's discrimination tasks in a learning set experiment. (B) Graph of the results of the first six trials of these discriminations. Each curve represents a block of problems. The data for the first 32 discriminations are grouped for blocks of eight discriminations; the remaining discriminations are grouped for blocks of 100, 100, 56, and 56 problems. The top line shows that the monkeys could perform each problem in the series correctly on the second trial; they had learned how to perform discrimination tasks in general and could easily apply their knowledge to all similar problems. (A. Courtesy Harry Harlow, Regional Primate Research Center, University of Wisconsin; B. H. Harlow. The formation of learning sets. *Psychological Review*, 1949, **56**, 51–65. Copyright © 1949 by the American Psychological Association. Reprinted by permission.)

learning-to-learn—first in monkeys and then in children—and labeled the phenomenon *learning set*. Monkeys were trained on a very large number of two-choice discriminations; they were presented with two dissimilar objects, one of which had a food reward under it. They were given six trials on each set of objects. On the first few problems they performed badly. However, after about 300 problems, they invariably scored almost perfectly after the first trial. They had no way of knowing which object was correct on the first trial of each problem. The first response is either correct or incorrect, a 50–50 chance of success. Whichever they choose, there is no question which is correct on trial two. If the food is not under the first object, it must be under the second. Skilled monkeys seem to show "insight"—they perform the first trial indifferently and then immediately go after the correct object on trial two. They clearly "know" the answer after the first trial. Very young children perform much like monkeys on learning-set problems. However, by the age of five they seem to catch on more quickly than do 5-year-old monkeys. Harlow notes that the very rapid learning of such simple problems by older children might lead us to conclude that some kind of new or insightful learning process occurs in humans; however, the well-trained monkeys do as well. The only difference is that we have controlled the past training of the monkeys.

Adult humans show clear learning sets when learning new types of verbal materials. Thune (1950) trained college students on three lists of paired adjectives per day for five days. (The adjectives are shown as pairs, for example, red—soft; the subject is asked to recall the second word of the pair after seeing only the first word. The pairs have no meaning; they must be learned by rote.) The subjects got progressively better each day even though they had to learn new lists each day. They were developing a learning set for this kind of learning task.

Insight

One of the classic observations in psychology was made by Wolfgang Köhler (1926) when he described insightful behavior in a chimpanzee. Köhler, a German psychologist and a pioneering figure in Gestalt psychology, was studying the behavior of apes. One chimpanzee was given the problem of reaching with two sticks a banana outside his cage; each

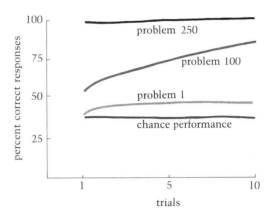

Graph showing how learning set affects performance. Although each problem is slightly different, all 250 problems can be solved by the same technique. By problem 100, the subject achieves 85 percent correct responses on trial 10. By problem 250, the subject is 100 percent correct on all trials. (Adapted from Bourne, 1966)

6-27
In a classic experiment, Köhler placed his prize chimpanzee Sultan in a cage with two sticks; outside the cage were two more sticks and an object that interested the chimp. Neither of the sticks held by the chimp was long enough to reach the object. Through insight and trial and error, the chimp discovered that one stick could reach the first outside stick; that stick could be inserted inside the other and together, the sticks were long enough to reach the final stick, which when inserted in the third stick allowed Sultan to reach the object. (Yerkes Regional Primate Center)

stick alone was too short. The chimp tried each stick for a while and gave up. Later, while playing with the sticks, he accidentally discovered that they could be fitted together to form a long stick. With an expression that seemed to say "Eureka!" he rushed to the edge of the cage and retrieved the banana. The ape had gained an _insight._

The insightful type of learning exhibited by Köhler's chimp is often contrasted with the emphasis on trial-and-error progress in earlier studies of learning—for example, Thorndike's cat in the puzzle box. Harlow's studies of learning set suggest that the truth may lie somewhere in between. Insightful learning—resulting in a sudden improvement in performance—does indeed occur, but it requires a long background of previous learning and learning-to-learn. Learning set may form the base for insightful learning.

Contemporary cognitive psychologists tend to adopt this general view. The development of learning capacities in children consists of several stages, as described so extensively by Piaget and his students (see Chapter 14). These stages require previous learning. Similarly, the development of intellectual capacities and learning abilities builds upon a hierarchy of past learning and learning sets.

Summary

1. Although we are often unaware it is happening, learning suffuses our waking lives. It may occur as an incidental impression, as an association of stimuli and responses, as a cognitive reorganization of our ideas, and in several other ways.

2. Two simple forms of learning are habituation, a decreased response to irrelevant stimuli, and sensitization, an increased response to meaningful stimuli. Both are essential to the organism's survival.

3. The decreased or habituated response to a repeated stimulus will increase or sensitize if any aspect of the stimulus changes.

4. Classical conditioning, developed by Pavlov, occurs when a stimulus associated with a meaningful event substitutes for the event itself and elicits similar responses.

5. In classical conditioning, an unconditioned stimulus is paired with a conditioned stimulus to elicit a conditioned response similar to the unconditioned response. The most effective time relationship between presentation of the CS and US is delayed conditioning (almost immediate); trace, simultaneous, and backward conditioning (usually ineffective) also are used.

6. First developed by Thorndike in his law of effect and further elaborated by Skinner, operant conditioning refers to the learning of behaviors that must be carried out in order to obtain reward or to avoid pain or punishment.

7. Shaping involves reinforcement of successive approximations of the desired response.

8. The four most common schedules of reinforcement are the fixed interval, variable interval, fixed ratio, and variable ratio. The variable-ratio schedule is the most effective because the subject never knows when to expect reinforcement.

9. Reinforcement may be positive, strengthening the activity that led to the presentation of the stimulus, or negative, strengthening the responses that led to the withdrawal of the stimulus.

10. Escape learning involves an organism's activity to escape from an unpleasant stimulus or situation.

11. In avoidance learning, the organism can escape the unpleasant stimulus or situation by responding to a cue that punishment is forthcoming. The organism may acquire a conditioned fear of neutral stimuli as a result of their being paired with a fear-producing stimulus.

12. Punishment, used to discourage a response, is a conditioning tool that most effectively controls behavior when accompanied by the learning of new responses to replace the old ones.

13. Autonomic conditioning, in which organisms can demonstrate direct control over their bodily functions, has great significance for the treatment of psychosomatic illness.

14. A fundamental element of learning is contiguity, the closeness in time of the stimuli to be associated.

15. The nature and amount of reinforcement are important to the learning process and can differ from subject to subject. Some reinforcers, such as money or praise, are conditioned as a result of their prior association with unconditioned reinforcers, such as food.

16. If reinforcement is eliminated or a CS is presented alone for several trials, a learned behavior extinguishes but may spontaneously recover at a later period.

17. Humans and other animals may generalize a learned response to objects similar to the original stimulus. They also are able to discriminate or differentiate between similar stimuli. Discrimination may be learned by selective reinforcement.

18 Thinking, problem-solving, and insightful learning are examples of complex intellectual activities called cognitive learning.

19. Incidental, or latent, learning occurs without the subject's active effort to retain information; the more meaningful and absorbing a stimulus is to a person, the more readily that person will achieve latent learning of the information.

20. Practicing a particular kind of learning produces a learning set for that task, which greatly facilitates success at all similar tasks.

21. Learning set may form the base upon which insightful learning—a sudden improvement in performance—occurs; however, a long background of previous learning and learning-to-learn is necessary.

Important Terms

learning

orienting response

habituation

sensitization

dishabituation

classical conditioning

unconditioned stimulus

unconditioned response

conditioned stimulus

conditioned response

interstimulus interval

trace conditioning

backward conditioning

delayed conditioning

simultaneous conditioning

operant or instrumental conditioning

trial-and-error learning

experimental chamber (Skinner box)

cumulative recorder

shaping (successive approximations)

reinforcement

fixed-interval schedule

fixed-ratio schedule

variable-interval schedule

variable-ratio schedule

positive reinforcement

negative reinforcement

escape learning

avoidance learning

conditioned fear

autonomic conditioning

contiguity

law of effect

conditioned reinforcer

unconditioned reinforcer

extinction

spontaneous recovery

generalization

discrimination

cognitive learning

incidental or latent learning

learning set (learning-to-learn)

insight

Suggested Readings

DEESE, J. E., & HULSE, S. H. *The psychology of learning*, 3rd ed. New York: McGraw-Hill, 1967.

An intermediate text presenting an overview of contemporary theory, often in historical perspective. Animal and human learning are given equal attention.

GAGNÉ, R. M. *Conditions of learning*, 2nd ed. New York: Holt, Rinehart and Winston, 1970.

A discussion of current learning theory, with special emphasis on its applications to education.

HILGARD, E. R., & BOWER, G. H. *Theories of learning*, 3rd. ed. New York: Appleton-Century-Crofts, 1966.

A thorough exposition of the major learning theories of the last century, from Thorndike to contemporary mathematical models.

KIMBLE, G. A. *Hilgard and Marquis' conditioning and learning*, rev. ed. New York: Appleton-Century-Crofts, 1961.

An advanced text, thoroughly covering conditioning experiments and theories through 1960.

LOGAN, F. A. *Fundamentals of learning and motivation*. Dubuque, Iowa: Brown, 1969.

A fast-moving, informal introduction to learning and motivation theory.

PAVLOV, I. P. *Conditioned reflexes* (1927). New York: Dover, 1960.

An unaltered republication of the original translation by G. V. Anrep. The pioneering work in conditioning by the noted Russian physiologist, it is often technical and difficult to read.

RACHLIN, H. *Introduction to modern behaviorism*. San Francisco: Freeman, 1970.

A concise and clear presentation of the behaviorist's approach to learning phenomena, with summaries of some of the more important experiments.

SKINNER, B. F. *About behaviorism*. New York: Knopf, 1974.

In this book, Skinner responds to the critics who took issue with some of the controversial theories and conclusions he advanced in *Beyond freedom and dignity*.

SKINNER, B. F. *Beyond freedom and dignity*. New York: Knopf, 1971.

A controversial statement of Skinner's beliefs about human nature and their implications for society.

SKINNER, B. F. *Cumulative record*, 3rd. ed. New York: Appleton-Century-Crofts, 1972.

A compendium of articles and papers spanning the career of the leading authority in behavioral psychology.

Chapter 7   Memory and Language

At a banquet given by a nobleman of Thessaly named Scopas, the poet Simonides of Ceos chanted a lyric poem in honour of his host but including a passage in praise of Castor and Pollux. Scopas meanly told the poet that he would only pay him half the sum agreed upon for the panegyric and that he must obtain the balance from the twin gods to whom he had devoted half the poem. A little later, a message was brought in to Simonides that two young men were waiting outside who wished to see him. He rose from the banquet and went out but could find no one. During his absence the roof of the banqueting hall fell in, crushing Scopas and all the guests to death beneath the ruins; the corpses were so mangled that the relatives who came to take them away for burial were unable to identify them. But Simonides remembered the places at which they had been sitting at the table and was therefore able to indicate to the relatives which were their dead. The invisible callers, Castor and Pollux, had handsomely paid for their share in the panegyric by drawing Simonides away from the banquet just before the crash. And this experience suggested to the poet the principles of the art of memory of which he is said to have been the inventor. Noting that it was through his memory of the places at which the guests had been sitting that he had been able to identify the bodies, he realised that orderly arrangement is essential for good memory.

—Francis A. Yates
(*The Art of Memory*)

Memory and Language

This chapter was drafted by Timothy Teyler, Department of Psychology and Social Relations, Harvard University.

If learning and language are the most distinctive of man's characteristics, memory is probably the most bewildering. The well-educated adult human has billions of items of information stored in his memory. By comparison, today's most advanced computer has a tiny—although more accurate—memory capacity. How can a couple of pounds of brain matter acquire, store, and retrieve this incredible amount of information? The evolution of the brain and the capacity for increased learning and memory go hand in hand. Simpler animals, like invertebrates, adapted to their environments by developing instinctive or permanent behavior patterns determined by fixed connections among neurons. Higher animals, mammals, and ultimately *Homo sapiens*, developed quite different means of adapting to their worlds. In place of instinctive or innate behavior patterns, learning and memory provide most of the controls of behavior.

In this chapter, in addition to describing what we know about memory, we shall examine the nature and origin of language. In ordinary life, words are the bulk of what we learn and remember. More than that, a considerable amount of the information we store is coded in the form of words and language. Although memory and language are obviously not the same and can be separated experimentally, they overlap a great deal. Language would not be possible unless we could learn and store in memory the sounds, words, phrases, and even the grammar and syntax of speech. Most of what you learn and remember from this text will be learned in the form of language.

Types of Memory

Every normal human has absolutely perfect and infallible memory—over short time spans. Listen to a short sentence spoken by a companion. You can repeat it easily without error. Look at a telephone number, then look away and repeat it. If you attend to the task you will never make an error. William James, the American psychologist, defined this process as *primary memory*. He distinguished between it and the recollection of things past, so-called secondary memory:

The stream of thought flows on; but most of its segments fall into the bottomless abyss of oblivion. Of some, no memory survives the instant of their passage. Of others, it is confined to a few moments, hours, or days. Others, again, leave vestiges which are indestructible, and by means of which they may be recalled as long as life endures. Can we explain these differences? (James, 1890)

Primary Memory

Primary memory is often called *short-term memory*. It is the immediate memory of visual or auditory stimuli. Primary memory has two important characteristics. One is its short duration. Primary memories fade in seconds. Look for several seconds at the first row of eight numbers below this paragraph. Now look away and after 3 seconds, try to recall the numbers. Next, look at the second row of eight numbers. Look away and after 30 seconds, try to recall the numbers. While waiting, let your mind "idle," without focusing on the numbers. You will find that you remembered the first set after 3 seconds very well, but made errors on the second set after a lapse of 30 seconds.

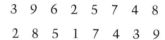

Peterson and Peterson (1959) analyzed the time course of short-term memory in a series of experiments similar to the above. They asked subjects to remember groups of three consonants, such as NLT. To prevent subjects from rehearsing between presentation and recall, they asked them to count backward by 3's during the interval. The result is illustrated in Figure 7-1. Primary memory was low after 10 seconds and disappeared after 18 seconds. Critics could say that, in this study, counting backward by 3's interfered with primary memory since both the numbers and three consonants must have been in primary memory.

An interesting study of such interference effects on primary memory was conducted by Reitman (1971), who filled the 15-second interval between presentation of a word and test for memory of the word with either a verbal task—repeating a syllable—or a tone judgment task—listening to pure tones and making judgments about them. A nice feature of her experiment was the fact that she could determine from the subjects' performance on the tone detection task that they were not rehearsing the word in primary memory. The results were striking. The decay or loss of primary memory occurred as expected when subjects repeated a syllable. However, there was *no* decay of primary memory when the subjects made tone judgments, even when they did not rehearse the word in primary memory. It seems that interference of certain kinds of stimuli is a major factor in the decay of primary memory.

The second important characteristic of primary memory is its limited capacity. A telephone number has seven digits. Add an unfamiliar three-digit area code and you will begin to make mistakes. If you were asked to glance at ten telephone numbers and then repeat them all,

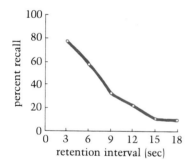

7-1
Graph showing that recall of a series of three-letter syllables decreases as the time interval between the original learning and recall increases. For intervals of 15 seconds, or more, recall was only about 10 percent (Peterson & Peterson, 1959)

you probably wouldn't even try. Such a task is beyond the capacity of primary memory.

The Magic Number Seven. The same memory limitation applies to other visual stimuli. If you look at a picture containing many different objects, then look away for a few seconds and try to remember the objects, you probably can name only about seven correctly. George Miller (1956) quantified the importance of the number seven in a classic paper entitled, "The Magical Number Seven, Plus or Minus Two." Miller analyzed how much information the human can process and transmit. The answer: about seven digits or seven items at a time. When we try to process more than seven, we make more and more errors. Thus, the numerical limit seven would seem to be the natural limit of primary memory.

However, Miller emphasizes that we are not limited to seven elementary bits of information. We can group or *chunk* information by using other knowledge and associations already well learned. A single key piece of information can serve to code a substantial chunk of material. We can hold up to seven such keys in primary memory. This "trick" has been known to memory experts for centuries. You memorize a few keys, each of which chunks much more information via previously well-learned associations. For example, if you are given the numbers 3, 7, 8, 4, 6, 2, 9, 1, you can remember only those seven numbers. If you group them—37, 84, 62, 91—you now have four chunks and have room for more numbers in your primary memory store.

Even with chunking we are still limited to about seven keys in primary memory. As Miller notes, there is something special about the magical number seven!

And finally, what about the magical number seven? What about the seven wonders of the world, the seven seas, the seven deadly sins, the seven daughters of Atlas in the Pleiades, the seven ages of man, the seven levels of hell, the seven primary colors, the seven notes of the musical scale, and the seven days of the week? What about the seven-point rating scale, the seven categories of absolute judgment, the seven objects in the span of attention, and the seven digits in the span of immediate memory? For the present I propose to withhold judgment. Perhaps there is something deep and profound behind all these sevens, something just calling out for us to discover it. But I suspect that it is only a pernicious, Pythagorean coincidence. (Miller, 1956)

The severely limited capacity of primary memory contrasts sharply with that of permanent or secondary memory, which is vast, perhaps limitless. In a sense, primary memory can be identified with consciousness or awareness, because the momentary stimuli we are aware of are our continuous primary memory. Many items in primary memory pass through our awareness and are forgotten. However, many other items that pass through primary memory are stored permanently in *long-term* or *secondary memory*. When you glance at a new telephone number, you rapidly forget it. However, you hold your own telephone number—and perhaps a few others—in your permanent memory store.

An interesting aspect of short-term or primary memory is its apparent independence of the stimulus mode. We remember equally well items that we see and those that we hear, although Norman and others suggest that the things we hear may go more directly into short-term memory than those that we see or feel.

Secondary Memory

Memories are formed in various ways. When you acquire a new phone number, how do you store it permanently in long-term or secondary memory store? The most common ways are by repeating it to yourself and by using it over a period of time. Of course, we learn and remember information in many other ways. Strong reinforcement as well as vivid emotional experiences can create enduring memories. Everyone can remember his or her first sexual experience. Can you remember your tenth? Many items fit so naturally into material already in store that they are easily remembered. A chess grand master has no trouble remembering every move in the game he has just played. A novice, whose memory store of chess is virtually nil, remembers only certain isolated moves. Later in this chapter, we shall return to the various factors that influence memory storage and recall.

The physical basis of secondary memory in the brain is completely unknown. Presumably, secondary memory is caused by permanent changes in the physical-chemical structure of the links among nerve cells. The nature of these changes is one of the great mysteries of the brain.

In contrast to short-term memory, secondary memory has an infinite amount of space for storing information. No individual ever completely "fills up" his brain with long-term information. However, incoming new material does seem to interfere with older stores. You may have heard of the renowned old professor of ichthyology. He refused to learn the names of his new students because, he said, "Every time I learn a new student's name, I forget the name of a fish."

We do not as yet know whether information placed in long-term memory is ever removed. Obviously, we forget things that have been placed in long-term memory. But we have not determined if such memories have actually been erased or whether the retrieval process that extracts such information is incomplete or gradually impaired. However, considerable evidence does suggest that long-term storage is relatively permanent and impervious to destruction. Retrieval failure seems, at this point, to be the more likely cause of memory loss (Norman, 1970).

Exact or Photographic Memory

Iconic Memory.   All normal humans possess a form of photographic visual memory. However, we all possess these photographic memories for only a *very short time.* George Sperling analyzed this form of "perfect" memory in the course of several experiments he reported in 1960. It is called *iconic* memory from the Greek word *icon,* meaning image. Iconic memory is the briefly retained visual image of a visual stimulus.

In one experiment, Sperling presented an array of letters for 1/20th of a second. Then, at varying times after the letters vanished, he projected a

"I don't understand you," said Alice. "It's dreadfully confusing."

"That's the effect of living backwards. It always makes one a little giddy at first—"

"Living backwards!" Alice repeated in great astonishment. "I never heard of such a thing!"

"—but there's one great advantage in it, that one's memory works both ways."

Through the Looking Glass
Lewis Carroll

Model of Sperling's concept of iconic memory. The large rectangle in color represents the subject. Letters flashed before the subject, for example, enter the visual information storage (VIS) system as a light pattern. The information is passed to a "translator," which converts the input to an output, a series of motor actions. These result in a written representation of the letter. (Sperling, 1960)

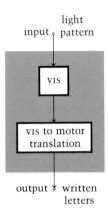

Look at this drawing for a few seconds. Turn away and try to recall as many details as you can. The person with eidetic imagery remembers everything, down to the smallest detail.

circle onto the part of the screen where one letter had been. The subject's task was to correctly identify that letter. At very short intervals, people have virtually perfect visual memory—they almost always identify the letters correctly. However, performance deteriorates into guessing in less than one second.

We cannot explain this short duration of iconic memory as a persistence of the retinal image. The bleaching of the eye's visual pigments does not last long enough. Rather, it is a central, as yet unknown, brain process.

Eidetic Imagery. You may have heard stories of people with photographic memory. They can glance at a complex picture, diagram, or page of a book, then glance away and recite it almost without error. This special ability, called *eidetic imagery,* is very rare. Although about 10 percent of all children possess eidetic imagery, very few individuals retain the power into adulthood. Children who have eidetic imagery can look at a picture for a few seconds, and then, while looking away, "see" the image before them for several minutes. They can scan this "picture" and note additional details, such as the number of buttons on an individual's coat (Haber & Haber, 1964).

Little is known about eidetic imagery or why it occurs primarily in children. Nor do we know why a person must view an item for several seconds before he can retain the item as an eidetic image. Often, the image is rather fragile. If a child blinks excessively or looks around the room, the image will disappear (Haber, 1969). The similarity of eidetic imagery to iconic memory suggests that the brain processes responsible for iconic memory may be somehow prolonged in some children, and in a very few adults, to provide a more persistent neural image of the visual stimulus, thus producing the eidetic image.

Most of us are not blessed with eidetic imagery. It would be a mixed blessing. As we shall see, normal humans appear to categorize information and then place it into long-term store. We sort what we remember in terms of its meaning, significance, and similarity to other learned materials. Eidetic imagery might tend to interfere with these organizational processes in memory.

Schematic of the possible relationship between primary and secondary memory. Items enter primary memory and are either forgotten (lost to primary memory) or passed on to secondary memory. Only those items that are rehearsed are passed on to secondary memory. The arrow reentering primary memory represents the rehearsal buffer. (Waugh & Norman, 1965)

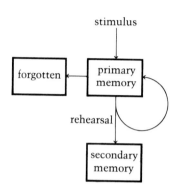

Several Kinds of Memory or One?

Relations between primary and secondary memory might occur as shown by the model in Figure 7-4, adapted from Waugh and Norman (1965). At a given moment, visual information passes through a very brief iconic phase when it is held *in toto*. About seven items of the information are then passed to primary memory. On the other hand, auditory information seems to pass more directly into primary memory. If the subject then repeats or rehearses the material in primary memory, all or some of it transfers to permanent secondary storage. Any material in primary memory that is not rehearsed is forgotten.

Visual stimuli, then, are received by three time-dependent phases of memory: iconic, primary, and secondary. Are these really three different processes? Iconic memory and its rare variant, eidetic imagery, do seem to differ from the other two. For although iconic memory is extremely brief and eidetic imagery is more lasting, both the iconic and the eidetic image are virtually total recreations of the original image—unlike primary or secondary memory. The differences among the three phases may reflect quite different kinds of processes in the brain in response to visual stimuli.

Some psychologists (Norman, 1969; Atkinson & Shiffrin, 1968) view primary and secondary memory as two distinct processes, rather than as separate phases of the same process. Norman further argues that primary memory is necessary for secondary memory. On the other hand, Melton (1963) has argued forcefully that primary and secondary memory have no basic differences. He notes that the variables influencing one influence the other equally. Both primary and secondary memory improve with repetition. Both are equally subject to interference from other learned material. For Melton, the distinction between primary and secondary memory is simply the result of how long after experience the memory is tested. However, we might remember William James' distinction: Primary memory is continuously present in awareness for a brief period. By contrast, secondary memories are not continuously present in awareness; they appear when we actively try to recall them or when an association brings them to mind. We will return to this issue after reviewing some of the information on measures and properties of memory.

Measures of Retention

There were three witnesses. Each claimed that he had seen the person who snatched the woman's purse. They were all positive that they could identify the thief. When questioned closely the first witness described a nervous little man who darted out, grabbed the purse and ran down the street. The second witness saw an athletic man wearing blue pants and a white shirt forcefully rip away the purse and knock the woman down. The last witness claimed that the assailant was a woman of rather stocky build wearing black shorts and a blouse.

Three witnesses each saw something different in the same situation. Or did they? Undoubtedly, if they were watching, they all *saw* approximately the same thing. However, they *remembered* different things. We cannot be sure whether the information was placed incorrectly in their memories or they recalled the information erroneously. The measure of memory is the measure of *retention*, determining what is remembered out of all that an individual experiences. Four basic methods for gauging retention have been used in laboratory investigations of memory. They are *redintegration*, *recall*, *recognition*, and *relearning.*

Redintegration or Reconstruction

A *redintegrative memory* is the prompted recall of a past event that is triggered by a stimulus from that past event. Many of us collect souvenirs, ticket stubs, banners proclaiming the wonders of Yellowstone National Park, tassels from the Pink Pussycat, photographs of friends, and the like. These stimuli redintegrate complete memories. Redintegrative memory depends on the subject's ability to "relive" an experience.

Recall

What is your name, your telephone number, your license plate number, and your Social Security number? We are periodically asked to use these pieces of information. In other words, we are asked to recall what they are. *Recall* is the ability to extract from memory a specific bit of information, usually devoid of context. Few of us have any trouble recalling our names, but we may have considerable difficulty recalling our Social Security numbers. Basically, two reasons explain this wide range of recall ease. First, your name is a meaningful stimulus, and second, it is a well-learned response. On the other hand, we are less often asked to use our Social Security numbers, and for many of us it may have no personal meaning. In fact, some individuals thoroughly dislike being categorized in terms of a number.

Whereas redintegrative memory has not been studied much in the laboratory, recall has been investigated extensively. The ability to recall specific items diminishes rapidly as time passes, with the most dramatic loss occurring immediately after learning. A man who had learned the names of six or seven strangers he had met at a wedding party probably will not recall the names in 2 weeks; in only 2 days, he probably will have forgotten all but the first names of three or four of the wedding guests.

One of the factors that exert a very powerful effect on recall is the interfering effect of other learning. Suppose you learn the capitals of all the states. Later you learn the name of the largest city in each state. Then you are tested on your memory of state capitals. Your memory of the largest cities will to some extent interfere with your recall of the capitals. New learning's interfering effect on past memories is called *retroactive inhibition* (which we shall discuss in greater detail later in this chapter). One of the most important variables that determine how much retroactive inhibition or interference will occur is the similarity between the original material (first) and the subsequent material (second). When the first and second materials are virtually identical, there is

The relationship between efficiency of recall and the degree of similarity of material to be recalled. When the subsequent material to be recalled is identical to the original material, and the required responses are the same, recall is most efficient (A). As the subsequent material becomes less similar to the original material, a point is reached (B) where recall is least efficient. After this point, recall becomes better but never as efficient as it was at A. (Robinson, 1927)

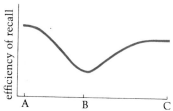

degree of similarity between subsequent material and original material—descending scale

actually facilitation rather than inhibition in recall of the first material. When there is some degree of similarity, as in state capitals and largest cities, there is maximum interference. When the materials are very different, there is relatively little interference. Learning the names of stars would not interfere with your prior memory of state capitals.

Recognition

Most students prefer objective to essay examinations. The most familiar objective tests are those composed of multiple-choice questions. On such a test, the average student can perform better than he can on an essay exam, which requires the student to answer by examining his memory and recalling the correct solution. Multiple-choice questions, on the other hand, resemble recognition memory tasks, which usually are less demanding. _Recognition_ is simply identifying an item one has experienced rather than wholly recalling that item from one's memory. When buying a can of coffee, a person may not be able to recall the brand name or even the look of the can itself. However, once in the store he can recognize it easily. Consistently, recognition memory is more accessible than recall.

Multiple-choice examinations are easier than recall tests but they may still be quite difficult. The alternatives may seem almost equivalent unless the material is thoroughly understood.

Laboratory researchers study recognition memory by presenting a series of stimuli and following them with a test in which the stimuli are interspersed with new stimuli. Subjects must identify the initial stimuli. The ability to do so of course declines as the interval following the first presentation grows longer.

Most laboratory studies of recognition memory have used lists of words or meaningless syllables that in themselves are difficult to learn. Nonetheless, recognition memory is surprisingly good. But because laboratory studies use abstract materials, they sometimes miss the most common and important recognition learning that people do. What is one of the easiest things to recognize? A human face. We have all had the experience of meeting someone who looks familiar. We have seen his or her face before, even though we often cannot remember the name. Our recognition memory for faces is much better than our memory for names. We might not recognize the name, even when told.

Actually, until some recent and dramatic studies by Shepard (1967) and Haber (1970) we had no idea just how remarkable our visual picture memories are. In one study, Haber showed subjects 2,560 pictures of people, objects, and scenes, each viewed for 10 seconds. On a subsequent day they were shown 2,560 pairs of pictures; one picture in each pair had been seen before and one had not. Subjects remembered correctly in 90 percent of the cases! A remarkable performance.

Relearning

As a measure of memory, the technique of relearning is somewhat different from the other three. _Relearning_ determines how efficiently an individual can re-acquire material he has previously mastered. This measure

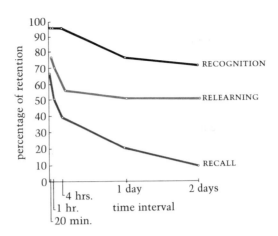

7-6
Graph comparing the relative efficiencies of three of the four measures of retention. Subjects learned lists of 12 nonsense syllables and were tested by each measure after certain intervals of time. As expected, recognition memory showed the best retention. (From C. W. Luh, "The conditions of retention." *Psychological Monographs*, 1922, **31,** No. 142, 22. Copyright © 1922 by the American Psychological Association. Reprinted by permission.)

of retention—also called the *savings method* because relearning takes less time than learning completely afresh—assumes that previously learned material, although apparently forgotten, can be readily relearned due to the fact that at least some of the material learned earlier remains in long-term memory. Relearning tasks are conceptually more complex than other measures of memory, in part because they involve *learning variables* in addition to *memory variables*. One must take great care to control relearning experiments to neutralize the effects of learning set, fatigue, and motivation. Relearning, which has been studied primarily in the laboratory, is not a very common memory technique in daily life.

The effectiveness of the various methods of measuring memory were compared in a classic study by Luh (1922); see also McGeoch and Irion (1952). Subjects learned lists of 12 meaningless syllables and were then tested for retention at various times by the different methods. Recognition was by far the most effective method and recall the least effective; reconstruction or redintegration and relearning give intermediate performances. These results are not particularly surprising. In recognition you are given the learned material again, whereas in recall you must reproduce the memories with no cues or aids.

Some memory authorities have suggested that these four different ways of testing memory—redintegration, recall, recognition, and relearning—may actually reflect different processes of memory. The test methods certainly differ in *how* a subject demonstrates his memories, and in how *well* he demonstrates them. Other experts argue that the four methods are merely different ways of testing the same underlying phenomenon. The different methods may involve somewhat different cognitive strategies for retrieving memory. Yet all involve the same basic memory system.

Factors Affecting Memory

Several factors determine how well material is remembered. In this section, we will discuss three of the most important factors—overlearning, organization, and retrieval.

7-7

Mnemonics involves the use of associations between key words and words to be recalled Following is a typical rhyme of the kind used by mnemonists. Memorize the rhyme and then have a friend read ten words to you, waiting approximately 5 seconds between words. For each word, you should form a bizarre association between it and that line of the rhyme. For example, if the tenth word is phonograph, imagine a hen laying eggs on a phonograph turntable. A minute or two after you have learned the entire list, have your friend ask for each of the words by number (in random order). How many can you recall? (From Miller, 1956)

one is a bun,
two is a shoe,
three is a tree,
four is a door,
five is a hive,
six are sticks,
seven is heaven,
eight is a gate,
nine is a line, and
ten is a hen.

Overlearning

To be well remembered, material must first be well learned. This does not mean simply learning a task or bit of information until it is mastered. Rather, it refers to a more extensive exercise that psychologists call overlearning. Once something is learned, *overlearning* requires that it be repeated and practiced until it is firmly established in the central nervous system. Thus, "practice makes perfect" could be modified to read "overlearning makes memory."

Although most of us must practice a good deal to establish information in our memory banks, rare exceptions are known. The Russian psychologist Luria (1968) has documented the case of a man who apparently was incapable of *not* storing things in his memory. He could learn extremely complicated material by being exposed to it only once. The material did not have to be meaningful to him. For example, he could learn perfectly, in one presentation, a long table of numbers. Even after several months he could recite the digits forward, backward, and in any order. We call an individual with such extraordinary memory power a *mnemonist*. Anyone can substantially improve his visual memory through the use of mnemonic techniques. One that might be used, for example, is the trick of reducing the number of elements by imposing an organizing scheme. Thus, your Social Security number is much easier to remember as 347-45-7701 than as 347457701.

The capacity to forget can be adaptive. We forget items that are meaningless or unimportant to us; and it is well that we do. Luria's mnemonist subject was severely hampered by his phenomenal memory. For example, he could not perform any kind of conceptual operation. While he could memorize and *recall* perfectly *the steps* in a complex mathematical problem, he was completely *unable to solve* the problem. In addition, his memory seriously handicapped him in his personal relations and in his ability to hold a normal job. Consequently, he earned his living by performing his memory feats and by lecturing on mnemonics.

Organization

If you were asked to design an organizational scheme for memory, how would you go about it? The problem is analogous to the file clerk's job of organizing the boss's files. One approach would be to use the *random pigeonhole*. Each file drawer would contain whatever papers the clerk arbitrarily thought appropriate for it. No particular order would be followed. The clerk might find this an efficient way to store information. As material came across his desk, he would simply put it in an empty pigeonhole. However, when he wanted to retrieve information, he would find it very difficult, if not impossible, to find the right data.

A better filing system would be the *classified pigeonhole*. One file drawer would be reserved for letters received, another for letters sent, another for budgets, and so forth. While this system is better than the random pigeonhole system, it has a flaw. Within each major classification, information would still be filed randomly. A more efficient filing system would add *clustered concepts;* items would be filed according to their nature. Personal letters, for example, would be filed with personal dossiers and job summaries. One difficulty with any filing system is

7-8

Write each of these nine words on a separate card. Have a friend look at each card, and later repeat the words that he can recall. Note that in recalling the words, he is likely to group them into concept categories—in this case, probably astronomy, animals, and plants.

planet
chlorophyll
lemur
star
aardvark
daffodil
elephant
asteroid
chrysanthemum

7-9

This passage from *Moby Dick* can be used to test memory organization.

overlap in meaning and import. The solution is cross-referencing. If the clerk added cross-references to the budget and the long-range planning file categories, they would tell where to find related data.

Human memory seems to operate on the cross-referenced, clustered-concept system. However, the cross-referencing is complex and multidimensional. Words are associated by meaning and also by rhyme, sound, syllabic similarity, pronunciation accents, by private associations gathered from the idiosyncrasies of individual learning—and yet more factors.

You can do a simple study to demonstrate the concept-clustering of words in human memory. Figure 7-8 describes a brief experiment to test for memory categorization. When the subject repeats as many words as he can recall, he will very likely group them into the three general categories—astronomy, zoology, and botany—to which they belong. Instead of repeating the words back to you in the order he saw them he will recite them by category—giving all the astronomy terms together, and so on. He has retrieved the words from general concept categories in his memory. This process works quite well. On the other hand, if you require him to repeat the words in the order in which he learned them, he will perform less well.

This loss in memory performance brought about by an imposed sequence of recollection indicates that individuals, when left to their own devices, organize what they learn and use this organization in the memory storage process. In addition, each person's organizational schema seems to be different. This finding suggests, for example, that a student's outline of this chapter would be more efficient in terms of his own learning than one organized by his instructor.

You can use the excerpt from Herman Melville's novel *Moby Dick* shown in Figure 7-9 to illustrate a feature of memory organization. Ask several friends to read the passage and then to retell it several times over a period of days or weeks. As retelling proceeds, your friends will omit some of the original details and embellish the passage with new ones.

MOBY DICK

Returning to the Spouter Inn from the Chapel, I found Queequeg there quite alone. He, having left the Chapel before the benediction sometime, was sitting on a bench before the fire with his feet on the stove hearth and in one hand was holding close up to his face that little negro idol of his, peering hard into its face and with a jackknife gently whittling away at its nose. Meanwhile humming to himself in his heathenish way.

But being now interrupted, he put up the image and pretty soon going to the table, took up a large book there and placing it in his lap, began *counting the pages with deliberate regularity. At every fiftieth page, as I fancied, stopping for a moment, looking vacantly around him and giving utterance to a long drawn gurgling whistle of astonishment. He would then begin at the next fifty, seeming to commence with number one each time as though he could not count more than fifty. And it was only by such a large number of fiftys being found together that his astonishment at the multitude of pages was excited.*

With much interest I sat watching him. Savage though he was and hideously marred about the face, at *least to my taste, his countenance had yet a something in it which was by no means disagreeable. You can not hide the soul. Through all his unearthly tattooing, I thought I saw the traces of a simple honest heart and in his large deep eyes, firey black and bold, there seemed tokens of a spirit that would dare a thousand devils. And besides all this, there was a certain lofty bearing about the Pagan which even his uncouthness could not altogether maim. He looked like a man who had never cringed and had never had a creditor. (H. Melville, Chapter 10)*

These new details usually will amplify and fit the passage's general meaning. This occurs because, when reading such a narrative, an individual organizes the material into a meaningful schema. Metaphorically, his memory of the story *plan* serves as a fixed pattern from which he derives the details. Thus, rather than reflecting complete rote memorization, memory often consists of a recollection of concepts which the individual then uses to reconstruct the details of the past event.

Retrieval

What do we mean when we say that we can't remember something? Is the item no longer in memory storage? Or, has the retrieval process simply failed to bring it forth? As we noted earlier, failure to retrieve something seems to be the more plausible explanation of forgetting.

Many who have studied memory phenomena claim that we never forget events that we have learned or experienced; they are always potentially available to recall. We have all found ourselves unable to remember something that we were thinking of only a few minutes before. It might have been our errands for the day, or a letter we were going to mail. Sometimes we can overcome these frustrating losses of memory by going back to the room or situation in which we had planned our day. Often, this step will make the memory "come back." This technique of recreating the conditions that existed at the time of learning so as to facilitate the retrieval of memory is employed sometimes by police when they take witnesses and suspects back to the "scene of the crime." They hope the stimuli at that place will trigger latent memories that may help to resolve the case.

The Tip-of-the-Tongue Phenomenon. Another common failure of memory retrieval occurs when a word is "on the tip of the tongue." The experience can be irritating, especially when we are relatively familiar with the word. The *tip-of-the-tongue phenomenon* (or TOT) illustrates another of the brain's organizational processes. Imagine a gardener telling his neighbor about the lawn seed he has just planted. The seed is Bermuda grass, but the name has escaped him. He knows what it is, he is familiar with the term, but it eludes him—it is on the tip of his tongue. Groping, he may think of Tahitian, Hawaiian, Burma, and so forth—an interesting clue to the brain's organizational processes. Within the brain, we tend to classify things into functional categories. So, in the TOT state, we "thumb through" a memory category as we try to find the missing word. Research on the TOT state also indicates that in addition to functional categories, at least one other organizational category, namely "sound" and "form" classification, is used in memory search. Thus, the searcher produces "groping" words which are similar in sound or form, but not necessarily in meaning. It is likely that the brain organizes the storage of words both by sounds of words and categories of meaning. *Sounds* retrieved from memory enable us to recognize speech, and *meanings* allow us to say what we want to say.

Typically, the memory traces are strong in the TOT state. The missing memory is well known. We *know* what it is, which is why TOT is so frustrating. This strong feeling that we clearly *can* remember the material we cannot remember suggests another kind or level of memory storage. Some process "knows" that the required information is there. Hence the missing trace must be strong. The failure to find it is probably due to the use of incorrect memory search strategies. In one experiment (Atkinson & Shiffrin, 1969), a student was asked the capital of the State of Washington. He experienced very strong TOT—he *knew* that he knew, but he could not remember. He was later asked the capital of Oregon. He answered correctly "Salem" and then immediately said that the capital of Washington was Olympia. He had learned both at the same time and associated them both temporally and geographically. Since he remembered Oregon's capital better, the proper strategy for Washington would have been to search first in neighboring states. However, he did not do this. His search strategy, not his memory, was at fault.

Retrieval of Short-Term Memory Store—Parallel or Serial? The tip-of-the-tongue experience is a phenomenon of search through our long-term or permanent memory store. What about search through short-term memory? Suppose you glance at a new phone number and then a few seconds later are asked if the number "3" was part of it. Do you search through the numbers one at a time serially or do you hold the entire number in short-term memory and compare it at once against "3" (parallel search)? This issue was resolved a few years ago.

In a remarkable and simple experiment, Sternberg (1966) presented subjects with a series of single digits one at a time; each digit was shown for 1.2 seconds. The number of digits in a series varied from one to six in a random order. Two seconds after a given series was completed a test digit was shown. If the number was shown in the series, the subject pulled a "yes" lever and if not, a "no" lever. Sternberg simply measured how long the subject took to make his response; that is, he measured the subject's *response latency*. The results were strikingly clear. Response latency was a virtually perfect straight line increasing as a function of the number of symbols in memory. Short-term memory search is a series process. The more items in memory, the longer the search, for *both* yes and no correct responses. Sternberg was even able to estimate the rate of the search process. It averages between 25 and 30 symbols per second.

Short-term memory search is a rapid process. Thirty symbols per second is about 33 milliseconds (33 thousandths of a second) per symbol. We flick through the short-term store at a high speed but must "examine" each element in the store in turn. This rapid search time rules out an older notion that short-term memory search was done by saying the items to oneself (subvocalizing). The serial nature of short-term memory search must be contrasted with long-term or permanent memory search.

A direct serial search of permanent memory, beginning with the first thing we ever learned and proceeding to the present, is impossible. We would die of old age before we got through one complete search. However, evidence indicates that search through permanent memory may in some ways be serial, although highly organized (Anderson & Bower, 1973). Permanent memory takes us directly to the right "filing cabinet," in effect, but we then may have to search through the file to find the specific memory we are trying to recall.

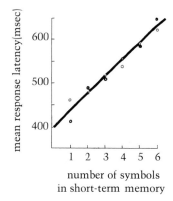

7-10
Graph of the relationship between the number of items in short-term store and response latency. The more items there were, the longer the subject took to search his memory to locate an item. In addition, as the number of items in memory increased, so did the number of negative responses (errors); negative responses are black circles; positive responses are colored circles. (From S. Sternberg, "High speed scanning in human memory." *Science*, 1966, **153**, 652–654. Copyright 1966 by the American Association for the Advancement of Science.)

MEMORIZING WITH IMAGINARY MAPS

Gordon H. Bower *Stanford University*

Most of us would like to have better memories—and we can, because memorizing is a set of learned skills rather than an inborn ability. One powerful memorizing skill—called the method of loci—exploits our map-making ability, which we use constantly.

People construct mental maps of their environments by integrating information from diverse sources—their senses, symbolic diagrams, and verbal descriptions. Your mental map tells you where places are, relative to a frame of reference and to each other. Your map also has a location for "myself here and now," which is your reference point for many spoken phrases, such as "here," "nearby," and "in front of me." The scale of your mental map is adjustable at will. For example, compare the level of detail as you visualize progressively the planet Earth, North America, the United States, your city, your house, and finally, your own room. Locations that are tiny subparts at one level become whole scenes at other levels.

We use new information to alter our mental maps, updating the location of objects as they move about. When a friend who has borrowed your car returns it, he will tell you where he parked it. His description enables you to update your map's entry for the location of your car, so you can find it easily in its new place.

This ability is a vital aid to individual adaptation and the survival of our species. Individuals who could not remember how to find good things (food, water, sexual mates, shelter) or avoid bad things (predators, cliffs, poisoned water) would not survive the evolutionary process of natural selection. All primates have well-developed abilities to find objects and locations. If a hungry chimpanzee watches you hide food at various places in his familiar terrain, he can later find the food unerringly, starting from any point. Like a salesman visiting customers, the chimpanzee will take a route that is almost a "minimum distance" path (Menzel, 1973), regardless of his starting point and the order in which he was shown the food sites. A child watching you hide Easter eggs will perform similarly. From such simple foundations have evolved man's more elaborate skills of hunting, trail-blazing, map-making, and navigating. Even in so-called "primitive" cultures, these skills are astonishingly sophisticated. Illiterate tribesmen regularly sail between tiny Pacific islands hundreds of miles apart; Eskimos find their way home across a wilderness of snow and ice.

Research has shown that map-making can be used to improve memory. One efficient way to learn

A

Levels of details in a cognitive map of our environment. The diminishing circle reflects the relative "size" of one subpart in differing contexts.

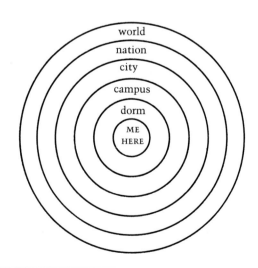

B

Schematic map of the chimpanzee's familiar terrain, showing some landmarks. The chimp saw food being hidden in the order indicated numerically. He starts his forage at the bird bushes (8) and traverses the route indicated by arrows. (Adapted from Menzel, 1973).

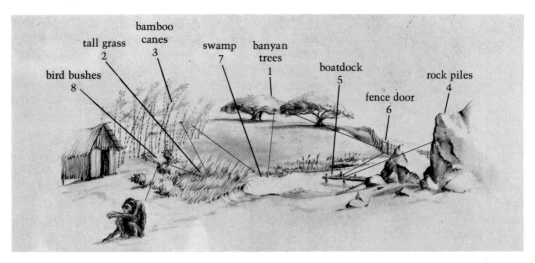

almost any new information is to imagine it as an object located at a familiar place. The ancient Greeks handed down this powerful method of *loci* (locations). As noted in the quote at the beginning of this chapter, Cicero asserted that the poet Simonides had invented the method. The loci method became the prescribed technique for improving memory in the Greek schools. It was extremely useful; in those days before cheap paper and pencils, students not only had to study all their orations, they also had to memorize them.

Today, you might use the loci method to remember your shopping list, errands, assignments or appointments, geographical facts, sets of scientific laws or phenomena, or the main points in this chapter. To use the method of loci, you first memorize a series of "mental snapshots" of locations familiar to you, selecting places that follow each other in some familiar order. Imagine the distinct

places you pass as you walk to your house or to your psychology class. Or you might think of the sequence of familiar locations you see each morning—your bed, the bathroom sink, the cafeteria line, and the breakfast table. The series can be quite long, though fifteen to thirty locations are adequate for most memory tasks. When selecting locations for your series, pick those for which you can form vivid mental images.

These locations are to serve as pigeonholes for any information you want to learn. First, you must convert the information into visual images. If you wish to remember a shopping list—toothpaste, aspirin, Kleenex, and dental floss—you can place an image of each item in a specific location on your mental map. First, you might imagine a big tube of toothpaste lying in your bed; then an enormous bottle of aspirin tablets being poured into the sink; then Kleenex wrapped around each person

in the cafeteria line; and finally, strands of dental floss crisscrossing the top of the breakfast table. The more striking the interaction between object and location, the easier it will be to remember. Visualize each image in its own location for about 10 seconds as you learn the list. When you want to remember the list, just call to mind the successive locations of your series and "see" what you have placed in your imagination.

Besides serving as filing cabinets for the images, the loci also act as reminders or cues. This procedure exploits the fact that human memory is associative. Stored information is retrieved by cues which we associated with the information when we first learned it.

College students using the method of loci are able to remember items on a list two or three times more accurately than students who learn the items by rote memory. Students using the method also recall items in

C

The four location images and their use in learning a shopping list for the drugstore.

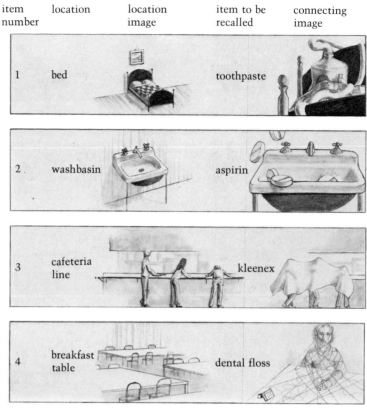

item number	location	location image	item to be recalled	connecting image
1	bed		toothpaste	
2	washbasin		aspirin	
3	cafeteria line		kleenex	
4	breakfast table		dental floss	

Connecting images:

1. Toothpaste squirting all over bed
2. Large aspirin pills pouring into the washbasin
3. Huge kleenex covers people in the cafeteria line
4. Strands of dental floss criss-crossing the breakfast table

their proper sequence rather than in the semirandom order in which most control subjects remember the items on their lists. One reason for the method's success is its built-in "retrieval plan," which tells you where to "find" each item and how to move from item to item in memory; the plan also monitors your recall, so that you can tell when you have forgotten something; and it tells you when you are finished with your recall.

Though we have illustrated the method with concrete objects, you also can use it—and just as effectively—to remember abstract ideas. The one essential is that you must render the idea into a concrete image or picture that suggests the abstract idea. For example, you might represent "classical conditioning" as one of Pavlov's dogs in your bed hearing the dinner bell and drooling on your pillow. Such far-fetched and bizarre images help make the pairings memorable—but of course, they must remind you of the abstract idea as well. These criteria exclude from the loci method such items as lists of numbers, foreign words, and anatomical terms having unknown referents. To learn such items, you must first convert them into meaningful images (Young & Gibson, 1962).

You can re-use the same memory sequences to learn new lists of items—provided you are willing to risk losing the images you placed there earlier. Frequently, this is all right; we often wish to remember items only long enough to use them once (for example, a waitress remembering lunch orders or a person remembering a shopping list). We weaken the connection between a location and its first item when we make new associations with that same location. This is the "retroactive inhibition" phenomenon, which is discussed on page 234 of this chapter.

You can overcome this problem in two ways. First, you can simply prepare multiple series of location images. You could select twenty loci from around your bedroom for learning your psychology course and another twenty from your campus for your physics course. In this way,

D
Strengths of associations between an imaginary location, i, and corresponding items (from different sets) being placed at that location. Darker arrows represent stronger associations. Progressive elaboration of a composite imaginary scene results in strong interconnections and good recall of all items.

UNLEARNING AND RETROACTIVE INHIBITION:

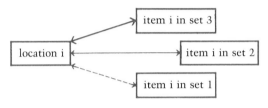

PROGRESSIVE ELABORATION:

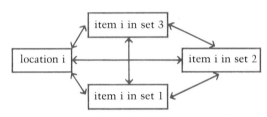

you avoid the unlearning created by placing several item images at the same locus. The second way to overcome the multi-list problem is to deliberately re-imagine each earlier item in its location while you are placing the corresponding new item there. In short, you elaborate a grand imaginary scene of interacting objects at each location; in our example, Pavlov's dog is now salivating over the big toothpaste tube. In laboratory experiments, such progressive elaboration has proven much more effective than simply trying to image each new set of items at the loci without deliberately re-imagining the items placed there earlier.

While the method of loci has many variants, it also has limitations as a memory aid. However, you can use other methods to help with other specific memory problems (Young & Gibson, 1962). Research on such memory devices has a twofold advantage. First, the research has practical significance — for example, improving the memory of the retarded child or the amnesic "stroke" victim. Second, the research has provided important new scientific theories about the representation, assembly, and storage of linguistic and imaginal information in memory. For our purposes, it is enough to note that the method of loci is an imaginative extension of man's everyday ability to alter the cognitive maps with which he guides himself through a vast and complex world.

Verbal Learning and Memory

We have discussed memory largely as a *verbal* phenomenon. Indeed, most human learning and memory does involve words and numbers, basically verbal materials. The study of verbal learning began with the work of the German psychologist *Hermann Ebbinghaus* in the late 19th century. Ebbinghaus believed that the association between verbal stimuli provides a way to study man's learning and memory processes.

Ebbinghaus's study of verbal learning employed one subject—Ebbinghaus himself. He chose to study verbal learning via poetry, plus a special set of <u>nonsense syllables</u> that he developed. Ebbinghaus realized that the words of a language, while otherwise entirely appropriate stimuli for learning, have one undesirable characteristic: They have meaning, and the meanings differ among people. Almost every word in the English (or German) language has more than one meaning. "Tart" can mean a small pie, a prostitute, or sour; to others it may simply be an unfamiliar word. The number and kind of associations people have for words also differ from person to person. In a learning experiment, all subjects must start on an equal plane. So, Ebbinghaus invented the nonsense syllable or nonsense word. Normal syllables such as cat may consist of a consonant-vowel-consonant letter sequence. Ebbinghaus's nonsense syllables consisted of the same letter pattern. However, his syllables had no meaning. He developed hundreds of nonsense syllables, such as YEF, ROG, and BOS

Ebbinghaus soon discovered that even these nonsense syllables, which carry no intrinsic meaning, often sound enough like real words to create a problem. For example, BOS, while meaning nothing, is pronounced like the English word, boss. Therefore, Ebbinghaus eliminated such words from his list of nonsense syllables.

Serial Learning

The first verbal learning task that Ebbinghaus devised became known as <u>serial learning</u>. In this task, 10 to 15 nonsense syllables are presented at random intervals, either orally or visually. Time and time again, the list is repeated in the same sequence. The subject attempts to anticipate the next word before it appears. The time the subject requires to correctly anticipate every word on the list is a measure of his learning.

In such serial learning, the so-called *serial position effect* makes subjects tend to remember items at the list's beginning and at the end much better than those in the middle. The serial position effect has prompted some interesting theories. The idea of <u>contiguity</u>, which we discussed in Chapter 6, predicts that since all the associations formed between adjacent nonsense syllables have been equally reinforced, they all should be equally well remembered. This, however, is not the case. It is conceivable that subjects remember items at the beginning and end of the list better simply because they are the most noticeable items. Most of us have experienced similar phenomena in daily life. We often can recollect the prefix of a telephone number while forgetting the rest. Similarly, in a sing-along, we commonly can start a stanza, but then cannot remember the rest of the lyrics. In a typical serial learning task, the subject first learns the nonsense syllables at the beginning and end of a 12-word string; he makes more errors in the middle of the list. The subject would also be better at recalling the beginning and ending words if he were to take a retention test the next day (Jensen & Roden, 1963).

Paired-Associate Learning

The second research tool in the study of verbal learning is *paired-associate learning*. The subject's task is similar to learning a foreign vocabulary with flash cards. On one side, the cards have a foreign word; on the other side are the same word and its English equivalent. The paired-associate procedure is simple. First, the foreign word is shown, followed by the foreign word and its English equivalent. The subject must identify the English equivalent of the word while seeing only the foreign word. Early paired-associate learning studies used the same stimuli that are used in serial learning, namely, nonsense syllables. Rather than associate a foreign word with its English equivalent, the subject had to associate one nonsense syllable with another. When he could correctly anticipate the second word of the pair, the subject had learned the task.

Forgetting

Much of modern verbal learning has been concerned with the factors relating to memory and forgetting. Forgetting is a basic issue. Why should material be forgotten once it is well learned? Initially, researchers thought that the mere passage of time allowed memory traces to decay. We shall review this theory of forgetting first.

Decay and Disuse. The hypothetical memory traces in the brain have been termed *engrams*. While no one has ever seen an engram, it is thought to be the physical base of memory in the central nervous system. According to the *decay theory*, engrams laid down in long-term storage in the brain simply fade away in time. This seems to be true. As we grow older, we can no longer readily recall experiences from the past. On the other hand, the decay theory also would suggest that an elderly person would not be able to remember the details of his youth. Yet this is not true. An elderly person may forget totally what he did yesterday while the details of some youthful experience remain precise and vivid.

A special aspect of the decay theory is the importance of use in memory. The *disuse hypothesis* maintains that memories are lost because they are not used. If an engram is laid down and is consistently used, the brain will, according to this explanation, retain the engram. But if the engram is not used, it will be deleted from the brain's permanent memory stores. Plausible as this theory may sound, little evidence has been put forth to support it. Again, the memories of youth are not consistently practiced, yet they can pop up years later.

Interference. Another explanation of forgetting is based on *interference* theories. They contend that the subject's learning of consecutive events can be either helped or hindered by his intervening activities. Similarly, depending on the nature of the learning task and the intervening activities, the subject's later memory performance may be facilitated or ham-

7-11

Graph of the effect of retroactive inhibition on recall. Subjects who learned the material immediately before sleep and were awakened and tested at specific intervals thereafter recalled more of the information than subjects who learned the material at the beginning of the day, when interference from other stimuli were more abundant. (Jenkins & Dallenbach, 1924)

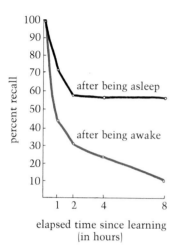

elapsed time since learning
(in hours)

pered. The similarity of established and newly acquired tasks seems crucial. It is easy to see how a new task could interfere with a similar, learned task.

Interference has its effects both forward in time (*proactive inhibition*) and backward in time (*retroactive inhibition*). In other words, the learning of one response can interfere with the memory of a response yet to be learned or with the memory of a previously learned response.

An experiment done years ago dramatically illustrates this effect (Jenkins & Dallenbach, 1924). Subjects learned lists of nonsense syllables immediately after they woke in the morning and immediately before they went to bed at night. After the learning task, they were either questioned during the day or awakened during the night and questioned. Subjects who were trained and tested during the day quickly forgot most of the syllables; several hours after learning they could recall less than 10 percent. But subjects who were trained immediately before retiring and tested when they were awakened during the night could recall many more nonsense syllables. During the day, it would seem, retroactive interference was acting on the memory process, resulting in the subject's reduced ability to recall the nonsense words. During sleep, there is much less interference.

Apparently, similar interfering processes affect permanent memory and its retrieval. One implication is that interfering memory may change the engram's details.

Learning, Memory, and Information Processing—a Synthesis

Modern study of human memory has made impressive advances, largely because it has been done in the context of information processing: How do people deal with, or process, the sensory and experiential information they continuously receive? The development of modern computers has aided this analysis. There are some important ways in which computers and humans are alike (as well as very important ways in which they differ). Both must receive and process information. Both must hold some of this information temporarily—short-term memory in humans and a "buffer" in a computer. It would be impossible for either humans or computers to process information if they did not have a temporary store or buffer to facilitate information flow in from the environment and out from permanent store. Both must place some of this information into permanent storage.

A recent model of human memory developed by Atkinson and Shiffrin (1968) summarizes our current knowledge of human learning, memory, and information processing. Their view elaborates the general scheme of information processing shown in Chapter 4. External input in the form of sensory stimuli enters the first stage of memory—the *sensory register*. This is the locus of iconic memory, our memory for visual stimuli that decays completely in less than a second. As we noted, iconic memory seems to be predominantly visual. (But, we must add, other senses have not been studied much.) Some portion of the information is selected and

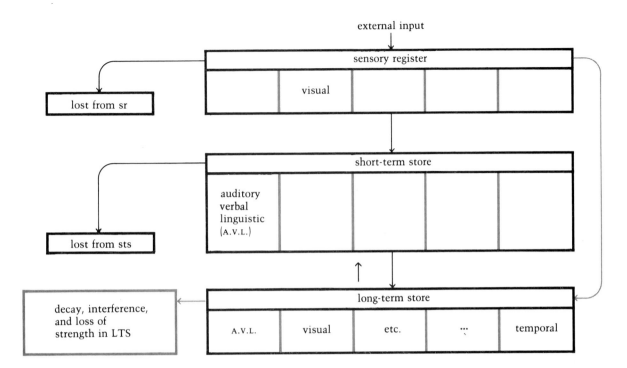

external input

sensory register

visual

lost from sr

short-term store

auditory
verbal
linguistic
(A.V.L.)

lost from sts

decay, interference,
and loss of
strength in LTS

long-term store

A.V.L.   visual   etc.   ...   temporal

7-12
The Atkinson-Shiffrin model of the structure of the memory system. Information from sensory stimuli first enters the sensory register. Only visual stimuli are listed in the model because memory for the other senses has not been as fully investigated. Meaningful material from the sensory register is coded and categorized and passed either into short-term store or directly to long-term store. The coding of memory in short-term store seems to be entirely in auditory, verbal, or linguistic terms. However, in long-term store, visual, taste, olfactory, tactual, and even temporal modes seem to exist. (Atkinson & Shiffrin, 1968)

transferred to short-term store—the short-term primary memory of our "conscious present."

In short-term store, information seems to be recoded into auditory, verbal, and linguistic terms. If the information in short-term store is rehearsed or repeated, it can actually be maintained for as long as we like. If it is not rehearsed or practiced, it decays and is permanently lost from short-term store. This type of forgetting process occurs in a period of perhaps 10–30 seconds.

Finally, some information is selected from short-term store (or even from the sensory register) and transferred into long-term store. The coding of memory in long-term store is often quite different from that in short-term store. It can be in auditory, verbal, or linguistic terms, and also in visual, taste, olfactory, and even temporal terms (memory of when past events occurred or how long they lasted). For example, the remarkable human ability to remember faces, as demonstrated in Haber's experiment, appears to reflect a process of transferring visual information directly from the visual sensory register to visual long-term store.

Atkinson and Shiffrin emphasize that the flow of information among the three systems is largely under the control of the individual person, rather than being automatic. Information from one store is copied and transferred to another store more or less at will, depending on such factors as attention, rehearsal, and motivation. This copying does *not* remove the information from the initial store. In both the sensory register and the short-term store it decays in characteristic time periods.

A person normally will scan information in the sensory register—together with searching of long-term store—and select certain material to hold in short-term store. Some of this material also may be selected to be permanently stored in long-term memory, again largely under the person's control. A final process of great importance is the transfer from long-term store back to short-term store, a procedure that also is largely under the deliberate control of the individual. This process is in great part what happens when we solve problems, test hypotheses, think, and even daydream.

Until very recently, virtually all research in human memory had been concerned only with long-term store. Most of the information about human learning and memory that we have reviewed in this chapter relates to permanent memory—measures of recall and recognition, effect of similarity, interference effects, and so on. This is valuable information, but it only taps a part of the human memory process. As an example, it was not until Sternberg's 1966 study of memory search through short-term store that we discovered how rapid the search is—30 characters per second—and that it is serial, in marked contrast to the search through long-term store.

We raised the question earlier of whether short-term and long-term memory are different processes or different aspects of the same process. The most direct evidence that they are fundamentally different processes comes from studies in the psychobiology of learning. The most compelling investigation is an extensive case history done over a period of years on a patient, Mr. H.M., who had both temporal lobes of his brain removed to treat a severe epileptic condition. The treatment succeeded in curing the epilepsy, but caused H.M. to develop a profound memory defect. He permanently lost the ability to place information in long-term store. His short-term store was normal and his permanent memories up to the time of the operation continued. However, he was unable to form new permanent memories. In Milner's words (1966):

This young man (H.M.) . . . had had no obvious memory disturbance before his operation, having, for example, passed his high school examinations without difficulty. (He sustained) a minor head injury at the age of seven. Minor (seizures) began one year later, and then, at the age of 16, he began to have generalized seizures which, despite heavy medication, increased in frequency and severity until, by the age of 27, he was no longer able to work. . . ; his prospects were by then so desperate that the radical bilateral medial temporal lobe (surgery) . . . was performed. The patient was drowsy for the first few post-operative days but then, as he became more alert, a severe memory impairment was apparent. He could no longer recognize the hospital staff, apart from (the surgeon), whom he had known for many years; he did not remember and could not relearn the way to the bathroom, and he seemed to retain nothing of the day-to-day happenings in the hospital.

His early memories were seemingly vivid and intact, his speech was normal, and his social behaviour and emotional responses were entirely appropriate.

There has been little change in this clinical picture during the years which have elapsed since the operation . . . there (is no) evidence of general intellectual loss; in fact, his intelligence as measured by standard tests is actually a little higher now than before the operation. . . . Yet the remarkable memory defect persists, and it is clear that H.M. can remember little of the experiences of the last . . . years. . . .

Ten months after the operation the family moved to a new house which was situated only a few blocks away from their old one, on the same street. When examined . . . nearly a year later, H.M. had not yet learned the new address, nor could he be trusted to find his way home alone, because he would go to the old house. Six years ago the family moved again, and H.M. is still unsure of his present address, although he does seem to know that he has moved. (The patient) . . . will do the same jigsaw puzzles day after day without showing any practice effect, and read the same magazines over and over again without finding their contents familiar. . . .

Even such profound amnesias as this are, however, compatible with a normal attention span. . . . On one occasion, he was asked to remember the number "584" and was then allowed to sit quietly with no interruption for 15 minutes, at which point he was able to recall the number correctly without hesitation. When asked how he had been able to do this, he replied.

"It's easy. You just remember 8. You see 5, 8, and 4 add to 17. You remember 8; subtract it from 17 and it leaves 9. Divide 9 in half and you get 5 and 4, and there you are: 584. Easy."

In spite of H.M.'s elaborate mnemonic scheme he was unable, a minute or so later, to remember either the number "584" or any of the associated complex train of thought; in fact, he did not know that he had been given a number to remember. . . .

One gets some idea of what such an amnesic state must be like from H.M.'s own comments. . . . Between tests, he would suddenly look up and say, rather anxiously,

"Right now, I'm wondering. Have I done or said anything amiss? You see, at this moment everything looks clear to me, but what happened just before? That's what worries me. It's like waking from a dream; I just don't remember."

Though H.M. had lost the ability to acquire new permanent memories, his iconic memory and short-term or primary memory were intact and seemingly normal. Furthermore, he retained his permanent memory for well-learned events prior to surgery. But he could no longer convert immediate memory into long-term storage.

The syndrome exhibited by H.M. is of great interest both in terms of what abilities he lost and what abilities he retained. Jerry Konoski, a Polish neuropsychologist, developed a method of testing memory for single events, termed "delayed paired comparisons," which Milner used

Graph of H.M.'s recall ability as compared with normal subjects. In each trial, the subject is presented with successive stimuli and must say whether a stimulus is the same as the preceding one. Normal subjects average one error per 12 trials. H.M.'s error rate varied as a function of time. With 0 seconds delay, he made only one error; with 60 seconds delay, he made an average of 4.5 errors in 12 trials. (Milner, 1966)

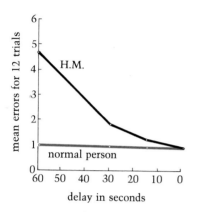

on H.M. Successive stimuli are presented one at a time with variable times of up to 60 seconds between presentations; the subject is asked each time whether the last two are the same or different. Among the stimuli that can be used are tones, color shades, nonsense forms, and words. Normal subjects average about one error for every 12 trials even when time intervals between stimuli are as long as 60 seconds. H.M.'s error score increased dramatically as the time interval was increased, and at 60 seconds he was performing not much better than chance (6 errors in 12 trials is chance). Thus, H.M. can register new perceptual information quite normally in short-term store. However, the information ceases to be available to him in about 30 seconds—the approximate maximum time limit for short-term store duration.

Another kind of evidence to distinguish short-term and long-term store comes from psychobiological studies of memory consolidation. It has been known for some time that severe electric shocks to the brain—the so-called electroconvulsive shock (ECS) therapy given to some psychiatric patients—interferes with memory. In a classic experimental study of this phenomenon, Duncan (1949) discovered that the ECS appears to prevent short-term store from consolidating into long-term store. He trained rats to avoid shocks to their feet by running in a shuttle box (a compartmentalized box in which the rat receives shocks from the grids on one side; he escapes the shocks by pushing the lever and running into the second compartment). A light came on 10 seconds before the foot shock and served as a conditioned stimulus. Animals were then given ECS at various times after the training trials. The closer the ECS is to the learning trial, the greater effect it has on memory. Rats that received an ECS almost immediately after receiving the foot shock did not remember that the light, the conditioned stimulus, was a warning that a foot shock was imminent. Although the memory consolidation literature is large and complex, there seems now to be little doubt that ECS, if given immediately after a learning experience, prevents the learned information from being retained in long-term store—it "uncouples" the normal link between short-term and long-term store (McGaugh & Herz, 1972).

In sum, both studies of information processing and memory in humans and psychobiological studies of humans and animals seem to support the idea that the three processes of information storage—sensory register, short-term store, and long-term store—may be fundamentally different from each other.

Motor-Skill Learning and Memory

Memory for motor skills appears to differ from memory for verbal material. For one thing, we do not seem to forget motor skills.

Humans learn literally thousands of motor skills—typing, playing a piano, operating a key punch, an adding machine, or a cash register, writing, tying shoelaces, driving a car, tapping out Morse code, knotting a tie, knitting, to name a few. These various kinds of motor learning share common elements. First, the subject must coordinate his muscle responses to produce a coherent and consistent pattern. Second, he must

7-14
Motor skills are learned after hours, months, or years of practice. Feedback is an important factor in motor-skill learning. The skill of rock climbing obviously must be learned with a particularly high degree of intensity. (Gaston Rebuffat, Rapho Guillumette)

direct patterns of motor movements toward some goal. That goal may involve all the body's muscles, as swimming and running do, or it may involve only certain muscles, as in typing. Third, he uses the results of his behaviors to adjust and control the responses as he continues to make them. For example, as he assesses the effects of his responses, he may dribble a basketball less vigorously, swing a bat higher, or pump a bicycle harder. This feature of motor-skill learning is termed feedback. We shall discuss it later in detail.

Motor skills are much more than simple collections of previously learned responses. They are, as we have noted, complete, integrated patterns of muscle action aimed at a goal. A pattern of responses seen as a whole takes on an entirely new meaning. For example, virtually everyone can strike single keys on the piano keyboard. However, only when a person coordinates these individual motor responses into a meaningful pattern can we say that he is playing the piano. The whole of the response pattern is considerably more than the sum of its parts.

Most of us have not skipped rope recently. However, if we tried it, we would find it surprisingly easy. Motor skills, once well learned, are very resistant to loss. Laboratory studies of motor-skill learning have tested well-trained subjects more than two years after their initial training. They showed virtually no loss in skill performance. While we do not know the reasons for this high retention, motor-skill learning could involve brain mechanisms unlike those used in other forms of learning. On the other hand, we might retain these skills well simply because they are unusually well perfected before we abandon them. You never forget how to ride a bicycle, for example. Another possibility is that we do not forget a motor skill because no activity is similar enough to interfere with our memory of it.

Factors Affecting Verbal and Motor-Skill Learning

Most of us learn verbal and motor skills without analyzing why we learn them, or why we learn some faster than others. But research has indicated that several factors bear importantly on our learning of motor and verbal skills.

Meaningfulness

As we might expect from what we already know about learning, we tend to learn and retain *meaningful* items—those that have significance for us—before we learn others. If you were to read an article about small towns in America, including your home town, you would learn first what was said about your home town and remember it in much greater detail. It has more meaning for you. This also can work in reverse. A single nonsense syllable in a list of real words often will be learned faster than the "meaningful" stimuli. The reason for this effect is similar to the reason for the beginning-end effect in the serial position phenomenon. Like the items at the beginning and end of a list, a nonsense sylla-

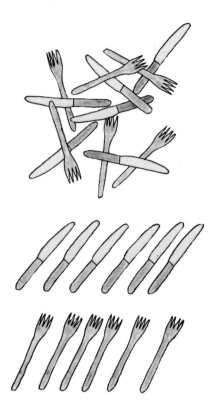

7-15

Chunking increases the amount of recall. We can keep approximately seven items in short-term memory. If we have a collection of different kinds of silverware — knives and forks, for example — we only have single items in memory. If, however, we chunk all the knives together as one category, and forks as another, we have room for five other categories.

ble stands out in a context of meaningful words. Apparently, anything that is distinct from its context will be learned better.

Studies of free recall have unearthed yet another feature of meaning. If several words in the same general conceptual category are randomly scattered through a list of other, disparate words, the subject will tend to recall most of the list's related words as a group. Clustering or chunking in this way is still another dimension in the process of verbal learning.

Distribution of Training

How frequently and lengthily an individual practices a verbal or motor skill affects his performance. The performance record of a person acquiring a motor skill shows the typical learning curve. This curve is not always smooth; it does not always show steady improvement up to a final maximum performance level. Instead, there are plateaus in the learning curve; at these points, continued practice does not bring immediate improvement. Plateaus can seriously impede response learning. However, the subject who realizes that plateaus are normal in motor-skill learning will persevere and eventually see his performance improve. Figure 7-16 shows an individual's rate of development of typing skills in terms of hours practiced. This graph, which plots the total number of correct characters typed during each practice session, illustrates the plateaus the individual encountered in learning this motor skill.

In this experiment, the subject practiced typing for about 85 hours over 5 months. We do not know from typing studies what would have happened if the 85 hours of practice had been spread over several weeks. But we can refer to the results of laboratory experiments. Basically, we want to know the relative merits of _massed_ versus _distributed practice_ — that is, practice that is conducted in a short time period versus the same amount of practice spread over a longer period of time. A classic experiment uses the task of drawing a geometrical figure while viewing the drawing hand in a mirror. This procedure reverses the hand's apparent movements and requires some experience to master (Lorge, 1930). Three groups performed the task. One group of subjects drew the figure over and over as fast as they could; the second group had a one-minute rest

7-16

Graph of motor-skill learning. The subject improves his typing ability at a steady pace until he achieves a certain level of competence. He remains at that level for a time and then continues to improve again. This sequence of improvement, leveling off, improvement, and so on is typical of most motor-skill learning. (After Book, 1908)

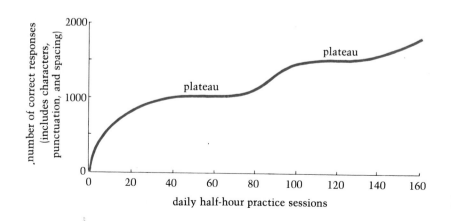

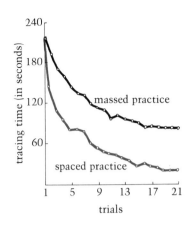

240

180

120

60

tracing time (in seconds)

massed practice

spaced practice

1   5   9   13   17   21

trials

7-17
Graph of the relative efficiency of massed and spaced practice. The subjects improved on the mirror-drawing task with both types of practice. However, improvement was greater and faster when practice was spaced. (From I. Lorge, *Influence of regularly interpolated time intervals upon subsequent learning.* Copyright 1930 by Teachers College, Columbia University. Reprinted by permission of the publisher.)

between successive attempts at drawing the figure; and the third group had a one-day wait between attempts. The group that had no rest at all between trials mastered the skill far more slowly than the group that had a one-minute rest between attempts. The group receiving one-day intervals learned the motor skill fastest, in terms of actual time spent drawing. These results, repeated many times in many different motor-skill experiments, have proved consistent. Distributed practice leads to faster learning. While subjects trained in massed practice sessions do eventually reach the performance level of subjects trained under distributed practice, it takes them many more trials.

Verbal learning also occurs faster under a regimen of distributed practice. A student studying for an exam can't cram all of the semester's information into one session. He would be better off taking breaks between periods of study. Over a longer time span, he could perform better on the final exam if he studied regularly throughout the semester instead of cramming the night before. Thus, both motor and verbal skills are learned faster with distributed practice.

Part Versus Whole Learning

Motor skills can be learned in pieces or as whole response patterns. We do not know whether it is more efficient to learn a skill in parts and later chain those parts together, or to attempt to master the entire task at once. The efficiency of the procedure depends largely on the task at hand. Each procedure has advantages and disadvantages. The piecemeal approach has the advantage that each individual component is worked upon alone until the point of mastery. Partial learning has an additional psychological advantage; the mastery of each part of the skill gives the subject considerable periodic reinforcement. On the other hand, it can be rather difficult to piece the parts together in a unified whole. The "all-at-once" approach has a drawback, too; motor skills are often long and complex. Learning to assemble and dismantle a car engine would be a challenging task, no matter how it was done. But it would be much more demanding to simultaneously learn the details of carburetion, transmission, suspension, and drive-train.

For some motor-skill tasks, one approach is definitely superior. In typing, for example, it would be foolish to train one hand at a time. Conversely, a subject could learn golfing quite efficiently by the part method. He first could perfect his technique of driving the ball down the fairway. Then he could work on his putting. He could complete his training by learning how to get the ball out of the rough.

As we noted, the choice of technique depends almost entirely on the task. Typing is an integrated activity, involving "parallel processing" of information. Golfing involves the mastery of a number of separate motor skills that are brought into play in a sequence. Similarly, certain verbal learning tasks can be learned better all at once. For example, when attempting to master a complex theory, it is better to approach it as a total unit so that you understand the relationships within the theory. On the other hand, a student attempting to memorize a long poem will learn it faster if he breaks the poem into meaningful sections and then combines the sections.

Feedback

There has never been a blind neurosurgeon nor is there likely to be one. One reason, among others, is that a blind neurosurgeon could never gain *feedback* or *knowledge of results* of his work so that he could later make corrections on the basis of this visual information. It is not only sight that provides feedback information. Depending on the task, feedback may come from hearing or from the joint and tendon receptors that tell our brain where our muscles are in space. Thus, feedback provides us with sensory information we can use to adjust and control our behavior. Feedback also provides positive and negative reinforcement. We are reinforced positively when feedback says that our responses were correct, and negatively when we are "told" our responses were incorrect.

Many homes in America have at least one feedback device—the thermostat that controls the furnace. The thermostat contains a device sensitive to temperature. If it detects that the room's air is cooler than the pre-selected temperature, the thermostat will turn on the furnace. When the room air reaches the selected temperature, the thermostat will turn the furnace off. Thus, the room gradually will cool again, the furnace will come on, heat the room, and be shut off again. In motor-skill learning, feedback operates like a thermostat.

Verbal learning also relies on feedback. For example, if a student gets a corrected exam back quickly, he can learn from his errors. However, if the teacher holds the exam for two or three weeks, the student may have forgotten the exam questions and why he answered them as he did. He will probably learn considerably less from such greatly delayed feedback. Operant conditioning of heart rate (see Chapter 6) contains a clear example of the efficiency of feedback coupled with reinforcement. You will recall that the procedure was to detect the autonomic response, be it heart rate or blood pressure, and use this information as positive reinforcement when the response changed in the desired direction. Thus, heart rate or blood pressure was the feedback.

Experiments in delaying feedback to subjects have dramatically illustrated the importance of feedback in directing motor-skill behavior. Even delays as short as a fraction of a second have devastating effects on performance. Some subjects are so severely disrupted that they cannot perform the task. Another example is an acoustically "live" room in which the loud and almost instantaneous echo feedback makes conversation difficult, if not entirely impossible.

Transfer of Training

A veteran salesman, who has dealt with scores of business contacts, can easily remember the names and titles of new individuals he meets. Past learning has resulted in a *positive transfer* to new learning situations. However, this is not always the case. A second experienced salesman may find that he cannot remember the names of last year's customers as well as he can those of customers from 5 years ago. For him, the memory of the earlier names seems to prevent the learning of the new names. Interference by previously learned responses is called *negative transfer.* Since the value of an education can presumably be measured in terms of the application of the acquired knowledge to real-world situations, the entire academic establishment is, in a very real sense, based upon the transfer of training.

Transfer of training can occur in two situations. In the first, the *stimuli* of two training tasks are similar, invoking a basic rule of transfer of training: similar stimuli require similar responses. A person who has learned to drive a Chevrolet sedan can readily transfer these responses to a Plymouth compact model. Automobiles are all quite similar. The steering wheel, gas pedal, brake pedal, and speedometer are all in roughly the same locations. Because the stimuli of the two automobiles are similar, transfer of training is positive and rapid. Negative transfer would occur if the average driver were asked to test-drive a new model car in which the driver lies flat on his back, observing the road ahead through a system of mirrors.

Positive transfer of training also occurs when the *responses* of two tasks are similar. We would expect positive transfer from one automobile to the other simply because they require similar responses. Negative transfer would occur if the responses were considerably different. If a manufacturer modified his car's braking system, substituting a "dead man" system, we might expect negative transfer. With a dead man braking system, the automobile is stopped when the foot is lifted from the brake pedal. This change would prompt negative transfer because the lifting response is diametrically opposed to the pedal-pressing response learned in the initial driving training. Backing up a car with an attached trailer is a common example of the tendency to transfer an apparently similar response. If you try to back the trailer as you would back the car alone, the results may be disastrous. In backing a trailer, you must turn the steering wheel in the "wrong" direction.

The significance of transfer in learning and memory is not simply in specific tasks like badminton and tennis. Harry Harlow's important demonstration of learning set—learning how to learn—is a much more general aspect of transfer. We discussed this phenomenon in the last chapter. Animals and humans do not merely transfer specific knowledge and skills from one task to another; they also transfer more general features, like the ability to learn certain kinds of tasks.

Comparing Verbal and Motor-Skill Learning

We have seen that such factors as distribution of training, part-versus-whole learning, and transfer of training have similar effects on both verbal and motor-skill learning. However, as we noted above, verbal and motor-skill learning are in many ways quite different. The most striking evidence of this comes again from Brenda Milner's unfortunate patient H.M. Remarkably enough, H.M. has normal long-term memory for newly learned motor-skill tasks, even though he has no long-term memory for other kinds of new information.

Milner used the mirror drawing task described earlier. The subject must draw a line with a pencil all the way around a star between two border lines. Each touch of a border line is an error. However, the sub-

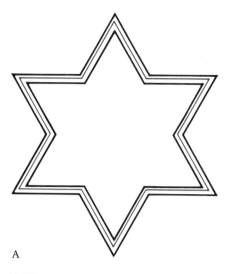

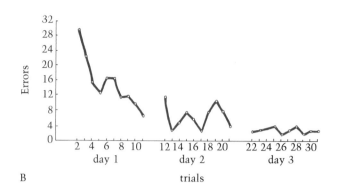

7-18

(A) Star used in the mirror drawing task. (B) Graph showing that H.M.'s ability to do the mirror drawing task improved with each day of practice. However, from day to day he was unable to recall the nature of the task. His verbal memory was impaired, but his motor-skill memory was not. (Milner, 1966)

ject sees the star and his hand and pencil only through a mirror, which reverses movements toward and away but not left and right. The interested reader is urged to try the task—it is not at all easy at first! Figure 7-18 shows H.M.'s performance on three successive days. His rapid learning and much better performance each day are essentially normal. However, even on day three, when his performance was virtually perfect, he was totally unaware that he had ever done the task before and it had to be explained to him again! A normal subject remembers the task in terms of his verbal report as well as his motor performance.

In essence, H.M. has normal abilities to develop long-term storage of learned motor skills. There appears to be a complete disassociation between his "perceptual-verbal-awareness" memory and his "perceptual-motor" memory. This is a most important finding deserving great emphasis. It seems to indicate that the brain substrates for motor-skill learning and memory are entirely different from those for verbal awareness. Does H.M. remember the mirror task or not? By one measure—his verbal report—not at all. By another measure—his motor performance—perfectly.

Programmed Learning

One of the major challenges in education is the search for the most effective method of exchanging knowledge between teachers and students. Education involves more than the transfer of a teacher's knowledge to a student. Ideally, an effective education would find the student possessing knowledge and insights beyond the teacher's. The student would learn not only a set of facts and definitions, but an ability to combine facts and insights into original concepts. In short, the student would learn how to learn.

In recent years, psychologists have developed a new approach to the learning challenge; _programmed learning_ applies to the academic situation the basic psychological principles underlying behavioral change. B. F. Skinner deserves primary credit for developing this approach to education. Emphasizing the effects of immediate reward or reinforcement on behavior, he developed methods of operant training with rats and pigeons in the laboratory, and then applied these methods to the human educational process.

Skinner observed that a behavior which is immediately followed by a positive reinforcement will tend to be repeated. Conversely, behavior immediately followed by punishment will tend not to be repeated. The educational process deals with behavioral *changes*. Test-taking, verbal recitation, and report writing are all forms of verbal behavior in the academic context; technical training includes motor-skill behaviors as well. The psychological principle of reinforcement requires some behavioral response to these behaviors. For example, consider a student's first recitation before a class. If the teacher and other students seem attentive and complimentary, the student will probably recite again. If he is criticized, laughed at, or otherwise negatively reinforced, he will not want to recite again.

Over the years, individualized instruction has proven to be the most effective method of education. But when there are large numbers of students in a class, individualized instruction by a teacher becomes difficult or impossible. Attempts to solve this problem have included automatic teaching machines, programmed instruction, and computer-assisted instruction.

In each of these approaches, the student is presented one item of material at a time—generally, a statement followed by a question about it. The student writes the answer to the question and then compares his answer to the correct answer, which has been hidden from view until then by the machine or a hand-held card. In this way, he is immediately reinforced for learning. *Computer-assisted instruction* is slightly different; the student types his answer, and the computer compares it to the correct answer. The computer reinforces the student by telling him if the answer is correct or incorrect—often with a certain humorous flair.

The advantage of teaching machines, including computers, is that they eliminate other forms of behavior, which may also be successful in

7-19
The student presses a button to indicate his answer (all questions are multiple-choice). The teaching machine automatically shows him whether his answer is correct or incorrect. (Paul Conklin, Monkmeyer)

selecting the correct answer—such as glancing ahead in a programmed text. They also require a written or typed answer, which keeps the student from advancing to another level of material when he has in his head only a poorly formulated response to the question at the preceding level.

A disadvantage of automated teaching is that, while it can easily handle single-item answers, it cannot deal with more complex forms of response, such as short-sentence or essay answers. Scientists are working to develop natural language processing in computers so that they can identify meanings in sentences and paragraphs. This is an extremely complex challenge, however; it will probably not be solved for many years.

Personalized Self-Paced Instruction

One of the more exciting approaches to education, employing some of the above methods but going beyond their limitations, has been developed by Fred S. Keller. Keller's method is founded on the principles of immediate reinforcement and grew out of military technical training procedures. Unlike teaching machines and computer-assisted instruction, it teaches large numbers of students without sacrificing individualized instruction. Keller (1968) summarizes the features of his method, which distinguish it from conventional teaching methods, as follows:

1. The go-at-your-own-pace feature, which permits a student to move through the course at a speed commensurate with his ability and other demands upon his time.

2. The unit-perfection requirement for advance, which lets the student go ahead to new material only after demonstrating mastery of that which preceded.

3. The use of lectures and demonstrations as vehicles of motivation, rather than sources of critical information.

4. The stress upon the written word in teacher-student communication; and finally

5. The use of proctors, which permits repeated testing, immediate scoring, almost unavoidable tutoring, and a marked enhancement of the personal-social aspect of the educational process.

Keller's method involves a close interaction between the professor, teaching assistants, proctors, and students. The proctors are undergraduate students who have previously mastered the course; as students, they have a unique understanding of the special problems of a student. They provide the first and closest instructional contact with the students. Each proctor has the tutorial responsibility for eight to ten students. For a student to advance to the next level of instructional material, he must demonstrate mastery of the current set of materials. He does this through readiness tests, which the proctor administers and evaluates. The student has an opportunity to explain any answers which the proctor questions. The graduate teaching assistants provide

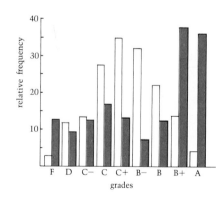

7-20
Graph comparing the grades of students taught by the Keller method (colored bars) with students using standard instructional methods. (Keller, 1968).

7-21
Students need to have motivation to learn. The material to be learned should be challenging and relevant. (Erich Hartmann, Magnum; Charles Harbutt, Magnum)

detailed assistance to the proctors and prepare various laboratory demonstrations as well.

When a specified number of students have demonstrated mastery of a certain level of material, the instructor will provide a lecture or other demonstration as a "vehicle of motivation" for further progress. These lectures and demonstrations may be videotaped for later viewing by students who missed them originally.

Several important points stand out with Keller's method. First, there is a clearly defined set of terminal skills or levels of understanding for each course. Indeed, these goals are made clear at the start of the course and the entire course is designed to guide each student to that level of capability. In contrast, conventional classes too often have ill-defined objectives. In addition, they often lack a clear organization for the presentation of information.

The other important features of Keller's method are that the student masters material at his own speed and that this mastery is verified before he advances to the next level. The importance of the latter cannot be overemphasized. Education and the development of independent critical thinking is a serial process in which basic concepts must be mastered before more complex concepts can be acquired. Too often, students are pushed to successive levels of complexity without an adequate foundation. Their understanding of a subject comes to be as fragile as a house of cards.

With the Keller method and several other similar approaches to teaching (see Ferster & Perrot, 1968; Postlethwait & Novak, 1967), the instructor's role changes from that of a transmitter of "knowledge" to that of a motivator, facilitator, and director of learning in his students (Keller, 1968).

Education, after all, is a process which occurs *within* an individual. The instructor's goal should be to facilitate that process. The methods of Keller and others promise to help instructors reach that goal while dealing with large numbers of students who have differing abilities.

Language Defined

"Hurry!" "Gimme toothbrush!" "Please tickle more!" "You me go there in!" "Please hurry!" "Sweet drink!" No one would be surprised to learn that the speaker of these utterances was a small child. The intended meaning is clear, but the grammatical structure is primitive. It may surprise you, however, to learn that the "speaker" was a chimpanzee.

Two Nevada psychologists, Beatrice and Robert Gardner (1969), obtained Washoe, a 1-year-old female chimpanzee, from the wilds of Africa and raised her in a trailer "apartment." During her waking hours, Washoe was constantly with human companions. Washoe did not learn to speak English; in fact, Washoe did not learn to "speak" at all. The chimpanzee was taught American Sign Language, the language used by deaf humans. Other idiosyncratic signs were included because they seemed natural for Washoe. Many other experimenters had attempted verbal language training of chimpanzees and had failed. The Gardners reasoned that such failure was not due to the chimpanzees' innate intellectual inability to learn language; it was due, they believed, to the limitations of the animal's vocal apparatus. There was another reason to use sign language; observations of chimpanzee behavior in the wild has shown that they use many hand gestures.

From the very beginning, the Gardners "talked" to Washoe only in sign language. They started with a very limited vocabulary of the most important or meaningful objects in Washoe's environment, such as concepts of self and food, and gradually built the vocabulary. Rather than adopt any particular learning theory bias, they used a variety of training techniques from cajoling to reinforcing to punishing. Molding Washoe's fingers into the correct signs, combined with her imitation of the experimenter's hands, proved the most efficient way to teach Washoe the sign language.

The Gardners used operant shaping techniques to teach the first signs. Washoe was rewarded first for trying to manipulate her fingers in imitation of the Gardners, and then for making signs that were successively more like the desired one. Finally, Washoe was rewarded only for making the desired sign. Washoe learned rapidly. After several months' training, she had mastered 10 syllables. In three years, her vocabulary had increased to more than 100 words. Even more important, Washoe showed an amazing ability to generalize the signs to many situations other than the teaching situations. Gradually, she began to combine the signs into rudimentary phrases and sentences, using the signs spontaneously and appropriately. For example, when she wanted to go outside and play, she would make the appropriate sign with her hands. Another sign, pantomiming "peek-a-boo," indicated that she wanted to play a particular game. In the end, she was using the articles of speech in the proper combinations and forming sentences of up to 6 words.

Was Washoe exhibiting "real" language? In some ways, this is

7-22

The Gardner's successfully taught Washoe to communicate with American Sign Language. At the Yerkes Regional Primate Center, a computer is used to teach another chimp, Lana, to communicate. Lana has apparently grasped the concept that she can ask not only for concrete objects by the names she has been taught, but also that she can ask for the abstractions, the names that represent objects whose names she does not know.

In the Yerkes language, dubbed Yerkish, questions begin with a ? and name-of is a single word. A Yerkish conversation is carried out using an electric keyboard in which each key represents a word. When keys are pressed, the words are projected in sequence on a display panel above Lana's keyboard. Lana and her teacher must read the projected images to get the message. (Yerkes Regional Primate Center)

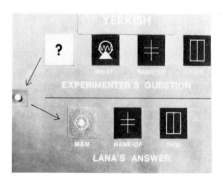

an academic question. She certainly was communicating her wants, needs, desires, emotions, and reactions. She was able to carry on two-way communication with her experimenters. However, her language behavior was not at all like that of a child. Washoe was just as likely to say, "Hurry! Gimme! Toothbrush!" as she was to say, "Gimme! Hurry! Toothbrush!" We do not know whether Washoe's failure to exhibit grammar and *syntax* (the proper ordering of words) is innate to the chimpanzee, or results from her training. With additional training, Washoe might develop a more consistent syntax. Since this was the first attempt to teach a chimpanzee to talk in sign language, many training errors may have occurred. We also must remember that the Gardners are not deaf; and although they are facile in American Sign Language, a deaf instructor might achieve better results. Finally, syntax is not as important in American Sign Language as it is in spoken English.

Syntax or word order is the key to language. After all, it makes a great deal of difference whether Kathryn hit Elizabeth or Elizabeth hit Kathryn. To date, Washoe does not exhibit clear evidence of syntax and therefore cannot be said to exhibit language in the human sense. Extensive communication, yes, but language, not yet.

Language and Speech. We must distinguish between speech and language. *Speech* is the physical sign of both the cognitive processes and the formal, grammatical structure called *language*. We can see, hear, evaluate, and respond to speech. Language is different. It is a hypothetical property of the mind and the grammar books which shows itself in speech. The speech-language relationship is similar to the relationship between learning and performance. While we can readily measure an organism's performance of a task, we must *infer* learning from the performance. We must infer language meaning from speech. As we observed in Chapter 3, people with certain types of brain damage will utter speech quite freely, using proper English words and even phrases. However, there is no language—the speech is utter gibberish. We must remember, nevertheless, that chronologically, language developed entirely through speech, together with certain gestures and noises. Written language and grammar books came much later.

Varieties of Communication

While man is certainly the most endlessly communicative of all animals, many nonhuman animals communicate in sophisticated ways. Invertebrates often communicate via chemicals. A foraging ant leaves behind a trail of chemicals known as *pheromones*. The chemicals are signals to other ants, which follow them like a path.

Some forms of chemical communication are exquisitely sensitive. When ready to mate, many winged insects exude an odor into the air. The male Bombyx moth can detect the female odor five miles downwind. Pheromones communicate a great deal of information to other members of the species, directing them to food stores and warning them of dangers, in addition to bringing a male and female together for mating. More advanced organisms also use chemical stimuli. Just about everyone has observed a dog marking telephone poles, fences, and

7-23

(A) As soon as they are able to talk, children replace their crying and arm-waving with verbal communication. (Arthur Freed) (B) The honeybee communicates to her fellow workers the location of a food source with reference to the position of the sun. If she performs her dance outside the hive (left), the central run of the dance will point directly toward the food source. If she performs her dance inside the hive on the vertical sides of the honeycomb (right), she orients herself by gravity and the point directly overhead takes the place of the sun. The angle shown is the same for both dances. The distance of the food source from the hive is indicated by the rate at which she performs the dance pattern.

A

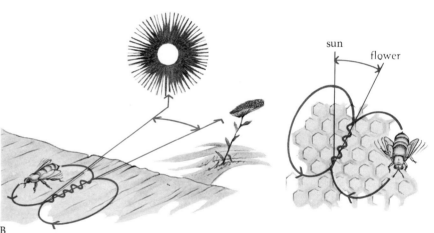

B

fire hydrants with small amounts of urine. This olfactory stimulus is a "boundary marker" that informs other dogs of this particular dog's presence.

Many animals use visual signs to communicate. One species of arboreal monkey, for example, has a black face with white eyelids. These monkeys frequently sit in adjacent trees and blink their eyes at one another using them much like semaphores. Von Frisch, an Austrian naturalist, observed that when a foraging honeybee returns to the hive, it goes through an elaborate ritual dance. During the dance, other bees gather around closely and learn the "road map" to the food source that the bee has discovered (Von Frisch, 1955).

Animal cries are another, more obvious kind of communication. An animal's loud, high-pitched distress cry conveys definite meaning to species members and to other animals as well. In the wilds, baboon troops often live with zebra herds. A hunting lion will provoke the alarm cry of either baboon or zebra, and both species can correctly interpret the other's cries. Some people believe that whales and dolphins have a rather well-developed language. An underwater microphone will record a dolphin school's wide variety of sounds. If a particular dolphin's sounds are tape-recorded and later played to another dolphin, they will elicit the same kinds of sounds from the "listener." While these sounds could have definite meaning, experimenters so far have no clear evidence that they do. Nonetheless, some form of primitive dolphin language may exist.

Thus, while language may be uniquely human, communication certainly is not. In fact, much of our nonverbal communication involves precisely the same kinds of behavior that occur in animal communication. We wrinkle our brow, snap our fingers, squint our eyes, shift our stance, shrug our shoulders, scowl, frown, smile, laugh, and gesture. While they are not formal language, these behaviors definitely do communicate information from one human to another.

Structure of Language

Language can be analyzed at several levels. At one extreme, we can examine the smallest units of language and how they are combined. At the other extreme, we can focus on _semantics,_ the study of the meaning or interpretation of language. We will consider both levels of linguistic analysis. We also will survey descriptive linguistics, that is, how frequently various language components appear, their sequencing, and their redundancy.

Phonemes. The smallest possible unit of language identifiable as a discrete sound is the _phoneme._ The p in pot, generally written /p/, and the s in say, written /s/, are phonemes. English has approximately 40 phonemes. A review of all human languages present and past has uncovered the fact that all of them are based on various combinations of about 90 phonemes. Any one language uses about 40 of them.

A phoneme's sound changes in relation to its context. In the words _cow_ and _keep_ one might assume that the initial letters in these words are different phonemes as well. However, this is not the case. While the "k" sound is slightly different in each of these two words, they actually represent the same phoneme, /k/. They "sound" different because of the letters or phonemes that follow them. In English, about 10 phonemes are used with great frequency, constituting half of our phoneme production. The most common phoneme, /i/, as in _sit,_ is used 100 times more often than the least commonly used phoneme, /z/, as in _has._

Morphemes. The next level of language is the morpheme. Morphemes are made up of a variable number of phonemes and may correspond in a rough way to words. A _morpheme_ is the smallest linguistic unit that can have an independent meaning, but a morpheme does not have to be a word. The word "cars" has two morphemes, the class name car and the s which indicates the plural.

English has more than 100,000 morphemes, which, arranged in various combinations, produce the one-million-word English vocabulary. Most individuals, of course, know and use a considerably smaller vocabulary—about 40,000 words. An exceptional person might have a 100,000-word vocabulary. Actually, such numbers are misleading; we do not use anywhere near this number of words in everyday conversation. In fact, well over half of our ordinary speech uses less than 150 words.

Syntax. The rules by which people speak and understand a language are its *syntax*. Syntax or grammar rules specify how morphemes are connected and ordered to produce larger units—phrases and sentences. While most of us have learned English grammar (or at least have been exposed to it), we might not be able to reconstruct all the rules of grammar. Nevertheless, our speech shows that we have internalized these rules. Few of us use grossly erroneous grammatical constructions.

Semantics. As we have noted, the study of the meanings implied by speech sounds and written language is called *semantics*. Understanding another person's intended meaning requires basic skills. To communicate, the individuals must be roughly equal in their fluent use of common phonemes, morphemes, and syntax. In addition, the meaning of a word or phrase depends on the associations it has acquired, its immediate context, and the emotion with which the speaker infuses the word or phrase.

Semantic interpretations are perhaps the greatest obstacles to clear communication. Two individuals can listen to a third person speak the same sentence and arrive at two entirely different meanings. The ambiguity present in language makes this possible. A large proportion of the English words that we use every day have two or more meanings. The word "walk" can have several meanings, for example: "I took the dog for a walk," or "I walked downtown," or "Don't slip on the walk!" Different as these uses of "walk" are, the meaning of the word is obvious from its context. Frequently, only such an examination of the surrounding content will reveal the intended meaning.

Minor as this problem may seem, a person without considerable experience in the use of a particular language may have semantic misunderstandings. Britons and Americans often have difficulties with a presumably common language. In England, it is quite proper to "knock up" a guest in the morning, but don't try it in the American semantic.

Descriptive Linguistics. While English is a rich and versatile language, the average American, as we have noted, uses less than 150 words in various combinations to produce more than half of his daily speech. One of the huge chunks of the English vocabulary he virtually ignores is made up of technical jargon, unique to particular trades or professions. As for the tens of thousands of other words he might use, he simply has not learned them—presumably for lack of a need.

Writers usually know more words than other people. But even writers find that they do not use their writing vocabulary in their everyday conversations. People who begin using a dictating machine are at first amazed at their dictation. When they compare a dictated paragraph with one of their long-hand passages, they are appalled to find that the dictation's sentence structure and vocabulary are much simpler and often grammatically wrong.

7-24
The Morse code and its referent English letters. Note that the letters occurring most frequently in English words have the smallest code symbols (see e, a, and t).

INTERNATIONAL MORSE CODE

A	.–	N	–.
B	–...	O	–––
C	–.–.	P	.––.
D	–..	Q	––.–
E	.	R	.–.
F	..–.	S	...
G	––.	T	–
H	....	U	..–
I	..	V	...–
J	.–––	W	.––
K	–.–	X	–..–
L	.–..	Y	–.––
M	––	Z	––..

7-25A
The first paragraph of *Hawaii* by James Michener has been put into code. See if you can crack the code and put the paragraph back into English. Turn to page 257 for the solution.

Frequency in Language. The most common word in English usage is "the." A count of the frequency of word appearances in magazine articles resulted in "the" accounting for about 5 percent of the words used. The least used word in English is anybody's guess.

Letters as well as words vary in their frequency of appearance in languages. Samuel Morse, inventor of Morse code, knew this and designed his telegraphic code to turn the idiosyncrasies of the English language into corporate profit. He assigned the most commonly occurring letter, e, the shortest code—the single dot. From top to bottom, the code's order corresponds roughly to each letter's frequency of occurrence.

The unequal usage of letters in normal speech and writing has spawned a specialized branch of inquiry among code breakers. For centuries, sensitive material has been coded so that if it falls into unfriendly hands, the message will remain hidden. If a message is coded so that every alphabet letter is simply assigned some arbitrary symbol, a cryptologist can soon "crack" the code. His first step in breaking such a code is to count how often each character appears in the message. The most common character will undoubtedly stand for the letter e. He also knows that the most common word will be the trigram "the." By looking for sequences of three symbols, the last one being the letter e, he can rapidly break the code. Figure 7-25A will give you a chance to practice your code-breaking skills. The coded section is the first paragraph of James A. Michener's *Hawaii*.

HAWAII IN CODE

Yussubcn qgbc yussubcn bo lwmfn meb, jzwc gzw tbcgucwcgn jwfw msfwmkl obfywk mck gzw rfucturms owmgqfwn bo gzw wmfgz zmk xwwc kwtukwk, gzwfw whungwk, gzwc mn cbj, bcw mnrwtg bo gzw jbfsk gzmg kjmfowk mss bgzwfn. Ug jmn m yuezgl btwmc, fwnguce qcwmnusl gb gzw wmng bo gzw smfewng tbcgucwcg, m fwngswnn wdwf-tzmceuce, euemcgut xbkl bo jmgwf gzmg jbqsk smgwf xw kwntfuxwk mn rmtuout.

Language is *redundant.* Consequently, many letters within a word and many words themselves can be eliminated from a message without seriously impairing its content. By choosing any work and deleting every eighth letter you can markedly alter the form of written language. Yet even with this random deletion of about 12 percent of the material, you can still understand the passage. Such redundancy may seem inefficient, but it actually is helpful. If we had to take into account every utterance as well as every written letter, we would have to work much harder at deciphering language. Thanks to redundancy, we can get the message without having to register all of the language elements. Without redundancy, speed reading would be impossible since you could not skim and pick out key phrases and words. Instead, you would have to register every written element. Speech would be similarly affected. We would have to hear and take into account every utterance; communicating in noisy or distracting situations would be virtually impossible.

UNDERSTANDING UNDERSTANDING

Eric Wanner *Harvard University*

Language sometimes lies about itself. The lies are not big ones, but they still cause problems. For instance, many people feel dissatisfied with human communication; we speak, but we are not understood, or so we feel. There are probably many reasons for these feelings of dissatisfaction, but one of them may be that we simply expect too much from language. Ironically, language itself may be to blame.

When we talk about communication, we usually talk about sending someone a message. Language makes it convenient to talk that way. But the convenience is misleading. Messages aren't sent anywhere during communication; we send signals. When I talk to you, the only thing that literally travels from me to you is a sound wave. If this sound wave communicates anything, it is only because a set of conventions we call language associates it with a message. For communication to work, the speaker must use his knowledge of language to *produce* the signal appropriate to his message; then the listener must use *his* knowledge of language to *identify* the signal and *interpret* its message. This sequence is portrayed schematically in Figure A.

When we look at communication in this way, we begin to see that the process leaves a lot of room for error. The listener doesn't just receive a message; he identifies and interprets a signal. How does he do it? Again, ordinary language gives a misleading answer.

To see this, suppose that you have just attended a difficult lecture delivered in barely audible tones. As you leave, you ask a friend whether he understood the lecture. If he replies, "I couldn't understand it because I couldn't hear it," you would probably find nothing odd about his reply, perhaps because implicitly you believe, as he does, that a signal must be identified before it can be interpreted. But now suppose instead that you asked your friend whether he could *hear* the lecture. If he replies, "I couldn't hear it because I couldn't understand it," you may think that he is playing games with you. Why? Probably because you believe that identifying a signal does not depend upon interpreting its message. If so, you are wrong; and

you can prove it to yourself with a tape recorder and a pair of scissors. Make a tape recording of an ordinary conversation. Then cut out several pieces of tape which contain all the sounds representing a single word or short phrase. Now splice these snippets onto a blank tape and play them to some friends. The results should be a bit surprising: most of the words and phrases will be quite unintelligible.

When psychologists conducted this experiment carefully, using high quality recordings and computer-controlled splicing techniques, they found that phrases must be five to six words long before they become generally intelligible. Figure B shows some representative results.

Why should words be so difficult to hear out of context? Why don't speakers—most of whom certainly can speak clearly—pronounce words precisely so that they can be identified in isolation? Perhaps the reason is that when words are produced in a context, the speaker knows the listener can use his interpretation of the ongoing message to make a pretty good guess about the current

A
A schematic view of communication.

SPEAKER
language
message ⟶ production process ⟶ signal ⟶

LISTENER
language
identification process ⟶ signal ⟶ interpretation process ⟶ message

B
Accuracy of identification as a function
of the amount of context provided.
(After Pollack & Pickett, 1964)

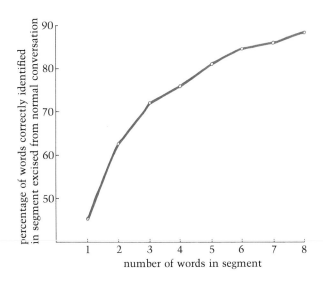

signal. If the listener can narrow his alternatives down to a few possibilities, he may not need much acoustic information to identify the signal. Speakers seem to know this and consequently get lazy about the signals they produce.

Contrary to common sense, then, what we hear *does* depend upon what we understand. In a way, it is wrong to say that the listener hears what the speaker has to say by listening. Instead, he actively figures out what the speaker is likely to say and then listens only enough to check his hypothesis. Small wonder, then, that comprehension sometimes goes astray, and with it communication.

A similar point can be made about the process of interpretation. Apparently, the listener does not content himself with passively determining the speaker's message. Instead, he uses the speaker's message for his own purposes, to update his understanding of the world. The evidence comes from studies of memory.

How many times have you heard someone say, usually in the course of an argument, "I remember exactly what you said." Chances are he is wrong. Again, you can make the test yourself. Read a friend a paragraph. Then pick a sentence from the paragraph and read it again to test your friend's memory. If you change the test sentence in a way which alters meaning, he should spot the change right away. However, if you only change the wording without altering the meaning, he will find it harder to tell you whether the test sentence differs from the sentence that actually occurred in the original paragraph. Now try the test again. This time, choose a test sentence which differs in meaning from any sentence in the paragraph, but which makes a statement that you might easily infer from the meaning of the paragraph. If your friend behaves like subjects in a series of recent psychological experiments (Barclay, 1973), he should find it hard to tell whether this sentence was in the paragraph. Why? Perhaps because he himself drew the

inference stated in the test sentence while he was listening to the paragraph and stored it away during comprehension.

So we return to where we started. Human communication is not what language says it is. We don't send messages; we produce sounds. Those sounds provide an occasion for the listener's mind to go into action. He makes guesses about our signals and he draws inferences from our messages that we may or may not have intended. On one hand, we should appreciate his efforts. They allow him to identify signals that we may have produced poorly and to make inferences about things we meant to say but didn't. On the other hand, we should understand that the active process the listener engages in is bound to produce some errors. Indeed, the more I understand about the process of understanding, the more it seems to me that the appropriate attitude toward successful human communication should be something close to utter amazement.

Understanding Understanding   **255**

Development of Language

How humans acquire language is a major question. Clearly, the child does not suddenly spring forth with a full-blown adult language. On the other hand, he does not have to attend a special school to acquire the complex skills of language. Language develops in the child over several years. We will describe how this development occurs later, when we describe two opposing schools of thought: one believing that language develops primarily through learning, and the other believing that language development is an outgrowth of brain structures that contain linguistic rules.

Speech development seems to follow a fairly standard timetable in human infants. Most babies begin babbling at around 6 months of age and produce their first words by their first birthday. Next, they combine words into rudimentary phrases, usually before 2 years of age. By 5, they have mastered the basic grammar and style of adult speech.

Sounds

Until he begins to babble fairly regularly, the infant's verbal repertoire includes a variety of sounds. Just as the infant's motor development is characterized by seemingly random thrashings and kickings, his verbalizations are varied and extreme. During his first 6 months, the infant produces sounds that are used in every known language. One cannot distinguish the sounds of a Japanese baby from those of an American or an African baby. Regardless of culture and language, all infants produce p, m, b, or t sounds and the vowel sounds e or a (McNeill, 1970). We do not know why these particular sounds are used, but the reasons may be related to the neuromuscular development of the throat and mouth. All children also babble very similar sounds: Mama, baba, dada, and the like. Thus, it is not surprising that the infantile forms of mother and father are similar in all languages.

During the first 6 months, the child becomes more sophisticated about the sounds of his language. At the same time, he eliminates "foreign" sounds from his vocabulary. Like the acquisition of any other motor skill, the development of speech requires practice. Infants spend long hours practicing the rudimentary speech sounds before they actually use the sounds in anything resembling words.

Although the child shows no ability to use words during the first 6 months, many studies have demonstrated that the child can respond to verbal stimuli. Usually, the child responds by turning toward the speaker; he clearly reacts differently to an angry voice than he does to a loving voice. In both cases, the child is responding to the intonation, rather than the words.

Words

Between the infant's 6th and 12th month, *babbling* appears. Many of the sounds he makes at this stage are completely unrelated to any English words. When, however, the child produces sounds similar to

KEY TO CODING OF HAWAII:

Alphabet	Code symbols
a	m
b	x
c	t
d	k
e	w
f	o
g	e
h	z
i	u
j	p
k	a
l	s
m	y
n	c
o	b
p	r
q	v
r	f
s	n
t	g
u	q
v	d
w	j
x	h
y	l
z	i

HAWAII DECODED

Millions upon millions of years ago, when the continents were already formed and the principal features of the earth had been decided, there existed, then as now, one aspect of the world that dwarfed all others. It was a mighty ocean, resting uneasily to the east of the largest continent, a restless ever-changing, gigantic body of water that would later be described as pacific. (James A. Michener, *Hawaii*, 1959)

English words, or at least similar to "accepted babbling standards," his parents usually will reinforce him for those sounds. When a parent praises an infant for saying dada, the reinforcement has its effect—it increases the probability that the infant will say dada again. Positive and negative reinforcers are partly responsible for the child's elimination of non-English sounds from his "vocabulary."

It is difficult to know whether an infant understands the meaning of a word he produces. A certain percentage of these "words" are presumably trial-and-error vocalizations. However, even if the child is completely unaware of the "meaning" of his utterances, parental reinforcement soon makes him aware that some words are favored and others are not.

The infant's first words gradually become more correct and discriminating. At first, dada might refer to anything that is not "mother." Gradually, however, the infant eliminates the milkman and the postman as he sharpens his discrimination. His first words are nouns, names of meaningful objects in his environment: parents, pets, or toys. The developmental progression appears to be nouns, verbs, adjectives, and finally pronouns.

Phrases and Sentences

Between 1 and 2 years of age, the child sharpens his language skills. His first phrases and sentences are very simple—they may be only one word. Depending on the situation, "Go!" can mean "I want to go," "The dog went outside," or "You go away." Next, the child begins to string words together into phrases of two, three, and four words. Nouns still predominate; they constitute about half of the 18-month-old's vocabulary.

Combining words, especially nouns and verbs, to form even simple phrases is an immensely complex learning task. At the time that the child begins combining words, the child's grammatical structure is rather rudimentary. It has been called *telegraphic speech* (see Table 7-1). For example, the child's translation of "The dog is going outside" might be "Dog go out" or "Dog out." "Where is your ball?" might be translated "Where ball?" This grammatical form of speech, while certainly not the adult form, serves the child well at this stage of his development. As he learns more and more words and generalizes the rules of grammatical structure, he perfects this form until it reaches the structural level of adult language.

The length of the child's utterances becomes dramatically longer between 18 months and 2 years. At this time, the child is assembling brief phrases and rudimentary sentences from his ever-increasing store

Table 7-1   Telegraphic Speech (Words On the Left are Combined with Words On the Right)

allgone byebye big more pretty my see night-night hi	boy sock boat fan milk plane shoe vitamins hot Mommy Daddy . . .

of words. By age 5, adult grammatical form is fairly well established and the child may have a vocabulary of 2,000 words.

To summarize, both maturation and learning appear to be important in the child's development of language. Positive and negative reinforcement of the child's utterances by adults and the child's imitative behavior are involved in learning language.

Factors in the Development of Language

Children of upper- and middle-class parents usually begin speaking sooner than the children of lower-class parents. There are several possible explanations. Homes of well-educated and financially secure people are generally filled with books, pictures, color televisions, stereos, and a variety of other objects from which the child can learn. Such families also travel more and expose their children to more activities. Diet is another possible factor; children of well-to-do parents eat more protein foods. Furthermore, the emphasis that these parents place upon intellectual development could be a factor. They work with their children, encouraging them to develop verbal behavior, and the parents themselves are more verbal and therefore expose their children to a richer verbal environment.

Some people believe that the early development of language reflects high intelligence. However, there appears to be no correlation whatever between adult intelligence and the age at which speech first occurs in normal people. Severely retarded children *are* slow to develop speech, but this relationship does not hold for the normal population. Those of us who may have been slow to begin speaking as infants can take comfort from the fact that Albert Einstein is reputed to have spoken his first word when he was 3 years old.

Theories of Language Development

How is language learned? The question is far ranging; an understanding of language acquisition affects one's understanding of the higher mental functions. We can formulate the question in terms of the "nature-nurture" problem. Are linguistic mechanisms primarily genetic and inborn? Or do we develop them as a result of learning and environmental factors?

Learning Theory of Language

Learning theorists, such as B. F. Skinner and O. H. Mowrer, believe that a person learns language in much the same manner that he learns any other behavior. He acquires it through his interactions with the environment, that is, through reinforcement and punishment. The infant gradually acquires language skills that are reinforced by the people around him. He first learns words in this manner and later strings them together to form phrases and sentences that adults do or do not reinforce, depending on their correctness.

In a normal family, the infant receives an enormous amount of reinforcement for uttering proper morphemes. When an infant's sounds imitate adult speech, his mother's response is clear. Most mothers make a terrific fuss when their babies emit their first words and they continue to reinforce the infants throughout their formative stages. (Incidentally, if parents refrain from talking baby talk to an infant, he will develop his language skills more rapidly.) In addition, the child gains a good deal of reinforcement simply by being able to express his wants and needs. If the child can convey that he wants a cookie by uttering the words, "Want cookie," he will be reinforced not only by the parent's approval, but by the cookie as well.

Skinner (1957) has emphasized that reinforcement of initially random babbling is the fundamental mechanism in language learning. The child's first words are closely related to reinforcement—Skinner calls these words *mands* (short for demands). "Bot" produces the bottle. At a later stage, the child is more influenced by secondary or social reinforcement, such as parental approval, and begins to learn *tacts* (short for "contacts," as in verbal contacts with the world). "There bot" would be a simple tact, locating but not demanding the bottle. Finally, more complex classes of utterances, the *intraverbals*, develop, again through social reinforcement. "Little bot" would be a simple intraverbal description of the bottle. As opposed to this simple, trial-and-error learning, Mowrer (1958) has emphasized the importance of *imitation* in the learning of appropriate language sounds. Such learning-theory views gain support from evidence that shows an utterance can be increased or decreased in frequency by use of positive or negative reinforcers.

Many criticisms have been leveled at the learning theory approach to language acquisition. One of the most telling is that language is too complex and varied for a child to learn it through the reinforcement of specific language behaviors. Moreover, a child's language is only crudely similar to his parents'. He uses a more rudimentary sentence structure and his use of pronouns does not begin until well along in his speech development. However, his use of syntax is amazing. Though he is not formally taught the rules of language, he nevertheless produces words in the correct sequences.

If the learning theory notion of language acquisition is correct, children in environments lacking feedback or opportunities to imitate language should suffer severe language impairment. To explore this point, several studies focused on the development of linguistic skills in the normal children of deaf parents. These studies found that when such children are several years old, they are indeed deficient in language production and recognition. However, during the first months of life, the stage in which normal children are practicing all the universal phonemic sounds, these children showed *no* impairment in language development. Lenneberg (1969) concludes that the earliest development phases of human vocalization are relatively independent of environmental reinforcers.

Linguistic-Relativity Hypothesis

"Language itself shapes a man's basic ideas." This quotation summarizes one extreme of psycholinguistic theory. Whorf (1956), a student of American Indian languages, has observed that it is often impossible to translate directly from one language into another. From this observation, he inferred that the world is perceived differently by individuals with dissimilar language structures. Exact equivalency between languages often is impossible because individuals see the world as their language dictates. As Whorf notes:

We dissect nature along lines laid down by our native languages. The categories and types that we isolate to form the world of phenomena (are not things) we find there because they stare every observer in the face; on the contrary, the world is presented in a kaleidoscopic flux of impressions which has to be organized by our minds—and this means largely by the linguistic system in our minds. We cut nature up, organize it into concepts, and ascribe significances as we do, largely because we are parties to an agreement to organize it in this (way)—an agreement that holds throughout our speech community and is codified in the patterns of our language. . . . Hopi (an Indian language of Southwestern North America) has one noun that covers every thing or being that flies . . . the Hopi actually call insect, airplane, and aviator all by the same word, and feel no difficulty about it. . . . This class seems to us too large and inclusive, but so would our class "snow" to an Eskimo.

What surprises most is to find that various grand generalizations of the Western world, such as time, velocity, and matter, are not essential to the construction of a consistent picture of the universe. (Whorf, 1956)

These ideas have come to be known as the *linguistic-relativity hypothesis*. However, the notion that our thought and our perception of the world are relative to the language of our culture has not been accepted without reservation. While critics also see a relationship between

Whorf's linguistic-relativity hypothesis proposes that man's language is directly related to his culture. Tribesmen of Bechuanaland perceive the world differently from businessmen in America; however, some of their communication patterns are quite similar. (Nat Farbman, Time-Life Picture Agency)

the structure of language and the conception of the physical world, they argue that meaningful events in the world also tend to modify the way in which we use language.

Genetic Theory of Language

Other linguists, most notably Lenneberg (1967), have stressed the importance of biological determinants in language production and interpretation. Lenneberg notes that all evidences of communication within the animal kingdom are *species specific*. Each animal species has developed its own form of communication. He also has observed that communicative abilities tend to be what he terms "species uniform." In other words, all known human cultures have developed languages that contain about 40 phonemes and have many basic similarities. From these observations, Lenneberg concludes that genetics determines many of our linguistic abilities.

Innate Capacity Theory of Language

Noam Chomsky, a leading figure in modern psycholinguistics, emphasizes that language develops largely because certain innate rules that determine language production and interpretation emerge as the child develops physically. Chomsky maintains that language development occurs when experiences with particular linguistic elements interact with the genetically determined functioning of the brain. The child needs only experience and learning to form his specific, native language out of the universal language. In this respect a specific language is, as the learning theorists contend, culturally determined and learned through interactions with the environment. Thus Chomsky argues that we are innately equipped with certain basic linguistic principles, and that to develop our specific, native language, we must learn the particular semantic and syntactic rules that our culture sets forth.

Chomsky emphasizes that all languages have two kinds of structure: surface structure and deep structure. *Surface structure* refers to the physical aspect of speech or language—the sounds that we hear, the phonemes and morphemes and the grammatical rules that govern their combination. *Deep structure* refers to meaning and the more basic processes of syntax and conceptual organization. In Chomsky's view, certain features of deep structure are universal and equally represented in every culture. The thoughts that an individual wishes to convey come from his deep structure. The individual translates his deep structure into a physical sequence of sounds or letters by using a system of *transformational rules* that have both innate and learned components.

Figure 7-27 might serve as an example of such transformations from deep structure. Here we see various transformations. While this example has not included all possible transformations of the concept, "Virginia ate candy," we still do quite a bit with it. We can phrase the concept in active or passive voice, negate it, or pose it as a question—all of which may alter the meaning without changing the concept. However, the last entry, "The candy ate Virginia," involves changing not only the surface structure of the sentence but the deep structure, or the concept, as well.

An important point in Chomsky's psycholinguistic theory is that the meaning conveyed by a sentence's surface structure may not bear any immediately obvious relationship to the meaning of the sentence's deep structure. The deep structure, an abstract conceptualization, cannot always be easily discovered from the surface structure. When we say "Virginia did not eat the candy," that means something quite different from saying "Virginia did eat the candy." But these meanings are part of the surface structure of these two superficially different sentences. A deeper meaning connects both sentences—they have the same deep structure—for both convey the same relationship between Virginia and candy. That is, Virginia is able to eat the candy, whether or not she actually has done so. Whereas, the candy cannot eat Virginia.

For Chomsky, the development of language is a form of theory construction. The child, using his innate linguistic framework, quickly learns the theory of his parents' language; then he uses this theoretical scheme of language as a framework upon which to fit the words that he is learning. The assumption that the child constructs or develops this theory without any kind of formal instruction is implicit in the psycholinguistic argument. As you might expect, this point has been challenged by writers offering other explanations of how the child acquires the mysterious power of language.

Recent research on the development of language in young children suggests that there is some truth in both the "learning" theories of lan-

7-27
The deep structure of any sentence can be transformed into a number of surface structures. All but the final sentence are transformations of the same deep structure concept.

BASIC SENTENCE:
Virginia ate candy.

POSSIBLE TRANSFORMATIONS:
Candy was eaten by Virginia.
Virginia didn't eat candy.
Did Virginia eat candy?
Virginia would not eat candy.
Wouldn't Virginia eat candy?
Virginia was eating candy.
Virginia has been eating candy.
Hasn't Virginia eaten candy?
Has Virginia eaten candy?
Virginia has eaten candy.
* The candy ate Virginia.

guage (Skinner's theory, for example) and Chomsky's "innate" theory. Thanks in large part to the work of Roger Brown and his associates at Harvard, it is now clear that children develop general rules for language even though they are not taught these rules. Every parent has heard his small child saying things like "I digged a hole." The child has never heard an adult say "digged," only "dig" or "dug." Yet the child follows the proper rule for forming the past tense of a regular verb. He has never learned the word digged, nor learned explicitly the past tense rule, yet he applies it. Brown gives another example:

Both (children and adults) were shown a picture of a man swinging something about his head and were told: "This is a man who knows how to gling. He glings every day. Today he glings, Yesterday he _____." Adults hang suspended between glinged, glang, glung, and even glought, but children promptly say glinged (Brown & Fraser, 1963)

Roger Brown and his students conducted the most systematic and intensive study of the development of child language to date (Brown, 1969, 1973). They virtually lived with three children, Adam, Eve, and Sarah, and taped many long sequences of their spontaneous speech. The children were just beginning to speak multi-word utterances. The results of these studies are rather complicated but some of the general conclusions are striking and of great importance. All children pass through an initial Stage I where grammar or syntax is very oversimplified. During Stage II they develop clear grammar and syntax. Some fourteen "grammatical morphemes" were studied. These are combinations of words that are necessary or obligatory for proper English. An example is the present progressive: make, mak*ing*. When her father was at work at Harvard, Eve said he was "making pennies." The general rule (or grammatical morpheme) is to add "ing" to the root verbs. Eve, of course, was never taught this rule in any formal way. Her correct use of the rule simply occurred at a particular stage in her development.

Remarkably, all three children developed the use of the fourteen grammatical morphemes in the *same order.* This has subsequently been verified in studies of a number of other children. The development of grammatical usage in English follows a virtually invariant sequence, al-

7-28
Berko also made up nonsense words and gave them to children in sentences. Even without prior training, the children supply the correct morpheme in the correct syntax. (Berko, 1958)

This is a wug.

Now there is another one.
There are two of them.
There are two _____.

7-29
Graph of the relationship between utterance length and age. There is a natural progression from 18 to 50 months of age. The slight regressions and pauses represent in a sense the child's pauses to digest what he or she has learned. (Brown, 1969)

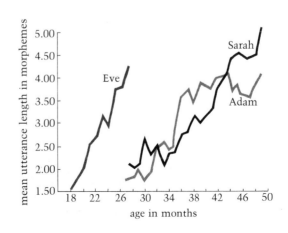

most as though the progression were predetermined or preprogrammed.

Thus, it would seem that children do not simply learn individual words and phrases by saying them and receiving reinforcement. Obviously, learning is critically important—but children learn rules and learn them in an inflexible sequence. Further, these rules are not taught explicitly; children simply pick them up. The portions of the human brain that have to do with language appear to be at least partly programmed or set to develop language in particular ways.

The development of language for every human being is an immensely complex undertaking. The young child does not experience formal schooling, tests, or well-prepared teachers. The subject matter is not constant, but varies from one individual to another and the child is not coached in abstract "rules of communication." Yet every normal child develops language—and does so with amazing rapidity and skill. The discovery of the biological and psychological forces underlying this process are certainly among the most profound challenges to the science of psychology.

Summary

1. All higher animals cope with life through the capacity for learning and memory, rather than through the instinctive, fixed behavior patterns of simpler animals.

2. Primary or short-term memory is the immediate memory of sensory stimuli. It is characterized by short duration (a matter of seconds) and by limited capacity (approximately seven items).

3. Secondary or long-term memory storage is relatively permanent and impervious to destruction. Repetition, use, strong reinforcement, vivid emotional experience, and other factors are important in the process of permanent acquisition.

4. Two other forms of short duration memory are iconic memory, which refers to the very briefly retained visual image of a visual stimulus, and eidetic imagery, occurring mainly in children, which involves the retention of complex material through a persistent neural image of the visual stimulus.

5. A basic issue in the study of memory is whether iconic, primary, and secondary memory are really different processes or are separate phases of the same process. Psychobiological and information-processing studies indicate they are different processes.

6. Four basic methods of gauging retention—the measure of memory—are redintegration, recall, recognition, and relearning. Redintegrative memory is the re-experiencing of a past event that is triggered by a stimulus from that past event. Recall is the ability to extract information from memory. Recognition is the ability to realize that one has experienced an item before. Relearning is based on how efficiently an individual can re-acquire material he has previously mastered; it is also called the savings method.

7. Overlearning, an important factor affecting how well material is remembered, involves the repetition and practice of something learned until it is firmly established in memory.

8. Organization of long-term memory seems to rely on a cross-referenced filing system in which information is organized according to its nature in a clustered-concept system.

9. One form of the failure to retrieve information from memory is the tip-of-the-tongue phenomenon (TOT), in which a piece of information eludes the person, although he has a strong sense of knowing it.

10. Short-term memory search is a rapid series process, in which the human mind can search an estimated 25 to 30 symbols per second.

11. The study of verbal learning began with serial and paired-associate learning tasks developed by Ebbinghaus. He utilized a special set of nonsense syllables for his studies. Subjects tend to remember items at the beginning and end of lists better than those in between (the serial position effect).

12. Three explanations of forgetting are decay theory, disuse theory, and interference, in which the learning of one response interferes with the memory of a response yet to be learned (proactive inhibition) or with the memory of a previously learned response (retroactive inhibition).

13. A model of human memory developed by Atkinson and Shiffrin suggests that sensory stimuli enter a sensory register (iconic memory); some portion of iconic memory is selected and transferred to short-term store; if not rehearsed it decays; if rehearsed, the information will be coded and transferred into long-term store.

14. To acquire motor skills, the subject must coordinate his individual muscle responses to produce a coherent response pattern, direct the patterns of motor movements toward some goal, and use the results of his behavior to adjust the responses as he continues to make them. Once well learned, motor skills are very resistant to loss.

15. Factors affecting verbal and motor-skill learning are meaningfulness, distribution and frequency of practice, amount of material to be learned at one time, feedback or knowledge of results, and transfer of training.

16. Past learning can assist learning in new learning situations (positive transfer), or it can interfere with new learning (negative transfer). Positive transfer occurs if the stimuli or the responses of the two training tasks are similar. Negative transfer occurs if the stimuli are similar but the required responses are not.

17. Research evidence shows that brain substrates for motor-skill learning and memory are entirely different from those for verbal learning and memory.

18. Language is a hypothetical property of the mind and the grammar books which shows itself in speech. Speech is the physical sign both of the cognitive processes and of the formal, grammatical structure called language.

19. A phoneme is the smallest possible unit of language identifiable as a discrete sound. A morpheme is made up of phonemes and is the smallest linguistic unit that can have independent meaning.

20. Syntax is the set of rules by which people speak and understand a language. It specifies how morphemes are connected and combined into phrases and sentences.

21. Semantics is the study of the meanings implied by speech sounds and written language.

22. Speech development seems to follow a fairly standard timetable in human infants. During the first 6 months all infants produce p, m, b, or t sounds and the vowel sounds e or a. Between 6 and 12 months, babbling begins. Between 1 and 2 years of age, simple phrases and sentences are uttered, though rudimentary in grammar; by 5, adult grammar is fairly well established.

23. Whether linguistic capabilities are the result of learning and environment or are primarily genetic is a question not yet answered. Some learning theorists believe that language is learned like any other behavior, through experience, reinforcement, and punishment.

24. Whorf's linguistic-relativity hypothesis states that our thoughts and our perception of the world are dependent upon the language of our culture.

25. A theory posed by Noam Chomsky states that language develops largely because certain innate rules which determine language production and interpretation emerge as the child develops physically. He believes that we are innately equipped with certain basic linguistic principles and need only learn the particular semantic and syntactic rules of our culture.

26. Recent research, notably by Roger Brown and associates, indicates that learned and innate factors contribute to the development of language in young children. Children learn rules and learn them in a regular and invariant sequence, though they have not been taught these rules explicitly.

Important Terms

primary memory
(short-term memory)

secondary memory
(long-term memory)

iconic memory

eidetic imagery

retention

redintegration

recall

recognition

relearning
(savings method)

overlearning

mnemonist

tip-of-the-tongue (TOT)
phenomenon

nonsense syllable

serial learning

paired-associate learning

forgetting

decay theory

disuse hypothesis

interference

proactive inhibition

retroactive inhibition

sensory register

motor-skill learning

feedback

chunking

massed practice

distributed practice

part learning

whole learning

transfer of training

negative transfer

positive transfer

programmed learning

semantics

phoneme

morpheme

syntax

descriptive linguistics

babbling

telegraphic speech

learning theory of language

linguistic-relativity hypothesis

genetic theory of language

innate capacities theory of language

surface structure

deep structure

transformational rules

Suggested Readings

BROWN, R. *A first language, the early stages.* Cambridge: Harvard University Press, 1973.
A fascinating account of how three children learned language, by the foremost authority in the field.

CHOMSKY, N. *Language and mind.* New York: Harcourt Brace Jovanovich, 1969.
A pioneer in psycholinguistics discusses the impact on psychology of his linguistic theory. Important, if sometimes difficult.

DEESE, J. *Psycholinguistics.* Boston: Allyn & Bacon, 1970.
A brief introduction to various psychological investigations of grammar and language development. No psychology background is presumed.

EBBINGHAUS, H. *Memory* (1885, trans. 1913). New York: Dover, 1964.
The classic experimental research on verbal learning.

KAUSLER, D. H. *Readings in verbal learning.* New York: Wiley, 1966.
A collection of some of the most important research in the area of human learning and memory.

KINTSCH, W. *Learning, memory and conceptual processes.* New York: Wiley, 1970.

Theoretical approaches to these areas of psychology are discussed with great emphasis on recent (1960–69) laboratory research. Minimal training in psychology is assumed.

MCNEILL, D. *The acquisition of language.* New York: Harper & Row, 1970.

A well-integrated and up-to-date presentation of a number of areas of language acquisition, with good background material on the biological bases of language. An appendix explains all the linguistic theory needed for understanding the book.

NEISSER, U. *Cognitive psychology.* New York: Appleton-Century-Crofts, 1967.

Integrated treatment of a wide variety of research areas and methods; clearly and interestingly written.

NORMAN, D. *Memory and attention.* New York: Wiley, 1969.

A clear treatment of the cognitive approach to these basic processes. Clearly written, this book presents excerpts from the most significant research papers in this area.

SKINNER, B. F. *Verbal behavior.* New York: Appleton-Century-Crofts, 1957.

The radical behaviorist approach to language and language acquisition.

SLOBIN, D. I. *Psycholinguistics.* Glenview, Ill.: Scott, Foresman, 1971.

A brief and lucid treatment of a number of issues concerning the psychology of language. Presumes a background in introductory psychology.

Chapter 8   Thinking

. . . In my own mind I make a sharp distinction between two types of concentration: one is immediate and complete, the other is plodding and only completed by stages. . . . These two opposite processes are vividly illustrated in two examples drawn from music: Mozart and Beethoven. Mozart thought out symphonies, quartets, even scenes from operas, entirely in his head—often on a journey or perhaps while dealing with pressing problems—and then he transcribed them, in their completeness, onto paper. Beethoven wrote fragments of themes in note books which he kept beside him, working on and developing them over years. Often his first ideas were of a clumsiness which makes scholars marvel how he could, at the end, have developed from them such miraculous results.

—Stephen Spender
(*The Making of a Poem*)

Thinking

Perception provides us with information; memory stores this information for future use. Thinking utilizes the knowledge provided by perception and memory and combines and organizes it into new patterns and combinations. Perception represents the *present*; memory reinstates *past* experiences; thinking reaches toward the *future*, toward something that has yet to be brought into existence. Customarily, all three of these mental processes are going on at the same time; together they constitute what is called *cognition*, a group of processes by which man achieves knowledge and command of his world.

If man possessed only the ability to perceive, he would be bound to the immediate present. Add memory to perception, and he becomes a creature with a past as well as a present. By adding the power of thought, man is able to project himself into the future. Through thought, man can rearrange the world to suit his fancy and his needs. There is no more important mental process than thinking, unless it be that of transforming thought into appropriate activity. To perceive the world correctly, to remember accurately, to think effectively, and then to act appropriately—these are processes that define a rational, intelligent human being.

Thinking is an active search for something that the person wants and needs. It is an internal trying-out process, a testing of and an experimenting with reality. It reflects a need to explain and to understand, and a desire to create.

If you are asked, "Where does thinking take place?" you will probably respond, "In my head" or "In my brain" because that is where you experience it. But if you are asked, "What is going through your mind while you are thinking?" you will probably find it difficult to answer. Though we sometimes think in words, and occasionally think in images or pictures, the form of most thinking is difficult to pin down. There is nothing concrete to describe except the subject matter of our thinking—for example, "I am thinking about getting a job." This characteristic of thinking has led many psychologists to conclude that thinking is imageless, that it has no describable content. Others say that it is a symbolic activity, but these people are unable to specify the nature of the symbols. It is safe to say that thinking is some sort of shorthand process. In this sense, it is symbolic, but the form of the shorthand still eludes us. Much of our thinking takes place unconsciously.

In this chapter, we shall briefly describe various types of thinking including reasoning and problem-solving, discriminating and judging, abstracting and generalizing, predicting and controlling, expecting and hoping, worrying, imagining, and daydreaming. We shall then describe conceptual thinking and problem-solving in some detail. We shall also discuss the uses of thinking and the distinctions between realistic and wishful thinking, concrete and abstract thinking, and creative and critical thinking. Finally, we shall point out some of the relationships between thinking and bodily processes, and between thinking and computers.

Types of Thinking

Thinking takes many forms. Let us consider some of the varieties and their distinguishing characteristics, bearing in mind, however, that no fixed boundaries separate these types of thought.

Reasoning or Problem-Solving

Reasoning is probably the easiest form of thinking to describe, although it is not necessarily the most prevalent. _Reasoning_ is highly conscious, directed, controlled, active, intentional, forward-looking, and goal-oriented thought. Reasoning usually starts with a specific problem and continues until a solution is found—unless the pursuit is interrupted or abandoned. A problem is anything that creates a feeling of tension in a

_8-1_
Logic applies formal rules to the principles of reasoning. Logic involves the use of _syllogisms_—sequences of statements that derive their truth from a relationship between a major and a minor premise. These Euler circles depict some possible relationships.

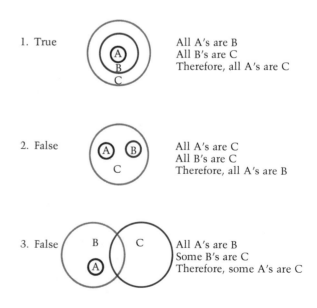

1. True

All A's are B
All B's are C
Therefore, all A's are C

2. False

All A's are C
All B's are C
Therefore, all A's are B

3. False

All A's are B
Some B's are C
Therefore, some A's are C

person, and a solution is something that discharges the tension. The tension is not necessarily an unpleasant sensation; a problem may be a challenge to a person, and if he can meet the challenge successfully, he feels good. If he is interrupted or has to give up, the tension remains and he may return to it again and again. Recall, for example, how you feel when you have mislaid something you want. You look everywhere, you think about where you last saw the object, you ask others if they have seen it, and so forth. The tension may remain for days, and you may find yourself thinking about the problem at odd moments. If there is a great deal of emotional involvement, such problems may become long-lasting preoccupations or obsessions.

Reasoning that leads from the problem to a solution involves trying out various ideas, hunches, or hypotheses, and has been called *mental trial-and-error.* In general, the more ideas a person has, the greater are his chances of reaching a solution. Such *flexibility* contrasts with *rigidity*, which is an inability to produce many alternative ideas. The flexibility-rigidity dimension is one on which people show large individual differences. Some people are, on the average, quite flexible; others are quite rigid. But a person may show flexibility on some occasions, and rigidity on others. Or he may be flexible in regard to certain issues and inflexible about others.

Discriminating and Judging

Because most problems have several alternative solutions, a person has to *discriminate* among the alternatives and *judge* which is the correct or most effective one. Ordinarily he does this by comparing the alternatives presented to him, noting their differences, and deciding which is the most appropriate for achieving the desired result. There are many familiar examples of this type of thinking—such as choosing among cuts of meat and styles of dress.

The problem may require the person to discriminate among simple stimulus characteristics—which object is larger, heavier, or brighter. It may require him to make an intellectual judgment, as in a multiple-choice examination. He may have to make a moral discrimination and judgment—which course of action is the right one. Or he may have to make an esthetic discrimination and judgment—which object is the most beautiful or pleasing.

We make countless discriminations and judgments every day. We make many of these so quickly and so automatically that we are not even aware of making them. A person driving in heavy traffic or playing a game of tennis is forced to make innumerable split-second discriminations and judgments. This suggests that consciousness is not necessary for most discriminating and judging. In fact, if we have to be conscious of them, it slows us down, often with unfortunate results.

Abstracting and Generalizing

The world, as Lewis Carroll's Walrus reminds us, is made up of many things. No two of them are exactly the same; and all of them change

8-2
In most fast-moving sports, discriminative thinking is automatic, and the individual is hardly aware of it. This photograph of Billie Jean King illustrates the split-second decision-making necessary to play a good game of tennis. (Wide World Photos)

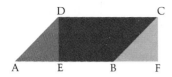

8-3

The Gestalt psychologist Max Wertheimer used the following technique to lead children to think in a logical, systematic way, so that they might be able to solve novel problems. The children were taught to find the area of certain rectangles by considering each of them to be the sum of the areas of several rows of squares. The children then were asked to find the area of the above parallelogram, ABCD. A 5-year-old girl cut the parallelogram along the line between D and E. She moved ADE to the right of the figure (making section BCF). The parallelogram was transformed into a rectangle, and the problem was easily solved. (Wertheimer, 1945)

with the passage of time. Some things deteriorate, others grow; our awareness of things often changes too. To cope with the world's infinite variety and incessant change we must impose stability and constancy on it. We do this by identifying a common feature which various objects share; we then assign to a single class all objects that possess this common characteristic. The class *dog* consists of many different breeds and many individual differences among the members of each breed, but they can all be identified as dogs because of features they share in common. To make such an identification, we must have a _concept_ or general idea of dogs.

In order to identify a common characteristic, we must _abstract_ it from the welter of perceptual information that is available. Once we have done this, we can make a _generalization_ by saying that all objects having this characteristic belong to the same class. For example, we say that all animals with backbones are vertebrates.

As a consequence of the mind's ability to abstract and generalize, man comes to live in a world of generalities instead of a world of particularities. By abstracting and generalizing, he develops concepts, principles, and laws that have universal application. Instead of having to start from scratch in thinking about each new problem, man tries to fit the problem into the familiar context of a general cognitive framework. If you have learned the general principles of levers, you can solve *any* lever problem — once you recognize that it is a lever problem.

Predicting and Controlling

Earlier we said that thinking is oriented toward the future. We think about what we want to have happen, and then try to bring it about. The scientist *predicts* what he will find if he does an experiment; the manufacturer and the farmer attempt to anticipate the demand for their products; and Joan tries to decide whether John will make a good husband. Man's desire to look into the future is as old as man himself.

We can distinguish two different attitudes regarding the future. One may be called the *ancient* attitude, though many people still have it. It regards the future as something predestined; what will be will be. Man may attempt to thwart fate but his attempts are fruitless. The *modern* attitude (although some people of the ancient world held it) is that man can shape the future. He can make things come true by exercising *control* over events.

In ancient times, certain wise men and women, called oracles or seers, were thought to possess the power of prophecy. They could foretell what was bound to happen, but they could not forestall it. These oracles were consulted by people who wanted to know what fate had in store for them. For many of us, the scientist has taken the place of the oracle. Scientific predictions are made by projecting present relationships into the future. Polls taken weeks before an election can usually predict the outcome, because most people do what they say they are going to do. Vocational tests taken at age 18 can forecast vocational success at age 30. And if a psychologist knows how a person has behaved in the past in a given situation, he usually can predict how the person will behave in that situation in the future.

8-4
In ancient Greece, the people sought advice from oracles, individuals thought able to predict the future. Pythia, the female oracle at Delphi, called upon snakes for her psychic powers. Her screams were heard by the priests in the cave with her; they transmitted her message to the people above ground. (New York Public Library)

Every man, whether he is a scientist or not, tries to anticipate and plan for the future, because he desires certainty in his life. In fact, the stability and security of man's existence depend to a considerable extent on his ability to project himself into the future. He predicts in order to control his life, and he bases his future on the information presently available to him.

Expecting and Hoping

Expecting is first cousin to predicting, the difference being the degree to which we believe something will happen. We predict with a confidence born of experience. To say we *expect* something implies there is a fair chance it will not occur. When we *hope* for something, we have even less confidence that it will come to be. Consequently, our disappointment is small when our hopes are unrealized, and it is great when our predictions fail. But if a hope does come true, we are far more elated than when something predictable happens. The greater our confidence that something is going to happen, the greater our disappointment when it does not occur and the less our elation when it does.

By a curious kind of cognitive magic, some people adopt very pessimistic attitudes about the future while secretly believing that it cannot be as black as they publicly declare it to be. This is the same kind of magic that deters people from voicing their expectations because they fear that "the fates" will punish them for being presumptuous. Some people even knock on wood or cross their fingers to placate "the fates."

This relation of cognitive attitudes to feelings demonstrates that thinking does not go on in a vacuum. It is intimately related to our needs and wishes, and to our emotions as well.

Worrying

When we hope that something will happen, we look forward with pleasurable anticipation to its happening. When we *worry* about the future, we are fearful that something unavoidable and unpleasant is going to occur. Unlike problem-solving, which progresses toward a solution, worrying dwells upon the dreaded event instead of trying to cope with it. Apprehension tends to immobilize our reasoning powers. A student who worries about an impending examination can become so preoccupied with thoughts of failing that he cannot study effectively. Since worrying prevents him from doing the very thing that would reduce his fear, he worries even more, and a vicious circle is started.

Worry may represent an unconscious desire to have that which is dreaded come true. A student who worries about failure may have an unacknowledged wish to fail; perhaps his hidden wish is to punish his parents for demanding that he get good grades. Indeed, Freud said that behind every fear there is a wish for the very outcome that is feared. For example, Freud would say that a person who is afraid to get too near the edge of a cliff because he is afraid of falling has an unconscious wish to destroy himself.

1. *Why am I going to college? What will it do for me?*

2. *Will the courses be interesting? Is the professor a stimulating lecturer?*

3. *Is the subject matter useful to my major? to my life in general?*

4. *What will be asked on the exam?*

5. *Will I pass the exam? Will I do as well as I want (or need) to?*

6. *Will I be satisfied with my grades? Will my parents be satisfied?*

7. *Will he or she call me tonight? or this week?*

8. *Will I have a date for the big game (dance, prom, etc.)?*

9. *Should we get married? If so, should we get married now or wait until we finish school?*

10. *Should I smoke pot (even though it is illegal) because my friends do? Should I experiment with stronger drugs?*

11. *Can I make the team (basketball, football, etc.)?*

12. *Can I live off campus? Can I afford to? Will the school let me?*

13. *Should I live with her or him or will it cause complications?*

14. *Can I get a job that will pay enough to cover the rising cost of college today?*

15. *What will I do with the rest of my life?*

16. *Who am I? What do I want from life?*

17. *Is our political system the best one? What might be better?*

18. *Is there a God?*

Imagining

The kind of thinking called *imagining* has two distinct characteristics: freedom from conventional thought patterns and a dissatisfaction with things as they are. When you imagine something, you create something new, something you have not experienced before in exactly the same way. To imagine is to picture new possibilities. When an inventor creates a new machine, a scientist discovers a new law of nature, or a painter devises a new way of representing an object, each of them first creates an image of what he wants to make or discover. Columbus had to imagine the world as round before he could set off on his voyage of discovery. Einstein, before he could come up with his special theory of relativity, had to imagine a universe in which someone traveling at nearly the speed of light would return from his trip having aged less than those he left at home. While imagining frequently is visual, it may also involve auditory, tactual, or other sensory stimuli. For example, Einstein said, "I very rarely think in words at all" (Wertheimer, 1945).

Daydreaming

Daydreaming is a type of imagining in which one casts off realistic restraints and conscious control and lets the mind wander in a free-

8-6
Scientists, and artists as well, have for years imagined man landing on the moon. Without the freewheeling thinking of imaginative people, many of our most important discoveries might never have been realized. Contrast (A) the drawing for a 1937 edition of Cyrano de Bergerac's *The Comical History of the States and Empires of the World of the Moon* with (B) an actual landing in 1971. (A. New York Public Library; B. NASA)

A

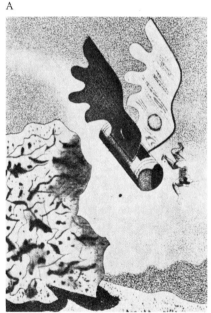

B

wheeling manner. Creative thinking usually leads to action (the artist paints a picture or the inventor devises a new machine), but daydreaming often is done for its own sake and may have no consequences other than personal satisfaction. One may be as unrealistic as one chooses because there is no need to test the fantasy in the world of reality.

Questionnaire studies reveal that almost everyone daydreams every day (Singer, 1966). Young adults (ages 18–29) do more daydreaming than other age groups. The favorite time for daydreaming is just before going to sleep, and most people consider it an enjoyable pastime.

Two major kinds of daydreaming have been differentiated. In one type, the person thinks over plans for the future, such as a vacation or buying a car or he thinks about his relations with other people—what girl he is going to ask to a party. These topics are realistic, and perhaps do not even deserve to be called daydreams. The other type is much more imaginary, wishful, and unrealistic. Such daydreams are about good fortune (inheriting a million dollars), sex, power, and aggression. The first type of daydreaming clearly serves the function of planning and rehearsing for some future event. The function of the second type is to provide visions of pleasures that cannot be obtained in reality.

Dreaming

Aristotle defined dreaming as thinking during sleep. It is an unusual form of thinking, because during sleep one's thoughts are represented by pictures and images rather than by words or thoughts. The sleeping person sees what he is thinking. Unlike daydreaming, which is recognized as fantasy, night dreaming usually seems like reality while it is going on. Because of the importance of dreaming, we shall devote the next chapter to this type of cognitive activity.

The Uses of Thinking

People often complain that thinking is hard work. To solve problems is difficult and wearing, to worry is unpleasant, and to dream bad dreams is terrifying. Why then do we think? One answer might be that we think because we have a brain; that it is a function of the brain to think, just as it is a function of the intestines to digest food and a function of the heart to pump blood. Another answer is that we think because the results of thinking are rewarding to the individual and therefore reinforce the process of thinking.

First Thoughts

The usefulness of thinking is most obvious when we observe the conditions under which thinking first makes its appearance. A newborn baby's brain is not developed sufficiently to enable him to think. He depends on other people for the satisfaction of his needs. He is a reflex apparatus, reacting automatically to stimuli impinging upon him from the outside world and from within his own body. He cries, squirms, sucks, and urinates unthinkingly. However, even the youngest baby can perceive. He feels the painful tension of an empty, contracting stomach; he sees and feels the bottle as it is put into his mouth; he tastes the milk; and he has a sense of well-being and gratification when the milk reaches his stomach and banishes the pangs of hunger. Cognitively speaking, the baby lives only in the present; for him, there is no past and no future.

A baby has the capacity for remembering what he experiences, however. Consequently, he soon acquires a past. When he feels hungry, he forms an image of the bottle, because it was the bottle that brought him satisfaction before. Obviously, this mental picture or whatever it is cannot satisfy his hunger. What can he do? This is the problem. The moment he realizes that the memory-image of an object is not the same thing as the object itself, the stage is set for the appearance of thinking. For the purpose of thinking is to produce that which will satisfy a need. In this situation, the baby has to formulate a plan to obtain a bottle. The plan may be to get his mother to bring it. So he cries. The mother hears him, assumes he is hungry, brings the bottle, the baby sucks, and the hunger disappears. The problem is solved. At first, of course, the crying is purely reflexive and not planned. As he grows older, the baby's aimless, reflex crying becomes more intentional, signalizing crying, as every mother knows. Later, when the young child learns to talk, speech is substituted for crying.

In this way, the baby acquires a sense of the future. He looks ahead to something not now present which can be brought into existence. Obviously, his ability to conceive of a future depends not only on his awareness of the present but also on his awareness of the past. He plans—thinks—in such a manner as to reinstate the past.

More Complex Thoughts

Since the example of a hungry baby involves such a simple form of thinking, let us go up the age scale a few years for a more complex example. A young child wants a drink of water, but he is not tall enough to reach the faucet. The first solution that occurs to him is to call his mother. This has worked many times in the past, but this time his mother replies that she is busy and he will have to wait. The child goes into the kitchen and looks at the faucet. He stands on tiptoe, but it is still beyond his reach. He tries to climb up on the sink but fails. He thinks, "How can I bring myself close enough to the faucet to turn it on?" Then it dawns on him that he can climb up on the kitchen chair. He pulls the chair to the sink, mounts it, and reaches the faucet. Then he discovers he has no glass. He gets down from the chair, moves it over to the closet where the glasses are kept, and mounts once again. But the chair is too low; he cannot reach the shelf. Again he is in a quandary. What should he do? He looks around the kitchen again and sees a stool, which is taller than the chair. He pulls the stool over to the closet, and it proves to be tall enough. He gets the glass, takes the stool back to the sink, climbs on it, turns on the faucet, fills the glass, and drinks. The uncomfortable feeling of thirst disappears and the thinking-acting sequence is terminated.

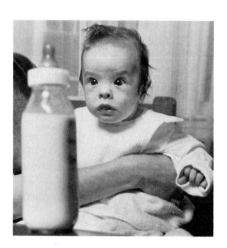

8-7
At a relatively young age, an infant develops a past and thus an ability to perceive relationships—for example, between the bottle of milk and the hunger in his stomach. (Lew Merrim, Monkmeyer)

Looking back over this account, we see that there is a beginning, the feeling of thirst, and an end, the disappearance of the feeling. The intervening steps consist of thinking out solutions, testing them with action, finding that some solutions do not work, thinking of other solutions, and trying them until a suitable one is found. The cognitive processes of perceiving, remembering, and thinking, combined with action, produce a satisfying outcome.

As a person grows older, he tends to replace action with thought; he tries out solutions mentally before acting upon them. Thinking becomes a substitute for action because it is more economical and more efficient. When an action is performed, it may be difficult to undo if a mistake is made; but a mistake in thinking can be corrected before any harm has been done. A person who acts impulsively—without thinking—often gets into hot water, which he might have avoided if he had taken a moment's thought. On the other hand, a person may postpone action until it is too late to do whatever is necessary. Effective thinking requires just the right balance between impulses and constraints on action. One can think too little or too much.

Concept Formation

If we are to function efficiently, we must somehow impose some stability on a world of endless diversity and change. We must learn to identify and classify objects.

The most common question is, "What is that?" and the most common answer is one that places the unfamiliar object into a familiar class. Everything is unique, yet everything can be placed in a group of objects and assigned a name. When a person can group together certain objects and exclude others, he has a _concept_. Thus if a person is confronted with an array of colored yarns and is able to pick out all those that are of a greenish hue, and not include any that are red, yellow, or blue, he is said to have a concept of greenness. When he can give the correct name

Seek simplicity and distrust it.

Alfred North Whitehead

8-8
Subjects are shown the drawings in each of these series, one at a time. Their task is to determine which nonsense syllable belongs with each picture. After each attempt, the experimenter calls out the correct nonsense syllable. Naturally on the first series it isn't possible to guess correctly, but eventually, on subsequent trials with later series, people are able to name the picture correctly. Since all the drawings are different, they have not learned to identify particular drawings; they have learned to associate the nonsense syllables with concepts. In these series, the concepts were: face = relk; bird = silm; hat = glif; 3 = joft; 4 = perg; 6 = mank. (Adapted from Heidbreder, 1947)

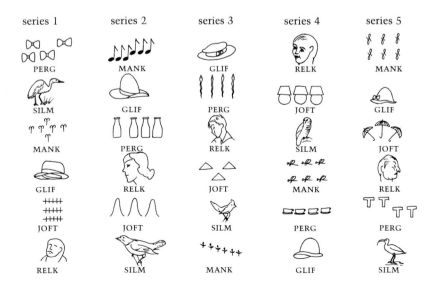

series 1	series 2	series 3	series 4	series 5
PERG	MANK	GLIF	RELK	MANK
SILM	GLIF	PERG	JOFT	GLIF
MANK	PERG	RELK	SILM	JOFT
GLIF	RELK	JOFT	MANK	RELK
JOFT	JOFT	SILM	PERG	PERG
RELK	SILM	MANK	GLIF	SILM

for the class, he is said to have a *concept-name*. People may have a concept without knowing the name of it. Young children can often distinguish colors they cannot name, for instance. And people frequently misunderstand concepts. A person may use the word *rectangle* to denote various geometrical forms, only some of which are rectangles.

How do we form a concept? We abstract some common feature from among a group of objects and then we assign to that class any object which possesses that feature. Thus, any three straight lines in the same plane which are joined together to enclose a space are said to form a triangle. We learn the concept of triangularity by observing this property of a geometrical form. It may be learned by seeing only one triangle but usually we must see several triangles before the concept is fixed. A test of the concept requires that the person be able to pick out all the triangles in a group of forms that includes not only triangles but other shapes as well.

Type of Concepts

Four types of concepts have been identified by Bruner and his associates (1956). They are: simple concepts, conjunctive concepts, disjunctive concepts, and relational concepts.

1. *Simple concepts.* When the objects to be discriminated and classified have one element in common, the subject forms a <u>simple concept</u>. For example, a person who can discriminate those objects in a group that are triangular from those that are not has formed the simple concept of triangularity.

2. *Conjunctive concepts.* When the objects to be discriminated and classified have two or more characteristics in common, the subject forms a <u>conjunctive concept</u>. The concept woman is conjunctive because all women share more than one common characteristic that differentiates them from men or anything else.

3. *Disjunctive concepts.* A <u>disjunctive concept</u> is one that embraces many different items, none of which, at first glance, has anything obviously in common with the others. For example, the legal concept of a felony includes murder, arson, forgery, armed robbery, kidnapping, and rape. None of these has anything in common with any of the others, except that they are all serious offenses. Disjunctive concepts are difficult for a person to learn. Many abstract concepts like freedom, justice, beauty, and truth are disjunctive. That is why there are so many arguments about them. People have different opinions about what should be included under each of these concepts.

4. *Relational concepts.* "Larger than" describes a relation between two objects; it is an example of a <u>relational concept</u>. The two objects need have nothing in common other than a relative comparison.

Focusing on Positive Instances

Studies of concept formation demonstrate that it is more effective to show the person *positive instances* of the concept than to show him

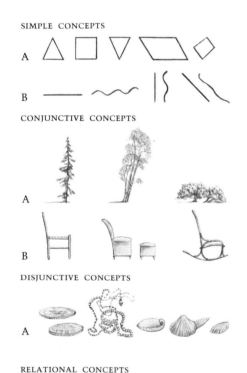

SIMPLE CONCEPTS

CONJUNCTIVE CONCEPTS

DISJUNCTIVE CONCEPTS

RELATIONAL CONCEPTS

8-9
Examples of each of the four types of concepts.

negative instances. For example, he will learn the concept of triangularity faster if he sees only triangles, rather than triangles mixed with squares, circles, and octagons. This finding may appear self-evident, but many parents and teachers persist in teaching children by the method of negative instances. They say, "That is not a dog" while pointing at a cat instead of saying, "That is a cat." Or they say, "That is not the right thing to do" when they should say what *is* right. Positive examples are more effective because the things that fall within a class are far fewer than the things that fall outside the class. It would take a very long time to teach someone the concept of triangularity or goodness by listing all of the things that are not triangles or are not good.

It is easier to learn a concept if the common features that define it are made to stand out. Yet for rapid identification of a complex object — an airplane flying overhead, for example — it is better to recognize the total shape, rather than take the time to analyze several identifying features. We probably categorize most of our concepts on the basis of total impressions. Of course, if the total impression leaves the identity uncertain, then we must resort to detailed analysis.

All of us have concepts we are not consciously aware of. This has been demonstrated repeatedly in experiments such as the following one by Rees and Israel (1935). Subjects were asked to rearrange the letters of nonsense words so that they made meaningful words. Of the first 15 nonsense words, each had one, and only one, possible solution. *Nelin* could be rearranged to make *linen; sdlen* to make *lends.* The transformation in each case was uniform. The first letter of the nonsense word became the last letter of the meaningful word, the second letter became the fourth, and the third, fourth, and fifth became the first, second, and third, respectively. The second group of 15 nonsense words had two possible solutions, one of which used the same transformed letter order as the first group while the other did not. Thus, the nonsense word, *nolem,* could be changed into either *lemon* or *melon.* Practically all of the subjects carried over the letter-order pattern learned from the first 15 words, although more than half of the subjects were unaware that they were doing it. They were not conscious of having a particular concept, yet their behavior showed they did have one.

Evaluation of the Use of Concepts

The advantages of thinking in terms of concepts are obvious. They enable us to transform a world of infinite appearances into a world of finite essences. Instead of having to react to each object as something unique, we learn to make generalized responses to classes of objects. Thus, the repertoire of responses required for our adjustment to the world is vastly reduced. These generalized responses function as principles or laws. When we learn the principles of geometry, for example, we are able to solve many problems involving physical shape. Concept formation makes for economy of thought and behavior.

However, some very real dangers arise from reacting to dissimilar things as though they were the same. It is easy to make the false assumption that because dissimilar things are alike in some respects they are alike in all respects. For example, the class woman is a biological

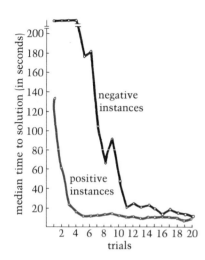

8-10
This graph shows the results of a study in which two groups of subjects were directed to solve 20 concept problems. Concepts were formed much faster by subjects presented with positive instances than by those given negative instances only. (Freibergs & Tulving, 1961)

concept based upon certain physiological structures and processes exclusive to females. Such a concept has many uses. But the very existence of woman as a class makes it easy to generalize other responses to women—to say that all women think or act in certain ways when, in fact, the concept does not justify such generalizations. Vast social harm can also be done by dividing human beings into races, nationalities, and religions, and then generalizing about these groups. We shall examine this process more closely when we explore the roots of prejudice in Chapter 18.

Problem-Solving

At 6 p.m. the well marked 1/2 inch of water and at daybreak 7/8 of an inch. By noon of the next day there was 15/16 and on the next night 31/32 of an inch of water in the hold. The situation was desperate. At this rate of increase few, if any, could tell where it would rise to in a few days.

Stephen Leacock

Because problem-solving is such an important part of everyday life, psychologists study it in great detail. Laboratory studies of problem-solving employ intellectual problems of varying complexity. One basic requirement is that the problem must be new to the person so that he cannot reproduce an answer he has learned previously. Usually the problem is clearly identified for the subject and has a solution, although studies occasionally involve unsolvable problems. Different types of problems have been employed. One popular type is the mechanical or wire puzzle; another is the thought problem, like those found in mathematics and physics. Picture puzzles also have been used. Less widely used, but probably more relevant to most people's lives, are personal and social problems. Assuming that subjects in a problem-solving experiment are well motivated and understand what they are supposed to do, their modes of attack may be classified under three general categories.

Trial and Error

How often have I said to you that, when you have eliminated the impossible, whatever remains, however improbable, must be the truth.

The Sign of Four
Sir Arthur Conan Doyle

The first mode of problem-solving, called *trial and error*, is characterized by a more or less blind groping for the solution. Confusion and a baffled or hopeless feeling often accompany this haphazard behavior. When and if the person finds the correct solution by trial and error, he may not comprehend the solution or even be able to tell how he found it. If the same problem is presented again, he may not be able to solve it any faster than he did the first time—or even as fast. In fact, he may not be able to do it at all the second time.

Gradual Analysis

The second mode of problem-solving is one of *gradual analysis* and understanding. Progress is made step-by-step in a reasonably systematic manner. Each step is checked before proceeding to the next, and a sense of calm satisfaction usually prevails.

Insight

In the third type of problem-solving behavior, the solution comes to mind suddenly, but unlike the trial-and-error discovery, the person understands the solution. The person is said to have had an *insight.* The insight usually occurs after a period of groping or gradual analysis.

ALBERT EINSTEIN: THE INSIGHT OF GENIUS

Born in 1879 to a modestly successful German businessman and his wife, Albert Einstein was not a remarkable child. Unlike many other geniuses, this slight, quiet boy showed little, if any, early evidence of the idiosyncratic insight that would lead to his theories of relativity, the foundation of modern physics. On the contrary, to the casual observer he may have seemed slow to develop. He did not begin speaking until the age of three. Shunning the physically active life of his schoolmates, Albert began early to prefer the solitude in which he could pursue his inner life of abstract thought.

Despite this internal world of reflection, Albert was sharply aware of and interested in the objects of his external environment. Late in his life he recalled how, at age 4 or 5, he had been awestruck and fascinated by a rather unexceptional gift—a magnetic compass. The regularity with which the instrument's needle sought out and fixed the earth's magnetic north pole may have sparked in the child the first inklings of Einstein's lifelong belief in an all-inclusive but hidden order in the universe.

At about 12 years of age, Einstein was introduced to algebra and geometry by the same uncle who had given him the compass. With rare exception, Einstein had little use for instruction, which he generally seemed to consider rather restrictive and plodding; he preferred to work alone.

Like his early musings on the oddly faithful ways of the compass, many of Einstein's later pursuits of physical mysteries began with simple observations. For example, when he was 16 years old Einstein posed this question: What would happen if I could move at the speed of light (186,000 miles per second)? This simple inquiry led to a highly abstract contemplation of the properties of light—a mental examination that finally brought Einstein to the conclusion that the 17th century English physicist, mathematician, and philosopher, Isaac Newton, had been wrong in several assertions which had by that time—1895—become the pillars of the science of physics.

For 10 years after he posed his question about light, Einstein worked at a fresh way of viewing this phenomenon. The result was his Special Theory of Relativity. Eleven years later, he produced the General Theory of Relativity and Gravitation. It seems that Einstein experienced sudden, integrating insights as a result of total immersion in the problems he sought to solve. He usually required absolute solitude when working out his concepts.

Paul Ehrenfest, a good friend and scientific colleague of Einstein's, described an incident in which Ehrenfest and the 29-year-old Einstein were visiting H. A. Lorentz, who was then reputed to be the world's outstanding theoretical physicist:

In his usual way, Lorentz saw to it first at dinner that Einstein felt himself enveloped in a warm and cheerful atmosphere of human sympathy. Later, without any hurry, we went up to Lorentz's cozy and simple study. The best chair was carefully pushed in place next to the large work table for the esteemed guest. Calmly, and to forestall any impatience, a cigar was provided for the guest, and only then did Lorentz begin quietly to formulate a finely polished question concerning Einstein's theory of the bending of light in a gravitational field. Einstein listened to the exposition, sitting comfortably in the easy chair smoking, nodding happily, taking pleasure in the masterly way Lorentz had rediscovered, by studying his works, all the enormous difficulties that Einstein had to overcome before he could lead his readers to their destination, as he did in his papers, by a more direct and less troublesome route. But as Lorentz spoke on and on, Einstein began to puff less frequently on his cigar, and he sat up straighter and more intently in his armchair. And when Lorentz had finished, Einstein sat bent over the slip of paper on which Lorentz had written mathematical formulas to accompany his words as he spoke. The cigar was out, and Einstein pensively twisted his finger in a lock of hair over his right ear. Lorentz, however, sat smiling at an Einstein completely lost in meditation, exactly the way a father looks at a particularly beloved son—full of secure confidence that the youngster will crack the nut he has given him, but eager to see how. It took quite a while, but suddenly Einstein's head shot up joyfully; he "had it." Still a bit of give-and-take, interrupting one another, a partial disagreement, very quick clarification and a complete mutual understanding and then both men with beaming eyes skimming over the shining riches of the new theory.

(Charles Haas, Magnum)

But when insight does come, everything falls into place and the problem is solved. The insight is often accompanied by a feeling of elation.

People do not fall into strict problem-solver categories corresponding to trial and error, gradual analysis, and sudden insight. The same person may use all three modes in solving a particular problem, and he may shift from one mode to another in solving various problems. The novelty of the problem determines, to some extent, the kind of strategy he uses. When a person confronts an unfamiliar kind of problem, he may do considerable groping; but if he has solved a number of similar problems his approach will be more systematic.

The experienced person possesses a fund of usable knowledge and a clear idea of the direction to be taken. He also has developed _heuristics,_ techniques or strategies that a person finds helpful for solving problems. An experienced chess player, dressmaker, surfer, cook, or sculptor has learned a number of strategies and can select the one that will work best in a particular situation at a particular time. A simple example of a heuristic solution is one used in playing ticktacktoe. An experienced player knows that if his opponent starts by placing an X in a corner he should respond by placing an O in the center, for only this maneuver will avoid defeat.

The experienced person also has developed an attitude of self-confidence based on his successful performance in the past. On the other hand, repeated failure can so discourage a person that he is licked before he starts. Confronted by a problem involving numbers, a person says, "I'm no good at math," and then proceeds to demonstrate the truth of his statement.

Factors Influencing Problem-Solving Ability

Many practical problems require _improvisation_—making do with the materials at hand—because the customary means for solving the problems are not available. Everyone who has had a car break down far from any garage or telephone knows what it means to improvise. Improvisation requires a broad and flexible understanding of the ways in which objects can be used. A person who cannot recognize the various possible uses of an object is said to be _functionally fixed._ He may not realize that a stone, for example, can be used as a prop, a hammer, a weapon, a weight, a grinding tool, a step, a wedge—to name only a few of its many potential uses—and so he may be unable to solve a problem requiring the novel use of a stone. Studies of problem-solving show that a wide knowledge of the functional properties of common objects is very helpful.

In one such study (Saugstad, 1955), the subjects, all college students, were asked to blow out a candle from a distance of six feet. Each subject was given six glass tubes, a solid metal rod, and a lump of putty. Before they were told what they were expected to do, they were shown the objects one at a time and asked to list all the conceivable functions of each object. Three functions would be necessary for solving the candle problem: (1) the glass tubes had to conduct an air stream when blown through, (2) the putty had to seal the joints between the tubes, and (3) the rod had to support the glass tubes in a horizontal position.

8-11
Functional fixedness often prevents us from discovering alternate uses for familiar objects. A little thought and a determination to hear the end of the concert prompted this man to think of converting his newspaper into a rain hat. (Henri Cartier-Bresson, Magnum)

All of the subjects who listed at least two of the three essential functions were able to solve the candle problem when it was presented to them. (The solution consisted of placing the rod through the glass tubes laid end-to-end, and sealing the joints between the tubes with the putty.) Only about half of the subjects who failed to list two functions solved the problem.

8-12

Some typical brain teasers. Try to solve each before you check the answers at the bottom of this figure.

PROBLEMS:

1. Horse problem. *A man bought a horse for $60 and sold it for $70. Then he bought it back for $80 and sold it again for $90. How much money did he make on the transactions?*
   The answer is among the following alternatives:

   He lost $10
   He broke even.
   He made $10.
   He made $20.
   He made $30.

   After you have selected an answer, try to solve this problem: A man bought a horse for $60 and sold it for $70. Later he bought another horse for $80 and sold it for $90. How much money did he make on the transactions?

2. Train problem: *A train leaves Detroit bound for Chicago every hour, and a train leaves Chicago for Detroit every hour. The trip takes 6 hours. How many trains will you meet coming from Chicago if you board the train in Detroit bound for Chicago?*

3. Hotel problem: *Three men take a room in a hotel. The clerk charges them $30 — $10 each. After they go upstairs, the clerk realizes that he charged too much; the rate is $25, and he should return $5 to them. But he can't divide $5 evenly, so he decides to return $1 to each man and pocket the rest. The men are now paying $9 each. Three times $9 is $27; the clerk kept $2; what happened to the other $1?*

ANSWERS:

1. *The answer to the second part of the problem should be obvious — $20. This is also what the man made in the first statement of the problem, but few people get the right answer when it is stated in that way. Talking about the same horse being sold and bought back creates a set which goes something like this: "he made $10 on the first transaction, but then he lost it by buying the horse back for $10 more than he had sold it for. At that point he is just even. When he sells it for $90 he makes $10"—which is the incorrect answer that many people give.*
2. *Either 12 or 13 is accepted as correct. As your train moves toward Chicago, the Chicago train moves toward you at the same speed. Thus your velocity relative to the Chicago trains is twice as great as your velocity relative to the tracks, and you will meet an oncoming train every half hour.*
3. *The men are not paying $9 each for the room. They are paying $8.33 each (1/3 of $25) plus $.67 each for the clerk's "tip" (1/3 of $2). The problem is carefully phrased to mislead you into assuming that all $9 is rent money.*

Improvisation is hindered when the object is originally identified with another use. For example, the problem of making a board stay in position across an open doorway was presented. The materials given included a cork, which had to be used as a wedge between one end of the board and the door jamb in order to keep the board in place. When the cork was serving as the stopper in an inkbottle, the problem was harder to solve than when the cork was left lying on the table.

Set. Although successful experience is undoubtedly the chief factor in producing efficient problem-solving, it may on occasion be detrimental to achievement. A <u>set</u>—a habit of responding in a fixed way because of experience—can blind a person to a more efficient means of reaching a solution. Dramatic examples of the adverse effects of habit are found in experiments conducted by Luchins (1971). He first asked his subjects to solve the following problem: If you had three empty jars that held 21, 127, and 3 quarts respectively, how might you measure accurately 100 quarts of water? To solve the problem, fill the largest container, draw off 21 quarts with one jar, and 3 quarts, twice, with the other jar. After his subjects solved several problems of this type, Luchins presented the following problem: Given three jars that hold, respectively, 23, 49, and 3 quarts, how would you get 20 quarts? The obvious economical solution is to fill the 23-quart jar and draw off 3 quarts. Most of the subjects, however, continued to use a cumbersome three-jar solution. They filled the 49-quart jar, drew off 23 quarts leaving 26 quarts. They then drew off 6 quarts by filling the 3-quart jar twice. When faced by a problem that could not be solved using the 3 jars but could be solved with 2 jars (to get 25 quarts, given three jars of 28, 76, and 3 quart capacity), most of the subjects could not solve the problem in the time allowed. This is an amazing demonstration of the rigidifying effects of habit and bears out what so many of us know from experience: it is easy to get into a rut in solving a particular type of problem. Table 8-1 contains the figures for all of Luchins' problems; use them to test your friends on this concept.

Table 8-1   Water-Jar Problem (after Luchins, 1959, 1971)

Problem	Capacity of Empty Jars			Required Capacity
	A	B	C	
1	21	127	3	100
2	14	163	25	99
3	18	43	10	5
4	9	42	6	21
5	20	59	4	31
6	23	49	3	20
7	15	39	3	18
8	23	76	3	25
9	18	48	4	22
10	14	36	8	6

Realistic Thinking and Wishful Thinking

Realistic and wishful thinking differ in the degree to which fact and fancy determine the course of one's thoughts. If thinking is in accord with actuality—with things as they are—it is said to be _realistic_. If it is influenced by wishes and fancies, it is said to be _wishful_ or _autistic_. In truly autistic thinking, fantasy is mistaken for reality. For example, a person wants to believe that he can communicate with the spirit world, and so he convinces himself that he is receiving messages from deceased friends and relatives.

But is there a simple and straightforward distinction between realistic and wishful thinking? Consider some of the issues involved. One universal assumption is that thinking, even that which is freest and most spontaneous, is always motivated. A person invariably has a reason for thinking, namely, his desire to solve a problem. The thought is there because of a wish that seeks fulfillment. Whether the thought accords with reality is unrelated to the underlying motivation. Consequently, it may be argued that all thinking is wishful.

If we are to distinguish clearly between realistic and unrealistic thinking, we need to define reality. A popular definition is that reality is what exists; the real world is the world of actuality. But how do we know what exists? Our senses give us information about the real world. If something exists it can be seen, heard, touched, tasted, or smelled. But is that all there is to reality? Hardly. Much of what we think is real has to be _inferred_ from evidence that is presented to our senses. We cannot see embarrassment but we can and do infer that a person is embarrassed when he blushes. We cannot see another person's pain but we can infer it from his actions. Pain and embarrassment are as real as a book or a chair. For that matter, all of the sciences deal with a world of abstract reality that is not immediately present to the senses.

How do we know that an inference is correct? One criterion is its acceptability. If a number of people agree that what is inferred is real, the inference is said to be true. But this social criterion of reality is suspect because even a great number of people can be wrong, as history amply demonstrates. Agreement, even among experts, does not make something true. The final test of the truth of an inference is its consistency with other lines of evidence. A very simple example of this is to test the inference that someone is embarrassed or in pain by asking him how he feels. If he acknowledges that he is embarrassed or feels pain, the inference is said to be confirmed. Of course, he may not be telling the truth, so other evidence is desirable. But if all of the evidence is consistent, we can be reasonably certain that the inference is valid.

The harmful effects of wishful thinking are not inherent in the thought, since all thinking starts with our needs and wishes. Wishful thinking becomes harmful only if it causes us to ignore or distort evidence that contradicts our wishful ideas. Obviously, if we accept only that which confirms our hypotheses and reject that which runs counter to them, we can prove practically anything. In short, the wishful factor in thinking cannot be avoided, so it is necessary to control it by critical thinking.

Delusions

The foregoing discussion may be sharpened by considering delusions. A _delusion_ is a false belief, just as an _illusion_ is a false perception. Many of us harbor delusions because (1) we are gullible and accept what someone tells us without putting it to the test of critical examination; (2) we are ignorant and do not possess sufficient knowledge to detect that a belief is a delusion; or (3) we have a strong urge to believe that something is true.

Delusions are prominent in people who are seriously disturbed psychologically. Their most frequent delusions are those of grandeur and persecution. A person who has _delusions of persecution_ believes that other people are conspiring against him. A person who has _delusions of grandeur_ imagines that he is an exceptional individual of outstanding merit and ability. He may be so deluded that he believes that he is Napoleon or Jesus. Nothing anyone can say will convince him other-

8-13B
To solve the problem on page 287, you must abstract (in your mind's eye) each horse into its component parts, recombine the parts, and then rotate one of the two drawings 90 degrees. (From Martin Scheerer, "Problem-Solving." Copyright © 1963 by Scientific American, Inc. All rights reserved.)

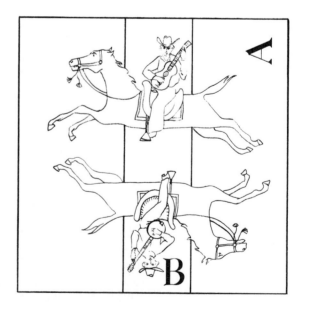

8-14

Superstitions are mild forms of delusional thinking. This artist is painting hex signs, which Pennsylvania Dutch farmers traditionally hang on their barns and homes to keep away evil spirits. His business has increased substantially during the past few years. (Wide World Photos)

wise; in fact, argument usually strengthens his delusions. Robert Lindner (1954), a practicing psychologist, treated a man who believed he could travel through space to another planet where he was accorded great respect and was showered with honors and favors. To no avail Lindner pointed out to the man, who was a scientist of some standing, that this was sheer fantasy. Lindner admitted that he almost became convinced of the reality of his patient's interplanetary explorations and was becoming as deluded as the man he was treating. Fortunately for both of them, the patient renounced his fantasies when Lindner began to share his patient's beliefs and to discuss them as one believer to another. Why did the patient give them up? Because he was unwilling to have another person share them. If another person could duplicate his feats, their grandeur would be diminished.

It is easy to see why delusions of grandeur are satisfying. But why are there delusions of persecution? Delusions of this type would seem to make one feel miserable. And yet they are just as common as delusions of grandeur and the two kinds of delusion often appear together. By thinking he is being persecuted, a person confirms his belief that he is exceptional and the world is jealous of his greatness. Was not Christ crucified? Moreover, delusions of persecution can rationalize failures. A man's inability to hold a job is explained on the grounds that the boss and fellow workers are jealous of him because he is superior. They see to it that he makes mistakes and is involved in accidents. He knows this because he saw them talking about him, pointing at him, and looking at him in an unfriendly manner. Of course, the real reason he cannot hold a job is apt to be that he is a poor worker and a troublemaker.

Delusions of grandeur are usually harmless; but delusions of persecution may be dangerous to the person and society if he decides to get even with his fancied persecutors.

Probably everyone experiences minor delusions of grandeur and persecution at one time or another, partly because our accomplishments do not live up to our expectations, and partly because we have to explain our inadequacies and inferiorities to ourselves. For example, some people are injustice-collectors. They make note of every wrong that is done to them and apparently aspire to be martyrs.

Delusions of all kinds are part of everyone's psychological baggage. Surveys show that virtually all of us believe in some *superstitions* —which, as we discussed in Chapter 6, are beliefs not based on reason or knowledge—or at least act as though we do. Common examples are refusing to light three cigarettes with a single match or being reluctant to walk under a ladder or step on cracks in the sidewalk. Of course, some people are more superstitious than others; usually, a better-educated person is less superstitious than a poorly educated one.

Concrete Thinking and Abstract Thinking

Every thought has an object. The object of one's thought may be something *concrete*—something that can be seen or heard or felt; or the object may be something *abstract*—a set of relationships, for example.

When a carpenter thinks about his work, his thoughts may be about specific planks of wood. However, such things as beauty or democracy or love are abstract objects of thought; they do not exist as things that can be lifted and weighed.

Abstract thinking involves thinking not about things themselves but about their relationships. It is also concerned with the way things are organized into patterns and systems. By means of abstract thinking, laws are discovered and theories are formulated. Planning ahead requires abstract thought. Thus, an architect thinks abstractly in designing a house, and a carpenter thinks in concrete terms when he saws the beams and nails them together.

The differences between abstract and concrete thinking become clearer if we compare the behavior of normal people with the behavior of people who have suffered extensive damage to the frontal portion of the brain—the area which ordinarily mediates abstract thinking (Goldstein & Scheerer, 1941). For example, if it is raining, such a brain-injured person cannot be induced to repeat the sentence, "The sun is shining," because he can only think about things as they are, not as they might be. Thus, although each case is somewhat different, a person with this kind of brain damage generally is unable to think abstractly. In addition, he is to varying degrees unable to perform several other tasks:

1. He cannot perform sequential acts. When asked to set the hands of a clock to a certain hour, he cannot do it, although he can recognize what time it is when shown a clock.

2. He lacks the ability to react to an organized whole, to break the whole into parts, and to synthesize them again. When he is shown a picture and asked to make up a story to go with it, he is unable to tell an organized story. He can only name some of the things in the picture.

3. He cannot abstract the common properties of a series of objects or form any part-whole relationships. This means that he is unable to complete an analogy like "shoe is to foot as what is to hand?"

4. He is unable to plan ahead, to take into account the probability of something happening in the future, or to think in symbolic terms. He may be able to find his way around in a familiar environment but he cannot draw a map or give a verbal account of how he gets from one place to another.

Although people with such frontal-brain injuries are limited to concrete thought, certain normal but literal-minded people also may have trouble dealing with abstract notions. When a literal-minded person is asked to tell what he sees in an inkblot, he says he sees an inkblot and that is all. Such people may fail to see the point of a joke that involves a play on words, because they take the words in their literal sense only and ignore their figurative sense. Similes and metaphors also are likely to leave the literal-minded person cold.

8-15
The Watts Towers. This incredible structure was begun in 1921 by Simon Rodia in the Watts section of Los Angeles. Born in Italy, Rodia was an uneducated (by American standards) immigrant who worked as a lumberman, miner, and finally tile-layer. He spent 30 years single-handedly creating this 104-foot structure and its surrounding towers and passageways. He worked with only small hand tools and a window-washer's belt to hoist himself to each level of the towers. For material, he used scrap steel (no bolts), cement, sea shells, broken bottles, tiles, plates, and anything else he could rescue from junk yards and scrap heaps. (Clarence John Laughlin)

Creative Thinking and Critical Thinking

Creative thinking is thinking that results in the discovery of a new or improved solution to a problem. *Critical thinking* is the examination and testing of suggested solutions to see whether they will work. Creative thinking leads to the birth of new ideas, while critical thinking tests ideas for flaws and defects. Both are necessary for effective problem-solving, yet they are incompatible—creative thinking interferes with critical thinking, and vice versa. To think creatively we must let our thoughts run free. The more spontaneous the process, the more ideas will be born and the greater the probability that an effective solution will be found. A steady stream of ideas furnishes the raw material. Then critical judgment selects and refines the best ideas, picking the most effective solution out of the available possibilities. Though we must engage in the two types of thinking separately, we need both for efficient problem-solving.

Brainstorming

If you want to think creatively, you must learn to let your mind go and not try to steer it along a definite course. This is known as *free association*. The free-associating person says everything that comes to mind, no matter how absurd it may sound. Although free association has been used primarily in psychotherapy, it also has been adapted for group problem-solving—an application called *brainstorming*.

Industry and government have used brainstorming to turn up new ideas for improving products, methods, and services. The procedure is simple. A group of people meets to "free-associate" about a problem: how to speed up the sorting of mail; how to raise money to build a community center; or how to sell more prunes. Every participant says whatever comes into his mind, even if it sounds unrelated to the problem or a bit crazy. Criticism is forbidden. The goal is sheer quantity of ideas, because the more ideas that are suggested the greater the chance that a really good idea will emerge. Following a brainstorming session, the recorded ideas are critically evaluated, preferably by a second group.

Group creative thinking rests upon the following psychological principles (Osborn, 1957):

1. The group situation stimulates the free flow of ideas. This is an example of *social facilitation* (see Chapter 19). It has been found that the average person can think up about twice as many ideas when working with a group as when working alone. In a group he is exposed to many different ideas; one person's idea may stimulate another, and so on. However, several experiments suggest that a schedule that intersperses periods of individual thinking with group thinking produces optimal results.

2. The group situation also stimulates competition among group members. As long as competition does not arouse critical and hostile attitudes, it acts as an incentive to creative thinking. Each participant tries to outdo the others in making suggestions.

3. The quality of the ideas improves as more ideas are suggested. The last 50 ideas are usually more useful than the first 50. Evidently, the ideas get better as the participants warm to the task.

4. Brainstorming works best when the group gets together for a second session a few days later. In this follow-up meeting, the ideas are often superior to the first session's. Apparently, some ideas require a period of incubation or "sleeping on" before they are ready to be born.

5. Having a second group screen the ideas makes good psychological sense. People have more difficulty seeing the weaknesses in their own ideas than in someone else's.

Inhibitions of Creative Thinking

Conformity—the desire to be like everyone else—is the foremost barrier to creative thinking. A person is afraid to express new ideas because he thinks he will make a fool of himself and be ridiculed. This feeling may date back to his childhood, when his spontaneous and imaginative ideas may have been laughed at by parents or older people. During adolescence, conformity is reinforced because young people are afraid to be different from their peers. Then, too, history teaches us that innovators often are laughed at and even persecuted.

Censorship—especially self-imposed censorship—is a second significant barrier to creativity. External censorship of ideas, the thought-control of modern dictatorships, is dramatic and newsworthy; but internal censorship is more effective and dependable. External censorship merely prevents public distribution of proscribed thoughts; the thoughts may still be expressed privately. But people who are frightened by their thoughts tend to react passively, rather than think of creative solutions to their problems. Sometimes they even repress those thoughts, so that they are not aware they exist. Freud called this internalized censor the *superego.*

A third barrier to creative thinking is the rigid *education* still commonly imposed upon children. Regimentation, memorization, and drill may help instill the accepted knowledge of the day, but these classroom methods cannot teach students how to solve new problems or how to improve upon conventional solutions. On the other hand, the progressive movement in education often has been criticized on the ground that its emphasis on creative thinking also encourages intellectual nonconformity and radicalism. Such critics fear that new ideas may threaten the established order. Others simply believe that creative thinking must be balanced by critical thinking if it is to be useful.

A fourth barrier to creative thinking is the great *desire to find an answer quickly.* Such a strong motivation often narrows one's consciousness and encourages the acceptance of early, inadequate solutions. People tend to do their best creative thinking when they are released from the demands and responsibilities of everyday living. Inventors, scientists, artists, writers, and executives often do their most creative thinking when they are not distracted by routine work. The value of a vacation is not that it enables a person to work better on his return but rather that it permits new ideas to be born during the vacation.

The daydreamer often is criticized for wasting his time. Yet without daydreams, society's progress would be considerably slower, since daydreaming often leads to the discovery of original ideas. This is not to suggest that all daydreaming or leisurely contemplation results in valid and workable ideas—far from it. But somewhere, among the thousands of ideas conceived, one useful idea will appear. Finding this one idea without having to produce a thousand poor ones would achieve a vast saving in creative thinking. But such a saving seems unlikely, especially since creative thinking is generally enjoyable whether its results are useful or not.

Critical Thinking

Creative thinking must be followed by critical thinking if we want to sort out and refine those ideas that are potentially useful. Critical thinking is essentially an idea-testing operation. Will it work? What is wrong with it? How can it be improved? These are questions to be answered by a critical examination of newly hatched ideas. You may be highly creative, but if you cannot determine which ideas are practical and reason-

8-16A
Various tests have been designed to measure creativity. In one such test, subjects are provided with the simple line drawings above and asked to elaborate on them. Take the test yourself and compare your drawings to those shown in Figure 8-16B on the following page. (Barron, 1958)

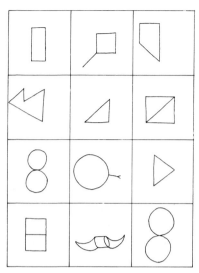

8-16B
Some sample drawings. The two drawings on the right were done by subjects identified as creative. (Barron, 1958)

able, your creativity will not lead to many fruitful consequences. In order to make such distinctions, you must maintain some distance and detachment, so that you can appraise your own ideas objectively.

Critical thinking requires some criteria by which to judge the practicality of the ideas. For example, if a community wants to do something about crime, it must decide what limitations are to be imposed upon the measures that are suggested. One limitation is the amount of money available; many proposals for curbing crime cost more than the community is willing or able to pay. Critical thinking must always take such realities into account.

What barriers stand in the path of critical thinking? One is the *fear of being aggressive and destructive.* We learn as children not to be critical, not to differ with what someone else says, especially an older person. To criticize is to be discourteous.

A closely related barrier is the *fear of retaliation.* If I criticize your ideas, you may turn about and criticize mine. This often involves yet another barrier, the *overevaluation* of one's own ideas. We like what we have created, and often we are reluctant to let others take apart our creation. By and large, those who are least secure hang on most tenaciously to their original ideas.

Finally, we should note again that if too much emphasis is placed upon being creative, the critical faculty may remain undeveloped. In their zeal to stimulate creativity in their pupils, teachers often are reluctant to be critical. One unintended result is that their students do not learn to think critically. This is unfortunate, since for most people life requires a balance between creative and critical thinking.

Critical Attitudes. There is an important distinction between critical thinking and a *critical attitude.* Critical thinking tries to arrive at a valid and practical solution to a problem. However much it may reject and discard, its final goal is constructive. A critical attitude, on the other hand, is destructive in intent. A person with a critical attitude tends to criticize solely for the sake of criticizing. Such an attitude is emotional rather than cognitive.

The Creative Person

In recent years, psychologists have studied creativity intensively. The first challenge they faced was how to define and recognize creativity. One common solution to this problem is to ask knowledgeable people to name the most creative individuals in their own field. Architects are asked to identify the most creative members of their profession or authors are asked to name the most creative writers. These highly creative people then are studied by means of interviews, questionnaires, tests, and other devices to see how they differ from less creative members of the same profession. These studies show that exceptionally creative people are characteristically:

1. flexible
2. intuitive
3. perceptive
4. original
5. ingenious
6. dedicated
7. hardworking
8. persistent
9. independent
10. unconventional
11. courageous
12. uninhibited
13. moody
14. self-centered
15. self-assertive
16. dominant
17. eccentric

Creative people often have vivid and sometimes even flamboyant personalities. They prefer complexity to simplicity. And those who are males accept the feminine side of their nature without being effeminate (Barron, 1959).

Isolating such characteristics of highly creative people may be useful. If these traits are related to creativity, child training and educational procedures may be tailored to produce more creative people. Still, we are only assuming that these traits have anything to do with being creative. They may merely be associated with creativity, rather than being determinants of it. Or, they may be necessary but not sufficient conditions for being creative. Flexibility, originality, and hard work, for example, may be requirements for creativity but they certainly are not sufficient to insure it. The creative genius displayed by Shakespeare, Leonardo da Vinci, Einstein, and Beethoven remains a mystery that has so far eluded scientific analysis.

Born nearly 100 years apart, Johann Sebastian Bach and Ludwig van Beethoven nontheless have a few things in common. Both were Germans born into the post-Luther era, both had unhappy childhoods —Bach's parents died when he was 9; Beethoven's father was a hopeless drunkard—and today both are dominant figures in the history of Western music. Bach is renowned for his deeply felt church music, such as his masterwork, *Mass in B Minor*. Beethoven is famous for his towering orchestral compositions.

But the similarities between the two men are outnumbered by the differences. Bach, born into a musical family, was inevitably exposed to music from infancy. A humble, religious, and dependable man, Bach also was enormously industrious—his collected works fill 60 large volumes, and still more works may never have been found. His interest in music appeared early, though he had relatively little formal instruction. Instead, Bach learned as he copied, imitated, and modified any music he could find. He experimented constantly, seeking his own style of expression. Starting in his 20s, this prodigious composer produced a steady flow of music that coursed on until his death in 1750; it included organ, choral, chamber, orchestral, and piano music.

Bach summed up his life, toward its end, in a rare self-evaluative remark. "I worked hard," he said. Despite his great talent and industry, Bach was little appreciated by his contemporaries or even his own children (he fathered 20 children; many died very young) several of whom became famous composers. He died blind at 65 and was buried in an unmarked grave in a Leipzig churchyard.

Beethoven was anything but humble. Driven by his failed and ruthless father to pretend to be a 6-year-old piano prodigy (he was actually 8), the boy withdrew into himself, becoming resentful at both the sufferings and the responsibilities his father inflicted on him. Already a

Bach, autograph of the Organ Prelude in B Minor

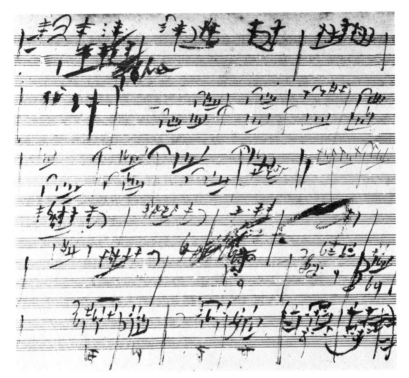

Beethoven, sketch of the Ninth Symphony

shy, uncouth, and ugly boy, Beethoven grew increasingly isolated from others. He avoided his schoolmates and they avoided him. As an adult he was fiercely proud, impatient, and intolerant of criticisms or slights, real or imagined. The result seems to show in the stubborn, thrusting vigor of his scores. And in his "musical attitude." Rather than focus almost exclusively, as Bach had, on church music, Beethoven turned to a celebration of man; even his *Missa Solemnis* has been said to elevate man to a godlike status rather than praise God.

A constant theme of Beethoven's life as a composer was the need to break with the traditional forms in music. He continually sought new styles and combinations, including such techniques as dissonance and free tonality. Like Bach, Beethoven produced orchestral, piano, chamber, and choral music; he also wrote *Fidelio*, an opera in which justice triumphs over oppression. While Beethoven was not as incredibly prolific as Bach, he clearly evolved as a composer, passing through new phases in which his music changed notably. His nine major symphonies spanned 20 years of his adult creative life, the Ninth being completed in 1824, three years before his death at 57 years of age. Even in death, Beethoven—by now stone deaf—was defiant. Lying mortally ill, he is said to have raised a clenched fist and then fallen back dead.

While many aspects of these two towering geniuses are interesting to compare, their handwritings alone reveal a great deal about their temperaments and musical styles. Bach's flowing crowded staff filled with rounds and curls strongly evokes the fluidity of his baroque melodies. The density of his measures creates a remarkable image of the music as it might be imagined visually by a listener. The overall impression of the manuscript is one of an integrated, productive, and congenial personality. Beethoven's musical handwriting presents another personality profile. His impetuous and struggling nature is evident in the rushed and seemingly haphazard and sketchy notations. While the Beethoven sample is admittedly a rough draft and the Bach sample a finished manuscript, the comparison of the two nonetheless suggests the differences in their persons and their music. (The John Herrick Jackson Library, Yale University, New Haven, Conn.; Beethoven-Haus, Bonn, slg. H. C. Bodmer)

Beliefs and Ideology

The more enduring features of a person's cognitive life are his beliefs. A *belief* is an idea that a person feels is true, that he acts upon when an appropriate situation arises, and that tends to persist over long periods of time. A belief is often accompanied by an emotional state.

Beliefs usually are organized into systems that relate to such subjects as religion, politics, sex, and race. Put together, these systems constitute one's *ideology*. Psychologists have been studying belief systems and ideologies for many years. They have been particularly interested in such ideological dimensions as liberal-conservative and democratic-authoritarian.

The usual method of studying beliefs is to formulate a set of statements about some topic and ask people to agree or disagree with each statement. In a study by Adorno, Frenkel-Brunswik, Levinson, and Sanford (1950), the statements used were devised to measure (1) a person's belief in social and political authoritarianism as opposed to an acceptance of a democratic ideology, (2) *ethnocentrism* or the belief in the superiority of one's own country and race and the inferior status of other races, (3) conventional religious beliefs, and (4) beliefs in a traditional family pattern.

A person who agrees with the following statements is said to have authoritarian beliefs:

1. What the youth needs most is strict discipline, rugged determination, and the will to work and fight for family and country.

2. Young people sometimes get rebellious ideas, but as they grow up they ought to get over them and settle down.

3. The best teacher or boss is the one who tells us exactly what is to be done and how to go about it.

A person who agrees with the following statements is said to be ethnocentric or prejudiced:

1. The danger to real Americanism during the last 50 years has come from foreign ideas and agitators.

2. The only way peace can be maintained is to keep America so powerful and well armed that no other nation will dare attack us.

3. It is only natural and right for a person to feel that his country is better than any other.

A person who agrees with the following statements is said to have conventional religious beliefs:

1. Life would hardly be worth living without the promise of immortality and life after death.

2. Every person needs a church—a place where he can go for prayer, moral uplift, and a feeling of security.

3. In addition to faith we need help from God in order to resist temptation.

A person who agrees with the following statements is said to believe in the traditional family pattern:

1. Some equality in marriage is a good thing, but by and large the husband ought to have the main say-so in family matters.

2. A child should never be allowed to talk back to his parents, or else he will lose respect for them.

3. There is hardly anything lower than a person who does not feel a great love, gratitude, and respect for his parents.

These statements tell us what a person *says* he believes. The difficult task is to determine whether what a person says is the same as what he *does* in actual life situations. Does a person who says he believes in democratic values actually practice them in his daily life? This is a complicated question for which there is no ready answer; but we can examine some of the issues involved. A person may say that he believes in democracy only because he feels that it is expected of him. Or he may believe in democracy but be swayed in the direction of undemocratic behavior by the pressure of his social group. Or he may practice democracy in some situations and not in others, depending on his current needs and circumstances. As a general rule, it is more accurate to evaluate a person's beliefs from what he does than from what he says.

Belief systems are usually interrelated. You can usually predict a person's beliefs about a subject if you know his beliefs about another subject. For example, a person who is politically conservative tends to be conservative with respect to social, economic, educational, and religious questions.

The intensity with which a person holds on to his cherished beliefs in the face of criticism, argument, and even clear-cut evidence against them has been observed by everyone—about someone else! A fact that may be less obvious is that beliefs tend to grow in strength as one has to make sacrifices for them. People who are harassed for their beliefs often are willing to suffer for them, even to the extent of giving their lives. We also can see in initiation rites the strengthening of beliefs through adversity. The more severe the tests, up to a certain point, the stronger becomes the initiate's belief in the ideology of the club or organization initiating him. The practical significance of this principle is that punishment and persecution are not effective ways to change beliefs.

How can a person's beliefs be changed? Social persuasion is effective under certain conditions. If the person who is trying to persuade us is like ourselves, we are more likely to change our beliefs than if he is quite different. College students are more readily influenced by the opinions of other college students than by those of older people. Our beliefs also tend to change when we become familiar with those beliefs held by the group of people with whom we associate. Very likely this accounts for many of the changes in beliefs that occur after students come to college. If you are attracted to a person, his influence on your views will be greater than if you are indifferent to him. Appeals to one's self-interest can also be effective. We are often influenced by people who have authority and power, or who have characteristics we admire and would like to possess. You may find it interesting to consider some of your beliefs that have changed during the last few years and why they have changed. We will have more to say about beliefs in Chapter 18.

The Physical Correlates of Thinking

As we have seen, damage to certain parts of the brain impairs perception, memory, and thought. Experimental studies with animals reveal that the efficiency of problem-solving is correlated, not with a particular zone in the cerebral cortex, but with the *total* cortex. The larger the amount of cortical tissue removed, the greater the reduction in the ability to reason and, often, in purposeful physical action as well.

Suppose, for example, we ask a person to think about bending his right elbow and simultaneously record changes in electrical currents (called *action potentials* and described in the Appendix to Chapter 3) in the muscle fibers of his right arm. We will find that action potentials occur in the muscles that would participate in actual elbow bending, but they do not occur in other muscles. These experiments show that thought and muscular action are synchronized. No thoughts, no action potentials, and hence no physical movement.

One investigator (Max, 1937) studied the muscular accompaniments of thinking in deaf-mutes who talked in sign language. Max reasoned that there would be more action potentials in their hands and arms when they were thinking than in the hands and arms of a control group of subjects who could hear and speak. His hypothesis was confirmed. When deaf-mutes were given problems to solve, action potentials in their arms were much larger and more frequent than those in the arms of the control subjects.

Do these studies mean that we think with our muscles as well as with our brains? Not at all. For example, an amputee will sometimes feel sensations that seem to be coming from his missing limb. This would be impossible if muscles were necessary for mental activity. Furthermore, completely paralyzed persons are capable of normal thinking. Undoubtedly we can think with our brain alone if connections between the brain and other parts of the body are broken.

If they are not broken, impulses generated by the thinking brain will pass into those motor channels that are associated with that idea. A particular action often follows a particular idea, so that when the idea recurs either the action or the action potentials will also recur in the muscles. This is known as *ideo-motor activity*. When no motor outlet has been established for an idea, or when the customary outlet is blocked, thinking is often accompanied by diffuse motor activity.

Thinking and Psychosomatic Illness

Thinking's physical correlates have received much attention because of the growing interest in *psychosomatic* (mind-body) *ailments*. Psychosomatic theory maintains that we can think ourselves into an illness. For example, if a person grows preoccupied with saving money, accumulating possessions, protecting himself from robbery, and keeping his ideas and feelings to himself, then these ideas may well be accompanied by physical retention, specifically of the feces; the person will become constipated. Do the thoughts cause the constipation or does the constipation cause the thoughts? Neither. Rather the thoughts and the physical symptoms are coordinated. Each organ of the body has its own specialized functions, but all of the organs are component parts of the total organismic system. If the total system is focused on the idea of retention, then each of the various organs will respond to this idea in its own way. The bowels will hold on to their contents by tightening the anal sphincter; the mouth will be firmly and tightly shut; the muscles will be flexed rather than extended; the breathing will be shallow; and the thoughts will be retentive in content. As we shall see in Chapter 20, there are several types of illness that may be psychosomatic in origin.

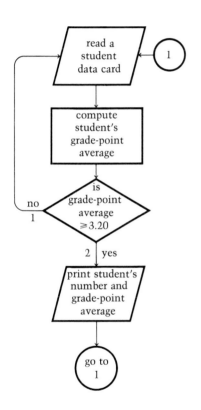

8-17
According to information-processing theories, humans solve problems in a manner similar to the way a computer processes data. This flow chart diagrams a simple computer information-processing model for compiling a list of those students who have made the honor roll. (Emerich & Wilkinson, 1970)

Computers and Thinking

Can machines be constructed that will do our thinking for us? The answer, of course, is yes. Computers already figure payrolls, run factories, solve complex mathematical problems, grade examinations, diagnose illnesses, predict election results, play chess, and even act as psychotherapists!

Marvelous as they are, computers can only perform those tasks for which they have been programmed. They cannot think for themselves.

By programming a computer to *simulate* (imitate) thinking, we attempt to discover how we think. We must translate our hypotheses about how thinking works into a set of instructions that the computer can follow. One important consequence of this search for effective computer programs to simulate thinking is that psychologists have been stimulated to learn a great deal more about how we think. As we gain more knowledge of thinking, we can devise better programs.

Some people are disturbed by the thought of machines doing their thinking for them. If we don't watch out, they protest, machines will soon be making love for us. They fear greater regimentation and a loss of freedom, associating computers with brainwashing and thought control. Others regard computers as labor-saving devices that give people time to engage in other, more satisfying activities.

Summary

1. Thinking includes reasoning and problem-solving, discriminating and judging, abstracting and generalizing, predicting and controlling, expecting and hoping, worrying, imagining, daydreaming, and dreaming.

2. A concept is formed by noting some common feature that a number of different objects share. There are simple, conjunctive, disjunctive, and relational concepts. They are learned more easily when a person is shown positive instances of the concept and when its common feature stands out.

3. Three modes of solving problems can be distinguished. These are trial and error, gradual analysis, and insight. Problem-solving ability may be inhibited by functional fixedness and set.

4. Realistic thinking tries to stick to the facts; wishful or autistic thinking tends to ignore or to distort reality.

5. Delusions are unrealistic beliefs. Two extreme types are delusions of grandeur and delusions of persecution.

6. Concrete thinking deals with things that can be directly perceived. Abstract thinking deals with relationships, inferences, and general ideas.

7. Creative thinking consists of finding new and better solutions to a problem by letting our thoughts run freely and spontaneously. Brainstorming is a technique to enhance creative thinking through group interaction. Creative thinking may be impeded by fear of ridicule, conventionality, self-censorship, regimentation, and pressures for fast decisions.

8. Critical thinking consists of examining the ideas obtained by creative thinking to see whether they will work.

9. Barriers to critical thinking include fear of being overly aggressive, fear of retaliation, and overevaluation of one's own ideas.

10. Ideologies are organized systems of beliefs. Two ideological dimensions that have been extensively studied by psychologists are liberal-conservative and democratic-authoritarian.

11. A person's beliefs tend to become stronger when he has had to defend them or make sacrifices for them.

12. Although an intact brain is necessary for thinking, thinking is accompanied by other bodily changes. According to the ideo-motor activity theory, muscular activity usually accompanies thinking.

13. Computers can be programmed to simulate thinking. A successful program helps us to improve our problem-solving skills.

Important Terms

cognition	hoping
thinking	worrying
reasoning	imagining
problem-solving	daydreaming
discriminating	concept
abstracting	simple concept
generalization	conjunctive concept
predicting	disjunctive concept
expecting	relational concept

trial and error

gradual analysis

insight

heuristics

functional fixedness

set

realistic thinking

autistic thinking

delusion

delusion of grandeur

delusions of persecution

superstition

concrete thinking

abstract thinking

creative thinking

critical thinking

brainstorming

critical attitude

belief

ideology

ethnocentrism

action potentials

ideo-motor activity

Suggested Readings

BARRON, F. *Creative persons and creative process.* New York: Holt, Rinehart and Winston, 1969.
  A study of creative persons in various vocations and an analysis of the creative process, by an outstanding authority on creativity.

BRUNER, J. S., GOODNOW, J. J., & AUSTIN, G. A. *A study of thinking.* New York: Wiley, 1956.
  An influential series of studies on concept attainment.

DEWEY, J. *How we think.* New York: Heath, 1933.
  A classic account of how we think and solve problems by a famous American psychologist, philosopher, and educator.

DUNCAN, C. P. (ED.) *Thinking: Current experimental studies.* Philadelphia: Lippincott, 1967.
  A collection of articles on various aspects of cognitive activities. The discussions are fairly technical.

MAIER, N. R. F. *Problem solving and creativity in individuals and groups.* Monterey, Calif.: Brooks/Cole, 1970.
  An account of 40 experimental investigations of creative problem-solving by individuals and groups, carried out by the author and his associates. Fairly technical.

SINGER, J. L. *Daydreaming.* New York: Random House, 1966.
  An original and readable account of a series of investigations conducted by the author on the contents and functions of daydreaming.

THOMSON, R. *The psychology of thinking.* Baltimore: Penguin, 1959.
  An elementary introduction to the psychology of thinking. This book is comprehensive and readable.

VINACKE, W. E. *The psychology of thinking.* New York: McGraw-Hill, 1952.
   A standard textbook, which systematically surveys the various types of human thought processes and the experimental work that has been done on them.

WERTHEIMER, M. *Productive thinking* (rev. ed.) New York: Harper, 1959.
   A classic analysis of thinking by one of the founders of Gestalt psychology. Contains many original ideas about ways of solving problems.

Chapter 9　Dreams and Symbols

Sleep takes off the costume of circumstance, arms us with terrible freedom, so that every will rushes to a deed. A skillful man reads his dreams for his self-knowledge; yet not the details, but the quality. What part does he play in them—a cheerful manly part, or a poor, driveling part? However monstrous and grotesque their apparitions, they have a substantial truth.

—Ralph Waldo Emerson
(*Emerson's Essays*)

A dream which is not understood is like a letter which is not opened.

—The Talmud

I reflected that dreams would sometimes in this way bring nearer to me truths or impressions which would not come through my own unaided effort or even through natural contingencies, and that they would awaken in me a desire, a longing for certain nonexistent things, which is the prerequisite for creative work, for getting out of the rut of habit and getting away from the concrete.

—Marcel Proust
(*Remembrance of Things Past*)

Blake inv:

Perry. sc:

O! how I dreamt of things impossible.
Of Death affecting Forms least like himself;
I've seen, or dreamt I saw the Tyrant dress,
Lay by his Horrors, and put on his Smiles;

Treacherous he came an unexpected Guest,
Nay, though invited by the loudest Calls
Of blind Imprudence, unexpected still;
And then, he dropt his Mask.

Alter'd from Young

Dreams and Symbols

Dreaming is a distinctive, unusual, and puzzling form of cognitive activity. Because it is so puzzling, many theories of dreaming have been advanced. One ancient explanation is that dreams are *actual* and not imaginary experiences. According to this belief, during sleep the soul leaves the body and roams around, having various adventures, which the person sometimes remembers when he awakes. Another old explanation is that dreams are omens or *messages* to the sleeper from supernatural beings, gods, or ancestors in the spirit world. More recently, theorists have tended to view dreams as messages from the dreamer himself. In this chapter, we shall discuss several modern theories.

Two of the most influential psychologists of the 20th century—Sigmund Freud and Carl Jung—studied dreams and dreaming extensively. Both Freud and Jung saw dreams as symbolic messages. Freud called the dream the "royal road" to the domain of the unconscious mind, and he considered his research on dreams to be his greatest achievement.

9–1
Some people hold that dreams are messages from the outside world. "Out-of-body" experiences during sleep are suggested as one of the ways in which such messages are transmitted to the sleeper. This drawing is an artist's conception of the experience reported by a subject in a laboratory investigation of such paranormal (not within the range of normal, scientifically explainable) phenomena. In a "nightmare," the subject, wearing a checked skirt she did not recognize as her own, was being followed while walking on a dark, deserted street. Her pursuer raped her and stabbed her to death. The next day the local newspaper reported that such a crime had occurred nearby to a girl wearing a checked skirt. A coincidence? Clairvoyance? Investigations of paranormal phenomena are discussed later in the chapter. (Tart, 1968)

Freud's *The Interpretation of Dreams,* published in 1900, is regarded as one of the most influential books of the modern era. Jung's work on symbolism, not only in dreams but in waking life as well, has inspired great and continuing interest in this subject.

The Scanning Hypothesis

As you will remember from Chapter 4, research on dreaming increased greatly after 1953, when Aserinsky and Kleitman made their chance discovery that the eyeballs of a sleeping person move periodically throughout the night. Guessing that REMs (rapid eye movements) accompany dreaming, they developed the *scanning hypothesis,* which says that REMs correspond to what a person is looking at in his dream. If, in a dream, a person were watching someone climb a ladder, his eyes would move upward; if he were looking at a parade, his eyes would move back and forth horizontally.

It was easy to test the hypothesis that REM periods were dream periods, simply by waking the subject when he was in such a stage and asking him if he had been dreaming. Nearly every time this was done, a dream was remembered. When subjects were awakened during periods of non-REM sleep, few dreams were reported. Since people average four or five REM periods a night, it was easy to assume that they also average four or five dreams a night. Even individuals who rarely remembered their dreams under normal conditions were able to recall several dreams a night in the laboratory when they were awakened during REM periods.

The scanning hypothesis was tested by correlating the direction of movement of the eyes with direction of looking in the dream. Early studies found such correspondences, but subsequent ones have not. More recently, the scanning hypothesis has been challenged by most experts in sleep-dream research. Why, then, are there eye-movements during sleep? Considerable evidence now suggests that REMs maintain the efficiency of coordinated eye movements and the accuracy of binocular depth perception when awake (Berger, 1969).

Dreaming and REM Sleep

The assumption that one dreams *only* during REM periods has not fared any better than the scanning hypothesis. Recent studies show that dreams are sometimes reported when the eyes are not moving. Dreaming, it seems, can take place at any time during sleep and may even continue throughout the night. Differences in the frequency of recall may be related to the quality of the particular stage of sleep from which a subject is awakened. For example, subjects seem less alert and more confused when awakened from one of the non-REM stages of sleep. The ability to recall a dream may also be due to the nature of the dream. There is some evidence that REM-period dreams are more dramatic, intense, and vivid than dreams that occur during non-REM periods, and that is why the REM dreams are more apt to be recalled.

Despite all the recent work in sleep laboratories, using such sophisticated "hardware" as the *polygraph,* which constantly records eye movements, brain waves, heart rate, respiration, and other physiological responses, we still do not know much about dreaming. No dependable relationships between the electrophysiological phenomena of sleep and the cognitive activity of dreaming have yet been firmly established, except that more numerous and vivid dreams are recalled from REM awakenings than from non-REM awakenings. Nonetheless, these laboratory studies have stimulated an interest in dreams that goes beyond the clinical studies of patients' dreams made by Freud and Jung.

Distinctive Characteristics of Dreaming

What characteristics distinguish dreaming from other cognitive processes? First, dreaming, by definition, occurs while we are asleep. The state of sleep differs in many physiological respects from the state of wakefulness. The brain, in particular, displays patterns of electrical waves that are not ordinarily found in a waking state. We know that sleep's different or "altered" physiological state is accompanied by an "altered" state of consciousness, even though we have not yet learned just how the physical and mental states relate to each other.

Dream Imagery

Another distinctive feature of many dreams is their vivid *imagery*. Most of this imagery is visual, but other types of imagery—sound, touch, movement, smell, and taste—also occur. The imagery of dreams is often much more vivid than the memory images of normal waking life. In fact, dream images are more like perceptions than memories. When we dream, our experiences seem immediate and actual. If we dream we are

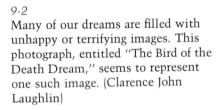

9-2
Many of our dreams are filled with unhappy or terrifying images. This photograph, entitled "The Bird of the Death Dream," seems to represent one such image. (Clarence John Laughlin)

being chased by a wild animal, it is as real and as terrifying an experience as if it were actually happening. When we awaken from such a dream, we are likely to feel strong emotions for some time. People who have heart conditions may suffer mild heart attacks during bad dreams (Nowlin, 1965). And it has even been suggested that an intensely emotional dream may be fatal, though, of course, this hypothesis cannot be directly tested.

An image that we react to as if it were real is called an *hallucination*. Dreams are actually hallucinations, and this fact also distinguishes dreaming from waking cognition. Dreams are a universal and normal experience, but similar hallucinations during waking life may be symptoms of a serious mental disorder. While we dream, then, we react as though our dream experience is real; that is, the dream seems like a perception. Occasionally, people report that they knew it was a dream while they were dreaming. They think to themselves, "Oh, it's only a dream." One suggested explanation is that their sleep period was punctuated by brief awakenings. Such wakeful periods usually are so brief that the person does not know he has awakened. But during such awakenings a person may become conscious of dreaming.

Bizarre Dreams

Another characteristic of dreams is that they are often bizarre. In dreams, the impossible or the highly improbable happens; space and time are frequently distorted. The dreamer is in one place one moment and in a distant place the next. Dream time may not accord with real time. Even stranger are some of the characters who enter our dreams. A person we have not seen or thought of for years suddenly appears in a dream; people long dead appear alive and well. We perform feats in our dreams that we cannot achieve in waking life. Some dreams violate all the rules of logic and reason. Yet while we are having a fantastic dream, it seems perfectly natural; only later, when we are awake and recalling it, does it seem nonsensical. This may be why many people dismiss dreams as meaningless and unworthy of serious consideration.

Theories of the Functions of Dreams

Freud and Jung did more than study the meaning of dreams. They also launched a continuing investigation into the function of dreaming. They were not content to learn what dreams meant to the dreamer; they also wanted to know what dreams *did* for him. In this section, we will examine several theories, including those of Freud and Jung.

The Tension-Reduction Theory

An early theory about the function of dreams was modeled upon sleep's *restorative function*. Dreaming, it was thought, gets rid of the mental tensions that have accumulated during the day, just as sleep gets rid of physical tensions. Consequently, both the mind and body awaken in the morning refreshed and alert.

This was an attractive theory, but for many years it seemed impossible to prove or disprove. Then came the discovery of REM sleep, and its accompanying belief that dreaming occurred *only* during REM periods. Researchers quickly assumed that if REM periods could be eliminated from sleep, there would be no dreaming. If a person were deprived of his dreams, night after night, the *tension-reduction theory* predicted that he would become progressively more tense and nervous in his waking life. To test this hypothesis, individuals slept in a laboratory and every time their eyes began to move, they were awakened. As a control for the stress of being awakened and for losing sleep, other individuals were awakened equally often during non-REM periods. The early experiments indicated that individuals deprived of REM periods did become more nervous and upset, whereas those awakened at other times did not. But later experiments failed to confirm the earlier results. This is not surprising if we consider recent evidence that dreaming is not restricted to REM periods, so that preventing REM sleep does not eliminate all dreaming.

So an apparently effective test of the tension-reducing function of dreaming turned out to be an inadequate test after all. If dreaming does occur more or less continuously throughout the night, we would have to eliminate *all* sleep to eliminate *all* dreaming. Consequently, we could not know whether the observed effects were due to dream deprivation or sleep deprivation.

Freud's Theories of Dream Function

On the basis of his extensive studies of dreams, Freud proposed that dreaming serves two functions. One function is to prevent the person from awakening; "The dream is the *guardian of sleep*" (our italics). Our own observations tell us that dreams sometimes awaken us, especially dreams that are very emotional or frightening. To this objection, Freud would reply that just because some dreams awaken us, it does not follow that *most* dreaming does not guard sleep. Freud's theory seems supported by the fact that minor disturbances during the night are often incorporated into a dream and thus do not awaken us. A loud noise, a change in temperature, hunger pangs, or bladder pressure may be woven into our dream either directly or symbolically. While such disturbances may eventually awaken us, we have unconsciously attempted to preserve sleep by incorporating the disturbance into a dream.

Freud also proposed a second and more important psychological function of dreaming—his famous *wish-fulfillment* theory. Simply stated, this theory says that dreams attempt to fulfill our wishes. If you have an unsatisfied sexual urge, you will have a sexual dream. If you become hungry while asleep, you will dream of food. If you are feeling angry with someone, you may dream of attacking him. Students dream of passing examinations or of being admitted to graduate school. Children dream of receiving presents. Even the guardian-of-sleep function can be included in the wish-fulfillment theory by saying that we dream because we wish to remain asleep.

Much can be said for this theory. Everyone has had some wishes gratified in dreams. In this connection, a college student performed the fol-

With the theory of dreams, psychoanalysis passed from being a psychotherapeutic method to being a psychology of the depths of human nature.

Freud, *New Introductory Lecture*

9-3
The Spanish painter Goya (1746–1828) vividly depicted the nightmarish quality of many dreams—"The Sleep of Reason Produces Monsters" (El Sueño de la Razón Produce Monstruos). (The Metropolitan Museum of Art, gift of M. Knoedler & Co., 1918)

lowing heroic experiment on himself. He decided to see if the number of nocturnal emissions he experienced would increase if he remained completely celibate. During the 157 nights of celibacy he had 22 nocturnal emissions. The frequency increased greatly throughout the period until he was having about one nocturnal emission every third night. The incidence of wet dreams fell off sharply when he resumed his normal sexual activities. This one experiment, which is not likely to be repeated very often, appears to support Freud's wish-fulfillment theory. But what about the bad dreams—dreams of being chased and attacked, of suffering a calamity, of failure, of losing something, of friends and relatives dying, of falling? Surveys of dreams prove conclusively that dreams of this sort outnumber pleasant, wish-fulfilling ones by a large margin. We can easily understand how a dream of aggression toward an enemy could be wish-fulfilling. But dreamers are far more frequently the victims of aggression than the aggressor. This holds true for both sexes, at all ages, and throughout the world.

Freud recognized that such anxiety and punishment dreams refuted a *simple* wish-fulfillment theory. His explanation was that another part of the personality produces anxiety dreams. For example, the superego (conscience) punishes the dreamer for his aggressive wishes by having him dream that he is the victim of aggression. Freud also conjectured that a person may wish to be punished because it gives him *masochistic* pleasure; he enjoys suffering. Freud's theory of dreaming is closely tied to his theory of personality, which will be discussed in Chapter 16.

Jung's Theory of Dream Function

Jung is said to have analyzed over 100,000 dreams during his lifetime as a psychoanalyst. Jung's vast experience led him to propose a *compensatory theory* of dreaming. He theorized that a person compensates in his dreams for the things that are lacking in his waking life. This sounds similar to Freud's wish-fulfillment theory, and in some respects it is. But just as Freud's theory of dreaming is tied to his theory of personality, so is Jung's and therein lies the difference. For Jung, the personality consists of a number of parts or subsystems (see Chapter 16). The goal of personality development is to unify these parts into a coherent, integrated whole. To achieve wholeness of personality—or *selfhood*, as Jung called it—each part must become fully developed or *individuated*. The part of the personality whose development has been neglected will express itself in dreams. For example, Jung identified a region of the personality that he called the *shadow*. The shadow comprises the animal side of man's nature—his sexual and aggressive impulses in particular. If the shadow remains undeveloped because it is repressed, it will find expression in primitive sexual and aggressive dreams.

We mentioned an ancient theory that dreams are messages or warnings from the gods. Jung has given a modern twist to this theory; dreams are indeed messages—not from supernatural sources, but from the dreamer's own psyche. Dreams are to be respected, Jung says, as communications from the neglected portions of our being. They demand that we listen to them and act upon them—but of course we must first learn how to interpret them.

The Problem-Solving Theory

Still another view of dreams is that they serve the same function all thinking does. Dreaming is merely a continuation of thinking about the same problems that beset us during the day—how to deal with our needs and wishes, with our interpersonal relations, and with the impersonal world. Of course, by themselves dreams cannot solve anything. They are imaginary happenings and can have no impact upon our real world unless we act upon them in waking life. What they can do is help us define our problems more clearly. That is why the analysis of dreams has proved to be so useful in the treatment of people with psychological problems. Dreams reveal problems the patient has not been conscious of. But you do not need to be in psychotherapy to benefit from dream analysis. Anyone can analyze his own dreams; they provide a means for expanding self-knowledge. We will examine several methods of dream analysis later in this chapter.

Some Frequent Questions About Dreams

People have always been curious about dreams and constantly ask the same questions about them. We will discuss some of these questions.

Why Can't I Remember My Dreams?

This is a common question, often expressed as "Why don't I dream?" As we have seen, the answer to the latter question is that *everyone dreams every night.* Evidently, some people cannot remember dreaming at all, while others remember they had a dream but cannot recall the details.

The reason for this forgetfulness is not clear. Some authorities believe that people who cannot recall many dreams actually repress them because they are too threatening. Little evidence exists to support this view. Others report that the recall of dreams can be improved if the dreamer makes an effort. You can prove this for yourself by keeping a dream diary. If you do, you may notice another reason for forgetting dreams that we mentioned earlier. Dreams are often unrealistic and bizarre, and these qualities can make them look foolish in the light of day. We tend to forget embarrassing things rather quickly, and so we may simply be burying our foolish dreams. Of course, dreams can seem pointless and dull, too. There is no reason why you should remember a boring dream that occurred hours before awaking, any more than you can remember a boring moment that occurred hours ago in waking life. Dramatic dreams are more memorable than dull ones. Dreams we have shortly before awaking in the morning are more apt to be remembered than dreams we have earlier in the night. In short, the laws of memory apply to dreams as well as to waking experiences.

And whatever be the pursuit to which one clings with devotion, whatever the things on which we have been occupied much in the past, the mind being thus more intent upon that pursuit, it is generally the same things that we seem to encounter in dreams.

Lucretius, *De Rerum Naturae*

Can We Learn to Control Our Dreams?

Ann Faraday, the author of *Dream Power*, cites a number of instances in which people have been able to control their dreams. Here is one example. A man dreamed he was walking through a wintry landscape, shivering with cold. He thought how pleasant it would be if it were warm. At that moment he realized he was only dreaming and that he had the power to change his dream. So he changed the winter landscape into a spring one and felt warm instead of cold.

Is it necessary to wake up momentarily in order to change a dream? Not necessarily. Faraday tells about one of her own experiences. She had been bothered by a recurring dream of being chased by murderous strangers. She resolved one night before going to sleep that she would turn on her attackers and say "You have no power over me." She did so, and gradually the frightening dreams disappeared.

You may be interested to see if you can influence your dreams.

Do People Dream in Color?

Most people report that there is *some* color in *some* of their dreams. A few people say they dream exclusively in color, and a few say their dreams are never in color. One investigation (Kahn, Dement, Fisher, & Barmack, 1962) indicates that all dreams are in color, but the color is forgotten by the time a person awakens and recalls the dream. These results were obtained by awakening the subjects during the night and questioning them closely about the presence of color in their dreams.

Some people have claimed that various colors have fixed meanings in dreams—white represents purity; black, evil or death; red, passion; green, vitality—but there is no adequate evidence to support this view. Red may stand for passion in one dream, danger in another, and anger in another, or it may not mean anything.

Do Animals Dream?

We cannot say with absolute certainty that animals do or do not dream. The only reason we know that other people dream is because they are able to tell us about their dreams. Many animal species show periods of rapid eye movements during sleep but as we have seen, REMs are not a guaranteed sign of dreaming. Many people believe that animals dream because they have observed a dog twitching its legs and making barking sounds while asleep. C. J. Vaughn (1964) conducted the following ingenious experiment to attempt to answer the question of whether animals dream. While they were awake, monkeys were trained to avoid shock by pressing a lever whenever pictures were flashed on a screen. Later, when they were asleep, the monkeys pressed the lever during REM periods, but not during non-REM periods. This suggests that they were responding to visual dream images during REM periods.

Do Paranormal Phenomena Occur During Dreaming?

Dreaming has always been associated with the mysterious, supernatural world of *precognition* (prophecy), *mental telepathy*, and *clairvoyance*

If I may trust the flattering truth of sleep,
My dreams presage some joyful news at hand:
My bosom's lord sits lightly in his throne:
And all this day an unaccustomed spirit
Lifts me above the ground with cheerful thoughts.
I dreamed my Lady came and found me dead,
(Strange dream that gives a dead man leave to think,)
And breath'd such life with kisses in my lips,
That I reviv'd and was an Emperor.
Ah me, how sweet is love itself possess'd,
When but love's shadows are so rich in joy.

Romeo and Juliet by William Shakespeare
Romeo, Act V, Scene 1.

(second sight). History is filled with tales of prophetic dreams. For example, Abraham Lincoln dreamed he entered the East Room of the White House and saw a coffin. When he asked who had died, the reply was "The President." A few days later the President was dead, the victim of an assassin's bullet. Was Lincoln's dream precognitive? Did Lincoln actually foresee his own death in the dream? This is a difficult question to answer. Any president is vulnerable to attack, as history shows, and Lincoln was particularly vulnerable during the Civil War. Moreover, Lincoln was said to have been preoccupied with death. The dream and its subsequent realization could have been coincidence. Lincoln might have had many similar dreams and not reported them; we simply do not know. How many people dream of calamity or death befalling them *without* its happening subsequently? It is human nature to note the positive evidence for any belief and to overlook evidence to the contrary.

The following investigation (Murray & Wheeler, 1937) points out the problems of determining whether a dream contains _paranormal_ (scientifically unexplainable) influences. In March 1932, a few days after the Charles A. Lindbergh baby was kidnapped, a request for dreams relating to the kidnapping appeared in newspapers throughout the country. The request brought in over 1,300 dreams. Murray and Wheeler's study compared all the dreams with the facts as they were eventually established. The facts were that the baby had been murdered; its mutilated and naked body was later discovered in a shallow grave in the woods near a road several miles away from the Lindbergh home. Death had been instantaneous and had occurred before the dreamers dreamed. In approximately 5 percent of the dreams sent in before the baby's death was known, the baby appeared to be dead. In seven dreams, the actual location of the body, its nakedness, and the manner of its burial were more or less accurately portrayed. The following dream was the most faithful of the seven:

I thought I was standing or walking in a very muddy place among many trees. One spot looked as though it might be a round, shallow grave. Just then I heard a voice saying, "The baby has been murdered and buried there." I was so frightened that I immediately awoke.

Only four of the seven dreams included the three items: death, burial in a grave, and a location among trees.

Were these seven dreams clairvoyant? Or is it statistically probable that 7 dreams out of 1300 would get some of the details correct? We would need to know the probabilities of the child's being either dead or alive; and if dead, whether in water, above ground, or below ground, and whether inside a house, in an open field, or in the woods. The investigators acknowledged that they did not have the necessary information for estimating these probabilities, but they felt that on the basis of chance alone more than 7 out of 1300 dreams should have referred to these critical features.

The fact that only 5 percent of the dreams pictured the baby as dead argues against any widespread prevalence of clairvoyant dreams. On the other hand, it could be argued that only a very few people (*sensitives*, as they are called) have clairvoyant powers, so that one would expect to find only a few clairvoyant dreams.

A team of scientists at Maimonides Hospital in Brooklyn, New York is conducting systematic studies of thought transmission to sleeping subjects (Ullman & Krippner, 1970). The design of the experiment is as follows: The sender is in a room far down a corridor from the room in which the subject is sleeping. A set of prints of modern paintings is used as the stimulus material. The prints are concealed in envelopes, and one is selected at random to be "sent" on a particular night. The sender alone knows which print has been chosen, and he does not know that until he opens the envelope after the subject is asleep. When the subject is in his first REM period, the sender takes the print from the envelope and concentrates on it. An assistant (who does not know what picture has been used) awakens the subject, and the subject reports his dreams into a tape recorder. This is done for subsequent REM periods so that a set of dreams is collected during the night.

9-4
One of the prints used by Ullman in his investigation of telepathy was "Trees and Houses," by the French artist Paul Cezanne. One dreamer's reports in response to the "sending" of this picture were as follows:

In the first dream report he mentioned ". . . seeing . . . a house." In his fourth dream report he said, "There was just this sort of toy or doll house. There were no people involved and nothing is going on." Other reports contained these descriptive elements: "a dirt road," "dingy building," "a lonely shack sitting on a hillside," and "orange clay of a dirt road." In addition, he referred a number of times to intersections, including one that looked like two legs joining the trunk of the body.

The dreamer also was struck by the fact that his dreams this night, unlike most of his dreams, were almost completely devoid of people.

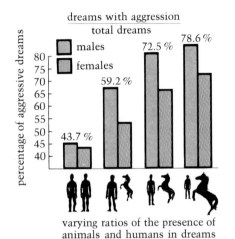

dreams with aggression
total dreams

varying ratios of the presence of
animals and humans in dreams

9-5
The silhouettes below the bar graphs indicate the extent to which animals were present in the dreams reported. When animals were absent (left), the average of male and female aggressive dreams to total dreams was 43.7%. At the far right, with animals predominant, aggressive dreams rose to 78.6% of the total. (From Robert L. Van de Castle, *The Psychology of Dreaming.* © 1971, General Learning Corporation. Reprinted by permission.)

The procedure is repeated for a number of nights with the same subject, using a different randomly selected picture each night. The sets of dreams and the pictures are then given to a panel of judges who are ignorant of the experiment's details. They try to match each set of dreams with its corresponding picture. Certain statistical techniques can determine whether their successful matches exceed the number that would be expected on the basis of chance or coincidence. Better than chance matches by *some* of the judges for *some* of the subjects have been found. This indicates that certain people may be able to receive thoughts while dreaming. Further work in sleep laboratories should settle the question of whether dreams can be influenced by the "sending of thoughts." If even a few such transmissions can be firmly established, then researchers will face the challenge of discovering how such messages are sent and received.

What Do People Dream About?

Dreams are infinitely diverse; their contents are inexhaustibly varied. This is probably why all modern theories of dreams, as well as some ancient ones, contain at least some truth.

Aggression. Amid the welter of dream images, some common themes can be identified. Aggression is one. In nearly half the dreams reported by young American adults, at least one aggressive interaction takes place. Such aggressions range from feelings of hostility to outright murder. Table 9-1 shows the different kinds of aggression and the frequencies with which they occurred in the dreams of 500 young adult males and 500 young adult females.

The murder rate in dreams is nearly 100 times higher than the actual murder rate in the United States—1 for every 150 dream characters as compared with 1 in every 14,000 persons in the United States. Other studies indicate this high rate of aggression in dreams is similar throughout the world. As we have already pointed out, the dreamer is more frequently the victim than the aggressor.

Friendly interactions occur less frequently, and they are less intense

Table 9-1 *Aggression in Dreams: Type and Frequency*

Subject of Dream	Dreams of Males	Dreams of Females
Murder	24	7
Physical attack	89	49
Being chased or held prisoner	62	43
Destructiveness	26	15
Serious threat	19	15
Rejection-disobedience	71	122
Quarreling	70	50
Feelings of hostility	41	36
Total:	402	337

and dramatic than aggressive interactions. Our feelings about a person who appears over and over in our dreams are apparently a mixture of hostility and friendliness, a condition known as *ambivalence* of feelings.

Misfortune. Misfortune also is common in dreams. Good fortune, on the other hand, is very rare. The dreamer or another character becomes ill, is injured, dies, loses something, is threatened by the environment, falls, loses his way, encounters an obstacle, misses a bus, is late for a class. Death by natural causes in dreams is much higher even than the incidence of murder.

We were astonished to find in the dreams of the Mount Everest climbers so many negative feelings about climbing. Failure, misfortune, resentment, and a desire to get the whole expedition over with and return home plagued their dreams. Here are a few examples:

"We failed miserably on the mountain so we went back to the village."

"The four men who were in the summit area were blown off the mountain by Communist Chinese jets."

"I was back home. I had come home early. I couldn't see why we had failed but we had. We were tired of living up there."

"I was climbing with a man up the West Ridge. I looked back and saw a child fall off the cliff. The child's father was the man I was climbing with."

Hall & Nordby, 1972

Sex. Young adults report fewer overt sex dreams than might have been forecast, given the emphasis placed on sex in dreams by some psychologists. About one in every ten dreams reported by young adult males, most of them unmarried, contains sexual imagery (Hall & Van de Castle, 1966). The corresponding figure for young adult females is about one in thirty dreams. It may be argued that sex dreams, even though remembered, may not be reported, or that sex dreams are disguised by symbolism.

An interesting observation made in laboratory studies of sleeping males is that they periodically have erections, usually during REM periods. For example, a group of men 20 to 26 years old averaged about four erections during the night. The total time of these erection episodes was about ½ hour (Karacan, Hursch, Williams, & Thornby, 1972). Adolescent males 13 to 15 years old averaged about seven erection periods for a total of 2½ hours during the night (Karacan, Hursch, Williams, & Littell, 1972). Erections during sleep also have been observed in infants and animals.

Do erections during sleep influence dreams or do dreams, perhaps, cause the erections? We do not know the answers to these questions. Penile tumescence may be only one feature of the general activation pattern that characterizes REM sleep and may have nothing to do with dream content. Since only one dream in ten contains an overtly sexual element and erections occur during virtually all REM periods, any specific correspondence between erections and dream content seems unlikely.

Some other common dream themes are eating, finding money, being nude in public, getting married, being dressed inappropriately, losing a tooth, swimming, and traveling (see Table 9-2).

9-6
As Table 9-2 shows, falling is one of the most common themes in dreaming. Falling may represent any number of things, including the fear of failure, of being unable to cope with a situation. (Lawrence Weissmann)

Table 9-2 *The 20 Most Common Dreams of College Students and the Percentage Having Each Type of Dream (Griffith, Miyago, & Tago, 1958)*

Type of Dream	Percentage of Students
Falling	83
Being attacked or pursued	77
Trying repeatedly to do something	71
School, teachers, studying	71
Sexual experiences	66
Arriving too late	64
Eating	62
Being frozen with fright	58
A loved person is dead	57
Being locked up	56
Finding money	56
Swimming	52
Snakes	49
Being inappropriately dressed	46
Being smothered	44
Being nude in public	43
Fire	41
Failing an examination	39
Seeing self as dead	33
Killing someone	26

More interesting to psychologists than dream topics is the *pattern* of themes that runs through an individual's dream series. Although most people dream about many of the things we have already discussed, each person has a unique pattern of recurrent themes.

Where Do Dreams Come From?

When we ask where dreams come from, we really want to know the source of the images that constitute a dream. Various sources have been postulated. We have mentioned that dreams have been attributed to supernatural beings or ancestors. We also have noted that some dream imagery may result from thought transference or precognition. However, there are simpler answers to this question.

Day Residue. We can easily trace many dream images to recent experiences during waking life. This source is called *day residue*. A problem,

KEKULÉ'S DREAM

Friedrich Kekulé, Professor of Chemistry in Ghent, Belgium, was the first to discover that carbon compounds can form rings. For some time, he had been pondering the nature of the structure of benzene, but to no avail. One afternoon in 1865, he turned away from his work:

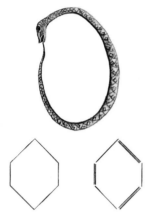

Benzene rings

I turned my chair to the fire and dozed. Again the atoms were gambolling before my eyes. This time the smaller groups kept modestly in the background. My mental eye, rendered more acute by repeated visions of this kind, could now distinguish larger structures, of manifold conformations; long rows, sometimes more closely fitted together; all twining and twisting in snakelike motion. But look! What was that? One of the snakes had seized hold of its own tail, and the form whirled mockingly before my eyes. As if by a flash of lightning I awoke and this time also I spent the rest of the night working out the consequences of the hypothesis.

The snake grasping its own tail was Kekulé's clue to the benzene ring. His dream is an excellent example of the role of the creative subconscious in scientific discovery.

---

worry, or preoccupation of waking life often appears in our dreams, either directly or in symbolic form. Intellectual problems may even be solved during sleep, though such instances are relatively rare. Here are some famous examples: Friedrich August Kekulé, a German chemist, literally dreamed up the structure of the benzene ring, and thus arrived at one of the landmark discoveries in chemistry. The Danish physicist Niels Bohr dreamed of being on a sun composed of burning gas while planets attached by thin filaments revolved about it. This image led Bohr to the radically new idea that electrons orbited the nucleus of an atom only at fixed distances from it. Experiments confirmed the theory; it became one of the foundations of modern physics and led to many other discoveries. Otto Loewi, who discovered the chemical nature of nerve impulses, acknowledged that the original idea for his discovery came in a dream. In each of these examples, the day residue consisted almost entirely of the problem the scientist was trying to solve.

Day residue is certainly an important source of dream material. It may be more important than we think; even a passing perception, memory, feeling, or thought, though scarcely noticed at the time, may find its way into a dream that night. We wonder, for example, why we dream about a person we have not thought of for years. The explanation may be that the day before the dream we saw someone or something that unconsciously reminded us of the person—perhaps someone who walked the same way.

Past Experience. Memories of experiences, even those of early childhood, also may contribute material to dreams. Anything—a stimulus from the body or the environment during sleep, a recent experience, an element in the dream, or any number of other events—may revive a memory of the distant past, which then appears in the dream. Some writers on the subject have even suggested that memories laid down in the fetal brain or during birth can appear in a dream.

Jung theorized that some dreams contain *archetypal* material— memories that are derived not from the dreamer's life but from his ancestral past. Jung argued that the brain of modern man contains features that link him to early man and even to his prehuman ancestors. Therefore, certain dream images reflect these inherited predispositions. For example, since Jung's shadow archetype represents man's animal impulses, he proposed that animals appearing in dreams symbolize the shadow. When the shadow is repressed in waking life, it expresses itself in dreams, according to Jung. A common shadow dream is one in which the dreamer is being pursued or attacked by a wild animal.

In this connection, it may be significant that children often dream about animals; the younger they are, the more frequently they dream about them (see Figure 9–7). For example, animals appear in about two-thirds of the dreams of 4-year-old children. By age 15, the proportion of animal dreams has decreased to about one in ten (Van de Castle, 1971). Is the great number of animal dreams in children due to remnants of the ancestral or even animal past? It is conceivable, but so are other explanations.

External Stimuli. One obvious source of dream imagery are the stimuli that act upon the person while he is sleeping. If they do not awaken the sleeper, they may be incorporated into a dream. We say "incorporated" because there is little reason to suppose that such stimuli *cause* us to dream. Many experiments have been conducted in this area since the initial ones were performed over 100 years ago. A variety of stimuli have been used, including touch, sound, light, vibration, odor, cold and warm objects, words, hunger, and thirst. The consensus of these experiments is that some stimuli are more effective than others in influencing the contents of dreams, but that in nearly all instances the influence on the dream is slight or unimportant.

9-7

Graph of the relationship between age and the percentage of animal dreams. N = the total number of dreams reported. (From Robert L. Van de Castle, *The Psychology of Dreaming,* © 1971, General Learning Corporation. Reprinted by permission.)

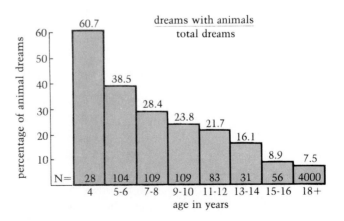

Physiological States. Special conditions in a person's life may affect his or her dreams. Dreams collected from pregnant women and from women during their menstrual cycles have been analyzed (Van de Castle, 1971). Women do not begin to dream about their pregnant condition until the last few months of pregnancy. They often dream then that the baby is magically delivered (wish fulfillment?) and that it possesses the ability to walk and talk. Pregnant women also may have terrifying dreams that their baby is born dead or deformed or is animal rather than human. Dreams during menstruation reflect preoccupation with the body and with babies, an identification with mothers, and friendly feelings toward other females together with a decrease in friendly feelings toward males.

In conclusion, we may say that many different sources—events of the day, memories, external stimuli, physiological states, and maybe even ancestral experiences—contribute to the formation of dreams.

Symbolism

Throughout history, people have believed that dreams contain a great deal of symbolism. Dream interpreters and dream books have claimed the ability to decode the symbolic elements of dreams, often for the purpose of forecasting the future. The first dream book appeared nearly 2,000 years ago and such books are still being published. Official dream interpreters still practice in many parts of the world. For example, the Cuna Indians, who live on the San Blas Islands near Panama's east coast, have dream interpreters called *Neles* (see Figure 9-8).

Freud and Jung are the modern authorities on dream symbolism. Indeed, the term "Freudian symbols" has become synonymous with sexual symbols. Snakes, guns, trees, bananas, pens, swords, towers, poles, to name only a few objects, are considered "Freudian symbols" for the penis; rings, caves, flowers, tunnels, rooms, and doorways are "Freudian symbols" for the vagina. This is a very oversimplified conception of Freud's treatment of symbols in dreams. He identified many other kinds of symbols in addition to sexual ones—for example, an authority figure such as an army officer or judge for father; cow for mother; black for death; room for woman; loss of a tooth for birth. Moreover, Freud did not emphasize the process of symbolization in dreams as much as some of his followers. In fact, Jung had much more to say about symbolism than Freud.

Denotative and Metaphorical Symbols

Before considering Freud's and Jung's views on symbolism, let us first define a _symbol_ as something that stands for something else. A word is a symbol because it stands for something—an object, an activity, a quality, or an abstraction. Numbers also are symbols; so are pictures, facial expressions, and gestures. Thoughts, memories, and perceptions also may be symbols because they stand for something else. Dream

9-8
Nele Obaldia is a Cuna Indian from Tigre Island. He uses the Uchus figures for dream interpretations. The Uchus, or boot shoe as they are also called, lead Nele to the underworld, where the dream is interpreted.

images, too, stand for something else: they are pictures of people and things and activities.

The "something else" that a symbol stands for is called the _referent_ for the symbol. The referent for the word _cat_, or a picture of a cat, or a dream image of a cat, is an animal with certain physical characteristics. The referent for a plus sign is the act of adding. The referent for a perception is the object that is perceived or the act of perceiving. This kind of symbolism, which refers specifically and literally to an object or event, is called _denotative symbolism_; that is, the symbol denotes a particular object, process, or event.

But denotative symbolism is _not_ what we mean when we refer to dream symbolism. To say a snake is a symbol for the penis is obviously not the same as saying that an image of a snake represents a snake. A snake is not a penis—a snake _resembles_ a penis in some respects, and consequently becomes a symbol for the penis. This is called _metaphorical symbolism_. A metaphorical symbol is one that stands for something other than what it appears to be. If you say black is a symbol of death, white is a symbol of purity, and red is a symbol of passion, you are speaking in metaphors. Metaphors are often referred to as figures of speech.

We use metaphors in waking life when we wish to communicate a meaning, a feeling, an idea, or an attitude about something. King Macbeth, stricken with grief by the sudden death of his queen, expresses his view of life's futility in metaphoric language: "Life's but a walking shadow, a poor player, That struts and frets his hour upon the stage, And then is heard no more. It is a tale told by an idiot, full of sound and fury, signifying nothing."

A metaphor is particularly useful when we wish to connote a complex of meanings and feelings with a simple, economical expression or image. Jung, for example, regarded the ocean as a symbol for the unconscious. The ocean is large and deep, its depths are hidden, and it contains many creatures dangerous to man. In Jung's eyes, large, deep, hidden, and dangerous also characterize the unconscious.

Metaphor is the language of poetry, art, and drama. By writing metaphorically, a poet can compress several meanings into one word or phrase, enabling the reader to infer and experience a wide variety of moods and emotions while reading a poem. Denotative symbols, on the other hand, are the language of science, practical affairs, and everyday discourse.

Let us refine this distinction between the two kinds of symbols, denotative and metaphorical. Here is a simple example. In the sentence, "The dog chases the cat," the words _dog_ and _cat_ stand for two kinds of animals. One can point to them or draw pictures of them. They are purely denotative symbols without any surplus meaning. But if one says of a person, "He is a dog," or "She is a cat," it is clear that the words are being used metaphorically and not denotatively. By using the name of an animal, the speaker intends to express a particular attitude about the person. What this attitude is depends on the speaker's conception of the animal. If he conceives of a dog as a lowly, brutish creature, then the person he calls a dog is regarded by him as having these qualities.

9-9
Poets frequently use metaphorical symbols drawn from nature to describe the female body. An extravagant example is a passage from Shakespeare's *Venus and Adonis*, in which Venus is trying to entice Adonis to make love to her. She likens her body to a park and Adonis to a deer:

Feed where thou wilt, on mountain or in dale;
Graze on my lips; and if those hills be dry,
Stray lower, where the pleasant fountains lie.
Within this limit is relief enough,
Sweet bottom-grass, and high delightful plain,
Round rising hillocks, brakes obscure and rough,
To shelter thee from tempest and from rain.

To Venus's dismay, Adonis is not moved by her poetic images and leaves her to go boar hunting. (National Museum, Stockholm)

The expression "son of a bitch" conveys this disparaging attitude in even stronger language, since the insult implicates the person's mother. When a woman is called a cat or catty, it is clearly intended to be uncomplimentary. Pussy, however, carries a sexual connotation, as does the term "cathouse." Kitten, on the other hand, implies cuteness.

To call a man a fox means he is sly and cunning because those are supposed to be attributes of a fox. Wolf has become a standard expression for a man who is sexually aggressive; chicken symbolizes a coward, hawk a warlike person, dove a peace-loving person, owl a wise individual, and goat a victim, as in scapegoat. The distinction between a denotative symbol and a metaphorical symbol is depicted in Table 9-3.

Table 9-3   Comparison of Denotative and Metaphorical Symbols

Symbol	Example	Referent
denotative	The word *fox*	The animal *fox*
metaphorical	The idea of a person as being crafty (foxy*)	The idea of a fox as being crafty

* Foxy also is used to refer to girls as a variant of sexy

The relation of a denotative symbol to its referent is usually arbitrary. A fox could be called by another name, and is in other languages. The relation of a metaphorical symbol to its referent is not arbitrary. Some recognizable identity must exist between the idea of the symbol and the idea of the referent. A person's conception of someone whom he calls a fox agrees with his conception of that animal's characteristics. Misunderstandings arise among people when their ideas of the referent object differ. For example, a goat is sometimes thought of as a lecherous animal—hence, the expression "He's an old goat"—and sometimes as a victim. Such different views could lead to misunderstanding.

Freud's Theory of Symbolism

Why do dreams contain metaphorical symbols? Freud gave two answers. One answer is his famous *disguise theory*. Dream symbols serve to conceal the true meaning of the dreamer's thoughts from himself. If he were to dream openly of sexual or aggressive referents, it would make him feel so anxious that he would awaken. In other words, symbols are the guardians of sleep. Freud's other answer was that an idea or attitude cannot appear in a dream unless it is converted into a visual image. Therefore, abstract thoughts and feelings must be represented in concrete terms. For example, a person's conception of the male sex organ as something frightening is abstract. Thus, that person may dream of a more concrete image, such as a gun. If the dreamer's conception of the penis is that it is something natural, growing, and sturdy, then the dream may be about a tree. Both gun and tree, in this context, can be seen as disguise symbols for the penis as well as visual representations of abstract attitudes.

Slang Expressions and Dream Symbols

Varying conceptions of the same object are common, not only in dreams but also in the slang we use in everyday speech. Slang is almost entirely metaphorical, and the metaphors of slang also are found in dreams. To show this relationship, an investigator (Hall, 1964) went through a dictionary of slang and noted every expression for the male and female genitals. Classified under a number of headings, he found 200 such terms for the male and 330 for the female. Next, he obtained a long list of dream symbols for the sex organs from published psychoanalytic reports. The dream symbols, he discovered, were classified in the same way that the slang words were classified. The two lists turned out to be remarkably similar.

In the largest class of slang words and dream symbols were those that focused on the similarity in shape between the metaphor and its referent. Phallic slang words and dream images emphasize length and hardness, while the female metaphors stress the vagina's enclosurelike quality.

Implements and machinery form a large class of phallic slang and dream symbols, but only a small class of symbols for the female. *Tool* has been a favorite expression for the penis since the middle of the 16th century and was standard English until the 18th century.

Among slang words for the male organ, there is only one (skyscraper) that refers to a building or an enclosure, but there are many such references for the female genitals (box, for example). Many more slang expressions and dream symbols for the penis have aggressive overtones than do those for the female. On the other hand, expressions and dream images drawn from the world of nature are much more frequent for the female organs than for the male organs (deflower, for example).

Slang expressions and dream symbols for sexual intercourse also have many parallels. The three most common classes of such metaphors in both slang and dreams are:

1. words or images that have an aggressive connotation,

2. words or images describing a mechanical action,

3. words or images referring to the physical work involved.

This study suggests that the metaphorical images of dreams and the metaphorical meaning of words *reveal* the thoughts and feelings rather than conceal them. This is what Jung thought. He did not believe in the disguise theory.

Jung's Theory of Symbolism

Jung's theory of symbolism applies not only to dream symbolism but to symbolism in waking life as well. He described the basic theory in this statement:

The symbol is not a sign that veils something everybody knows. Such is not its significance; on the contrary, it represents an attempt to elucidate, by means of analogy, something that still belongs entirely to the domain of the unknown or something that is yet to be. (Jung, 1916)

What is this "unknown or something that is yet to be"? It is man's psyche—his whole personality, or his selfhood, as Jung preferred to call it. As we noted earlier, Jung saw dream symbols as attempts to clarify the psyche's needs and point the way to its complete development and integration. To achieve a degree of selfhood, Jung prescribed that all aspects or components of the personality must become fully individuated (developed). The interpretation of symbols, whether they appear in dreams or waking life, can help us become more familiar with the unknown or neglected aspects of our personality.

Suppose, for example, a merchant spends his waking life being friendly and congenial, assisting and pleasing his customers, never offending them, and accepting criticism with a smile. However, when he dreams at night, his dreams are violent and aggressive; he shouts at people, insults them, and even assaults them. Jung would say that such dreams express an aspect of his personality that is not allowed expression in waking life. As long as this side of him is kept from individuation, he will be unable to achieve complete selfhood.

Techniques for Analyzing Symbols

Freud and Jung deserve major credit for counteracting the view that dreams are meaningless. They believed that every dream, no matter how senseless it might seem, has a meaning. What is more important, they developed methods for discovering the meaning of dreams. Freud distinguished between two types of dream content. _Manifest content_ is the dream as dreamed and recalled; _latent content_ consists of the thoughts and feelings out of which the manifest content is constructed. During the formation of the manifest dream, the latent thoughts and feelings undergo condensation, displacement, and symbolization. The object of Freud's technique of free association is to undo the condensations, displacements, and symbolizations, and by so doing to disclose the latent thoughts and feelings. Such latent elements constitute the dream's real significance. In other words, free association reverses the process of dream formation. Free association starts with the elements of the dream as dreamed and ends with the latent elements. Dream formation starts with the latent elements and ends with the manifest dream.

Freud's Free Association Method

Freud's method of dream interpretation is called _free association._ Free association also is used to disclose the symbolic significance of experiences in waking life. Both uses are vital to psychoanalysis.

In free association, a dream is broken down into its basic elements, and then the dreamer says whatever comes to mind about each element, providing clues to the significance of the dream elements. Using the free-association method, a young unmarried girl who was undergoing treatment for anxiety attacks related the following dream:

An elephant was chasing me. I ran home but the door was locked and I couldn't get in.

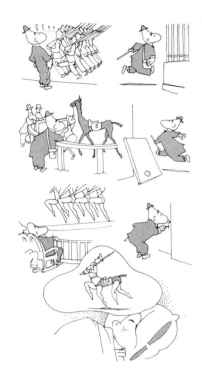

9-10
Cartoon depicting Freud's theory that day residue is condensed in dreams. (Angel Garma, 1966)

Her associations to the first sentence were as follows:

I'm afraid of elephants. Their long, snakelike trunks and little mean eyes terrify me. My father took me to a circus when I was little. There were lots of elephants. They climbed on each other's backs. They waved their long trunks in the air and made loud trumpeting noises. I was scared and I cuddled close to my father. His breath smelled bad and his eyes were half-closed and bloodshot. I guess he was drunk. He often was. I cried and wanted to go home. My father was a great big man. He had dark gray hair and a long red nose. I used to be afraid of him.

To the second sentence she gave the following associations:

I guess I was running home to my mother. She used to protect me from my father when I was a child. When I became older, she didn't seem to care about me anymore. She didn't care about anything except her little dog, Snooky. She shut us all out of her life.

From these associations, the dreamer arrived at the following interpretation of the dream:

The elephant is my father who is chasing me. I run to my mother for protection but she has locked me out.

Jung's Method of Amplification

Jung developed another method for interpreting dreams. *Amplification* requires the person to concentrate on a dream element and to produce a set of responses that are directly related to that element. The result is a cluster of associations around a dream element instead of a line of associations — as in free association — that may lead far afield from the original element.

In free association, the dreamer alone produces the associations. In amplification, the analyst also may contribute material. Ancient writings, mythologies, religious texts, fairy tales, and other sources may be consulted to provide additional information about the dream element.

Here is an example in which the analyst performed all of the amplification (Meier, 1959). The patient dreamed that he was fishing in a reservoir divided into compartments, but he was not catching anything.

Becoming exasperated, I took up a three-pronged spear and immediately succeeded in spearing a fine fish.

The element to be amplified was the three-pronged spear. A three-pronged spear, called a trident, is associated with the Greek god Poseidon (Neptune in Roman mythology). Poseidon has many roles; he is god of the sea and co-equal with Zeus and Hades in ruling the Cosmos. He is also the god of earthquakes, which he produces by driving his trident into the earth. Every time he uses the trident, something creative happens; a spring wells out of the earth, or a valley opens between the hills. Poseidon is the god of storms and a stormy lover. He has affairs with all sorts of creatures, producing many offspring. He is the god of the earth, responsible for the fertility of the soil. He created the first

9-11
Poseidon (or Neptune) depicted as god of the sea. With his trident he controls all natural events, according to Greek mythology. (New York Public Library)

horse by using his trident. He is called the father of men. In short, Poseidon is a creative god, and the trident is his creative tool. Although in this case, the analyst interpreted the significance of the three-pronged spear, it is clear that the patient must also have unconsciously associated this symbol with creative powers, since, in his dream, use of the spear allowed him to "create" a solution to the frustrating fishing problem.

Amplification of this dream element was a key step in individuating the patient's creative abilities, symbolized by the trident. The development of his abilities began a healing process which led to his recovery from a serious, three-year depression.

Analysis of dreams by free association and amplification provided Freud and Jung with useful information with which to help their patients recover from disturbances and lead richer lives.

Dream Series Method and Content Analysis

Another method has been developed for analyzing the dreams of any person, whether in psychotherapy or not. In the _dream series method_, the dreamer keeps a record of his dreams until he has accumulated 50 to 100; he then looks for recurrent themes and preoccupations, checking one dream against the others until a meaningful pattern emerges, much as you complete a jigsaw puzzle.

You also can use another kind of analysis that yields more quantitative and objective information than a purely impressionistic or qualitative analysis. _Content analysis_ uses sets of categories into which the dream elements can be placed. For example, many different characters will appear in a series of dreams. They can be classified as males and females; relatives, friends, and strangers; children and adults; fictional and supernatural characters; and animals. After classifying the characters in a series of dreams, you can determine what kinds of interactions you have with each of these classes of characters, or with specific individuals who appear frequently in the dream series. The interactions may be friendly, aggressive, quarrelsome, sexual, or neutral. Presumably, the more often you dream about a person or a class of people, the greater your preoccupation with that person or class. Your dream interactions with these recurring types of people will reveal your feelings about them.

Objects appearing in dreams and the dreamer's interactions with them can be analyzed in the same way. This reveals how the dreamer conceives of the world of physical objects. For example, a young surfer's dream diary contained many dreams of the ocean, most of which were frightening. He dreamed of being attacked by sharks, of losing his surfboard, of crashing on rocks, and other catastrophes. Rarely did he have a good time in his surfing dreams. These dreams suggest that behind his avid interest in surfing lay a fear of what might happen to him in the water.

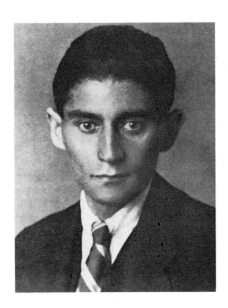

9-12
Franz Kafka (1883–1924), author of *The Castle, The Trial, The Metamorphosis, The Penal Colony,* and many other writings, recorded 37 of his dreams in his diaries and letters. A content analysis of these dreams revealed seven major themes:

1. Preoccupation with the body
2. Body disfigurement
3. Emphasis on clothing and nakedness
4. Looking (voyeurism)
5. Passivity
6. Ambivalent feelings toward men and women
7. Masculinized women

Kafka's preoccupation with these subjects spilled over into waking life and into some of his writings.

Methods for Detecting Symbols

Most authorities agree that dreams contain metaphorical symbols just as do poetry and slang. But how do we know whether a dream element is a symbol or simply what it appears to be? In general, any bizarre or unusual image, or anything that is illogical in the dream, may be symbolic. Animals in general, except for one's own pets, often are symbolic. But to say that a dream image is symbolic is merely to state a hypothesis that must be verified. Next, we will look at some methods for detecting and interpreting symbolism in dreams.

Hypnosis

One method for detecting and deciphering symbols employs *hypnotism* (Moss, 1967, 1970). It is suggested to a person under hypnosis that he will have a dream in which a referent will be represented by a metaphor. The type of metaphor is not suggested to him. For example, a hypnotized man was told he would have a dream of sexual intercourse. He reported the following dream:

This fellow and girl go horseback riding. They're taking it easy, just riding along. Then, the girl decides to race her horse. He races his. They race for a mile. Both horses are foaming. The fellow and the girl are laughing.

Another hypnotized man was told to dream about masturbation. He dreamed as follows:

This fellow's taking an exam. It's a very hard exam. He gets tense. As he looks at the paper he gets more tense. His face gets flushed and his hand begins to shake. He knocks the paper and pencil off the desk and drops his head on the desk from exhaustion.

Such experiments help to confirm the reliability and accuracy of dream interpretation by reversing the process—that is, they move from explicit meaning to metaphor, while dream interpretations move the other way.

Another procedure is to take an element from an actual dream and ask a hypnotized person to decipher it. Some people are able to do this. A young woman was given the following instructions after she had been hypnotized: "Dreams have meaning. Now that you are asleep you will be better able to understand them. A girl dreamed that she was packing her trunk when a big snake crawled into it. She was terrified and ran out of the room. What do you think the dream means?" The hypnotized girl replied, "Well, I guess she was afraid of being seduced. The snake would be the man's sex organ and the trunk hers."

Several hypnotized individuals were given this dream to interpret: "A boy was sitting at his desk studying when the wastebasket caught fire. He ran and got a pitcher of water and put the fire out." Their responses were "He wet the bed," or "He should have gone to the bathroom."

The Occurrence of Wet Dreams

Another indication of the referents of symbols is found in some dreams that accompany nocturnal emissions ("wet dreams"). A man dreamed that he removed a large cap from a fire hydrant and water gushed out; he

9-13

This graph shows that single males between the ages of 16 and 20 who have been to college have almost three times as many wet dreams as those who have been only to elementary school. Kinsey offers the explanation that more imaginative people have more wet dreams. He also notes that those who have been to college have fewer outlets for sexual intercourse than those with only an elementary school education. (Kinsey, Pomeroy, & Martin, 1948)

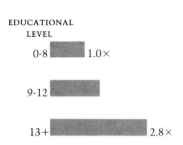

EDUCATIONAL
LEVEL

0-8 1.0×

9-12

13+ 2.8×

woke up having an emission. The emission proves pretty conclusively that the water gushing out of the hydrant is sexual symbolism. However, most wet dreams are not metaphorical—they occur when a person is dreaming about having sexual relations. Nor does a gushing fire hydrant necessarily refer to sex in every dream in which it appears. Most dream images are probably not symbolic in a metaphorical sense. They are usually literal denotations of referent objects and events.

Word Derivations

Sometimes the derivation of a word may give a clue to the symbolism of a dream image. A young woman dreamed she went with her boyfriend to a dance. He bought her a carnation. They entered the ballroom in high spirits, attracting everyone's attention. To her dismay, the dreamer saw blood on her white evening gown and found that it was dripping from the carnation. The flower was bleeding! They left the ballroom in great embarrassment.

Even the etymology of the word *carnation* suggests that this dream image refers either to menstruation or to defloration. Carnation is derived from the Latin *carnis,* which means flesh. Other English words from the same root are *carnal* and *incarnation.* The flesh was bleeding and staining her purity and virginity, as represented by the white dress. You may be interested in looking up the etymology of another flower name, the *orchid,* a flower which is given by a man to a woman as a token of affection.

How Many Meanings May a Symbol Have?

Many dream books assume that a symbol has only one meaning or referent. It is not difficult to prove this is incorrect. One person's dream image often has different meanings in successive dreams. An image is even less likely to mean the same thing for two different dreamers.

For example, the automobile is commonly thought of as a sex symbol; advertisements often stress this theme. The dream series method is one way to test whether the automobile is *solely* a sex symbol or whether it has other meanings as well. In one series of 652 dreams, automobiles figured in 77. In these dreams, themes of destruction and obstruction predominated. In 25 dreams, there was a threatened accident or an actual accident. Cars skidded, ran off the road, plunged over cliffs, overturned, caught fire, collided, and ran into objects or pedestrians. In 21 dreams, an automobile was unable to proceed or reach its destination. It was stopped by a traffic light, halted by police, had a flat tire, lost a wheel, ran out of gas, lacked power, or encountered an obstacle. Sexual activity took place in 12 of the automobile dreams. In the rest, the automobile played neutral or varied roles. In several dreams, the car was associated with pleasant activities.

If the automobile is regarded strictly as a sexual symbol, it could be argued that even the themes of destruction and obstruction are related to sexuality. An accident could represent punishment to the dreamer for having sexual thoughts; a defect in the car could signify the dreamer's feeling of sexual impotence or inadequacy or inferiority. An obstruction could mean that the dreamer felt blocked or inhibited in his sexual life. If these interpretations were correct, it would still indicate that the dreamer has various conceptions of his sexuality, including feelings that it is bad, pleasant, satisfying, inadequate, defective, or dangerous. But any highly charged symbol, such as the automobile seems to be, probably stands for many other things in addition to sexuality.

Semantic Differential Technique

Words, as we have said, are denotative symbols. They have specific, meaningful referents. But words also can have associations in addition to their literal, explicit referents. For example, the word *lion* may not only bring to mind a specific animal but also carry such meanings as strong, dominant, majestic, and ferocious. Such associations or *connotations* underlie and make possible the use of the word or image of a lion as a metaphorical symbol. We saw earlier how a young woman had free-associated elephants with her father. Her connotations of "elephant" agreed with her connotations of "father," so she could use an image of an elephant in a dream to stand for some frightening characteristics of her father.

A special technique has been devised to measure the connotative meanings of words. The *semantic differential technique* (Osgood, Suci, & Tannenbaum, 1957) consists of locating a word (usually a noun) on a number of descriptive 7-point scales. The ends of each scale are bipolar adjectives (they have opposite meanings). Here are some examples:

1	2	3	4	5	6	7
rough						smooth

1	2	3	4	5	6	7
ugly						beautiful

1	2	3	4	5	6	7
small						large

To discover what connotative meanings a word has for a person, he rates the word on each of the scales. For example, he might give lion a rating of 2 on the rough—smooth scale, a rating of 5 on the ugly—beautiful scale, and a rating of 6 on the small—large scale. The word lion has for him the connotations of being fairly large, rough, and somewhat beautiful. The semantic differential scale can accurately determine what words have similar connotations for a person. Thus it provides another method for decoding metaphorical symbols in dreams by showing that the connotations for the symbol are the same as the connotations for the referent.

Research using the semantic differential technique has turned up an interesting finding: the innumerable scales of contrasting adjectives can be reduced to three basic dimensions of meaning. The three dimensions are *evaluation* (good—bad, pleasant—unpleasant, homely—pretty); *potency* (strong—weak); and *activity* (active—passive). Other dimensions exist, but they do not carry much weight. For every person, *any* word

9-14

A large number of people of both sexes were asked to rate the words *man* and *woman* on the scale at the right. These ratings were correlated along the three dimensions of meaning: evaluative (good—bad), potency (strong—weak), and activity (active—passive). The averages of all the ratings were as follows (Jenkins, Russell, & Suci, 1958):

	Evalu-ative	Potency	Active
man	.44	.81	.94
woman	.99	−.71	1.67

Note that women are viewed as being better, less strong, and more active than men. It is interesting that when the words *male* and *female* are rated, males are viewed as more active than females. And when the words *masculinity* and *femininity* are rated, masculinity is rated as being slightly better than femininity.

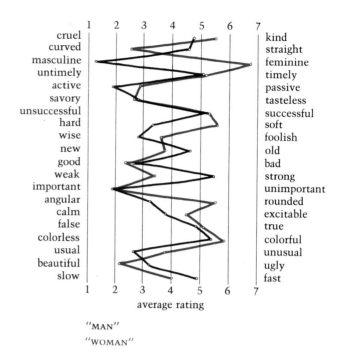

"MAN"

"WOMAN"

9-15

The Yin-Yang symbol, which represents the union of opposites. To Jung, this symbol represented the integration of each person's masculinity and femininity.

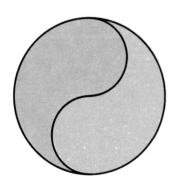

has some degree of goodness or badness, strength or weakness, and activity or passivity. By averaging the ratings made by a large number of individuals, a word can be located in three-dimensional semantic space—that is, along the dimensions of evaluation, potency, and activity. In a recently published semantic atlas (Snider & Osgood, 1969), one can look up the three connotative dimensions for each of 550 common words (mostly nouns). Many words seem to have about the same connotations in various languages.

An investigation of the meanings ascribed to the ancient Chinese Yin-Yang symbol (Craddick, Thumin, & Barclay, 1971) proved to be an interesting application of the semantic differential technique. In Chinese lore, this symbol represents the union of opposites, especially masculinity and femininity. In Jungian psychology, the Yin-Yang symbol represents the *anima* (femininity) and the *animus* (masculinity), which Jung regarded as inborn archetypes.

The symbol shown in Figure 9-15 was projected on a screen before 242 college students, who rated it on a 1 to 7 scale for each of 30 bipolar adjectives. When their ratings were averaged, the symbol was found to have the following connotations: good, beautiful, pleasant, happy, serene, relaxed, quiet, strong, and powerful. These are the feelings that the Yin-Yang symbol is supposed to arouse in the spectator. The average rating on the masculinity—femininity scale was right at the midpoint, which indicates that the figure does incorporate the concepts of both maleness and femaleness, just as it is supposed to.

Because it is objective, quantitative, and easily administered, the semantic differential technique should prove to be a very useful tool in studies of symbolism. Subjects seem to have no difficulty locating any word on the scales and even appear to enjoy the task.

The Status of Research on Dreams and Symbols

Until recently, dreams and dreaming have been surrounded by an aura of mysticism and superstition. The scientific study of dreams began as early as 1861 when a French scientist, A. Maury, published his experiments on the influence of external stimuli on dreams. But it was not until the appearance of Freud's *The Interpretation of Dreams* in 1900 that the subject began to interest psychologists. Even then, dreams were associated with the treatment of mentally disturbed people. Moreover, dreaming was thought to be too subjective for scientific study.

Starting in the 1950s with the discovery of REM sleep, various dream experiments now can be performed under laboratory conditions. As a result the study of dreaming has become more scientifically respectable.

The introduction of quantitative methods for the analysis of dream content has also helped to make the subject of dreams a more scientific enterprise. By using content analysis, investigators can dispense with the methods of free association and amplification, which are cumbersome to use outside the psychoanalytic situation.

Laboratory investigations of dreams and quantitative content analysis have shifted interest from the dreams of people in psychoanalysis to the dreams of all types of people.

Although psychologists have made considerable progress in this century toward an understanding of the meaning of dreams, much remains to be done on this frontier of contemporary psychology. When this frontier has been pushed back further, we shall have a clearer picture of how the mind and brain function. Meanwhile, the analysis of dreams can help us gain a better understanding of ourselves and of others.

Summary

1. Dreaming is a distinctive kind of cognitive activity. A dream consists of images, usually visual in character and often vivid. Dream events may be bizarre.

2. Dreams are hallucinations because they are experienced by the dreamer as if they were real perceptions.

3. Laboratory studies have proven that everyone dreams, but people differ greatly in their ability to recall dreams.

4. Many theories of the function of dreams have been proposed. These include tension-reduction, guarding of sleep, wish fulfillment, compensation, and problem-solving.

5. Common dream topics are aggression, misfortune, sex, eating, finding money, and being nude. Unpleasant dreams are more common than pleasant ones.

6. Each person has his own unique pattern of dream content. The content of these dreams comes from a variety of sources: day residue, early memories, external stimulations and bodily changes during sleep, and

possibly from paranormal sources, fetal experiences, and inherited archetypes.

7. There are two kinds of symbols: denotative and metaphorical. A denotative symbol is a reference to a specific object or event. A metaphorical symbol stands for something other than what it appears to be.

8. According to Freud's theory of symbolism, dreams are symbolic because the latent thoughts are too painful to be allowed into consciousness. Also, dreams must be symbolic because abstract ideas must be converted into visual images.

9. Jung's theory of symbolism states that symbols represent our psychic needs—the parts of our personality that need to become individuated in order for us to achieve selfhood, the full development and integration of our personality.

10. Several methods for decoding symbols have been used. In Freud's method of free association, the dreamer mentions everything that occurs to him in relation to each element of the dream. Freud analyzed dreams by determining the latent content underlying the manifest content.

11. Jung's method of amplification involves analysis, by patient and therapist, of each element of the dream or waking thought. Jung proposed that symbols represent elements of the individual's personality that are hidden from consciousness and inhibit individuation; the unconscious is attempting to elucidate these elements by means of analogy.

12. In the dream series method, the individual keeps a dream diary and attempts to identify recurring characters, events, and themes.

13. Content analysis is a more scientific version of the dream series method. The dreamer categorizes people and objects and the types of interactions he has with each category of people and objects.

14. To determine whether a dream element is actually symbolic, psychologists have used hypnotism, word derivations, and the semantic differential technique.

15. The semantic differential technique characterizes words along three connotative dimensions: evaluation, potency, and activity.

Important Terms

scanning hypothesis

REM period

non-REM period

imagery

hallucination

tension-reduction theory of dreaming

wish-fulfillment theory

compensatory theory

selfhood

individuation

shadow

problem-solving theory of dreaming

precognition

mental telepathy

clairvoyance

day residue

archetype

denotative symbol

metaphorical symbol

referent

disguise theory of symbolism

free association

amplification

dream series method

content analysis

hypnosis

semantic differential technique

Suggested Readings

FARADAY, A. *Dream power.* New York: Coward, McCann 1972.

FARADAY, A. *The dream game.* New York: Harper & Row, 1974.
These two books present a clear account of how a person can constructively analyze and interpret his own dreams for use in his waking life.

FREUD, S. *The interpretation of dreams* (1900). Standard edition, vols. IV & V. London: Hogarth Press, 1953.
This book is considered to be one of the most influential books of the 20th century. It contains not only a theory of dreams but also a theory of the mind. Freud felt it was his most significant work.

HADFIELD, J. A. *Dreams and nightmares.* Baltimore: Penguin, 1954.
A very readable and compact survey of the literature on dreams.

HALL, C. S. *The meaning of dreams.* New York: McGraw-Hill, 1966.
A nontechnical explanation of how dreams can be analyzed. Dream reports are used to enhance the discussion. A number of common themes and conflicts that are expressed in dreams are described.

HALL, C. S., & NORDBY, V. J. *The individual and his dreams.* New York: New American Library, 1972.
A nontechnical description of how the elements of a series of dreams can be analyzed quantitatively. It also deals with the question of symbols in dreams and their relation to symbols in waking life.

JUNG, C. G. *Man and his symbols.* New York: Doubleday, 1964.
The first chapter in this book contains an excellent description of Jung's ideas about dreams and symbols. Readable and beautifully illustrated.

LUCE, G., & SEGAL, J. *Sleep.* New York: Coward, McCann, 1966.
A nontechnical exposition of recent discoveries regarding the nature of sleep and its relation to dreaming.

MACKENZIE, N. *Dreams and dreaming.* London: Aldus, 1966.
An excellent survey of the subject. This book is written for the general reader and is well illustrated.

OSWALD, I. *Sleep.* Baltimore: Penguin, 1966.
A general discussion of sleep, by a leading figure in laboratory studies of sleep.

VAN DE CASTLE, R. L. *The psychology of dreaming.* Morristown, N.J.: General Learning Corp., 1971.
A short, authoritative survey of contemporary dream research, written for the beginning student. The author has made many important contributions to our knowledge of dreams.

WITKIN, H. A., & LEWIS, H. B. *Experimental studies of dreaming.* New York: Random House, 1967.
An interesting description of a number of recent experiments on dreams. Particular attention is paid to the effects of presleep experiences on dream content.

Chapter 10 Motivation

And a homeless hungry man, driving the roads with his wife beside him and his thin children in the back seat, could look at the fallow fields which might produce food but not profit, and that man could know a fallow field is a sin and the unused land a crime against the thin children. And such a man drove along the roads and knew temptation at every field, and knew the lust to take these fields and make them grow strength for his children and a little comfort for his wife. The temptation was before him always. The fields goaded him, and the company ditches with good water flowing were a goad to him.

And in the south he saw the golden oranges hanging on the trees, the little golden oranges on the dark green trees; and guards with shotguns patrolling the lines so a man might not pick an orange for a thin child, oranges to be dumped if the price was low.

He drove his old car into a town. He scoured the farms for work. Where can we sleep the night?

—John Steinbeck
(*Grapes of Wrath*)

Motivation

In order to prepare yourself for the subject matter of this chapter on motivation, you may wish to give some thought to the following questions or others like them. Why are you reading this book? Why are you attending college? Why are you planning to go home this weekend? Why do you like to drive fast? Why are you attracted to some people and not to others? Why do you like to do some things and not others?

All of these questions have one thing in common: They ask you to think about your motives or reasons for doing something. The answers to some of these questions are quite simple, or at least appear to be simple. For other questions, the answers are more complex. Some activities satisfy a number of different desires. Climbing a mountain, for example, may give us a sense of well-being, fulfill our cravings for physical activity, achievement, recognition, and adventure, and compensate for feelings of inferiority and frustration.

Exploring motives is a fascinating and difficult task, for they can be so obscure that we are not aware of them. Sometimes we think we are doing something for one reason when actually we are doing it for another reason. Sometimes we misrepresent our motives to other people because we want to make a favorable impression on them. Psychologists call this _rationalization_, an attempt to justify our actions by giving socially acceptable reasons for them. Through rationalization, we may even deceive ourselves about the real motives for our behavior.

In this chapter, we shall examine the nature of human motives and the role they play in determining our behavior. We shall begin by presenting some of the definitions and characteristics of motivated behavior, then we shall discuss the major issues and theories that have grown out of scientific studies of human motivation.

Motivation Defined

A _motive_ is anything that initiates behavior. There are two classes of motives: _drives_ (or _needs_) and _incentives_. Drives are incitements to action. Drives that have their origin in identifiable, internal organic processes are called _primary_ or _unlearned drives_. Hunger is an example.

Other drives are acquired through learning; competition is an example of a _learned drive_. As we shall see, many motives involve both learned and unlearned components.

Incentives are objects or conditions in the environment that stimulate behavior; they are inducements to action.

Drives and incentives usually are two sides of the same coin. Hunger causes us to look for food, and food when found invites us to eat. When we are not hungry, food ordinarily has no incentive value. But incentives also can arouse us to action without the presence of a drive. For example, we may not be hungry but the sight of strawberry shortcake or apple pie can stimulate our appetite, or we may not be feeling erotic but the sight of an attractive person can stir our interest.

Primary drives keep a person alive and healthy by satisfying the needs of the body. Learned drives serve to adjust the individual to his social environment. Desires for approval and achievement are examples of learned drives that are acquired through reinforcement from parents, teachers, and other reinforcing agents. The reinforcers that are used to implant drives in a person are incentives. Incentives are offered by our society to encourage or discourage a person from acting in a particular way; they may be either positive or negative. Positive incentives are rewards; negative incentives are punishments.

The three major characteristics of motivated behavior are arousal, direction, and a feeling of wanting or desiring. _Arousal_ is the energizing of behavior. A motive makes us more active and restless. Motivated behavior also has purpose or intention. The motivated person has _direction_, an aim or goal. The feeling of _wanting or desiring_ is experienced as tension, strain, and expectation. When the aim is achieved, tension and strain disappear, and so does the energetic activity.

Now that we have become familiar with the chief concepts of motivation, let us turn our attention to some of the major issues and investigations in this interesting and important area of psychology.

The Pleasure-Pain Principle

One of the oldest and most persistent ideas about motivation is that man pursues pleasure and avoids pain—_the pleasure-pain principle_. Freud initially made this the basis of his theory of motivation. But, like other psychologists, Freud eventually looked beyond the pleasure principle for something more basic in human nature.

The most obvious objection that psychologists have to the pleasure-pain principle is that people often behave in ways that apparently violate the principle. They seem to avoid pleasure and seek (or at least tolerate) discomfort. Martyrs are an extreme example. Joan of Arc suffered death by burning, although she could have avoided it by renouncing her beliefs. Why didn't she save herself? Because the thought of giving up her beliefs was more painful to her than her terror of the flames?

Joan of Arc's choice explains many apparent violations of the pleasure-pain principle. Pain or discomfort is endured because it is less painful or uncomfortable than the alternative. In short, pain and pleasure are relative terms; there are degrees of pain and pleasure. Two behaviors may both involve pain, yet one may be less painful than the other. A person whose death sentence is commuted to life imprisonment may be overjoyed, but a person who expects a fine may be horrified by a six-month prison sentence.

Most of us accept temporary discomforts to reap greater pleasures. Students endure the rigors of medical school to qualify for a satisfying and rewarding profession. Others practice self-denial and save their money so they can buy a car. All of us weigh discomfort *now* against pleasure *later*. For some, even a lifetime of suffering can be compensated for by the thought of an eternity of heavenly bliss.

Pleasure is often enhanced by a period of discomfort. One reason for this is the *contrast effect;* pleasure is heightened when we can contrast it with discomfort. Another reason is that some people feel guilty when gratification comes easily. They feel they should suffer discomfort before they can enjoy themselves. Such people have been taught that a person should work hard before he indulges himself. To them, pleasure requires a sacrifice; and if it is not paid before the pleasure, it has to be paid afterward.

Some people appear to have a need to suffer. They undergo unnecessary trials and tribulations, and even seek them out. Such people are called *masochists.* Their opposite numbers—those who derive pleasure from inflicting pain on others—are called *sadists.* Many people possess both masochistic and sadistic tendencies to some degree.

As our examples have demonstrated, pleasure is not limited to gratification of the senses or simple enjoyment. Working on a difficult mathematical problem may give a male mathematician much more pleasure than looking at the centerfold in *Playboy.* A lecture on atomic physics may be more pleasurable than a party to a physicist. This leads us to our next observation: One person's pleasure may be another person's pain. Pleasure and pain are subjective feelings; they cannot be observed.

The subjective, individual natures of pleasure and pain make it difficult to investigate them. Psychologists have thought of several solutions. One is to ask the person when he feels pleasure and when he feels pain or discomfort. This method is not entirely satisfactory. Not only can it be difficult to communicate subjective states, but dishonest reporting also can distort results. People often hide their private feelings when they think they are being asked to conform to someone else's expectations.

Another method psychologists have tried is to search for objective indicators of pleasure and pain. Usually the search leads the investigator into the realm of physiological variables, such as blood pressure, respiration rate, and muscle tone, all of which are thought to be associated with pleasure and discomfort. Such variables can indicate the presence of an emotional state, but they cannot tell investigators *which* emotion a subject is feeling.

Subjective states may be inferred from expressive behavior, but how accurate are the inferences? If we see a woman frowning, biting her pencil, uttering harsh words, and looking for all the world like a tormented soul, we may think she is in great pain—until we find that she is enjoying herself working out a difficult crossword puzzle. A man laughing uproariously at a party may be hiding his despair. Expressive behavior is not a dependable indicator of inner feelings.

10-1

In Old's experiments, electrodes were implanted in a rat's hypothalamus. Once the rat learns that pressing the lever will produce a pleasurable sensation, it presses the lever repeatedly, hour after hour. (James Olds)

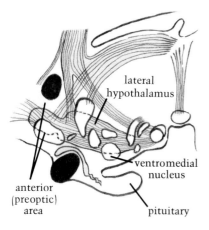

10-2

Schematic of the hypothalamus of the human brain. The lateral hypothalamus, which runs the entire length of one side of the hypothalamus, produces the greatest amount of pleasure from electrical self-stimulation.

Nor does it clarify the situation to say that pleasurable activities are those that a person engages in and painful activities are those that a person avoids. This reasoning is circular. A person does those things that give him pleasure. How do we know they give him pleasure? Because he is doing them.

Pleasure and pain are widely held to be strong motivating forces, but as we have noted, they present certain difficulties to the scientific investigator. For this reason, most psychologists prefer to use such concepts as drive, need, incentive, reward and punishment, tension reduction, and reinforcement. Nonetheless, it is virtually impossible to write about motivation without using the terms pleasure and pain or equivalent words. Moreover, recent experiments indicate that there are specific "pleasure" zones in the brain.

"Pleasure" Zones in the Brain

In 1953, James Olds, a psychologist, provided the first evidence that "pleasure" zones exist in the mammalian brain. Olds placed electrodes in certain parts of a rat's brain. When the rat was allowed to stimulate these regions with a brief electric current by pressing a lever, it would bang away at the lever hour after hour. Olds found that even a hungry rat will prefer electrical self-stimulation to eating.

Whether the rat experiences pleasure when it stimulates its brain is known only to the animal, but it is a reasonable inference—particularly since experimental stimulation of the same regions of the human brain produces pleasurable feelings. Like rats, humans will continue to shock their brains for a long time because, as they say, it feels good.

The region of the brain giving the greatest pleasure from self-stimulation is the *lateral hypothalamus*. Since this region also contains the centers for eating and drinking, the pleasure or reward value derived from electrical stimulation was first thought to be associated with the pleasures of eating and drinking. A recent experiment (Olds, Allen, & Breezy, 1971) raised some questions about this explanation. The investigators used very small electrodes and very weak currents so that the stimulus activated only a tiny region of brain tissue. The overall results were clear-cut. Stimulating one region of the hypothalamus yielded only drinking behavior. Eating behavior was induced by stimulating another region of the hypothalamus. Electrical self-stimulation was obtained from a fairly wide area which *did not overlap* completely the eating and drinking areas. This study suggests that the hunger and thirst centers in the lateral hypothalamus may be somewhat separate and distinct from the "pleasure" zone. The regions just happen to be close together anatomically, so that stimulation with large electrodes activates several regions at once.

The existence of specific "pleasure" zones in the brain—and of identifiable "pain" zones as well—suggests that the pleasure-pain doctrine may have an objective, organic basis after all.

Primary Organic Drives

Much of our daily behavior is motivated by recurrent bodily conditions that upset our equilibrium and produce discomfort. The itch-scratch reflex will illustrate and clarify the basic features of organically motivated behavior. First, a specific part of your body becomes irritated. When you feel the irritation, you scratch. The scratching removes the irritation. And you stop scratching.

Thus, organically motivated behavior progresses in a sequence of events with a well-defined beginning and end. For the sake of clarity, let us label each event in the sequence:

> Itching is the *drive source.*
>
> Scratching is the *instrumental act.*
>
> Cessation of itching is the *drive aim.*

This simple example may be generalized for all organic drives:

> Discomfort is the drive source.
>
> An instrumental act removes the discomfort.
>
> Removal of discomfort is the drive aim.

Actions motivated by the drive are called *instrumental acts* because they are instruments with which the drive aim is achieved. When objects are required to satisfy the drive source, they are called *instrumental objects*. For example, the instrumental act of scratching your itching back may require a back-scratcher as an instrumental object.

This formula applies to all organically motivated behavior. A parched throat motivates you to drink, pangs of hunger motivate you to eat, and a toothache motivates you to visit the dentist.

An organic drive's source and aim are constants; the source is always an irritation or discomfort and the aim is always to obtain relief from the irritation or discomfort. Of course, the irritation's intensity may vary from mild to extreme. The relief from irritation also may vary from slight to complete. But these are quantitative differences.

Instrumental acts and objects, on the other hand, may vary both in quality and quantity. People place virtually no limits on the means they will employ to reduce a specific discomfort. Even such a simple act as scratching may be done in various ways. The possible instrumental acts and objects for satisfying hunger are almost infinite. Consider, for example, the elaborate arrangements people make to get enough to eat or to satisfy their sex drive. Source and aim are the same for hunger and sex throughout the world, but the instrumental acts and objects vary

10-3
An astonishing variety of instrumental acts and objects are used to satisfy organic drives. These photos illustrate food-gathering techniques in three cultures. (Nancy Flowers, Bethel; Arthur Freed; Ken Heyman)

from culture to culture, from individual to individual, and even from day to day for the same individual.

The reasons for the great variation in acts and objects are numerous. They include cultural traditions, sanctions and taboos, specific learning experiences, climate and geography, availability of objects, skills and aptitudes, individual requirements, and much more. For instance, a hungry Moslem will not eat pork, and a hungry Hindu will not eat beef, because their religious beliefs forbid it. Custom is an important factor in shaping particular ways of satisfying the primary drives. When hunger becomes acute, however, food preferences tend to break down; some starving people will eat anything, even human flesh.

When a drive source, an instrumental act, and a drive aim are constants for all members of a species, usually the behavior they produce is called an _instinct_. When birds of a given species all build the same kind of nest, nest-building is said to be instinctive to them. Do human beings have instincts?

The Instinct Doctrine

Several decades ago, the British psychologist William McDougall declared that "the instincts are the prime movers of all human activity" (1921). He defined an instinct as an innate disposition "which determines its possessor to perceive, and to pay attention to, objects of a certain class, to experience an emotional excitement of a particular quality upon perceiving such an object, and to act in regard to it in a particular manner, or, at least, to experience an impulse to such action. . . . Take away these instinctive dispositions with their powerful impulses, and the organism would become incapable of activity of any kind." He then proceeded to identify the principal instincts of man: flight from danger, disgust, curiosity, pugnacity, submissiveness, self-assertion, parental care, reproduction, gregariousness, acquisition, and constructiveness.

McDougall's view of human instincts embraced two distinct concepts. First, instincts _arouse_ activity; second, they _direct_ that activity into specific instrumental ways of satisfying the instinct.

Psychologists today generally accept McDougall's arousal concept. Hunger, thirst, and sex do arouse or invigorate activity. However, they are now called _drives_ or _needs_ instead of instincts. McDougall's idea of inborn behavior patterns was rejected for a number of years in favor of a learning explanation. Humans must learn what objects to attend to and what acts to perform before they can remove the drive source. Recently, psychologists have again been asking whether primary drives inherently direct behavior as well as arouse it. Although the question is by no means settled, some evidence indicates that a primary drive state may determine the perceptions we will have and the acts we will perform _before_ any learning has taken place. For example, even before a baby learns how his actions relate to hunger pangs, hunger may focus his attention on food or food-related objects, and thus direct his efforts toward obtaining them. Some instrumental acts have been shown to be inborn. The newborn baby does not have to learn to suck—in fact, thumb-sucking has been observed in fetuses (we assume fetuses are not

10-4
This photo of a fetus sucking its thumb indicates that some behaviors are innate. (Roberts Rugh & Dr. Landrum B. Shettles)

able to learn this behavior). Future research may disclose a number of other ways in which primary drive sources are innately connected with instrumental acts and objects.

In short, we can say that some inborn primary drive sources exist, and that very likely so do some inborn instrumental ways of achieving drive satisfactions. We will explore this question further in Chapter 13. Now we will examine some of the primary drives.

The Hunger Drive

What causes a person to eat and what causes him to stop eating? The common sense answer is that he eats because he feels empty and he stops eating because he feels full. Most people think these feelings of emptiness and fullness begin in the stomach—and for a long time psychologists did too. Then people who had had their stomachs removed surgically were observed to experience perfectly normal hunger. Recent experimental findings indicate that switching centers in the brain turn eating behavior on or off. Presumably, these centers also activate the sensations of emptiness and fullness. These eating switches are triggered by blood sugar levels, body temperature, and probably other bodily conditions. The thirst centers are activated by the amount of water in the body cells.

The switches for hunger and thirst are located in the hypothalamus. Anand and Brobeck (1951) demonstrated that injury to the *lateral hypothalamus* can abolish both eating and drinking behavior. Conversely, electrical stimulation of the lateral hypothalamus in an animal that has eaten to satiation causes it to start eating again. A significant drop in blood sugar level dramatically increases the activity of neurons in the lateral hypothalamus. Thus, *decreased* blood sugar appears to stimulate activity in the lateral hypothalamus, which, in turn, switches on hunger and eating behavior.

Another important consequence of destroying the lateral hypothalamus is that the animals appear to lack general motivation. They are apathetic and inactive. Evidently, such destruction impairs motivation itself, rather than just eating and drinking behaviors.

The switch that turns *off* eating is located in another part of the hypothalamus, the *ventromedial* region. Lesions (injuries) in this region cause an animal to eat so voraciously that it becomes very fat, but stimulation of the ventromedial area through implanted electrodes inhibits eating in hungry rats. Furthermore, this part of the hypothalamus is normally activated by an *increasing* level of blood sugar. All of these observations indicate that the ventromedial hypothalamus acts as a *satiation center*. It turns off hunger and eating when sufficient food has been consumed to increase the blood sugar level.

Eating and drinking are affected by a number of other factors: habitual mealtimes, characteristics and availability of the food, family customs regarding food and drink, and many other types of learned instrumental behaviors. A person who says he is full may be tempted to eat more if he is offered something appealing. A hungry person may refuse food he finds distasteful.

10-5
The hyperphagic (fat) rat. When the lateral hypothalamus is stimulated continuously—or the ventromedial region is lesioned—the rat eats too much. It is unable to experience sensations of satiation. (Courtesy Neal E. Miller)

10-6
Humans sometimes find an advantage in being overweight. These brothers are professional wrestlers, weighing in at 700 and 720 pounds. (Wide World Photos)

Overeating. People differ in the amount of food they consume each day. Some people eat much more than their bodies require and become obese (overweight). Obesity is a hazard to health; it also can lead to personal and social maladjustments. The huge popularity of reducing programs testifies to the magnitude of the obesity problem.

Why do people overeat? One popular theory says that eating is a substitute gratification for some other unsatisfied need. A person who does not receive sufficient love and affection may make up for it by eating excessively. In one dramatic case treated by Lindner (1954), an obese young woman continually gorged herself with food. In her case, analysis revealed that she was trying to fulfill an unconscious fantasy of having a child by her father; overeating made her look pregnant. Another hypothesis is that people overeat because they are anxious, and eating reduces their anxiety.

Recently, another hypothesis has been tested both in the laboratory and in natural situations (Schachter, 1971). The hypothesis maintains that, unlike normal eaters who eat as a response to such internal cues as stomach contractions (hunger pangs) and low blood sugar, the overeater's eating is triggered by external cues. Such external cues include time of day, the appetizing sight, smell, or taste of food, the amount of food available, and the ease with which the eater can obtain food.

Several experiments were designed by Schachter to test this hypothesis, with the following results.

1. Normal eaters feel hungry only when stomach contractions are registering on the experimenter's recording instruments. The obese show no correlation between stomach contractions and hunger. They are as likely to feel hungry when their stomachs are quiet as when they are active. Neither group, of course, could see the record that was being made of their stomach contractions. This experiment proves that obese people are not responding to a normal physiological indicator of hunger, namely, stomach contractions.

2. Overweight subjects placed on an unappetizing diet for several weeks decrease their food intake, whereas those of normal weight do not. This suggests that the palatability of food is more important for the obese than it is for normal eaters. Overeaters like to eat, but they like to eat well. Restricting overweight people to an uninteresting diet is one method that helps them reduce.

3. The amount of food obese people eat is determined by the amount available. Overeaters consume everything on their plates, provided it is tasty. Normal eaters are not influenced by the amount of food available. They eat until their hunger is appeased, and do not feel obliged to "lick the platter clean."

4. If, by speeding up a clock in the experimental room, subjects are led to believe that it is mealtime, overweight subjects will eat more than normal eaters. Presumably, people of normal weight respond to the state of their stomachs rather than to the clock.

5. Fear stops stomach contractions, causing a frightened person to lose

his appetite—if he is a normal eater. Overeaters eat as much when they are in a frightening situation as when they are not.

Schachter also found that obese people will not work as hard to obtain food as normal eaters. In one experiment, overweight subjects ate fewer nuts when they had to be shelled than when they were already shelled (see Table 10-1). In another experiment, Schachter observed the eating behavior of diners in Chinese restaurants in New York City. Unless a Westerner is practiced in the use of chopsticks, it is much easier for him to use silverware. As each patron entered the restaurant Schachter and his colleagues characterized him as being overweight or normal, and then observed whether he ate with chopsticks or with silverware, both of which were equally available. Among Westerners, normal-weight people were five times more likely to eat with chopsticks than over-weight people.

Table 10-1 *Effects of Work on the Eating Behavior of Normal and Fat Subjects*

	Normal Subjects		Fat Subjects	
	eat	don't eat	eat	don't eat
nuts with shells	10	10	1	19
nuts without shells	11	9	19	1

S. Schachter. Some extraordinary facts about obese humans and rats. *American Psychologist*, 1971, 26, 129–144. Copyright 1971 by the American Psychological Association. Reprinted by permission.

These experiments show that *external* conditions are important regulators of the food intake of overweight people. The studies also show the importance of *internal* conditions in the regulation of the food intake of normal-weight people. External factors also may play an important role for those who overindulge in other ways. A person who is exceptionally active sexually may be responding more to external cues than to internal ones. (We will examine this and other aspects of sexual behavior in Chapter 13.) The same may be true for alcoholics, smokers, and gamblers. If this is the case, removing the external cues that activate the compulsion or removing the person from the external cues should effectively limit the compulsive behavior. In fact, dieting camps use both techniques. Another technique is to recondition the compulsive eater or drinker to the external cues so that the cues produce aversive or withdrawal reactions in place of approach ones.

Starvation.   What happens when people are placed on a semistarvation diet for a long period of time? This question was explored by a group of Minnesota investigators (Keys, Brôzek, Henschel, Michelson, & Taylor, 1950). Thirty-six healthy male volunteers between the ages of 20 and 33 were restricted for six months to a diet that contained less than half the necessary number of calories. Some of the observed changes were:

1. The consumption of coffee increased so much that a limit of nine cups per day had to be imposed.

2. Those who smoked, smoked more, and many of those who had not smoked previously began the habit.

3. Gum-chewing increased noticeably.

4. The men spent much time collecting recipes and kitchen utensils, and planning menus.

5. They talked, thought, and dreamed about food.

6. They displayed more sympathy for starving people.

7. Some of them grew concerned about saving money for a rainy day while others collected odds and ends of junk.

This and other, similar studies indicate that an essential drive like hunger, when it is not satisfied, tends to monopolize one's thoughts, fantasies, and behavior. Sometimes, however, a hungry person tries to banish all thoughts of food because it only makes him unhappy to think about what he does not have.

Specific Nutritional Needs. The body needs more than just the energy calories furnished by food. It also requires specific nutrients, such as proteins, minerals, and vitamins. Some evidence exists that young children can select a balanced diet for themselves. One experimenter let groups of children eat what they wanted from a wide range of nutritious foods. She found that the children almost always ate a healthy and balanced variety of foods in the course of a few days (Davis, 1939). Other studies have shown that children will rectify a nutritional deficiency by eating the appropriate food. One child, for example, began to eat extraordinary amounts of salt. His dismayed parents took the child to a doctor, who found that the child needed the salt to correct an imbalance caused by a glandular condition.

Adults do not seem to retain this ability to select a balanced diet, probably because cultural considerations like habit, convenience, and price are more influential in determining what they eat. In fact, for all too many of us, little correlation exists between what our bodies need and what we eat. Motives other than nutritional needs direct our eating habits. As a result, nutritional deficiencies are widespread.

Recently, a growing awareness of the importance of nutrition has produced a number of dietary fads and practices and the proliferation of health-food stores. Many of these, like vegetarianism, are inspired by ethical, religious, or weight-loss considerations. Others, like the organic food movement, are built on opposition to chemical fertilizers and preservatives.

Other Primary Drives

Satisfaction of the hunger and thirst drives is vital to human survival. Several other primary drives also must be satisfied. In the following paragraphs we will discuss the drives for sleep, temperature regulation, and oxygen.

The Need to Sleep. All human societies recognize the need for regular periods of sleep. Even the months-long arctic "day" does not keep Eskimos from sleeping on a regular 24-hour cycle very close to our own. We all know from experience that we cannot function for more than a few days without sleep—but science has not been able to discover why this is so. We assume that sleep meets some essential physiological need, such as the revitalization of bodily functions. However, so far experiments have failed to pinpoint any specific, invariant change of a physiological or biochemical nature that occurs when a person is deprived of sleep. Certainly, performance on tasks requiring vigilance and alertness deteriorates following sleep loss, but we cannot attribute this deterioration to any identifiable bodily change. Experiments show that extra sleep affects performance adversely in the same way that loss of sleep does. This finding fits the common observation that everyone has his own individual sleep needs; some people need only five hours while others need ten. But even this idea has not yet been proven scientifically.

At present, we cannot say with certainty that sleep serves any measurable restorative function. Some have suggested that sleep's purpose is to conserve energy when food is limited. Presumably, this is why bears hibernate in winter. If energy conservation was the original function of sleep, then sleep should not be necessary now that food is plentiful. Its persistence in man, according to this view, is merely a genetic remnant from our animal past.

Temperature Requirements. In our air-conditioned, centrally-heated society, we can easily forget that regulating our temperature is as vital a need for us as food and water. But our elaborate, expensive, and highly efficient methods of temperature control are a clear indication of just how important to us our temperature requirements are. We employ a vast variety of instrumental objects and activities—clothing, blankets, heating, and air conditioning, among other things—to regulate our temperature needs. We have elaborate bodily mechanisms to keep our temperature within the narrow limits necessary for survival. Though we tend to take it for granted, control of our body temperature is definitely a primary drive.

The Need for Oxygen. Our need for oxygen is crucial, but it is satisfied automatically. Thus our oxygen need has not posed much of a problem for us until recent years, when air pollution began to increase at an alarming rate. The needs for clean air, clean water, and unadulterated food have become powerful motivating forces in contemporary society, and it seems likely that these concerns soon will alter our society's behavior in significant ways.

As we have seen in this section, the means we use to satisfy primary drives vary greatly due to learning and custom. The importance of primary drives is obscured by the elaborate arrangements that modern societies have made for their satisfaction. However, when these arrangements break down—as in massive power failures, floods, and famines—the primary needs of the body for food, water, oxygen, and warmth assert their priorities over our learned drives.

10-7
All animals have a basic need for oxygen. With the increase in air pollution today—as evidenced by these photos of a power plant in New Mexico (top) and a smoldering garbage dump in California—people are no longer so inclined to take the satisfaction of this need entirely for granted. (UPI; National Air Pollution Control Administration)

Learned Drives

Nearly everyone acknowledges that a person acquires many motives through learning. He learns to want to be productive and creative, to be sociable, to be altruistic, to seek power, and to compete.

The possible sources of learned motives form a complex and controversial topic. We must analyze them carefully to avoid confusion over contradictory hypotheses and beliefs. Let us consider the various hypotheses in relation to a particular form of behavior, the pursuit of political power. Because political power is a strong motive for some people, they pursue it with "consuming" passion. They "hunger" for power, they "feed" on it, and when they are without it they feel "starved" for it. Their "appetite" can be insatiable. When Alexander the Great realized there were no more worlds to conquer, he wept with frustration. Where is the drive source for power? Various answers have been given.

Bodily Tensions

One answer—the _bodily tensions theory_—asserts that all drives originate in physical discomforts. The source of the drive for power is a bodily "itch," like that of hunger, sex, or thirst. According to this theory, everyone has this hunger for power, just as everyone has a hunger for food. In some people, the craving for power is intense and it takes a large amount of instrumental behavior to satisfy the craving. In others, the irritation is moderate or weak, and is more easily assuaged. Thus, according to this view, learned drives do not exist. Drives are innate. One simply learns the best (or most socially acceptable) ways of satisfying the basic, innate drive, in this case the drive for power.

This answer has prompted several objections. In the first place, no bodily source of the drive for power (or for other learned drives, for that matter) has yet been located. A second objection is that some people do not manifest a power drive. Their behavior may even express just the opposite wish—to be dominated by others. They have a drive to submit rather than to govern. If there is a bodily source for the power drive, then this source should be common to everyone, as is hunger.

Although we cannot rule out the possibility that the body has a specific seat of tension—perhaps in the brain—that energizes the power drive, we do not have adequate evidence to support such an assumption.

Displacement

A second attempt to explain the location of the drive source for power states that the power drive is not a drive at all, but a set of instrumental acts motivated by another drive source. The craving for power is a substitute for another craving.

Substitution of a less direct form of satisfaction for a more direct one is called _displacement._ For example, sexual tension often is displaced into nonsexual channels, such as a job, a sport, or a hobby. The energy is not altered, but the activity performed is. Examples of displacement are quite common—especially in aggressive behavior, which we will discuss in Chapter 12.

10-8
Displacement may involve substituting a socially acceptable instrumental behavior for a less acceptable one. Dancing, for example, is considered one of many common displacements for sexual impulses. (Ken Heyman)

One frequent suggestion is that political conquests are a substitute for sexual conquests. Some evidence indicates that both Napoleon and Hitler were sexually frustrated. Thus, their desire for world domination could have been a compensation for their sexual frustration. Freud often has been criticized for attributing too much of man's behavior to the sex impulse. Whether this criticism is justified or not, Freud was a leading exponent of the view that all of man's far-flung activities are powered by a few basic, organic sources. To Freud, motives like the craving for power were really instrumental activities. Freud's theory can be diagrammed as follows:

Source	Instrumental Acts	Aim
Sexual impulses	Substitute, nonsexual acts	Sexual relief

Since, according to Freud's theory, power-seeking behavior does not fully satisfy the sexual impulse, more of the substitute behavior is required to achieve a satisfaction equivalent to that which would be gained by sexual activity.

Instrumental acts associated with a basic drive like sex may also satisfy a learned drive. For example, sexual conquests often satisfy the craving for power as well as the sex drive. Similarly, as we have already noted, people who overeat and become obese sometimes are trying to satisfy other needs, such as the need for love.

The theory that all the motives of man can be reduced to a few basic bodily conditions has the virtue of economy and simplicity. In the hands of some psychologists, including Freud, it has considerable explanatory power. Other psychologists believe it is an oversimplification and does not do justice to the complexities of human motivation. But if someone proposes a new drive—such as curiosity, exploration, activity, power, or achievement—he first must show that this new drive is more than an instrumental activity satisfying a primary drive.

Conditioning

Like the displacement concept, the conditioning explanation emphasizes the existence of only a few basic drives; each drive is satisfied in many different ways. Unlike displacement theories, which refer to substitution of drives, the _conditioning theory_ states that a person learns particular ways to satisfy his few basic drives because of the reinforcers he receives for engaging in that behavior. For example, he learns to seek power because the exercise of power brings him various material rewards. When these rewards are no longer forthcoming or when the dissatisfactions outweigh the satisfactions, he quits playing the power game and learns to satisfy his basic needs in other ways.

Many psychologists favor this theory because it accords so well with modern learning theory. However, we should point out that one can apply the conditioning principle without even considering motivation. Power-seeking behavior can be conditioned by reinforcing it when it occurs; we need not assume an underlying motivation—a view associated with B. F. Skinner (see Chapter 6).

Functional Autonomy

According to the *functional autonomy* hypothesis, an acquired drive originally consists solely of instrumental behavior, but repeated use and association with pleasurable outcomes converts it into a motive in its own right. For example, a person is persuaded to run for public office on the ground that it is his social obligation. He is elected and learns to exercise the power of his office. At the end of his term, he is motivated to run again or to run for a higher office because he has learned to enjoy the sense of power that the position gave him. Social obligation is no longer a consideration; he is now motivated directly by the drive for power. In other words, the functional autonomy theory says, a drive is created merely by doing something rewarding over and over again; habits become drives (Allport, 1961).

This theory is appealing. Many examples support it. A person begins to smoke out of a need to conform and continues the habit because it is satisfying in its own right. A child practices the piano out of a desire for approval and learns to enjoy his ability to make music. The noted psychologist Erich Fromm maintains that society must make a person want to act as he has to act if the society is to function. Thus, in a capitalistic economy, people must learn to want to save money.

Despite its apparent validity, this theory has some weaknesses. Not all repeated acts become habits and not all habits become drives in their own right. Not every child who practices the piano learns to love playing it; not every politician learns to love power for its own sake.

Why do some habits become drivelike while others quickly vanish when their instrumental value disappears? It may be that a habit persists, not because it has acquired its own motive power, but because it satisfies a basic drive. This basic drive is not necessarily the same drive that motivated the habit originally. For example, a person may practice the piano to please his parents and then discover that it is an effective way to reduce several other tensions. No piano-playing drive has been created; it is still an instrumental activity, but now it is in the service of other drives. For example, playing the piano may make the individual feel popular with his friends, give him a means to earn money, or allow him to express his feelings through music.

Furthermore, a well-entrenched habit often can disappear with apparent suddenness. A person who has wielded power for many years suddenly stops. What shuts off the motor? If you view habits not as drives but as instrumental activities, then you would say that the motor has not been turned off. Instead, its energy has been shunted into new instrumental acts that promise to furnish greater relief. A veteran smoker's fear of lung cancer may finally outweigh whatever relief from other irritations the smoking gave him. The fear of defeat or the yearning for a peaceful retirement may persuade a politician to retire from public life. On closer examination, most "sudden" decisions like these turn out to be the result of gradual changes in a person's aims.

Anxiety

The final answer we will consider is the view that the principal energy source for learned motives is *anxiety*. For example, a person engages in

10-9
The drive for political power often becomes functionally autonomous. Whatever the original reasons for seeking office—money, prestige, etc.—the politician eventually may desire power for its own sake. (M. S. Stern, Black Star)

10-10
Philippe Petit, a Parisian acrobat, has been walking tightropes since he was 15. In 1971 Petit balanced on a steel cable strung between the Notre Dame cathedral towers (see chapter opening photo). In 1974 he spent over 30 minutes cavorting between the twin towers of the World Trade Center in New York. Petit is motivated, he claims, by the thrill of conquering the "impossible." His mother asserts that his walks enable him to dominate his anxieties (J. A. Pavlovsky, Sygma)

power-seeking behavior because he has learned that such activities help to alleviate his anxiety, just as for the same reason he might learn to smoke cigarettes or marijuana, drink, play games, go to the movies, work crossword puzzles, or make love. The motivating force is anxiety, and the behaviors are merely instrumental acts for reducing anxiety. The assumption is that everyone carries within him a fund of unresolved anxiety, and that he seizes on anything that will reduce this anxiety. The reduction of anxiety reinforces the tendency to engage in the activity that reduces the anxiety.

This view of the pervasive drive quality of anxiety has been applied not only to the learned motives but to the basic organic drives as well. Hunger or the threat of hunger arouses anxiety, and the anxiety, not the physiological condition of hunger, motivates food-seeking behavior. Much sexual and aggressive behavior also has been attributed to anxiety.

A Look to the Future

Each of these theories of learned motives has its advocates among psychologists. Each is supported by experimental evidence. Perhaps all of them are correct to some degree, so that any final theory of learned motives will have to bring them together in a meaningful synthesis.

Meanwhile, the one basic difference among these viewpoints is the number of drives acknowledged by each. Do only a few basic, organic drives provide the motivating force for all human behavior? Or are there innumerable drives? We are not likely to find the final answer to this crucial question for a long time. Until then, it probably is wise to maintain an open mind and to consider all the theories.

Some Learned Drives

Numerous learned drives have been identified and psychologists have extensively investigated some of them. We will discuss three of these learned drives—the approval motive, the achievement motive, and task motivation.

The Approval Motive

The desire for *approval* is just about as universal a learned drive as you can find. From an early age, children actively seek praise from their parents. During adolescence, the approval of one's peers becomes an extremely important incentive. Adults may be less concerned about approval but the need, however disguised or discounted, is still there. Because the drive for approval and esteem is so strong, parents and others regularly use the giving and withholding of approval as incentives to control behavior.

Crowne and Marlowe (1964) extensively investigated the approval motive, using a *need-for-approval scale*. A person's approval-motivation score is based on the number of "good" or socially-sanctioned answers he gives. Sample items are "I always try to practice what I preach," "I never resent being asked to return a favor," and "I am always willing to admit it when I make a mistake." There are 33 extremely virtuous statements like these, and the subject is asked to answer "true" or "false" to each. The more "true" answers he gives, the stronger is his drive to create a good impression and win approval.

In order to learn more about the people who scored high and low on their scale, Crowne and Marlowe gave their subjects various other tests as well. Their subjects took part in an experiment that was designed to be very dull and boring. The experimenter was described as a person high in status and prestige. Subjects who had a strong need for approval (as measured by the test) told the experimenter that his experiment was interesting and enjoyable. Those who had a low need for approval were more realistic in their appraisals. Among other things, the researchers found that:

1. People high in approval motivation are more likely to conform to group standards.

2. In a learning situation, individuals with a strong drive for approval learned more rapidly when the experimenter approved of correct responses than when he said nothing.

3. In a dart-throwing situation, the subjects were permitted to stand at any distance from the target. Individuals scoring high on the approval measure chose intermediate distances. By so doing, they were conforming to the socially desirable middle ground, neither making things too easy for themselves nor showing off by selecting a great distance.

The authors concluded from these and other results that a strong need for approval arises from the desire to bolster one's low level of self-esteem. People of this type deny or avoid awareness of their personal shortcomings. They find it difficult to act in an independent, self-assertive manner because they fear disapproval.

The Achievement Motive

No learned drive has been more extensively studied than the *achievement* motive. David McClelland did the first studies in the 1950s; since then, he and many other investigators have given us a much better understanding of this economically useful motive.

McClelland began his studies by developing a way to measure achievement motivation. He showed pictures to his subjects and asked them to tell stories about them. He assumed that a person who was strongly motivated to achieve would tell stories that emphasized achieving behavior. His assumption proved to be correct; people who told such stories were found to be high achievers in school and in other situations.

10-11
Drawings such as this one are used to test for achievement motivation. Subjects are asked to make up a story about the picture. Subject 1 obviously shows more achievement motivation than Subject 2. (From C. P. Smith & S. Feld *Motives in Fantasy, Action and Society* © 1958 by Litton Educational Publishing, Inc. Reprinted by permission of Van Nostrand Reinhold Company)

Subject 1

1. This brings to mind T. Edison who is dreaming of possible inventions rather than turning to his studies. A poor student, Edison is probably worried about his future.

2. Probably he is doing poorly in school or is thinking of his girl or perhaps he is being reprimanded by the teacher for inferior work.

3. I think he is dreaming of some childhood invention that he would much rather be working on than studying the boring subjects of grammar school.

4. He is destined to become one of the greatest of American inventors devoting his entire life to things such as the light bulb, phonograph.

Subject 2

1. The boy is in a classroom daydreaming about something.

2. He is recalling a previously experienced incident that struck his mind to be more appealing than being in the classroom.

3. He is thinking about the experience and is now imagining himself in the situation. He hopes to be there.

4. He will probably get called on by the instructor to recite and will be embarrassed.

Several other measures of the achievement motive have been devised. One study (McClelland, 1965) collected children's readers from various countries and analyzed them for achievement themes. The results were compared with the economic growth rates of the countries, as shown by the yearly increase in electricity-generating capacity. As expected, there was a strong correlation between a country's economic growth and the number of achievement themes in its readers. Evidently, a country that places a high value on productivity will implant this value in children through the stories written for them.

A similar study was made of folk tales collected from 45 primitive societies. Those societies that produced more than they could consume emphasized themes of hard work, persistence, and productivity in their folk tales.

Achievement behavior is not restricted to economic productivity. It may express itself in many other areas, such as art, writing, science, sports, social service, teaching, and politics. Most of the great artists and writers, for example, have been unusually hard workers. The achievement-oriented person characteristically applies himself diligently to increasingly difficult and challenging tasks.

The achievement motive originates in early childhood, as do most of the other learned motives. For example, it was determined that the strength of the achievement motive measured in childhood correlated with its measured strength when the children had become adults.

What experiences predispose the child to become a high achiever? Studies show that the parents of achieving children are themselves achievement-oriented and value hard work. They are the primary models for the child. High-achieving parents tend to encourage their children to do well and praise them when they do, thus reinforcing achievement behavior.

Probably the most important influence is the type of training the child receives. Children who are taught to be independent and self-confident are most likely to become high achievers. One study found that when fathers specified achievement goals for their sons, the boys did not show high achievement. Evidently, children achieve more if they are encouraged to set their own goals. Tasks set for the child should not be so easy as to give no sense of achievement, nor so difficult that the child continually fails at them. However, tasks should be frustrating to an ex-

10-12

Persons judged to be high achievers tend to set more rigorous goals for themselves and expect more in return for their efforts. In this study, high achievers set consistently larger monetary rewards than did low achievers when asked to determine suitable prizes for success at each distance in a ring-toss game. (From a study by Lewin reported in McClelland, 1961)

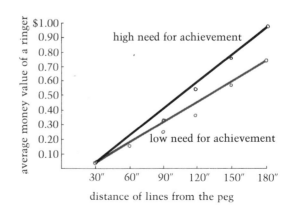

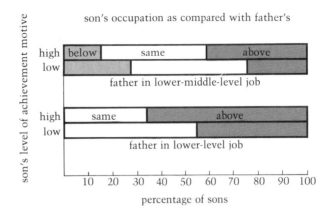

son's occupation as compared with father's

son's level of achievement motive

father in lower-middle-level job

high — below | same | above
low — | | above

father in lower-level job

high — same | above
low — | above

10   20   30   40   50   60   70   80   90   100

percentage of sons

10-13
A high achievement motive increases the likelihood that a child will rise above his father's socioeconomic level. This graph shows, as we would expect, that a greater proportion of high achievement-oriented sons rose above their fathers' occupation level (Crockett, 1962)

tent, so that the child can learn to tolerate frustration. They also should be increased gradually in difficulty so that the child is being challenged continuously. A stimulating environment, in which the child learns to master a number of different skills and problems, also helps to develop a generalized orientation to achievement.

Task Motivation

Some tasks create their own motivation. A task that has a specific, predictable end—putting together a jigsaw puzzle, climbing a mountain, reading a mystery story—often arouses a drive to complete it once it is begun. The drive to finish a task becomes stronger as we approach the end of the task; thus, it has been named the *goal gradient.*

A person who is interrupted as he nears completion of a task feels quite frustrated and annoyed; he returns to the task as soon as the interruption ceases. The goal gradient principle of motivation applies not only to short tasks but also to long projects such as obtaining a college degree or writing a book. Experimental evidence indicates that uncompleted tasks are better remembered than completed ones, which suggests that the drive to complete has a persisting effect (Zeigarnik, 1927). The uncompleted projects of childhood may continue to motivate a person for many years.

Psychological Drives as Basic Needs

Throughout this chapter we have used the terms *drive* and *need* interchangeably. However, they are different in one important way. Drive refers more to the source of motivated behavior, and need to the goal. When we talk about the hunger drive, we mean those processes within the person that drive him to action. When we talk about the need for food, we are specifying a goal object that is necessary for good health and survival. A person may need food without being motivated to seek food. For example, the science of nutrition is concerned with nutritional needs and not with the hunger drive.

Must a person also satisfy certain psychological needs to be psychologically healthy? This exceedingly important question is very difficult to answer. First, we have no satisfactory model of psychological health;

thus, we find it hard to say which needs really must be satisfied. To develop such a model, we would have to deprive people systematically of certain types of behaviors, one at a time, to see what effect the deprivation would have. For ethical reasons, deprivation experiments are difficult to perform on human beings, although we did see earlier that psychologists have studied the effects of food and sleep deprivation in the laboratory. Deprivation sometimes occurs as a result of social conditions, but these "natural" experiments often lack adequate controls, making it difficult to say which need actually was deprived.

A second difficulty is that a person can rather readily substitute one psychological need for another. We can compensate for deficiency in one need by satisfying another need.

Third, research has suggested that psychological needs form a hierarchy; some needs have priority over others. When our high-priority needs have been satisfied, new needs appear, which suggests that man is never completely satisfied, that he is always reaching out for something new.

Murray: Twenty Basic Needs

Despite the difficulties involved in deprivation studies, many psychologists have tried to define and list man's essential psychological requirements. One of the most influential lists of human needs was drawn up by the Harvard psychologist Henry Murray (1938). From an intensive study of a small group of people, Murray identified twenty distinctive needs. His list (see Table 10-2) has stimulated a great deal of research. You will notice that although Murray's list of needs resembles McDougall's list of instincts (see page 344), Murray does not insist upon the inborn nature of needs.

Table 10-2   Murray's Twenty Basic Needs

Need	Brief Definition
Abasement	To submit passively to external force. To accept injury, blame, criticism, punishment. To surrender. To become resigned to fate. To admit inferiority, error, wrongdoing, or defeat. To confess and atone. To blame, belittle, or mutilate the self. To seek and enjoy pain, punishment, illness, and misfortune.
Achievement	To accomplish something difficult. To master, manipulate, or organize physical objects, human beings, or ideas. To do this as rapidly and as independently as possible. To overcome obstacles and attain a high standard. To excel oneself. To rival and surpass others. To increase self-regard by the successful exercise of talent.
Affiliation	To draw near and enjoyably cooperate or reciprocate with an allied other (an other who resembles the subject or who likes the subject). To please and win affection of a cathected object. To adhere and remain loyal to a friend.

Table 10-2 (*Continued*)

Need	Brief Definition
Aggression	To overcome opposition forcefully. To fight. To revenge an injury. To attack, injure, or kill another. To oppose forcefully or punish.
Autonomy	To get free, shake off restraint, break out of confinement. To resist coercion and restriction. To avoid or quit activities prescribed by domineering authorities. To be independent and free to act according to impulse. To be unattached, irresponsible. To defy convention.
Counteraction	To master or make up for a failure by restriving. To obliterate a humiliation by resumed action. To overcome weaknesses, to repress fear. To efface a dishonor by action. To search for obstacles and difficulties to overcome. To maintain self-respect and pride on a high level.
Defendance	To defend the self against assault, criticism, and blame. To conceal or justify a misdeed, failure, or humiliation. To vindicate the ego.
Deference	To admire and support a superior. To praise, honor, or eulogize. To yield eagerly to the influence of an allied other. To emulate an exemplar. To conform to custom.
Dominance	To control one's human environment. To influence or direct the behavior of others by suggestion, seduction, persuasion, or command. To dissuade, restrain, or prohibit.
Exhibition	To make an impression. To be seen and heard. To excite, amaze, fascinate, entertain, shock, intrigue, amuse, or entice others.
Harm avoidance	To avoid pain, physical injury, illness, and death. To escape from a dangerous situation. To take precautionary measures.
Infavoidance	To avoid humiliation. To quit embarrassing situations or conditions which may lead to scorn, derision, or indifference of others. To refrain from action because of the fear of failure.
Nurturance	To give sympathy and gratify the needs of a helpless object: an infant or any object that is weak, disabled, tired, inexperienced, infirm, defeated, humiliated, lonely, dejected, sick, mentally confused. To assist an object in danger. To feed, help, support, console, protect, comfort, nurse.
Order	To put things in order. To achieve cleanliness, organization, balance, tidiness, precision.
Play	To act for "fun" without further purpose. To like to laugh and make jokes. To seek enjoyable relaxation of stress. To participate in games, sports, dancing, drinking parties, cards.

Table 10-2 (*Continued*)

Need	Brief Definition
Rejection	To separate oneself from a negatively cathected object. To exclude, abandon, expel, or remain indifferent to an inferior object. To snub or jilt an object.
Sentience	To seek and enjoy sensuous impressions.
Sex	To form and further an erotic relationship. To have sexual intercourse.
Succorance	To have one's needs gratified by the sympathetic aid of an allied object. To be nursed, supported, sustained, surrounded, protected, loved, advised, guided, indulged, forgiven, consoled. To remain close to a devoted protector. To always have a supporter.
Understanding	To ask or answer general questions. To be interested in theory. To speculate, formulate, analyze, and generalize.

Adapted from *Explorations in Personality* edited by Henry A. Murray. Copyright 1938 by Oxford University Press, Inc.; Renewed 1966 by Henry A. Murray. Reprinted by permission of the publisher.

Fromm: Five Existential Needs

Erich Fromm specified five universal human needs. They are (1) the need for *relatedness*, (2) the need for *transcendence*, (3) the need for *rootedness*, (4) the need for *identity*, and (5) the need for a *frame of orientation*. The need for relatedness stems from the fact that man in becoming man has been torn from the animal's primary union with nature. In place of the animal's instinctive ties with nature, man has to create his own relationships; the most satisfying ones are based upon mutual care, responsibility and respect for others, and sympathetic understanding.

The urge for transcendence refers to man's need to rise above his animal nature, to become a creative person instead of remaining a creature of instincts. If his creative urges are thwarted, man tends to become a destroyer.

The need for rootedness reflects man's desire to be an integral part of the world, to feel that he belongs. Man finds his healthiest and most satisfying roots in a feeling of communion with other men and women.

But man also has a need for personal identity, to be a unique individual. If he cannot attain this goal through his own creative efforts, he may obtain a certain mark of distinction by identifying himself with a prominent person or group.

Finally, man needs to have a frame of reference, a stable and dependable way of perceiving and comprehending the world.

For Fromm, these needs are purely human and purely objective. They are not found in animals and they are not derived from observing what man says he wants. Nor are these strivings created by society; rather they have become embedded in human nature through evolution. In other words, they are inborn needs.

Maslow: Basic Needs and Metaneeds

Scientific psychology has been criticized for overemphasizing man's bodily and psychological needs and neglecting his spiritual needs. Abraham Maslow (1967) has attempted to make up for this neglect. He considers man to have two kinds of needs: *basic needs* and *metaneeds*. _Basic needs_ are those that most psychologists accept: hunger, thirst, sex, security, achievement, and the like. _Metaneeds_ are for spiritual qualities, such as justice, goodness, beauty, order, and unity. Man's basic needs are deficiency needs; a person who is hungry lacks something. Metaneeds are growth needs. When they are properly satisfied, a person grows into a completely developed human being. Basic needs take precedence over metaneeds; they must be fulfilled before a person can turn his attention to his metaneeds. Maslow believed that metaneeds are inherent in man, and when they are not fulfilled a person may suffer alienation, anguish, apathy, and cynicism. Maslow's theory of motivation is an important feature of his humanistic approach to psychology.

Work, Love, and Self-Actualization

In the preceding sections, we described several lists of human needs proposed by various psychologists. Freud also identified what he felt were the basic human needs. He said that to be contented a person requires just two things—*work* and *love*. A number of psychologists believe man has only one need—*self-actualization*. Every person possesses the imperious and inherent need to develop all aspects of his being to the greatest degree. All of the so-called motives are merely separate manifestations of the sovereign need to realize oneself, to become a fully developed person. Kurt Goldstein (1963), the founder of organismic psychology (an area of psychology based on the belief that everything must be considered in terms of the entire organism) was the first to put forward this concept, which is one of the pillars of humanistic psychology.

Incentives: External Motivators

As we said earlier, an incentive is an *external* inducement to act in a certain way. Incentives can be divided into two general types. Incentives that help a person satisfy his needs and realize his potential are called _facilitative incentives_. Incentives that attempt to impose on him behaviors alien to his needs and potential are called _coercive incentives_. Notice that this distinction is not the same as the distinction between rewards and punishments. Rewards may be used either to facilitate *or* to coerce; so may punishments.

What incentives, whether facilitative or coercive, effectively arouse and direct behavior in specific, predictable ways? This very practical question is important for parents, teachers, advertisers, employers, coaches, political candidates, and anyone else who wants to influence another person's behavior. No universal answer exists; to learn what incentives will be effective in a particular situation, we must still rely on trial and error.

Money is a fairly dependable incentive for getting most people to work. But some people do not see it as an incentive at all, and for many others money loses its incentive value after they reach a certain income level. Freedom is supposedly a strong incentive, but considering how readily men give up their freedom and submit to authority we must question the importance and universality of this incentive. Security is said to be a strong incentive, but a situation that is secure for one person is stifling for another. Praise and approval as well as their opposites, criticism and disapproval, often are used as incentives. They are effective for many people, but not for all. Much depends on the person who is giving the praise or the blame, as well as the activity in question.

Incentives often have short-term effects. After a while, they lose their power to influence behavior; adaptation sets in, and a new incentive must be employed. Industry recognizes this basic principle of motivation by making innovations in its products and by devising new appeals in its advertising.

Often, an incentive's short-term effect is all we care about. For example, when we have persuaded a person to vote for our candidate, the incentive has served its purpose.

In other circumstances, people are more interested in achieving a long-term effect. A mother who uses incentives to get her child to keep his room in order hopes that eventually he will develop an intrinsic desire to be orderly. As noted earlier, some behaviors established by incentives acquire a drivelike character in their own right. But we cannot predict beforehand which behaviors will become drives and which will not.

Summary

1. A motive is anything that initiates behavior.

2. Motives take the form of either drives, which are internal incitements to action, or incentives, which are external inducements to action.

3. There are two classes of drives: primary drives and learned drives.

4. One of the earliest theories of motivation was Freud's pleasure-pain principle, which he later rejected.

5. The source of a primary drive is an identifiable, inborn, organic disturbance. The primary drive's aim, the removal of the organic disturbance, is realized by instrumental acts and objects.

6. Hunger and thirst are controlled by switchlike centers in the lateral and ventromedial hypothalamus that respond to such factors as blood sugar level, body temperature, and amount of water in the body cells. Our eating and drinking drives are also influenced by a number of external factors, such as custom and the availability of food and water.

7. Obese people are influenced more by external environmental circumstances; normal eaters are influenced more by internal bodily conditions.

8. The source of the primary drive for sleep has not been identified, but it may be related to the body's need to conserve energy.

9. The needs for warmth and oxygen are important primary drives.

10. Five important hypotheses regarding the origin of the learned drives are (a) learned drives are not really drives at all, but rather displacements: instrumental behaviors motivated by primary drives; (b) learned drives are originally instrumental behaviors, but through repetition and reinforcement they become functionally autonomous; (c) all learned drives originate in bodily tensions; (d) once a person learns particular ways to satisfy his few basic drives, he is conditioned to continue these reinforced behaviors; and (e) all behavior is motivated by anxiety.

11. Three learned drives—those for approval, achievement, and task completion—have been extensively investigated by psychologists.

12. Murray, Fromm, Maslow, and others have proposed various lists of psychological needs that must be fulfilled if a person is to be psychologically healthy.

13. There are two types of incentives: facilitative incentives and coercive incentives.

Important Terms

rationalization

motive

drive

need

incentive

primary drive

learned drive

pleasure-pain principle

masochist

sadist

self-stimulation

drive source

instrumental act

drive aim

instrumental object

instinct

arousal

hunger drive

satiation center

overeating

starvation

thirst drive

temperature requirements

bodily tension theory of learned drives

displacement theory of learned drives

conditioning theory of learned drives

functional autonomy theory of learned drives

anxiety theory of learned drives

approval motive

achievement motive

task motivation

goal gradient

Murray's basic needs

Fromm's existential needs   Maslow's basic needs

relatedness   Maslow's metaneeds

transcendence   self-actualization

rootedness   facilitative incentives

identity   coercive incentives

frame of orientation

Suggested Readings

COFER, C. N. *Motivation and emotion.* Glenview, Ill.: Scott, Foresman, 1972.
> A survey of research and theory written for the beginning student.

COFER, C. N., & APPLEY, M. H. *Motivation: theory and research.* New York: Wiley, 1964.
> A comprehensive and critical review of the experimental and theoretical literature on motivation. A standard reference book. Technical.

CROWNE, D., & MARLOWE, D. *The approval motive: studies in evaluative dependence.* New York: Wiley, 1964.
> An interesting account of a number of studies showing differences between people with high and low needs for approval.

MCCLELLAND, D. C., ATKINSON, J. W., CLARK, R. A., & LOWELL, E. L. *The achievement motive.* New York: Appleton-Century-Crofts, 1953.
> A classic study of a very important social motive.

MCCLELLAND, D. C., & STEELE, R. S. (EDS.) *Human motivation.* Morristown, N.J.: General Learning Corp., 1973.
> A book of readings.

MURRAY, E. J. *Motivation and emotion.* Englewood Cliffs, N.J.: Prentice-Hall, 1964.
> A comprehensive introductory textbook.

SCHACHTER, S. *Emotion, obesity, and crime.* New York: Academic Press, 1971.
> A fascinating account of some innovative investigations.

Chapter 11 Emotion

Letter to an actress: "From what you told me last night I see that you do not know your power. You are like a person who consumes herself in love and giving and does not know the miracles that are born of this. I felt this last night . . . , that you were whatever you acted, that you touched that point at which art and life meet and there is only BEING. I felt your hunger and your dreams, your pities and your desires at the same time as you awakened all of mine. I felt that you were not acting but dreaming; I felt that all of us who watched you could come out of the theatre and without transition could pass magically into another Ball, another snowstorm, another love, another dream. Before our very eyes you were being consumed by love and the dream of love. The burning of your eyes, of your gestures, a bonfire of faith and dissolution. You have the power. Never again use the word exhibitionism. Acting in you is a revelation. What the soul so often cannot say through the body because the body is not subtle enough, you can say. The body usually betrays the soul. You have the power of contagion, of transmitting emotion through the infinite shadings of your movements, the variations of your mouth's designs, the feathery palpitations of your eyelashes. And your voice, your voice more than any other voice linked to your breath, the breathlessness of feeling, so that you take one's breath away with you and carry one into the realm of breathlessness and silence. So much power you have, Sabina!

— Anäis Nin
(A Spy in the House of Love)

Emotion

During most of our waking hours, our mood follows a fairly even course. From time to time, however, we are thrown off balance by a moving or disturbing experience. Everything is running smoothly when suddenly we encounter an obstacle and our composure is broken by exasperation or anger. An uneventful day becomes a day of rejoicing when we receive word of an unexpected honor or a wish fulfilled. Or, we may be walking along, minding our own business, when something threatens us and we are gripped by fear. We hear of the death of a friend and are plunged into grief. Out of the blue, we become infatuated and fall in love. Seeing someone we love flirting with a rival rouses our jealousy. An offensive taste ruins a pleasant meal. A succession of failures leads us to despondency and depression.

If you stop to think about each of these common emotional experiences, you will notice that all of them contain three elements. The most prominent one is a strong feeling; as the word emotion implies, it is a *moving* experience. This feeling may be one of excitement or sorrow (for the present, we shall focus on the exciting emotions.) If the emotion is strong enough, you will notice that your heart beats faster, your breathing speeds up, the palms of your hands sweat, and your muscles tense. This is called the *arousal* element of an emotion.

The second common element among emotions is the *label* we attach to particular aroused states—fear, anger, joy, grief, or love. How do we know what emotion we are experiencing? The labeling of our emotional experiences may seem self-evident, but as we shall see, some basic questions have been asked about how we accomplish this identification.

Finally, you will notice that emotion strongly incites you to *do* something, unless the emotion is so traumatic that it immobilizes you. We have an automatic tendency to run when we are afraid, to strike out when we are angry, to jump up and down when we are joyful, and to hug and kiss when we are in love. But emotion also can make us engage in more complex, long-term activities. Anger can launch a person on a long campaign of revenge. Blood feuds may last for generations. Fear can motivate a person to develop elaborate defenses to fend off the dangers that seem to threaten him. The motivating powers of love, hate, and jealousy form popular themes in literature. Emotions can and usually do express themselves in action. This _behavioral_ or _motivational_ element is the third common element shared by emotions.

The Arousal Element of Emotion

There are many different ways to measure arousal; unfortunately, they do not always agree. The most widely used yardsticks are the electroencephalogram (EEG); peripheral autonomic responses such as heart rate, blood pressure, and electrical resistance of the palms; and of course, the general behavior of the organism.

Donald Lindsley (1950) pioneered the exploration of the concept of arousal in a laboratory setting. He discovered that the low-voltage fast EEG characteristic of alert waking states gave a reliable indication of the level of arousal. The diagram in Figure 11-1 shows the relationship between the degree of arousal and the degree of successful or integrated behavior. A simple experiment illustrates this _"inverted-U" function_. A person is asked to perform a repetitive task, perhaps mental arithmetic, while squeezing a spring-handled device that measures the strength of the squeeze. If the subject squeezes very weakly, his squeeze will have little effect on his mental arithmetic performance. If he squeezes moderately, his performance on the task will improve. However, if he squeezes very hard, his performance on mental arithmetic will deteriorate. We all can think of examples closer to home; recall your feelings while taking a test. If you are extremely nervous about it, you are likely to do poorly. If you don't care at all, you are also likely to do poorly. However, if you have a moderate degree of arousal or anxiety, you probably will perform most effectively.

Berlyne (1960) performed a variety of experiments in which he varied the arousal level of his subjects systematically. He used nonthreatening conflict situations that consistently caused arousal. For example, if the subjects were trained to push a lever one way when a light on the right was flashed and the opposite way for a light on the left, they would experience conflict if both lights were flashed simultaneously. Berlyne found that such conflicting visual stimuli resulted in heightened arousal and improved performance on subsequent tests. More complex visual

11-1
The "inverted-U" function. At low arousal—sleep being the extreme—efficiency is relatively poor. Similarly, at high levels of arousal, efficiency is minimal; the individual is immobilized by strong emotion, just as a person confronted by a bear may freeze in his tracks. At levels of moderate arousal, efficiency is best; the individual is neither too apathetic nor too excited to respond. (After Hebb, 1972)

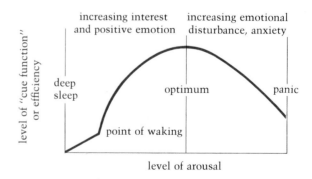

stimuli produced more arousal than simple stimuli. In other words, arousal and complexity may be related and a moderate degree of each may improve performance. The lower end of the waking-arousal continuum, represented by sensory deprivation, was discussed in Chapter 4. As we saw, performance deteriorates markedly under abnormally low conditions of arousal.

Arousal is an inferred or hypothetical construct. EEG records cannot be considered direct measurements of any general state of arousal. They are simply measurements that apparently reflect levels of arousal. The current approach to defining arousal is to measure brain activity, autonomic nervous system responses, and behavioral indicators. Psychologists then use these measurements to characterize an arousal pattern and to determine how this pattern changes in different situations.

Perhaps the best-known attempt to specify a consistent pattern or syndrome of arousal was Pavlov's definition of the *orienting response.* The contemporary Soviet scientist Ye. N. Sokolov (1963) has studied this response in detail. The normal human response to the sudden presentation of a novel stimulus consists of a relatively clear pattern of physiological changes: pupil dilation, temporary arrest of breathing, a brief slowing of the heart rate, increased muscle tone, decreased blood flow in the limbs but increased blood flow in the head, and an EEG pattern of arousal. When the stimulus is repeated, these response patterns rapidly diminish as the subject habituates to them. If the stimulus is more intense or threatening, a different pattern, termed the *defensive syndrome,* will occur. This syndrome includes all the physiological reactions and behaviors an organism must employ to fend off or escape an attacker. It is also known as the fight or flight response.

11-2
Schematic of the orienting response. The horizontal lines at the left indicate that the individual has become habituated to a dark room. A light is turned on and—as the dips in the lines show—he exhibits an orienting response: his pupils contract, his galvanic skin resistance shows a brief decrease, and his production of alpha waves and his visual sensitivity are diminished. After a short time, the individual habituates to the light. When the light is turned off, he exhibits an orienting response to the dark and again soon habituates to it. (Adapted from Sokolov, 1957 and 1958, in Berlyne, 1960)

11-3
Sokolov's defensive syndrome. The three areas show an individual's responses to different intensities of electrodermal shock stimuli. Very low intensities produce no response (zone 1). The middle intensities, from 2 to 17, produce an orienting response (zone 2), but with repeated presentation the subject either habituates to them or (for intensities of 7 and above) the stimuli eventually cause a defensive reaction (zone 3). Intensities above 17 produce an immediate defensive syndrome. (From Ye. N. Sokolov, *Perception and the Conditioned Reflex.* © 1963. Reprinted by permission of The Macmillan Company.)

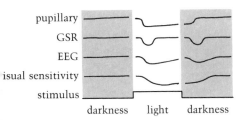

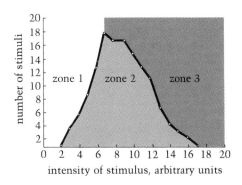

CONTROL OF BODILY FUNCTIONS THROUGH BIOFEEDBACK

Neal E. Miller   *Rockefeller University*

Immediate rewards and punishments are more effective than delayed ones. A person who is trying to learn a new skill learns faster if he sees the results of his actions right away. For example, if he is learning to shoot a basketball from the foul line, seeing the ball swish down through the net is a reward which increases the probability that he will repeat his successful set of movements. Seeing the ball miss is a punishment that lessens the probability of repeating the unsuccessful set of movements. Thorndike called this information about a response's success "knowledge of results." He showed that without it people do not learn to improve, just as one would not expect a blindfolded basketball player to learn to sink foul shots. More recently, this information has been called "feedback."

For some responses the feedback is readily perceived and unambiguous; the basketball player promptly sees the ball go through the hoop or miss. Other responses give poor feedback. For instance, tension can build up gradually in certain muscles of the forehead without a person realizing it; later he feels tired or has a dull ache. Similarly, a person can stand or sit in a bad posture without realizing it until, eventually, his body becomes deformed.

Feedback from many of the actions of our internal organs is especially poor. Most people cannot detect moderate changes in their blood pressure, heart rate, or intestinal contractions. The person trying to learn to control such functions is like the blindfolded basketball player; he does not learn. Furthermore, the Western belief that learning to control such functions is impossible has persuaded people so well that they do not even try.

Today, however, modern recording devices can give people better immediate information about what is happening inside their bodies. Such information has been called "biofeedback." With its help, people apparently can learn to gain better control of these processes.

Evaluating the effects of biofeedback, however, turns out to be tricky. It illustrates the importance of using the scientific skills that psychologists have developed for the study of complex behavior.

Feedback from Muscle Tension

One of the most straightforward uses of biofeedback is to teach better control over skeletal muscles — the muscles over which we ordinarily have considerable voluntary control. When muscle fibers contract, they produce electrical potentials. These can be picked up by suitable electrodes and amplified to produce an electromyograph, abbreviated EMG. The subject can see the EMG on a meter or hear it as a series of clicks that become faster as the muscle contracts. When subjects receive such information about the activity of single motor units in a muscle, they can learn to fire these units without contracting the rest of the muscle, something they otherwise cannot do.

While most people can relax most of their muscles quite successfully, tense people have more difficulty, especially with such muscles as the frontalis muscles in the forehead. Experiments have shown that such people can learn to relax better if they receive EMG feedback from the activity of these muscles. Tension headaches apparently are caused by contraction of the frontalis muscle. Biofeedback, used to train people to relax these muscles, can pro-duce relief in a larger proportion of cases than can relaxation without feedback. Similarly, EMG feedback has helped certain patients suffering from torticollis, a condition in which the neck and head are held twisted far to one side. These individuals were trained, with EMG feedback, to relax their spastically tensed muscles and then to contract their atrophied opposing ones.

Placebo Effects

Evaluating the therapeutic effect of any specific treatment requires us to rule out the relief a patient often will feel simply because he believes something important is being done for him. Such relief, called a "placebo effect," might be produced by giving a patient an impressive-looking sugar capsule and telling him it contains a powerful drug. Headaches are notoriously subject to placebo effects. In the work on tension headaches, the experimenters attempted to control for placebo effects by showing that the group given EMG feedback gained greater relief than a group merely instructed to practice relaxing. This is not a perfect control, however, since the EMG procedure probably was more impressive and may have been given with more enthusiasm than the relaxation one. Placebo effects are known to be increased by an impressive procedure and by an enthusiastic therapist.

In testing drugs, a "double-blind" procedure is used to control for placebo effects. All the patients believe they are getting the drug and the physician giving the pills does not know which patients receive drugs and which receive sugar pills. In one study evaluating a drug's effectiveness against high blood pressure, the 48 patients getting only the

A

Voluntary control over heart rhythm. Large spikes indicate premature ventricular contractions (PVCs); the absence of large spikes denotes normal sinus rhythm. Line above the electrocardiogram indicates skin conductance. R: period of rest. S: patient instructed to suppress PVCs. B: patient instructed to produce bigeminy or the alternation of PVCs and normal beats. The strips are a continuous record of a single 16 minute session. (From work by Dr. Thomas Pickering in the author's laboratory)

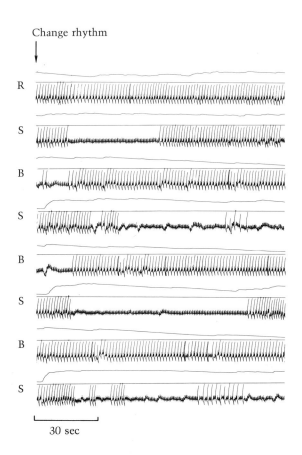

Change rhythm

R

S

B

S

B

S

B

S

30 sec

B

The top edge of the wide black band represents the blood flow at the peak of the pulse; the bottom of the band represents the blood flow at the trough. The line beneath is the average blood flow with the pulse fluctuations filtered out, and the line at the top of the graph is the temperature. As you will note, the command "Cool your hands" produces a prompt reduction in blood flow and pulse amplitude followed by a decrease in temperature. (From work by Dr. Wesley Lynch and Mr. Sorel Kohn in the author's laboratory)

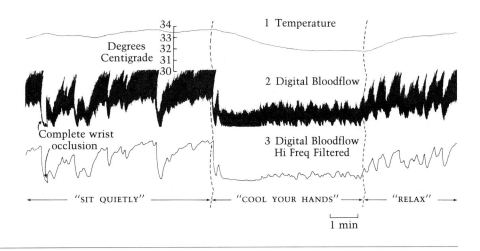

1 Temperature

Degrees Centigrade 34 33 32 31 30

2 Digital Bloodflow

Complete wrist occlusion

3 Digital Bloodflow Hi Freq Filtered

← "SIT QUIETLY" → "COOL YOUR HANDS" → "RELAX" →

1 min

Considerable evidence indicates that the normal syndrome of arousal can be dissociated—that is, we can separate some components of the arousal pattern from others. A simple method for doing this is to give subjects a drug called *atropine*. Following moderate doses of atropine, the EEG becomes strongly synchronized, showing typical slow brain waves indicative of relaxation and sleep, even though the subject remains behaviorally awake. In fact, even strong sensory stimulation does not produce EEG arousal after atropine is administered. Bradley and his associates (1964) demonstrated that animals given sufficient atropine to produce strong EEG synchrony showed no difference in learning behavior from animals not given atropine. In other words, although EEG measurements indicated that one group of animals was totally unaroused and the other was highly aroused, both groups performed equally. This experiment warns us that we cannot presume that arousal does not exist merely because one measurement, such as the EEG pattern, indicates that it does not.

Behavioral tasks also can dissociate the various measures of arousal. John Lacey (1967) has done careful studies of autonomic responses and arousal in man. Lacey's results provide a less clear picture than our brief description of the orienting response implies. For example, in a test where the foot is immersed in ice water for several seconds, some subjects showed changes in the electrical resistance of the palms (due to sweating), but no heart rate change, while others showed increases in both palmar resistance and heart rate. These experiments indicate that the arousal pattern or orienting response may vary from individual to individual, with age, and with the complexity of the task.

Arousal and the Autonomic Nervous System

The physical aspects of arousal are controlled by the autonomic nervous system. As we discussed in the Appendix to Chapter 3, the autonomic nervous system consists of two divisions: the sympathetic and the parasympathetic. The sympathetic division acts as the body's arousal mechanism; it prepares the organism for vigorous action. You need not actually engage in vigorous activity to experience these arousal effects; thoughts alone can activate the sympathetic division. If you even think of a frightening or dangerous situation, your heart rate increases and you breathe more deeply; gastrointestinal activity ceases as blood is shunted away from the *viscera* (internal organs) and into the muscles; glucose (blood sugar) is released into the bloodstream; and glands in the skin exude sweat. The parasympathetic system, in contrast, provides recuperative, protective, and nutritive functions—for example, it maintains digestion and tissue health.

The organization of the sympathetic and parasympathetic portions of the autonomic nervous system is shown in the Appendix to Chapter 3. The sympathetic motor nerves have their cell bodies in the spinal cord. Their axons terminate in a series of ganglia close to the spinal cord, called the *sympathetic ganglia*. Here they synapse on nerve cell bodies whose axons stimulate such organs as the heart and stomach. These peripheral sympathetic ganglia are interconnected. Indeed, they permit the sympathetic system to operate as a unit. The symptoms of sympathetic activity—pounding heart, dilation of the pupils, inhibition of stomach activity, and so on—form a coherent pattern of responses to prepare us for emergency action. Table 11-1 contains a list of symptoms experienced by pilots in combat; note how the sympathetic division acts during such "emergency" situations.

Table 11-1   Bodily Expression of Fear as Reported by World War II Pilots (Shaffer, 1947)

Symptom	Often	Sometimes	Total
Pounding heart and rapid pulse	30	56	86
Muscles very tense	30	53	83
Easily irritated, angry, or "sore"	22	58	80
Dryness of the throat or mouth	30	50	80
"Nervous perspiration" or "cold sweat"	26	53	79
"Butterflies" in the stomach	23	53	76
Sense of unreality, that this couldn't be happening	20	49	69
Need to urinate very frequently	25	40	65
Trembling	11	53	64
Confused or rattled	3	50	53
Weak or faint	4	37	41
After mission, not being able to remember details of what happened	5	34	39
Sick to the stomach	5	33	38
Not being able to concentrate	3	32	35

The parasympathetic division has a different organization. The initial fibers also have their cell bodies in the central nervous system, but the fibers themselves pass out directly from the brain through the cranial nerves to ganglia near the target organs. For example, there is a small ganglion near the heart that activates other nerve fibers terminating on the heart musculature.

Most organs of the viscera have both sympathetic and parasympathetic nerves. Thus, increased sympathetic activity results in a faster heart rate, for example, while increased parasympathetic activity results in a lowering of the heart rate. In this way, the autonomic nervous system maintains a double control over the responses of the viscera. The heart rate can be increased either by an *increase* in sympathetic input or a *decrease* in parasympathetic input. The heart's response is simply the net result of the inputs. The autonomic nervous system is under the direct control of groups of neurons in the brainstem, which, in turn, are controlled by the hypothalamus and limbic forebrain structures. The autonomic nervous system is at the command of the brain structures that most directly mediate the emotional and motivational aspects of behavior.

Autonomic Measures of Emotionality.   As we have noted earlier, a change in skin resistance due to changes in sweat gland activity is called

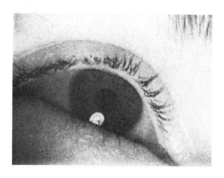

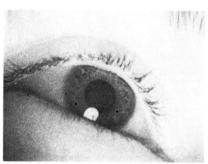

11-4
Pupil size increases as interest in the subject being viewed increases. The pupil diameter of this male subject increased in size 30 percent while he was being shown a photograph of a pinup girl. (Eckhard Hess)

11-5
The lie detector. Bands around the chest and wrists detect changes in breathing and pulse rate. These changes are recorded by the polygraph, which the examiner observes closely for clues to the information he seeks.

the galvanic skin response (GSR). [Another term for it is *electrodermal response* (EDR)]. Sweat glands are innervated by the sympathetic division. Such innervation is normally an involuntary response to an emotional stimulus. A study of GSR response in several 1-day-old humans showed a high correlation between the level of their GSR and their degree of arousal as measured by the amount of crying and movement. But the GSR is not a perfect reflection of emotional activity since it also reflects such influences as environmental temperature and physical activity.

Changes in blood pressure can also provide valuable clues to emotional states. Since emotional behavior requires activity, it causes the hypothalamus to direct the sympathetic division to increase the blood supply to the skeletal muscles. As a result, blood pressure increases often reflect the existence of underlying emotions.

Hess and Polt (1960) studied the pupil size of the human eye as it is exposed to arousing visual stimuli. Pupil size is another sign of arousal that is not under voluntary control. Of course, pupil size is largely determined by the amount of light present; the brighter the light, the smaller your pupil will be. However, the pupil also responds to arousing or emotional stimuli. Hess and Polt showed slides of sexual and neutral objects—such as a baby, a nude male, a nude female, a landscape, and a woman holding a baby—to adult subjects. The male subjects' pupils increased sharply in size only when they were viewing the nude female. The female subjects' pupils increased at the sight of the baby, the woman with the baby, and the nude male. They also increased a little at the sight of the nude female and constricted somewhat when the landscape appeared.

Considering the complexities of human autonomic responses, it is surprising that lie detectors can be used at all. A *lie detector* is simply a

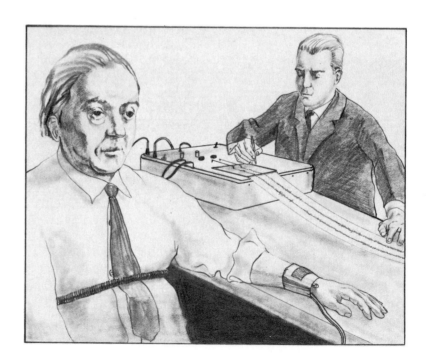

"polygraph," which, as we mentioned earlier, is a device that graphs the heart rate, the blood pressure, the GSR, and other autonomic responses. The lie detector does this while the subject answers questions. When the subject tells a lie, he may exhibit marked autonomic responses, even though he attempts to cover them up by subsequent responding. Surprisingly little careful work has been published on the validity of lie detector results.

Stress and the Adrenal System

Many of the bodily changes accompanying short-term emotional reactions in trying situations also can occur over much longer time spans. A variety of "stressful" stimuli and situations can require the body to mobilize its reserves to cope with the stress. In this section, we will emphasize the chronic, long-lasting stresses that are most familiar. A stress response does not require a disaster. In the human, fear of an upcoming examination, daily bickering with one's mate, or the thwarted desire to beat your neighbor in a game of bridge can produce stress. Obviously, these are not physical stresses like electric shock or confinement. However, the accumulated effects over long periods of these "psychological" stresses can be as powerful and devastating as the most severe physical stress. Psychological stress is not limited to man; under the appropriate conditions, it can be produced in many animals.

Hans Selye (1950, 1956) has studied the response to chronic stress extensively and has termed the stereotyped stress response the *general-adaptation-syndrome*. The first stage of the three-phase response is the *alarm reaction*. Typically, this phase consists of the bodily changes that occur with emotional responses—pupil dilation, increased heart beat, increased pulse, and an increase in GSR. Under prolonged stress, the organism enters the second stage, *resistance to stress*. During this stage a human recovers from the emotional alarm reaction and attempts to cope with the situation. Physiologically, the sympathetic output decreases, the endocrine glands resume a lower, more normal rate of secretion, and the organism seems to adapt successfully to the stress. This is deceptive, for this endurance seems to consume whatever resources are available and if the stress continues the organism reaches the terminal stage, *exhaustion*. Rarely do psychological stresses result in exhaustion. However, stresses of disease, exposure, or injury can often result in exhaustion. The first-stage symptoms reappear and the organism will die unless treated.

The *adrenal gland* plays a major role in the stress syndrome. It really is composed of two glands, the *adrenal cortex* and the *adrenal medulla*. The adrenal medulla is regulated directly by sympathetic innervation which causes it to secrete large amounts of epinephrine and norepinephrine into the blood. They release energy stores and increase metabolism.

The adrenal cortex is necessary for life. Its proper functioning depends on a hormone from the pituitary gland called ACTH. The adrenal cortex manufactures over 40 hormones, known as *adrenocortical steroids*. The steroids' functions are best described by the changes that follow removal of an animal's adrenal glands. It loses its appetite, experiences gastroin-

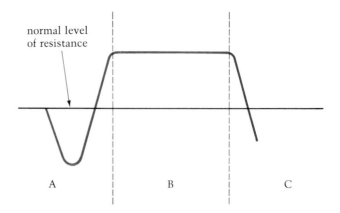

11-6

A graphical characterization of Selye's general-adaptation-syndrome. Descriptions of each of the three stages appear below the graph. (From *The Stress of Life* by Hans Selye. Copyright 1956 by McGraw-Hill Book Company. Used with permission of McGraw-Hill Book Company)

normal level of resistance

A   B   C

A. Alarm reaction. The body shows the changes characteristic of the first exposure to a stressor—pupil dilation, increased heart beat, increased pulse, and an increase in GSR. At the same time, its resistance is diminished and, if the stressor is sufficiently strong (severe burns, extremes of temperature), death may result.

B. Stage of resistance. Resistance ensues if continued exposure to the stressor is compatible with adaptation. The bodily signs characteristic of the alarm reaction have virtually disappeared, and resistance rises above normal.

C. Stage of exhaustion. Following long-continued exposure to the same stressor, to which the body had become adjusted, eventually adaptation energy is exhausted. The signs of the alarm reaction reappear, but now they are irreversible, and the individual dies.

testinal disturbances, reduced blood pressure and body temperature, and kidney failure, and if not treated it will soon die. When a person is subjected to physical or psychological stress, the pituitary gland will secrete more ACTH, resulting in more circulating steroids, which then "turn off" the pituitary ACTH (Selye, 1950). One experimenter discovered that exposing young animals to mild stresses (handling or weak electric shock) enables them to resist the deleterious effects of stress as adults. In general, they grow up to be stronger, larger, and more adapted to survival than their littermates that were not subjected to stress as infants (Levine, 1960). They also have larger adrenal glands, which seems to indicate that it is beneficial, rather than harmful, to expose developing organisms to mild environmental stresses. The finding further suggests that by protecting human infants from mildly stressful situations we may be doing them a disservice.

In modern society man is confronted with a number of simultaneous psychological stresses, accompanied by occasional acute stresses. Selye has observed, in connection with this multiplicity of stresses, that if during the stage of resistance the organism encounters a second stress—a stress that by itself could be handled—the entire adaptive mechanism may break down and the stage of exhaustion set in. This reaction has important consequences for medicine. Multiple or continuous stress situations are thought to be contributing factors in such diseases as hypertension, arthritis, allergies, and ulcers. Brady and his associates (1958) produced ulcers in monkeys by presenting them with a stressful situation. For six-hour periods over a span of weeks, the animals had to press a lever every few seconds to avoid a shock. The monkeys developed severe ulcers; several had to be removed from the experiment. This experiment has an interesting sidelight. The control monkeys received shocks at the same times as the experimental monkeys, but the control animals had no lever and no way of controlling the shock. These animals did not develop ulcers. This indicates that while both animals were subjected to the same physical stimuli only the lever-pressing monkey felt the added psychological stress that apparently arose out of having to press the lever to avoid the pain.

Labeling Emotions

Is there a unique pattern of bodily changes for each emotional state, so that we can tell from these changes alone what emotion we are experiencing? The answer is no. Of course, variations exist in the intensity of the physiological reactions, but they give us little indication of the specific emotion. Pleasant and unpleasant emotions show some differences; even more differences can be seen between exciting and depressive emotions. And a few subtle distinctions between fear and anger have been found. Nonetheless, you cannot ordinarily tell whether a person is experiencing anger or fear or joy from his bodily changes alone. Nor can you be certain of a person's emotion from his facial expressions. Even weeping is not a good indication of grief; people sometimes weep for joy or from exasperation. What, then, leads us to identify an aroused state as anger, fear, or joy?

William James, the famed American psychologist, and a Danish scientist named Lange were the first to suggest (in 1884) that the emotions we feel grow out of bodily experiences. Of course, most of us do not experience it that way. We say, "My stomach churns when I get angry"—but the James-Lange theory reverses the sequence, saying in effect that we experience the churning sensation first and then identify it as anger. The James-Lange theory implied that each emotion was preceded by a specific physiological state of arousal, but Cannon (1929) demonstrated that this was not so. The same internal state accompanies different emotions, and many internal states change too slowly to keep up with fast-changing emotions. Nonetheless, aroused states do interact with perceived emotions, and many theorists have sought to explain how this process works.

The best current answer is that the labeling of an emotion depends on the person's interpretation of the situation that arouses him. Suppose that a person crossing the street is almost struck by a car. His physiological response is the state of arousal described earlier. If he thinks the near miss was the driver's fault, he will feel angry, but if he thinks it was his own fault, he will experience fear. Or he may feel afraid initially and then become angry.

11-7A
It is difficult to label an emotion. Try to determine the emotions being expressed by these people and then turn to page 380 for a view of the context in which each emotion is being expressed. (A. Jan Lukas, Rapho Guillumette; B. Christa Armstrong, Rapho Guillumette)

Their surroundings provide clues about what emotions are being expressed, but it is still hard to be sure. The man at the left is telling a joke; the girl is engaged in a staring contest. (Jan Lukas, Rapho Guillumette; Christa Armstrong, Rapho Guillumette)

Fear often turns into joy when a threat of danger is removed, and joy into anger when a pleasurable activity is interrupted. The aroused state remains the same but the experience and the behavior are different.

The following experiment was performed to demonstrate that a person's perception of a situation determines what emotion he will experience (Schachter & Singer, 1962; Schachter, 1971). All the subjects were told they were being injected with a drug called "Suproxine" (a fictional name) which would improve their performance on certain tests of visual-motor skills. The control group (half the subjects) actually was given a *placebo*—an inactive substance that has no physiological effect whatever; in this case, it was saline. The experimental group (the other half) was given norepinephrine, a hormone secreted by the adrenal glands; norepinephrine produces the same bodily changes that occur during strong emotion. Different groups of subjects received two types of instructions: informative or uninformative. The informed subjects were told that a few minutes after injection of the drug, they would feel "side effects"—their hands would shake, their hearts would start to pound, and their faces would get warm and flushed. In short, these subjects were given a complete explanation of *how* they would feel and *why* they would feel that way. The uninformed subjects, on the other hand, were told that the injection would have no side effects at all.

Subjects of each group, informed and uninformed, were placed in two different situations immediately after injection. In one situation, called "euphoria," the subject was placed alone in a room with a stooge who had been introduced as a fellow subject. The stooge then behaved in an exuberant fashion, flying paper airplanes, jumping about, and generally acting exceedingly happy. In the other situation, "anger" was induced in the subject by asking him to fill out a long and infuriating personal questionnaire that asked such questions as "With how many men has your mother had extramarital relations—4 and under, 5–9, or 10 and over?" Filling in the questionnaire beside the subject was a stooge who displayed more and more irritation at the questionnaire and finally ripped it up in rage, threw it to the floor, yelled, "I'm not wasting any more time; I'm getting out of here," and stamped out of the room.

The results were unusually clear. Uninformed subjects given the nor-

11-8
Is this skateboarding chimpanzee delighted or terrorized? Not only is it hard to tell from this picture but many scientists hold that it is wrong to attribute human emotions to any animals except humans, that when we do so we are guilty of anthropopathism. (UPI)

epinephrine injection experienced and exhibited the same emotion the stooge was portraying, whether it was euphoria or anger. Clearly, these uninformed subjects interpreted their own bodily sensations—pounding heart, flushed face, and so on—in terms of the emotional feeling appropriate to the situation. The informed norepinephrine subjects did not report any emotional experience in either situation, because they attributed their bodily sensations to the effects of the drug. The control subjects, receiving no bodily sensations from the placebo, were unmoved in either situation.

These findings have important implications. If people are forewarned about the physiological changes caused by certain medicines, drugs, or bodily processes, they can attribute their feelings to these changes, rather than to external factors. For example, a person who can identify the early symptoms of a developing cold is not so likely to look for the cause of his distress in the environment. Furthermore, if the people around him know what is causing his tension, they can take this into consideration when responding to his heightened irritability. When we feel the internal source of certain feelings but attribute them inappropriately to some external source, we may well cause needless interpersonal conflict.

However, correct identification may not eliminate the expression of feelings. The person who does not feel well is more vulnerable to irritation. He may vent his irritation on people around him even though he knows why he is feeling irritable and knows that they are not at fault. Knowledge is helpful in understanding the reasons for one's emotions, but it is not a cure-all for the expression of unwarranted ill-feelings.

Some theorists believe that a similar kind of evaluation plays a part in determining emotional responses generally. For example, Arnold (1960) has proposed a *cognitive appraisal theory* of emotional response. According to this theory, external stimuli are appraised and judged as essentially good or bad. This judgment determines which emotion we feel, and we then express this emotion in our physiological responses and in our overt actions as well. According to Arnold, then, appraisal precedes the arousal state; but like Schachter, Arnold holds that we give emotional meaning to our states of physiological arousal. And both Arnold and Schachter agree that states of arousal lead us to organize and channel our behavior.

Behavioral Elements of Emotion

Although states of arousal evidently serve to organize and direct behavior, just how any particular person will act in the grip of a specific emotion is determined by a number of factors. Cultural mores are one. A traveler who journeys from northern to southern Europe will certainly notice the various ways in which different nationalities express their emotions. Another factor is that of parental influence. In the chapter on aggression (Chapter 12), you will find many examples of how parents serve as models for their children. Through trial and error, a person learns the approved methods of expressing his emotions in different situations and with different groups of people.

Different facial expressions are supposed to accompany the different emotions. Most people believe, for example, that the facial expression in anger is different from that in fear, joy, or disgust. Experimental evidence appears to disprove this belief; people are not very accurate in judging what emotion is being expressed from the face alone. However, investigations by Schlosberg (1954) show that three dimensions of emotion can be judged quite accurately from facial expressions. Pleasant expressions can be distinguished from unpleasant ones; intense emotions can be distinguished from mild emotions; and attentive, interested expressions can be distinguished from disdainful, indifferent expressions.

Finally, we should note that emotion can either facilitate or disrupt behavior. Whether an emotion will have positive or negative effects on behavior depends on three factors. The primary factor is *intensity*. All emotions begin to disrupt behavior when they exceed a certain level of intensity. This level or threshold is not a constant for everyone, or even for the same person on different occasions. When the threshold is exceeded, the higher centers of the brain appear to lose control, as though they are flooded with impulses from the lower centers, preventing the person from thinking straight. We say he has "lost his head" or "gone to pieces."

Below this level of intensity, emotion often is useful in invigorating and organizing behavior. A state of moderate emotional stress makes one more alert and effective. For example, numerous laboratory experiments have shown that people with moderate levels of anxiety can learn some tasks faster than can those with only a low level of anxiety.

The second factor is *unexpectedness*. A person who suddenly and unexpectedly encounters an extremely emotion-provoking situation may be overwhelmed by it. His response is likely to be confused, and he may go into a state of shock. People have even been known to die from fright. But if a person can anticipate emotional stimulation, he can usually prepare himself for it.

The third factor that determines whether emotion will be disruptive or facilitative is the *character of the responses* it evokes. If the responses interfere with adaptive behavior, the effect will be harmful. We all have seen how embarrassment can make a person behave awkwardly and inappropriately in social situations. But if the responses are adaptive, the effect of emotion is beneficial. Strong emotion has enabled many people to perform feats of strength that are beyond their capacity under ordinary circumstances. More than one man has single-handedly lifted a car to free an accident victim.

We shall have more to say about the behavioral aspects of emotion when we discuss specific emotions.

Types of Emotion: Their Causes, Consequences, and Control

It is time that we considered some of the common emotions. Several of the more powerful emotions are dealt with elsewhere in this book. Anger is discussed in the chapter on aggression, and love, jealousy, and the sexual emotions are discussed in the chapter on human sexual behavior. But here we shall discuss several emotions that all of us experience fairly regularly—fear, anxiety, disgust, and joy. Psychologists have paid particular attention to anxiety because it can have such devastating effects on mental and physical health. By contrast, little is written about joy in the psychological literature because it has no dire consequences.

Fear

Fear is an emotional response to a specific, perceived threat or danger. Common causes of fear in young children are loss of support and falling, unfamiliar objects and people, animals, darkness, separation from parents, strange places, loud noises, and pain. Many of these things also cause fear in adults.

A strong fear can be acquired from just one frightening experience. For example, a baby is taken to the doctor for the first time to have a routine inoculation. The prick of the needle evokes a fear reaction. This one experience can make the baby fear hypodermic needles thereafter. Moreover, fear generalizes to other aspects of the situation in which the fear was first experienced. The child's fear of the needle may spread to the doctor or anyone who looks like him; to all doctors, white coats, the doctor's office, and even to the building in which the doctor's office is located.

Once established, a fear is difficult to eradicate. One reason for this is that fear produces avoidance behavior. Consequently, the person does not have an opportunity to learn that the conditioned stimulus—a white coat, for example—is really not dangerous. So he continues to make withdrawal responses to situations that are not harmful.

In general, we have two ways to control the spread of fear. One is to prevent the occurrence of the original fear stimulus that acts as the source of the fear. Since pain is one such original cause, we can try to eliminate or minimize the pain. The generalization of fear also can be controlled by manipulating the consequences of the fear. By following painful experiences with pleasant ones, the effects of the pain can be nullified. Many people are apprehensive about going to the dentist, but when they suffer from a raging toothache, the relief promised by the visit to the dentist may more than offset the prospect of the painful treatment.

Are There Any Inborn Fears? Is fear of the dark, for example, inborn? The following argument makes a good case for its inheritance. Before man had the power to illuminate his environment at night, he lived in danger of nocturnal attack from enemies, both human and animal. Men who feared these dangers probably exercised more caution and prudence than people who were not afraid. Thus, the fearful ones would be more likely to survive. In other words, fear of the dark had survival value when our ancestors were living in a primitive state and consequently this useful fear became a part of our inheritance. Although there is no way to prove the validity of this explanation, it agrees with what we know about evolution. Moreover, it would account for fear of the dark, which is almost universal.

11-9
Demagogues take advantage of the emotional state of the people they seek to influence. Adolph Hitler played on the German people's needs and emotions—their angers, their fears, their economic woes—to strengthen his own power. He provided them with a scapegoat; they could blame the Jews for their own misery. (The Bettmann Archive)

Anxiety

Anxiety is closely related to fear; in fact the two words often are used interchangeably. A common distinction made between fear and anxiety is that fear is a response to a definite and specific threat or danger, while *anxiety* is a fear of something unknown or indefinite. You can be anxious without knowing why you are anxious, which is not true of fear. Moreover, anxiety usually lasts longer than fear, although fear is apt to be more intense while it lasts. Anxiety's persistence means that it can have more disastrous effects on one's physical well-being than fear. Persistent anxiety—often referred to as the stress and strain of modern living—is an important factor in high blood pressure, asthma, peptic ulcers, arthritis, constipation, and many other disorders. A new field of medicine, *psychosomatic* medicine, has been developed to treat such anxiety-related disorders, which are both physiological and psychological in nature.

Investigations of anxiety reveal that the scources are generally internal. The "enemy" is within, rather than outside as in the case of fear. A student is anxious about an upcoming exam because he is afraid of his own inadequacy and the possible loss of self-esteem. A worker becomes anxious because he feels he cannot measure up to the demands of his job.

Our impulses provide another source of anxiety—especially the impulses of sex and aggression, which could get us in trouble if expressed. Since we cannot flee from these inner sources of anxiety, as we can flee from external dangers, anxiety tends to build up and persist.

Our conscience is another internal source of anxiety; it can cause moral anxiety or guilt feelings. Because we cannot always live up to the moral dictates of our conscience, guilt feelings are common. Even when we do act in accordance with our moral principles, temptations always present themselves. If we do not yield to the temptation, the mere fact that we felt tempted sometimes is enough to make us feel guilty. On the other hand, not yielding can give us feelings of pride.

Anxiety's function is the same as fear's: to warn us of danger. In the case of fear, the danger is external. With anxiety, the danger lies within, amid unrecognized or indefinite threats from our inadequacies, our impulses, or our moral standards.

Trait Anxiety and State Anxiety. Psychologists usually distinguish between enduring anxiety, called *trait anxiety*, and anxiety that is a transitory response to a specific situation, called *state anxiety*.

Psychologists have been particularly concerned with trait anxiety because so many people suffer from its adverse effects—including both physical ailments and *anxiety neuroses*. People with trait anxiety typically restrict their lives to avoid anything that might arouse anxiety; they also experience a narrowing of consciousness and a loss of flexibility. Chronic anxiety predisposes a person to seek relief in a variety of potentially harmful addictions—alcohol, drugs, tranquilizers, and smoking, to name but a few.

State anxiety, on the other hand, can serve to energize our behavior and make our reactions more effective. For example, moderate anxiety about a forthcoming examination can cause a student to study harder and achieve a better grade. But excessive state anxiety will interfere with a student's attempts to study for an exam. His lack of preparation then heightens his anxiety, and by the time he takes the exam, whatever knowledge he has may fly completely out of his head. He has a mental block, and the pen freezes in his fingers.

Students who suffer from such intense test anxiety have been found to have strong apprehensions about being evaluated or judged. They worry about inadequacy, loss of status, a blow to their self-esteem, and punishment, and they want to escape the testing situation. Naturally, these feelings make it hard for them to respond appropriately to the test questions. Highly anxious students achieve poorer grades in college than less anxious students—but strangely, this is true only for the middle range of scholastic ability. Students with superior aptitude perform well, and students with inferior aptitude perform poorly, no matter what level of state anxiety they have.

Test anxiety can be reduced by the following procedure. The anxious student first is taught how to relax his muscles. While they are relaxed, he is told to visualize a series of situations that evoke gradually increasing anxiety. The first situations presented to him are so mild that they do not disturb his relaxed state. Each successive situation raises the anxiety level slightly, but this is done so gradually that the subject's relaxed state is not disturbed. Eventually, he is able to visualize calmly those test situations that previously aroused great anxiety. From that point, he has little trouble applying the relaxation techniques to actual test situations. This anxiety-reducing technique, called *systematic desensitization,* is used to treat fears and phobias of various sorts (see Chapter 21).

Of course, trait anxiety must be identified in a person before it can be treated. So psychologists have developed tests that measure trait anxiety with considerable accuracy, using true-false questions such as these (the answers in parentheses are those given by anxious people):

I have very few headaches.	(false)
I practically never blush.	(false)
I have nightmares every few nights.	(true)
I sweat very easily even on cool days.	(true)
I do not have as many fears as my friends.	(false)
I cannot keep my mind on one thing.	(true)

Fear and Gregariousness. The truth of the old saying "misery loves company" has been demonstrated in a series of experiments by Schachter (1959). In each of the experiments, a small group of young women, strangers to one another, volunteered for an unspecified experiment. They were led to a laboratory filled with complicated electrical equipment; an imposing man in a white coat introduced himself as a physician. He told the women they were going to be subjects in an experiment on the effects of electric shock. In some experiments the group members were told they would receive severe, painful, but not injurious shocks. In other experiments they were told that the shocks would be mild, producing only a slight tickle. The subjects then were given a questionnaire to measure the degree of their fear. As might be expected, those who were told they would receive a strong shock were more fearful than those who were told they would receive a mild shock. Next, they were told there would be a delay before the experiment began, and that they could wait *alone* in a comfortable room with magazines and books, or in a classroom with other subjects. They also were given a choice between staying for the experiment and leaving. Many members of the high-shock groups left.

About two-thirds of the women in the high-shock groups chose to wait with others, whereas only one-third of the young women in the low-shock groups preferred to wait with others. (The experiment ended after the subjects expressed their preferences for waiting alone or with others. They were not given any shocks, and the nature of the experiment was explained to all of them.) It appears from these experiments that being with others who are also fearful about a forthcoming danger helps to alleviate our fears.

Disgust

Place a small piece of garlic on a baby's tongue and observe the resulting discomfort. In infancy, the reaction is one of agitated squirming. As the child grows older, his reactions to an offensive stimulus become more directed and purposeful. If the offensive object is food, he spits it out; if it is an odor, he holds his nose; if it is a noise, he covers his ears; and if it is a sight, he closes his eyes. *Disgust* is evoked by anything that offends. In childhood, the offensive situations are closely associated with sights, sounds, smells, and tastes; the word disgust derives from Latin roots meaning "offensive taste." Adults are offended by a much wider variety of situations, including such abstract stimuli as newspaper editorials, higher taxes, and coarse language. But common gestures of disgust toward intellectual or artistic objects are also to hold the nose, close the eyes, or cover the ears. Such actions demonstrate the close kinship between adult and infantile disgust. They also show how we try to exclude disgusting stimuli by barring the sensory pathways by which we receive the stimuli.

Joy

Anger, fear, anxiety, and disgust often are called negative emotions because they are disturbing; consequently, we usually try to avoid them. *Joy* is a positive emotion: wanted, sought, and, once possessed, cherished. Unfortunately, joy is relatively short-lived. Several causes of joy have been identified. One is relief from discomfort. The child is elated when he has finished his homework, eaten his vegetables, or escaped a visit to the dentist. Under these conditions, joy passes rapidly because it is merely an immediate reaction of relief.

Another cause of joy is obtaining something one wants very much—new clothes or a new automobile, a promotion or a prize, an invitation, or admission to graduate school. This joy also fades quickly because the acquisition rather than the possession causes it.

A third cause of joy or exuberance is the esthetic experience. Seeing lovely scenery, beautiful works of art, handsome people; listening to music, smelling a pleasant odor, tasting delicious food—these experi-

11-10
Joy—young boys at play. (N. R. Farbman, Time-Life Picture Agency)

Alone or with others, an individual's feelings of joy are somewhat impulsive and transitory—a sudden thought about a particular event or simply a general feeling of well-being. (Arthur Freed)

11-12

Some children are taught emotional restraint at an early age. This child retires to his own room to let flow the unhappiness he feels. (Charles Harbutt, Magnum)

ences, as well as such activities as playing tennis, tinkering with machinery, swimming, surfing, and dancing, can bring us joy.

Joy is not complex, like anger and fear. We do not need to displace it or find disguised outlets for it. Obviously, joy is not a cause of conflict, nor does society frown upon it—unless the exuberant person becomes too rowdy. Joy, like other emotions, is often experienced vicariously; we enjoy seeing others act joyfully. When we identify with a character in a movie, play, or novel, we live his joys with him. Parents frequently experience vicarious joy when they see their children enjoying themselves.

The Depressive Emotions

Some emotional states do not invigorate behavior but have just the opposite effect of depressing activity. *Depressive emotions* include feelings of *discouragement, dejection, despondency,* and *despair.*

Depression varies in intensity and duration from a slight, transitory mood of discouragement to a severe, persistent feeling of despair. Severe depression is a common feature of neurosis and psychosis, and all too often it can lead to suicide. Changes in mood between elation and dejection are quite normal, however, and may be cyclical in nature.

Depressive reactions include a loss of interest in the outside world, apathy, pessimism, loss of appetite, loss of the capacity to love, lowering of the vital functions (pulse rate, blood pressure, and breathing), and complaints of imaginary bodily ailments (*hypochondria*). These reactions correlate with the presence of a low level of the adrenal hormone, norepinephrine, in the hypothalamus. This low hormonal level slows down nervous activity; as we saw earlier, a high concentration causes excitement. Pep pills (amphetamines) increase the amount of norepinephrine in the brain, while tranquilizers reduce the amount.

What circumstances make a person feel depressed? Among the most frequent causes are failure, loss of a job, divorce. Generally, any frustration that makes one feel inadequate or hopeless will evoke some degree of depression. Embarrassment, shame, and guilt feelings also may produce depression. Insecure people are especially susceptible to depression when a sudden reversal occurs. Although depression may lead to suicide, most depressed people live out their lives in a chronic state of quiet resignation.

Serious depression can be treated by antidepressant drugs, electroshock treatment, and psychotherapy (see Chapter 21).

Grief

Grief resembles the depressive emotions in many respects. A grieving person, like a depressed person, may grow withdrawn, suffer insomnia and loss of appetite, appear apathetic, and experience a sense of despair. But grief and depression differ in several important ways. Grief is not due to a loss of hope and self-respect, as depression is, but to a loss of a loved one or something one values. Grief is a process of adjustment. It enables the bereaved person to express the emotions of loss, to accept the finality of it, and to find alternatives to the ties that have been broken. Grief is a healing process; it leads the grieving person back

Where there is war, there is grief. The grief of war encroaches on all people — the soldiers on the battlefield and the civilians who happen to get in the way. (U.S. Signal Corps, Al Chang)

to action, which the depressive emotions rarely do. Moreover, grief — unlike depression — is not regarded as a pathological condition unless it continues indefinitely. Perhaps the most important difference between grief and depression — one that Freud pointed out — is that the grief-stricken person feels that the world has become impoverished, but the depressed person feels he himself has become depleted and inadequate.

In addition to sorrow, the death of a loved one may bring on feelings of guilt and remorse. The bereaved person may feel that he failed to express affection or neglected his responsibilities toward the deceased person. Such guilt feelings may stir an unconscious need for punishment. For example, a young man, whose father died suddenly from a heart attack, soon began to have symptoms of heart trouble, although physicians could find no organic basis for them.

The emotions of grief usually run a predictable course. Numbing despair, shock, and inconsolability gradually give way to an acceptance of death's irreversibility. The bereaved person slowly develops new interests and attachments to fill the void left by the loved one's death and to provide new outlets for the love he had given to the deceased person.

Boredom

Boredom is more of a mood than an emotion, although it resembles a mild form of depression and apathy. Sometimes it is difficult to tell whether a person is bored or depressed. Unlike depression, boredom can be distinctly motivating. When bored, we tend to look for excitement. Young people who have gotten into trouble often explain their misconduct by saying, "We were looking for something to do." Some psychologists believe that the need for excitement or stimulation is a very important motive, perhaps as important as anxiety.

If having nothing to do is boring, so is having to do the same thing over and over again. Office and factory workers who are engaged in repetitive tasks often become so bored that they quit. As a result, firms are experimenting with various measures to relieve the tedium of working on assembly lines. As parents well know, young children are especially susceptible to boredom. They have what has been called a need for novelty or stimulation. In general, the more complex a situation is, the less it is likely to be boring. Even babies will look longer at complex figures like faces than they will at simple figures like squares and triangles (Caron & Caron, 1968). The need for novelty, stimulation, and complexity has been called the *curiosity motive*.

Emotions: Some Conclusions

We can draw some general conclusions about emotions from the various ideas and investigations we have discussed in this chapter. Emotions, except for the depressive emotions, are states of psychophysiological arousal, agitation, and excitement. They are produced by a variety of external and internal stimuli. Emotional reactions can easily be conditioned to neutral stimuli that happen to be present when a person is experiencing an emotion.

Emotions also are motives. They direct our behavior into specific motor channels, unless the emotion is so intense that it simply disrupts behavior. But an emotion can direct behavior only if we have interpreted the perceived situation and decided which emotion we are experiencing. Then we behave in accordance with the label we have given to our excited state.

Summary

1. An emotion has three elements: arousal, identification of the emotion, and behavior.

2. The arousal element consists of activation of the brain and various bodily organs, and a heightening of consciousness. Arousal involves increased heart rate, blood pressure, and GSR, and dilated pupils.

3. These physiological reactions are under the control of the sympathetic division of the autonomic nervous system.

4. The lie detector is simply a polygraph that measures heart rate, blood pressure, GSR, and other autonomic responses.

5. Selye termed the body's response to stress the general-adaptation-syndrome, which includes three phases: alarm reaction, stage of resistance, and exhaustion.

6. The adrenal glands play an important role in enabling the body to respond to stress.

7. The James-Lange theory of emotion stated that emotions were preceded by physiological responses. Cannon argued the reverse. However, according to Schachter and Arnold, identification or labeling of the specific emotion depends on the person's interpretation or appraisal of the situation that caused the arousal.

8. A person's facial expression is not always a good indicator of the emotion he is experiencing.

9. Emotions are motives: They not only invigorate behavior; they also direct behavior.

10. What a person will do when emotionally aroused depends primarily on how he interprets the situation and the name he gives to his feelings.

11. Other factors that determine the direction of emotionally aroused behavior are cultural norms, parental influences, and trial-and-error learning.

12. Moderate emotional intensity can make a person's actions more effective; conversely, intense and unexpected emotional stimulation can disrupt behavior.

13. Fear is an emotional response to a specific external threat or danger.

14. Anxiety is a fear of some unknown or indefinite danger; the fear of being overwhelmed by one's impulses; or, in moral anxiety, guilt about violating the dictates of the conscience. Psychosomatic medicine deals with anxiety-related illnesses.

15. Trait anxiety is an enduring disposition of a person; state anxiety is a more transitory response to a specific situation.

16. Fear and anxiety are prevalent largely because they are so easily conditioned to many different stimuli.

17. Disgust is an inborn or learned emotional reaction to an offensive stimulus.

18. Joy is a positive emotion; it usually lasts a relatively short time.

19. Depression consists of feelings of hopelessness and despair brought on by a series of frustrating experiences. In depression, the bodily processes and behavior are slowed down rather than aroused.

20. Grief results from the loss of someone or something a person values.

21. Boredom is a mild form of depression that results from lack of novelty and stimulation.

Important Terms

emotion	stage of exhaustion
arousal	James-Lange theory
"inverted-U" function	Cannon's theory
orienting response	cognitive appraisal theory
defensive syndrome	fear
autonomic nervous system	anxiety
sympathetic division	trait anxiety
parasympathetic division	state anxiety
viscera	disgust
lie detector	joy
general-adaptation-syndrome	depressive emotions
alarm reaction	grief
stage of resistance	boredom

Suggested Readings

ARNOLD, M. B. (ED.) *Feelings and emotions.* New York: Academic Press, 1970.
   A collection of papers by specialists in the study of emotions.

BECK, A. T. *Depression: causes and treatment.* Philadelphia: University of Pennsylvania Press, 1972. 2 vols.
   A readable and comprehensive survey of the literature on depression by a leading authority.

SPIELBERGER, C. D. (ED.) *Anxiety: current trends in theory and research.* New York: Academic Press, 1972. 2 vols.
   A collection of technical papers by leading investigators of anxiety.

Chapter 12   Human Aggression and Conflict

We're living in an era of unspeakable horror–of Biafra, of East Pakistan, of My Lai. Of course, events of this kind are not peculiar to the present decade. A friend once showed me a very thin book—only ten or fifteen pages long—that purported to be a capsule history of the world. It was a chronological listing of the important events in recorded history. Can you guess how it read? Of course—one war after another, interrupted every now and then by a few other events, such as the birth of Jesus and the invention of the printing press. What kind of species is man if the most important events in his brief history are situations in which people kill each other en masse?

Man is an aggressive animal. With the exception of certain rodents, no other mammal so consistently and wantonly kills members of his own species. We have defined social psychology as social influence—that is, one person's (or group's) influence on another. The most extreme form of aggression (physical destruction) can be considered to be the ultimate degree of social influence. Is aggression part of the nature of man? Can it be modified? What are the social and situational factors that increase and decrease aggression?

—Elliot Aronson
(*The Social Animal*)

Human Aggression and Conflict

Man's inhumanity to man has been the subject of countless sermons and moral essays. War has always been a favorite topic in historical writings. Crime and strife rank high as themes in literature and in the newspapers, television, and movies. Accounts of human conflict and cruelty attract as much attention as do those of love and sex. At an early age, we begin to act out our aggressive fantasies. As adults our acts of aggression are frequent and take many forms. We argue, compete, criticize, discriminate, quarrel, fight, steal, destroy, and kill. We also engage in many self-injurious practices. Even our dreams and daydreams are filled with conflict. Man, it is said, is the cruelest, most destructive, and most violent of all the species.

In recent years, social scientists have taken up the study of aggression and conflict in an attempt to identify the causes of destructive behavior. Such investigations seek to provide understanding and knowledge that can be used to reduce human destructiveness and violence. Among the first things that psychologists learned about aggression and conflict is that they usually are intertwined with a feeling of frustration. For this reason, we will look at all three subjects together. Moreover, since a good deal of aggression is directed against oneself, we also will deal with the topic of self-aggression in this chapter.

What Is Aggression?

Aggression is any act performed with the intention of destroying, injuring, degrading, coercing, or subjugating a person (including oneself), a group of people, or a material object. Aggressive acts run the gamut from an unfriendly look, an unkind word, or a slap — to suicide, murder, or total destruction of a city and its people.

Of course, many injurious and destructive acts happen without anyone's intending them. Accidents on the highway, in the home, and at work take a substantial toll in human life; but accidents generally are not considered to result from willful aggression. Pollution of the environment is destructive, but it is not done with destructive intent. Carelessness with fire is not aggressive, though arson is. If society finally succeeded in controlling willful aggression, a lot of unintentional harm still would be inflicted on people and things.

Before we can limit our discussion to those aggressive acts that are intentionally harmful, we must deal with the subjective nature of the word *intentional*. Does it mean that a person has to be *aware* of his intention? Or does it also include intentions of which a person is not aware? Psychologists have found the concept of unconscious motivation useful. For example, many accidents are discovered, upon analysis, not to be accidents at all but the result of a person's unconscious wish to harm himself or others. Researchers have examined the backgrounds of the more than 50,000 drivers killed in auto accidents each year in the United States, and they estimate that as many as 8,000 of those deaths are actually conscious or unconscious suicides. Table 12-1 lists some of the major causes of death, both accidental and intentional.

Hostile aggression also can masquerade under such guises as social control, discipline, and consideration for the victim's own welfare. Punishment often is justified on the ground that it teaches the punished person a useful lesson. Psychologists have discovered that the one lesson it certainly teaches is how to be aggressive.

We also must distinguish between intentionally aggressive acts motivated by anger and those that result from other causes. For example,

Table 12-1   *Causes of Death for Americans, 1972 (The World Almanac and Book of Facts, 1974)*

Causes	Contributory Data	Total Number
Intentional Death		
War (Vietnam)	96,120*	
Homicide	18,880	
Suicide	24,280	
		139,280
Death from Disease		
Heart disease	1,028,560	
Cancer	346,930	
Tuberculosis	4,550	
Other diseases	305,770	
		1,685,810
Accidental Death		
Traffic accidents	56,600	
Drowning	7,600	
Fire	6,800	
Firearms	2,400	
Other types of accidents	40,270	
		113,670

* Average total figure per year, based on data for 1961–1973. All other figures pertain only to 1972.

12-1
The extreme of aggression is war. Many people believe that war is not a true indicator of aggression because soldiers are "ordered" to behave aggressively and are simply protecting their own lives. However, the products of war—death and destruction—are equally devastating regardless of the emotions of the participants. (Sergeant L. Chetwyn, Courtesy Imperial War Museum, London; Soviet Life from Sovfoto)

two of the most destructive forms of behavior are crime and war. But a burglar who breaks into a house and steals a television set ordinarily bears the owner no ill will. He simply needs money or a television set. A soldier who shoots an enemy is rarely angry at him; he is merely doing his duty as a soldier. Crime and warfare are caused primarily by economic and political considerations and not by the emotion of anger.

Of course, some crimes and probably some wars are motivated by anger and a desire for revenge. More than one discharged worker has burglarized his former employer's office. Most murders in this country are committed in the heat of angry family quarrels. For example, *The New York Times* (1974) reported the arrest of a man who had set fire to his home while his wife and seven children were asleep. Earlier that evening he and his wife had had a fight. And Hitler led the Germans into World War II with angry speeches calling for revenge (although his motives were far more complex than simple revenge).

To avoid confusion, therefore, we must say that *aggression is the performance of an act whose intent, whether conscious or unconscious, is to cause injury, harm, or destruction to others or to oneself.*

Studying Aggression In the Laboratory

One of psychology's chief contributions to understanding aggressive behavior has been its experimental studies of the phenomenon. We shall briefly describe some of the methods devised for this purpose.

Great ingenuity is required to produce genuine aggression in the laboratory. In one widely used method, a confederate of the experimenter interferes with the subject while he is trying to complete a task, such as putting together a jigsaw puzzle. The frustrated subject then is given an opportunity to express his aggression. He is instructed to administer electric shocks to a person (not the confederate) as punishment for that person's making mistakes in a learning situation. The subject may select a weak, medium, or strong shock. No shocks are actually given, but the subject does not know this. The intensity of the shock chosen is used as a measure of the intensity of the subject's aggression.

This standard situation can be varied in a number of ways. A film can be shown between the frustration and the opportunity to express aggression, to see whether the film increases or reduces the intensity of the subsequent punitive acts. Or the confederate's characteristics can be varied to see what effect they have on the level of aggression. In one experiment, the confederate pretended to be hard of hearing, which was supposed to account for and excuse his interference with the subject's performance.

Albert Bandura and his associates (1973) used a method of studying aggression in children. Nursery school children saw an adult exhibit aggressive acts, both physical and verbal, toward a large toy doll. Other children saw an adult sitting quietly in the experimental room paying no attention to the doll. Later, each child was mildly frustrated and then placed alone in the room with the doll. The children behaved like the adult model they had been exposed to. The children who had seen the aggressive adult performed more aggressive acts than a control group of

12-2
These film sequences show the aggressive adult model in Bandura's experiment and the resulting aggressive behavior of two children. (Bandura, 1973)

children who had not seen any adult with the doll, and made many responses that were exact imitations of the model's behavior. In contrast, the children who had observed the nonaggressive adult made even fewer aggressive responses than the control subjects. Children who saw the adult model being rewarded for aggressive behavior were much more likely to imitate the model's behavior than children who saw the model punished for aggression. Bandura concluded that the children identified strongly with the adult models' rewards and punishments as well as their actions.

One advantage of studying aggression in the laboratory is that we can isolate factors and see how each raises or lowers the amount of aggression. Another advantage is that we can employ controls to make sure that the factor under consideration actually is having an effect. For example, a film of a prize fight was shown to subjects to see how it would affect their aggressiveness (Geen & O'Neal, 1969). Another group of subjects was shown an exciting film of a long-distance race in which no physical aggression occurred. The subjects who saw the prize fight subsequently punished subjects more severely for making mistakes than those who saw the race film. Such experiments, which duplicate real-life situations, have considerably increased our knowledge of the factors that determine aggression.

12-3
In an experimental study of aggression, subjects were asked to tell a story about each picture. Those who experienced conflict over the expression of hostility told stories involving hostility about the neutral picture (top); a comparison group told stories that were appropriate for each picture. Similar results were obtained on a word-association test and on physiological measures. The investigators thus showed that a measureable difference exists between the physiological and psychological responses of people who are in conflict over the expression of hostility and those who are not. (Nelson & Epstein, 1962)

Aggression also can be studied experimentally in nonlaboratory situations. Goldstein and Arms (1971) studied the effect of a football game on the spectators' level of aggression. They gave a hostility questionnaire to 150 male spectators before and after a hard-fought Army-Navy game and found an *increase* in the amount of hostile feelings expressed, whether the spectator had rooted for the losing or the winning team. A comparison group of spectators at a gymnastic meet were given the same questionnaire before and after the meet; their hostility did not change significantly.

Is There an Instinct for Aggression?

Many writers believe that man has an instinct for aggression. Given an appropriate stimulus—frustration, for example—a person will naturally react aggressively. He does not have to learn to be aggressive, although he does learn specific, culturally prescribed *ways* of being aggressive. This view, which was out of favor for a number of years, has recently been taken up again by psychologists and biologists. Often the term drive, motive, or need is substituted for the term instinct.

The argument in favor of the *instinctivist position* rests on the following considerations:

1. the prevalence of human aggression throughout history

2. the prevalence of aggression in almost all species of animals

3. the appearance of aggressive acts early in childhood

4. the survival value of aggression

Prevalence of a specific form of behavior does not in itself prove that the behavior is instinctive. More convincing, perhaps, is the observation that young children bite, pinch, hit, and kick when they are frustrated and angry. But even this obviously aggressive behavior may have been learned by watching others behave in these ways. Children are very impressionable, and much covert learning takes place early in life.

Does aggression have survival value for the individual? This is a complicated question. If a person can kill an enemy before the enemy kills him, he will survive. But survival in this instance does not depend on being aggressive; it depends on the ability to win the fight. This ability may require physical strength, cunning, agility, or other personal characteristics. In short, aggressive acts seem to be more of a threat than an aid to an individual's survival, because they will put him in dangerous situations he might otherwise avoid. Moreover, much aggression consists of self-destructive acts, which obviously diminish the chances for survival.

Freud proposed that aggression or destructiveness is not itself an instinct but is a byproduct of the death instinct. The death instinct, Freud believed, resides in all species of animals, including man, as a result of the evolution of living matter out of inorganic matter. The *death instinct* represents the tendency within organic life to return to its original, inorganic antecedents. This is what Freud meant when he wrote that "the goal of life is death."

In 1932, Albert Einstein wrote to Freud on the question of why men wage war. Einstein came to the conclusion that "man has within him a lust for hatred and destruction," that he has an "aggressive instinct." Freud concurred with this view:

I can only express my entire agreement. We who believe in the existence of an instinct of that kind have in fact been occupied during the last few years in studying its manifestations. . . . As a result of a little speculation, we have come to suppose that this instinct is at work in every living creature and is striving to bring it to ruin and to reduce life to its original condition of inanimate matter. Thus it quite seriously deserves to be called a death instinct. . . . The death instinct turns into the destructive instinct when it is directed outwards. . . . The organism preserves its own life, so to say, by destroying an extraneous one. Some portion of the death instinct, however, remains operative within the organism, and we have sought to trace quite a number of normal and pathological phenomena to this internalization of the destructive instinct. (in Freud, 1940)

Why, in Freud's view, is the energy of the death instinct channeled into aggressive behavior? Because life instincts conflict with the death instinct. Self-destruction is turned into aggression toward other people and things when our urge to live outweighs our urge to die. Freud's idea of a death instinct has not been widely accepted, although some writers take it very seriously. Norman O. Brown's book, *Life Against Death*, is perhaps the best-known current work on this theme.

The instinct doctrine assumes that everyone is born with a propensity to be aggressive. Common observation tells us, however, that people vary widely in the number of aggressive acts they perform and they also differ in the expressed intensity of their hostile feelings. Our conversation reflects these perceived differences when we describe one person as "filled with hostility" and say of another that "he doesn't have a mean bone in his body." Some authorities have suggested that these differences among people have a genetic basis, but no hard evidence as yet exists to support this theory.

Aggression and the Brain

Considerable evidence indicates that aggressive behavior is governed by regions in the brain. Of necessity, most of the work in this area has been done with animal subjects.

Aggression and the Hypothalamus

A number of years ago, Philip Bard (1928) removed various portions of a cat's brain to determine the effects of their loss on rage behavior. He found that if all brain tissue above the level of the hypothalamus were removed, it was still possible to elicit rage behavior. If the hypothalamus were removed, only isolated bits of rage behavior remained—the cat might hiss or its hair might rise—but no integrated rage occurred.

In a series of studies, Hess and Akert (1955) developed the technique of stimulating the brain and eliciting behavioral patterns. They showed that electrical stimulation in the general region of the hypothalamus could produce full-blown rage in the cat. The rage was very similar to that shown by a normal cat: hissing, hair raised on back, claws out, and a directed attack. Hess emphasized that the experimenter could even be the object of the attack: "A slight movement on the part of the observer is sufficient to make him the object of a brisk and well-directed assault. The sharp teeth and claws are effectively utilized in this attack." In other words, the elicited rage was real; the cat was genuinely angry and attacked whatever was available, including the experimenter.

More recently, John Flynn (1962, 1963) has undertaken a systematic series of studies on the brain mechanisms of rage. Flynn felt that rage elicited by electrical brain stimulation provided a very important model for the study of aggression, with direct bearing on human aggression. Flynn was able to replicate and refine Hess's original observations. He found that stimulation of the more lateral portion of the hypothalamus elicits directed rage and attack. Moreover, Flynn observed two quite different forms of directed attack. In one, called *affective* attack, the animal shows full-blown rage with all of the side effects of hissing, salivation, back hair raised, and so on. In another form of attack, which Flynn called *quiet biting* attack, the cat quietly stalks the prey, pounces, and kills. (The prey used in Flynn's experiments was typically a deeply anesthetized rat.)

In the affective attack, as the intensity of the electrical stimulus is increased the general alerting occurs. The back hair rises, the tail becomes bushy and fluffed out, the ears lie back on the head, the cat paces with low growls, facing its prey. If the cat is sitting, it leaps to its feet, head lowered, hissing, snarling, salivating profusely, and breathing deeply. It either moves directly to the rat or approaches it by circling to the rear of the cage. At first, it stands poised, watching the rat intently. After a second or two, it raises a paw with claws unsheathed and strikes a series of swift accurate blows. If the rat is moved, attack is immediately triggered, but the attack occurs even if the rat is lying motionless. In some instances, the cat pounces with a high-pitched scream and tears at the rat with its claws and teeth.

The quiet biting attack contrasts markedly with the apparent rage of the affective attack. It reminded Flynn of an animal carefully stalking a prey. At lower stimulus intensities, the cat is alerted. It often leaps to its feet almost with the onset of the stimulus and looks attentively around. At higher stimulus intensities, the cat moves swiftly with its nose low to the ground and hair slightly on end. The cat usually goes directly to the rat in a quiet and efficient manner and bites at its head and neck using its paws to knock the rat on its back and hold it down. The rat is immediately dispatched. In this quiet biting attack, the cat gives only minimal signs that it is angry. Its behavior is much more that of a hunting predator than that of an angry animal.

Stimulation of slightly different regions in the hypothalamus elicits these two different forms of attack. The affective rage seems to resemble human rage, as when we suddenly "blow up." A full-blown rage attack in humans resembles very much the affective attack of the

12-4
The affective attack described by Flynn. (Mary E. Browning, National Audubon Society)

cat. The quiet biting attack of the cat resembles hunting behavior in humans. Nonetheless, it is unlikely that we have many built-in behavior sequences for predatory hunting, although we may have some. The cat seems to have a good many innate behavior tendencies that combine to form the sequence of the integrated, quiet biting attack. In any event, the important point is that these two forms of aggressive behavior, quite different in their emotional tone, result from activation of slightly different regions of the lateral hypothalamus, that critical region in the depths of the brain that is concerned with so many essential aspects of emotion and motivation. It is also in the lateral hypothalamus that pure pleasure can be elicited by using Olds' electrical self-stimulation technique (see Chapter 10).

In the natural state, animals often must choose between fight and flight. The situational and physiological conditions for attack and escape are not too different—and in fact, electrical stimulation of the hypothalamus has sometimes produced flight behavior. One possible interpretation of rage and flight is simply that the stimulus hurts. The animal tries to get away from the painful stimulus, and so becomes enraged by it. But several investigators have succeeded in dissociating flight and fight. The different responses seem to depend on exactly where the electrodes are placed in the hypothalamus. In studies on brain

12-5
Dr. José Delgado has implanted electrodes in an area of the bull's brain (caudate nucleus). A push of the button on his transmitter activates the electrodes, prompting the bull to turn its head suddenly sideways, thus stopping the animal in its tracks.

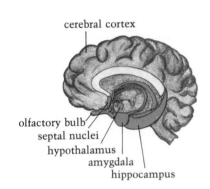

cerebral cortex

olfactory bulb
septal nuclei
hypothalamus
amygdala
hippocampus

12-6
Diagram of the limbic system (color)
in the human brain.

stimulation in dogs, Fonberg (1958) showed that with one point of stimulation, fear seemed to predominate. The dogs whined and bit, not at the experimenter, but at the restraining straps. Furthermore, they quickly learned to raise a paw to avoid the brain stimulation. They behaved as though it were simply a painful stimulus from which they were trying to escape. On the other hand, animals that showed directed rage from stimulation of a slightly different region of the hypothalamus could not be trained to avoid the stimulus. Instead, they would bite the experimenter or anything else within reach. Evidently, rage is not simply an attempt to get away from something painful. It is a directed, positive form of behavior in itself, and therefore an animal cannot be trained to perform instrumental responses to avoid the stimulus that elicits rage.

The studies of Flynn and the earlier work of Hess and Bard all portray the hypothalamus as critical for the elicitation of integrated rage behavior. Rage and aggression in their normal form require an intact, functioning hypothalamus. Furthermore, it seems to be the *only* structure that is essential to elicit integrated rage behavior. Most of the particular aspects of rage behavior, such as raising of hair and growling, involve various reflex brain systems in the lower brainstem. The motor behavior of the directed attack itself, of course, involves the higher brain regions, the visual system, the auditory system, the motor areas of the cerebral cortex that control actual movement, and presumably association areas of the cerebral cortex as well. But the hypothalamus is the critical place where all of this is put together. The other higher brain systems that are most intimately involved in rage and emotional behavior are the limbic forebrain structures. However, no single one is essential for rage; rather, they all seem to act to modulate the expression of rage.

Aggression and the Limbic System

The first experiment to implicate the limbic system in emotional behavior was Kluver and Bucy's (1937) famous study in which they removed bilaterally the entire temporal lobes in monkeys. This operation's results have come to be called the *Kluver-Bucy Syndrome.* The animals exhibited marked increases in oral behavior, putting all kinds of objects, whether they were edible or not, into their mouths; they also showed greatly increased sexual behavior. The animals attempted to mate not only with other monkeys but with animals of other species, including even the experimenters. They also seemed totally without fear or aggressiveness. The Kluver-Bucy Syndrome has since been produced with lesions limited to the *amygdala.* The amygdala also is involved in the social dominance behavior of monkeys, which further confirms its role in emotional aspects of behavior. Rosvold, Mersky, and Pribram (1954) showed that when the amygdala of the most dominant monkey in a hierarchical group of monkeys was removed, the animal lost its dominance and dropped to the bottom of the social ladder.

The amygdala is actually a very complicated structure consisting of three different subdivisions: anterior, medial, and lateral. The anterior portion of the amygdala is related to olfactory input and may be important in directing aggressive behavior in lower vertebrates. Killer rats—rats that seem genetically impelled to kill prey whenever the opportunity arises—will distinguish clearly between rat pups and mice in their aggressive behavior, killing only mice under normal conditions. They fail to make the discrimination if their olfactory bulbs are removed or if the anterior amygdala is damaged.

Kaada and his associates (1954) demonstrated that stimulation of the amygdala's lateral region elicited aggressive responses in animals. Cutting the link between this part of the amygdala and the hypothalamus abolishes the aggressive effect of amygdala stimulation. Evidently, this region of the amygdala projects to the hypothalamus to stimulate aggression.

Finally, Ursin (1960) showed that lesions in the medial region of the amygdala result in an increase in aggressive behavior. Cutting the nerve fibers linking this region to the hypothalamus also results in increased rage behavior. Thus, it appears that the amygdala's medial region acts as a "flight" zone and inhibits rage behavior in the hypothalamus.

The *septum* is another portion of the limbic system involved in aggressive behavior. Animals that have had the septum destroyed display a consistent syndrome. They become wild and ferocious and enormously jumpy. A septal rat jumps a foot when you touch it. Such behavior declines over time. However, if the amygdala is destroyed after a septal lesion, the aggressive behavior is immediately abolished. Septum and amygdala seem to act oppositely on aggressive behavior.

Human Destructiveness and the Cerebral Cortex

Man's brain structures for motivation and emotion represent an ancient heritage from his primitive ancestors. Man is the most lethal and destructive of all predators and the only one to kill his own kind systematically. We probably must blame that most recently evolved structure of the forebrain, the cerebral cortex, for the evil as well as the good in human nature. The hypothalamus and limbic forebrain structures provide the neural basis for motivation and emotion in all vertebrates. They are the source of the motivational drives that compel us to need and seek, and they provide us with emotional experiences and reactions. However, what we do in response to drives and emotions is the result of our large cerebral cortex. Popular writers commonly assume that man's lower and more primitive brain structures are responsible for his more base and "animalistic" instincts and behaviors. We do the animals an injustice. The overpowering destructiveness of *Homo sapiens* can be traced to a large cerebral cortex. We are the most dangerous and lethal species *because* we have much greater intellectual abilities, not in spite of them.

X Y Y Genotypes

The cells of the human body normally contain 46 chromosomes, two of which are the X and Y chromosomes that determine a person's gender. The female has two X chromosomes, and the male an X and a Y chromosome. Very rarely, a male has an extra Y chromosome.

In 1965, a group of investigators (Jacobs, Brunton, Melville, Brittain, & McClemont) discovered an association between the XYY genotype and a phenotype of tall stature, mental retardation, and violent behavior. Several men convicted of brutal slayings were found to have an extra Y chromosome. The total frequency of XYY genotypes in the institutionalized criminal population is about 2 per 100 as compared with about 1 or 2 per 1,000 in the general male population (Jarvik, Klodin, & Matsuyama, 1973). In other words, the chance of a male being sent to prison is much greater if he has an extra Y chromosome than if he has only one Y chromosome. However, only a very small percentage of the criminal population has an extra Y chromosome; thus, this genetic anomaly cannot be a very important contributing factor in antisocial behavior. Moreover, the conclusion that XYY males tend to be violently aggressive has not gone unchallenged (Shah & Borgaonkar, 1974), so the issue is still undecided.

Learning and Aggression

Whether or not researchers eventually will demonstrate the biological bases for aggression, it is a well-established fact that reinforcement will increase both the number of a person's aggressive acts and their intensity. If parents encourage or approve of their child's aggressiveness, the child will become increasingly aggressive. The reinforcement need not even be direct. Merely watching another person's aggressiveness being rewarded or approved is enough to make a subject more aggressive. Bandura's study, described earlier, is one of many demonstrations of this principle, which is known as *vicarious reinforcement*.

In short, if a person discovers that he can achieve his goals by harming others, he probably will do so. He may not even be angry with them. Most people are pragmatists; they will do whatever is necessary to achieve their ends.

Physically punishing a child for being aggressive is not an effective way to curb aggression, since punishment itself is an aggressive act. Children who are frequently punished learn to be aggressive, although they may not show their aggression toward their parents; instead, they displace it onto other children or toys. Several studies have found that the aggressiveness of adults was related to the amount of physical punishment they had received from their parents. Teenage youths arrested for such aggressive offenses as breaking windows, shooting out street lights, and attacking other boys were found to have been physically punished and deprived of privileges more often than their law-abiding peers.

Another study found that aggressive children had experienced no more frustration in the home than their less aggressive classmates. Their aggression in school and on the playground therefore could not be attributed to the displacement of frustrations at home. Rather, it was discovered that the aggressive children had aggressive parents who actually approved of their children's aggression outside the home. The mothers and fathers of the less aggressive children generally discouraged aggression in their children.

12-7
Aggression is thought to occur more frequently in young people whose parents are themselves aggressive or who encourage aggressive behavior in their children. (W. Eugene Smith)

Psychologists distinguish between physical and psychological punishment. Psychological punishment involves the withdrawal of love or approval; usually it is experienced as rejection. These two kinds of punishment produce quite different results. Children who are habitually spanked grow up to be either aggressive and violent or submissive and fearful. Children who are punished psychologically develop strong, internalized consciences. They tend to feel guilty when they are tempted to express aggression, or they turn the aggression on themselves.

Sources of Aggression

Aggressive behavior occurs for various reasons. The individual may be frustrated or angry, or he may be responding to aggressive behavior. In this section, we shall discuss several of the more common sources of aggression.

Anger-Motivated Aggression

Many psychologists believe that aggression is not a motive in its own right. Rather the motive for aggression is anger. What causes a person to become angry and hostile? One cause that psychologists have studied extensively is *frustration*, the product of thwarted efforts. If a person wants something and is prevented from obtaining it, he is very likely to feel angry and to express his hostility through some form of aggressive or destructive act. Thus, the typical sequence is frustration, anger, aggression. Of course, frustration may produce feelings other than anger, and aggression may be caused by conditions other than anger.

Displaced Aggression. The typical target for aggression is the frustrating agent, who may possibly retaliate with aggression, in which case either a conflict will ensue or the angry, frustrated person will withdraw because he is afraid. The person who withdraws from a conflict is likely to remain angry and frustrated; he will tend to vent his anger on a substitute target. This is called *displaced aggression*.

Like frustration, displacement of aggression has been intensively investigated by psychologists. They have shown that aggression is generally displaced onto a person who resembles the original frustrating agent in some respect. People frequently displace aggression from their fathers to other people who exercise authority—teachers, supervisors, policemen, army officers. These father-figures, as they sometimes are called, are often frustrating agents in their own right; but the intensity of the angry reaction to them is amplified by early paternal frustrations.

Scapegoating. *Scapegoating* is a form of displaced aggression that involves a mechanism called *projection*. We project on our victim those qualities in ourselves that we are unconsciously ashamed of. This makes us feel self-righteous and allows us to believe that "He is the sinner, not I." Scapegoating operates according to a set of rules, the two most important of which are (1) The case against the scapegoat must be justified by some vices that are attributed to the scapegoat; and (2) the

12-8
The classic example of scapegoating occurred in Nazi Germany and in some of the countries allied with or conquered by Germany in the 1930s and 40s. This photo shows a Jew, who refused to clean the streets and white-wash the walls of the town of Chemnitz, Czechoslovakia, being paraded through the streets in a refuse wagon. (Culver Pictures)

scapegoat must be weak enough so that he cannot retaliate effectively, but not so weak that he is easily victimized. The justification usually consists of the simple alibi, "He deserved it." A scapegoat who tries to fight back "deserves what he gets," namely, additional punishment for trying to defend himself.

Another important consideration is the availability of a scapegoat. When a person is frustrated and angry he often directs his wrath at the first accessible person or thing. Afterward he looks for excuses to justify his aggression—and he usually finds them. We also tend to notice in other people the embodiment of our own weaknesses, and since often they actually do possess those weaknesses, we feel justified in attacking them. Projection, like displacement, occurs unconsciously.

Prejudice and discrimination against classes of people are malignant forms of scapegoating that exist in every society. Prejudice is very difficult to eradicate because of its deeply unconscious roots.

Self-aggression. If the aggression cannot be displaced, it may be turned inward in the form of *self-aggression.* However, if a person feels that his own inadequacies are keeping him from a desired goal, he becomes angry with himself directly and the self-aggression is not a displacement.

The three stages—direct aggression, displaced aggression, and self-aggression—are exemplified in the following case of a boy in an institution. First, he displayed unusually strong aggression against adults—biting, pinching, and hair-pulling. When he was punished for this expression of his anger toward adults, the boy then began to bite, pinch, and pull the hair of other children. When these displays of anger were eliminated by punishment, the child began to pinch himself, bang his head against the wall, and pull out his hair. These self-aggressive acts created bad sores on his body and bald spots on his head.

The intent to harm oneself, which is usually unconscious, can take many forms. We may mistreat our bodies by overeating, excessive drinking, heavy smoking, taking harmful drugs, not getting sufficient sleep, and not exercising. We expose ourselves to all kinds of stresses and strains that could be avoided. Psychosomatic ailments, in which emotional stress plays a large role, are widespread and their incidence appears to be increasing. Years ago, the prominent psychiatrist Karl Menninger wrote a book entitled *Man Against Himself,* in which he spelled out the many varieties of self-aggression.

Suicide. The epitome of self-aggression is *suicide,* a subject that has been closely studied in recent years. Suicide is one of the ten leading causes of death in the United States. Among American college students, suicide is the third ranking cause of death, being exceeded only by accidents and cancer. A Center for Studies of Suicide Prevention has been established by the federal government at the National Institutes of Health. Many communities have suicide prevention agencies. These agencies provide around-the-clock counseling, usually by telephone, for a person who is contemplating suicide.

Why does a person take his own life? Guilt feelings and self-hatred are among the reasons, but they are not the only ones, and they may not be the most important. Loneliness is the chief cause of suicide among college students. Relief from intolerable, hopeless, or painful conditions is often the suicidal person's goal. Suicide also can be a way of taking revenge upon someone else. It is useful to differentiate between the wish to die (bringing one's life to an end) and the wish to kill oneself (active self-destruction). Incurable cancer might cause one to wish to die; self-hatred might cause one to wish to kill oneself. Table 12-2 presents some facts about people who attempt suicide.

Some other facts about suicides are grimly interesting. Three times as many men as women commit suicide; men prefer to shoot themselves,

12-9
Police are attempting to rescue a man who climbed a cable almost to the top of a tower of the Brooklyn Bridge. It took them an hour to coax him to come down. When first approached, the man had cried out, "I need somebody"—which in a limited way verifies the idea that people who attempt suicide often are looking for attention and a sense of being cared about. (UPI)

Table 12-2   Facts and Fables on Suicide

FABLE:	People who talk about committing suicide do not do so.
FACT:	Of ten persons who kill themselves, eight have given definite warnings of their suicidal intentions.
FABLE:	Suicide happens without warning.
FACT:	Studies reveal that the suicidal person gives many clues and warnings regarding his suicidal intentions.
FABLE:	Suicidal people are fully intent on dying.
FACT:	Most suicidal people are undecided about living or dying, and they "gamble with death," leaving it to others to save them. Almost no one commits suicide without letting others know how he is feeling.
FABLE:	Once a person is suicidal, he is suicidal forever.
FACT:	Individuals who wish to kill themselves are "suicidal" for only a limited period of time.
FABLE:	Improvement following a suicidal crisis means that the suicidal risk is over.
FACT:	Most suicides occur within three months following the beginning of "improvement," when the individual has the energy to put his morbid thoughts and feelings into effect.
FABLE:	Suicide strikes much more often among the rich—or, conversely, it occurs almost exclusively among the poor.
FACT:	Suicide is neither the rich man's disease nor the poor man's curse. Suicide is very "democratic" and is represented proportionately among all levels of society.
FABLE:	Suicide "runs in the family."
FACT:	Suicide does not run in families. It is an individual pattern.
FABLE:	All suicidal individuals are "mentally ill."
FACT:	Studies of hundreds of suicide notes indicate that although the suicidal person is extremely unhappy, he is not necessarily mentally unbalanced.

From "The Cry for Help" by N. L. Farberow & E. S. Shneidman. Copyright 1961 by McGraw-Hill. Used by permission of McGraw-Hill Book Company.

women prefer poison. The suicide rate for married men is lower than for single men. The suicide rate for college students is much lower than for their noncollege-age peers. More whites than blacks commit suicide. The suicide rate is highest in the spring and lowest in the winter. It is highest in late afternoon and lowest in the early morning hours. Monday is the favorite suicide day, at least for males.

The Reservoir Concept of Anger-motivated Aggression. Anger that cannot be expressed or displaced accumulates through repeated frustrations to form a reservoir of angry emotion. This *reservoir concept* of stored anger explains the sudden and unpredictable outbursts of temper tantrums in children, the angry rebellion of adolescents against their parents and other authorities, and the outbreaks of violence by frustrated individuals or groups within a society. It also explains why some people fly off the handle at the least provocation. Whenever rage is out of proportion to the provoking stimulus, we can assume that the dam has broken and a flood of pent-up anger is bursting forth from the reservoir.

Much of the aggression and violence by blacks in the United States has been attributed to the rage accumulated over years of repression and frustration by whites. Ironically, increased aggression often accompanies attempts to improve the conditions of a coerced minority. This phenomenon has been called "the revolution of rising expectations." As long as oppressed people have no hope of a better life, privation and deprivation do not lead them to revolt. Instead, they tend to withdraw from the society and live their lives within the family or ghetto. But when improving conditions provide a basis for hope, rebellious actions begin to look practical rather than futile. If progress suffers a setback, or if expectations are not realized as rapidly as possible, then the tendency to revolt is strengthened.

The reservoir-of-rage concept suggests that a person should be given opportunities to dissipate his resentments in harmless aggressive acts before the anger builds up and results in harmful acts. The trouble with this suggestion is that the expression of anger in aggressive acts is habit-forming, so that the person actually will become more aggressive. We shall discuss this question more fully later in this chapter.

Societies generally treat angry aggression more leniently than aggression performed in a deliberate, unemotional manner. The law does not punish impulsive murder as severely as it punishes premeditated murder. It is not difficult for us to understand and forgive a person who commits a crime of passion, because we have all experienced similar feelings. But we are horrified by a person who commits a brutal crime in cold blood, and we tend to regard him as less than human.

Aggression Caused by Aggression

A great deal of aggression is the product of aggression; in fact it may be the most important cause of aggression in adults. A basic principle of behavior states that we tend to react in the same way that we are acted upon. If someone smiles at me, I smile back. If someone yawns, I yawn. If someone shoves me, I shove back. And if someone hits me, I will want to hit back. The behavior of two people toward each other tends to match or be symmetrical.

12-10
The urban ghetto sets the scene for aggressive behavior. Young people, frustrated because they cannot find work and with little to occupy their time, become hostile and aggressive. The promise of something better may only increase their frustration and anger if it fails to live up to the expectations it has raised. (Gamma)

The tendency to act in the same way that another person is acting should not be confused with imitation or identification. Imitation implies an effort or intention, unconscious though it may be, to be like someone else. This effort is ordinarily practiced over a long period. A beginner at tennis tries to imitate the expert; children identify with their parents. Symmetry reactions, in contrast, are immediate, automatic, and lacking in intent or effort. They do not have to be learned because they are already a part of the person's behavioral repertoire.

The *principle of symmetry* accounts for much aggressive behavior. Force is met by force, argument by argument, and insult by insult. "It takes two to make a fight." By the same principle, of course, friendliness is matched by friendliness, grief by grief, and fear by fear.

What happens when an asymmetrical or discordant response occurs—for instance, when a pleasant smile is returned for an angry accusation? The attacker may become angrier because his expectation of picking a fight or of making the other person feel bad is frustrated; he may become angrier because he thinks the other person is mocking him; he may match his behavior to that of the other person by returning the smile; or he may simply be confused. This confusion is called *cognitive dissonance* (see Chapter 18).

Matching of behavior is not restricted to the interactions between two people. If a person is watching two people fight, he tends to make incipient or outright bodily movements that match theirs. (Recall the study of nursery school children, who began to act aggressively after they were exposed to an adult who was behaving aggressively toward others.) Even the presence of an object associated with aggression—a gun, for example—can by itself evoke aggressive reactions.

Conversely, experimenters have discovered that the matching of aggressive behavior can result in a subsequent *decrease* of aggression. The following experiment was performed. A subject who had been frustrated was told to shock a second subject for making mistakes in a learning task. Each time the learner was shocked he was allowed to give a shock in return. The learner could return the same intensity of shock he had received, or return a shock of lower or higher intensity. Only when the intensity of the shock returned by the learner was the same as he had received did the frustrated subject reduce his subsequent shocks. Evidently, it is difficult for a person to reduce aggressive behavior until it has been matched by an equivalent response.

Catharsis versus Symmetry. The widespread violence on television and in movies has prompted a great deal of public discussion about aggression. The question is: Does viewing aggressive acts cause the spectator to become aggressive, or does it provide a harmless, vicarious release (*catharsis*) for stored-up aggression? If the principle of symmetry holds true, then aggression on the screen will build up aggression in the spectator so that he is subsequently more aggressive. But if the reservoir concept is correct, the expression of aggression while watching violent scenes should lower the level in the reservoir and leave the person less aggressive. Each of these viewpoints has its proponents.

One leading investigator of aggressive behavior declares that, "An increasing body of experimental research has demonstrated that the observation of violence can increase the likelihood of subsequent aggres-

12-11
Symmetry of aggression may involve a harsh word for a harsh word, a punch for a punch, and so on. The legal, public form of such symmetry takes place in the boxing ring, as shown by Muhammed Ali and Joe Frazier. (Wide World Photos)

sion" (Berkowitz, 1969). Other investigators of aggression (Feshbach & Singer, 1971) give evidence that either the active expression of aggression or the passive observation of it will reduce the tendency to be aggressive.

These opposing viewpoints can be reconciled in the following manner. If a person has performed an aggressive act or watched one being performed, his impulse to be aggressive will probably be weakened temporarily. "Blowing one's top" clears the atmosphere for a while. This illustrates the general psychological principle that a nonresponsive period follows the performance of any act or even concentrated thinking about it. After eating, one does not eat again for several hours; after sexual intercourse, sexual desire abates for a while. Performance of an act temporarily inhibits repetition of the act.

Although aggression may be reduced temporarily by an act of aggression or by watching a violent movie, the disposition to be aggressive is strengthened by each act or observation of aggression (Berkowitz, 1971, 1973). Thus, every time a person successfully carries out an aggressive act or watches aggression being rewarded, his tendency to be aggressive is increased, according to the reinforcement principle.

One objection to experimental investigations of the effects of violence is that the effects have been observed only over short periods of time. Aggression may increase or decrease when children watch violent programs on television, but how long does the effect last? A study by Eron, Lefkowitz, Huesmann, and Walder (1972) indicates that the effect can last as long as ten years. In 1960, they obtained ratings of aggressiveness for the entire third-grade population of a semirural county in New York State. The ratings were made by the children themselves. Each child was asked to name those classmates who performed various aggressive acts, for example, "Who pushes and shoves other children?" and "Who starts a fight over nothing?" Each child's preference in television programs was obtained by asking each mother to name her child's three favorite television programs. All programs mentioned then were categorized as violent or nonviolent. It was found that boys named as aggressive by their classmates preferred more violent programs.

Ten years later, about half of the children in the original study were located. Again they were rated for aggressiveness by their classmates. This time, the subjects themselves listed their four favorite television programs. A preference for violent programs *at age 9* was correlated with aggressive behavior *at age 19*. After examining various hypotheses, the investigators concluded that "a preference for watching violent television in the third grade contributes to the development of aggression." An alternate explanation might be that because some parents teach and reward violence in their children, a preference for violent television shows can be explained as resulting from a heightened proclivity for violence, rather than a cause.

In explaining their findings, the investigators adopted a theory of aggression developed by the Stanford psychologist Albert Bandura (whose experiments we discussed at the beginning of this chapter):

Bandura and his associates have demonstrated that aggressive behaviors new to the subject's repertoire of responses, as well as those already well established in his repertoire, can be evoked by observation of models performing such aggressive behaviors. The likelihood of performance of the observed aggressive behaviors is stronger when the model is rewarded for his aggressive behavior. (Eron, Lefkowitz, Huesmann, & Walder, 1972)

The fact that leading television characters often are shown obtaining desirable goals by violent means (see Table 12-3) would strengthen the viewer's tendency to be aggressive.

Table 12-3   Violent Acts on Television During an Average Week (U.S. National Commission on the Causes and Prevention of Violence, 1970)

Situation	Percentage
Plays containing violence	80%
Cartoons containing violence	95%
Comedies containing violence	67%
Major characters exhibiting violence	50+%
Leading character killing someone	10%
Leading character being killed	5%
Character attempting to stop violence	8%
Violence not being subject to legal due process	80%
Lawmen initiating violence	40%
Lawmen contributing to violence	70%
Lawmen responding nonviolently to violence	10%

TOTAL NUMBER OF VIOLENT ACTS: 600

Why was there no correlation between television viewing and aggression in girls? The investigators suggest that girls learn early in life that physical aggression is not a desirable form of behavior for their sex. Consequently, they do not imitate aggressive behavior when they see it on television as boys do. Moreover, relatively few violently aggressive females appear on television, so that girls have fewer aggressive models to imitate. However, when girls are reinforced for aggressive acts, they do become more aggressive.

Sex differences in *physical* aggression have been observed throughout history. Females are less violent than males—even in their dreams. Females of college age have fewer dreams of physical aggression than males do.

One argument defending violent television programs maintains that such programs teach the lesson that "crime does not pay;" the "good guys," representing law and order, kill the "bad guys." If this view is correct, the spectator should become less aggressive. But the following experiment undermines this argument. Subjects trying to accomplish a task were interrupted and thus frustrated by the experimenter. Then they were shown a film of a prize fight. Some of the subjects were told that the fighter who was badly beaten was an unmitigated scoundrel (implying that he deserved what he got). Other subjects were told that the defeated fighter was really a decent fellow at heart and was trying to mend his bad ways. All of the subjects then were given an opportunity to rate the annoying experimenter on a number of characteristics. Those who had been told that the defeated fighter was really a bad fellow gave the experimenter more negative ratings than those who had been told that the defeated fighter was really a decent fellow. This study indicates that the television industry could minimize the effects of violence on spectators by showing programs in which the "bad guys" are not all that bad and are repentant for what they have done.

Factors That Determine Aggressive Behavior

Various factors determine whether a person will react aggressively in a specific situation—for example, when someone steps on his foot. For the sake of simplicity, we will call the person stepped on the "victim" and the other the "aggressor." Note that a single situation can involve *all* of the following factors:

1. The victim's interpretation of the aggressor's intention. Was it deliberate, playful, careless, or an unavoidable accident? A deliberate attack is more likely to arouse hostility than an accidental one.

2. The aggressor's subsequent behavior. If he apologizes, the victim is less likely to express his anger aggressively.

3. The amount of harm done. If it is very irritating, perhaps because the victim is suffering from corns or wearing new shoes, his anger will be strengthened.

4. The characteristics of the aggressor. A good friend, a woman, or a child ordinarily arouses less aggression than a stranger or an enemy. The size of the aggressor and his status also are important variables. One might even feel proud to have his foot stepped on when the aggressor is a famous person.

5. Characteristics of the situation. In a crowd, the chances of being stepped on are increased, and a victim usually takes these situational factors into account.

6. Internal state of the victim. These influences may be either temporary or more permanent. Temporary variables include such things as the victim's mood at the moment, his state of fatigue or preoccupation, and so on. Permanent variables include such general traits as his aggressiveness, impulsiveness, "good-nature," and so forth.

All of these factors combine in various ways so that it is difficult if not impossible to predict when a person will become aggressive. And of course the victim may feel aggressive but not show this feeling either by words or actions. Some psychologists believe that the only reasonably sure basis for predicting whether a particular person is going to act aggressively in a particular situation is to ascertain how he has acted in the past in that situation.

12-12
Disputes may be avoided if one of the two participants responds calmly and somewhat apologetically. Meeting anger with anger simply intensifies the problem and is unlikely to help in reaching an equitable solution. (Leonard Free, Magnum)

Control of Aggression

Suppose you were asked to draw up a plan for reducing the incidence of maladaptive physical aggression and violence in the world today. What could you learn from psychological research and speculation that would be applicable to this task? Your plan might include the following prescriptions, all of which, especially the first three, are based on psychological findings:

1. Eliminate all needless *externally imposed* frustrations, deprivations, privations, injustices, inequities, coercions, and punishments.

2. Stop reinforcing aggressive behavior and start reinforcing nonaggressive behavior.

3. Eliminate objects associated with aggression and scenes and stories depicting brutality and cruelty.

4. Provide alternatives for physical violence. Alternatives might include strenuous interactions with the physical environment and reasonable discussions and analyses of the situations that arouse anger.

5. Find nonaggressive ways of reacting to aggression. Such ways might include "a soft answer," "turning the other cheek," reasonable discussion, and restitution.

6. Instruct people on ways to avoid or overcome frustration.

7. Allow parents only minimal use of physical punishment.

8. Avoid situations that make one angry.

Frustration

Whenever we pursue a goal, we are likely to encounter frustration. It may be due to external factors, or to factors within ourselves. A certain amount of frustration is inevitable in any major undertaking—but several forms of frustration can hinder even the simplest pursuit.

For example, consider what can happen if you decide to call a friend from a pay phone. If you have no change, you will suffer from *privation*—a lack of something necessary for fulfillment of a goal. If vandals have stolen the phone, you will feel *deprivation*—the removal of something that is needed for your purpose. If you cannot remember your friend's number, you are suffering from *blocking*. If you reach your friend but traffic noises drown out his voice, you are being blocked again—but this time the frustration is environmental, not internal. Often, frustration is a combination of both environmental and personal obstacles.

Whether a frustrated person will persist in his efforts to reach a desired goal depends upon several factors: the strength of his motive, his desire for the goal and how close he is to attaining it, the magnitude of the obstacle, and his estimate of his ability to overcome it. If he thinks he has no chance of success, he will give up. He acquires such expectations through his previous experiences with the obstacle or with similar obstacles. A person may not even begin a task if he feels his chance of success is poor.

12-13
The frustrated and angry child who is not permitted to express his feelings may behave aggressively toward inanimate objects. Hurling a rock at a broken-down piano helps the child relieve his feelings of anger. (Philip Jones Griffiths, Magnum)

12-14
Although the expression of aggressive feelings may temporarily help a person reduce his feelings of aggression, each aggressive act actually strengthens such tendencies.

Self-confidence is an important variable in determining whether a person will undertake and pursue a task in the face of obstacles. He acquires confidence through previous successes—that is, his confidence is a product of positive reinforcers, just as are all of the traits and habits he has learned. Similarly, he fails to acquire confidence because of the discouraging effects of negative reinforcers.

As we have noted, frustration does not always make a person angry and even if it does, an angry person does not always behave aggressively. Frustration has other effects. It may persuade the person to give up his goal-directed activity. It may cause him to regress to an earlier and more immature form of behavior. It may lead him to repeat the same activity over and over again, even though his action is ineffective. Or it may inspire him to try to overcome the obstacle by adopting a problem-solving attitude.

Many people overcome serious personal handicaps or environmental privations and become outstanding successes. The psychoanalyst Alfred Adler made *compensation* for frustrating weaknesses and defects one of the cornerstones of his viewpoint. He also developed the concept of the *inferiority complex.* A person with an inferiority complex lacks confidence and feels that he is a failure. Adler believed that childhood training determined whether a person would compensate for a defect by outstanding accomplishments or be burdened with an inferiority complex.

The poverty-stricken boy who becomes a millionaire and the physically weak boy who becomes an Olympic athlete are not just myths. Some people can tolerate a lot of frustration without giving up. In fact, many people prefer to pit themselves against the challenge of difficult tasks, as we saw in discussing the achievement motive. What they do *not* like is to be interfered with arbitrarily and unnecessarily while they are engaged in goal-directed activity.

Frustration is a fact of life that can never be completely eliminated from the world, although it could be drastically reduced. For this reason, many psychologists now stress the importance of teaching effective and reasonable methods of overcoming obstacles. Many of the most serious frustrations arise in the context of intimate relationships—marriage and the family, for example—or at work. Special counseling techniques have been devised to deal with these frustrations. Among the best known is the *encounter group*, in which involved people reveal and discuss their frustrations with the guidance of an experienced leader (see Chapter 21). People obtain considerable relief by expressing their feelings in this way. More importantly, they learn from the rest of the group specific ways of dealing with a particularly stubborn frustration. Pooling the resources of a group of people faced with similar problems is often a great help in resolving interpersonal frustrations.

Inner Conflicts

Conflict is both a form of aggression and a frustration. When we say that a person is in conflict with another person, his family, or society, we mean that feelings of hostility and antagonism exist between them. The person may express these feelings by aggressive acts ranging from silent disapproval to murder. Most of these conflicts are caused by frustration; the person wants something and he is prevented from getting it by another person or a group of people.

Another kind of conflict exists within a person—an *inner conflict.* Inner conflicts are frustrating because they prevent a person from getting what he wants, and they also involve aggression. But an inner conflict is like a civil war, because the conflict is between two contrary forces within the person. Commonplace inner conflict arises when a person wants something but his conscience says he should not have it.

Approach-Avoidance Conflicts

Inner conflicts are clashes between the two incompatible response tendencies of approach (desire) and avoidance (fear). A person wants something, which means in behavioral terms that he tends to approach it, but he is afraid of what might happen should he get it, meaning that he also tends to avoid or withdraw from it.

A simple example of an *approach-avoidance conflict* is often seen at the beach. A young child is fascinated by the waves and runs toward them (approach). When a wave breaks and swirls around his feet, he runs back up the beach to safety (avoidance). He approaches again as the water recedes, and withdraws as a new wave breaks. He may continue this behavior for some time. Running back and forth is a characteristic response to all inner conflicts. In adults the conflict usually is expressed in thoughts, worries, and fantasies rather than in the physical act of running to and fro.

If you continue to observe the young child at the beach, you probably will notice that he starts running rapidly toward the water and gradually slows down until he comes to a halt at the water's edge. His behavior is the result of two *gradients*, approach and avoidance. The approach gradient is stronger to begin with, hence the fast running. But as he nears the waves, the avoidance gradient increases in strength resulting in a gradual slowing down until it overtakes the approach gradient and causes the child to stop or run back up the beach to safety. In general, the greater the desire and the more attractive the goal, the stronger is the approach gradient. The greater the fear, the stronger is the avoidance gradient. We can see the effects of these differences in strength in the behavior of the child. One child who is very afraid of the waves stays well back on the beach. Another child who is only mildly frightened advances quite far into the water. Should the second child be pushed over by a wave and become frightened, we can be sure that a weak avoidance gradient will suddenly become very strong. Not only will he stay far back on the beach but he may demand to leave it and not come back.

Approach-avoidance conflicts have been studied at some length in the laboratory, usually with animals, and these experiments have corroborated all that we have said about the child's behavior at the beach. We can summarize the major principles as follows:

1. The tendency to approach a positive incentive becomes stronger the nearer one comes to it.

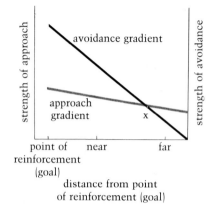

12-15
Graph of an approach-avoidance conflict. Starting at the far right of the graph and moving left, as the goal is approached both attraction and fear increase. Because the avoidance gradient is steeper than the approach gradient, a point X is reached at which attraction (strength of approach) equals fear (strength of avoidance). As one continues to move nearer to the goal, the tendency to turn back becomes ever stronger as fear mounts much more rapidly than attraction.

2. The tendency to withdraw from a negative incentive also increases in strength the nearer one comes to it.

3. The avoidance gradient increases more rapidly than the approach gradient when a subject nears a goal that has both positive and negative features.

4. The tendency to approach or avoid something varies with the strength of the drive to reach the goal.

The approach-avoidance conflict can take one of two forms. One may have to endure some hardship or unpleasantness *before* reaching the desired goal, or one may experience the unpleasantness *after* the goal is reached. Psychologically, the two situations are quite different, since the stronger response tendency in the first case is that of withdrawal and in the second case that of approach. Consider, for example, what would happen if people were paid for work before they did it.

Approach-Approach and Avoidance-Avoidance Conflicts

The psychological literature often mentions two other types of inner conflicts—approach-approach and avoidance-avoidance. In the *approach-approach conflict*, a person is presented with two desirable goals, but cannot have both. For example, a man is invited to two parties on the same night and must decide which invitation to accept. In trying to make up his mind, he runs back and forth mentally between the two parties, weighing their relative merits. This same situation can become a *double approach-avoidance conflict*, if each party also has some negative features compared with the other. For instance, one party may be some distance away, while the other party—though nearby—will include a couple of disagreeable guests. In this situation, too, approach and withdrawal will alternate between the two choices until the person decides.

When a person is presented with two choices and both are distasteful, his natural response is to avoid both. This *avoidance-avoidance conflict* also is called "leaving the field." If another person coerces him into choosing, the conflict becomes an external one. But his conscience may force him to choose one of the disagreeable alternatives. If he finally is forced to choose, his decision then turns into an approach-avoidance conflict as he tries to decide which choice is less distasteful. We conclude, therefore, that all types of conflicts can be reduced to variations on the single theme of approach-avoidance.

Basic Approach-Avoidance Conflicts

The many approach-avoidance conflicts can be reduced to three basic types: impulse versus reason, desire versus fear, and desire versus guilt. *Impulse versus reason* involves any situation in which we want something immediately but must delay and plan to get it. We learn the capacity to postpone satisfaction. Young children cannot tolerate delays in the satisfaction of their desires. As they grow older and learn to appreciate the greater satisfactions that can result from reasonable planning, they also learn to tolerate longer and longer delays. Perhaps the most common example of delayed satisfaction is saving money for some large acquisition like a car or a house. The temptation is great to spend the money before it is accumulated, and many people yield to it.

Desire versus fear is an inner conflict that expresses itself in virtually limitless ways. We may be afraid of the path we must take to reach the goal, or we may fear some characteristic of the goal or of the consequences of attaining it. For instance, we may want to learn to ski but fear various consequences. Learning to ski may seem painfully embarrassing, and so we avoid it. Or we may fear that becoming a regular skier will increase our chances of breaking a leg, or distract us from more serious but less enjoyable pastimes. In some cases, we can become afraid of the desire itself, because it leads to painful consequences.

The conflict between *desire and guilt* is a special case of desire versus fear. Fear is being afraid of something in the external world such as parental punishment, loss of one's job, dismissal from school, or imprisonment. Guilt is the result of transgressing or being tempted to violate one's moral and ethical principles. Desire says yes, conscience says no.

Some people still believe that the moral sense is inborn, but psychologists agree that we have to learn our moral standards. Each individual's moral code is constructed on a foundation of rewards and punishments established by his parents during early childhood. What is defined by the parents as being good is rewarded (or at least not punished); what they consider bad is punished (or at least not rewarded).

As a result the child takes over his parents' moral principles — interpreting them, incorporating them within his personality, and making them his own. Thereafter, when he is tempted to do something bad (in his own terms) or actually does it, he feels guilty. He is no longer afraid of what his parents will do to him — they may be completely out of the picture — but he suffers from a guilty conscience. Everyone who has a well-developed conscience knows how painful guilt can be.

Paradoxically, behaving in a manner consistent with our moral standards does not spare us from guilt. Simply feeling tempted, even without acting upon it, often makes a person feel guilty. In fact, a person who is tempted to violate his principles may feel even guiltier than a person who actually commits a misdeed. This phenomenon was borne out by the following experiment (MacKinnon, 1938). College students were placed one at a time in a problem-solving situation in which they could cheat by consulting the answers in the back of the booklet. They were told not to look at the answers, and then they were observed through a one-way window to see if they violated the instructions. About half of them did. A subsequent test showed that those who did *not* cheat felt more remorse than those who did. Their remorse was due to a conscious temptation to cheat. Those who cheated did so because they had less severe consciences to begin with and, as a consequence, less guilt at the end.

Moral Standards: A Special Case of Conflict

Many investigators have tried to identify precisely what is most effective for moral training. They have discovered that the *types* of rewards and punishments used by parents are of paramount importance.

As mentioned earlier in this chapter, two main types of reward and two main types of punishment are available. Rewards may be either _material_ (giving the child candy or a toy) or _psychological_ (giving love, affection, praise, and approval). Punishments may be either _coercive_ (spanking, taking away privileges, or depriving of a valued possession) or _psychological_ (disapproval, rejection, or withholding affection). Psychological rewards and punishments are much more effective in developing a strong _internalized_ conscience. A child or an adult with an internalized conscience polices his own behavior and punishes himself. A child or an adult with an _externalized_ conscience resulting from material rewards and coercive punishments behaves as long as someone is around to police his conduct. If he thinks he can get away with something, he does so without a twinge of conscience to deter him.

Love as a reward and withdrawal of love as a punishment do not suffice to develop a strong conscience. The parents must persuade the child that they want him to behave morally and that they themselves act that way. Psychological discipline thus requires reasoning with the child and explaining to him why he should not do certain things. Moreover, a child tends to incorporate the moral standards of the adult who controls his access to love, security, or mastery. Direct parental approval will encourage a child to modify his behavior — but a child will change his moral judgments _more_ readily when he sees an adult approving of another adult for behavior that runs contrary to the child's principles.

As the child grows older, he sees people he admires or respects behaving in ways that do not fit his moral principles. This often throws a young person into conflict and forces him to reconsider or change his principles. When he goes to college, his conscience often is severely strained because his classmates and some of his professors have standards of conduct that differ from his. He begins to doubt the "rightness" of his principles and gradually he may acquire new ones. But this process of conversion may be painful and disturbing. Such a reevaluation of moral principles is one of the chief causes of nervous strains and internal confusion among students.

Resolution of Conflicts

If all inner conflicts can be represented as opposing forces within the person, or response tendencies of approach and avoidance (withdrawal), then the resolution of these conflicts may proceed in several ways.

The tendency to approach may be strengthened or the tendency to withdraw may be weakened or both may be done at the same time. For example, a child who is afraid of the waves may be taken by the hand and led slowly into the water while being reassured and encouraged by his adult guide. If this is done slowly and carefully so that the child's withdrawal tendencies are not increased, and if it is repeated from time to time, the fear will be weakened or disappear, and the conflict will be resolved. The adult's role is to reinforce the approach tendencies and weaken the withdrawal ones.

Many life situations are dangerous and must be avoided. For these situations, withdrawal must be strengthened and approach weakened. The child learns soon enough to avoid the hot stove or the scratching cat.

But teaching a child to stay off a busy street is not so easy because the direct reinforcement of avoidance behavior—being struck by a car—is obviously too dangerous for the child. Threats, appeals, explanations, the example of others, and punishment all are employed to weaken such dangerous approach tendencies.

Some Defense Mechanisms

Many inner conflicts are resolved effectively—that is, they disappear or a satisfactory compromise is made. But many others are handled in ways that eventually may result in greater trouble for the individual, and may even contribute to the development of a neurosis. Psychologists have identified some of the ineffective ways—commonly called _defense mechanisms_—of handling inner conflicts. They are called renunciation, repression, projection, reaction formation, vicarious satisfaction, and displacement, which was discussed earlier in this chapter. The final defense mechanism we shall discuss is sublimation; unlike the others, it often seems to be quite successful and productive.

Renunciation. Many proponents of "character-building" and "clean living" philosophies advocate _renunciation_, or foregoing, of a drive or desire; undoubtedly, renunciation is a widespread method of dealing with inner conflicts. Renunciation, we are told, helps us to build a strong character—but this seems not to be its chief outcome. More often, it results in depression, melancholy, lowered vitality and sponta- neity, a "martyr complex," and an envy of others who are satisfying _their_ desires. The renounced drive does not disappear. Its continued pres- ence is a constant reminder to the person of the sacrifice that he is making. Moreover, the desire often grows in strength so that stronger ef- forts are needed to renounce it. People who renounce their desires while others are satisfying theirs feel unjustly treated, envious, and vindictive. This is the source of much social conflict.

Repression. Another conflict-resolving technique, related to renuncia- tion, is _repression_ or submergence of a desire. While renunciation is a conscious, intentional act, repression takes place unconsciously. The person is not even consciously aware that he _has_ the desire. These repressed desires are persistent and they affect behavior in ways that are devious and often destructive.

Projection. Attributing a repressed desire to another person is called _projection_. We see in others what is hidden within ourselves—and not surprisingly, our projected perceptions are sometimes accurate. But whether they are accurate or not, projections are a way of handling conflicts. They also can be a very devious way of satisfying the repressed drive. For example, a person who is unconsciously hostile toward some- one projects the hostility onto the other person and then feels justified in "defending" himself aggressively. It is an elaborate, unconscious deception. Nations as well as individuals use projection to justify their aggressive acts.

Reaction Formation. The appearance in consciousness and behavior of the exact opposite of a repressed motive or feeling is called _reaction for-_

mation. Hostility, for example, is replaced by friendliness. The friendliness, however, is exaggerated, and appears to an objective outsider to be hypocritical. Reaction formation, like projection, is a devious and unconscious way of satisfying the repressed feeling.

For instance, a mother's conscience may not permit her to express or even recognize her hostile feelings toward her child, so she buries these feelings under a great display of affection. By overprotecting and smothering the child, she releases her aggressive feelings under the guise of maternal concern. Because this is all done unconsciously, she deceives herself, even though her hostility is often apparent to the child and others.

Any form of fanaticism concerning moral standards is probably a reaction formation. The fanatic who denounces sin actually is fighting his own repressed "sinful" desires.

Vicarious Satisfaction. Many people seek _vicarious satisfaction_ of their desires by imaginatively participating in the experiences of others. Stories, plays, movies, and television programs may provide vicarious outlets for repressed desires. We have already examined this question in connection with aggression. Although the evidence is contradictory, the bulk of it seems to support the view that the spectator's drives are increased in strength rather than decreased. Watching public displays of aggression seems to weaken inhibitions and may allow repressed hostility to express itself. Indulging one's fantasies may simply strengthen the urge to behave in ways that are contrary to one's moral standards.

Our society evidently believes that vicarious satisfaction is socially useful. Our mass media offer almost unlimited opportunities for vicariously experiencing aggression and sex while society denies, condemns, and restrains the direct expression of these same drives.

Sublimation. Displacement is an unconscious process, as it must be to permit the satisfaction of drives without arousing the conscience and causing feelings of guilt. Displacement of a drive into channels of expression that make an ally of the conscience is called _sublimation._ Through sublimation, the energy from a repressed drive is used for creative, socially useful, or spiritual activities. Freud believed that romantic and spiritual love are sublimations of repressed sexuality. For example, he suggested that Leonardo da Vinci sublimated repressed sexual desires for his mother by painting pictures of the Madonna. From this viewpoint, the farmer who breaks the soil, plants the seeds, cultivates the plants, and harvests the crop is sublimating his repressed incestuous wishes for union with the mother. Jung was an ardent advocate of sublimation as a method for resolving inner conflicts. The animal instincts in man (the shadow, in Jung's terminology) provide the energy for artistic and spiritual activities. The sculptor who chips away at hard stone all day may be getting rid of a lot of repressed aggression at the same time that he is producing something beautiful. Of course, other motives, conscious and unconscious, are also at work in such cases, since any activity that is important to the individual satisfies a variety of motives.

Of all the defense mechanisms used for resolving conflicts, sublimation seems the best. It alone can simultaneously satisfy the demands of the drive, the demands of reason, and the demands of conscience.

Summary

1. Aggression is the performance of an act whose intent, whether conscious or unconscious, is to cause injury, harm, or destruction to others or to oneself.

2. Some authorities believe man has an inborn propensity to be aggressive; others feel that aggression is largely learned behavior.

3. There appears to be a center in the brain (the amygdala) that elicits aggressive behavior when stimulated. The hypothalamus and other parts of the limbic system are also involved in aggressive behavior.

4. The number of aggressive acts performed by a person can be increased by positively reinforcing him for being aggressive.

5. Frustration that arouses anger is one of the chief causes of aggressive behavior.

6. When a frustrated person cannot express his anger against the frustrating agent, he often will displace hostility, directing it at other people, objects, or himself. Scapegoating is a form of displaced aggression which involves the defense mechanism of projection.

7. Self-aggression takes many forms, including abuse of the body, self-destructive acts, exposure to stressful situations that could have been avoided, and suicide.

8. Repressed anger can accumulate until the pressure becomes so great that it explodes in extremely aggressive behavior. Such outbursts have a short-term cathartic effect, making the person less likely to be aggressive for a time after the outburst.

9. Aggressive behavior is often a response to aggression. A person tends to match his behavior symmetrically with the behavior of others.

10. A child whose parents engage in aggressive behavior, who is rewarded for being aggressive or sees others being rewarded, and who watches violent television programs and movies will most likely become aggressive.

11. Frustration is any condition that prevents a person from reaching a desired goal. Some people compensate for frustrating personal handicaps; others may develop inferiority complexes.

12. Responses to frustration include aggressive behavior, giving up, regression, fixation, and problem-solving.

13. Types of inner conflicts are approach-avoidance, approach-approach, avoidance-avoidance, and double approach-avoidance. Basically, all consist of the two opposing response tendencies of approach-avoidance.

14. Both approach and avoidance become stronger the closer one gets to a goal that has positive and negative aspects. But the avoidance gradient increases more rapidly than the approach gradient.

15. A person feels guilty when he violates or is tempted to violate his moral standards.

16. Moral standards become incorporated into the child's personality by means of parental rewards, punishments, and examples. These internalized standards constitute his conscience.

17. Approval and love, which are psychological rewards, and disapproval and rejection, which are psychological punishments, have been found to be more effective in developing a strong internalized conscience than material rewards and coercive and physical punishments.

18. Inner conflicts may be resolved by reinforcing either approach behavior or avoidance behavior or by the defense mechanisms of renunciation, repression, projection, reaction formation, vicarious satisfaction, and sublimation. Sublimation is the only one of these that can simultaneously satisfy the demands of the drive, of reason, and of conscience.

Important Terms

aggression

affective attack

quiet biting attack

Kluver-Bucy syndrome

amygdala

septum

XYY genotypes

displaced aggression

death instinct

vicarious reinforcement

frustration

self-aggression

scapegoating

projection

anger

reservoir concept of anger

principle of symmetry

catharsis

compensation

inferiority complex

inner conflict

approach-avoidance conflict

approach-approach conflict

avoidance-avoidance conflict

double approach-avoidance

gradient

repression

renunciation

reaction formation

displacement

vicarious satisfaction

sublimation

Suggested Readings

BANDURA, A. *Aggression: A social learning analysis.* Englewood Cliffs, N.J.: Prentice-Hall, 1973.
  Compendium of the author's many important experiments on how people learn to be aggressive by social imitation.

BERKOWITZ, L. (ED.) *Roots of aggression.* New York: Atherton, 1969.
A series of fairly technical articles by leading authorities on the sources of aggression.

COLE, J. K., & JENSEN, D. D. (EDS.) *Nebraska symposium on motivation.* Lincoln: University of Nebraska Press, 1972.
A series of technical articles by experts in the area of aggression.

ERON, L. D., WALDER, L. O., & LEFKOWITZ, M. M. *Learning of aggression in children.* Boston: Little, Brown, 1971.
A description of a 5-year investigation of the relation of children's aggression in school to the behavior of their parents in the home.

FESHBACH, S., & SINGER, R. D. *Television and aggression: an experimental field study.* San Francisco: Jossey-Bass, 1971.
An analysis of experiments on the effects of watching violent television programs on aggressiveness in boys. The results suggest that there is a reduction in aggressive behavior.

JOHNSON, R. N. *Aggression in man and animals.* Philadelphia: Saunders, 1972.
A readable, comprehensive survey of the scientific literature on aggression.

LORENZ, K. *On aggression.* New York: Harcourt Brace Jovanovich, 1966.
An interesting and provocative essay on the instinctual roots of aggression by the celebrated Nobel-laureate ethologist.

MAPLE, T., & MATHESON, D. W. (EDS.) *Aggression, hostility, and violence: nature or nurture?* New York: Holt, Rinehart and Winston, 1973.
A comprehensive collection of readings on aggression.

MILGRAM, S., & SHOTLAND, R. L. *Television and antisocial behavior: Field experiments.* New York: Academic Press, 1973.
Description of the authors' experiment in which they produced three versions—differing in antisocial content—of an episode of a popular television serial, and then carried out field studies to assess the effects of these different versions on viewers.

SINGER, J. L. (ED.) *The control of aggression and violence.* New York: Academic Press, 1971.
Several psychologists discuss various methods for controlling aggression.

STORR, A. *Human aggression.* New York: Atheneum, 1968.
An elementary introduction to current issues regarding aggression.

Chapter 13 Human Sexual Behavior

*Love-thoughts, love-juice, love-odor, love-yielding, love-climbers, and
   the climbing sap,
Arms and hands of love, lips of love, phallic thumb of love, breasts of
   love, bellies press'd and glued together with love,
Earth of chaste love, life that is only life after love,
The body of my love, the body of the woman I love, the body of the
   man, the body of the earth,
Soft forenoon airs that blow from the south-west,
The hairy wild-bee that murmurs and hankers up and down, that grips
   the full-grown lady-flower, curves upon her with amorous firm legs,
   takes his will of her, and holds himself tremulous and tight till he is
   satisfied;
The wet of woods through the early hours,
Two sleepers at night lying close together as they sleep, one with an
   arm slanting down across and below the waist of the other,
The smell of apples, aromas from crush'd sage-plant, . . .*

—Walt Whitman
("Spontaneous Me")

Human Sexual Behavior

The sexual impulse is a strong and insistent human motive that has pervasive effects on behavior and personality. Sexual maladjustments are widespread and cause much suffering and discord. In recent years the taboos that once hindered open discussion of sex have been put aside, so that we are not obliged to skirt a subject of such immediate and urgent concern to young men and women who are learning to come to terms with it in their individual lives.

In this chapter, we attempt to present an objective, balanced discussion of the sex drive and its manifestations. Though our discussion is based on scientific findings, it may sound sensational at times, because sex *is* a sensational and controversial topic.

We begin by surveying the various methods that have been employed to discover what people do sexually and why they do it. We shall examine some of the findings that these methods have produced. We then shall discuss the underlying factors that shape and determine sexual behavior, and conclude with a section on sexuality's sometime companions, love and jealousy.

Studies of Sexual Behavior: Methods and Results

Human sexual behavior is such an intimate and private activity that it is difficult to investigate it scientifically. Moreover, the subject has been so closely associated with morality and sinfulness that it is hard to be objective about it. Consequently, much of the vast literature on sex and sexual themes—which has grown ever larger as legal restrictions on pornography have been relaxed—consists of opinion, speculation, moralizing, and sensationalism rather than solid evidence. In fact, the hard scientific data on human sexual behavior is probably sketchier than the data available on the sex life of the elephant seal.

Furthermore, much that is known about sexual behavior has been obtained from studies of atypical groups—unhappy people who seek professional help for sexual problems, disturbed people who have been confined in mental institutions, or men who have been convicted of sexual offenses. This information is important, but it cannot tell us much about the sexual activities of ordinary people. However, the inhibitions on sexual studies have finally been relaxed in recent years, and some first-rate studies of typical sexual behavior are now available.

The Fathers of the Sexual Revolution

We will mention two early classics in the literature on sex because of their enormous influence. These are Havelock Ellis's *Studies in the Psychology of Sex* and Sigmund Freud's *Three Essays on Sexuality*. Havelock Ellis (1859–1939) was trained as a physician but he did not practice medicine. Instead, he devoted his life to describing what had been learned and thought about sexuality since the days of the ancient Greeks. The first volume of his *Studies* appeared in 1896; his final, revised edition, containing seven volumes, was published 40 years later.

In his introduction to the 1936 edition, Ellis describes the feelings that led him to the lifetime study of sexual behavior:

I was a youth of sixteen when I formed the resolve to undertake the exploration of this matter (sexual behavior); I can still recall the moment and the spot where the inspiration came to me. It was in Australia where I had lately arrived, and in the neighborhood of Sydney. Like many other boys of my age brought up in a good religious home protected from the world, I was much puzzled over the phenomena of sex. I had already acquired a sceptical outlook; I viewed with contempt the hypocritical ultra-Puritanic, sentimental, or obscurantist teaching on sex, supported by the most varied theories, often fantastic, put forward by the few writers who at that time ventured even to touch on the subject. Where could I find real help and guidance in this difficult yet so vital field? I was already in wide touch with the cultural and scientific literature of various lands. But the answer, so far as I could see, to this question was: Nowhere. I determined that I would make it the main business of my life to get to the real natural facts of sex apart from all would-be moralistic or sentimental notions, and so spare the youth of future generations the trouble and perplexity which this ignorance had caused me.

Ellis's seven volumes are a compendium of practically everything that was known or thought about sexuality at the time. One valuable feature of the work is the many case histories and subjective accounts written at Ellis's request. The influence of Ellis's work can be attributed not only to its substance but also to its clear and graceful style.

The other classic, Freud's *Three Essays on Sexuality*, was published in 1905 and revised a number of times. Although it is scarcely over 100 pages in length, it has had as much influence on attitudes toward sex as any book written in the present century, with the possible exception of the more recent Kinsey Reports and Masters-Johnson studies. Freud's three essays deal with sexual aberrations, sexual development during childhood, and the changes that occur during pubescence. Freud's original contribution was to analyze the normal development of the sexual

13-1

Freud proposed that each person passes through several stages of psychosexual development. During the oral stage, the mouth is the primary source of pleasure (A); during the anal stage sexual interests are diverted to the buttocks and anus (B); during the phallic stage the child discovers his or her genitals as sources of satisfaction and becomes curious about the opposite sex (C) and (D). (A. Wayne Miller; B. Erika; C. Ray Brown, Jr., dpi; D. Hella Hammid, Rapho Guillumette)

A

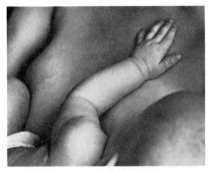

impulse, especially during infancy and early childhood. Freud took the very unpopular position that the child was not as sexually innocent as had been thought. The outlines of sexual development, he maintained, are well established by the age of six, and the sexuality that emerges during adolescence and adulthood has its roots in early childhood.

Freud also broadened the concept of sexuality by noting that sexual feelings involve other parts of the body in addition to the genitals. In his essay, he observes that the young child passes through successive *psychosexual stages*: the oral (first year), the anal (second year), and the phallic (ages 3–5). During the *oral stage*, the mouth is the primary source of pleasure; the child enjoys being fed, sucking on a bottle or pacifier, and so on. In the *anal stage*, the buttocks and anus become the focus of sensual pleasure as the child learns that he can control his impulses to defecate. During the *phallic stage*, the child discovers that the genitals can provide sensual pleasure. These three stages are said to be auto-erotic and narcissistic (deriving pleasure from admiration of one's own physical attributes) because the child obtains pleasure by self-stimulation of the mouth, anus, and genitals. The final stage of sexual development usually occurs during early adolescence. This is the *genital stage*, when the individual begins to be sexually attracted to members of the opposite sex and to feel the first pangs of romantic love. Remnants of the preceding stages remain, however, and combine with the genital stage to produce the whole gamut of lovemaking.

Freud also described how sexual motivations permeate much of man's behavior. This doctrine of *pansexualism*—sex is everywhere, though often in disguised form—is largely responsible for the tremendous emphasis upon sex in contemporary society. Thus, Freud's theories and Ellis's vast documentation jointly launched the so-called sexual revolution, which first emerged during the 1920s and culminated in the sexual freedom movement of the 1960s.

B

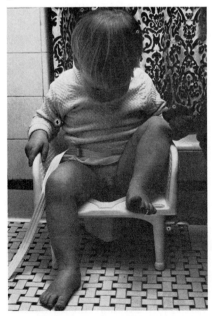

C

D

Studies of Sexual Behavior: Methods and Results **427**

Case Studies

Both Freud and Ellis frequently employed case studies in their researches, and the method is widely used today. A *case study* is a descriptive account of the past and present status of an individual. It usually contains the following information: family background, relations with members of the immediate family, education, medical history, vocational experience, religion, institutional record if any, physical characteristics, sexual history, expressed feelings and attitudes, and critical events of the person's life history. It also may contain the results of psychological testing. Case studies are compiled by professional people—psychologists, social workers, psychiatrists, or sociologists. If such a study is written by the person himself, it is called a subjective account.

The case study may explore only the sexual feelings and behavior of the individual and their probable determinants, or it may treat the person's sexuality as one aspect of his total behavior. If it is the latter type, one can see how a person's sexuality interacts with and reflects other features in his personality. For example, a group of Harvard psychologists did intensive case studies of the personalities of several student volunteers (Murray, 1938). Each case demonstrated that the person's sex life paralleled other aspects of his behavior. One young man's chief satisfaction in all areas of his life came from conquering-hero fantasies, which almost completely substituted for activity and achievement. His sexual life typified this pattern. He did not have dates or any other contacts with girls, preferring to masturbate to the accompaniment of grandiose daydreams. In one such fantasy, he saw himself flying over a city and impregnating hundreds of women with a downpour of semen.

Case studies that focus on sexuality usually involve subjects who have sexual disorders or inadequacies. Such studies try to determine what caused the disorder. For instance, an investigation was made of a middle-aged man who had been arrested a number of times for molesting children (Bell & Hall, 1971). It was determined that he had tried but had never completed coitus with a woman. Information obtained from interviews, psychological tests, and a dream diary that the man had kept for a number of years strongly indicated that he was an immature, childlike person. His preference for children was evidently a reflection of his own immaturity. Moreover, his dreams indicated that he had been seduced by his own father when he was a young child (this suspicion was confirmed by other sources of information). When he grew up, he attempted to seduce children just as his father had seduced him. (Large-scale studies of child-molesters indicate that most do not attempt intercourse with children; they are more likely to restrict their behavior to fondling the child and exhibiting themselves, and they are seldom physically aggressive or brutal.)

A well-written case study often provides welcome relief from the mass of tables, diagrams, technical terminology, abstractions, and hypotheses that make up a typical scientific report. Reading a good case history is like reading a novel; one can identify and emphathize with the person, and see theories, concepts, and other abstractions come to life.

Case studies have deficiencies, however. Information provided by the subject may be inaccurate. People tend to be deceitful when they think they can gain some advantage by falsifying—as is often true when one has been charged with an offense. Forgetfulness, embellishments, exaggerations, and vanity also contribute to the inaccuracy of self-reports.

Given a reasonably accurate record, the investigator still faces the difficulty of providing a causal relationship between a person's history and his present behavior. In the above example, we cannot be completely sure that the son's seduction by his father was the reason for the son's subsequent child-molesting behavior. Nor can we assume that this case has anything to tell us about normal sexuality—and case studies almost inevitably focus on unusual patterns of behavior.

Probably the greatest value of case studies is that they provide suggestions and leads for large-scale studies. Having learned that a particular child-molester was seduced by his father, one can then examine whether other child-molesters were sexually assaulted by their fathers or by older males, in comparison to a control group of men who have never molested children.

Subjective Accounts. Closely related to the case study are the *subjective accounts* of sexual feelings and experiences. These sexual autobiographies or confessions have all the defects of the case-study method and few of the merits. They sometimes do provide valuable leads for understanding the role of sexual motivation in a person's life. But more often, subjective accounts are written to justify and boast about the writer's sexual excursions, and to entertain and excite the reader in the process.

Historical Studies. In an age in which sexual behavior is so openly discussed, it is not surprising that historians and literary critics should study the sexual practices and sentiments of the past. Ancient Greece has been extensively mined, probably because of the Greeks' relaxed attitudes toward sex. The classic study of Greek sexuality is Hans Licht's *Sexual Life in Ancient Greece* (1963).

Closer to our day are the recent exposés of sexuality in Victorian England, a society outwardly committed to prudishness, sentimentality, and silence regarding sexual matters. That not all Victorians practiced what they preached is brought out by Steven Marcus's *The Other Victorians* (1964). Using materials collected by Kinsey, Marcus had no trouble showing that extensive underground sexual literature (pornography) was in circulation during the nineteenth century, as in every other century. The classic of this period is the anonymously authored *My Secret Life*, which, in its 4,200 pages, gives an astonishingly frank account of sexual practices. "*My Secret Life* shows us," Marcus writes, "that amid and underneath the world of Victorian England as we know it—and as it tended to represent itself to itself—a real, secret social life was being conducted, the secret life of sexuality."

Cross-Cultural Studies

The classic *cross-cultural study* of sexual behavior is *Patterns of Sexual Behavior* (1951) by Clellan Ford, an anthropologist, and Frank Beach, a psychologist. Ford and Beach did much of their research in the Yale University Human Relations Area Files, which contain information about all aspects of life for many different people in all parts of the world. They assembled a study comparing sexual behavior in 190 different contemporary societies, many of which are preliterate. The only complex, modern society included was the United States. The book is so comprehensive that we can present only a few of its outstanding conclusions.

Cultural Similarities and Differences. Virtually every kind of sexual activity with every kind of sexual partner is countenanced by at least one society, although heterosexual relations between adults are the accepted norm everywhere. The preferred position for intercourse in most societies is the man on top of the woman but some groups prefer other positions. In some societies, the woman is supposed to be passive, while in others she is expected to be aggressive and active.

The customary length and kinds of foreplay vary a great deal. Kissing, for example, is unacceptable in some societies. Manual and oral stimulation of the partner's genitals is the rule in some groups. A desire for privacy during sexual intercourse is practically universal.

Most groups permit a man to have more than one wife at a time, but rare is the group that permits a woman to have more than one husband. Incest—whether betweens parents and offspring or brother and sister—is *universally* prohibited. Various kinds of sexual liaisons outside of marriage are approved by over one-third of the groups.

Many societies consider masturbation a natural activity for children and adolescents, but it is almost universally frowned upon or ridiculed when practiced by adults. Sexual play among children is permitted in many of the groups. Homosexual relationships or acts, under some circumstances and for certain classes of people, are acceptable in nearly two-thirds of the societies.

Whatever the sexual customs of a group may be, they are transmitted to children and youths by the adult members of the society in unmistakable terms. Since many primitive societies consist of small groups in villages, detecting and punishing any deviations from the society's norms are fairly easy. Moreover, birth-control methods are rarely available, so that the risk of pregnancy acts as a strong deterrent to prohibited sexual liaisons.

Despite the apparent strictness of the sexual code in many primitive groups—for example, premarital or extramarital intercourse may be punished by death—it is usual for a society to permit alternative sexual outlets before or after marriage. Thus, where young men are forbidden to interact with young women prior to marriage, they are allowed to have sexual relations with each other. These sexual acts cease after marriage. In some societies, *monogamy* (marriage with only one person at a time) is strictly enforced but married men are allowed to engage in sexual activities with boys. Some groups sanction sexual intercourse with concubines who have been imported from other groups.

The sexual mores in primitive societies are not based upon moral considerations as they often are in western countries. Rather, they serve to maintain the identity of kinship groups, which are vital for mutual assistance and defense. Kinship groups are preserved by a rigid system of relationships that specifies whom one can marry and have children with. The birth of an illegitimate child is a disaster because it upsets the kinship system; for this reason a bastard often is aborted or killed. But societies that insist on such harsh measures often will encourage certain extramarital sexual relationships that do not endanger the kinship rules.

This vast array of facts leads to one obvious conclusion: although the sex drive is universal, sexual behavior is heavily influenced by customs and tradition. Except for the *incest taboo,* behavior that is condemned in one society may be condoned or encouraged in another.

Observational Studies in Natural Settings

Observational studies of human sexual activity in natural settings are rare for obvious reasons. Even if a scientific observer were to gain admission to a bedroom, his presence would change it into an unnatural setting for the sexual partners. Despite the obstacles, however, a few ingenious and intrepid investigators have found ways to overcome them.

An anthropologist, Gilbert Bartell (1971), made a study of married couples who engage in sexual activities with one or more other couples. Such people call themselves "swingers." The several hundred people in Bartell's sample were white, middle-class, primarily middle-aged Protestants living in the Chicago suburbs. Nearly all of them had two or three children. Bartell and his wife attended parties (although they did not participate sexually), placed advertisements in publications catering to swingers, and interviewed couples about their experiences.

The Bartells found that these middle-aged swingers followed definite rules and customs.

1. The couples meet through advertisements or through other couples. The first meeting between couples is merely to get acquainted; it does not involve sex. The second meeting culminates in sex but only after a long period of socializing and drinking.

2. The typical couple has sex with each new couple just once. This prevents the development of emotional involvements that might threaten the marriages.

3. Unmarried couples and single males or females are not welcome; nor are nonwhites, long-haired men, people wearing unconventional clothes, or those who use bad language. Drugs are strictly taboo. If a couple wants to bring another couple to a party, they must ask the host and hostess for permission. In other words, the swingers' behavior is governed by middle-class amenities and attitudes.

4. Couples may pair off and go to separate rooms, or they may have group sexual activities. A woman may refuse an invitation to have intercourse if she is not attracted to the man, but she has to make up a good excuse so as not to hurt his feelings.

5. Two women can have sex together, and they often are encouraged to do so by their husbands, who may enjoy watching—but any physical contact between males is strictly forbidden.

Most of the couples felt that participating in group sex had improved their own sexual life and compatibility. They had acquired a new interest that they could share and that brought them closer together. In fact, planning, arranging, and talking about swinging activities occupied much of their free time.

Another example of an observational study in a natural setting was conducted by a sociologist, Laud Humphreys (1970). He observed several hundred sexual acts between men in a number of public restrooms in a large city. Most of these acts occurred in the morning when the men were going to work and in the late afternoon when they were returning home.

Humphreys was interested to learn what kind of men engaged in this hasty and wordless sexual activity with strangers. His investigations revealed that participants are of all ages and of all economic classes from factory workers to physicians. Most are married and have children. When 50 participants were compared with a control group of 50 nonparticipants matched for occupation, race, section of the city in which they lived, and marital status, no significant differences were found.

What is their motivation for obtaining sexual gratification in this way? Humphreys believes their motives are:

1. to obtain sexual relief quickly

2. the easy availability of sexual partners

3. the excitement of "playing with fire" (they may be arrested or beaten up)

4. the novelty of having sex with a different person each time

Humphreys confirmed his beliefs by interviewing many of the participants directly (of course, the men did not know about Humphreys' observations of them or the real reason for his interview). Humphreys was able to locate the men by tracing the license plates of their cars through the local license bureau.

Laboratory Studies

In 1966, a book entitled *Human Sexual Response* was published. It immediately became a best seller, and its contents were widely discussed. *Human Sexual Response* is a sober, scientific study written by a medical doctor, William H. Masters, and his associate (now his wife), Virginia E. Johnson. Unlike the earlier Kinsey reports, Masters and Johnson's work depended entirely on *laboratory studies* conducted under precisely controlled conditions.

Why did this highly scientific account become a best seller? The answer is obvious when one reads the book. Masters and Johnson brought married couples and single men and women into the laboratory and observed them while they engaged in intercourse or masturbation. Special instruments, cameras, and recording equipment were developed to find out what changes take place in the genitals and other organs of the body before, during, and following an orgasm. Although this was not the first time sexual relations had been observed under laboratory conditions, it was the first large-scale study. The investigation began in 1954 at the Washington University School of Medicine in St. Louis. By 1966, the authors had recorded observations and measurements during more than 10,000 male and female orgasms. The research population consisted of 276 married couples and 142 unmarried males and females, 98 of whom had been married. They ranged in age from 18 to 89. The sample included all social classes and educational levels, but it was heavily weighted with well-educated people.

The standard research procedures involved (1) masturbation with hand or finger, (2) sexual intercourse with the man on top or the woman on top, (3) artificial coition with a transparent probe, and (4) stimulation of the breasts alone. The transparent probe enabled the investigators to see more clearly what changes were taking place in the female genitals.

The Basic Pattern of Sexual Responses. Masters and Johnson discovered a basic pattern of sexual response for both women and men. Although minor variations occur, this basic pattern falls into four distinct phases:

1. *The excitement phase.* The first physiological change in the male is erection, which occurs almost immediately. In some males, the nipples also become erect. The first change in the female is the moistening of the vaginal lining with a lubricating fluid. The nipples also become erect and the breasts swell.

2. *The plateau phase.* The testes of the male increase in size about 50 percent and they are pulled up high in the scrotum. In the female, the tissues surrounding the outer third of the vagina swell, reducing the diameter of the vaginal opening by as much as 50 percent. The deeper portion of the vaginal cavity becomes distended. The clitoris retracts under the hood that covers it. These changes result from the filling of vessels and tissues with extra blood or from increases in muscle tension.

3. *The orgasmic phase.* The penis throbs in rhythmic contractions. Sperm cells collect in the seminal vesicles, which then contract, discharging the semen into the urethral bulb. Contractions of the bulb and the penis project the semen out of the urethra under great pressure. Semen may be expelled as far as 2 feet.

   In the female, there are rhythmic muscular contractions of the outer third of the vagina and of the uterus. Other muscles, such as the anal sphincter, may also contract rhythmically.

   In both sexes, muscles throughout the body contract in various patterns. The heart beats faster, blood pressure is elevated, and respiration is increased.

4. *The resolution phase.* The organs and tissues return to their unstimulated condition, some slowly, some more rapidly.

Masters and Johnson drew several conclusions from their observations and measurements. We shall discuss two of these. First, penis dimension is of little importance for sexual satisfaction. Precise measurements showed that small penises enlarge with erection relatively more than larger penises do. This means that the sizes of erect penises vary less than nonerect penises. Moreover, the vaginal contraction grips the penis irrespective of its size.

Second, Masters and Johnson found no difference between the orgasms produced by clitoral stimulation and vaginal stimulation. Prior to the

THE BASIC SEXUAL PATTERN FOR MALES

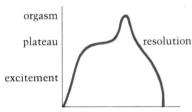

orgasm
plateau
resolution
excitement

THE BASIC SEXUAL PATTERN FOR FEMALES

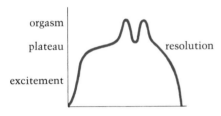

orgasm
plateau
resolution
excitement

13-2
Graphic representation of the typical sexual response patterns in males and females. Although no single response pattern is typical of all females, the lower graph describes one of the three most common patterns. As the graphs show, the sexual arousal of both male and female steadily increases until at a certain phase (plateau) it begins to level off. The orgasm is a brief and sudden surge of total arousal. The male begins to return to his original level of arousal immediately after orgasm; the female may peak twice or more before the onset of the resolution phase. (Masters & Johnson, *Human sexual responses.* 1966. Reprinted by permission of Little, Brown and Company)

investigation, the role of the clitoris in sexual stimulation was hotly disputed. Some authorities, including Freud, argued that female orgasms produced by clitoral stimulation were less mature and less satisfying than orgasms produced by stimulation of the vagina. In fact, stimulation of the clitoris is almost always indirect. The hood that covers the clitoris is moved back and forth, and this movement stimulates the clitoris. Direct contact with the clitoris is often painful rather than stimulating.

Masters and Johnson are now using the knowledge they have acquired to help men who suffer from premature ejaculation or impotence and women who are frigid or unable to respond sexually (1970). Although their laboratory studies were physiologically oriented, their treatment of people with sexual difficulties is primarily psychological in character. Sexual attitudes and feelings are changed by psychotherapy and guidance, so that a person may function more effectively and thereby receive more satisfaction from sex.

Quantitative Studies

In 1948, a book of over 800 pages, crammed with tables and charts and all the formidable methodology of science, became a best seller overnight. *Sexual Behavior in the Human Male* is better known as the Kinsey Report, after its senior author, Alfred C. Kinsey, an Indiana University zoologist. It presented a highly detailed statistical description of the sex lives of 5,300 white American males ranging in age from 10 to 90. All of the data were gathered by personal interviews between 1938 and 1947. During the two-hour interview, a trained interviewer asked each person about 300 questions.

The Kinsey Report is a famous example of the *quantitative study* technique. Like public opinion polls, quantitative studies question hundreds or thousands of people to get a representative sampling of an entire group's thoughts or behavior.

Kinsey's survey was not without flaws. His 5,300 subjects were not representative of the male population in the United States. His sample was deficient in children and in males over 50, those living in the country, and manual laborers and factory workers. Most of the males interviewed lived in the East or Midwest. Despite these deficiencies, it remains the most comprehensive study of human sexual behavior ever undertaken. It is equaled only by its companion volume, *Sexual Behavior in the Human Female*, which appeared in 1953 and gave a quantitative description of the sexual practices of 6,000 American females.

Both volumes analyzed sexual behavior in terms of the subject's age, marital status, education, occupation, religion, rural-urban background, decade of birth, and onset of adolescence. Nine classes of sexual behavior were distinguished: masturbation, nocturnal emissions, petting to climax, premarital intercourse, marital intercourse, extramarital intercourse, intercourse with prostitutes (for the male sample only), homosexual contacts, and animal contacts.

It is impossible to summarize 1,700 pages of text and tables here. Instead, we will give a few of the highlights and some of the more surprising findings, especially about the sexual behavior of those informants who had attended college.

13-3
The frequency by age of premarital intercourse engaged in by males who eventually attended college in 1948 and 1970. (Based on Kinsey, 1948 and Hunt, 1974)

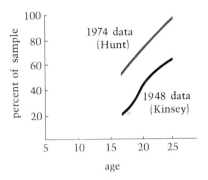

Kinsey's Report on Male Sexual Behavior. The average male has from one to four orgasms a week. The incidence gradually declines after the age of 30. Married men have more orgasms per week than single men do, and college graduates fewer than those who did not attend college. Masturbation, nocturnal emissions, and petting to climax are more frequent outlets for college graduates than for those who did not attend college. Premarital, extramarital, and homosexual outlets are more frequent for those with less education than for college graduates. The frequency of intercourse with wives is about the same for all educational levels. Relations with one's wife make up between 80 and 90 percent of all sexual outlets at all ages and educational levels. College graduates show an increasing proportion of extramarital intercourse with age, whereas those with less education show a decreasing proportion as they grow older.

Patterns of sexual behavior vary with social class. Professional men engage in more kissing, embracing, and foreplay activities than do mechanics and factory workers. The better-educated also are more apt to be nude when they copulate, and to experiment with different sexual positions.

About two out of every three male college students will have had premarital intercourse by the time they are graduated. The incidence of premarital intercourse is much higher for males of comparable age who have only finished grade school.

One of Kinsey's figures astonished many people and cast doubt on the accuracy of all his findings. One-third of his male respondents reported that they had at least one sexual interaction with another male. Considering the amount of sexual experimentation that takes place among adolescent boys, plus the sexual segregation that exists in the armed services, prisons, and jobs in isolated places, perhaps the occurrence of at least one homosexual contact reported by a third of the respondents is not so surprising. It may help to place the incidence of homosexual acts in perspective by considering the following figures: 63 percent of males have never engaged in a homosexual act; only 4 percent engage exclusively in homosexual relations; 33 percent have had varying proportions of heterosexual and homosexual outlets.

Kinsey's Report on Female Sexual Behavior. Comparing Kinsey's statistics for female sexual behavior with those for males is difficult. The criterion used for male sexual behavior was any activity that led to an

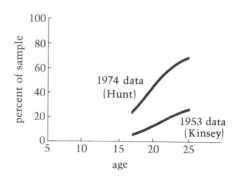

13-4
Recent figures indicate that the percentage of females above about 16 years of age who have had premarital intercourse has almost doubled since the publication of the Kinsey report. (Based on Kinsey, 1953 and and Hunt, 1974)

orgasm. An *orgasm*, as defined by Kinsey, consists of the abrupt and virtually instantaneous release of tension, following a period of increasing tension. This release of tension is quickly followed by a series of muscular spasms or contractions, and in the male by the ejaculation of semen. In some females most of the time, and in all females some of the time, sexual activity does not culminate in an orgasm. For example, 10 percent of the sample of married women had never reached orgasm at any time in sexual intercourse with their husbands, and one-quarter of the wives had not had an orgasm during the first year of marriage.

When college women are compared with less-educated women, masturbation is more frequent for college women and premarital intercourse more frequent for those with less education. About one college woman in five had premarital intercourse compared with almost two in five for those with grade-school education. This difference disappears after the age of 30, however. College graduates have more marital intercourse leading to orgasm than high school graduates do. After the age of 25, more of the college graduates are having extramarital intercourse than are those with less education.

About 2 out of 100 women are exclusively homosexual (as compared with 4 out of 100 men); about 5 out of 100 are predominantly homosexual. College graduates have fewer homosexual relations before the age of 20, and more such contacts after that age than do women who have not attended college. One noteworthy finding is that homosexual contacts lead to orgasm in women more often than heterosexual contacts do. Kinsey and his associates attribute this to the fact that women know better than men what excites another woman.

In spite of the difficulty of comparing male and female sexual behavior, one can glean from Kinsey's figures that men have more sexual outlets and are more promiscuous than women. More men than women masturbate, experience nocturnal emissions, engage in premarital and extramarital intercourse, and have homosexual and animal contacts. Women outnumber men in only one category: petting to climax.

Table 13-1, based on the Kinsey Report, shows the average number of total orgasms per week for single men and women and for married men and women.

The Kinsey reports indicate that men are sexually aroused by a wider range of stimuli than are women. They engage in more sexual fantasies and have more sex dreams; they react more to erotic stories and pictures; they talk more about sex; and they more often are aroused by

Table 13-1   Total Orgasms per Week (Based on Kinsey, Pomeroy, (Martin & Gebhard, 1953)

Age	Single		Married	
	Males	Females	Males	Females
16–20	2.9	.4	4.7	2.9
31–35	2.4	1.0	2.7	2.3
46–50	1.9	.9	1.8	1.4

watching others in erotic activities. Kinsey's group made a special study of graffiti (writings on walls, usually in public toilets, often of a sexual nature) which indicated that many more men than women make such inscriptions. According to Kinsey's figures, women are not as interested in the male body or the genitals as men are in the female body. Women prefer to have various parts of the body stimulated before being touched in the genitals.

When the Kinsey reports first appeared, they seemed to confirm the general belief that men are more sexually oriented or have a stronger sex drive than women. In recent years, quite a few writers have challenged the notion that this is an inborn difference. Many people now believe that women are just as sexually oriented as men, but that parental and social prohibitions have repressed their sexual expression. Leaders of the women's liberation movement are strongly urging women to free themselves from the sexual bondage to which society has committed them.

The figures in the two Kinsey reports were gathered a generation ago; do they still hold true today? Or has there been a radical change in sexual practices, as some people maintain? These are exceedingly difficult questions to answer. Because sex has become such an open subject for discussion and portrayal, it would be a mistake to infer that our sexual practices have changed. What we talk about does not accord necessarily with what we do. An avid interest in the erotic may be more symptomatic of frustration than of sexual freedom.

Moreover, there has been no recent survey of sexual behavior comparable to those of Kinsey and his associates. The limited surveys that have been made recently indicate that more women engage in premarital sex today than did in Kinsey's day. How much more varies from survey to survey. Male sexual behavior has changed less than female's and the incidence of homosexual acts has not increased according to these studies. It has been suggested that bisexuality (having sexual relations with both sexes) is becoming more commonplace, but according to Kinsey's figures bisexuality was fairly common among men prior to 1940. Caution should be exercised in drawing any firm conclusions about the incidence of various types of sexual behavior today. The most recent survey of the sexual attitudes and practices of 2,026 Americans (Hunt, 1974) provides some interesting similarities and contrasts with the earlier Kinsey findings. The incidence of masturbation has not changed appreciably but adolescents start masturbating at an earlier age, do it more often, and continue it over a longer period of years. The

13-5
College students were asked the following question: "Would it be important to you that the person you marry be a virgin, or not so important?" The view that men and women should remain virgins until marriage was held most strongly by students at denominational (church-affiliated) schools. (Gallup, 1970)

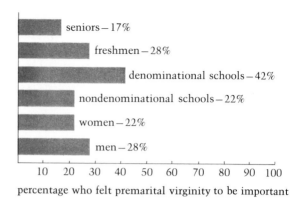

percentage who felt premarital virginity to be important

proportion of females who engage in premarital coitus has doubled since Kinsey's time, but the increase for males is slight. There is little evidence that casual sex or promiscuity is very widespread. The frequency of coitus for married couples has increased, but there has been no change in the amount of extramarital sex, except among young married females. Finally, there has been no change in the incidence of homosexuality.

Having completed our survey of methods used to study sexual behavior, now we shall consider the sources of the sex drive.

Determinants of Sexual Behavior

Despite the wide range of possible sexual acts and sexual partners, the most frequent outlet for adults throughout the world is heterosexual lovemaking. Obviously, the survival of the species depends on heterosexual intercourse. But most acts of intercourse occur because a man and a woman desire it and expect to derive pleasure from the act itself. This desire is independent of a desire to have children; in fact, measures are taken in most acts of mating to prevent pregnancy. What, then, are the sources of sexual desire?

Hormones or Learning?

Scientists assume that any universal pattern of behavior has a neurophysiological basis. The human species, like most others, is divided into males and females. Biological gender is determined at the moment of conception. If the fertilizing sperm carries an X chromosome, the offspring will be female; if it carries a Y chromosome, the offspring will be male. This is inevitable, except for the rare genetic or fetal anomaly in which the offspring has reproductive features of both sexes or undifferentiated genitals.

In lower animals, the mating impulse is governed largely, though not completely, by the male and female sex hormones secreted by the testes and ovaries, respectively. Human beings also have sex hormones, and the surge of erotic interest during adolescence closely follows the maturation of the sex glands and the sexual apparatus. Nonetheless, most authorities on human sexual behavior minimize the role of hormones in determining human mating patterns. No other important physiological basis for the sex drive has been discovered. But undoubtedly an individual's early experiences and training heavily influence his or her sexual feelings, preferences, and activities. For these reasons, many psychologists believe that the whole pattern of human sexual activity is a learned one. Boys *learn* to be aroused by girls, and girls by boys.

Before we accept a completely environmental or cultural explanation, we should consider another possibility: the learning of the heterosexual pattern may itself be influenced by the differing biological makeup of males and females. In other words, learning to be heterosexual may be easy because of hormonally controlled predispositions.

Gender Identity.   Although ethical reasons make it difficult to perform sexual experiments on humans, nature occasionally provides experimental subjects. Some individuals, called *hermaphrodites,* are born with ambiguous reproduction structures, so that their gender cannot be clearly defined as exclusively male or exclusively female. Such individuals are sometimes raised in contradiction to their sex as determined by their genetic and hormonal make-up, the morphology of the internal reproductive organs, or the morphology of the external genitals. For example, an individual may have the male Y chromosome, more male than female hormones, and testes, but if he is identified and reared as a girl, he will develop and maintain a feminine role and a feminine identity. Such mistakes have taught us much about the ways in which gender identity is normally established.

To establish a firm sexual identity for children with ambiguous sex characteristics, three conditions usually are necessary. First, cosmetic surgery to define the external genitals as either male or female should be performed soon after birth. This is important because the visual appearance of the sex organs determines how other people will perceive the child—and even more important, how the child will perceive itself. Once a sexual identification has been imprinted on the child's mind, it is difficult to alter this conception. The critical age for gender identity is about one and a half, when language learning begins. As one authority on sexual differentiation put it:

One must make the inferences that psychosexual differentiation takes place as an active process of editing and assimilating experiences that are gender-specific and that derive ultimately from the genital appearance of the body. These experiences include direct apperception—visual, tactile, and proprioceptive—of one's own sexual organs. They also include the multitudinous and cumulative experiences that derive from genital appearance as it has determined the sex of assignment and rearing—experiences that are defined by the gender of personal nouns and pronouns, clothing style, haircut, and a thousand other gender-specific expectancies and attitudes. (Money, 1965)

A second key to sexual identity is that the parents must feel completely convinced that the child is definitely of one sex or the other. They will transmit to the child any doubts they harbor and will thus obstruct the development of a clear-cut gender identity. Finally, the child should be treated with the appropriate hormone at puberty to insure the development of the appropriate secondary sex characteristics. If the child has been classified as a boy, administration of the male sex hormone will cause a deepening of his voice, the growth of facial hair, and the development of a masculine physique.

Psychologists who have studied hermaphrodites find that their sexual identification sometimes contradicts their sex of assignment and rearing. A hermaphrodite who has been raised as a boy still may think of himself as a girl and behave accordingly. Even people with normal sexual attributes occasionally identify very strongly with the opposite sex. A man feels that he was meant to be a woman, or a woman feels she was meant to be a man. Such people are known as *transsexuals*. Several hundred transsexuals have had hormone treatments and then have had their genitals changed surgically so that their bodies will agree with their feelings. Others choose less drastic methods. (Transsexualism is discussed more fully later in this chapter.) These cases indicate that gender identity is not solely governed by the structure of the genitals.

The Brain and Sexuality

Another possible factor in the development of sexual identity is the central nervous system. Recent research with animals suggests that the brains of males and females may differ in some important respects that affect their perceptions, feelings, preferences, and arousal and mating patterns. If gender-specific processes do exist in the central nervous system, they conceivably could facilitate the learning of different patterns of sexual behavior by human males and females.

Does the brain have a region that funnels sexual feelings and mating impulses into appropriate motor outlets? Recent research indicates that such a region exists in the *anterior hypothalamus* (Levine, 1966). Destruction of this area appears to obliterate sexual behavior.

External Stimuli and Sexual Arousal

Any part of the body, any kind of sensory stimulation, any object or condition, either fantasied or perceived, can be erotically stimulating. Practically everyone has a collection of potentially arousing images and associations, though these stimuli can vary a great deal with changing conditions. Although the sex impulse is virtually universal, each individual has a unique arousal pattern.

Of course, almost everyone finds certain things sexually stimulating, including caresses and erotic pictures, movies, and books. But other stimuli become sexualized only for certain individuals and have no sexual association for most people. A person who develops a strong sexual fixation on an object that is not usually thought of as being erotic is said to have a *fetish*. For example, a man may be sexually stimulated by women's shoes and keep a large collection of them to look at and handle while masturbating.

How does a stimulus acquire the power to be sexually exciting? The simplest answer is that it coincides with a satisfying experience. This experience may be overtly sexual or it may be related to sexual activities only indirectly; but by *association* and *reinforcement*, a neutral stimulus acquires a sexual charge. The same explanation can account for the acquisition of aversions. Any stimulus present during a disagreeable sexual experience gains the power to inhibit rather than to excite. If the inhibitory stimuli become stronger than the arousal ones, the person may become impotent or frigid or may lose interest in sex. Masters and Johnson in their book *Human Sexual Inadequacy* (1970) describe many specific experiences that have resulted in impotence and frigidity. Among the more common ones are a repressive religious orthodoxy; fear of pregnancy; maternal or paternal domination; painful or disgusting first sexual experiences; and disappointment with a sex partner. Masters and Johnson observe that for their patients, "Frequently, one particular event, one specifically traumatic episode, has been quite sufficient to terminate the individual male's ability to, facility for, interest in, or demand for ejaculating intravaginally."

Strength of the Sex Drive

Some people believe the sex impulse is a very strong force that influences many aspects of life. Others feel that the importance of sexual motivation has been grossly exaggerated.

Whether sex has great or little influence on behavior, the strength of the sex drive varies widely from person to person. According to Kinsey, the extremes of frequency of male orgasms range from complete absence to as many as 33 per week over a 30-year period. The frequency of orgasms is a good operational definition of the strength of the sex drive, but other equally useful measures have been proposed. A person may think, fantasize, and dream about sex much of the time, or expend considerable energy in overcoming obstacles to sexual fulfillment, or he may displace most of his sexual energy into other activities and thus have few orgasms. The strength of the sex drive, as measured by number of orgasms, is affected by many conditions, both temporary and permanent, age being one of the more important ones. But the sex drive does not disappear after a certain age. Men and women in their 80s can still have active sex lives.

Homosexuality

Some people are aroused erotically by members of their own sex, and for many of them, arousal culminates in some form of sexual interaction. Strong affectional feelings often accompany the sexual aspects of such homosexual relationships, and sometimes these love relationships are maintained for years.

In any discussion of homosexuality, we must distinguish between homosexual *acts* and homosexual *persons*. Kinsey showed that homosexual acts are fairly common, but that only a small percentage of males and females can be classified as homosexual. Kinsey defined a _homosexual_ as a person whose sexual outlets are mostly with individuals of the same sex over a long period of time. That is, a person should be called a homosexual only if he has a fairly permanent erotic preference for his own sex. Some authorities have suggested that persons who have sexual relations with both sexes with about equal frequency be called _bisexual_ or _ambisexual_.

Despite the relatively small number of people who are exclusively homosexual, the subject is now widely discussed, written about, and portrayed in movies and plays. Homosexual organizations, magazines, and bars, and an active "gay" liberation movement, demanding the same rights as heterosexuals, all have emerged in the last few years. Research on homosexuality has increased also. Some is primarily descriptive, while other investigators are attempting to identify the causes of homosexuality.

Descriptive Analysis of Homosexuality

An excellent descriptive study of homosexuality has been done by Evelyn Hooker (1965). Starting in 1954, she observed and interviewed a group of older males (their average age in 1954 was 35) who were exclusively homosexual with the exception of three who had a few heterosexual experiences. She selected them as being normal; that is, they were not seeking psychological help, they were gainfully employed, and they displayed no signs of psychological disturbance. Many had lived with the same homosexual partner for a number of years, although they usually did not remain monogamous.

Hooker was particularly interested in the relation between the kind of sexual activity they engaged in and their feelings about their own masculinity and femininity. A common misconception about homosexuals is that they can be divided into those who play an active, masculine role ("husbands") and those who are passive and effeminate ("wives"). Hooker found that most of her subjects did not limit themselves to any fixed sexual role; they varied their activity with the same partner and with different partners. The majority thought of themselves as being completely masculine.

Studies of the physiques of homosexuals indicate that they show the same range of builds as heterosexuals. Distinguishing a representative sample of homosexuals from a representative sample of heterosexuals is impossible on the basis of physical build—or any other characteristic, for that matter. The only thing that sets homosexuals apart from heterosexuals is that they are sexually attracted to their own sex.

However, some homosexual males prefer to play the feminine role, and some prefer a masculine role. A number of years ago, Terman and Miles (1936) devised a test for measuring masculinity and femininity. The test consisted of a number of questions relating to interests, opinions, preferences, information, and word-associations to which males and females gave different answers. This test was given to a group of homosexuals, some of whom were classified as passive (played the feminine role in sexual interactions) and some as active (played the masculine role). The scores of the active homosexuals matched those of heterosexual males, while the scores of passive homosexuals were closer to those of heterosexual females. Neither passive nor active homosexuals differed from heterosexuals in physical characteristics, though the passive homosexuals had the mannerisms of females. Many of the passive homosexuals reported they had always thought of themselves as feminine.

13-6
In recent years gay liberation movements have become more vocal in demanding equal rights for homosexuals. (Mimi Forsyth, Monkmeyer)

Possible Causes of Homosexuality

Why should 4 out of every 100 males and about 2 out of every 100 females (Kinsey's figures) be exclusively homosexual throughout their lives? Many hypotheses have been advanced but most of them will fit under one of the following headings: (1) heredity, (2) hormonal balance, (3) early childhood experiences, (4) arrested development, (5) seduction, and (6) segregation of the sexes.

Heredity. At first glance, it is difficult to see how heredity could play much of a role. Homosexuals ordinarily do not have children, and whatever genes are supposed to incline the person toward homosexuality therefore would tend to disappear from the gene pool. Still, some homosexuals do marry and have children, and for these children, heredity *may* be a contributing factor. But most homosexuals have heterosexual parents, which suggests either that heredity plays no role in causing homosexuality, or that recessive parental genes for it combine to produce homosexual children.

A study of twins provides some interesting information that may point to a genetic basis for homosexuality (Kallman, 1952). Twins, it will be recalled, are either monozygotic (identical) or dizygotic (fraternal). All of the monozygotic twin brothers of 37 homosexual males were found to be either exclusively homosexual or bisexual. *None* of the dizygotic twin brothers of homosexual males were homosexual or bisexual. This is not conclusive evidence for the inheritance of homosexuality, because we do not know what role the environment may have played in causing the identical twins to be more alike than the fraternal twins. Nonetheless, it is suggestive and should be studied further.

Hormonal Balance. The discovery of male and female sex hormones and the presence in varying proportions of *both* kinds of hormones in *both* sexes suggested a hormonal basis for homosexuality. Male homosexuals, some writers suggest, secrete relatively more female sex hormones, and female homosexuals secrete relatively more male sex hormones. This is an attractively simple theory, but unfortunately research findings do not substantiate it. Hormone balance appears to be independent of sexual object choice. Individuals who have a high proportion of the opposite sex hormone may be either homosexual or heterosexual. Similarly, individuals who have a high proportion of the sex hormone of their own sex may be either homosexual or heterosexual. Treatment of homosexual adult males with the male sex hormone heightens the sex drive but does not change their sexual preferences.

Occasionally, a female fetus is masculinized by a biochemical condition of the mother. Studies of girls who were fetally *androgenized* (received male sex hormones in the prenatal state) showed that 80 percent of them became tomboys. They engaged in vigorous sports, preferred to play with boys, were indifferent to dolls and feminine clothes, and as adults they subordinated marriage to a career. But none of them developed a homosexual orientation.

Childhood Experiences. Ever since Freud first described how the child's early experiences influence his later character and behavior, investigators have been examining parent-child interactions to see how they might affect the individual's sexual patterns. These studies have turned up evidence that a dominant, possessive, and indulgent mother combined with an aloof, absent, hostile, or deceased father, may predispose a boy toward homosexuality. Psychologists theorize that such circumstances make it difficult for a boy to identify adequately with the masculine role, and so he is likely to identify with the mother. But most such boys grow up to be heterosexual. Apparently, these early childhood experiences make it easier for a boy to become homosexual, but they do not necessarily cause it to happen.

Arrested Development. Freud theorized that growing children pass through a series of psychosexual stages. In the final or genital stage, a person's sexual impulses become directed toward members of the opposite sex. Some people, Freud argued, become fixated at earlier stages and do not achieve full psychosexual maturity. According to this view, homosexuals are victims of arrested development as a result of traumatic or deforming experiences. A person may become fixated at the stage of fascination with his or her own genitals, and subsequently require a sex partner who has the same kind of sex organs. Or a boy may be so frustrated in his attempts to gain the exclusive love of his mother that he develops a hostility toward women. A girl may develop a hostility toward men because of her frustrated love for her father. For others, guilt over sexual desires for the parent of the opposite sex and fear of the parent of the same sex may instill a long-lasting homosexual orientation. Or a person may become fixated on anal or oral stimulation.

Seduction. A common justification for laws against homosexual acts is that adolescent boys are said to be seduced into homosexuality by older men. Though such seductions do take place, no investigator has yet studied the problem, so we do not know how much of it can be attributed to subtle or overt invitations by the boys. Whether the seduced boy becomes a homosexual and whether he would have become homosexual in the absence of seduction are also not known.

The concepts of imprinting and reinforcement may be relevant in connection with the seduction theory. If sexual object-choice is undifferentiated during childhood and early adolescence, and if the boy's or the girl's first sexual experiences are homosexual and satisfying, and if subsequent heterosexual relations are less satisfying, then the individual may be inclined toward homosexuality.

Segregation. Homosexual acts are known to increase when the sexes are kept apart, as they are in prison. But no evidence is available to indicate that homosexual acts under such circumstances cause a person to become homosexual. Nor do heterosexuals continue such homosexual behavior after release from prison. Clearly, sexual segregation leads to temporary adaptations rather than permanent changes in sexual orientation.

Association and Reinforcement. Patients in psychotherapy report innumerable incidents and fantasies, dating back to early childhood, that led them to prefer certain sexual partners and practices and to avoid others. The learning principles of association, reinforcement, avoidance conditioning, and imprinting are sufficient to explain the great variety of heterosexual practices and preferences. They also can account for the equally great variety of homosexual practices and preferences. What a person will learn probably is influenced by his hormonal balance and other physiological variables. While hormones evidently play an important role in animal sexual behavior, it is difficult to obtain solid evidence about their influences on human sexual behavior.

The reinforcement theory of the origin of homosexuality is reflected in a technique designed to change a homosexual orientation into a heterosexual one. This technique gives the patient negative reinforcement in the form of mild electric shock whenever he has homosexual fantasies or urges or engages in homosexual behavior. It also provides positive reinforcement by instructing him to feel pleasure when his fantasies, urges, and acts are heterosexual. Here is an actual case (Gray, 1970).

A young homosexual wanted to become heterosexual. He had a girlfriend but could not bring himself to touch her, even though they often slept in the same bed. Treatment consisted of the following instructions: He was told to stand close to her when he was having pleasant thoughts, and to move closer to her as long as he did not feel anxious. He also was told that when he was masturbating, he should switch his fantasies from homosexual to heterosexual ones at the moment of the orgasm. He was instructed to think about disgusting things while having homosexual fantasies. He was to think about sexually arousing heterosexual books or movies while in close proximity to his girlfriend. After 21 sessions with the psychotherapist, he was able to enjoy sexual relations with the girl.

Such _behavior therapy_ has been used to treat other symptoms of sexual disorders, including exhibitionism, transvestism, child-molesting, premature ejaculation, impotence, and frigidity.

Is Homosexuality a Disease?

In 1973, the American Psychiatric Association's board of trustees voted to describe homosexuality as a "sexual orientation disturbance" rather than to continue to call it a "mental disorder." In effect, this decision allows homosexuals the freedom to decide whether or not their homosexuality represents a psychiatric disorder to them. If they wish to be "cured" of their homosexuality, psychiatrists will attempt to help them to convert to heterosexuality. If they do not wish to change, they now have the option of being treated for other disorders while retaining their homosexual orientation.

While homosexuality is no longer classified as a mental disorder by the APA, it remains a criminal offense in 43 states, even when practiced between consenting adults in private. Some psychiatrists and many laymen still regard it as a disorder. If it is a disorder, it has a cause and possibly a cure. One psychiatrist (Bergler, 1956) staunchly maintains that all homosexuals, _without exception,_ are neurotic, that the neurosis began during the first year or two of life, and that homosexuality can be cured by psychoanalysis provided the patient wishes to be cured. His views have been criticized on many grounds; the most important is that the homosexuals he treats come to him because they are neurotic.

"Normal" or healthy homosexuals do not go to psychiatrists any more than "normal" or healthy heterosexuals do.

Evelyn Hooker, using several types of psychological tests that measure adjustment to the stresses of adult life, could not find any significant differences between a group of homosexual males and a matched group of heterosexuals, nor were experienced clinical psychologists able to distinguish the two groups on the basis of their test records. It must be remembered, however, that Hooker selected only reasonably well-adjusted homosexual persons.

Transsexualism

Most people's sexual feelings and motivations match their biological gender. Whether they are heterosexual or homosexual, most men think of themselves as men, and most women think of themselves as women. However, some individuals have sex-linked self-concepts that are contrary to their biological sex. A male yearns to be a female; a female yearns to be a male. As we have noted, such people are called *transsexuals*.

In recent years, surgeons have been reasonably successful in transforming transsexual males into females. Somewhat less success has been achieved in transforming females into males, because it is more difficult to make a functional artificial penis than a functional artificial vagina. Whether it will be possible to give a man a uterus and ovaries so that he can bear children, or give a woman testes so she can father children, remains to be seen.

The first transsexual clinic in the United States was started at the Johns Hopkins University Medical School in 1965; since then, many such clinics have been established. People seeking sex change have beseiged these clinics despite the treatment's relatively high cost.

The first step in changing the sex of a male consists of treatment with the female sex hormone for a number of months. This makes the testes and prostate much smaller and develops the breasts.

The second step involves removing the penis (except for the urinary canal) and the testes, and creating an artificial vagina. Six to eight weeks after the operation, the transsexual can perform sexual intercourse as a woman. Some of these transsexuals have married males and live completely as women. Others have not adjusted well to their new gender, and a few have become prostitutes.

Reversing the sex of a female also starts with hormone treatment. Testosterone (one of the male sex hormones) is injected for some months. This treatment causes a deepening of the voice, a decrease in the size of the breasts, enlargement of the clitoris, appearance of a beard, and an increase in muscular strength. The breasts, uterus, and ovaries are then removed. The creation of a penis is the last and most difficult step. If it succeeds, these transsexuals can live as men, and several have since married women.

Females who become men seem to make better adjustments than males who become women. This may simply indicate that transsexual females are generally better adjusted before they become men. Males

13-7
The transformation of a transsexual male into a female is produced by hormone injections, surgery, and makeup. Two brothers are now two sisters. (UPI photo)

seem to expect more from the operation and are less satisfied with their womanhood as a result. Transsexuals are urged to have psychotherapy for a period following the operation to help them adjust to their new gender role.

What produces such a strong desire to be of the opposite sex that a person will undergo a painful, lengthy, and expensive operation? Many theories have been advanced. Some propose inherent or congenital causes; others favor environmental determinants, especially childhood experiences that cause an identification with the opposite sex. Transsexuals generally report that their preference for the opposite sex role appeared early in childhood. Both heredity and environment probably interact; for some, the genetic factor may be more important, while for others, environmental influences may predominate.

Love and Jealousy

We have discussed many topics related to sexual motivation and behavior; but so far we have paid little attention to the emotion of love. Although love often is independent of any conscious sexual attraction, and sexual relations can proceed without love, the two feelings are customarily intertwined.

In Western societies (and probably throughout the world), marriage symbolizes the union of a man and a woman who are in love and sanctions a sexual relationship between them. Although alternatives to marriage and the prevalence of divorce are discussed a great deal today, a lasting, primarily monogamous marriage between two people is still the rule in most of the world.

Needless to say, sexual acts occur prior to marriage; they also occur after marriage with partners other than the spouse. Kinsey's figures revealed that about 20 percent of females and 80 percent of males who marry at age 25 had engaged in premarital intercourse (the figure for women is higher today). By the age of 40, about one-fourth of married women and one-half of married men will have had extramarital sexual relations.

We should note that, although the *incidence* of extramarital intercourse is quite high, the *frequency* is fairly low. As a result, sexual relations with one's spouse account for more than 80 percent of all sexual acts, while extramarital sexual relations account for only 10 percent (the remaining 10 percent is accounted for by masturbation, wet dreams, and so on). In short, the typical husband and wife either have no relations outside of marriage, or have only a few transient affairs. These affairs often occur when the husband and wife are separated for a period of time.

What does it mean to fall in love? We experience it as a desire to be close to the loved one, to engage in physical intimacies, to do things together, and to share our private feelings and ambitions. People in love want to do things for each other and to make sacrifices if necessary. Love is called the tender emotion because of the affection and consideration that people in love feel for each other.

In the world of love, no boundaries, impediments, or insecurities intrude; everything becomes possible. A man and a woman in love compose a union of male and female that forms a complete whole. As Jung put it, the female element in a male (the *anima*) finds fulfillment in loving a woman, and the male element in a female (the *animus*) finds fulfillment in loving a man. Since people in love feel secure and whole, they are capable of appreciating and realizing the abundance of possibilities in the world. Although this view of love may sound overidealized, it accurately describes what many people experience; the world does indeed open up to them.

Falling in love is accompanied by physiological reactions that are like those for other states of arousal. These reactions include an accelerated heartbeat, increased blood pressure, and shallower, faster breathing. Some psychologists believe that love causes these physiological changes; others say love is merely the name we give to the feelings we have when these changes occur. People in love are generally too busy enjoying their feelings to care about such questions.

Exclusivity, another aspect of love, leads to the emotion of jealousy. _Exclusivity_ is the desire to have sole possession of the loved one. When this possessiveness is threatened by a third person or by a competing interest, _jealousy_ may spring up. Since exclusive possession is an impossible goal, jealousy often goes hand in hand with love. It has been called love's shadow.

Characteristically, jealousy appears during early childhood when the first-born child sees the next-born child as a competitor for the mother's love and attention. This is responsible for the well-known phenomenon of _sibling rivalry_.

Falling in love, like so many other common human psychological behaviors, is programmed. It appears at a specific age in the life-cycle—typically, shortly after puberty, when the sex glands, the reproductive apparatus, and the secondary sex characteristics have matured.

What determines our choice when we fall in love? Obviously, proximity plays a major role. We fall in love with someone who lives nearby or goes to the same school, or with someone we meet at a party or during a vacation. We also tend to fall in love with someone of the same social class and family background.

Given these limitations, what determines the choice of a mate? One explanation of marital choice is that the needs of two people who fall in love complement each other. For instance, a person who has a need to be protected and taken care of will fall in love with someone who has a need to protect and take care of another. Some studies of married couples support this _complementarity hypothesis_. This hypothesis is a particular example of the popular idea that "opposites attract." The contrary belief is that "likes attract." Evidence also supports this view; married couples often share many of the same interests, attitudes and traits.

Given the complexities of human nature, it is not surprising that both hypotheses are partially correct. We can be attracted to a person who is the same in some respects and different in others. Empirical studies support our common sense assumption that sexual attraction is an important component of falling in love. Happily, both *mutuality* of desire and *complementarity* of the sexual organs are involved.

To the question "Why do you like him," a wise man replied, "Because he likes me." This is probably the crucial factor in friendship or love. Although one can fall in love with someone who does not return love, the chances of the relationship's lasting are slim. A person who is attracted to another person sends out signals to communicate his feelings. If these signals go unanswered or produce a negative response, they soon will cease. A person who is rebuffed loses interest. But if the signals get a positive response, the attraction takes root and culminates in a love affair or marriage. However, two people often give each other both positive and negative reinforcement. This ambivalence creates feelings of insecurity and uncertainty and is the cause of much discord between couples.

Another theory attributes the choice of a mate to childhood imprinting experiences, which become fully developed during adolescence. For a boy, the most important influences are derived from his feelings about his mother. For a girl, the father is the chief imprinting agent. These feelings, imprinted during childhood, are assumed to govern the kind of person a boy or girl will fall in love with during and after adolescence.

Do the observable facts support this theory? Is there any correlation between the characteristics possessed by husbands and their wives' fathers, or between wives and their husbands' mothers? The answer is yes and no. In some ways they are alike; in other respects they are different. One difficulty with such studies is that a person's imprinted conception of his or her mother may differ noticeably from an objective observer's impression of the parent's personality. Another difficulty is that a boy who is on bad terms with his mother or a girl who resents her father may select mates who are unlike the objectionable parent. This could result in negative correlations between husbands and wives' fathers or wives and husbands' mothers—but even in this situation, the results are seldom unequivocal.

One may wonder why brothers and sisters rarely fall in love with each other and try to marry. The usual explanation is that they are prevented from doing so by the incest taboo and legal prohibitions. However, observers have noted that unrelated individuals who grew up together in the same Israeli kibbutz did not fall in love and marry each other, although community attitudes did not forbid it. And American college students report that when men and women are assigned rooms on the same dormitory floor, friendships are frequent but love affairs develop only with "outsiders" who live elsewhere. Cynics claim that too much familiarity ruins the possibility of romance. Others theorize that love affairs are tacitly forbidden because they might disrupt the close-knit group. We need to know more about this intriguing phenomenon before we can evaluate these theories.

The difficulties of trying to understand one person's behavior are multiplied when we try to understand the behavior of two people interacting with each other. Surely no simple rules will be generally applicable. Jung summed up the situation in a letter to a friend: "Man is a most peculiar experiment of nature and particularly in erotic respects simply anything is possible."

13-8
Old, as well as young, can enjoy the benefits of a warm, sharing, love relationship. (Brassai, Rapho Guillumette, Kosti Ruohomaa, Black Star)

Summary

1. Many approaches are used to study sexual behavior: the case study method, subjective accounts, historical methods, cross-cultural investigations, naturalistic observation, observations of people engaging in sexual activities in the laboratory (the studies by Masters and Johnson, for example) and large-scale quantitative studies (as exemplified by the work of Kinsey and his associates).

2. Different studies reveal considerable variation in the nature of sexual activities from culture to culture and from individual to individual.

3. Hormones are less important than learning in determining human sexual behavior.

4. Recent evidence indicates that a region of the anterior hypothalamus channels sexual impulses into appropriate motor outlets.

5. The sex impulse is universal but the stimuli that arouse the sex drive are virtually limitless. People differ greatly in the strength of their sex drive.

6. A homosexual person is one whose sexual outlets are predominantly with those of the same sex; homosexual acts are engaged in occasionally by people who also have heterosexual relations. Homosexuals do not differ physically from heterosexuals.

7. Some evidence shows that heredity may be a factor in predisposing a person to become homosexual, but the relative proportion of male and female sex hormones secreted by a person does not appear to be a factor. Childhood experiences and learning are probably the most important factors. Other explanations are arrested development and seduction of a younger person by an older person.

8. People who have the organs of one sex and the thoughts and feelings of the other are known as transsexuals. Today they can have their gender changed from male to female or from female to male by hormone treatment and surgery.

9. Loving a person is usually (but not always) accompanied by a wish to express that love sexually.

10. Falling in love usually occurs for the first time shortly after sexual maturation has been completed.

11. Jealousy arises out of a desire to have exclusive possession of the loved one.

12. According to one theory, we fall in love with a person who complements our own personality. Another theory states that similar people are attracted to one another. A third theory is that people imprint an image of their opposite-sex parent in childhood and later fall in love with people who match this image.

Important Terms

psychosexual stages	plateau phase
oral stage	orgasmic phase
anal stage	resolution phase
phallic stage	quantitative study
genital stage	homosexuality
pansexualism	bisexual (ambisexual)
case study	androgen
subjective account	testosterone
historical study	gender identity
cross-cultural study	fetish
observational study	transsexual
laboratory study	anima
excitement phase	animus

Suggested Readings

BEACH, F. A. (ED.) *Sex and behavior.* New York: Wiley, 1965.
> A collection of fairly technical articles by experts. Both animal and human studies are included.

ELLIS, H. *Studies in the psychology of sex.* New York: Random House, 1936.
> A pioneer work in seven volumes on every aspect of human sexual behavior. Many case histories are included. Fascinating reading.

FORD, C. S., & BEACH, F. A. *Patterns of sexual behavior.* New York: Harper & Row, 1951.
> An authoritative review of patterns of sexual behavior in lower animals and in various human societies. The presentation is fairly technical.

FREUD, S. *Three essays on sexuality.* Standard edition, vol. VII. London: Hogarth Press, 1953, pp. 135–243.
> A short, provocative book, containing Freud's thoughts about the development of sexuality in the individual and the various ways the sex impulse can express itself.

KINSEY, A. C., POMEROY, W. B., & MARTIN, C. E. *Sexual behavior in the human male.* Philadelphia: Saunders, 1948.
KINSEY, A. C., POMEROY, W. B., MARTIN, C. E., & GEBHARD, P. H. *Sexual behavior in the human female.* Philadelphia: Saunders, 1953.
> These two volumes are packed with statistics about the sexual activities of American males and females.

MASTERS, W. H., & JOHNSON, V. E. *Human sexual response.* Boston: Little, Brown, 1966.

A fairly technical, but interesting and informative, step-by-step account of the physiological changes in males and females during the sexual act.

MASTERS, W. H., & JOHNSON, V. E. *The pleasure bond.* Boston: Little, Brown, 1975.

An analysis of sexual successes and failures, based on seminars with newlyweds, married couples with extramarital experience, individuals engaged in group sex, and many others.

MILLER, H. L., & SIEGEL, P. S. *Loving: a psychological approach.* New York: Wiley, 1972.

A well-written, stimulating account of the psychology of love relationships as seen primarily from the standpoint of learning theory. Useful for understanding and improving one's interpersonal relationships.

MONEY, J., & EHRHARDT, A. A. *Man and woman, boy and girl: the differentiation and dimorphism of gender identity from conception to maturity.* Baltimore: Johns Hopkins University Press, 1972.

A fascinating, scientific account of how human beings establish their identities as men or women.

MURSTEIN, B. I. (ED.) *Theories of attraction and love.* New York: Springer, 1971.

A fairly technical collection of papers which presents an excellent picture of what psychologists know and think today about love and attraction.

Chapter 14 Development

There is no steady unretracing progress in this life; we do not advance through fixed gradations, and at the last one pause: through infancy's unconscious spell, boyhood's thoughtless faith, adolescence' doubt (the common doom), then skepticism, then disbelief, resting at last in manhood's pondering repose of If. But once gone through, we trace the round again; and are infants, boys, and men, and Ifs eternally. Where lies the final harbor, whence we unmoor no more?

—Herman Melville
(*Moby Dick*)

Development

This chapter was written by Sandra Scarr-Salapatek, Institute of Child Development, University of Minnesota.

Imagine that a person standing at a bus stop with you suddenly screams, throws himself down, kicks, and sobs. If he were 2, you might think that he was excessively tired, hungry, or frustrated but generally behaving normally for his age. If he were 6, you might think he needed help to overcome such infantile behavior by developing greater self-control and more constructive ways to express his anger and frustration. Were he 26, you would regard his behavior as very unusual, and probably as evidence of a serious behavioral disturbance. This sequence illustrates the basic tenet underlying the idea of development: Behaviors that are normal at one age are abnormal at another. Behaviors change across the lifespan.

In this chapter we shall discuss the development of human behavior—why it changes as people mature and gain more experiences, how psychologists study it and attempt to explain it, and what behaviors are typical of infancy, childhood, adolescence, and adulthood. Development is one of psychology's most fascinating aspects. Like a flowing river, a human being is changing constantly and yet remains the same person from birth to death.

Characteristics of Development

Psychologists define development as an _orderly sequence of behavioral change_. Developmental changes are (1) _directional_, (2) _cumulative_, and (3) characterized by _increasing differentiation_ and _integration_.

The directional nature of developmental changes is apparent in most behaviors, such as language. When babies begin to talk in their second year, they use single words and then two-word sentences. By 5 years, most children are using sentences containing most of the elements of adult speech.

Development's cumulative nature means that a behavior depends on one or more earlier behaviors. A child cannot walk until he can stand alone and move his legs in alternating fashion while holding on. Many behaviors develop in similar sequences. Before a child can fully develop his reading skills, he must recognize the 26 letters of the alphabet and know the sounds of each letter. Some adult skills are largely an expansion of childhood abilities. With increasing experience and maturity, most people become more accomplished at almost any skill.

Development also is characterized by increasing differentiation and complex organization—a process one can see if one studies the growing embryo. As development of the early fetus proceeds, cells specialize and differentiate more and more; previously identical cells become distinct from each other. As the fetus matures, some cells organize into complex units to form organ systems. Similarly, behavioral development becomes more differentiated and complex. One example is the development of an action pattern, which the developmental psychologist Jean Piaget calls a *scheme*. At birth, infants possess unlearned motor patterns for such behaviors as sucking, grasping, and moving their limbs. But they do not know how their behaviors relate to the external world. After a few months, infants begin to learn how to affect their environments. They repeat actions that have interesting effects, such as kicking the crib to make a mobile move or thrashing out at an object that makes noise. They later develop more differentiated and elaborated schemes; striking out becomes differentiated into such behaviors as patting, throwing, slapping, tapping, and fingering. Soon an infant can combine these schemes into action sequences that help him find out about the world. Still later, he learns which schemes are appropriate for which objects. As behaviors develop they usually become more specialized and differentiated; they also become more highly organized into complex patterns and sequences.

Development: The Interaction of Genes and Environment

Development depends on genes and environment. Genetic determinants often are expressed as important maturational changes in the brain—for example, the enlargement of the cerebral cortex, which controls complex behaviors. The environmental factors that affect development often are expressed as opportunities to learn. The human capacity to learn from experience is itself an evolved, genetic characteristic. How well we learn from our environment depends on our capacity to learn, our maturational level at the time, our past experiences, and the material immediately available to us.

Some people believe that such developments as physical growth depend more on genes than on environment, and that psychological development, such as the development of social behavior, depends more on environment than on genes. These people forget that, in the case of physical growth, food obviously is an essential environmental component. In the case of social behaviors, genetic determinants affect how people respond to others. Normal physical growth and social development both depend on having a normal genetic makeup *and* an adequate environment. As we shall see, some developments require *specific* environmental stimulation while others require *general* stimulation.

All of us know that every child is the product of both parents' genes. However, we do not yet know which characteristics and traits will be inherited from which parent. One is reminded of the lady who proposed marriage to George Bernard Shaw, the brilliant British dramatist.

"You have the greatest brain in the world," she pointed out, "and I have the most beautiful body; so we ought to produce the most perfect child." Shaw unhesitatingly refused, replying that he was entirely unwilling to run the parallel risk of having a child with his looks and her intelliigence.

An important question in psychology today is, How much do genetic and environmental determinants contribute to the development of *individual differences?* Currently, a controversy about genes and intelligence centers on how much *genetic differences* contribute to differences in IQ scores. Although both genes and environment are required for development, one or the other can be primarily responsible for differences among individuals. If we all were reared in exactly the same environment, any differences among us would clearly be due to our genetic differences. If we all were genetically identical but reared in different environments, any differences among us would result from our different environments. Since both genetic and environmental differences exist among members of human populations, the question is, How much does each factor determine the large observable differences in IQ?

Sequences and Stages

Nearly all developmental psychologists recognize *sequences* in behavioral development. Flavell (1972) has suggested three reasons for sequences in development: (1) the structure of the organism, (2) the structure of the environment, and (3) the structure of the behavior.

An organism must mature neurologically to a given level before it can perform a particular behavior. Creeping precedes walking in infant motor development largely because walking requires greater neurological maturity. Babbling always precedes speech, and concrete intelligence always comes before formal, abstract logic; the maturity of the central nervous system is important to all of these sequences.

The environment's structure determines sequences of development by arranging experiences according to age. In general, the number of experiences increases with age. In addition, sociocultural norms determine which experiences are appropriate for which ages. Although many 13-year-olds can perform adult sexual behaviors and reproduce, most cultures do not grant them full adult status until years later. The adoles-

14-1
The course of human development—infancy, childhood, adolescence, adulthood, and old age.

cent dating game is a precursor to adult mate selection. At the other end of the life span, in this society most workers must retire in their middle sixties when they are still active and capable adults. Cultural norms regarding retirement thrust older adults out of the social mainstream, and, as a result, they often experience social isolation, poverty, and a sense of purposelessness. Many other societies revere their older people as wise advisers. Because we usually do not, we know that some developmental changes we observe in old people, such as mental deterioration and social withdrawal, result in part from the structure of the environment.

The structure of the behavior is determined by the sequences within it; the earlier and later behaviors are logically related. If being able to add and subtract is an essential part of learning to multiply and divide, then the former will always precede the latter. Knowing the names of some objects is essential to speech, and later language development depends on earlier naming skills. Sequences generally are recognized in the development of most kinds of behavior, and their origins lie in one or more of the three causes that Flavell has suggested.

Although the idea of stages of development enjoys less consensus, it still has considerable acceptance among psychologists and the general public. Parents often will say, "Oh, that's just a stage he's going through," to excuse a child's misbehavior. The implication is that the problem behavior will go away in time because the child will enter a new stage with different behaviors. In psychology, the concept of a stage usually means that (1) behaviors at a given age are *organized* around a dominant theme; (2) behaviors at the new stage are *qualitatively different* from behaviors at other stages; and (3) development proceeds in *spurts* that mark transitions to new stages *and plateaus* that represent the stages themselves.

How well does the stage concept characterize development? If you compare a 2-year-old with a 12-year-old, you will notice many cognitive, linguistic, and social differences. The 2-year-old's thinking is not logical by 12-year-old standards; his speech does not follow the same rules, and his social behaviors are selfish and uncontrolled in comparison to the 12-year-old's. The 12-year-old is nearly an adult in his modes of thinking, his language, and even his social relationships. While the 2-year-old can think about things that happened in the past and imagine things that may never happen, his understanding of the world is strongly influenced by apparent changes that older children can ignore. From a linguistic point of view, the 2-year-old is in the *two-word* or *three-word* stage, meaning that he can express his thoughts only in short utterances not typical of adult speech ("Go bye-bye car"). From a social point of view, he is at the *autonomy* stage because he has begun to battle with his parents for the right to control his own actions ("Me do it!").

If you watch—as parents do—the 2-year-old become a 3-, 5-, and 10-year-old, you will notice that for particular behaviors some ages have more rapid changes than others. Important shifts in intellectual development tend to occur around 7 and 11. For language development the years from 2 to 5 mark an amazingly rapid shift from a few words to nearly complete mastery of the child's native language—from "Go bye-bye car" to "Please, Mommy, let's go for a ride in the car because I want to visit the zoo again." For social development, the years 2 to 6 include the child's development of self-confidence and considerable independence from direct parental control and his entrance into the larger social worlds of peer groups and the school.

Thus, from several points of view, behaviors at different ages can be organized around dominant themes; they differ qualitatively from behaviors at other ages; and they show rapid shifts from one period to another, followed by relatively long periods without dramatic changes.

The problem with the stage concept is its overgeneralization. No one theme can adequately characterize all of 2-year-old behavior, or behavior at any life stage. Qualitative shifts do not occur simultaneously for all aspects of behavior. And the rapidity with which spurts occur and the presence of plateaus in development are debatable points. In many cases, a seemingly dramatic shift from ignorance to understanding will have been preceded by many quantitative changes in the necessary components of that shift. In a relatively brief period, the child may have been able to put those components together in a new way, but one cannot ignore the many less obvious preparatory steps that preceded the shift. Nor can one ignore the many important applications of the new skill that the child must work out after the shift has occurred.

Some theorists, such as Jean Piaget and Erik Erikson, argue that development consists of an invariant sequence of stages, each one qualitatively different from preceding or succeeding stages and each with a dominant mode of thinking or developmental step to be taken. Other theorists, such as Albert Bandura and B. F. Skinner, disagree. For them, development is a continuous process of acquiring new behaviors through learning. They do not recognize qualitative shifts in development. Can both stage and anti-stage theorists be correct? The answer is that the usefulness of the stage concept depends on which behaviors the theorist finds interesting and how willing he is to infer mental structures from observed behaviors. As we shall see in the next section on theories, the usefulness of the stage concept remains undecided.

Theories of Development

When a child shakes his fist and yells at another child, some people infer that the child is angry or that he is an "aggressive" child; others maintain that something in the immediate environment provoked this behavior and that nothing should be inferred about the child.

In psychology, two principal groups of theories attempt to explain development: the _structuralists_, who infer internal rules (or structures) from observed behaviors, and the _behaviorists_, who see the environment as the determinant of behaviors. The behaviorists see development as the accumulation of learned responses; the structuralists see learning as an observable product of internal changes in the rules and organization that determine behavior. Since both observe the same human organism behaving and changing over time, how can they disagree so fundamentally on the nature of development? Part of the answer is that structuralists and behaviorists do not ask the same questions about development.

The Behaviorist Position

Behaviorists are interested primarily in discrete behavioral responses in particular situations. The followers of B. F. Skinner focus on changing observable behaviors through the manipulation of rewards. If a nursery school child plays alone for most of the day, he can be shaped—as we discussed in the learning chapter (Chapter 6)—to emit more social behaviors if his every attempt to get close to another child and to engage in reciprocal interaction is rewarded. His antisocial behaviors can be extinguished if they are ignored. As we mentioned in the chapter on aggression and conflict (Chapter 12), other behaviorists, such as Albert Bandura, point to the importance of imitation and modeling in shaping social behaviors. Children learn new ways of behaving by observing models, such as parents, teachers, and older children, being rewarded. They learn that they will be rewarded for similar behaviors. Behaviorists seldom ask *why* some behaviors are emitted and others are not. They are interested in *how* the frequencies of behaviors change.

The Structuralist Position

The structuralists ask *why* behaviors are emitted, especially why at some ages and not at others. They observe discrete behaviors and try to deduce the *rules* that produce those behaviors. Structuralists believe that internal rules guide all behavior and that the rules change as the person develops.

Jean Piaget best represents the structuralist position on learning and intelligence. Piaget (1951) observed the behaviors of his own children, noting shifts in the organization of their behaviors and inferring rules that would produce the behaviors he observed. The action patterns or schemes of infancy are gradually internalized, coordinated, and elaborated until in adulthood much of our intelligent behavior is mental activity. Adults can *think* about complex solutions to problems while younger children must try them out in concrete ways. Piaget postulated three distinct stages of intellectual development, each of which spans several years and is characterized by a different set of rules. Later in this chapter, we shall discuss these—the sensorimotor, the operational, and the propositional—in some detail.

Erik Erikson is another important structural theorist. His theory of psychosocial stages is concerned primarily with emotional and social development from infancy to old age. Each stage has a principal problem to be solved, a dominant theme that characterizes many of the behaviors we observe at that stage. Discrete behaviors are generated by attempts to solve internal conflicts between one's innate drives and demands in the social environment. We shall also examine Erikson's views in detail later.

Structural theories prompt two major questions. The first is, Where do the rules come from? We have no completely satisfactory answer. Chomsky believes that knowledge about the general form of linguistic rules may be "given" or innate, and that the genetic, species-specific capacity to acquire language matures rapidly in early childhood. If any effective language exists during those years (that is, if the child is not totally isolated or deaf), the child will acquire speech. Piaget follows an evolutionary perspective on the development of intelligence. Cognitive rules represent man's evolved capacity to think. Across age, cognitive abilities change in accord with the child's developmental level. Maturation pushes the child into new experiences, and new experiences lead to new development. A child's environment changes because the child selects new information and stimulation from his environment as his cognitive capacities mature. Erikson depends on maturation and culture to explain the origin of rules of behavior. New conflicts arise from both increasing maturity and social demands. Structural theorists tend to accept an evolutionary account of man's capacities and the framework that evolution provides for understanding human behavior. In their attempts to explain development, they take an *interactionist* point of view; that is, they believe both maturation and learning are essential to development.

The second question provoked by structural theories is, Why do linguistic rules change? The answer is that the child has achieved all of the solutions he can with the first set of rules. Yet he realizes that other problems exist. Dissatisfaction or, in Piaget's term, disequilibrium, is the result. Piaget's theory of _equilibration_ proposes two processes by which learning occurs: _assimilation_ and _accommodation_. Assimilation is the acquisition of new information through the application of the existing set of rules or structures. Accommodation is the stage-to-stage process of changing rules to acquire new information that does not fit existing structures.

Behavioral Observation

Developmental research uses most of the methods and designs we have encountered in other areas of psychology. The scientific method, with its rules of experimentation, applies to developmental studies, too. However, developmental research places more emphasis on observational methods.

Behavioral observation is particularly important to the study of children for two reasons. First, many experiments possible with subhuman species cannot be carried out ethically with children. Second, young children cannot report on their own experiences as easily as adults can. By watching children of different ages, and the same children across time, developmental psychologists can infer many interesting ideas about the nature of development.

The first principle of behavioral observation is that observations must be _sampled_; you cannot see everything that happens in a continuous stream of behaviors. The two basic sampling methods are the _event_ and _time_ samples. For an event sample, the observers decide in advance on the behavior that interests them. Then they record only those events—for example, each time one child hits another—regardless of when they occur. By focusing on only one, two, or three behaviors, they have time to record their observations. Time-sampling involves taking behavior samples at regular intervals during an hour, day, week, month, year, or years. It requires careful attention because behaviors vary by time of day, month of the year, and so forth. School children's behaviors change dramatically from school hours to afterschool hours, from Monday to Friday, from winter to summer, from the beginning of the school year to the end, and from grade to grade. Separating developmental changes from other temporal shifts requires a carefully planned observation schedule. To give himself time to record what he has seen, the observer usually views the subject for a brief span. He usually has a strict time schedule of, say, 15 seconds to observe and 15 to record. Otherwise, he may only report the "interesting" events that catch his eye.

The second principle of behavior observations is that what is recorded must be exactly what is observed: *judgments about behaviors are not observations*. If the basic data are not exclusively the child's behaviors, the observer's biases creep in. Television tape and inexpensive film recordings have made it possible to avoid biases by having many observers "score" the behaviors.

The third principle of behavior observations is that they must be *reliable*. Two or more observers must agree on what was seen. In event sampling, the two observers must agree on the number of times the chosen behaviors occurred. In time sampling, the observers must agree on the frequencies and types of behaviors observed during the chosen times.

From such careful observations, psychologists can describe typical behaviors at different ages. They also can look for consistencies in individual behavior across time. Is the child who hits and pushes excessively in nursery school the same child who fights more than other children in third grade? How does the social organization of children's play groups change from middle to late childhood? Scientific behavioral observations can answer these and many other questions.

Developmental Phases

You can best appreciate the course of human development when you know people of different ages. If you observe and interact with newborns, toddlers, 8-year-olds, young adolescents, adults, and old people, you will quickly see that nothing can replace an intimate knowledge of their actual behavior. In this section, we shall introduce people at several developmental levels and discuss some of the facts developmental psychologists have discovered about them. A portion of the scientific information will merely confirm what you already believe about development, but some of it may surprise you. In recent years, psychologists have discovered, for example, how very competent infants are at perceiving and exploring their worlds; how universal are the stages of moral development; and the importance of play in the intellectual development of children.

Several ways to divide the life span into periods or phases have been proposed. For convenience, we have adopted a scheme based on contemporary Western ideas about life periods; it consists of *infancy, childhood, adolescence,* and *adulthood.* Until the late 18th century, the

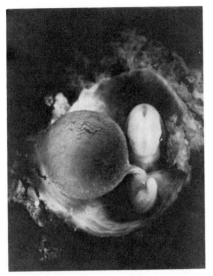

A

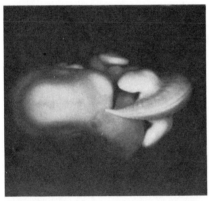

B

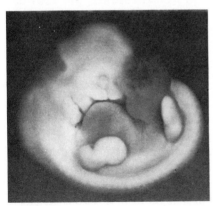

C

14-2
Development of the fetus. (A) 28 days; (B) and (C) 39 days; (D) 42 days; (E) 55 days. (Roberts Rugh & Dr. L. B. Shettles)

period that we call adolescence had not been recognized as separate from adulthood. Some contemporary cultures, especially preindustrial groups, still do not recognize a period of adolescence. Even childhood was not separated from infancy until the Renaissance (Aries, 1962). Before that, the period of early dependence lasted for about 7 years, at which time people moved into the social and economic world of adults. Not until the 20th century did childhood become fully established as a separate period for all children. The advent of child labor laws and compulsory school attendance mark the final recognition that youth of all classes has a right to special protection in childhood.

Infancy — From Fetus to First Words

The most rapid changes of the entire lifespan occur between conception and birth. A single fertilized cell with 23 pairs of chromosomes develops into a fully functioning newborn baby in only 38 to 40 weeks. During the first 16 weeks of the gestation period in the womb, nearly all of the essential metabolic and sensory systems of what is to become the human infant take form and begin to function. The later weeks of gestation put the finishing, maturational touches on these systems. Before it is 26 to 28 weeks of age, a fetus cannot survive outside the uterus. The final functioning of many systems, including respiration and digestion, is perfected in the last 4 to 6 weeks of gestation. Premature infants often have difficulty with their breathing and in maintaining their body temperature and the acid-alkaline balance of their body fluids. After 38 to 40 weeks, the average newborn of European descent weighs 7 to 7½ pounds (girls are slightly smaller than boys) and measures about 20 inches. Newborns of Asian and African descent are somewhat smaller but equally mature.

The newborn baby is a surprisingly efficient organism. He has a large array of reflexive behaviors and a well-developed sensory apparatus. Some of his behaviors, such as "rooting" toward his mother's nipple and sucking, serve to obtain food. Other behaviors, like eye-blinks, body turning, and limb flexing, allow him to escape noxious stimuli such as bright lights and sharp pricks. Still other responses to visual and auditory stimuli show that he is alert to and can follow changing patterns in his environment. And, finally, he shows some rudimentary social responses, such as quieting when he is held.

D

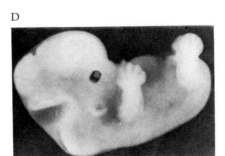

E

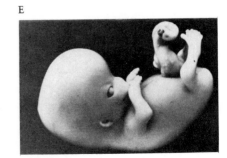

Early Adaptation

The newborn period, from birth to one week, is a triumph in adaptation. From a fetus completely dependent upon the mother, he becomes an independently breathing, digesting, eliminating, and temperature-maintaining infant. Babies come into the world with relatively mature sensory systems. Unlike many mammals, such as puppies and kittens—which are blind at birth—the human newborn perceives much of his environment. Although his visual acuity is not nearly as good as it will be at 6 months (at birth he has about 20/200 acuity) he can focus clearly on objects about 10 inches from his eyes. Because his lenses do not accommodate well to depth, he sees distant objects out of focus. He does not always see with binocular vision; for several weeks each eye tends to operate independently. In the last decade, research has proved conclusively that despite his visual limitations, the newborn does see; that he prefers to view patterned stimuli rather than blank fields; and that he actively inspects his visual environment.

Hearing also is highly developed in the infant. As soon as the fluid in which he floated as a fetus has drained from his ear canals, the newborn responds to sounds of 40 to 60 decibels, the range of a normal speaking voice. Although he has had no opportunity to learn to make fine tone discriminations, some newborns can detect a difference of one note on a musical scale (Bridger, 1961). The newborn baby's senses of taste and smell are not nearly as acute as an adult's, but he does detect and withdraw from noxious odors and strong saline solutions. A few weeks after birth, his abilities to smell and taste improve markedly.

After the first week of life, the infant has recovered from the stresses of delivery, and his eating and sleeping patterns become more stable. He sleeps as many as 20 hours a day, and he may cry often. Between one week and about two months, the baby is settling down and becoming more regular in his behavior patterns; but he is not yet a very interactive creature. He smiles sometimes when he is drowsy and well-fed, just before falling asleep. Although this is not social smiling, the baby can smile at faces in this period—if he is fully alert, engaged in eye-to-eye contact with an adult, and otherwise content. With considerable effort social smiles can be evoked about once a day at 2 to 3 weeks of age; the frequency of social smiling continues to increase until about 8 weeks.

Social Responsiveness and Learning

By 2 months of age the baby seems to enter a new period that lasts until he is 7 or 8 months old. Two important changes in this 6-month period are his increased social responsiveness and his improved learning ability. Babies smile readily at human features, particularly when the faces are smiling and the heads nodding. At 2 to 3 months infants will smile at many facelike configurations, even flat cardboard faces and those with scrambled features. Smiling reaches its peak when the baby is about 4 months old (Gewirtz, 1965). Later in this period, and certainly by 7 months, most babies will smile more readily at real human faces, and particularly at familiar people rather than at masks or two-dimensional representations of faces.

14-3
At 4 months of age, the infant already prefers faces to other objects — even when the faces are made of cardboard. As the shape of the faces becomes less and less like a human face, the infant's fixation time grows shorter. (R. A. Haaf & R. Q. Bell. A facial dimension in visual discrimination in infants. *Child Development*, 1967, **38**, 895. Copyright 1967 by the Society of Research in Child Development, Inc. By permission.)

stimulus				
degree of faceness	1	2	3	4
amount of detail	3	1	4	2
percent fixation time	.33	.28	.19	.20

Babies learn important discriminations in this period. One of the most acute discriminations a 2-month-old can make is between the sounds of human speech. He can respond to a minimal phoneme contrast, such as the difference between "pa" and "ba" (Eimas, Siqueland, Jusczyk, & Vigorito, 1971). Psychologists now regard this early ability to discriminate speech sounds as an essential feature of later language acquisition.

In the first 2 months a baby can be conditioned to suck at different rates and strengths and to turn his head (Lipsett, 1963). But most psychologists would agree that the ease and frequency with which learning occurs increases dramatically after 2 or 3 months of life. Operant conditioning and discrimination learning are fairly easy to demonstrate in infants older than 3 months. In large part this change is the result of greater cortical maturity and the decline of reflexive behaviors. The baby is born with many reflexes, such as the Moro startle response (flailing of the arms in response to loss of support) and the Babinski reflex (a fanning of the toes when the sole of the foot is stroked). Many of these reflexes are mediated by subcortical regions of the brain. As the cortex begins to mediate more complex behavior in the first few months of life, these reflexes are "covered over" and disappear. They only reappear in severely brain-damaged persons who have lost most of their cortical control.

The 3-month-old's brain is better developed for learning than a newborn's (Conel, 1939, 1941, 1947). By 3 months of age, infants also are alert for longer periods of time, without internal interruptions or the continual need to eat, a physiological need that seems to interfere with smooth functioning during the first 8 weeks. Voluntary control over muscles also improves markedly. Hand-eye coordination, reaching, and grasping become useful behaviors for exploration at 5 to 6 months. With these skills, the infant can learn about his world much more rapidly.

Walking, Talking, and Attachment

By 7 or 8 months, three new developments begin: the baby makes significant progress toward independent locomotion; he develops strong attachments to particular people; and he begins to babble in language sounds. Most babies pass the major motor milestones of sitting alone, creeping, standing, and walking between the ages of 7 and 15 months. This invariant sequence of motor skills depends on increasing neurological and muscular maturity and on numerous opportunities to try out locomotion.

14-4

14-4
Stages of infant motor development—from lifting head and shoulders to crawling to standing to walking. (Gerry Cranham, Rapho Cuillumette)

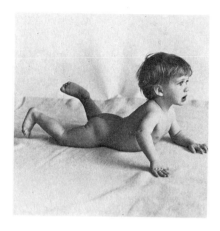

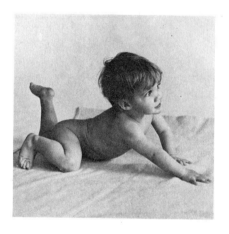

In the social realm, the infant frequently develops a fear of strangers. Instead of smiling at everyone as he did at 4 months, he actually may break into tears at the approach of a stranger, despite the new person's overt friendliness and smiling face. A baby of 7 to 12 months often looks away from strangers, glancing fleetingly to see if they are still there and burying his face in his mother's shoulder if the stranger comes too near. It is easy to win over a baby at this age if you keep your distance and let him approach you—good babysitters and some psychologists know that fear often is replaced by curiosity if the baby is allowed to pace the experience himself (Rheingold & Eckerman, 1970). The baby's fear of strangers is part of his attachment to his parents and other familiar adults. When they leave him alone or with unfamiliar people, he protests loudly. He wants to be with them and only them.

Until an infant is 6 or 7 months old, he "coos" but does not make many of the consonant sounds used in adult speech. In the second half of the first year, the infant begins to babble, emitting sounds that occur in all languages. "Ga, ca, ba, ma, pa, da" are the first consonant sounds spoken by babies. Babies of English-speaking parents make perfectly good French u's and German r's. Babbling seems to be a product of maturation at first. Even deaf babies babble. By the end of the first year, however, deaf babies almost stop babbling, while normal babies are using the sounds they hear about them more frequently than sounds that are rare or completely absent from their environments. Clearly, feedback and reinforcement play an important role in maintaining the infant's flow of sounds.

At the beginning of the second year the baby starts to understand simple commands ("No, No!" and "Come!") and to use a few object names ("Mama," "baba" (bottle?), "cookie") that stand for ill-defined action concepts and expressions of his feelings about objects and situations ("Mmm," "Dididi"). He can walk alone and is generally considered to be "into everything." Between 12 and 15 months the toddler explores but doesn't talk much. Around 15 to 18 months his language skills increase sharply. He begins to name everything and to use single words to stand for action sequences, or to make requests. "Bye-bye?"

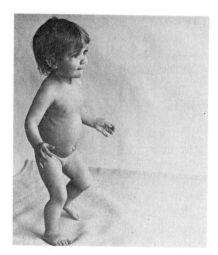

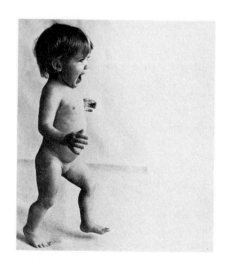

14-5

By 7 or 8 months of age the infant has learned by trial and error how to manipulate objects in his environment. (George Zimbel, Monkmeyer)

said with rising intonation at the end is a request for information about whether the parents are going out and whether the baby is going to go with them. "Car! Car!" said while the baby points out the window at a shiny red automobile means "Look at the car, Mommy." Underlying this sharp transition in the use of language is a still more stunning change in the infant's intelligence. He has become a symbol-user. Words and images stand for events remembered. He can code memories and recall them at a later time. This transition from a mind bound to immediate experience to a symbolic thinker usually marks the end of infancy and the beginning of childhood.

This brief discussion of infant development has set the stage for two topics: infant intelligence and infant social attachments.

Infant Intelligence

The foremost spokesman for the infant as a competent learner is Jean Piaget, the eminent Swiss psychologist. Piaget refers to infant intelligence as the _sensorimotor_ stage, which is characterized by a practical "let's-try-it-out-and-see-what-happens" kind of intelligence. This is the first of Piaget's three stages of intellectual development. The sensorimotor stage itself is divided into six substages. The first of these substages is dominated by the newborn's reflexes: during the first month of life he becomes particularly efficient in using such reflexes as sucking. In the second substage, the baby repeatedly practices such motor actions as moving his legs and waving his arms, but he does not seem to see any connections between his actions and what happens in the environment. Not until the third substage, called _secondary circular reactions_, does the baby show that he recognizes the effects of his actions. At 3 or 4 months, many infants learn that if they kick their legs they can shake their cribs enough to make their mobiles move above them. They will repeat this action sequence over and over while watching the mobile. The baby seems to _want_ to make interesting things happen. The baby also may learn at this stage that if he cries briefly to signal his mother, she will come. Thus, he no longer cries the whole time she is preparing his food.

By 7 or 8 months, the baby begins to use more specific goal-oriented strategies. In the fourth substage he coordinates the secondary reactions of the third stage to find hidden objects that he wants and to overcome simple obstacles in his path toward a goal. By 10 months a baby is able to keep a goal "in mind" and to pursue it with a persistence that can drive his parents to distraction. Around the end of the first year, in the fifth sensorimotor stage, the infant becomes a more innovative experimenter. Once he discovers that he can make an interesting event happen in one way, he tries many other ways to repeat that event and others like it. Give him a long bead necklace and a cup. He picks up one end of the necklace and pushes it segment by segment into the cup. He pours it out and starts again. At times his fingers fail to disengage the beads and he pulls a part of the necklace out again. He tries to push the middle in first, then the other end. He inverts the cup over the necklace and picks up the (empty) cup to see if the necklace crawled inside. He puts the necklace around his head and tries to fit the cup over

14-6
Between 6 months and 2 years, the child begins to make playful responses to a mirror. (Anna Kaufman Moon)

1.5 months. Social smile; talks and smiles.

5.7 months. Picks up cube deftly and directly.

6.2 months. Playful response to mirror. Credit if child plays with mirror image, with such responses as laughing, patting, banging, playful reaching, leaning toward the image, "mouthing" the mirror, etc.

7.9 months. Listens selectively to familiar words. Says, "da-da" or equivalent.

11.8 months. Puts 3 or more cubes in cup.

14-7
Sample test items from the Bayley Scale (Bayley, 1969, The Psychological Corporation).

his head. A baby may practice variations on the same theme for 20 or 30 minutes at a time. What most adults fail to see in a baby's play is the vast amount of trial-and-error learning that he achieves from these simple experiments. He coordinates his existing action patterns; discovers a variety of ways to reach his goal; discovers the nature of objects (cups do not fit in necklaces but necklaces fit in cups); and invents new action sequences to use in his explorations.

In the last half of the second year the infant's explorations become even more inventive, but he no longer has to try out every new action before using it to solve a problem. He can symbolize or imagine action sequences *before* trying them out. His behavior at this sixth stage looks like insight learning. He can observe a problem situation, pause, and then apply an appropriate solution that he has never practiced before. The baby also can imitate actions that he has seen earlier but are not now present in his immediate environment. This new ability means that he has mental representations of events. Piaget gives a charming example of his daughter, Jacqueline, at 16 months, imitating a temper tantrum.

Jacqueline had a visit from a little boy of (18 months) whom she used to see from time to time, and who, in the course of the afternoon got into a terrible temper. He screamed as he tried to get out of a playpen and pushed it backward, stamping his feet. Jacqueline stood watching him in amazement, never having witnessed such a scene before. The next day, she herself screamed in her playpen and tried to move it, stamping her foot lightly several times in succession. (From Ginsburg & Opper, 1969)

Infant Intelligence Tests. Tests, as well as observation, are used to assess an infant's intelligence or developmental level. One test, developed by Uzgiris and Hunt (1974), is based on Piaget's ideas about infant intelligence. The test's six scales measure the baby's progress in understanding object concepts, means-ends relations, imitation, causality, action sequences (schemes), and objects in space. Some babies develop more rapidly than others, but all pass through the invariant sequence of six sensorimotor stages.

Bayley (1968) developed another widely used test to measure an infant's mental level compared with that of other babies of his chronological age. *The Bayley Scale of Mental Development* is based on *norms* or average behavioral achievements at each month level from 1 to 30 months. Although no developmental theory explicitly underlies the Bayley scales, many of the items measure the same behaviors tested by the Uzgiris-Hunt Scales. The overlap in the two tests is due, in part, to the common definition of intelligent behavior in infancy. Everyone would agree that such behaviors as a baby's understanding of cause-effect relations and of the continued existence of absent objects is part of intelligence in the first two years of life.

Although infant intelligence can be assessed reliably (the same baby achieves approximately the same score on two successive days), the baby's score on the infant test does not predict his later IQ very well. Babies who are advanced in sensorimotor development are not necessar-

14-8

Graphs showing the correlation between (A) 21-month, (B) 3-year, and (C) 6-year-old children's IQ scores and their scores at later ages. In each instance the correlation decreases substantially as the child grows older. This is due in part to the fact that tests of infants and young children are more visual than verbal, while verbal items (the prime measure of intelligence) are emphasized in later years. Thus, early IQ scores are not good indicators of later intellectual ability. (Honzik, MacFarlane, & Allen, 1948)

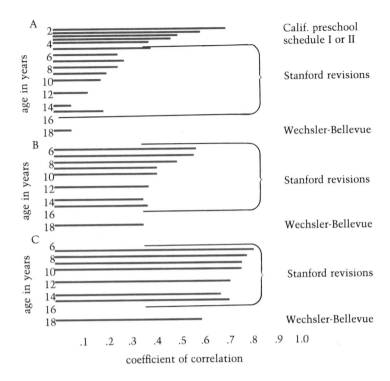

ily precocious in the school years. Babies who are seriously retarded in infancy do tend to be retarded in later years, and more often if they are reared in poor homes (Willerman, Broman, & Fiedler, 1970). Not until children are at least 4 years old do their scores on intelligence tests become even moderately good predictors of their later IQs.

Why isn't precocity in infancy related to higher IQ scores in later life? One reason is that tests of babies under 2 years of age have very few items that call for symbolic skills, the very skills that later tests weigh most heavily. Virtually no vocabulary or reasoning items are on the infant tests, because, as we have seen, infants do not use symbols. Another reason may be that while nearly all homes are adequate to develop sensorimotor skills, many do not sufficiently encourage verbal and conceptual skills in older children. Thus, the basis for individual differences in infancy would be different from the basis for differences in childhood. A third reason could be that genes responsible for some developmental differences among infants are not the same genes that affect later intellectual growth. If the gene locations are uncorrelated, then the behavioral differences may be unrelated. But, whatever the reasons, infant intelligence does not correlate highly with later IQ (McCall, Applebaum, & Hogarty, 1973).

Basic Trust and Social Attachments

A newborn baby depends totally on his parents for his survival. He can cry to signal his needs, but he cannot independently feed, change, or warm himself. He must trust his parents or others to care for him. Erik Erikson (1963) describes the crisis of infancy as basic *trust versus mistrust*. Babies whose parents respond quickly and reliably to their needs

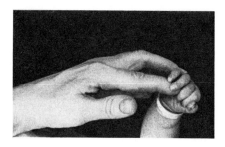

14-9
The infant is totally dependent upon his mother for everything he needs and wants. (Eve Arnold, Magnum)

14-10
The attachments between mother and child are mutually reinforcing. (V. Bystricky, Rapho Guillumette)

develop a sense of basic trust in people, a feeling that people will not fail them. As they grow older they can tolerate delays and frustrations because they are optimistic about people and events. Babies whose caretakers are neglectful or indifferent to their signals are said to develop a sense of mistrust and suspicion toward people. They find it hard to tolerate everyday frustrations without feeling an overwhelming helplessness and rage toward those who have left them to suffer.

All normal babies become attached to their principal caretakers, but some babies develop a kind of hostile dependence on their parents. Ainsworth and her colleagues (Ainsworth, 1973; Ainsworth & Bell, 1970) have studied the relationships that babies form with their mothers. Most 1-year-old babies are securely attached, happy to be with their mothers, and distressed when their mothers go away. The babies with insecure relationships become distressed when their mothers leave, but do not show delight and relief when they return.

Harlow and his colleagues (Harlow & Harlow, 1966) studied the attachments of baby monkeys to their neglectful and abusive mothers, who themselves had been reared in isolation. The mothers had not been properly mothered, and they were unable to mother their babies. The mothers sometimes held their newborn babies upside down, pushed them away, and slapped them—all very unusual behavior for mother monkeys, who normally protect and nurture their babies. Despite this abuse the babies clung to their mothers; when thrown to the ground they returned over and over again only to receive more abuse. The babies seemed to be attached to their mothers, despite their neglectful and hostile caretaking. Since the babies had to be rescued soon after birth to prevent serious injury, we do not know what kinds of relationships they would have developed with their mothers. Would they have been like the insecurely attached babies that Ainsworth described? Children who have been abused by their parents often are very attached to them, although they surely mistrust them to some degree (Sameroff & Chandler, 1974).

Why do infants and their mothers form strong bonds or attachments? Bowlby (1969, 1973) points out that the mother-infant twosome has a long evolutionary history in which the behaviors of both members have evolved toward mutual regulation. Both mother and infant behaviors maintain proximity. The infant's behaviors elicit caretaking responses in the mother, and the mother's caretaking elicits further attachment behaviors in the offspring. Without attachments, mothers would not care for their infants, and infants would wander away from the protection of their mothers.

Bowlby's theory would predict that Harlow's abused baby monkeys would return again and again to their abusive mothers because, ironically, the mother's behavior itself constitutes a *threat* to the infant's proximity to her. Her abuse evokes proximity-seeking in the baby; the baby clings furiously to her; she throws him down again, which evokes more clinging by the baby. The mother is at once the origin of the threat and the only possible relief for the infant's anxiety.

In the early months, the baby cries to signal his needs; his cries make the mother anxious and she responds to reduce his distress and her own. She picks him up, cuddles and feeds him. The baby stops crying, relaxes, and goes back to sleep. Later when he can creep, the baby not only signals for proximity, he maintains proximity by creeping after his mother from room to room, babbling, and smiling at her.

Attachment and proximity-seeking behaviors result from substantial physical distances between mother and infant and from threats. The baby uses the mother as a safe base from which to explore, returning to her whenever he is alarmed by too great a separation or by too novel an event. The mother quickly brings him to her when she perceives a threat or a potential threat from too much distance between them. The close physical proximity that represents attachment in infancy wanes as infants feel secure enough to explore at greater distances and as mothers treat them as children rather than as infants.

Childhood — From Toddler to Teenager

For many people, infants are a bit mysterious. After all, one cannot *talk* with them to find out how they feel or what they think. However, children do talk and think—although in some rather odd ways by adult standards. The 2-year-old has his own rules of grammar, logic, and social relations; they are idiosyncratic and egocentric. As children develop, they become able to learn the ways adults use language, think, and form relationships. The rate of development is slower than it was in infancy, but dramatic shifts in behavior occur during childhood.

The 2-year-old is a headlong, willful explorer. He asks endless questions (although his speech often is difficult to comprehend); defies his parents ("No" is a frequent response); and makes unreasonable demands. You may have heard of the "Terrible Twos." However, unless adults are expecting him to behave like an older child, he actually is a charming baby-child whose new language and intellectual skills open up to him a universe of possibilities. He is learning to regulate his own behavior, and he demands the right to do so. Parents often have difficulty blending permission for the decisions that the child can manage with prohibition of actions that he cannot yet regulate. He can be permitted to decide which shirt to wear that day and whether he wants a peanut-butter-and-jelly sandwich or a hot dog, but he cannot be permitted to cross the street alone or to play with matches. The 2-year-old

14-11
The toddler needs to try everything, to find out for him or herself what the world is all about. (Inge Morath, Magnum; Alice S. Kendall, Rapho Guillumette; Richard Swanson, Time-Life Picture Agency)

typically does not distinguish among the decisions he wants to make. Erikson calls this stage a struggle for _autonomy_. Parents demand more mature social behavior; the child resists and asserts his right to control himself.

The child from 2 to 3 years old is an imaginative person. He can play at adult roles, imagine fearsome ghosts and monsters, and pretend to be almost anything. However, he can easily frighten himself with his thoughts. He often mistakes dreams for real experiences because the 2-year-old does not distinguish between the dream and reality. In short, while his mental life is full of images and symbols, he actually is not able to deal with them very effectively.

By age 3, most children are well on the way to being socialized. They can obey without losing their sense of autonomy. They can begin to play _with_ other children, not merely beside them. Their curiosity about the world is less egocentric; now they can observe events and understand them apart from their own roles in them.

Children 4 and 5 years old are increasingly independent of direct parental control. They usually spend part of each day in school where they can observe the behaviors of their peers, as well as those of adults other than their parents. Conceptual learning, classification skills, and operational logic change rapidly from age 3 to age 5. Sex-typed behaviors and culturally sanctioned sex-roles are learned during this period.

School-age children often are concerned with achievements; they want to learn new skills and to demonstrate their competencies on school tasks and in other ways. Their greatly improved understanding of the physical world is based on new logical principles. They play elaborate games with rules and roles for the participants. Six- and seven-year-olds form friendships with particular children, and older school-age children often have enduring relationships. Peer groups formed during childhood exert their own socializing force on children's behaviors, sometimes supporting parental influences and sometimes not. Predelinquent and even delinquent behaviors can be a serious problem in the school-age group. Children in the later elementary grades develop moral reasoning that reflects their new capacity for logical thinking, but neither is yet mature by adult standards.

In the following sections, we shall review the development of language and intelligence in more detail.

14-12
Children learn a great deal from imitating those around them. While they have great fun following the baton twirler, they also may learn something about social roles from him. (Alfred Eisenstadt, Time-Life Picture Agency)

Language Development

Between the second and fifth years of life, children's speech develops from one-word utterances to a nearly adult command of the rules of their native language. Since rule systems in all natural languages are so complicated that no linguist can specify them adequately, and since young children are not great logicians, it is astounding that they learn to speak at all. How do they do it?

Children hear sentences spoken by adults and older children around them. Adults often simplify and shorten their speech for young children, but the young child still hears thousands of different utterances. However, he does not learn thousands of sentences. He learns the rules of his language for producing correct sentences.

Nearly every sentence an adult constructs is unique. This also is true of a child's speech. A 2- or 3-year-old constructs sentences that not only are unique in the words they put together, but are based on rules that differ from the rules of adult speech. A typical toddler will say "All gone cookie" or "Cookie all gone." No adult uses the first sentence because it is an inversion of English word order ("The cookie is all gone"); similarly, the latter sentence omits those important "little words." Children's use of rules is demonstrated by the extensive recordings of children's speech made by Brown (1973). These records reveal important developments in speech regularities. Only certain word combinations appear, such as "All gone shoe" and "Pretty shoe" but never "All gone pretty." Even at the beginning of speech, children use rules to assemble classes of words. While the rules are idiosyncratic to each child at the start, at 3 to 4 years of age they become more and more like those of adult speakers.

Children of ages 2 to 4 often make errors that signal their acquisition of a grammatical rule. In English, past tense verbs are usually made by adding "ed" (kick, kicked), plural nouns by adding "s" or "es" (dog, dogs; dish, dishes). Toddlers often use irregular, past tense verbs correctly because they learn them as vocabulary items, not as exceptions to a rule. When rules are learned, the child begins to make errors on irregular forms. For example, a 2-year-old may say "*Went* home." When he has learned to make regular past tense verbs, he may say "We *goed* home." "He *brought*" becomes "He *bringed*." "*Mice*" becomes "*mouses*;" "feet" becomes "foots." At this stage children are relatively impervious to correction; they do not give up newly won regularities easily. Only later, when the proper rules of the language are well established, can they incorporate exceptions into their speech.

The learning of grammatical rules is so rapid that, as we discussed in Chapter 7, Chomsky (1972) and other psycholinguists have proposed an innate language ability to account for it. The exact nature of the evolved language capacity is unknown, but it must include an ability to analyze speech into categories and an ability to develop rules of combination. The child's task is to *understand* adult speech and to *produce* his own utterances.

To understand another's speech, the child must decode the meaning of the sentences he hears. The situations in which particular sentences are spoken often help the child grasp the meaning of the words. Children also learn meanings by attaching words to external referents like actors, actions, and objects. Contexts within sentences can give the child clues to meanings, too. If one speaks of *a* boy and *some* water, they are both subjects or objects but not verbs. The first is a "count" noun, the second a "mass" noun. In addition, English has constructions and inflections that help to signal meaning.

The word order of many simple declarative sentences ("Mary broke the dish") gives children an easily identifiable actor—action—object sequence that they can decode and code earlier than any other kind of utterance. Many children 3 to 4 years old cannot understand passive sentences. ("The dish was broken by Mary") because they violate the actor—action—object word order. To ask "Wh–" (for example, why or what) questions, young children simply put the wh– word at the front and keep the rest of the sentence in the declarative order: "Where we should put it?" or "Why he goed home?" Early negative sentences also retain the simple, declarative form with the addition of "no" or "not" ("He not like me" or "No play that").

Child language has its own rules, which the child presumably extracts from the speech he hears. At first his rules are simpler versions of adult rules, without the subtleties of any natural language. As he gets older his rules approximate more closely the enormously complex set of rules that speakers use (without knowing it) to generate speech. How the child acquires such proficiency in two or three years remains a mystery.

Intellectual Development

The young child's thought is *egocentric* and focused on a *limited* aspect of any problem. As he grows older he becomes able to take more aspects of the problem into account and to consider others' needs and points of view. A major developmental trend in children's thinking is what Piaget calls _decentration_, a focus that turns more and more away from oneself and toward a broader perspective. Piaget divides the second, or _operational_, period of children's intellectual development into two sub-periods, called _preoperational_ and _concrete operational_.

From the end of infancy until the first or second grade, the child's thought is said to be preoperational. He focuses on a limited amount of information in seeking a solution to any problem. Asked to judge the equivalence of two rows of ten poker chips, both of which are arranged in lines 12 inches long, he can say that they are the same. If one line is spread out to 20 inches, the 4-year-old is likely to say that the longer line has more chips. He attends to length but ignores density. Asked to judge the equivalence of two identical beakers of water, he can say that they are the same. But if one beaker's contents are poured (in his view) into a tall, thin container, the 4-year-old probably will say that the new one has more liquid because it is taller (or higher or bigger). His thought centers on only one essential part of the problem; he cannot coordinate two dimensions at once.

Since the child cannot simultaneously consider two points of view, he uses his own perspective solely. Thus, his communications to others often center on himself (egocentric). The 3- or 4-year-old uses many indefinite referents ("*He* hit me." "Give *it* to me.") even though the person to whom he is speaking has not observed the hit or does not know what "it" is.

Conservation. The school-age child develops an appreciation for transformations. He can discriminate unimportant from important changes, changes in appearance from changes in quantity. He has developed a mental operation, _reversibility_, to solve problems like those involving the poker chips and the beakers. A 6- or 7-year-old can negate or reverse the operation of spreading the poker chips out by mentally compressing the line. Realizing that the two lines were equivalent before, he imagines that the chips in the 20-inch line are bunched back in a 12-inch line and sees that they must still be equivalent. The logical imperative—*must* be equivalent—is a hallmark of the concrete operational child. He has achieved _conservation,_ the understanding that numbers of

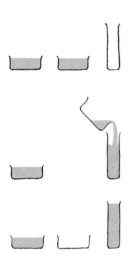

14-13

Piaget's concept of conservation. The child has achieved conservation when he realizes, for example, that if water is poured from a short, wide jar into a tall, narrow jar, the amount of water does not change. The child also can imagine the process being reversed.

items and total quantities remain the same though they may appear to increase or decrease. During the years from 6 to 12, children apply their logical operations to more and more conservation problems. Number usually is achieved earlier than liquid measurement, which is earlier than weight and volume. Although the logical operations involved in conservation problems are the same, a developmental sequence marks their achievement because some of the problems are inherently more difficult than others.

Another aspect of concrete operational thought is the ability to coordinate more than one dimension. With the liquid in beakers, the older child realizes that the second container is both taller *and* narrower than the first container. The two properties of the new container are reciprocal; their effects cancel each other out. The school-age child also develops hierarchical classifications. Given a pile of animal figures he can sort them. He can form a class, "animals," that includes "dogs" and "cats"; a subclass, "dogs," that includes "Great Danes" and "collies," and so on. Children in the early elementary grades become very adept at forming classes, knowing their defining properties, deciding which objects to include and exclude, and making sure that they classify all of the objects presented. They do not yet fully understand the relations among levels of the hierarchy. Asked whether there are more "Great Danes" or "dogs," a child of 7 is likely to answer "Great Danes" if there are more "Great Danes" than "collies." He cannot think simultaneously of the several levels and subclasses of his hierarchy. Part-whole relations still escape him. An older child typically knows that there *must* be more "dogs" than "Great Danes" because "Great Danes" are a subclass of "dogs."

Other examples of concrete logical operations include *transitivity* and *symmetrical relations*. Transitive reasoning takes this form: If A is greater than B and B is greater than C, then A ? C. If Mary is taller than Jane, and Jane is taller than Sue, who is taller, Mary or Sue? School-age children usually can reason transitively. Reciprocal or symmetrical relations are exemplified by kinship: If John is Mike's brother, then Mike must be John's brother. If Jean is Joe's daughter and Sue is Joe's daughter, then Jean and Sue must be sisters.

The ages at which children go through Piaget's operational stages vary widely. Some individuals are 3 or 4 years ahead of others in achieving concrete operations. Cultural differences also can significantly affect the ages at which children solve problems. Compared with children in Geneva, children in Martinique lagged 4 years behind in achieving conservation (Piaget, 1970). Outside of mentally defective people, virtually everyone achieves concrete operational thought. However, *teaching* concrete operations to children who are not yet ready to acquire them has proved difficult. Numerous experiments have failed to teach preschool children what 8-year-olds understand about the laws of the physical world. We do not yet know the factors that determine the rate at which a child acquires concrete operations.

The concrete operational child is quite logical by adult standards, but he still is tied to the manipulation of concrete materials to solve problems. He has not yet developed the ability to deal logically on an imaginary or hypothetical level. That skill usually emerges at adolescence.

PSYCHOLOGICAL DIFFERENCES BETWEEN THE SEXES—AND THEIR IMPLICATIONS

Eleanor Emmons Maccoby and Carol Nagy Jacklin *Stanford University*

Are boys more analytical than girls? Are girls more verbal and less adept at spatially-oriented tasks than boys? Are girls more eager than boys to have the approval of others? These are a few of the questions to which we have sought fuller answers. For those answers we reviewed a very large body of evidence on the subject of the differences between males and females (Maccoby & Jacklin, 1974).

Most reports on the psychology of men and women emphasize studies that have found *differences* between the sexes. Besides these studies, we were interested in those that *might* have found differences but did not. Such results are harder to find, as they tend to be hidden in footnotes or buried in tables. Since a review that included primarily the positive findings would present a partial—and biased—picture, we systematically looked through research that used subjects of both sexes, and included in our review the studies that found *no* differences.

Did consistent sex differences in psychological functioning emerge when we tabulated both positive and negative findings? Some, but far fewer than many people believe. Certain allegations about the psychology of the sexes may safely be labeled myths, since clear evidence was discovered against them. Other claims are solidly based in fact. And still others remain in doubt, requiring more conclusive evidence.

Perception

While infant boys are thought by some psychologists to be especially interested in visual stimulation and girls in sounds, we found in our survey that male and female responses to visual and auditory stimuli are similar. Male and female infants quickly develop a more sustained interest in social than in nonsocial events. For example, both sexes will look longer at faces (real or pictured) than at nonhuman objects (see page 465).

Relatively little work has been done on the senses of touch and smell. While some early studies indicate that newborn girls are more sensitive to touch than boys, subsequent studies have not yielded consistent findings. Girls and women seem to be more sensitive to certain odors and tastes (specifically bitter tastes), but more research is needed.

Learning

Broverman and his colleagues (1968) have argued that females are superior to males in "simple, overlearned, repetitive behavior," while males excel in "complex behaviors requiring problem-solving, delay, or reversal of usual habits." Accordingly, they list conditioning as a learning process at which females should excel. Our overall survey findings disagree. After examining studies on conditioning in infants and preschoolers, as well as the conditioning of verbal responses in children and adults, we conclude that the two sexes respond to conditioning in a remarkably similar way. Very few differences can be found in the speed with which males and females acquire a conditioned response, or in the rate at which their responses extinguish. Eyelid conditioning (blinking to a stimulus) among adults is the single exception: women condition more readily. As Spence and Spence (1966) have shown, however, subjects who score high on the Manifest Anxiety Scale condition faster to the eyelid responses. Women on the average score higher than men on this scale. When eyelid conditioning is "masked"— that is, when it is incidental to procedures that seem to be measuring something else—the sex differences disappear, as do the correlations with manifest anxiety. Thus we appear to be dealing with a sex difference in manifest anxiety, not with a difference in ease of conditioning.

Paired-comparison learning might be another candidate for the Broverman category of simple rote learning, although we know that subjects frequently complicate this process by imposing on it their own elaborate hypotheses. In any case, we found no consistent difference between the sexes in the speed or accuracy with which they learned paired associates.

What about learning tasks involving problem-solving, delay, or the reversal of habits? Such tasks should give an advantage to males, according to Broverman's hypothesis. Finding agreement on which tasks call for the inhibition of acquired response tendencies is not easy. To our minds, even such a simple process as discrimination learning requires inhibition; sex differences seldom are found in this task. The reversal shift, in which a choice previously labeled correct is made systematically incorrect, would be a clearer case. No sex differences have been found in studies of reversal shifts. Delay-of-reinforcement studies also call for response inhibition. Only four of the delay-of-reinforcement studies we located analyzed results for the subject's sex. None found a difference between the sexes. Since it also involves inhibition, the Stroop Color-Word test (1935) might be considered an excellent instrument for testing the Broverman hypothesis. When a subject looks at the test word "green" printed in red ink, for example, and is asked to "read" the color of the ink, he must inhibit his strong, learned tendency to read the printed word. While few recent studies seem to have used this test, the initial reports from investigators using it state that male and female subjects did not differ in their skill on the task.

In sum, we found no evidence to support the theory that girls perform on intellectual tasks in a rote repetitive way while boys use more complex problem-solving strategies which involve the inhibition of old responses to acquire new ones. As they grow older, of course, both sexes do shift toward higher level problem-solving strategies. But they shift at the same rate and with the same success.

Intelligence

Tests of general intelligence do not show sex differences—because they were designed not to. Several such tests minimize sex differences by choosing mostly items on which the sexes are known to perform similarly, or by balancing the test items, choosing some that give males an advantage, some that aid females. However, in subtests of special abilities, sex differences do emerge. On the average, girls excel at verbal tasks and boys at mathematical and visual-spatial ones. Work done on verbal abilities in the 1930s and 1940s indicated that the girls' verbal advantage begins very early. More recent work casts doubt upon this conclu-

sion. Not many new large-sample studies have been done with children under 2½ years of age. Consequently, we do not know conclusively whether today's boys and girls say their first words or their first short sentences at different ages. But the recent studies that are available for children under 3 do not report a sex difference. Similarly, among preschool children, girls are not more verbal, except perhaps among disadvantaged children. Among children of middle- and upper-income families, consistent sex differences in verbal ability begin to emerge only at about age 10. At this age, girls forge ahead not only in verbal fluency but also in complex, high-level verbal skills. Studies vary greatly in how large a sex difference is found during the teen years, but a reasonable estimate on most measures would place the girls' score about one-fourth of a standard deviation higher than the boys' (see the Statistics Appendix for an explanation of standard deviation).

On measures of mathematical ability, no differences between the sexes appear before early adolescence—except, again, among disadvantaged children. In this group, girls perform better on number concepts and arithmetic skills. Among unselected populations of adolescents, boys generally score higher than girls. How much higher is very difficult to say from present evidence. Thus, our survey agrees with the solidly established conclusion that boys do excel in math. However, the

research shows that the differences between boys and girls do not emerge until relatively late in development, and the size of these differences has not been established.

In a similar vein, the sex difference in visual-spatial ability can be easily demonstrated. These skills are involved, for example, in tasks that ask the subject to rotate a figure mentally to see if it fits into another figure. Figure A shows an item from the Primary Mental Abilities subtest on spatial ability. The subject's task is to identify which of the four figures on the right would make a complete square if fitted with the figure on the left. "Embedded Figures" tests also require spatial ability. In these tests, the subject is shown a simple figure, whose outline he must find when the figure is embedded in a larger, more complex figure (See Figure B).

After age 10 or 12, boys perform better on the average than girls on such tests, although, of course, some girls obtain very high scores and some boys do poorly. "Embedded Figures" tests also have been developed for younger children. While some children solve them much more easily than others, such variations in ability usually are not related to sex.

An adolescent boy's greater skill on the visual-spatial "Embedded Figures" test should not be read as a general male superiority in analytic thought. In other forms of disembedding or "decontextualization," girls do as well—or better; their difficulty seems to be confined to the visual-spatial sphere.

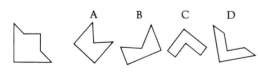

A

Sample item from the Primary Mental Abilities subtest on spatial ability. The subject must determine which figure on the right, when fitted onto the figure on the left, would make a complete square.

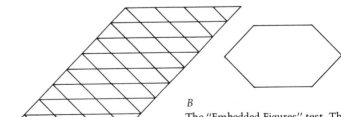

B

The "Embedded Figures" test. The subject must locate the figure on the right in the more complex figure on the left.

Achievement Motivation

Performance in the intellectual sphere is directly related to achievement motivation. Many people believe that the relatively small number of women among the very high achievers in intellectual pursuits reflects a lower level of achievement motivation among women—perhaps a disinterest in achievement that begins during childhood. Yet we have found no evidence in the research that girls lack achievement motivation. Indeed, during the school years, girls on the average maintain a fairly high level of academic motivation, while boys are less school-oriented. While a boy's achievement motivation does respond more than a girl's to competitive challenge, we have every reason to believe that girls care as much as boys about mastering the intellectual content of their school work. For example, the sexes score similarly in task persistence. Occasionally, a theorist will contend that girls achieve for the praise and approval of others, while boys achieve solely because of the task's intrinsic interest. Evidence to date, however, lends no support to that theory. Both sexes are influenced about equally by the reactions of parents, teachers, and others to their performance.

Can we trace the different levels of the sexes' adult achievement levels to other aspects of their motivation—to self-confidence or self-esteem, for example? Our review indicates that on a variety of measures of self-esteem, boys and girls are essentially equal through childhood and adolescence. During the college years, the situation changes somewhat. When college women are asked how well they think they will do on a new task or how good their grades will be at the next grading period, they are less optimistic than college men, even on tasks that they perform as well as men. In contrast to males, they have a dimin-

ished sense of control of their own destinies. The so-called "locus-of-control" measures reveal higher internal control scores for men than women of college age. The male college student's self-concept contains a sense of personal potency and optimism about his ability to perform tasks. Obviously, this self-concept may relate to his subsequent achievement.

Sociability and Affiliation

Many people believe that girls and women are especially concerned that others like or love them. Supposedly, this concern appears early in life as a greater tendency among little girls to cling to others and to remain close to their attachment figures. At later ages, girls are thought to be more sensitive to the opinions of others, and more sociable; more likely to seek the company of others, less comfortable alone.

We were surprised at how little factual support we could find for these beliefs. No studies have shown that infants of either sex have more interest than the other in social stimuli. Nor, as we have already noted, are members of one sex more susceptible to praise or criticism for their performance on intellectual tasks. Beyond this, our review has uncovered no consistent tendency of little girls to be more attached to their parents or dependent upon them. Children of both sexes seek to be close to their parents, particularly when they are under stress. However, males and females are equally ready to leave their parents to explore a new environment. Some evidence indicates that young boys are more likely to cry when a parent leaves them alone; but even this sex difference, if it is confirmed in further studies, is a transitory tendency of early childhood.

In play with age mates, girls are *not* more social than boys in terms of the amount of time they spend playing

with other children as contrasted with solitary play. Indeed, boys interact more with their playmates than girls do, at least during the preschool years. Boys and girls do have different social interests during childhood, but the differences seem to be qualitative rather than quantitative. Boys congregate in larger groups, while girls tend to prefer pairs and trios, especially after they enter school.

Girls are widely believed to be more empathic—that is, more attuned to the emotional states of others—and more likely to help others. But the evidence does not support this belief. In the little research done so far, the two sexes have proved equally adept at identifying the emotional states of others. Furthermore, neither sex shows a greater overall tendency to alleviate another's distress or to gratify others.

An exceedingly important, unanswered question is whether the care of young children is more "natural" for women because of an inborn disposition that makes competent child care easier for them. Among lower animals, the hormones associated with pregnancy and childbirth do "prime" the mother to feed, retrieve, and nurture her young. We do not know if hormones play such a role in human child care. But we do know that among humans and other animals, contact with the young and responsibility for their care powerfully influence the production and maintenance of nurturing behavior. Both males and females can be influenced in this way, and some research indicates that boys with baby-sitting experience are less aggressive with their own playmates.

Aggression and Dominance

So far, our review has discovered more myths than realities. We turn now to an area in which sex differences are clear and quite consistent with popular beliefs: namely, aggression. Boys *are* more aggressive than girls, starting at about 2 years of age. The finding is the same in a wide range of situations—from free play in naturalistic settings to laboratory conditions. Furthermore, the results do not seem to depend on how the aggression is measured. Boys are thought to show more physical aggression and girls more verbal aggression, but this is not the case. Boys display a higher level of verbal as well as physical aggression. An exchange of verbal insults frequently precedes an exchange of blows, and boys often use verbal taunts or threats as they work out dominance relations in their play groups.

Another popular belief holds that the two sexes may be equal in their potential for aggressive behavior, but that fear inhibits girls' displays of aggression because they are more likely than boys to be punished for aggression. Bandura and his colleagues (1965) have provided evidence for this point of view. They have shown that girls are less likely to imitate an aggressive model spontaneously; however, if offered a reward for imitating as many of the model's responses as they could remember, the girls proved they had learned the model's aggressive behavior. This finding is supposed to imply that without the restrictions on their aggression, girls would be as aggressive as boys. We have several objections to this view. First, no evidence exists to show that girls are punished more often for aggression. Indeed, boys may well be punished more. Nursery school observation indicates that boys draw more negative reactions to their aggression, both in absolute numbers of reprimands and punishments, and in proportion to the number of aggressive acts they commit. Furthermore, if it were true that the female's normally low level of aggression did result from inhibitions imposed upon a fairly high aggressive potential, we would expect to find displacement. That is, we

would expect girls to be aggressive in ways and situations that would not entail punishments. But we find that boys practice more attenuated and displaced aggression—in fantasy aggression, playful aggression (a punch on the shoulder accompanied by a grin), and probably in bullying younger children and animals. A finding by Titley and Viney (1969) is relevant. They used the Buss shock technique, in which the subject administers shocks to a learner when the learner makes a mistake. The shocks' duration and intensity are the subject's aggression score. Male subjects characteristically administer longer and stronger shocks to their victims than female subjects. In one experimental trial, Titley and Viney used a physically handicapped learner. They found that the victim's obvious helplessness increased the intensity of shocks delivered by males and decreased the shocks given by females. These findings simply do not fit the picture of a female with a high level of bottled-up aggression, who is waiting only for a safe outlet. We believe that the female's readiness to aggress, either overtly or covertly, is simply not as great as the male's.

Biology may explain the sex difference in aggression. Several kinds of evidence support our belief. First, the sex difference has been found in all human societies in which aggression has been studied. Second, greater male aggression is found consistently among the animals closest to man in the phylogenetic series. Third, levels of aggression are linked to the amount of male hormone in the subject. In this connection one must be wary of using only correlational evidence. For example, one can take blood samples from a group of males and analyze them for current levels of androgens. Rose and his colleagues (1971, 1972) have found that with both monkeys and human beings, such scores correlate positively with some (but not all) behav-

ioral measures of aggression. However, a high androgen level can be both a result and a cause of aggressive behavior. When a normally meek animal is placed with a cagemate that it can dominate in aggressive encounters, its testosterone level goes up and remains up until it is placed with a cage-mate that defeats it. The causal contribution of male hormones to aggression is demonstrated more clearly by studies in which male hormones have been experimentally administered; in such studies, the higher aggression levels of both sexes testify to the male hormones' power to increase aggressive behavior.

The choice of victims provides an interesting sidelight on aggression. Not only do females initiate aggressive encounters less often; females, both animal and human, are chosen less often as victims. Males aim their aggression primarily at other males. Patterson and his colleagues (1967) have analyzed in detail several aggressive sequences between pairs of children in nursery school. They found that, in general, an aggressor will become more aggressive if his victim cries, yields a disputed toy, or otherwise reinforces the attacker's aggressive actions. On the subject of sex differences the data yielded some anomalies. Girls, when aggressed against, did not reinforce the behavior of their aggressors any more or less frequently than boys; nevertheless, aggression toward them usually was not continued or repeated. In other words, they were chosen less often as victims despite the fact that they reinforced aggression as often as boy victims did.

To many people, aggression and dominance (control and leadership) are linked closely. We know that among apes, dominance is achieved and maintained either through aggression or through threats of it. If the human male is the more aggressive sex, must he dominate the female? The answer is complex but

C
Traditionally, boys are taught the more "masculine" games—soldier, cowboys and Indians, and so on. Today they are more often encouraged to try whatever interests them, whether or not it is considered by some to be a feminine task or game. (Left: Frees, Photo Researchers; Right: Erika)

mainly negative. While boys try to dominate others more frequently than girls, most of the boys' dominance attempts are directed toward one another, or (less often) toward adults. They seldom attempt to dominate girls; when they do, the evidence as to their success is contradictory. Most evidence shows that girls do not yield readily to boys' dominance attempts. Among children from age 4 or 5 up to adolescence, play groups tend to be segregated by sex. Dominance issues occur more frequently in boys' play groups; and among young boys at least, dominance appears to depend on "toughness," including fighting ability.

As children grow older, finding a single dominance hierarchy becomes harder and harder. A leader in one activity is not especially likely to be a leader in another. Furthermore, fighting ability declines in importance (in most kinds of groups) as a criterion for a leader. In adulthood, dominance and aggression do not seem to be related. To summarize, little boys appear to achieve dominance, or leadership, primarily by aggressive means. With increasing maturity, the linkage between leadership and aggression weakens.

The little boy's greater aggressiveness appears to be accompanied by other characteristics, including a greater tendency to resist adult demands or intrusions. The few existing studies suggest that when a parent or teacher says, for example, "Stop that" or "Put that down," a girl is more likely to comply immediately, while a boy is likely to continue in his behavior until the adult pressure increases. Does this imply that boys persist more at tasks, or that they tend to try more vigorously to overcome barriers placed in their path? The research on "barrier behavior" is not extensive, but studies to date show no consistent differences between the sexes. On the whole, girls are just as likely as boys to attack a barrier vigorously, at least when adults permit such an attack. In addition, the two sexes are equally persistent at tasks they undertake spontaneously.

Activity Level. How, then, can we explain boys' greater aggressiveness and their stronger tendency to resist adult demands? A popular hypothesis for greater male aggression is that boys are simply more active. In moving more freely through their environment they are more likely to bump into others or invade their play space, prompting more frequent aggressive encounters. We had high hopes for this hypothesis, but the evidence on activity level left us with more questions than answers. No consistent sex difference in activity level is evident during the first year of life. From the second year onward, many studies continue to find no sex difference; those that do almost always find boys more active. We have tried to examine the situations in which the children were observed for specific conditions under which males are more active. A clue can be found in the study being conducted at the National Institute of Mental Health by Halverson and Waldrop (1973). They recorded the activity level of 2½-year-old children in a nursery school setting. They analyzed their results separately by sex of subject, and separated activity scores for group and solitary play. Although the sex of the playmates in social groups was not recorded, a preponderance of play at this age tends to be with partners of the same sex. They found that boys and girls were about equally active when playing alone. At play with other children, however, the boys' activity level increased substantially, while the girls' did not.

This finding is reminiscent of an experiment that found that when infant monkeys are tested alone or caged with their mothers only, male and female infants are equally active. But when two mother-and-infant pairs are placed in cages separated only by a glass panel, the activity level of male infants is higher, and the activity involves a good deal of play-imitating and threats by one infant toward the other. We suggest that while activity level is not a "cause" of male aggression, both increased activity levels and aggression derive from a common factor still to be defined.

Young males are excited by each

other's presence. Their activity level goes up when they encounter each other, play rough-and-tumble, make attempts to dominate each other, or fight. Neither females nor male-female pairs stimulate one another in the same way. Psychologists would be very interested to know the signals boys use to elicit these behaviors from one another and why girls do not use the same signal system. The methods used by ethologists could help answer such questions. We suspect the sexes may differ both as to the signals that arouse them, and in their readiness to be aroused. Frustration is a major source of arousal. Goodenough's classic work in the 1930s shows that subjects of both sexes at 18 months of age and younger made about the same number of emotional outbursts in frustrating situations. After 18 months of age, the frequency of the girls' outbursts declined dramatically but the boys' did not. Recent work in Holland confirms this age trend quite precisely. Van Leishout (1974) observed children at 18 and 24 months of age. During the experimental session, an attractive toy was taken from the child and put into a plastic box whose latch was difficult to open. At 18 months, the sexes were similar in the frequency and intensity of their frustration reactions. By 24 months, the girls were considerably less upset by this frustrating situation than they had been 6 months before. However, the boys' frustration reactions remained at a high level. Does the boy's greater readiness to be emotionally aroused lead to his increased activity and rough-and-tumble play? At this point we do not know. But we believe some underlying temperamental qualities differentiate the sexes and help to determine their reactions to their life experiences. Some recent work at Stanford with pairs of 18-month-old children (who are too young to be clearly aware of one another's sex) has indicated that even at this early age, certain behaviors occur primarily in male pairs. Thus, we are inclined to believe that the temperamental differences and sex-specific social interactions are not solely a product of social shaping.

Nature and Culture

As we have seen, in many respects the male and female are much alike. Among the differences there appear to be some that are not due to social shaping, as well as some that are. Even for those differences that imply biological predispositions, the variation within the sex is extremely large, so that many individuals share characteristics more commonly associated with the opposite sex; and the individual must learn even those behaviors that he is biologically "primed" to acquire. Because he must learn those behaviors, they become subject to social shaping.

Does the existence of some biological dispositions compel us to believe that the two sexes are destined to have different statuses, roles, and occupations? We would be hard pressed to prove that most men's occupations require spatial or mathematical ability, and most women's require verbal ability. With rare exceptions, work seems to be assigned to the two sexes on an entirely different basis. In some instances (for example, professional prizefighter), we can see that the activity requires the male's greater strength and aggressiveness, making it inevitable that men will continue to predominate in the occupation. However, it is surprising how often the division of daily labor between the sexes demands greater feats of physical strength from women than from men. In some cultures, for example, only the women bear heavy burdens upon their heads or do the taxing agricultural work. Perhaps women, with their lower levels of strength and aggression, have been less willing, or less able, to protest onerous tasks.

It has been argued (see Goldberg, 1973) that wherever a biological difference exists, societies will—and should—socialize individuals so as to emphasize the difference. Girls should be trained to be submissive, Goldberg holds, because as adults they otherwise would be destined for frustrating encounters with men, who inevitably would dominate them because of their biological advantage in strength and aggressiveness. Perhaps in a culture where authority is maintained by brute force, a submissive course would be wise for women. But group leadership of mature human beings is exercised increasingly through persuasion, inspiration, and competence. In these domains, neither sex has an intrinsic advantage. Human social groups can make choices concerning the kind of society they want to have. In the interests of adaptation between the sexes, a society could either train its girls to accept male coercion, or train its boys to moderate their aggression, and teach both sexes the skills of positive social interaction. We see no reason why one approach should be regarded as more "natural" than the other. Social institutions and social practices are not merely reflections of the biologically inevitable. A variety of social practices are possible within the framework set by biology. Human beings are less driven by predetermined behavior patterns than lower animals and can select the socializaation processes that foster the life styles they value most.

Adolescence: Apprenticeship to Adulthood

Adult attitudes toward adolescents show remarkably little consensus. Some adults regard adolescents as dangerously impulsive trouble-makers, out to wreck society with their protests for change. Others see adolescents as irresponsible, fun-loving faddists in the heyday of life. Still other adults view adolescents as the hope of the future, the next generation who will rescue society from its current ills. All of these views reflect more about the adults who hold them than about the nature of adolescents. As John Conger has said, adolescents are a kind of projective test for adults. "We see in youth not merely what is actually there, but the mirror of our own desires, hopes, satisfactions, frustrations, fears, and disappointments" (1973).

What are adolescents really like? First, we must distinguish young adolescents from older ones, girls from boys, adolescents in industrial nations from those in preliterate groups, adolescents in school from those out of school, contemporary adolescents from those in the past, and so forth. We can no more characterize all adolescents in a single sweep than we could all adults. However, we can describe some general characteristics of the adolescent period.

Adolescence begins with puberty, the physiological achievement of sexual maturity, and ends with adult social status. In girls, the start of adolescence usually is marked by the biological changes of menarche (the beginning of menstruation), and in boys by the appearance of pigmented pubic hair. On the average, these changes occur around age 13. However, since the early 1900s the age of menarche for girls in the United States has been declining about 4 months in every decade. Girls begin their growth spurt earlier and achieve sexual maturity earlier, presumably because of better nutrition than in former times. For the same reason, boys also are growing to full adult stature at an earlier age. No one thinks that this trend toward larger size and earlier maturation will continue once optimum nutritional levels have been reached; if it is continued, we might eventually have 8-foot giants who mature sexually at the age of 3!

Associated with these changes, of course, are many other hormone-produced developments such as breast and hip development in girls, increased musculature and voice changes in boys. Social expectations and experiences also change at puberty, and, as we shall see, important behaviors develop. The end of adolescence is marked by changes in the social roles that people play. When the adolescent has become economically independent and has established a residence of his own, he generally is considered an adult. It is very difficult to attach any age to the end of adolescence because some people assume adult roles at 18 and others at 25. And some people never seem to become adults!

G. Stanley Hall, the first American psychologist to write about adolescence, characterized the period as one of "storm and stress" (1904). The biological changes of puberty and the new cultural expectations of their behavior seem to plunge some young people into behavioral oscillations between high activity and lethargy, excitement and depression, selfishness and selflessness, conceit and humility, tenderness and cruelty, curiosity and apathy. Psychoanalytic theory holds that adolescence is a period of renewed conflicts, a time when current problems and social pressures with the regulation of sex drives may combine with unresolved attachments to parents, conflicting identifications, and other problems of childhood to produce emotional upset, and behaviors that would be viewed as mental disorders in an adult. However, out of the adolescent upheaval comes new psychological growth (A. Freud, 1968).

Contemporary research on adolescents suggests that most young people are not experiencing extreme "storm and stress." They are, in fact, about as well adjusted as most adults. Some adolescents do feel anxiety, depression, and urges to "act out" their confusions in socially unacceptable ways, but the amount of psychopathology in adolescence does not exceed that in adulthood. Three studies of adolescent adjustment (Offer, 1969; Douvan & Adelson, 1966; Hathaway & Monachesi, 1963) support the view that, despite the major changes in biological and social forces at adolescence, most young people are flexible, consistent, stable, in touch with their feelings, and able to establish rewarding relationships with others.

Physical Growth

Young adolescents between 12 and 16 are rapidly changing people. They grow suddenly; boys can grow 5 to 6 inches taller in a single year, girls 4 or 5 inches. Their body proportions change from childhood to adult dimensions. Girls' bodies become more rounded, boys' more angular. Physical strength becomes far greater than in childhood, especially in boys, whose musculature now increases more than their fatty tissues. Throughout childhood, boys and girls have roughly the same size and body proportions; at adolescence, sexual dimorphism (differences in bodies) becomes prominent. After about 2 years, the growth spurt slows and in 2 or 3 more years, stops altogether. The average age of maximum adolescent growth in girls is 12, in boys 14.

As with all other developments, a great deal of normal individual variation occurs in physical growth. Some girls begin their growth spurt as early as 8; some boys as late as 16. Early and late maturing both have psychological consequences. Early maturing boys reach socially prestigious positions before their peers, being stronger, taller, and more mature in behavior. By junior high, early maturing girls are more popular with both boys and girls. Late maturers are treated like children for a

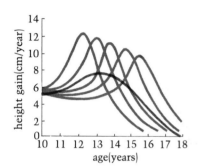

14-14
Graph of the height gains of five boys between the ages of 10 and 18. The colored line represents the mean (average) of their annual increases in height at each age. The mean curve is a more rounded bell-shaped curve because each boy's rate of growth peaked at a different age. (Tanner, Whitehouse, & Takaishi, 1966)

14-15
While the average age for maximum growth is 12 for girls and 14 for boys, there is great variation in the timing and the rate of this growth spurt—as this drawing of four subjects shows. (Tanner, 1969)

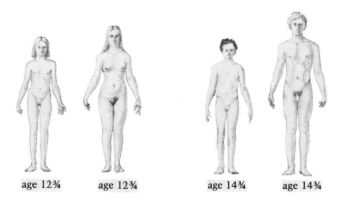

age 12¾   age 12¾   age 14¾   age 14¾

longer period, are not considered leaders by their peers, and are rated by teachers as being less mature in their behavior. It is hardly surprising that early maturers have higher self-esteem (Jones & Bayley, 1950).

Sexual maturity follows the adolescent growth spurt. Young adolescents usually are not reproductively mature when the girl begins to menstruate and the boy to ejaculate. Often many months, even years, pass before the girl's menses are accompanied by ovulation and the boy's ejaculation contains live sperm. Attraction to the opposite sex frequently is preceded by a period of "crushes" on same-sex peers, a normal transition from same-sex friendship to heterosexuality.

Intellectual Development

At the beginning of adolescence a profound change takes place in children's thinking. In the concrete operational period the grade-school child's problem-solving still is tied to the manipulation of concrete materials and to reality. Around 11 or 12 (later for many children) young adolescents begin to reason formally or propositionally in "If . . . then" statements. They can imagine all of the logical consequences of a hypothesis and systematically reason about them to reach a solution to a complex problem. At adolescence intelligence is abstract, flexible, and effective; in Piaget's terms, it has reached a high degree of *equilibrium*. Although it will be a few years before the adolescent can apply abstract logic to many different kinds of problems, he now uses the formal operations of an adult.

Typically, young adolescents criticize their parents and society. Because their abstract logic can imagine ideal possibilities, their parents' actual beliefs and behaviors suffer by comparison. Adolescents can argue endlessly about minute details of parental errors, prejudices, and perceived foolishness. This activity seems to serve several purposes: It helps them to loosen bonds to their parents and become more independent; it sharpens their ideas about the kind of person they do and do not want to become; and it gives them an opportunity to try out new ideas in a safe environment.

Young adolescents also are very critical of themselves and are easily shamed and embarrassed. Elkind (1967) says that the intellectual changes at adolescence bring a new kind of egocentrism. Because adolescents can conceptualize their own thoughts, they also can contemplate the thoughts of others. Adolescents' thoughts often are focused on themselves, and they tend to believe that other people's thoughts are similarly focused. As a consequence, an adolescent frequently is "playing" before an imaginary audience, all of whose eyes are focused on him. When he dislikes the way he looks or behaves, he is sure that everyone else is similarly critical of him. When he is pleased with his appearance, he will be especially elated because he sees everyone else as admiring him, too. As they mature, adolescents gain perspective on themselves and others by *decentering*. They realize that others do not necessarily share their thoughts and feelings. This realization is necessary to form mutual relationships; otherwise, each member of the pair projects his own feelings on his partner and is unable to perceive the other's needs.

Older adolescents of approximately 16 to 19 have passed the period of rapid physical growth, but they are faced with crises in forming a mature identity, choosing a future vocation, developing lasting relationships, and becoming independent of their parents. This age group is commonly romanticized in contemporary advertising and criticized by conservative adults. On the brink of adulthood, they have not yet assumed adulthood's alleged burdens, but they are socially and sexually mature enough to enjoy many adult privileges. In considering this stage of late adolescence, we shall discuss identity formation and the development of moral reasoning.

Identity Formation

Everyone must come to terms with himself, with who and what he is as a person. A child spends little time contemplating his character; neither his intellectual level nor his social concerns are sufficient to the task. But, as most of us are aware, both from personal experience and from observation, adolescents do tend to be introspective. According to Erik Erikson, the adolescent's paramount problem is to develop a consistent sense of self, an ego identity to serve as a standard for his behavior. He will have to face and make decisions on his own, based on a coherent sense of who he is and what he wants in life. No longer can parents protect the adolescent and make decisions for him. The term ego identity implies *individuality, coherence,* and *integration* of a person's self-concept. Adolescents must develop a sense of themselves as different from anyone else yet sharing many characteristics with others. Individuality is not isolation; it is being "put together" in a unique way. Coherence or consistency in the way one is put together is essential because unless a consistent set of needs, goals, and ideals underlies a person's decisions, they will move in random or confused directions.

Initially, identity in adolescence is based on identifications formed with others during childhood. Young children identify with (become like) their parents in many ways. Later, children often identify with older siblings, teachers, coaches, sports heroes, movie stars, and many others. While one's identity is based partially on these earlier identifications and on those made in adolescence, identity is not the mere sum of one's identifications. If it were, a person's identity would have no coherence. Rather, the adolescent can isolate the select features from these varied models and combine them into a unique identity for himself.

Identity formation is not a totally conscious process. Erikson believes that most of the process occurs without the adolescent consciously asking, "Who am I?" Although he may consciously try out different ways of behaving (and being)—one month he's on his way toward early marriage and a stock brokerage; the next he's disenchanted with that course and has decided to join a commune—underlying these behavior vacillations is a persistent but unspoken need to find a consistent sense of self. A great deal of the unsettled behavior that does occur in adolescence is the young person's attempt to arrive at a consistent and satisfying identity.

Why is identity formation a problem of adolescence and not childhood? First, because in Western cultures, as a person becomes sexually

14-16
During adolescence, boys and girls learn to live with their new-found sexual identities—and those of their friends as well. (Hella Hammid, Rapho Guillumette)

and socially mature, he must make life decisions for himself; and, second, his new intellectual level allows him to reason abstractly about himself. Identity formation is in part a culturally conditioned process. If a young person's adult status and life style were predetermined in childhood, as they are in many other cultures, he would know who and what he was going to be. A member of such a society has neither need nor opportunity for much individual identity formation. Because Western societies offer opportunities for social mobility based on individual characteristics, one must decide what one is going to be. The individual has both a personal need and cultural opportunity in adolescence to arrive at a sense of individual identity.

The ability to form an individual identity is rooted in formal operational intelligence. The adolescent can reason about himself, just as he can reason about scientific problems; he can ruminate about what, in the realm of possible-but-not-actual selves, he can become. Unlike a child who finds it difficult to imagine possibilities that are not real, the adolescent can dream about ideal political systems, ideal life styles, and an ideal self. This newly found ability to reason about unrealized ideals disturbs some adults, especially those who unquestioningly support the status quo.

Not everyone achieves a full sense of individual identity in adolescence or even adulthood. Just as identities are prescribed in traditional, preliterate groups, many people in our society are drawn into socially prescribed definitions of themselves. Sometimes this means doing exactly what one's parents or peer group expect; sometimes it means defying significant adults and being exactly what they despise. In either case, the person is tied to others' definition of him. Some adolescents and young adults cannot develop consistency in their definitions of themselves. They shift from job to job, relationship to relationship, and life style to life style. They become 35-year-old "adolescents" who are still trying to "find themselves." Still others arrive at an early self-concept without considering other possibilities. They are defensive and anxious about the ambiguities that adolescents must endure to arrive at an individually consistent self. Neither premature consolidation of oneself nor extremely delayed identity formation is as adaptive in our society as a period of adolescent self-examination and experimentation followed by the formation of the consistent individuality called an identity.

Moral Development

Adolescents, more than members of any other age group, are concerned with moral values. They are faced with personal, moral decisions about political, social, and sexual behavior—all of which press them to arrive at personal, moral standards. And they are intellectually able to raise and examine moral issues on an abstract level that was not possible in childhood. Kohlberg (1968, 1969, 1973) believes that children proceed through six stages of moral reasoning that are tied to Piaget's stages of cognitive development. Progress from preoperational to concrete operational to formal operational thought is the necessary but not sufficient condition for advances in moral judgment. Cultural values and parental behaviors also contribute to the way people think about moral problems. Although individuals and groups differ greatly in their rates of moral development, the sequence of stages that people all over the world go through in thinking about morality is surprisingly consistent.

Kohlberg is less concerned with *what* they think than with *how* they reason about a problem. To assess levels of moral judgment he poses moral dilemmas, such as the following:

Before the Civil War, we had laws that allowed slavery. According to the law, if a slave escaped he had to be returned to his owner like a runaway horse. Some people who didn't believe in slavery disobeyed the law and hid the runaway slaves and helped them to escape. Were they doing right or wrong? (from Turiel, 1974)

When this dilemma is posed to grade-school children 5 to 10 years old, they tend to respond to cultural labels of good and bad and to the physical power of those who define good and bad. They are oriented toward punishment and unquestioning obedience to those in authority. Many 10-year-olds respond that both the slave and the one who hid him were wrong because they both were defying authority and will be punished. This reasoning is at Stage 1 of the _preconventional_ level. At Stage 2 of the preconventional level "right action consists of that which satisfies one's own needs and occasionally the needs of others. Human relations are viewed in terms like those of the marketplace." (If the slave was a friend it might be okay to help him, if you didn't get caught.) Notions of reciprocity are present but they are instrumental in the sense of, "You do something for me, and I'll do something for you." Ideals of justice, fairness, or loyalty are absent.

By the early teens many adolescents have developed to the *conventional* level. The two stages at the conventional level can be characterized respectively as the "good boy—good girl" orientation and the "law and order" mentality. In Stage 3, the first conventional period, good behavior is what pleases and helps others and what is approved by them. For the first time behavior is judged by its intentions rather than by its consequences. Kohlberg points to Charlie Brown in *Peanuts* as an example of Stage 3 morality; being nice and meaning well are not especially impressive virtues but they are important changes from the marketplace morality of the earlier stage. At Stage 4 adolescents still are oriented toward authority, but they now have a personal investment in maintaining the social order. Duty to society, respect for the existing law, and support for law enforcement are the virtues of this period. Law is not yet considered a social contract that can be changed; it is an immutable fact. (Slavery may be wrong but the law against escape must be enforced, lest all laws fall and chaos overcome us.)

Two final stages at the _postconventional_ level are characterized by higher order values and the questioning of the legal system as it exists. In Stage 5 a social-contract orientation appears in which constitutional rights and legal procedures are recognized values, while other personal opinions and values are clearly relative. "The result is an emphasis upon the 'legal point of view'; but with an emphasis upon the possibility of *changing* law in terms of rational considerations of social utility, rather than freezing it in the terms of Stage 4 'law and order'." Kohlberg says that Stage 5 reasoning is the official morality of the United States Government and is expressed in the Constitution. (Helping an escaped slave would be right if it helped to change an unjust law.) Some, but not a majority, of late adolescents reach this level of moral reasoning. The final stage is achieved by very few people. Stage 6 is characterized by self-chosen, abstract ethical principles like the Golden Rule. They are not prescriptions for behavior but universal principles of justice, reciprocity, and equality of human rights, and respect for the dignity of human beings as individual persons. Mahatma Gandhi, Martin Luther King, Jr., Henry David Thoreau, and Abraham Lincoln represent similar commitments to ethical-moral principles beyond the immediate social contracts of the societies in which they were reared. Kohlberg ascribes this uniformity of principles to the fact that ". . . the ideal principles of any social structure are basicallly alike. . . . And most of these principles have gone by the name of justice" (Kohlberg, 1968).

The adolescent's increasingly abstract thought makes it possible for him to espouse universal principles of justice. However, most adolescents do not. Although no one's thought is totally at a single level, most adults in our society can be assigned to Stages 4 and 5. In other societies, Stages 3 and 4 predominate. The social context in which people are reared, Stage 5-American Government and Stage 4-local standards of conduct, are strong learning influences. The content of most people's morality represents the ethical-moral-religious values with which they were reared. They need not—and often do not—apply their intellectual skills to further moral development. Research studies have shown that people understand examples of moral reasoning at their own level and at one level above their own. They do not comprehend moral reasoning two levels above (Turiel, 1974). Thus, if many people operate at Stage 4 moral reasoning, they do not really grasp the universal principles of Stage 6; those who can use Stage 5 cannot necessarily move on to Stage 6.

14-17
Graphs of the development of Kohlberg's six stages of moral thinking in boys of 10, 13, and 16 years of age from five cultures. All of the ten-year olds exhibited Stage 1 thinking predominantly, with each of Stages 2 through 6 being exhibited by a decreasing percentage of boys. At age 13, in the United States, for instance, Stage 1 thinking had dropped down to just over 10% of the boys, whereas almost 30% exhibited Stage 3 judgments. By age 16, Stage 5 thinking was the most common for the U.S. boys, with the other stages following in reverse order—except for Stage 6, which maintained its bottom position in every group tested. (Kagan & Moss, 1962)

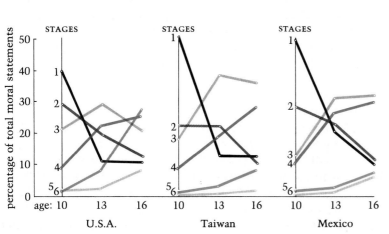

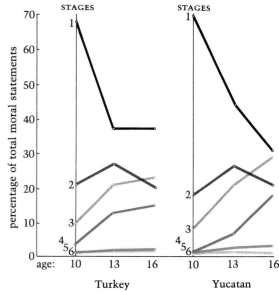

Adolescence is a time of apprenticeship for adulthood, a time for self-definition and preliminary commitments to a life course. Commitments change, even into middle adulthood, but for the healthy person adolescence brings an increasing sense of wholeness. The adolescent has developed an identity and a morality that give him personal-ethical standards by which to evaluate his own and others' behavior.

Adulthood

Imagine being exactly the same person at 25 and 75. It is almost unthinkable that one would not develop emotionally, intellectually, and socially over 50 years. The rate of change is surely slower than in earlier years, but since most of your life is spent as an adult, you have plenty of time for development. Young adults of perhaps 20 to 40 years of age are usually in the process of establishing themselves, making adjustments in their commitments, beginning families, and making progress in their jobs and communities. Adults in the middle period of life, from 40 to 60, are likely to be more established; they reap the benefits and problems of earlier years as they continue to invest themselves in their families, jobs, and society. Older adults, past 60, have a varied course of development or decline: Some remain actively invested in work, family, and society; others retire to a more relaxed and self-indulgent life; and many others are relegated to poverty and isolation by enforced retirement and social neglect.

As they are at any other life stage, developmental changes in adulthood are rooted in both biological and social causes. Some people call these changes decline rather than development because, physically at least, the person is past his peak of strength and sexuality. But he continues to gain in self-consistency, self-assurance, understanding of himself and others, intellectual knowledge, and judgment. In short, people *mature* as they move from adolescence through adulthood. Even in sports we can find outstanding examples of mature experience compensating for declining agility and quickness. Frank Tarkenton (football), Hank Aaron (baseball), Ken Rosewall (tennis), and Gordie Howe (hockey) are all well past the usual prime age for their sports, but they have remained respected competitors as much for the mature judgment they bring to the task as for their physical qualities. In other life endeavors that require less physical prowess, adults—even older adults—often perform considerably better than the inexperienced young. The maturing of personality and intelligence is an important development in adulthood.

Intelligence

After adolescence, intelligence passes through no new developmental stages. The adult forms of logical thought are extensions and applications of earlier skills, according to Piaget. Improvements in intellectual skills that occur in early adulthood result from greater facility in using the available logical operations and increased experience in applying them to a variety of problems.

Better-educated adults continue to gain in IQ scores through early and middle adulthood; the IQs of those with more limited educational experiences and interests begin to decline in their 30s and 40s (Bayley, 1933). In part these patterns of gain and decline reflect the skills sampled by IQ tests. Better-educated people compensate for declines in some skills by increasing their scores on other parts of the test. Subjects who are less well educated cannot compensate.

What skills decline with age? Considerable research on the intelligence of aging adults suggests that *speeded performance* begins to fall off in middle adulthood. People do not respond as quickly to problems and thus lose points on timed IQ tests. Since the solutions to most of life's problems are not gauged in seconds but by the quality of the outcome, the loss of speed in performing may not be an important loss.

Cattell (1971) has divided intelligence into two components: fluid and crystallized. *Fluid intelligence* is "a capacity for insight into complex relations that is independent of sensory mode or cultural content in which the intelligence is expressed." Fluid intelligence, according to Cattell, is neurologically determined. *Crystallized intelligence* results from the use of fluid intelligence to learn whatever higher-level cultural skills the person is exposed to. Crystallized intelligence is the sum of culturally conditioned acquisitions like social information, common factual data, school skills, and the like. Most IQ tests are a mixture of the two types of intelligence.

Fluid intelligence, according to Cattell's model, declines steadily after age 15, while crystallized intelligence increases slowly with age. Because the former declines more rapidly than the latter increases, most people lose IQ points as they grow older. Better-educated subjects can compensate better for the loss of fluid intelligence by increases in their culturally conditioned skills.

At the very end of a person's lifespan biological changes may cause loss of memory and general intellectual decline. Arteriosclerosis, the hardening and narrowing of the vascular system, including those arteries that supply nutrients to the brain, is frequently a factor. Shortly before a natural death from arteriosclerosis, intellectual functioning often registers a marked decline. But up to that point, the person probably has been functioning at or near the level he maintained in his middle adult years.

Social factors also hasten the intellectual decline of many older people in our society. After retirement, and perhaps the death of a spouse, the older adult is increasingly isolated from meaningful contact with others. His children have grown to maturity and do not want the responsibility of caring for him. His grandchildren often consider his "wisdom" an

14-18
Growth curves of fluid and crystallized intelligence. As hypothesized by Cattell, fluid intelligence declines with age. Its loss is to a greater or lesser extent compensated for by increased crystallized intelligence. (Cattell, 1971)

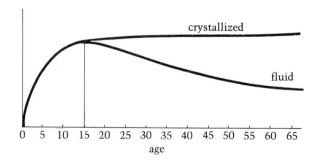

irrelevant intrusion into their lives. In a rapidly changing society, the older person's experiences, accumulated in a context that no longer exists, may seem passé to the young. In other societies older people are respected, even venerated, for their wisdom.

Today many older people are judged by our society's standards to have outlived their usefulness, and we do not hesitate to relegate them to the corners of society—the institutions and nursing homes that are merely holding areas where residents await death. The mythology that aging leads inexorably to mental incompetence comforts us in our current practices, but the developmental facts for most aging people do not support this view. Most would remain far more competent if they were in the mainstream of life. When Sigmund Freud was asked what a competent adult should be able to do well, he replied simply, "To work and to love." Under our social system, many older adults have lost the opportunity to do either.

An Overview of Development

Throughout this chapter we have emphasized development as change. It is time to emphasize continuity. An individual is, after all, the same person from birth to death—the same but different in each developmental phase. Werner (1961) has said that development is a dialectic process, the synthesis of two opposing forces: *adaptive change* and *organized stability*. True to a dialectic process, continuity imposes constraints on change and change imposes constraints on continuity. On the one hand, the person is capable of only certain kinds and amounts of change at any point in his development. What he is determines what he can become next. His genes and his experiences define his ability to take the next step in development. On the other hand, he cannot remain the same; he is a developing biological organism, propelled toward change by his genetic heritage and his increasing experience. As an "open" system he takes in new experiences that provoke modifications in his organization; as a maturing system he uses new experiences in ever more complex and adaptive ways.

The level of a person's intelligence, his physical growth status, and some of his personality traits have been shown to be fairly stable across developmental periods. As an individual he tends to score in about the same rank relative to his age mates as they and he change across time. In the case of IQ and personality, the actual behaviors that provide evidence for these traits change from childhood to adulthood.

Several longitudinal studies have shown continuity in social behaviors from childhood to adolescence and from adolescence to adulthood (Scarr, 1969). Children who are more outgoing and sociable earlier in life tend to be more outgoing and sociable at a later period. But the child behaviors that are called "sociability" are far different from the adult behaviors that are given the same label. The same continuity-but-change can be observed in IQ scores. The test items are different at each age level. What constitutes "intelligent" behavior at one age does not represent it at another. For example, only about one out of two 3-year-olds can follow simple directions without making an error. All but the most retarded 10-year-olds can. Thus, at the 10-year level more difficult items are needed to measure what we mean by intelligent behavior. Nonetheless, scores on IQ tests show some correlation between ages 3 and 10. Over comparable age spans at later ages, the scores correlate even more highly, despite the fact that all of the items are different.

Stable individual differences depend both on the person's genetic background, which has its own developmental patterns, and on continuity in his experiences. Severe deprivation or unusual enrichment can alter the developing person's rank in his age group. Many studies have pointed to the large longitudinal changes that occur in children's IQ scores, depending on personality factors (Kagan & Moss, 1962) and family influences (McCall, Applebaum, & Hogarty, 1973). High achievement motivation, a stable family, and a good deal of intellectual stimulation in the home are associated with rising IQ scores. Continuities and discontinuities in personality are less well understood.

And so a person changes but retains, relative to his peers, some continuities. We still have much to discover about development, and research in the field has increased tenfold in the last two decades.

Summary

1. The concept of development as change over time involves a need to specify how much change, what kinds of change, and over how much time.

2. Development may be defined as an orderly sequence of permanent change in behavior that is directional, cumulative, and shows increasing differentiation and integration.

3. Behavioral development depends on both genetic and environmental determinants. Their relative contributions to individual differences have caused controversy, particularly regarding intelligence.

4. Sequences in behavioral development occur, according to Flavell, because of the neurological maturity of the organism, the structure of the environment, and the structure of behavior. Behavioral stages are organized around a dominant theme, are qualitatively different from behaviors at other ages, and show a spurt in development followed by a period without dramatic change.

5. Two principal groups of theories about development are the structuralist, which infers internal rules from observed behaviors, and the behaviorist, which contends that the environment determines which behaviors a person acquires.

6. Behaviorists are concerned with how behaviors can be changed. Skinner focuses on the manipulation of rewards; Bandura emphasizes the importance of imitation of rewarded models, such as parents and older children.

7. Structuralists are concerned with why behaviors occur. They believe that all behavior is guided by internal rules and that development is the joint product of maturation and experience. Jean Piaget posed three

stages of intellectual development: the sensorimotor, the operational, and the propositional. Erik Erikson postulated psychosocial stages based on conflicts arising from increasing maturity and social demands.

8. Three principles of behavioral observation are that you cannot see everything that happens in a continuous stream of behaviors; that judgments are not observations; and that observations must be reliable.

9. The newborn infant has a large array of reflexive behaviors and a well-developed sensory apparatus. A newborn can see clearly objects 10 inches away, respond to sounds in the 40 to 60 decibel range, and withdraw from noxious odors and the taste of strong saline solutions.

10. By 2 months, an infant shows increased social responsiveness and improved learning ability; by 3 months, more alertness and improved voluntary control over muscles; by 7 or 8 months, more independent locomotion, strong attachments or fears of people, and babbling in language sounds; and by 17 to 18 months, improved language skills and use of symbols.

11. Piaget describes six sensorimotor stages in which infant intelligence proceeds from reflexive actions, to practicing of motor actions, to recognizing the effects of these actions, overcoming obstacles toward a goal, attempting variations and new action sequences, and insightful learning. Two tests of infant intelligence are the Bayley Scales and the Uzgiris-Hunt Scales. IQ scores of infants are not necessarily related to IQ scores in later life.

12. Erikson describes basic trust versus mistrust as the crisis of infancy. Infants and their mothers form strong bonds, possibly because attachments have important survival functions.

13. The rate of development in childhood is slower than in infancy. The 2-year-old begins struggling for autonomy; the 3-year-old begins to become socialized and his mental life becomes full of images and symbols not easily distinguished from reality; the 4- or 5-year-old seeks independence and achieves conceptual learning, classification skills, and operational logic; the school-age child is concerned with achievements and special friendships.

14. The rapid development of language between a child's second and fifth year has led some psycholinguists to propose an innate language ability involving skills in analyzing speech into categories and developing rules of grammar. Child language possesses its own rules, basically simpler versions of adult rules.

15. Young children focus on a limited aspect of any problem and on its relationship to themselves. One developmental trend is toward a broader perspective through an appreciation of transformation, logical necessity, hierarchical classifications, and transitive and symmetrical relations.

16. Adolescence, which begins with puberty (around age 13) and ends with adulthood, is a period when most young people accelerate in physical growth, gain sexual maturity, and achieve abstract, flexible, and effec-

tive intelligence. Although critical of adults and of themselves, adolescents begin to perceive the needs of others, to face the crisis of forming a mature identity, and to become independent.

17. A major problem of adolescence is to develop a consistent sense of self or an ego identity. The ability to form this identity is rooted in formal operational intelligence, which enables the person to reason about himself introspectively and abstractly.

18. Adolescents encounter personal, moral decisions about political, social, and sexual behavior. Kohlberg has posed six stages of moral reasoning, including preconventional levels of unquestioning obedience to authority and satisfaction of one's needs; conventional levels of thinking intended to please others and satisfy law-and-order morality; and postconventional levels of higher-order values, which lead to questioning of the laws in light of social utility and such abstract ethical principles as justice and human dignity.

19. Developmental changes in adulthood are marked by a decline in physical strength and sexuality, but also by gains in self-consistency, self-assurance, understanding of oneself and others, intellectual knowledge, and judgment.

20. Improvements in adult intellectual skills result from better facility in using the available logical operations and from increased experience with their application to a variety of problems. Speed of performance declines with age as does fluid intelligence, which is the capacity for insight into complex relations. However, crystallized intelligence—the sum of the culturally conditioned skills and information the person is exposed to—increases slowly over age.

21. Continuity is also an important aspect of development. Heinz Werner has called development a dialectic process, the synthesis of two opposing forces: adaptive change and organized stability.

Important Terms

development

scheme

structuralist theory of development

Jean Piaget

Erik Erikson

behaviorist theory of development

B. F. Skinner

equilibration

assimilation

accommodation

infancy

childhood

adolescence

adulthood

fetus

sensorimotor stage

secondary circular reactions

Bayley Scale of Mental Development

trust versus mistrust

autonomy	puberty
decentration	equilibrium
egocentrism	ego identity
operational stage	preconventional level
preoperational stage	conventional level
concrete operational stage	postconventional level
conservation	fluid intelligence
transitivity	crystallized intelligence
symmetrical relations	

Suggested Readings

ARIES, P. *Centuries of childhood: A social history of family life.* Trans. from the original by R. Baldrick. New York: Vintage Books, 1962.
> A historical account of the ideas about children and family life in Europe from medieval times to the present, using evidence from paintings, literature, and accounts of educational practices and family-oriented customs.

BROWN, R. *A first language.* Cambridge: Harvard University Press, 1973.
> A leading social psychologist's detailed description of the development of language in young children, based on several longitudinal studies. Some background in psychology and linguistics is assumed.

CONGER, J. J. *Adolescence and youth: Psychological development in a changing world.* New York: Harper & Row, 1973.
> A thorough, scholarly, research-oriented textbook for undergraduates. Such aspects of adolescent development as value systems, moral development, alienation, and commitment are discussed in the light of contemporary social issues and trends.

ERIKSON, E. *Childhood and society.* New York: Norton, 1963.
> A psychosocial approach to human psychological development. Both general principles of development and specific patterns to be expected from living in other cultures are deduced from case studies.

GINSBURG, H., & OPPER, S. *Piaget's theory of intellectual development: An introduction.* Englewood Cliffs, N.J.: Prentice-Hall, 1969.
> The ideas and findings of the leading contributor to the field of psychological development are presented in a form designed to help clarify a complicated and difficult body of work.

KAGAN, J., & MOSS, H. A. *Birth to maturity: The Fels study of psychological development.* New York: Wiley, 1962.
> A discussion of the methods and conclusions of a longitudinal study of the psychological development of 89 children from birth through early adulthood.

MUSSEN, P. H. (ED.) *Carmichael's manuel of child psychology* (3rd ed.). New York: Wiley, 1970.

A two-volume overview of the major thinking and research in the psychology of human development. This edition reflects the current emphasis on explaining, rather than describing, development.

REESE, H. W., & LIPSITT, L. P. (ED.) *Experimental child psychology.* New York: Academic Press, 1970.

An intermediate-level text in which major research topics, such as basic learning processes, perceptual development, language acquisition, and intelligence, are discussed from various viewpoints.

Chapter 15 Intelligence and Its Measurement

Man is an organism that seeks and demands explanations. He has sought to understand the mysteries of his environment. He has asked questions, and searched for answers, about his origin and the meaning of his existence. . . . Man asks these questions and seeks their answers because he is an intelligent being who is not limited to mere behavioral interactions with his environment. He is a conscious, reflective, evaluative, anxious being who is required to be as responsive to the realities of his [imagined] and created environments as to his physical and biological environments. The fact of human intelligence demands this. Human intelligence also provides the key to the answers to the questions it is capable of raising. Man believes that he has survived as a species and will continue to survive in spite of his [comparative physical] weakness because he has the intelligence necessary to probe, to seek to understand, and to control the environmental forces that threaten him.

So far, his experience supports this intellectual circularity and pervasive human chauvinism.

The critical question of this period of human history—the answer to which must also come from the critical use of man's mind—is whether or not human intelligence as traditionally defined offers any reliable assurance of human survival. This question may seem hopelessly abstract, even trite. But nothing could be more concrete. Is pure intelligence enough to protect man from self-inflicted destruction?

—Kenneth Clark
(*Pathos of Power*)

Intelligence and Its Measurement

This chapter was drafted by Timothy Teyler, Department of Psychology and Social Relations, Harvard University.

It is safe to say that every student reading this book has taken an intelligence test sometime in his or her life. It is also safe to assume that you are in college reading this book because you made above a certain score on an intelligence test. How much you comprehend of what you are reading now and how well you will do on examinations in this course is somewhat related to your intelligence test score. If you aspire to go to a graduate school or professional school, you can be fairly sure that your chances of being accepted will be enhanced by a superior performance on an intelligence test. For those of you who apply for a job instead of going to graduate school, your chances of getting the job, especially if it is one in a large company or in the civil service, will often be determined by the results of an intelligence test. Not many of you will go into one of the armed services, but many young men and women do, and their opportunities for specialized training and advancement depend in part on their scores on an intelligence test.

So you can see that your performance on an intelligence test is an important factor in your life. Whether it should be so important is a question many people are asking today. Intelligence tests are being criticized on a number of grounds. They are accused of favoring individuals who have grown up in an intellectually stimulating environment; that is, one that enables them to do well on intelligence tests. They certainly do favor such individuals, as all studies show. Since the amount of intellectual stimulation provided children depends largely on the income and education of their parents, children from poorer homes are clearly at a great disadvantage. This results, it has been suggested, in the development of an exclusive intellectually elite class that perpetuates itself from generation to generation. Those who are handicapped by an unfavorable home or school environment are permanently excluded from this elite class.

Intelligence tests also are criticized because they place heavy emphasis on language, thus penalizing those whose knowledge of the language is limited. This, too, is a well-documented fact. Another criticism is that the questions asked on intelligence tests are limited in scope. They may measure one's ability to learn school subjects, but do they tap other abilities just as important as book learning? A person lacking a large vocabulary, a knowledge of mathematics, and a great fund of information may lead a satisfying and productive life and excel at many endeavors.

In order to discuss these questions intelligently, it is necessary to know just what an intelligence test is, how it is constructed, what it is supposed to measure and what factors influence the test scores. Later we will discuss how the tests can be improved, and how intelligence, as measured by the tests, can be increased.

How Is Intelligence Measured?

We must understand the historical development of intelligence testing if we are to appreciate current concepts of intelligence and the means by which it is studied. The field is quite new. A hundred years ago, scientists showed virtually no curiosity about intelligence. The first faint interest was expressed in the latter half of the 19th century by Sir Francis Galton and others. They measured and studied a vast array of sensations, reflexes, and responses, only to discover that these measures had little to do with superior mental characteristics. It fell upon a French psychologist to provide the basis for the modern field of intelligence assessment.

The Binet Tests

It all began in 1904 when the prominent French psychologist Alfred Binet was appointed to a committee that was to investigate the causes of retardation among public school pupils. As a consequence of this work, Binet saw the need for a test that would identify children who were incapable of learning the ordinary grade school subjects in the standard length of time. If such children could be identified, they could then be placed in special classes where more appropriate methods of instruction would be employed and more time would be devoted to learning a subject. Binet made what proved to be an insightful basic assumption. He reasoned that a child who is a slow learner will not have acquired as much knowledge as the average child of the same age. In other words, if a child is 10 years old but knows only as much as an 8 year-old, he must be a slow learner and will need more time to learn a new subject.

Working on this assumption, Binet set out to discover what the average child at each age level knows. Obviously, he could not hope to measure the complete range of a child's knowledge. He had to be selective. Accordingly, he chose commonplace items of knowledge to which all children are exposed. Table 15-1 gives some of the questions and problems used by Binet. After assembling many such questions and problems, Binet gave them to a large number of children at various ages.

Table 15-1   Sample Items from Binet's Intelligence Test

Are you a boy or a girl?
How old are you?
What are the names of these four colors?
Hand me five blocks from that pile.
Repeat these numbers after me.
What is the opposite of the word *large?*
Define the word *pride.*
Which one of these objects is different from the rest?
Point to your nose.

He then computed the number of children at each age level who answered each question or solved each problem correctly. If about 75 percent of the children at a given age level and more children at a higher age level answered it correctly, the item was classified as belonging to that given age. In other words, if three-quarters of the 6-year-olds tested could hand to the tester five blocks from a pile of blocks, and if only half of the 5-year-olds and over 75 percent of the 7-year-olds could perform the same task correctly, the ability to do this task was said to be typical of 6-year-olds. A number of items were assigned to each age level.

The result of Binet's work was the first intelligence test. Let us consider this word *test*. As used in everyday speech it means a critical trial. "He was put to the test and found wanting." In psychology, a test is a measure of behavior in a standard situation. The word *standard* characterizes the test as exactly the same for everyone. Furthermore, a test is only a sample of behavior. It does not cover the entire range of knowledge in a given domain. These two characteristics of a test—that it is the same for everyone and that it is a sample of the whole universe of knowledge—are well known to every student because he takes hundreds of such tests in the course of his school life.

After constructing his test, Binet hit upon another very useful idea—the concept of *mental age*. If a child answers all questions up to and including those at the 8-year level and fails all of the items beyond that age, he is said to have a mental age of 8. Mental age is a psychological scale and every child can be located on this scale. In actual practice it does not work out quite so neatly; a child is not likely to pass all the items up to a particular age and fail all those beyond it. Suppose there are six questions at each age level. Then the number of questions answered correctly will be more like the following example:

A child answers all of the 7-year-old questions, five of the 8-year-old questions, three of the 9-year-old questions, one of the 10-year-old questions, and none of those above the tenth year level. Two months' credit is given for each question answered. It is assumed that since he answered correctly all the questions at the 7-year level he could do as well at the lower age levels. Thus, his mental age is computed as follows:

Seven is his basal mental age. To this basal age are added ten months for the five questions passed at age 8, 6 months for the three questions at age 9, and 2 months for the one question at age 10. The sum is 8 years and 6 months, and this is his mental age. Now suppose the child is 8½ years old. His mental age is exactly in keeping with his chronological age. He is neither advanced nor retarded for his age, and he should be able to learn the school subjects as quickly as most children of his age.

Revisions. Binet did not take the next logical step. It was taken by a German psychologist, William Stern, when he divided the mental age by the chronological age and multiplied this quotient by a hundred. The resulting figure is known throughout the civilized world as the *IQ (Intelligence Quotient)*. IQ has become a synonym for intelligence. Suppose an 8-year-old child has a mental age of 10. We find his IQ by the following formula.

$$\frac{\text{MA (mental age)}}{\text{CA (chronological age)}} \times 100 = \text{IQ (intelligence quotient)}$$

The quotient is multiplied by 100 to get rid of the decimal point and make the IQ a whole number. To illustrate:

$$\frac{10}{8} = 1.25 \qquad 1.25 \times 100 = 125, \text{ which is the IQ.}$$

It is obvious that if the IQ is above 100, the child is advanced for his age; if it is below 100, he is retarded.

Did Binet's test—or, as it is more properly called, the *Binet-Simon Intelligence Test* because Binet was joined in the enterprise by Thomas Simon—do what Paris school authorities hoped it would do, namely, identify the slow learners? In order to find this out, the Paris teachers were asked to identify the slow learners in their classes. Those who gave the tests were not told which pupils had been designated as slow learners by their teachers. Tests were given to all children, and the test scores (mental ages) identified those children who were expected to be slow learners. Many were the same children who appeared on the teacher's lists of slow learners.

The Concept of "Normal." Binet and Simon noted that the use of mental age allowed one to classify the entire range of intelligence—from the handicapped to the superior individual. A 5-year-old with a mental age of 6 would have an IQ of 120 (6/5 × 100 = 120). The French pioneers also saw that most pupils fell into the "normal" range; at either extreme was a smaller group of handicapped students and an equally small group of superior students. Later in this section we shall examine more closely the distribution of intelligence in the population.

"Normal" is an important label; it must be clearly understood. It is not a classification based on an absolute standard. Psychologists determine normal behavior by giving a set of test items to a large group of children who are as similar as possible to the children who later will take the same test. The average score, or more usually a range of scores, of the large test group becomes the "normal" value.

A child's IQ status is not always correctly understood. For example, if a child's IQ score remains at 100 from year 7 to year 8, it does not mean that his intellect has not expanded in that year. It most certainly has. At

8 he can perform operations that were difficult or impossible for him at 7. His *absolute* amount of intellect has definitely increased; however, his *relative* standing in his norm group remains the same. Similarly, a child whose IQ score falls from 100 to 95 over a year is not, in most cases, becoming absolutely less intelligent. Rather, his rate of intellectual growth is not equal to that of the average child, so he is becoming *relatively* less intelligent.

The Stanford-Binet Test

In 1916, a test similar in content and style to the Binet and Simon was devised by Lewis Terman, the Stanford University psychologist who popularized the use of intelligence tests in America. In 1937, this test was revised, incorporating a number of changes. Known as the *Stanford-Binet*, this test then was standardized on a large group of students.

Unlike the original Binet, the Stanford-Binet includes scales that make it possible to determine the IQ of adults. Previous tests had shown that mental age increases with chronological age at a fairly constant rate up to the age of 12 or 14. Thereafter, mental age grows more slowly. Thus, to divide the mental age performance by chronological age (MA/CA $\times$ 100 = IQ) past the early teens leads to an apparent, and false, decline in intelligence with age. Using the standard formula, the IQ of an older man would be half of his younger counterpart (15/15 $\times$ 100 = 100 versus 15/30 $\times$ 100 = 50). A far better solution is to obtain representative samples of persons of all ages and assign the score of 100 to the average performance of persons of *any* age. Thus, the IQ score in its final form is a standard score based on the range of performances of any age group. In 1960, the Stanford-Binet test was again revised to incorporate the standard score derivation of IQ. Table 15-2 shows the descriptive categories originally assigned to the various Stanford-Binet scores.

A Drawback. While the sample on whom Terman standardized the Stanford-Binet consisted of males and females, rural and urban dwellers, and individuals of different socioeconomic classes proportionate to their

Table 15-2   Distribution of IQ Scores on the Stanford-Binet Test

IQ Score	Category	Percent of Children Ages 2–18
140 and above	very superior	1%
120–139	superior	11%
110–119	high average	18%
90–109	average	46%
80–89	low average	15%
70–79	borderline	6%
below 70	mentally handicapped	3%

Source: Adapted from M. A. Merrill, The significance of IQ's on the revised Stanford-Binet Scales. *Journal of Educational Psychology*, 1938, **26**, 641–651. Copyright © 1938 by the American Psychological Association. Reprinted by permission.

numbers in the population, it included only American-born white children. If only white American-born children are to be tested, this is not a problem. However, if a black, Hispanic-American, or foreign-born child takes this test, his score represents only how well he has done relative to the norm of American-born white children. Often, because of cultural or educational differences, he will earn a lower score—and whatever consequences may accompany it. We shall discuss this problem in more detail later in the chapter.

The Wechsler Scales

Binet and Simon began one tradition of intelligence testing, most recently represented by the Stanford-Binet test. These tests, administered by one examiner working with one student, use mostly verbal instructions and responses. As such, they are time-consuming and somewhat difficult to score because the child can answer in any way he chooses. The Binet tests also assign a single value—the IQ— as the result of the test's procedure. But as we will see, another approach—parceling the overall intelligence measure into component factors—may be a greater aid to understanding and measuring intelligence. With this goal in mind, psychologists have devised tests that analyze intelligence as a complex phenomenon composed of many interacting abilities.

The 1958 *Wechsler Adult Intelligence Scale* (WAIS) was the first widely-used test to incorporate several measures of intelligence. The scale items resemble those in the Binet test but they are classified into two categories—*verbal* and *performance.* Verbal items deal with such elements as points of information, comprehension, vocabulary, arithmetic, and similarities. Performance items include object assembly, picture arrangement, block design, picture completion, and other nonverbal problems in spatial relations. Table 15-3 gives sample items from the Wechsler Adult Intelligence Scale. The final WAIS score is a combination of the scale's verbal and performance subsets. This composite measure is roughly comparable to the measure that the Stanford-Binet provides.

The WAIS was designed to measure adult intelligence. A later version was prepared for the measurement of school and preschool children's intelligence. Known as the *Wechsler Intelligence Scale for Children* (WISC), this scale also divided overall intelligence into verbal and performance subcategories. By observing patterns of scoring on the various verbal and performance items, it was hoped that examiners could develop diagnostic profiles for persons with brain damage, behavior disorders, or other psychological problems. To some extent, the Wechsler scales have been helpful in this regard.

The Wechsler scales differ from the Binet tests not only because they break the intelligence measure into two categories, but also because they measure intelligence over a wider age range. Like the Stanford-Binet, the scales are administered by one examiner to one person at a time, so it is a slow process. It is also affected by the subjective nature of the person's response—although we can, of course, argue that open-ended responses allow a person to express his individuality while multiple-choice items do not.

Table 15-3   Questions Similar to Those Found in the Wechsler Adult Intelligence Scale

General Information
1. Where does coffee come from?
2. Who wrote *Macbeth?*
3. What is anthropology?
4. How far is it from New York to San Francisco?
5. Who invented the steam engine?

General Comprehension
1. What would you do if you were on a boat and a person fell overboard?
2. Why does the state require automobile drivers to have drivers' licenses?
3. Why do we have graduated income tax so that the rich pay a higher rate than the poor?

Arithmetical Reasoning
1. How many apples can you buy for eighty-one cents if each apple costs nine cents?
2. Three men can finish a job in nine days. How many men will it take to finish the job in three days?
3. An automobile goes twenty miles in thirty minutes. How many miles can it go in three minutes?

Digits Forwards and Backwards
1. (The subject repeats the following numbers in the order that they are read to him.) 3, 8, 4, 6, 2, 9, 1
2. (The subject repeats the following numbers in the reverse order that they are read to him.) 6, 4, 1, 8, 2, 5, 7

Similarities
(The subject is asked to tell in what way each of the following pairs of words is alike.)
1. Apple and Peach
2. Novel and Painting
3. Airplane and Train
4. Law and Command
5. Whale and Porpoise

Group Tests

You may not be familiar with the tests we have mentioned — although most college students have been exposed to intelligence testing — because they are individually administered while most general intelligence measuring is done with *group tests*. The military initially developed group tests during World War I to evaluate draftees' intellectual abilities. Individual tests would have been far too time-consuming. Two types of group tests were given: the *Army Alpha Test*, which was designed for those who could read, and the *Army Beta Test*, which was designed for draftees who did not speak English or were illiterate. Figure 15-1 gives examples of items from the Alpha and Beta tests.

Because of their experience with group tests, the military developed a more sophisticated group test during World War II. This test, the *Army*

15-1
Examples of test items from the Army Alpha and Beta tests. The Alpha test was intended for literate draftees. The Beta test was intended for non-English-speaking draftees and illiterates. (Yerkes, 1921)

ALPHA TEST: SAMPLE QUESTIONS

1. If it takes 6 men 3 days to dig a 180 foot drain, how many men are needed to dig it in half a day?

2. Freezing water bursts pipes because a) cold makes the pipes weaker; b) water expands when it freezes; c) the ice stops the flow of water.

3. Is the meaning of repress *the same as/opposite to the meaning of* restrain?

4. "certain some death of mean kinds sickness" When unscrambled is this sentence true or false?

5. 8 1 6 1 4 1 _ _ What numbers come next?

6. establish *is to* begin *as* abolish *is to slavery/wrong/abolition/end.*

Answers: 1. 36; 2. (*b*); 3. *same as;* 4. *Some kinds of sickness mean certain death — true;* 5. *2 and 1;* 6. *end.*

BETA TEST: SAMPLE QUESTIONS (*instructions given verbally and visually*)

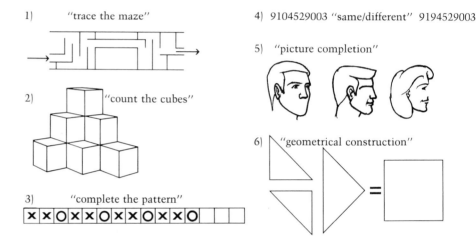

1) "trace the maze"

2) "count the cubes"

3) "complete the pattern"

4) 9104529003 "same/different" 9194529003

5) "picture completion"

6) "geometrical construction"

General Classification Test (AGCT), contained subscales on verbal material, spatial relations, arithmetic, and numerical reasoning. These tests are valuable research tools because they have been applied to literally millions of men, offering the researcher an enormous experimental population. Unfortunately, however, their sample is not necessarily representative of the entire population of men. In any event, the military, which is continually revising its tests (the latest being the *Armed Forces Qualification Test*), uses intelligence testing on an enormous scale, surpassed only by school testing.

The military use of intelligence scores is representative of testing in general. Below a certain intelligence score, draftees are rated as unfit for military duty and rejected. Those who surpass the minimum score should be placed in positions based on their abilities. Yet almost every veteran of military life knows about drafted accountants who are put to work repairing engines while mechanics are assigned work as accountants. In the great majority of cases, however, the military combines the scores obtained on intelligence tests with interest profiles, aptitude scales, personality evaluations, and interviews to determine the most suitable job for an individual.

Many group tests have been patterned after those of the military. Probably the most familiar to students is the *Scholastic Aptitude Test* (SAT), commonly known as the "College Boards," which is taken by many students who want to go to college. You also may be familiar with the *School and College Ability Tests* and the *Graduate Record Examination* for prospective graduate students.

Intelligence tests are constantly being modified and changed as a result of experience with the tests and new data compiled by research psychologists. The test you took is probably not the same as that taken 10 or even 5 years ago. Within 10 years, today's test also will have been altered. However, while the instrument will have changed to provide more detailed, accurate, or reliable results, the meaning of the intelligence measures will remain the same.

The Distribution of Intelligence

Measurement of intelligence, like that of so many other human qualities, finds most of us neither genius nor dunce, but firmly in the middle. As we have noted, IQ is a comparative figure, based on the individual's score in relation to a norm. The range of IQs forms a *bell-shaped* or "normal" curve; that is, most people are distributed around the middle (they are average) and relatively few are at either extreme. Distributions of height, weight, strength, running speed, and many other measurements resemble the same bell-shaped curve. This distribution makes the curve symmetrical around the *mean* or average (which is determined by adding all the scores and dividing by the number of scores). While natural phenomena usually do not fit a normal curve perfectly, they come quite close. The distribution of intelligence scores is not perfectly "normal" in that more individuals cluster at each extreme than would be expected.

Under the distribution of intelligence curve in Figure 15-2 are noted the *standard deviation* and the corresponding college board scores and percentile rankings for this distribution. The degree to which scores cluster close to the mean can be expressed by calculating a standard deviation (see Statistics Appendix), a descriptive statistic that expresses

15-2
The distribution of intelligence scores. The correspondence between IQ scores, standard deviation scores, college boards, and percentile rankings is shown below the graph. Note that a standard deviation from the mean, from 0 to 1 on the SD axis, is equivalent to the range from 100 to 116 in IQ, from 500 to 600 in college boards, and from 50 to 84 in percentile rankings. The percentages under the curve point out that 68% of the population falls within standard deviations of −1 to +1, 95% within −2 to +2, and about 99% within −3 to +3.

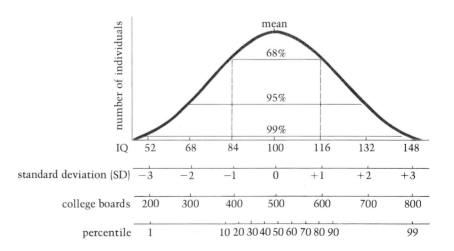

				mean			
				68%			
				95%			
				99%			
IQ	52	68	84	100	116	132	148
standard deviation (SD)	−3	−2	−1	0	+1	+2	+3
college boards	200	300	400	500	600	700	800
percentile	1			10 20 30 40 50 60 70 80 90			99

Two normal distributions with equal
means but unequal variances.

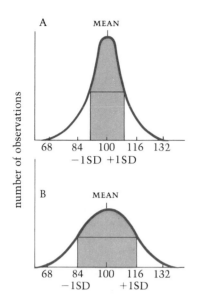

the deviation from the mean that accounts for approximately 34 percent
of all the observations or scores.

Figure 15-3 shows two bell-shaped distributions with approximately
the same range, from just under 68 to just over 132, and the same mean.
In this example, the shaded area under each curve includes two standard
deviations, one on either side of the mean (68 percent of all the observations). You can see that the range of scores that falls within the shaded
area is not the same for each curve. This is due to the greater variability
about the mean of curve B. Using mathematical methods, the dispersion
or *variance* of scores can be measured quite accurately. With a small
variance (A), most of the individual scores are close to the mean. With
large variance (B), the mean is not a very satisfactory representation of
the individual scores.

Limitations of Testing

Few of the tools devised by man are perfect. Intelligence-measuring
tools are no exception. Most of the reasons why these tests are not perfect have been identified and we shall discuss each briefly.

Validity

A prime requirement of any test is that it must demonstrably measure
what it claims to measure. If it does so, we call it a *valid* test. The lack
of a universally accepted definition of intelligence might seem to prevent an assessment of an intelligence test's validity. But in fact, we do
not rely on definitions. We know that the mental abilities that determine one's test performance also are used in school, work, and similar
settings. Thus, we can validate a test by the performance of people in a
specific setting.

For example, if you wanted to measure people's bicycle-repairing skills
you could do it in several ways. You could give a large number of people
a test of various mechanical, spatial, and logical abilities. You could
then compare the scores with the individuals' bicycle-repairing performances to see how many high scorers were good at repairing bicycles and
how many low scorers were inept at the task. In this setting, several results are possible. The higher scorers might be the best bicycle mechanics and the low scorers the worst. There might be no relation between
test scores and ability to repair bicycles. Alternatively, the low-scoring
people might be the best bicycle mechanics while the high scorers
might be the poorest. In the second case, the test is invalid because
you cannot predict mechanical ability from the test results. In the first
and third cases, the test scores predict performances and thus have validity, although the third test indicates the ability in an inverse manner.

A second way to validate a test would be to search out people skilled
in bicycle repair and administer the test to them and to a random
sample of the population. Test scores and demonstrated mechanical
abilities then could be compared, as in the first method. If the skilled
repairmen did better on the tests than the average of the random
sample, this, too, would indicate the validity of the tests.

Several issues become important at this point. Judging mechanical prowess—or any performance variable—is far from foolproof. Many factors besides the directly relevant mental abilities can interact to produce a good mechanic. The individual may have unremarkable abilities but he may work twice as diligently or twice as long as his fellow workers. He may be judged as excellent by those who have only experienced the very poor mechanic. To these people, he would appear to be excellent, when in fact he is average. Many other factors can distort an evaluation. Validity-testing relates two sets of judgments, one from a test and one from a real-life situation.

Consider school grades. A prime source of intelligence-test validation is children's academic performance, presumably reflected in their grades. Yet every student knows that his school performance depends on a vast array of interacting pressures and situations. A student may do poorly on an exam because of a quarrel, an illness, fatigue, an upsetting breakfast, or a hangover. He may do well because of a morale-boosting personal victory, an instructor's encouraging word, a good night's sleep, or because he relaxed at a movie the night before. Considering such factors, it is rather surprising that intelligence tests predict academic success as well as they do.

Can we assume that a test proved valid for bicycle repairing is valid for automobile repairing? Yes, if we *know* that automobile repairing requires abilities similar to those needed for bicycle repairing. Although we could make good guesses, this kind of information is not available. Therefore, the only way to extend the test's validity is to validate it on automobile mechanics. Remember, of course, that validity is not concerned with statements such as "You must have a high IQ to be a good auto mechanic." While that statement might be statistically true, many good mechanics don't have high IQs. Instead, validity says, "Intelligence test scores are related to and can predict to some extent performance in auto repairing or computer programming, for example."

Correlation Coefficient. Central to the concept of validity is the correspondence between the test scores and performance in the real-life situation. Correspondence between two sets of data can be mathematically expressed by a statistic termed a *correlation coefficient* (see Statistics Appendix). When applied to two sets of data, this statistic describes the degree of relationship between the sets of data. The statistic, called the *Pearson product moment* (r), has a value ranging from -1 through 0 to $+1$. A perfect positive correlation would receive an r of $+1.00$. In such a relationship, each individual would occupy the same rank order in the two sets of data (see Figure 15-4D). Zero correlation means that the scores are not related, permitting no predictions. A negative correlation of -1.00 means that the individual with the highest score on one scale received the lowest score on the other. Intermediate values simply mean varying degrees of positive or negative relation between sets of scores. Demonstrations of a test's validity usually are based upon correlation coefficients between test scores and some referent, such as school or work success. Most intelligence tests correlate with school performance at around $+0.6$, a degree of correlation that is far from perfect.

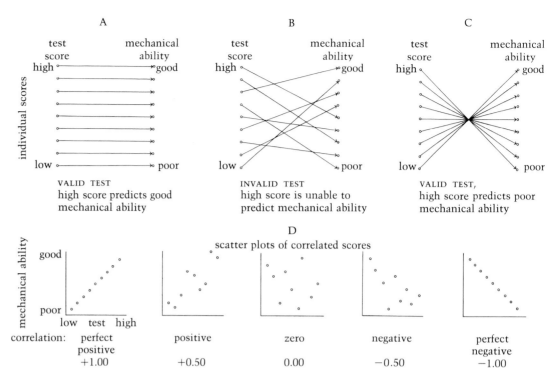

A

test score — mechanical ability
high ○———————→● good

individual scores

low ○———————→● poor

VALID TEST
high score predicts good
mechanical ability

B

test score — mechanical ability
high ○   ● good

low ○   ● poor

INVALID TEST
high score is unable to
predict mechanical ability

C

test score — mechanical ability
high ○   ● good

low ○   ● poor

VALID TEST,
high score predicts poor
mechanical ability

D

scatter plots of correlated scores

mechanical ability
good

poor
low   test   high

correlation: perfect   positive   zero   negative   perfect
               positive   negative
               +1.00   +0.50   0.00   −0.50   −1.00

15-4
Diagrammatic representations of valid (A and C) and invalid (B) tests. (D) shows five graphs of the correlations between two sets of data. In the perfect positive test ($r = 1$), low scores accurately predict poor mechanical ability. For the perfect negative test ($r = -1$) the correlation is just the reverse: low scores correlate to good ability and high scores to poor ability.

Reliability

If a test can consistently measure the same factor in the same subject and produce a similar score when it is repeated, it is a _reliable_ test. Any test's reliability can be measured by comparing the results obtained from two equal tests of an individual. The two equal tests can be (1) two forms of the test, (2) halves of the test produced by dividing the test items into two equal groups, or (3) a test and a subsequent retest using the same set of test items. Most intelligence tests have a reliability correlation coefficient of +0.9 or higher—much higher than for validity, indicating that it is much easier to construct a reliable test than a valid one.

Standardization

Upon whom should intelligence tests be standardized? The _standardization_ group should resemble in its characteristics the individuals who will be given the test. Such obvious characteristics as age, sex, racial background, educational level, height, and eye color are relatively easy to identify. But temperament, personality, and environmental variables often are hidden and more difficult to determine. Then, too, we are not sure that all of the relevant characteristics have been identified. In any event, the sample should represent the population as closely as possible. An alternative strategy is to select individuals purely at random. If the sample is truly random and large enough, it will represent the entire population.

Theories of the Structure of Intelligence

Attempts have been made to clarify the concept of intelligence by identifying the components of its total structure. Is its structure simple, consisting of one or two components, or is it more complex? A number of theories relating to this question have been developed.

Spearman's Factor Theory

An English psychologist, Charles Spearman, observed in 1927 that the interrelations between scores on a number of intelligence tests suggest that two "factors" affect the performance on any test item, or for that matter any real-life mental operation. One factor is a *general mental facility* ("g") necessary for any kind of intellectual functioning. Performance on any task requires the operation of an additional *specific mental capability* ("s") which is specific to that task. Excellence of performance on a given test depends on the possession of a general mental capability plus the operation of a more specific mental endowment. An individual's performance on a few items might be based on having a few exceptionally high "s" factors, whereas overall performance excellence is best understood as being related to a high "g" factor.

Spearman based his notions on analyses of test results using *factor analysis* (a statistical method that defines the intercorrelations between two sets of data), and he provided some evidence supporting his idea of a general intellectual capacity. However, his greatest contribution was that he opened the door for research into the idea of intelligence as a family of component factors.

Thurstone's Primary Mental Abilities

L. L. Thurstone, an American engineer turned psychologist, examined the same kind of test results as Spearman had. Thurstone determined that a combination of factors could better explain the test results. Using factor analysis, Thurstone examined various test forms given to a subject and found that seven common factors could account for the results. Essentially, Thurstone discarded Spearman's "s" and replaced his "g" with a set of factors, which he called *primary mental abilities* (Thurstone, 1938). These abilities are verbal comprehension, perception, visual spatial relations, numerical ability, memory, inductive and deductive reasoning, and verbal fluency. A subject's performance on any test item depends to varying degrees on one or more of these factors.

Thurstone was able to extract a profile of factor weightings on the basis of his factor analysis. Figure 15-5 shows a hypothetical profile for John Doe, from which we can make certain predictions about him. For example, we might expect that he would make a better salesman than an accountant.

Thurstone has presented evidence that common elements exist among the factors, which suggests the operation of an independent process, perhaps akin to Spearman's "g." Many persons exhibit groupings of factors that seem to go together, as in the case of John Doe's verbal abili-

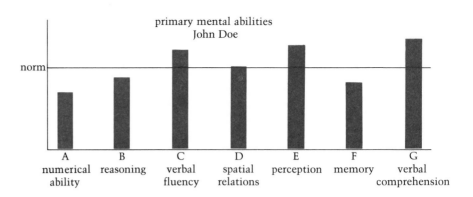

15-5

A hypothetical mental abilities profile as obtained on Thurstone's Primary Mental Abilities test.

FACTOR	DESCRIPTION
numerical ability	to manipulate numbers quickly and accurately
reasoning	to extract commonalities, to discern relationships and rules, to proceed logically
verbal fluency	to be facile with words
spatial relations	to visualize and manipulate objects in space
perception	to observe subtle stimuli quickly and accurately
memory	to remember symbols and relations
verbal comprehension	to understand words

ties. This has led some observers to suggest that these groupings be considered factors. Others have tended to whittle away at the factors as proposed by Thurstone, subdividing them even further.

Guilford's Structure of Intellect

Guilford views the _structure of intellect_ as the interaction between three processes: contents, operations, and products; each is subdivided into various elements. _Contents_ refers to what the individual deals with, the inputs and the materials he knows. _Operations_ refers to what the individual does with these things, his processing of the inputs. _Products_ refers to the end results, the individual's output.

In Guilford's three-dimensional multicomponent scheme, 120 separate factors (4 content factors × 5 operation factors × 6 product factors = 120) make up the whole of intellect (see Figure 15-6). If this model accurately reflects the structure of intellect, we should be able to find examples of all the postulated factors. Factor analysis is used to identify factors from the results of an intelligence test. Well over 100 have been identified. Is this the structure of intelligence? While we cannot firmly answer yes, we can say that the structure of intelligence, however formulated, is consistent with many such contemporary ideas.

On a practical level, investigations into the structure of intelligence have produced sweeping changes in intelligence assessment, particularly in such mass testing situations as schools, industry, and the military. The days of a single IQ score as the sole measure of intelligence probably are gone forever. In their place are testing instruments that provide subcomponents and factors. Scores are broken down into verbal,

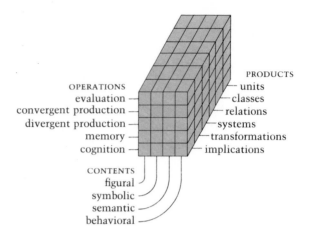

15-6
A diagram of Guilford's structure of intellect. Listed below are the subdivisions of Guilford's categories. (From *The Nature of Human Intelligence* by J. P. Guilford. Copyright 1967 by McGraw-Hill Book Company. Used with permission of McGraw-Hill Book Company)

CONTENTS
1. figural — concrete objects
2. symbolic — nonverbal concepts, e.g. number
3. semantic — verbal concepts
4. behavioral — interpersonal relations

OPERATIONS
1. evaluation — reflecting on past events
2. convergent production — determining the best solution for a problem
3. divergent production — devising multiple solutions for a problem
4. memory — storing or retrieving memories
5. cognition — understanding

PRODUCTS
1. units — single items of information
2. classes — multiple units with a common element(s)
3. relations — interdependences between two units
4. systems — more complex relations between many units
5. transformations — changing of information from one form to another
6. implications — the potential effect of information.

quantitative, and, other scales in an attempt to characterize the individual's intellectual abilities. We can expect that, as laboratory investigations delve further into the domain of intellect, their findings will quickly be translated into tests that will be used throughout this nation and the world.

Development of Intelligence

The environment interacts with a person's genetic endowment to modify the expression of the genes. To put it another way, nature provides a range of potential intelligence, but nurture determines the individual's location within the range. At present, the genetic component cannot be changed. However, the environmental component can

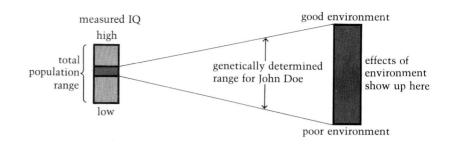

A diagram representing the interaction between genetic (nature) and environmental (nurture) factors in determining an individual's performance on an intelligence test. In a good environment, a person will score at his highest possible level; but, under the influence of a poor environment, he will score at the lower end of his genetically determined range.

be changed, often without great difficulty. In short, the chief hindrances to improving the environment and thus IQ scores are political and economic ones.

Genetic Factors in Intelligence

We are the products of an immense amount of genetic information transmitted from our parents. They, in turn, received genetic information from their parents. Any individual having offspring is contributing his gene set to the gene pool of the total population. From this pool, endless new combinations are made. If an individual does not have offspring, his genetic contribution to the total gene pool is lost forever. Genetically handicapped individuals are often unable to create offspring, and therefore do not contribute their genes to the pool. Thus, certain gene sets are eliminated and others are selected to endure. Behaviors, to the extent that they are genetically determined, are retained by this procedure of natural selection.

Genetic information in man is encoded in about ten million genes. While many genes operate singly, making their functions easier to study, such complex operations as intelligence probably involve thousands of genes operating in unison. While we do not know how these genes interrelate, we can guess that the relationship is highly complex. Nevertheless, a single gene can have a powerful effect on the operation of all the other genes affecting a polygenic (many genes) trait. The PKU genetic defect provides an especially clear illustration of this. This disease is due to a single flawed gene, which causes an enzyme to increase the conversion of one amino acid, phenylalanine, into another, tyrosine. The result is that abnormal chemicals build up in the body level, causing mental retardation. Luckily for the victims, this genetic deficiency can be overcome by restricting them to foods that contain no phenylalanine. The point is that while intelligence is a polygenic trait, it can be markedly affected by a single gene.

Performance on intelligence tests depends on many factors. Among them are the capacities to learn and to remember. What role does genetics play in these abilities? Studies suggest that memory, as measured on common intelligence tests, is not primarily under genetic control. Vandenberg (1967) made statistical comparisons of the variation between the intelligence scores of identical and nonidentical twins. The instruments used included the Wechsler Intelligence Scale for Children and Thurstone's Primary Mental Abilities (PMA) Test. Since the twins all were reared in similar environments, any statistical difference between their scores was presumed to be primarily due to genetic factors. Of the seven PMA scales (number, verbal, spatial, word fluency, reasoning, perception, and memory), only reasoning and memory failed to show strong heritability components. Thus, genes do not seem to play a role in these two aspects of intelligence.

In many instances, the environment greatly influences a gene's expression. The defective gene responsible for PKU only causes trouble when the diet (that is, the environment) contains phenylalanine. With intelligence, too, the interaction of genes, environment, and environmental history is critical. Thus, one can simultaneously hold both nature and nurture interpretations of intelligence—that is, one can hold to an *interactionist* viewpoint. At some point, the argument becomes pointless. After all, an environment must act upon an organism and the organism is specified by genetic conditions—but on the other hand, a genetic endowment has meaning only in relation to an environment.

Twin Studies. As we noted in Chapter 2, nature has provided science with a neat experimental situation for investigating the relative contribution of genes and environment: twins. Because identical (monozygotic) twins are derived from a single fertilized egg, they have *identical genetic structures.* In most cases, their environmental history is similar since they live with the same parents. While fraternal (dizygotic) twins do not have identical genes, they too usually have similar environmental histories. If a psychologist compares the intelligence factors of identical and fraternal twins, he can estimate the degree to which their genes determine their intelligence.

Figure 15-8 shows the results of many experiments, involving over 30,000 pairings of twins and nontwins. The people tested ranged from

15-8
The results of many experiments on the role of genetics in determining intelligence are summarized here. The colored areas are the range (± one standard deviation) of correlations of IQ scores for people of varying degrees of genetic similarity. The lines connect the median (most frequently occurring) scores from each group. (Erlenmeyer-Kimling, L., & Jarvik, L. F. Genetics and intelligence: A review. Science, 1963, **142,** 1477–1479. Copyright 1963 by the American Association for the Advancement of Science)

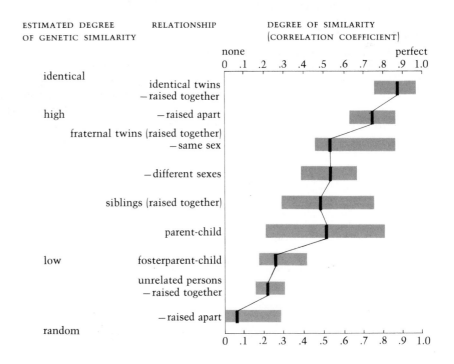

twins with identical genetic structure who were raised together, to unrelated people raised apart. These categories are listed from top to bottom in order of *decreasing* genetic similarity. The degree of IQ similarity for each pair of people tested is represented by a correlation coefficient. The identical twins raised together (identical genetics, very similar environment) have close to perfect correlations: +0.87. The correlations are not perfect due to slight differences in the twins' environments and the tests' own inherent imperfections, which are relatively minor. A retest correlation coefficient of 0.90 (obtained by giving a test twice to the same person and comparing the two scores) indicates a very reliable test.

Looking at Figure 15-8, we can see a definite pattern. Intelligence scores become more similar as the degree of genetic similarity increases. There is virtually no relationship between the intelligence test scores of unrelated persons raised together. By contrast, there is almost a perfect relationship between the scores of identical twins who have been raised together.

In an experiment in which over 1,500 English school children were tested (Burt, 1966), the results also indicate a high correspondence between genetic and intellectual similarity (see Figure 15-9). Interestingly, the various educational attainments that were examined varied primarily according to environmental features. Few investigators in this area deny the importance of environmental input.

15-9
The degree of similarity (expressed in correlation coefficients) in IQ scores, educational attainments, and weight for English children of varying degrees of genetic similarity. (Burt, 1966)

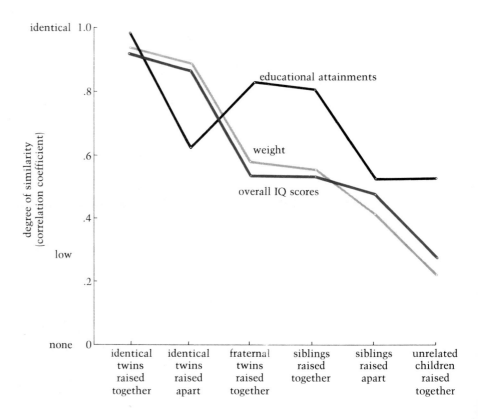

Environmental Factors in Intelligence

A great many environmental factors influence intelligence: income level, social class, culture, and education. Psychologists have studied many of these factors in the light of racial differences. The ambiguity of the concept of race is a concern common to any interpretation of racial intelligence scores. Race, per se, is a biological concept that takes into account a genetic history that diverged from a common ancestor, and because of selection pressures, now possesses some distinguishing characteristics. These characteristics include anatomical proportions, stature, skin color, eye color, hair type and color, facial structure, and surface fat distribution.

One of the great racial myths which endures today in this country is that blacks generally have inferior intelligence. Research has shown that the overlap in intelligence between the white and black populations is much greater than some authorities had believed. Tests to date have indicated an average difference of 15 IQ points. However, the range of variation of intelligence scores *within* the white population, or within the black population, far exceeds any average difference *between* whites and blacks. Intelligent as well as unintelligent persons can be found in both populations; only the frequency within the population differs. There are several possible reasons for this difference in frequency.

Education. It is generally accepted that the schooling of American blacks has been inferior to that of white students, particularly in the South. Given this situation, it seems likely that the chances to attend better schools would result in higher IQ scores for blacks — reasoning that is borne out in studies comparing southern and northern school children. The northern black child invariably scores higher on the average than the southern black child. Another interpretation of this fact is that many of the most intelligent and able blacks migrated to the North and as a result their children appeared in the northern schools. The Army Alpha tests of World War I indicated that the intelligence of the northern black recruit (from New York, Ohio, Illinois) surpassed that of the southern black recruit (*and* the southern white recruit) from Arkansas, Kentucky, and Mississippi. This difference may indicate that environmental stimulation can raise IQ scores appreciably. The converse — that an impoverished environment will lower IQ scores — probably also is true, though research can support it only indirectly since no scientist would place a person from a good environment in a poor environment for a long period simply to study the results of such deprivation.

In a now-classic experiment, Lee (1951) tested the intelligence of black children in Philadelphia according to how long they had lived and attended school in that city. He followed the same children through several years of schooling and evaluated the school exposure's effect on their intelligence scores. Table 15-4 presents the average IQs of the various groups of black children. This table clearly shows that the length of exposure to northern schools relates to increased IQ scores, suggesting that the black children's IQs rose due to Philadelphia's superior educational environment.

Table 15-4 Measured IQ (Lee, 1951)

Group	First Grade	Fourth Grade	Ninth Grade
Philadelphia born —kindergarten	96.7	97.2	96.6
Philadelphia born —no kindergarten	92.1	94.7	93.7
Southern born —attended Philadelphia school at grade			
—one	86.5	91.8	92.8
—one and two		88.6	90.5
—three and four		86.3	89.4
—five and six			90.2
—seven through nine			87.4

Culture. Black Americans make up a large part of the nation's poor. Some observers have argued that this relative cultural and class handicap has resulted in lower IQ scores. Such a possibility clearly exists, given the disparity between black and white family income and the fact that stimulating experiences (books, travel, museum trips), which presumably affect intellectual development, are often costly. One study attempting to equate economic and social status (at the low end of the spectrum) found that about one-third of the black/white difference could be eliminated by equalizing the groups' socioeconomic status (Bruce, 1940). This indicates that cultural handicaps may be substantial obstacles to IQ parity between individuals.

Intelligence tests in common use in America were designed for and standardized predominantly on white, middle-class, American-born children. If it is correct to speak of the "black subculture" as a distinct entity, then cultural differences between black and white may be responsible for any IQ score differences. The black subculture uses a somewhat different vocabulary and grammar and professes somewhat different values and priorities. In addition, the experiences and knowledge that form a base for intelligence test items may be somewhat different for blacks and whites. While the cultural differences are not huge or applicable to all Americans, overall, the cultures are not identical, a fact that can produce inaccuracies in intelligence assessment. Essentially, blacks and whites are similar in "real" intelligence, but cultural bias in test standardization puts blacks today at a disadvantage on standard IQ tests. To illustrate the point of cultural differences, consider the Eskimo. His language contains over 20 words describing various snow and ice conditions. A test standardized on Eskimo culture and experiences might well contain questions relating to these natural phenomena. American children—white or black—being foreign to these experiences, would do poorly on such a test. Would it be correct to conclude that the American children were less intelligent than the Eskimo—or vice versa? Similar mechanisms may be operating on the black child, although surely not to the same degree.

15-10

The relationships between the environments in which students live and their reading abilities in comparison to the national averages (upper chart) and the relationships between the educational levels of the students' parents and the students' reading abilities (lower chart). (*The New York Times*, 1974)

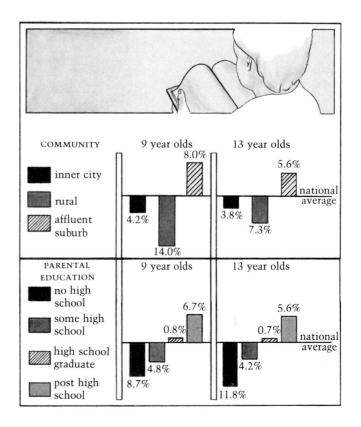

The cultural-bias argument also relates to racial differences in verbal abilities, temperament, and motivation. When intelligence testing first started in the United States, illiteracy was much more common among blacks than whites (who also were quite illiterate compared to today). While the black/white illiteracy imbalance is dramatically reduced today, blacks may remain less literate due to differing cultural emphases on verbal abilities. Such a difference would handicap blacks, since most intelligence test items rely heavily on verbal skills.

Racial differences in temperament also have been cited as contributors to IQ score differences. Most intelligence tests operate with a time limit, which makes speed an important indicator of intellectual performance. Across racial groups, the differing emphasis on speed may lead to inconsistent results.

A generally similar argument says that motivation differences between the races account for IQ differences. For example, the cultural framework for white motivational pressures to succeed in competition draws from such wellsprings as the Puritan Ethic. The black subculture does not have this degree of culturally determined motivational pressure.

Social Class.   America today is not a classless society. Social classes do exist and all classes do not have an equal distribution of measured intelligence. Higher socioeconomic status usually implies higher intelligence scores. Figure 15-11 shows the average IQs of children of various social classes listed by parental occupational level. These averages represent an enormous range of scores. The numbers on the

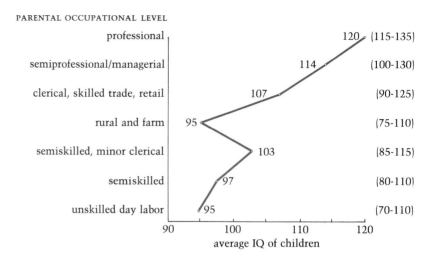

15-11
The average IQs of children of various socioeconomic classes as defined by occupational category. The figures in parentheses indicate the IQ range of the central 75% of each group. (Adapted from McNemar, Q. *The Revision of the Stanford-Binet Scale,* Houghton Mifflin, 1942; Johnson, 1948; and Harrell & Harrell, 1945)

right are estimates of the IQ range of the central three-quarters of the people in each occupational category. The range narrows near the top of the socioeconomic scale because of a nonsymmetrical relationship: mentally handicapped people cannot be professional people but intelligent people can be laborers. Thus, the upper occupational groups have built-in range-limiting factors but the lower ones do not.

Socioeconomic status, high or low, carries with it certain implications. The environmental constraints or benefits deriving from low or high status are fairly obvious. These advantages and disadvantages pervade all facets of a developing child's life: nutrition, availability of educational materials in the home, varied experiences, contact with stimulating individuals and events, medical care, status-connected values, and others. What may not be so obvious are the genetic implications of socioeconomic class membership. Our political-social system is basically a meritocracy; most Americans earn their positions through performance. An individual's social class position depends heavily on his genetically determined merits or abilities. The result is social class membership that is associated with particular genetic endowments. According to some (Herrnstein, 1973), these genetic determinants will become more and more important in our increasingly technological world.

Biological Factors

Heredity's sizable role in determining intelligence could lead naturally to the belief that observed differences between racial or ethnic groups are due partially to genetic differences between the groups. Indeed, discussion of this possibility has produced some of the liveliest and, on occasion, most violent debate ever known in the world of social science. The term "Jensenism" entered our vocabulary as a result of the writings of Arthur Jensen, who has generally defended the position that genetic factors may well play a significant role in producing observed IQ differences between blacks and whites in our society.

We have little reason to question the considerable importance of genetic factors as determinants of measured intelligence. However, heredity's possible role in producing *group* differences in intelligence presents an enormously more complicated situation. Although a massive array of evidence bears at least indirectly upon this question, that evidence does not definitively prove that hereditary factors influence ethnic differences in IQ. No doubt, further studies will help resolve the current ambiguity.

For now we should recall that average differences between groups in measured IQ tell us nothing about individual performance. Further, the great overlap in performance between ethnic groups prompts one to think in terms of the individual rather than his ethnic background. Moreover, social policy (government programs of compensatory education or adequate nutrition for all citizens, for example) does not depend on the relative importance of environmental or genetic factors as determinants of intelligence. Almost anything that might enhance the intellectual performance of groups that currently are below the national average should be done, regardless of whether the groups' observed deficiency is rooted in their genes or in their environment.

Does Intelligence Decline With Age?

If intelligence tests measure mental characteristics that are inherited at conception and developed primarily during youth, then it seems reasonable to assume that an individual's measured intelligence should remain constant throughout life. Indeed, evidence does suggest that IQ remains constant or increases slightly from the preschool to subteen years. Data on over 600 children tested at age 2 and again at age 10 show that IQ scores increased only 5 points (Werner, Honzik, & Smith, 1968). A similar longitudinal study of 600 children tested at 8 months and again at 7 years indicated no change in IQ for the average child (Goffeney, Henderson, & Butler, 1971). There is some doubt about these data. The subjects' age-related abilities require that different tests be used at test (8 months) and retest (7 years), thus hampering comparisons between the performances at the two ages.

Preschool tests also are of questionable validity. Figure 15-12A shows one difficulty associated with making IQ measurements on preschool children. The IQ determined at age 3 is highly correlated with only the fourth- and sixth-year IQ measures and not beyond those ages. This means the third-year IQ measure is not a very good basis for prediction. Figure 15-12B shows the correlation between various test ages up to year 12. Again, the same phenomenon occurs — a relative failure of preschool tests to predict future IQ scores accurately.

After school years, IQ remains relatively constant and may continue to increase slowly until 20 or 30 years of age. Thereafter, full-scale IQ declines. However, if we separate out the verbal and the performance-related items, verbal abilities remain constant while performance measures decline (Jones & Conrad, 1933). Since most intelligence tests are closely timed, any slowing of response produces a lower IQ score. Old people may be working at a disadvantage due to physical ailments, poor

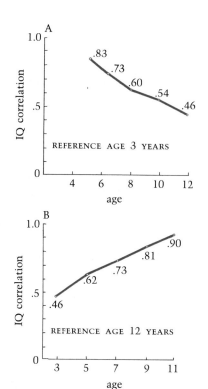

15-12
(A) Correlation coefficients between intelligence scores obtained at age 3 and scores obtained later in childhood. (B) Correlation coefficients obtained between various ages when the reference age is 12 years. The data are from a longitudinal study of the same individuals. (Sontag, Baker, & Nelson, 1958)

sight, or the general debilitating effects of aging. If a subject has an unlimited time to complete the test, significantly less decline occurs. Another common problem with age-related studies on intelligence is that older people were educated when schooling was not as available or as good as it is today. Intelligence test items depend on and are related to educational experiences. So, here too, older people may be operating under a handicap. The solution: a longitudinal study following a group of people from childhood into old age. For reasons of time and cost primarily, such studies have not been done.

Aging may have yet another effect on measured intelligence. Every day of our lives, neurons are being destroyed; the cumulative effect over time must be large. Many old people suffer minor strokes that destroy small portions of the brain. As most of us know from personal experience, the effects of aging on intelligence vary a great deal from person to person. Some individuals have agile, "bear-trap" minds at 95; others seem "dotty" in their late 60s.

Extremes of Intelligence

Most of us by definition have average intelligence. However, as we have noted, there are relatively small groups at each extreme of the normal curve for intelligence: the mentally gifted and the mentally retarded. Both groups require society's attention because both have special needs that require special treatment.

Mentally Gifted

About 3 percent of the world's population has an IQ over 130. These individuals receive society's rewards; their educational achievements, professional and social standing, income, health, and general happiness are all higher than average (Terman, 1959). The Terman investigation is a longitudinal study of over 1,000 children with an average IQ of 150, who were selected in 1922 from school children in the vicinity of California's Stanford University. Ever since, these children have been "followed." Periodically, the current custodians of this long-lived experiment issue evaluations of their subjects' progress and status.

The gifted children were drawn primarily from the families of professional and managerial people; less than 10 percent were from working-class families. This was not an intentional bias, merely a reflection of where high intelligence is concentrated in society. The sample's 800 males achieved much higher educational levels than the average for 800 men selected at random. Nearly 125 men held M.D. or Ph.D. degrees; 85 held law degrees and over 100 had engineering degrees. By 1959, the group had produced 60 nonfiction books, more than 2000 scientific papers, more than 30 novels, over 350 short stories and plays, and at least 230 patents—a level of activity clearly superior to a "more typical" group of people.

The subjects of the experiment were heavier at birth; as children they were healthier and taller than their peers. They generally walked and talked at an early age and were leaders in social groups. As children and adults, they did not fit the stereotype of the brilliant "bookworm" who is sickly, introverted, and dull. Their histories also belied the myth that genius and madness are closely related; their incidence of mental illness and suicide were below the national average. In short, these individuals appear to be well adjusted socially and intellectually, and have reaped society's rewards of money and prestige for their accomplishments.

Mentally Retarded

About 6 million Americans have IQs below 70. About 5 percent of these people are so mentally incapacitated—having an IQ below 25—that they require institutional care. Table 15-5 lists typical achievement and developmental characteristics of the mentally handicapped. This list intentionally omits such descriptive labels as imbecile, moron, profoundly retarded, feebleminded, and subnormal. While there is nothing inherently wrong with such labels, in practice they almost always devolve into slang expressions of insult.

Table 15-5 is related primarily to intellectual and sensory-motor skills. It also alludes to the social development of mentally handicapped individuals. In general, social handicaps correlate with mental ones. Individuals do continue to learn social skills throughout life and will attain a higher "social age" equivalent than their mental age equivalent. A mentally handicapped man of 25 may have a mental age of 10 years; his social age may be 12 or 13 years.

Few mentally handicapped individuals ever assume social or career positions of importance and influence. Indeed, many are fortunate to be employed at all. One characteristic of our technological society has been the machine's elimination of tedious and repetitive jobs. Unfortunately, these are the very jobs that the mentally handicapped person can do well. Charity often is the last thing the handicapped person wants or needs. He much prefers a sense of personal worth, of belonging and being needed; often, these feelings are very difficult for him to achieve. The frequent lack of such feelings among the mentally handicapped may help explain why so many of these people gravitate toward antisocial activity, such as delinquency, prostitution, and crime.

In rare cases, some mentally handicapped individuals, known as *idiot-savants*, can perform prodigious mental feats. One such individual has been reported to be able to recite correctly the day of the week for any date over a range of thousands of years. He also can tell, for example, all of the years in which November 25 fell on a Wednesday. These feats are amazing, especially when one knows that the subject cannot add, subtract, multiply, or divide even simple numbers (Horwitz, Kestenbaum, Person, & Jarvik, 1965). Another such individual could remember a page of numbers for months after looking at it only briefly (Luria, 1968). While they are astounding in their contrasts, these examples also emphasize our almost total ignorance of the brain's functioning in either the handicapped or the normal person.

Primary and Secondary Retardation. By and large, modern medicine cannot "cure" the mentally handicapped individual. While he can be helped to develop to his utmost capacity, we usually cannot correct his basic disability. However, it is possible that in the future others like him will be cured if we can finally understand the brain mechanisms that underlie the individual's handicap.

There are two broad kinds of mental handicap: primary retardation and secondary retardation. _Primary retardation_ reflects the operation of genetic mechanisms. In individuals with primary retardation, no medical defects, accidents, diseases, or traumas are responsible for the handicap. As we have seen, measured intelligence has a sizable genetic com-

Table 15-5   _Typical Achievement and Developmental Characteristics of the Mentally Handicapped_

Measured IQ	% of Population (est.)	Birth–5 yrs.	6–20 yrs.	21 yrs.–Death
50–70 (equiv. to an avg. 8–12 year old)	2.1 *(4,200,000)	Rarely distinguished from normal at this age; slight deficit in sensory-motor skills; can develop language & social skills.	Maximal school achievement is 6th grade by late teens; can benefit from special education.	Can hold job and maintain social relations in structured, stable environment; needs help under severe stress.
35–50 (equiv. to an avg. 6–8 year old)	0.6 *(1,200,000)	Poor social awareness; can learn to communicate; moderate sensory motor deficits; can benefit from self-help training; needs moderate supervision.	Maximal school achievement is 4th grade by late teens if given special help.	Can hold semi- or unskilled job in stable environment; needs help under mild stress.
20–35 (equiv. to an avg. 3–6 year old)	0.2 *(400,000)	No social awareness; minimal benefit from self-help training; poor sensory-motor development; little communication.	Cannot benefit from traditional schooling; can learn to communicate; can benefit from systematic, special training in areas like personal hygiene.	Can help contribute to self-support under total supervision; can function in stable, controlled environment.
Below 20 (equiv. to an avg. newborn to 3 yr. old)	0.1 *(200,000)	Requires nursing care; severe sensory-motor retardation; little or no communication; unable to benefit from self-help training.	Needs complete care; may develop some communication; cannot benefit from special training.	Some motor skills and speech development; incapable of self-maintenance; requires total care and supervision.

* Estimated number of Americans in each category.

Adapted from J. F. Kennedy, "Mental illness and mental retardation: a message from the President of the United States." _Amer. Psychol._ **18**:280–289, 1963. W. Sloan & J. W. Birch, "A rationale for degrees of retardation." _Am. J. Ment. Deficiency,_ **60**:262, 1955. R. L. Masland, S. B. Sarason, & T. Gladwyn, _Mental Subnormality._ New York: Basic Books, 1958. G. W. Kisker, _The disorganized personality._ New York: McGraw-Hill, 1964.

ponent. We also have seen that a population's distribution of IQ is nearly statistically "normal"—that is, the bulk of cases lie in the middle range with a few high and a few low cases. Thus, from our knowledge of the normal distribution of intelligence we can expect some persons of low intelligence to be born. As expected, the parents of handicapped individuals often are themselves handicapped. In many of these cases, the family history is replete with mentally handicapped individuals.

Secondary retardation results from brain injury. It may have occurred in the womb, during birth, or at any time after birth (although a brain-injured adult or older child is rarely labeled "retarded"). Brain injury may arise from a number of sources. An infection in a pregnant woman, such as syphilis or measles, can produce brain damage in the fetus. Several other prenatal influences can result in fetal brain damage. A few of these are excessive exposure to radiation, drugs such as the infamous Thalidomide (which resulted in many varied birth defects as well as mental handicaps), and poor nutrition. Child delivery holds several possibilities for brain damage, including mechanical damage to the brain from forceps and lack of oxygen. Once born, the child still is not safe. Infection and high fever, drug poisoning, and transmitted genetic defects, such as phenylketonuria (PKU, see page 514) and mongolism (a genetic defect giving the child 47 rather than the normal 46 chromosomes) can take their toll.

Nothing short of "genetic surgery" can prevent primary retardation. Prospects for eliminating secondary retardation are quite a different story. As the causes of mental handicaps become known, they can be guarded against. Today, we know much about what women should and should not do during pregnancy. We also know that much of the brain damage that occurs after birth is avoidable. In many cases, we need only apply our knowledge to reduce secondary retardation. This effort has several social implications. It means that *all* citizens should have access to prompt medical attention, adequate diet, and sufficient education so that they can develop their capacities to their full potential. In addition, medical research will undoubtedly uncover more examples of genetic or biochemical defects, such as PKU, which can be counteracted, thus preventing brain damage. Overall, the long-range outlook for the reduction of secondary retardation is quite bright.

Summary

1. The concept of intelligence has no precise and widely accepted definition.

2. The first test of intelligence was devised by Alfred Binet and Theodore Simon in 1905. Its aim was to identify students who were intellectually impaired.

3. Later revisions included the concepts of chronological age (CA), the subject's actual age in years, and mental age (MA), his performance at tasks for which age norms for competence had been set. Using MA and CA, Stern developed a formula for IQ: MA/CA × 100, which allowed classification of the entire range of intelligence.

4. In the United States, Lewis Terman developed the Stanford-Binet test, which includes scales to determine the IQ of adults. A drawback of this early test was that only American-born white children were sampled.

5. The Wechsler Adult Intelligence Scale (WAIS) was the first widely used test to incorporate several measures of intelligence, classified into verbal and performance categories. A later version, known as the Wechsler Intelligence Scale for Children (WISC), also used this approach.

6. For purposes of efficiency, group tests were developed, initially by the military during World War I. A more sophisticated Army General Classification Test (AGCT) was developed during World War II, containing subscales on verbal material, spatial relations, and numerical reasoning. Recently, the Armed Forces Qualification Test was introduced. Group tests for students include the familiar Scholastic Aptitude Test (SAT).

7. The distribution of individual scores in relation to a norm forms a bell-shaped curve, symmetrical around the average. The degree to which scores cluster close to the mean can be expressed by calculating a standard deviation.

8. The validity of a test is the degree to which it measures what it is supposed to measure. Demonstrations of a test's validity are usually based upon correlation coefficients between test scores and some referent in a real-life situation.

9. The reliability of a test is its ability to measure consistently the same factor in an individual on different occasions.

10. Intelligence tests may be standardized by selecting a sample, or standardization group, that resembles the individuals who will take the test. Another method is to select a large number of individuals purely at random.

11. An early theory of the structure of intelligence was developed by Charles Spearman. He suggested two factors: a general mental facility ("g") necessary for any intellectual functioning and a specific mental capability ("s") for specific tasks.

12. L. L. Thurstone suggested a set of factors called primary mental abilities. They are verbal comprehension, perception, memory, reasoning, spacial relations, verbal fluency, and numerical ability.

13. A more elaborate theory by J. P. Guilford views intelligence as composed of the interaction between three processes: contents (what the individual knows), operations (what the individual does to process the material), and products (the individual's output). According to Guilford, the whole of intellect involves 120 separate factors.

14. The range of an individual's potential intelligence is determined in part by genetic factors. Environment can greatly influence a gene's expression.

15. Differences in the quality of education, in cultural exposure, values and priorities, and in socioeconomic status—affecting nutrition, medical care, and other elements—present obstacles in the use of intelligence

tests that have been standardized on white, middle-class, American-born children.

16. Evidence suggests that IQ remains constant or increases slightly from the preschool to subteen years, remains constant or increases slowly until 20 or 30 years of age, then declines in terms of performance measures while verbal abilities remain constant. Physical ailments, poor eyesight, fewer opportunities for schooling, and the destruction of neurons are some factors that may account for an IQ decline in the elderly.

17. Mentally gifted individuals, with IQs over 130, comprise about 3 percent of the world's population.

18. Mentally retarded individuals, with IQs below 70, number about 6 million Americans. Some mentally handicapped individuals, known as idiot-savants, can perform prodigious mental feats. Two broad kinds of mental handicap are primary retardation (people who are born with low intelligence due to genetic factors), and secondary retardation (people with some form of brain injury, occurring either in the womb, during birth, or at any time after birth).

Important Terms

norm

Binet & Simon Test

mental age

chronological age

intelligence quotient (IQ)

Stanford-Binet Tests

Wechsler Adult Intelligence Scale (WAIS)

Wechsler Intelligence Scale for Children (WISC)

normal distribution (bell-shaped curve)

mean

standard deviation (SD)

variance

validity

correlation coefficient

reliability

standardization

Spearman's factor theory

Thurstone's primary mental abilities

Guilford's structure of intellect

primary retardation

secondary retardation

Suggested Readings

ANASTASIA, A. *Psychological testing.* 3rd ed. New York: Macmillan, 1968.
    An introduction to the principles of psychological testing, including discussions of the major types of tests in current use. Assumes no statistics background.

BUROS, O. K. (ED.) *The mental measurements yearbook.* Highland Park, N. J.: The Gryphon Press, 1938–1972.

Seven editions of this "yearbook" have been published since 1938. They contain up-to-date bibliographies of all work done in psychological testing, and critical reviews of tests and books on testing.

CRONBACH, L. J. *Essentials of psychological testing.* 2nd ed. New York: Harper, 1960.

A basic course in testing, discussing test development, history, effectiveness, and validity. For undergraduates and beginning graduate students.

GUILFORD, J. P. *The nature of human intelligence.* New York: McGraw-Hill, 1967.

A presentation of the author's research into the multifactor nature of intelligence. Mathematically difficult reading.

MATARAZZO, J. D. *Wechsler's measurement and appraisal of adult intelligence.* Baltimore: Williams and Wilkins, 1972.

A comprehensive, up-to-date, and stimulating discussion of intelligence and Wechsler's approach to its measurement.

MUSSEN, P. H. *Carmichael's handbook of child psychology.* 3rd ed. New York: Wiley, 1970.

Vol. I, Chapter 16, by Nancy Bayley, is a synthesis of the work done in the past three decades on theories of intelligence, types of intelligence testing, and the effects of heredity and environment on the development of intelligence.

VERNON, P. E. *The structure of human abilities.* Rev. Ed. London: Methuen, 1960.

A historical, theoretical discussion of intelligence and ability testing, based on the principles of factor analysis. Assumes knowledge of elementary psychology and statistics.

HERRNSTEIN, R. J. *IQ in the meritocracy.* Boston: Atlantic-Little, Brown, 1973.

The author contends that intelligence is heritable and that, consequently, egalitarian social programs (if they are successful) will lead to a hereditary aristocracy. A challenging and stimulating book.

Chapter 16 Personality: Theories and Issues

Woman must come of age by herself. This is the essence of "coming of age"—to learn how to stand alone. She must learn not to depend on another, nor to feel she must prove her strength by competing with another. In the past, she has swung between these two opposite poles of dependence and competition, of Victorianism and Feminism. Both extremes throw her off balance; neither is the center, the true center of being a whole woman. She must find her true center alone. She must become whole. She must, it seems to me, . . . follow the advice of the poet to become "world to oneself for another's sake."

In fact, I wonder if both man and woman must not accomplish this heroic feat. Must not man also become world to himself? Must he not also expand the neglected sides of his personality; the art of inward looking that he has seldom had time for in his active outward-going life; the personal relationships which he has not had as much chance to enjoy; the so-called feminine qualities, aesthetic, emotional, cultural and spiritual, which he has been too rushed to fully develop? Perhaps both men and women in America may hunger, in our material, outward, active, masculine culture, for the supposedly feminine qualities of heart, mind and spirit—qualities which are actually neither masculine nor feminine, but simply human qualities that have been neglected. It is growth along these lines that will make us whole, and will enable the individual to become world to himself.

—Anne Morrow Lindbergh
(*Gift from the Sea*)

Personality: Theories and Issues

Two girls are discussing a boy; one asks, "What kind of a personality does he have?" and the other replies, "Oh, he has a very nice personality." What does her reply mean? Very likely it means she sees him as being friendly, considerate, dependable, and responsive. Now imagine that the same boy is being discussed by two boys, and the boy who knows him is asked the same question by the other boy. He replies "Oh, he just hasn't any personality at all." This means he lacks those characteristics that would impress another boy. In these contexts, personality is defined as the impression a person makes on others. When it is defined this way, personality lies in the eyes of the beholder rather than in the individual. Consequently, a person may have a number of personalities depending on who is describing him.

Psychologists regard personality in a different way. For them, personality is not a measure of one's popularity, although the question of why some people are popular, attractive, and well liked and others are not is an interesting area of psychological investigation. Nor is personality considered to be something some people have and others do not. The psychological view is that everyone has a personality that can be objectively described.

Although psychologists have many theories about personality, they generally agree that _personality_ is an organization of qualities that reside in and characterize an individual. What these qualities are, how they originate and develop, how permanent they are and what affects them, and how they are organized—these are questions for which we have many answers. In no other field of psychology are there so many contrasting theories. Why is this? Because personality is such a complex entity. It encompasses the whole person and not just a single process like perception, memory, and thought; it can be viewed from many perspectives.

Each theory has its adherents and its defenders, as well as its critics. More important, these theories have had practical consequences. They have influenced the practice of psychotherapy and counseling, affected the ways in which children are raised and educated, led to the construction of many types of tests and other methods for assessing personality, and generated an immense amount of research. Well-thought-out theories of personality, based on careful observation and experiment, can be extremely useful and practical.

In this chapter, we shall describe a number of modern theories of personality. You probably will find some of these theories more appealing than others, but we urge you not to take sides before giving them all a fair hearing. If you do this, you may find something of value for you in every one of the theories. Remember that each theory has grown out of the experiences of a person who has devoted his life to observing people in the clinic and consulting room, or to performing experiments and devising personality measures in the laboratory. Every theory to be presented here represents an organization and systemization of the theorist's experiences. For that reason alone, each merits our close attention.

Psychodynamic Theories

Psychodynamic theories emphasize the impelling unconscious, inborn, and often irrational motives that direct and control our behavior. They stress the dramatic interplay among man's instinctual life, the stark realities of his environment, and the restraints of society. These theories portray the age-old conflict between impulse and reason. They descend into the underworld of nightmares and dreams, nameless terrors, neurotic conflicts, symbols, rituals, taboos, myths, and occult phenomena, to reach the ultimate roots of human nature.

Psychodynamic conceptions of man are exemplified by the theories of Sigmund Freud, C. G. Jung, and Henry Murray.

Freud's Psychoanalytic Theory

Freud was the founder of *psychoanalysis*, which, as we noted earlier, is a way of examining the psychic mechanisms and content that an individual usually cannot explore through a rational examination of his own consciousness. Trained as a psychiatrist, Freud spent his life treating maladjusted people. From his experiences in the consulting room, he gradually formulated a far-reaching and influential theory of personality.

Central to his theory is the division of the personality into three major systems: the id, the ego, and the superego.

The Id. The *id* (a Latin word meaning *it*) is the original, inborn system of personality from which the other two systems emerge. It is the reservoir of psychic energy which furnishes the power for the operation of the whole personality. The id is in close touch with the bodily processes, from which it derives its energy.

The id contains the basic instincts of sex and aggression (also called the life and death instincts) which we discussed in Chapters 12 and 13.

16-1
The founder of psychoanalysis, Sigmund Freud, was born in a small town in Moravia (in what is now Czechoslovakia) on May 6, 1856 and died in London on September 23, 1939. For nearly 80 years, however, he resided in Vienna, leaving that city when the Nazis took over Austria in 1938. His father was a wool merchant. After receiving a medical degree from the University of Vienna and studying for a year in Paris with the great French psychiatrist Jean Charcot, Freud entered the practice of psychiatry. Dissatisfied with the methods of treatment then used, Freud adopted the free-association method originated by a Viennese colleague, Joseph Breuer. This was the beginning of psychoanalysis. Freud attracted a number of disciples through his writings, and the psychoanalytic movement soon became worldwide. In 1909, Freud brought his theories to the United States in a series of lectures at Clark University in Worcester, Massachusetts. He is now acclaimed as one of the dominant architects of 20th century thought.

The contents of the id are not directly available to consciousness. They are said to exist in a state of *repression*, which means that active forces oppose their becoming conscious. To explore these unconscious contents and processes, Freud developed the methods of free association and dream analysis, which we discussed in Chapter 9.

The id cannot tolerate painful increases of tension. Consequently, when the tension level is raised either by external stimulation or internally produced excitations, the id tries to discharge this increased tension immediately, impulsively, and often irrationally. This impulsive method of tension-reduction by which the id operates is called the *pleasure principle* (see Chapter 10).

The contents of the unconscious id change very little after the age of six. Consequently, the id is an infantile formation filled with infantile complexes. The most important of these complexes are the *Oedipus complex* and the *castration complex*. The Oedipus complex comprises the child's sexual desire for the parent of the opposite sex and his hostility toward the parent of the same sex. The castration complex in the boy consists of a fear that he will be emasculated by the father for desiring the mother. In the girl, the castration complex consists of her envy of the male's more prominent genitals. She also feels she was castrated early in life as punishment for desiring her father and hating her mother. This feeling is reinforced by the bleeding that occurs during menstruation. These two complexes have a tremendous influence on our feelings and interactions with the same and the opposite sex throughout our lives.

The Ego. The *ego* comes into existence because the id is incapable of satisfying the needs of the organism through appropriate, rational transactions with the objective world of reality. The ego operates in accordance with the *reality principle*, whose aim is to prevent the discharge of tension from the id until an object appropriate for the need has been discovered in the external world. The ego makes use of perception, memory, and thought in its dealings with the environment.

The ego is called the executive of the personality because it controls the gateways to action, selects the features of the environment to which it will respond, and decides what instincts will be satisfied and in what manner. In performing these very important executive functions, the ego has to try to integrate the often-conflicting demands of the id, the superego, and the external world. This is not an easy task and sometimes causes the ego to become anxious. To prevent the occurrence of anxiety attacks, the ego learns to employ various defenses, including those of repression, displacement, reaction formation, projection, denial, rationalization, and sublimation, which we discussed in Chapter 12.

The ego is the seat of consciousness, although many of its processes and contents exist in a state of preconsciousness. This means they readily become conscious when the need arises. It is not difficult to summon from the preconscious a memory for a name or a telephone number because—unlike the contents of the id—they are not held in the grip of repression. Everyone has had the experience of not being able to recall a familiar name no matter how hard he tries. The name has not been forgotten; it has been repressed out of the preconscious into the unconscious. Often the name pops back into consciousness after we have given up trying to recall it (see the essay on the tip-of-the-tongue, or TOT, state on page 536). This occurs because the repression has been lifted. The next time this happens to you, you may find it interesting to figure out why you repressed the name. Usually it is because you associate the name with something unpleasant.

Although Freud regarded the ego as the executive of the personality, he believed it always remained the servant of the id. "This oldest portion of the mental apparatus remains the most important throughout life" (Freud, 1940). Some recent psychoanalytic theorists have granted the ego a status in the personality which makes it independent of the id. According to this new view, which is often referred to as "ego psychology," the ego does not emerge out of the id. It has its own inherent predispositions, its own energies, its own satisfactions, and its own lines of development. The aims of the ego can become quite independent of instinctual objectives. In short, the ego is autonomous. Essentially, what ego psychology states is that man need not be a slave to instinct and impulse; he can become a fully conscious and fully rational human being.

The Superego. The third and last system of personality to develop is the *superego*. It is the internal representative of the traditional values and ideals of society as interpreted to the child by his parents, and enforced by means of rewards and punishments imposed upon the child. The superego is the moral arm of personality; it represents the ideal rather than the real, and it strives for perfection rather than pleasure.

The superego tries to inhibit the impulses of the id, especially those of sex and aggression, since these are the impulses whose expression society most highly condemns. It also tries to persuade the ego to substitute moralistic goals for realistic ones. With the formation of the superego, self-control is substituted for parental or outside control.

In concluding this brief account of Freud's theory of personality, we should point out that the id, ego, and superego are not manikins ("little men") that dwell within the person and control his behavior. They are merely names for various psychological processes which obey different system principles. Under ordinary circumstances, these different principles do not collide with one another nor do they work at cross-purposes. On the contrary, they usually work together as a team under the ego's administrative leadership. The personality normally functions as an integrated whole rather than as three separate segments. When it does not, the person is in trouble.

In a very general way, we may think of the id as the biological component of personality, the ego as the psychological component, and the superego as the social component.

Jung's Analytic Theory

For years, Jung was closely associated with Freud in the development of psychoanalysis. Their association ended when Jung's ideas diverged from Freud's. Jung then developed his own viewpoint, which is known as *analytic psychology*.

16-2
The iceberg can represent the relationship between the conscious and unconscious mind. Conscious material makes up only the exposed tip of all that the mind contains.

16-3

Carl Gustav Jung, the founder of analytical psychology, was born on July 26, 1875 in Kesswil, a village on Lake Constance in Switzerland, where his father was a pastor. After receiving his medical degree in 1900 from Basel University, Jung became an assistant in a mental hospital in Zurich, a city where he was to live the rest of his life. Jung read Freud's *Interpretation of Dreams* soon after it was published; several years later, following correspondence with Freud, he went to Vienna to meet him. This was the beginning of a close personal and professional relationship between the two men that lasted for six years. Jung broke with Freud because he felt that Freud overemphasized the role of the sex impulse. He then developed his own psychoanalytic viewpoint. Like Freud, Jung's writings attracted a number of students and his influence became worldwide. He wrote not only on psychological and psychiatric subjects but also on such occult matters as alchemy, astrology, telepathy and clairvoyance, yoga, spiritualism, fortune-telling, and flying saucers. Jung and Freud are often considered to be the two most influential figures in modern psychology. Jung died on June 6, 1961 at the age of 85.

Early in his career as a psychiatrist, Jung began experimenting with the word-association test. This test consists of a list of words which are read to a person one at a time. He is told to respond as quickly as possible with the first word that occurs to him. A sample of the 100 words used by Jung are *bread, green, water, death, money, child, fur, woman, happiness, quarrel, marry, box,* and *old.* Signs of emotional disturbance produced by some of the words are (1) prolonged reaction time or an inability to respond at all, (2) responding with more than one word, and (3) repeating the same response to a number of different words. These signs Jung called *complex-indicators.* A *complex* consists of a cluster of disturbing feelings, often unconscious, about some aspect of a person's life. For example, a young married woman to whom Jung gave the word-association test displayed signs of disturbance in her reactions to the following words: *pray, marry, happiness, unfaithful, anxiety,* and *contented.* All of these words had some connection with her unhappy married life. At first she denied that her marriage was an unhappy one, but when Jung confronted her with the evidence from the word-association test, she finally admitted that she was discontented with her husband.

For a number of years, the complex was one of Jung's chief theoretical concepts, and the identification and treatment of complexes in patients were his chief therapeutic aims. Everyone has one or more complexes, be it a father complex, a mother complex, a money complex, a power complex, a sex complex, or whatever, which tend to dominate his thoughts and actions. The complexes of a neurotic person are just more intense and more influential in the personality than those of a normal person. Many other psychologists, including Freud, Adler, and Murray, also have used the term.

Then Jung discovered the collective unconscious, which was a brand-new idea. Freud, it will be recalled, conceived of the unconscious mind as being formed by the repression of disturbing childhood experiences. Evidence obtained from the analysis of patients' dreams and from a study of myths, symbolism, and religion convinced Jung that part of the unconscious mind is predetermined at birth and that it is the same for everyone. Thus, he called it the *collective unconscious.*

The collective unconscious consists of inborn predispositions to react to the environment in certain ways. These inborn predispositions are called *archetypes.* For instance, because children have always had mothers, the brain has evolved in such a way that the infant's brain is attuned to respond to his mother as a distinctive person in his environment. This is called the *mother archetype.* We discussed archetypes in Chapter 9, so we will mention them only briefly here.

Primitive man's close association with animals, as well as his evolution from lower forms, has implanted in the brain of every person an animal archetype, which Jung called the *shadow.* We are predisposed to fear animals—and by analogy, our own animal impulses—because wild beasts often threatened the lives of our primitive ancestors and because man's evolutionary ancestors were lower animals.

The anima is the feminine archetype in the male and the animus is the masculine archetype in the female. These archetypes have become a part of human nature by virtue of the long association of the sexes. Men

ON THE TIP OF MY TONGUE: TWO APPROACHES TO MEMORY FAILURE

Phillip Shaver *Columbia University*

Sigmund Freud was one of the earliest and most outstanding personality psychologists, and his work is still highly influential. Nevertheless, many experimental psychologists believe that his ideas must be replaced by theories that are grounded more firmly on research evidence. Such people say that while Freud's case studies may be brilliant and intriguing, they contain conjectures and interpretive leaps that are dangerously speculative, if not downright bizarre. Some of this criticism may be justified, but I believe much of it is due to a failure to distinguish between *studying a particular person* and *studying many people in order to establish general principles.* Freud's ideas are, for the most part, completely compatible with the principles established by laboratory researchers, but his emphasis was different. Like a geologist, he tried both to discover general principles and to use them to explain particular, naturally occurring incidents. Specifically, he was interested in the motives and meanings behind particular human actions, and in the unique configurations of needs, experiences, and fantasies that made each of his patients a special case.

Differences between Freud and the experimentalists can be seen in their respective examinations of the well-known "tip-of-the-tongue" phenomenon, a situation in which one knows a name or a word but cannot quite recall it (see page 226 in Chapter 7). Laboratory researchers have devised ingenious procedures to create this feeling in subjects. They can thus explore the phenomenon and summarize their findings in the form of group averages and percentages. In one such study, Roger Brown and David McNeill (1966) had 56 undergraduate subjects listen as definitions of 49 words were read from a dictionary. The words were carefully selected to be familiar to college students but not so familiar that they would be used in everyday conversation. If, as a particular definition was read, the students could recall the corresponding word immediately or felt quite sure they did not know the word, they were instructed simply to sit and relax for a few minutes. If they felt they knew the word but couldn't quite recall it—that is, if they found themselves in the mysterious tip-of-the-tongue (TOT) state—they filled out a special response sheet. This questionnaire asked them to try to specify the number of syllables and initial letter of the lost target word, and also to write down words of *similar sound* and *similar meaning* that came to mind but were recognized as incorrect.

From 2744 possible instances (56 people times 49 words), Brown and McNeill obtained 233 usable TOT reports. Most of the incorrect words that came to people's minds proved to be similar in sound to the target word, although some were similar in meaning rather than sound. When the definition of the word *sampan* was read, for example, subjects produced the following similar-sounding words: Saipan, Sian, Cheyenne, sarong, sanching, and sympoon (not all of which are real words). The similar-meaning words were barge, houseboat, and junk. Guesses about the number of syllables in the target word were surprisingly accurate: Subjects were correct 57% of the time and were close to correct in most of the remaining cases. They guessed the correct initial letter 57% of the time, too, which is quite good considering that there are 26 possibilities. By comparing the accent patterns of guessed words and target words, the psychologists discovered that these matched about 75% of the time and also that the first and last few *letters* often corresponded, especially if the target word contained a common suffix. Thus, strange as it may seem, *subjects could report the number of syllables and even match the sounds in a word that they could not quite recall.*

The experiment clearly demonstrates that a person in the TOT state has, somewhere in memory, enough of the lost word available to guess its structure. It is as if the definition activates an incomplete trace of the word in memory, but the trace is too weak to produce a correct answer. To account for the results of their experiment, Brown and McNeill developed a general model of word memory, which, although too complex to be described here, has certain notable features. First, the model was based on data from many subjects, and so ignored unusual associations and unique reasons for forgetfulness; individual quirks got buried in the averaging process. Second, the reason for forgetting a word, according to the model, is that too little information about the structure of the word is stored in memory—probably because the person hasn't used the word very often in conversation. Third, the model ignores motivation. It proposes a mechanical, motivationally neutral process to account for memory failure, never even hinting that one might forget a word at a particular time because, at some level, one does not *want* to remember it.

Freud's analysis of the TOT phenomenon, by contrast, emphasized uniquely patterned associations and motives and, typically, began with an incident in his own life:

[He] who strives for the escaped name brings to consciousness others—substitutive names—which, although immediately recognized as false, nevertheless obtrude themselves with great tenacity. The process which would lead to the reproduction of the lost name is, as it were, displaced, and thus brings one to an incorrect substitute. Now it is my assumption that the displacement is not left to psychic arbitrariness, but that it follows lawful and rational paths. In other words, I assume that the substitutive name (or names) stands in direct relation to the lost name, and I hope, if I succeed in demonstrating this connection, to throw light on the origin of forgetting of names. In the example which I selected for analysis in 1898 I vainly strove to recall the name of the master who made the imposing frescoes of the "Last Judgment" in the dome of Orvieto. Instead of the lost name—Signorelli—two other names of artists—Botticelli and Boltraffio—obtruded themselves, names which my judgment immediately and definitely rejected as being incorrect (Freud, 1914).

In trying to understand why he had forgotten the name Signorelli, Freud mulled over the entire incident many times, searching for clues. The memory failure occurred when Freud was riding with a stranger in a carriage bound for Herzegovina. The two men were discussing customs of the Turks who lived in Herzegovina and the neighboring state of Bosnia. Freud told his traveling companion that one of his colleagues, a doctor, had mentioned that his Turkish patients placed a surprising amount of confidence in him. When he admitted that he could not save a certain person's life, for example, they would say: "Sir (which in Freud's native German is *Herr*, and in Signorelli's Italian is *Signor*), what can I say? I know that if he could be saved you would save him." At this point in his story, Freud hit upon a train of thought that he did not want to express. He remembered that this same doctor friend had told him that the Turks value sexual pleasure highly and seem to be more concerned about losing that than about dying. One of the man's patients had said: "For you know, sir (*Herr*, in the version told to Freud), if that ceases, life no longer has charm."

Freud realized that besides not wanting to discuss sex with a stranger, a natural enough reservation in Victorian times, he had also wanted to avoid thinking about the theme of *death and sexuality.* For he had recently heard, while visiting *Trafoi*, that one of his former patients had committed suicide because of an incurable sexual problem. At this point in the conversation, as Freud changed the topic to traveling in Italy, he found himself unable to recall the name Signorelli. He interpreted his forgetfulness as an example of repression and attempted to explain it in the following way:

The name Signorelli was . . . divided into two parts. One pair of syllables (elli) returned unchanged in one of the substitutions (Botticelli), while the other has gained, through the translation of Signor *(sir, Herr), many and diverse relations to the name, contained in the repressed theme, but was lost through it in the reproduction. Its substitution was formed in a way to suggest that a displacement took place along the same associations—Herzegovina and Bosnia—regardless of the sense and acoustic demarcation.* (Freud, 1914)

Notice that Freud's analysis is quite compatible with the results of Brown and McNeill's experiment. One of the incorrect words, *Botticelli*, is structurally similar to the target word—they have the same suffix, the same number of syllables, and the same accent pattern. But Freud recognized an additional factor: He wanted to forget about death and sexuality, which were connected in his memory with the words Trafoi and *Herr*. In his own words: "I wanted to forget something, I *repressed* something." Unintentionally he also repressed *Signor*, the Italian word for *Herr*. As he struggled to recall the name Signorelli, pieces of the puzzle came into consciousness—"Bo" from Bosnia, "elli," the correct number of syllables, and the accent pattern from the repressed target word, and "traffio" from Trafoi—but the pieces did not form the desired pattern because "Signor" was unavailable.

Freud adopted a similar method in studying other psychological phenomena. According to his account, the compromise words Botticelli and Boltraffio are functionally similar to compromise symbols that appear in dreams (innocent objects representing sexual objects, for example) and to psychosomatic symptoms, such as paralysis of an arm or temporary blindness, that symbolize the sources of strong intrapsychic conflict. Experimental psychologists are interested in these phenomena also, and they have discovered a great deal about sleep, dreams, and psychopathology that was unknown in Freud's time. Nevertheless, their general principles are rarely sufficient to explain the details of a specific case. As individuals, we are not satisfied with a science that ignores our individuality. And in order to understand a particular person, psychologists still need to know about the person's unique structure and dynamics—including his or her hopes, fears, dreams, and fantasies. Freud designed the process of psychoanalysis to ferret out that kind of information, and it seems unlikely that his insights and methods will be made obsolete, even by the most spectacular of experimental psychology's future discoveries.

have become feminized by their age-old association with women, and women have become masculinized by their association with men. Thus, one sex's attraction for the other is due partly to the male finding expression for his anima in relationships with women, and women finding expression for their animus in relationships with men.

The *persona* is another important archetype. As the name implies, the persona is the mask we wear to hide our true feelings from others. Ever since the first human society, man has had to conform to its dictates. Because of this long history of conformity and because of its survival value, man developed an innate tendency to be conventional.

Perhaps the most important archetype is the *self*. It is the unifying force in the personality and represents man's eternal quest for unity and wholeness. Man can no more refrain from trying to achieve completeness than he can refrain from breathing.

When Jung discovered the collective unconscious and its archetypes, complexes became of secondary importance. In fact, a complex owes its existence to an archetype. The archetype is like a magnet in the brain; it attracts to itself any relevant personal experiences to form a complex. The mother archetype attracts the child's actual experiences with the mother, for example. Archetypes are universal structures in the personality; complexes are personal structures. In other words, a complex is the individual manifestation of the archetype. Because we all have different experiences, we have different complexes.

Jung also developed a system of character types, which we will discuss later in this chapter.

Murray's Personology

The American psychologist Henry Murray was deeply influenced by Freud and Jung and adopted many of their ideas in developing his theory of personality, which he called personology. Murray was primarily concerned with a full understanding of the lives of individuals. He established a clinical setting in which normal individuals, often college students, could be observed, interviewed, tested, and also measured on a variety of physiological, physical, and behavioral scales. When all of the data for an individual were assembled, a team of psychologists formulated an overall personality sketch. The results of these studies are fully described in the fascinating book, *Explorations in personality* (1938).

Central to Murray's *personology theory* of personality are his concepts of need and press. A *need* is a motive that arouses and maintains activity until the need is satisfied. (A list of Murray's needs is presented in Chapter 10 on page 358.) A *press* is some aspect of the environment that impedes or facilitates the efforts of the individual to satisfy his needs. Press include family discord or support, poverty or affluence, rejection or acceptance, affection or antagonism, and cooperation or competition.

The analysis of behavior consists of identifying the specific need and the specific press that are acting upon a person. The interaction between a need and a press is called a *thema*. For example, a person may try to

16-4

Henry Alexander Murray was born in New York City on May 13, 1893. Like many others who have made important contributions to psychology, Murray was not formally trained in psychology. He majored in history at Harvard, received a medical degree in 1915 from the Columbia College of Physicians and Surgeons, an M.A. in biology from Columbia, and a Ph.D. in biochemistry from Cambridge University in 1927. During those years he was much influenced by Freud and Jung.

In 1927 Murray became an instructor in psychology at Harvard, where he remained until his retirement in 1962. For a number of years, Murray was director of the Harvard Psychological Clinic, where he conducted research on personality with the cooperation of a number of colleagues and students. Their joint efforts culminated in a very influential book, *Explorations in Personality* (1938). He also collaborated with Christiana Morgan in developing the *Thematic Apperception Test,* a widely used projective test.

make friends with another person but be given the cold shoulder. The thema can be described as need affiliation/press rejection.

If we observe a person over a long period of time, we often find that the same pattern of related needs and press keeps repeating itself. This is called a *unity thema*. For instance, a person's efforts to succeed may inevitably end in failure. A unity thema has its roots in childhood experiences and is often unconscious.

Murray's theory has been popular with academic psychologists because it has stimulated experimental research—for example, McClelland's extensive studies of need achievement (see page 354). It also has been popular with clinical psychologists, because it has provided them with useful diagnostic tools, such as the Thematic Apperception Test (see page 587). Moreover, Murray's theory and work have made Freudian theory more palatable to American psychologists. One reason for this is that Murray's personology emerged from investigations of normal rather than neurotic individuals.

Social Psychological Theories

In the eyes of psychodynamic theorists, man's character and behavior are largely determined by unconscious instinctual forces and by infantile complexes. A number of psychoanalytically oriented theorists, feeling insufficient attention had been paid to the social determinants of personality, introduced new concepts which would correct for this oversight. We shall discuss the views of several socially oriented theorists.

Alfred Adler

The earliest psychoanalyst to focus on social variables was Alfred Adler. He had been associated with Freud from the inception of psychoanalysis. Like Jung, he severed his connection with psychoanalysis and developed his own viewpoint.

Early in his theorizing, Adler stressed the aggressive nature of man and his compulsive drive for superiority to overcome deep feelings of inferiority. Criticized for belaboring selfish motives, Adler began to turn his attention to man's social nature. He came to appreciate that the individual is embedded in a social context from the first day of his life. The relationship between baby and mother is a completely social one. From that early point, the individual is continuously enmeshed in a web of personal relations.

At first, his social relations provide outlets for personal ambition and selfish gain. Ultimately, however, *social interest* displaces selfish interest. Private gain becomes subordinated to public welfare. Adler wrote that "Social interest is the true and inevitable compensation for all the natural weaknesses of individual human beings" (1929).

Although Adler believed social interest is inborn, he recognized that it must be nurtured by guidance and training. Toward this end, Adler became active in establishing child guidance clinics, improving education, and lecturing and writing on proper methods of rearing children. Adler was what we would call today a "social activist."

16-5
Alfred Adler was born in Vienna in 1870 of a prosperous middle-class family. He died in 1937 in Aberdeen, Scotland, while on a lecture tour. He received a medical degree in 1895 from the University of Vienna. At first he specialized in ophthalmology, and then, after a period of practice in general medicine, he became a psychiatrist. He was one of the charter members of the Vienna Psychoanalytic Society and later its president. However, Adler soon began to develop ideas which differed from those of Freud and others in the Vienna Society. When these differences became acute, he was asked to present his views to the Society. This he did in 1911, and his ideas were denounced. Adler resigned as the Society's president and later severed his connection with Freudian psychoanalysis.

In 1935 Adler settled in the United States, where he continued his practice as a psychiatrist and served as professor of medical psychology at the Long Island College of Medicine.

Karen Horney

Another psychoanalyst who strongly objected to Freud's biological orientation was Karen Horney. She did not believe in the castration and Oedipus complexes as described by Freud, nor did she accept the psychosexual stages of oral, anal, and phallic. She rejected Freud's concept of penis envy as the determining factor in the psychology of women. She held that aggression is not inborn as Freud stated, but is a means by which the individual tries to protect his security.

Horney believed that above all else, the child needs a sense of security for healthy psychological growth. The child has to feel that his parents love him and will protect him. When he feels isolated, unwanted, and helpless, he becomes anxious. The insecure, anxious child develops various neurotic strategies to cope with his feelings of insecurity. He may become hostile and seek to avenge himself against those who have rejected him. Or he may become overly submissive to win back the love he feels he has lost. He may develop an unrealistic, idealized picture of himself to compensate for his feelings of inferiority. He may wallow in self-pity to gain people's sympathy.

All of these neurotic actions, which are only a few of the many discussed by Horney, result from the disturbances in the individual's social relationships that make him feel insecure.

Erich Fromm

A third psychoanalyst who has argued strenuously for society's great importance as a molder of personality is Erich Fromm, whose theory of man's needs we discussed in Chapter 10. Fromm was strongly influenced by Karl Marx as well as by Freud.

If a particular society is to function smoothly and maintain itself, the child's character must be shaped to fit the society's needs. The task of the parents and of education is to make the child want to act as he has to act to maintain the society's economic, political, and social systems. In a capitalistic system, the desire to save money must become second nature in the individual so that capital will be available for an expanding economy. A society that has evolved a credit system must see that people feel an inner compulsion to pay their bills promptly.

By making demands upon the individual which are too contrary to his nature, society warps and frustrates both men and women. It alienates them from their humanness. Fromm does not hesitate to brand a whole society as sick when it fails to recognize and satisfy the basic needs of man. He has condemned both capitalism and communism for trying to make man a robot of the state, a wage slave on a monotonous assembly line or a nonentity behind a typewriter, a victim of propaganda, deceit, and "brainwashing."

Fromm points out that when a society changes in any important respect—such as when feudalism was supplanted by capitalism or when the factory system replaced the individual artisan—the change is likely to produce dislocations in the social character. This is because the old character structure does not fit the new society. Man is cut off from traditional values, and until he can develop new ones, he feels lost.

16-6
Karen Horney was born in Hamburg, Germany, on September 16, 1885. She studied at the University of Berlin, where she received her degree in medicine. She then became associated with the Berlin Psychoanalytic Institute and obtained her training in psychoanalysis from two of the leading figures in the field, Karl Abraham and Hanns Sachs.

Dissatisfied with the orthodox approach to psychoanalysis, Horney and others who shared the same convictions founded their own association, the Association for the Advancement of Psychoanalysis, and their own training institute, the American Institute of Psychoanalysis. Horney held the position of dean of the Institute until her death on December 4, 1952.

16-7
Erich Fromm was born in Frankfort, Germany, on March 23, 1900. He studied psychology and sociology at the Universities of Heidelberg, Frankfurt, and Munich. After obtaining his Ph.D. in 1922 from the University of Heidelberg, he went to Berlin to receive training in psychoanalysis at the Psychoanalytic Institute there. Before coming to the United States in 1933, Fromm was associated with the influential Institute for Social Research in Frankfurt.

In the United States, he joined the International Institute for Social Research in New York City and established a private practice in psychoanalysis. Fromm now divides his time between Mexico City, where he lectures at the National University, and New York City, where he is a fellow of the William Alanson White Institute of Psychiatry, Psychoanalysis, and Psychology and a professor at New York University.

During such transitional periods, he becomes prey to all sorts of panaceas and nostrums, which promise him a refuge from loneliness.

Man's relation to society is of great concern to Fromm. After much thought and study, he feels the following statements are true: Man has an inborn nature; society is created by man to fulfill this basic nature; no society which has yet been devised meets the basic needs of man; such a society can be created.

Fromm has tried to imagine a society

. . . in which man relates to man lovingly, in which he is rooted in bonds of brotherliness and solidarity . . . a society which gives him the possibility of transcending nature by creating rather than by destroying, in which everyone gains a sense of self by experiencing himself as the subject of his powers rather than by conformity, in which a system of orientation and devotion exists without man's needing to distort reality and to worship idols. (1955)

Fromm even suggests a name for this perfect society: Humanistic Communitarian Socialism.

Harry Stack Sullivan

Harry Stack Sullivan created a radically new conception of personality which states, in effect, that personality cannot be isolated from interpersonal relations. Personality cannot be the object of study because the individual does not and cannot exist apart from his relations with other people. Personality is a "relatively enduring pattern of recurrent interpersonal situations which characterize a human life" (1953).

The unit of study is the *dynamism*. A dynamism is a relatively enduring form of interpersonal behavior. A person who behaves in a habitually hostile way toward people is said to have a dynamism of malevolence. A man who seeks out sexual relationships with many different women has a dynamism of lust. A child who is afraid of strangers or of animals has a dynamism of fear. All people have the same basic dynamisms, but a dynamism's mode of expression varies with the individual's situation and life experiences.

Another of Sullivan's concepts is personification. A *personification* is a complex of feelings, attitudes, and conceptions that an individual has concerning himself or another person. They develop out of the individual's experiences with need-satisfaction and anxiety. For example, the baby develops a personification of a good mother by being nursed and cared for by her. The personification of a bad mother results from experiences with her that evoke anxiety in the baby.

The personifications that we carry around in our heads are rarely accurate descriptions of the people to whom they refer. They are first formed to cope with people in fairly isolated interpersonal situations. But once they are formed, they usually persist and influence our attitudes toward other people. Thus, an individual who personifies his father as a mean and dictatorial man may project this same personification onto other older men. Consequently, a psychic activity that reduced anxiety in early life may interfere with one's interpersonal relations later in life.

16-8
Harry Stack Sullivan was born on a farm near Norwich, New York, on February 21, 1892. He received his medical degree from the Chicago College of Medicine and Surgery in 1917. In 1922 Sullivan went to Saint Elizabeth's Hospital in Washington, D.C., where he came under the influence of William Alanson White, a leader in American neuropsychiatry. From 1923 until the early thirties, he was associated with the Medical School of the University of Maryland and with the Sheppard and Enoch Pratt Hospital in Towson, Maryland. It was during this period of his life that Sullivan conducted investigations of schizophrenia which established his reputation as a clinician. He left Maryland to open an office on Park Avenue in New York City for the express purpose of studying obsessive patients. At this time he began his formal training in psychoanalysis. In 1933 he became president of the William Alanson White Foundation, and in 1936 he helped found the Washington School of Psychiatry, which is the training institution of the Foundation.

Personifications of the self, such as the good-me and the bad-me, follow the same principles as personifications of others. The good-me personification results from interpersonal experiences that are rewarding, the bad-me personification from anxiety-arousing situations.

Personifications that are shared by a number of people are called *stereotypes*. Common stereotypes in our culture are the absent-minded professor, the unconventional artist, and the hard-headed businessman.

Sullivan's ideas about anxiety and about the development of the self are quite original. Anxiety is transmitted to the baby by the mother whenever she becomes anxious. She does not have to do anything to the baby to make him anxious, such as pushing him away from her nipple; if she is anxious, the baby will become anxious. Anxiety reactions then spread to other features of the environment in which the baby first experienced anxiety. The individual develops various security measures that protect him from feeling anxious. These security measures form the *self-system*.

Sullivan believes that the self-system is a product of the irrational aspects of society. By this he means that the child is made to feel anxious for reasons that would not exist in a more rational society. The self-system tends to become isolated from the rest of the personality, and this isolation prevents the person from having constructive interpersonal relations. Moreover, a strong, unrealistic self-system blocks favorable changes in the personality.

Sullivan's ideas have been very influential, especially in the practice of psychiatry. He was a founder and director of the Washington School of Psychiatry, which is an important psychiatric training institute.

Trait Theories

We all know that people differ from one another in the observable traits of their behavior. John is easy going, friendly, and generous while Bill is conscientious, hard-working, and thrifty. Joan is shy, withdrawn, and moody while Betty is outgoing, gregarious, and high-spirited. We also believe that a trait resides within the person and causes him to behave as he does. Barring some unusual frustration, failure, traumatic experience, or radical change, the traits of a person tend to remain fairly constant throughout life. Mary's shyness is often as characteristic of her at 40 as it was at 10.

Two prominent psychologists, Gordon Allport and Raymond Cattell, have developed their theories of personality around the central concept of *trait*. Traits, for them, are the "real" units of personality. The theories of the two men differ mainly in the methods they employ to identify an individual's basic traits.

Allport's Trait Theory

Allport defines personality as "the dynamic organization within the individual of those psychophysical systems that determine his characteristic thought and behavior" (1961). The psychophysical systems to which he pays the most attention are traits.

16-9
Gordon Willard Allport, a prominent figure in the areas of personality and social psychology, was born in Montezuma, Indiana on November 11, 1897. His father was a physician. Allport received his A.B. and Ph.D. from Harvard University and was associated with that university until his death on October 9, 1967. Allport's primary interest was in the psychology of the individual; he is respected by psychologists for the clarity and elegance with which he expressed his ideas in his numerous and influential publications.

For Allport, a trait is more than a characteristic way of behaving. It is an actual force, motive, or disposition within the individual that initiates and guides a particular form of behavior. The expression of the trait of generosity, for example, consists of an individual's performing generous acts, but the performance of these acts is governed by a disposition of the person to act generously. A person with a marked disposition to be generous does not wait for a suitable situation in which to express this trait; he actively seeks out or creates situations in which he can be generous.

Allport distinguishes among different kinds of traits. One distinction is between common and individual traits. A _common trait_ is one that is shared by many people. Common traits can be measured by personality tests (see Chapter 17). An _individual trait_ is one that is peculiar to the person; it must be determined by observation of behavior and by the analysis of such personal records as letters, diaries, and autobiographies. There are also cardinal, central, and secondary traits. A _cardinal trait_ is general; almost every act of a person who possesses a cardinal trait can be traced to its influence. You probably know a person who is very contrary. He takes exception to everything you or anyone else says. If you want to do something, he wants to do just the opposite. Allport believes that few people have cardinal traits, however.

More typical are _central traits_. A central trait is highly characteristic of an individual but it is not as general as a cardinal trait. Allport suggests that the number of central traits by which a person can be fairly accurately described is surprisingly small—perhaps five to ten. In a study of the letters written by a middle-aged woman, Allport (1965) found that her personality could be described by eight central traits. They were

1. quarrelsome-suspicious

2. self-centered

3. independent

4. dramatic

5. artistic

6. aggressive

7. cynical

8. sentimental

The consistency with which a person behaves is due to his central traits.

A _secondary trait_ is one that is more limited in its occurrence and narrower in scope than a central trait. In some situations and under certain conditions a generous person may behave selfishly but it is not a consistent feature of his behavior. In fact, we often are astonished to see a friend who is usually generous act in a selfish manner. The fact that inconsistency surprises us indicates that we are used to having our friends behave consistently. However, psychologists have argued for years over just how consistent people really are. Considerable evidence can be summoned for each side of the argument. Allport argues persuasively that central traits are constants in the personality.

16-10
Raymond B. Cattell was born and educated in England. He emigrated to the United States in 1937, and in 1944 he assumed his present position as research professor of psychology and director of the Laboratory of Personality and Group Analysis at the University of Illinois. Cattell is an indefatigable researcher and a prolific writer. He also has devised a number of psychological tests which are widely used.

Cattell's Trait Theory

Cattell's approach to the study of personality differs from Allport's in one respect. To identify the traits of a person, Cattell uses a very sophisticated statistical method known as *factor analysis*. The first step in this complex method is to obtain a large number of scores for each of a large number of individuals. These scores may be obtained from questionnaires, ratings, tests, or any other source that provides a significant and quantifiable measure of behavior. Ideally, these measures should tap many different aspects of behavior. Given these scores, the investigator then applies the technique of factor analysis to discover the fewest possible underlying factors or traits that account for differences among individuals. Once the basic traits have been identified by factor analysis, the investigator can construct new measures which will assess these traits more efficiently.

Cattell's extensive investigations using factor analysis have enabled him to unearth various types of traits. Central to Cattell's viewpoint is the distinction between surface traits and source traits. A *surface trait* is easily observed; a *source trait* lies behind and determines the surface manifestations. Source traits must be inferred since they are not directly observable. For example, we can directly observe nervousness but we have to infer the underlying cause of a person's nervousness. Factor analysis helps one to make such inferences. Cattell has been able to distinguish between source traits that are primarily innate (*constitutional traits*) and those that are primarily determined by the environment (*environmental-mold traits*). He accomplished this by comparing twins and siblings raised together in their own homes with those adopted into different homes. Cattell also classified traits as dynamic traits, ability traits and temperament traits. A *dynamic trait* is one that acts as a motive; it initiates and guides behavior. Some dynamic traits are much like the instincts described by McDougall (see page 344). Cattell called these traits *ergs*. So far he has identified the following ergs: sex, gregariousness, parental protectiveness, curiosity, escape, self-assertion, and self-indulgence. Dynamic traits that result from social conditioning are called *sentiments*. Patriotism is a sentiment.

Ability traits refer to the effectiveness with which a person reaches a goal. General intelligence, special aptitudes, and skills are examples of ability traits. *Temperament traits* are those that describe such behaviors as speed of reaction, energy output, and emotional reactivity.

As you can see, Cattell's view of personality is a very broad one, embracing many facets of the personality.

Type Theories

Type theories are closely allied to trait theories. A *type* is a name for a group of traits found together in an individual. For example, when psychoanalysts speak of an anal character, they refer to an individual who possesses a cluster of traits originating in the second year of life, when the child ordinarily is learning to control his bowel movements. Three traits that describe the anal character are orderliness, stubbornness, and

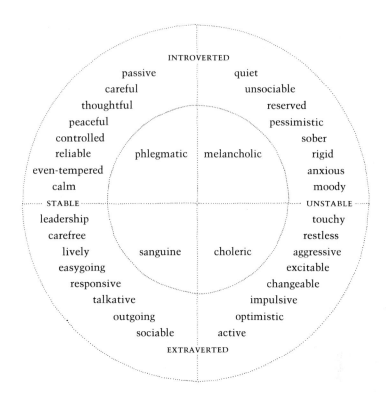

16-11
Using the factor analysis method, Eysenck has identified two general dimensions or types of personality. One dimension is that of introversion-extraversion, the other of stability-instability (neuroticism). As the illustration shows, the characteristics of each type can be compared with the four types of temperament recognized by ancient Greek physicians. According to this ancient doctrine, one's temperament is determined by the fluids of the body. Too much blood causes a person to be sanguine, too much phlegm causes him to be phlegmatic, too much choler or bile causes him to be choleric, and too much black bile causes him to be melancholic. Although the explanation of temperament in terms of body fluids is not accepted today, Eysenck's findings indicate that the classification of temperaments by the ancients contained some valid insights. (Eysenck & Eysenck, 1963)

miserliness. Another example of a type theory is Jung's distinction between extraverts and introverts, which we will discuss in the next chapter. The most prominent type theory, however, is one developed by William Sheldon.

Sheldon's Type Theory

Sheldon started his investigations by seeing whether he could identify types of physique. He examined a large number of full-length photographs of nude males and made many physical measurements of their bodies. Sheldon concluded that there are three basic types of physique: fat (*endomorph*), muscular (*mesomorph*), and skinny (*ectomorph*). Of course, few pure types exist; most physiques are blends of the three types in differing proportions. To classify individuals, Sheldon devised a *somatotype* (body-type) index, which consists of ratings from 1 (low) to 7 (high) for each of the three components. The first number in the index stands for endomorphy, the second number for mesomorphy, and the third number for ectomorphy. Thus, a person with a somatotype index of 362 is a little below average (an average rating is 4) in endomorphy, above average in mesomorphy, and has little ectomorphy in his physical makeup. In other words, he is a husky individual.

Sheldon then asked whether personality types correspond to the physical types. To answer this question, he drew up a list of 50 basic personality traits. By observing and interviewing a group of young men over a period of a year, he was able to rate each on the 50 traits. A statistical analysis of the ratings revealed three clusters of traits. The first cluster,

ENDOMORPH

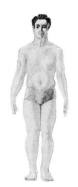

MESOMORPH

ECTOMORPH

16-12
Sheldon's constitutional theory of personality. The drawings represent the three body types. The table relates physique to temperament.

Physique	Temperament	Personality Traits
Endomorphy	Viscerotonia	Sociable, relaxed, even-tempered, easy to get along with, generally loves comfort
Mesomorphy	Somatotonia	Aggressive, tends to be callous of the feelings of others, loud, noisy, loves physical adventure and risk-taking, has a strong need for vigorous physical activity
Ectomorphy	Cerebrotonia	Restrained, inhibited, desires concealment, secrecy, and solitude

16-13
William Herbert Sheldon was born in Warwick, Rhode Island on November 19, 1898 and grew up on a farm. He attended Brown University, the University of Colorado, and the University of Chicago, from which he received a Ph.D. in 1925. After teaching psychology in several universities, Sheldon enrolled in the Medical School of the University of Chicago and obtained an M.D. in 1933. After studying in Europe, he became professor of psychology at the University of Chicago and then moved to Harvard University, where much of his work on body types was done. He became Director of the Constitution Laboratory at the College of Physicians and Surgeons in New York City, where he remained until 1959. During this period, Sheldon was actively engaged in studying the relationships between organic disease and physique. He was then associated with the University of Oregon Medical School, from which he retired in 1970.

which he called *viscerotonia*, includes such traits as sociability, love of physical comfort, relaxation, desire for social approval, pleasure in eating, complacency, and an even disposition. The second cluster is called *somatotonia* and consists of such traits as a need for vigorous physical activity, a love of adventure and taking risks, aggressiveness, courage, competitiveness, callousness, and indifference to pain. The third cluster, called *cerebrotonia*, is characterized by such traits as restraint, inhibition, love of privacy and solitude, fear of people, self-consciousness, and secretiveness.

Ratings from 1 to 7 for each of these three components were assigned to each person to establish his personality type. The first rating is for viscerotonia, the second for somatotonia, and the third for cerebrotonia. A person with a personality index of 362 is high in somatotonia and below average in the other two.

Having found three types of physique and three types of personality, Sheldon then looked for a relationship between physical type and personality type. Does a person with a somatotype of 362 have a personality index of 362? The answer, according to Sheldon, is yes—there is a close relationship. Other investigators have usually agreed that physique and personality are related, but the relationship is not nearly as close as that found by Sheldon. Thus, the popular stereotypes of the jolly, fun-loving, fat person; the energetic, aggressive, muscular person; and the shy, withdrawn, skinny person are true to some extent. However, neither physique nor personality is limited to three types; many more can be identified.

For Sheldon, a person's physique is a manifestation of his whole biological constitution, which determines the kind of personality he will develop. Physique determines personality in several ways. First, a person's physique sets limits to the behavior that he can engage in successfully. A mesomorph can engage in rough sports without getting hurt; an ectomorph cannot. The fat person is adapted for sitting around and socializing, and not for climbing mountains. Second, the type of physique a person has determines what others will expect of him. A muscular person is expected to be an athlete, and a fat person is expected to be the "life of the party." These expectations help to shape the traits a person will acquire. Third, the relation between body build and personality may be accounted for by the common influence of biological factors. Thus, one may argue that both physique and personality are largely determined by hereditary factors, which provide the linkage between the two.

Cognitive Theory

Many of the theories we have considered so far stress the emotional, impulsive, and often irrational side of man's nature. We noted, however, that even psychoanalytic theory increasingly has focused its attention on the rational, cognitive functions of the ego.

Kelly's Personal Construct Theory

An example of this trend toward the rational is George Kelly's _personal construct theory_. For Kelly, man is—or can be taught to become—a more fully rational animal.

A _personal construct_ is the way in which an individual construes, interprets, or attaches meaning to some aspect of the world, including himself. A construct is like a belief or attitude. For example, a person may have the construct that college students are radicals or that snakes are dangerous or that he himself is a failure.

A personal construct determines what and how a person will perceive, remember, learn, think, and act toward the class of elements encompassed by the construct. If he thinks that all snakes are dangerous, he will be alert for them when he goes walking in the woods.

A construct may be thought of as a working hypothesis which is validated or invalidated by the test of experience. One tends to revise his constructs in the general direction of greater validity, although sometimes a person stubbornly clings to a construct in the face of evidence to the contrary. Constructs that are validated tend to remain fairly constant. They can change, however, and new constructs are added as a consequence of new experiences that cause us to look at the world in fresh ways.

According to Kelly, the chief aim of psychotherapy is to change the constructs of a person, either because they are incorrect or because they

16-14
George Alexander Kelly was born in Perth, Kansas on April 28, 1905. For a brief period following graduation from college he was an aeronautical engineer. Kelly then took a master's degree in educational sociology at the University of Kansas and a Ph.D. in psychology at the State University of Iowa in 1931. For ten years after receiving his doctorate Kelly was on the faculty of Kansas State College at Fort Hayes. During the war he served as an aviation psychologist. He then became head of the clinical psychology program at Ohio State University, where he wrote his important book, _The Psychology of Personal Constructs_ (1955). In 1965 Kelly went to Brandeis University. He died in 1966.

are too narrow or too broad. Change is accomplished by using *fixed-role therapy*. For example, a man may come to a therapist with the complaint that he cannot get along with women. His personal constructs toward women are examined, and it is found that he views women as avaricious, demanding, insincere, and fickle. He is given a new role to play in which he is required to treat women in a warm, friendly manner. By acting this new role, his attitudes toward women undergo a radical change because he learns that they are not what he previously thought they were.

Behavior Theories

Behavior theories of personality grew out of the pioneer work of the great Russian physiologist I. P. Pavlov, the discoverer of the conditioned reflex, and the American psychologist E. L. Thorndike, whose studies of animal learning led him to formulate the famous law of effect. Behaviorism as a wholly new and radical psychological viewpoint was proclaimed by J. B. Watson about the time of World War I. Thereafter, a number of versions of behaviorism evolved, but all of them have two elements in common: a commitment to the observation, measurement, and analysis of overt behavior; and an emphasis on the acquisition of new habits and the breaking of old ones.

Behavior theories are simpler than all other theories of personality. The modern behavior theorist is not interested in inferring or imagining internal psychological structures like the id, ego, superego, instincts, archetypes, traits, personal constructs, dynamisms, needs, or the self. He is interested only in behavior that he can observe and measure, preferably under highly controlled laboratory conditions. Lower animals, such as rats, cats, dogs, pigeons, and monkeys, are often used as subjects, because their lives can be more strictly controlled than those of human subjects.

We will describe three closely related behavior theories: Miller and Dollard's stimulus-response theory, Bandura and Walters' social learning theory, and Skinner's operant reinforcement theory.

Miller and Dollard's Stimulus-Response Theory

Habit is the key concept in Miller and Dollard's theory. A *habit* is a learned association between a stimulus and a response. All habits are acquired in the following manner, according to Miller and Dollard. First, the experimental subject—be it rat, cat, or man—must be appropriately motivated. This can be accomplished in a number of ways: by depriving the subject of food, water, or sex; by shocking him; or by offering him an incentive, such as money. The motivated subject is then placed in a situation containing a stimulus object or cue which, if responded to correctly, terminates the drive condition. This is called reinforcement or reward. The four requirements for the acquisition of a habit are *motive* or *drive*, *stimulus* or *cue*, *response*, and *reinforcement*.

Imagine the following situation: A hungry cat is placed in a box which has barred sides. Outside of the box is a dish of food which the cat can see and smell. To get out of the box, the cat must pull a rope hanging from the ceiling of the box. When it makes this response, a door opens and the cat gets out and eats the food. The first time it is in the box, the cat wanders around until it happens to claw at the rope and the door opens. The next time it is placed in the box, it claws at the rope sooner than it did on the first occasion. On each successive trial, the time taken to make the correct response declines, until finally the cat makes the response as soon as it is put in the box. The cat has formed an association between the stimulus object, the rope, and its response of pulling on the rope.

What has this to do with personality? Miller and Dollard believe that personality consists of patterns of specific stimulus-response units (habits) to which trait names have been given. A person is described as aggressive because he responds to various stimuli (people or objects) by kicking, hitting, or giving verbal abuse. He has acquired this trait of aggressiveness because he has been reinforced for making aggressive responses. As we saw in the chapter on learning, conditioned responses generalize so that a person who has been reinforced for being aggressive toward a particular individual tends to be aggressive toward all others who resemble that individual.

One of the useful features of stimulus-response theory, as well as other behavior theories, is that habits can be broken as well as formed by applying its principles. In other words, personality can be changed. This is accomplished in several ways. Since habits are maintained by reinforcing them, the habit will gradually disappear when reinforcement is no longer given. This is known as experimental extinction. A cat will stop pulling the rope to get out of the box when food is no longer available outside or when pulling the rope no longer opens the door. It also will cease responding to the rope when it is well fed. A second method of breaking the habit is to give the cat an electric shock whenever it pulls the rope. This is called *aversive conditioning* and is used in the treatment of behavior disorders.

Bandura and Walters' Social Learning Theory

Bandura and Walters emphasize the importance of <u>social imitation</u> in learning new habits and breaking old ones. As we noted in Chapter 12, when nursery school children watched an adult behave aggressively, they also behaved aggressively (Bandura, 1973). As this experiment demonstrates, children can learn novel responses (form new habits) merely by observing others, without necessarily having had the opportunity to make the responses themselves and without either the model or themselves having been reinforced for the behavior. However, if the model is reinforced for his behavior, the children are much more likely to copy him than if he receives no reinforcement. This is known as <u>vicarious reinforcement</u>. A child is less likely to copy the model if the model is punished for being aggressive. This means that a habit can be strengthened or weakened depending on whether the model's behavior is rewarded or punished. Bear in mind, however, that habits can be formed without reinforcement.

16-15
Albert Bandura was born in Canada on December 4, 1925, and earned his B.A. in 1949 at the University of British Columbia. His M.A. and Ph.D. (1952) were obtained at the University of Iowa. Since 1953, he has been a member of the psychology faculty at Stanford University.

Habits also can be eliminated through social learning. Thus, a person who is afraid of an object can have his fear eliminated or substantially reduced by watching a model deal fearlessly with the object in a nonthreatening situation.

One of Bandura and Walters' major contributions has been their extensive efforts to introduce into the laboratory setting conditions that resemble real-life social situations.

Skinner's Operant Reinforcement Theory

Skinner has reduced behavior theory to a bare minimum of essential concepts. While Miller and Dollard use four concepts—drive, stimulus, response, and reinforcement—to explain the acquisition and elimination of habits, Skinner uses only two, *response* and *reinforcement*. Skinner points out that the stimulus that causes the response need not be identified. The response need only operate upon the environment in such a way as to produce a reinforcement; that is why Skinner's theory is called *operant reinforcement*. The cat's pull on the rope, for example, operates on the environment to enable the cat to get to the food.

We can sum up Skinner's position in the following statements: When a response occurs, reinforce it and the subject will tend to respond again in the same way. Withold the reinforcement or punish the subject and the response will tend to disappear.

Often the most difficult problem in eliciting a novel response is to get the response to occur in the first place. For example, the experimenter may have to wait a very long time for the cat in the box to pull the rope. It may never pull it—in which case, that cat has to be discarded as a subject. Skinner has shown how the desired response can be elicited using reinforcement alone. The method, which we described in Chapter 6, is called *shaping*. Basically, the subject's response is shaped by reinforcing successive approximations of the desired behavior. Eventually, by means of these successive approximations, the cat will pull the rope, the pigeon will peck the disc, or the rat will press the lever for the first time. A reinforcement at this point will confirm the subject's response and make it likely to occur again.

Behavior also can be shaped by varying the schedule of reinforcements. In the plain shaping exercise, the pigeon is reinforced every time it pecks—continuous reinforcement. Suppose, however, that the bird is reinforced after every tenth peck. Under this schedule of reinforcement, the rate of pecking is greatly increased.

Again we ask, what has this to do with personality? If we think of personality as an assembly of behavior traits, and if each trait describes a set of related learned responses, then clearly the principle of operant conditioning can account for personality. If a baby is picked up and hugged *only* when he cries, then surely he will become a cry-baby. If an adolescent *only* gets approval from his parents when he submits to their wishes, he soon will develop the trait of submissiveness. Generosity can be instilled in a person by rewarding him for generous acts. If we withdraw reinforcement for a certain class of acts—those, for example, that are aggressive—such acts will tend to decline in number.

16-16

The outstanding behavioristic psychologist, Burrhus Frederic Skinner, was born in Susquehanna, Pennsylvania on March 20, 1904. His father, a lawyer, wanted his son to follow in his footsteps—but Skinner wanted to be a writer and majored in literature at Hamilton College in Clinton, New York. After graduating in 1926, he spent several years writing but the results were not productive. Deciding to study psychology, Skinner entered Harvard University, where he received his Ph.D. in 1931. After several university appointments, Skinner returned as a professor to Harvard where he has remained. Primarily a research psychologist, Skinner has worked mostly with animals, especially the pigeon. He is generally regarded as the greatest living American psychologist.

Operant reinforcement is an extremely powerful means of shaping personality. Skinner and his followers have applied it to a number of important practical problems, including programmed learning ("teaching machines") and the treatment of behavior disorders. In *Walden Two* (1948), Skinner has even drawn up a blueprint for a utopian society based on his methods of behavior control. Skinner's willingness to apply his methods of shaping behavior through reinforcement to an extremely wide range of behaviors and beliefs and his talent for expressing his views to a general audience (see, for example, *Beyond Freedom and Dignity*, 1971) have made him a controversial figure.

Theories of the Self

Many psychologists, beginning with the pioneer American psychologist William James, have considered the *self* to be the central structure of the personality. Adler spoke of the creative self as the sovereign power in the personality. McDougall had his concept of the self-regarding sentiment. Sullivan recognized a self-system that acts as a guardian of one's security. Jung's archetypal self strives for unification of the total personality. For Jungians, it is the center of the personality around which all the other systems revolve; it holds these systems together and provides the personality with unity, equilibrium, and stability. But before the self can emerge as an active force, the personality's other components must be fully developed. For this reason, the archetype of the self does not become evident until middle age.

Some recent personality theorists have a great deal to say about the self. Among these are Kurt Goldstein, Abraham Maslow, and Carl Rogers.

Goldstein's Self-Actualization Theory

For Goldstein, self-actualization is the master driving force in personality; in fact, it is the individual's only motive. What appear to be different drives, such as hunger, sex, power, achievement, and curiosity, are merely manifestations of the sovereign purpose of life, to actualize oneself. When a person is hungry, he actualizes himself by eating; when he craves power, he actualizes himself by obtaining power.

Self-actualization is the creative force of human nature. It is the organic principle by which the organism becomes more fully developed and more complete. A person who desires knowledge feels an inner emptiness; he has a sense of his own incompleteness. By reading and studying, he fulfills his desire for knowledge and the emptiness disappears. His desire has become an actuality. Any need is a deficit state which motivates the person to fill the deficit. This fulfillment of a need is self-actualization.

Although self-actualization is universal, the specific ends toward which people strive vary from person to person. This is because people have different innate potentialities, as well as different environments and cultures to which they must adjust and from which they must secure the necessities for growth.

16-17
Kurt Goldstein was born in Upper Silesia, Germany (now Poland), on November 6, 1878. He earned a medical degree in 1903. During the First World War, he became director of the Military Hospital for Brain-Injured Soldiers and was instrumental in establishing an institute for research on the aftereffects of brain injuries. It was in this institute that Goldstein carried out the studies that laid the foundation for his organismic viewpoint. Goldstein was also deeply influenced by Gestalt psychology, which was being developed in Germany at that time. In 1930, he went to the University of Berlin as a professor of neurology and psychiatry. When Hitler took over Germany, Goldstein was jailed and then released on condition that he leave the country. He went to Amsterdam, where he wrote his most important book, *The Organism* (1939).

Goldstein came to the United States in 1935. During the war years, he published a book on the aftereffects of brain injuries. In his later years, Goldstein became more closely associated with phenomenology and existential psychology. He died in New York City on September 19, 1965, at the age of 86.

16-18
Abraham Harold Maslow was born in Brooklyn, New York, on April 1, 1908. All of his degrees were earned at the University of Wisconsin, where he did research on primate behavior. For fourteen years (1937–1951) he was on the faculty of Brooklyn College. In 1951, Maslow went to Brandeis University, where he remained until 1969, when he became resident fellow of the Laughlin Foundation in Menlo Park, California. Maslow suffered a fatal heart attack on June 8, 1970.

How can an individual's potentialities be determined? Goldstein says this can best be done by finding out what the person prefers and what he does. His preferences correspond to his potentialities. Most famous artists—Picasso is only one of many examples—show their preference for drawing at a very early age. The same is true of musicians, writers, actors, athletes, scientists, mathematicians, inventors, engineers, and mechanics. Thus, if parents or teachers want to help their children or pupils actualize themselves, they must pay attention to what they like to do and what they have gifts for doing.

Maslow's Self-Actualization Theory

Maslow approached self-actualization from a different perspective. He sought out people who had developed their potentialities to the utmost and studied them intensively to see how they differed from more ordinary people. Self-actualizers are characteristically

1. realistically oriented

2. accepting of themselves, other people, and the world

3. spontaneous

4. problem-centered rather than self-centered

5. detached

6. independent

7. democratic

8. creative

9. nonconformists

Most self-actualizers have had profound mystical or spiritual experiences, although these were not necessarily religious in character. Their relationships with the few people they love are profound and deeply emotional rather than superficial. Their sense of humor is philosophical rather than hostile.

Maslow also has investigated what he calls *peak experiences*. He asked a number of people to think of the most wonderful experience of their lives. He found that during a peak experience, people felt more integrated, more at one with the world, more their own master, more spontaneous, less aware of space and time, and more perceptive.

We have already discussed Maslow's theory of motivation in Chapter 10. He points out that to actualize yourself fully you must not only satisfy the basic needs of hunger, sex, and security, but also the metaneeds or growth needs of justice, goodness, beauty, and order.

Like Goldstein, Maslow postulates that the drive for actualization of one's potentialities is inborn, although this impulse for growth and self-realization may be frustrated by external obstacles. In such cases, the individual becomes psychologically stunted or mentally disturbed. Certainly Maslow was one of the most eloquent spokesmen for a growth psychology. Another eloquent spokesman is Carl Rogers.

16-19
Carl Ransom Rogers, the founder of nondirective or client-centered counseling, was born in Oak Park, Illinois on January 8, 1902. He grew up on a farm in a highly religious home. After receiving his bachelor's degree from the University of Wisconsin in 1924, he enrolled at the Union Theological Seminary in New York City. While taking courses in psychology at Columbia University, he decided to give up his religious studies and become a clinical psychologist. After receiving his Ph.D. in 1931 from Columbia, Rogers worked in a guidance clinic in Rochester for nine years. An appointment as professor of psychology at Ohio State University in 1940 enabled him to develop his ideas on counseling in collaboration with a number of graduate students. From there, he moved to the Counseling Center at the University of Chicago and then to the University of Wisconsin, where he did important work on psychotherapy with schizophrenics. Rogers is presently resident fellow at the Center for Studies of the Person in La Jolla, California.

Rogers' Self Theory

Although Rogers accepts the idea of self-actualization and growth needs, his principal contribution to personality theory has been to show how the self or self-concept emerges out of the experiences of the total organism and how this emergent self then can distort or deny the organism's experiences.

Rogers' chief concept, and the bedrock upon which the personality rests, is that of experience. *Experience* is everything that is potentially available to the organism's awareness. This totality of experience constitutes the person's *phenomenal* (experiential) *field*. The experiences of the organism are always valid, and as long as one acts in accord with them the personality will not be disturbed.

Within this phenomenal field a region develops which Rogers calls the *self* or *self-concept*. The experiences of this self system are those that refer to the "I." They are the ways in which I experience myself. Statements such as the following are expressions of the self's experiences: "I am unattractive." "I am honest." "I am intelligent." Note that these statements are self-evaluations. Unfortunately, these experiences of the self may not be correct because the self-concept is heavily influenced by evaluations made by other people, especially by parents when the child is growing up.

Because such evaluations are sometimes positive and sometimes negative, the child learns to differentiate between actions and feelings that are worthy (approved) and those that are unworthy (disapproved). Unworthy experiences tend to be excluded from the self-concept even though they are organismically true. This results in a self-concept that is in part out of tune with organismic experiences. The child tries to be what others want him to be instead of being what he really is. For example, a boy has a picture of himself as a good boy, loved by his parents, but he also enjoys teasing his little sister, for which he is punished. This punishment calls upon him to revise his self-image in one of the following ways: (a) "I am a bad boy," (b) "My parents don't like me," (c) "I don't like to tease my sister." Each of these self-attitudes contains a distortion of the truth. He is not a bad boy, his parents do love him, and he does like to tease his sister. Suppose he adopts the attitude "I don't like to tease my sister," thereby denying his real feelings. Denial does not mean that the feelings cease to exist; they are just no longer available to his consciousness. A conflict then will exist between the spurious, conscious feeling "I don't like to tease my sister" and the genuine, denied one "I like to tease my sister."

When more and more of the true organismic experiences are displaced by values taken over from others and perceived as being one's own, conflicts between self and organism will increase. Self-deception makes a person tense, uncomfortable, and dissatisfied. He feels as if he does not know what he is and what he wants. He feels constantly threatened by his true organismic feelings.

How can this breach between false self-evaluations and true organismic experiences be healed? Rogers proposes the following remedy.

Under certain conditions, involving complete absence of any threat to the self-structure, experiences which are inconsistent with it may be perceived, and examined, and the structure of self revised to assimilate and include such experiences (1951).

Rogers developed a method of counseling which provides just such conditions for revising the self-concept. Originally named nondirective counseling, it now is called client-centered counseling. In client-centered counseling, the person finds himself in a nonthreatening situation because the counselor unreservedly accepts everything the client says with absolutely no hint of evaluation or interpretation. Either he remains silent, occasionally saying "uhm," or he calmly reflects what the client is saying—"so you don't feel happy with yourself?" The counselor's accepting attitude encourages the client to explore his unverbalized feelings and to make himself aware of them. In the safety of the therapeutic situation, the formerly threatening feelings can be assimilated into the self-structure. The assimilation may require rather drastic renovation of the self-concept to align it with the reality of organismic experience. An important social benefit of this renovation is the person's greater understanding and acceptance of other people.

Rogers deserves great credit for developing a method of psychotherapy that is consonant with his theoretical viewpoint. He constantly is testing his theories in the counseling situation and improving his counseling practices. No psychologist has done more research on the process of psychotherapy.

Existential Theory

The *existential* viewpoint has been introduced into psychology only recently. Adapted from a prominent school of philosophy, existential psychology is still more of a European movement than an American one—although it is gaining headway in the United States. Existential theory bears a faint resemblance to Rogers' self theory, in that both viewpoints recognize experience as the source of psychological knowledge. Existential theory also recognizes self-actualization as the goal toward which the individual strives.

Boss's Existential Theory

The leading exponent of existential psychology is the Swiss psychiatrist, Medard Boss. We will synopsize some of the basic tenets of existential theory.

Man is a being-in-the-world. This hyphenated noun is intended to describe the individual as embedded in the world. Person and world cannot be separated. Man is neither subject nor object. He is thrown into the world and remains inseparable from it.

The world is disclosed in the individual and the individual discloses the world. These disclosures or experiences constitute the whole realm of existence. Nothing lies behind these experiences. Nothing causes them; they just *are,* in all of their immediacy.

16-20
Medard Boss, one of the founders of existential psychology, was born in St. Gallen, Switzerland on October 4, 1903. When he was two years old his parents moved to Zurich, where Boss has lived ever since. He received his medical degree from the University of Zurich in 1928. Analyzed by Sigmund Freud and trained in psychoanalysis in London and Germany, Boss also had contact with his fellow townsman, Carl Jung. In 1946 he became acquainted with the existential philosopher Martin Heidegger; under his influence, Boss developed a new viewpoint regarding treatment. Two visits to India also had an impact on his thinking. Since 1954 Boss has been professor of psychotherapy at the University of Zurich and the leader of the existential movement in psychiatry known as Daseinsanalysis.

Man carries within himself an almost infinite number of possibilities for disclosing the world. He, and he alone, is responsible for realizing as many of these possibilities as he can. When he accepts this responsibility, he is exercising his freedom as a man. Man is free to be what he wants to be.

When the individual fails to use his freedom to realize all of his possibilities, he experiences a sense of guilt. Guilt is an inescapable aspect of the human condition, however. The individual cannot avoid it because he is always in debt to the myriad possibilities for disclosing the world. Every choice he makes means that for the time being he has rejected all other possibilities.

Another consequence of the failure to realize all of one's possibilities is nonbeing or nothingness—that which is not realized. The individual is always in danger of falling into the void of nothingness and ceasing to exist as a being. His dread of nothingness hangs over man like a dark cloud.

Existence is never static; it is always becoming something new, or transcending itself. The goal of existence is to become completely human, that is, to actualize as many ways of being-in-the-world as are humanly possible.

As you can see by this brief excursion into existential psychology, it holds both hope and despair for man; hope because he is free to realize himself, despair because he never can realize all of his possibilities.

Issues in Modern Personality Theory

Now that we have surveyed many of the prominent theories of personality, let us turn to some of the more controversial issues regarding the nature of personality. Since much of the controversy stems from the theorists' dissimilar backgrounds and the different types of work they do, let us examine this matter first.

Clinical Versus Laboratory Settings

Some of the theorists developed their conceptions of personality out of their experiences in treating patients afflicted with various types of psychological disorders. We may call this a clinical setting. Included in this group are Adler, Boss, Freud, Fromm, Goldstein, Horney, Jung, Kelly, Rogers, and Sullivan. With the exception of Fromm, Kelly, and Rogers, all were medically trained psychiatrists.

Other theorists developed their ideas from observations and experiments they made in university laboratories. Included in this group are the theories of Allport, Bandura and Walters, Cattell, Maslow, Miller and Dollard, Murray, Sheldon, and Skinner. With the exception of Murray, they hold doctorates in psychology. (Sheldon also has a medical degree.) Murray was medically trained but during his years at Harvard as director of the Psychological Clinic he was much more research-oriented than clinically oriented.

The primary data for the clinical theories consist of patients' verbal and expressive behaviors while undergoing treatment. The primary data for the laboratory theories consist of behaviors performed in controlled experiments or of scores on standardized tests.

Clinical theories are based on the intensive study of individuals who are seen several times a week, often for a number of years. Laboratory theories often (but not always) are based on the study of large groups of individuals for short periods of time, often for only an hour or two. A clinical investigation's aim is to try to understand all aspects of a person. A laboratory investigation's aims are to measure carefully limited aspects of the person, and to determine how personality characteristics can be altered by manipulating variables in the environment or in the individual. The objective of some laboratory studies is to see how traits fit together by correlating them with one another.

Statistical techniques, some of them very complex, are used to analyze the results obtained from laboratory investigations. Clinical findings often are not subjected to any kind of statistical treatment. One looks in vain through the writings of Adler, Boss, Freud, Fromm, Horney, Jung (except for Jung's early research on complexes using the word-association test and a later astrological investigation), and Sullivan for any statistical analysis, even the most elementary. The clinician prefers verbal descriptions to numbers.

Laboratory studies often use animals and children as subjects, whereas clinic patients are usually adult humans. Another difference is that laboratory subjects are typically "normal" individuals and clinical subjects are troubled people.

Sometimes, laboratory investigations are considered more "scientific" than clinical studies but this depends on how one defines science. Virtually all of the clinical theorists received rigorous scientific training.

We may have given the impression that the two groups of theories, derived as they are from different settings, have little in common. This is not entirely true. Hypotheses and insights obtained in the clinic have stimulated a great amount of laboratory research, and clinicians have generously applied the findings of experimental investigations. Moreover, some of the clinic-based theorists have done laboratory research or have performed well-controlled experiments in the clinic. Rogers' studies of the changes that take place during psychotherapy are fine examples. Some of the laboratory theorists have had personal experience in the clinic, and one of them, Henry Murray, established a simulated clinical environment in which he studied a nonpatient population. This interpenetration of the clinic and the laboratory has begun to blur the distinctions between the two kinds of theories.

Now let us discuss some of the substantive issues on which theorists differ.

Conscious Versus Unconscious Determinants of Personality

Prior to Freud, psychology was primarily a science of the conscious mind. Although Freud was not the discoverer of the unconscious, he was the first person to develop and use methods—free association and dream interpretation—to explore it in depth. Freud and Jung both assigned great importance to the unconscious determinants of personality and behavior. At the opposite end of the unconscious-conscious continuum are Allport, Boss, Kelly, and Rogers. They are interested primarily in analyzing the role of conscious, rational experiences in determining behavior. Somewhere between these two poles we find many of the other theorists—but the behavior theorists do not concern themselves with the question. They reject all mentalistic concepts, preferring to formulate their theories in terms of observable, overt behavior alone.

Each position on the importance of conscious and unconscious determinants fosters different research and clinical practices. Therapists who believe the unconscious can control behavior concentrate their efforts on bringing the unconscious into consciousness; they use such techniques as free association, active imagination, amplification, and dream interpretation. Theorists who attribute a leading role to consciousness attempt to use rational analysis to describe its structure and its various modes of experiencing the world. Theorists who reject mentalistic concepts, such as consciousness or unconsciousness, employ reinforcement, aversive conditioning, systematic desensitization, and other behavior-modification methods based on learning principles. Partisans of each position claim that their methods are therapeutically effective, as indeed they are for *some* patients with *some* specific problems.

In doing research, those who believe in unconscious determinants use *projective* tests of personality whereas those who believe in conscious determinants employ *objective* tests or questionnaires. We shall describe both kinds of tests in the next chapter.

The Role of Heredity

Another issue on which personality theorists differ is the role they assign to inborn determinants of personality. Freud's instincts and id, Jung's archetypes, Sheldon's somatotypes, Goldstein's self-actualization, Rogers' organism, and Maslow's basic needs are all aspects of man's innate nature. He is born with them and they continue to influence him throughout his life, these theorists believe. Some theorists, particularly the behaviorists, say that however strong man's innate nature may be, experience, education, and manipulations of his environment can modify it. Others, such as the self-actualization theorists Goldstein and Maslow, argue that the individual should be allowed to develop in accord with his inborn potentialities. They believe the organism has its own integrity; if an individual's integrity is deformed by externally imposed modifications, his personality will be seriously damaged.

While many psychologists will concede that man has an inborn nature, the kinds of investigations that would establish this inborn nature are unequivocally difficult to conduct with human subjects. As we have mentioned, one method used to estimate the influence of heredity on various aspects of personality and behavior is to compare the performance of identical (monozygotic) twins with the performance of fraternal (dizygotic) twins. Identical twins are, of course, generally more similar than are fraternal twins. However, identical twins are *less* alike in personality traits than in intellectual and physical traits. This suggests that the environment usually influences personality traits more than it influences our intellectual and physical characteristics. Cattell's research indicates that the genes affect some personality traits more than others. The influence of genetic factors on personality is a fascinating area of research that is now attracting many psychologists.

Situational Determinants

When several people with different personalities encounter the same situation, they tend to react differently to it. For example, John, Bill, and Alex are hiking in the mountains when they hear a strange noise in the underbrush near the trail. John, who is curious, fearless, and impulsive, immediately dashes into the underbrush to see what is making the noise. Bill, who is cautious, anxious, and lacking in self-confidence, retreats down the path away from the noise. Alex, who is meditative and withdrawn, pays no attention to the sound and keeps on walking.

Because the reactions of the three young men are so varied, one could argue that the situation is not an important determinant of their respective responses. Some personality theorists—Jung, for instance—do pay little attention to situational factors. They feel that the environment is merely a stage on which individuals perform actions and interactions; or that it is a neutral background on which individuals project their wishes, fears, conflicts, and personality traits.

In our example, however, it is interesting to note that neither John nor Bill would have reacted as they did unless they had heard a noise. They would have continued on the path as Alex did. Consequently some psychologists, including the behavior theorists, argue that to understand and predict behavior we must take into account the situational variables.

Some theorists try to solve the problem by formulating concepts that bridge or eliminate the gap between personal and situational variables. Existential psychologists deny a gap; for them, the person is always in the world and cannot be separated from it. He *is* his world. Murray's concept of thema unites personal need and situational press. Cattell suggests that a person's response in a particular situation can be predicted by what he calls the *specification equation*. In this equation, each of a person's traits is weighted by its relevance in a given situation. Some traits will be very relevant and receive a strong weighting, others will be less relevant and receive a moderate weighting, and still others will be irrelevant and receive no weighting at all. The specification equation readily lends itself to application. Thus, employment offices might describe jobs in terms of situations requiring certain kinds of personality traits. In this way, they could test a job applicant and match the profile of his traits with the requirements of the various jobs until they find one that he is suited for.

Kurt Lewin, whose theory we have not discussed, proposed that behavior results from the person *and* the environment. He then developed concepts that describe personal and environmental variables and their relations to one another. Two of Lewin's concepts are *vectors* and *valences*. A vector is an inner motivational state or "push;" a valence is an environmental incentive or "pull." The behavior or *path* (as Lewin

Diagram of Lewin's field theory of
personality. Either the vector (the
push from within) or the valence (the
pull from the environment) must be
strong enough for a person to cross the
barrier to obtain the desired object.

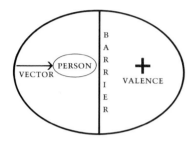

called it) that a person takes is determined by the vectors' relation to the
valences, and also by any barriers between the person and the object
that has valence.

If a person is to break through the barrier and obtain the desired object,
the vector must be strong enough to give him the necessary push or the
valence must be strong enough to give him the necessary pull.

The Development of Personality

Does personality develop only to a certain age and then stop or does personality continue to grow throughout one's life? Does personality
develop in fairly distinct stages? Personality theorists answer these
questions in widely divergent ways.

One of Freud's more astonishing observations was that the scaffolding
of personality is erected by the age of 5 or 6. How the individual behaves
later is prefigured by his early development. From what evidence did
Freud draw this conclusion? Not primarily from observations of children growing into adults, although Freud did have six children of his
own to observe. Nor did he treat children in his practice as a psychoanalyst, except on one occasion, and in that case the child's father acted
as an intermediary between Freud and the child.

Freud's chief sources of information were the memories and associations of his adult patients. Inevitably, they began to talk about their
childhood experiences in connection with their present difficulties.
Even their nocturnal dreams contained many direct or symbolized
memories of childhood. Freud then began to understand that not only
did neurotic symptoms have their origins in childhood, but so did the
normal character traits of adults. Thus, an adult who is thrifty may possess that trait because of the kind of toilet training he experienced.

Freud's version of personality development, stressing the importance
of childhood experiences, has been widely accepted—perhaps because
many people believe the popular sayings "The child is father of the
man" and "Just as the twig is bent the tree's inclined." However, other
personality theorists have not left his theory unchallenged. Gordon Allport espouses a theory of development diametrically opposed to Freud's.
He believes a sharp division separates the young child, who is motivated
largely by biological drives, and the mature adult, who is motivated by
conscious, rational purposes. Allport does acknowledge that some of the
infant's behavior is recognizable as a forerunner of subsequent personality traits. He also admits that some adults do not become fully mature
but retain infantile characteristics in their personalities.

The self-actualization psychologists view personality as continuously
developing. Self-actualization is never completed, nor does it ever stop.
Existential psychologists do not pay much attention to development
because, in their view, the individual's whole history is always present
at any given moment.

Behavior theorists have a different view. They believe that personality
changes but does not necessarily develop or grow. Changes in personality in the sense of acquiring new habits or breaking old ones can
take place at any time during one's life, depending on what responses
are reinforced or not reinforced.

Stages of Development.   Many psychologists disagree over the stages of development. As we have already noted, some theorists believe personality development is a continuous process. Those who do believe in recognizable stages do not agree on the nature of the stages or their length. Freud identifies three stages—the oral, anal, and phallic—that take place before the age of 5 (see Chapter 13). Jung sees two important periods—before middle age (35 to 40) and after middle age. Before 35, the person is energetic, vigorous, and extraverted. He expends his energies in such practical activities as learning a vocation, getting married and having children, and participating in social, political, and community affairs. After 35, the individual becomes more introverted, less energetic, and wiser. His values become more cultural and spiritual. Jung observes that some people do not make this transition smoothly. As a consequence, they are dissatisfied and restless, often becoming neurotic. In his practice, Jung treated many middle-aged people who were having difficulty shifting their values.

Sullivan delineates six stages in the development of personality prior to the final stage of maturity. These are (1) infancy, (2) childhood, (3) the juvenile period, (4) preadolescence, (5) early adolescence, and (6) late adolescence.

The period of infancy extends from birth to the appearance of speech. It is the period in which the mouth is the primary zone of interaction between the baby and his environment. Nursing provides the baby with his first interpersonal experience. He acquires his first personifications, such as the bad, anxious, rejecting, frustrating mother and the good, relaxed, accepting, satisfying mother.

The transition from infancy to childhood is made possible by the learning of language. Among other things, language permits the fusion of different personifications—for instance, the fusion of the good mother and bad mother, and the integration of the self-system into a more coherent structure. The growth of symbolic ability enables the child to play at being a grown-up; Sullivan calls these performances *dramatizations.* One dramatic event of childhood is the *malevolent transformation,* the feeling that one lives among enemies. The malevolent transformation distorts the child's interpersonal relations and causes the child to isolate himself. The malevolent transformation is caused by painful and anxiety-arousing experiences with people, and may lead to a regression to the less threatening stage of infancy.

Childhood extends from the emergence of articulate speech to the appearance of the need for playmates. This begins the juvenile stage, which lasts throughout the grammar-school years. The individual becomes social, competitive, and cooperative; yet he learns the meaning of ostracism, disparagement, and group feeling.

The relatively brief period of preadolescence is marked by the need for an intimate relationship with a peer of the same sex, a chum in whom one can confide and with whom one can collaborate in meeting the tasks and solving the problems of life. This is an extremely important period because it marks the beginning of genuine human relationships on a level of equality, mutuality, and reciprocity. Lacking an intimate companion, the preadolescent becomes desperately lonely.

16-22
Erik Homburger Erikson was born of Danish parents on June 15, 1902, near Frankfort, Germany. Upon completing high school, Erikson spent a year wandering through Europe, trying to find out what direction his life should take. Eventually he decided to become an artist and to teach art. While teaching in a small private school in Vienna, Erikson became well acquainted with the Freud family and began analysis with Anna Freud. Through her encouragement, he began to study psychoanalysis at the Vienna Psychoanalytic Society. He also studied the Montessori method of education, which stresses the development of the whole child.

In 1933, Erikson departed for the United States, where he became the first child psychoanalyst in Boston. He also held positions at Harvard and the Massachusetts General Hospital. Years later he went to live on a Sioux reservation and observe Sioux Indian children. At the end of that year, he became associated with the Institute of Child Welfare of the University of California in Berkeley, where he published a very influential book, *Childhood and Society* (1963). Erikson later returned to Harvard University as a professor of human development. He retired in 1970.

The main task of early adolescence is the development of heterosexual relationships. The youth experiences the physiological changes of puberty as feelings of lust; out of these feelings the lust dynamism emerges and begins to assert itself in the personality. Erotic need diverges from the need for intimacy; the erotic need takes as its object a member of the opposite sex while the need for intimacy remains fixated upon a member of the same sex. If these two needs do not become divorced, the young person displays a homosexual rather than heterosexual orientation. Sullivan points out that many of the conflicts of adolescence arise out of the opposing needs for sexual gratification, security, and intimacy.

The period of late adolescence constitutes a rather prolonged initiation into the privileges, duties, satisfactions, and responsibilities of social living and citizenship.

One of the best-known descriptions of stages of personality development was formulated by the psychoanalyst Erik Erikson. Although strongly influenced by Freud (as noted in Figure 16-22, he studied at the Vienna Psychoanalytic Society), Erikson describes his stages in *psychosocial* rather than in psychosexual terms. Moreover, Erikson sees personality developing throughout the whole life cycle rather than ending in all essential respects at the age of 6.

Erikson identifies five stages between birth and adolescence. During infancy, the first stage, the baby and the mother recognize, or acknowledge, each other many times a day. This mutual recognition is the basis for an emergence of *trust* in the infant. Lacking trust, the baby would be severely handicapped in the following stages. This stage corresponds to Freud's oral stage.

When the child trusts his environment he can develop *independence* and a sense of his own *autonomy*. If the parents criticize and frustrate his attempts to examine and test the objects in his environment, they hinder the development of autonomy and cause the child to feel ashamed and harbor doubts about his adequacy. This period corresponds to Freud's anal stage.

Later in childhood, but before he enters school, the child acquires *initiative*. He learns to do things for himself without being told, and he begins to practice various roles which he will have to play later in life. If the parents interfere with his freedom, the child may respond by feeling guilty. This period corresponds to Freud's phallic stage.

During the early school years, the fourth stage, the child learns how to work and to be *industrious*. If his efforts are criticized or ridiculed, he may develop a sense of inferiority. This period corresponds to Freud's latency period when the child's sexual impulse is at a low level of expression.

The feelings of trust, autonomy, initiative, and industry must develop before the crucial period of adolescence. During this time, the individual acquires his own *identity* as a unique human being with his own inherent characteristics, preferences, and aspirations. He now gains control over his own life. He defines who he is and what he wants to be.

During the stage of *identity formation*, the adolescent is apt to suffer more deeply than ever in his life from a confusion of roles, or what

Comparison of theories of personality development.

Theorist	Stages		Ages
Freud	oral		birth–2
	anal		2–5
	phallic		5–12
	genital		12+
Jung	stage 1		birth–35 (or 40)
	stage 2		35+
Sullivan	infancy		birth–1½
	childhood		1½–3
	juvenile		3–11
	pre-adolescence		11–13
	early adolescence		13–15
	adolescence		15–19
Erikson	trust vs. mistrust		birth–1
	autonomy vs. doubt		1–3
	initiative vs. guilt		3–5
	industry vs. inferiority		5–11
	identity vs. role confusion		11–18
	intimacy vs. isolation		early adulthood
	generativity vs. self-absorption		middle age
	integrity vs. despair		old age

Erikson calls *identity confusion*. This confusion can make the young person feel isolated, empty, anxious, and indecisive. He feels he must make important decisions but he cannot. He also feels that society is pushing him to make decisions, and he becomes resistant. His behavior is inconsistent and unpredictable. At one moment, he does not feel like committing himself to anyone in a friendly relationship for fear of being rejected, disappointed, or misled. In the next moment he may want to be a follower, lover, or disciple at any cost. A person who does not form a stable identity during adolescence will encounter one problem after another during his adult life.

During young adulthood, an individual forms *intimate* relationships with others; if he does not, he feels isolated. In middle age, the person develops what Erikson calls *generativity*. This means he looks beyond himself and his own interests to the future and to things outside of himself—his family and his country. In old age, if a person has fulfilled his potentialities, he can enjoy a sense of *integrity*. But if his life has been a misdirected, unfulfilled one, he will experience despair and depression.

Are Personality Theories Useful?

Having completed a survey of many of the leading conceptions of personality and some of the issues on which theorists divide, some readers may expect an evaluation of each theory, spelling out where it is true and where it is false. This is an impossible task for several reasons.

In the first place, the evidence is so incomplete that we would be premature to draw any final conclusions from it. Second, the evidence we do have often conflicts so strongly that it is difficult to say where the truth lies. Third, psychologists do not always agree on what constitutes evidence. Data that one psychologist has accepted are rejected as spurious by another. For example, evidence obtained in the clinic often is dismissed as implausible by experimental psychologists. Conversely, evidence obtained from laboratory experiments often is criticized as irrelevant and trivial by clinical psychologists.

Finally, because different theories address themselves to different aspects of the total personality, we cannot compare them, except when they have different views on the same subject. Therefore, it is probably most useful to regard theories as sources of ideas for testing by observation and experiment. A good theory, by this criterion, is one that generates a number of testable hypotheses.

Summary

1. Although there are many conceptions of personality, psychologists generally agree that personality refers to an organization of more or less permanent qualities that characterize an individual.

2. Personality theories can be classified as psychodynamic, social-psychological, trait, type, cognitive, behavior, self, and existential.

3. Psychodynamic theories stress inborn predispositions, unconscious motivation, and infantile complexes.

4. Central to Freud's psychoanalytic theory are his concepts of the id, which operates according to the pleasure principle; the ego, which operates according to the reality principle; and the superego, which is our conscience.

5. Jung, in his theory of analytic psychology, described the role of complexes and their appearance through complex-indicators. Jung also described the collective unconscious, which contains the archetypes that exist in all people.

6. Social psychological theories, such as those developed by Adler, Fromm, Sullivan, and Horney, accentuate the role of social and cultural factors and interpersonal relations, especially within the family, in determining personality.

7. Trait theories describe personality in terms of traits, which are innate or learned dispositions to behave in particular ways. Allport distinguishes between common and individual traits, and between cardinal, central, and secondary traits. Cattell emphasizes surface and source traits.

8. Sheldon's type theory recognizes three dimensions of personality that are correlated with three dimensions of physique.

9. George Kelly's cognitive theory states that personal constructs are the central feature of personality. A personal construct is defined as the way in which a person interprets some aspect of his world.

10. Habit is the key concept of the behavior theories. Acts become habitual if they are reinforced. Miller and Dollard refer to the sequential roles of drive, stimulus, response, and reinforcement. Bandura and

Walters stress the role of social imitation. Skinner concentrates on response and reinforcement.

11. The self and its actualization are prominent features of the viewpoints of Goldstein, Maslow, and Rogers.

12. Existential theory, such as that of Boss, regards man as a being-in-the-world who is free to be whatever he wants to be and who has the responsibility for fulfilling all of his possibilities.

13. Personality theories may be divided into those based on observations made in the clinic and those based on experiments performed in the laboratory.

14. Some of the issues on which personality theories take different positions include (a) the role of conscious and unconscious processes, (b) the influence of heredity, (c) the importance of situational factors, and (d) the way in which personality develops.

15. Stages of personality development have been proposed by Freud, Jung, Sullivan, Erikson, and others. Each of Erikson's eight stages is characterized by a psychosocial conflict.

Important Terms

personality

Freud's psychoanalytic theory

id

pleasure principle

Oedipus complex

castration complex

ego

reality principle

superego

Jung's analytic psychology

complex-indicators

collective unconscious

archetypes

Murray's personology

need

press

thema

unity thema

Adler's theory

Horney's theory

Fromm's theory

Sullivan's theory

dynamism

personification

stereotypes

self-system

Allport's trait theory

common traits

individual traits

cardinal traits

central traits

secondary traits

Cattell's trait theory

factor analysis

surface traits

source traits

dynamic traits

ability traits

temperament traits

sentiments

Sheldon's type theory

endomorph

mesomorph

ectomorph

somatotype

viscerotonia

somatotonia

cerebrotonia

Kelly's personal construct theory

Dollard and Miller's stimulus-response theory

habit

motive (drive)

stimulus (cue)

response

reinforcement

Bandura and Walters' social learning theory

social imitation

Skinner's operant reinforcement theory

Goldstein's self-actualization theory

Maslow's self-actualization theory

peak experiences

Rogers' self theory

experience

phenomenal field

self-concept

Boss's existential theory

Kurt Lewin's theory

vectors

valences

pathway

barriers

Freud's psychosexual stages of personality development

Sullivan's stages of personality development

dramatizations

Erikson's stages of personality development

identity formation

Suggested Readings

HALL, C. S. *A primer of Freudian psychology.* New York: New American Library, 1955.

An introduction to the principal concepts of Freudian psychology written for the beginning student. A brief biography of Freud is included.

HALL, C. S., & LINDZEY, G. *Theories of personality.* 2nd ed. New York: Wiley, 1970.

A standard textbook in which thirteen theories of personality are presented.

HALL, C. S., & NORDBY, V. J. *A primer of Jungian psychology.* New York: Taplinger, 1973. (Paper: New York: New American Library, 1973.)

An introduction to the chief concepts of Jungian psychology written for the beginning student. A brief biography of Jung is included.

LINDZEY, G., HALL, C. S., & MANOSEVITZ, M. (EDS.) *Theories of personality: primary sources and research.* 2nd ed. New York: Wiley, 1973.

> Selections from the writings of a number of personality theorists, and representative studies that have been stimulated by each of the theories.

NORDBY, V. J., & HALL, C. S. *A guide to psychologists and their concepts.* San Francisco: W. H. Freeman, 1974.

> A survey of the concepts of many of the psychologists discussed in the present chapter. It includes brief biographies.

SARASON, I. G. *Personality: an objective approach.* 2nd ed. New York: Wiley, 1972.

> A standard textbook which stresses the empirical approach to personality.

Chapter 17   Assessment of Personality

It is the mark of an educated man to look for precision in each class of things just so far as the nature of the subject admits.

Aristotle

I have made a ceaseless effort not to ridicule, not to bewail, nor to scorn human actions, but to understand them.

Spinoza

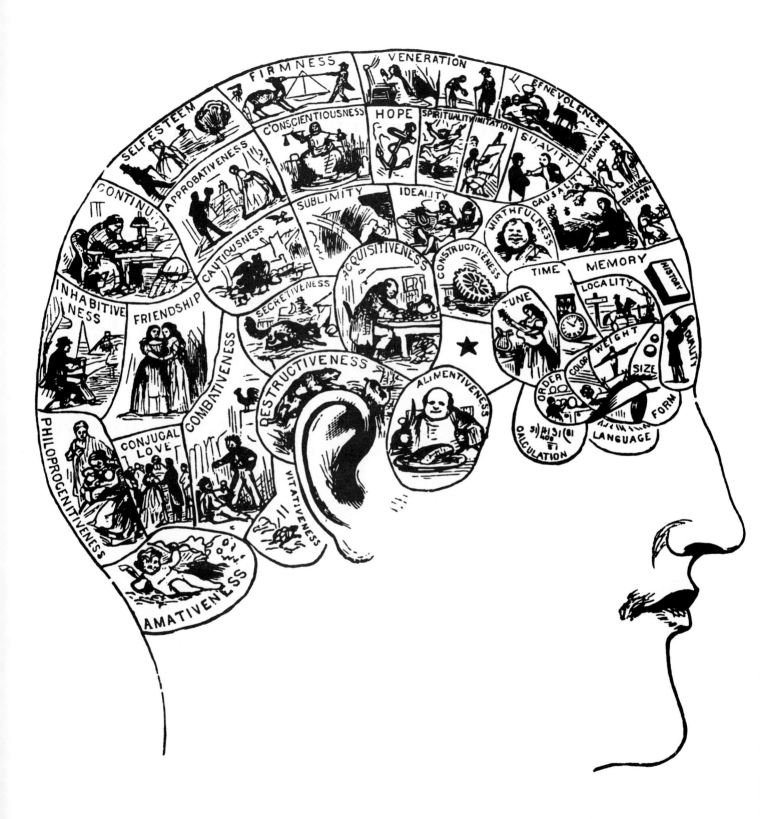

Assessment of Personality

Just as there are many theories of personality, so there are many concepts of how we can best describe, measure, and evaluate personality. Of course, we cannot measure personality as a whole. It is not a physical entity like the body that can be weighed and measured. Each theory of personality identifies and describes *dimensions* or aspects of personality, and it is these dimensions that have been subjected to various kinds of measurement. The dimensions may be instincts or drives (McDougall, Freud), archetypes, complexes, and character types (Jung), needs and press (Murray), temperament types (Sheldon), modes of being-in-the-world (existentialism), traits (Allport, Cattell), vectors and valences (Lewin), self-concept (Rogers), personal constructs (Kelly), or habits (behaviorism).

Common sense tells us that people differ with respect to any of these personality characteristics. We know from experience that one person is more or less aggressive or achievement-oriented than another. But to estimate the *degree* of a person's aggressiveness, we must devise a yardstick or *scale* for measuring aggressiveness. Many types of personality scales have been devised; in this chapter, we shall describe some of these types and the assumptions underlying them.

How Personality Tests Are Constructed

To demonstrate how we construct a scale for measuring a dimension of personality, let us consider Jung's dimension of introversion-extraversion. The first question is, how did Jung happen to identify introversion-extraversion as a significant aspect of personality? He did so by observing the expressive behavior and verbalizations of his patients, other people, and himself. He noticed that some of the things they said and did referred to the external world, to their interactions with other people, to their occupations and recreations, and to qualities of the environment that interested them. Other things they said and did referred to their inner life, to their thoughts and feelings, and to their private experiences and fantasies.

He named these two observed orientations extraversion (turning outward) and introversion (turning inward). He also observed that some people engaged in more extraverted behavior, whereas others engaged in more introverted behavior. These two types of people he called *extraverts* and *introverts,* respectively. Jung did not believe, however, that all of mankind could be placed in one or the other of these two categories. Extraversion and introversion were for him a matter of degree, not absolute types. Introversion-extraversion is a dimension of personality just as height and weight are dimensions of the body; and this trait has many gradations, as do all traits.

Scales for measuring introversion-extraversion have been developed. They consist of questions concerning one's preferences and activities. Each question has two answers. One reflects an extraverted attitude, the other an introverted attitude, as defined by Jung. The subject must make a choice; he cannot mark both answers or skip a question. Figure 17-1 shows some examples from the Gray-Wheelwright Jungian Type Survey (1964). The I or E in parentheses indicates an introverted or extraverted answer.

The test score consists of the number of items for which a person selects the extraverted answer and the number for which he selects the introverted answer. Since the Gray-Wheelwright test has 34 questions, the highest possible score for either introversion or extraversion is 34. Such extreme scores are rarely, if ever, found. Most people score somewhere near 17–17, because most people behave in an extraverted manner sometimes and in an introverted manner at other times. Jung

17-1
Sample questions from the Gray-Wheelwright Jungian Type Survey. Although the sample is relatively small and not necessarily conclusive, try taking the test and score yourself along the dimension of introversion-extraversion. (Gray & Wheelwright, 1964)

In general company do you like to
    a. Listen   (I)
    b. Talk   (E)
How many friends do you have
    a. Few   (I)
    b. Many   (E)
Granting you like both, which do you prefer most of the time
    a. Reflective people   (I)
    b. Lively people   (E)
Is your temperament
    a. Serious   (I)
    b. Cheerful   (E)
In pictures, which attracts you more
    a. Form   (I)
    b. Color   (E)
Are you eager to join in the plans of others
    a. Seldom   (I)
    b. Usually   (E)
Do you enjoy meeting strangers
    a. No   (I)
    b. Yes   (E)
Is your nature to
    a. Think and feel about life   (I)
    b. Throw yourself into active experience   (E)
At home are you conversational
    a. Not very   (I)
    b. Rather   (E)

himself felt that a balance between the two attitudes was desirable.

Let us consider some of the assumptions that underlie this type of scale. The first assumption is that extraverted and introverted attitudes are expressed in many ways, and the items in the scale are only a sample of all the questions that might be asked. The sample should include enough items to assess a wide variety of preferences but not so many as to make the questions repetitious.

Second, each answer is assumed to carry the same weight. We can merely add up the extraverted answers and the introverted answers to obtain the total score for each attitude. Some personality tests give differential weights to various answers; one answer might count for five points while another answer counts for only one.

Third, each question is assumed to reflect what Jung meant by introversion-extraversion. Test-writers attempt to insure this by consulting Jung's writings on introversion-extraversion and formulating questions that they think coincide with his ideas. Questions derived in this manner are said to have _face_ or _content validity_. They are direct, valid instances of Jung's concepts of introversion-extraversion. Gray and Wheelwright are both trained Jungian analysts who drew upon their broad knowledge of Jungian psychology when they devised their questions.

Sometimes the validity of a test of a personality trait is determined by correlating it with another test of the same trait. For example, Myers and Briggs devised a measure of introversion-extraversion. The scores of a group of people on the Myers-Briggs test were found to correlate perfectly with their scores on the Gray-Wheelwright scale. This result proves that the two scales are measuring exactly the same trait.

Fourth, it is assumed that the person answering the questions knows what his real preferences are and will state them truthfully. On many personality scales, it is relatively easy for a person to give deceptive answers. In many situations, a person might gain an advantage by creating a false impression. For instance, if a job applicant is given the Gray-Wheelwright test, he often will be able to figure out that it is an introversion-extraversion test. If he thinks that a high extraversion score will increase his chances of obtaining the position, he will be tempted to give extraverted answers. This is a serious fault of many personality tests, including the Gray-Wheelwright. You can test this yourself by reading the questions in Figure 17-1 to a friend and then asking him what traits are being tested.

Even if a person tries to be honest in answering the questions, he may be unaware of his actual behavior. His answers would not give a valid picture of his personality. Discrepancies between his answers and his behavior can be determined in a number of ways. Information about his behavior can be obtained from those who know him. For example, if a person is asked "At home are you conversational?" and he replies "Not very," his family can be queried. If they say he talks quite a bit, a discrepancy exists.

Another check is to observe how a subject actually behaves. If a woman says she prefers muted colors (an introverted answer) but is wearing brightly colored clothes and came to the test in a red car, the discrepancy is obvious.

If a great many discrepancies are found between what people say they do and what they actually do, the test is not a valid one, and its results cannot be trusted. Psychologists have often debated the problem of the validity of personality tests.

A final assumption is that the person will answer in terms of his most frequent behavior, because a person does not always behave identically in similar situations. For example, a person may react one time to a painting's form and another time to its color. His answer on a test should represent his *most frequent* behavior in the situation described.

Suppose a person takes an introversion-extraversion test one day, and the next day he takes a different but equivalent test of introversion-extraversion. He may obtain about the same scores on successive days, or he may obtain quite different scores, so that on the first test he is more introverted than extraverted and on the second test he is more extraverted than introverted. This lack of consistency is sometimes considered a serious problem in personality testing. It *is* a serious problem if you assume that a person's position on the introversion-extraversion dimension must be stable or fixed. If an extravert can become an introvert overnight and switch back again the following day, what are we measuring?

Actually, the problem becomes less serious if we can demonstrate that the changes are systematically related to changes in some other variable or variables. A person's introversion may wax and wane with a change in his blood chemistry or the barometric pressure, or with a change in his life situation. This would be an important finding. But if changes in a person's introversion-extraversion scores cannot be related to any other variable, the test would be of little value. As a matter of fact, a person's relative degree of introversion and extraversion does seem to be a fairly constant and enduring feature of his personality; conspicuous changes are seldom found. When changes do appear, they usually can be related to changes in the person's life situation or physical condition.

Once a dimension of personality has been identified and a scale has been constructed to measure this dimension, we can relate it to other dimensions of the person and to situations in his environment. If we can establish many relationships, we usually can assume that the dimension plays an important role in his personality. The dimension of introversion-extraversion appears to be involved in a number of behaviors. Here is a partial list of them (Eysenck, 1970).

As compared with extraverts, introverts:

1. are more accurate in their work

2. are more persistent

3. have a larger vocabulary

4. have a lower appreciation of jokes, especially sexual jokes

5. make more compact designs

6. have a higher level of aspiration

7. are more rigid

8. are more anxious

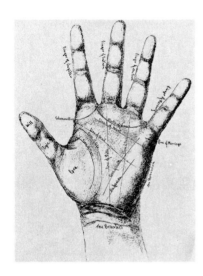

17-2
A palmistry chart. To the palmist, the length, depth, and other characteristics of the lines running across the person's palm describe his character and predict his future. (The Bettmann Archive)

17-3
According to phrenologists, bumps on the head indicate various aspects of the individual's personality. Charts such as the one shown at the beginning of the chapter are used to interpret the bumps. (The Bettmann Archive)

9. work more slowly

10. are more easily conditioned

11. are more reactive to stress

12. are more likely to be physically skinny (ectomorphs)

13. have lower thresholds for sensory stimulation

14. have a higher level of cortical arousal

When a scale measures some aspect of personality that is related to many other forms of behavior, it has *construct validity*. A test measuring a trait that did not relate to any other behavior would not be a very useful test.

Character Analysis

Before we discuss the types of tests psychologists have devised, we shall look briefly at the prescientific methods of character analysis. The "reading" of character, using various outward manifestations or signs, has a long history. *Palmistry* (reading character from the lines on the palm), *graphology* (reading character from handwriting), *phrenology* (reading character from the bumps on the head), and *astrology* (reading character from birth dates and the stars) are only a few of the methods of character analysis that have been popular for centuries and still are practiced widely. Most of these methods not only provide an analysis of a

person's character; they also prophesy what is going to happen to him or warn him what to do or avoid doing at a given time.

Astrology

The most popular of these methods is astrology. Almost every newspaper carries a horoscope column. For many people, the question "What are you?" means "What is your astrological sign?" The answer is Taurus, Virgo, or whichever of the twelve signs of the zodiac a person was born under. Many people, including some prominent ones, will not make an important decision until they have consulted a professional astrologer.

We will not go into all of the ramifications of astrology here; it is a complex subject that requires years of study to master. Nor do we intend to make a critical analysis of its claims. Most psychologists, with the notable exception of Carl Jung, are skeptical of its validity for analyzing character or predicting the future.

One feature of astrology deserves mention here because it is common to many character analysis systems, including some that claim to be "scientific." Consider these statements taken at random from a serious, professional book on astrology (Lynch, 1962).

The Taurean shows himself exceptionally capable of faithful and enduring friendship and affection.

These people (Gemini) generally enjoy their work.

At times they (Sun in Gemini and Moon in Pisces) are erratic, but always inventive and original.

Nevertheless the nature (Cancer) is loving, loyal, and sympathetic.

They (Virgo) give freely and ungrudgingly of their time and strength . . . but nevertheless they know how to say no.

Though somewhat reserved he makes acquaintances easily. (Sun in Virgo and Moon in Cancer)

There is good general mental ability with, in some cases, special aptitude in some one direction. (Sun in Libra and Moon in Virgo)

This combination gives much independence and self-reliance. (Sun and Moon in Scorpio)

For in spite of their tendency to regard mankind as one great family, they recognize that . . . we are not all free and equal. (Saggittarius)

The chief characteristic of the typical Aquarian is his extraordinary breadth of vision.

Statements of this kind, which are sufficiently general and desirable to be accepted by almost anyone who is having his horoscope cast, have *universal validity*. Surveys show, for example, that most people do enjoy their work. Who is not erratic at times? What person would deny that he has breadth of vision, good general mental ability, independence and self-reliance, loyalty and sympathy? All of us like to think that we are somewhat reserved and yet capable of making new acquaintances.

Universal Validity of Character Analyses

Universal validity's effect on the acceptability of a character analysis was demonstrated in a college classroom experiment (Forer, 1949). After a personality measure called the Diagnostic Interest Blank was described by the instructor, the students asked to be given the test and to be furnished with personality evaluations on the basis of the test results. The instructor gave the test and later furnished each student with a sketch of his personality. The students were asked to rate how well the sketch fit them; most thought it fit them very well. In fact they had all received exactly the same evaluation. Here are a few of the statements that appeared on all the evaluation sketches.

You have a tendency to be critical of yourself.

While you have some personality weaknesses, you are generally able to compensate for them.

Your sexual adjustment has presented problems for you.

At times you have serious doubts as to whether you have made the right decision or done the right thing.

You have found it unwise to be too frank in revealing yourself to others.

At times you are extraverted, affable, sociable, while at other times you are introverted, wary, reserved.

The point is that these statements are true of virtually everyone, because there is a core of human nature that is common to most people. It is an interesting and valid problem to determine just how large the core is. Most of us prefer to think we are unique individuals. But the truth is that we are alike in many ways. People who analyze character using handwriting, palmistry, phrenology, and astrology usually formulate their analysis in such general terms that it will match the experiences, hopes, and fears we all have in common. Their prophecies, too, are often so general in character that they inevitably come true. "You are going to have a misfortune." "You are going to receive some good news." "You are going to meet a tall, dark, handsome man." Psychologists speak of *self-fulfilling prophecies*, meaning that a person who has been told something will happen unconsciously arranges conditions so that it does happen. The girl who expects to meet that tall, dark, handsome man is unlikely to turn down any party invitations, for example.

Personality Inventories

Two main strategies are used in devising personality tests. One strategy starts with a theoretical concept and proceeds to develop a scale for measuring it. These are called *theoretical scales*. The introversion-extraversion test is an example of a theoretical scale because it measures concepts developed by C. G. Jung. The other strategy consists of assembling a number of questions, giving them to two groups who are clearly different in some way, and determining which of the questions differentiate the groups. These differentiating questions constitute the final scale, which is called an *empirical scale* because it is not based on any theoretical preconceptions.

Theoretical Scales

A theoretical type of test that is widely used is the *Study of Values* constructed by Gordon Allport, Philip Vernon, and Gardner Lindzey (1960). This test is based upon a theory developed by the German psychologist Edward Spranger. Spranger identified six types of people: the theoretical, the economic, the aesthetic, the social, the political, and the religious. The dominant interest of the *theoretical man* is the discovery of truth, whereas the *economic man* values that which is practical and useful. For the *aesthetic man*, the highest values are those of form and harmony, and for the *social man* the chief values are altruism and love of mankind. The *political man* aspires to power, and the *religious man* seeks a sense of unity with the world.

The test has two parts. Part 1 consists of 30 statements, to be answered in one of two ways. Here are some examples. (You may want to answer them before looking at the scoring key.)

1. Assuming that you have sufficient ability would you prefer to be: (a) a banker (b) a politician?

2. Which of the following branches of study do you expect ultimately will prove more important for mankind? (a) mathematics (b) theology.

3. If you had some time to spend in a waiting room and there were only two magazines to choose from, would you prefer: (a) *Scientific Age* (b) *Arts and Decorations?*

4. If you were engaged in an industrial organization (and assuming salaries to be equal), would you prefer to work: (a) as a counselor for employees, (b) in an administrative position?

17-4
Graph showing sex differences as scored on the Study of Values test. Males score higher on the theoretical, economic, and political scales, while females score higher on the aesthetic, social, and religious scales. (Reproduced by permission of the Houghton Mifflin Company)

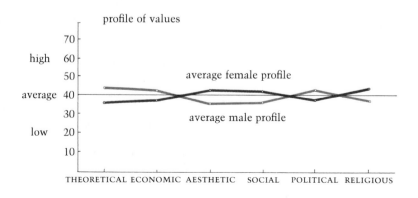

The values for the two possible answers to the questions are:

1. (a) economic (b) political

2. (a) theoretical (b) religious

3. (a) theoretical (b) aesthetic

4. (a) social (b) political

Part 2 consists of 15 multiple-choice questions. The person taking the test ranks the four choices 4, 3, 2, and 1, with the most appealing choice rated 4. Here are two sample test questions:

1. If you had sufficient leisure and money, would you prefer to—

    a. make a collection of fine sculptures or paintings
    b. establish a center for the care and training of the feeble-minded
    c. aim at a senatorship, or a seat in the Cabinet
    d. establish a business or financial enterprise of your own

2. At an evening discussion with intimate friends of your own sex, are you more interested when you talk about—

    a. the meaning of life
    b. developments in science
    c. literature
    d. socialism and social amelioration

The values for the answers to these questions are:

1. (a) aesthetic (b) social (c) political (d) economic

2. (a) religious (b) theoretical (c) aesthetic (d) social

The total number of points for the whole test is 240. If these points are evenly divided among the six values, the score for each value is 40. College students, as a group, average close to 40 on each of the six values. Thus, a score of 50 or more on a value is unusually high, while a score below 30 is very low.

Of course, no one will belong exclusively to one of these types. Most people who take the test score high on one or two values and low on one or two others. Whether a person's score for a value is considered high or low is determined by comparing it with the *norms* for that value. Norms are the distribution of scores made by a large group of people. This distribution approximates a bell-shaped curve in most cases. The center of the distribution (under the highest point on the curve) is the *average,* also called the *mean* (see the Statistics Appendix). The distribution from the lowest score to the highest score made by a large group of people may be divided into units. One such unit is called the *standard deviation* or *sigma.* For most distributions, there are six of these standard deviation units between the lowest and highest scores. Three of these units are below the average, and three are above the average, as was shown in Figure 15-2 on page 507.

Suppose a person takes the Study of Values test and makes a score of 54 on the economic value. This score is one standard deviation above the average, which for this value is 43. In other words, his score exceeds the scores of about 84 percent of the norm group; he stands high on the economic value. If he should make a score of 32, which indicates a low economic value, he exceeds only about 16 percent of the norm group. Scores on scales are nearly always expressed in terms of the percentage of the population that a person's score exceeds. If his score falls right in the middle of the distribution, what percentage of the population does he exceed? The answer, of course, is 50 percent.

The Study of Values test has face validity, because the questions measure directly what they are supposed to measure. The test also has *predictive validity* because, from the scores on the test, you can make predictions that you can later confirm. For example, it was predicted that women, on the average, would have higher scores on religious, social, and aesthetic values than men, and that men would have higher scores on the theoretical, economic, and political scales. This proved to be the case (Allport, Vernon, & Lindzey, 1960). Predictions also were made as to the dominant values of various majors in college as well as occupational groups. Table 17-1 shows the results.

Table 17-1   Dominant Values of Students Majoring in Different Subjects

Students by Major	Highest Value
Engineering students	theoretical
Business majors	economic
Medical students	theoretical
Art students	aesthetic
Air Force officers	political
Clergymen	religious
Nurses (female)	religious
Guidance workers (female)	social

The long-range predictive validity of the Study of Values test was confirmed in a study (see Allport, Vernon, & Lindzey, 1960) in which college women were given the test, and 15 years later their occupational status was determined. Those who had scored high on the economic value in college were in business; those who had scored high on the theoretical value were in medical work; and those who had scored high on the social value were in social work. This study shows that one's values remain fairly stable over the years; it also suggests that one's values influence one's choice of work.

Empirical Scales

Unlike theoretical scales, empirical scales make no assumptions about what comprises a particular personality dimension; the dimension itself may not be identified with personality theory. The intent is to discover what kinds of behaviors constitute a dimension of personality.

In Chapter 15, we saw that the first intelligence tests were devised by finding questions that differentiated children who were doing well in school from those who were doing poorly. These tests were empirical ones, since their questions were not derived from any theory of intellectual functioning.

Masculinity-Femininity Test. An example of an empirical personality test is a masculinity-femininity test. The first step in constructing such a test is to write a large number of questions or items that sample many different types of behavior—interests, attitudes, traits, moods, feelings, wishes, motives, emotional reactions. This battery of questions then is administered to many males and females. Their answers to each question are tabulated separately for each sex. If significantly more males than females answer "yes" to a given question, that answer is considered to be a male-oriented or masculine one. If more females than males answer "yes" to a question, it is classified as a female-oriented or feminine answer. The larger the difference in the way the sexes answer a question, the greater is the weight given to the answer. Questions that both sexes answer in approximately the same way are eliminated. The remaining questions that actually differentiate between males and females now can be used to measure the dimension of masculinity-femininity as empirically defined. A person who answers a high proportion of questions as males do has a high degree of masculinity. If the person's answers are mostly the same as those of females, the person has a high degree of femininity. Such a test can appraise all degrees of masculinity-femininity.

Notice that a masculinity-femininity test makes no assumptions about how males and females *should* behave. Nor is it based on any preconceptions of how males and females do behave. It is derived entirely from the different ways in which males and females answer questions about their behavior.

If age, education, socioeconomic status, or any other factor affects the dimension of masculinity-femininity, that factor must be considered when interpreting a person's test score. For example, since males over 30 score significantly lower on the masculine scale than those under 30, a man taking the test should be compared with his own age group. If he is under 30, he should be compared with a reference group that is under 30. Since women with a college education make less feminine scores than women with only a high school education, a college woman taking the test should be compared with a reference group of college women.

Time is another factor that apparently influences a scale such as the one for masculinity-femininity. Some items that differentiated men from women a generation ago no longer do so. For that reason, an empirical test should be revised periodically to keep it up to date.

The Strong-Campbell Interest Inventory. An empirical test that is widely used in job counseling is the *Strong-Campbell Interest Inventory (SCII)*. The occupational scale of this test was constructed by presenting a battery of questions to a number of occupational groups. Those questions that members of a given occupational group answered in a distinctive way constitute the pattern of interests for that reference

	scale	std. score	very low	low	average	high	very high
			30 35	40	45 50 55	60 65	70
R-THEME	agriculture						
	nature						
	adventure						
	military activities						
	mechanical activities						
I-THEME	science						
	mathematics						
	medical science						
	medical service						

17-5

The Strong-Campbell Interest Inventory consists of both basic interest and occupational scales. As we noted in the text, the occupational scale is based on the interests of a sample of happily-employed members of each occupation; the interest scale is based on a sample of 600 men (shaded bar) and women (open bar) from the population in general. The person taking the test answers "like" or "dislike" to a large number of items that relate to the interests being tested.

The Strong-Campbell Interest Inventory is a form of the original Strong Vocational Interest Blank. This version includes males and females on the same scales; the original did not. (From the Strong-Campbell Interest Inventory, Form T325 of the STRONG VOCATIONAL INTEREST BLANK, by Edward K. Strong, Jr. and David P. Campbell. Reprinted with permission of the publisher. Stanford: Stanford University Press, 1974)

group. A person who is trying to choose a line of work fills out the SCII, and his answers are compared with each of the occupational scales. The test assumes that if a person's answers generally agree with those of a certain occupational group, he is qualified for that occupation in terms of shared interests. This assumption has proved at least partially valid.

Minnesota Multiphasic Personality Inventory. One of the most popular personality tests is the *Minnesota Multiphasic Personality Inventory* (*MMPI*). An *inventory* is a test that measures either a single trait or a number of personality dimensions (for example, depression). The MMPI consists of 550 true-false questions. It is called multiphasic because it provides measures along a number of different dimensions. The authors of the inventory assembled hundreds of questions from a variety of psychiatric sources and gave them to 800 psychiatric patients with various diagnoses. The responses of each psychiatric group (the *criterion* group) were compared with those of a nonpsychiatric group (the *control* group). For example, the answers given by people diagnosed as having a paranoid personality were compared with the answers given by the control group. Questions that were answered differently by the two groups constituted the paranoid scale. The authors produced a number of scales from these comparisons, including the following:

Depression. The subjects in this criterion group are characterized by intense unhappiness, poor morale, and lack of hope about the future.

Psychotic Deviate. These are people with notable difficulties in social adjustment, and with histories of delinquency and other antisocial behavior.

Paranoia. These subjects typically demonstrate symptoms of suspiciousness, feelings of persecution, and delusions of grandeur.

Psychasthenia. The subjects in this criterion group showed unreasonable fears, high general anxiety, feelings of guilt, and excessive doubts.

17-6
Graph of the scores of a 20-year-old female on an MMPI test. Each raw score is converted to a T–score, which is based on the scores of a normal reference group. For example, a T score of 50 equals the average score of the reference group. The letters stand for the three control scales and the ten personality scales: L(Lie — tendency to falsify); F(careless answers); K(defensiveness); Hs(Hypochondriasis); D(Depression); Hy(Hysteria); Pd(Psychopathic deviation); Mf(masculinity-femininity); Pa(Paranoia); Pt(Psychasthenia); Sc(Schizophrenia); Ma(Hypomania); and Si(Social introversion). The numbers below the letters indicate the ten personality scales. To the right is a printout of the computer's written analysis, that is, an interpretation of the graph. (Adapted from Fowler & Miller, 1969)

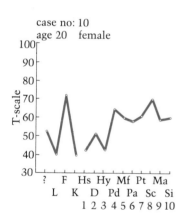

case no: 10
age 20   female

The patient's responses to the test suggest that she understood the items and followed the instructions adequately. It appears, however, that she may have been overly self critical. The validity of the test may have been affected by her tendency to admit to symptoms even when they are minimal. This may represent an effort to call attention to her difficulties to assure obtaining help. This suggests that she feels vulnerable and defenseless, which may reflect a readiness to accept professional assistance.

This patient has a test pattern which is often associated with serious personality disorders. Psychiatric patients with this pattern frequently show obviously deviant behavior. They are usually diagnosed as having a personality disorder or psychotic reaction. Usual manifestations are poor social adjustment, and unusual or bizarre thinking and behavior, frequently in the sexual area. Medical patients with this pattern are characterized by vague physical complaints and considerable anxiety. Many appear to be early psychotic reactions, although they rarely show frankly bizarre behavior.

In general, people with this test pattern are seen as odd or peculiar. It should be emphasized that the presence of this pattern is not conclusive evidence of a personality disorder. However, the high incidence of unusual behavior among patients with this pattern suggests that the patient should be carefully evaluated.

She is a rigid person who may express her anxiety in fears, compulsive behavior and rumination. She may be chronically worried and tense, with marked resistance to treatment despite obvious distress.

This person feels unable to deal with the environmental pressures facing her, or to utilize her skills or abilities to full advantage. At present she feels unable to cope with life as she sees it. She may respond to her feelings of inadequacy with increasingly rigid behavior or withdrawal depending upon individual factors.

The test results on this patient are strongly suggestive of a major emotional disorder. Appropriate professional evaluation and continued observation are suggested. Psychiatric care may be required.

In practice, the Minnesota Multiphasic Personality Inventory scores on the various scales are combined into *patterns* to obtain a comprehensive picture of an individual's personality.

California Psychological Inventory. The *California Psychological Inventory (CPI)*, an empirical test, is much like the Minnesota Inventory and even has many of the same questions. However, it was designed for the multidimensional description of *normal* personality. The scales measure such traits as dominance, responsibility, achievement potential, and intellectuality. Criterion groups were obtained in various ways. For example, the dominance scale was developed by asking fraternity and sorority members to nominate their five most dominant and five least dominant members. Questions that were answered differently by the most dominant and least dominant people constituted the measure of dominance.

PSYCHOLOGY AND JURY SELECTION

Phillip Shaver   *Columbia University*

The individual personality is a decisive element in many significant encounters and decisions. For this reason, an accurate assessment of personality can be highly valuable in predicting how people will behave in any given situation. One important situation calling for personality assessments is the selection of jurors before a trial. Jury members supposedly make their decisions on the basis of evidence presented in the courtroom. However, these decisions also are affected by the composition of the jury and by their measurable psychological characteristics. Some jurors are conservative and some are liberal; some defer to authorities, others do not; some tend to be natural leaders whose statements carry extra weight with their fellow jurors, others prefer to follow. My colleagues and I (Schulman, Shaver, Colman, Emrich, & Christie, 1973) believed that defense lawyers would be greatly aided if they could assess these characteristics and foresee how they would affect the jury's decision.

The 1972 Harrisburg conspiracy trial gave us a chance to see whether psychologists could help lawyers choose jurors who were unlikely to be predisposed against their clients. Seven antiwar activists, including the well-known Father Philip Berrigan, had been accused of conspiring to raid draft boards, to bomb heating tunnels in Washington, and to kidnap Henry Kissinger, then adviser to President Nixon. The indictment of the Harrisburg Seven seemed to many of us to be an attempt by the Justice Department to weaken the antiwar movement. J. Edgar Hoover, at that time director of the FBI, had said in a highly publicized statement that the defendants were guilty. The government's case was based on evidence provided by an informant who

had been paid by the FBI to infiltrate antiwar organizations. The government had chosen Harrisburg, the most conservative of several available cities, as the site for the trial. Moreover, the Federal District judge in Harrisburg was a recent Nixon appointee. Conspiracy is a vague concept which leaves a great deal of room for interpretation by a jury. If the jurors in the Harrisburg case were predisposed against the defendants, the government would not find it difficult to make "conspiracy" sound plausible.

Working with volunteers from the Harrisburg area, we first conducted phone interviews with a random sample of registered voters. We checked our results against a summary of the current jury panel's characteristics. We found that young voters were underrepresented in the panel—a fact that might hurt the Harrisburg defendants since the missing younger people were more likely to sympathize with the defendants' antiwar views. The defense attorneys presented this evidence and other information to the judge. As a result, a new group of prospective jurors, which included more young people, was chosen.

The volunteers then conducted more extensive interviews with a subset of our sample. In these interviews the volunteers explored the beliefs, attitudes, values, life styles, organizational memberships, and news sources of the kinds of people who would be on the jury panel. No one on the panel itself was interviewed because such action might have been declared "jury tampering."

We used the results in several ways. We submitted some of the survey questions to the judge when he asked us to suggest issues he should explore in his initial examination of

prospective jurors. The judge used several of the survey questions. Second, the defense lawyers asked our other important questions. We had found, for example, that religious beliefs were strongly related to political attitudes (for example, conservative religious beliefs correlated with conservative political attitudes). Consequently, the lawyers asked each prospective juror what church he or she attended, how regularly, and so on. Because of the pertinence of our questions—and no doubt because of the lawyers' skill—the judge excused 22 people whom the defense believed were predisposed against the defendants. He also allowed the defense 28 peremptory challenges (challenges for which no stated reason is required). Our survey findings were especially important in deciding how to use these challenges.

During the questioning, some of us attempted to take notes on each person's answers to key questions, and on their clothing style, personal manner, and reactions to the judge and the attorneys on both sides. When the defense team was deciding whether to challenge or retain a given person, they sometimes would refer to these rough notes. Unfortunately, interpretations of both survey findings and scrawled notes left considerable room for confusion, opinion, and argument. In some cases, the defendants' intuitions about people as well as their unsystematic consideration of "sense of humor" or "sexual vibes" were given greater weight than the survey predictions.

After one of the longest deliberations in history, the jury announced that it was hopelessly deadlocked on the conspiracy charges; ten voted for acquittal, two for conviction. Because the government did not request a new trial, the decision freed the defendants. Most members of the defense team considered this a victory for our methods, although they remained painfully aware that we had made at least two mistaken choices (the two jurors who voted for conviction in the face of what seemed to us an overwhelming case for acquittal).

In an effort to understand those mistakes, we analyzed post-trial interviews with seven of the jurors, with prospective jurors who had been excused for various reasons, and with some members of our original survey sample. We concluded that if *both* predictors—the survey variables and the subjective courtroom ratings—agreed, we had classified a juror correctly—either "good" or "bad" from our point of view. Mistakes occurred when these two predictors conflicted. In some instances, this happened because prospective jurors misrepresented themselves and fooled us; in other instances it happened because their attitudes differed from those of other people in the Harrisburg area who shared their characteristics. We decided that in future trials we should establish an informal social network that could quickly gather additional information to resolve such ambiguities. We also decided that the courtroom ratings should be more precise to avoid later misinterpretations and disagreements. In addition, these ratings, we agreed, should assess nonverbal behavior—as did those made by the psychologists working for Angela Davis (see Sage, 1973).

Gradually our methods are being improved. In the Pentagon Papers trial, for instance, a psychiatrist devised a much more detailed courtroom rating procedure (Gould & Gould, 1974). In the Gainesville trial of the members of the Vietnam Veterans Against the War who were accused of conspiring to disrupt the 1972 Republican Convention, Schulman, Christie, and some talented volunteers developed a prediction equation, based on survey results. The equation assigned a "favorability rating" to each prospective juror.

Of course, the Justice Department did not simply ignore all of this activity on behalf of the defense. In Gainesville, Justice Department attorneys requested a change in the jury-selection procedures that would make it difficult to use the personality-assessment techniques used in Harrisburg. The judge obliged them by personally asking all the questions and by withholding names of prospective jurors until the last possible moment.

When my colleagues and I decided to work with the Harrisburg defendants, we were aware of the ethical issues involved. We were particularly worried by the possibility that in the future the government, or defendants with whom we did not sympathize, could use the jury-selection methods we had developed. In the short time since that initial effort, our concern has proved justified; already, market-research firms are selling the results of social psychological surveys to clients who can afford them. And several newspaper articles, including an editorial entitled, "Science: Threatening the Jury Trial?" (Etzioni, 1974), have questioned the wisdom of the entire procedure, regardless of who uses it.

In my opinion, our work has helped to improve the jury system. Across the country, lawyers and social scientists are looking more carefully at jury-selection procedures. In many areas the list of prospective jurors is out of date, and young people and minority group members are underrepresented. In some places women are not as likely to serve as men. Constant scrutiny of jury-selection procedures will reduce such inequities.

Perhaps every prospective juror should fill out an official questionnaire; its results would be stored in a computer available to attorneys on both sides of a case. Any other information, such as FBI files, tax records, military service records, and credit ratings, also would have to be made available to both sides. (Defense attorneys with whom I've discussed the matter say that the government currently uses such sources, which are inaccessible to defendants.)

When I was a student, I wondered whether psychology was at all relevant to "real life." The work on jury selection convinces me that it is. It also shows that the methods and findings of psychology, like those of other sciences, can be used for good or bad ends. If psychology is to be used wisely, psychologists—and an informed public—must remain constantly aware of their work's political and ethical implications.

Projective Methods

Personality scales, as we have seen, consist of *structured* questions. The person taking the test must choose one of the answers presented to him. He cannot make up his own answers, alter the answers that are printed on the form, or refrain from answering any questions. This rigid structuring is designed to make the test situation the same for everyone.

Other methods of measuring personality provide the person more freedom to respond. These usually are called *projective methods* because the person is said to project his personality characteristics into his answers. This will become clear after we discuss some of these methods.

Sentence Completion Test

One widely used projective method is called *Sentence Completion*. The person is given a list of incomplete sentences (called stems) which he is to complete in any way he wishes. He is told that there are no right or wrong answers. Here are some stems that have been used:

The happiest time _____

My mother _____ .

My greatest fear _____ .

The future _____ .

My father _____ .

My mind _____ .

People _____ .

The problem for the tester is to decide what the subject's responses indicate about his personality. Sometimes this is relatively easy. Consider, for example, a subject who makes the following completions:

The happiest time *is when I am doing something well.*

My mother *has always encouraged me.*

My greatest fear *is that I will fail.*

The future *is a challenge.*

My father *is a successful man.*

My mind *is clear and strong.*

People *are fun to be with.*

These answers indicate that the person who gave them is well-adjusted and achievement-oriented. Some answers are more difficult to interpret, as in the following example:

The happiest time *is now.*

My mother *is a woman.*

My greatest fear *is yet to come.*

The future *is tomorrow.*

My father *is a businessman.*

My mind *is in my brain.*

People *come in all shapes and sizes.*

The person who gave these answers appears to be exceptionally literal-minded—or perhaps he is trying to conceal something about himself.

This type of test generally has a scoring manual to help the tester interpret the answers. Such manuals classify answers under various headings: positive, dependent, erotic, friendly, anxious, and so on. The Sentence Completion test often is used as a prelude to psychological counseling, because it reveals some of the client's conflicts and anxieties. Ordinarily, the person taking the test is aware of his feelings, and if he cares to, he can make a false impression by slanting his completions.

In a more sophisticated type of projective test, the subject does not know what he is revealing about himself. Such a test might ask the subject to describe what he sees in certain pictures or to make up stories about the pictures. Instead of saying things about himself, as he does when he answers a personality inventory or completes sentences, he is describing an external situation. This creates sufficient distance between the person and the situation so that he is less guarded in what he says. Moreover, these projective methods often reveal unconscious material the person is not aware of. This is their real importance for understanding personality. The two most famous tests of this type are the Rorschach Inkblot Method and the Thematic Apperception Test (TAT).

The Rorschach Inkblot Method

The *Rorschach inkblot test* consists of ten cards; a symmetrical inkblot
is printed on each card. Some inkblots are in color, others are not. The cards are presented one at a time to a person, always in the same order, and he is asked to tell what he sees or what they remind him of. He may give as many responses to each inkblot as he wishes. The time he takes to make his first responses to each card is recorded. His answers are scored using a system that is very elaborate and complex, so that we will present here only a few of the scoring categories and some of the inferences drawn from each.

In looking at an inkblot, a person may perceive it as a whole or he may select a certain feature of the blot and respond to it. Responses to the whole blot reflect the ability to organize material and relate details to one another, and an interest in the abstract and theoretical. Responses to details of a blot indicate an interest in the specific and concrete, and a practical, commonsensical intelligence.

Responses may be determined primarily by the blot's shape, or they may be more influenced by its color. Responses to shape denote the ability to exercise control without becoming emotionally involved.

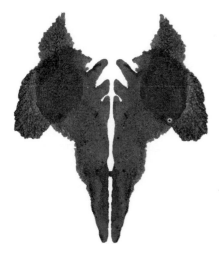

17-7
An inkblot similar to those used in the Rorschach projective test. The patient is asked to describe what he sees in the inkblot or what the inkblot reminds him of. The examiner transcribes the patient's comments verbatim and then analyzes them for patterns of responses.

Responses to color are more emotional, and disclose in particular the person's emotional relationships with people.

Although the inkblots are static pictures, one may read movement into them. Three kinds of movement are scored: movement of perceived human figures, movement of perceived animal figures, and movement of inanimate objects. Human movement suggests a high level of mental functioning, integrative ability, and creativity. Animal movement symbolizes the less acceptable part of a person's basic impulses, that is, the sexual and aggressive desires condemned by society. Inanimate movement indicates tension and conflict.

The total number of responses that a person gives to the ten blots reveals his productive capacity. The average length of time it takes for a person to make his first response to each blot is a measure of his alertness. A response that many people make to a particular card is called a popular response. A large number of popular responses indicates conformity. A number of original responses signifies mental superiority.

Rorschach testers compute scores for each of these types of response, but they are concerned primarily with *relationships* among the scores. Testers compute many ratios and proportions between the single scores before they draw any inferences about a subject's personality. For example, one important measure is the ratio of human movement responses to color responses. If human movement exceeds color, this is indicative of an introverted personality; if color exceeds movement, this is indicative of an extraverted personality. Configurations among the scores disclose much other information about the individual's personality and mental functioning.

Inferences also can be drawn from the content of the responses. Repeated perception of heads and faces in the blots may indicate a concern about intellectual ability. Seeing a lot of fierce animals may refer to aggressive tendencies in the individual, while seeing a lot of domestic animals may show passivity and dependence. Anatomy, geography, or science responses are often given by people who are trying to show off intellectually or trying to hide their emotions. Seeing masks in the blots may symbolize a desire to cover up feelings.

The scores obtained from the various categories, the patterning of scores, and content analysis all contribute to the tester's conclusions about the subject's personality. A personality analysis derived from the Rorschach is illustrated in the following report.

Tony, a ten-year-old male

The Rorschach reveals that Tony's intellectual status is probably above average, but because of severe emotional difficulties he cannot function up to his capacity. His vocabulary is meager, his ideas few, and there is no evidence of originality. He is struggling with many problems, and he is a very insecure child. He fears attack from others, and he fears his own impulses. He is very confused about himself. He is easily distracted. His problems are bound up in his unsatisfactory relationship with his parents. Neither parent offers a source of comfort or security. Since he cannot relate to people and his own feelings are so threatening to him, he withdraws into an immature fantasy world that provides little relief for him. He is an unhappy, immature child with potential strengths who should benefit from psychotherapy. (Abridged from Klopfer & Davidson, 1962)

Here is another report, based on the Rorschach given to a middle-aged woman who was having marriage problems.

May, a middle-aged female

May is a fairly well-adjusted person with no disabling characteristics which would interfere with her getting along with other people. She is emotionally outgoing, can relate well to people, and has her emotions and impulses under control. She is quite sensitive to social demands. She has a passive and submissive conception of her role in life. Under stress, she functions a little less efficiently than usual, but she recovers quickly. She is evasive about a male figure in her life, or perhaps it is the masculine side of her own personality that she is avoiding. (Modified from Allen, 1966)

How valid is the Rorschach for evaluating personality and predicting behavior? This is a controversial question. Attempts to find positive relationships between Rorschach scores and other measurements of the same personality and cognitive characteristics have sometimes succeeded but they also have failed. Qualified psychologists disagree about the validity of the Rorschach. Their considered judgments range from the bleak statement that it has no validity whatsoever, to the optimistic conclusion that its usefulness has been demonstrated in the diagnosis of personality characteristics and psychiatric conditions, as well as in the prediction of behavior and the outcome of psychotherapy. Despite the abundant criticism directed against the Rorschach Method, it is still the most widely used projective test of personality in clinics and hospitals.

The Thematic Apperception Test

The *Thematic Apperception Test (TAT)* consists of 20 black and white pictures, but instead of inkblots the pictures contain people and objects. The pictures show ambiguous scenes that can be interpreted in a number of ways. In one picture, for example, a figure who might be either a girl or a boy crouches beside something that looks like a bed; on the floor is an object that might be a gun, a toy, or a number of other things.

The subject is asked to tell a story about each picture. He is told that the story should include what has led up to the scene on the card, what is happening at that moment, what the people in the story are feeling and thinking, and the outcome of the story.

After the subject has told 20 stories, the psychologist must interpret them. He usually assumes that the main character in the story represents the storyteller himself or some significant person in the storyteller's life (mother, father, spouse, sibling). What these characters do and what happens to them is assumed to reflect something about the storyteller's preoccupations, concerns, wishes, needs, and other private or even unconscious states.

17-8
One of the pictures used in the Thematic Apperception Test. Like the Rorschach, the TAT is administered by a psychologist who keeps a verbatim record of the subject's responses. (Harvard University Press)

The stories may be analyzed for various personality characteristics. The test was originally devised by Murray and Morgan to obtain measures of Murray's list of needs. As we saw in Chapter 10, McClelland and his associates used the test to measure one particular need, achievement.

One question often asked about the Thematic Apperception Test is: How close are the actions performed by the characters in the stories to the actual behavior of the storyteller? Specifically, does a very aggressive person tell stories in which the characters perform many aggressive acts? The answer is, he may or he may not. If his aggressive impulses make him feel anxious, he may have private aggressive fantasies which he projects into his stories, and yet display little aggressive behavior in his daily life. But if he accepts his aggressive feelings and does not inhibit them, he will tell stories with aggressive themes and act aggressively as well.

The question of the Thematic Apperception Test's general validity has been answered in various ways. Some psychologists feel that its validity has not been adequately demonstrated; others believe that it is valid for certain purposes. Like the Rorschach, the TAT is used widely in clinical settings to gather information that cannot be obtained easily by other methods.

Projective methods may be used not only to measure dimensions of personality but also to unearth specific conflicts, anxieties, complexes, and preoccupations that an individual may not be aware of. Information of this sort often is used in conjunction with counseling and psychotherapy. It is a quick way of locating possible trouble spots in the personality.

Behavior Ratings

A personality trait is a name that describes a class of behaviors. When we say a person is very aggressive, we mean that he gets into a lot of fights, quarrels with everyone, tries to hurt people, and is generally destructive. Such aggressive acts are usually easy to observe. But it is extremely time-consuming to observe the behavior of even a few individuals and to record the aggressive acts that each individual performs in a given period. Moreover, unless the observer is exceptionally unobtrusive, observation itself may affect the subjects' behaviors.

One solution is to find people who, by the nature of their work, have observed the behavior of many individuals in varying situations. Such people generally have acquired a great deal of knowledge about how individuals differ in aggressiveness, submissiveness, altruism, timidity, and other traits. Schoolteachers probably have the best opportunity to make such observations. They see their pupils in a variety of situations over a long period of time, and they usually are trained to be observant and objective. A veteran teacher has observed the conduct of a large number of pupils, and generally is familiar with the entire range of trait expressions.

For these reasons, teachers often are asked to make *ratings* of their pupils' personality traits. Such ratings are made by locating each child on a scale for a specific trait. The scale is divided into units, usually five or seven, and each unit represents an increasing amount of the trait. Here is an example.

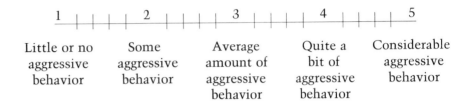

1	2	3	4	5
Little or no aggressive behavior	Some aggressive behavior	Average amount of aggressive behavior	Quite a bit of aggressive behavior	Considerable aggressive behavior

The teacher may place a mark for a particular child anywhere on this scale. Before making the ratings, the teacher has been told exactly what kinds of behavior define the trait in question.

Other methods are used to obtain information about personality traits from teachers. They may be asked to rank their students from the most aggressive to the least aggressive. Or the experimenter can present a list of pairs of children's names, in which each child is paired with every other child, and ask the teacher which child of each pair displays more aggressive behavior. This method of _paired comparisons_ yields very precise measurements but it is tedious to do if many children are involved. A class of 20, for example, will make a list of 190 pairs. If you only want to identify the extremes of a trait dimension, you can ask teachers to name the pupil who is most aggressive and the pupil who is least aggressive.

All of these methods also can be used to obtain information about personality characteristics from the children themselves. These are called _peer ratings_. Children in the same class usually know each other fairly well and have a pretty good idea of how their classmates stand on various traits.

Some pitfalls appear whenever one person appraises the personality traits of others. A serious pitfall is the _halo effect._ The presence in an individual of an outstanding, highly desirable characteristic may push up the ratings he receives on other desirable traits. The opposite of the halo effect is the _horns effect._ A person who has a very undesirable trait may be rated correspondingly low on other traits. The strong influence of the halo or horns effect is easy to demonstrate. Suppose that you give two groups of people lists of adjectives that describe a person. The lists are identical except for one pair of words. Here is an example.

intelligent	intelligent
skillful	skillful
industrious	industrious
warm	_cold_
determined	determined
practical	practical
cautious	cautious

Of course, the critical words, cold and warm, are not italicized in the actual presentation.

After the two groups have looked over their respective lists, they are given another list of adjectives and are asked to check those that apply to the person. The group who had *warm* in their list check more favorable adjectives—for example, generous, good-natured, popular—than the group who had *cold* in their list. *Warm* creates a halo effect; *cold* a horns effect (Asch, 1946).

Two raters may give quite different ratings to the same person. In this case, you cannot know which rater is more accurate. Some traits are very difficult to rate accurately because they cannot be defined clearly. Raters also may have different standards of judgment. One rater may habitually rate certain traits high, and another may rate them low. Human judgment is always fallible, but various safeguards can be used to reduce the amount of distortion.

Situation-Specific Behavior

One problem that arises in measuring any dimension of personality is the impact of the prevailing situation. A person's behavior often depends on his situation. A man may behave like an introvert at home and be the "life of the party" at social gatherings. Parents often are astonished to learn from a teacher that their rather irresponsible, rebellious, untidy adolescent is dependable, cooperative, and orderly in school. A timid, nervous young man becomes a hero in a critical situation. When a person's behavior is determined by the situation, we call it *situation-specific*.

Many years ago, a character study of school children demonstrated that honesty is highly situation-specific. A child might be honest in one situation and dishonest in another. Another study carefully recorded the punctuality of college students in arriving at six destinations. The six places were eight o'clock classes, breakfast in the cafeteria, conference appointments with instructors, extracurricular activities, chapel, and athletic contests and entertainments. A few students were found to be generally punctual, fewer were consistently tardy, but most were inconsistent overall. These findings make it impossible to speak of a general trait of honesty or punctuality for most people.

One way to work with these fluctuating traits is to look for consistent relationships between types of situations and behavior. A person may be consistently dominant in some situations and consistently submissive in others. Unfortunately, several studies indicate that a person is not even consistent in the same situation from day to day. For example, counselors at a summer camp for boys kept a daily behavior record on 30 such items as these:

Did he speak before the group at campfire?

What percent of the time did he play or work alone?

Did he get into fights with other boys?

A boy's consistency from day to day was the first factor to determine. If he worked alone one day, would he be likely to work alone the next? The answer is no. Only a few boys behaved consistently from day to day. Next, the 30 items were grouped under 10 headings that were more general. Each heading was a different aspect of the same behavior trait. Again, little consistency was found. A boy who cooperated in one group activity might not cooperate in another group activity. Finally, the 10 traits were grouped under the most generalized heading of all, introversion-extraversion. Could the boys be classified as being consistently outgoing or consistently withdrawn? Three of the 51 boys were classified as consistent extraverts and two as consistent introverts, but the other 46 fell into neither class.

Another way to meet the problem of inconsistency is to sample a person's behavior in a great many situations and to strike an average for him. This is how you construct a personality inventory. Questions are asked about various expressions of a particular dimension of personality. The resulting score enables us to say, for example, that a person expresses introverted behavior a certain proportion of the time. One difficulty with this solution is that not all acts are equivalent in terms of their consequences to the person or to others. Consider, for example, a few of the many ways of being aggressive: "dirty looks," harsh words, physical blows, and killing. How many harsh words equal a killing? The question is absurd. Different acts of aggression obviously cannot be evaluated on a single scale of intensity. About all we can say is that murder is a lot more serious than a slap in the face and, in most cases but not all, a slap in the face is more serious than an unkind word. We cannot say that fifty slaps equal one murder or that ten unkind words equal one slap.

Uses of Personality Tests

Most of us are aware that personality tests are used often to diagnose behavior disorders. But personality tests are used in several other settings besides the clinical—in research laboratories, schools, and industry, for example. In this section we will discuss some of the many uses of the personality test.

Research

Personality tests often are constructed primarily for research purposes rather than practical application. An investigator who proposes to study individual differences in anxiety requires an objective measure of anxiety. If a measure is not available, he has to construct one. In this way, researchers open new areas of investigation. Advances in our understanding of personality depend to a large extent on objective, standardized, demonstrably valid measures. The investigation of how to devise useful tests is an independent research area called _psychometrics_.

Assessment

Although a psychologist can evaluate specific aspects of an individual—such as femininity or extraversion—by using a single personality test, he must administer a number of tests, tapping various components, to obtain a more complete and well-rounded picture of the person. From the test results and other sources of information about the person—family background, education, work history, hobbies, and so forth—he attempts to assess the total personality structure and dynamics. This is a large task and usually is done only when the person must make an important decision or when others must recommend treatment for the person.

Personality assessment may help a person plan his career. People who are being considered for positions that require a particular type of personality may have to undergo extensive assessment. Whether a patient is to be discharged from a mental hospital or an inmate paroled from a penitentiary often depends on the results of personality assessment.

Predicting Behavior

Psychologists often are asked to predict a person's future behavior from his performances on personality tests. The questions may be very specific ones, such as, is this person likely to:

commit suicide?

become insane?

become a criminal?

make a good policeman?

have his marriage end in divorce?

have a serious automobile accident?

break down under stress?

become an alcoholic?

become a talented writer?

benefit from psychotherapy?

Obviously, being able to predict such developments with some confidence would be a valuable skill. If psychologists could tell from personality tests which people are likely to become insane, delinquent, suicidal, or accident-prone, they could take measures to forestall such misfortunes. Similarly, if they could tell a person that he probably would be happy and successful in a particular occupation, he could be guided by, and benefit from, their prediction.

Unfortunately, present measures of personality do not, in general, enable psychologists to make precise predictions. This means, for example, that in predicting suicide from indications on personality tests, many people who are identified as suicidal will never commit suicide (such indications are called *false positives*). What is worse, some who are identified as not being suicidal will take their own lives (such indications are *false negatives*). The objective is to reduce the false negatives and positives to a negligible number. This distant goal can only be reached through persistent, creative research activities.

Counseling and Psychotherapy

Both theoretical and empirical personality scales can expedite counseling and psychotherapy by providing information about the client or patient more quickly than it can be obtained in other ways. That is, personality tests have *diagnostic* value, as contrasted with *prognostic* or predictive value. Exact diagnoses or precise measurements are not essential in the clinical situation. Tests like the California Personality Inventory or the Thematic Apperception Test can indicate problem areas; the counselor or therapist then may focus attention on those areas.

Self-Knowledge

"Know thyself"; many people think it is wise counsel, but it is also a difficult task. Personality tests can make it less difficult. One benefit of standardized tests is to show an individual how he compares with others in his feelings, motives, attitudes, and emotional reactions. Suppose a young man is troubled because he thinks of himself as feminine. He takes a masculinity-femininity test and his score shows that he is no more feminine than the average male of his age. This knowledge can be very reassuring to him. Or a young woman may consider herself neurotic but discover after taking personality tests that she is better adjusted than many other young women. Of course, just the opposite may occur—a person may discover disturbing things about himself. That is why some psychologists feel that only well-trained professionals should administer, score, and interpret personality tests.

Personality inventories are an invaluable aid to self-analysis. They can reveal a person's strengths and weaknesses in comparison with other people, so that he is better able to use his strong points and to try to correct his weak ones.

Projective tests like the Thematic Apperception Test also can be used for self-analysis. Without the presence of an examining psychologist, a person can tell stories about the pictures and see how the material in the stories relates to his own life and personality. If he does this objectively, intelligently, courageously, and without any preconceptions of what he is going to find, he will discover many interesting and enlightening aspects of himself.

Criticisms of Personality Tests

Psychologists themselves have been the most fervent critics of personality tests. They criticize them in the expectation that personality measures can be improved by future research.

One criticism of the use of personality tests that cannot be overcome by research involves the rights of the individual. Many people have complained that such tests are an invasion of privacy. Two congressional inquiries have investigated the possible abuse of psychological tests and some public support exists for the view that personality tests should be prohibited. A school board in Houston burned the answer sheets to six psychological tests that had been administered to 5,000 ninth graders because a number of parents objected to some of the test questions.

Many people, psychologists included, feel that the criticism is justified when individuals are *required* or *pressured* to take a personality test and the results are then placed in files that are accessible to others. No one doubts that personality tests do ask for information that could be damaging to the person if misused. An old rule of law says that a person cannot be required to testify against himself, and in a sense, this is what he does when he takes a personality test. Naturally, a person is not inclined to tell the truth about himself if he feels it will be used against him. However, as we have mentioned, some personality tests elicit potentially damaging information without the person knowing what he is divulging.

From this viewpoint, the best solution is to administer a personality test only when a person specifically requests it or when he *freely* volunteers to act as a research subject. Even under these conditions, he should be fully informed of what is involved, and be assured that he can be guaranteed complete anonymity. Anything less *is* an invasion of privacy and should not be tolerated.

This is not the only viewpoint, however. The other side of the question is that society has a right to protect itself and that it can use any legal methods to do so, even if these methods invade the individual's privacy. Some commentators on the subject believe that certain classes of people—those convicted of crimes or judged insane, for example—have lost their right to privacy. Others argue that job applicants, employees, civil servants, military personnel, and candidates for public office must place the interests of their employers or the public before their own right to complete privacy.

This extremely controversial issue surely will be debated for a long time to come.

Summary

1. Personality tests or scales have been devised to measure many different dimensions or traits of personality.

2. Palmistry, graphology, phrenology, and astrology are prescientific methods of analyzing character. Self-fulfilling prophecies are nonscientific predictions that come true because the person unconsciously arranges conditions so that the predicted event will occur.

3. Statements about personality may have face or content validity, construct validity, and universal validity.

4. Some personality inventories—for example, the Gray-Wheelwright Jungian Type Survey and the Study of Values test—measure a single trait and are based on concepts derived from theories of personality. Other tests, such as the Strong-Campbell Interest Inventory, are empirical in character.

5. Some inventories, such as the Minnesota Multiphasic Personality Inventory (MMPI) and California Psychological Inventory (CPI), measure

a number of personality dimensions at the same time. Like other inventories, they consist of questions with fixed or structured answers.

6. Projective tests consist of material that allows the individual to project his personality into his answers. The two most popular projective tests are the Rorschach Inkblot Method and the Thematic Apperception Test.

7. Personality traits also may be assessed by the rating method. Ratings of an individual are made on a scale by a person who is familiar with the individual.

8. Personality measures are used for (a) research, (b) assessment, (c) predicting behavior, (d) counseling and psychotherapy, and (e) self-knowledge.

9. Personality tests have been criticized as an invasion of personal privacy.

Important Terms

Gray-Wheelwright Jungian Type Survey

face (content) validity

construct validity

universal validity

self-fulfilling prophecies

theoretical scale

empirical scale

Study of Values test

norm

mean

standard deviation (sigma)

predictive validity

inventory

Strong-Campbell Interest Inventory

Minnesota Multiphasic Personality Inventory (MMPI)

California Psychological Inventory (CPI)

projective tests

Sentence Completion test

Rorschach test

Thematic Apperception Test

behavior ratings

paired comparison

peer ratings

halo effect

horns effect

psychometrics

Suggested Readings

BUROS, O. K. *Personality: Tests and reviews.* Highland Park, N.J.: Gryphon Press, 1970.

An invaluable reference book, containing descriptions, evaluations, and references for 513 personality tests.

LANYON, R. I., & GOODSTEIN, L. O. *Personality assessment.* New York: Wiley, 1971.

A clear, simple account of the methods and techniques employed for measuring personality.

RABIN, A. I. *Projective techniques in personality assessment.* New York: Springer, 1968.

A description of various projective methods and their uses for analyzing and assessing personality.

Chapter 18   Attitudes and Their Measurement

I have often thought that the best way to define a man's character would be to seek out the particular mental or moral attitude in which, when it came upon him, he felt himself most deeply and intensely active and alive. At such moments there is a voice inside which speaks and says: "This is the real me!"

—William James
(*The Letters of William James*)

Attitudes and Their Measurement

This chapter was drafted by Hazel Markus and Robert Zajonc, Department of Psychology, University of Michigan.

The world we confront is bristling with labels. We have categorized it, mostly as a result of our language and culture, into distinct objects, concepts, and events. We have identified tables and windows and war and books and walls and corners and failures and scratches and hysterectomies and poverty and the military-industrial complex and, above all, people. It is striking that our perception of the world is so heavily directed toward people, and that our perception of objects is largely determined by their significance for us. All of us have learned personal responses to the significant individuals, objects, and events in the world around us, responses that are evaluative (arising from our value judgments) and affective (arising from our emotions). Psychologists define these responses as *attitudes*. Let us look at them more closely.

To know that something is an object means we know its function. Each table is an entity in itself, with a certain shape, texture, color, hardness, mass, location, and orientation. But above all it is a thing at which *people* eat, or write, or play chess, or something people sit around for conferences. A chair is mostly to sit upon, but in the hands of a lion tamer it becomes a shield. To the extent that we perceive objects in terms of their functions, we perceive them in their relation to human needs, wants, or actions. Unless an object can be related to something human, knowledge of it appears to be incomplete.

We can readily perceive an object's physical and spatial properties and an event's temporal properties. But it is the object's function or the event's origin and consequences that really identify it for us. Since objects are perceived in terms of their functions, and since function is a matter of value, our perceptions of objects are filtered through our evaluative and emotional reactions to them. We see an *attractive* table, we meet a *likable* person, we speak about a *hateful* war. A rock is smooth or sharp, small or large, but we are likely to perceive it as especially good for skipping over water, or for a flagstone path. A chair may be heavy or light, large or small, but we will tend to see it as comfortable, awkward, solid, wobbly, or expensive; all of these perceptions are value judgments.

Our evaluations of and emotional reactions to an object are as inseparable from our total perception of the object as are the object's physical properties. Just as we cannot separate a table's shape from our perception of the table, we find it extremely difficult and perhaps impossible to separate completely our feelings about the table from our perception of it. Both our perception of the table's shape and our feelings toward it are fairly permanent because our perception is based upon the physical reality of the table and our affective and evaluative reaction depends on a lifetime of accumulated experiences.

Characteristics of Attitudes

People have attitudes toward every class of object and every specific object (natural or artificial, concrete or abstract), toward every class of issue and every particular issue (political, moral, scientific, or social), toward every class of human being and every particular person (real or fictitious). In short, we have an attitude toward almost every entity we can perceive or conceive of in our imaginations. Attitudes, of course, differ in complexity, determinants, origins, implications for behavior, and intensity. Some attitudes represent a single evaluative or affective response to an object while others are built up through many experiences. But above all, attitudes are convenient summaries of our reactions to the objects about us. An individual's attitude includes all his reactions, overt and covert, to the object itself, as well as those he experiences when he talks, writes, or thinks about the object.

Attitudes and Habits

If we were to observe an individual over a number of years we would readily discover certain recurrent actions. He chews on his pipe stem when working on a problem; he always comes home the same way although there are five alternate routes; he always brushes his teeth before getting dressed; he begins most sentences with "You know . . ." These are _habits_—recurrent patterns of acquired behavior.

Habits and attitudes have common features but they are not to be confused with one another. Whereas habits classify behavior according to responses (for example, chewing), attitudes classify behavior according to objects. Even though pipe-chewing behavior is recurrent and involves an object (pipe-stem) or classes of objects (hard things that can be put into one's mouth), it is not an attitude because the effect of this behavior is not a significant factor in our analysis. We are primarily concerned with what the individual is doing, not with the consequences of his action. The emphasis is on chewing, not on the pipe.

Attitudes and Causes of Behavior

Attitudes are *inferred from* observations of behavior; they are not classes of behavior themselves. Nor, in the strict sense of the word, are attitudes causes of behavior. An attitude is a predisposition to respond positively or negatively to an object or an event.

Yet attitudes do help us to organize and give meaning to our actions, and to the actions of others. As summaries of our past encounters with people, concepts, and objects, attitudes express enduring preferences. If we know that Joe preferred Mary to Jennifer in the past, we will guess that Joe will continue to prefer Mary. Attitudes allow members of a society to make predictions about their own and others' future choices and reactions. Often, attitudes also serve as "explanations" and "accounts" of action. Our own behavior often is influenced by an appeal to our attitudes and so is the behavior of others: "Why don't you want to go to Joe's party?"—"I don't like him." "Would you be interested in contributing some money to the Audubon Society?"—"Yes, I like birds."

Reactions can indicate whether a person's attitude is positive or negative. For example, measure two classmates' reactions to people smoking cigars. Determine the degree to which each reaction is positive or negative. If you count the number of times their various reactions occur—taking into account only the extent to which any reaction is positive or negative—you will obtain a frequency distribution.

Many of A's feelings are positive although he shows a few negative reactions. B's feelings toward the smokers, however, are mostly negative. Still, A and B do overlap somewhat: over years of observation, a few of A's reactions may seem more negative than some of B's reactions. Thus, while A's attitude toward the smokers is generally positive and B's attitude is negative, neither attitude actually causes their behavior. If B admires a particular smoker, he may forget his general dislike of cigar smokers.

While attitudes do not cause behavior directly, attitudes and behavior are related. For example, authoritarian attitudes, which are characterized by seeking security in authority and regimentation, frequently do predict behavior. High scorers on the California F-scale, which measures authoritarian attitudes, are more likely to vote for conservative political candidates, to raise their children in a traditional authoritarian manner, and to prefer more regimented leadership on the job. Although such general correlations can be found, several experimental investigations of the

18-1

Frequency distribution of the attitudes of two people toward a particular object. The curve leaning to the right of neutrality represents predominantly positive attitudes; the curve to the left represents negative attitudes.

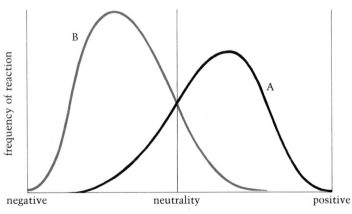

affective polarity of reaction toward a given object of attitude

attitude-behavior link show that no simple one-to-one correspondence exists between expressed attitudes and subsequent behavior.

One of the first studies to draw attention to the attitude-behavior inconsistency was done in 1934 when many Americans harbored negative feelings toward various minority groups, including Orientals. A sociologist, La Piere, toured the country by car with a Chinese couple. All three stopped at 250 hotels and restaurants where they almost always were accepted without question. Later, La Piere wrote letters to the same hotels and restaurants asking if they would serve Orientals. Their responses were almost all negative. This study was said to show that prejudiced attitudes do not predict actual discriminatory behavior. Later, similar investigations found the same attitude-behavior inconsistency. For example, in a study in the Northeast, Kutner, Wilkins, and Yarrow (1952) used a procedure similar to La Piere's but employed one black female and two white females. In every restaurant in which the women ate, the service was "exemplary" even though none of the restaurants had replied to earlier letters asking for reservations for an interracial party.

Numerous studies indicate that people will behave according to their attitudes only *in certain situations.* Why don't attitudes predict behavior more consistently? One answer, of course, is that they do not predict behavior because they do not cause behavior. Another reason for the divergence of attitude and behavior is that a person's responses to conceptualized objects may vary from his responses to specific objects. In the La Piere study, the restaurant and hotel owners' letters may have been reflecting some negative Oriental stereotype, while the couple involved in the actual behavioral test was well dressed and well mannered. A further reason is that any single behavior may be determined by a variety of factors, not the least of which are the pressures inherent in the situation. In almost any situation, the individual's perception of the social consequences of his actions will greatly influence his behavior. In the La Piere study, the owners may have served the Chinese couple because they did not want to run the risk of disrupting business with a public refusal that might have been followed by a vigorous protest from the couple.

Stability of Attitudes

Attitudes are *relatively enduring and stable*—although not unchangeable—across a variety of situations and contexts, and for fairly long periods of time. This relative durability and persistence exists for several reasons. First, the affinities and aversions we express toward objects or persons are *rooted in our emotions.* Once emotional responses, especially those of aversion, are acquired they are quite difficult to extinguish. One reason for this is that we tend to avoid a second encounter when the first produced a negative attitude. For instance, if you took a dislike to a teacher because he embarrassed you on the first day of class, you might change classes to avoid him. Even if his offensiveness had been a misunderstanding on your part, you would have no opportunity to revise your initial unfavorable impression.

The second reason for the durability of attitudes is that *feelings cannot be separated readily from our perceptions.* Our feelings direct our attention and perceptions only to certain aspects of the world, so that the world we perceive does not violate too many of our expectations, impose on us new feelings, or contradict our previous experiences. Thus, not only does the individual protect himself from contact with objects for which he has negative attitudes, but when such contact is imminent, or when information about such objects is available, he attends to it selectively or distorts it. For example, he probably will not notice evidence of good sportsmanship by a despised opponent.

A third reason for the longevity of attitudes is our *social environment,* a very powerful force in maintaining the individual's attitudes. Our attitudes are continually reinforced by the groups with which we associate. Because of this rewarding aspect of contact with people of like minds, we tend to seek them out and avoid those who share few of our values or actively oppose them. In an effort to become accepted by certain groups, we adopt what we believe are attitudes valued by these groups. The neophyte and the convert are especially vulnerable in this regard.

Attitudes, Beliefs and Opinions

Beliefs are made up of the information we accept about an object, concept, or event—whether or not that information is accurate. Beliefs are the cognitive aspects of attitudes, the factual components as distinguished from the emotional components, although not all beliefs imply an attitude. An *opinion* can be defined as a lightly held belief.

Many beliefs simply consist of a proposition that is widely regarded as true. For example, the statements that smoking causes cancer, that out-of-state students should pay the same tuition as in-state students, and that space programs cost altogether too much money are all beliefs. On about the same plane are the beliefs that we cannot divide numbers by zero, there is no Heaven or Hell, no baseball team can ever win the World Series five times in a row, and there are extrasensory phenomena. Of course, a relationship may exist between an attitude's cognitive components (beliefs) and its affective components: If we accept the possibility that smoking causes cancer, then we may have an unfavorable attitude toward smoking. And if the smell of cigarette smoke repels us we may be more ready to believe that smoking causes cancer.

Very often, the emotional and cognitive components of an attitude are so closely bound up with each other that they cannot be distinguished clearly. This is particularly true of controversial beliefs, whose acceptance or rejection has powerful emotional consequences. If you were to accept as fact your suspicion that your best friend has betrayed your trust, your feelings toward him are likely to change radically.

Prejudice: A Prevalent and Harmful Attitude

Beliefs may correspond or conflict with facts or they may not be capable of verification at all. The belief that New York lies in the eastern United States corresponds to the known facts. The belief that the price of gold is determined by the phases of the moon does not correspond to known facts. The belief that animals do not have souls cannot be verified. But a belief's correspondence to known facts has little to do with the tenacity with which it is held. Some of the most stubbornly-held beliefs have been impossible to verify in fact. The belief that those who are good on earth will be rewarded in an everlasting afterlife cannot be proved or disproved. Conversely, some facts which are now readily ascertained were for centuries denied by most of the world. Examples of this are particularly abundant in the physical sciences: one has only to recall Galileo's trial and imprisonment by the Inquisition for advocating that the solar system is centered about the sun rather than the earth.

Whether they are true or false, beliefs have a strong influence on those who hold them. Beliefs about people may have even more influence on those who are their targets. _Prejudice_ is a belief, generally about other racial, ethnic, or social groups, which has no adequate factual basis. Prejudice exists in all societies, and beliefs about others' or one's own place in the "scheme of things" are fraught with false assumptions and specious reasoning. Because many of our social beliefs justify a certain pattern of living and make it invulnerable to change, the beliefs themselves are almost unassailable. The tenacity of such beliefs is further strengthened by the fact that all prejudices contain some element of truth, however small. They involve _overgeneralization, oversimplification,_ and _distortion_ of reality. Because of these features, centuries often pass before some beliefs, often totally absurd, are changed. Informal communication networks or the mass media continually reinforce them; they are substantiated by false evidence or given the authority of scientific proof or the blessing of the church. _The Medical and Surgical Journal_ of 1851 contains an interesting illustration of this. The _Journal_ published a report to the Medical Association of Louisiana—written by a physician, Samuel A. Cartwright. In his report, Dr. Cartwright discusses the "diseases and physical peculiarities of the negro race" and bemoans the medical profession's neglect of this field of pathology. He outlines a number of physiological and anatomical differences between whites and blacks:

From the diffusion of the brain . . . into the various organs of the body, in the shape of nerves to minister to the senses, everything partakes of sensuality, at the expense of intellectuality. Thus, music is a mere sensual pleasure with the negro. There is nothing in his music addressing the understanding; it has melody, but no harmony; his songs are mere sounds, without sense or meaning—pleasing the ear, without conveying a single idea to the mind. The great development of the nervous system . . . is associated with a deficiency of red blood in the pulmonary and arterial systems, from a defective atmospherization or arterialization of the blood in the lungs—constituting the best type of what is called lymphatic temperament, in which lymph, phlegm, mucus, and other humors, predominate over the red blood. It is this defective hematosis, or atmospherization, of the blood, conjoined with a deficiency of cerebral matter in the cranium, that is the true cause of the debasement of mind which has rendered the people of Africa unable to take care of themselves. . . .

18-2
The Ku Klux Klan represents an extreme form of prejudiced behavior. For many years members of the Klan terrorized Southern blacks—burning their homes, maiming, and killing them. (Burk Uzzle, Magnum)

Dr. Cartwright goes on to "demonstrate" how these "facts" explain beliefs that the Louisiana slave holders "knew" all along and how they relate to the controversial issue of the abolition of slavery. On this subject, Dr. Cartwright says:

. . . in a country where two races of men dwell together, both born on the same soil, breathing the same air and surrounded by the same external agents—liberty, which is elevating the one race of people above all other nations, sinks the other into beastly sloth and torpidity; and slavery, which the one would prefer death rather than endure, improves the other in body, mind and morals; thus providing the dogma false and establishing the truth that there is a radical, internal, or physical difference between the two races, so great in kind as to make what is wholesome and beneficial for the white man, as are liberty and republican or free institutions, etc., not only unsuitable to the negro race, but actually poisonous to its happiness.

This preposterous report was not the first of its kind, nor unfortunately the last. It demonstrates clearly how people—even those who might in their own minds be honest citizens and objective scientists—can marshal beliefs in the service of political and social ends. In addition, the quote illustrates the power of one's social environment. Dr. Cartwright's medicine and physiology seem totally absurd to us today, but they went unquestioned in 1851, not because Dr. Cartwright offered solid evidence for them but because the social climate of the time made his assertions all too acceptable, and therefore plausible.

No doubt, similar reports are made today. Like Dr. Cartwright's audience, we may be unaware of their falsity because they fit comfortably with our existing prejudices. As recently as April 1973, a current textbook by J. Robert Willson, another physician, was publicly burned by a campus group objecting to its derogatory view of women. In *Obstetrics and Gynecology*, Willson, like Cartwright supporting his statements with physiological "facts," asserts that categorical differences exist between the "feminine" and "masculine" personality. A woman, according to Willson, manifests maturity only when she can display a balance of the three essentially "feminine traits": narcissism, masochism, and passivity.

Origins of Prejudice. The origins of prejudice are not mysterious. As we shall see, attitudes are formed and maintained in a predictable and relatively well-understood manner, and prejudice is neither more nor less than a particular type of attitude. Thus, an understanding of the formation and change of attitudes provides a general understanding of how prejudice is instilled and sustained.

As a foretaste of what is to come, however, let us examine a few of the major findings concerning prejudice against minority groups. We know that prejudice emerges gradually during development; in our society, the first signs appear at about nursery school age (Goodman, 1964). Many studies have shown that the individual's prejudices are influenced heavily by the norms of his culture and the significant groups to which he belongs (see Harding, Proshansky, Kutner, & Chein, 1969). Many of

	% of whites agreeing with statement	
Statement	1963	1971
Blacks are inferior to white people.	31	22
Blacks have less ambition.	66	52
Blacks smell different.	60	48
Blacks have lower morals than whites.	55	40
Blacks breed crime.	35	27

18-3
The results of 1963 and 1971 surveys on the perception of blacks by whites. While attitudes are fairly resistant to change, they can be altered. (The Harris Survey, October 4, 1971)

these same studies demonstrate that parents play a significant role in determining the prejudices of their children. And as even a casual observer would predict, the nature and extent of prejudice vary with socioeconomic status, education, and religious affiliation.

Somewhat less compelling evidence suggests that various personality factors play a role in determining prejudice. Some investigators consider that the displacement of aggression is a major cause of prejudice against minorities. Proponents of this point of view, sometimes called the *scapegoat theory of prejudice*, believe that a prejudiced individual is frustrated in the expression of some significant wish or impulse and that his frustration arouses aggression which he cannot express against the appropriate target (because of the target's greater power or status). He displaces this pent-up aggression upon a substitute object (scapegoat), in this case the minority group member. Evidence for the theory is, however, not decisive (Berkowitz, 1961; Lindzey, 1950).

Changing Prejudice. Given the fact that an individual of any age is prejudiced, how can this state of affairs be changed? The very factors that help instill prejudice also can help undo or alter prejudicial attitudes. Thus, education that points out the irrational component in a prejudice has a significant influence (Stember, 1961), as does changing the social groups to which the individual belongs. Perhaps the most extensive evidence on changing prejudice against a minority group can be found in contacts between prejudiced individuals and members of the minority group. Such contact usually has a liberalizing effect—but not always. The greatest "loosening" of attitudes occurs under conditions that encourage or require intergroup cooperation and equality. One of the best known examples is Star, Williams, and Stouffer's study (1965) of United States Army riflemen. They found that 64 percent of the white riflemen who had served in platoons with black riflemen believed that it was a good idea to have mixed platoons; while only 18 percent of the white riflemen who had not served in an integrated platoon believed that racially mixed groups were desirable.

We have considered the general nature of attitudes, something about their relationship to behavior, their stability, and their relationship to other psychological concepts. We also have used the example of prejudice as a particular class of attitudes that, because of its implications for society and the individual, has been a matter of special interest to psychologists. Now, we shall turn to the matter of measuring attitudes.

Attitude Measurement

Attitudes are complex phenomena with many manifestations. An individual's attitude toward an object or idea could be inferred by noting all of his reactions and all of his thoughts about the topic over a period of time. While the result would be an extraordinarily rich description, the task of collecting the relevant information about even one attitude in only one person would be too enormous to be practical. Even if this kind of data could be collected, their complexity would make it difficult to compare individuals or to characterize groups of individuals and compare one with another.

Because of these problems, most attempts to measure attitudes have been based on a severely limited set of observations. A common procedure is to rely on a structured kind of self-report in which the person is asked directly about his beliefs and behavior. Typically, a statement or series of statements is presented, and the person is asked to indicate his agreement or disagreement with them. We shall describe more indirect methods of assessing attitudes later in this section.

Also in the interest of simplification, psychologists treat an attitude as if it were a single, quantifiable dimension, similar to a physical dimension, such as height, weight, or speed. Just as we can measure a person's height (or weight or speed of reaction) and assign it an index number (inches, centimeters, or whatever), so we should be able to assign people an index number that reflects the strength or intensity of an attitude, as well as its direction—favorable or unfavorable.

Measuring attitudes is far trickier, however, than measuring a physical attribute such as height. Physical properties are directly observable, while attitudes must be inferred from a more or less complex set of external signs. The instruments available to measure physical properties are highly accurate and reliable: that is, if the same object is measured by several different instruments or on repeated occasions by the same instrument, the results will be exactly the same. The "human yardstick," particularly when assessing psychological characteristics, is subject to fluctuations and uncertainties, which makes reliable measurement far more difficult.

Still another problem concerns the meaning of the numerical representation of an attitude. The numbers used to indicate physical attributes, such as height, have the same properties as the number system itself. If A is 70 inches tall, for example, and B is 35 inches, we know that A is twice as tall as B. If C is 60 inches tall, and D is 45 inches, we know that the difference in height between A and C is the same as between D and B. Attitude scales have only a few of the properties of physical measurements. Numerical scores can be used, for example, to order individuals according to the degree of their favorable or unfavorable attitude toward some matter, but rarely to specify exactly how much difference in attitude exists between any pair of individuals.

18-4
Frequency distribution of the attitudes of 10 people toward a particular object. The fact that the range of attitudes of just 10 people is so diverse demonstrates the difficulty of measuring the attitudes of an entire, large population.

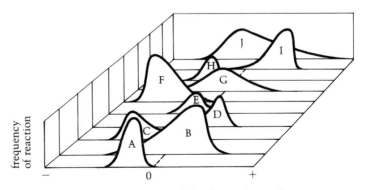

affective polarity of reaction toward the object of attitude

Attitude Scales

Despite the oversimplified assumptions underlying attitude scales and the many problems associated with attempting to measure any psychological phenomenon, psychologists have devised a number of reliable, useful instruments.

Rating scale techniques attempt to assess an individual's attitude by asking him to express that attitude as a categorical or numerical rating. The rating scale may require a simple yes or no (agree or disagree) or may ask the individual to check his degree of endorsement or nonendorsement on a scale with many gradations.

The rating scale method that is most frequently used in attitude measurement is the *Likert technique*. A series of single statements is presented; each statement describes an aspect of the attitudinal complex and is accompanied by a rating scale on which the individual is to indicate his reaction.

For example, a scale designed to measure attitudes toward American foreign policy might make statements on such subjects as trade with Communist countries and nuclear bomb treaties. The individual is required to indicate his reaction to each on a rating scale like the one shown below.

The index number used to characterize the person's attitude is obtained by summation; that is, each of his ratings is given a numerical value (in our example, from −2 to +2), and these numbers are added to give the person's overall score.

Far more complicated scaling methods have been devised. An example is the *Guttman Scalogram*, in which a person's response to a particular statement determines his answers to subsequent items tapping the same attitudinal dimension. The scale is an extension of an idea from intelligence testing in which a person who has successfully answered a difficult question of a specific type (for example, an arithmetic problem) is expected to be able to answer all easier questions of that type. Scalogram analysis applies this notion to attitudes. An attempt is made to order items along a continuum of acceptability, so that acceptance of, or agreement with, a given item results in acceptance of all other items that reflect a less extreme attitude. Conversely, a person's disagreement with an item implies that he also will reject all more extreme items. Scalogram items are presented in unvarying order, and each person's position on the dimension is described by the pair of adjacent items representing the highest on the dimension he has found acceptable and the lowest he has found unacceptable.

The *Bogardus Social Distance Scale* (Bogardus, 1959) is the classic example of a Guttman scale. Bogardus thought that the more prejudiced an individual is, the more social distance he will want between himself and members of the group he dislikes. The instructions in the Bogardus scale are: "According to my first feeling reactions, I would willingly admit members of each race (as a class, and not the best members, nor the worst member) to one or more of the following classifications under which I have placed a cross:

1. close kinship by marriage;

2. my club as personal chums;

3. my street as neighbors;

4. employment in my occupation;

5. citizenship in my country;

6. my country only as visitors;

7. exclude them from my country."

If we know the person's most extreme response, we know how he responded on all the items. If a respondent says he is willing to admit a Chicano to employment in his occupation, we expect that he would not exclude this person from his country, would allow him to be a visitor in his country, and would allow him to hold citizenship in his country. On the other hand, if the respondent would not have the Chicano as a neighbor, it is doubtful that he would accept him as a personal chum, or a relative by marriage.

Indirect Measures of Attitudes

The measuring techniques we have discussed rely on the person's awareness of his attitude and his readiness to communicate it verbally. With such techniques, the person also knows that his attitude is being assessed; this knowledge may affect his responses. In such self-report measures, the person may distort his responses to please the interviewer, to appear psychologically "healthy," or for any number of other reasons.

Some psychologists have been attempting to develop measures that are less liable to these sorts of distortions (Campbell, 1950; Webb, Campbell, Schwarz, & Sechrest, 1966). *Indirect techniques*, in which the subject does not know that his behavior or attitude is being assessed, are of two types. A subject's behavior may simply be observed without telling the subject. Or the subject may think he is being tested for some other purpose, for example, intellectual function, when actually the test is measuring his emotional reactions to certain objects. Indirect techniques are especially useful if the respondent seems reluctant to express his attitudes candidly.

In one indirect technique, the experimenter gives the subject pictures and asks him to tell a story about them (Proshansky, 1943). The subject's reply is scored for the attitude toward the person or situation in the picture. Thus, if a subject consistently and repeatedly interprets pictures of similar objects in the same way, his stories are believed to be determined by something *in him* (his attitude) and not by something in the picture. Here is how two subjects responded to the same picture in a measure of prejudice regarding poverty and the races:

Subject A:

Home of a man on relief . . . shabby—dresses poorly. Scene is probably in a shack down South. Also might be the home of some unemployed laborer. Horrible housing conditions. Why don't the government provide for these people. The ordinary worker is always forgotten and allowed to rot.

Subject B:

Picture of one room, very messy, stove in the center, woman on the left, man standing next to the stove, couple of children near them. This is a room of what we call "poor people." They seem to be messy, sloppy people, who seem to enjoy dwelling in their own trash.

These responses obviously indicate very different attitudes toward poverty and its causes.

In another indirect method used to study prejudice, the subjects are given male and female figures cut from black and white felt and are asked to arrange them any way they wish on a felt board (Kuethe, 1964). The resulting organizations of figures can be classified according to how many segregated groupings are made. Studies using this technique have found that it relates closely to some self-report techniques for ethnocentrism and prejudice.

There are many other indirect techniques. They include memorization of favorable and unfavorable material about the object, completion of syllogisms (All men are foolish; Smith is a man; therefore Smith is foolish.) with favorable and unfavorable conclusions, or judging characteristics of test items for their plausibility. All of these indirect techniques present the task as cognitive or intellectual, while the experimenter actually is interpreting the subject's attitudes as revealed by his perceptions, memory biases, and faulty logic.

While specific tasks are frequently used, a subject's attitudes often can be assessed just by secretly observing his behavior. One psychologist measured museum visitors' interest in various displays by noting how often the tiles in front of each exhibit had to be replaced (Melton, 1936). He assumed that the more times the tiles had to be changed, the more popular the exhibit. He took into account the fact that visitors had a right-turning bias after entering the museum and tended to drag their feet toward the end of their tour. Validating this study, Chicago's Museum of Science and Technology found that the tiles around the exhibit of live, hatching chicks had to be replaced every six weeks, while the tiles around other less engaging displays had gone for years without being replaced.

Another indirect measure is the "lost letter" technique (Milgram, Mann, & Harter, 1965) devised to measure people's attitudes toward various groups. Stamped letters addressed to organizations like the Young Communist League or Citizens Against Gun Control are "dropped" throughout a city—in stores, in telephone booths, on sidewalks. The number of letters that are picked up and mailed is taken as

Photos such as this one are used in indirect tests to measure attitudes. How would you describe this scene? Try to analyze your description. (Charles Harbutt, Magnum).

an indication of positive attitudes toward the cause or the organization mentioned in the address.

Indirect measures of attitudes raise some important issues for psychologists. To what extent does assessing an individual's attitude, when he is not aware of it, represent an invasion of his privacy? Is deception or concealment of purpose a breach of ethics? Do we always need the consent of the respondent? Psychologists and citizens in general differ widely among themselves on these questions, which are of concern not only for those doing indirect attitude testing, but also for almost everyone doing psychological research.

Some of the most recent studies of attitude measurements stress that direct and indirect tests may be tapping different aspects of attitudes. This suggests that ideally both direct, self-report measures and indirect measures should be employed to assess or measure complex, multifaceted attitudes. Using two or more independent measurements should allow us to interpret a particular attitude more accurately and completely.

Physiological Measures of Attitudes

Yet another approach to attitude measurement is to measure physiological responses. While the subject is viewing or thinking about the object of his attitude, his heartbeat, galvanic skin response (GSR), or pupil dilation is measured. Usually, individuals cannot alter or easily control their physiological responses. Although we need much more research to establish the evidence firmly, these physiological responses show some correspondence to the person's emotional state.

Several studies have related changes in galvanic skin response (GSR) to racial prejudice. People whose verbal responses are unfavorable to blacks show different GSRs to blacks than do people who report favorable attitudes. Prejudiced individuals display greater GSRs when favorable re-

18-6
Physiological measures of an attitude
are good indicators of the strength
rather than the direction of that attitude. However, these men obviously
hold a positive attitude toward the
"object" they are staring at. (Jan
Lukas, Rapho Guillumette)

marks are made about the objects of their prejudice or when slides of
these people are presented (Westie & Defleur, 1959; Cooper & Pollack,
1959). In another area of prejudice, subjects with both pro- and anti-
church attitudes displayed proportionately higher GSRs to statements
that clashed with their measured attitudes.

Eye-pupil response is another attitudinal measure that has generated
interest and speculation. Changes in eye-pupil diameter accompany
many activities. A person's pupils tend to dilate (enlarge) when he is
viewing a particularly interesting sight and to contract when he is
bored. One investigator found that the pupils of culturally pro-black
subjects dilated significantly more in response to pictures of blacks than
did the pupils of anti-black subjects. Another investigator reported substantial pupil dilation when male subjects viewed photographs of nude
females.

Of course, such measures have their shortcomings. If we observe a
strong physiological response, we can assume that it corresponds to a
strong feeling. However, we cannot be certain of the attitude's nature
or direction, although some research does suggest, as we have noted,
that pupil dilation and contraction correspond to positive and negative arousal, respectively. Since a person usually has a strong physiological reaction if he feels that the attitude's object is either very good
or very bad, physiological measures probably are best used in cases
where one knows the direction of attitude but also wants to know its
strength.

Public Opinion Polling

Public opinion pollsters have developed some useful and highly
predictive measurement techniques. Public opinion survey techniques,
especially those concerned with voting behavior, are quite precise. Ever
since the polls appeared on the morning of President Truman's election,

predicting that New York Governor Thomas Dewey would win, pollsters have progressively narrowed their margin of error. In the 1972 presidential election, the Harris poll predicted shortly before the election that Richard Nixon would attract 61 percent of the votes and George McGovern 39 percent. The Gallup poll predicted 62 percent for Nixon and 38 percent for McGovern. Election night totals gave Nixon 60.7 percent of the vote and McGovern 37.7 percent. Considering all the complicating factors, this result is a powerful validation of current polling techniques.

Typically, _opinion polling_ involves interviewing a sample of people which is representative of the whole population. Such polls are used to compile information on everything from voter attitudes to toothpaste preferences. Regardless of the topic, the polling steps are essentially the same. First, the pollster outlines the study's major objectives. He specifies both the questions and the type of information he needs to satisfy the objectives. Next, he selects the sample of people to be interviewed. If he is surveying women workers in a particular factory, the group interviewed must be representative of _all_ of the factory's women employees. If the survey concerns American attitudes on divorce, the sample must represent the entire adult population: each adult in the population must have the same chance of being included.

Getting a _representative sample_ of a factory's women employees is relatively easy. Usually, a given number of names can be drawn at random from a complete and accurate list of personnel. But there are no lists of the entire adult population of the United States. How can we draw a _representative national sample?_ We may use _area sampling_, a method developed by the Institute for Social Research in Ann Arbor, Michigan. To draw a sample of American adults, the method samples households, selected on the basis of very detailed maps. All the cities and towns and all United States farmland are divided into small segments, "weighted" by their population. The segments are counted off; a small number is selected at random to comprise the sample. This procedure insures that every type of household, representing every type of attitude on a particular subject, has an equal chance of being included in the sample. The next step is to divide the segments to be sampled into blocks. Interviewers then visit every "nth" household in each block. The similarity of the people to be surveyed and the precision desired determine the sample's size. Usually, errors in opinion polling occur not because the sample is too small, but because the sample did not represent the population.

After a sample is selected, the next step is the writing of the _questionnaire._ A great deal of research has shown that people may be influenced by the wording of a question and that seemingly straightforward questions often evoke anything but straightforward answers. Questions must be understood by everyone in the sample and mean approximately the same thing to all of them. Questions have to be worded to encourage the respondent to talk freely and not distort his answers. Questionnaire writers must be constantly alert for people who respond falsely because they want to please (or spite) the interviewer, or because they are worried about what might be done with their answers.

Sample questions used by a pollster in analyzing attitudes toward various subjects related to government activity. (Harris, 1973)

26. Now I want to ask you about some situations involving government. For each, tell me if you personally object to the government doing that, or would you just accept it as something that had to be done for the good of the country or the community? (Read list and record below for each item.)

	Would object	Would accept	Not sure
a. If the government allowed people to own a gun, but said it had to be kept at a local police station and signed in and out, with a pass given each time it was used.	———	———	———
b. If the government said every family had to pay $50 a year more in taxes to clean up air and water pollution	———	———	———
c. If the government imposed and enforced a stiff fine for littering public places with trash	———	———	———
d. If the police made spot checks at traffic lights to see if people had their safety belts on in cars and imposed stiff fines if they didn't have them on	———	———	———
e. If the government required all auto owners to bring in their car every three months for an inspection to be sure it wasn't burning too much gasoline during the gas shortage	———	———	———
f. If the government raised taxes for each family $50 a year to make sure the streets were safe to walk on at night	———	———	———
g. If the government said the price of bread had to go up 5 cents in order to send wheat to China and Russia as a way to keep peace in the world.	———	———	———
h. If the government asked that all demonstrations against the government be called off so that government leaders could get the work of government done.	———	———	———
i. If the government required that every residence had to be inspected once a year for cracks and leaks that wasted heat or fuel.	———	———	———
j. If police said they needed the right to come into your home without a search warrant to control drug abuse	———	———	———

Attitude Formation

Attitudes develop because humans learn from each other. The first, and perhaps most effective, teachers of attitudes are a child's parents. Other adults, peers, schools, and the mass media also influence attitude formation. In addition, repeated contact with an object, opinion, or belief usually affects an individual's attitude.

Direct Contact with the Attitude Object

At the beginning of this chapter, we saw that attitudes are determined by the relationship between the object and the action. In part, this is true. If everything else holds constant, repeated contact with a given object—assuming no noxious consequences—will result in a more favorable attitude. Repeated exposure alone, without rewards or other favorable circumstances, is all that is necessary (Zajonc, 1968).

Research in this area has explored minimal conditions for the formation of favorable attitudes. In one experiment, photographs of men's faces were shown, some just once, others as many as 25 times. Then the photographs were shown again and the subjects were asked if they thought they would like the person. The more often subjects had seen a picture, the more they thought they would like the person. The exposure-liking effect has been detected with other stimuli, such as nonsense words, Chinese ideographs, and Pakistani music.

Many animals are affected in a manner similar to humans. In an ingenious experiment (Cross, Halcomb, & Matter, 1967), one group of rats was raised hearing musical selections from Mozart, 12 hours a day for 52 days, while another group grew up with selections from Arnold Schönberg. A third group heard no music. The investigators then tested the rats for their musical preference by putting each rat in a chamber with a floor that was hinged at the center and suspended over two switches, one on each side of the hinge. A rat's weight was enough to push down one side of the floor and depress a switch that would activate a recording. Selections the rat had not heard before were used, but they were either from Mozart or Schönberg. The results clearly indicated that exposure to one kind of music led the rats to "prefer" that kind of music. Human Mozart lovers may resent these cross-species tests of musical preferences and rightfully argue that *their* musical attitudes are differentiated and based on intellectual and aesthetic considerations, but at least some part of the emotional component of the attitude seems well developed in rodents.

Implications of the exposure phenomenon reach into many human activities. Advertisers and political campaigners know very well the importance of exposure. Much of the $20.5 billion spent annually on advertising in the United States is spent just to gain public exposure. An unwritten rule of political campaigning states that a candidate should not mention his opponent's name when attempting to demonstrate the superiority of his own stand on various policies and programs. Every mention of the name gives his opponent additional exposure.

In advertising, we usually assume that the colorful, novel, or dramatic print ads, and the catchy tunes on radio and television, gain the customer's attention so that the ad copy can inform him about the advertised product and persuade him to buy it. In some cases, this probably is true. But for products that are highly similar, such as aspirin or cigarettes, it may be exposure to the product, and not the accompanying information, that establishes a favorable attitude toward the product.

An example, both funny and frightening, of the power of exposure appeared in a news article in *The New York Times:*

FOOTPOWDER PRODUCES HEADACHES IN ECUADOR

Quito, Ecuador, July 17, 1969 (Reuters)

Controversy is raging here because a foot powder called Pulvapies was elected mayor of a town of 4,000 people. The company that manufactures the foot deodorant decided during recent campaigns for municipal offices to use the slogan: "Vote for any candidate, but if you want well-being and hygiene, vote for Pulvapies." On the eve of the election, the company distributed a leaflet the same size and color as official voting papers, saying: "For Mayor, Honorable Pulvapies." When the votes were counted, the coastal town of Picoaza had elected Pulvapies by a clear majority.

Social Interaction and the Formation of Attitudes

While mere repeated exposure to a novel stimulus can produce an initially favorable emotional reaction, the intensity of such reactions is quite low. Yet, in everyday life, we encounter attitudes so powerful that acts of violence or supreme sacrifices on their behalf do not seem exceptional. Obviously, contact alone cannot instill such intense attitudes. We must look to the host of other factors that bear on the acquisition and development of attitudes. Social influences, including family, social class, and ethnic background, provide an initial orientation within which a child develops his characteristic way of responding. *Parents* are the predominant shapers of a child's early attitudes.

Parental Influence. Children's attitudes toward political, economic, and religious affairs generally resemble their parents' attitudes, despite the estrangement within many families (Syman, 1959; Horowitz & Horowitz, 1938). The most recent national survey of high school students and their parents (Jennings & Niemi, 1968) found that 74 percent of the students and their parents had the same religious affiliation. Sixty percent of the students chose the same political party as their parents. Of the others, some students identified themselves as independents and less than 10 percent switched to the opposite party.

Although only 60 percent of the students choose their parents' political party, many more move in the same general political direction – toward liberalism or conservatism. One study of student activism (Braungart, 1966) surveyed delegates attending a convention of the left-wing Students for a Democratic Society and students attending a convention of the right-wing Young Americans for Freedom. Right-wing students were predominantly middle-class Protestant children of Republicans who were not college graduates. In marked contrast, the left-wing students were Jewish or nonreligious and came from upper-class parents who were more likely to be college graduates and usually belonged to the Democratic or Liberal party. Several other studies confirm the finding that left-wing student activists consistently have more liberal parents than students who are not activists.

Parent-child agreement decreases substantially when investigations move from general issues to more specific attitudes, such as those toward minority groups, labor unions, or big business. Here, parental influence appears to fade. For instance, mother and daughter may identify with the Democratic party but diverge widely on particular issues, such as welfare or busing. This lack of specific attitude correspondence coincides with the stereotype of the generation gap. The absence of parent-child attitudinal correspondence on many issues suggests that other factors besides the family have a substantial impact on attitudes.

Peer-Group Influence. Starting the preschool period, the *peer group* exerts an important influence on an individual's attitudes. As the individual grows older, he spends more and more time away from home with his friends. While friends seldom seem to attempt explicitly to change one another, they do share experiences and confidences and provide acceptance and support. Similarities in interests and values that develop as a result of a friendship lead to the increasing convergence of attitudes and opinions.

In this context, school assumes special importance, not only as a source of education and information, but as the source of most friendships. A well-known investigation of peer influence (Newcomb, 1943) studied women students from wealthy, conservative backgrounds entering a small liberal college. The longer the women participated in the activities of the college and the community, the more liberal they became. The women who participated least in their peers' activities did not change their attitudes substantially, if at all. A follow-up study conducted 20 years later showed that the women continued to hold the changed attitudes they had held as college seniors. Several other studies have shown that the early college years often produce striking changes in attitudes as students are exposed to a variety of experiences and attitudes they had not previously encountered (Freedman, Carlsmith, & Sears, 1970; Feldman & Newcomb, 1968).

18-8
As we grow older, we spend more and more time with our peer group and less and less time at home. Peer group influence on attitudes thus becomes quite strong. A person who is accepted by his peer group usually adopts its members' attitudes, their ways of behaving, even their style of dress. (Ken Heyman, Bruce Davidson)

The peer group is more important to attitude formation in such settings as the Israeli kibbutzim and the child-rearing collectives of the Soviet Union. In these collective child-rearing settings, the peer group induces its members to feel socially responsible for the other group members and to take the lead in attempting to help them. The peer group is the most potent reinforcer because of the limited individual attention that the caretakers can give to each child. Most of the affection, approval, and material rewards come from other group members.

Within his peer group, a child's attitudes are determined by the attitudes of his peers. If group norms call for achievement, responsibility, and adherence to adult patterns of behavior, the members will perform accordingly. If the peer group is viewed as an escape from parental authority, groups may devalue achievement or call for violation of adult norms. In one study (Bronfenbrenner, 1970) American and Russian children were asked to fill out a questionnaire about how they would behave if some of their friends urged them to steal fruit from an orchard, accidentally break a window and run away, or go to a movie disapproved of by their parents. The American children were far more inclined to perform the acts than were the Russian children. And when the Russian children believed that their peers would see their answers, they were less likely to admit an inclination toward the acts than when they thought no one would see their answers.

Adoption of peer-group attitudes is not necessarily automatic and complete. The peer group involves a set of relationships from which the individual partially draws his own identity and self-concept. If an individual is on the fringe of his peer group, he may feel little identification with its attitudes. So, he may maintain his attitudinal independence. Acceptance by the group and status within the group substantially increase the individual's adoption of his peers' attitudes.

The Influence of Education. Apart from the peer influences evident at school or college, *education* is itself a significant factor in forming permanent attitudes. For instance, education relates strongly to the holding of liberal attitudes. One study (Sears, 1969) showed that 66 percent of college graduates but only 16 percent of grade school graduates held a liberal attitude toward civil liberties. Other studies show that education correlates negatively with authoritarianism, dogmatism, prejudice, and conservative attitudes toward public issues. However, individuals who go to college may already be different from those who do not. Thus, other variables besides the college's academic program may account for attitude differences. College's impact upon attitudes depends on the college's size and type, the student's psychological makeup, the extent to which the student interacts with peers and faculty, and his major field. However, the information provided by the educational experience has more impact upon attitudes when higher education is less universal than is common in this country. For example, mass education has brought about impressive attitude changes in less developed countries.

The Influence of the Mass Media. The *mass media* also may influence and form attitudes. But most research indicates that the media play more of a reinforcing than a converting role. People attend to content that agrees with, rather than opposes, their own beliefs and opinions. Thus, the media usually are viewed as standardizing and integrating forces; they have been considered virtually ineffective in producing large-scale changes in attitude. However, some notable exceptions have been recorded. The classic example of media influence is the widespread panic caused by Orson Welles' radio broadcast of "an invasion from Mars" in 1938. Most people who tuned in late thought they were hearing an actual radio broadcast of the invasion. A study of the reactions shows that people had great faith in radio commentators and many blindly accepted the unbelievable account. A recent example of such continued faith in the media appeared in a *Newsweek* magazine survey, which named news commentator Walter Cronkite as the most trusted man in America. Americans' newly acquired or newly awakened regard for a clean environment and nourishing natural foods is further evidence of the media's influence in our attitudes.

Psychological Processes Involved in Attitude Formation

As we have seen, the most elementary process of attitude formation is repeated contact with the object. This process is easiest to understand when an object is relatively novel, since familiar objects are seldom neutral—we already have attitudes toward them.

When positive reactions grow stronger after repeated exposure to an object, it is primarily because the successive contacts are resolving a conflict that arose at the first encounter with the object. At first, an individual does not know what a new object is or whether it has positive or negative consequences for him. This overall state of uncertainty may be associated with mildly negative emotional reactions. He fears and shuns novel objects to some extent—a reaction that has significant survival value. Until he has assessed the possible danger in the novel object, caution is a reasonable response.

We face many everyday situations involving novel objects. We feel mildly ill at ease among strangers at a party, confused in a strange building, perhaps conspicuous in a group composed solely of members of the opposite sex. All these reactions represent a conflict between the individual's avoidance reactions and his desire to discover just what the object or the situation is like (approach). It is a conflict between caution and curiosity. As his encounters with the novel object recur—assuming no particularly negative events follow the encounters—his negative emotional reactions diminish. The object has ceased to be novel and he is now more favorably disposed to it. If, on the other hand, noxious consequences follow, the individual may undergo typical aversive conditioning that results in a strong negative attitude toward the object—and probably its surroundings as well.

Advertising relies on building favorable attitudes toward a product by presenting it with highly attractive "stimuli." The logic is that the individual will associate his positive reaction to the attractive "companion" stimulus that appears in the advertisement together with the product. If this strategy works, the product eventually will evoke positive reactions, even without the "companion" stimulus. As we noted in Chapter 10, advertisers for car manufacturers, knowing that most car buyers are men, regularly use beautiful women in their advertisements because they hope to associate their cars with sexually desirable females.

Conditioning and learning leading to the acquisition of attitudes occur within a complex social process. In this process, an individual's peers, superiors, friends, and parents control the reinforcers that shape the individual's reactions to objects. Hence, *conformity* to a group's norms or *imitation* of admired individuals can play a significant role in attitude formation. The impact of college on the student's attitudes results in part from conformity and imitation. Only by association with these powerful social processes, and only in matters central to the individual's social and psychological life—his identity, his view of the world and of himself—can basic attitudes be transformed—or confirmed.

Attitude Change

An attitude, once acquired, is a fairly permanent predisposition to react in a particular way to an object. Eventually, successive encounters with the object generate a distribution of reactions that is fairly uniform and consistent.

Before we discuss how attitudes change and what procedures produce this change, we must discuss briefly just what we mean by attitude change. An analogy with changes in weather seems appropriate. Like weather, attitude is not a unitary phenomenon. We can think of weather as temperature, wind velocity and direction, humidity, cloud cover, and barometric pressure. If we say that the weather in California is better than the weather in Maryland, we mean that the "average weather"—all of these aspects of weather averaged over a period of time—produces a more pleasant climate. If we say that the weather is improving, we probably mean that the amount of sunshine will increase, the temperature will become more moderate, and the humidity will decline. Similarly, if we say that college graduates are more liberal than those who did not attend college, we are looking at a frequency distribution of one population and representing it by its mean (average) and its standard deviation (variation). We compare the values of this population to the corresponding values of the other population. We use a similar alignment when we compare an individual's attitudes on two different occasions—which, of course, is exactly what we compare when we measure attitude change.

Attitudes can change in several ways. First, the individual's average attitude may become more positive or more negative. Usually, this is what we mean by attitude change. But other changes are possible. The variability of his reaction may change. If he has been exposed to a fairly uniform view of the military service as the duty of every citizen, and then he encounters pacifists and gradually acquires their attitudes, his views will become generally more liberal. He isn't quite as positive toward military service as he had been. But, his response is less dogmatic as well as less positive. He may recognize various circumstances under which the draft definitely should be dropped, for example. His emotional reactions to military service are now more widely distributed—not only the mean but the standard deviation has increased. Such an individual may in fact manifest attitude change not simply by a change in his general attitude but also by a more variable response, depending on the particular setting or issue. For example, he may still have a strong positive attitude toward the draft in the context of World War II and yet have an equally strong negative attitude toward it in the context of the war in Southeast Asia.

Attitude change is, of course, the goal of propaganda and persuasive communication. Such messages are designed to induce the recipient to change his attitude. Studies of persuasive communications have generally been concerned with one or more of the variables we shall discuss in this section. They are (1) the effectiveness of different sources of communication, (2) the nature of the communication, and (3) the characteristics of the audience.

Source of Communication

Our attitude toward the *source of a message* has an effect on whether we will change our attitudes after receiving a message. If we think the sender of a message is credible, we are likely to believe him. Credibility depends on the speaker's prestige and the credentials he presents. Many studies show that an experimenter can vary the amount of attitude change a message produces by ascribing it to sources that differ in education, age, intelligence, and social status.

For example, Hovland and Weiss (1951) presented subjects with a communication arguing that the building of atomic-powered submarines was a practical undertaking. (The study was conducted when there were serious doubts about the project, before the first atomic sub was built.) For some subjects, the argument was attributed to J. Robert Oppenheimer, an internationally known and respected physicist. For others, it was attributed to a Soviet newspaper. The results showed that the message was more effective in changing opinions when it came from Oppenheimer, who was viewed as an expert and trustworthy source.

Even irrelevant characteristics of the source's status have an effect on attitude change. In a study by Aronson and Golden (1962), an attempt was made to promote the virtues of arithmetic. The subjects were white sixth graders, and four communicators were used: (1) a white engineer, (2) a black engineer, (3) a white dishwasher, and (4) a black dishwasher. Aronson and Golden found not only that the relevant characteristics of the source (engineer vs. dishwasher) influenced the effectiveness of the communication, but that the irrelevant characteristics (white-black) also had an effect. Racially prejudiced students changed less in their opinions of arithmetic when the communicator was black than when he was white. The advertising industry has not overlooked the persuasive influence of such irrelevant communicator characteristics. Shaving creams are not endorsed by dermatologists, chemists, or barbers—they are endorsed by admired athletes or attractive women.

Two traits of the communicator affect his success. First, a communicator's effectiveness can be increased if he appears to argue a position contrary to his own self-interest. For example, a noted mobster influenced subjects more when he argued for stricter and more powerful courts than when he argued for less severe sentences and lenient courts (Walster, Aronson, & Abrahams, 1966). Similarly, a communicator's effectiveness increases if he appears to be uninterested in influencing our opinions. In one experiment, overheard conversations between persons who seemed unaware of the subjects' presence influenced their opinions more than when they seemed aware of the subjects' presence (Walster & Festinger, 1962).

The Sleeper Effect. We know little about the permanence of attitude changes brought about by experimental persuasion. Caution is especially important here since experimental studies of persuasion normally focus on attitudes that are vulnerable to change simply because the individual has very little psychological investment in them—such as the argument about the feasibility of atomic submarines. Yet, one aspect—the so-called sleeper effect—appears to be a stable finding.

Discovered in the 1950s, the _sleeper effect_ describes an attitude change that shows itself only after some time has elapsed. Immediately after a persuasion attempt, no change appears. But if the subject is tested again in 2 or 4 weeks, his attitude shows a shift toward the persuader's point of view. The explanation for the sleeper effect may be that over time the message's content and the communicator's credibility become separated. Thus, if a message that, in itself, is quite effective is presented by a barely credible source, the listener's total immediate attitude change is minimal, since the source's negative effects prevent the message's content from exercising its reasonable influence on him. However, when the listener has forgotten where the message came from, the message can operate at full force; a delayed change in attitude is the result.

Nature of the Communication

A message's persuasive force depends on many factors; these include the intelligibility, length, elaboration, logical content, and emotional appeal of the message. Early studies showed that, of the _emotional_ and the _logical_ components, the emotional are more powerful. More recently, in his history of the 1968 presidential campaign, McGinniss (_The Selling of the President, 1968_) reports that Nixon's adviser, Joe Gavin, said:

Voters are basically lazy, basically uninterested in making an effort to understand what we're talking about. Reason requires a high degree of discipline, of concentration; impression is easier. Reason pushes the viewer back, it assaults him. The emotions are more easily roused, closer to the surface, more malleable . . . get to the gut reactions which are unarticulated, non-analytical, a product of the particular chemistry between the voter and the image of the candidate.

The content's effect depends on the emotion aroused, under what conditions, and how intense it is. Emotional content that arouses _fear_ works under some conditions, depending on how much fear is aroused. The fear appeal makes the listener feel that something undesirable will happen to him if he fails to heed the message. This topic first aroused interest when an experiment required high school students to listen to lectures on dental hygiene (Janis & Feshbach, 1953) under one of three conditions: strong fear, moderate fear, and no fear. The higher the level of fear aroused by the communication, the _less_ likely students were to accept the communicator's point of view.

Messages with extremely high fear content may provoke anxiety and thus prompt the individual to avoid the message. Paradoxically, people who can cope better with anxiety-provoking situations should be more influenced by fear appeals than persons who are easily disturbed. Studies by Leventhal (1970) suggest that this is true. He has further shown that fear messages that exactly spell out the remedial action to be taken work much better than other fear appeals. For example, a campus campaign to encourage the taking of tetanus shots included the time and place where the shots were being given (a map was distributed showing the location of the student health center). Under these conditions, high-

18-9
Some messages are communicated effectively through symbolic acts. The gas mask warns us of the dangers of pollution. Because the message arouses fear, many people prefer to ignore it. (WHO Photo by J. Mohr)

fear appeals produced a more favorable response to tetanus shots than did low-fear appeals—a result that contradicted the findings of Janis and Feshbach. It was the specific instructions that made the difference: Of those who received instructions, 28 percent got shots. Of those who simply received the persuasive messages with fear appeals (although knowing from other sources that shots were available at the health service), only 3 percent got shots.

Characteristics of the Audience

The *characteristics of the audience* or the person who receives the message also are important in attitude change. Some individuals are more susceptible to persuasive influences than others. Research indicates that women are more readily influenced than men; poorly educated people more than the well educated. However, this research may be saying only that people can be more easily influenced about topics that they don't care or know about. The subjects chosen may have been interesting only to men or to the well educated. If the topics had been of interest to women or poorly educated people, the results might have been exactly the opposite.

In general, moderate attitudes can be changed more easily than extreme attitudes. Tannenbaum (1956) had greater success changing the attitudes of people who differed in their middle-range attitudes toward such issues as legalized gambling and abstract art than in changing the attitudes of those who held extreme views. More recently March and McGinnies (1968) presented college students, previously classified as doves, moderates, or hawks, with a tape recording that advocated the unilateral withdrawal of the United States military from Vietnam. Students with moderate opinions regarding U.S. involvement in Vietnam shifted their attitudes most toward agreement with the recorded argument.

Since attitudes often are anchored in the groups to which individuals belong, attempts to change attitudes must consider the social context. Two methods of changing group-related attitudes immediately suggest themselves: (1) change the individual's identification from the reference group sharing his attitudes to another reference group with different attitudes; (2) change the social norms of the group that is the source of his attitudes. A good example of changing reference groups is Newcomb's study of women at Bennington College, which we discussed earlier. The study demonstrates how political attitudes change when a student moves from his family reference group to a liberal college peer group.

A study by Lewin (1952) carried out during World War II is a good illustration of how to change attitudes by changing group norms. In the study, which changed the attitudes of women toward cooking and serving unpopular cuts of meat, such as sweetbreads, beef hearts, and kidneys, one group of women received a lecture on the health value of the meats, their economy, and attractive ways to prepare them. The second group did not receive a lecture; the members simply discussed the relationship between the uses of various meats, the war effort, and general health. The women in the discussion group convinced each other and thus changed the prevailing social norms; they displayed considerably more attitude change toward serving the meats than did the women who received a lecture on the meats' positive qualities.

Attitudes and Cognitive Consistency

Attempts to change attitudes often fail. Failure is particularly likely when we deal with attitudes central to the individual's psychological functioning. Here we are attempting to change one element in a complex organization of intimately related parts. Any change has repercussions, for attitudes do not exist in isolation. Our view of the United States economy is related to our view of the individual's place in the political process; and our view of school busing is related to our views on the rights of minorities. We hold a coherent system of thoughts and beliefs that are subjectively and psychologically consistent. Theories stemming from this idea are labeled *cognitive consistency theories*. They maintain that conflicting attitudes are intolerable to man and that inconsistency stimulates change. As a rational and rationalizing animal, man seems compelled to eliminate illogical or conflicting attitudes and beliefs. Thus, when we believe that something is true, we convince ourselves that it also is wise and desirable. A recent study (Dion, Berscheid, & Walster, 1972) shows that attractive persons of either sex are judged from their photographs alone to have more socially desirable personality traits; to be more likely to attain higher occupational status; to be less likely to be divorced when married; and to experience greater total happiness than less attractive persons. Both men and women gave these consistency ratings.

Balance Theory. Heider's *balance theory* is one type of consistency theory. This theory assumes that we like consistency in our relationships with other people and in our environment. In Heider's theory, person P is perceiving person O and one other entity, X, which can be an idea, a person, or an attitude object. Heider wanted to know how P organizes the relationships among P, O, and X. These relationships can be either balanced or unbalanced; in a balanced state, the relationships are harmonious. Thus, P is a female graduate student who believes that a woman's place is anywhere but in the home, and who is in charge of the local campaign for pro-abortion legislation. She meets O, a male graduate student, and finds that he is a bright, interesting, likable person. Some time later, P discovers that O is strongly opposed to abortion on demand. Balance theory predicts an unbalanced state. P likes O and approves of X, but O disapproves of X. Heider predicts that forces toward balance will arise. If P can induce O to change his attitude or if P decides she no longer likes O, she will achieve balance.

Dissonance Theory. The consistency theory that has stimulated the most controversy and research is *dissonance theory*, which, as we noted in Chapter 12, Festinger developed in 1957. *Cognitive dissonance* is the state of tension that results when an individual holds two cognitions (ideas, attitudes, beliefs, opinions) whose implications are psychologically inconsistent. Cognitive dissonance is unpleasant and people are motivated to reduce it. The classic example is the person who enjoys smoking and also knows of the well-documented research that links smoking to lung cancer and respiratory diseases. He feels dissonance because his cognition "I smoke cigarettes" clashes with his cognition that "Smoking causes cancer and I do not want to contract cancer." He can reduce dissonance by giving up smoking; the cognition "I do not smoke" would be consistent with the cognition "Smoking causes cancer." Other measures to reduce dissonance include trying to find flaws in the scientific evidence linking cigarette smoking to cancer, switching to a filter-tip brand in the hope that the filter will trap the cancer-producing materials, or making friends with other seemingly intelligent people who smoke. The confirmed smoker even may try to add new cognitions to his system, such as, "Smoking is important because it relieves stress and makes life more enjoyable." Any action that reduces or tones down the inconsistency prompted by pursuing an activity that is clearly life-endangering reduces dissonance.

An outside observer may not always detect an inconsistency in another person's belief system. Depending on a person's underlying premises, a behavior that seems blatantly inconsistent to one individual may be completely consonant for another.

According to Festinger's theory, all decisions are likely to generate dissonance. If one has to choose between two alternatives, the more equal they are in overall attractiveness, the greater the resulting dissonance. Specifically, dissonance derives from the individual's knowledge that he chose an alternative that had negative aspects and rejected other alternatives that had positive aspects. Research has shown that such a subject attempts to reduce dissonance by changing (making more negative) his original opinion about the rejected alternative and increasing his liking for the chosen one. Dissonance arises whenever we feel we have done something without sufficient justification.

Justifying such an action to restore consonance often requires new cognitions. An experiment with children shows how such cognitions may operate. Contrary to some common beliefs, obedience may be more readily gained through mild warnings than harsh threat. Children who were mildly admonished not to play with an attractive toy refrained to a

18-10
Graph of the results of an experiment in which subjects were paid to write an essay advocating opinions contrary to their own. Those who were paid the least changed their opinions the most. They needed to justify having written the essay—and the amount of money they received was not enough justification. (L. Festinger, "Cognitive Dissonance." © 1960 by Scientific American Inc. All rights reserved.)

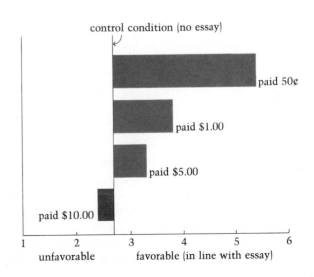

control condition (no essay)

paid 50¢

paid $1.00

paid $5.00

paid $10.00

1   2   3   4   5   6
unfavorable   favorable (in line with essay)

greater extent than children who received severe threats (Aronson & Carlsmith, 1963). Even after 2 months, the prohibition was effective. In this procedure, once a mild threat has prevented the behavior, the child must somehow justify to himself *why* he is not playing with what seems to be a rather attractive toy. His justification is a reduction of the toy's attractiveness—a change in attitude that will reduce the likelihood of his wanting to play with the toy again.

Such effects are especially dramatic if the initial decision or action is difficult to revoke, or if the person has made a heavy commitment to an attitude. Similarly, if a government is strongly committed to a line of action—perhaps military intervention in a small foreign country—and if the result is a fiasco, dissonance may arise. Since the government has committed itself to the action and the initial decision has been supported, the only way to resolve the dissonance is to find new justifications. Often, they will be deceiving to others and self-deceiving as well. Government officials will find reasons why the fall of the small country threatens the larger country's national security. They conjure up images of the disasters that would threaten the beleaguered foreign population if we withdrew. They appeal to our honor and other higher principles. In this setting, the government commitment actually may be increased. The accumulation of successive "justifications" makes it increasingly difficult to extricate the military forces, as we have seen in our own recent history.

Note that in these examples, attitude change *follows* behavior. We normally think that attitudes predict or "cause" behavior. However, as we noted early in this chapter, this causal link is rather tenuous. Moreover, the causal relationship between attitudes and behavior may operate in the opposite direction. The child *first* chooses the toy, and only then revises his attitudes; the government first decides to become involved in a remote and contested territory, and only then asserts how vital that territory is, with its importance growing in proportion to the increasing commitment.

This need for cognitive consistency is pronounced. Evidence shows that individuals will deny or distort the amount of pain or hunger they experience under conditions of dissonance (when they have freely decided to suffer a painful experience or to refrain from eating). In one study (Zimbardo, Cohen, Weisenberg, Dworkin, & Firestone, 1966), the subjects not only reported less change in felt pain when they had voluntarily agreed to undergo painful exposure, but also the psychophysiological indicator (GSR) agreed with the self-report.

On some occasions in which attitudes result from behavior, the actual determinants of behavior may be quite different from the apparent ones. Suppose that on June 14 we observe a member of a society that predicted the end of the world on June 13, and he is vigorously engaged in recruiting new members. When asked about the now overdue end of the world, his response is that it will come soon nevertheless, that he had made a slight error in determining the date. His belief is unshakable, and he trusts the prediction more than before. This individual's proselytizing efforts could be regarded as motivated by his loyal attitude toward his fellow adherents. But dissonance theory argues that the individual engages in proselytizing *to resolve his own dissonance.* All the commitment on his part that preceded June 13 now appears wasted. Unless he can find new justification and buttress his previous (false) belief, dissonance will result. If he can recruit additional members who come to believe in the new doomsday, he cannot have been totally wrong and his efforts were not wasted after all. Moreover, his new commitment (the renewed effort in recruiting members) is itself a behavior that seeks justification; thus, his attitude toward the doomsday society becomes even more positive. In this way, the doomsdayer can reduce the dissonance resulting from the behavior (proselytizing) that he performed initially without sufficient justification.

Attribution Theory

Accounts of the manner in which we commonly attribute or assign attitudes (as well as traits and abilities) to others is called _attribution theory._ Attribution theory also is an explanation of how people organize behavior and make it meaningful; it focuses especially on the attribution of causes, motives, abilities, and predispositions. An individual attributes attitudes and traits under conditions of uncertainty, when he knows only a few relevant facts. Usually, he observes only a small sample of behavior, such as a few verbal assertions. On the basis of these limited data, he often is willing to infer some pervasive underlying trait, belief, or ability. A person makes a $100 contribution to a pacifist organization. Is he a pacifist? Suppose he is a highly placed executive in industry with a six-figure income. Suppose further that his company makes military aircraft. Do we begin to wonder? He still could be a pacifist. But his motives are suspect. Perhaps the donation is a form of gift to his rebellious son, a way of ingratiating himself across the generation gap, or a form of personal atonement. A Catholic sees a minister entering a brothel. He takes it as evidence of the low morals of the Protestant clergy. Then he sees a Catholic priest go in. He now suspects that a dying person is inside in need of the Holy Sacrament. If we see only behavior and action, we construe causes and motives from whatever information we have. Thus, social judgments rest on an inference process that frequently is based on very limited information. Each of us, every day, makes decisions on just such meager evidence.

Our readiness to infer "facts" from insufficient information—in fact, our inability to refrain from making such inferences—has profound social and individual consequences. Attribution theory has examined some of these consequences. Storms and Nisbett (1971), for example, provided several subjects with a temporary relief from insomnia. The investigators began with the assumption that one part of the insomnia problem is that even before going to bed, a person may begin to worry about how difficult it will be for him to fall asleep; his self-diagnosis becomes increasingly pessimistic; a train of troubled thoughts develops and they nettle him still more. Storms and Nisbett sought to have the person attribute the causes of his sleeplessness to external factors, reducing his self-concern and possibly allowing him to fall asleep. A pill was administered to two groups of insomniacs. Although the pill was a placebo, it was described to members of one group as having calming effects which would soon allow them to fall asleep. Members of the other group were told the pill was an excitant, that they would experience a state of excitation, that it would at first be *more* difficult for them to fall asleep, but that in the long run, the pill might help. The subjects who received the "calming pill" found themselves, as usual, troubled with sleeplessness. They discovered themselves not sleeping *in spite of* the medication and concluded that they must have especially serious cases of insomnia. The individuals who received the "excitant" also were unable to sleep. However, they did not worry about the gravity of their condition. They could attribute their sleeplessness to an external cause—the "stimulant." Hence, they worried less and fell asleep sooner.

While attitudes are not the ultimate causes of behavior, they do summarize and account for consistency across broad areas of behavior. For this reason, they have proved to be important tools for organizing and giving meaning to individual and group behavior. In addition, techniques for attitude measurement have proved useful in many other areas of psychology; and theories developed to account for the origin and change of attitudes have helped to account for diverse aspects of behavior as well. All in all, the study of attitudes can confidently be regarded as central not only to social psychology but to all of psychology.

Summary

1. Attitudes are our evaluative (arising from our value judgments) and affective (arising from our emotions) responses to individuals, objects, and events.

2. Although our attitudes differ in complexity, determinants, origins, implications for behavior, and intensity, we have attitudes toward almost every entity we can perceive directly or conceive of in our imaginations. Attitudes serve to summarize conveniently our general reactions to individuals, objects, and events.

3. Habits are recurrent patterns of behavior. The principal difference between a habit and an attitude is that emotion or affect is not involved in a habit.

4. Though they may be inferred from observing behavior, attitudes do not cause behavior. Attitudes and behavior may differ from one another because a person's responses to conceptualized objects may be different from his responses to specific objects. Attitudes and behavior may also differ because a person's behavior in a given situation may be influenced by the situation's inherent social pressures or consequences.

5. Although changeable, attitudes are relatively enduring and stable in a variety of situations and contexts. Attitudes are persistent because they are rooted in our emotions, because we cannot readily separate our feelings from our perceptions, and because the social environment is a reinforcing influence.

6. Beliefs are made up of the information we accept about an object, concept, or event—whether or not that information is accurate. Beliefs are the cognitive components of attitudes. Opinions are lightly-held beliefs.

7. Prejudice is a belief that has little or no factual basis to support it and some good evidence against it. While it may contain some element of truth, a prejudice involves overgeneralization, oversimplification, and distortion of reality. Prejudice against minority groups is an attitude that appears in early childhood and is heavily influenced by the norms of a culture, by parents, and possibly by factors in the individual's personality.

8. Attitudes are measured in various ways, including rating-scales, which ask the subject to express his attitude as a categorical or numerical rating or ranking. The Likert scale rates single statements and then sums them up for an overall score. The Guttman Scalogram orders items along a continuum of acceptability.

9. Indirect techniques are often used to measure attitudes. For example, the subject's behavior is observed without his knowledge, or his emotional reactions to certain objects are studied when he believes he is being tested for another purpose.

10. Attitudes also may be measured by physiological responses, such as heartbeat, galvanic skin response, or pupil dilation. Such measures reveal something about the attitude's strength but nothing about its nature or direction.

11. Opinion polling involves interviewing a sample of people that is representative of the whole population being studied.

12. Direct contact with the attitude object is one way attitudes are formed. Increased exposure is believed to encourage the formation of favorable attitudes.

13. Social factors that influence the formation of attitudes include parents, peer groups, schools, and the mass media.

14. Novel objects arouse a conflict in the individual between avoidance reactions (caution) and approach reactions (curiosity). With repeated encounters, attitudes will form on the basis of the positive or negative consequences resulting from those encounters.

15. Attitudes can change by becoming generally more positive or negative or by becoming more widely distributed or variable, depending on the particular setting or issue.

16. The credibility and prestige of the source of a message will affect the probability of our changing our attitudes after receiving the message. A communicator's effectiveness can be increased if he appears to argue a position contrary to his own self-interest and/or if he appears uninterested in influencing our opinion. The sleeper effect is an attitude change that shows itself only after some time has elapsed.

17. The persuasive force of a message depends on its intelligibility, length, elaboration, logical content, and emotional appeal. The impact of emotional content depends on which emotion is aroused, the conditions under which it is aroused, and the intensity of the emotion. Messages that arouse a great deal of fear may provoke anxiety and thus avoidance of the content of the message.

18. Audience characteristics affect attitude change. People with moderate attitudes toward a particular object or issue can be influenced more easily than people with extreme attitudes. Two group-related means of changing attitudes are to place the individual in a different reference group or to change the group's norms.

19. Humans generally possess coherent systems of thoughts and beliefs which are logically and psychologically consistent. Cognitive consistency theories maintain that man finds conflicting attitudes intolerable and that such inconsistency stimulates change.

20. Two prominent consistency theories are Heider's balance theory and Festinger's dissonance theory. Heider's theory states that humans like consistency or harmony in their relationships with other people and the environment and seek to achieve balance in situations. Festinger's dissonance theory states that tension results when an individual holds two cognitions whose implications are psychologically inconsistent and that the person will act to reduce the dissonance.

21. Attribution theory studies the manner in which we commonly attribute attitudes and traits when our social judgments are based on limited information.

Important Terms

attitude

habit

belief

opinion

prejudice

scapegoat theory of prejudice

rating scale

Likert technique

Guttman Scalogram

Bogardus Social Distance Scale

indirect techniques of attitude measurement

opinion polling

representative sample

area sampling

conformity

imitation

source of a message

sleeper effect

nature of the communication

cognitive consistency theories

balance theory

cognitive dissonance

attribution theory

Suggested Readings

BEM, D. *Beliefs, attitudes and human affairs.* Belmont, Calif.: Brooks/Cole, 1970.

   A short, readable discussion of the way people form beliefs and attitudes and the effect this has on their behavior. Emphasis is given to the view that attitudes follow behavior.

DAWES, R. M. *Fundamentals of attitude measurement.* New York: Wiley, 1972.

A clear, nontechnical presentation of the basic techniques for attitude measurement. Each method is illustrated with an example from attitude research.

FISHBEIN, M. (ED.). *Readings in attitude theory and measurement.* New York: Wiley, 1967.

A compilation of classic readings, including historical foundations, attitude measurement, and attitude theory.

GREENWALD, A. G., BROCK, T. G., & OSTROM, T. M. (EDS.). *Psychological foundations of attitudes.* New York: Academic Press, 1968.

A collection of articles emphasizing the role of learning in attitude formation. Several theories of attitude change—in addition to the consistency theories discussed in this chapter—are described.

INSKO, C. *Theories of attitude change.* New York: Appleton-Century-Crofts, 1967.

A comprehensive explanation and critique of all the major attitude-change theories, including balance, cognitive dissonance, functional, and reinforcement theories. Each chapter contains a description of the theory, a thorough review of relevant experiments, and an analysis of the logical properties of the theory and its empirical support.

JONES, E. E., KANOUSE, D. E., KELLEY, H. H., NISBETT, R. E., VALINS, S., & WEINER, B. *Attribution: perceiving the causes of behavior.* Morristown, N.J.: General Learning Press, 1972.

A broad survey of theory and empirical work in attribution theory; a common-sense approach to the way people evaluate themselves, other people, and events.

KIESLER, C. A., COLLINS, B. E., & MILLER, N. *Attitude change: a critical analysis of theoretical approaches.* New York: Wiley, 1969.

A review of theories of attitude change, similar in purpose to, though somewhat less comprehensive than, Insko's book. Emphasis is placed on critical examination of the theories.

LINDZEY, G., & ARONSON, E. (EDS.). *Handbook of social psychology.* Vols. 1–5. 2nd ed. Reading, Mass.: Addison-Wesley, 1969.

The most complete compendium of social psychology theory and research available. Especially relevant chapters are W. McGuire, "The Nature of Attitudes and Attitude Change," a comprehensive summary of research on the factors influencing attitude change, and W. A. Scott, "Attitude Measurement," a detailed discussion of the many methods of measuring attitudes.

ZIMBARDO, P., & EBBESON, E. B. *Influencing attitudes and changing behavior.* Reading, Mass.: Addison-Wesley, 1969.

A simplified discussion of techniques of persuasion, attitude change, and behavior change with an emphasis on relevant social issues.

Chapter 19   Groups and Social Interaction

No man is an island, entire of itself; every man is a piece of the continent, a part of the main; if a clod be washed away by the sea, Europe is the less, as well as if a promontory were, as well as if a manor of thy friends or of thine own were; any man's death diminishes me, because I am involved in mankind; and therefore never send to know for whom the bell tolls; it tolls for thee.

—John Donne
Devotions XVII

Groups and Social Interaction

This chapter was drafted by Robert Zajonc, Department of Psychology, University of Michigan.

All humans are characterized by their relationships to groups. We belong to some groups and not others. We admire certain groups and are contemptuous of others. We enhance our self-esteem by joining particular groups, and we protect our status by avoiding other groups. Membership in certain groups is almost inescapable—such as belonging to a family, a neighborhood, or a nation—while membership in other groups can be achieved only with extraordinary effort—such as becoming a world class tennis player, a sculptor, or a Nobel Prize winner. Every group membership exerts some influence upon the individual member. In some cases this may be a minute effect while in others it is a deep and pervasive influence. All in all, it is fair to say that each individual's psychological makeup is heavily dependent upon the groups to which he now belongs or once did belong.

To sustain itself as a group, every population goes through a series of *integrations* (group formations, affiliations, interpersonal choices) and *differentiations* (competition, group conflict and tensions, and interpersonal rejection). Forces and pressures, both inside and outside a group, maintain it, whether the group is a family, a street gang, or a symphony orchestra. Such memberships are fairly *enduring*. New members do not join at will, nor can old members readily leave. At the same time, one will seldom confuse the members of one group with the members of another. Family surnames, the jackets of street gangs, and the formal dress of orchestra members prevent such a confusion of group identities. *Identification* also means that movement between groups is not quite as easy as it is within groups. Groups define "strangers," prevent the entry of outsiders, assign themselves areas of territorial supremacy, and develop a complex internal structure, which they maintain over time.

In this chapter, we shall focus on several psychological factors and mechanisms involved in the integration and differentiation of human groups. We shall concentrate on attraction, affiliation, and attachment as mechanisms of integration; and categorization, aggression, and competition as mechanisms of differentiation. Then we shall turn to the relationships between the individual and the group.

Integration

Affiliation, attachment, and attraction among individuals are significant mechanisms of integration because they maintain physical proximity. Enduring bonds between particular individuals create order, and while other forces of cohesion also prevent the disruption of the group, these mutual emotional bonds are the basic ties that keep group members together. The group's integrity and permanence does not require that every member be attached to every other member, but that each is attached to at least one other.

Attraction, Attachment, and Affiliation

The affective bonds among individuals and those between an individual and his environment are bonds formed by attraction, attachment, and affiliation. All three terms imply that if these bonds exist, the individuals involved will attempt to gain and maintain proximity to each other. *Attraction* deals primarily with *gaining* proximity; it focuses our attention on the properties of the object and on its capacity to elicit approach behavior. *Attachment* and *affiliation* are terms that imply the maintenance of proximity. Attachment is the more general term, and it covers attempts to maintain proximity to all sorts of targets, animate and inanimate. Affiliation has to do only with attachment of individuals to one another.

Affiliation and mutual attachment are the basic forces promoting group stability. Individuals who share a positive emotional relationship learn to seek each other out to satisfy various needs, develop cooperative relationships, give each other confidence and support, share scarce resources, confide in each other in times of stress, prefer the same material objects, and seek the same environment.

Affiliation implies *differential* preferences among individuals. It implies that if A likes or loves B, C, and D, then inevitably there are individuals, X, Y, and Z whom A does not love. Thus, attachment also is a form of differentiation for it divides groups into subgroups. As we saw when we discussed attitudes in Chapter 18, group membership promotes favorable attitudes toward individuals within a group and negative attitudes toward strangers. Hence, the bonds among individual members are, to some extent, exclusive; new bonds, especially with "strangers," cannot be formed easily. Groups also reduce chances for contact with strangers. Thus, events that would support the formation of new bonds do not take place readily.

Attachment between just two people (known as a *dyad*—the smallest group) is very common. Dyad members may be friends, lovers, mates, or relatives. If attachment between A and B keeps them near each other, neither A nor B can often get close to other individuals. Similarly, if A and B have a relationship that satisfies many of their needs, they will not try to satisfy those needs elsewhere. Consequently, they will be less likely to form outside relationships. These aspects of attachment pro-

19-1
The ultimate attachment is love. Photographers and artists frequently portray a young couple in glowing, romanticized surroundings to show the "wonderful aura of togetherness." (Bruce Roberts, Rapho Guillumette)

mote its stability. Thus, it may not be primarily legal sanctions that maintain a marriage. Marriage, when successful, is self-perpetuating, as are most human associations, including scout groups, committees, political organizations, social, national, and ethnic groups, business corporations, neighborhood gangs, and athletic teams.

Origins of Attachments

Attachment between parent and offspring seems to be essential to the survival of many species. A human infant will not survive without the help of an adult who provides nourishment, safety, warmth, and instruction. But why does the mother stay with her offspring? The very fact that attachment is necessary for the survival of the species means that it was selected for during the species' evolution.

Reinforcement. We can gain a deeper understanding of attachment by inquiring both into its immediate behavioral consequences for the individuals involved and into the forces that tend to maintain the attachment. Bowlby (1958) has argued that such infant responses as clinging, following, sucking, crying, and smiling support the affiliative bonds between infant and adult. These responses lead to parent-infant interactions, from which both participants receive reinforcement. For example, crying can produce distress in the mother; she is reinforced when, in response to her comforting, the baby stops crying. For the child, on the other hand, the effectiveness of crying is reinforced by his mother's response to it.

Crying and parental arousal may be complementary mechanisms that evolved together (Freedman, 1968). In many species, including humans, the offspring will exhibit distress when separated from its parents. Puppies yelp when alone, chicks peep when separated from the mother hen, and human infants cry and suffer separation anxiety when parted from their parents. At the parents' return, the offspring, whether chick or child, stops its distress call. Such mutually reinforcing reunions maintain the parent-offspring affiliative bonds.

While reinforcement plays an important role in establishing and maintaining early attachments, by itself reinforcement is not an adequate explanation. Parent-offspring events will not always be pleasurable. So it would be difficult to demonstrate that drive-reduction and need-satisfaction provide the complete explanation for approach-seeking.

Another explanation maintains that early attachments are formed automatically in accord with hereditary predispositions. Among domestic chickens, ducks, geese, and quail a form of attachment occurs early in life, in fact a few hours after hatching. In this attachment, which is called *imprinting*, the role of reward is minimal. In the initial research on imprinting, its foremost exponent, Konrad Lorenz, considered it an innate mechanism released by a set of stimuli, often visual. Usually, the stimuli belong to a person or object similar to the individual's parent—but this is not always the case, as was proved to Lorenz's dismay when a family of goslings imprinted on him!

WHAT IS THIS THING CALLED LOVE?

Zick Rubin *Harvard University*

To the poet, love is "a spirit all compact of fire" or "a sickness full of woes," or "the pearl of my oyster," depending on which poet you consult. To the philosopher, it is "a greater law unto itself" or "a centrifugal act of the soul" or "a state of perceptual anesthesia." To the social psychologist, love is an attitude. It is a constellation of thoughts, feelings, and behavioral predispositions that one person has for another person.

A few years ago, when I was searching for an unspoiled topic for my doctoral dissertation, I decided to try to measure this attitude. Using attitude-scaling techniques similar to those described in the previous chapter, I developed a thirteen-item love scale. A person is asked to indicate the extent to which each item accurately reflects his or her feelings toward a particular other, usually a girlfriend or a boyfriend. Love, as defined in my scale, has three components. I call them *attachment* (the desire to be near the other), *caring* (the concern for the other's well-being), and *intimacy* (the desire for close and confidential communication with the other).

The attitude of love is a close relative of the attitude of liking, which results largely from a favorable evaluation of another person. But loving and liking are by no means synonymous. Among a large sample of couples that I tested, loving and liking (as measured by my love scale and a parallel liking scale) correlated only moderately. Interestingly, the two sentiments were distinguished more sharply by women than by men.

Perhaps women, by virtue of their traditional specialization in "social-emotional" matters, have developed more finely tuned interpersonal sentiments, while men are more likely to blur such fine distinctions. Love

scale scores also agreed with a well-known nonverbal measure of love: The more the two partners loved one another, the more eye contact they made in a laboratory situation, while being surreptitiously observed through a one-way mirror (Rubin, 1973).

Where Does Love Come From?

Throughout history, spokesmen for love have offered answers to this question. Among the best known sources are Cupid's arrows, love potions and other aphrodisiacs. Few of today's psychologists favor any of these explanations. Instead, they look to affiliative needs, secondary reinforcements, and social pressures. People come to love others because they have strong needs to make contact with other people (as discussed in this chapter), because they have learned to expect rewards (such as sexual pleasure, emotional support, or just having a good time) in the other's presence, and because their families, friends, and culture

Love-Scale and Liking-Scale Items

(The more often a person's name appears on the scale, the more likely it is that you love or like him or her.)

Love Scale

1. If _____ were feeling bad, my first duty would be to cheer him (her) up.
2. I feel that I can confide in _____ about virtually everything.
3. I find it easy to ignore _____'s faults.
4. I would do almost anything for _____.
5. I feel very possessive toward _____.
6. If I could never be with _____, I would feel miserable.
7. If I were lonely, my first thought would be to seek _____ out.
8. One of my primary concerns is _____'s welfare.
9. I would forgive _____ for practically anything.
10. I feel responsible for _____'s well-being.
11. When I am with _____, I spend a good deal of time just looking at him (her).
12. I would greatly enjoy being confided in by _____.
13. It would be hard for me to get along without _____.

Liking Scale

1. When I am with _____, we almost always are in the same mood.
2. I think that _____ is unusually well-adjusted.
3. I would highly recommend _____ for a responsible job.
4. In my opinion, _____ is an exceptionally mature person.
5. I have great confidence in _____'s good judgment.
6. Most people would react favorably to _____ after a brief acquaintance.
7. I think that _____ and I are quite similar to one another.
8. I would vote for _____ in a class or group election.
9. I think that _____ is one of those people who quickly wins respect.
10. I feel that _____ is an extremely intelligent person.
11. _____ is one of the most likable people I know.
12. _____ is the sort of person whom I myself would like to be.
13. It seems to me that it is very easy for _____ to gain admiration.

(From *Liking and Loving* by Zick Rubin. © 1973, by Holt, Rinehart and Winston. Reprinted by permission.)

all tell them that falling in love is the appropriate thing to do. Sometimes a sexual experience makes it easier for an individual to decide that he or she loves the other person. One student told an interviewer that she was surprised to discover that she enjoyed making love with her boyfriend, because until that time she hadn't known that she loved him. The pleasant surprise helped to convince her.

Paradoxically, love also may arise from experiences that are, at least on the surface, negative rather than positive. Experimental evidence suggests, for example, that fear can heighten romantic attraction. Ovid had this idea in mind 2,000 years ago when he advised Romans to take their dates to the arena to watch the gladiators. Donald Dutton and Arthur Aron (1975) demonstrated the principle in a dramatic experiment conducted on two foot bridges over the Capilano Canyon in British Columbia—one a narrow, rickety construction that swayed in the wind hundreds of feet above the rocks, the other a solid structure a few feet above a shallow stream. An attractive female experimenter approached men who were crossing one bridge or the other. Those encountered on the swaying bridge were more sexually aroused and more attracted to the woman, as measured by the amount of sexual imagery in stories they wrote and by the likelihood of their telephoning the experimenter afterward (ostensibly to get more information about the study). The best explanation, suggested by Stanley Schachter's theory of emotion (see Chapter 11) is that inner stirrings of fear sometimes are relabelled as sexual arousal and attraction.

How Does Love Grow?

In the Court of Love, presided over by Eleanor of Aquitaine in the 12th century, the love relationship had four stages—first, the giving of hope; second, the granting of a kiss; third, the enjoyment of an embrace; and fourth the yielding of the whole person. More recently, a Scandinavian psychologist named Gerhard Nielsen identified 24 clearly demarcated steps in the "courtship dance" of the American adolescent. The steps and countersteps, which ordinarily proceed in a fixed order, include: Boy holds girl's hand; she presses his hand, signalling a go-ahead; he allows his fingers to intertwine with hers; he puts an arm around her shoulder and approaches breast from side; she blocks with upper arm against side; and so on.

When we leave the strictly sexual domain, reliable descriptions of the growth of love are much harder to come by. However, computer simulation of such relationships may help investigators. L. Rowell Huesmann and George Levinger (1975) have developed a unique computer program called RELATE. Using its built-in set of rules, plus some additional input provided by two role-playing students, RELATE did a creditable job of predicting the romantic relationship of two hypothetical individuals, John (who was described in the computer language equivalent of "attractive, but shy and introverted") and Susan (portrayed as "attractive and extraverted"). RELATE predicted that after a period of time in which they interacted at a superficial level, "John learns that Susan is willing to disclose intimacies in response to his disclosures, and he confides in her completely. This leads the pair into active striving for a deep romantic involvement." By the end of RELATE'S love story John and Susan both are oriented toward a permanent relationship, although neither has proposed marriage.

As it presently is programmed, however, RELATE's simulations are greatly oversimplified. Although its scenarios are intuitively reasonable, they are at best pale reflections of real-life love stories. The longitudinal research that might provide RELATE with an improved set of rules is still in its infancy.

My coworkers and I (Rubin, Peplau, & Hill, in preparation) are currently analyzing the results of one such study, in which we tracked the progress of 231 student dating couples in the Boston area over a two-year period. Among other things, our data provide empirical support for one aspect of an "exchange model" of love relationships put forth by sociologist Peter M. Blau and others. In Blau's words, "It seems that commitments must keep abreast for a love relationship to develop into a lasting mutual attachment. If one lover is considerably more involved than the other, his greater commitment invites exploitation and provokes feelings of entrapment, both of which obliterate love . . . Only when two lovers' affection for and commitment to one another expand at roughly the same pace do they tend mutually to reinforce their love" (Blau, 1964). The couples in our study who reported that they were "equally involved" in their relationship came to love each other more, and were much more likely to stay together, than the couples who reported that one partner was more involved than the other.

The idea of studying love systematically deeply disturbs some people. At a recent convention, one psychologist went so far as to declare that "The scientist in even attempting to interject love into a laboratory situation is by the very nature of the proposition dehumanizing the state we call love." He is entitled to his opinion, but I couldn't disagree more. I am much more persuaded by the words of the late Abraham Maslow, one of the most human of modern psychologists: "We *must* study love; we must be able to teach it, to create it, to predict it, or else the world is lost to hostility and to suspicion" (Maslow, 1970).

Konrad Lorenz receives affectionate
pecks from his "children"—the
goslings imprinted on him. (Nina
Leen, Time-Life Picture Agency)

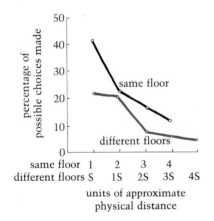

19-3
Graph of the relationship between
proximity and attachment. The
closer the neighbors' apartments
were to each other (next door on the
same floor being the closest), the
more likely they were to form friendships. As distance increased, degree
of friendship decreased proportionately. (Festinger, Schachter, & Back,
1950)

Human attachments are not necessarily shaped by the same processes
and mechanisms that form animal attachments. Nor is there reason to
suppose that attachments are the same in all species. On the contrary,
behavioral mechanisms and processes clearly differ among species. It is
possible however, that a single, basic process may be common to all
species and may operate side by side with the mechanisms specific to
each species. Attachment as a result of exposure or proximity is a good
candidate for such a process.

Proximity. Persons or objects that surround an individual are more
likely to impress him than those in another neighborhood, town, or
state. Hence, you may marry the girl or boy next door, love your
mother's cooking, adore your home-town band—all because you know
these things well. The proximity-attachment relationship is self-perpetuating. Proximity can create attachment, which then prompts the individual to seek continued proximity.

Newcomb (1961) carried out several studies of students living in
the same house. In one study, students were assigned rooms according
to their attitudes. Some pairs of roommates held compatible attitudes
and others incompatible ones. Newcomb's measures of attraction
among the students show, above all, that contact and proximity played a
decisive role. Even when they held incompatible attitudes, roommates
liked each other a good deal. An earlier study (Festinger, Schachter, &
Back, 1950) investigated an entire housing project and showed that
friendship patterns emerged primarily among people who were close
neighbors. Of those mentioned as friends, 65 percent lived in the same
building. Among women, more than two-thirds of their friends lived on
the same floor of their building.

Similarity. An important requisite for attachment is *similarity.* A number of studies (Byrne, Clore, & Worchel, 1966; Byrne, Griffit, & Stenfaniak, 1967; Byrne, 1969) have measured liking for hypothetical people, about whom the subject of the study knows only their opinions. Results seem to show that the more the attitudes of hypothetical strangers resemble our own attitudes, the better we like them. Behind this research is the theory that having our beliefs and attitudes supported by someone else, especially a stranger, is rewarding. We are attracted to, and like, those who validate our beliefs.

These findings are not true without exception, as Newcomb's study—which found as much attraction between roommates with incompatible attitudes as between those with similar attitudes—demonstrates. Other exceptions to Byrne's findings can be cited. For example, we are not fond of a rival, even though he likes exactly the same things we like. A study by Jones, Bell, and Aronson (1971) has shown another aspect of attraction—we find it more pleasing to be liked by someone who disagrees with our opinions than by someone who agrees with them. The explanation for this finding is that if somebody likes us in spite of our beliefs, he must like us for some more fundamental reason.

We all like to be around people who somehow satisfy our needs, help us, do us favors, and who are themselves likable. If we are praised by a person who we believe has no ulterior motive, we will place high value on the praise and be inclined to hold the person in high esteem and feel friendly toward him. In this regard Jones (1964) showed that praising (ingratiation) is an effective way to make friends.

However, such reinforcement is not a necessary condition for attachment. Lott and Lott (1960) conducted an experiment in which children followed successful and unsuccessful leaders through an imaginary minefield. Successful leaders—those who led them with a minimum of "explosions"—were liked best. In a study of reactions to radio programs, Zajonc (1955) found that children liked and identified with successful leaders, regardless of whether they were autocratic or democratic. Hence, with children, success was important for forming attachments.

The theory of cognitive dissonance, which we discussed in Chapter 18, makes predictions about attraction and reward. But we should note an interesting twist. We sometimes get to like someone after we have given him a reward, rather than after he has rewarded us. The question asked by Jecker and Landy (1969) was: If we perform a favor for a person, will we change our feelings toward him? Dissonance theory predicts that when we have no good reason to have done a favor, we must justify it. One way of justifying it is to increase our attraction toward the person. We convince ourselves we did the favor because we like him, because he is a "nice guy."

The Need for Social Attachment

Social attachments are inevitable. Cases of physical isolation demonstrate the importance of human contact. It is uncommon for any person to spend more than a day or two alone. Soon, he or she feels a need for

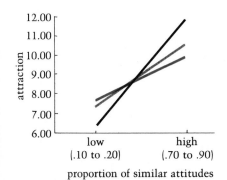

19-4
The relationship between attraction towards a new acquaintance, similarity of attitudes, and level of arousal. The black line indicates moderate arousal; gray, low arousal; and color, high arousal. Our attraction is greater for those with similar attitudes at all three levels of arousal; however, at moderate arousal, attraction and similarity of attitudes correlate most closely. (After Byrne & Clore, 1967 in Byrne, 1969)

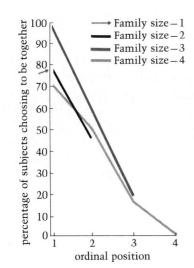

human contact. It is no accident that solitary confinement is used as punishment. Prisoners in solitary frequently show psychotic symptoms as a result of being alone for a year or more. Complete, enforced solitude is unquestionably painful, stressful, and damaging—and not only for humans. A bee cannot survive alone for more than 48 hours, even if all the physical conditions of its environment are made optimal for its survival.

Infants and young children feel the loss of human contact most intensely. They feel anxious and afraid when left completely alone during waking hours. Solitude combined with threat or stress from other sources is even more likely to produce anxiety. In an experiment described in Chapter 11, Schachter (1959) has demonstrated the important role of affiliation in response to stress. Subjects threatened with severe electric shocks wanted the company of others much more than subjects who anticipated mild shocks.

As we mentioned in Chapter 13, love is the extreme attachment. Unfortunately, the present research data on this universal and perhaps

Table 19-1 Student Affiliation Preferences in Thirteen Situations

Situation	Percentage of students who:		
	Wished to be with others	Wished to be alone	Had no preference
When depressed	42	48	10
When worried about a serious personal problem	52	44	4
When physically tired	6	85	9
When mildly ill (e.g., with a cold)	32	49	19
When very happy	88	2	10
When feeling very guilty about something you have done	45	43	12
When embarrassed	16	76	8
When you want to cry	8	88	4
When in a good mood	89	0	11
When busy	12	70	18
After an extensive period of social contact—after being with others for a long time	12	75	13
On Saturday night	85	1	14
When you are in a strange situation or doing something you've never done before	77	13	10

(From *Social Psychology and Modern Life* by Patricia Niles Middlebrook, Copyright © 1973 by Alfred A. Knopf, Inc. Reprinted by permission of the Publisher.)

uniquely human attachment is inadequate. Love apparently occurs in all human societies, but the lack of systematic research on the topic leaves us largely ignorant, in scientific terms, of the profound emotional experience associated with love relationships.

We already know that similarity enhances interpersonal attachments and attractions. Thus, in studying a specific social group, the nature and source of similarities among its members are important factors. In the following sections, we shall describe several factors that produce similarity among individuals and therefore result in attachments.

Genetic Determinants of Similarity

Often, group members come from a somewhat restricted gene pool (see Chapter 2), and many of their similarities are determined by their genes. Various physical characteristics of a particular population are transmitted over generations. Because the group's members have few or no opportunities to mate with members of other communities, their own population becomes somewhat homogeneous—obviously in its visible physical characteristics but also in its behavioral components.

The similarity of such groups—for example, an isolated Brazilian Indian tribe or the recently discovered Tasaday tribe of the Western Pacific—binds them together. Aristotle probably was not the first to observe that "we like those who resemble us, who have come to regard the same things as good and the same things as evil. . . ." As we have seen, a great deal of research has explored the impact of similarity on the attraction of one individual for another (Lindzey & Byrne, 1968). For example, if a person believes that a hypothetical stranger lives at a similar economic level, the person likes the stranger more than when his economic level differs (Byrne, Clore, & Worchel, 1966). Similar personality characteristics also produce more attraction (Byrne, Griffit, & Stenfaniak, 1967).

While genetic determinants contribute to a population's general outward uniformity, other identifiable common traits cannot be ascribed to genetic factors. For example, the people of a given community dress more or less alike. The residents of an American college town dress similarly, as do villagers from the Chinese province of Sinkiang. But the dress styles of the two populations differ. Many other common traits exist *within* each of these populations, and many differences, other than dress, exist *between* them. To name a few: architecture, food, methods of farming, patterns of shopping, child rearing, courting, music, and art. Genes do not determine these similarities and differences; instead, social psychological forces develop and maintain them. The two that contribute most to widespread uniformities within a community are imitation and conformity.

Imitation

Imitation is one individual's copying of another individual's behavior, as we discussed in Chapter 6. Imitation's contribution to social life can hardly be exaggerated. Its importance is most obvious in the acquisition

19-6
Groups are distinguished by various outward uniformities—speech, mannerisms, dress, and so on. In many cases the distinctions are not clear cut. However, as shown here, this family obviously belongs to a culture different from our own. (Nat Farbman, Time-Life Picture Agency)

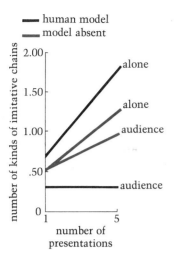

human model
model absent

number of kinds of imitative chains

2.00
1.50
1.00
.50
0

alone
alone
audience
audience

1   5
number of
presentations

19-7
Graph showing that subjects are more likely to imitate a model when they are alone with the model than when an audience is present. Imitation is also more likely when a human model is present than when it isn't—in the case of a film, for instance. (Fouts & Parton, 1974)

of the responses that protect an individual from harm. If a person by imitating another individual, can learn that certain areas of the environment are dangerous, that certain substances are harmful, or that certain actions cause disaster, he may avoid doing a great deal of damage to himself or to members of his community. A person can learn by imitation to fear fire without ever being burned, to drive at reasonable speeds without ever having an accident, and to avoid jumping off high buildings without ever having done so.

Early theories of imitation considered primarily the "pure" examples of the phenomenon. For instance, Miller and Dollard (1941) viewed this situation: One individual, the "leader," makes a choice between two alternatives (finds a candy bar under one or another box). A second individual, the "follower," observes the leader, then makes the choice himself. Miller and Dollard's analysis involved four concepts: drive, cue, response, and reward. The learner had to be motivated to do something (drive). He had to have cues (the leader's responses) to guide his behavior. And for learning to occur, he also had to choose between the boxes (response) and receive candy (reward)—an event that would strengthen the link between the leader's cue and his own action. Such a situation is arranged so that the follower receives candy only when he makes the response the leader made. Withholding of the reward discourages independent behavior. In this way, the child *learns* to imitate, according to the early theories.

However, a number of recent experiments suggest that the follower can learn a great deal without participating very actively at all. According to these studies, the follower does not have to make the response or receive the reinforcement. He can learn through simple observation. He can anticipate the consequences, seeing the right and wrong things to do in each case. As we said in Chapter 12, this process is referred to as observational learning. In his social learning theory, Bandura (1971) attempts to account for this process systematically.

Vicarious Learning.   The efficiency of the imitative process is most dramatically illustrated in *vicarious learning.* As we discussed in Chapter 12, vicarious learning differs from classical imitation because the vicarious learner does not make the appropriate response and is not reinforced. Instead, the situation gives him total or partial information regarding the cues, the appropriate responses, and the consequences of one or another response. Vicarious learning accounts for much of our everyday learning and is especially common in situations in which it would be either inefficient or dangerous for the learner to try again and again until he eventually discovered the right behavior sequence. For example, surgeons trained by the direct reinforcement technique would make four or five incisions in their patients to discover eventually what to do when a patient complains of severe pains in the area of his appendix. The surgeon would be reinforced negatively by all his failures and positively by all his successes. But his successes would be few, and he probably would fill the local morgue before perfecting his technique. In practice, by allowing him to observe and by giving him the opportunity to make *only* the safe responses under the strict direction of the instructor, most of the danger for the patient is avoided. On another level, the ability to learn from the experience of a few makes a group, such as a human society or organization, much more efficient.

The typical experiments on vicarious learning compare people who are exposed to a model engaged in the acquisition or performance of a task, or in responding in a certain manner, and receiving either reward or punishment as a consequence (see discussion of Bandura's experiments in Chapter 12). But there are other types of experiments as well. Berger (1962) measured the galvanic skin response (GSR) of subjects who observed models jerking their arms sharply—supposedly as a result of an electric shock. Other subjects saw models who made the same jerks but who presumably did not receive shocks. The shock followed a buzzer, which became the "conditioned stimulus" for the subjects as well as the models. Although they themselves were never subjected to an electric shock, observers who saw the jerk as a reaction to a shock rather than as a voluntary muscle movement showed a higher GSR to the buzzer.

More recently, Kravetz (1974) went one step further to see if vicarious conditioning could occur without the subject's actually viewing the model. He told his subjects he was collecting physiological reactions—particularly the subject's heart rates. Some subjects were to be the "controls" while others (actually the experimenter's confederates) were described as the experimental subjects. The "experimental subjects" were either to receive shocks or to do push-ups. The actual subject was placed in one cubicle and the confederate in another. The subject was told that, to keep all other factors constant, he would receive the same cues as the experimental subject. Thus, the subject heard the signals that either announced shock or gave instructions for push-ups. He heard both the shock generator (white noise) and the "experimental subject's" heart rate as it changed in a typical emotional reaction. For example, for 10 seconds after the signal for shock (or for push-ups), the subject heard a noticeable increase in the "experimental subject's" heart rate. When changes in the subject's own heart rate were measured, the results showed that he had reacted emotionally by increasing his own heart rate only when he heard the signal that indicated an electric shock was being given. Subjects who were paired with the "experimental subject" doing push-ups registered no changes in heart rate. This experiment shows that vicarious conditioning can be produced even when the model is not visible to the subject and the subject has only auditory cues about the model's actual behavior or circumstances.

Conformity

Imitation and vicarious learning can be shortcuts to a number of useful, often vital, skills. But we also may acquire habits and tendencies of more questionable usefulness. For example, the wearing of ties hardly can be justified as having survival value or any other value, nor can the 18th century custom of wearing wigs. Yet, just as a young Madison Avenue executive today would be unlikely to appear at a staff meeting without his tie, a pre-Revolutionary French nobleman would not have stepped from his bedchamber without his wig. Certain social uniformities among members of a community are signaled by the absence of certain responses—some things just are not done. People do not ordinarily go around naked, tell ribald stories to children, or openly covet their neighbor's spouse. While many such uniformities are acquired through vicarious learning, these forms of imitation contain specifically social elements. When imitation prominently involves social elements, it is called *conformity*. Conformity differs from imitation in that it is nearly universal for members of a community. Conformity also differs from ordinary imitation because the community generally agrees that the particular behavior is desirable, necessary, or morally justified—or just the reverse. Such auxiliary verbs and adverbs as *should, must,* or *must never,* are commonly used to describe behavioral uniformities that are under conformity's control. These words are not idle semantic variations; the community can enforce conformity. Social sanctions and pressures are the forces that compel deviants back into line.

While one imitates *somebody,* one conforms *to* something. That something is a social *norm.* It includes a uniformity of behavior, the social expectations regarding that behavior, and the social methods of controlling it.

Much of the more interesting research on conformity deals with the individual's willingness to yield to social pressures. For example, are people ready to act against their own better judgment if sufficient pressure urges conformity? Early experiments concerned conflicts between the individual's own sensory information and information offered by group consensus. A variety of experiments, following Asch (1952), used as stimuli three lines, clearly different in length. The subject was to match one of the lines against a standard line. The investigator's confederates judged the lines publicly and then the subject made his judgment. On many occasions, the group consensus (controlled by the experimenter) as to which of the three lines matched the standard was not correct. In one case, the three lines were 10, 3, and 2 inches long and the standard line was 10 inches long. The confederates maintained that the 3-inch line matched the standard. Remarkably, even under the best viewing conditions, 26 percent of the subjects agreed with the false consensus. In contrast, individuals who made their choices without hearing the group's judgments were nearly always correct.

Many studies have focused on the tendency to yield to a false majority. These investigations have produced a number of significant results. For example, individuals who feel competent in the behavior being exam-

19-8
Conformity among members of a group involves similar dress, hair style, and so on. Various situational and socioeconomic factors determine the style that is adopted. (Sygma; Cornell Capa, Magnum)

19-9
Most of us are simultaneously conformists and nonconformists. We want to be accepted by our peer groups, but we want to be recognized as individuals as well. The girl on the left wears a ring in her nose to distinguish herself. At the same time, she is identifying with her heritage—the tribal women of Africa who wear larger rings to symbolize their marital status. (Joel Gordon; Paolo Koch, Rapho Guillumette)

19-10
Graph showing that overall conformity increases slightly from grades 3 and 5 to grades 9 and 11, while conformity to parental behavior diminishes pretty steadily from grade 3 on. (Utech & Hoving, 1969)

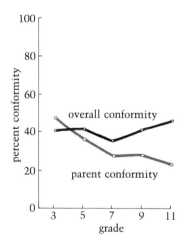

ined are not as readily influenced by the false group consensus as those who feel less competent. Poets will not be easily influenced to praise a poem they think is metrically poor; however, one probably could influence their judgment on the efficiency of fuel-injection systems in the modern internal combustion engine. When a group consensus is presented as the opinion of experts, it influences the subjects more readily. Personal attractiveness as well as any attribute of the consensus group that promises, or even suggests, benefits, approval, or affection also can affect an individual's willingness to agree with the group.

Obedience. Every individual is pressured to conform. Even before the infant can exercise freedom of choice, a basis for later conformity is being established. By two years of age, pressures to conform to norms in such behavior as time of eating and sleeping are quite strong. Eventually, prohibitions emerge; the mother prevents the child from hurting himself and later from hurting others. He must not hit sister on the head, cannot pull the dog's hair or poke the cat's eyes. When he is called he must come, and when told to stop jumping on the couch, he must comply. Even in a permissive family, much of the infant's life must fit into the family's schedule. In general, he is expected to obey.

<u>Obedience</u> is a kind of conformity. The authority of those issuing the command represents the social norm. Obedience is compliance with such social controls as sanctions, threats, and promises of reward. Under what conditions will an individual *disobey* authority? The justifications invoked to explain the hideous cruelties inflicted on the innocent victims of the Nazi concentration camps, the atomic bombing of Hiroshima, and the massacre at My Lai dramatize the question. The commandant of Auschwitz, the infamous World War II concentration camp, accounted for his actions as obedience to his superiors' commands. He was only an administrator carrying out their orders. Killing the inmates wasn't his idea; he did not devise the methods of extermination; and the pressures on him to speed up the extermination rate often surpassed the capacity of the facilities at his disposal.

Blind obedience is a matter of moral concern, and the blind obedience that was required of the soldiers of the 19th century and earlier is gradually disappearing. Yet, what about the atrocities committed 25 years ago in the Korean War, or those in Vietnam only 5 years ago? Are they exceptional cases? We tend to believe that Americans—depicted in World War II films as friendly GIs distributing candy and chewing gum to the outstretched hands of French and Italian children—are different. We find it hard to imagine that one of "our boys" could commit such acts. Yet, at My Lai one of our boys was found guilty of the mass slaughter of civilians. Since this case, many Americans have asked themselves whether he was an extraordinary and deviant case or whether he was the typical American in Vietnam reacting to alien circumstances, the terrors of war, and social pressures. Was the man or the conformity-demanding situation the major factor? Can we explain such cruelty as the product of a disturbed personality or could anyone (including any one of us) commit these atrocious acts?

In a series of experiments, Stanley Milgram (1963) showed that, in fact, American males—from New Haven and surrounding communities, in these studies—were quite capable of inflicting considerable pain on others. Milgram's experiments consisted of asking a subject to give strong electric shocks to another individual whom he could not see. The subject controlled a simulated shock generator with 30 clearly visible voltages ranging from 15 to 450. Fifteen volts was labeled "Slight Shock" and 450 volts, "XXX-Danger! Severe Shock." The entire exercise was presented to the subject as a learning experiment in which he—the subject—acts as a teacher who punishes wrong responses by the learner. The "victim," a confederate of the experimenter, was trained to respond in a certain manner, depending on the conditions of the experiment. The experimenter explained that he was interested in punishment's effects on memory. As the series of trials progressed, he asked the subject to give the victim increasingly strong shocks.

The "victim" was strapped in his seat and an electrode was attached to his wrist with a great deal of paste "to avoid blisters and burns." The subject was assured that although "the shocks can be extremely painful, they cause no permanent tissue damage."

The victim-learner's task in paired-associate learning was to learn to anticipate the second of two words when he heard the first word. Whenever the learner erred, the subject was to administer shock. The learner, the subjects were told, could appreciate the level of shock because he had been given a mild shock earlier. The confederate was instructed to make three times as many errors as correct responses. When being shocked, he was to make no sound until the subject administered the 300-volt shock. At this time, the subject heard agitated pounding from the victim's room.

The subject could see the victim's responses in the form of four lights, one of which was the "correct" answer on each trial. However, when the pounding occurred, the lights stopped flashing. The experimenter told the subject that this meant the learner had failed to respond to the questions, and that "no response" should be treated as an ordinary error. The subject was then told to give the learner about 5 to 10 minutes, and if he still made no response, to administer shock. When the subject gave the 315-volt shock, he again heard pounding from the adjacent room. But the shocks subsequently administered by the subject were followed by ominous silence: The light panel did not indicate that the victim was responding to the task; nor was there any pounding.

When the subject showed hesitation, the experimenter prodded him: "Please continue" or "The experiment requires that you continue," or finally, "You have no other choice, you *must* go on."

When a number of psychiatrists had been asked what proportion of adult American males would obey the experimenter under these conditions, they replied that no more than 10 percent would comply with the experimenter to the point of giving the victim a shock of 450 volts, marked "XXX-Danger! Severe Shock." In fact 26 of the 40 did. None of the subjects refrained from giving shocks marked "Intense Shock": 255, 270, and 285 volts. After hearing the pounding on the wall, only five subjects refused to go on beyond the 300-volt level:

I think he's trying to communicate, he's knocking. . . . Well it's not fair to shock the guy—these are terrific volts. I don't think this is very humane. . . . Oh, I can't go on with this; no, this isn't right. It's a hell of an experiment. The guy is suffering in there. No. I don't want to go on. This is crazy. (Subject refused to administer more shocks.)

He's banging in there. I'm gonna chicken out, I'd like to continue, but I can't do that to a man. . . . I'm sorry I can't do that to a man. I'll hurt his heart. You take your check. . . . No really, I couldn't do it.

An additional four subjects stopped at 315 volts, two at 330, and one each at 345, 360, and 375, for a total of 14 out of 40. Thus, the majority complied with the experimenter's command and administered to a stranger what was ostensibly a very severe pain.

Milgram's experiments drew considerable criticism because of the stress they placed upon his subjects, who thought they were administering real shocks. While these studies point up the importance of ethical considerations in behavioral research (human or animal), they also point to the unexpected capacity of "ordinary" members of our society to commit reprehensible acts if they are encouraged by an apparently legitimate authority, and are paid for doing it.

Differentiation

Any circumstance or process that results in the bonding together of entities, whatever they might be, results simultaneously and necessarily in separating them from others. An atom that becomes part of one molecule cannot at the same time be part of another. A Democrat cannot also be a Republican, a Midwesterner cannot also be a Southerner, a junior cannot be a freshman, and a Hell's Angel cannot be a Blue Devil. The mechanisms of integration—such as attachment, attraction, imitation, and conformity—all form, maintain, and reinforce bonds among individuals. Contact through exposure results in attachment; attraction is fostered by similarity; and imitation and conformity produce similar individuals who behave in similar ways because their actions are con-

19-11
Integration implies differentiation. Attachment to one group automatically results in detachment from another group. In any crowd, you can pick out the various groups. Even the pigeons form their own groups. (Robert Doisneau, Rapho Guillumette)

strained by rules and norms that generate social uniformity. But at the same time, these processes, which create groups, societies, communities, cliques, friendships, and marriages, also create cleavages and distinctions. Hence, they are simultaneously instruments of social differentiation. While contact and proximity lead to friendships, they also lead to the exclusion of some who will not become "friends." If John spends most of his time near three of his classmates, he is clearly not spending much time near many of his other classmates. John defines them as "strangers" and treats them differently. And they will treat him differently than his three "chosen" classmate-friends will. Similarly, John will have different attitudes and feelings toward his three friends and toward the "others"—the rest of his class.

Social Categorization

The arbitrary classification of individuals into groups is called *social categorization*. Such social differentiation, attributed to differential contact alone, exists throughout the animal world. Zajonc, Wilson, and Rajecki (1973) found that even day-old chicks can distinguish between "friends" and "strangers." During incubation, eggs were injected with red or green vegetable dye so that chicks would be colored when they hatched. Upon hatching, some chicks were caged in pairs. Some of the pairs were the same color and some were mixed. They were kept together for a number of hours and then placed with other chicks in an "arena." The experimenters observed each chick's pecking of the others, a sensitive indicator of chicks' social response.

When two cage-mates were placed together, they did very little mutual pecking. But "strangers," chicks that had not been housed together, displayed considerable pecking even during the first minutes of their encounter. One might suppose that the differential dye explains the ease of this social differentiation. However, the experiment shows that chicks of identical color can discriminate between "strangers" and "companions," and that a green chick that lived with a red one for as little as 16 hours will distinguish between its companion and a red stranger as easily as between its companion and a green stranger. It appears that neither the chick's own coloring nor the coloring of its companion can overcome the effects of the brief period of close association.

What is true of chicks need not be true of humans. However, a number of experiments show a compelling resemblance between animal and human results. Rabbie and Horwitz (1969) brought 15-year-old boys and girls to the laboratory, eight at a time. Seated at a table partitioned lengthwise, four were on one side of the partition and four on the other. The experimenter called one group the "blue group" and the other the "green group." Members of the two groups wore blue or green identification cards, wrote with blue or green ballpoint pens, filled out blue or green blanks, and were consistently addressed and spoken about as "blues" and "greens." The subjects were told that the study dealt with first impressions and each was given two photographs to judge. Other forms were filled out as well, and in some instances a transistor radio was given for the most accurate judgments. Afterward, all subjects were asked whom, among the seven others, they liked the most and whom they liked the least, and they rated each participant on a number of characteristics. In the control condition (in which no radios were given as prizes) there were no differences in liking between the ingroup and the outgroup ratings. But providing one group (and not the other) with a prize created an opportunity for invidious comparison and produced reliable differences between a subject's assessment of his ingroup and the outgroup. Ingroup ratings were higher than outgroup ratings on various personal characteristics, such as responsibility, consideration, fearfulness, cordiality, openness, familiarity, and soundness of judgment. Ingroup ratings exceeded outgroup ratings on social choices. Each of the seven individuals was ranked by every subject as to his or her desirability as a friend or a work partner. Members of the ingroup received substantially higher choices than members of the outgroup. Rabbie and Horwitz concluded that allocation of a scarce resource (the radio) among people so that some become "haves" and others "have-nots" is a sufficient condition for generating biases.

In a later study by Tajfel, Billig, Bundy, and Flament (1972), the opportunity for invidious comparisons was excluded as a possible contributor to ingroup-outgroup biases, yet these biases still were observed. Apparently, having the experimenter classify individuals arbitrarily into two groups is alone enough to generate differential attitudes. Rather than using judgments of personal characteristics or sociometric choices, they studied the way rewards or "profits" were divided between the two groups. The investigators reported that the subjects strove "to achieve a maximum difference between the ingroup and the outgroup . . . ." Not surprisingly the subjects rewarded the ingroup more.

Aggression

As we saw in Chapter 12, aggression is an inescapable fact of our lives. Moreover it is a fact of life that is as important to the social psychologist as it is to the personality psychologist.

The city of Detroit averages more than two homicides per day, and other American cities have similar records: countless rapes, break-ins, robberies, and assaults. During World War II, 15 million military personnel were killed or missing in action. Obviously, these phenomena are not limited to any one society. Violence rages around the world: terrorism, skyjacking, guerrilla war, gang fighting, all are reported daily in our newspapers. Some authors claim that more aggression occurs now than during the Dark Ages, and some claim that aggression is more common in some regions of the world than in others. Many of these claims cannot be substantiated upon close scrutiny. But within a group, aggression does lead to differentiation or to a breakdown of the group's integrative forces.

The universality of violence and aggression has prompted some writers to assume that man's aggressive urges are innately determined. Perhaps the leading proponent of an instinct view is the German ethologist, Konrad Lorenz. He has proposed a theory in which aggression is featured as a necessary part of personality, human or animal. In this concept, the release of aggressive impulses is as natural and inevitable as feeding or mating.

Lorenz begins with the assumption that aggressive energy originates within the organism. He believes that there are stimuli that are particularly prone to act as releasers of this aggressive energy. There exists, in his view, "a mechanism akin to a filter, letting through only certain stimuli while strictly excluding others, or a complicated lock which can only be unlocked by a very specific key." In his book on aggression (1963) he asserts, for example, that ". . . geese and ducks 'know' by very selective, innate releasing mechanisms that anything furry, red-brown, long shaped and slinking is extremely dangerous . . . ," meaning, presumably, a fox.

As an example of innate releasing mechanisms, the case of the three-spined stickleback, studied by Tinbergen and his colleagues, often is cited. They saw that a male stickleback patrolling near its nest would attack a red-colored intruder much more aggressively than a fish of another color. They noticed, to their amazement, that "even a red mail van passing our windows at a distance of 100 yards could make the males in the tank charge the glass sides in that direction" (1952). A number of experiments with models have convinced ethologists that the theory of innate releasers has much to offer. However, other evidence raises questions about the theory, especially in regard to the specificity of the releasers.

The stickleback mates during the early spring. During the course of this activity, his belly changes from inconspicuous grey to pink and then to bright scarlet. He attempts to attract the female to the nest he has made, and once she is over the nest, he prods her tail with a series of rhythmic thrusts. She lays eggs and leaves the nest, whereupon the male fertilizes the eggs and begins to look for another female. In the course of mating, three to five females may be induced to enter the nest and lay eggs. Eventually the male loses sexual interest, returns to his original grey color, and devotes his time to guarding the nest. While guarding his nest, he attacks all intruders.

You may by now have noticed something puzzling. If the innate aggression-releasing mechanism has evolved because of its survival value, and if it causes the release of an aggressive reaction upon the appearance of a particular stimulus, what survival function is served by having the red-scarlet belly of the mating male stickleback become a target for aggression from other males? What survival value is there in inducing attacks upon a member of the community who is in charge of bringing up the brood? Note that the male stickleback doesn't acquire a red belly until he has made some progress in building his nest. From an evolutionary point of view, wouldn't it be best for the stickleback who is interested in establishing a family to be as inconspicuous as possible? The red belly may be a fine stimulus for attracting females, but if it is also a releaser for aggression in other males, the mating season of sticklebacks should be nothing short of Armageddon. Yet it isn't.

Recent work by Muckensturm (1969) casts doubt on the theory of innate releasing mechanisms, especially in the stickleback. In a series of experiments, in which aggression toward violet, red, grey, and yellow models was observed, she was able to show that considerable differences exist among individual sticklebacks. Some show a great deal of aggression, others none. In two consecutive tests, separated by a substantial interval of time, she also demonstrated that these differences among sticklebacks were not accidental or peculiar to the given situation, but that they persisted over the two tests. A fish that attacks a target on the first test, also attacks it on the second. And she also found that red was *not* the preferred target of aggression. Rather it was violet and yellow. Grey was never the preferred target but occasionally it did elicit aggressive attacks. How can these results be reconciled with the notion of innate releasers?

It appears on the basis of all the results thus far collected that the one major determinant of aggression in the stickleback is novelty. The fact that red is attacked means simply that a red belly is a less frequent experience for the ordinary stickleback than grey. And yellow and violet are attacked *more* because these two colors are even less familiar. Muckensturm also reports that a great deal of aggression occurs *before* any coloring appears—aggression that might be related to the establishing of a dominance structure in which "winners" gain access to choice spots. The coloring changes only *after* reproductive aggression has taken place. These facts are indeed difficult to reconcile with the theory of innate releasers.

The early version of the aggression theory prompted many scholars to view aggression in man as an instinctive force. But if the story of instinctive determinants of aggression is not yet understood in animals, it is undoubtedly less clear in man.

What then are the factors that make man aggress against man? One of the important theories is the *frustration-aggression hypothesis*, discussed in Chapter 12 and published in its best known form more than three decades ago (Dollard, Doob, Miller, Mowrer, & Sears, 1939). The theory holds that frustration (blocking of the individual's progress toward a given goal or thwarting of the satisfaction of certain needs) has several consequences. One is the tendency to aggress against the agent perceived to be blocking attainment of the goal. Research findings have supported the theory. For instance, a recent study by Rule and Percival (1971)—similar to Milgram's obedience experiments—showed that the subject's frustration led him to give the "learner" a greater number of electric shocks.

Our discussion in Chapter 12 emphasized the importance of cues in eliciting aggressive responses in humans (Berkowitz, 1962). Consistent with the ethologists' concept of "releasers," some cues appear to be especially well suited to eliciting aggression. If the subject is angered or frustrated, he will aggress even more when his arousal is increased by another means, such as the surrounding context (Zillman, 1971). The reason frustration can instigate aggression may be that frustration is accompanied by heightened arousal. We shall see later that heightened arousal is capable of enhancing any *dominant response* (the response most likely to be made in any given situation). If the situation makes aggressive responses dominant, frustration, acting to increase arousal, will result in heightened aggression. But by this theory *any* increase in arousal—frustration, hunger, sex, strong stimulation, or the ingestion of stimulants—could enhance aggression when the individual was in a situation in which aggressive responses were dominant.

The problem of aggression is as important as it is complex, and it would be foolish to imply that psychologists fully understand the phenomenon and its determinants. A great deal more work is required, work which is made especially difficult because it is often unethical or impractical in laboratory situations to conduct studies that would be particularly informative. No one doubts, however, that aggression exists to a greater or lesser extent in practically all societies and in all species, and that its universal consequence is *social differentiation*. Among a large number of species, aggressive responses lead to the establishment of dominance hierarchies in which individuals gain particular social positions and thus a preferential access to scarce resources. Outcomes of aggression categorize individuals by placing them in privileged and underprivileged classes or segregating groups into separate factions. In all cases of aggression, especially among animals, the achievement of a stable structure, be it a dominance hierarchy or a clique, leads to a reduction of aggressiveness and hostility.

Competition

A powerful force promoting the differentiation or division of existing groups is *competition*. The competition may be between individual members of the group or between subgroups; in either case, the effect of competition is to separate the group into distinct parts.

Competition is an ever present ingredient of social living. And as we discovered in Chapter 16, some personality theorists, particularly Alfred Adler, believe competition for power, status, and wealth lies at the core of human nature. Such personality psychologists view competition and the related issues of dominance and submission as central to our understanding of the individual personality. Moreover social psychologists have long viewed competition within and between groups as an essential factor in understanding group processes.

In an early and influential investigation by Deutsch (1949) a group of

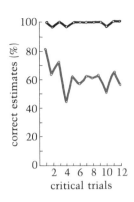

19-12
Graph showing the effect of social pressure on accuracy of judgment. The bottom line shows judgments in the presence of six to eight competitors; the top line shows accuracy of judgment when the person is not under pressure. (Solomon E. Asch. *Social Psychology.* © 1952. Reprinted by permission of Prentice-Hall, Inc., Englewood Cliffs, New Jersey.)

five individuals worked under two conditions. In the first condition, performance was evaluated solely in terms of what the total group did (cooperation); in the second condition, the contribution of each member of the group was individually evaluated (competition). The results indicated that the effect of competition was to:

1. increase the difficulty in communicating and paying attention to other group members;

2. decrease the readiness to accept the ideas of other group members;

3. decrease division of labor and productivity.

A comparable study by Smith, Madden, and Sobol (1957) compared cooperative and competitive groups in the quality of a discussion concerning how to deal with a human relations problem. One group was told that its discussion would form the basis for judgments of *individual* intelligence while the other group was told that its discussion would provide the basis for assessing the *group's* intelligence. The discussion within the cooperative groups was judged to be more productive than within the competitive groups.

The studies we have just discussed involved the experimental creation of groups under competitive and cooperative conditions. Other studies have investigated naturally occurring groups characterized by varying degrees of internal competition. Kelley and Thibaut (1969) reviewed both types of studies; the results make clear that competition has a general deleterious effect upon group performance and that, in extreme cases, competition may lead to the group's dissolution.

The Group and the Individual

We have reviewed some of the lasting relationships and dependencies that exist between the group and the individual. We noted that groups achieve social integration by processes that are a part of every individual's psychological makeup. These processes affect "strangers" as well as members of the group. All feel the group's impact. Through attachment and affiliation, powerful emotional bonds form among individuals—some so powerful that their dissolution may cause serious psychological disturbance.

By imitation and conformity the individual assumes the habits, values, and attitudes of his group. He sees himself as sharing much with the group and believes that the other group members see him in the same way. He is grieved when any damage is done to his fellow members; proud when his class or ethnic group is credited with some achievement; and delighted when, in a strange environment, he comes across someone like himself. He may be an individual but his identity is imbedded in his group memberships, and his uniqueness invariably derives in part from them. When he is interacting with citizens of his own country, he sets himself off from them by stressing his regional or state origin. When he is with residents of his own city, he associates himself

19-13
The individual's behavior is greatly influenced by the group to which he belongs. Not only his attitudes, as we discussed in the last chapter, but also his motor-skill responses are either facilitated or inhibited by the presence of others. How well he performs depends on the task itself and on the extent to which he feels accepted by the group. (Arthur Freed)

with the area or street where he lives. With people of the same profession he sets himself apart by reference to his particular specialization. Among musicians, the musician is a cellist or second violinist with the Philadelphia Orchestra, a composer or an arranger for a Nashville group. But among his neighbors, he is again a musician. Among Englishmen, the Englishman becomes a Londoner, a Northerner, or a Liverpudlian. The individual achieves uniqueness only temporarily and only on a comparative level. The Liverpudlian is singular among Londoners and even more so among New Yorkers. But when in Liverpool, he must find another attribute that will distinguish him from others around him. Perhaps his visit to New York affords him some distinction. Few people are socially unique, since someone always can be found who resembles them. Perhaps those few with extraordinary achievements, like the scientist who discovers the newest subatomic particle, or Hank Aaron, who broke Babe Ruth's home run record, have some extraordinary attributes that others do not share. But the vast majority of us derive our individuality partially from a group, class, or category membership. It does not come solely from within us.

In the last analysis, of all the factors that influence the individual's behavior, *social* influences are perhaps the most significant and far-reaching. Even such factors as habits, attitudes, or values, which we usually assume to be internal, can be traced largely to some reference group or to some of the individual's personal group memberships and identifications. In the individual's immediate environment, the significant stimuli that elicit responses are mainly social—the responses of other people around him. Often, they need not even make responses. Their anticipated responses are sufficient to determine the individual's behavior. Indeed, the mere presence of other people may discourage the mugger or encourage the exhibitionist.

In this section, we shall examine some of the effects that other people around an individual have on his behavior. In contrast with the previous section, we are not concerned with permanent effects that derive from social contact or social interaction. We are concerned only with momentary, albeit recurrent, influences.

Social Facilitation

The simplest and the most primitive social influence is the impact that the mere presence of others has on an individual's behavior. This effect acts jointly with other social influences, such as control of the individual's reinforcements, the giving of informative cues, or the possibility that the other people present might compete with the individual.

Considerable evidence suggests that the mere presence of passive spectators or of others engaged in the same activity has a detectable impact on the individual's behavior. This *social facilitation* research shows that the individual's performance either improves or deteriorates in the presence of others. It would seem that the term social *facilitation* would characterize only findings that show improvement; however, it applies to both improvement and deterioration. The term arose during the early

1900s, when most of the findings did indicate that performance improved in the presence of others.

This early evidence suggested that some form of facilitation occurs in such tasks as word association or the solving of simple arithmetic problems. The first experiment was performed by Norman Triplett in 1897 — perhaps the first formal experiment in social psychology. An avid fan of bicycle racing and well acquainted with record race times, he noticed a gross discrepancy between the speeds that riders achieved when racing in competition and when racing alone against a stopwatch. By changing from a race against time to a competitive race, a racer could better his time by 20 percent. Triplett reviewed an enormous mass of racing records and compared the times achieved under various conditions. He finally concluded that the mere presence of other riders is enough to make bicyclists ride faster. He also devised an experiment in which children wound fishing reels alone and in the presence of others and obtained a clear facilitation effect. His conclusion, stated with reference to the bicyclists, was:

. . . the bodily presence of another rider is a stimulus to the racer in arousing the competitive instinct; that another can thus be the means of releasing or freeing nervous energy for him that he cannot of himself release; and, further, that the sight of movement in that other, by perhaps suggesting a higher rate of speed, is also an inspiration to greater effort.

He named his explanation the dynamogenic theory of performance. Interestingly, Triplett wasn't the first to speak of social facilitation and its generality. The origin of this quote may surprise some readers:

Apart from the new power that arises from the fusion of many forces into one single force, mere social contact begets . . . an emulation and a stimulation of the animal spirits that heighten the efficiency of each individual workman. Hence, it is that a dozen persons working together will, in their collective working day of 144 hours, produce far more than twelve isolated men working 12 hours, or than one man who works twelve days in succession. The reason for this is that a man is, if not as Aristotle contends, a political, at all events a social animal. (Karl Marx, 1867)

The information collected on social facilitation, beginning with Triplett's experiment, appears inconsistent. For example, Triplett did find that the speed with which the children wound the fishing reels increased when they were working in the presence of others. Allport (1924) found that performance on a word-association task improved when other persons were present. But Innes and Sambrooks (1969), who asked subjects to learn difficult lists of paired associates in the presence of others, found that on the whole their performance deteriorated. An even more recent study by Fouts and Jordan (1973) showed that when subjects were given unassociated words (table-kangaroo, day-house) as opposed to words whose associations come readily to mind (table-chair, day-night), they did better alone than in the presence of others.

A close scrutiny of the results shows both *facilitation* and *deterioration* in the presence of others and suggests that these tasks can be divided into two distinct categories. Facilitation is achieved on simple tasks and well-learned skills. Deterioration occurs primarily on complex assignments. Hence, in the presence of others, difficult maze learning is impaired, as is other learning that involves the discovery of appropriate responses. Ader and Tatum (1963) brought medical students to a laboratory, strapped electrodes to them, and then, without saying a word, left the room and locked the door. From then on, the individual received a shock at regular intervals. He did not know it, but he could have avoided the shock if he had located a push-button on the table. A press of the button would delay the shock for a fixed interval of time. If it were pressed again within a prescribed time limit, he got no shock at all. But the subject had to discover the button and its effects. Ader and Tatum found that individuals learn to avoid shock within a few minutes, but that pairs of individuals learn much more slowly. Of the twelve pairs in the experiment, only two succeeded in avoiding the shock before the one-hour experiment ended. Thus the presence of another person distinctly impaired performance.

The presence of others also seems to cause arousal in the individual. Several studies, using physiological measures, such as degree of palmar sweat or heart rate, show that arousal does increase when other persons are present. Research indicates that one consequence of arousal is the facilitation of the dominant response. Conversely, therefore, subordinate responses are not likely to occur. They become even less likely as arousal is heightened, because to gain expression they have to compete more intensely with the dominant response. In simple tasks and in the performance of highly learned skills the "correct" responses are dominant. This is true for simple addition problems. It also is true that whatever the response, if it is strong and dominant, the subject will make it sooner and with greater vigor when he is aroused. For example, if subjects were to try making less obvious association responses to such words as table or day (that is, responses other than chair and night), most people would think of very little at first. A host of weak responses to these words would lose out under conditions of high arousal in competition for expression with the dominant response. A similar situation occurs in the early stages of learning. If a maze is complicated, with several alternatives at each point of choice, and only one choice is correct, the subject will hesitate when he has to choose. Of course, he is not likely to make the correct response, since it is only one of many possibilities. Dominant responses prevalent during learning are very likely to be incorrect. The child learning to multiply may respond as he would to an addition problem when he first hears the words, "How much is two times three?" His dominant response, assuming he is mistakenly thinking of the familiar addition process, would be "five"—an incorrect response. Learning is the substitution of appropriate responses for inappropriate ones. The consistent difference that allows us to relate facilitation and impairment to task difficulty and type of performance also suggests a resolution of the apparent conflict (Zajonc, 1965). When the correct response is the obvious or dominant response, arousal (social facilitation) will facilitate the correct response (performance). When the correct response is not dominant, social facilitation will make it less likely that the correct response will be made and thus impair performance.

While arousal does seem to play a definite role in social facilitation, the extent of its role is not completely clear. Cottrell (1972) proposed that mere presence of others is not enough to enhance dominant responses. Instead, he contended, human expectations, especially those associated with being evaluated by others, create the state of heightened arousal. In this experiment, Cottrell had subjects perform tasks of varying complexity while a blindfolded spectator entered the room. Since he could not see the subjects, and therefore could not evaluate their performance, his presence was neutral; it neither facilitated nor inhibited their performances.

The incidence of *stuttering* may be a sensitive index of the mere presence of others upon performance. Research has shown that the stutterer increases his rate of stuttering when any stimulus increases his arousal. Unaroused and alone, the stutterer can speak quite well. If stuttering is caused by evaluation alone, then stutterers who recite or read in isolation but who know that their speech is being recorded and that others will listen to it, should falter more than stutterers who are alone and are convinced that no one is listening or recording their speech. On the other hand, if stuttering is caused by the mere presence of others, these two groups should not differ and both should outperform a group whose members speak and read in the presence of another person. Svab, Gross, and Langova (1972) performed an experiment under just such conditions. Their results showed that the stutterer's oral performance deteriorated only when another person actually was present. When he thought someone was in the next room listening to him, or that his performance was recorded and would be heard later by others, he stuttered as little as when he was in total isolation and believed that no one, then or ever, would be monitoring his speech. Thus, Cottrell's formulation does not appear to be supported uniformly.

Helping Others

As we have seen, the problem of social facilitation is generally examined by observing performance in paired-associate learning tasks, maze running, or motor tasks. How does the presence of others affect social behavior? One behavior that is typically "social" is helping, especially helping another in distress.

Many observers of city life have noted that in large urban centers people generally are not very kind or helpful. Some have remarked that while an epileptic seizure or heart attack might bring spectators, help should not be expected. In New York City in 1964, a young woman struggled with an assailant for half an hour while at least 38 people nearby had some awareness of the attack. Not only did no one help her; no one even called the police. Critics of urban life often cite small communities as a contrast, noting that they pride themselves on being friendly, helpful, sociable, and cohesive. While rural life is generally more open, as these observers suggest, it too has its formal social rules and structures, which govern group and individual behavior; strangers are certainly treated differently from citizens even in the friendliest rural community.

Social psychologists have studied the phenomenon of seeming social indifference. Darley and Latané (1967) invited college students to their laboratory for what they described as a discussion of personal problems associated with college life. To "avoid embarrassment," they talked over an intercom system, with each individual in a separate cubicle. The discussion went normally until one student appeared to undergo an intense seizure. (In the course of the discussion, he had mentioned that he was prone to seizures, especially when studying for exams.) He grew louder and incoherent, saying in a choking gurgle that he was having a seizure, that he needed help, and that he was going to die.

I er I think I I need er if if could er er somebody er er er er er er give me a little er give me a little help here because I er I'm er er h-h-having a a a a real problem er right now and I er if somebody could help me out it would er er s-s-sure be sure be good . . . because er there er er a cause I er I uh I've got a a one of the er sei . . . er er things coming on and and and I could really er use some help so if somebody would er give me a little h-help uh er er er er er c-could somebody er er help er uh uh uh (choking sounds). . . . I'm gonna die er er I'm . . . gonna die er help er er seizure (chokes, then quiet).

The experimenters wanted to know if the subject would help and, if so, how long he would wait before helping. Three experimental combinations were used: the subject and the "epileptic victim"; the subject, the victim, and another confederate; and the subject, the victim, and four confederates, all presumably healthy.

Darley and Latané found that when only the subject and the victim participated, 85 percent of the subjects helped the victim. When the subjects thought that there was one other person, only 62 percent helped, and when they thought that four other subjects were present, 31 percent helped. The speed with which help was given, too, varied inversely in relation to group size: 52 seconds for the lone subject, 93 for groups of three, and 166 for groups of six.

Darley and Latané suggest that the subject in these situations suffers a conflict. He is torn between feelings of guilt for his hesitation about helping, and feelings of restraint because he may make a fool of himself by running out of his cubicle without knowing exactly what to do next. If he is aware that other people are waiting nearby, it is easy to assume that someone else will help, and his conflict is resolved. Subsequent research has generally confirmed these results, finding that the fewer people are involved, the more likely that any one of them will give help. Thus, the unfriendliness of large urban centers probably is due not so much to "alienation" or the "anomie" of the urban dweller, as to *diffusion of responsibility*. An individual feels less responsibility for an act of omission, even if immoral, when he can share his guilt with others or shift responsibility to others.

19-14
An experimental setup to test helping behavior. This experiment indicated that helping behavior is affected by both the number of other people present and the condition of the person in need of help. As shown in the table, a person who was obviously ill was helped more often and faster than a person who appeared to be drunk. And, contrary to situations in which subjects could not see each other, the speed of response increased as the number of people present increased. This was because the subjects could see each other and could not justify not helping by assuming that someone else surely would do so. (Adapted from Piliavin, Rodin, & Piliavin, 1969)

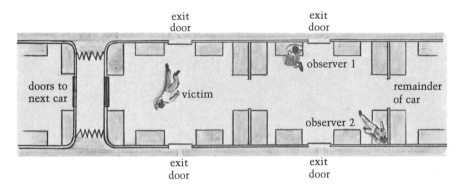

The Effects of Group Size on the Average Speed of Helping

Number of Males in Immediate Area	Average Time Taken to Help Ill Victim (in Seconds)	Average Time Taken to Help Drunk Victim (in Seconds)
1–3	15	309
4–6	18	149
7 or more	9	97

Source: Adapted from Piliavin, Rodin, and Piliavin, 1969, Table 5.

The Risky Shift

Diffusion of responsibility also has been thought to be an important factor when a group makes a decision that has significant consequences. Suppose that a bank's board of directors is deciding how to invest the money of its depositors. The decision involves risk. The alternatives can be categorized into conservative and risky investments. A conservative investment is virtually certain to yield some moderate profit. On the other hand, the risky investment may yield a large profit, but the company also may suffer serious losses. If we compared such a group decision to an individual decision, and if diffusion of responsibility is a factor, we would predict that groups would make riskier decisions than individuals working alone because several individuals would share the risk and its possible consequences.

The early group risk research led to this conclusion, supported by considerable data. Typically, a number of individuals were given a series of "choice dilemmas"—questionnaire items with two alternatives. One alternative was generally risky and one conservative; the subject's task was to assess the risky alternative's chances of success before making his recommendation. One such item was:

The captain of a losing football team must, on the last play of the game, decide between a play that will almost certainly lead to a tie and a more risky play which will win the game if successful, but lead to a certain defeat if unsuccessful.

The subject then must recommend for or against the risky play, explaining to the captain its chances of success.

Graph showing that helping behavior
is much more likely to occur when
the individual in need of help is a
friend. (After Latané & Rodin, 1969)

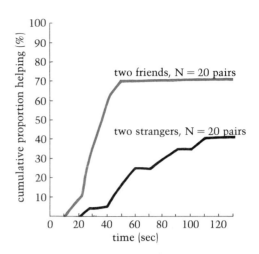

Another situation given was:

A couple considering whether or not to get married have had a number of arguments. Consultation with a marriage counselor has indicated that a happy marriage, while possible, is certainly not assured.

Developed to study personality effects in *individual* risk-taking, these problem situations have been used by Stoner (1961) to investigate *group* decision-making. Stoner's finding, later replicated by Wallach, Kogan, and Bem (1962), was that group decisions are more inclined toward risk-taking than individual decisions, and that once an individual participates in a group decision, the level of his own risk-taking rises. He retains the level of risk of the group choice—a phenomenon called the *risky shift*. Some social psychologists considered the findings alarming. They had only to think of the National Security Council, for example, making a decision regarding nuclear attack.

But the cause for alarm, it became clear, was exaggerated. First of all, the subjects in these studies did not really make decisions; they recommended which alternatives a hypothetical person should choose. None of the subjects had to suffer any consequences of the decision. While they might be held responsible for giving bad advice, even that possibility was remote. After all, the decision-maker, whether the captain of the football team or the engaged couple, decides on the basis of his or their own information in addition to the subject's advice. We do not know how much the subject's advice weighed in the captain's or the couple's decision. Hence, even though the decision involved a shared, hypothetical responsibility, the magnitude of that responsibility was far less than is the case for the actual decisions made by the National Security Council. However, in some studies in which the subjects did suffer some minor consequences—usually a slight gain or loss of money or a small success or failure—the risky shift was also seen to occur.

One critical result turned researchers away from a diffusion-of-responsibility interpretation of the risky-shift effect. It was the finding of a consistent shift toward greater conservatism on some items. For example, in one study after another, the choice dilemma of the engaged couple shows a shift toward greater conservatism. That is, when discussing the problem at length, the group usually recommended that the couple not marry.

A number of theories have emerged to explain the discrepancy between shifts to risk and shifts to conservatism. For example, it is a replicable finding—using the choice dilemma procedure—that the group's need to agree generally results in shifts to risk. But if the individuals can discuss the dilemmas freely, without having to come to any joint decision, their individual scores also shift toward greater risk. The lack of a joint decision calls into question a diffusion-of-responsibility interpretation. Worse yet, when subjects are allowed to observe others discussing these problems, they too shift toward greater risk.

One of the earlier theories on the risky shift was proposed by Brown (1965), who explained it in terms of *social values.* Brown's basic idea was that in dealing with an ambiguous situation, the subject sees himself as taking a fair risk; and since, in our culture, risk-taking is valued, he wants to be at least as inclined to take risks as the average person. Frequently, when subjects find out in conversations or by other means, that they are below average in risk-taking, they quickly conform to their new perception of the group norm or value. Brown's theory proved inadequate, however, in dealing with the items that consistently shifted toward greater conservatism. To revise the theory, we would have to assume that some decisions involve a value toward risk and others toward conservatism. Then we would have to determine which decisions fit into each category.

More recent theories on the risky shift emphasize the *role of the arguments* that emerge in discussion. For items that eventually shift toward greater risk, the most persuasive arguments usually support a greater risk; for items that shift toward less risk, the most defensible arguments favor greater caution. For example, some arguments that emerge when the group discusses the engaged couple point out that the couple had already had some difficulties, that the two people themselves have a question about marrying and are uncertain enough to see a marriage counselor. These facts must mean, at least, that they have mixed feelings about each other. Their past relationships suggests future difficulties that will be more serious. All of these arguments favor caution.

We are far from a full understanding of the process of group decision-making. We cannot expect the combining of individual preferences into a simple average to predict consistently the group consensus. Nor can we always expect groups to engage in the risky shift. Despite these uncertainties about behavior in social settings, we have learned a good deal about man as a social animal through the investigations that social psychologists have carried on for more than half a century.

We have seen that an essential feature of human life is group membership. There are many regularities in the relation between the individual and the group, including identifiable factors that tend to maintain or integrate groups and other factors that tend to differentiate or subdivide groups. As examples of integrative forces we have discussed attraction, affiliation, and attachment; and we considered categorization, aggression, and competition as factors that favor differentiation. We have also considered the impact of the group on the individual, including such matters as social facilitation (and social deterioration), willingness to help others, and changes in the readiness to choose alternatives involving a high degree of risk (risky shift).

Summary

1. All human populations form groups, which are maintained by internal and external forces and pressures. Groups are fairly enduring and provide a means of identification for their members.

2. Three mechanisms of integration are attraction, which deals primarily with the gaining of proximity; attachment, which covers attempts to maintain proximity to all types of targets; and affiliation, which refers to specific attachments to individuals rather than to parts of the environment. Both affiliation and attachment strengthen group stability.

3. Among the origins of attachment are its survival value, reinforcers that are mutually fulfilling, proximity that produces opportunity for contact and exposure, and similarity of attitudes.

4. Social attachments are both inevitable and necessary for the individual's psychological health. While love occurs in all human societies, its exact nature is far from fully understood.

5. Widespread uniformities within a group result from the group's restricted gene pool, producing somewhat homogeneous physical and behavioral components, and from the processes of imitation and conformity.

6. Imitation—one individual's copying of another's behavior—may involve active participation, simple observation, or vicarious learning.

7. Imitation that involves social norms is called conformity. A social norm includes uniformity of behavior, social expectations regarding this behavior, and social methods of controlling it. Obedience to social norms may be induced by the use of sanctions, threats, or promises of reward.

8. Any process that creates a group also simultaneously acts as an instrument of social differentiation by separating that group from others.

9. The arbitrary classification of individuals into groups is called social categorization. Differential classification alone is sufficient to generate differential attitudes between group members and nonmembers.

10. Aggression leads to a breakdown of the integrative forces within groups, causing social differentiation and dominance hierarchies.

11. Competition is another force promoting the differentiation or division of existing groups. The general effect of competition is to interfere with group performance and, in some instances, to dissolve the group.

12. The vast majority of humans derive much of their individuality and identity from their memberships in groups, classes, or categories.

13. The simplest social influence is the impact of passive spectators on an individual's behavior. Social facilitation may occur in simple tasks and well-learned skills, while social deterioration may occur in complex tasks.

14. The phenomenon of social indifference is related to the diffusion of responsibility. An individual feels less responsible for assisting others when he can share his guilt with others and less likely to act when he believes someone else can help.

15. In certain settings, group decisions may be more inclined toward risk-taking than are individual decisions. A phenomenon in which the individual retains the level of risk of the group decision is called the risky shift. However, the shift that may occur due to a decision's being made by a group is not always in the direction of greater risk.

Important Terms

integration

differentiation

attraction

attachment

imprinting

affiliation

social norm

conformity

social categorization

competition

innate releasing mechanism

social facilitation

dynamogenic theory of performance

risky shift

Suggested Readings

BANDURA, A. *Social learning theory*. Morristown, N.J.: General Learning Press, 1971.
    A discussion of the development of social behavior (primarily aggressive behavior) based on the principles of behavioral learning. Imitation is seen as the chief determinant.

BOWLBY, J. *Attachment and loss*. Vol. I, *Attachment*. New York: Basic Books, 1969.
    A study of the nature of the child's tie to his mother; it uses a psychoanalytic frame of reference. Information from observations of children in real-life situations, as well as from animal studies, is included.

BROWN, R. *Social psychology*. New York: Free Press, 1965.
    An integrated, personal view of the field of social psychology. Unusually well written and wise.

DEUTSCH, M., & KRAUSS, R. M. *Theories in social psychology.* New York: Basic Books, 1965.

A summary and criticism of the major social-psychological theories.

HARLOW, H. F. *Learning to love.* New York: Albion, 1971.

A readable summary of the research findings by this major primate researcher.

KOGAN, N., & WALLACH, M. A. *Risk-taking: a study in cognition and personality.* New York: Holt, Rinehart and Winston, 1964.

Descriptions of selected research in group decision-making, including the first explorations of the risky shift phenomenon.

MEHRABIAN, A. *Tactics of social influence.* Englewood Cliffs, N.J.: Prentice-Hall, 1970.

A short, readable discussion of the principles of behavior modification and their applications to familiar social problems. No psychology background is assumed.

NEWCOMB, T. M. *The acquaintance process.* New York: Holt, Rinehart and Winston, 1961.

A report on a two-year study concerning social interaction, group formation, and attitudes, using data collected in an experimental university housing unit.

RUBIN, Z. *Liking and loving.* New York: Holt, Rinehart and Winston, 1973.

A highly entertaining discussion of the ways in which interpersonal attraction (friendship, mate selection, and intergroup relations) have been studied by social psychologists.

SCHACHTER, S. *The psychology of affiliation.* Stanford: Stanford University Press, 1959.

The first major exposition of the psychological bases of affiliation, which prompted research on the significance of birth-order.

Chapter 20   Behavior Disorders

It seems to come out of nowhere. I've tried to discover what touches it off, what leads up to it, but I can't. Suddenly, it hits me. . . . It seems I can be doing anything at the time—painting, working at the Gallery, cleaning the apartment, reading, or talking to someone. It doesn't matter where I am or what's going on. One minute I'm fine, feeling gay, busy, loving life and people. The next minute I'm on an express highway to hell.

I think it begins with a feeling of emptiness inside. Something, I don't know what to call it, starts to ache; something right in the center of me feels as if it's opening up, spreading apart maybe. It's like a hole in my vitals appears. Then the emptiness starts to throb—at first softly like a fluttering pulse. For a little while, that's all that happens. But then the pulsing turns into a regular beat; and the beat gets stronger and stronger. The hole gets bigger. Soon I feel as if there's nothing to me but a vast, yawning space surrounded by skin that grabs convulsively at nothingness. The beating gets louder. The sensation changes from an ache to a hurt, a pounding hurt. The feeling of emptiness becomes agony. In a short while there's nothing of me, of Laura, but an immense, drumming vacuum.

—Robert Lindner
(*The Fifty-Minute Hour*)

Behavior Disorders

This chapter was drafted by Irwin Sarason, Department of Psychology, University of Washington.

The study of abnormal behavior is of vital concern to each of us. Behavior that is deviant or abnormal poses critical problems for every individual as well as for our society. It would be difficult to find a single person who has not been affected either directly or indirectly by problems of mental disorder. Just about everybody has among his family and friends someone who is undergoing psychological treatment or is very much in need of it. Thus, problems related to mental disorders are by no means confined to the therapist's office or contained within the walls of the psychiatric hospital.

Psychopathology, or mental disorder, is important to study not only in its own right but also because of the light it sheds upon normal behavior. We have seen that the insights of Freud and many other influential psychological theorists were based upon observations of disturbed individuals. These observations give clear evidence of the continuity between normal and abnormal — all of us can recognize aspects of ourselves in descriptions of various forms of mental disorder. Cleanliness is a virtue, alert concern for possible threat in the environment is adaptive, happiness is something we all seek. But an excessive amount of any of these traits disturbs normal functioning and may lead to the diagnosis of a *neurosis* (moderate mental disorder) or *psychosis* (severe mental disorder).

A Historical Note

The present-day view of abnormal behavior is that it is understandable, predictable, and can be subjected to scientific study. To most of us, this seems only reasonable — yet such an objective view of abnormal behavior is surprisingly new.

To be sure, certain ancient Greek, Roman, and Arabic scholars viewed abnormal behavior much as we do today. Hippocrates (450–377 BC) and Plato (429–348 BC) urged their students to interpret mental deviations as natural phenomena. Unfortunately, their enlightened approach did not

20-1

"The doctor thinks that no well-regulated institution should be unprovided with the circulating swing." This illustration, dated 1818, depicts a method of treating "lunatics" in the 18th and 19th centuries. One hundred revolutions per minute was the recommended speed, and an unlit room was suggested. (Culver Pictures)

20-2

An engraving by William Hogarth (1697–1764) of Bedlam, the hospital of St. Mary's of Bethlehem, an asylum in London, illustrates the horrors of the early mental institutions and several of the more common symptoms of the inmates—such as delusions of grandeur, delusions of persecution, and mania. (Culver Pictures).

prevail. During the Middle Ages, the scientific approach was unknown. Superstition and belief in magic, alchemy, and witchcraft challenged the vast power of religion. To combat what it saw as the devil's work, the church arbitrarily labeled specific types of behavior as sinful, attributed such behavior to possession by demons, and tortured those "possessed" in an effort to exorcise the demons from their bodies.

The humanistic spirit of the Renaissance brought with it a gradual decline in the importance of such ideas as possession by the devil. The idea of dealing rationally and humanely with disordered behavior took centuries to emerge, but a general positive trend became evident in the 1500s. By the middle of the 1800s, a vigorous reform movement in several countries urged that disordered behavior be treated as a sign of "insanity" or mental illness. As the concept of insanity became accepted, reformers began demanding more humane conditions in the "madhouses" where persons with severe disorders were confined. In 1792, in keeping with the ideals of the French Revolution, Phillipe Pinel removed the chains of patients at a mental hospital near Paris. By the 19th century, the focus had definitely shifted from the pursuit of demons to a search for the causes and proper treatment of insanity. By 1840, Samuel Hitch had improved the training of nurses who worked in English mental hospitals. In America, a Boston schoolteacher named Dorothea Dix visited hundreds of penitentiaries, jails, and almshouses and revealed the terrible conditions that existed in those institutions. As a result of her efforts, 32 mental hospitals were constructed to provide better care for the insane. Another significant figure in America was Clifford Beers (1876–1943). His moving, autobiographical account of the experiences of a manic-depressive psychotic, combined with his personal efforts to promote reform, led to the founding of the mental hygiene movement.

The 20th century has seen a continuation of such humanitarian efforts

to help disturbed individuals, and there also has been more questioning of traditional concepts and methods. For example, Thomas Szasz has attacked the whole idea of "mental illness," saying it leads to the erroneous conclusion that behavioral derangement is caused by mysterious inner entities called mental illnesses. Growing numbers of researchers and clinicians, agreeing at least in part with Szasz, have focused their attention on *problems in living* and their recognizable causes and correlates. According to Szasz (1960):

Our adversaries are not demons, witches, fate or mental illness. We have no enemy whom we can fight, exorcise, or dispel by "cure." What we do have are problems in living—*whether these be biologic, economic, political, or sociopsychological. My argument was limited to the proposition that mental illness is a myth, whose function it is to disguise and thus render more palatable the bitter pill of moral conflicts in human relations.*

Modern Approaches to Abnormal Behavior

Problems in living are numerous and complex. They are not necessarily limited to the biological, economic, political, and sociopsychological factors Szasz mentioned. Experts argue over definitions and the relative importance of various factors, but they agree that careful, scientific inquiry is the best way to settle their differences. In their research, students of abnormal behavior use many approaches. One common approach is to observe subjects' responses to naturally occurring conditions. Another method is to manipulate the conditions under which behavior is observed.

Whatever approach he adopts, the observer will be influenced by the theory of abnormal behavior he favors. Such theories are simply special applications of the personality theories discussed in Chapter 16.

Psychodynamic Approach

A *psychodynamic theory*, such as psychoanalysis, emphasizes the importance of internal events of which we are unaware. These theories hold that most behavior, including dreaming, is an expression of unconscious thoughts which would arouse anxiety if brought to awareness in undistorted form. Early childhood events are considered to be of primary importance in understanding adult behavior—including behavior disorders.

Learning Approach

Another group of psychological theories has grown out of the learning laboratory; it relies partially on the results of experiments performed on animals. Most *learning theorists* concentrate their research on directly observable events rather than inferred internal states. Learning theories are perhaps best known for their explorations of stimulus-response relationships.

When learning-theory psychologists explore abnormal behavior, they often study the effects of reinforcement or reward on behavior. Since severely disturbed persons show conventional behavior less frequently than normal persons, it is important to ask whether reinforcement or rewards will increase the frequency of conventional responses. The following case, of a 43-year-old man who had not spoken for 14 years, shows that objectively definable reinforcements (in this case, chewing gum) can be used to strengthen conventional behavior (in this case, verbal responding).

This patient, with a combative history prior to mutism, habitually lay on a bench in the day room in the same position, rising only for meals and for bed. Weekly visits were begun by E (experimenter) and an attendant. During these visits, E urged S (subject) to attend group therapy sessions which were being held elsewhere in the hospital. E offered S chewing gum. This was not accepted during the first two visits, but was accepted on the third visit and thereafter. On the sixth visit, E made receipt of the gum contingent upon S's going to the group room and so informed S. S then altered his posture to look at E and accompanied him to the group room, where he seated himself in a chair and was given the gum. Thereafter he came to this room when the attendants called for him.

Group Sessions 1–4. Gum reinforcement was provided for coming to the first two weekly sessions, but starting with the third, it was made contingent upon S's participation in the announced group activity. The group (whose other members were verbal) was arranged in a semicircle. E announced that each patient would, when his turn came, give the name of an animal. E immediately provided gum to each patient who did so. S did not respond and skipped his turn three times around. The same response occurred during the fourth session.

Group Session 5. The activity announced was drawing a person; E provided paper and colored chalk and visited each patient in turn to examine the paper. S had drawn a stick figure and was reinforced with gum. Two other patients, spontaneously and without prior prompting by E, asked to see the drawing and complimented S. Attendants reported that on the following day, S, when introduced to two ward visitors, smiled and said, "I'm glad to see you." The incident was followed by no particular explicit consequences.

Group Session 6. The announced activity was to give the name of a city or town in Illinois. S, in his turn, said, "Chicago." He was reinforced by E, who gave him chewing gum, and again two members of the group congratulated him for responding. Thereafter he responded whenever his turn came.

After the tenth session in the group, gum reinforcement was discontinued. S has continued to respond vocally in the situations in which he was reinforced by E but not in others. He never initiates conversations, but he will, however, respond vocally to questions asked on the ward, even when put by E. (Isaacs, Thomas, & Golddiamond, 1960)

Social Psychological Approach

Learning theorists focus on the immediate, day-to-day events in the life of the individual under study; most of us would see these events as important determinants of what we do. Psychologists with *social psychological* and *sociological* orientations explore somewhat larger environments involving more than one individual. Typically, they will examine a specific social group, neighborhood, or town. Research on the topic of suicide illustrates this approach. Suicide rates vary widely, depending on such factors as religion, social class, and nationality (Sarason, 1972). Protestants commit suicide significantly more than Catholics, and suicide is more common among the upper and middle classes than among the lower class. People discharged from mental hospitals are 34 times more likely to commit suicide than the general population. Studies of groups of cities and countries have revealed noticeable differences. Japan, Germany, and Sweden have high rates of suicide; Spain, Ireland, and Egypt have relatively low rates. San Francisco has the highest suicide rate in the United States, which ranks in about the middle of the distribution of nations indexed. The suicide rate in San Francisco County is about three times the national rate. More research will be needed to uncover the reasons for these particular differences. However, such sociological methods produce clear evidence that socioeconomic and cultural factors affect human behavior.

Biophysical Approach

A fourth approach to abnormal behavior, and one that is becoming increasingly important, emphasizes *biophysical* events as they relate to disordered behavior. Currently, the influences over behavior of the central nervous system and the ductless glands of the endocrine system are being explored intensively.

Researchers also have been examining the role of heredity in behavior disorders. One way to evaluate the extent of this influence is to use twin studies, which compare identical (monozygotic) and fraternal (dizygotic) twins. These studies seek to determine the relationship between twins and other family members with respect to a given characteristic or trait. As we discussed in Chapter 2, schizophrenia has been studied in exactly this way. In general, the *concordance rate* (given one twin with the diagnosis, the likelihood of its occurring in the other twin) of schizophrenia in a family with one schizophrenic parent is high for identical twins. Thus, if one twin is schizophrenic, the other twin probably will be schizophrenic too. The rate drops precipitously for dizygotic twins of the same sex (Gottesman & Shields, 1972). The drop is even greater for dizygotic twins of the opposite sex. Since the rate of schizophrenia does not approach 100 percent even in identical twins, the role of environmental influences, and perhaps other factors, must be evaluated. Still, the available evidence suggests the presence of an important genetic component in schizophrenia.

While the theories we have mentioned may seem like competing approaches to a particular problem, they usually are applied to different aspects of the total behavior. Consequently, the theories are complementary rather than competitive. For example, in certain cases of mental retardation, identifiable endocrine deficits or brain anomalies appear. On the other hand, a psychodynamic or learning approach would probably be more effective in cases of neurotic behavior which give no indication of being related to bodily defects.

The Range of Abnormal Behavior

One of the problems that confront clinical workers is the lack of universally accepted standards of abnormal behavior. According to a _statistical criterion_, it is behavior that occurs infrequently. According to a _consensual criterion_, it is behavior that society generally perceives as dangerous, anxiety-provoking, or socially disruptive. Although this standard provides a useful guideline for many clinicians, they do not accept such social evaluations as anything more than value judgments about behavior. In short, consensual as well as statistical criteria of abnormality are relative standards, not absolute measurements.

Personal criteria vary widely, because they include any behavior that an individual labels as "problem behavior" for himself. Many neurotics enter psychotherapy, not because they feel socially or vocationally unsuccessful, but because they feel anxious and unhappy despite their accomplishments. Each of these criteria—statistical, consensual, and personal—has its practical uses, but no single one can fully define abnormal behavior.

Figure 20-3 shows the incidence of several types of abnormal behaviors, as reflected in the rates of first admissions to mental hospitals in 1965. The rates are classified according to the patient's age and the type

20-3
Incidence of mental disorders according to age among patients admitted for the first time to United States county and state mental hospitals in 1965. Those hospitalized each year represent only a portion of the total number of people who seek help. (Kramer, 1969)

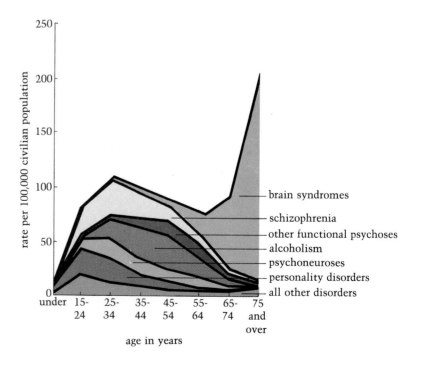

of disorder. Notice that different disorders reach their peak during different age periods. One clear example is abnormal behavior linked to brain defects (brain syndromes). Behavioral adequacy, like physical health, tends to deteriorate in old age; thus a high percentage of patients in mental hospitals are old people. Their problems range from extreme psychosis to a mild behavioral incapacity complicated by the absence of family or friends who might provide sufficient emotional support for the individual to maintain himself in the community.

This figure does not give a comprehensive picture of the incidence of behavior disorders because it is limited to hospitalized people. Many psychiatrists and other physicians, clinical psychologists, and social workers devote most of their time to people with less debilitating conditions—most notably, those with neuroses that do not require the individual to live in a mental hospital. For example, in a study of one English town, 81 out of every 1000 residents sought help from general practitioners for apparently neurotic problems, 44 out of every 1000 residents sought the help of a psychiatrist, and only 1.9 out of every 1000 residents were hospitalized for psychiatric treatment (Taylor & Chase, 1964). While most clinical psychologists are employed by nonprofit agencies (state hospitals, community mental hygiene clinics), the majority of psychiatrists are in private practice and their clients consist of those who can afford to pay fees ranging from $20 to $100 per hour of consultation.

Abnormal behavior may be major or minor. It may involve intellectual inadequacies, dissatisfaction with oneself, pent-up or uncontrolled emotions, or a combination of these factors. It may reflect poor social relationships, bodily defects, maladaptive tendencies acquired through learning, or combinations of these influences. But whatever the causes may be, the total cost of behavior disorders is staggering. It is impossible to estimate the personal and social costs—the unhappiness and disruption caused by abnormal behavior. However, we do know that half of all hospital beds in daily use in the United States are occupied by psychiatric patients. Estimates of the annual economic cost of behavior disorders range upward from $20 billion.

Such cost estimates include one special kind of behavior disorder—the mammoth problem of crime and its consequences. Millions of serious crimes are committed every year in the United States; over a million juveniles are arrested each year. But if society responds to crime with alarm, other forms of disorder evoke less vigorous responses. The particular problems of living associated with poverty and old age often are compounded by social isolation and neglect.

Assessment and Classification

Any abnormal behavior raises questions about its causes, the conditions that maintain it, and the treatment that might reduce or eliminate it. What is the history of the problem? Do the people involved—the patient, his relatives, his co-workers—agree on the nature of the problem and its severity? How severely incapacitated is the patient? Why is professional help being sought *now*? What course of action might be effective?

20-4
A drawing by Pieter Brueghel (1525–1569) of women afflicted with St. Vitus' Dance. The symptoms—falling down, twitching, and jerking about—were previously considered to be signs of madness. It later was learned that St. Vitus' Dance is a nervous disorder that involves involuntary muscular contractions. (The Bettmann Archive)

Several assessment procedures are used to answer such questions. The usual purpose of assessment is to form a _diagnosis_ of the problem. Diagnosis places a given case within a classification system that groups behavior disorders according to noticeable similarities. The most commonly used classification system is that of the American Psychiatric Association, published in its _Diagnostic and Statistical Manual_ (1968). Classification provides a basis for communication among clinical workers; it enables them to keep statistical records of the incidence of various types of problems and to plan therapeutic programs.

Classification is nothing more than an attempt to identify various behavioral disorders in terms of their similarities and differences. Despite its usefulness, classification of abnormal behavior is in a primitive stage of development. Moreover, many leading psychologists and psychiatrists oppose the whole idea of classification. Why is this so?

First, many maintain that classification violates the individuality and uniqueness of the person who should be the focus of attention in abnormal psychology. Second, these critics suggest that individual differences are essentially a matter of degree. People do not fit neatly into categories and consequently any classification system creates artificial distinctions. Some psychologists feel that the differences between behavior disorders are simply quantitative rather than qualitative. That is, the difference between two disturbed individuals is a matter of degree of disturbance rather than a difference in kind. Rather than try to categorize a person as psychotic or neurotic, schizophrenic or depressive, it is better to examine the extent to which his normal adaptive behavior has been disrupted.

Those who believe that mental illness is a myth point to a recent study by Rosenhan (1973). In this controversial study, a small number of normal subjects were trained to describe themselves as having subjective symptoms indicative of psychosis. They easily convinced psychiatrists that they were "mentally ill," and as a result they all were hospitalized. Once hospitalized, they behaved normally, but this did not lead to a change in diagnosis or release from the hospital. Those opposed to diagnosis say that this study demonstrates the lack of validity and lack of underlying reality of the classification system. Experienced clinicians see the study as demonstrating the obvious—a patient can mislead an internist, a neurologist, or a psychiatrist if he lies about his symptoms. Moreover, symptoms do not exist in a constant state. Consequently, their temporary disappearance does not ordinarily lead to an immediate change in diagnosis.

The Psychoses

The _psychoses_ are the most serious forms of mental disorder. They are the types of disturbance that the public links with "insanity" and "mental illness," because they are characterized by the most extreme and dramatic departures from normal behavior. While psychoses appear in tremendous variety some of their leading characteristics are:

1. The individual is likely to be _institutionalized_. Most of the patients

20-5
Many psychotics are divorced from reality. They sit or lie by themselves, focusing on personal fantasies. They may be unaware of anyone or anything around them. (Ken Heyman)

who find their way temporarily or permanently into mental hospitals are diagnosed as psychotic.

2. Typically, the individual has *little or no insight* into the nature or severity of his disorder.

3. *Interference with normal perception of reality* is severe. The individual has difficulty in accurately perceiving the world around him; he often confuses internal feelings and memories with his perceptions of the outer environment.

4. Somatic or *physical therapies* are used more often to treat psychoses than other forms of mental disorder. Psychotherapy is often ineffective because many psychotics are unable to sustain meaningful and close personal relationships.

5. Typically, *anxiety does not play a key role* in these disorders.

6. The individual often frankly expresses his *acceptance of impulses and emotions* that would *normally be completely unacceptable.* As this suggests, he cannot distinguish clearly between that which would normally be unconscious and that which is conscious.

7. *Interference with normal thought processes* is present to some degree in all psychoses. This ranges from an inability to speak coherently or rationally to a single, highly specific irrational belief; but in all cases the person displays some degree of disturbed or irrational thinking.

Although psychotic disturbances can be categorized in many ways, a fundamental distinction often is made between organic and functional disorders. *Organic psychoses* are related to identifiable damage to the nervous system. Psychoses resulting from brain injuries are perhaps the clearest examples. *Functional psychoses* are not connected with known physical damage to the nervous system, although many believe that eventually evidence for such damage will be found; if this should happen, the distinction between functional and organic will be eliminated.

We shall discuss several functional psychoses, in particular the varieties of schizophrenia and affective or emotional disturbances.

Schizophrenic Reactions

Schizophrenia is by far the most frequent form of serious mental disorder; in many respects it is the strangest, most baffling, and most difficult to understand. Of all the functional psychoses, it is one of the most resistant to cure and generally the most incapacitating. Little wonder that schizophrenia has been the focus of research and theoretical attention for many decades.

Schizophrenics occupy almost two-thirds of the beds in mental hospitals. The incidence of all forms of schizophrenia has been estimated to be about 150 per 100,000 population per year (Crocetti & Lemkau, 1967). This is probably an underestimate, as many schizophrenics (especially of the simple type) live marginally—undiagnosed and untreated—outside institutions. Most schizophrenics admitted to mental hospitals are between 20 and 40 years of age, the 25 to 34 age group having the highest incidence of all age groups (Yolles & Kramer, 1969). First hospitalizations tend to average 4 to 5 months and total hospitalization throughout the schizophrenic's lifetime may be 10 years or longer.

Most observers agree that schizophrenia represents a family of disorders rather than a single, unitary process. How this family should be divided and labeled is another matter, however, and here disagreement often arises. One recent classification system focuses upon the probable outcome of the disorder. Patients with a poor prognosis are referred to as *process schizophrenics.* They show life-histories characterized by inadequate adjustment, withdrawal, social isolation, and gradual onset of the disabling symptoms. On the other hand, people classified as *reactive schizophrenics* show a more rapid onset of the disease and a higher likelihood of return to relatively normal functioning. They also have a past history of relatively successful social-personal adjustment prior to the start of the disorder, which is often associated with some identifiable traumatic experience.

The more traditional system classifies schizophrenia according to symptoms. *Simple schizophrenia* is distinguished by a progressive deterioration in normal functioning and a gradual loss of interest in the surrounding world. The disorder frequently is first observed during adolescence or young adulthood, a time when normal individuals are concerned with developing plans for the future and actively participating in various social roles. In general, the patient appears apathetic, uninterested, and relatively contented. He displays none of the violent or acute psychotic symptoms, nor any of the dramatic delusions, hallucinations, or motor symptoms of the other varieties of schizophrenia.

The following case history describes a 23-year-old former Air Force officer who was diagnosed as exhibiting simple schizophrenia:

Kent recently finished his bachelor's degree at a state university with a major in agriculture. Through an R.O.T.C. program he was able to enter military service with a commission. His first six months in service were uneventful although he seemed to be quite listless and indifferent toward his career. He was likeable enough to his peers, mainly because he asked little of them but was always himself a "soft touch." Loaning out money without being repaid did not seem to disturb him; in fact, he seemed to have become quite isolated from his surroundings. The other officers and enlisted men often made jokes at his expense, but could stir no reactions other than a mild smile every now and then. Emotional display seemed entirely absent. As his first year of service reached its end, Kent came to the attention of his superiors because of his "eccentric" behaviors. He had taken to talking to himself, sometimes quietly muttering, at other times speaking aloud. His sleeping habits were sometimes altered and he would spend part of the evening sitting with a stray dog that he had found. His ability to carry through an order or to delegate a task became increasingly more impaired as he appeared barely to take notice of commands. He was referred for a psychiatric evaluation and diagnosed as a schizophrenic reaction, simple type.

*Kent had always seemed to his immediate family an unusually with-
drawn person. In fact, he was laughingly dubbed "The Shy One"
during childhood, a nickname which seemed so appropriate even later
in life that it stuck. In elementary school he participated in few group
sports or activities, preferring to be alone. While the other children enjoyed remaining at the school playground when classes were over, Kent
left school by himself and spent most of his hours in his room at home.
In high school he was a model student in the sense that he never was a
disciplinary problem, knew enough to get by, and was always polite.
Few teachers felt that he was reachable, none noticed any topic about
which he could become "fired-up." At the university he spent more of
his time with the animals and in the fields than with his fellow
students. He joined a fraternity but this seemed more for the convenience of the living arrangement. Parties generally found him a quiet
observer, although he occasionally allowed himself to be prompted into
participating. He soon became the butt of many jokes because of his
tendency to work in the yard while others were busy meeting and chat-
ting with coeds. The joking barbs never seemed to penetrate his almost
too even-tempered disposition. None of his friends ever felt they knew
him in any real sense, and most of them found it difficult to explain
how he ever decided to volunteer for advanced R.O.T.C.*

*Kent was given a medical discharge from the military. He made an
abortive attempt to enter outpatient treatment on the request of a
friend. However, this lasted for one session. He was last heard of
leaving the state in his car, heading toward farming land where he
thought of seeking intermittent employment in soil conservation.*
(Suinn, 1970)

The main symptom of *hebephrenic schizophrenia* is silliness. Such patients appear childish and immature; they show plentiful evidence of
bizarre thoughts and peculiar overt acts. Giggling and silly mannerisms and gestures are common, and emotional responses are often
inappropriate. Such patients sometimes display "word salad" or "word
hash" in which words are spoken without any apparent coherence or
logical connection. Thus a 20-year-old hebephrenic girl uttered the following:

*Losh, I don't know what it is. You see—she says—I don't know, I'm
sure. There Cinderella. There is a much better play than that. "I don't
know," I said. He is an awful idiot. Oh dear God, I'm so stupid. That's
putting two and two together—saying I really don't know—saying
Cathie, and so I observe and—flowers. An orange and shoe laces. The
gabardine skirt. They like my hair bobbed but I'm so stupid. Contrary
Mary. Statues at Copland and Lye's. "Oh," I said, "Yes, yes, yes." "I'd
go off to sleep immediately afterwards." I said, "I know quite well."
"Nothing," I said. I forget all that I saw next. The next thing was—eh?
The poor man's mad. They'll be chopping off our heads next, and—ca-
lendars tied with blue ribbons. . . .* (Henderson & Gillespie, 1956)

Catatonic schizophrenia is usually distinguished by bizarre motor
symptoms (physical movements and gestures) and by the alternation of

20-6
Letters and drawings by schizophrenics illustrate the patients' loss of contact with reality. To the trained observer, handwriting characteristics of personality disintegration also are apparent. (Thea Stein Lewinson and the *American Journal of Psychiatry;* UPI)

excitement and stupor. Patients often swing from extremes of motor inhibition to motor agitation. While in a stuporous state, patients may stay almost completely immobile and appear indifferent to everything going on around them. Such patients sometimes display stereotyped patterns of motor behavior such as *echopraxia* (compulsive repetition of the actions of someone he is observing); *echolalia* (compulsive repetition of the speech of an observed person); *waxy flexibility* (holding his body in a particular position—even one that is uncomfortable and difficult to maintain—for as long as several hours). Often, the motor symptoms are associated with hallucinations (perceptions in the absence of an adequate stimulus) and delusions (a false belief system). The disorder usually has the most rapid onset of all the varieties of schizophrenia and the likelihood of recovery is consistently more favorable.

Paranoid schizophrenia is characterized by an array of hallucinations and delusions. Some clinicians distinguish between paranoid schizophrenia and paranoia, pointing to the greater general deterioration and loss of function of schizophrenic patients. We shall consider them as a single disorder with varying degrees of general intactness and capacity to behave adaptively.

While the delusions of a paranoid person can take any form, we can identify four common types. If he has _delusions of self-reference,_ an individual feels that everything that goes on around him, no matter how coincidental or apparently unrelated, actually is directed at or refers to him. If he sees his behavior as subject to the control of external forces such as electrical currents, voices, or spiritual beings, he has _delusions of control._ You will recall that we discussed delusions of persecution and grandeur in Chapter 8. A person with _delusions of persecution_ believes that some person or group is determined to bring about his downfall and destruction, even though their actual relationship may be one of neutrality or even love. _Delusions of grandeur_ lead a person to consider himself far more gifted, famous, or influential than is actually the case. Such delusions often are coupled with hallucinations, which are typically auditory. Thus, voices may control his behavior, they may assert that he is Napoleon or Jesus, or they may warn him of the danger he faces from an associate or even a stranger. This combination of strong delusional systems and hallucinations makes the paranoid the most dangerous of all psychotics. Indeed, many of the well-known mass murderers of past years are known or suspected to have been paranoid.

Paranoia tends to appear somewhat later in life than other forms of schizophrenia and usually involves less intellectual and emotional deterioration than other schizophrenias.

Infantile Autism

In 1944, Kanner suggested that a severe form of childhood psychosis, associated with a variety of bizarre symptoms, might be a different disorder rather than a form of childhood schizophrenia. Though complete agreement has not yet been reached, the dominant point of view today is that *infantile autism* does constitute a separate disorder (Rimland, 1964). Children showing autistic symptoms are generally healthy and are considered to possess a high degree of intelligence. The actual IQ is often difficult to ascertain, because all such children show some interference with normal language and many are totally unable to use language for ordinary communication. Perhaps the disorder's most distinctive feature is the child's inability to form relations with people—indeed, a primary symptom is strong resistance to physical or social contact, even with parents. At the same time, the child often is fascinated by physical objects and obsessively concerned that everything in the environment be preserved unchanged.

The fact that these children appear physically healthy, have normal motor skills, show signs of unusual intellectual ability, and typically come from families with no history of mental illness has created a special interest in the syndrome. It has also led to many attempts to treat the disorder by a variety of techniques, most of which have been quite unsuccessful. Early researchers thought the disorder resulted from a severe deprivation of maternal affection, but in recent years there has been a growing belief in the likelihood of a physical-biological basis for the disorder. The following case history illustrates many of the symptoms that characterize this puzzling psychosis.

A boy of five was brought for initial consultation because his school could not accept his behavior. The history taken from his parents revealed that from early infancy he was considered an incredibly "good" child. He never cried, never fussed, and was content to be alone in his crib for as long as the parents would permit. They then noted that he seemed oblivious to them and nonresponsive. Their first concern was for his hearing. He was evaluated by the family physician and referred to pediatric examination for possible deafness. Subsequent examination ruled this out, and careful neurological examinations were completed to rule out the possibility of brain damage. His behavior became more bizarre, with hand-clapping, twirling, jumping and bouncing, and peculiar posturing. The family was unable to toilet-train the child or teach him any verbal communication. Yet he seemed very bright—almost gifted in certain ways. For example, he developed highly skilled fine-motor coordination in playing endlessly with small toys and subsequently developed phenomenal skill in ball throwing and catching. He never developed speech and subsequently had to be institutionalized in a special school, where he was able to achieve a good institutional adjustment. (Lustman, 1966)

Determinants of Schizophrenia. Given the widespread interest in schizophrenia, it is not surprising that many theories exist concerning its causes. According to the psychodynamic position, the irrational thoughts and bizarre behavior of a schizophrenic person represent the intrusion of unconscious, illogical material into conscious awareness and overt behavior. Psychodynamically, the schizophrenic's inhibitions and fear of close interpersonal contacts result from profoundly frustrating, pathological contacts with other significant individuals (usually his parents) during the early years of life. While the schizophrenic's withdrawal into himself may proceed unnoticed for many years, symptoms appear when life crises unleash previously controlled thoughts and fantasies.

To learning theorists, the distinctive feature of schizophrenia is the extinction or lack of development of conventional responses to social stimuli. Accompanying this social impoverishment is the acquisition of a highly personalized response repertory that, no matter how unusual, has been learned in the same way as conventional responses. In this view, hallucinations take the place of conventional social rewards. Because the individual has deprived himself of the rewards of meaningful personal relationships, his hallucinations may take on considerable value—as comforting companions, perhaps. A similar process takes place when normal people are subjected to extreme isolation, as we saw in Chapter 4.

From a sociological or social psychological perspective, the schizophrenic person responds to stress with (1) personalized reactions, such as self-degradation and distorted self-images and (2) an inability to shift from one social role to another. This inability, believed to arise from inadequate early childhood socialization, prevents the schizophrenic from seeking new ways of responding to conflict. One sociological variable that has been linked quite definitely to schizophrenia is social class. Little doubt exists that a disproportionate number of schizophrenics come from lower socioeconomic strata. However, this relationship has been interpreted in various ways. Sociologists believe the high correlation indicates that the pressures of poverty cause schizophrenia. Other theorists offer the social drift explanation: schizophrenics tend to collect in the lower strata because they are unable to earn an adequate living or maintain personal relationships.

Much of the current research on schizophrenia involves the exploration of possible biophysical causes of the disorder. Several signs indicate that chemical substances may cause the bizarre behavior of schizophrenics. For example, mescaline and LSD can bring on temporary psychotic reactions—that is, they can produce visual and auditory hallucinations and feelings of unreality in normal people. Certain common substances are chemically similar to LSD. This has led to the theory that schizophrenics somehow convert these common substances into LSD. Researchers now are looking for evidence of such chemical transformations.

To determine the extent to which each of the above factors influences the development of schizophrenia, a number of investigators have looked for possible differences between the identical twin who becomes schizophrenic and the twin who does not. Research on this question has yielded the following:

1. The twin who later became schizophrenic weighed less at birth.

2. When he was an infant, his parents—particularly his mother—frequently perceived him as vulnerable. His survival was occasionally thought to be imperiled.

3. He was the focus of more worry and attention than his twin.

4. He developed more slowly than his twin.

5. As a child he was perceived to be less competent and weaker than his twin.

6. He tended to be the more docile and compliant of the two and he was generally less independent.

We have seen that schizophrenia is a thought disorder characterized by psychotic behavior. Many variations occur among individual cases, but social withdrawal, self-containment, and irrationality are especially noticeable in most schizophrenics. Research continues at many hospitals and universities into the determinants of the disorder and its possible cures. At the present time, no definitive cure for schizophrenia exists, although some people recover from it without treatment and there continue to be individual therapists who make strong claims for the success of their particular method of treatment.

Affective (Emotional) Disorders

Affective disorders are mood disturbances that often reach psychotic proportions. They can take several forms, including simple depression, mania, involutional depression, and circular or manic-depressive psychosis. All of these disorders disrupt normal emotional responses to such an extent that the individual's contact with reality is impaired and his capacity to adjust to the external world is limited. These disorders can lead to hospitalization. Most patients with affective disorders are characteristically either depressed or elated. One estimate suggests that, of such patients, about 40 percent are depressed, 35 percent are manic, and only 25 percent are circular or manic-depressive.

Mania. The _manic_ individual is characterized by flights of ideas; his words and thoughts appear irrational because they rush out in such a rapid and uncontrolled manner. He also displays heights of euphoria or elation, with extremes of happiness and self-confidence. Moreover, he is typically overactive, talks spontaneously, and is unable to remain quiet for even brief periods of time. Such a person's boundless energy, together with his lack of normal inhibitions, can easily lead him into unwise and even dangerous acts. The following conversation between a doctor and his 46-year-old female patient typifies the manic person's style of conversation:

Doctor — *Hello, how are you today?*

Patient — *Fine, fine, and how are you, Doc? You're looking pretty good. I never felt better in my life. Could I go for a schnapps now? Say, you're new around here, I never saw you before — and not bad! How's about you and me stepping out tonight if I can get that old battleship of a nurse to give me back my dress? It's low cut and it'll wow'em. Even in this old rag, all the doctors give me the eye. You know I'm a model. Yep, I was Number One — used to dazzle them in New York, London, and Paris. Hollywood has been angling with me for a contract.*

Doctor — *Is that what you did before you came here?*

Patient — *I was a society queen — entertainer of kings and presidents. I've got five grown sons and I wore out three husbands getting them . . . about ready for a couple more now. There's no woman like me, smart, brainy, beautiful, and sexy. You can see I don't believe in playing myself down. If you are good and know you're good you have to speak out, and I know what I've got.*

Doctor — *Why are you in this hospital?*

Patient — *That's just the trouble. My husbands never could understand me. I was too far above them. I need someone like me, with savoir faire you know, somebody that can get around, intelligent, lots on the ball. Say, where can I get a schnapps around here — always like one before dinner. Someday I'll cook you a meal. I've got special recipes like you never ate before . . . sauces, wines, desserts. Boy, it's making me hungry. Say, have you got anything for me to do around here? I've been showing those slowpokes how to make up beds but I want something more in line with my talents.*

Doctor — *What would you like to do?*

Patient — *Well, I'm thinking of organizing a show, singing, dancing, jokes. I can do it all myself but I want to know what you think about it. I'll bet there's some schnapps in the kitchen, I'll look around later. You know what we need here . . . a dance at night. I could play the piano, and teach them the latest steps. Wherever I go I'm the life of the party. (Coleman, 1964)*

Depression. <u>Depressive disorders</u> are characterized by negative emotions and reduced physical activity. The individual appears sad, careworn, discouraged, and manifests little interest in what goes on about him. His speech tends to be slow and infrequent and he is often physically immobile for long periods of time. Usually he feels unworthy and blames himself for past misdeeds. He tends to have little interest in eating, and consequently he loses weight. Of all the forms of mental disorder, depression is most likely to lead to self-injury or self-destruction; institutionalization is often necessary to prevent suicide. Depression occurs in many forms, ranging from mild disturbances that leave the individual in relatively good contact with the outer world (neurotic depression) to severe depressions in which the individual appears to have lost all capacity to relate to reality.

The following case illustrates several features of psychotic depression. One such feature is that events ordinarily leading to understandable, temporary mourning and grief result instead in long-term immobilization, thought and behavioral disturbances, and bizarre fears:

Mr. T. S., aged 40, married and the father of three children, was hospitalized after a consultation between his family physician and a psychiatrist. In the hospital, if left to his own devices, he would spend most of his time sitting on a chair by the side of his bed, moaning and wringing his hands. His facial expression was one of the deepest dejection, and his eyes were reddened from weeping. At times, he would get up and pace the floor heavily. . . . Mr. S. had no appetite, and, if left to himself, would not eat. He was severely constipated. He tended to ignore his personal appearance and hygiene completely. He was insomniac although appearing to be fatigued.

As a rule, Mr. S. would not speak unless spoken to, but occasionally he would address another patient or a member of the ward staff. At such times he would usually blame himself in the harshest terms for having "ruined his family," saying that he did not deserve to live. Now and then, paradoxically, he would express fears of dying, saying that he was certain that he had some incurable disease, the nature of which the doctors were concealing from him.

The physical and laboratory findings were essentially negative except for indications of rather marked recent weight loss and mild dehydration.

The patient was unable to give an adequate history of the present illness, but Mrs. S. gave a rather full statement which included the following relevant material. The couple had been married for 12 years, and the marriage, for the most part, had been reasonably satisfactory. Mr. S. was the proprietor of a small business; he worked hard and was a good provider. He was a careful, conscientious, and methodical person, very fair in his dealings with others. He placed great emphasis upon routine and was disconcerted by departures from it. He seldom took a vacation, and when he did, he was apt to become restless after a few days, finding it difficult to relax. He was lacking in a sense of humor, although he tried to be a good sport about things. His business judgment was usually sound, but he was evidently an insecure person, for he seldom expressed confidence in himself.

About three months before the present admission, Mr. S. had experienced a minor business reverse. A month later, while he was still endeavoring to cope with this situation, his mother died of a heart attack. The patient was terribly distressed. He appeared to grieve deeply. He was restless and agitated. He became anorexic (lost his appetite) and increasingly insomniac. For a time he strove to carry on his business, but he was quite ineffectual and had had to turn the management over to an assistant. At first the family had interpreted his condition as one of deep mourning, but they realized that something more serious was

20-7
A therapist who detected suicidal tendencies in this painting by a depressed patient was able to foil a suicide attempt. The therapist interpreted the rising white figure as symbolic of the patient's desire to leave this world. (Edward Adamson, Director of Art, Netherne Psychiatric Hospital, England)

taking place as his self-reproach became increasingly intense and unrealistic. (He spoke of himself as having thrown away the family resources and having caused his mother's death and the impoverishment of his wife and children.) Mrs. S. had become increasingly frightened but had not known what to do. When the patient had begun to speak of himself as not deserving to live, his wife had sought medical assistance. (Hofling, 1968)

Manic-Depressive Disorders. <u>Circular</u> or <u>manic-depressive disorders</u>—characterized by alternating periods of manic excitement and depression—are the least common of the affective reactions. Sometimes a period of normal behavior separates the manic and depressive stages of the disorder. In other cases, the patient swings directly from one psychotic state to the other. Such an alternation can continue for years; one individual, admitted to a mental hospital in a state of depression, continued for 35 years (until his death) to alternate between periods of mania and depression.

Involutional Melancholia (Depression). In most respects, <u>involutional melancholia</u> is simply a form of psychotic depression. Its distinguishing features are the particular period of life at which it appears and its lower incidence of recurrence. Typically, it occurs in women during menopause (ages 40 to 50) and in men when they are likely to be undergoing changes in their sexual adequacy (ages 50 to 65). The apparent relationship between the onset of this disorder and the occurrence of significant hormonal changes has led many to suspect that it has a hormonal basis. However, current evidence for this is inconclusive. Moreover, changes in reproductive and sexual adequacy have important psychological implications, so it seems likely that involutional melancholia stems more from psychological stress than from hormonal changes.

Causes of Affective Disorders. It is generally agreed that situational factors play a major role in the onset of affective disorders—particularly the loss, real or fancied, of a loved person or object. The disturbance may follow the death of a loved one or it may be associated with some apparently trivial loss. The psychodynamic view is that the individual is really responding to an infantile or childhood loss (for example, loss of a parent or a parent's love) that is symbolized by the current event. Moreover, such theorists consider states of mania or elation to be functionally very close to depressive states. That is, the individual attempts to ward off his despondency by a desperate and unrealistic flight into elation. In psychoanalytic terms, mania represents the use of reaction formation to avoid depression (see Chapter 11, which describes this and other defense mechanisms). This explains why the extremes of mania are just as rigid, unswerving, and desperate as the extremes of depression.

As we have mentioned, many researchers believe that affective disorders are associated with biological factors. The hormonal changes that accompany menopause, the fact that various pharmacological agents induce changes in mood states (even of psychotic proportions), and the clear demonstration of genetic influences, all add up to substantial support for the biophysical position. For example, Kallman reports a concordance rate for monozygotic twins in manic-depressive psychosis of 100 percent, while for dizygotic twins the rate is only 24 percent and for siblings 23 percent. Virtually all comparable studies have provided strong evidence that genetic factors play a role in this disorder (Rosenthal, 1970).

The evidence for biological determinants in affective disorders, and the indications that situational factors and early experience also play an important role in them, does not rule out the role of learning in this disorder. Indeed, the association of current situational factors with early experiences strongly suggests that some kind of conditioning mechanism is also at work.

The Neuroses

More frequent and less severe than the psychoses are the so-called moderate mental disorders—the <u>neuroses</u>. Neurotics suffer, and they function at less than an optimal level—but they function. They maintain relations with the real world and usually do not have to be institutionalized, even though they may be fearful and inhibited and find it difficult to sustain rewarding interpersonal relations.

Estimating the incidence of neurosis is difficult because the lesser forms of neurotic behavior seldom receive attention from agencies, such as clinics and hospitals, that maintain careful records. One group of investigators (Srole, Langner, Michael, Opler, & Rennie, 1962) found that 30 percent of a metropolitan population had mild neurotic disturbances and 22 percent had moderately severe neurotic symptoms. Neurotic disorders can occur at any age but they appear most often between adolescence and the mid-30s.

*Table 20-1   Comparison of Neurotic and Psychotic Disorders
(Coleman, 1964)*

Factor	Psychoneuroses	Psychoses
General behavior	Mild degree of personality dysfunction; reality contact and social functioning impaired	Severe degree of personality dysfunction; reality contact markedly impaired; patient incapacitated in social functioning
Nature of symptoms	Wide range of psychological and somatic symptoms but no hallucinations or other extreme deviations in thought, feeling, or action	Wild range of symptoms with delusions, hallucinations, emotional blunting, and other severely deviate behavior
Orientation	Patient rarely loses orientation to environment	Patient frequently loses orientation to environment
Insight	Patient often has some insight into nature of his behavior	Patient rarely has insight into nature of his behavior
Social aspects	Behavior rarely injurious or dangerous to patient or to society	Behavior frequently injurious or dangerous to patient or to society
Treatment	Patient rarely needs institutional care	Patient usually needs institutional care

Anxiety States

The most frequent and characteristic neurotic symptom is anxiety. Thus, we can consider the *anxiety reaction* to be the prototype neurosis. The anxious individual suffers chronic or acute anxiety attacks that often involve a large variety of somatic and psychological symptoms. The physical symptoms may include heart palpitations, breathlessness, lack of appetite, constipation, diarrhea, twitching of muscles, weakness of limbs, blurring of vision, and so on. Besides anxiety, the psychological reactions may include an inability to concentrate, depression, irritability, and excitability. The person often feels that some dire event is impending but cannot specify what it is or explain his anxious feelings.

The following case illustrates an anxiety reaction. If you compare it with the cases of psychosis given earlier, it will help you to clarify some of the differences between major and minor mental disorders.

Twenty-five-year-old Harvey A. was a man with superior intelligence (verbal I.Q. over 130 as estimated from a short form of the Wechsler Adult Intelligence Scale) when he sought help at a psychological clinic. He had performed poorly in high school and had to repeat his junior year. After graduation, he held a succession of temporary jobs for a year or two, and then enrolled in, and successfully completed, two years at a junior college. He was subsequently admitted to a state university, where he experienced great difficulty with his academic work. He spent long hours in inefficient studying, read very slowly, and was particularly distressed by a severe difficulty in spelling. A course in remedial spelling did no good. Harvey A. dropped out of school after a year, and has since held a number of unskilled jobs.

He has had as many difficulties in his social relations as in the academic and vocational areas. His father died when he was 14. Shortly thereafter his mother began to have a series of affairs that eventuated in a brief marriage to a man who was apparently an alcoholic. This stepfather was belligerent and assaultive when drunk, and Harvey recalled several incidents in which his mother called on him to protect her from the stepfather's rages. In one instance a physical fight ensued in which Harvey knocked the older man down. Following his mother's divorce from this man and a period of further instability in the family situation he moved in with his recently married older sister. For a short while he experienced a more relaxing home situation, obtaining "more mothering from my sister than I ever got from my mother."

More currently Harvey reports generalized feelings of tension and apprehension. He is especially sensitive to being jeered or laughed at by working men such as construction workers. He has a mustache, and this results in his being the occasional target of taunts of the kind directed by working men toward university students. He and his roommate were also pushed around a bit by four marines one night, and Harvey has since been very fearful of walking the streets after dark.

His relationship with his roommate has been a source of some distress. Harvey fears that his roommate could "destroy" him, if he chose to do so, by a sustained verbal assault. He has dated several girl friends, and has a continuing involvement with one including sexual relations. He nevertheless is apprehensive about his relationship with this girl, and worries that she may reject him.

On a checklist of fears he reported strong fear of being alone, speaking in public, failure, one person bullying another, being criticized, being rejected by others, being disapproved of by others, making mistakes, and looking foolish.

In summary, Harvey A. presented a picture of chronic inability to master academic and vocational goals, chronic difficulty in achieving satisfying interpersonal relationships, and continuing fearfulness in many situations that seem to have in common a potential for criticism and ridicule. In addition, he reports feelings of loneliness, discouragement, and depression—hardly surprising in view of the above. (Martin, 1971)

Phobic Reactions

Anxiety neurotics seem perpetually to be anticipating vague misfortunes or disasters. The *phobic* person suffers from highly specific anxieties that are also irrational. Among the more common phobias are acrophobia (fear of high places); claustrophobia (fear of enclosed spaces); and zoophobia (fear of animals). Of course, most of us have a "favorite" fear. Phobias reach serious proportions only when they interfere with the individual's life. A clinical worker who wants to understand a particular phobia must explore several contributing factors. These include the individual's present status in life, his history of interpersonal experiences, and other personality characteristics.

The history of the individual seems especially important because of the likelihood that irrational fears may be conditioned responses. Phobias tend to generalize and get progressively broader with time. A phobic reaction to spaniels, say, might develop into a reaction to all dogs. The phobic individual usually develops ways of reducing his fears (by avoiding all contact with dogs, for example). Phobic fears often develop so gradually that it is difficult to tell whether or not specific precipitating factors are involved. The following case history vividly illustrates the role of conditioning in the development of phobias:

A young woman of good heredity developed during her childhood a severe phobia of running water. She was unable to give any explanation of her disorder which persisted without improvement from approximately her seventh to her twentieth year. Her fear of splashing sounds was especially intense. For instance, it was necessary for her to be in a distant part of the house when the bathtub was being filled for her bath, and during the early years it often required the combined efforts of three members of the family to secure a satisfactory washing. She always struggled violently and screamed. During one school session a drinking-fountain was in the hall outside her classroom. If the children of the school made much noise drinking, she became very frightened, actually fainting on one occasion. When she rode on trains, it was necessary to keep the shade down so that she might not see the streams over which the train passed. (When she was 20 years old an aunt visited her and, upon hearing of her condition, responded: "I have never told." This provoked a recall of the following events that took place when she was seven years of age.) The mother, the aunt, and the little girl . . . had gone on a picnic. Late in the afternoon, the mother decided to return home but the child insisted on being permitted to stay for a while longer with her aunt. This was promptly arranged on the child's promise to be strictly obedient and the two friends (aunt and niece) went into the woods for a walk. A short time later the little girl, neglecting her agreement, ran off alone. When she was finally found she was lying wedged among the rocks of a small stream with a waterfall pouring down over her head. She was screaming with terror. They proceeded immediately to a farm house where the wet clothes were dried, but, even after this the child continued to express great alarm lest her mother should learn of her disobedience. However, her aunt reassured her with the promise "I will never tell . . ." As the older woman left the next morning for a distant city, the girl had no one in whom she could confide. On the contrary she repressed all thought of her accident and presently she was unable to recall the facts even when a serious effort was made to have her do so. (Badby, 1928)

Hysteria

Hysteria is the oldest known, most extensively studied, and most dramatic of all the neuroses. It is also a disorder that can appear in countless different forms. Typically, the hysteric displays some mixture of the following characteristics: (1) a physical symptom, defect, or deficiency in the absence of any organic or physiological cause; (2) a relatively bland and unconcerned reaction to the symptoms, no matter how serious they may appear to be; (3) the existence of dissociative tendencies, so that some portion of the individual's personality appears to operate without the awareness or cooperation of the remainder of the personality.

When the disorder consists primarily of physical symptoms without an organic basis, it is referred to as *conversion hysteria.* Any organ or function of the body may be involved, including all motor and sensory spheres. Thus, the individual may show loss of speech, paralysis of any portion of the body, or convulsions, or he may report deafness, blindness, or anesthesias (total or partial loss of sensation); or the symptoms may be no more than headaches, shortness of breath, or tremors. In conversion hysterias, the physical symptom evidently bears some relation to an unconscious wish or memory which is denied conscious expression.

Dissociative phenomena include *amnesia,* in which the individual loses his sense of identity and the capacity to recall his past; *somnambulism,* in which the individual walks or carries out other acts while apparently in a sleeping stage; and *multiple personality,* in which the individual displays two or more relatively well-organized personalities that function more or less independently of each other. These personalities ordinarily differ in important respects and often have no awareness of each other's existence. Almost everyone is familiar with *Dr. Jekyll and Mr. Hyde,* which is a fictional interpretation of the phenomenon. The factual account of the *Three Faces of Eve,* in book and film versions, is equally well known. A somewhat simpler case was reported by Erickson and Kubie (1939). A young college girl, Miss Damon, suffered from an obsessive concern that doors to the icebox, kitchen, college laboratory, locker, and such had been left open; this concern led to a compulsion to re-examine the doors. She also had an intense hatred of cats. She participated in some hypnotism experiments and then agreed to try automatic writing (writing that is not under the conscious direction of the writer). It soon became clear that she had another personality of which her conscious personality was unaware.

After she had scrawled some illegible automatic writing, she was asked to interpret it. She had a great deal of difficulty reading what she had written; while studying it, she laughingly remarked "Did I really write that nonsense?" The investigators replied lightly that she had. Without her noticing it, an investigator had slipped a new sheet of paper under her hand, which was still holding the pencil. At that moment her hand, which was out of her range of vision, wrote "No." The investigators asked "What do you mean?" and while Miss Damon puzzled over this meaningless question, her hand wrote "Can't." When asked "Why?" her hand wrote "Damon doesn't know these things." Miss Damon continued to act like a confused bystander, while the writing hand and the investigators carried on an exchange that went like this:

"Why?"
"Don't know, afraid to know."
"Who?"
"D (Damon)."
"Who does?"
"Me."
"Me?"
"Brown."
"Who?"
"Me — Brown — B."
"Explain?"
"D is D; B is B."
"B know D?"
"Yes."
"D know B?"
"No. No."
"B part of D?"
"No. B is B. D is D."
"Can I talk to B?"
"Are . . . what do you want?"
"Help D."
"Why?"
"D afraid. Do you know what D is afraid of?"
"Yes; D, no."
"Why?"
"D afraid, forgot, don't want to know . . ."

Miss Damon was then shown the questions and answers and after studying them remarked, "Why that really must mean I have a dual personality." She was startled when her writing hand responded "Right." When Miss Damon asked "Can I talk to you?" the hand replied "Sure." "Can you talk to me?" "Yes." "Is your name really Brown?" "Yes." "What is your full name?" "Jane Brown."

Further study revealed that Brown was a well-integrated, separate personality who sometimes was willing to argue actively with both the investigators and Miss Damon. In general, Brown was strongly protective of Miss Damon and in various ways tried to secure help for her, encourage her, and assist her. B's feelings could be hurt, and when D made derogatory remarks about her on several occasions, B refused to write anything except "Won't" until D apologized. Eventually Miss Damon, aided by B, recalled an early traumatic experience; with this, her initial symptoms disappeared — and so, in time, did B.

Generally, multiple personalities, like other dissociative states, are believed to represent a failure of the personality's integrative function. Some powerful conflict, involving tendencies or impulses that are denied expression, leads to the expression of these repressed tendencies through the alternate personality. Thus, a direct confrontation between the customary self and the unacceptable tendencies is avoided.

Obsessive-Compulsive Disorders

No neurosis comes closer to normal behavior than the obsessive-compulsive disorder. Modern society demands and rewards regularity, dependability, order, cleanliness, and persistence, and it is just these qualities, malignantly magnified, that typify this class of disorders.

An _obsession_ is a recurrent thought that the individual cannot put out of his mind even though it causes him pain and anxiety. It may be a simple idea, an impulse, or a complicated chain of thought. The behavioral equivalent of an obsession is a _compulsion_—an act or series of acts that the individual feels compelled to carry out, even though it may be senseless, inconvenient, or even repugnant to him. Many compulsions take the form of ritualistic behavior, such as repetitive hand-washing or stepping over every crack in the sidewalk. More pathological compulsions involve elaborate actions that must precede even the most routine acts. In extremes of this disorder, the individual may be quite literally immobilized. The following case typifies a temporary compulsive immobilization:

A young man, uncertain as to whether or not his calling up a well-to-do girl for a date would advance his cause with her, spent an anxious, miserable hour in a telephone booth, unable either to put the dime in the slot and call, or to pocket it and go home. Each time his hand approached the coin box he developed anxiety lest his calling her might ruin his chances with her; each time he let his hand fall again he developed anxiety over the possibility of his throwing away a golden opportunity. He matched every good positive argument with a good negative one, going into all the intricate ramifications of his contradictory motives, imagining everything the girl and members of her family might think about his attentions to her and about his neglect of her. He fantasied in detail, as he sat there, every possible consequence of his decision, to him and to her, on and on into remote contrasted futures.

This patient was, in fact, caught in a common compulsive dilemma. He needed a far greater degree of certainty than the ordinary person before embarking upon a given course of action. But his technique of guarding against every conceivable mischance, by imagining it as it might occur, actually drove him farther and farther from his goal the longer he employed it. In the end he had to give up the ambivalent debate and go home, feeling exasperated, chagrined and worn out. He later developed the conviction that, in not making the telephone call, he had missed the chance of a lifetime for gaining happiness and security. (Cameron, 1963).

Determinants of Neurosis

Neurotic behavior may be interpreted from several standpoints. Psychodynamic theorists see neurotic behavior as an outgrowth of mental conflict and unconscious motivations. Anxiety is the core problem; the symptoms represent defenses against anxiety or, in some cases, the failure of these defenses. To these theorists, neurotic behavior is the result of defense mechanisms erected against anxiety-inducing unconscious impulses. Most psychodynamic theories state that neurotic tendencies have their origins in the formative years of life. Although the research evidence is not conclusive, it suggests that a neurotic mother greatly increases the probability that her children will develop neuroses later in life. Neurotic behavior has been linked by many psychoanalytic writers to maternal overprotection, domination, and rejection. Separation of the child from its mother in infancy also seems related to neurosis in adult life, as do poverty and broken homes.

To learning theorists, neuroses are learned responses and response tendencies. They believe that both adaptive and neurotic behavior are learned according to the same general principles. Thus, neurotic behavior may be interpreted as operant responses that have been strengthened through systematic or unsystematic schedules of reinforcement. Neurotic behavior also may be seen as responses that are conditioned along Pavlovian lines, but in any event, conditioning is considered the key to understanding neuroses. Neurotic behavior also may be acquired through vicarious learning; the child may behave neurotically because he has observed a member of his family behave in a similar way.

The observer who believes in an organic basis for neurotic behavior can point to the effectiveness of various drugs in reducing neurotic symptoms, as well as evidence indicating a substantial genetic component in the disorders (Rosenthal, 1970).

Personality or Character Disorders

Many observers feel that neuroses are decreasing in American society and that simultaneously a striking increase in _character_ or _personality disorders_ is occurring. These disturbances lack the focal conflict and distinctive symptoms of the neuroses. They are less a reaction to stress and more a chronic mode of inadequate adjustment. While anxiety plays a key role in neurosis, being either directly expressed or defended against, character disorders typically are not associated with anxiety. These individuals simply display inadequate or ineffective patterns of behavior—indeed, they are sometimes referred to as "inadequate personalities."

An example of a personality disorder is the _hysterical personality_. An individual with this diagnosis tends to show excitability, emotional instability, and a tendency to be overly dramatic in social relationships. He is self-centered and at the same time heavily dependent upon others. Another example is the _schizoid personality_. These individuals respond with seeming detachment and indifference to stresses that most of us would find highly frustrating and conflict-laden. They tend to be shy, seclusive, and self-oriented daydreamers. The personality disorder that has received the most public attention is the _psychopathic_ or _sociopathic personality_. Psychopaths seem incapable of feeling anxiety, shame, or guilt and consequently they have few reservations about lying, cheating, and even murdering. These individuals are often socially adept and display a considerable surface charm, but this masks a basic indifference for the feelings of others and an inability to form close and enduring personal relationships.

People diagnosed as having personality disorders have been compared with both neurotics and psychotics, depending on their symptoms. Increasingly, personality disorders are viewed as characteristic modes of coping with the major and minor stresses of life. Some psychologists think that these disorders, especially the milder ones, are signs of a potential for more serious, "traditional" psychiatric disorders. They list a number of indicators of this potential for serious disturbances, such as inflexibility in adapting to situations. An individual with a personality disorder seems to perpetuate his difficulties and promote new ones for himself; he restricts his opportunities for new experiences. Another indicator is his fragility under stressful conditions. He seems to lack *ego strength*, the ability to rebound from difficulties. Thus people with personality disorders often reveal inflexibility, a tendency to stereotyped interpersonal relationships, and a tenuous stability under stress.

Despite these handicaps, most people with mild personality disorders manage a passable adjustment to life. Dramatic pathology is not characteristic of them. Instead, they usually settle into jobs and social routines that do not push them beyond their limitations. For example, schizoid personalities are generally insensitive to the feelings and thoughts of others, but many jobs demand very little in the way of interpersonal sensitivity. The same is true of other personality characteristics, such as passivity and a lack of spontaneity in dealing with others. But these characteristics provide the soil in which more serious problems may grow if conditions change.

These cases pose problems for the clinician because, while they suggest the possibility of severe derangement, no such derangement has yet occurred. Is the schizoid personality a potential schizophrenic? While some of the personality traits seen in full-blown cases of schizophrenia may be present, sufficient evidence to diagnose the individual as schizophrenic is not available. After all, he remains able to function in society despite some limitations.

The following case describes George, a man of young middle age, who has been divorced. He might well be diagnosed as a schizoid personality, as he tends to retreat into his own private world for prolonged periods. His social stability seems much reduced, and his tendency toward behavioral deterioration under stress is substantial:

George was picked up as a vagrant in a town 70 miles from his home. He had been drinking, caused considerable commotion outside a bar, made lewd comments to passersby and seemed unclear as to his whereabouts. In police headquarters he seemed stuporous and apathetic, and was minimally communicative; he remained so for the following week, during which time he was sent to a state hospital for observation.

Family history showed George to be the third of seven children; his mother, a hardworking woman, died when he was 11, and his father, a drifter and periodic drunkard, died when George was 16. George was the "queer" member of the family, always by himself, teased by his siblings, and shunned by his peers. He left school at 16, wandered for a year, took odd jobs to sustain himself, joined the Navy for a four-year tour of duty, did not care for it and has lived by himself since then in a rundown part of the city, working irregularly as a dishwasher, cook and park attendant. He married a "pick-up" while in the Navy, and lived with her "miserably" for a few months. Upon his discharge, his wife disappeared; he has not seen her since, although he heard that she was remarried; she never legally divorced George.

When not in "trouble," George does not bother people; he simply prefers to be alone. Every couple of months he goes on a binge, a wild spree in which he spends all of his money, gets into a drunken brawl and usually lands in jail. Between these episodes, he does not drink and is quiet and unobtrusive.

Psychological tests and interviews with George showed that he was of better than average intelligence, had great mistrust of others and felt humiliated by his low status in life and the shame he brought to his more successful brothers in town. He admitted being suspicious of everyone's motives, having been made a fool of so much of the time. As he put it, "nobody gives a damn about you, especially if you're not worth a damn."

With regard to his wild sprees, he claimed that he "had to do something" every so often, so as "not to go crazy doing things that don't mean nothing." When his isolation and monotony became unbearable he would "hit the bottle, and start feeling some life again." (Millon, 1969)

The prospects for successfully treating personality disorders are not good, especially in relatively disturbed individuals such as George. This is because they involve deeply ingrained habits and attitudes that pervade the whole fabric of life. In short, these individuals have failed to learn effective and adaptive means of adjustment (defenses) and consequently they function at a marginal level.

Psychosomatic Disorders

We have already mentioned one group of patients, hysterical neurotics, who have physical symptoms (for example, paralysis) but no detectable organic defects. In _psychosomatic_ or _psychophysiological disorders_, the patients suffer actual organic damage. What is particularly intriguing about these disorders is that psychological conditions evidently lead to disturbances in bodily functioning, which then cause physical damage to body tissues. Clinicians believe that the following major groups of disorders originate largely from stress or emotional conflict:

1. respiratory disorders, such as bronchial asthma;

2. cardiovascular disorders, such as high blood pressure;

3. skin disorders, such as eczema; and

4. gastrointestinal disorders, such as peptic ulcers.

Specialists do not assume that these conditions always represent an interaction between mind and body. And even when a physical disorder seems to have a clear psychological basis, medical treatment is given promptly to relieve the physical symptoms. The following case describes a patient suffering from an ulcer that seemed to have a psychological basis:

A businessman, aged 35, had been working hard under great pressure to build up his advertising agency. He was a typical "achiever" or "go-getter," full of energy, initiative and push, never able to relax, and driving himself to the limit. When one of his close associates left the firm to establish a rival agency, the patient developed a peptic ulcer. To a psychiatric consultant he at first presented a bland picture of indifference; but after reaching the point where he was able to express angry resentment over what he considered a betrayal by his former associate, his medical course showed marked improvement. (Cameron, 1963)

Determinants of Psychosomatic Disorders

Are different personality characteristics associated with specific types of psychosomatic reactions? This question has inspired efforts to isolate problems and conflicts peculiar to particular disorders. For example, persons with stomach ulcers have been described as being overtly ambitious and covertly needing to depend on others. Cases of high blood pressure have been described in terms of chronic underlying hostility associated with overt friendliness and self-control. Although these interpretations may often prove accurate, any specific disorder represents a combined function of the individual's biology, his personality development, and his various social roles. Moreover, the relative influence of these three factors is likely to vary as circumstances change. Despite these qualifications, research into psychosomatic disorders has shown that intense emotional reactions can lead to irreversible physical symptoms; subjective experiences, thoughts, feelings, and conflicts measurably affect the way in which the body functions.

Some evidence suggests that social and cultural forces help bring about some types of physical disorder. In one study, illness rates were tabulated for the crew of a naval vessel (Rubin, Gunderson, & Doll, 1969). Most illnesses occurred in a relatively small group of crew members; 29 percent of the men developed 75 percent of the illnesses. The rate of illness showed a consistent elevation during combat periods as compared with in-port periods. The illness rates were highest among men whose jobs appeared to be the most stressful. Provocative cross-cultural differences, whose causes are not obvious, suggest yet another dimension of the relationship between personality and illness. For example, Japan has one of the lowest rates of heart disease in the world; the United States has one of the highest. Dietary, climatic, and other differences complicate the interpretation of this type of finding. Yet one general relationship does emerge: Life stress and physical illness do seem to be linked, although the precise nature of the linkage is unclear at this time.

Researchers have found that people have individual patterns of autonomic response; eventually, these may help to explain why a person will develop a particular disorder. However, *why* our response patterns differ is not known. One hypothesis is that response tendencies are inherited. Another is that a symbolic association links the underlying conflict and the particular symptoms that appear. No strong evidence supports either hypothesis. We do know that individuals react to stress differently. The notion of somatic susceptibility suggests that particular organs may be vulnerable to the physiological effects of stress due to damage, genetic weakness, or early psychological experiences. Such factors as exercise and diet also may influence psychosomatic disorders. One theory is that a homeostatic mechanism may fail to reduce high-tension reactions in certain individuals. But whatever the causes, the chief components of psychosomatic disorders are stressful life conditions, strong emotional reactions, and physical symptoms.

The following account of a 23-year-old graduate student with an ulcer shows the close relationship between the individual's personality attributes, the occurrence of life crises, and physical symptoms:

This passive-ambivalent graduate student was admitted to the college infirmary following a recurrence of an old ulcer ailment. Peter's early history showed intense rivalries with an alcoholic but "brilliant" father who constantly demanded superior performances on the part of his son in both academic affairs and athletics. However, no matter how well Peter would perform, his father demonstrated "how much better he could do it now—or did it when he was young." Although Peter "quietly hated" his father, he dared not express it for fear of "being publicly humiliated by him."

In recent weeks, Peter's thesis proposal had been severely criticized by his departmental advisor. Peter believed that the professor was completely wrong in his judgments and suggestions, but dared not express these thoughts for "fear of further condemnation." Unable to vent his resentments, which were so much like those he felt toward his father, Peter's repressed emotions churned away inside and resulted in a flareup of his ulcer. (Millon, 1969)

Organic Disorders

A large and growing group of psychiatric patients have organic brain damage. However, the behavioral consequences of tissue damage to the brain are quite different from the consequences of conditions like peptic ulcers and asthma. Among the major results of brain damage are the following symptoms:

1. Perceptual distortions, in which the individual has difficulty in recognizing common stimulus patterns in his environment;

2. Memory disorders, in which the individual has trouble remembering past events and previously learned responses;

3. Impairment in attention, problem-solving, and the ability to express oneself in conventional ways and to maintain normal locomotion;

4. Organic psychoses, whose severe personality aberrations are characterized by distortions of mood and thought.

An important question in any case of brain disorder is whether the condition is acute and reversible or chronic and irreversible. Acute cases usually involve a sudden onset of rapid behavioral deterioration. The major symptoms are delirium (a profoundly agitated and confused mental state marked by hallucinations, delusions, and incoherence), stupor, and sometimes coma. Chronic cases, on the other hand, usually show a gradual onset with slow, progressive deterioration. The major symptoms are decline in interest, motivation, self-concern, and intellectual ability. Acute conditions are usually reversible if they are due to temporary disturbances in brain function, such as an infection or metabolic or toxic disturbance. Chronic conditions are irreversible; they are brought about by diffuse and permanent destruction of brain tissue. The causes of the destruction may be insidious brain lesions or chronic degenerative or vascular conditions.

Alcoholic Psychoses

One group of disorders includes both acute and chronic conditions and stems from long periods of excessive alcoholic intake. These are the *alcoholic psychoses* (see also the essay on alcoholism on the following page). *Delirium tremens* ("the d.t.'s") is an acute brain condition characterized by delirium, tremors, and terrifying visual hallucinations. Delirium tremens may not appear until after the person has stopped drinking; it can last longer than a week. Some chronic alcoholics suffer substantial and irreversible damage to brain tissue. In these cases, behavior becomes so disorganized that the alcoholic requires continuing hospital supervision.

General Paresis

A historically significant discovery in the scientific study of abnormal behavior was the finding, at the turn of the century, that syphilitic infection causes progressive deterioration in brain tissue, resulting eventually in a vegetative level of existence. Before its cause and therapy were discovered, patients with *general paresis*, as the disease is called, represented up to one-third of all admissions to mental hospitals. Within two years of infection, most untreated syphilitics will show a positive cerebrospinal fluid Wasserman test, which indicates the presence of syphilitic antibodies in the blood serum. If diagnosed in the early years, the syphilitic infection can be treated with drugs, usually penicillin. Though the infection can be cured, any damage to neural tissue is irreversible.

Senile Dementia

A common type of disorder today, and one that represents a growing social problem, is *senile dementia* or *senile brain disease*. This is a progressive organic deterioration seen in people over the age of 60. Of first admissions to public mental hospitals, 25 percent are persons over the age of 65, and 80 percent of these patients are diagnosed as having senile brain disease. The causes of senile brain disease are not known.

20-8
At Mount Sinai Hospital in New York baboons were used as models in studying the effect of alcohol on the body. Two baboons became so addicted that they experienced d.t.'s upon the withdrawal of alcohol. (The New York Times/Larry Morris)

ALCOHOLISM

Daniel X. Freedman *University of Chicago*

Perhaps it is a mischievous trick of nature that people who use chemicals for a pleasurable change of mental state risk serious adverse consequences. "Alcoholism" is a blanket term for patterns of alcohol consumption that are linked to these adverse consequences. They range from unwanted loss of control in acute intoxication and subsequent hangover to different degrees of physical and psychological dependence on the drug. Alcohol can have many social, psychological, and physical consequences as well. These include violent and impulsive crimes, marital and family discord, job failure, and other frustrations of social expectations, as well as injuries and deaths on the highway. Psychological consequences include a high rate of suicide and depression. Among the psychophysiological and organic consequences are delirium tremens, hallucinosis, gastritis, poor nutrition, and vitamin B deficiencies. Moderate deficiencies of Vitamin B have reversible effects on peripheral nerve fibers. Severe deficiencies affect the brain, leading to Korsakoff's psychosis—a disorder characterized by an inability to register external events or consolidate them in the memory. This leads to disorganized speech and confabulation—the jumbling together of fact and fantasy in memory. Finally, there is cirrhosis—the inflamation, scarring, and hardening of the liver—which is frequently fatal.

Most consumers of alcohol manage to avoid these pitfalls well enough so that drinking remains a social and personal pleasure, and most cultures provide implicit guidelines for the occasions and patterns of its use. Since frequency and amounts consumed vary in different cultures (as they also do among individuals and in the same individual from time to time), no absolute criterion can define alcoholism and tell us what degree of consequences or consumption merit inclusion in that category.

In *The Lost Weekend*, Charles Jackson wrote that the alcoholic is one who can take it or leave it—but takes it! In practical terms, alcoholism is a condition in which the drinker has serious problems about drinking and drinks anyway. E. M. Jellinek, who pioneered alcohol research, defined alcoholism as use that causes damage to the individual or society. In the United States, by the best (though imprecise) estimates, over 9 million people are alcoholics at any one time, and 5 million of these are in serious trouble. The numbers of alcoholic women and young people are increasing noticeably. The average alcohol consumer has about a 6% chance of becoming a problem drinker or alcoholic, but it is noteworthy that about 20 percent of America's 9 million alcoholics enter and leave that category every year. While alcoholism is not necessarily a life-long disorder, it commonly is, and life expectancy (though somewhat greater for moderate drinkers than for abstainers) is distinctly less for problem drinkers and even ex-alcoholics. In short, it is not alcohol itself, but the way it is used—or not used—that affects longevity.

The down-and-out skid row drunk represents only a small proportion of those with serious drinking problems. Most definitions of alcoholism include two key concepts: the inability to abstain and the degree of control over intake. These concepts can distinguish both individual and cultural patterns of alcoholism. The Finnish pattern is characterized by regular episodes of poor control over intake, separated by intervals of abstinence. The

French pattern consists of an inability to abstain, combined with relative control over steady daily intake. Some American patterns are characterized by an inability to stop once drinking starts, but, of course, it is the individual drinking pattern that is of central interest in any one case.

Many people who could not be classified as problem drinkers value their habit; they look forward to their daily drink or two and miss it if circumstances interfere, but they can abstain without severe distress or alcohol-seeking behavior. The key factor is not the quantity of alcohol consumed but how the individual weaves the use of alcohol into the fabric of his or her life. It is not easy to detect when drinking becomes a problem. The alcoholic may begin with social drinking and then subtly over-value the tension reduction, gradually increasing his consumption, using a drink for courage or to avoid internal stress or external demands. Thus he generalizes and learns to use alcohol for more and more varied occasions of minor frustration. As use becomes heavier, "blackouts" or amnesia for events during intoxication occur. Periods of depression, remorse, and guilt increase, marked by sneaking and gulping drinks. Lies and alibis to explain away the drinking are commonplace. Depression and hangover after drinking lead to more drinking and a pattern of dropping out. The so-called "crucial phase" is a definite loss of control over drinking, characterized by solitary consumption, uncontrolled benders, subsequent apologies, and loss of self-esteem. At this stage, the alcoholic begins secretly organizing the day around the need to protect the alcohol supply. Near-paranoid resentments and displacement of blame onto fate and family are common. This situation may develop over a period of ten years or longer, building up until crises mount in frequency and intensity and the user "hits bottom," reluctantly "facing the facts" at last.

The family's role in protecting or provoking drinking has often been observed; alternations of angry blame and subsequent placating are common. Non-alcoholic spouses may actually feel a sense of increased self-esteem and self-justification through the burden they endure. As a result, they devote their energies to handling repeated crises rather than to the more difficult task of finding the self-awareness and consistency necessary for solutions.

Perhaps 10 to 15 percent of alcoholics are psychiatrically disturbed; for them, alcohol is a misdirected self-treatment. Some people are highly sensitive to small quantities of alcohol and quickly lose control over their aggressive impulses. For others, a single drink leads to a loss of control over subsequent drinking behavior. As Alcoholics Anonymous members put it, "one drink is too many and 20 are not enough." They call this lifelong vulnerability an allergy—a kind of built-in temptation—which means there is no permanent cure for alcoholics, but only one more day of successful abstinence. Both AA and some experts speak of alcoholism as a disease. It certainly is a behavioral dysfunction—and to speak of it in these terms enables us to apply enlightened scientific and rehabilitative approaches rather than useless moralizing.

The search for causes of alcoholism has not led to a distinctive weighting of the complex variables that seem associated with it; nor is it reasonable, given the different kinds of people and drinking problems, to hope that one theory would fit all the patterns of consumption and consequences. As a result, theories abound. Various researchers have seen abnormal drinking as a form of learned behavior linked to uncon-

scious internal conflicts and early emotional deprivations, or to social pressures and prohibitions, as well as to constitutional genetic factors and biochemical mechanisms. A range of biobehavioral factors could predispose a person to drink, or precipitate an episode of drinking, or reduce the ability to control intake once it has begun. But the search for distinctive personality variables that predispose a person to drink has not been productive; we cannot forewarn someone on the basis of his or her personality profile.

However, clinicians have identified some clusters of personality characteristics in some alcoholics. Alcoholics frequently come from broken homes, and male alcoholics often identify with an alcoholic parent. Many alcoholics are described as displaying sexual immaturity, latent homosexual strivings, suppressed anger, markedly self-destructive activities, and a low frustration tolerance coupled with a strong perfectionist drive. Some alcoholics also show traits of excessive shyness, or gregariousness linked with a strong moralistic inhibition from which alcohol may be a relief. Such observations describe the psychology and personality patterns commonly encountered, but they do not distinguish cause or consequence. In identifying precipitating stresses rather than predisposing factors, some observers have noted the sensitivity of many alcoholics to frustration and to minor rebuffs to their self-esteem. This highly sensitive and vulnerable pride seems to characterize a good many alcoholics.

There is strong evidence that alcoholism can be a familial disease. For 75 years, psychiatrists have noted this tendency, reporting rates of alcoholism in the fathers and brothers of a patient that were five times the normal. Recent controlled studies of alcoholic patients' family histories indicate that male members of the patient's family will show alcohol-

ism and female members, depressive disorders (Winokur et al., 1970). A strong interest in possible genetic factors in alcoholism was stirred by animal experiments in which specific strains of mice were found to metabolize alcohol faster than others.

Twin studies indicate that if one twin is an alcoholic, the identical twin's chances are 60% of being alcoholic compared with 20% for the dizygotic twin. A recent study in Denmark indicates that the son of an alcoholic parent, though reared from infancy in an adoptive family, nevertheless had a four times greater chance of becoming an alcoholic than if his biological parents were not alcoholic. Obviously, more work is required, but this predisposing factor is impressive, no matter how it operates to produce the ultimate outcome we call alcoholism.

One fact is amply clear: For the vulnerable, alcohol is an enormously potent reinforcement, even more potent than the drastically punitive consequences alcoholics endure. Alcohol's reinforcing power may explain why it is so extraordinarily difficult for many alcoholics to give it up. The alcoholic's power to self-administer relief, to privately revise reality with a single gulp and thus avoid consequences and demands, is a powerful motive indeed. All addicts find comfort in a familiar experience: the very act of puffing on a cigarette or swallowing a pill is a way of exerting control over what the next few seconds or minutes will bring. Such acts serve as slight but obviously highly valued barriers against intrusion and the unexpected.

This overvaluation of private control reflects a high degree both of insecurity and wishful thinking. It seems to rest on a deep-seated notion of personal omnipotence—an idea that one can be invulnerable to an act's ordinary consequences. This wishful approach includes a notion that is common to all risk-taking: "It can't happen to me." It is characteristic of addicts to believe that they can take the risks and somehow avoid the consequences that are so evident to others. This occurs because the addict's attention is focused on the moment-to-moment pseudo-control of his own state—a control he values enormously.

This intrinsic capacity to escape reality and manipulate pleasure states is at least partially shaped by learning and experience during growth and development. Many formal and informal tutoring systems help the growing child as well as the adult to regulate pleasure and pain; maternal behavior provides infants with comfort and barriers against the unexpected until they gain some capacity to deal with it. These family practices and beliefs provide models and taboos for the consumption of "good" and "bad" foods and chemicals and define the occasions for their use. This is one reason why the consumption of alcohol is accompanied by so many group reinforcements. For example, rites and rituals attend the consumption of wine in religious ceremonies. The slight change of state induced by alcohol disposes one to regard the occasion in a special way, to put one in a different frame of mind and to share an understood communion. The group thus defines the occasion for drinking, the reason for feeling different, and the appropriate response to that difference. The group's definition of what is appropriate largely governs what may happen before, during, and after drinking. In a culture highly censorious of intoxication, the errant drinker may suffer guilt and even ostracism for just one misstep. Many American Indians have come to believe in their legendary vulnerability to "fire water;" in some tribes, an Indian may be drunk before he takes his first drink, because his very decision to drink defines the occasion for him: He has reached the end of his rope and intends to let go. Set and expectation, then, are key to many drug

effects. What to do about physiological dependence is also socially defined: For example, does one take more alcohol for a hangover or resort to stoic endurance? It is the way we hope to manage the effects of drugs, and the personal or social uses to which we put drugs that largely shape the pattern of drug effects, whether we speak of drug use or abuse.

Psychopharmacological studies of alcohol—viewing it as a drug—are of limited help in understanding some of the behavioral phenomena seen in alcoholism. Alcohol is, of course, a drug. While little knowledge is available on the effects of the congeners (the non-alcoholic chemicals in distilled beverages), ethanol is the active ingredient. It is a nutritive substance producing 7.1 calories per gram, but it is of little nutritive value, partly because it is rapidly metabolized. Alcohol slows the intestinal absorption of essential amino acids; this effect and the neglect of a good diet may account for the frequency of multiple B-vitamin deficiencies in alcoholics. The level of alcohol in the blood can be directly ascertained. The "breath analyzers" used by the police reflect blood levels of alcohol with fairly reasonable accuracy. A concentration of 0.15 percent is closely correlated with diminished reality control and reaction time, while 0.2 percent corresponds with heavy intoxication. A blood-alcohol level of 0.5 percent could kill the drinker by directly depressing the activity of the brain cells that control respiration. The details of the effects of alcohol on the brain are still not well known; some cellular biochemical processes are impaired, but only with exceptionally high doses. Significantly, alcoholism cannot be diagnosed with microscopic brain-cell analyses at autopsy. Occasionally, but not always, the severe vitamin-B deficiency typical of acute alcoholism produces lesions in the deep structures of the brain.

About 90 percent of consumed al-

cohol is broken down by enzymes, especially in the liver. The ethanol becomes acetaldehyde which is further metabolized to products that can be easily excreted. A drug—disulfiram, or antabuse—blocks the destruction of acetaldehyde. If alcoholics can be induced to take the drug daily and then drink, the high levels of acetaldehyde will lead to reddening of the face, headache, palpitation, faintness and nausea—a response which, for some, may help to reinforce abstinence.

Some cultures prize the ability to "hold your liquor"—to drink large quantities of alcohol without acting intoxicated or falling unconscious. Some estimates say that an alcoholic can drink, at the very most, no more than twice as much as a teetotaler in terms of subjective and objective measures of intoxication. But many heavy drinkers lack metabolic tolerance. Unfortunately, there is still no reliable data on central neuronal adaptations to alcohol and individual differences. Rats intoxicated for a long time do about 5 percent better on a performance test than naive rats given alcohol; learning may be a factor in this slightly increased tolerance.

Some tests of intellectual functioning show impairment on so-called "deductive" tasks, but enhanced performance in tests requiring "inductive reasoning." Many drinkers claim that the impairment is less important than the decrease of intellectual inhibition; they believe that drinking helps them to function more creatively or freely. In general, decreased inhibition—the so-called "release" effect of alcohol—accounts for both the transient feelings of well-being and the freer expression of previously suppressed or conflicted needs (in Vino Veritas). Alcohol does not, however, compel verbosity. People who are not neurotically pushed to "spill the beans" can maintain instructions not to reveal a secret, even under heavy doses of amytal (the so-called "truth serum" and a drug with effects quite similar to those of alcohol). Alcohol has been called the aphrodisiac of the newly wed — again, probably because of the mild release of inhibition — but the most common effects of heavy intake are retarded ejaculation and potency disturbance in the male.

Many studies of the drug show some state-dependent learning; for example, certain word associations learned in an alcoholic state are recalled better during intoxication. Indeed, many alcoholics have noted that when sober they forgot where they had hidden various caches of liquor, but when intoxicated they recalled the hiding places again.

Alcoholics seldom recognize how they really feel and behave when drunk. Many remember the alcoholic episode as they wish it to be — as a great relief. When they are shown videotapes of their drunken behavior, they are shocked by it and by their expressions of misery. Direct studies of alcohol's effects on memory function have not yet produced definitive findings, but the drug clearly has some differential effects. Clinically, this is most evident in the "blackout." The alcoholic who repeats himself when drunk is not really tracking or registering what is going on.

Despite all that is known about the drug, it is hard to prove that it has direct or enduring toxic effects on any cells. With heavy drinking, slight fatty infiltration of the liver will appear in most people (and disappear with cessation). But this condition cannot be linked to cirrhosis. All that we know is that the majority of Americans with cirrhosis are alcoholics; but most alcoholics seen in alcohol treatment units do not have cirrhosis — perhaps only 5 to 10 percent. (No animal model was available until recently, when Charles Leiber induced baboons to consume two quarts a day for four years. Only two

of 13 baboons showed the authentic pathology of cirrhosis.) The Finns show a low incidence of cirrhosis with heavy but intermittent drinking, while the French have a high incidence and a pattern of steady, often heavy, drinking. Most experts believe that pattern of drinking alone is not sufficient and that there is an uncommon or X factor for vulnerability to cirrhosis that is yet to be defined. In the cirrhotic, however, complete abstinence is required or alcohol will soon be lethal to the already-impaired liver.

Alcohol tends to produce tissue dependency or addiction, so that its withdrawal brings on tremors, jitteriness, and anxiety. Such effects are exaggerated opposites of the calm, sedation, and pleasure associated with the first drink. The body's cells overreact to the absence of the drug to which they have adapted. These symptoms can be relieved by other sedative, antianxiety drugs such as librium, valium, barbiturates — or by alcohol. This indicates ethanol's close link with sedative drugs and emphasizes its sedative effect — one which many users deliberately exploit. It also explains why the heavy drinker who also takes barbiturates is risking death; the two sedative drugs have an additive effect that can be lethal. For severe alcoholics, abrupt withdrawal can lead to delirium tremens — a state of hypervigilance, tremor, excessive sweating, and terrifying hallucinations — which is fatal to about 5 percent of those stricken.

The success of any treatment of alcoholism usually depends on the alcoholic's motivation to take advantage of the treatment. Industry has employed individualized counseling with some success. Group therapies seem enormously potent — as one would expect in view of the social reinforcement that successfully regulates normal drinking behavior. Self-help groups such as AA merit the attention of specialists because of

their acute perception of the specific behaviors — especially the alibis and rationalizations — of fellow problem drinkers. Further, direct authoritarian relationships, to which many alcoholics seem sensitive, are avoided by the sharing processes of the AA group, which can maintain self-esteem while sharing vulnerability and shame. Counseling and psychotherapy for some alcoholics is aided by disulfiram. Other treatment is symptomatic — helping the alcoholic to "dry out" and regain a clear head, health, and perspective. Family treatment is frequently helpful in revealing destructive patterns that have formed between husband and wife and other family members. No one treatment has been markedly successful, especially over the long term. Probably the most powerful force toward a successful treatment is belief and a form of religious conversion. AA stresses that the alcoholic must acknowledge something bigger than himself (thus dealing with the omnipotence drive of the addict, to which we have referred).

The consumption of alcohol, then, is closely linked to cultural and moral beliefs and their implementation — fundamentally, to how a society wishes to regulate the intake of substances and pleasure and pain. It is no wonder that attitudes about what we should consume create violent opinions and extreme responses, as the great American Prohibition experiment, the fluoridation controversy, and the organic-food fad all demonstrate. As a case study in which the operation of genetic, biochemical, psychological, behavioral, and cultural factors interact, the study of alcoholism provides a rich and complex field. As a major public health problem, it is an extraordinary challenge to the biomedical, rehabilitative, and social sciences.

But its incidence is increasing. Cases of senile dementia may show a marked arteriosclerotic brain condition—a thickening and hardening of arterial walls that reduces the amount of oxygen reaching the neurons in the brain. Hereditary, vascular, and endocrine factors all seem to contribute to the condition. In a sizable percentage of senile brain disease cases, profound personality changes occur. Over half the cases show such symptoms as agitation, paranoid thought, schizophreniclike behavior, and depression. The following passage illustrates a number of features typical of senile dementia:

Five years before the patient's admission, her adopted son, with whom she resided, noted that she was becoming forgetful, especially concerning her usual household duties and recent accidents. She hoarded articles and sometimes said that someone had stolen them. She remembered events of her childhood quite well and at times was somewhat boring in her accounts of early experiences. Her adopted son noted that she became increasingly neglectful of her personal appearance. For many months prior to her admission she would not bathe unless reminded to do so. Recently she often went to bed without removing either clothing or shoes. At times she put on her clothing inside out. For four years prior to admission she seemed to find it difficult to prepare meals at accustomed times.

On many occasions she completed the preparation of the midday meal at 8 A.M. and insisted that the family should eat at that time. In preparing coffee she often put sugar instead of coffee in the coffee pot but failed to recognize her error. In a few instances she wished to pay bills that she had already paid. She was restless at night but often slept during the day. The patient became increasingly confused in surroundings with which she had formerly been quite familiar. Often, when crossing the street, she paid no attention to approaching automobiles. At times she wandered away from home.

There were periods during which she constantly packed and unpacked her clothing. During recent months she had often failed to recognize friends. She became increasingly suspicious, and said that neighbors were talking about her, spoke of them in extremely derogatory terms, maintained that her son lied to her and had tried to poison her, and that her neighbors had threatened to kill her. She claimed that her son and an elderly woman who had been employed to give her protective care had been secretly married. She complained that everyone was trying to control her activities and threatened to commit suicide if not permitted to do as she wished.

When the patient was brought to the mental hospital, she rose to meet the admitting physician, shook his hand, asked him where she was and if there was anything she could do for him. She knew her name but could not give her address or other identifying data. She claimed that her son, who had really been extremely devoted to her, had ejected her in order to secure possession of her house, which was located "down the hill." After her admission, affectless and placid, she sat in a rocking chair all day, paying little or no heed to her environment. Her existence had become but little above a vegetative level. (Kolb, 1968)

We need to know much more about the physical, nutritional, and genetic events that lead to such deterioration. We also must examine the personal and social contexts in which such deterioration takes place. Some evidence indicates that psychodynamics influence both the form of organically caused psychosis and the individual's response to it. Learning theorists have developed many special programs to help rehabilitate patients, especially those whose organic conditions are reversible. In many cases, they have been able to restore a variety of adaptive functions (such as the capacity to feed oneself or to remain continent) that had been lost.

In this chapter, we have examined the major varieties of abnormal behavior and the theories and research that have attempted to explain them. In the next chapter, we will examine the methods of treatment and rehabilitation that have been developed to aid people suffering from these disorders.

Summary

1. Abnormal behavior has been variously viewed through the ages as either possession by demons, mental illness, or a result of the problems in living. Today, it is regarded as a process that has a rational basis and therefore can be studied scientifically.

2. The psychodynamic approach to abnormal behavior holds that most symptoms are associated with an expression of unconscious and unacceptable thoughts, particularly as a result of childhood events, which would arouse anxiety if brought to awareness in undisguised form.

3. Learning theorists emphasize the effects of reinforcement on behavior and deal with the current situation of the patient.

4. The biophysical approach to disordered behavior emphasizes the influence of biochemical and physiological functions and systems as well as the influence of heredity.

5. There are no universally accepted standards of abnormal behavior. Both statistical criteria and consensual criteria are relative standards and not absolute measurements. Personal criteria also vary widely according to the individual's own concept of abnormal behavior.

6. Diagnosis of a behavior disorder simply means that an individual is classified as displaying symptoms typical of a particular disorder. Objections to this procedure include its lack of consideration for the uniqueness of each individual, the fact that categories do not always fit exactly, and the fact that certain disorders seem to vary in degree rather than in kind.

7. The most extreme and serious forms of mental disorders are the psychoses. Psychotics often require institutionalization, show little insight into their illness, have a confused perception of reality, and experience interference with normal thought processes. Unlike functional psychoses, organic psychoses involve damage to the nervous system.

8. Schizophrenia may be classified in terms of simple (deterioration in normal functioning), hebephrenic (childish and silly behavior), catatonic (extremes of motor inhibition and agitation), and paranoid (hallucinations and delusions). Process and reactive schizophrenia are classifications based on the onset of the disease.

9. A severe form of childhood psychosis is infantile autism, in which the child is unable to form relationships with people and tends to exhibit language and other communication disorders.

10. Several theories attempt to explain the causes of schizophrenia. The psychodynamic theory is that schizophrenic behavior represents the intrusion of unconscious, illogical material into conscious awareness and overt behavior. Learning theorists believe that such behavior arises from a lack of development of conventional responses to social stimuli. Sociologists trace it to an inadequate early childhood socialization, and biophysical theorists seek the causes in biochemical and genetic factors.

11. Affective disorders disrupt normal emotional responses so that contact with reality is impaired and adjustment to the external world is limited. These conditions include mania (extreme elation and self-confidence), depression (strong negative feelings, infrequent speech and movement), manic-depressive (alternating moods), and involutional melancholia (depression associated with hormonal changes and accompanying psychological stress—at menopause, for example).

12. Theories concerning the cause of affective disorders include the psychodynamic view that the individual is really responding to a childhood loss that is symbolized by a current event. The biophysical view holds that biochemical and genetic influences are responsible.

13. The neuroses are mental disorders that are less serious than the psychoses; neurotics can maintain relations with the real world but cannot function at an optimal level because of excessive anxiety and inhibitions.

14. Anxiety reactions are the most frequent and characteristic symptoms of neuroses. They include physical symptoms and psychological manifestations associated with fear, in the absence of physical danger.

15. Phobic reactions include highly specific anxieties centered around irrational fears. They tend to generalize and broaden and may interfere seriously with a person's life.

16. Hysteria is characterized by physical defects without organic cause (conversion hysteria), indifference to symptoms, and personality dissociation, including amnesia and multiple personality.

17. Other neurotic disorders are obsession (a recurrent thought that the individual cannot put from his mind) and compulsion (an act that the person is compelled to carry out even though it may be senseless, inconvenient, or repugnant to him).

18. Theories on the cause of neurotic behavior include the psychodynamic view that it results from defense mechanisms erected against

anxiety-inducing unconscious impulses; the learning theory view that it involves operant responses that have been strengthened through reinforcement; and the biophysical theory that neurotic behavior has a substantial genetic component.

19. Character or personality disorders reflect a chronic mode of adjustment in which a person displays inadequate or ineffective patterns of behavior, including adaptive inflexibility, stereotyped interpersonal relations, and tenuous stability under stress. Examples are the hysterical, the schizoid, and the psychopathic personalities.

20. Psychosomatic disorders occur when psychological conditions lead to disturbances in bodily functioning which then cause actual tissue damage.

21. Although the causes are unclear, psychosomatic disorders represent a joint function of the biology of the individual, his personality development, and his various social roles. The chief components of these disorders are stressful life conditions, strong emotional reactions, and physical symptoms.

22. Organic disorders that involve tissue damage to the brain are characterized by perceptual distortions, memory disorders, impairment in attention, and distortions of mood and thought. Acute conditions, marked by sudden onset, are usually reversible; the opposite is true for chronic conditions.

23. Alcoholic psychoses may be acute or chronic. Delirium tremens, an acute condition, is characterized by delirium, tremors, and terrifying hallucinations.

24. General paresis is an organic disorder caused by syphilitic infection. It results in progressive deterioration of brain tissue.

25. Senile dementia is an organic condition that affects people late in life. Marked arteriosclerotic brain damage, agitation, paranoid thought, depression, and schizophreniclike behavior typify the disease.

Important Terms

psychopathology

psychosis

organic psychoses

functional psychoses

process schizophrenia

reactive schizophrenia

simple schizophrenia

hebephrenic schizophrenia

catatonic schizophrenia

paranoid schizophrenia

infantile autism

affective disorders

manic-depressive disorders

involutional melancholia

neurosis

anxiety reaction

hysteria

conversion hysteria

multiple personality

phobia

personality (character) disorder alcoholic psychosis

hysterical personality   general paresis

schizoid personality   senile dementia

Suggested Readings

BEERS, C. W. *A mind that found itself.* New York: Doubleday, 1948. Clifford Beers (1876–1943), the founder of the mental hygiene movement in America, suffered from manic-depressive psychosis for much of his life. This book—first published in 1908—is an early presentation of a patient's thoughts during various phases of psychosis.

COLEMAN, J. C. *Abnormal psychology and modern life.* Chicago: Scott, Foresman, 1964.
One of the most popular books in this field; the treatment is elementary, but thorough.

GREEN, H. *I never promised you a rose garden.* New York: Signet, 1964. A beautifully written, compassionate novel about a young schizophrenic girl who lives in her own private world. She has lost touch with reality; the book describes her fight to regain it.

KISKER, G. W. *The disorganized personality.* New York: McGraw-Hill, 1972.
An abnormal psychology textbook reflecting the author's 25 years of experience as a clinical psychologist. The author goes beyond theory and devotes much of his book to detailed case reports and taped interviews with his patients.

LINDNER, R. *The fifty-minute hour.* New York: Bantam Books, 1956. This book launched a new literary genre—part documentary, part interpretation. The author relates case histories of his patients, presenting the intricacies and human drama of the disturbed mind in layman's language.

SARASON, I. G. *Abnormal psychology: The problem of maladaptive behavior.* New York: Appleton-Century-Crofts, 1972.
A recent, comprehensive text on the varieties of abnormal behavior, including material on diagnosis, symptoms, and treatment. Clearly written with many good examples.

WHITE, R. W. *The abnormal personality.* New York: Ronald Press, 1972. A classic text in this field; the author covers the major topics in abnormal psychology in a literate, well-organized manner.

Chapter 21   Treatment of Behavior Disorders

> *. . . she was speaking from a place in which she had been before.*
> *"There are no colors, only shades of gray. She is big and white. I am*
> *small and there are bars between. She gives food. Gray. I don't eat.*
> *Where is my . . . my . . ."*
> *"Your what?"*
> *"Salvation!" Deborah blurted.*
> *"Go on," the doctor said.*
> *"My . . . self, my love."*
> *Dr. Fried peered at her intently for a while and then said, "I have a*
> *hunch—do you want to try it with me?". . . . "Your mother had*
> *trouble with a pregnancy when you were very small, did she not?"*
> *"Yes, she miscarried. Twins."*
> *"And afterward went away to rest for a while?"*
> *The light struck the past and there was a seeming sound of good,*
> *strong truth, like the pop of a hard-thrown ball into a catcher's glove.*
> *Connect. Deborah listened to the sound and then began to tumble over*
> *her words, filling the missing features of the ancient nightmare . . .*
> *"The white thing must have been a nurse. I felt that everything warm*
> *had left. The feeling comes often, but I thought it could never have*
> *been true that I ever really was in such a place. The bars were crib bars.*
> *They must have been on my own crib. . . . The nurse was distant and*
> *cold . . . Hey! Hey!" The now-friendly light struck something else and*
> *its suddenness made the small, prosaic connection seem like a revela-*
> *tion full of greatness and wonder. "The bars . . . the bars of the crib*
> *and the cold and losing the ability to see colors . . . it's what happens*
> *now! It's part of the Pit—it's what happens now, now! When I am*
> *waiting to fall, those bands of dark across my eyes are the old crib bars*
> *and the cold is that old one—I always wondered why it meant more*
> *than just something you could end by putting on a coat."*
> *The rush of words ended and Dr. Fried smiled. "It is as big, then, as*
> *abandonment and the going away of all love. . . ."*
>
> —Hannah Green
> (*I Never Promised You a Rose Garden*)

Treatment of Behavior Disorders

This chapter was drafted by Irwin Sarason, Department of Psychology, University of Washington.

Given the enormous variety of behavior disorders, it is not surprising that attempts to cure or alleviate these disorders take many forms. Perhaps the only elements common to all the different therapies are the presence of a person judged to be in need of psychological help and a therapist who offers such help. The training of the therapist, the setting in which the therapy is conducted, the length of time consumed by the therapy, the particular agent believed to produce the desired change, the cost of the therapy, even the number of persons involved, all vary greatly among therapists and institutions. We cannot even specify as a common element a significant personal relationship between patient and therapist, because the most widely used methods of treatment involve physical and pharmacological agents.

Although theory and therapy are not necessarily linked directly, they do correspond generally. People who adopt a theory emphasizing unconscious motivation, interpersonal events, and conflict as determinants of behavior disorders are likely to favor psychoanalysis, client-centered therapy, or some related technique that emphasizes personal relationships. Those who view behavior disorders as learned, maladaptive patterns of behavior would naturally prefer one of the behavior therapies. And a strongly biophysical view of the origins of behavior disorders would predispose one to search out some form of somatic therapy.

In this chapter, we shall discuss six therapeutic approaches which, though logically distinct, often are used in combination. The first, called psychodynamic therapy, uses methods derived primarily from psychoanalysis. The second is based on Carl Rogers' self theory. The third consists of the various techniques developed for treating people in groups rather than individually. The fourth, behavior therapy, is closely related to learning theory. The fifth technique—less developed than the others—attempts to modify deviant behavior through manipulation of the social environment. These five therapies, despite their differences, have one thing in common: they are all forms of psychotherapy—that is, each relies on psychological intervention to aid the patient. In contrast, the sixth approach uses somatic methods such as electroshock treatment and psychoactive drugs.

Psychodynamic Therapy

Freud described *psychodynamic therapy* as "talking therapy." The psychodynamic therapist talks with his clients to help them identify and resolve their conflicts and make adaptive changes in their behavior.

Psychodynamic therapists generally agree that an individual's conscious and unconscious thoughts determine his observable behavior. Therefore, they seek to help him modify his view of himself and others as a necessary first step toward changing his overt behavior. However, therapists have differing views of the individual's inner world—and these views will influence each therapist's choice of tactics.

Psychodynamic therapy is practiced in all kinds of settings—offices, clinics, hospitals, and churches. But because of overcrowding, most hospitals—especially state and federal institutions—provide only limited opportunities for "talking therapy."

Psychoanalysis

In his earliest therapeutic efforts, Freud used hypnosis as a means of bringing unconscious material to awareness. But eventually he concluded that the hypnotic technique had undesirable features and the same result could be achieved through *free association.* As we explained in Chapter 8, this technique requires the patient to express his thoughts freely, without concern for right, wrong, or logical connections, and without hesitation or reflection. Freud felt that having the patient recline on a couch, with the therapist out of sight, helped to relax ordinary controls and censorship. By reducing the degree of rational control and normal inhibition, Freud believed he could gain a clearer picture of the hidden impulses and conflicts underlying the patient's unhappiness and deviant behavior.

Freud emphasized the importance of dreams, believing that they were the "royal road" to the unconscious. Consequently, clinical psychoanalysts often stress *dream interpretation (dream analysis)* and the relationship of dreams to those unconscious wishes and impulses that are responsible for symptoms, and for much normal behavior as well. Basically, free association and dream interpretation are means of bringing unconscious and unacceptable impulses and conflicts to the conscious level, where they can be re-experienced and analyzed.

This re-experiencing of past events refers particularly to *transference*—the tendency of the patient to transfer onto the analyst feelings, impulses, memories, and wishes associated with significant people in his past, especially such key figures as members of his family. Thus, within the analytic setting, the patient relives old emotions and frustrations with an intensity that often rivals that of the original experience. But the therapeutic setting is neutral, and the analyst does not respond

21-1
The couch has been associated with psychoanalysis since Freud first placed his patients on the one in his consulting room, shown here. (Edmund Engelman)

as the key figures once did. This makes it possible to re-experience the transferred memories and emotions from the past in such a manner that they lose their traumatic or harmful impact. Then they are not only brought to consciousness, they are also subjected to rational analysis and understanding. The repressed and maladaptive experiences of infancy and childhood become part of the individual's conscious self and lose their pathological effects. The analysis of these transference responses, both positive and negative, is generally looked upon as the key to a successful psychoanalysis.

The "analysis" in psychoanalysis actually takes four different forms. The first is the interpretation or analysis of dreams reported by the patient. The second is the analysis and understanding of the material that is brought to awareness as a result of free association. The third is the analysis of the patient's resistances, so that the material being defended against can be brought to consciousness. Finally, there is the analysis of the transference—reactions originating in the past that are transferred into the analytic session and onto the analyst. In spite of this emphasis upon analysis, the actual role of the traditional psychoanalyst is passive. He does vastly more listening than talking.

While the past few decades have seen efforts to extend psychoanalytic therapy to a wider variety of disorders, the great majority of people receiving psychoanalytic therapy have lesser problems—either neuroses or personality disorders. Freud himself felt that psychoses could not be treated successfully with psychoanalysis.

Psychoanalysis is not widely used; it takes a long time and costs a great deal, and psychoanalysts are relatively scarce. Nonetheless, Freud's theories and procedures have greatly influenced the way almost all therapists carry out their therapy today.

Client-Centered Therapy

Many neo-Freudians, such as Adler, Horney, and Sullivan, have derived their theories and therapies substantially from Freud's. Carl Rogers, however, has developed a theory and therapy that oppose both Freudian and neo-Freudian approaches; it often is referred to as a self or self-actualizing theory.

At the center of Rogers' theory, as we discussed in Chapter 16, is his belief in the importance of the phenomenological world—the world as seen and experienced by the individual, as contrasted to the objective world. Each person (self) is the center of his own changing world of experience; the nature of this personal self accounts for most of his behavior, normal and pathological. The person's *self-concept,* the relatively stable patterns of self-perceptions that he has acquired in interaction with the world around him, largely determines how he will relate to other people and objects. Generally speaking, the more positive the individual's self-concept, the more likely he is to be adaptive and successful in his transactions with the environment. A key assumption of Rogers' position is the "growth hypothesis"—an assumption that every person has within him a strong motivation for positive change and growth and that, given the proper setting, every individual will tend to realize the positive aspects of himself.

The task of the client-centered therapist is to provide a setting that will encourage the growth or actualization of those potential strengths that every individual possesses. The creation of this setting or *therapeutic climate* is the essence of *client-centered therapy*. Rogers believes that this climate must have three major components. The first component is the therapist's congruence with the patient. That is, the therapist must feel a strong empathy with the patient's feelings and beliefs and must express an openness toward the client in order to establish a genuine relationship between them, a relationship that is not limited to the particular therapeutic setting. Second, it is essential that the therapist communicate a strong *unconditional positive regard* for the patient. In Rogers' words, this implies that:

> . . . the therapist communicates to his client a deep and genuine caring for him as a person with human potentialities, a caring uncontaminated by evaluations of the patient's thoughts, feelings, or behavior. The therapist experiences a warm acceptance of the client's experience as a part of that person and places no conditions on his acceptance and warmth. He prizes that client in a total, rather than conditional, way. He does not accept certain feelings in the client and disapprove of others. He feels an unconditional positive regard for this person. . . . It involves as much feeling of acceptance for the client's expression of painful, hostile, defensive, or abnormal feelings as for his expression of good, positive, mature feelings. (Rogers, 1966)

Third, the therapist must have an *accurate empathic understanding* of his client. He must be at home in the inner world of the client, sensitively understanding just what the client intends, feels, or experiences.

Recently, Rogers has become increasingly interested in applying client-centered techniques in group settings and in sensitivity training.

Group Therapy

Currently, group therapy is widely used to bring psychotherapy and counseling to larger numbers of disturbed people. Group therapy also is valued as a way to make therapeutic techniques more efficient. Group therapy comes in many varieties, including those based on Freudian, Rogerian, and behaviorist principles, among many others. *Family therapy* typifies the basic approach. Instead of being treated individually, the family members are encouraged to deal as a group with their feelings toward each other and with their resistances to cooperation, sharing, and mutual affection.

Two factors have accelerated interest in group approaches. One is the scarcity of specialists who are trained to provide individual therapy. The second is the focus on interpersonal influences that can mold and sustain abnormal attitudes and behavior. Group therapists contend that when several patients with similar disorders are treated together, they can quickly spot each other's—and therefore their own—maladaptive attitudes, habits, and response patterns. The group members' interplay

21-2
In encounter sessions, a form of group therapy, members strive to heighten awareness by relating freely and honestly with each other. (Bob Nadler, dpi)

gives them valuable opportunities to observe obvious distortions in perception and social behavior. Such interplay is therapeutic, group therapists maintain, because the patients can learn new and more adaptive interpersonal tactics while actually relating to a segment of the real world—a group of peers.

In individual psychotherapy, the patient relates to the sometimes authoritarian therapist. But in the group he relates primarily to his peers. He learns to accept criticism and to provide more effective social support for others. He comes to respect the feelings of others—and, it is hoped, his own as well. These assertions, reflecting the views and experiences of group therapists, have not yet been confirmed by scientific research. Nevertheless, they govern group therapists' efforts to help psychologically troubled people.

Encounter Groups. A type of group therapy that has come to be of special interest—and occasional concern—to many people is the *encounter group.* These groups attempt to facilitate their members' positive change and growth and greater achievement of potential. They are variously known as *T* (for training) *Groups, Sensitivity Training Groups, Integrity Groups, Marathon Groups, Encounter Groups, Nude Encounter Groups,* and so on. The origins of these approaches are as varied as their labels; they range from psychoanalysis in all its forms to Kurt Lewin's interest in group dynamics. At present, we have too little firm evidence to evaluate the effects of such group encounters. We do know, however, that the number of encounter groups has increased dramatically in recent years. Many observers feel that their great popularity is a reflection of the anonymous, alienated, and impersonal nature of our society. It is at least possible that, for many participants, a group may provide a contrived intimacy that is lacking in their daily existence.

Encounter groups characteristically focus on improving the individual's capacity to relate to others, rather than trying to rid him of specific symptoms or failures of adjustment. In fact, many leaders of encounter groups specifically deny that they are engaged in therapy, and most could substantiate this claim by pointing to the fact that they have had no formal training as therapists.

Virtually all of these groups start with a leader who provides the rules that the members of the group are to follow. In some groups, the leader may provide no further guidance, thus leaving it to the members of the group to decide how they will go about relating to one another. In other groups, the leader may be extremely, even harshly, authoritarian, demanding that members relate to the group in ways that are intensely embarrassing. Groups may vary in size from as few as a half dozen people to 20 or more. In some cases, the group meets periodically for months or even years; the other extreme (the marathon group) is a single, extended meeting ranging virtually nonstop for 24 to 72 hours.

The following report by a participant in a marathon group shows the intensity of feeling that can be generated in such groups, as well as some of the techniques that are employed:

For me the marathon was a real breakthrough, which came about mostly through the games. From early childhood I had a kind of phobia about touching, in any affectionate way, another person except my mother and grandparents. I was an only son. I wouldn't show physical affection even for my two younger sisters. If another person, even family or friends, put their arms around me I was embarrassed and uneasy and would draw away. . . .

The game that affected me most was when Nicholas was asked to affirm his deformed leg as a part of him even if unsightly because of the paralysis. He was asked to sit in the center of the room without his shoe and sock and let us all see it. His deep resentment of this as a shame was about to preclude him from continuing when, almost as one, the group went to him to give him their love and encouragement. At this point I sat behind him and when somebody first touched his foot, he fell back almost in agony into my arms. He was encouraged to speak words of acceptance to his leg as they finally bared it and laid their hands on it and caressed it. After a while I laid his head in the lap of one of the women and continued to stroke his shoulder as others in the group used physical touch to affirm their support of him and their loving acceptance. I had never expressed love in a physical way to a man before this day. I myself, in a certain sense also "crippled" by my phobia against physical contact, was freed to experience its rightness and genuine human warmth. My "homo hang-up" disappeared as a result of this experience. It was the involvement of the entire group that made it possible for me to act and feel as I did. (Mintz, 1971)

As this excerpt shows, body awareness and physical contact between participants often play an important role in the encounter group.

Behavior Therapy

Psychodynamic and learning theories agree that behavior must be understood in terms of its causes. But they disagree about the nature of the causes. As we have seen, psychodynamic theories and their psychotherapeutic offshoots stress unconscious motivation and infantile determinants of abnormal behavior. Learning psychologists, on the other hand, focus on acquired responses. While the importance of learning principles in understanding abnormal behavior has long been recognized, a broad spectrum of learning-oriented therapies has been developed only recently. These treatments generally are labeled the _behavior therapies._ Because their goal is simply to reduce or eliminate undesirable learned behaviors without delving into their specific origin, these therapies are often referred to as _behavior modification_ procedures.

Therapies Based on Operant Conditioning Techniques

B. F. Skinner's scientific contributions have greatly influenced the development of behavior therapy. As you will recall from Chapter 6, Skinner's theoretical orientation grew out of research in the 1930s and 1940s on the behavior of rats and pigeons in his now-famous experimental chamber, the so-called Skinner box. Skinner studied behavior as expressed through lever-pressing and other specific responses. A central idea in Skinner's work is *reinforcement*. Any manipulation or event (stimulus) that increases the probability that a given response will be made is a reinforcement. Techniques for treating depression, childhood disorders, and stuttering will be used to illustrate the reinforcement or *operant conditioning* approach to behavior disorders.

Depression. According to learning theory, depression is a reaction to a severe loss of reinforcement—a sharp drop in personal status, for example. Some depressions begin slowly, and in these cases it is not always easy to identify the precipitating stimulus. Nevertheless, the individual's history of reinforcement would seem to be a potent determinant of his self-perception and perception of others. Depressed people, for example, may acquire self-debasing attitudes through behaviors for which they were reinforced earlier in their lives. Using learning principles to modify depression, the patient's self-concept may be strengthened by reinforcing him—with praise or whatever else he values—when he acts on his own initiative or tells of one of his own ideas. Shaping, too, may be required to elicit the desired behavior.

Childhood Disorders. Therapists working with disturbed children often use operant techniques. Autistic children, for example, present a real challenge to therapists. They show inadequate language development, motor disturbances, seclusiveness, and a diminished emotional responsiveness. They do not look others in the eye, fail to communicate adequately, and may even be mute; they frequently respond to objects as normal children respond to people—with anger, affection, and other emotions.

The technique used in treating a seven-year-old boy in a hospital ward illustrates the learning approach to such childhood disorders (Brawley, Harris, Allen, Fleming, & Peterson, 1969). In this case, adult attention in the form of praise and a second reinforcer—potato chips—was given when the boy behaved in ways that were socially appropriate and desirable. These reinforcements were withheld after inappropriate responses. Before the child came under operant conditioning, he hit himself frequently and withdrew totally from others. He rarely spoke. (The hospital staff paid more attention to such bizarre behavior than to his acceptable behavior, thus probably reinforcing the bizarre behavior.) During the reinforcement sequence, his comprehensible verbal responses increased from 2 percent of his speech to 46 percent. Withdrawal and other inappropriate behavior diminished sharply. When the reinforcers were stopped, his appropriate behavior dropped significantly; when they were restored, his behavior returned to the previous reinforced levels. Figure 21–3 shows the course of appropriate behavior during the several stages of treatment.

Stuttering. The treatment of stuttering provides another example of an operant approach to abnormal behavior. Stuttering is a speech disorder in which hesitations or rapid repetitions of word elements interrupt the flow of speech. Does stuttering reflect an unfortunate history of reinforcement? Some evidence supports this view. But whatever the cause, studies have shown that direct manipulation of reinforcements can

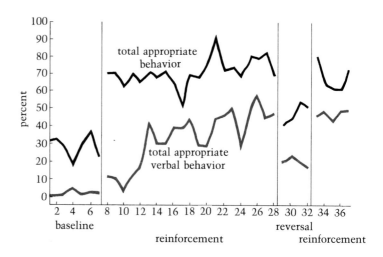

21-3
Total appropriate responses recorded in the study of a disturbed 7-year-old boy whose appropriate behaviors were reinforced with praise and food. (After Brawley, et al., 1969)

reduce stuttering. In one experiment (Martin, 1968), a stutterer was given a mild electric shock whenever he stuttered. Stuttering declined substantially during the experiment, compared with the subject's normal speech. Similarly, the occurrence of the speech interruption, "uh," declined markedly when the experimenter simply indicated to the subject that he had made a wrong response. Figure 21–4 traces the subject's "uh" responses in relation to the use of the negative reinforcer, "wrong."

Though operant conditioning now is used in clinics, the processes involved are not fully understood. Much more research must be done to provide this information. Meanwhile, reinforcement schedules that seem theoretically workable often are ineffective in practice. The choice of the reinforcement is vital—this much we do know. Stimuli that are meaningless or irrelevant to the subject cannot effectively modify his behavior. Often, the major clinical task is identifying the reinforcer that will work. For example, social reinforcers (approval of others, friendliness, and so on) may be very powerful stimuli for some individuals but not for others. In addition, the reinforcer will not be effective unless the subject understands that the reinforcement is dependent upon the desired response.

Token Economies. Many mental-hospital programs for schizophrenics and other chronic patients use operant methods of behavior modification. One popular program is called a *token economy*. In a token economy:

1. Tokens are presented to the patient as payment for work he has performed; the number of tokens is proportionate to the amount of reinforcement; and the reinforcers are received when the tokens are cashed in (for candy, special privileges, and so on).

2. Work performed by the patient must be socially appropriate, adaptive behavior. It can be helping to clean a hospital ward, using eating utensils properly, or simply making conventional verbal responses.

In one well-known study (Ayllon & Azrin, 1965), the primary reinforcers that could be purchased with tokens included privacy, leave

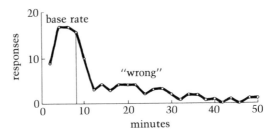

21-4
A marked drop in "uh" responses follows the negative reinforcement (begun after 8 minutes) of taking "uh" to be an incorrect response and immediately indicating "wrong." The number of "uh" responses occurring over two-minute intervals was recorded. (After Martin, 1968)

from the ward, social interaction with the staff, recreational opportunities, and specific items from the commissary. Tokens also could be earned for a wide variety of activities or jobs, including assisting in the kitchen or dining room, serving as a tour guide, or grooming or bathing oneself. All of the activities for which tokens were awarded had one thing in common: They related to normal, self-sufficient functioning.

Therapies Based on Classical Conditioning Techniques

The Pavlovian learning concepts underlying classical conditioning also have stimulated research inquiries and clinical applications. As you know, in classical conditioning a conditioned stimulus is paired with an unconditioned stimulus. The two stimuli are presented in very close sequence to associate the conditioned with the unconditioned stimulus. The unconditioned stimulus elicits a response naturally. After a number of trials, the conditioned stimulus evokes a similar response. Specific reactions may arise accidentally because of classical conditioning. A child who has been bitten by a dog may fear all dogs and, through generalization, other types of animals as well.

Systematic Desensitization. One therapeutic technique that employs classical conditioning is called *systematic desensitization.* This procedure has been used widely with phobic patients—persons with irrational and maladaptive fears. The first step is to teach the patient to become aware of deep muscle relaxation and to concentrate on relaxing when he develops tension. The therapist conveys the idea of relaxation to the patient in this way:

Even the ordinary relaxing that occurs when one lies down often produces quite a noticeable effect. It has been found that there is a definite relationship between the extent of muscle relaxation and the production of emotional changes opposed to those of anxiety. I am going to teach you how to relax far beyond the usual point, and this will enable you to "switch on" at will the greatest possible emotional effects of an "anti-anxiety" kind.
 I am now going to show you the essential activity that is involved in obtaining deep relaxation. I shall again ask you to resist my pull at your wrist so as to tighten your biceps. I want you to notice very carefully the sensations in that muscle. Then I shall ask you to let go gradually as I diminish the amount of force I exert against you. Notice as your forearm descends that there is decreasing sensation in the

biceps muscle. Notice also that the letting go is an activity, but of a negative kind—it is an "uncontracting" of the muscle. In due course, your forearm will come to rest on the arm of the chair, and it may then seem to you as though relaxation is complete. But although the biceps will indeed be partly and perhaps largely relaxed, a certain number of fibers will still be contracted. I shall therefore say to you, "Go on letting go." Try to continue the activity that went on in the biceps while your forearm was coming down. It is the act of relaxing these additional fibers that will bring about the emotional effects we want. Let's try it out and see what happens. (Wolpe, 1966)

After the individual has learned this method of muscular relaxation, he is presented, one at a time, with stimuli known to produce anxiety. The therapist begins with the mildest stimuli and works his way up an *anxiety hierarchy* to the most anxiety-provoking stimulus. For a person who is afraid of snakes, the hierarchy of stimuli might range from reading a book about snakes to being in the same room with a snake, to actually handling a snake. When a presentation elicits no anxiety response, the therapist introduces the next stimulus in the anxiety hierarchy. This goes on until the most intense stimulus elicits no anxiety. Systematic desensitization may be described as a deconditioning process. A fear response is reduced in a gradual, step-by-step fashion because when the subject encounters the fear-arousing stimuli, they are paired with a relaxed state. Thus his fear response is not evoked.

In the following case, a 24-year-old art student sought help because of her anxieties about examinations, which interfered with her preparation for and performance on tests. After she was taught to relax, the following procedure was employed:

I am now going to ask you to imagine a number of scenes. You will imagine them clearly and they will generally interfere little, if at all, with your state of relaxation. If, however, at any time you feel disturbed or worried and want to attract my attention, you will be able to do so by raising your left index finger. First I want you to imagine that you are standing on a familiar street corner on a pleasant morning watching the traffic go by. You see cars, motorcycles, trucks, bicycles, people and traffic lights; and you can hear the sounds associated with all these things. (Pause of about 15 sec.) Now stop imagining that scene and give all your attention once again to relaxing. If the scene you imagined disturbed you even in the slightest degree I want you to raise your left index finger now. (Patient does not raise finger.) Now imagine that you are at home studying in the evening. It is the 20th of May, exactly a month before your examination. (Pause of 5 sec.) Now stop imagining the scene. Go on relaxing. (Pause of 10 sec.) Now imagine the same scene again— a month before your examination. (Pause of 5 sec.) Stop imagining the scene and just think of your muscles. Let go, and enjoy your state of calm. (Pause of 15 sec.) Now again imagine that you are studying at home a month before your examination. (Pause of 5 sec.) Stop the scene and now think of your own body. (Pause of 5 sec.) If you felt any disturbance whatsoever to the last scene raise your left index finger now. (Patient raises finger.) If the amount of disturbance decreased from the first presentation to the third do nothing, otherwise again raise your finger. (Patient does not raise finger.) *Just keep on relaxing.* (Pause of 15 sec.) *Imagine that you are sitting on a bench at a bus stop and across the road are two strange men whose voices are raised in argument.* (Pause of 10 sec.) *Stop imagining the scene and just relax.* (Pause of 10 sec.) *Now again imagine the scene of these two men arguing across the road.* (Pause of 10 sec.) *Stop the scene and relax. Now I am going to count up to 5 and you will open your eyes, feeling very calm and refreshed.* (Wolpe, 1966)

Again, the therapist has combined relaxation with an imaginary recreation of the anxiety-evoking situation until the fear situation — both real and imaginary — no longer evokes anxiety.

While desensitization may not apply to all behavioral problems, it does seem to be an effective, efficient, and relatively brief way of modifying intense fears and anxieties. As in other forms of psychotherapy, further investigation is needed, not only into its successes and failures, but also into the details of how it operates. For example, do the effects of desensitization vary with the client-therapist relationship or with the therapist's personality and expectations?

Implosive Therapy.   Desensitization contains a strong cognitive component. The subject must imagine a variety of scenes and progressively relax when thinking about them. Another technique that has a strong imaginative element is *implosive therapy.* It is based on the belief that many behavioral problems are due to painful prior experiences; to resolve these problems, the original painful situation must be recreated so that the individual can learn to cope with his fears. This form of therapy has been used most frequently with anxiety neuroses.

In implosive therapy (implying an inward-directed explosion), the therapist encourages the client to imagine events related to his conflict and to recreate the anxiety he felt in those scenes. By creating an atmosphere devoid of the original threatening conditions, the therapist helps the patient to respond more neutrally to the anxiety-provoking situation. The old threat is recreated but under supportive circumstances. Research suggests that this procedure is effective in a significant percentage of cases of intense anxiety.

The implosive procedure assumes that the anxiety can be extinguished most effectively by repeatedly eliciting intense emotional responses without punishment or negative reinforcement. As we have seen, the emotional responses are evoked symbolically. Thus, a person with a dirt phobia — an extreme dread of being dirty or of handling dirty objects — may be instructed to imagine himself in a septic tank surrounded by all of its undesirable contents. The implosive procedure assumes that someone who can learn not to be anxious about being in a septic tank will find it relatively easy to overcome his fear of dirty floors or depositing rubbish in a garbage can. Like most behavior modifiers, implosive therapists spend relatively little time ferreting out the sources of the client's anxieties. They focus primarily on extinguishing the specific anxiety, whatever its origins. The following case illustrates the steps used in a clinical application of implosive therapy:

A female college student of 19 with a lifelong fear of spiders was introduced to two therapists and given a general idea in her first session of the purpose and procedure of implosive therapy. Returning a few days later for her second session, she was asked to close her eyes and imagine herself in her room alone, suddenly confronted with a spider on her window curtain. Following that, one of the therapists suggested that she visualize seeing several spiders surging rapidly out of the hole in the wall next to the window. . . .

Hundreds of them begin to creep over her furniture, around the walls and up the ceiling. She can't escape them—the door is bolted and covered with menacing spiders. One by one, the spiders crawl toward her. The first spider, a particularly large creature, creeps onto her leg—another suddenly lands on her head. Then 5, 20, 50, 100 of them creep all over her—into her eyes, nostrils, up her dress, into her mouth—fat, hairy, monstrous spiders swarming on her body, into her clothes, down her throat, into her vagina, anus, intestines, stomach. . . .

Needless to say, the patient is extremely tense, at her wit's end. Then suddenly, the patient is "awakened" from her nightmarish vision. The spiders are gone—she's all right—nothing, in fact, has happened to her. (Millon, 1969)

The fact that the subject never actually suffers any negative consequences while imagining the intensely fearful situation eventually reduces or extinguishes her fears.

Modeling

In recent years, the phenomenon called _modeling_ has attracted an increasing amount of research. In modeling, a subject learns or modifies his behavior after observing the behavior of others. The subject does not himself have to make the response he observes, or be reinforced for making it, to learn the new behavior. The term modeling often is used interchangeably with _observational learning._

The behavior-modification possibilities of modeling are suggested in a study using boys and girls, 3 and 5 years old, who had strong fears of dogs (Bandura & Menlove, 1968). In this experiment, the children watched films in which models displayed progressively closer contacts with a dog. In the first sequences, the model simply looked at and occasionally patted the dog, which was confined in a playpen. Later movies showed the model walking the dog on a leash, grooming it, holding it in his arms, and serving it canine snacks. In the final sequences, the model's behavior was more venturesome. He climbed into the playpen with the dog, played with it, and even rested his head on the dog for a short time. This progressive modeling treatment alone led to stable reductions in the children's fear and avoidance behavior.

Psychodynamic and Behavior Therapies

Over the years, psychodynamic therapists have differed strongly with behavior therapists about the principles underlying their separate ap-

21-5

In a series of experiments, Bandura (1965) compared the effectiveness of three different techniques in curing people of a snake phobia. Subjects were divided into four groups: group I was systematically desensitized; group II watched a film of people playing with snakes; group III observed live models playing with snakes and group members were encouraged to imitate the model; and group IV was not treated at all. Subjects in Group III clearly were least afraid of snakes at the end of the sessions; they could sit still while a snake crawled all about them.

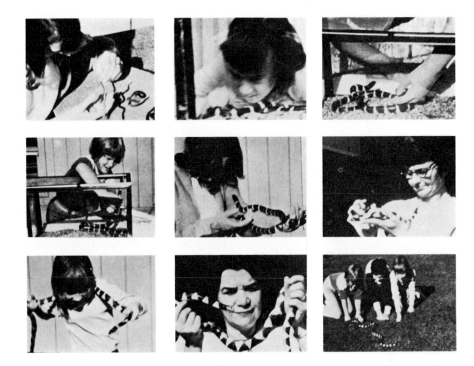

proaches. As learning-based therapeutic methods grew more common, several writers contended that psychodynamic therapy was declining. They viewed psychodynamic therapy as inefficient, overly complicated, unrelated to its own basic theories, and poorly validated by proven successes. On the other hand, these critics saw the learning-based therapies as rational, direct, and clear outgrowths of their theory. Other writers, undaunted by the apparent successes of the behavior therapies, observed that these therapies could be used only on a few disorders within the psychopathological spectrum. They also argued that treatments such as desensitization and implosive therapy were superficial because these treatments did not basically restructure the personality, a step that was considered essential for a lasting cure. In addition, these critics complained that desensitization and implosive therapy had little relation to learning theory.

In recent years, this psychodynamic therapy–behavior therapy cold war has moderated somewhat. Two views have gained acceptance. The first is that the behavior therapist's attitudes and personality may well be inextricably bound up with the therapy itself, so that therapy sessions may involve many more subtle psychological factors than extinction or reinforcement of specific responses. The second view that has gained wider acceptance holds that the psychodynamic therapist frequently and unwittingly functions as a behavior therapist—for example, when he praises a patient to reinforce him for producing impulse-laden and conflict-laden dreams and fantasies.

If psychodynamic and learning therapies do, in fact, have some similarities, it would seem helpful to access the relative importance of the similarities and differences. Also, clinical workers might be well advised to be flexible in their use of therapeutic techniques.

Among the developers of behavior therapy is Arnold Lazarus. In a revealing glimpse into his life as a clinical worker, he reflected on his growing awareness of the need to be flexible and ready to use the best technique available:

Many trainees who were acquainted with my writings expressed some surprise after observing me with patients. Although my previous publications had stressed such features as interpersonal considerations and other "nonspecific" factors, the extent to which these aspects often dominate my therapeutic interactions had not been sufficiently emphasized. . . .

As an ever-increasing number of therapeutic systems mushroom into existence, it becomes impossible to keep pace with the field. Theorists who try to integrate assumptions from divergent systems often end up embracing incompatible notions. Those who identify exclusively with one or two schools of thought often find that their devotion eventually leads to diminishing returns. But those clinicians who are willing to employ any technique that has been shown to be effective empirically, regardless of its point of origin, manage to extract the active ingredients from a vast array of different systems. (Lazarus, 1971)

In his book, Lazarus gives an excellent example of the need for clinical flexibility. A patient came to Lazarus ostensibly concerned with a bridge phobia. Before using desensitization (the usual choice in such a case), Lazarus conducted an intensive interview. In it, the problems of the patient, the youngest of five children, expanded considerably beyond his bridge phobia:

Patient: *I have a fear of crossing bridges.*
Therapist: *Do you have any other fears or difficulties?*
Patient: *No.*
Therapist: *Well, in what way has it affected your life?*
Patient: *I had to quit an excellent job in Berkeley.*
Therapist: *Where do you live?*
Patient: *San Francisco.*
Therapist: *So why didn't you move to Berkeley?*
Patient: *I prefer living in the city.*
Therapist: *To get to this institute, you had to cross the Bay Bridge.*
Patient: *Yes, I was seeing a doctor in San Francisco. He tried to desensitize me but it didn't help so he said I should see you because you know more about this kind of treatment. It's not so bad when I have my wife and kids with me. But even then, the Golden Gate, which is about one mile long, is my upper limit. I was wondering whether you ever consult in the city?*
Therapist: *No. But tell me, how long have you had this problem?*
Patient: *Oh, about four years, I'd say. It just happened suddenly. I was coming home from work and the Bay Bridge was awfully slow. I just suddenly panicked for no reason at all. I mean, nothing like this had ever happened to me before. I*

felt that I would crash into the other cars. Once I even had a feeling that the bridge would cave in.

Therapist: Let's get back to that first panic experience about four years ago. You said that you were coming home from work. Had anything happened at work?

Patient: Nothing unusual.

Therapist: Were you happy at work?

Patient: Sure! Huh! I was even due for promotion.

Therapist: What would that have entailed?

Patient: An extra $3,000 a year.

Therapist: I mean in the way of having to do different work.

Patient: Well, I would have been a supervisor. I would have had more than fifty men working under me.

Therapist: How did you feel about that?

Patient: What do you mean?

Therapist: I mean how did you feel about the added responsibility? Did you feel that you were up to it, that you could cope with it?

Patient: Gee! My wife was expecting our first kid. We both welcomed the extra money.

Therapist: So round about the time you were about to become a father, you were to be promoted to supervisor. So you would face two new and challenging roles. You'd be a daddy at home and also big daddy at work. And this was when you began to panic on the bridge, and I guess you never did wind up as a supervisor.

Patient: No. I had to ask for a transfer to the city.

Therapist: Now, please think very carefully about this question. Have you ever been involved in any accident on or near a bridge, or have you ever witnessed any serious accident on or near a bridge?

Patient: Not that I can think of.

Therapist: Do you still work for the same company?

Patient: No. I got a better offer, more money, from another company in the city. I've been with them for almost 1½ years now.

Therapist: Are you earning more money or less money than you would have gotten in Berkeley?

Patient: About the same. But prices have gone up so it adds up to less.

Therapist: If you hadn't developed the bridge phobia and had become foreman in Berkeley at $3,000 more, where do you think you would be today?

Patient: Still in Berkeley.

Therapist: Still supervisor? More money?

Patient: Oh hell! Who knows! (laughs). Maybe I would have been vice president.

Therapist: And what would that have entailed?

Patient: I'm only kidding. But actually, it could have happened.

As a result of this interview and Lazarus's later discovery that the patient's mother had influenced him to think he would never amount to anything, Lazarus designed a mixed treatment. He combined elements of psychodynamic and learning theories. Thus, although Lazarus is a firm advocate of desensitization techniques, he also finds it helpful to understand the context in which symptoms appear. In this case, the bridge phobia did not simply "occur." Instead, Lazarus believed, the bridge was closely associated with the new responsibilities of his job and his fatherhood, which the patient did not feel he could face. A Freudian or Jungian therapist would have an even more "dynamic" view of the events surrounding the bridge.

A Case Study

What actually happens during the course of various kinds of therapies? In this essay, we shall follow Ginny's progress as her neurotic conflicts are treated through psychoanalysis, behavior modification, and client-centered therapy. Though Ginny is fictitious, her problems are commonplace and her treatment, in each case, is representative of the form of therapy being described (Adapted from R. W. Heine, *Psychotherapy.* Englewood Cliffs, N.J.: Prentice-Hall, 1971).

Psychoanalysis

Ginny is a prime candidate for psychoanalysis. At age twenty-six she is having serious difficulty in establishing her independence from her hypochondriacal and domineering mother and in contemplating marriage in opposition to her mother's wishes. Nevertheless, she has functioned well most of her life, graduated from college, and has worked productively without undue anxiety.

At first glance, we might be inclined to say that all of Ginny's problems were created by her mother, and that if her mother changed, Ginny could change. However, while Ginny contends with her mother's disagreeable maneuvers on a realistic basis, she also uses her mother as an excuse while attempting to resolve her own ambivalent feelings about marriage.

Thus, there is much that Ginny could change in herself to enable her to meet her current and future problems more effectively.

Before the analysis begins, the analyst obtains a case history, explains the need for free association, and works out a plan for appointment times and payment of fees. When the analysis begins, the analyst sits behind the couch on which Ginny is relaxing and waits for her to speak.

Tentatively at first, and then with feeling, Ginny expresses her anger at her mother, vividly recounting the ways in which she has made life in their family difficult. The pleasant, neutral analyst gives largely silent assent to Ginny's diatribe, in sharp contrast to her mother who argues vigorously if she is opposed or criticized. Thus Ginny begins to feel very attached to the analyst. If he is a male, she finds in him some of the good characteristics of her father, greatly enlarged, and none of the negative features. Moreover, she feels very well, having unburdened herself, and more competent to face problems than ever before. Shyly, she confides her affection for the analyst and alludes to his great skills in helping her to achieve remarkable improvements in so short a time. She may suggest termination, saying that she has gained what she came for and would not profit from further sessions.

At this point, the analyst's tactics may include appropriately timed observations that Ginny has not commented at any length about herself and her own problems, that her reports of her handling of difficult situations suggest that she may identify with her mother's hypochondria, since she also develops physical symptoms in periods of crisis; that she handles some aspects of her relationship with her mother in ways that evoke the very behavior she claims to fear and resent; and so on. In this way, the analyst suggests that their work has really just begun—that Ginny's good feelings are in part the product of her not really looking at herself closely, and that there are, quite possibly, some complicated truths about her relationship with her family that remain to be uncovered. Since Ginny in one sense already knows that there are undisclosed and conflictual elements in her feelings toward significant people in her life, and also knows that examination of these elements would be painful and anxiety-provoking, she is not eager to pursue them. Moreover, she has given the analyst a rare gift of trust, approbation, and even affection, and he seems to spurn her.

What can we reasonably conjecture about the prisoners Ginny holds in repression? Some, such as a far-reaching dependence-independence conflict, are shared with most people, simply because all of us were once weak and small and necessarily dependent. In the same category would be wildly unrealistic, comprehensive solutions to conflicts associated with early psychosexual development — fantasies of total control of significant others or of completely unbounded impulse expression. Given Ginny's history, we can infer an inordinate fear as a young child that she had the capacity to kill her hypochondriacal mother, coupled with some relish at possessing such power. We may also conjecture that her surface antagonism to her mother is matched by hidden admiration for the strength reflected in her mother's capacity to terrorize the household. We can guess that as a girl she had a deep attachment to her father, competing with intense anger at the impotence that made him incapable of protecting her. We note Ginny's ambivalence with respect to marriage, which may be linked to the equation: disobedience equals mother's death, but could also be tied to profound unconscious fears of loss of dependency. She, like her mother, might have to be dominant because men are weak. But domination requires independence and threatens potential loss of love.

The analyst's gentle nudging toward exploration of these highly emotion-laden unconscious conflicts leaves Ginny feeling depressed, angry, and anxious. She now perceives the analyst as rejecting, unhelpful, and incompetent. Again, she thinks of terminating the relationship, now so painful.

In the next phase, the diffuse feelings of antagonism toward the analyst begin to coalesce around particular issues. For long periods, she inveighs angrily against the analyst's impotence (like her father's) and then is equally upset at his controlling, dominating, critical behavior (like her mother's). As Ginny replays these poignant episodes from her childhood, the analyst remains his professionally decent, discerning, neutral self and, as the occasion seems to demand, interprets the transference. In effect, Ginny has the experience of reliving the traumatic events of her life, but with a different outcome. Instead of evoking real or imagined anger, rejection, abject dependency, or lonely independence, her fantasies and emotions evoke only warm support to examine them in the light of her adult capabilities for understanding.

As Ginny works through the release of one imprisoned fear, conflict, or fantasy after another, she can see that they do not place her in the desperate jeopardy she feared in childhood, but are simply distortions that can now be corrected. At the conclusion of analysis, Ginny will still have to cope with her mother, the responsibilities of marriage, and personal ambitions. All of these will be realistically difficult to handle, and there will be much unhappiness as well as gratification in the process. But Ginny will be free of intense, disabling anxiety and ambivalence in the face of realistic problems and free of the tendency to respond impulsively and erratically when decisions must be made. She will have a realistic view of her own capacities, and will see herself neither as a malevolent force nor as an omnipotent, saving angel.

Behavior Modification

What would happen if Ginny had seen a behavior therapist instead? Ginny's manifest symptoms (chest pains, headaches, and stomach upsets) are not those commonly treated by behavior therapists. Nor are her chronic interpersonal difficulties with her mother or her conflicts about marriage readily approachable by simple conditioning procedures. Therefore, Wolpe's technique will be our treatment of choice (the technique of systematic desensitization as described in the text).

It is clear what Ginny's life-long problem has been in behavioral terms. Her mother, for reasons that need not concern us here, has persistently and effectively used her hypochondriacal illness to manipulate Ginny's behavior with regard to independence and marriage. She simply became seriously ill and "threatened" to die if Ginny moved in any significant way toward independence. Thus, in order to achieve independence or to marry, Ginny would have had to sustain the intense anxiety associated with the idea of causing her mother's illness or even her death. Her mother's punishing behavior would not necessarily make independence less attractive, but it would make painful any move toward independence. If Ginny's mother had systematically rewarded dependent behavior, as some mothers in similar situations do, Ginny's moves to be free of her mother might have been weakened over time and her conflict lessened.

The therapeutic task is to desensitize Ginny to her mother's threats and enhance the rewards of independence. The physical symptoms (with the exception of Ginny's chest pains) present no serious problem, since they represent physiological reflections of intense anxiety and will disappear if the dependence-independence conflict is resolved. The chest pains, in contrast, may have been learned by modeling on her mother's device for managing others. Reluctant either to give up the possibility of marriage or to go through with it, Ginny may try to stop the flow of events by offering a valid physical excuse for temporizing. If her fiance is impressed by this physical ploy, it would reinforce Ginny's use of chest pains to delay indefinitely the resolution of her conflict.

The behavioral therapist begins by eliciting Ginny's report of her current situation. Then he asks her to list in hierarchical order, from the most to the least upsetting, as many recurrent, anxiety-arousing encounters with her mother as she can.

This rank order may include similarly anxious encounters with her fiancé. Once this hierarchy is formed, the therapist starts with the least anxiety-arousing problematic situation—perhaps a situation in which some minor step toward independence is met by strong resistance from Ginny's mother.

Ginny is first trained to achieve complete relaxation, either by a method that systematically focuses on one muscle group after another or by a light hypnotic trance. Once she is completely relaxed, the therapist asks her to imagine the encounter with her mother as vividly as possible and to make it turn out differently. That is, he asks her to imagine herself being assertive in the face of her mother's threats and resistant to her mother's efforts to arouse guilt. According to Wolpe's theory of reciprocal inhibition, Ginny's state of relaxation will make it difficult if not impossible for her to experience anxiety. Thus, she will become desensitized to her mother's manipulative attempts.

Once Ginny had been led through her hierarchy of anxiety-evoking encounters, she will presumably be able to confront her mother and assert her rights to independence (including marriage and the move to another city) with minimal anxiety. Free of the need to give in to her mother's threats, she will also be free to test more fully the potential delights of independence. If independent decision-making leads to gratifying experiences, the behaviors that comprise this orientation to self and others will be strengthened, and the possibility of a relapse will be reduced correspondingly. There seems to be evidence that Ginny would find independence exceptionally gratifying.

Client-Centered Therapy

If Ginny turned to a Rogerian client-centered therapist, her treatment would progress in still another manner.

Based on our knowledge of Ginny's long-standing conflict with her mother, we can anticipate that she will spend a great deal of time in the first hours defining her difficulty in breaking away from her mother's influence in order to be married. She will describe how sad she feels that life is slipping away from her and castigate herself for being weak, dependent, and easily intimidated. Ginny will also criticize her mother for being so domineering, unfair, and selfish; her father for having been so weak, and hence failing to protect her.

Key exchanges around these issues might go as follows:

GINNY (angrily): Just about every time in my life that I have tried to do something *I* wanted to do when and how I wanted to do it, my mother would either criticize my plans until I gave them up or, if that didn't work, she would become very ill because of my obstinacy. Then I would get scared.

THERAPIST: It seems to have been very upsetting to you to learn that you had the power to make your mother ill.

GINNY: Yes, it was very upsetting, but sometimes it seems that mother is just using her illness to keep me tied to her.

THERAPIST: So even though it often seems as if it is your behavior that is affecting your mother's health, you sense that it is really she who is controlling you.

GINNY: Yes, but it would still be terrible if I somehow caused her death.

THERAPIST: Deep down you are really frightened by the thought that you actually could kill her by opposing her.

GINNY: About my fiancé and the plans for marriage, I feel all mixed up. I love him and want to marry him. I'm embarrassed that I appear so changeable and uncertain. Yet at the same time I'm angry because he doesn't seem to be sympathetic about the spot I'm in with my

mother. He ought to be more patient while I work things out.

THERAPIST: You would really be relieved if your fiancé saw your problem with your mother in the same way you do.

GINNY: In one sense, maybe. In another, I like his ability to make firm decisions and stick with them. He seems stronger than my father was—my father always gave in to my mother. But I'm just not ready to take the leap of both marrying *and* leaving the city when my mother is so opposed.

Later in therapy we might conjecture an exchange as follows:

GINNY: Still, when I think back, I have accomplished a good deal in spite of my mother. I've been away from home and on my own twice and really enjoyed it when I could stop thinking about how reproachful my mother would be if she knew I was enjoying myself. My mother complained endlessly about her health, but nothing actually happened to her when I went away from her.

THERAPIST: You believe that once *you* have the courage to oppose your mother, she may accept it better than she says she will.

GINNY: Yes, I see that it is *really* my *own* lack of conviction about what is the right thing to do that holds me back. In this sense, I blame my mother for a fault that is at least half mine.

Then, toward the end of the therapy, we might hear the following:

GINNY (cheerfully): Well, it's all set. I'm leaving in two weeks to be married.

THERAPIST: Finally making the decision really makes you pleased with yourself.

GINNY: It certainly does. I've talked everything over with my fiancé, and he agrees that mother can visit us from time to time. Meanwhile, I've talked with her doctors—something I could never bring myself to do before—and they tell me that basically she's in very good health for a person of her age. She is bitching a lot, but I just tell her that I've decided and that's it.

THERAPIST: It is really a relief to have reassurance about her condition even though you suspected she was exaggerating.

GINNY: Yes, it certainly is. But I couldn't really bring myself to find out until I had solved my own problem about being independent. As long as I needed her, I had to believe she really needed me.

THERAPIST: Yes, that certainly seems to be the way it is.

In these illustrative exchanges, we can see Ginny's original anxiety, depression, and self-criticism give way to a more realistic appraisal of herself and finally to a self-satisfied planning for the future. The therapist, true to his theory, stayed with Ginny as closely as he could. He did not reassure her when she was self-deprecating, nor did he attempt to interpret her mother's or her fiancé's behavior to her. Rather, the therapist showed complete respect for the client's capacity to bring out and effectively confront any thoughts, feelings, and attitudes that were creating emotional turmoil.

Other Methods of Psychotherapy

We have examined a wide spectrum of distinctive approaches to altering or eliminating disturbed behavior. Diverse though these techniques may appear, they are but a small sample of the approaches that have been advocated and, in some cases, applied extensively. And like Lazarus, many therapists often adopt an eclectic approach, combining elements of different therapeutic techniques and selecting the particular pattern of treatment that appears best suited for each individual patient—rather than employing a single, rigid therapeutic procedure regardless of the symptoms, age, education, and socioeconomic status of the patient.

Freud first treated hysteric patients by using hypnosis to elicit the unconscious memories or impulses that he believed lay at the root of the neurotic disorder. Today, some therapists use hypnosis as a part or even as a principal feature of their therapeutic efforts. When combined with techniques from classical psychoanalysis, this approach is referred to as *hypnoanalysis*. More common is the use of hypnosis to eliminate specific symptoms through posthypnotic suggestion. Some therapists rely almost solely upon hypnotic suggestion, particularly in connection with such apparently isolated problems as smoking, difficulty in concentrating when studying, or insomnia.

Play therapy is a therapeutic technique with a rather long history. It is particularly useful for work with children, and it takes place in a setting that includes toys and dolls as well as other commonplace objects. The child is encouraged to use the objects to act out impulses and wishes that are not expressed in his ordinary world. Sometimes this approach is called *release therapy* because the child is encouraged to release impulses that usually are kept pent up. The manner in which the child manipulates (and talks to) the mother, father, and sibling dolls can be interpreted by the therapist, so the technique can be incorporated into a "talking therapy." The technique also is used for diagnostic purposes; the observer can infer the nature of the disturbance by watching the child play with the toys.

Closely related to play therapy is *psychodrama*, which was developed almost 50 years ago by J. L. Moreno. This method also involves play-acting, but it is acting with real people rather than dolls. The patient may participate with other patients who are also projecting their problems and conflicts into the drama. The drama may unfold with little structure and with the therapist playing a relatively passive role, or the patient may be asked to play a specific role in a particular play or sequence. Therapists using psychodrama believe that patients secure some release by acting out the forbidden and unacceptable. They also interpret the psychodrama with the patient, to help him gain greater insight into the underlying causes of his problems.

Social Therapy

Psychotherapy and behavior therapy both deal with the patient's personal relationships. Typically, the vehicle for their improvement is the therapist-patient relationship. Thus, the base of the therapy is social. *Social therapies* build on knowledge gained in psychodynamics and learning research, and they emphasize how the environment in general and community experience in particular contribute to a person's psychological development. Thus, large group participation and group problem-solving occupy center-stage in social therapy.

Social therapy is distinct from other forms of therapy only in the size of the groups it attempts to work with. To date, relatively few attempts have been made to modify behavior in large social units, such as neighborhoods and cities. Why then give it separate treatment? Primarily because clinical workers today are recognizing that many purely "personal" problems have important roots in the community. As we understand more about the relationships between "personal" problems and characteristics of communities and societies, we may be able to prevent as well as treat certain abnormal behaviors in the community. For example, evidence suggests that poverty and lack of social interaction help create many behavior problems that are especially evident in urban ghettos.

Earlier we described token economies in mental hospitals. We might well have described the token economy as a social or community program, since the token economy usually is directed at an entire community—though it may be a small one, such as a hospital or even a single ward.

Community Mental Health Programs

Efforts to increase human effectiveness on a relatively large, community-wide scale have already been put into effect. Compensatory educational programs, such as Head Start—which is designed to enrich the preschool learning of underprivileged children and to teach mothers to train their own children in the use of adaptive behavior—are widespread. Halfway houses represent another form of social therapy, as we shall see.

Community-wide programs have been encouraged recently because of society's increasing acceptance of responsibility for educating, planning, and changing the community for optimal use of human potential. Levine and Levine (1970) succinctly expressed this growing social acceptance:

The contemporary community mental health movement must also be considered from the perspective of its place in American society. Its broad goals must be viewed as a product of the growing acceptance by American society of the responsibility for the total welfare of all individuals. The contemporary period reflects trends that began with the industrial revolution, which were accelerated with the rapid social changes induced by the processes of industrialization and urbanization, and which continue today, powered by scientific and technical developments.

The question of society's responsibility for the maladjusted echoes a topic we discussed at the beginning of the preceding chapter—changing social attitudes regarding mental health. We pointed out that over the past several centuries, society has come to treat disturbed persons more kindly. This change in attitude is reflected in the improvement in public hospitals' physical plants, the attitudes of their staffs, and the humanity with which they treat patients. This progress has been dramatic. However, the treatment programs of these institutions could be still more effective and more considerate of the patient's human needs.

The Social Community of the Hospital.   Recent studies of the effects of long-term hospitalization, as well as the effects of other possible methods of treatment, make one point clear: Hospitalization, whether long- or short-term, is usually a negative social experience. Individual behavior is closely linked to the hospital's immediate social environment in a cause-effect pattern. If hospital authorities become more aware of this relationship, they may be able to change conditions that

21-6
By 1890, most mental institutions no longer treated the mentally disturbed as freaks. Asylums were modernized and recreation rooms were provided for the patients. While the institutions themselves still were very dismal and depressing, these changes signalled enormous advances in the treatment of the mentally disturbed. (Culver Pictures)

currently promote chronic maladaptive behavior in psychiatric patients. Approximately two-thirds of the patients now in U.S. public mental hospitals are chronic cases. About 40 percent of those newly admitted to these hospitals will never leave. So a large number of people are permanently affected.

A major problem in many large hospitals is the extreme regimentation of life and the accompanying loss of dignity for patients. One way to improve the hospital environment is to replace the word "patient" with "resident." Perhaps more important are the steps taken to give residents more responsibilities and to encourage them to develop social interaction and social skills. Reformers also have added opportunities for residents to earn rewards—perhaps through a token economy. Such programs encourage hospital residents to take steps toward independence in preparation for life outside the institution.

Halfway Houses. When the resident returns to the community, he faces many problems. For this reason, a number of hospitals discharge individuals to *halfway houses.* These are special community institutions in which the individual is a participating, decision-making resident. Most residents of these increasingly common facilities use them as a transitional point; they usually leave within a year. However, not all people with mental afflictions can learn to accept the greater social responsibilities of life "on the outside." These people need houses designed for permanent residents.

Just as the settlement houses, common in the United States at the turn of the century, were intended to provide an easier transition between two cultures or nations, the halfway house is intended to provide a smoother transition between the world of the mental hospital and existence in the outer world. The following description by Rausch and Rausch (1968) provides a picture of life in a halfway house:

The typical resident of the typical halfway house is an ex-hospital patient, at one time diagnosed as schizophrenic. Directly or shortly after leaving the hospital, he came to the house, perhaps after some visiting. He finds the house very different from the hospital ward. For one thing it is in a residential area of the city. It is a many-roomed place, dating from the twenties or thirties, in town rather than in the suburbs. It is a house, and it looks like a house and not like a hospital. Aside from staff, there are only about ten other residents. The resident has his own room or he shares a room with just one other person; also, unlike the hospital, the house has no locked rooms. While there are lots of things to do at the house, he has to go outside for any special entertainment. Moreover, he pays for his room and board. These cost him about $90 a month [in 1963], a fee that covers little more than half of the expenses that the house requires for his care. At the halfway house the resident receives no written rules. Still, he finds out that there are some things he must not do—such as drink on the premises, and some things that he must do—such as to tell staff when he goes out, come to meals promptly, keep himself and the premises clean and obey his doctor's orders. He must care for his own room and he is usually expected to do some extra work of his own choice around the house. If he *doesn't live up to these requirements, considerable social pressure will be placed on him and he may even be threatened with having to leave the house. In some ways then it isn't like living independently at a boarding house; it is much more closely supervised, and there is much more interaction with staff and with other residents. But it isn't like a hospital either; for example, he doesn't have to get "passes," and no one threatens to remove his "privileges."*

Preventing Mental Health Problems

In keeping with this increasing concern for the disturbed individual, the attitude toward psychological treatment has taken a new turn—preventive community care. Many clinical workers who have devoted most of their careers to personal relationships with their clients have now begun to apply their psychological knowledge to the community. They are trying not only to rehabilitate people but also to prevent the development of community-related mental health problems. A loosely organized discipline of mental health workers oriented to community problems (*community psychology*) is taking this new approach.

One accepted role for such community psychologists is that of dispassionate observer and analyst of social systems and processes. For example, a psychologist observing a school system from the outside can see problems and patterns that teachers or students are "too close" to see. If such objective observations were available to school officials, some school policies might be improved and a source of behavior disorders eliminated.

Milieu Therapy. Few large-scale applications of therapies based on social-psychological concepts have been attempted. However, clinical workers are increasingly applying these therapies on relatively restricted—but still very complicated—environments, such as mental hospitals. For example, *milieu therapy* programs stimulate patients to maintain and even improve their interpersonal skills and social responsibilities. Ordinarily the mental patient lives in a quiet, supportive, tolerant environment, removed from normal environmental stresses. In a word, he is sheltered. Milieu therapy attempts to broaden the patient's experience—to "unshelter" him somewhat. In today's progressive institutions, patients commonly participate in activities such as "open ward" meetings and patient government. Such programs, designed to enrich the patient's world, directly involve him in the conduct of daily routines and recreational activities. In some cases, self-organized and supervised groups—the level of supervision is proportionate to the patients' condition—have responsibility for community planning within the hospital. Special patient committees may handle some part of the job of orienting new patients to hospital life and its particular routines.

Milieu therapy programs usually are combined with other programs, such as *occupational therapy* and *educational therapy.* In occupational and educational therapy, patients work and learn for recreation but also to strengthen skills related to their social adjustment in and out of the hospital.

21-7
Occupational therapy has long been used to help institutionalized mental patients prepare themselves for the world outside. In the early 19th century in Leipzig, Germany, a Dr. Segert already was beginning to use a rudimentary form of occupational therapy. (The Bettmann Archive)

Somatic Therapies

The study of abnormal psychology has demonstrated that biophysical factors are associated with, and are perhaps the primary cause of, much disturbed behavior. We mentioned this link in the previous chapter, in the discovery, for example, that general paresis is caused by a syphilitic infection. Not only are there organic causes of abnormal behavior, but also *somatic* (or *organic*) *therapies.* Many times over the years, enthusiastic researchers have proclaimed the discovery of a drug or some other organic treatment that appeared to cure mental disorders. All too often, the hopes of professional workers and the general public subsequently were dashed by more thorough research showing that early reports were overly optimistic. Despite these setbacks, some of these therapies—especially those involving psychoactive drugs—have turned out to be useful in treating (if not curing) mental disorders. Certain other organic therapies have turned out to be harmful.

Psychosurgery

When new techniques are discovered in almost any discipline, they may at first be used too readily and, therefore, inappropriately. As we saw in Chapter 5, when morphine first became available, it was widely used as a painkiller—until its addictive properties were discovered. Another example of overuse is the enthusiasm in the 1930s for lobotomies. A *lobotomy* is a brain operation in which the surgeon severs the neural pathways to the patient's prefrontal lobes. Shortly after its first use on a human, the lobotomy was seen as a quick and easy means of treating illness. For a number of years, lobotomies were performed frequently, especially on chronically hospitalized mental patients. We now know that many people respond poorly to such *psychosurgery.* They may sink into stupor, confusion, and a vegetablelike existence. In other words, lobotomies not only failed to help some patients; they actually harmed them. The early enthusiasm stemmed from the lobotomy's effect of markedly reducing the anxiety of some mental patients. Today, lobotomies rarely are performed in clinical practice, but other forms of psychological brain surgery have been developed and have also provoked considerable controversy (see the essay on page 736).

Electroshock Therapy

Another somatic therapy, electroshock or electroconvulsive therapy, also came into use in the 1930s. Unlike lobotomy, electroshock is still used fairly often. *Electroshock therapy* consists of brief electric currents passed through the brain; the shocks produce convulsions and often result in a coma. Such therapy frequently has dramatic effects on a patient's behavior. After less than a dozen shock treatments, a deeply depressed person may become cheerful and active. While this effect is readily apparent, how electric shock brings it about is not known. Moreover, many patients have suffered some loss of memory and other unfortunate side effects from shock treatment. In a few extreme cases, the treatment has produced irreversible brain damage. For these reasons, electroshock treatment is employed less often than formerly; it now is used primarily with severely depressed patients.

Psychopharmacology

Since 1955, the resident population of public hospitals has declined steadily. To a considerable extent, the decline is due to the development and widespread use of *psychoactive drugs.* These drugs have led to a revolution in the care and treatment of the mentally ill. Thousands of patients, who just a few years ago were condemned to spend their entire lives in the back wards of state mental hospitals, now can live and function in society when they use certain psychoactive drugs. The study of the effects of these drugs on behavior—as we noted in Chapter 5—is called *psychopharmacology.*

Antipsychotic Drugs. The psychotherapeutic agents in widest use today are the *antipsychotic drugs. Chlorpromazine* is the most prominent of the drugs used to treat major psychoses, such as schizophrenia. Chlorpromazine, first produced in France in 1952, is preferred over other drugs because it does not make the user as sleepy as many other such drugs and yet tends to reduce the most extreme psychotic symptoms. Another significant drug is *reserpine,* which was first used in the United States in 1954 to lower blood pressure, but was discovered also to reduce the agitation common in mental patients. Reserpine tends to depress the patient's mood (chlorpromazine does not) and also causes a significant decrease in the brain's content of biogenic amines (chemicals that act as transmitter substances at the synapse). Researchers are exploring the possible connections between these effects of reserpine.

These and other *tranquilizers* are used extensively both in and out of institutions. In addition to alleviating and even eliminating agitation, hallucinations, and delusions, the drugs also may reduce the social withdrawal that severely disturbed people frequently exhibit. Research is continuing in order to clarify how the tranquilizing drugs work and to reduce such known side effects as dependency, liver problems, and skin reactions. One point well understood by researchers and clinicians alike is that these drugs do not result in permanent cures. They treat the symptoms and not the cause of a behavior disorder. When the medication is withdrawn, the symptoms tend to return.

Antianxiety Drugs. The *antianxiety drugs* are *minor tranquilizers,* and are of little value in treating psychoses. However, they do produce a pleasant and relatively anxiety-free state similar to that induced by alcohol. Minor tranquilizers are prescribed and taken widely in today's culture. Indeed, brand names such as Miltown and Valium have become a part of our common idiom. In moderate doses, they have only minor effects. They slightly alter the brain waves so that they are more sleep-like and they reduce anxiety, according to those who use them. How antianxiety drugs work is unknown, but their many users testify to their value.

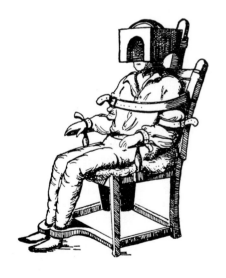

21-8
Today patients are calmed with tranquilizing drugs. During the 19th century the tranquilizing chair was used to restrain unmanageable cases. (The Bettmann Archive)

PSYCHOSURGERY

Elliot S. Valenstein *University of Michigan*

Discussions of psychosurgery frequently elicit two opposite points of view. One is that these brain operations can alleviate crippling and otherwise intractable mental illnesses. The other is that they are brain mutilations that eliminate troublesome behavior only by changing human beings into emotional and intellectual "vegetables." Debates usually degenerate into emotional outbursts that may be cathartic for the participants but are hardly insightful. Because this controversy contains many types of decisions that will have to be faced more frequently in the future, I should like to set down the arguments and the evidence as clearly and thoroughly as I can manage within the space available to me in this short essay. (For a fuller discussion of the history, the experimental and clinical data, and the social implications of psychosurgery, see *Brain Control: A Critical Examination of Brain Stimulation and Psychosurgery* (Valenstein, 1973). Shapiro (1974) presents an excellent treatment of legal questions.

The notion of destroying a part of the brain for psychiatric reasons can be such a horrifying thought that it obscures all historical perspective. Until recently most people were convinced that research would trace genius, personality traits, and mental illness to features of the brain. Even though investigation revealed no reliable correlation between gross development of any part of the brain and personality, the conviction remained that excessive activity in some region of the brain could produce psychiatric disorder. The development of more sophisticated techniques for studying the microscopic structure of brain tissue prompted the hope that the origins of mental illness might be found in the fine

connections between neurons, if not in gross anatomical differences. The Portuguese neurologist Egas Moniz was certainly not alone in entertaining the idea that excessive activity in some portion of the brain could result from synaptic changes that occurred during learning. Although he was not the first to try psychosurgery, Moniz was the first to operate on the prefrontal region of the cerebral cortex. His reports of dramatic improvements in some patients brought him a Nobel Prize in 1949.

Moniz's selection of prefrontal cortex areas for his operation was not surprising. It was the only subdivision of the cerebral cortex to which a specific sensory or motor function had not been attributed. Therefore, the higher integrative processes were commonly thought to take place there. Studies demonstrating that animals became aggressive or impulsive after destruction of that brain region suggested emotions also might be regulated there. Moniz was encouraged to try psychosurgery by Carlyle Jacobsen's report of the learning deficits that followed destruction of primates' prefrontal areas. Jacobsen included a description of an unusual chimp, Becky, who threw a temper tantrum every time she made an error. After destruction of the prefrontal area of her brain, however, she became quite calm and accepted all her errors with equanimity. Obviously impressed, Moniz logically asked: If frontal-lobe removal prevents the development of experimental neuroses in animals, why would it not be feasible to relieve such states in man by surgical means?

In 1935 Moniz and a neurosurgical colleague performed their first psychosurgery—an operation designed to

interrupt some of the nerve fiber connections between the frontal lobes and the rest of the brain. By 1937, Moniz had performed 38 operations and was able to draw conclusions about the technique in general. He observed that although some patients deteriorated, other patients improved substantially and could go back to work after being discharged from the hospital. In reality, the patients had not been studied in great depth. But Moniz's optimistic description of his results and the confirming reports by Freeman and Watts in the United States and other neurologists and neurosurgeons around the world contributed to the large-scale adoption of psychosurgery. Two other factors contributed to the sudden popularity of psychosurgery: there were relatively few psychiatrists as compared with the large numbers of severely disturbed veterans of World War II, and psychopharmacological drugs were not yet available as a possible alternative treatment.

After 1955, the number of operations performed declined drastically because drugs became more available and because there were reports that the operations produced damaging side-effects. More recently, as surgical techniques became more precise and it became clear that some patients were not helped by psychotherapy, drugs, or any other treatment, interest in psychosurgery revived. A flood of arguments against psychosurgery has met this revival. Some of these arguments are valid while others may reflect more emotion than logic.

The most common argument against psychosurgery is that the brain should never be violated because it is the organ that gives us our humanness—our personality, creativity, and our capacity to learn and

A
Diagram of the older Freeman-Watts lobotomy technique.

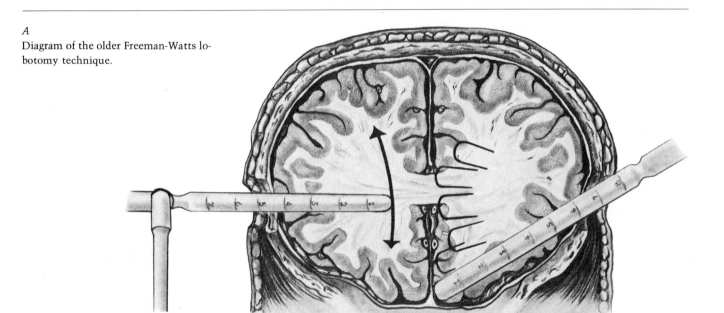

to experience emotion. How critical an argument is this? Undoubtedly, the brain as a whole is the seat of all these attributes, but no psychosurgical procedure involves more than a small part of the brain. We must talk about particular parts of the brain and the functions that are regulated by these parts. Many people have had localized brain tumors removed with little, if any, detectable loss in these human capacities. Although the sentiment expressed and the underlying concerns motivating such remarks are admirable, general assertions about the whole brain are not very helpful in making decisions about a particular brain operation. At best, these assertions force us to keep in mind—should it ever be forgotten—that surgeons always should exercise extreme caution before destroying any part of the brain; deficits may be produced that are difficult to detect with conventional tests.

Psychosurgery is said to be unique because healthy brain tissue is destroyed for a presumed therapeutic purpose. Actually, however, it is not the only kind of operation that destroys healthy tissue. Healthy tissue also has been destroyed to alleviate physiological disorders. Dr. Irving Cooper, for example, has destroyed a small brain area in over 10,000 patients suffering from such muscle or movement disorders as Parkinsonian tremors and various types of spasticity (Cooper, 1969, 1973). In all likelihood, the brain tissue Cooper destroyed was normal. Cooper reports a high percentage of success with these operations despite some risk of other deficits. Also, in some cases of intractable epilepsy, for which drugs have proved ineffective, the cutting of the corpus callosum—the most extensive fiber connections between the two sides of the brain—has significantly decreased the incidence of seizures. No one believes that the corpus callosum in these patients was abnormal. Here, too, the surgery produced deficits, but special testing is required to reveal them (see Gazzaniga, 1970; Sperry, 1968; and pages 53 through 58 of this text). In fact, these "split-brain" patients may function quite well in normal life—certainly much better than when they were plagued by a number of intense epileptic seizures every day. Even though such operations are controversial and carry the possibility of deficits, the advocates of psychosurgery argue that what is gained more than compensates for what is lost and that this loss-gain ratio justifies the use of psychosurgery, particularly when, without it, the patient is totally unable to cope with life. The dilemma, of course, is that psychiatric disorders do not allow you the luxury of being certain that you have exhausted all other more conservative treatments.

Perhaps the charge that psychosurgery has been, or may be, used as a political instrument to control social "troublemakers" has provoked the most concern. Many people believe this charge but there is no clear evidence to support it. The concern appears to be primarily over *potential* political use of psychosurgery. We cannot dismiss completely this disconcerting possibility; psychosurgery has been proposed as a socially useful alternative to lifetime prison terms. In addition, the suggestion that brain pathology may cause a significant amount of violence (Mark & Ervin, 1970) has initiated some studies of the incidence of neuro-

Diagram of the present-day procedure for psychosurgery.

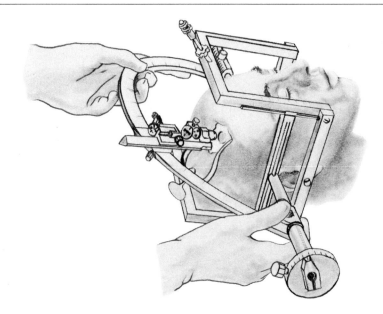

logical disorders among prison inmates with the possible implication that psychosurgery may be a sensible way to calm down incorrigibly violent prisoners. All of this prompts concern that people in positions of power might become convinced that biological solutions are readily available for problems that may be, in fact, mainly social.

Pointing out the logical or factual weakness of some arguments against psychosurgery does not constitute support for psychosurgery itself. It does, however, focus our attention on the main issue—namely, can destruction of a part of the brain be justified on therapeutic grounds? A difficult question. Even if all the data on the consequences of a particular psychosurgical procedure could be set forth before an operation began, two people, after examining this data, might still reach opposite conclusions. This happens simply because people are unable to agree about the relative importance of the physical and mental gains and losses the patient would experience after he had undergone the operation. For example, is a dulling of emotional responsiveness a reasonable price to

pay for freedom from crippling anxiety? Another problem is that the results of any brain operation probably will never be totally predictable, regardless of any increase in precision. In part, this is true because the behavioral effect of destroying any part of the brain depends on the patient's total personality, an entity so complex that it will probably always defy exhaustive analysis.

The earlier operations yielded varied results; evidence can be found to support almost any conclusion. The medical literature contains data demonstrating that after prefrontal lobotomy, patients suffer blunted emotional responsiveness, lower performance on at least some parts of IQ tests, an inability to maintain goal-directed behavior, and epileptic seizures or other neurological problems. On the other hand, a number of studies report significant psychiatric improvement, no IQ loss, and an increased ability to hold a job. All these studies can be criticized on various methodological grounds. The tests were probably insensitive to important changes in behavioral capacities. Estimates of improvement often stressed the elimination of

behavior troublesome to the hospital staff or society in general while paying little attention to the ways in which the operation may have reduced the patient's abilities and affected his relationships with others.

There are considerably fewer reports on the results of modern "fractional" operations. In the older operations (Figure A), surgical knives rotated inside the prefrontal area damaged that area of the brain extensively. Today's techniques (Figure B) are more precise, often destroying an area only three to five millimeters in diameter. While earlier psychosurgery disconnected large parts of the prefrontal area from the rest of the brain, present-day operations destroy either very specific parts of the prefrontal area or such parts of the limbic system as the amygdala, anterior thalamus, or hypothalamus. The smaller area of destruction and the added precision of the newer operations probably have resulted in considerably fewer instances of gross behavioral deterioration, or neurological side-effects, such as epilepsy. However, we have only very limited information about the emotional and intellectual changes produced by the newer procedures.

Neurosurgeons have neither the training nor the time to conduct the type of studies that would adequately evaluate the changes produced by their brain operations. Post-operative changes usually are reported in gross terms, listing percentages of patients exhibiting different degrees of improvement in poorly defined categories ranging from "completely cured" to "no change." Few post-operative tests were designed to measure changes in those capacities that animal studies have shown are likely to be altered. Indeed, many neurologists and neurosurgeons have displayed an amazing "tunnel vision" toward animal studies. While quick to see clinical applications of animal studies, they often have been quite blind to data that should have cautioned them against an operation and influenced their evaluative procedures.

Throughout the entire history of psychosurgery, many striking examples illustrate this sort of selective perception. Moniz, for example, quickly perceived that one of Carlyle Jacobsen's chimpanzees was less emotional after destruction of its pre-frontal area. However, he apparently was not influenced by Jacobsen's main conclusion that prefrontal damage produced animals that no longer could perform adequately on some learning tasks, particularly those requiring a delayed response.

Destruction of the amygdala nucleus (a limbic structure located in the temporal lobe) in patients who are repeatedly violent and destructive provides another example of selective perception. The operation was undertaken partly because in some studies the animals became tamer following amygdalectomy. At the same time, proponents of the operation more or less neglected the reports that these animals also were blunted emotionally, often displayed very inappropriate hypersexuality, had a compulsive tendency to place any object in their mouths, and had difficulty recognizing objects or gestures that they perceived visually. The work of Kling and his colleagues recently demonstrated the extent of these deficits. Trapped wild monkeys in Africa were amygdalectomized, tested, and then returned to their wild groups. Although the monkey subjects seemed tamer when approached by the experimenters, they were completely unable to cope with the complexities of life back in the wild. They did not seem to understand the various ways monkeys communicate with one another and their behavior was often inappropriate—for example, they sometimes displayed aggression toward the dominant animals in their groups. After a short period, all the amygdalectomized animals either retreated from, or were forced from, their groups. Eventually, they died from starvation or fell to predators.

We do not know that humans would have the same deficits as monkeys after an amygdalectomy, but the data presented have not been collected in a way that can completely reassure us. Case reports that emphasize the decrease in disruptive behavior are no substitute for objective testing designed to assess changes in the patients' different capacities. Today's great apparent need is for a mechanism that will increase the interactions between clinicians and those scientists trained to evaluate changes in behavior, emotions, and thought processes following damage to the brain.

Antidepressant Drugs. These drugs, such as *imiprimine*, are particularly interesting because we have some clues about how they work. They seem to alleviate severe psychotic depressive states by blocking or inhibiting the MAO enzyme. This enzyme inactivates the brain's biogenic amines, or neurotransmitter substances. Hence the antidepressant drugs lead to increased brain content of biogenic amines. This discovery led Kety to develop the theory that the biogenic amines play an important role in the emotional aspects of human behavior.

Psychotomimetics. Another intriguing drug group is the psychotomimetics. As we discussed in Chapter 5, these drugs seem to mimic psychotic behavior—hence their name. *Mescaline, psilocybin,* and *lysergic acid dimethylamide* (LSD) fall within this group. Although some of the psychotomimetics have been used experimentally in conjunction with psychotherapy—particularly in the treatment of alcoholism—they cannot be considered a legitimate method of treatment. This restriction is due to the limited similarity between the drugs' effects and the natural psychotic states. For this reason, the psychotomimetics do not seem to be helpful in therapy or in aiding our understanding of psychosis. Moreover, as part of the drug movement of the past decade these drugs have, in the hands of uninformed users, produced brain damage, psychosis, and even death.

Lithium. While drugs to lift deep depressions, to alleviate tension and anxiety, and to quell aggressive tendencies make their contributions on a day-to-day clinical level, exploratory work with new physical procedures continues. The investigation of the effects of *lithium salts* is an example. In 1949, an Australian researcher named Cade found that lithium salts, used as a substitute for sodium salts in the diet of heart patients, seemed to relieve acute manic-depressive disorders. While these salts curb mania and overactivity, they do not do it by suppressing behavior as do sedatives.

One intriguing aspect of lithium is that a single dose does not affect behavior. Optimal dosages vary from person to person but, in any case, positive results require continued treatment over time. While studies have yielded highly encouraging findings, experts do not agree about how repeated doses influence mania, nor do we fully understand lithium's side effects; but the research continues.

Evaluating Treatment

We have reviewed a number of treatments for behavior disorders. Today, we need to know much more about how the various types of treatment relate to each other. This need is especially clear in the case of schizophrenia, which has been approached from every therapeutic viewpoint we have mentioned. Each approach has offered promise, yet it remains unclear how the major psychological, sociological, and biophysical variables combine to produce this disorder and how it can be alleviated.

In addition to integrated studies of behavior disorders, comparative studies of therapeutic techniques could yield useful information. Several studies have compared drugs, psychoanalysis, and Rogerian counseling, using the client's detectable improvement and his own reports as the supporting evidence for each method.

While such accounts are valuable, we also need objective information if we want to evaluate the effectiveness of psychotherapy. One way to obtain such data is to record changes in overt behavior as the therapy progresses. Does a compulsive patient indulge less in, say, compulsive handwashing as treatment continues? Does psychotherapy help a person do better work? Do their friends and co-workers find former psycho-therapy patients more capable and personable? Clearly, it is not easy to keep such questions and answers truly objective. Exploring the dimensions of therapeutic success is difficult; thus far, it has been only partially achieved. Another problem in assessing the effectiveness of therapy is the wide range of skills and experience—and therefore effectiveness—among therapists.

A third problem in such experiments is how to measure observed and reported improvement in response to therapy as against improvement that results from enthusiasm and placebos.

Enthusiasm can have significant effects distinct from the effects of therapy. If a hospital ward's staff believes that a new therapeutic program will greatly improve their patients' behavior, they themselves may act differently with the patients—perhaps more buoyantly or with greater vigor and hope. As a result, patients may show short-term improvements. For this reason, research must distinguish between the new treatment—a new drug, for example—and the possible effects of enthusiasm.

Placebo effects are similar to enthusiasm effects. An inactive substance—a sugar pill, for example—may, under certain conditions, produce noticeable improvement in patients. A placebo succeeds—when it does—because it has the same suggestive properties as a "real" treatment. A physician knows that the confidence with which he prescribes medicines can influence his patient's reactions. The behavior of a suggestible patient might improve if he were given a placebo that was presented to him as a powerful, highly effective drug. One way to discount placebo effects is to use two control groups. The test group receives the treatment of special interest; the first control group, a placebo; and the second control group, no treatment at all. In recent years, researchers have recognized that the doctor's involvement also must be taken into account. To eliminate this additional variable, investigators use the _double-blind method,_ in which the doctor does not know whether the drug he gives his patients is active or inert. Thus, he cannot, even unknowingly, influence his patients.

The study of abnormal behavior is a broad challenge. Few authorities doubt that treatment should be tailored to the particular disorder. Psychoanalysis might be most appropriate for the vaguely anxious neurotic while behavior therapy might prove the best approach for an individual with intense phobias. Tranquilizers might be most helpful to the schizophrenic. Only objective research into the various treatments—their intended effects, side effects, interactions with intelligence, socioeconomic status, education, and symptoms—can reveal which treatment will help the patient most. Clearly, the investigator faces a formidable task.

In the Future

In the previous chapter, we observed that behavior disorders occur in amazingly diverse forms and that agreement about the classification and the origins of these disorders is hard to find. Thus we should not be surprised that methods of treatment show a corresponding diversity, or that little is understood of the details of why a particular therapy is successful (when this can be demonstrated).

This is not necessarily a discouraging state of affairs. During this century, demonstrable progress has been made in almost every aspect of treatment. Attitudes toward mental disorders have changed from superstitious rejection to rational concern; the quality of care in mental hospitals generally has improved substantially; the number of patients in mental hospitals has decreased after decades of steady increases. Our understanding of the biogenetic determinants of behavior has taken significant steps forward. Research techniques in psychopathology are now highly refined and precise; we can realistically plan studies that will simultaneously measure such variables as type of disorder, type of treatment, personal characteristics of the therapist, and various changes in the patient's behavior.

All in all, it does not seem too ambitious to believe that in the next decade or two, we may find the basis for both understanding and treating many behavior disorders that are currently poorly understood and poorly treated. While we cannot expect *the* treatment or *the* understanding, a very significant increase in our general knowledge of the origins and proper treatment of the various mental disorders seems a challenging but attainable goal.

Summary

1. Because of the variety of behavior disorders, many different forms of treatment exist. Six major approaches to treatment are psychodynamic therapy, self therapies, group therapy, behavior therapy, social therapy, and somatic therapy.

2. Psychodynamic therapy is a "talking therapy" in which a patient is helped to identify and resolve his conflicts and to make adaptive changes in his behavior.

3. Through such methods as free association, dream interpretation, and analysis of transference reactions, psychoanalysis enables the patient to bring unconscious and unacceptable impulses and conflicts to the conscious level where they can be re-experienced and rationally analyzed.

4. Client-centered therapy involves the establishment of a setting that will encourage the patient to actualize his potential strengths and develop a positive self-concept. According to Carl Rogers, this can occur only if the therapist achieves and communicates an accurate empathic understanding and unconditional positive regard for the patient.

5. Group therapy includes family therapy, in which family members deal collectively with their feelings toward each other, as well as en-

counter groups, which focus on improving individuals' interpersonal skills.

6. Behavior or learning therapies, which focus on acquired responses rather than on unconscious motivation, are relatively new techniques based on the principles of operant and classical conditioning.

7. Therapy based on operant conditioning uses reinforcement to replace maladaptive responses with adaptive responses. Token economies reward patients for performing work related to normal, self-sufficient functioning.

8. A technique used in classical conditioning therapy is systematic desensitization, in which the patient is taught to relax and to imagine a range of stimuli, from mildly to intensely anxiety-provoking. When an imagined stimulus no longer causes anxiety, the therapist moves on to the next stimulus in the anxiety hierarchy. Another technique is implosive therapy, in which the patient is asked to imagine an intensely fearful situation related to his phobia. The fact that no negative consequences actually follow can lead to a gradual lessening of his fears.

9. In modeling the subject modifies his behavior after observing the behavior of others.

10. Although psychodynamic therapists and behavior therapists differ strongly in theory and practice, many practitioners urge clinical flexibility in the use of various methods of treatment.

11. Social therapy emphasizes the contributions of the environment and the community experience to a person's psychological development. Many personal problems are believed to have their roots in the community.

12. One reflection of society's acceptance of responsibility for educating, planning, and changing the community for optimal use of human potential is the growing number of community mental health programs. Greater patient participation in the work and social environment of mental hospitals, known as milieu therapy, and halfway houses to facilitate a patient's return to the outside world are two attempts to upgrade mental health care.

13. Psychosurgery is used occasionally for chronically hospitalized patients. In the earlier methods of psychosurgery, large parts of the prefrontal area were disconnected from the rest of the brain; present-day operations destroy either very specific parts of the prefrontal area or such parts of the limbic system as the amygdala, anterior thalamus, or hypothalamus.

14. Generally used with severely depressed patients, electroshock therapy consists of briefly passing electric currents through the brain.

15. The science of psychopharmacology studies the effects of psychoactive drugs on behavior. These drugs include antipsychotic varieties that reduce agitation and hallucinations in patients with major psychoses, antianxiety drugs that produce a pleasant feeling, antidepressant drugs that alleviate severe depression, psychotomimetics that mimic psy-

chotic behavior, and lithium salts which relieve acute manic-depressive disorders.

16. Carrying out comparative studies of the various therapeutic techniques involves questions of how to measure observed and reported improvements and how to account for the effects of enthusiasm and placebo effects. Only objective research into the effects of the various treatments now being used will help us gain an understanding as to which treatment, or combination of treatments, will be best able to assist in the cure of each patient.

Important Terms

psychotherapy

psychodynamic therapy

psychoanalysis

dream analysis

free association

transference

client-centered therapy

self-concept

group therapy

family therapy

encounter groups

behavior therapy

behavior modification

therapies based on operant conditioning techniques

token economy

systematic desensitization

anxiety hierarchy

implosive therapy

modeling (observational learning)

hypnoanalysis

play therapy

psychodrama

social therapy

halfway house

community psychology

milieu therapy

occupational therapy

educational therapy

somatic (organic) therapy

psychosurgery

lobotomy

electroshock therapy

psychopharmacology

psychoactive drugs

antipsychotic drugs

chlorpromazine

reserpine

tranquilizers

antianxiety drugs

antidepressant drugs

imiprimine

psychotomimetics

mescaline

lithium salts

psilocybin

lysergic acid dimethylamide (LSD)

placebo effects

double-blind method

Suggested Readings

ARIETI, S. (ed.). *American handbook of psychiatry.* vol. III. New York: Basic Books, 1966.

Devotes a section to psychodynamic therapy, including psychoanalysis; chapters by leading psychiatrists and psychologists discuss Freudian, neo-Freudian, client-centered, and group techniques. There are also sections relevant to somatic treatment and social therapies.

AYLLON, T., & AZRIN, N. *The token economy: A motivational system for therapy and rehabilitation.* New York: Appleton-Century-Crofts, 1968.

Tells how to establish and operate a token economy system within a mental hospital; describes successful applications of the system in clinical settings.

BARTON, A. *Three worlds of therapy: Freud, Jung & Rogers.* Palo Alto, Cal.: National Press Books, 1974.

An interesting and readable account of the therapeutic approaches of Freud, Jung, and Rogers. Each approach is described in terms of the underlying story and the methods of treatment that would be appropriate to a common patient, "Mary."

BERGIN, A. E., & GARFIELD, S. L. *Handbook of psychotherapy and behavior change: An empirical analysis.* New York: Wiley, 1971.

Organized around specific research issues and research projects; emphasizes empirical results and their possible practical applications. The authors believe that behaviorism is the most useful and valid therapeutic approach today and see a corresponding decline in the contribution of psychoanalysis.

FORD, D. H., & URBAN, H. B. *Systems of psychotherapy.* New York: Wiley, 1963.

Provides a theoretical framework in which various methods can be compared. It describes 10 systems, chosen to represent the great variety of theories in psychotherapy, including psychoanalysis, behavior therapy, will therapy, and client-centered therapy.

FREUD, S. *Introductory lectures on psycho-analysis.* Standard Edition. vols. 15 and 16. London: Hogarth Press, 1955.

Freud's own introduction to psychoanalysis for the beginning student. These volumes outline the major elements of the theory and discuss psychoanalysis as a method of treatment. This is still the best available introduction to psychoanalysis, both because of the authority of the author and because of his talent as an interesting and comprehensible writer.

KANFER, F. H., & PHILLIPS, J. S. *Learning foundations of behavior therapy.* New York: Wiley, 1970.

Analyzes the theories and research underlying the current applications of learning principles and techniques to therapeutic change. The authors also discuss problems arising in the practical application of these principles.

MARTIN, D. G. *Introduction to psychotherapy.* Belmont, Calif.: Brooks-Cole, 1971.

Describes the author's belief in client-centered therapy and his therapeutic applications of it. Leaning on Rogers' work and adopting a humanistic approach, he develops a theoretical model of psychotherapy that is capable of accounting for the therapeutic effectiveness of accurate empathy, warmth, and genuineness.

MINTZ, E. E. *Marathon groups: Reality and symbol.* New York: Appleton-Century-Crofts, 1971.

An interesting and nontechnical account of how marathon groups are conducted; contains a variety of intimate reports of experiences in such groups.

PATTERSON, C. H. *Theories of counseling and psychotherapy.* New York: Harper & Row, 1966.

An attempt to deal systematically with the problems and crucial issues that the student will encounter in preparing for a career in counseling.

ROGERS, C. R. *On becoming a person: A therapist's view of psychotherapy.* Boston: Houghton Mifflin, 1961.

Rogers' personal statement on client-centered therapy, written for the "intelligent layman." He deals with such concepts as self-actualization, becoming, and growth.

Appendix   Highlights of Descriptive and Inferential Statistics

This Appendix was written by Janet Spence, Department of Psychology, University of Texas, Austin.

Imagine a world without numbers. You would have to use such vague expressions as "many moons ago," "not very heavy," and "as long as this room" instead of such precise quantitative statements as 10 months ago, half a pound, and 22 feet. Numbers describe the properties of objects and events with much greater accuracy than purely verbal expressions. Without numbers, everyday communication would be hampered and the growth of science and technology stymied.

Although measurement, other than simple counting, can never be exact, scientists have developed ways of measuring some physical properties very accurately. (How accurate we attempt to be in practice depends on our purpose. For example, in describing the age of human adults it is usually sufficient to refer to age at the last birthday; in contrast, the half-life of a subatomic particle might be measured to the nearest millionth of a second.) Scientists are able to measure these properties precisely because they have invented measuring instruments that have a high degree of *reliability*; that is, repeated measurements of an object with the same device or simultaneous measurements by several instruments of the same type (such as clocks or rulers) produce highly similar results. Further, the measuring scales for most physical dimensions are made up of index numbers that have all the properties of the number system itself—the most important being the zero point (complete absence of the property being measured) and equal distances between adjacent numbers on the scale. Thus, we can know, for example, that if the number assigned to one object is twice as large as the number assigned to another, the first object has twice as much of the property as the second.

Measuring psychological characteristics is more challenging and attempts to do so have been less successful. The characteristics themselves are seldom one-dimensional or directly observable; they are typically convenient scientific fictions which must be inferred through a number of manifestations. Achieving a reliable measurement is often difficult, particularly with nonobjective methods of assessment. For example, how would you measure how "with it" your friends are? Despite the use of sophisticated psychometric techniques, no psychological scale has all of the properties of the number system, and many produce numbers that do little more than rank individuals in order.

Discussing the limitations of psychological measurement may reinforce the suspicions of humanist students who already question psychology's attempts to quantify human behavior. However, it should be recognized that both the scientist and the humanist, when they describe psychological phenomena, make implicit or explicit assumptions about the dimensions and categories into which these phenomena fall. Purely verbal descriptions of psychological events suffer from the same vagueness and lack of precision as do purely verbal descriptions of such physical dimensions as time, distance, and temperature. To discover the fundamental order assumed to underlie all natural phenomena, we must have a precise description of empirical events and theoretical concepts. Whenever possible, therefore, we seek numerical description.

The Role of Statistics

Variability is one of the fundamental facts of nature. People vary widely in almost every conceivable dimension—in their height, weight, and body build, in their attitudes and beliefs, in their cognitive skills, in their ways of reacting to situations. Thus, measuring a group of individuals or objects almost always produces a varied collection of numbers, which must be ordered and summarized in order to be made intelligible. For this job, statistics is an indispensable tool. In the following section, we shall discuss some of the major statistical techniques for describing masses of data.

Statistics is even more indispensable when we seek to infer the characteristics of an entire population from samples of that population. We want to assess the typical high school student's familiarity with the Constitution's Bill of Rights, and we devise an objective test. Testing *all* high school students (the _population_) is at best impractical and expensive, and probably impossible. But data could be obtained from a _representative sample_ of, say, several hundred students. This sample's results cannot be assumed to be identical to the entire population's. If we were to test additional samples of the same size, the results might be similar, particularly if the samples were large, but they would not be identical and might differ from one another quite a lot. None of the samples, then, can be assumed to mirror the population exactly. However, by using the appropriate statistical techniques we can make reasonable inferences or guesses about the population's characteristics from the sample's data.

Consider another example—testing a new drug intended to increase the mental alertness of senile patients. A group of such patients is given a battery of tests of mental functioning. The drug is administered to half of them (the experimental subjects) and the others (the control subjects) are given sugar pills. After several weeks, the patients are retested. Not surprisingly, few of the control subjects earn exactly the same scores on retest as they did initially. On the average, the control group improves slightly—but as a whole, the drug group exhibits greater improvement than the control group. Can we conclude that the drug is effective? No, since we cannot be certain that the differences between the groups are not due to unidentified, chance factors (*sampling errors*) or that a repetition of the experiment with new patients would produce similar results. However, statistical tests can be applied to the data to permit the experimenters to make *probability statements*—numerical estimates of the likelihood that the observed differences are genuine and not due to chance. Given this probability level, we can make an educated guess about whether the drug is useful. Most statistical techniques employed by research scientists were devised to permit this type of inference.

Descriptive Statistics

Frequency Distributions and Graphic Presentation

A researcher usually gathers data in the form of one or more collections of numbers. Each number reflects some measurable characteristic of members of the group or groups under study. As a first approach to describing the data, the investigator can put the numbers into rank order, from highest to lowest. If a large enough sample is involved and a number of tie scores have occurred, a simple *frequency distribution*, such as the one shown in Table A-1, affords a more concise presentation of the data. All possible scores on a psychology test, from the highest to the lowest, are listed in the left column; the right column shows the frequency with which each score occurred. By inspecting the frequency distribution, we can determine some of the group's characteristics, such as the range of scores, where the bulk of the cases fall, and the overall shape of the distribution. If the pattern of the distribution is of particular interest, it often may be discerned more easily—particularly if the group is large and heterogeneous—by casting the data into a *group frequency distribution*. An example of a grouped distribution is shown in Table A-2. Sets of adjacent scores are grouped together to form equal classes (for example, the 5 scores 45 through 49 and the 5 scores 50 through 54). Then, the frequency of the scores falling into each class is determined.

Presenting the data in graphic rather than tabular form reveals the properties of a frequency distribution even more clearly than does a table. In a graphic representation of a frequency distribution, the scores or classes of scores are shown along the horizontal axis or baseline and the frequencies along the vertical axis, as is illustrated in Figure A-1, which plots the data from the simple frequency distribution of Table A-1. Each case is represented by a bar placed above the appropriate score; the height of each bar thus indicates the total number of cases receiving the given score. This type of bar graph, or *histogram*, as it is traditionally called, is used occasionally. More typically, however, data are presented in the form of a *frequency polygon*. In a polygon, a point at the appropriate distance above each score indicates the frequency. The points then are connected by straight lines and, usually, the figure is

Table A-1 A Simple Frequency Distribution

Score	Frequency
13	2
12	4
11	5
10	9
9	12
8	10
7	6
6	7
5	4
4	1
	Total = 60

Table A-2 A Group Frequency Distribution

Class of Scores	Frequency
100–104	3
95–99	1
90–94	5
85–89	8
80–84	12
75–79	16
70–74	15
65–69	10
60–64	7
55–59	4
50–54	2
45–49	2
	Total = 85

A-1

Histogram and superimposed frequency polygon (in color) of the simple frequency distribution in Table A-1 (reproduced below).

Table A–1

Score	Frequency
13	2
12	4
11	5
10	9
9	12
8	10
7	6
6	7
5	4
4	1
	Total = 60

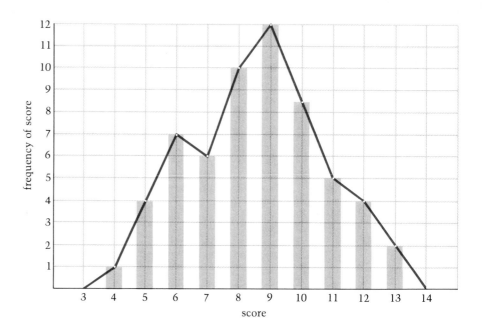

completed by dropping the curve to the baseline at the score points at either end (indicating the scores at which zero frequencies begin). These features are illustrated in Figure A–1, in which the polygon has been superimposed on the histogram to demonstrate the relationship between the two.

Shapes of Frequency Distributions

Frequency distributions (and the polygons or histograms based upon them) may take a variety of forms. Figure A–2 illustrates and labels several types of *symmetrical* polygons. (Actual research data—based on a limited number of cases—are rarely absolutely symmetrical but may closely approximate this idealized form.) Figure A-2a represents a *rectangular distribution*, in which each score occurs with equal frequency. Figure A-2b represents a U-shaped distribution, in which scores at both extremes occur more often than those in the middle of the score range.

Figure A–2c is a *bell-shaped curve*. One important member of the family of bell-shaped distributions is the so-called *normal probability curve*. While a number of psychological characteristics (such as IQ) approximate the normal distribution, the normal curve is used primarily in theoretical statistics; many sampling distributions, as we shall discuss, take this form. By inspection alone, it is almost impossible to tell whether a particular bell-shaped curve is normal; thus we must resist the temptation to label "normal" all polygons of this general shape.

Figure A–2c also is an illustration of a *unimodal* (one mode) curve. (The mode is technically defined as the score that occurs most frequently). Figure A–2d shows, in contrast, a *bi-modal* (two mode) distribution, one in which the scores cluster about two modal values rather than one.

Figure A–3 shows two examples of nonsymmetrical, *skewed* distribu-

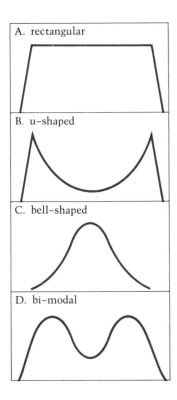

A-2
Four types of symmetrical distribution.

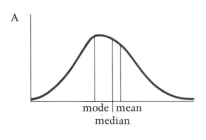

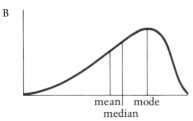

A-3
Two types of skewed distribution and the mean, median, and mode of each.

tions, both of them unimodal. Curve A–3b exhibits a greater amount of skew (that is, a greater departure from symmetry) than *a* and a different direction of skew. In distribution A–3a, the cases pile up at the lower end of the score scale and trail off at the upper end (*positive* skew); in A–3b, they concentrate at the upper end of the scale (*negative* skew).

Measures of Central Tendency

While investigators often look for information about the pattern of a collection of measures, they even more frequently seek a single number that characterizes the group as a whole. For example, they might ask how many cigarettes a person smokes each day or whether male and female first-year students at the local university differ on a standardized test of scholastic aptitude. A smoker's daily consumption may vary, so a figure that represents a usual day must be obtained. Similarly, students of both sexes differ in scholastic aptitude; it will be easier to compare the sexes if we first describe the typical man and the typical woman. A single representative number, used to characterize an entire distribution, commonly is found near the middle of the score range and hence is called a *measure of central tendency*.

Though a number of measures of central tendency have been devised, we shall describe only the three most commonly used—the *mode*, the *median*, and the arithmetic *mean*. The mode, as we noted earlier, is the value of the score that occurs most frequently. The mode can be determined simply by locating the most frequently occurring score in a distribution or by locating the peak of the hump in a frequency polygon. In polygons with two or more distinct humps or clusters of scores, more than one mode may be identified, even if the frequencies of each modal score are not identical.

The median is the score point that divides the upper and lower 50 percent of the cases. In the distribution of the numbers 3, 6, 8, 11, and 12, the median is 8. The median of the scores 15, 18, 20, 21, 26, and 29 is 20.5. (Three of the scores are 20 or below and three are 21 or above; since the median is a single point, the point midway between 20 and 21 is chosen as its value.) Of course, no such fractional value as 20.5 actually occurred among the six given numbers, a fact that illustrates an important aspect of measures of central tendency and many other statistics. These measures are convenient mathematical abstractions that have been invented, rather than real entities that must be discovered.

The median also can be described as the score point that divides a polygon in half. If the median is on the polygon's baseline and a vertical line is erected from that point up to the curve, the total area under the curve is divided into two equal parts. This relationship can be seen in Figure A–3.

The mean, popularly known as the average, is obtained by adding up all the individual scores and dividing by the total number of scores. For example, the sum of the scores 2, 6, and 9 is 17; if we divided this quantity by 3, we find that the mean is 5.67 (another nonexistent fractional value). The mean can also be defined as that point in a distribution from which the algebraic sum of the scores' deviations is zero. The scores 4, 20, and 21, for example, have a mean of 15. The first score is 11 points below the mean $(4 - 15 = -11)$, and the other two scores are 5 and 6 points above it. The sum of these deviations from the mean $(-11, 5, 6)$ is zero. Note also that except for reversal of signs, the sum of the deviations above and below the mean is equal. In terms of deviations, then, the mean is a kind of balance point in a distribution.

In a symmetrical, unimodal distribution, the mode, median, and mean will have the same value. That is, the same point will be the score that occurs most frequently, that divides the area under the curve in half, and that is the balance point, in deviation units, of the scores on either side of it. As distributions depart from symmetry, the three measures of central tendency become increasingly divergent. The mode remains at the hump, but the mean and median are drawn out toward the "tail" of the distribution. Because the mean alone among the measures is determined by the exact value of every score, it is sensitive to extreme scores and the point of algebraic balance is further out toward the tail than the median. Figure A–3 illustrates the relative positions of the three measures in skewed distributions.

Since the mean, median, and mode reflect different properties of a distribution, investigators must be careful when distributions are markedly skewed, both in determining which measure of central tendency is most appropriate and in interpreting the resulting values. In a highly skewed distribution, the mean, for example, does not represent the "typical" case. However, unless a distribution is markedly asymmetrical, the mean is the preferred measure of central tendency in research investigations. The mean fluctuates less from sample to sample than the median and the mode and over the long run, the mean provides us with more stable estimates on which to base inferences about population characteristics. Further, as we shall see, additional statistical manipulations of the data typically demand that the mean be calculated.

Measures of Variability

Frequency distributions differ not only in form and in the several measures of central tendency but also in the amount of _variability_ among the scores. For example, all the distributions in Figure A–4 have the same mean and involve the same number of cases. However, the individuals in Group A cluster closely about the mean and as a group are quite homogeneous. Group B is more heterogeneous; that is, the dispersion or variability of the scores about the mean is greater. Variability among the individuals of Group C is most marked of all. More specifically, the distributions might represent three football teams. The mean of the weights of all the players on each team is the same; the distribution of weights is the most homogeneous in Team A and the least in Team C.

The simplest measure of variability is the _range_ of the distribution, that is, the number of units between the highest and the lowest score. The range, however, is highly unstable from sample to sample since only the two extreme cases determine its value. Also, it does not reflect the dispersion of all of the intervening scores. Groups B and C in Figure A–4, for example, have the same range although Group C is considerably more heterogeneous. Except as a quick estimate of dispersion, the range therefore is seldom used as a measure of variability.

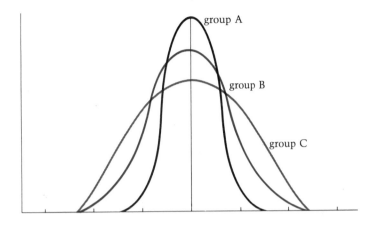

A-4
Three frequency distributions with the same mean and number of cases but differing in variability.

The most useful measure of variability and the one that is almost exclusively used in statistical analyses is the _standard deviation_. The standard deviation represents a kind of average or mean amount by which the scores differ from the overall mean of the distribution. The first step in calculating this statistic is to obtain individual deviations by taking each score and subtracting from it the value of the mean. For example, the set of 4 scores, 8, 13, 13, and 14, have a mean of 12; their deviations from the mean are -4, $+1$, $+1$, and $+2$, respectively. The mean of this set of deviations could be found by dividing their sum by their number; however, the result would give us no useful information because, as we explained earlier, the sum of the deviations from the mean _always_ equals zero and their mean will of course also equal zero. To avoid the cancellation of minus deviations (from scores below the mean) by plus deviations (from scores above it), each deviation is squared, and the mean of these squared deviations obtained. The resulting statistic is called the _variance_ of the distribution. The square root of the variance is the standard deviation. In our example, the variance is 5.5 $(-4^2 + 1^2 + 1^2 + 2^2 \div 4)$ and the standard deviation is 2.35. To repeat our earlier statement, the standard deviation represents a special kind of mean and essentially reflects the average amount (number of score units) by which individual scores in the distribution deviate from the mean.

Percentiles and z (or SD) Scores

Percentiles often are used to describe the position of individual scores in a distribution. Essentially, the rank of a score is determined, with 1 representing the best or the top score in the distribution, and this rank then is translated into the percentage that falls _at or below_ this score. For example, if a score falls at the 75th percentile, 25 percent of the group scored at or above this point and 75 percent at or below it. The score that falls in the middle of the distribution is the 50th percentile (also called the median); the score that divides the lower 10 percent and upper 90 percent of the cases is the 10th percentile, and so on. Any original _raw score_ can be translated into a percentile (and vice versa), so that percentiles are an alternative scale, using percent frequency rather than raw scores as the unit of measurement.

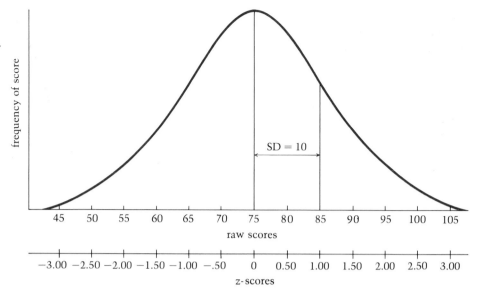

Frequency distribution with a mean
of 75 and a standard deviation of 10.
The baseline has been laid off in
raw score and z-score units.

Still another type of transformation of raw scores involves the construction of a scale that uses the distribution's standard deviation (SD) as the unit of measurement. Figure A-5 illustrates this process through a bell-shaped curve with a mean of 75 and an SD of 10. The curve's baseline is marked off not only in raw scores but in SD-units or what have come to be called *z-scores*.

In this scoring scheme, the scale's 0 point is set at the mean, and the baseline marked off into SD- or z-score units. In Figure A–5, one SD-unit above the mean (that is, a z-score of +1.00) is 10 raw score units above the mean and has a raw score equivalent of 85(75 + 10). Conversely, a z of −1.00 lies 10 raw score units below the mean and has a raw score equivalent of 65(75 − 10). By using the formula

$$z = \frac{\text{raw score} - \text{mean}}{\text{SD}}$$

the z value of any raw score can be determined. Thus, 55 has a z-score of −2.00 (55 − 75 divided by 10) and 90 has a z-score of +1.50.

Scores in SD-units are used to report the results of several nationally used tests, such as the Graduate Record Examination. (To avoid fractions and negative numbers, each z-score is multiplied by 100 and then added to 500, thus yielding a distribution with a mean of 500 and a standard deviation of 100.) The score distribution of the test-taking groups, on which these SD-related scores are based, is essentially normal in shape. Those familiar with the normal probability curve can interpret scores on these standardized tests as easily as percentiles, as the following section should make clear.

The Normal Probability Distribution

The normal curve (like any curve) is unique in the percentage of the total area that lies between the mean and any given z-score along the baseline, and its properties can be described by specifying these area relationships. Representative values are shown in the normal curve

A-6

Normal curve showing what percentages of the total area under the curve lie between selected z-scores. These area percentages are equal to percent frequency, that is, the percentage of the total population that falls within the indicated range.

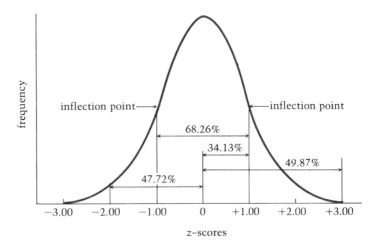

reproduced in Figure A–6. (Percent area, it should be recognized, is equivalent to percent frequency of cases.)

Notice first that the scores occurring one SD-unit from the mean (z-scores of ±1.00) fall at the *inflection point*, the point at which the direction of the curve changes. (Below the inflection point the curve is convex to the baseline; above it the curve is concave to the baseline.) The area beneath the curve between the mean and the z-score of +1.00 is 34.13% of the total area beneath the curve; 47.72% of the area lies between the mean and a z of +2.00, and 49.87% between the mean and +3.00. Since the curve is symmetrical, identical relationships are found with negative z scores. Thus, about 68% of the cases in a normal curve score within ±1.00 SD-units of the mean. Almost all (99.74 percent) fall between ±3.00 SD-units. One can specify the percentage that falls between the mean and *any* z-score in a normal curve. For example, 45 percent of the cases lie between the mean and a z of 1.65.

If we know the properties of the normal curve, we can describe normally-distributed events that have already occurred. But we also can make statements about the likelihood of some future or hypothetical event. We can illustrate this use of the normal probability curve with a widely used, well-standardized IQ test, the Stanford-Binet (see Chapter 15), whose score distribution closely approximates normality. The mean of the IQ distribution has been set at 100 and the SD has been found to be about 16. In a normal distribution, about 68 percent of the cases fall within the z-score interval of ±1.00—in this instance, within the interval of 84 to 116 IQ points. Suppose an individual, selected at random, takes the test. He has approximately 68 chances out of 100, a probability of .68 (out of 1.00), of scoring between 84 and 116. Another example: the z-score equivalent of the IQ score 124 is about 1.65; as we have noted, 45 percent of the cases in a normal distribution lie between the mean and this z-score. Thus, only 5 percent can equal or exceed this value. The probability that our randomly selected individual will earn an IQ of 124 or above is therefore 5 chances out of 100 or .05.

We shall refer again to the use of the normal curve to make probability statements when we discuss sampling distributions and statistical inference.

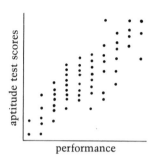

A. Clerical workers

B. Big 10 teams

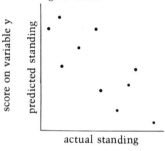

C. Women

score on variable x

A-7

Scatter diagrams of the hypothetical data described in the text illustrating variations in the degree and direction of the correlation between sets of paired measures (X and Y).

Correlation

So far, we have presented techniques for describing the properties of single frequency distributions. We turn now to a class of statistical techniques that describes the relationship or *correlation* between *two* groups of measures. For example, a sportswriter predicts the teams' final standings in the Big 10 conference and wants to know how accurate he was. A psychologist tries to determine whether physically attractive women are smarter or dumber than their less attractive sisters. A company's personnel officer wants to know whether an aptitude test designed to select clerical employees is valid, that is, whether test scores relate to actual job performance. All of these instances involve two sets of *paired* measures. The sportswriter has his predicted standing and the actual standing for each team. For each woman in his study, the psychologist has a rating of attractiveness and a measure of intelligence. The personnel officer also has a pair of measures for his group of clerical workers: test scores and an assessment of job performance. The sportswriter, the psychologist, and the personnel officer all are asking about both the *degree* of relationship between the pairs of measures, and the *direction* of the relationship—for example, if attractiveness is related to intelligence, are the beautiful dumber or brighter?

Plotting the pairs of measures on a *scatter diagram* can provide useful information. In this type of diagram, one variable lies on the horizontal axis and the second on the vertical. Each pair of measures is plotted as a point whose position is determined by its value on each axis. (The horizontal and vertical axes of any graph are identified as the X and Y axes, respectively, and the sets of measures that are being correlated as the X and Y variables.) Scatter diagrams for each of our hypothetical situations are shown in Figure A-7. Figure A-7a is a plot of the data from the sample of clerical workers. High scorers show a strong tendency to do well on the job and low scorers tend to do poorly. The data reflect a *high* degree of *positive* correlation between the variables. (Strictly speaking, the data reveal a high degree of *linear* or straight-line relationship. We will not discuss nonlinear correlations.)

The results of the sportswriter's prediction test are shown in Figure A-7b. We can see some relationship between the two sets of ranks, but the agreement is less than in the previous example. Unfortunately, the direction of the correlation is not what the forecaster had in mind; most of the teams he predicted would win ended up near the bottom, while those he thought would be "also-rans" performed well. The data thus illustrate a *moderate* degree of *negative* correlation.

Figure A-7c shows a *zero* correlation. In this group of women, beauty did not relate to brains, the distribution of intelligence scores being similar for those at every level of physical attractiveness.

Figure A-8 shows a scatter diagram of a perfect positive and a perfect negative correlation, that is, relationships that cannot be improved. All of the data points fall along a straight line, which indicates that the individuals receiving a given score on the X variable all receive exactly the same Y score (and vice versa). Further, each score in one distribution is paired with a score that occupies the same relative position in the other

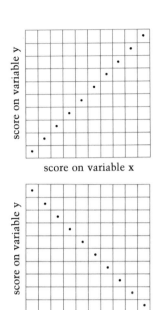

score on variable y

score on variable x

score on variable y

score on variable x

A-8
Scatter diagram of a perfect positive and a perfect negative correlation.

distribution in the case of a perfect *positive* relationship. That is, each pair of raw scores has identical *z*-scores. In the case of a perfect negative relationship we see the mirror image of that position. The score that ranks first in one distribution is last in the other, so that the pairs of *z*-scores are equal in absolute value but differ in sign.

While inspection of a scatter plot reveals something about the relationship between two sets of measures, we need a more precise specification of the degree of correlation. Two major techniques for describing linear relationships are the *Pearson product-moment correlation coefficient* (symbolized by the letter *r*) and the *Spearman rank-order correlation coefficient* (symbolized by the Greek letter ρ, pronounced "rho"). The Spearman ρ is used when the data consist of the ranks that each of the measures occupies within each set. (For example, the predicted and actual ranks of the football teams.) Both techniques produce coefficients that take the value of +1.00 when the correlation is a perfect, positive one, decrease in value until they reach 0 as the relationship weakens, and then proceed to a maximum of −1.00 as the relationship becomes increasingly negative.

The major practical use of correlation coefficients is in *prediction*. Predictions may be of *future* events (for example, estimates of how well a student will do in his college courses on the basis of his entrance test scores) or of *concurrent* events (for example, estimates of the degree of hostile suspicion a psychotic patient will exhibit in his day-to-day interactions on the basis of his behavior in a psychological interview). The prediction process is based on the following rationale: When a guess has to be made about some randomly selected individual with respect to some variable, the most reasonable estimate (assuming a symmetrical distribution) is the mean of the population to which the individual belongs. For example, we might predict that the height of an unseen 21-year-old female is 5′6′′, the approximate mean height of adult women in this country. If we were told the individual's weight (known to correlate with height), we would instead predict the mean height of all women of that weight. In more abstract terms, if information about X is given and Y is to be predicted, we predict that the person will receive the mean score on variable Y obtained by all individuals receiving that particular X score.

In the extremely rare instance in which two variables correlate perfectly (independent of direction), prediction also is perfect, as Figure A–8 demonstrates. In each column (that is, for each X score), the Y scores show no variability; every individual with that X has the same Y. In high but less than perfect correlations, errors will occur; but overall, we can make highly accurate predictions. In Figure A-7a, for example, the Y scores in each X column are not identical but the means of these Y scores tend to fall along a line the slope of which is roughly similar to the slope of the straight line of the perfect positive correlation. As the correlation between variables decreases, so does accuracy of prediction. When the correlation reaches zero, prediction is impossible; the mean Y score in the X columns shows no systematic variation and except for chance factors, each will be equal to the overall mean of the Y distribution. Thus, in the case of a group of women, each of whose height we are attempting to predict, being told how many books each read last year will not help, since these variables are unrelated. Whatever their reading habits, our prediction would remain 5 feet 6 inches for all the women, and this prediction would, of course, have some degree of error for most of them. If we were told the women's shoe sizes, we would, since the two do correlate somewhat, be able to make more accurate predictions of the height of each woman. Weight is even more highly correlated with height than shoe size, and, with this added information, the overall accuracy of each prediction would improve still further. Predictive accuracy falls off rapidly, however, as correlations drop below +1.00. A correlation coefficient of .90, for example, does not imply 90 percent accuracy, nor does it produce twice as much accuracy as a correlation of .45.

Correlation and Causality A correlation coefficient indicates the degree to which two variables co-vary, the degree to which changes in the value of one tends to be accompanied by changes in the value of the other. Although it often is tempting to infer a cause and effect relationship, the correlation shows only an association between the variables and not why it exists. We must look to additional kinds of information about the phenomena under study for explanations of a given correlation. The possibilities are many. In some instances, the two variables may indeed be causally linked, directly or through an indirect chain of events. But the causality does not run both ways; whether X is dependent upon Y or Y dependent upon X must be established. For example, seismographs can record the magnitude of earthquakes. The earthquake "causes" the change in the measuring instrument, but luckily, local manipulations of the seismograph (brought about by a clumsy technician, for example) do not set off earthquakes around the world; the causality is unidirectional.

In most instances, correlations between sets of variables occur because a common set of factors affects both. The identity of the factors may not be readily apparent and their path of influence may be complex. In the field of child development, for example, extensive data have been collected describing age-related changes in physical and psychological characteristics. The child's physical maturation and the cumulative influence of experience that bring about these developmental changes take place over time; passage of time per se is not responsible for the observed effects and does nothing to explain the correlation between age and the measured characteristics.

Several major scientific controversies involve the interpretation of correlations. For example, an association has been unambiguously established between cigarette smoking and the incidence of lung cancer and heart disease. What does this correlation mean? One group argues that it reflects the deleterious effects of smoking on the individual's health. Another denies it, claiming that heavy smokers have certain characteristics or find themselves in certain environments that cause both the physical disorders and their dependence upon tobacco. Both parties to the dispute cite volumes of evidence in their favor. But lacking conclusive experimental evidence of a causal connection, the controversy rages on. Another subject of public debate concerns the interpretation of the correlations between IQ scores of family members (between parents and their children, for example, or between fraternal or identical twins). Do these correlations result completely from environmental influences that family members tend to share, or are inherited, genetic variables at least partially responsible? Scientists disagree on the answer. These examples show that interpretations of any correlation must be offered cautiously and must be based on all the relevant evidence.

Inferential Statistics

The investigator uses descriptive statistics to organize and interpret data. He employs *inferential statistics* to make guesses about the properties of populations after having observed samples.

Populations and Samples

Scientific investigations seek knowledge about *populations* of objects or events, about *all* the members of a group who exhibit the properties under study. A pollster attempting to forecast the outcome of a presidential election is trying to predict the preferences of all who will vote in the election. An agricultural expert investigating the characteristics of a newly developed plant strain is concerned with reaching generalizations about all examples of the strain, those that have already been produced and those that may yet be produced. An educational psychologist investigating the effectiveness of a new technique for teaching first-grade arithmetic is concerned with its potential influence on all first graders, present and future. Populations, as demonstrated by these examples, may be finite or infinite, real or hypothetical. But, typically, populations that are of scientific interest are large.

With rare exceptions, it is impractical or impossible to measure populations in their entirety. Instead, to repeat what we stated earlier, one or more samples from the population are selected for study; inferences about the population are based on the sample results. Therefore, the method of selecting samples is crucial. Distorted, nonrepresentative samples will lead to distorted, erroneous conclusions about the population. A pollster, for example, would not confine his sample of voters to a single age group, occupational category, or geographical location, since each of these factors is known to have an association with political attitudes and preferences. Rather, he would attempt to obtain a sample that would represent the entire voter group in all factors that may correlate with voting behavior.

As we discussed in Chapter 18, *random sampling* is one method for selecting unbiased samples. It is essential to most of the statistical techniques that have been developed to obtain reliable inferences about populations from sample data. While the method does not guarantee that each sample will represent its population, it does permit the use of statistical techniques for estimating the likelihood of chance variations.

Obtaining truly random samples is difficult, however. First, identifying all members of the population is not always possible. (How does the pollster know, for example, which registered voters will go to the polls on election day? He is trying to predict the behavior of the population of actual, not potential, voters.) Second, assuming this formidable problem is overcome, the investigator cannot guarantee that every case chosen for the sample will be available for the study. So he frequently must compromise with ideal random selection procedures.

Random sampling is of importance, too, in the planning of many experiments. When conducting an experiment, a central concern is to begin with equivalent groups—that is, groups that would respond similarly if given identical treatments. These equivalent groups can then be assigned to different experimental conditions (for instance, one group would receive a drug and the other a placebo). Random sampling is one way to try to achieve this goal. A closely related technique that is easier to implement, and therefore almost exclusively used, is *randomization*. A pool of subjects is identified (for example, all the introductory psychology students who show up for an experiment) and members of the pool are assigned at random to the different conditions of the experiment. When randomization is used, investigators must be especially cautious about specifying the groups to which the results should be generalized.

Sampling Distributions and Hypothesis Testing

Suppose we have constructed a frequency distribution of 1,000,000 numbers, which is normal in shape, with a mean of 60 and a standard deviation of 15. If we draw a random sample of 100 numbers from the population of 1,000,000 and determine its mean, our best single guess is that the sample mean also will be 60. However, we would not be surprised if the actual value were somewhat above or below this figure.

If we repeated this procedure until we had, let us say, 5,000 of these random sample means, statistical theory indicates that the resulting distribution of sample means would be *normal* in shape and have a mean equal to the *mean of the population*. Statistical theory also shows that the standard deviation of the sample distribution is related in a specifiable way to the size of the population SD and the size of the individual samples. With a population SD of 15 and a sample size of 100, the standard deviation of the sampling distribution in our example would be 1.5. With these facts and with knowledge of the normal curve, we can make concrete statements about the sampling distribution of our 5,000 random sample means. For example, about 68 percent of the area under a normal curve lies within ±1.00 SD-units of the mean; therefore 68 percent of our sample means fall in the interval 60 ± 1.5. Another example: In a normal curve the extreme 5 percent of the area (2½ percent at either end) falls at or beyond z-scores of ±1.96. In our sampling distribution, therefore, the extreme 5 percent of the sample means deviates from the overall mean of 60 by 2.94 points or more [60 + (1.96)(1.5)].

We can use this theoretical knowledge about sampling distributions to test hypotheses about population characteristics from the data of a single sample. Suppose, for example, we did not know the mean and SD of a population, but we had reason to hypothesize that the mean was 60. We test a random sample of 100 cases and find that its mean is 57.0. We know that if we had tested not merely one but a very large number of samples and if the population mean were 60, as we have speculated, the hypothetical sampling distribution would be normal and have a mean of 60. We also can estimate, from our sample data, the SD of the sampling distribution; suppose that this estimate is 1.5. Now we ask ourselves this question: If the population mean is 60, how likely are we to obtain a sample mean that deviates from the population mean by as much as ours? Our sample mean of 57.0 lies 3 raw score units and therefore (with SD = 1.5) exactly 2 SD-units from the mean of the hypothetical sampling distribution. With a population mean of 60, we would expect to get a sample mean this much or more different less than 5 percent of the time. Have we obtained a sample mean this unusual by chance? Or, instead, is our hypothesis a poor one? No definitive conclusion can be reached. However, assigning a cut off at certain probability levels, most commonly the 1 percent or the 5 percent levels, allows us to offer a tentative answer. If an event would occur by chance less than 5 percent (or 1 percent) of the time if the hypothesis were true, we decide to *reject* the hypothesis, to conclude that it is probably false. Conversely, if the obtained difference could happen by chance more than 5 percent (or 1 percent) of the time, we would tentatively accept the hypothesis as true.

Differences between the hypothetical and the actual sample values that occur less than 5 percent or 1 percent of the time because of a sampling error also are called *significant* differences—they do not occur by chance; the probability figures are called the 5 percent and 1 percent *significance* levels. In our example, we can describe the obtained difference as significant at the 5 percent level; we would *reject* the hypothesis that the population mean is 60 at the 5 percent level of significance.

We have explained in some detail the sampling distribution of means and the general logic of testing a hypothesis about a population mean from the data of a single random sample. The same kind of logic underlies tests of hypotheses about other population statistics. The *null hypothesis*, concerns the difference between population means and hypothesizes that this difference is zero.

The Null Hypothesis and the t-Test   Experimental questions are typically posed in very general terms: Is one type of psychotherapy more helpful than another? Does one condition in a memory experiment increase acquisition more than another? Is one kind of message more persuasive than another? The statistical question asked in an effort to answer these queries typically involves a comparison of hypothetical *population means:* Would the mean of everyone who might be in one condition (mean of population 1) be the same as or different from the mean of everyone who might be in condition 2 (mean of population 2)?

To answer the latter question, we obtain data from two random or randomized samples, one from each population (that is, in an experiment, one sample is given condition 1 and the other condition 2). The *statistical* hypothesis we typically test states that the samples come from populations with identical means and that any difference between our pair of sample means is due to sampling error. Since the difference between population means is postulated to be 0, this hypothesis is known as the *null hypothesis.* (Our *experimental* hypothesis—what we actually believe about the relative influence of the conditions—may or may not correspond to the null hypothesis.)

If the null hypothesis were correct, and repeated pairs of samples were tested, the sampling distribution of the difference between pairs of sample means would be normal in shape (assuming adequate sample size). In some pairs, the mean for condition 1 would be higher than for condition 2 and for others the reverse; the mean difference (the mean of the sampling distribution of differences) would be 0. We can estimate the value of the standard deviation in this case from the data of the pair of samples we have actually tested. Thus we can state the probability that we would find a discrepancy of the size that occurred between the means of our samples if the null hypothesis were correct. If the probability is low (less than 5 percent or 1 percent), we *reject* the null hypothesis and conclude that our observed difference between the means is *significant,* occurring because of genuine differences caused by the conditions and not because of chance.

The symbol identifying the statistic computed to evaluate the null hypothesis is *t* and the procedure as a whole is known as the *t*-test. A *t*-test also may be used to evaluate other types of hypotheses.

Analysis of Variance. A major limitation of the *t*-test is that it can compare only two groups. A more flexible procedure that can be used to test the null hypothesis about any number of groups or conditions is known as *analysis of variance.* For example, we might ask female college students to rate the likability of other students who say that they want to have either 0, 1, 2, or 3 children, and then compare the mean ratings to see if number of children desired influences likability. The analysis of variance technique also permits us to study the *joint effects* of two or more variables. In the example above, we might get judgments not only from female college students but also from groups of women in their 40s and in their 60s. We would thus study the influence of *two* variables on likability: age of the judges and number of children wanted by the student being judged. A third variable might be the sex of the judges, male or female, and so on. These *factorial designs,* as they are called, allow us not only to test a null hypothesis about the effects of each variable but also a hypothesis about how the variables combine or *interact* to influence performance. Because of their flexibility, factorial designs and the analyses of variance used to interpret their results are frequently used in psychological research.

Generalizations abound in every chapter of this text, seldom qualified by reference to statistical tests and significance levels. With few exceptions, however, the data on which the generalizations are based had to be subjected to statistical tests before a conclusion about the results could be offered. We have deleted references to these tests to facilitate the flow of our discussion. The recognition that all of our conclusions are based on probability statements, not absolute certainty, emphasizes a characteristic that psychology shares with all of science: scientific principles are tentative and do not pretend to be final truths.

Glossary

ability traits Cattell's term for traits that describe the effectiveness of a person's behavior.

abstract thinking thinking about relationships among things; performing abstractions; planning and theorizing.

accommodation changing the curvature of the lens of the eye in order to provide cues to distance. Also, Piaget's term for the process of changing rules or schemes to acquire new information that does not fit existing schemes.

acetylcholine (ACh) a synaptic transmitter present at neuromuscular junctions.

action potential term for the nerve impulse that is transmitted down the axon of the nerve cell to the synapse to produce effects on other nerve cells; also called the spiked discharge.

addiction physiological and psychological dependence on a substance such as a drug.

additive mixture combining of light energies of different wavelengths. When complementary colors are mixed, the result is grey.

adrenal gland endocrine gland which releases hormones that energize the body to respond in emergency situations; situated above the kidneys; consists of the adrenal cortex and the adrenal medulla; secretes adrenalin and cortin.

affective reactions marked disturbances in feelings, emotions, moods, and emotionalized drives; abnormal excitement (mania) and depression (melancholia) are examples.

afferent (sensory) neuron a type of neuron found in the peripheral nerves which transmits information from the sense organ to the spinal cord or brain.

affiliation a form of integration involving the maintenance of proximity to other individuals.

aggression behavior aimed — consciously or unconsciously — at hurting someone, or the impulse to do so.

agraphia inability to write resulting from damage to the auditory-visual area of the cerebral cortex.

alexia inability to read resulting from damage to the auditory-visual area of the cerebral cortex.

all-or-none law the amplitude of the nerve impulse in a single nerve fiber is independent of the stimulus and depends only on the characteristics of the nerve cell axon itself; the nerve cell responds either completely or not at all.

alpha blocking a cessation of alpha waves that occurs when a relaxed subject is suddenly startled or aroused.

alpha waves ten second, unsynchronized brain waves which accompany a state of wakeful relaxation.

ambivalence feelings of both liking and disliking someone or something.

amphetamine a powerful stimulant, which affects the brain and the peripheral autonomic system.

amplification a method developed by Jung to get at the meaning of symbols; the person, together with his analyst, concentrates on an element of a dream and produces responses that are directly related to that element.

amplitude the degree of displacement of a sound wave; a physical property of sound. The psychological term for amplitude is loudness.

amygdala structure within the limbic system that is concerned with aggression and emotion.

anal stage Freud's second psychosexual stage, during which the anal region is the source of sensual pleasure.

analytic theory of personality Jung's theory of personality, which stresses the importance of complexes and the inborn archetypes in each person's collective unconscious.

androgen any of the hormones that develop and maintain masculine characteristics.

anesthetics substances that relieve pain.

anima Jung's term for the feminine side of the male's personality.

animus Jung's term for the masculine side of the female's personality.

antianxiety drugs the minor tranquilizers, such as meprobamate, which tend to produce a pleasant and anxiety-free state.

antidepressant drugs drugs that tend to relieve severe psychotic depressive states.

antipsychotic drugs tranquilizers such as reserpine and chlorpromazine that are used to calm and relax psychotic patients.

anvil one of the three bones of the middle ear; acts in transmitting vibrations across the middle ear to the inner ear.

anxiety a vague, persistent fear.

anxiety hierarchy in systematic desensitization, a sequence of imagined events that are increasingly anxiety-provoking for the patient. The individual progresses

through the list as each step fails to produce anxiety in him.

anxiety neuroses functional disorders resulting from trait anxiety; characterized by inability to cope adequately with the environment because of fear.

anxiety reaction neurotic disorder which involves apprehension, fear, and dread; accompanied by increased heart rate, raised blood pressure, sweating of palms, dryness of mouth, and rise in muscle tension.

aphasia a language defect, resulting from damage to the speech area of the brain.

apparent movement perception of movement of an object that is not actually in motion. It occurs when a series of objects are flashed in rapid succession (phi phenomenon) or when a single light in a dark area appears to move (autokinetic phenomenon).

approach-approach conflict situation in which a person is faced with the choice between two desirable goals.

approach-avoidance conflict situation in which a person wants something but is afraid of obtaining it; opposition between the two incompatible response tendencies of desire and fear.

archetype Jung's term for an inherent predisposition to perceive and react to the world in certain ways. Contained in the individual's collective unconscious, archetypes are derived from the experience of the race and represent the original model of someone or something—for example, the mother archetype.

area sampling a method of sampling by analyzing the population of small geographical segments and selecting a random group of representative units; used in poll-taking.

arousal the inciting and energizing of behavior by an internal or external stimulus.

assimilation Piaget's concept that new information is acquired through the application of existing rules or schemes.

association process by which a person connects related elements such as perceptions, memories, or ideas with each other.

association areas largest regions of the cerebral cortex which are thought to control such complex processes as the organizing and storing of information.

astroprojection the act of projecting the spirit (mind, soul) out of the body and into space.

attachment a form of integration involving the maintenance of proximity to both individuals and aspects of the environment.

attention a "filter" interposed between sensory input and the cognitive structure. Attention admits some information or sensations and excludes others.

attitude the evaluative and affective aspect of our responses and perceptions toward a given object or situation.

attraction a form of integration involving primarily the gaining of proximity and the capacity of an object to elicit approach behavior.

attribution theory accounts of the manner in which we commonly attribute or assign attitudes (as well as traits and abilities) to others.

auditory nerve fibers elements connected to the hair cells within the cochlea of the ear that must be stimulated in order that sound may be perceived.

Australopithecus the first precursor of modern man that appeared in Africa 4 million years ago.

autism, infantile severe childhood psychosis characterized by the inability to use language and form relations with people, despite normal health and a high degree of intelligence.

autistic thinking thinking that is guided by one's wishes without regard for reality or practical considerations.

autokinetic phenomenon type of apparent movement in which a single, stable light appears to move after the subject has stared at the light for a short period of time. (See apparent movement.)

autonomic conditioning operant conditioning technique for controlling autonomic responses (blood pressure, intestinal contractions, and so on) that are normally not under the organism's control.

autonomic nerves the nerves that connect to the smooth muscles, heart, and glands involved in responses commonly concerned with emotional and life-maintaining functions.

autonomic nervous system the part of the nervous system that controls involuntary actions, particularly of the smooth muscles and glands, and consists of the sympathetic and parasympathetic divisions.

autonomy stage stage of development proposed by Erikson during which the child begins to assert himself.

average evoked potential a process of averaging out background brain activity in order to isolate brain potential evoked by a stimulus.

aversive conditioning therapeutic technique in which a painful or discomforting stimulus (electric shock, for example) is paired with a stimulus in order to extinguish the undesirable response to that stimulus.

avoidance-avoidance conflict situation in which a person is forced to choose one of two undesirable goals.

avoidance learning conditioning technique in which the subject learns to avoid an unpleasant stimulus or situation.

awareness consciousness of various sensations and/or emotions. This is a difficult concept to measure, and psychologists must rely on verbal descriptions as well as elementary physiological recordings.

axon the long fiber of the nerve cell which transmits neural impulses across the synapse to other nerve cells.

backward conditioning in classical conditioning, the sequence in which the unconditioned stimulus is presented prior to the conditioned stimulus; usually it is ineffective.

balance theory of attitude change Heider's consistency theory in which people are believed to prefer a balanced or harmonious state in their relationships with other people and their environment.

barbiturates most commonly used sedatives and hypnotics; act as general depressants.

behavior genetics field of study that attempts to measure the extent to which heredity accounts for differences among people.

behavior therapy therapeutic technique based on the principles of learning; emotional problems arise because the individual has not learned effective responses or has acquired faulty behavior patterns because of inappropriate reinforcement contingencies. Behavior therapy includes a variety of classical and operant conditioning techniques.

behaviorism school of psychology which relies on objective observation of overt behavior.

behaviorist theory of development a theory that sees development as the accumulation of learned responses.

belief an opinion about something that a person considers to be true.

bell-shaped curve (See normal distribution.)

beta waves brain waves having a fast, low-voltage rhythm of 18 to 30 per second.

Binet-Simon intelligence test first intelligence test based on a comparison of mental age and chronological age to determine IQ (intelligence quotient).

binocular vision the fusion of the two separate retinal images as the two eyes function in unison.

biocybernetics a new area of research concerned with the ways in which man may become more aware of—and thus control—those biological events of which he is normally unaware. Computers are used to provide the necessary "feedback" to the subject.

biofeedback process whereby the individual can observe physiological processes of which he is normally unaware and, as a result, can learn to control those processes.

biophysical approach to behavior disorders the approach that considers the individual's biological-genetic makeup as the basic determinant of his behavior—normal or abnormal.

bisexual (ambisexual) a person sexually attracted to both males and females.

blind spot the point where the optic nerve leaves the eye. At this point there are no light receptors.

botulinus toxin a deadly food poison that blocks the release of ACh from the presynaptic axon terminal causing total paralysis.

brain the part of the central nervous system enclosed in the skull that coordinates and controls physical and mental activity.

brainstorming a technique in which a group of people freely express their ideas in a problem-solving situation.

brightness psychological property of color, usually determined by the amount of light energy emitted by an object.

Broca's area a major speech area located in the front of the left hemisphere of the brain.

cardinal trait Allport's term for a very general trait that characterizes the individual's behavior patterns.

case studies descriptive accounts of the past and present status of individuals.

castration complex a Freudian term that refers to a boy's fear of being castrated by his father and a girl's feeling that she has already been castrated and the penis envy she develops as a consequence of this feeling.

catatonic schizophrenia a type of schizophrenia characterized mainly by psychomotor manifestations such as stupor, repetitive movements, or automatic compliance.

catharsis the reduction in the strength of an impulse following expression of the impulse.

central fissure a major infolding of the cerebral cortex that separates the frontal lobe from the parietal lobe; also called fissure of Rolando.

central nervous system the part of the nervous system that includes the spinal cord and the brain.

central trait Allport's term for a trait that is highly characteristic of the individual but is not as general as a cardinal trait.

cerebellum a brain structure that lies below and behind the forebrain and seems to be specialized for movement control and sensory-motor coordination.

cerebral cortex the highest region of the brain which controls the more complex functions of the organism; composed of deep infoldings that cover parts of the forebrain.

cerebrotonia Sheldon's term for a temperament type that is characterized by restraint, inhibition, and a desire for solitude.

chlorpromazine antipsychotic drug (tranquilizer) used to alleviate or even eliminate agitation, hallucinations, and delusions.

chromosomes long, threadlike strands which contain the genes, the basic units of heredity.

chronological age the individual's actual age.

chunking grouping together of several related words to facilitate verbal learning.

circadian rhythms recurrence of biological events at approximately 24-hour cycles; for example, sleep.

clairvoyance literally "clear vision"; the power to perceive things that are outside the natural range of human senses.

classical conditioning a form of conditioning attributed to Pavlov, in which stimuli associated with naturally meaningful stimuli tend to become substitutes for the stimuli themselves and to elicit similar responses. Technically, the pairing of a CS with a US elicits a CR similar to the UR originally elicited by the US.

client-centered therapy nondirective therapeutic technique based on Rogers' theory of self-actualization; that is, that human nature is fundamentally sound and that every individual is capable of healthy adjustment and self-realization.

clinical psychology the diagnosis and treatment of psychological disorders, conducted in private offices, schools, clinics, hospitals, and so on.

cocaine type of drug which acts as a local anesthetic. Continued use of cocaine results in addiction.

cochlea a bony spiral in the ear that resembles a snail shell and is composed of 2½ convolutions wound around an axis in the form of a hollow cone that contains the cochlear vessels and nerves. Hair cells in the cochlea are stimulated by vibrations of the cochlear fluid and transform the sound waves into neuronal activity.

coercive incentives an incentive that is imposed upon a person to get him to behave in a certain way regardless of his needs.

cognition the mental processes—including perception, memory, and thinking—by which one acquires knowledge, makes plans, and solves problems.

cognitive dissonance Festinger's term for a state of tension that arises when a person holds two thoughts, attitudes, or beliefs that are logically inconsistent, motivating that person to reduce the dissonant situation.

cognitive learning complex learning which involves reorganization of one's perceptions or ideas.

cognitive maps mental images of locations.

collective unconscious Jung's term for that portion of the unconscious that is inborn and that is common to all of mankind. (See also archetype.)

color constancy tendency to perceive colors as the same, whether in bright or dim light.

community mental health the application of psychological principles to the environment to promote psychological well-being.

community psychology branch of applied psychology involving the full use of community resources in the identification, treatment, and rehabilitation of the psychologically disturbed; more concerned with social intervention than with interpersonal change.

compensation Adler's concept for overcoming a frustrating defect by concentrating on substitute activities with attainable goals.

compensatory theory of dreaming Jung's theory that dreams attempt to compensate for undeveloped or neglected parts of the dreamer's personality.

complementary colors colors directly opposite each other on the color wheel. For example, blue and yellow are complementary; when mixed they are seen as gray or white.

complex-indicators Jung's term for signs of emotional disturbance.

concept a general idea derived from observing similarities among different objects.

concrete operational stage according to Piaget, a subperiod of intellectual development in which the child can discriminate unimportant from important changes and changes in appearance from changes in quantity in relation to principles of logical necessity.

concrete thinking thinking about specific, concrete things.

conditioned fear anxiety which results from a neutral stimulus that has been associated with one that elicits fear.

conditioned reinforcer a reinforcer that derives its meaning as a result of its association with basic, unconditioned reinforcers.

conditioned response (CR) in classical conditioning, a response that develops to the conditioned stimulus after a number of pairings of the conditioned stimulus with an unconditioned stimulus . The conditioned response is similar to the unconditioned response.

conditioned stimulus (CS) in classical conditioning, a stimulus with which the unconditioned stimulus is paired; as a result of the pairing, the CS comes to elicit a response similar to the original response (UR) to the unconditioned stimulus (US).

conduction aphasia an aphasia in which a patient can produce fluent words and phrases without making any sense; caused by a lesion limited to the region interconnecting Wernicke's area and Broca's area.

cones receptors within the retina of the eye that transform light energy into nerve impulses. Cones are found predominantly in the fovea and are responsible for color vision.

conformity behaving in accordance with established social norms; it contributes to uniformity within a community.

conjunctive concept idea derived from discriminating and classifying objects that have two or more characteristics in common.

consensual criterion of abnormal behavior the criterion that uses society's standards of abnormal, harmful, or socially disruptive behavior; it is essentially a social value judgment.

conservation an achievement of the concrete operational period in which a person applies principles of logical necessity to problems of number, liquid, weight, and volume.

consistency theories of attitude change theories stemming from the view that people are usually motivated to make their thoughts, beliefs, and behavior consistent; inconsistency becomes a stimulus to change.

constancy perceptual compensation by which objects retain constant perceptual properties in spite of objective changes. (See also size constancy, shape constancy, and color constancy.)

constitutional theory of personality Sheldon's theory of personality which stresses the relations between physique and temperament.

constitutional traits Cattell's term for traits that are determined by heredity.

content analysis the analysis of various elements found in dreams by developing a set of categories into which the elements of a dream can be placed.

contiguity the closeness in time or space of the stimuli to be associated.

conventional level a stage of moral reasoning, described by Kohlberg, which defines good behavior as what is intended to please others at one substage to a belief in the maintenance of law and order at another substage.

convergence the process by which the eyes turn slightly inward to focus on an object.

corpus callosum the most important fiber band joining the two cerebral hemispheres (that is, the two halves of the brain).

corpus luteum a temporary endocrine gland formed in the ovary which secretes the sex hormones estrogen and progesterone.

correlation coefficient the mathematical expression of the degree of relationship between two sets of data, such as test scores and performance in real-life situations.

correlation techniques means of estimating the extent to which two variables or events are related.

counseling psychology the application of psychological principles to advise relatively normal individuals with problems usually pertaining to educational or vocational choices and interpersonal relations.

creative thinking thinking that results in the discovery of new ideas and solutions to problems.

critical thinking thinking that consists of examining and testing new ideas to see whether they will work.

Cro-Magnon a branch of *Homo sapiens*; invaded Europe 35 or 40,000 years ago.

crystallized intelligence according to Cattell, the sum of culturally conditioned acquisitions like social information, common factual data, and school skills.

cumulative recorder a device which records the organism's rate of response in a test of operant conditioning.

curare a poison that blocks acetylcholine from activating the postsynaptic receptor, causing total paralysis.

dark adaptation process by which the rods become fully sensitive to very dim light.

death instinct Freud's term for an inborn self-destructive tendency.

decay theory hypothesis that engrams in long-term storage fade away with the passage of time.

decentering an aspect of adolescent maturational development in which adolescents realize that other people do not necessarily share their thoughts and feelings.

decentration a major developmental trend in children's thinking described by Piaget as a focus increasingly away from oneself and toward a broader perspective.

deep structure according to Chomsky, the meaning and more basic processes of syntax and conceptual organization in any language.

defense mechanism technique for resolving inner conflicts. (See also renunciation, repression, reaction formation, sublimation, and projection.)

defensive syndrome pattern of arousal that results from the presentation of a threatening or intense stimulus; the organism's physiological systems prepare it for fight or flight.

delayed conditioning in classical conditioning, a sequence in which the unconditioned stimulus is presented after the conditioned stimulus has been turned off.

delirium tremens (*d.t.'s*) an acute brain condition that usually occurs after years of addiction to alcohol and is often precipitated by withdrawal of the drug. There is partial or complete disorientation, accompanied by hallucinations, delusions, and general restlessness.

delta waves brain waves that are very slow, synchronized, and of large amplitude, occurring 2 or 3 per second, only when a person is in slow-wave sleep or unconscious.

delusion a false belief.

delusion of grandeur a belief that one is an exceptional person; often found in psychosis.

delusion of persecution a belief that one is being talked about or plotted against by enemies; often found in psychosis.

dendrites fibers of a nerve cell that receive neural impulses from the axons of other nerve cells and transmit them to their axon.

dendritic spines synapses containing small bumps or knobs on the postsynaptic membrane that occur on the dendrites of nerve cells.

denotative symbolism a symbol that represents something directly; for example, the word "cat" is a direct symbol for a certain species of animal. (See also metaphorical symbol.)

deoxyribonucleic acid (*DNA*) a complex type of biochemical substance which determines the genetic composition of the organism.

dependent variable in an experiment, the variable which is measurably affected when the independent variable is manipulated.

depth perception perception of the distance of an object from the eye; enables us to see the third dimension.

development an orderly sequence of directional changes in behavior.

developmental psychology traditionally, the study of child development; currently also includes the study of development through adolescence, adulthood, and old age.

differentiation a type of social interaction in which individuals by virtue of forming affective bonds with certain individuals necessarily and simultaneously separate and segregate themselves from some others.

discrimination process by which the organism distinguishes between closely related items and thus responds differentially; an element in both classical and operant conditioning.

disguise theory of symbolism Freud's theory that dream symbols conceal the true meaning of the dreamer's thoughts from him.

dishabituation the reappearance of the initial level of response to a stimulus following a change in some aspect or feature of it.

disjunctive concept idea embracing many different items, which have been grouped together arbitrarily. For example, a felony is a disjunctive concept.

displaced aggression aggression directed against someone or something as a substitute for the original cause of one's anger.

displacement the substitution of a less direct form of satisfying a motive for a more direct one.

dissonance theory (See cognitive dissonance.)

disuse theory hypothesis that an engram, if unused, will be deleted from the permanent brain stores of memory (long-term memory).

dizygotic twins nonidentical twins; develop from two separate zygotes, thereby having different genetic compositions.

dorsal root a nerve at the back of the spinal cord that allows incoming sensory fibers to enter the cord. (See also ventral root.)

dorsal root ganglion a group of cell bodies of sensory nerves from the skin and body that lies outside the spinal cord.

double approach-avoidance conflict situation in which each desirable goal has both desirable and undesirable features relative to another goal.

dramatizations according to Sullivan, performances in which a child acts out his personifications.

dream analysis technique of psychoanalysis in which the manifest content of the patient's dreams is interpreted so as to reveal their latent content and thus the unconscious meaning.

dream series method method of detecting the meaning of a symbol by analyzing a series of dreams reported by an individual.

drive an incitement to action that has its origin in an internal bodily state (for example, hunger), or that has been learned (for example, the drive to obtain approval).

drug potentiation the tendency of some drugs to augment the effects of another. For example, a barbiturate taken with whiskey will have a much greater depressing effect than either taken alone.

dynamic traits Cattell's term for traits that are motivational in character.

dynamism Sullivan's term for a relatively enduring form of interpersonal behavior.

dynamogenic theory of performance Triplett's theory of social influence, in which the presence of a competing individual arouses the competitive drive, frees nervous energy, and inspires greater effort in the individual.

eardrum a membrane that lies between the external auditory canal and the middle ear. The hammer of the first auditory ossicle is joined to it.

ectomorphy Sheldon's term for that dimension of physique which is characterized by thinness.

educational psychology the study of behavior in the educational setting with emphasis on the principles of learning.

efferent (motor) neuron a type of neuron found in the peripheral nerves which transmits impulses from the brain or spinal cord to the appropriate muscles or glands.

ego Freud's term for the system of personality that interacts with the external world.

ego identity individuality, coherence, and integration of one's self-concept.

eidetic imagery a rare form of photographic memory in which a subject retains an unusually vivid visual image of a stimulus for a period of time; found mainly in children.

electro-dermal response (EDR) See galvanic skin response.

electroencephalogram (EEG) a recording of the brain waves detected by an electroencephalograph; a machine that amplifies and records the electrical activity of the brain from wires (electrodes) placed on the scalp. This record enables a doctor or scientist to diagnose how alert the brain is, how it is functioning, and whether there are any disturbances present.

electroshock therapy type of somatic therapy in which an electric current is passed briefly through the brain, producing changes in behavior. Also called electroconvulsive therapy, its widest use is for treating states of depression.

emotion any strong feeling, always accompanied by physiological activity of the internal organs.

encounter group a controversial form of group therapy in which individuals are encouraged to relate intimately with one another and to express themselves more fully than in ordinary interpersonal relations.

endocrine glands a system of glands that produce hormones and secrete them directly into the bloodstream, for example, thyroid, adrenals, and pituitary.

endomorphy Sheldon's term for that dimension of physique which is characterized by fatness.

engineering psychology the study of the relationship between men and machines.

engram hypothetical memory trace or physical representation of a memory in the central nervous system.

environmental-mold traits Cattell's term for traits that are environmentally determined.

epinephrine a hormone secreted by the adrenal medulla that releases energy, increases metabolism, and provides a mechanism for distributing the effects of sympathetic activity throughout the bloodstream; also called adrenalin.

equilibration according to Piaget, the processes by which a person learns to deal with problems that cannot be solved with his existing set of rules or schemes.

ergs Cattell's term for dynamic traits that are instinctive in man.

escape learning conditioning technique in which the subject learns to escape or terminate an unpleasant stimulus.

estrogen a female sex hormone that controls the development of secondary sex characteristics and the reproductive functions.

ethnocentrism belief in the superiority

of one's own country and race and the inferior status of other races.

eugenics the application of selective breeding to human beings to improve the species.

evolution a gradual process by which simple forms have significantly changed into those that are more complex.

existential theory of personality theory of personality that is concerned exclusively with immediate experience.

experimental chamber apparatus designed by B. F. Skinner to test operant conditioning techniques. It usually contains a lever, a food hopper, and wire grids for the passing of electric shocks; also known as a Skinner box.

experimental method the rigorous scientific process by which hypotheses are tested under laboratory conditions.

experimental psychology the study of different components of the behavior of humans and other animals under laboratory conditions, in which a variable or variables can be manipulated to determine their effect on another variable or variables.

extinction the gradual disappearance of a learned behavior when the reinforcement is removed. In classical conditioning, removal of the unconditioned stimulus causes extinction; in operant conditioning, removal of the stimulus that causes the emitted response to persist causes extinction.

extraversion Jung's term for an attitude that is oriented on the outer or objective world.

facilitative incentive an incentive that helps a person to satisfy his needs.

factor analysis a statistical method for identifying general factors—for example, personality traits.

factor theory of personality Cattell's theory of personality which considers traits—classified into five types—to be the main components of personality; traits are identified by the method of factor analysis.

fear an emotional reaction to threat or danger from specific stimuli.

feedback the process by which an individual gains information regarding the correctness of his response so that he can use that information to alter succeeding responses.

fetish (sexual) an object or part of the body that produces unusual sexual excitement; for example, a shoe fetish.

fetus an unborn, developing human being, usually from 3 months after conception to the moment of birth.

figure-ground relationship the Gestalt rule of perceptual organization that some part of the field stands out as a unified object while the rest recedes into the background.

filter model Broadbent's theoretical device developed to explain selective attention; that is, how the brain accepts and rejects messages. It is done, according to this theory, by a selective filter that "screens" incoming information.

fitness according to Darwin, the ability of a species to reproduce itself.

fixed-interval schedule a schedule of reinforcement in which organisms are reinforced for the first correct response that occurs after a fixed period of time has elapsed since the previous reinforced response.

fixed-ratio schedule a schedule of reinforcement in which the organism is reinforced after a set number of nonreinforced correct responses.

fixed-role therapy therapeutic technique, based on Kelly's personal construct theory of personality, which uses role playing to alter a person's constructs of himself and others.

fluid intelligence according to Cattell, a neurologically determined component of intelligence.

forebrain the highest region of the brain, containing the cerebrum, thalamus, and hypothalamus, and covered by the cerebral cortex.

fovea a recessed area of the retina, in which cones predominate. It is the region of greatest visual acuity in daylight.

free association a technique in which a person says everything that occurs to him; used in the analysis of dreams, particularly in psychoanalysis, to get at unconscious material.

frequency number of sound waves per second. Measured in hertzes, it is one of the objective, physical properties of sound.

frontal lobe the frontal region of the cerebral cortex that is presumed to serve very complex higher mental functions.

frustration environmental or personal obstacle that prevents one from obtaining a desired goal; also, a condition caused by the blocking of a goal.

functional autonomy Allport's term for motives that have become independent of their biological origins.

functional fixedness inability to recognize the various possible uses of an object.

functional psychosis psychosis in which there is no known organic basis. The individual often cannot think normally, work, or make decisions. He tends to lose interest in people, sex, and all social activities.

galvanic skin response (GSR) change in electrical resistance of the skin in response to certain stimuli.

gamma waves brain waves having a fast, low-voltage rhythm of 30–50 per second.

general-adaptation-syndrome Selye's term for a stereotyped stress response, consisting of an alarm reaction (bodily change), resistance to stress (an attempt to cope), and exhaustion.

general paresis a condition in which there is progressive deterioration of brain tissue as a result of syphilitic infection.

generalization process whereby the organism responds similarly to stimuli which resemble one another.

genes basic units of heredity; composed of the biochemical substance deoxyribonucleic acid (DNA) which provides the basic heredity information and controls.

genetic diversity variety of genetic composition of individuals within a species.

genetic drift relatively large increases or decreases in the frequencies of certain genes from generation to generation.

genital stage the final psychosexual stage, according to Freud, during which the individual obtains pleasure from sexual contact with other persons.

genotype the genetic constitution of the individual.

Gestalt psychology school of psychology in which the wholeness of experience forms the basis for understanding behavior.

glial cell a cell that makes up the supporting tissue of the nervous system.

goal gradient term used to describe the fact that as one approaches a goal, the drive to reach it becomes stronger.

gonads sex glands, either testes or ovaries.

group a number of individuals associated through feelings of attachment and affiliation; usually long term.

group therapy technique of therapy in which individuals work together to solve their mutual problems through social interaction. The term covers many techniques, such as encounter groups, non-directive group therapy, and family group therapy.

grouping process by which our visual field is organized into meaningful groups of objects, patterns, or stimuli.

guilt the feeling that results from doing something contrary to one's moral standards.

habit a recurrent pattern of behavior acquired through experience and made more or less permanent by various reinforcing events.

habituation the lessening or disappearance of a response with repeated presentations of the stimulus.

hair cells a series of columnar cells in the cochlea of the ear. Because they vary in length according to their location in the cochlear canal, they have been assumed to play a role in selecting sound waves of varying frequencies.

halfway house a temporary residence that provides a transition between the mental hospital and life in the community.

hallucination mental picture that is mistaken for reality, as in a dream.

hammer one of the three bones of the middle ear; acts as part of the mechanical transmission system between the external auditory canal and the cochlea of the inner ear.

hashish cannabis resin; the strongest of the hemp products used to produce a feeling of well-being.

hebephrenic schizophrenia a type of schizophrenia characterized by severe disintegration of the personality. The patient loses touch with reality, and all major functions become increasingly disorganized and distorted. Delusions and hallucinations are common.

hemispheres (*right and left*) two halves of the brain joined by the corpus callosum.

Hering-Hurvich opponent-process theory theory of color vision based on the assumption that there are three systems of receptors in the retina (one each for red-green, blue-yellow, and black-white); each system contains two opposing types of receptors.

heritability the ability to inherit genes that determine behavioral traits.

hermaphrodite a person having the sex organs and many of the secondary sex characteristics of both male and female.

heroin a semisynthetic morphine derivative (diacetylmorphine). It produces relief from pain and a state of well-being; chronic use is habit forming.

heuristics strategies developed for solving problems.

hindbrain the lowest region of the brain, primarily concerned with vital reflexes; it contains the pons, medulla, and cerebellum.

homeostasis processes that maintain balance in the operation of the internal bodily functioning.

Homo erectus a precursor of modern man that appeared 800,000 years ago.

Homo sapiens modern man; first appeared 50,000 years ago.

homosexuality a sexual preference for members of the same sex.

hormones chemicals produced by the endocrine glands that have a powerful and profound effect on bodily function and behavior.

hue a psychological property of color; the basis for the color's specific name.

humanistic psychology a contemporary school of psychology which emphasizes man's positive features and growth capacity.

hypersensitivity theory theory to explain drug addiction; whatever effect a drug has will appear in its opposite form during withdrawal.

hypnosis a temporary trancelike state of altered awareness. It is usually induced by a second person. As a result of increased susceptibility to suggestion, subjects exhibit a variety of behaviors either spontaneously or in response to verbal or other stimuli.

hypnotic regression technique of hypnosis in which the individual is made to behave as he did when he was younger.

hypnotic suggestion the adoption of specific ideas, attitudes, and behaviors by a patient under hypnosis.

hypothalamus a region at the bottom of the brain, just above the midbrain, that plays a critical role in the motivational and emotional aspects of behavior and also in endocrine gland functions.

hysterical neurosis disorder characterized by disturbances of normal integration of behavior (amnesia, multiple personality) or physical symptoms (paralysis, disturbances of the senses, tumors, tics) in the absence of an organic basis.

hysterical personality a personality trait disturbance that is characterized by immature, self-centered behavior that manifests itself in frequent emotional outbursts and histrionic display.

iconic memory the briefly retained visual image of a visual stimulus.

id Freud's term for the system of personality that includes the unconscious, basic, biological impulses or instincts.

identity formation according to Erikson, the stage of personality development in which the individual acquires his own identity as a person.

ideology a system of beliefs, for example, a democratic ideology.

ideo-motor activity an action that results from an idea.

idiot-savant a mentally handicapped individual who can nevertheless perform prodigious mental feats.

illusion an alteration of reality in perception; a mistaken perception of a given object.

imagining a type of thinking in which new ideas or images are formed.

implosive therapy type of behavior therapy in which anxiety responses are extinguished by presenting the patient with the fear-evoking stimuli in a comfortable, secure environment.

incentive an external inducement to act in a certain way; money and encouragement are common examples of incentives.

incest taboo practice of forbidding sexual relations between close blood relatives.

independent variable in an experiment, the variable which the experimenter can manipulate to determine its effects upon the dependent variable.

individuation Jung's term for the differentiation of personality into various systems, and the differentiation within each system.

industrial psychology the study of psychological aspects of the business and industrial environment.

inferiority complex Adler's term for feelings of inadequacy.

innate capacity theory of language Chomsky's theory that many aspects of our linguistic abilities are genetically determined.

insight in problem-solving, a solution that appears suddenly.

instinct an inborn predisposition to behave in a specific way when appropriately stimulated. Instincts are complex behaviors that the characteristic of a species.

instrumental acts acts motivated by an organic drive source through which the drive aim is achieved.

instrumental conditioning (See operant conditioning.)

instrumental objects in organically motivated behavior, objects required to satisfy the drive source.

integration a type of social interaction in which individuals form affective bonds through group affiliation.

intelligence the capacity of humans and other animals to deal effectively with the environment.

intelligence quotient (IQ) a measurement of intelligence expressed as a number derived from the formula mental age/chronological age $\times$ 100 = IQ.

intensity loudness, in subjective terms.

interference hindrance of learning and memory caused by intervening events. (See also retroactive inhibition, proactive inhibition.)

interneuron essentially all neurons in the central nervous system except sensory and motor neurons.

interstimulus interval in classical conditioning, the time elapsed between the conditioned stimulus and the unconditioned stimulus.

introspection process by which an individual closely observes his mental experiences.

introversion Jung's term for an attitude that is oriented toward the inner or subjective world.

inverted-U function term for Hebb's concept that emotional arousal directs behavior most effectively at some middle level of arousal.

iris an opaque diaphragm in the form of a thick disk of connective tissue that separates the anterior and posterior chambers of the eye; it regulates the opening and closing of the pupil and thus the amount of light that enters the eye.

isolation the separation of one group from another by physical barriers which causes inbreeding and separate development to occur within each group.

just noticeable difference (j.n.d.) the least amount of change in a stimulus necessary for the individual to be able to detect a difference.

kappa waves brain waves with a frequency of about 8 to 12 per second that are thought to be associated with intellectual processes.

language a formal means of communication that possesses a grammatical structure.

latent content Freud's term for the underlying (unconscious) meaning of a dream.

latent learning learning that does not become manifest until an incentive is introduced.

law of effect Thorndike's concept that an organism will tend to repeat and learn behavior that has a satisfying or reinforcing outcome; behaviors that cause pain or discomfort will not be repeated or learned.

learned drives drives that are acquired through learning; see also primary drives.

learning behavior that has been modified as a result of an organism's experience.

learning set learning how to learn a particular task.

learning theories of language theories that language is a behavior or skill acquired through the interaction of experience and the contingencies of the environment (reinforcement and punishment, for example).

lens an oval, transparent structure that lies between the iris and the pupil. It changes shape so that objects are sharply imaged on the retina.

light adaptation process by which the cones adapt to bright light.

limbic systems the higher brain structures concerned with emotional and motivational aspects of behavior.

limited channel capacity term used to refer to the sensory systems' inability to attend to more than one stimulus at a time.

linguistic relativity hypothesis a proposition which asserts that our thought and our perception of the world are relative to the language of our culture.

lobotomy a form of psychosurgery that involves cutting nerve fibers that connect the frontal lobes to the thalamus. Once considered suitable for those suffering from tension and psychotic symptoms but now is seldom used.

long-term memory (See secondary memory.)

loudness psychological property of hearing, determined by the intensity of a sound as judged by an individual; amplitude is the physical correlate of loudness.

lysergic acid dimethylamide (LSD) psychotomimetic drug which produces psychoticlike behavior; also called a hallucinogen.

malevolent transformation according to Sullivan, the felling that one lives among enemies.

mania type of affective disorder characterized by extreme excitation.

manic-depressive disorder type of affective disorder characterized by extreme mood disturbances—from mania to depression.

manifest content Freud's term for the dream as it is actually recalled by the dreamer.

marijuana a form of cannabis from the female hemp plant. It is smoked, and its effect is akin to that of hashish, only less strong.

masochism pleasure derived from pain inflicted on oneself by others. (See also self-aggression and sadism.)

mathematical psychology a subfield of quantitative psychology in which mathematical models are developed to represent (and predict) significant areas of behavior.

mental age the age corresponding to an individual's performance on an intelligence test in relation to a standardization group.

mentally retarded. individuals with an IQ below 70.

mescaline psychotomimetic drug derived from the peyote cactus.

mesomorphy Sheldon's term for that dimension of physique which is characterized by muscularity.

metaneeds Maslow's term for growth needs, such as justice, goodness, and beauty, whose proper satisfaction enables the individual to become a completely developed human being.

metaphorical symbol a symbol that stands for something other than what it appears to be; for example, a dog may stand for a lowly, brutish person; see also denotative symbolism.

midbrain the region of the brain that lies below the forebrain, containing relay nuclei for the visual and auditory systems; its parts are the tectum and tegmentum.

milieu therapy therapeutic technique in which the mental hospital establishes programs to stimulate the patients to maintain and enhance their interpersonal skills and social responsibility.

mnemonics techniques developed to facilitate learning by organizing unrelated items into artificial relationships.

modeling type of learning or relearning in which behavior is learned or modified as a result of observing the behavior of others; also called observational learning.

monocular cues visual cues of linear perspective, clearness, texture-gradient, and so on, which aid us in seeing depth with only one eye.

monozygotic twins identical twins; occur when a zygote divides once and each of the two cells with identical chromosomes develops as a separate individual.

morpheme the smallest unit of linguistic analysis that has independent meaning.

morphine addictive drug derived from the opium poppy; used to relieve pain.

motive anything that initiates behavior.

motor-skill learning ability to coordinate skills requiring the use of the muscles in an integrated whole pattern.

mutation change in the chemical composition of a gene.

myelin sheath a fatty substance that covers the fibers of the larger sensory and motor neurons.

narcotics class of opium alkaloids, such as morphine and heroin, which are addictive and may be fatal, if an overdose is taken.

natural selection principle by which those members of a species whose genetic makeup produces certain characteristics promoting adaptation to their environment constitute an increasing proportion of their species in the environment with each succeeding generation.

nature-nurture issue the question of the extent to which environment and heredity determine behavior.

Neanderthal race of man which first appeared 100,000 years ago in Europe, North Africa, and the Near East.

negative afterimage the appearance of a color's complement after looking at a color for a while and then looking away at a piece of grey paper.

negative discriminative stimulus (S$^\triangle$) in operant conditioning, the stimulus to which responses are nonreinforced or negatively reinforced.

negative reinforcer in operant conditioning, a stimulus whose withdrawal increases the probability that the response leading to its termination will persist.

negative transfer the interference of previously learned responses with learning in a new situation.

need an internal or external deficiency; often used as a synonym for drive.

nerve cell (See neuron.)

nerve tract a collection of nerve fibers inside the central nervous system.

neuron special type of cell which transmits nerve impulses; also called a nerve cell.

neurosis functional disorder involving an inability to cope appropriately, adequately, or satisfactorily with the environment. Anxiety plays an important role. Failure to maintain rewarding interpersonal relationships is characteristic.

neurotic-depressive reaction an acute depression precipitated by an intensely distressing situation such as the death of a loved one or the loss of a job.

nodes of Ranvier small interruptions in the myelin sheath covering the fibers of the larger nerve cells.

non–REM sleep (NREM) stages of sleep during which there are no rapid eye movements (REM).

nonsense syllable a set of verbal stimuli developed by Ebbinghaus consisting of three-letter syllables that carry no intrinsic meaning.

norepinephrine a hormone secreted by the adrenal medulla that decreases metabolism; also called noradrenalin.

norm a set standard of achievement derived from the average achievement of a large group.

normal distribution the bell-shaped curve formed by the distribution of scores from a random sampling of the population.

obsessive-compulsive reaction a neurotic reaction characterized by a persistent impulse to think certain thoughts (obsessions) and/or carry out certain actions (compulsions).

occipital lobe the back end of the cerebral cortex involved in processing visual information.

Oedipus complex a Freudian term that refers to a child's love for the opposite-sex parent and hostility toward the same-sex parent.

operant conditioning a form of conditioning in which the persistence of a response emitted by an organism depends on its effect on the environment; also known as instrumental conditioning.

operant reinforcement theory of personality Skinner's theory, which describes personality as a pattern of responses operating upon the environment in such a way as to produce a reinforcement.

operational stage according to Piaget, a period of intellectual development divided into the preoperational and concrete operational substages.

opium addictive drug that is composed of the juice of the opium poppy.

oral stage the first of Freud's psychosexual stages, during which the mouth is the source of sensual pleasure.

organic psychosis psychosis caused by pathological changes in the brain; it may be acute and reversible or chronic and irreversible. (See also functional psychosis.)

organic therapies forms of treatment based on the premise that psychological disorders have an organic basis. The therapy involves modification or treatment by means of drugs, surgery, electroshock therapy, or some other physical intervention. Also called somatic therapies.

orienting response a response to a stimulus in which the organism turns toward the source of the stimulus.

oval window an oval aperture between the middle and inner ears, which transmits vibrations to the inner ear.

ovaries the female reproductive glands that produce ova.

paired-associate learning a verbal learning task developed by Ebbinghaus, in which pairs of words or nonsense syllables are to be memorized. The first syllable serves as the stimulus for the response of its paired syllable.

pansexualism the idea, usually attributed to Freud, that the sex drive expresses itself in many different ways.

paradoxical sleep stage of sleep during which REMS occur. Called paradoxical sleep because, while the brain waves resemble those that occur during wakefulness, it is very difficult to arouse the sleeper.

paranoia disturbance characterized by delusional systems often related to grandeur and persecution; distinguished from paranoid schizophrenia by the lack of general disorganization and deterioration of thought and behavior.

paranoid schizophrenia a schizophrenic syndrome in which delusions and hallucinations usually predominate. The individual believes that he is being persecuted. Thought, volitional, and emotional disorders may also be present.

parasympathetic division a division of the autonomic nervous system that is concerned with the recuperative, restorative, and nutritive functions of the body.

parietal lobe a large portion of the cerebral cortex above the temporal lobe concerned in part with bodily sensations.

part learning an approach to verbal or motor-skill learning in which small parts of the whole are learned and later combined to produce the final behavior.

path Lewin's term for the direction of behavior in an environmental field.

peak experience Maslow's term for the rare events in which the individual feels more integrated, more at one with the world, more his own master, more spontaneous, less aware of space and time, and more perceptive.

perception a psychological function which—by means of the sense organs—enables the organism to receive and process information on the state of, and alterations in, the environment.

persona Jung's term for each person's mask of conformity.

personal construct theory Kelly's theory of personality, which stresses that man can be taught to be a more rational animal by altering his personal constructs; that is, how he construes, interprets, or attaches meaning to aspects of the environment.

personality the psychological makeup and characteristic behavior of the person as a whole.

personality (character) disorder pathological character structure that stems primarily from defective personality development. These disorders include a group of conditions characterized by deviant or maladjusted behavior, but without focal conflict or symptoms.

personality psychology the study of individuals and the similarities and differences between them.

personification Sullivan's term for a complex of feelings, attitudes, and conceptions that an individual has concerning himself and other people.

personology Murray's theory of personality, which stresses the interaction between needs and press, that is, between the individual's motives and aspects of the environment that hinder or facilitate satisfaction of those motives.

phallic stage the third of Freud's psychosexual stages, during which the genitals are the source of sensual pleasure.

phase the differential pressure exerted on the ear by a sound wave.

phenomenal field Rogers' term for the totality of experiences.

phenomenological approach an unstructured method of reporting experiences which concentrates on events occurring outside the laboratory.

phenotype the outward expression of the genotype.

phi phenomenon process in which two lights a short distance apart are flashed alternately in rapid succession; the light seems to move from one position to the other. (See apparent movement.)

phobic reactions reactions such as blushing, fainting, vomiting, or abnormal, compulsive behavior used to overcome irrational, strong fears (phobias) of objects or situations that are not usually thought of as frightening.

phoneme the smallest possible subdivision of language that can still be identified as a discrete sound.

physiological psychology the study of the relationship between biological processes in humans and other animals and behavior.

pitch psychological property of hearing, determined by the frequency of sound waves entering the ear.

pituitary gland endocrine gland (sometimes called the "master gland") which releases hormones that influence other organs to release hormones; also affects cellular growth. Consisting of a posterior and anterior gland, the pituitary is located at the base of the brain.

placebo inactive substance used as a control in drug experiments.

plasticity the capacity of an organism to modify its responses through changes in its neuron connections; the ability of learning and memory.

play therapy psychotherapeutic technique to treat disturbed children. The child is encouraged to express himself in relatively unstructured play.

pleasure-pain principle the principle that man is motivated to seek pleasure and avoid pain.

polling measurement technique that relies on interviewing a sample of people who are representative of the entire population in question.

polygraph literally "many graphs"; a device for measuring simultaneously a number of physiological processes such as heart rate, blood pressure, breathing, and so on.

positive discriminative stimulus (S^D) in conditioning, the stimulus to which responses are positively reinforced.

positive reinforcer in operant conditioning, a stimulus whose presentation increases the probability that the response leading to it will persist.

positive transfer the facilitation of the learning of responses in new situations as a result of past learning.

postconventional level according to Kohlberg, a stage of moral reasoning ranging from higher-order values to self-chosen abstract ethical rules.

posthypnotic amnesia forgetting what happened while a person was in a hypnotic trance, usually as a result of a suggestion by the hypnotist.

precognition knowledge of something before it occurs.

preconventional level a stage of moral reasoning described by Kohlberg as ranging from unquestioning obedience to authority at one substage to satisfaction of one's own needs first at another substage.

prejudice a belief which is characterized by the oversimplification, overgeneralization, and distortion of some small element of truth.

preoperational stage according to Piaget, a subperiod of intellectual development in which the child's thought focuses on a limited amount of information in seeking a solution to any problem.

press according to Murray, some aspect of the environment that impedes or facilitates the efforts of an individual to satisfy his needs.

primary drive an organic drive, such as thirst; also called unlearned drive.

primary memory storage system in which information is kept for only short periods of time; also called short-term memory.

primary mental abilities a set of factors described by Thurstone which influence a subject's performance on any intelligence test item.

primary retardation low intelligence as a normal consequence of heredity.

principle of symmetry concept that individuals tend to react in the same way that they are acted upon; for example, matching aggression with aggression.

proactive inhibition process whereby the retention of new learning is interfered with by previously learned material.

progesterone the maternal hormone.

programmed learning learning technique in which the student is guided through a curriculum step-by-step; it provides reinforcement while enabling him to work at his own pace.

projection defense mechanism in which the individual attributes to others his undesirable qualities, attitudes, and desires.

projection areas areas of the cerebral cortex, each of which regulates a specific activity—vision and hearing, for example.

prostigmine a drug that blocks the action of the enzyme AChE leading to prolonged and uncontrollable muscle contractions.

psilocybin psychotomimetic drug, derived from mushrooms.

psychiatric social worker one who is trained to work with the families of disturbed individuals as well as social agencies. He or she usually holds a graduate degree.

psychiatrist a medical doctor, with additional training in that branch of medicine that deals with the diagnosis and treatment of mental disorders.

psychoanalysis technique of psychotherapy based upon psychoanalytic theory; involving free association, dream interpretation, and analysis of transference responses. Developed by Freud and modified by his successors, it attempts to bring to awareness the patient's unconscious thoughts and conflicts and to integrate them with the conscious self.

psychoanalytic theory of personality Freud's theory of personality, which stresses the importance of unconscious motives.

psychobiology the scientific study of the biological bases of behavior.

psychodrama type of group therapy in which the patient re-enacts past events that were critical in the development of his psychological conflicts. Patients achieve insights and are able to alter behavior patterns through the acting out of various situations.

psychodynamic therapy approach that stresses unconscious events and early experience as the causes of disorders; typified by psychoanalysis.

psychology the scientific study of behavior.

psychometrics tests and other techniques for measuring various aspects of behavior.

psychopharmacology the study of drugs that act on behavior and experience.

psychophysics the study of the relationship between the physical properties of a stimulus and the individual's psychological experience of it.

psychosexual stages according to Freud, the sequence of stages through which each person passes in growing up; during each stage—oral, anal, phallic, and genital—sensual pleasure is obtained mostly by stimulation of a particular zone of the body.

psychosis a major disturbance that involves disorganization of the personality to the extent that the individual is unable to take care of himself and often is institutionalized. Typically involves disturbances of thought, emotion, and motor behavior.

psychosomatic (psychophysiological) disorders disorders in which psychological conditions contribute to actual organic damage or physical symptoms, as in ulcers, hypertension, or asthma.

psychotherapy a variety of psychological techniques used to modify behavior disorders. Distinguished from somatic and organic therapies.

psychotomimetics drugs like LSD and psilocybin that induce psychotic-like experience and behavior.

punishment presentation of a painful or discomforting stimulus which decreases the probability that the response leading to it will persist.

quantitative psychology the study of human behavior through the use of mathematical and statistical methods.

rapid eye movements (REM) sleep periods characterized by the movement of the eyes during desynchronized or activated sleep.

rating scale a form of index measurement that attempts to assess an individual's attitude by asking him to express it in terms of a categorical or numerical rating on some identified scale.

rationalization self-justification; a defense mechanism whereby the individual tries to give reasons for irrational behavior.

reaction formation defense mechanism whereby the individual's expressed desire is the opposite of the one that has been repressed.

reasoning a type of thinking which involves the systematic solving of a specific problem.

rebound effect the increase in the amount of time the eyes move during a night of uninterrupted sleep, following a night of REM deprivation; a similar rebound effect occurs for NREM deprivation.

recall a measure of retention whereby the individual is able to extract from memory a specific piece of information, usually devoid of context.

receptor cell a specialized cell connected to a nerve cell; it has a low threshold for one sort of stimulus and a high threshold for others. When activated, it initiates impulses in the associated afferent sensory nerves.

recognition a measure of retention whereby the individual is able to identify stimuli to which he has been previously exposed.

redintegration a form of memory in which the subject re-experiences a past event when triggered by a component stimulus of that event.

referent that which a symbol refers to.

reflex an involuntary spontaneous and unlearned bodily response to a stimulus.

reinforcement presentation of stimuli generally regarded as rewards or punishments. (See also reinforcer.)

reinforcement theory of personality B. F. Skinner's theory which defines personality as the totality of habits that have been formed as a result of positive and negative reinforcers.

reinforcer the unconditioned stimulus in classical conditioning; any stimulus that increases or decreases the probability of a response being emitted in operant conditioning.

relational concept idea involving a comparison between two objects.

relearning a measure of retention whereby the individual recommits to memory material or a skill already learned but apparently forgotten; also called the savings method.

reliability the ability of a test to measure something consistently.

renunciation defense mechanism involving the conscious, intentional denial of a desire.

repetition compulsion Freud's term for repetitive behavior patterns derived from unconscious material rooted in childhood experiences.

representative sample a scientifically selected number of people who are polled in place of the total population when the size of that group makes it impossible to interview everyone.

repression a defense mechanism in which undesirable or anxiety-provoking thoughts are excluded from consciousness.

reserpine antipsychotic drug (tranquilizer) which effectively lowers blood pressure and reduces agitation.

reservoir concept of anger theory that anger that cannot be expressed or displaced accumulates through repeated frustration to form a reserve of anger.

retention a construct of memory which is measured by various methods such as recall, recognition, and savings.

reticular formation a complex network of nerve cells extending through the brain stem; it plays a role in sleep, waking, and arousal.

retina the inner layer of the eye. Light must first penetrate a part of the retinal layers until it reaches the light-sensitive rods and cones. In the retina, stimuli are changed into nerve impulses that are then conducted to the optic centers.

retroactive inhibition process whereby the retention of previously learned material is interfered with by new learning.

ribosomes structures in a cell that contain RNA and carry out protein synthesis.

risky shift a phenomenon of social behavior in which an individual who has participated in a group decision retains the higher level of risk chosen by the group.

rods elongated elements in the retina of the eye that are sensitive to light, but not color. They function mainly in dim light.

Rorschach test projective test in which the subject is shown ten cards one at a time and is instructed to interpret the ink blots freely. The responses are interpreted according to one of many systems and lead to a personality description.

sadism pleasure derived from inflicting pain on others. (See also masochism and self-aggression.)

saturation psychological property of color, determined by the fullness of the hue. The degree of saturation of a color can be defined as its "distance" from grey—or the absence of color.

savings method (See relearning.)

scanning hypothesis theory that when the eyes move during sleep they are watching (scanning) what is taking place in a dream.

scapegoating aggression against an innocent victim, who is usually similar to the source of anger or frustration, but is less able to retaliate; a form of displacement.

scheme Piaget's term for an action pattern associated with behavioral development.

schizoid personality a personality disturbance characterized by shyness, introversion, and a tendency to avoid social contact and close relationships. Thought processes are disturbed and the individual may have delusions.

schizophrenia psychosis characterized by thought disorders, and often involving disturbances of emotion and motor behavior. Often results in hospitalization.

school psychology application of psychological principles to advising of individuals in primary and secondary school settings.

secondary circular reactions according to Piaget, the substage of the sensorimotor stage of intellectual development during which an infant relates his actions to the environment.

secondary drive (See learned drive.)

secondary memory storage system in which information is retained for long periods of time, sometimes forever; also called long-term memory.

secondary retardation retardation as a result of some form of brain injury occurring in the womb, during birth, or any time after birth.

sedatives class of drugs which relax physical functioning. In large doses they cause enormous depression.

self-actualization the need within each person to develop all aspects of his being to the greatest degree.

self-aggression behavior aimed at harming oneself. (See also masochism and sadism.)

self-concept Rogers' term for those experiences that are regarded as belonging to the person.

selfhood Jung's term for the wholeness of personality that results from unifying the parts into a coherent, integrated whole.

self-system Sullivan's term for the various security measures a person develops to protect himself from feelings of anxiety.

self theory of personality Rogers' theory of personality which stresses the development of the self or self-concept within the phenomenal field.

semantic differential technique a technique for measuring the connotative meanings of a word or concept by locating the word on a number of descriptive 7-point scales.

semantics the study of the meaning or interpretation given to language.

senile dementia a state of mental, emotional, and social deterioration resulting from degeneration of the brain in old age.

sensitization the intensifying of an organism's response to stimuli that do not ordinarily produce such strong reactions.

sensorimotor stage according to Piaget, a period characterized by the development of a practical kind of intelligence in the infant; divided into six substages.

sensory deprivation a situation in which an individual is denied all normal sensory stimulation. Hallucinations and other abnormal sensations often occur during such a period.

sensory register according to Atkinson and Shiffrin, the first stage of memory; the locus of iconic memory.

septum portion of the limbic system that is involved in aggression and emotion.

serial learning a verbal learning task developed by Ebbinghaus; each nonsense syllable serves as the stimulus for the response of the next nonsense syllable.

serial position effect in serial learning, the tendency of the subject to remember items at the beginning and at the end of the list better than those items in the middle.

set a fixed, rigid attitude or habit that determines how a person will approach a problem-solving situation.

sexual recombination process by which a sperm and an egg, each carrying half of the normal number of chromosomes, are combined.

shadow Jung's term for the animal side of man's nature.

shape constancy tendency to perceive objects as the same shape, no matter what the angle of viewing, and thus the retinal image, is.

shaping (*successive approximations*) operant conditioning technique for achieving a final behavior by reinforcing successive approximations of the desired response.

short-term memory (See primary memory.)

simple concept idea derived from discriminating and classifying objects that have one element in common.

simple schizophrenia a form of schizophrenia characterized by withdrawal from social contact, lack of initiative, and emotional apathy.

size constancy tendency to perceive objects as the same size, no matter how close or far away they are; we modify the actual size of the image on the retina to account for distance.

Skinner box (See experimental chamber.)

sleeper effect an attitude change that becomes evident after a period of time has elapsed. Believed to be associated with the tendency of communicator and message to become dissociated over time.

social facilitation a form of social influence in which an individual's performance is affected when carried out in the presence of others. For simple tasks, performance improves; more complex tasks are usually performed less efficiently in the presence of others.

social learning theory of personality Bandura and Walters' theory, which stresses the importance of social imitation in learning new habits and breaking old ones.

social norm a certain standard to which individuals strive to conform as a result of social pressure or sanction.

social psychology the study of the interaction of man with society.

social therapies therapies that seek to make changes in the patient's environment or conditions of life. Group participation and group problem-solving are emphasized. (See also milieu therapy.)

somatic nerves the nerves that connect to the striated or skeletal musculature of the body.

somatic therapy See organic therapies.

somatotonia Sheldon's term for a temperament type that is characterized by a preference for physical adventure and vigorous activity.

somatotyping Sheldon's method of measuring the physique of a person.

source traits Cattell's term for the underlying traits that determine overt behavior.

Spearman's two-factor theory the theory that two factors are involved in the performance of any test item or real-life mental operation: a general, nonspecific mental capacity ("g") and a more specific mental endowment ("s").

spiked discharge (See action potential.)

spike threshold the voltage level of the membrane at which the spike will develop and travel down the axon.

spinal cord the lower end of the central nervous system extending from the lower back up to the brain.

spinal reflex a reflex moderated by the spinal cord.

spontaneous recovery process whereby a conditioned response reappears after apparent extinction.

standard deviation a mathematical expression of the variability of a distribution.

standardization a means of establishing test validity and reliability by utilizing a representative group similar to the population of individuals that will take the test.

Stanford-Binet tests intelligence tests developed by Terman and his co-workers based on a revision of the Binet-Simon scales; provide for the measurement of adult IQs.

state anxiety anxiety as a transitory response to a specific situation.

Steven's power law theory that the size of the difference between the intensities of two stimuli is proportional to the intensity of the experience of the initial stimulus.

stimulants class of drugs which increase motor activity and awareness. Stimulants may be very mild, such as the caffein in coffee, or very powerful, as in cocaine.

stimulus-response theory of personality Miller and Dollard's theory, which stresses that patterns of stimulus-response units (habits) form the traits that constitute personality.

stirrup one of the three bones of the middle ear; acts in transmitting vibrations across the middle ear to the inner ear.

structuralism school of psychology in which introspection was used to reveal basic elements of consciousness.

structuralist theory of development a theory that sees development as an observable product of internal changes in the organization of behavior.

structure of intellect Guilford's model of intelligence, involves the interaction of three processes: operations, contents, and products. With their subdivisions, there are 120 factors.

sublimation defense mechanism in which the energy of a repressed desire is used for creative, socially approved, or spiritual activities that the conscience will approve; a form of displacement.

subtractive mixture combination of paint pigments; by absorbing some wavelengths and reflecting others, various colors are achieved.

successive approximations (See shaping.)

superego Freud's term for the conscience.

surface structure according to Chomsky, the physical aspect of language, including sounds phonemes, morphemes, and the grammatical rules that generate and govern their combination.

surface traits Cattell's term for observable, overt behavior patterns.

survey methods the tools through which the attitudes or opinions of sizable segments of a population are measured.

Sylvian fissure a major unfolding of the cerebral cortex that separates the temporal lobe from the parietal and occipital lobes; also called the temporal fissure.

symbol something that stands for something else.

symmetrical relations a type of concrete logical operations in the form of kinship: If John is Mike's brother, then Mike must be John's brother.

sympathetic division a division of the autonomic nervous system that acts as an arousal mechanism for the whole body.

synapse the close, functional connection between the axon of one neuron and the dendrite or cell body of another neuron.

synaptic vesicles small round vesicles in the axon's terminal bouton which are believed to contain a chemical substance important in synaptic transmission.

synesthesia the translation of one type of sensory experience into another; for example, hearing a sound evokes visualizing a color.

syntax the internalized rules by which a language is spoken and understood.

systematic desensitization behavior therapy in which classical conditioning techniques are used to reduce or eliminate anxiety. (See anxiety hierarchy.)

telegraphic speech a grammatical form of speech utilized by a child in which simple phrases substitute for complex adult structure.

telepathy communication from one mind to another without the intervention of any known sense organs.

temperament traits Cattell's term for traits that are primarily concerned with speed, energy, and emotional reactions.

temporal fissure (See Sylvian fissure.)

temporal lobe a region of the cerebral cortex including auditory information processing, speech and language comprehension, and other complex functions.

tension-reduction theory of dreams hypothesis that dreams rid the individual of mental tensions accumulated during the day.

terminal bouton a specialized structure at the end of the axon which releases a chemical substance to complete the synaptic transmission.

testes the male reproductive glands, the source of spermatozoa and of the male sex hormones. Also called testicles.

testosterone a male sex hormone.

thema Murray's term for the interaction between need and press.

theta waves brain waves with a frequency of about 5 to 7 per second that are particularly prominent in adolescents and younger children.

thinking a general term for a group of mental activities including reasoning, discriminating, abstracting, generalizing, planning, and imagining.

tip-of-the-tongue phenomenon inability to recall a word or idea with which a person is familiar.

token economy a therapeutic situation in which the patient performs carefully designed work and receives payment for it; the number of tokens received is proportionate to the amount of reinforcement desired.

tolerance the need for larger and larger doses of a drug to produce the original desired effect.

trace conditioning in classical conditioning, standard sequence whereby the unconditioned stimulus is presented after the conditioned stimulus, with an inter-stimulus interval of about 0.5 seconds.

trait a characteristic way of behaving; a predisposition to behave in a certain way.

trait anxiety anxiety as an enduring disposition (trait) of a person.

trait theory of personality Allport's theory of personality which stresses traits as the primary components of personality.

tranquilizers drugs that calm and relax the individual; commonly used to calm disturbed and excited mental patients. Extensively used in treatment of psychoses.

transcendental meditation a chain of reflections sometimes referring to religious or otherworldly subjects.

transfer of training the application of past learning to new learning situations.

transformational rules a system of rules that have both innate and learned components which govern the actual physical sequence of sounds or letters; rules whereby deep structures are changed into surface structures.

transitivity a type of concrete logical operations in the form of such problems as: If A > B and B > C, then A ? C.

transsexual a person who is physically one sex and psychologically the other. Transsexuals can change their physical gender by surgery and hormonal treatment.

trial and error type of problem-solving in which various ideas are tried until a solution is reached. It may be covert or overt.

type theories theories of personality based on groups of traits found together in an individual.

unconditioned response (UR) in classical conditioning, an unlearned and innate response to an unconditioned stimulus.

unconditioned stimulus (US) in classical conditioning, a stimulus that elicits an unlearned and innate response (UR).

unconscious as used by Freud, the unconscious comprises all the psychological material that has been repressed or that has never been conscious.

unity-thema Murray's term for the pattern of related needs and press that repeats itself in a person.

valences Lewin's term for an environmental incentive that attracts a person.

validity the degree to which a test measures that for which it was intended.

variable-interval schedule a schedule of reinforcement in which the organism is reinforced after a period of time that varies from one reinforcement to the next; reinforcement is independent of correct responses.

variable-ratio schedule a schedule of reinforcement in which the organism is reinforced after a number of nonreinforced responses; the number varies from reinforcement to reinforcement.

variance the spread of scores on a particular test.

vectors Lewin's term for an inner motivational state that determines the direction and intensity of behavior.

ventral root a nerve at the front of the spinal cord that allows outgoing motor fibers to exit the cord. (See also dorsal root.)

ventral root ganglion a group of cell bodies of motor nerves from the muscles and glands that lies outside the spinal cord.

vicarious reinforcement reinforcement obtained from watching someone else being rewarded for a particular behavior.

vicarious satisfaction defense mechanism in which a desire is satisfied by imaginatively participating in the experiences of other people.

viscera internal organs of the body.

viscerotonia Sheldon's term for a temperament type that is characterized by a love of comfort, sociability, and a good disposition.

visible spectrum the amount of electromagnetic radiation (the number of wavelengths) that the human eye can see.

visual acuity the ability to see fine details in the environment; sharpness of vision in daylight.

Weber's law theory that the amount a stimulus has to be increased before it can be detected as a j.n.d. is directly proportional to the initial stimulus intensity.

Wechsler Adult Intelligence Scale (WAIS) an intelligence test for adults using multi-scale measures of intelligence and test items classified into verbal and performance categories.

Wechsler Intelligence Scale for Children (WISC) an intelligence test for children measuring verbal and performance subcategories.

Wernicke's area a major speech area located in the temporal lobe of the left hemisphere of the brain.

wish-fulfillment theory of dreaming Freud's theory that dreams are attempts to fulfill the dreamer's unsatisfied or repressed wishes.

Yin-Yang an Oriental symbol for the union of opposites, especially those of femininity-masculinity.

Young-Helmholtz theory theory of color vision which assumed that there are three types of color receptors in the retina; any color in the visible spectrum can be reproduced by a combination of the three primary colors (red, blue, green).

zygote fertilized egg.

References

ADER, R., & TATUM, R. Free-operant avoidance conditioning in individual and paired human subjects. *Journal of Experimental Analysis of Behavior,* 1963, **6,** 357–359.

ADLER, A. *Problems of neurosis.* London: Kegan Paul, 1929.

ADLER, A. *The practice and theory of individual psychology.* New York: Harcourt Brace Jovanovich, 1927.

ADORNO, T. W., FRENKEL-BRUNSWIK, E., LEVINSON, D. J., & SANFORD, R. N. *The authoritarian personality.* New York: Harper, 1950.

AINSWORTH, M. D. S. The development of infant-mother attachment. In B. M. Caldwell & H. N. Riccuiti (eds.) *Review of child development research,* Vol. 3. Chicago: University of Chicago Press, 1973.

AINSWORTH, M. D. S., & BELL, S. M. Attachment, exploration and separation: Illustrated by the behavior of one-year-olds in strange situations. *Child Development,* 1970, **41,** 49–67.

ALLEN, R. M. *Student's Rorschach manual.* New York: International Universities Press, 1966.

ALLPORT, F. H. *Social psychology.* Boston: Houghton Mifflin, 1924.

ALLPORT, G. W. *Letters from Jenny.* New York: Harcourt Brace Jovanovich, 1965.

ALLPORT, G. W. *Pattern and growth in personality.* New York: Holt, Rinehart and Winston, 1961.

ALLPORT, G. W. The historical background of modern social psychology. In G. Lindzey & E. Aronson (eds.) *Handbook of social psychology* (rev. ed.) Vol. I. Reading, Mass.: Addison-Wesley, 1968.

ALLPORT, G. W., VERNON, P. E., & LINDZEY, G. *Study of values* (3rd ed.) Boston: Houghton Mifflin, 1960.

ANAND, B. K., & BROBECK, J. R. Hypothalamic control of food intake in rat and cat. *Yale Journal of Biological Medicine,* 1951, **24,** 123–140.

ANDERSON, J. R., & BOWER, G. H. *Human associative memory.* Washington, D.C.: V. H. Winston & Sons, 1973.

ARIES, P. *Centuries of childhood: A social history of family life.* New York: Vintage Books, 1962.

ARONSON, E., & CARLSMITH, J. M. Effect of the severity of threat on the devaluation of forbidden behavior. *Journal of Abnormal and Social Psychology,* 1963, **66,** 584–588.

ARONSON, E., & GOLDEN, B. The effect of relevant and irrelevant aspects of communicator credibility on opinion change. *Journal of Personality,* 1962, **30,** 135–146.

ASCH, S. E. Forming impressions of personality. *Journal of Abnormal and Social Psychology,* 1946, **41,** 258–290.

ASCH, S. E. *Social psychology.* Englewood Cliffs, N.J.: Prentice-Hall, 1952.

ASERINSKY, E., & KLEITMAN, N. Regularly occurring periods of eye mobility and concomitant phenomena during sleep. *Science,* 1953, **118,** 273–274.

ATKINSON, R. C., & SHIFFRIN, R. M. Human memory: A proposed system and its control processes. In K. W. Spence & J. T. Spence (eds.) *The psychology of learning and motivation: Advances in research and theory,* Vol. II. New York: Academic Press, 1968.

BACKMAN, M. E. Patterns of mental abilities: Ethnic, socioeconomic, and sex differences. *American Education Research Journal,* 1972, **9,** 1–12.

BAGBY, E. *The psychology of personality.* New York: Holt, 1928.

BAKER, J. *Race.* New York: Oxford University Press, 1973.

BANDURA, A. *Aggression: A social learning analysis.* Englewood Cliffs, N.J.: Prentice-Hall, 1973.

BANDURA, A. Influence of models' reinforcement contingencies on the acquisition of imitative responses. *Journal of Personality and Social Psychology,* 1965, **1,** 589–595.

BANDURA, A. *Social learning theory.* Morristown, N.J.: General Learning Press, 1971.

BANDURA, A., & MENLOVE, F. L. Factors determining vicarious extinction of avoidance behavior through symbolic modeling. *Journal of Personality and Social Psychology,* 1968, **8,** 99–108.

BANDURA, A., ROSS, D., & ROSS, S. A. Transmission of aggression through imitation of aggressive models. *Journal of Abnormal and Social Psychology,* 1961, **66,** 3–11.

BANDURA, A., & WALTERS, R. H. *Social learning and personality development.* New York: Holt, Rinehart and Winston, 1963.

BARCLAY, T. R. The role of comprehension in remembering sentences. *Cognitive Psychology,* 1973, **4,** 229–255.

BARD, P., & MACHT, M. B. The behavior of chronically decerebrate cats. *Ciba Foundation symposium, neurological basis of behavior.* London: Churchill, 1958.

BARRON, F. *Creative person and creative process.* New York: Holt, Rinehart and Winston, 1969.

BARRON, F. The psychology of imagination. *Scientific American,* 1958, **199** (50), 150–156.

BAUGHMAN, E. E., & DAHLSTROM, W. G. *Negro and white children: A psychological study in the rural south.* New York: Academic Press, 1968.

BAYLEY, N. *Bayley's scales of infant development.* New York: The Psychological Corporation, 1969.

BEARY, J. F., & BENSON, H. A simple psychophysiologic technique which elicits the hypometabolic changes of the relaxation response. *Psychosomatic Medicine,* 1974, **36,** 115–120.

BELL, A. P., & HALL, C. S. *The personality of a child molester: An analysis of dreams.* Chicago: Aldine, 1971.

BENNETT, E. L., DIAMOND, M. C., KRECH, D., & ROSENZWEIG, M. R. Chemical and anatomical plasticity of brain. *Science,* 1964, **146,** 610–619.

BENSON, H., BEARY, J. F., & CAROL, M. P. The relaxation response. *Psychiatry,* 1974, **37,** 37–46.

BENSON, H., ROSNER, B. A., & MARZETTA, B. R. Decreased systolic blood pressure in hypertensive subjects who practiced meditation. *Journal of Clinical Investigations,* 1973, **52,** 8.

BENSON, H., & WALLACE, R. K. Decreased drug abuse with transcendental meditation—a study of 1,862 subjects. In C. J. Zarafonetis (ed.) *Drug abuse: Proceedings of the international conference.* New York: Lea and Febiger, 1972.

BERGEN, A. E. Further comments on psychotherapy research and therapeutic practice. *International Journal of Psychiatry,* 1967, **3,** 317–323.

BERGER, R. J. Oculomotor control: A possible function of REM sleep. *Psychological Review,* 1969, **76,** 144–164.

BERGER, S. M. Conditioning through vicarious instigation. *Psychological Review,* 1962, **69,** 450–466.

BERGER, S. M. Drugs and Suicide. In *U.S. Clinical Pharmacology and Therapeutics,* 1967, **8**(2), 219–233.

BERGLER, E. *Homosexuality: Disease or way of life?* New York: Collier, 1956.

BERKO, J. The child's learning of English morphology. *Word,* 1958, **14,** 150–177.

BERKOWITZ, L. *Aggression: A social psychological analysis.* New York: McGraw-Hill, 1962.

BERKOWITZ, L. The contagion of violence: An S-R mediational analysis of some effects of observed aggression. In W. Arnold & M. Page (eds.) *Nebraska Symposium on Motivation, 1970.* Lincoln: University of Nebraska Press, 1971.

BERKOWITZ, L. (ed.) *Roots of aggression.* New York: Atherton, 1969.

BERKOWITZ, L. Some determinants of impulsive aggression: Role of mediated associations with reinforcements for aggression. *Psychological Review,* 1974, **81**(2), 165–176.

BERLYNE, D. E. Conflict and choice time. *The British Journal of Psychology,* 1957, **48,** 106–118.

BINET, A., & SIMON, T. *The development of intelligence in children.* (Trans. by E. S. Kite.) Publication of the Training School at Vineland, N.J., 1916, # 11.

BLAU, P. M. *Exchange and power in social life.* New York: Wiley, 1964.

BOGARDUS, E. *Social distance.* Yellow Springs, Ohio: Antioch Press, 1959.

BOOK, W. F. The psychology of skill: With special reference to its acquisition in typewriting. *University of Montana Publications in Psychology,* Bulletin 53, Psychology Series 1, 1908.

BORING, E. G. *A history of experimental psychology* (2nd ed.) New York: Appleton, 1950.

BOSS, M. *Psychoanalysis and Daseinsanalysis.* New York: Basic Books, 1963.

BOURNE, L. E., JR. *Human conceptual behavior.* Boston: Allyn and Bacon, 1966.

BOWER, T. G. R. The object in the world of the infant. *Scientific American,* 1971, **225**(4), 30–38.

BOWLBY, J. Attachment and loss. Vol. 1. *Attachment.* New York: Basic Books, 1969.

BOWLBY, J. Attachment and loss. Vol. 2. *Separation.* New York: Basic Books, 1973.

BRADY, J. V., PORTER, R. W., CONRAD, D. G.,

& MASON, J. W. Avoidance behavior and the development of gastroduodenal ulcers. *Journal of Experimental Analysis of Behavior*, 1958, **1**, 69–73.

BRAUNGART, R. G. *SDS and YAF: Backgrounds of student political activists.* Paper presented at the meeting of the American Sociological Association, Miami, 1966.

BRAWLEY, E. R., HARRIS, F. R., ALLEN, K. E., FLEMING, R. S., & PETERSON, R. F. Behavior modification of an autistic child. *Behavioral Science*, 1969, **14**, 87–97.

BROADBENT, D. *Perception and communication.* London: Pergamon Press, 1958.

BROADBENT, D., & GREGORY, M. Accuracy of recognition for speech presented to the right and left ears. *Quarterly Journal of Experimental Psychology*, 1964, **16**, 359–360.

BROGDEN, W. J. Sensory preconditioning. *Journal of Experimental Psychology*, 1939, **25**, 323–332.

BRONFENBRENNER, U. *Two worlds of childhood: U.S. and U.S.S.R.* New York: Russell Sage Foundation, 1960.

BROSSE, T. Altruism and creativity as biological factors of human evolution. In P. A. Sorokin (ed.) *Exploration in altruistic love and behavior.* Boston: Beacon Press, 1950.

BROVERMAN, D. M., KLAIBER, E. L., KOBAYASHI, Y., & VOGEL, W. Roles of activation and inhibition in sex differences in cognitive abilities. *Psychological Review*, 1968, **75**, 23–50.

BROWN, N. O. *Life against death.* New York: Random House, 1959.

BROWN, R. *First language: The early stages.* Cambridge. Harvard University Press, 1973.

BROWN, R. *The first sentences of child and chimpanzee.* Unpublished mimeo report. Harvard University, 1969.

BROWN, R. *Social psychology.* New York: Free Press, 1965.

BROWN, R., CAZDEN, C., & BELLUGI, U. The child's grammar from I to III. In J. P. Hill (ed.) *Minnesota symposium on child psychology*, Vol. II. Minneapolis: University of Minnesota Press, 1969.

BRUDNY, J., GRYNBAUM, B. B., & KOREIN, J. Spasmodic torticollis: Treatment by feedback display of EMG—a report of nine cases. *Archives of Physiological Medical Rehabilitation*, 1974, **55**, 403–408.

BRUNER, J. S. *The process of education.* Cambridge: Harvard University Press, 1960.

BUDZYNSKI, T. H., STOYVA, J. M., ADLER, C. S., & MULLANEY, D. J. EMG biofeedback and tension headache: A controlled outcome study. *Psychosomatic Medicine*, 1973, **35**, 484–496.

BURT, C. The genetic determination of difference in intelligence: A study of monozygotic twins reared together and apart. *British Journal of Psychology*, 1966, **57**, 137–153.

BUSS, A. Physical aggression in relation to different frustrations. *Journal of Abnormal and Social Psychology*, 1963, **67**, 1–7.

BYRNE, D. Attitudes and attraction. In L. Berkowitz (ed.) *Advances in experimental social psychology*, Vol. 4. New York: Academic Press, 1969.

BYRNE, D., CLORE, G. L., & WORCHEL, P. Effect of similarity-dissimilarity on interpersonal attraction. *Journal of Personality and Social Psychology*, 1966, **4**, 220–224.

BYRNE, D., GRIFFIT, W., & STENFANIAK, D. Attraction and similarity of personality characteristics. *Journal of Personality and Social Psychology*, 1967, **5**, 82–90.

CAMERON, N. *Personality development and psychopathology.* Boston: Houghton Mifflin, 1963.

CAMPBELL, D. T. The indirect assessment of social attitudes. *Psychological Bulletin*, 1950, **47**, 15–38.

CARTWRIGHT, D. Determinants of scientific progress: The case of research on the risky shift. *American Psychologist*, 1973, **28**, 222–231.

CARTWRIGHT, S. A. *Medical and Surgical Journal*, 1851.

CATTELL, R. B. *The scientific analysis of personality.* Chicago: Aldine, 1966.

CATTELL, R. B. The structure of intelligence in relation to the nature-nurture controversy. In R. Cancro (ed.) *Intelligence: Genetic and environmental influences.* New York: Grune & Stratton, 1971.

CHERRY, E. C. Some experiments on the recognition of speech, with one and two ears. *Journal of the Acoustical Society of America*, 1953, **25**, 975–979.

CHOMSKY, N. *Language and mind.* New York: Harcourt Brace Jovanovich, 1968.

CHOMSKY, N. *Syntactic structure.* S'Gravenhage, Netherlands: Mouton, 1957.

COLEMAN, J. C. *Abnormal psychology in modern life* (3rd ed.) Chicago: Scott, Foresman, 1964.

CONEL, J. L. *The postnatal development of the human cerebral cortex*, Vol. I, II, & III. Cambridge: Harvard University Press, 1939, 1941, 1947.

CONGER, J. J. *Adolescence and youth: Psychological development in a changing world.* New York: Harper & Row, 1973.

COOMBS, C. H. Psychological scaling without a unit of measurement. *Psychological Review*, 1950, **57**, 145–158.

COOPER, J. B., & POLLOCK, D. The identification of prejudicial attitudes by the galvanic skin response. *Journal of Social Psychology*, 1959, **50**, 241–245.

COTTRELL, N. B. Social facilitation. In C. G. McClintock (ed.) *Experimental social psychology.* New York: Holt, Rinehart and Winston, 1972.

CRADDICK, R. A., THUMIN, F. J., & BARCLAY, A. G. A semantic differential study of the Yin-Yang symbol. *Journal of Personality Assessment*, 1971, **35**, 338–343.

CROCETTI, G. M., & LEMKAU, P. V. Schizophrenia. II. Epidemiology. In A. M. Freeman & H. I. Kaplan (eds.) *Comprehensive textbook of psychiatry.* Baltimore: Williams & Wilkins, 1967.

CRONBACH, L. J. *Essentials of psychological testing.* New York: Harper, 1960.

CROSS, H. A., HALCOMB, C. G., & MATTER, W. W. Imprinting or exposure learning in rats given auditory stimulation. *Psychonomic Science*, 1967, **7**, 233–234.

CROWNE, D. P., & MARLOWE, D. *The approval motive: Studies in evaluative dependence.* New York: Wiley, 1964.

CUSTANCE, J. Mental hospitals and mental

treatment. *International Journal of Social Psychiatry*, 1955, **1**, 66–70.

DALAL, A. S., & BARBER, T. X. Yoga, "yogic feats" and hypnosis, in the light of empirical research. *American Journal of Clinical Hypnosis*, 1969, **11**, 155–166.

DARLEY, J. M., & LATANÉ, B. Bystander intervention in emergencies: Diffusion of responsibility *Journal of Personality and Social Psychology*, 1968, **8**, 377–383.

DAWES, R. M. *Fundamentals of attitude measurement*. New York: Wiley, 1972.

DEJERINE. L'agraphie. *Progres med.*, 1912, **40**, 344–347.

DELGADO, J. R. Social rank and radio-stimulated aggressiveness in monkeys. *The Journal of Nervous and Mental Disease*, 1967, **5**, 383–390.

DEMENT, W. C. The effect of dream deprivation. *Science*, 1960, **131**, 1705–1707.

DEMENT, W. C. *Sleep and the maturing nervous system*. C. D. Clement, D. P. Purpura, & F. E. Mayer (eds.) New York: Academic Press, 1972.

DEMENT, W. C., & COHEN, H. B. Sleep: Changes in the threshold to electroconvulsive shock in rats after deprivation of paradoxical phase. *Science*, 1965, **150**, 1318–1319.

DEMENT, W. C., & KLEITMAN, N. Cyclic variations in EEG during sleep and their relation to eye movements, bodily motility, and dreaming. *Electroencephalography and Clinical Neurophysiology*, 1957, **9**, 373–390.

DEUTSCH, M. An experimental study of the effects of cooperation and competition upon group process. *Human Relations*, 1949, **2**, 199–232.

DEVALOIS, R. Behavioral and electrophysiological studies of primate vision. In *Contributions to sensory psychology*. New York: Academic Press, 1965.

DION, K., BERSCHEID, E., & WALSTER, E. What is beautiful is good. *Journal of Personality and Social Psychology*, 1972, **24**, 285–290.

DOUVAN, E., & ADELSON, J. *The adolescent experience*. New York: Wiley, 1966.

DUNCAN, C. P. The retroactive effect of electroshock on learning. *Journal of Comparative and Physiological Psychology*, 1949, **42**, 32–44.

DUTTON, D. G., & ARON, A. P. Some evidence for heightened sexual attraction under conditions of high anxiety. *Journal of Personality and Social Psychology*, in press.

EBBINGHAUS, H. *Memory: A contribution to experimental psychology* (1885). (Trans. by H. A. Ruger and C. E. Bussenius.) New York: Teachers College, Columbia University, 1913.

ECCLES, J. C. *The physiology of synapses*. New York: Academic Press, 1964.

ECCLES, J. C. *The understanding of the brain*. New York: McGraw-Hill, 1973.

EIMAS, P. D., SIQUELAND, E. R., JUSCZYK, P., & VIGORITO, J. Speech perception in infants. *Science*, 1971, **171**, 303–306.

ELKIND, D. Egocentrism in adolescents. *Child Development*, 1967, **38**, 1025–1034.

ELLIS, H. *Studies in the psychology of sex*. New York: Random House, 1936.

ENGEL, B. T., & BLEECKER, E. R. Application of operant conditioning techniques to the control of the cardiac arrhythmias. In *Cardiovascular Psychophysiology* P. A. Obrist, A. H. Black, J. Brener, & L. V. DiCara (eds.) Chicago: Aldine, 1974.

ERIKSON, E. *Childhood and society* (2nd ed.) New York: Norton, 1963.

ERICKSON, M. H., & KUBIE, L. S. The permanent relief of an obsessional phobia by means of communications with an unsuspected dual personality. *Psychoanalysis Quarterly*, 1939, **8**, 471–509.

ERLANGER, H. S. Jury research in America: Its past and future. *Law and Society Review*, 1969, **4**, 345–370.

ERLENMEYER-KIMLING, L., & JARVICK, L. F. Genetics and intelligence: A review. *Science*, 1963, **142**, 1477–1479.

ERON, L. D., LEFKOWITZ, M. M., HUESMAN, L. R., & WALDER, L. O. Does television violence cause aggression? *American Psychologist*, 1972, **27**, 253–263.

ETZIONI, A. Science: Threatening the jury trial? *Washington Post*, May 26, 1974, C-3.

EYSENCK, A. S. & EYSENCK, S. B. G. *The Eysenck Personality Inventory*. London: University Press, 1963.

EYSENCK, H. J. The effects of psychotherapy. In H. J. Eysenck (ed.) *Handbook of abnormal psychology*. New York: Basic Books, 1961.

EYSENCK, H. J. *The structure of human personality* (3rd ed.) London: Methuen, 1970.

FABRIC, S. I. Emotional behavior of Long-Evans and Hall-Spence rats on walled and unwalled runways. Unpublished doctoral dissertation, University of Florida, 1965. In D. D. Thiessen (ed.) *Gene organization and behavior*. New York: Random House, 1972.

FANTZ, R. L. Form preferences in newly hatched chicks. *Journal of Comparative and Physiological Psychology*, 1957, **50**, 422–430.

FANTZ, R. L. The origin of form perception. *Scientific American*, 1961, **204**. 66–87.

FARBEROW, N. L., & SHNEIDMAN, E. S. (eds.) *The cry for help*. New York: McGraw-Hill, 1961.

FECHNER, G. *Elements of psychophysics* (1860). (Trans. by H. E. Adler.) New York: Holt, Rinehart and Winston, 1966.

FELDMAN, K. A., & NEWCOMB, T. M. *The impact of college on students*. San Francisco: Jossey-Bass, 1969.

FERSTER, C. B., & PERROT, M. C. *Behavior principles*. New York: Appleton-Century-Crofts, 1968.

FESHBACH, S., & SINGER, R. D. *Television and aggression: An experimental field study*. San Francisco: Jossey-Bass, 1971.

FESTINGER, L. *A theory of cognitive dissonance*. Stanford: Stanford University Press, 1957.

FESTINGER, L. Cognitive dissonance. *Scientific American*, 1962, **207**, 93–98.

FESTINGER, L., SCHACHTER, S., & BACK, K. *Social pressures in informal groups*. Stanford: Stanford University Press, 1963.

FINKLE, B. S. *Proceedings of the U.S. Senate*. Subcommittee on Juvenile Delinquency of the Committee of the Judiciary, May 17, 1972, **4**, 286.

FLAVELL, J. H. An analysis of cognitive-developmental sequences. *Genetic Psychology Monographs*, 1972, **86**, 279–350.

FONBERG, E. Transfer of instrumental avoidance reactions in dogs. *Bulletin of the Polish Academy of Sciences*, 1958, **6**, 353–356.

FORD, C., & BEACH, F. *Patterns of sexual behavior*. New York: Harper & Row, 1951.

FORER, B. R. The fallacy of personal validation: A classroom demonstration of gullibility. *Journal of Abnormal and Social Psychology*, 1949, **44**, 118–123.

FOUTS, G., & JOURDAN, L. The effect of an audience on free associations to emotional words. *Journal of Community Psychology*, January 1973.

FOWLER, R. D., JR., & MILLER, M. L. Computer interpretation of the MMPI. *Archives of General Psychiatry*, 1969, **21**, 502–508.

FREEDMAN, D. G. Personality development in infancy: A biological approach. In Y. Brackbill (ed.) *Infancy and childhood*. New York: Free Press, 1967.

FREEDMAN, J. L., CARLSMITH, J. M., & SEARS, D. D. *Social psychology* (2nd ed.) Englewood Cliffs, N.J.: Prentice-Hall, 1974.

FREIBERGS, V., & TULVING, E. The effect of practice on utilization of information from positive and negative instances in concept identification. *Canadian Journal of Psychology*, 1961, **15**, 101–106.

FREUD, A. Adolescence. In A. E. Winder & D. L. Angus (eds.) *Adolescence: Contemporary studies*. New York: American Book, 1968.

FREUD, S. An outline of psychoanalysis (1940). In *Standard Edition* (1953), Vol. 23. London: Hogarth Press, 1964.

FREUD, S. The interpretation of dreams. In *Standard Edition*, Vol. IV, V (1953). London: Hogarth Press, 1969.

FREUD, S. Three essays on sexuality. In *Standard Edition*, Vol. VII. London: Hogarth Press, 1953.

FROMM, E. *Escape from freedom*. New York: Holt, Rinehart and Winston, 1941.

FROMM, E. *The sane society*. New York: Rinehart, 1955.

FROMM, E., SUZUKI, D. T., & DE MARTINO, R. *Zen Buddhism and psychoanalysis*. London: Allen and Unwin, 1960.

GALTON, F. *Hereditary genius: An inquiry into its laws and consequences*. London: Macmillan, 1869.

GARCIA, J., & ERVIN, F. R. Gustatory-visceral and telereceptor-cutaneous conditioning-adaptation in internal and external milieus. *Communications in Behavioral Biology*, 1968, **2**, 389–415.

GARCIA, J., & KOELLING, R. A. Relation of cue to consequences in avoidance learning. *Psychonomic Science*, 1966, **4**, 123–124.

GARDNER, R. A., & GARDNER, B. T. Teaching sign language to a chimpanzee. *Science*, 1969, **165**, 664–672.

GATES, M. G., & ALLEE, W. C. Conditioned behavior of isolated and grouped cockroaches on a simple maze. *Journal of Comparative Psychology*, 1933, **13**, 331–358.

GEEN, R. G., & O'NEAL, E. C. Activation of cue-elicited aggression by general arousal. *Journal of Personality and Social Psychology*, 1969, **11**(3), 289–292.

GELBER, B. Investigation of the behavior of *Paramecian aurelia*: I. Modification of behavior after training with reinforcement. *Journal of Comparative and Physiological Psychology*, 1952, **45**, 58–65.

GESCHWIND, N. Disconnexion syndromes in animals and man: I, II. *Brain*, 1965, **88**, 237–294, 585–643.

GEWIRTZ, J. L. The cause of infant smiling in four child-rearing environments in Israel. In B. M. Foss (ed.) *Determinants of infant behavior*, Vol. III. London: Methuen, 1965.

GEWIRTZ, J. L. Mechanisms of social learning: Some roles of stimulation and behavior in early human development. In D. A. Goslin (ed.) *Handbook of socialization theory and research*. Chicago: Rand McNally, 1971.

GIDRO-FRANK, L., & BOWERS-BUCH, M. K. A study of the plantar response in hypnotic age regression. *Journal of Nervous and Mental Disease*, 1948, **107**, 443–458.

GINSBURG, H., & OPPER, S. *Piaget's theory of intellectual development: An introduction*. Englewood Cliffs, N.J.: Prentice-Hall, 1969.

GLADWIN, T. *East is a big bird*. Cambridge: Harvard University Press, 1970.

GLASS, D. C., & SINGER, J. E. *Urban stress*. New York: Academic Press, 1972.

GLOBUS, A., ROSENZWEIG, M. R., BENNETT, E. L., & DIAMOND, M. C. Effects of differential experience on dendritic spine counts in rat cerebral cortex. *Journal of Comparative and Physiological Psychology*, 1973, **82**, 175–181.

GOLDBERG, D., & COOMBS, C. H. Some applications of unfolding theory of fertility analysis. Emerging Techniques in Population Research. *Proceedings of the 1962 Annual Conference of the Milbank Memorial Fund*, 1963.

GOLDBERG, S. *The inevitability of patriarchy*. New York: William Morrow, 1973.

GOLDSTEIN, K. *The organism*. New York: American Book, 1939.

GOODENOUGH, F. L. *Anger in young children*. Minneapolis: University of Minnesota Press, 1931.

GOODMAN, L. S., & GILMAN, A. *The pharmacological basis of therapeutics* (4th ed.) London: Macmillan, 1970.

GOUGH, H. G. Minnesota Multiphasic Personality Inventory. In A. Weider (ed.) *Contributions toward medical psychology*, Vol. II. New York: Ronald Press, 1953.

GOULD, R. L., & GOULD, R. Jury selection: Pentagon papers trial. *American Journal of Psychiatry*, in press.

GRAY, H., & WHEELWRIGHT, J. B. *Jungian type survey*. San Francisco: Society of Jungian Analysts of Northern California, 1964.

GRAY, J. J. Case conference: Behavior therapy in a patient with homosexual fantasies and heterosexual anxiety. *Journal of Behavior Therapy and Experimental Psychiatry*, 1970, **1**, 225–232.

GREEN, R., & MONEY, J. *Transsexualism and sex reassignment*. Baltimore: Johns Hopkins University Press, 1969.

GRIFFITH, R. M., MIYAGO, O., & TAGO, A. The universality of typical dreams: Japanese vs. Americans. *American Anthropologist*, 1958, **60**, 1173–1179.

GROVES, P. M., & THOMPSON, R. F. Habituation: A dual-process theory. *Psychological Review*, 1970, **77**, 419–450.

GUILFORD, J. P. *The nature of human intelligence.* New York: McGraw-Hill, 1967.

GUILFORD, J. P. The structure of intellect. *Psychological Review*, 1961, 68, 1–20.

HAAF, R. A., & BELL, R. Q. A facial dimension in visual discrimination by human infants. *Child Development*, 1967, **38, 895.**

HABER, R. N. Eidetic images. *Scientific American*, 1969, **220**, 36–55.

HABER, R. N. How we remember what we see. *Scientific American*, 1970, **222**(5), 104–112.

HABER, R. N., & HABER, R. B. Eidetic imagery: I. Frequency. *Perceptual and Motor Skills*, 1964, **19**, 131–138.

HAILMAN, J. How an instinct is learned. *Scientific American*, 1969, **221**, 98–106.

HALL, C. S. *A primer of Freudian psychology.* New York: New American Library, 1954.

HALL, C. S. Slang and dream symbols. *Psychoanalytic Review*, 1964, **51**, 38–48.

HALL, C. S., & NORDBY, V. J. *A primer of Jungian psychology.* New York: New American Library, 1973.

HALL, G. S. *Adolescence: Its psychology and its relations to physiology, anthropology, sex, crime, religion and education,* Vol. 1. New York: Appleton, 1904.

HALVERSON, C. J. JR., & WALDROP, M. F. The relations of mechanically recorded activity level to varieties of preschool play behavior. *Child Development,* 1973, **44,** 687–81.

HARLOW, H. The formation of learning sets. *Psychological Review*, 1949, **56,** 51–65.

HARLOW, H., & HARLOW, M. K. Learning to love. *American Scientist*, 1966, **54,** 244–272.

HARRELL, T. W., & HARRELL, M. S. Army general classification test scores for civilian occupations. *Educational Psy-*

chological *Measurement*, 1945, **5,** 229–239.

HARRELL, W. A., & SCHMITT, D. R. Effects of a minimal audience on physical aggression. *Psychological Reports*, 1973, **32,** 651–657.

HARTMANN, D. P. Influence of symbolically modeled instrumental aggression and pain cues on aggressive behavior. *Journal of Personality and Social Psychology*, 1969, **11,** 280–288.

HATHAWAY, S. R., & MONACHESI, E. D. *Adolescent personality and behavior.* Minneapolis: University of Minnesota Press, 1963.

HEBB, D. O. *The organization of behavior.* New York: Wiley, 1949.

HEBB, D. O. Sensory deprivation: Facts in search of a theory. *Journal of Nervous and Mental Disorders*, 1961, **132,** 40–43.

HEBB, D. O. *A textbook of psychology* (3rd ed.) Philadelphia: Saunders, 1972.

HEIDBREDER, E. The attainment of concepts: III. The problem. *Journal of Psychology*, 1947, **24,** 93–138.

HELD, R., & FREEDMAN, S., JR. Plasticity in human sensorimotor control. *Science*, 1963, **142,** 455–462.

HELD, R., & HEIN, A. Movement produced simultaneously in the development of visually guided behavior. *Journal of Comparative and Physiological Psychology*, 1963, **130,** 133–141.

HENDERSON, D., & GILLESPIE, R. D. *A textbook of psychiatry.* New York: Oxford University Press, 1956.

HERBERT, M. J., & HARSH, C. M. Observational learning in cats. *Journal of Comparative and Physiological Psychology*, 1944, **37,** 81–95.

HERRNSTEIN, R. J. *IQ in the meritocracy.* Boston: Atlantic-Little, Brown, 1973.

HESS, E. H. Imprinting. *Science*, 1959, **130,** 133–141.

HESTON, L. The adult adjustment of persons institutionalized as children. *British Journal of Psychology*, 1966, **112,** 1103–1110.

HESTON, L. The genetics of schizophrenic and schizoid disease. *Science*, 1970, **167,** 253.

HILGARD, E. R. *Hypnotic susceptibility.* New York: Harcourt Brace Jovanovich, 1965.

HIRAI, T. *Psychophysiology of Zen.* Tokyo: Igaku Shoin, 1974.

HIRSCH, H. V., & SPINELLI, D. N. Visual experience modifies distribution of horizontally and vertically oriented receptive fields in cats. *Science*, 1970, **168,** 869–871.

HOCHBERG, J. *Perception.* Englewood Cliffs, N. J.: Prentice-Hall, 1964.

HOFLING, C. K. *Textbook of psychiatry for medical practice.* Philadelphia: Lippincott, 1968.

HOFFMAN, A. A discussion of his research with LSD. In J. H. Brenner, R. Coleges, & D. Meagher (eds.) *Drugs and youth.* New York: Liveright, 1970.

HOOKER, E. An empiricial study of some relations between sexual patterns and gender identity in male homosexuals. In J. Money (ed.), *Sex research: New developments.* New York: Holt, Rinehart and Winston, 1965.

HORNEY, K. *Neurotic personality of our times.* New York: Norton, 1937.

HOROWITZ, E. L., & HOROWITZ, R. E. Development of social attitudes in children. *Sociometry*, 1938, **1,** 308–338.

HORWITZ, W. A., KESTENBAUM, C., PERSON, E., & JARVIK, L. Identical twin—"idiot savants"—calendar calculators. *American Journal of Psychology*, 1965, **121,** 1075–1079.

HOVLAND, C. I. The generalization of conditioned responses. I. The sensory generalization of CRS with varying frequencies of tone. *Journal of General Psychology*, 1937, **17,** 125–148.

HOVLAND, C. I., & WEISS, W. The influence of source credibility on communication effectiveness. *Public Opinion Quarterly*, 1951, **15,** 635–650.

HUBEL, D. H., & WIESEL, T. N. Receptive fields, binocular interaction and functional architecture in the cat's visual cortex. *Journal of Physiology*, 1962, **160,** 106–154.

HUESMANN, L. R., & LEVINGER, G. Incremental exchange theory: A formal model for progression in dyadic social interaction. In L. Berkowitz & E. Walster (eds.), *Advances in experimental social psychology.* vol. 8. New York: Academic Press, in press.

HUMPHREYS, L. *Tearoom trade: Impersonal sex in public places.* Chicago: Aldine, 1970.

HUNT, M. *Sexual behavior in the 1970s.* Chicago: Playboy Press, 1974.

HURVICH, L. M., & JAMESON, D. Some quantitative aspects of an opponent-colors theory: II. Brightness, saturation and hue in normal and dichromatic vision. *Journal of the Optical Society of America*, 1955, **45,** 602.

HYMAN, H. *Political socialization: A study in the psychology of political behavior.* New York: Free Press, 1959.

HYPPA, M. The role of the hypothalamus in hormonal sex differentiation. *Revue Roumaine de Physiologie*, 1968, **5**(4), 289–299.

INNES, J. M., & SAMBROOKS, J. E. Paired-associate learning as influenced by birth order and the presence of others. *Psychonomic Science*, 1969, **16,** 109–110.

ISAACS, W., THOMAS, J., & GOLDIAMOND, I. Application of operant conditioning to reinstate verbal behavior in psychotics. *Journal of Speech and Hearing Disorders*, 1960, **25,** 8–12.

JACOBS, P. S., BRUNTON, M., MELVILLE, M. M., BRITTAIN, R. P., & MCCLEMONT, W. F. Aggressive behavior, mental subnormality and the XYY male. *Nature*, 1965, **208,** 1351–1352.

JAMES, W. *The principles of psychology.* New York: Holt, 1890.

JANIS, I. L., & FESHBACH, S. Effects of fear-arousing communications. *Journal of Abnormal and Social Psychology*, 1953, **48,** 78–92.

JARVIK, L. F., KLODIN, V., & MATSUYAMA, S. S. Human aggression and the extra Y chromosome: Fact or fantasy? *American Psychologist*, 1973, **28,** 674–682.

JECKER, J., & LANDY, D. Liking a person as a function of doing him a favor. *Human Relations*, 1969, **22,** 371–378.

JENKINS, J. G., & DALLENBACH, K. M. Oblivescence during sleep and waking. *American Journal of Psychology*, 1924, **35,** 605–612.

JENKINS, J. J., RUSSELL, W. A., & SUCI, G. J. An atlas of semantic profiles for 360 words. *American Journal of Psychology*, 1958, **71,** 688–699.

JENNINGS, M. K., & NIEMI, R. G. The transmission of political values from parent to child. *American Political Science Review*, 1968, **62,** 169–184.

JENSEN, A. R. How much can we boost IQ and scholastic achievement? *Harvard Educational Review*, 1969, **39,** 1–123.

JOHNSON, D. M. Applications of the standard-score IQ to social statistics. *Journal of Social Psychology*, 1948, **27,** 217–227.

JONES, E. E. *Ingratiation; A social psychological analysis.* New York: Appleton-Century-Crofts, 1964.

JONES, E. E., BELL, L., & ARONSON, E. The reciprocation of attraction from similar and dissimilar others: A study in person perception and evaluation. In C. G. McClintock (ed.), *Experimental social psychology.* New York: Holt, Rinehart and Winston, 1972.

JONES, H. E., & CONRAD, H. S. The growth and decline of intelligence: A study of a homogeneous group between the ages of ten and sixty. *Genetic Psychology Monographs*, 1933, **13,** 223–298.

JONES, M. C., & BAYLEY, N. Physical maturing among boys as related to behavior. *Journal of Educational Psychology*, 1950, **41,** 129–148.

JULIEN, R. *Drugs* (tentative title). San Francisco: Freeman, 1975.

JUNG, C. G. *Collected works.* Ed. by Sir H. Read, M. Fordham, & G. Adler. (trans. by R. F. C. Hull.) Princeton: Princeton University Press, 1953.

JUNG, C. G. *Man and his symbols.* New York: Dell, 1968.

JUNG, C. G. The structure of the unconscious (1916). In C. G. Jung. *Collected works.* Ed. by Sir H. Read, M. Fordham, & G. Adler. (Trans. by R. F. C. Hull.) Princeton: Princeton University Press, 1953.

KAGAN, J., & MOSS, H. A. *Birth to maturity: The Fels study of psychological development.* New York: Wiley, 1962.

KALLMAN, F. J. Comparative twin studies on the genetic aspects of male homosexuality. *Journal of Nervous and Mental Diseases*, 1952, **115,** 238–298.

KALVEN, H., JR., & ZEISEL, H. *The American jury.* Boston: Little, Brown, 1966.

KARACAN, I., HURSCH, C. J., WILLIAMS, R. L., & THORNBY, J. I. Some characteristics of nocturnal penile tumescence in young adults. *Archives of General Psychiatry*, 1972, **26,** 351–356.

KARLEN, A. *Sexuality and homosexuality—a new view.* New York: Norton, 1971.

KATZ, M. M., COLE, J. O., & BARTON, W. E. (EDS.) *The role and methodology of classification in psychiatry and psychopathology.* Washington, D. C.: U.S. Department of Health, Education and Welfare, Public Health Service Publication No. 1584, 1968.

KAUFMAN, L., & ROCK, I. The moon illusion. I. *Science*, 1962, **136,** 953–961.

KELLER, F. S. Good-bye teacher. . . . *Journal of Applied Behavior*, 1968, **1,** 78–89.

KELLEY, H. H., & THIBAUT, J. W. Group problem solving. In G. Lindzey & E. Aronson (eds.), *Handbook of social psychology,* Vol. IV. Reading, Mass.: Addison-Wesley, 1969.

KELLY, G. A. *The psychology of personal constructs.* 2 vols. New York: Norton, 1955.

KENNEDY, J. F. Mental illness and mental retardation: A message from the President of the United States. *American Psychologist*, 1963, **18,** 280–289.

KENNEDY, J. L., GOTTSDANKER, R. M., ARMINGTON, J. C., & GRAY, F. E. A new electroencephalogram associated with thinking. *Science*, 1948, **108,** 527–529.

KEYS, A., BRÔZEK, J., HENSCHEL, A., MICHELSON, O., & TAYLOR, H. L. *The biology of human starvation.* Minneapolis: University of Minnesota Press, 1950.

KINSEY, A. C., POMEROY, W. B., MARTIN, C. E., & GEBHARD, P. H. *Sexual behavior in the human female.* Philadelphia: Saunders, 1953.

KINSEY, A. C., POMEROY, W. B., & MARTIN, C. E. *Sexual behavior in the human male.* Philadelphia: Saunders, 1948.

KISKER, C. W. *The disorganized personality.* New York: McGraw-Hill, 1964.

KLOPFER, B., & DAVIDSON, H. H. *The Rorschach technique: An introductory* manual. New York: Harcourt Brace Jovanovich, 1962.

KLOPFER, P. H. An experiment on emphatic learning in ducks. *American Naturalist*, 1957, **91**, 61–63.

KLOPFER, P. H. Influence of social interaction on learning rates in birds. *Science*, 1958, **128**, 903.

KOGAN, N., & WALLACH, M. A. *Risk-taking: A study in cognition and personality*. New York: Holt, Rinehart and Winston, 1964.

KOHLBERG, L. A cognitive-developmental analysis of children's sex-role concepts and attitudes. In E. E. Maccoby (ed.), *The development of sex differences*. Stanford: Stanford University Press, 1966.

KOHLBERG, L. The child as a moral philosopher. *Psychology Today*, September 1968.

KOHLBERG, L. Stage and sequence: The cognitive-developmental approach to socialization. In D. A. Goslin (ed.) *Handbook of socialization theory and research*. Chicago: Rand McNally, 1969.

KOHLER, W. *The mentality of apes*. New York: Harcourt Brace Jovanovich, 1925.

KOLB, L. C. *Noyes' modern clinical psychiatry*. Philadelphia: Saunders, 1968.

KRAMER, M. Statistics of mental disorders in the United States: Current status, some urgent needs and suggested solutions. *Journal of the Royal Statistical Society* (Series A), 1969, **132**(3), 353–407.

KRAMER, M. Manifest dream content in normal and psychopathological states. *Archives of General Psychiatry*, 1970, **22**, 149–159.

KRAVETZ, D. Heart rate as a minimal cue for the occurrence of vicarious classical conditioning. *Journal of Personality and Social Psychology*, 1974, **29**, 125–131.

KUETHE, J. L. Prejudice and aggression: A study of specific social schemata. *Perceptual Motor Skills*, 1964, **18**, 107–118.

KUETNER, B., WILKINS, C., & YARROW, P. R. Verbal attitudes and overt behavior involving racial prejudice. *Journal of Ab-*

normal and Social Psychology, 1952, **47**, 649–652.

LACEY, J. I. Somatic response patterning and stress: Some revisions of activation theory. In M. H. Appley & R. Trumbull (eds.), *Psychological stress*. New York: Appleton-Century-Crofts, 1967.

LAPIERE, R. T. Attitudes vs. actions. *Social Forces*, 1934, **13**, 230–237.

LATANÉ, B. & RODIN, J. A lady in distress: Inhibiting effects of friends and strangers on bystander intervention. *Journal of Experimental and Social Psychology*, 1969, **5**(2), 189–202.

LAZARUS, A. A. *Behavior therapy & beyond*. New York: McGraw-Hill, 1971.

LECOMTE, J. L'interattraction chez l'abeille. *C. R. Seances Acad. Sci.*, 1949, **229**, 857–858.

LEE, E. S. Negro intelligence and selective migration. *American Sociological Review*, 1951, **16**, 227–233.

LEIBOWITZ, H. *Visual perception*. New York: Macmillan, 1965.

LENNEBERG, E. H. *Biological foundations of language*. New York: Wiley, 1967.

LENNEBERG, E. H. On explaining language. *Science*, 1969, **164**, 635–643.

LESSER, G. S., FIFER, G., & CLARK, D. H. Mental abilities of children from social-clan and cultural groups. *Monographs of Social Research in Child Development*, 1965, **30**, 1–115.

LESTER, D. Suicidal behavior in men and women. *Mental Hygiene*, 1969, **53**, 340–345.

LETTVIN, J. Y., MATURANA, H. R., MCCULLOCH, W. S., & PITTS, W. H. What the frog's eye tells the frog's brain. *Proceedings of the Institute of Radio Engineers*, 1959, **47**, 1940–1951.

LEVENTHAL, H. Findings and theory in the study of fear communications. In L. Berkowitz (ed.) *Advances in Experimental Social Psychology*, Vol. 5. New York: Academic Press, 1970.

LEVINE, M., & LEVINE, A. *A social history of helping services: Clinic, court, school, and community*. New York: Appleton-Century-Crofts, 1970.

LEVINE, S. Sex differences in the brain. *Scientific American*, 1966, **214**, 84–90.

LEWIN, K. *A dynamic theory of personality*. New York: McGraw-Hill, 1935.

LEWIN, K. Group decision and social change. In G. Swanson, T. M. Newcomb, & E. L. Hartley (eds.), *Readings in social psychology*. New York: Henry Holt, 1952.

LEWIS, M., & MCGURK, H. Evaluation of infant intelligence. *Science*, 1972, **178**, 1174–1177.

LICHT, H. *Sexual life in ancient Greece*. Ed. by L. H. Dawson. (Trans. by J. H. Freese.) New York: Barnes & Noble, 1963.

LILLY, J. C. Mental effects of reduction of ordinary levels of physical stimuli on intact, healthy persons. *Psychiatric Research Report*, 1956, **5**, 1–9.

LINDNER, R. *The fifty-minute hour*. New York: Rinehart, 1954.

LINDSLEY, D. B. Attention, consciousness, sleep and wakefulness. In J. Field, H. W. Magoun, & V. Hull (eds.) *Handbook of Physiology*, Section I: Neurophysiology, Vol: III. Washington, D. C.: American Physiological Society, 1960.

LINDSLEY, D. B. Emotion. In S. S. Stevens (ed.) *Handbook of experimental psychology*. New York: Wiley, 1951.

LINDSLEY, D. B., SCHREINER, L. H., KNOWLES, W. B., & MAGOUN, H. W. Behavioral and EEG changes following chronic brain stem lesions in the cat. *Electroencephalography and Clinical Neurophysiology*, 1950, **2**, 483–498.

LINDZEY, G., & BYRNE, D. Sociometric measurement and social attraction. In G. Lindzey & E. Aronson (eds.) *Handbook of social psychology*, Vol. II. Reading, Mass.: Addison-Wesley, 1968.

LINDZEY, G., LOEHLIN, J., & SPUHLER, J. N. Personal communication to the authors, 1973.

LIPSETT, L. P. Learning in the first year of life. In L. P. Lipsett & C. C. Spiker (eds.) *Advances in child development and behavior*. New York: Academic Press, 1963.

LORENZ, K. The comparative method in studying innate behavior patterns. *Symposium of the society for experimental biology*, New York: Academic Press, 1950.

LORENZ, K. *On aggression.* New York: Harcourt Brace Jovanovich, 1963.

LORGE, I. Influence of regularly interpolated time intervals upon subsequent learning. *Teachers College Contributions to Education,* 1930, #438.

LOTT, B. E., & LOTT, J. A. The formation of positive attitudes toward group members. *Journal of Abnormal and Social Psychology,* 1960, **61,** 297–300.

LUCE, G. G., & SEGAL J. *Sleep.* New York: Coward-McCann, 1966.

LUCHINS, A. S. Mechanization in problem solving: The effect of Einstellung. *Psychological Monographs,* 1959, 248.

LUCHINS, A. S. *Wertheimer's seminar recorded: Problem solving and thinking.* Albany, N.Y.: SUNY Student Faculty Evaluation, 1972.

LUH, C. W. The conditions of retention. *Psychological Monographs,* 1922, **31**(3), Whole No. 142.

LURIA, A. R. *The mind of a mnemonist.* New York: Basic Books, 1968.

LUSTMAN, S. L. Behavior in childhood and adolescence. In F. C. Redlich & D. X. Freedman (eds.) *The theory and practice of psychiatry.* New York: Basic Books, 1966.

LUTTGES, M., JOHNSON, R., BUCK, C., HOLLAND, J., & MCGAUGH, J. An examination of "transfer of learning" by nucleic acid. *Science,* 1966, **151,** 834–837.

MACKINNON, D. W. Violation of prohibitions. In H. A. Murray. *Explorations in personality.* New York: Oxford University Press, 1938.

MACNICHOL, E. F., JR. Three-pigment color vision. *Scientific American,* 1964, **211,** 48–56.

MCCALL, R. B., APPELBAUM, M. J., & HOGARTY, P. S. Developmental changes in mental performance. *Monographs of the Society for Research in Child Development,* 1973, **38**(3), Whole No. 150.

MCCLELLAND, D. C. *The achieving society.* New York: Van Nostrand, 1961.

MCCLELLAND, D. C., ATKINSON, J. W., CLARK, R. A., & LOWELL, E. L. *The achievement motive.* New York: Appleton-Century-Crofts, 1953.

MCDOUGALL, W. *Social psychology.* Boston: John Luce, 1921.

MCGEOCH, J. A., & IRION, A. L. *The psychology of human learning* (2nd ed.) New York: Longmans, Green, 1952.

MCGINNIS, J. *The selling of the president.* New York: Trident Press, 1969.

MCNEILL, D. Language development in children. In P. Mussen (ed.) *Handbook of child psychology* (3rd ed.) New York: Wiley, 1970.

MCNEMAR, Q. *The revision of the Stanford-Binet scale.* Boston: Houghton Mifflin, 1942.

MAIER, N. R. F. *Frustration: The study of behavior without a goal.* New York: McGraw-Hill, 1949.

MARCH, B. A., & MCGINNIES, E. *Communicator credibility and initial attitude as variables in persuasion.* Technical Report 13, Office of Naval Research, May 1966.

MARCUS, S. *The other Victorians.* New York: Basic Books, 1964.

MARTIN, B. *Anxiety and neurotic disorders.* New York: Wiley, 1971.

MARTIN, R. The experimental manipulation of stuttering behaviors. In H. N. Sloane, Jr., & B. D. MacAuley (eds.) *Operant procedures in remedial speech and language training.* Boston: Houghton Mifflin, 1968.

MARX, K. *Capital.* Vol. I. London: Lawrence and Wishart, 1954 (originally published in German in 1867).

MASLAND, R. L., SARASON, S., & GLADWYN, T. *Mental subnormality.* New York: Basic Books, 1958.

MASLOW, A. H. *Toward a psychology of being* (2nd ed.) New York: Van Nostrand, 1968.

MASTERS, W. H. & JOHNSON, V. E. *Human sexual inadequacy.* Boston: Little, Brown, 1970.

MASTERS, W. H., & JOHNSON, V. E. *Human sexual response.* Boston: Little, Brown, 1966.

MAX, L. W. Experimental study of the motor theory of consciousness. IV. Action-current responses in the deaf during awakening, kinesthetic imagery and abstract thinking. *Journal of Comparative Psychology,* 1937, **24,** 301–344.

MEIER, C. A. *Jung and analytical psychology.* Newton Centre, Mass.: Andover Newton Theological School, 1959.

MELTON, A. W. Implications of short-term memory for a general theory of memory. *Journal of Verbal Learning and Verbal Behavior,* 1963, **2,** 1–21.

MELTON, A. W. Some behavior characteristics of museum visitors. *Psychological Bulletin,* 1933, **30,** 720–721.

MENDELS, F. *Concepts of depression.* New York: Wiley, 1970.

MENNINGER, K. *Man against himself.* New York: Harcourt Brace Jovanovich, 1966.

MENZEL, E. W. Chimpanzee spatial memory organization. *Science,* 1973, **182,** 943–945.

MERRILL, M. A. The significance of IQ's on the revised Stanford-Binet scales. *Journal of Educational Psychology,* 1938, **26,** 641–651.

MILGRAM, S. Behavioral study of obedience. *Journal of Abnormal and Social Psychology,* 1963, **67,** 371–378.

MILGRAM, S., MANN, I., & HARTER, S. The lost-letter technique of social research. *Public Opinion Quarterly,* 1965, **29,** 437–438.

MILLER, G. A. The magical number seven, plus or minus two: Some limits on our capacity for processing information. *Psychological Review,* 1956, **63,** 81–97.

MILLER, N. E. Applications of learning and biofeedback to psychiatry and medicine. In A. M. Freedman, H. I. Kaplan, & B. J. Sadock, (eds.) *Comprehensive textbook of psychiatry* (2nd ed.) Baltimore: Williams & Wilkins, 1975.

MILLER, N. E. Studies of fear as an acquirable drive. I. Fear as motivation and fear-reduction as reinforcement in the learning of new responses. *Journal of Experimental Psychology,* 1948, **38,** 89–101.

MILLER, N. E., & BANUAZIZI, A. Instrumental learning by curarized rats of a specific visceral response, intestinal or cardiac. *Journal of Comparative and Physiological Psychology,* 1968, **65**(1), 1–7.

MILLER, N. E., & DOLLARD, J. *Social learning and imitation.* New Haven: Yale University Press, 1941.

MILLER, N. E., & DWORKIN, B. R. Visceral learning: Recent difficulties with curarized rats and significant problems for human research. In P. A. Obrist, A. H. Black, J. Brener, & L. V. DiCara (eds.) *Cardiovascular Psychophysiology.* Chicago: Aldine, 1974.

MILLER, N. E., & KESSEN, M. L. Reward effects of food via stomach fistula compared with those of food via mouth. *Journal of Comparative and Physiological Psychology*, 1952, **45**, 555–564.

MILLON, T. *Modern psychopathology: A biosocial approach to maladaptive learning and functioning.* Philadelphia: Saunders, 1969.

MILNER, B. Amnesia following operation on the temporal lobes. In C. W. M. Whitty, & O. L. Zangwill (eds.) *Amnesia.* London: Butterworth, 1966.

MILNER, B. Some effects of frontal lobectomy in man. In J. M. Warren, & K. Akert (eds.) *The frontal granular cortex and behavior.* New York: McGraw-Hill, 1964.

MONEY, J. (ed.) *Sex research: New developments.* New York: Holt, Rinehart and Winston, 1965.

MONOD, J. *Chance and necessity.* New York: Knopf, 1971.

MORGAN, C. T. *Physiological psychology.* New York: McGraw-Hill, 1965.

MORUZZI, G., & MAGOUN, H. W. Brain stem reticular formation and activation of the EEG. *Electroencephalography and Clinical Neurophysiology*, 1949, **1**, 455–473.

MOSS, C. S. *Dreams, images, and fantasy.* Urbana: University of Illinois Press, 1970.

MOSS, C. S. *The hypnotic investigation of dreams.* New York: Wiley, 1967.

MOWRER, O. H. An experimental analogue of "regression" with incidental observations on reaction formation. *Journal of Abnormal and Social Psychology*, 1940, **35**, 56–87.

MOWRER, O. H. Hearing and speaking: An analysis of language learning. *Journal of Speech and Hearing Disorders*, 1958, **23**, 143–151.

MUCKENSTRUM, B. La signification de la livree nuptiale de l'epinoche. *Revue de la Comportement Animal,* 1969, **3,** 39–64.

MUELLER, C. G. *Sensory psychology.* Englewood Cliffs, N.J.: Prentice-Hall, 1965.

MURRAY, H. A. *Explorations in personality.* New York: Oxford University Press, 1938.

MURRAY, H. A., & WHEELER, D. R. A note on the possible clairvoyance of dreams. *Journal of Psychology,* 1937, **3,** 309–313.

NAHAS, G. G., SUCIU-FOCA, N., ARMAND, J. P., & MORISHIMA, A. Inhibition of cellular mediated immunity in marihuana smokers. *Science,* 1974, **131,** 419–420.

NATIONAL ACADEMY OF SCIENCES. *Doctoral scientists and engineers in the United States.* Washington, D. C.: National Academy of Sciences, 1974.

NEISSER, U. *Cognitive psychology.* New York: Appleton-Century-Crofts, 1967.

NELSON, J. T., & EPSTEIN, S. Relationships among three measures of conflict over hostility. *Journal of Consulting Psychology,* 1962, **26,** 345–350.

NEWCOMB, T. M. *The acquaintance process.* New York: Holt, Rinehart and Winston, 1961.

NEWCOMB, T. M. *Personality and social change.* New York: Dryden Press, 1943.

NIELSON, G. *Studies in self-confrontation.* Copenhagen: Munksgaard, in press.

NORMAN, D. A. *Memory and attention.* New York: Wiley, 1969.

NORMAN, D. A. *Models of human memory.* New York: Academic Press, 1970.

NOWLIN, J. B. The association of nocturnal angina pectoris with dreaming. *Annals of Internal Medicine,* 1965, **63,** 1040–1046.

O'CONNELL, D. N., SHOR, R. E., & ORNE, M. T. Hypnotic age regression: An empirical and methodological analysis. *Journal of Abnormal Psychology,* 1970, **76** (Monogr. Suppl. No. 3), 1–32.

OFFER, D. *The psychological world of the teen-ager: A study of normal adolescent boys.* New York: Basic Books, 1969.

ORNE, M. T. The mechanisms of hypnotic age regression: An experimental study. *Journal of Abnormal and Social Psychology,* 1951, **46,** 213–225.

ORNSTEIN, R. E. The techniques of meditation and their implications for modern psychology. In C. Naranjo & R. E. Ornstein (eds.) *On the psychology of meditation.* New York: Viking Press, 1971.

OSBORN, A. F. *Applied imagination: Principles and procedures of creative thinking* (2nd ed.) New York: Scribner's, 1957.

OSGOOD, C. E., SUCI, G. J., & TANNENBAUM, P. H. *The measurement of meaning.* Urbana: University of Illinois Press, 1957.

OTIS, L. S. If well-integrated but anxious, try T. M. *Psychology Today,* 1974, **7,** 45–46.

PATTERSON, G. R., LITTMEN, R. A., & BRICKER, W. Assertive behavior in children: a step toward a theory of aggression. *Monographs of the Society for Research in Child Development,* 1967, **32,** Serial No. 113.

PAVLOV, I. P. *Conditioned reflexes.* (Trans. by G. V. Anrep.) New York: Oxford University Press, 1927.

PIAGET, J. *The child's conception of the world.* New York: Humanities Press, 1951.

PIAGET, J. Piaget's theory. In P. H. Mussen (ed.) *Carmichael's manual of child psychology* (3rd ed.) New York: Wiley, 1970.

POLLACK, I., & PICKETT, J. M. The intelligibility of excerpts from conversation. *Language and Speech,* 1964, **6,** 165–171.

POSTLETHWAIT, S. N., & NOVAK, J. D. The use of 8-mm loop films in individualized instruction. *Annals of the New York Academy of Science,* 1967, **142,** 464–470.

POSTMAN, L. Short-term memory and incidental learning. In A. W. Melton (ed.) *Categories of human learning.* New York: Academic Press, 1964.

PRIBRAM, K. H. *Languages of the brain.* Englewood Cliffs, N.J.: Prentice-Hall, 1971.

PROSHANSKY, H. M. A projective method for the study of attitudes. *Journal of Abnormal and Social Psychology,* 1943, **38,** 393–395.

RABBIE, J. M., & HORWITZ, M. Arousal of ingroup outgroup bias by a chance win or loss. *Journal of Personality and Social Psychology*, 1969, **13**, 269–277.

REES, H. J., & ISRAEL, H. E. An investigation of the establishment and operation of mental sets. *Psychological Monographs*, 1935, **46**(6), Whole No. 210.

REIFF, R., & SCHEERER, M. *Memory and hypnotic age regression: Developmental aspects of cognitive function explored through hypnosis*. New York: Universities Press, 1959.

REITMAN, J. S. Mechanisms of forgetting in short-term memory. *Cognitive Psychology*, 1971, **2**, 185–195.

REYNOLDS, G. S. *A primer of operant conditioning*. Glenview, Ill.: Scott, Foresman, 1968.

RHEINGOLD, H. L., & ECKERMAN, C. O. The infant separates himself from his mother. *Science*, 1970, **168**, 78–90.

RICHMAN, A., & ORLAW, R. Barbiturate mortality as an index of barbiturate use, Canada, 1950–1963. *Canadian Medical Association Journal*, 1965, **93**(26), 1336–1339.

RIESEN, A. H. Arrested vision. *Scientific American*, 1950, **183**, 16–19.

RIESEN, A. H., & AARONS, L. Visual movement and intensity discrimination in cats after early deprivation of pattern vision. *Journal of Comparative and Physiological Psychology*, 1959, **52**, 142–149.

RIMLAND, B. *Infantile autism*. New York: Appleton-Century-Crofts, 1964.

ROBERTS, A. H., KEWMAN, D. G., & MAC-DONALD, H. Voluntary control of skin temperature: Unilateral changes using hypnosis and feedback. *Journal of Abnormal Psychology*, 1973, **82**, 163–168.

ROBINSON, E. S. The "similarity" factor in retroaction. *American Journal of Psychology*, 1927, **39**, 297–312.

ROFFWARG, H. P. *et al.* Ontogenetic development of the human sleep-dream cycle. *Science*, 1966, **152**, 604–619.

ROFFWARG, H. P., DEMENT, W. C., MUZIO, U. N., & FUHER, C. Dream imagery: Relation to rapid eye movements of sleep. *Archives of General Psychology*, 1962, **7**, 235–258.

ROGERS, C. R. *Client-centered therapy: Its current practice, implications, and theory*. Boston: Houghton Mifflin, 1951.

ROGERS, C. R. The concept of the fully functioning person. *Psychotherapy*, 1963, **1**, 17–26.

ROGERS, C. R. *On becoming a person*. Boston: Houghton Mifflin, 1961.

ROSE, R. M., GORDON, T. P., & BERNSTEIN, I. S. Plasma testosterone levels in the male rhesus: Influences of sexual and social stimuli. *Science*, 1972, **178**, 643–45.

ROSE, R. M., HOLADAY, J. W., & BERNSTEIN, I. S. Plasma testosterone, dominance rank, and aggressive behavior in male rhesus monkeys. *Nature*, 1971, **231**.

ROSENHAN, D. On being sane in insane places. *Science*, 1973, **179**, 250–258.

ROSENQUIST, H. S. *Social facilitation in rotary pursuit tracking*. Paper read at the Midwestern Psychological Association Meetings, Cleveland, Ohio, May 1972.

ROSENTHAL, D. *Genetic theory and abnormal behavior*. New York: McGraw-Hill, 1970.

RUBIN, F. *Learning and sleep*. Bristol: John Wright, 1971.

RUBIN, R. T., GUNDERSON, E. K. F., & DOLL R. E. Life stress and illness patterns in the U.S. Navy. III. Prior life-change and illness onset in an attack carrier's crew. *Archives of Environmental Health*, 1969, 19, 738–747.

RUBIN, Z. *Liking and loving: An invitation to social psychology*. New York: Holt, Rinehart and Winston, 1973.

RUBIN, Z. PEPLAU, A., & HILL, C. T. *Becoming intimate: The development of male-female relationships*. In preparation.

RULE, B. G., & PERCIVAL, E. The effects of frustration and attack on physical aggression. *Journal of Experimental Research in Personality*, 1971, **5**, 111–188.

RUSHTON, W. A. H. Visual pigments in the color blind. *Nature*, 1958, **182**, 690–692.

SAGE, W. Psychology and the Angela Davis jury. *Human Behavior*, January 1973, 56–61.

SAMEROFF, A. J., & CHANDLER, M. J. Reproductive risk and the continuum of caretaking casualty. In F. D. Horowitz, E. M. Hetherington, S. Scarr-Salapatek, & J. Siegel (eds.) *Review of child development research*, Vol. 4. Chicago: University of Chicago Press, 1974.

SARASON, I. G. *Abnormal psychology: The problem of maladaptive behavior*. New York: Appleton-Century-Crofts, 1972.

SAUGSTAD, P. Problem-solving as dependent on availability of functions. *British Journal of Psychology*, 1955, **46**, 191–198.

SAWREY, W. L., CONGER, J. J., & TURRELL, E. S. An experimental investigation of the role of psychological factors in the production of gastric ulcers in rats. *Journal of Comparative and Physiological Psychology*, 1956, **49**, 457–461.

SCHACHTER, S. *Emotion, obesity, and crime*. New York: Academic Press, 1971.

SCHACHTER, S. *The psychology of affiliation*. Stanford: Stanford University Press, 1959.

SCHACHTER, S. Some extraordinary facts about obese humans and rats. *American Psychologist*, 1971, **26**, 129–144.

SCHACHTER, S., & SINGER, J. Cognitive, social and physiological determinants of emotional state. *Psychological Review*, 1962, **69**, 379–399.

SCHAIE, K. W. A general model for the study of developmental problems. *Psychological Bulletin*, 1965, **64**, 92–107.

SCHEERER, M. Problem-solving. *Scientific American*, April 1963, **208**, 118–128.

SCHILLER, P. H. Innate constituents of complex responses in primates. *Psychological Review*, 1952, **59**, 177–191.

SCHUELL, H., & JENKINS, J. J. Further work on language deficit in aphasia. *Psychological Review*, 1964, **71**, 87–93.

SCHULMAN, J., SHAVER, P., COLMAN, R., EMRICH, B., & CHRISTIE, R. Recipe for a jury. *Psychology Today*, 1973, **6**, 37–44, 77–84.

SCHWARTZ, G. E. *Meditation as an altered trait of consciousness: Current findings on stress reactivity and creativity*. Paper presented at the 82nd annual meeting of the American Psychological Association, New Orleans, 1974.

SCHWARTZ, G. E. *Pros and Cons of Meditation: Current findings on physiology and anxiety, self-control, drug abuse and creativity.* Paper presented at the 81st Annual Meeting of the American Psychological Association, Montreal, 1973.

SEARS, D. O. Political behavior. In G. Lindzey & E. Aronson (eds.) *Handbook of personality and social psychology* (2nd ed.), Vol. V. Reading, Mass.: Addison-Wesley, 1968.

SELYE, H. *The physiology and pathology of exposure to stress.* Montreal: Acta, 1950.

SELYE, H. *The stress of life.* New York: McGraw-Hill, 1956.

SHAFFER, L. F. Fear and courage in aerial combat. *Journal of Consulting Psychology,* 1947, **11,** 137–143.

SHAH, S. A., & BORGAONKAR, D. S. The XYY chromosomal abnormality: Some "facts" and "fantasies"? *American Psychologist,* 1974, **29,** 357–359.

SHAPIRO, A. K. A contribution to a history of the placebo effect. *Behavioral Science,* 1960, **5,** 109–135.

SHELDON, W. H. (with the collaboration of S. S. Stevens). *The varieties of temperament: A psychology of constitutional differences.* New York: Harper, 1942.

SHEPARD, R. Recognition memory for words, sentences and pictures. *Journal of Verbal Learning & Verbal Behavior,* 1967, **6,** 156–163.

SIDMAN, M. Two temporal parameters of the maintenance of avoidance behavior by the white rat. *Journal of Comparative and Physiological Psychology,* 1953, **46,** 253–261.

SINGER, J. L. *Daydreaming.* New York: Random House, 1966.

SIQUELAND, E. *Further developments in infant learning.* Paper read at the symposium in the learning processes of human infants. London: XIXth International Congress of Psychology, 1969.

SKINNER, B. F. *The behavior of organisms.* New York: Appleton-Century-Crofts, 1938.

SKINNER, B. F. *Beyond freedom and dignity.* New York: Knopf, 1971.

SKINNER, B. F. *Cumulative record: A selection of papers.* New York: Appleton-Century-Crofts, 1972.

SKINNER, B. F. *Science and human behavior.* New York: Macmillan, 1953.

SKINNER, B. F. *Verbal behavior.* New York: Appleton-Century-Crofts, 1957.

SKINNER, B. F. *Walden two.* New York: Macmillan, 1948.

SLOAN, W., & BIRCH, J. W. A rationale for degrees of retardation. *American Journal of Mental Deficiency,* 1955, **60,** 262.

SMITH, A. J., MADDEN, E. H., & SOBOL, R. Productivity and recall in cooperative and competitive discussion groups. *Journal of Psychology,* 1957, **43,** 193–204.

SMITH, C. P., & FELD, S. How to learn the method of content analysis for *n* Achievement, *n* Affiliation, and *n* Power. In J. W. Atkinson (ed.) *Motives in fantasy, action, and society.* New York: Van Nostrand, 1958.

SMITH, F., & MILLER, G. A. *The genesis of language.* Cambridge: The M.I.T. Press, 1966.

SNIDER, J. G., & OSGOOD, C. E. (eds.) *Semantic differential technique.* Chicago: Aldine, 1969.

SNYDER, F., HOBSON, J. A., MORRISON, D. R., & GOLDFRANK, F. Changes in respiration, heart rate, and systolic blood pressure in human sleep. *Journal of Applied Psychology,* 1964, **19,** 417–422.

SOKOLOV, YE. N. *Perception and the conditioned reflex.* New York: Macmillan, 1963.

SONTAG, L. W., BAKER, C. T., & NELSON, V. L. Mental growth and development: A longitudinal study. *Monographs of Social Research in Child Development,* 1958, **23,** Serial 68.

SOROKIN, P. *Contemporary sociological theories.* New York: Harper, 1928.

SPEARMAN, C. *The abilities of man.* New York: Macmillan, 1927.

SPELT, D. K. The conditioning of the human fetus in utero. *Journal of Experimental Psychology,* 1948, **38,** 338–346.

SPENCE, K. W., & SPENCE, J. T. Sex and anxiety differences in eyelid conditioning. *Psychological Bulletin,* 1966, **65,** 137–42.

SPERLING, G. The information available in brief visual presentations. *Psychological Monographs,* 1960, **74,** Whole No. 498.

SPERRY, R. W. Brain bisection and mechanisms of consciousness. In J. C. Eccles (ed.) *Brain and conscious experience.* New York: Springer-Verlag, 1966.

SPERRY, R. W. Hemisphere deconnection and unity in conscious awareness. *American Psychologist,* 1968, **23,** 723–733.

SPERRY R. W. The great cerebral commissure. *Scientific American,* January 1964, **210,** 42–52.

SPIEGEL, H., SHOR, G., & FISCHMAN, S. An hypnotic ablation technique for the study of personality development. *Psychosomatic Medicine,* 1945, **7,** 272–278.

SPIELBERGER, C. D. The effects of manifest anxiety on the academic achievement of college students. *Mental Hygiene,* 1962, **46,** 420–426.

SROLE, L., LANGNER, T. S., MICHAEL, S. T., OPLER, M. K., & RENNIE, T. A. C. *Mental health in the metropolis: The midtown Manhattan study.* New York: McGraw-Hill, 1962.

STANDING, L., CONEZIO, J., & HABER, R. N. Perception and memory for pictures: Single-trial learning of 2500 visual stimuli. *Psychonomic Science,* 1970, **19**(2), 73–74.

STERMAN, M. B. Neurophysiological and clinical studies of sensorimotor EEG biofeedback training: Some effects on epilepsy. *Seminar of Psychiatry,* 1973, **5,** 507–525.

STERNBERG, S. High-speed scanning in human memory. *Science,* 1966, **153,** 652–654.

STEVENS, S. S. The surprising simplicity of sensory metrics. *American Psychologist,* 1962, **17,** 29–39.

STONER, J. A. F. *A comparison of individual and group decisions involving risk.* Unpublished master's thesis, School of Industrial Management, M.I.T., 1961.

STORMS, M. D., & NISBETT, R. E. Insomnia and the attribution process. *Journal of Personality and Social Psychology,* 1970, **16,** 319–328.

STRODTBECK, F. L. Social process, the law, and jury functioning. In W. M. Evan (ed.) *Law and sociology.* New York: Free Press, 1962.

STRONG, E. K. *Vocational interests of men and women.* Stanford: Stanford University Press, 1943.

STROOP, J. R. Studies of interference in serial verbal reactions. *Journal of Experimental Psychology,* 1953, **6**, 643–62.

STRUPP, H. H., FOX, R. E., & LESSLER, K. *Patients view their psychotherapy.* Baltimore: Johns Hopkins University Press, 1969.

SUINN, R. M. *Fundamentals of behavior pathology.* New York: Wiley, 1970.

SULLIVAN, H. S. *The interpersonal theory of psychiatry.* New York: Norton, 1953.

SVAETICHIN, G., & MACNICHOL, E. F. Retinal mechanisms for chromatic and achromatic vision. *Annals of the New York Academy of Science,* 1958, **74**, 385.

SYLVA, K., BRUNER, J. S., & GENOVA, P. The relationship between play and problem-solving in children three to five years old. In J. S. Bruner, A. Jolly & K. Sylva (eds.), *Play: Its role in evolution and development.* London: Penguin, in press.

SZASZ, T. S. *Law, liberty and psychiatry.* New York: Macmillan, 1963.

SZASZ, T. S. The myth of mental illness. *American Psychologist,* 1960, **15**, 113–118.

TAJFEL, H., BILLIG, M. G., BUNDY, R. P., & FLAMENT, C. Social categorization and intergroup behavior. *European Journal of Social Psychology,* 1971, **1**, 149–178.

TANNENBAUM, P. H. Initial attitude toward source and concept as factors in attitude change through communication. *Public Opinion Quarterly,* 1956, **20**, 413–425.

TAUSER, H. A. *The settlement of Negroes in Kent County, Ontario.* Chatham, Ontario: Shepard, 1939.

TAYLOR, S. J. L., & CHASE, S. *Mental health and the environment.* Boston: Little, Brown, 1964.

TERMAN, L. M. (ed.) *Genetic studies of genius,* Vol. V. Stanford: Stanford University Press, 1959.

TERMAN, L. M., & MILES, C. C. *Sex and personality.* New York: Russell & Russell, 1936.

THIESSEN, D. D. *Gene organization and behavior.* New York: Random House, 1972.

THOMPSON, R. F. *Introduction to physiological psychology.* New York: Harper & Row, 1975.

THOMPSON R. F. *Foundations of physiological pschology.* New York: Harper & Row, 1967.

THORNDIKE, E. L. *Animal intelligence* (*1898*). New York: Macmillan, 1911.

TUNE, L. E. Warm-up effect as a function of level of practice in verbal learning. *American Psychologist,* 1950, **5**, 251.

THURSTONE, L. L. *Multiple factor analysis.* Chicago: University of Chicago Press, 1947.

THURSTONE, L. L. Primary mental abilities. *Psychometric Monographs,* 1938, **1**, 1–121.

THURSTONE, L. L. The measurement of change in social attitudes. *Journal of Social Psychology,* 1931, **2**, 230–235.

THURSTONE, L. L. & THURSTONE, T. G. Factorial studies of intelligence. *Psychometric Monographs,* 1941, 2.

TINBERGEN, N. The curious behavior of the stickleback. *Scientific American,* December 1952, **187**, 22–26.

TINBERGEN, N. *The study of instinct.* New York: Oxford University Press, 1951.

TITLEY, R. W., & VINEY, W. Expression of aggression toward the physically handicapped. *Perceptual and Motor Skills* 1969, **29**, 51–6.

TRIESMAN, A. Selective attention in man. *British Medical Journal,* 1964, **20**, 12–16.

TRIPLETT, N. The dynamogenic factors in pace-making and competition. *American Journal of Psychology,* 1897, **9**, 507–533.

TRUE, R. M. Experimental control in hypnotic age regression states. *Science,* 1949, **110**, 583–584.

TRYON, R. C. Genetic differences in maze-learning ability in rats. *Thirty-ninth yearbook of the national society for the study of education. Intelligence: Its nature and nurture. Part I. Comparative*

and critical exposition. Bloomington, Ill.: Public School Publishing, 1940.

ULLMAN, M., & KRIPPNER, S. Dream studies and telepathy: An experimental approach. *Parapsychological Monographs,* 1970, No. 12.

U.S. National Commission on the Causes and Prevention of Violence. To establish justice, to insure domestic tranquility: the final report. New York: Praeger, 1970.

UTECH, D. A., & HOVING, K. L. Parents and peers as competing influences in the decisions of children of differing ages. *Journal of Social Psychology,* 1969, **78**, 267–274.

UZGIRIS, I. C., & HUNT, J. MCV. *Assessment of infancy: Ordinal scales of psychological development.* Urbana: University of Illinois Press, 1974.

VAN DE CASTLE, R. L. *The psychology of dreaming.* Morristown, N.J.: General Learning Corp., 1971.

VANDENBERG, S. G. Hereditary factors in psychological variables in man, with special emphasis on cognition. In J. N. Spuhler (ed.) *Genetic diversity and human behavior.* Chicago: Aldine, 1967.

VAN LIESHOUT, C. F. M. Reactions of young children to barriers placed by their mothers. Unpublished manuscript, Stanford University, 1974.

VAUGHAN, C. J. The development and use of an operant technique to provide evidence for visual imagery in the rhesus monkey under "sensory deprivation." *Dissertation Abstracts,* 1966, **26**(10), 6191.

VERKES, R. M., & MORGULI, S. The method of Pavlov in animal psychology. *Psychological Bulletin,* 1909, **6**, 257–273.

VINOKUR, A. Review and theoretical analysis of the effects of group processes upon individual and group decisions involving risk. *Psychological Bulletin,* 1971, **76**, 231–250.

VON FRISCH, K. *The dancing bees.* New York: Harcourt Brace Jovanovich, 1955.

WADA, J. A. Interhemispheric sharing and shift of cerebral speech function. *Exerpta Medica, International Congress Series,* 1969, **193**, 296–297.

WALD, G. The photochemistry of vision.

Documents in Ophthalmology, 1949, **3,** 94–137.

WALLACE, R., & BENSON, H. Physiological effects of transcendental meditation. *Science,* 1970, **167,** 1751–1754.

WALLACH, M. A., KOGAN, N., & BEM, D. J. Group influence on individual risk taking. *Journal of Abnormal and Social Psychology,* 1962, **65,** 75–86.

WALSTER, E., ARONSON, E., & ABRAHAMS, D. On increasing the persuasiveness of a low prestige communicator. *Journal of Experimental Social Psychology,* 1966, **2,** 325–342.

WALSTER, E., & FESTINGER, L. The effectiveness of the "overheard" persuasive communications. *Journal of Abnormal and Social Psychology,* 1962, **65,** 395–402.

WATSON, J. B. Experimental studies on the growth of emotions. In C. Murchison (ed.) *Psychologies of 1925.* Worchester, Mass.: Clark University Press, 1926.

WATSON, J. B. *Psychological care of infant and child.* New York: Norton, 1928.

WATSON, J. B., & RAYNER, R. Conditioned emotional reactions. *Journal of Experimental Psychology,* 1920, **3,** 1–4.

WAUGH, N. C., & NORMAN, D. A. Primary memory. *Psychological Review,* 1965, **72,** 89–104.

WEBB, E. J., CAMPBELL, D. T., SCHWARTZ, R. D., & SECHREST, L. *Unobtrusive measures: Nonreactive research in the social sciences.* Chicago: Rand McNally, 1966.

WEBER, E. H. De pulsu, resorptione, uditu et tactu: Annotationes anatomicae et physiologicae (1834). In R. I. Herrnstein & E. G. Boring (eds.) *A source book in the history of psychology.* Cambridge: Harvard University Press, 1965.

WECHSLER, D. *The measurement and appraisal of adult intelligence.* Baltimore: Williams & Wilkins, 1958.

WECHSLER, D. *The Wechsler intelligence scale for children.* New York: Psychological Corp., 1949.

WEITZENHOFFER, A. M., & HILGARD, E. R. *Stanford hypnotic susceptibility scales, Forms A and B.* Palo Alto, Calif.: Consulting Psychologists Press, 1959.

WENGER, M., BAGCHI, B., & ANAND, B. Experiments in India on "voluntary" control of the heart and pulse. *Circulation,* 1961, **24,** 1319–1325.

WERNER, H. *Comparative psychology of mental development.* New York: Science Editions, 1961.

WESTIE, F. R., & DEFLEUR, M. L. Autonomic responses and their relationship to race attitudes. *Journal of Abnormal and Social Psychology,* 1959, **58,** 340–347.

WHORF, B. L. *Language, thought, and reality.* J. B. Carroll (ed.). New York: Wiley, 1956.

WILLERMAN, L., BROMAN, S. H., & FIEDLER, M. Infant development, preschool IQ, and social class. *Child Development,* 1970, **41,** 69–77.

WILLSON, R., BEECHAM, T., & CARRINGTON, E. R. *Obstetrics and gynecology.* St. Louis: Mosby, 1971.

WILSON, A. C., & SARICH, V. M. A molecular time scale for human evolution. *Proceedings of the National Academy of Science,* 1969, **63,** 1088–1093.

WOLPE, J. *The practice of behavior therapy.* New York: Pergamon Press, 1966.

WRIGHT, H., & HICKS, J. C. Construction and validation of a Thurstone scale of liberalism-conservatism. *Journal of Applied Psychology,* 1966, **50,** 9–12.

YATES, F. A. *The Greek art of memory.* Chicago: University of Chicago Press, 1966.

YERKES, R. M. (ed.) Psychological examining in the United States Army. *Memoirs of the National Academy of Sciences.* Washington: Government Printing Office, 1921, **15.**

YOLLES, S. F., & KRAMER, M. Vital statistics of schizophrenia. In L. Bellak & L. Loeb (eds.) *The schizophrenic syndrome.* New York: Grune & Stratton, 1969.

YOUNG, M. N., & GIBSON, W. B. *How to develop an exceptional memory.* Hollywood: Wilshire Book, 1962.

YOUNG, P. C. Hypnotic regression, fact or artifact. *Journal of Abnormal and Social Psychology,* 1940, **36,** 273–278.

ZAJONC, R. B. Attitudinal effects of mere exposure. *Journal of Personality and Social Psychology,* 1968, **9,** 1–27.

ZAJONC, R. B. *Animal social behavior.* Morristown, N.J.: General Learning Corp., 1972.

ZAJONC, R. B. Social facilitation. *Science,* 1965, **149,** 269–274.

ZAJONC, R. B. Some effects of "space" serials. *Public Opinion Quarterly,* 1955, **18,** 367–374.

ZAJONC, R. B., WILSON, W. R., & RAJECKI, D. W. *Affiliation and social discrimination produced by brief exposure in day-old chicks.* In preparation.

ZAJONC, R. B., WOLOSIN, R. J., WOLOSIN, M. J., & LOH, W. D. Social facilitation and imitation in group risk-taking. *Journal of Experimental and Social Psychology,* 1970, **6,** 26–46.

ZEAMAN, D. Response latency as a function of the amount of reinforcement. *Journal of Experimental Psychology,* 1949, **39,** 446–482.

ZEIGARNIK, B. Uber das Behalten von erledigten und unerledigten Handlungen. *Psychologische Forschung,* 1927, **9,** 1–85.

ZEIGLER, H. P., & LIEBOWITZ, H. W. Apparent visual size as a function of distance for children and adults. *American Journal of Psychology,* 1957, **70,** 196–209.

ZILLMAN, D. Excitation transfer in communication-mediated aggressive behavior. *Journal of Experimental Social Psychology,* 1971, **7,** 419–434.

ZIMBARDO, P. G., COHEN, A. R., WEISENBERG, M., DWORKIN, L., & FIRESTONE, I. Control of pain motivation by cognitive dissonance. *Science,* 1966, **151,** 217–219.

Name Index

Subject Index

Bogardus social distance scale, 608–609
botulinus toxin, 86
bouton, 81, 83, 84
brain, 69; and aggression, 398–403; anatomy of, 73–80; electrical activity of, 59–62; and engrams, 233–234; and form perception, 117; and hearing, 97; in infancy, 465; and language, 64–66; and long-term memory, 218; nerve and glial cells of, 51, 80–86, and perception, 89–90, 125; "pleasure" zones in, 342; and senile dementia, 704; and sense organs, 89; and sexuality, 440; size, 30, 31, 52; and thinking, 300. *See also* brain damage; cerebral cortex
brain damage: and amphetamines, 167; and behavior disorders, 698–705; and delta waves, 60; effect on language, 64–66; frontal, 290; and marijuana, 173; and secondary retardation, 525
brain stem, 74–76
brainstorming, 291–292
brightness, 101, 122–123

California Psychological Inventory, 581
case studies, 15–16; of sexual behavior, 428–429
catatonic schizophrenia, 679–680
cell body of nerve cell, 69, 81, 83
central fissure (fissure of Rolando), 53
central nervous system, 69–86. *See also* brain, spinal cord
central tendency measures, 751–752
cerebellum, 74, 76
cerebral cortex, 51–59, 62–63, 74, 75, 76, 78, 129, 402
character analysis, 573–575
child-rearing practices, 19, 20, 617–618
childhood, 471–475, 561; and homosexuality, 443–444; and psychological differences between sexes, 476–481. *See also* children
children: aggression in, 395–396, 403–404; development of thinking in, 277–279; EEG development in, 62; and eidetic imagery, 219; and emotional expression, 381; high achievers, 356; and infantile autism, 681–682, 717; language development in, 256–258; and selection of diet by, 348; and television violence, 408–411
chimpanzees: compared with humans, 27; insightful behavior in, 208–209; and mental maps, 228; and sign language training, 247–249
chromosomes, 37, 39, 173. *See* heredity
chunking, 217, 240
circadian rhythms, 140–141
clairvoyance, 314–316
classical conditioning, 19, 180, 184–188, 189, 200, 719–722
client-centered therapy, 554, 728–729
clinical personality theories, 555–556
clinical psychology, 11
clustering, memory and, 224–225
cocaine, 166, 168–169
cocktail party phenomena, 91–93
codeine, 168–169
cognitive-appraisal theory, 381

cognitive consistency theories, 624–627
cognitive dissonance theory, 624–627, 639
cognitive learning, 205–209
cognitive personality theory, 545–546
color: constancy, 122–123; dimensions, 103; dreams in, 314; mixture principles, 105–106; psychological dimensions of, 101
color blindness tests, 103
color solid, 101, 103
color vision, 98–100; theories of, 101; essays on, 102–113
communication: and attitude change, 621–623; and competition, 655; in science, 5; and sensations and perceptions, 112; species-specific, 261; use of language for, 254–255; varieties of, 249–251
community mental health, 11, 730–733
competition, 292, 654–655
computer-assisted instruction, 245–246
computers: and simulation of love, 643; and simulation of thinking, 301
concept formation, 274, 279–282
concordance rate in twin studies, 673, 687
concrete operational stage, 474–475, 484
concrete thinking, 289–290
conditioning theory, 197, 202, 203, 351, 621. *See also* classical conditioning; operant conditioning
conflicts, 413–414. *See also* inner conflicts
conformity, 292–293, 619, 643, 645–649, 659
consciousness, 18–19, 58–59, 139, 159, 384, 533–534
conservation, development of, 474–475
consumer psychology, 12–13
contact, attitudes and, 615–616, 619
contiguity, learning and, 200–201, 232
control group, 4, 13
corpus callosum, 53, 54, 737. *See also* split-brain experiments
correlation, 16–17, 756–758
correlation coefficient, 16–17, 510, 757
counseling psychology, 11–12
cranial nerves, 71, 74, 75
creative thinking, 291–297, 320
critical thinking, 291–297
Cro-Magnon, 30, 32
cross-tolerance, 86
culture: and achievement behavior, 356; and instrumental acts and objects, 343–344; and intelligence, 518–519; and language development, 256; and modes of consciousness, 58–59; of Neanderthal man, 31; and reinforcers, 202; and sex differences, 476–481; and sexual behavior, 430–431; and species-uniform communication, 261
curare, 85–86

dark: adaptation to, 114; fear of, 383; -reared animals, 127, 128
day residue, 319–320
daydreaming, 139, 276–277, 293, 393, 428
decay theory, 216, 233, 235

decentration, 474, 484
defense mechanisms, 418–419, 693–694
delirium tremens, 699, 701
delta waves, 60–61, 142
delusions, 288–289, 680–681
dendrites, 81, 83
dendritic spines, 63, 84
denotative symbolism, 322–324
dependent variables, 13–14
depression, 387, 684–686; and barbiturates, 159; grief and, 388; and lithium, 740; and operant conditioning, 717; and renunciation, 418; and sleep deprivation, 145
depth perception, 120, 121, 122
descriptive statistics, 749–759
development, 453–459; and behavioral observation, 461–462; and change, 491–492; of mentally handicapped, 524; phases of, 462–463; theories of, 459–461. *See also* adolescence; adulthood; childhood; infancy
developmental psychology, 7–8
differentiation: and development, 454; and group membership, 635
discrimination in learning, 204–205, 273, 465
disgust, 386
disjunctive concepts, 280
displacement aggression, 404, 405, 419
dissociative phenomena, 369–370, 691
distributed practice, 240–241
DNA, 37; and marijuana, 173
dog(s): amphetamine studies in, 106–107; and avoidance learning, 196; and chemical communication, 249–250; and classical conditioning, 184–185, 188; hypothalamic stimulation in, 400–401; and operant conditioning, 188–189
dominance (dominant responses): and arousal, 654; group influence on, 658–659; need for, 359; sex differences in, 478–481
dorsal root, 70, 71; ganglia of, 70, 73
dreaming (dreams), 141, 277; aggression in, 393; by animals, 314; and barbiturates, 160; bizarre, 310; of child molesters, 428; in color, 314; content of, 317–319, 326; control of, 314; and day residue, 319–320; and external stimuli, 321; forgetting, 313; Freud's and Jung's studies of, 307–308, 311–313; and imagery, 309–310; interpretation, 313, 322, 327–328; and paranormal phenomena, 314–317; and past experience, 321; problem-solving and, 313; and psychoanalysis, 714; and REM sleep, 308–309; scanning hypothesis of, 308; sources of, 319–322; and state of consciousness, 309; status of research on, 333; tension-reduction theory of, 310–311. *See also* symbolism; symbols
drug addiction, 164–165
drugs, classification and uses for, 158, 159, 168–169. *See also under types of, i.e.,* psychotomimetic drugs, etc.
dyads, 636–637
dynamism, 541

nerve membrane, 81, 82
nervous system: and barbiturates, 159; cells, 51; and color vision, 106–107; selective filter in, 92. *See also* autonomic nervous system; central nervous system; brain
neuroanatomy, 69–80
neuron, *See* nerve cell
neurophysiology, 80–86
neuroses, 188, 198, 445–446, 687–694
nodes of Ranvier, 81
nonsense words, 223, 232–233, 239–240, 281
norepinephrine, emotions and, 380–381, 387
NREM sleep, 141–143; deprivation, 145–146
nuclei, 69, 70
nucleus of nerve cell, 81
null hypothesis, 761–762

obedience, 625–626, 647–649, 654
obesity, overeating and, 346–347
observational studies, 431–432, 609. *See also* behavior observation
obsessive-compulsive disorders, 693
operant conditioning, 188–199; and behavior therapy, 716–717; and contiguity, 200; and discrimination, 204–205; as form of associative learning, 180; and reinforcement theory, 550–551; and superstition, 200–201; and teaching sign language to chimpanzees, 248
opinions, attitudes and 603–606
opium alkaloids, 161–162
organic disorders, 677, 699, 704–705
organic drives, 343
organismic psychology, 361
orgasm, 433–434, 435, 436, 437, 441
orienting response, 181, 369
overlearning, 224

pain: and dissonance, 626; habituation to, 181; and hypnosis, 147–148; perception of, 90, 162; and sound magnitude, 118; threshold, electric shock and, 118–119
paired-associate learning, 233, 476, 589
palmistry, 573
pancreas, 77
paranoid schizophrenia, 680–681
paranormal phenomena, 314–317
parasympathetic division of ANS, 71–72, 374, 375
parathyroid, 77
parents: and attitude formation, 616–617; as models, 381, 403–404, 417; and prejudice in children, 606
partial reinforcement, 192
Pearson product moment correlation coefficient, 510, 757
peer groups, 472, 589, 617–618
percentiles, 753–754
perception: and attention, 90–94; and attitudes, 599–600, 603; and barbiturates, 159; compared with thinking, 271; distorted, 129–130; emotions and, 380–381; events resulting in, 89–90; in infants, 278; learning and, 128–129; and

LSD, 137, 170–171; and marijuana, 171–172; of movement, 124–126; predetermined, 126–127; and sensory deprivation, 130–132; and sensory-motor integration, 126–130; sex differences in, 476; of simultaneous speeches, 91–92; and size constancy, 122; and transcendental meditation, 155. *See also* hearing; vision
performance: and age, 490; and approval, 354; and arousal, 368–369; group influence on, 656–657; and sensory deprivation, 131; and sleep, 349
peripheral nerves, 70–71
persona, 536
personality: dimensions of, 569; and instinct theory, 652; and marijuana, 173; maturing of, 489; and sex life, 428.
personality assessment: and behavior ratings, 588–591; and personality inventories, 575–581; projective methods for, 584–588. *See also* character analysis
personality disorders, 694–696
personality inventories, 575–581
personality psychology, 9–10, 654
personality tests, 569–573, 591–594
personality theories, 531–559; and clinical vs. laboratory setting, 555–556; conflict over, 559–562; controversial issues in, 555–563; existential, 554–555; and Jung, 312–313; operant reinforcement theory, 550–551
personality traits: of creative person, 295–297; and prejudice, 606; and psychosomatic disorders, 698; and risk-taking, 662–664; of self, 551–554; of self-actualizers, 552; similar, 641; and situational determinants, 558–559; theories of, 540–542
personalized instruction, 246–247
personification, 539–540
personology, 536–540
phenotype, 41, 47
phobias, 689–690; and desensitization, 719–721, 724–726
phoneme, 251
phrases, in language development, 257, 258
physical growth, and adolescence, 482, 483–484
physiological attitude measures, 611–612
physiological psychology, 9
physiological states: and dreams, 322; and falling in love, 448; and sexual behavior, 433–434. *See also* physiology
physiology: of mentally gifted, 522; and race, 604–605; and thinking, 300–301; and type theory, 542–545
pituitary gland, 76, 77
PKU genetic defect, 514, 515, 525
placebo effects, 172, 370–371, 741
play, development and, 359, 467–468, 472
play therapy, 729
pleasure-pain principle, 340–342, 533
pons, 74, 75
positive reinforcement, 195, 245, 413
power drive, 350–351, 352, 353
power law, 118–119

precognition, 314
predictions, 274–275, 578, 592, 601, 757
prejudice, *See* racial prejudice
primary drives, 339–340, 342, 349
primary memory. *See* short-term memory
primary mental abilities theory, 511–512
primary retardation, 523–525
problem-solving, 272–273, 282, 284–286; and dreams, 313; in infants, 278; sex differences in, 476
process schizophrenia, 678
programmed learning, 244–247
projective personality assessment, 584–588, 593
prostigmine, 86
proximity, attachment and, 448–449, 640
psilocybin, 168–169, 170–171
psychoactive drugs, 682–683, 735, 740
psychoanalysis, 20–21, 532, 712–713, 726–727
psychoanalytic theory, 482–483, 532–534
psychodrama, 730
psychodynamic theory, 532–537, 671, 682, 687, 694
psychodynamic therapy, 711, 712–713, 723–729
psychological drives, 357–361
psychology: and case studies, 15–16; fields of, 6–13; historical background, 17–22; methods of, 13–17
psychopathic personality, 694
psychoses, 170, 640, 676–687, 695
psychosexual stages, 427, 444
psychosocial stages, 561
psychosomatic disorders, 79, 198–199, 300–301, 384, 696–698
psychosurgery, 734, 736–739
psychotherapy. *See* behavior disorders treatment
psychotomimetic drugs, 168–169, 170–173, 745
public opinion polling, 612–614
punishment, 149, 197–198, 404, 417

quantitative studies, 4, 9, 434–438
questionnaires, 15, 613–614

race(s), 33, 35–36, 40, 407, 517–520
racial prejudice, 405, 602–606, 621
random sampling, 759
rat(s): and amygdala damage, 402; cerebral cortex growth in, 62–63; and cognitive maps, 206–207; and conditioned fear, 197; and electroconvulsive shock, 238; operant conditioning of, 200; selective breeding of, 32; startle response studies in, 182–183
raw scores, 753–754
reaction formation, 418–419
reactive schizophrenia, 678
realistic thinking, 287–289
reasoning, 415–416, 514. *See also* problem-solving
recall, 207, 221–223, 309
redintegrative memory, 221
reflex, spinal, 73
reinforcement, 13; aggression and, 403, 409, 410; attachment and, 637–638; ex-